FREE MONEY TO PAY YOUR BILLS

by

Matthew Lesko

and

Mary Ann Martello

Researchers
Cindy Owens, Jean Neuner,
Bev Matson, Chelsea Noble, Dixie St. John

Production
Beth Meserve

Marketing
Kim McCoy

Support
Mercedes Sundeen

Cover
Tom Ford

 Published by Information USA, Inc., P.O. Box E, Kensington, MD 20895; {www.lesko.com}.

FIRST EDITION

Library of Congress Cataloging-in-Publication date
Lesko, Matthew
Martello, Mary Ann

Free Money To Pay Your Bills

ISBN # 1-878346-65-2

Most books by Matthew Lesko are available at special quantity discounts for bulk purchases for sales promotions, premiums, fund-raising or educational use. Special books or book excerpts also can be created to fit specific needs.

For details, write Information USA, Special Markets, Attention: Kim McCoy, P.O. Box E, Kensington, MD 20895; or 1-800-797-7811, Marketing; {www.lesko.com}.

Other books available from Matthew Lesko:

Free Money To Change Your Life

Free Money To Change Your Life
6-hour instructional audio cassette/CD

Lesko's Info-Power III

Government Giveaways for Entrepreneurs IV

Free Legal Help

Free Health Care

Gobs and Gobs of Free Stuff

Free Stuff For Busy Moms

Free Stuff For Women's Health, Fitness and Nutrition

Free College Money And Training For Women

Free Money And Help For Women Entrepreneurs

Free Money to Change Your Life CD-ROM

Free Money For Your Retirement

How to Write and Get a Grant

For ordering information on any of Matthew Lesko's publications, call 1-800-UNCLE-SAM, or contact his web site at www.lesko.com.

TABLE OF CONTENTS

$$$ Pay Your Living Expenses (continued)

$$$ Pay Your Health Care Bills 120

$$$ Pay Your House and Apartment Bills (continued)

$$$ Pay Your College and Education Bills 462

INTRODUCTION

We all have bills. Some of us have more than others. We know all about our bills and how much we owe — each of us is an expert. And we all know our major source of income for paying our bills… it's our job. But what most people don't know is that there are thousands of government programs that provide money and other assistance to help average citizens pay their bills. So why don't most people know this? It's simple: THE GOVERNMENT DOESN'T ADVERTISE.

This year the government will distribute over $450 billion. You could use some of this windfall to:

- ☞ pay your mortgage and rent;
- ☞ pay your utility bills;
- ☞ pay your health care bills;
- ☞ pay your or your kids' education bills
- ☞ pay your food bills;
- ☞ pay your travel and entertainment bills; or
- ☞ pay your other living expenses.

The amount of money given out every year averages $4,000 for every family in the United States. Is your family getting your fair share? Are you?

Most of this money is completely free. It's money you don't ever have to repay, and it doesn't just go to poor people. Many of these programs go to middle class taxpayers making $40,000, $60,000, even $80,000 per year. Believe it or not, some programs have no income requirements at all.

These are difficult economic times. Credit card debt, bankruptcies, job losses and mortgage defaults are breaking records. It's time average Americans know about these government programs. Your tax dollars pay for these programs, whether you use them or not. Why not get your money's worth?

THERE'S NO SHAME IN TRYING TO BETTER YOURSELF

Some people don't feel right asking for help. They don't want to bother anyone with their problems. But neither should we impose on others by asking for a handout. We shouldn't make anyone feel awkward if they have to say "no" if they can't help. I once believed asking for any kind of help was bad. I don't anymore, but I have one condition: whether the help will help me help others.

I believe greedy, selfish people who abuse friendships or institutions, including government programs, should not be asking for help. But I don't believe that people who need help should worry about asking for it. Nor do I believe that people who want to better themselves should be afraid, embarrassed or feel guilty about asking for assistance. This isn't about pride — it's about prosperity.

Not only should you feel free to ask for help to better yourself, you have an obligation — to yourself, your loved ones and all of society. Everyone benefits when you help yourself.

Sometimes society, the system, or even our friends and loved ones can make us feel guilty or embarrassed for needing help. I know it's hard, but you have to ignore these people. The bottom line is that they're either stupid or forgetful. Maybe they can't remember the last time they needed help. But nobody's life is perfect. We all do dumb things, make lousy decisions and suffer the consequences. If we don't seek help we stay stuck in a bad situation forever, never able to contribute our best. Asking for help makes us better people. It means we want to move forward toward something better. And that's exactly what makes this country the greatest the planet has even known — above all, we move forward.

The programs in this book exist to help people overcome their problems: financial, personal, you name it. As a society we understand that everyone needs help at one time or another, and we have collectively decided to allocate resources to provide that help. You don't have to use these programs but remember: they exist to be used. They exist to help you solve your problems so that you can contribute to society. Think of it this way: by helping yourself, you're helping America.

Wealthy people have tax attorneys trying to figure out every tax break and available deduction. Although most of us aren't rich, and there are very few tax breaks for the middle class, there are plenty of government programs that offer help in the form of grants and other giveaways. Your right to these money programs is no different than the right a rich person has to every tax advantage they can find.

I'M SORRY, BUT THIS BOOK IS OUT OF DATE

I know you probably hate to hear this, but it's true. All printed material is out of date as soon as it is printed. Our world changes so fast that it's impossible for print materials to keep pace. Even the Internet, which has the capability of being updated instantly, is rarely completely up to date. I keep running into more and more outdated web sites because someone has to take the time to keep a web site current, and many organizations don't have the resources to keep someone dedicated to the task full time.

You may call an office in this book and inquire about a money program only to talk to a 16-year-old kid at some pizza delivery service. Things change. Phone numbers change. People move. Even the Yellow Pages are out of date before it is printed. Just order a pizza and keep moving. There are always other numbers. I know we are among the best sources of this information. We provide the most current research and contact information for each book, and we don't copy this data from secondary sources — we go right to the horse's mouth. We don't rely on government publications or even web sites. We contact the office directly to insure that we get the most current information about each and every program.

I know we are only as good as our information, but in our fast-changing society, time is our enemy. Here are some tips for handling some of the out-of-date problems:

Phone Number Is Wrong:
This does not mean the office went out of business. Believe me, even the toughest "small-government-is-better-government" lawmakers cannot get rid of these offices. Chances are excellent the program still exists and is still giving out money, but just

moved. Or the program stayed still and the phone moved. Or the program got a new phone system or even a new name. Wherever it is, you can contact the national information operator by dialing… 411. Just give the operator the agency name, city and state, and you will almost always be able get the new phone number.

Web Sites Won't Work:
Our web site descriptions of the programs may be lengthy because, when possible, we try to give you the address that goes directly to the page describing the program. If you have trouble connecting to the web site address, or it appears to be inactive, there are a number of things you can do before you start searching the Internet on your own. You may be able to get there by not using the complete address. For example if you put in {www.eren.doe.gov/buildings/home_weatherizing.html} and you receive a notice that "Page cannot be found", try putting in {www.eren.doe.gov} and work your way through the site to where you would like to go. Sometimes simply retyping the address in your web browser instead of clicking though an address in a document will work. Try these techniques before attacking the Internet's many unruly search engines.

CALL ME A LIAR

My mom's going to hate me for this. Politicians lie and rationalize that they're telling us the truth. The media lies and believes it's telling the truth. Even churches have even lied, believing they were telling the truth.

For instance, the Catholic Church once believed the earth was the center of the universe and put the genius stargazer Galileo under house arrest for preaching otherwise. When I was a young Catholic kid, the church told me I would go to hell if I ate meat on a Friday. Then the Vatican changed its mind and let us have our hot dogs and hamburgers. Even our parents lied to us, believing it was for our own good.

I know some people look at my work and call me a liar too. They take one of my books, call a few numbers, and become frustrated or even angry when they don't succeed in finding money. They may be told that:

> "the program ran out of money,"
> "they don't qualify for the money," or
> "Lesko's an idiot; there's never even been a program like that."

This can be frustrating, I know, and I'm sorry. I don't mean to purposely frustrate people. The mission of my work is to help people. Of course I want to make a few bucks by selling my books, but I do know that ultimately my books won't sell if people can't find the money programs I list and use them to help themselves and others.

A degree of lying — you know, white lies — seems to be inherent in all languages and all forms of communication. It's really not lying; it's more a matter of not presenting the downside of a situation. For example, a women or man going out on a date never shows up looking like they do first thing in the morning. They are going to try to look and act their best. This is what I do when I sell books. I point out all the good things my book has to offer, and not the problems people encounter before achieving their goals using the best program. I don't tell you "it may take a lot of effort" or "not every person who buys my book gets money."

I do know one thing, though. The truth is that you will never get any of this money if you don't know about the programs, do your homework, and apply to the right person.

There Certainly Is Money To Pay Off Your Credit Card Debt!

It's wise not to call the first government office in the book and ask for money to pay off your credit cards. Most government money programs are for specific kinds of bills, like rent, healthcare, child care and housing. The government doesn't have a category called "credit card bills" so when you call they will tell you there's no such program, to put it nicely.

But they're WRONG. There are plenty of programs that give out money that can be used to pay down your credit card debt; they're just not labeled as such. The programs in this book <u>can</u> be used to pay off credit card bills. Any program that offers cash to be used for living expenses can also be used to pay old bills. Like the extra money that is available from the Social Security Administration, or the extra money available from your local department of labor when you're out of work. Or the emergency money that is available from non-profit organizations. Or the money that some states make available to special groups like seniors or people with disabilities. And certainly you can use all the special tax credit money mentioned in this book to pay off credit card debt.

Most programs that fit this criteria are in the section titled, "Pay Your Living Expenses." But don't stop there. The money offered in the education and training sections does not have to be spent exclusively on education. Some can also be used for paying bills. Some money programs mentioned in the health section can even be used this way. Just make sure you check the requirements about restrictions.

EVERYONE IS ELIGIBLE FOR SOMETHING

Everyone is certainly eligible for something, but nobody is eligible for everything. Each program has different requirements that must be met in order to qualify for assistance, even though some have no income requirements at all.

You'd be surprised at the government's definition of "disadvantaged" for some of these. I even found a government program that requires you to have under $750,000 in the bank in order to qualify for business assistance. That's almost being a millionaire and the government thinks you need special financial help. And there are housing programs where you can qualify for help with an annual income of $83,000.

" THOSE ELIGIBLE MUST WEAR POLKA DOT BOW TIES, AND SUITS WITH QUESTION MARKS ON THEM. "

Many of the lower income programs that have strict income requirements can still include families making up to $35,000 a year. This represents about 30% of the country or about 30 million families.

Even millionaires like media icon Sam Donaldson are eligible for these programs. Donaldson had cancer surgery paid for by a program in this book. George W. Bush got a $200 million government grant for his baseball team, and Dick Cheney got over $3 billion in government money when he was running the Halliburton Company.

Remember Mohammed Atta, the suspected head of the 9/11 terrorist attacks? Peter Jennings ran a story on ABC News showing how the terrorist purchased my book, "Free Money To Change Your Life", from a TV commercial and walked into a government office in Florida asking for $600,000 to buy a crop dusting plane that could also be used for transporting passengers. He had a green card from the Immigration and Naturalization Service (INS) that made him eligible.

The government didn't give him the money because they thought his idea was unworkable, but he was eligible for the money.

It upsets me that a terrorist knew about and could apply for government money while the average citizen has no idea most of these programs even exist.

For Shame: Millions Are Eligible But Don't Apply

There are millions of people who are eligible for government money programs yet for some reason they never apply. For example:

- ✦ Over 100 million people are eligible to have their prescription drug bills paid, but only a very small percentage apply.
- ✦ Over 4 million kids are eligible for free health insurance, but their parents don't apply.
- ✦ Some 3 million seniors who can receive an extra $600 a year are not applying for their money.
- ✦ About 58% of people eligible for an extra $800 to pay their bills never apply for help.
- ✦ Millions of families that can get back up to $3,200 a year from the U.S. Treasury are not asking for their money.

Why don't people apply for this money? It's because they don't know about the programs. But even government experts only know a little about these programs. You can call a government office asking about a program and if it's not right under their nose they are not likely to know anything about it. Even if the office across the hall has such a program, the bureaucrat may not know it exists.

No single bureaucrat can possibly know about all 4,000 programs the government has in place. When we identified the program that offers free prescription drugs for people with incomes up to $40,000 a year, we conducted an undercover survey of doctors around the country to see if any knew about the program. We found that 94% of the doctors we surveyed were not aware of the free drug program.

If a doctor prescribes medication that costs you $300 each month and you ask if there is a program to help you pay for it, chances are they would sympathize but tell you no such program exists. BUT THERE IS.

HOW LONG DOES IT TAKE TO GET THE MONEY?

Some emergency money programs allow you to get cash within days or even hours, but these are very few and far between. It is more likely to be weeks or even months before you get any money, and many programs only accept applications at certain times of the year. If you just missed the application date, you have to wait another entire year.

But application deadlines and processing delays shouldn't trouble you. After all, if someone is going to give you $800 a month for the next 10 years of your life, you can certainly wait a few weeks. Or if someone will pay all of your college tuition bills, you can certainly wait even a few months for that to happen. You probably can't even remember exactly what you did on this day a month ago and look, here you are today, and no one is giving you money.

The good things in life always take a little time. Sure you may get lucky and make one telephone call and get a check in the mail within a few days. People have done it, but don't count on it.

What Are Your Chances Of Getting The Money?

The answer to this question is, "it depends." Every program has different requirements and qualifications. Some programs operate on a "first come, first serve" basis, while others limit help to only the most worthy of applicants. But if you're the only one applying, you're going to get the money. If 10 people apply and they only have enough money for 3, do the math. Your odds of getting the money may only be one in thirty-three, but ask anyone who plays the Lottery and they'll tell you about odds.

Still other programs are set up so that every eligible person gets their share, even if the country goes bankrupt. If you qualify, you're guaranteed the money — you just have to apply. Many programs in this book fit into this category, so don't be afraid to search. After all, this is money you and others have already paid in taxes and it's your elected officials who passed the laws making this money available.

FREE MONEY,
TAKE A CHANCE!

Isn't There A Lot Of Paperwork?

Red tape is overhyped. Most of the programs in this book require very little paperwork. Long applications are six or seven pages, but most average two to three. Of course, some money programs do require large amounts of paperwork, but they aren't listed in this book. Large applications tend to be for those looking for money for inventions or to improve communities.

So don't worry about paperwork. Everything you need to know about applying will be provided once you find the right office. They'll even help you fill out your application! Who cares how long it takes to get an extra $15,000 to live on? You can certainly spend a few minutes, hours or even days filling out the paperwork to get this money.

Can I Apply To More Than One Program?

Sure, what's the worst that can happen? Everyone gives you the money? That's a very nice problem to have. There may be some programs with multiple application restrictions but they are rare, so don't worry about it until someone brings up the issue. Remember this is a numbers game. The more programs you apply to the better your odds become. Chances are you will get the money.

You Can Find More Than What's In My Book!

That's right, you can out-Lesko Lesko. No single person knows everything about these programs, not even me. Sure I know a lot. I've been collecting information about government programs for over 25 years and over that time I've helped thousands of corporations and millions of consumers take advantage of these services. But I still can't know everything. The government is huge and constantly changing. We live in a big complex society and programs come and go. My researchers and I have tried to categorize every major program available but I know no matter how hard we try we still miss some, particularly at the local level and those offered by non-profit organizations.

We would never finish the book if we said that we wouldn't stop until we get every single program that exists. It would be like counting every grain of sand. This is why you can find programs that aren't in this book. I guarantee that if you use this book as a starter, and spend the next three days researching these programs, you will find opportunities that even we didn't know about (but please, let us know). There are over 3,000 counties in the United States. If we spent just one day researching every county program it would take us an additional 8 years to complete this volume, and by then the information would be outdated, right? But you should be able to research local programs in just a few days. We're sure we have well over 80-90% of what is available, because most of the money comes from federal and state sources. But that last 10% may well include the program that will change your life. As you go along, you will also discover newer programs that have been launched since we published the book. Then you can call us up and ask to be hired as a researcher.

GET FREE RESEARCH TO FIND MORE

Not only is there free money available to help solve your problems, there is also free research help if you have trouble finding the right office. Here are two of the best sources of free research if you need help figuring out who in the government can help you. When I was a Washington consultant I used to charge $100 an hour for the same services these offices provide for free.

For help with the federal government contact:

FEDERAL INFORMATION CENTER

This free government locator service can help you find the best office or program for your needs.

www.pueblo.gsa.gov/call
1-800-FED-INFO

For help with your state government contact:

YOUR STATE CAPITOL OPERATOR

Most government money initially comes from Washington and is then distributed by state and local governments. Your state capitol operator can help point you to the right local office. Or go to

http://www.piperinfo.com/state/index.cfm

THE EXPERTS ARE WRONG

I already confessed that I can be guilty of not giving you the complete story. So it's not a big stretch to also tell you that I also don't know everything. I may know more about government money programs than anyone else on the planet because I've been doing this for over 25 years and written over 100 books on the subject. But I certainly don't know everything. And neither does anyone else. Remember this when looking for money, especially when a government official or other self-appointed expert tells you there is no such thing as a government grant for business. THEY ARE WRONG.

I hear from people all the time who say they called the government and asked about business grants, but were told such programs don't exist. When I dig deeper into their query I usually find out that they called the Small Business Administration. There are many government grants for business but they are just not available from the Small Business Administration. You have to go to places like the U.S. Department of Agriculture and your state office of economic development to find them.

The world is too big and complex for any one person to know everything. If you are sick with an uncommon ailment you can see three different doctors and get three different diagnoses. I have seen many studies where consumer experts will have five different accountants compute income taxes owed by a fictitious family and get five different answers. The same holds true for government programs and resources.

Alan Greenspan, the head of the Federal Reserve Board, had no idea when the Wall Street bubble was going to burst, or even if it was a bubble at all. And this guy is treated in financial circles with more reverence than the Pope. The U.S. spends more on intelligence than any other country, yet we were taken by surprise on Sept. 11.

If a doctor diagnosed you with a condition that will stop you from living your life to its fullest, you would certainly get another opinion. Use the same skepticism when dealing with bureaucrats and their secretaries. When someone says you can't get the help you need, it pays to be distrustful. Don't listen. Get a second, third, fourth, fifth, sixth, seventh, eighth, ninth, tenth and even an eleventh opinion.

THE BEST WAY TO CONTACT A GOVERNMENT OFFICE

Face it, this isn't going to be as easy as going into the store for a loaf of bread. But it's probably going to be a lot easier than arranging for new phone service. Remember ours is a complicated system regardless of whether we're dealing with the government or a large corporation. To successfully navigate any large organization takes a certain attitude, I've found. When you contact a government office keep in mind these two facts:

Fact #1: Large Organizations Are Run By Rules Not People.
The people you deal with are not the ones who made the rules, usually a legislative body or a board of directors does this. They set the rules and regulations that must be followed. No matter how stupid the rules may seem, don't get mad at the person you are dealing with. THEY DID NOT SET THE RULES. And for goodness sake don't waste time and energy trying to get the organization to change its rules. If you want to change the rules, you have to go through the political process and if you need money or help now, that's going to take way too much time.

Fact #2: The People You Talk To Are Just Like You.
Many people have the wrong opinion about government workers. They aren't lazy bureaucrats, they're people just like you. They are paid to follow rules that have been set down by others. They have feelings. They want to help, but they have to be given the chance. I've found these to be the best 4 steps to take when contacting a government office:

Step #1: First Read Their Literature
The best thing you can do for yourself is to find out what a program says it has available. This can make everything happen more smoothly and increases the chances for getting all you need. Offices and programs can be so complex that it is often the case that many of the people working there are not aware of all the programs available. Employee turnover

also leads to misinformation. The more information you can review before discussing your needs with a program office the better. Go to the agency or program's web site for information or call the office to ask to have the information sent to you.

Step #2: Speak With Someone Who Knows About The Program
Even if you have all the information you need to apply to the program directly, be sure to talk with someone at the program office. Call the office and say something like:
"Hi. I'm Matthew Lesko and I'm thinking about applying to one of your programs — is there someone there who knows about this program?"
When you get an expert on the phone, describe your situation and ask if their program can help.

Step #3: Call Anyway
Even if the program described doesn't perfectly match your needs, or you doubt you qualify, call anyway. Talk with someone. Ask about the program. Ask if there is any way you might be able to qualify for help, and always ask if they know about any other programs that might be helpful.

Step #4: Obstacle Jumping
You are certainly going to encounter obstacles when trying to get through to some of the more popular programs. Don't get discouraged. It should be seen as a game. Ask yourself, "How am I going to get around, through or over this roadblock?" This is the fun part — the challenge. If someone makes things difficult, it just means you're probably on the right track. It probably means that most of your competitors turned back at this point. They quit, but not you. It's another little test for "How Bad Do You Really Want It." Are you going to let a little roadblock stop you from doing what you want in life?
Here are some ways I cope with the more common obstacles:

If you keep getting voice mail, call the information operator and ask for any other numbers they may have for that office. Call even if it's the office of the president or director.

See if you can get the name of someone from the web site or from the literature. It can be the name of anyone. As long as you have a name. Call the main number of the organization and ask to speak to that person and then ask them if they know....

You always have a last resort option. If the office you are trying to contact is a federal government office, you can contact the local offices of your Senator or Representative in Congress. If it's a state or local office, contact the office of your state senator and state representative. If you don't know how to find these people, your local library can help.

Here's what Henry Ford the founder of the first giant auto company said about getting around roadblocks: "Obstacles are those frightful things you see when you take your eyes off the goal."

THE BEST WAY TO GET A BUREAUCRAT TO HELP YOU

Cry a lot…. Well not exactly, but it probably won't hurt. What you really want to do is to make yourself notable and not just another number. Your mission is to try and NOT be:

- ➔ just another phone call today
- ➔ just another email to be answered
- ➔ just another letter to respond to
- ➔ just another person looking for money

Here's where creativity, personality, niceness and anything else that makes you special really counts. You have to try with everything you've got to set yourself apart from the other calls, emails, letters and applications that typically fill a bureaucrat's day. YOU HAVE TO MAKE YOURSELF HUMAN.

If you can get a bureaucrat to relate to you as a unique and interesting individual I believe that you increase your chance of success many times over,

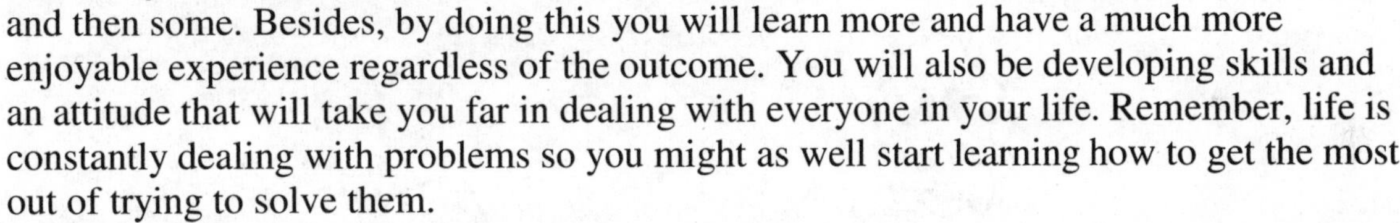

and then some. Besides, by doing this you will learn more and have a much more enjoyable experience regardless of the outcome. You will also be developing skills and an attitude that will take you far in dealing with everyone in your life. Remember, life is constantly dealing with problems so you might as well start learning how to get the most out of trying to solve them.

If you can get a bureaucrat to relate to you as an individual, they are always more likely to help you or direct you to someone who can help. Some will even share little tricks to help you get even more than you expected. And they are also more likely to make an exception for you if you are not completely qualified.

It is a basic instinct in most humans to want to help people who need it. We all want to help other people — the problem is trying to find someone in need of help. So if you contact a government office and begin by yelling and screaming that you've been trying to get through to them for over 2 hours, or that you've received the run-around for 3 days, believe me, you're off on the wrong foot.

Remember these bureaucrats will get the same paycheck if they work for you free for the next two weeks or if they hang up as soon as possible. Make them mad and they might even "accidentally" delete your email or lose your letter.

BUREAUCRATS CAN BREAK THE RULES

No matter what you've heard from me earlier, there are many occasions where a bureaucrat can change the rules just for you. Government officials have often told me they have the power to make exceptions to the rules. For example, if a program requires a maximum income under $30,000, some administrators can make special exceptions for applicants with incomes up to $40,000.

You will never be told that anyone has this power so it's very difficult to determine if exceptions can be made without asking. The bureaucrat usually has to get to know your case personally in order to make this type of exception. So this is just another reason to contact the office and speak to someone, even if you don't think that you qualify.

Remember that exceptions are one of the best reasons to follow my guidelines and recommendations. You can get in line with everyone else and expect the expected, or you can try to get into a line that appears beyond your reach and be pleasantly surprised. If you don't try for surprises, you will certainly not get any.

"NO" DOESN'T MEAN "NO"

The older I get, the more I believe that "no" seldom means "no" in most bureaucracies, including the government. There are times when bureaucrats will say, "no, you don't qualify," or "no, we don't give money for that," just because it's the path of least resistance. It's either the easiest thing to say or they don't really know what they are talking about.

Several years ago a young man from Boston saw me on the David Letterman show telling the audience about a government program that gives money to teenage entrepreneurs. Steven Stern contacted the appropriate office but they said that he couldn't apply for the money because it was only for teenagers who lived in small towns. Steven wouldn't take no for an answer. He tracked me down and asked what he could do. I wasn't sure, but I told him to get a copy of the program literature before giving up. When he got the literature he read it closely. It certainly said that the money was indeed for teens in small towns but a separate line also stated that it was also for teens that wanted to start a lawn mowing service. That was exactly what Steven wanted to do. He contacted the office and after he told them what their own literature said, they gave him the money. The $2,000 he received to start his lawn service earned him over $10,000 each year, money that he used to put himself through college.

Sometimes a "no" changes to a "yes" because an office is trying to get rid of money towards the end of the fiscal year because not enough people have applied for it. Or a "yes" may become a "no" because the official misunderstood your proposal or is simply not creative enough to understand how to bend the objective of your project to meet the objectives of the money program. It all takes effort.

What Do You Do When The Government Gives You The Run-Around?

Like it or not, sooner or later the bureaucratic run-around will get you. This is true in any large organization as well as the government. But you have some power over government bureaucrats when they mistreat you. Although your tax dollars pay the salaries of government workers, including bureaucrats, you do not have any direct power over them. But each government office is funded through the legislative branch of government, and that means letting your senator or representative go to bat for you when the going gets tough.

Every year the legislative branch passes laws to pay the salaries of the bureaucrats. The bureaucrats know this. This is why they tend to be especially kind to anyone from the legislative branch and maybe not so kind to taxpayers. When a member of Congress contacts a government agency, their messages go on different colored paper than ours. They even have separate offices just to handle requests from Congress.

What is interesting is that you have power over the legislators. They want your vote. Your vote is the only way they can keep their job. If a congressman or senator calls an agency for you and gets you something you want, you will vote for them forever, no matter what their politics are. They know this. You will also tell your friends what a great congressman you have. They also know this. This is why most incumbent legislators get reelected.

So if something goes wrong when you are dealing with a federal government program, you have three offices to contact for help, and you should contact them all. You have one member of the House of Representatives and two members of the Senate. Each has a local office near you and another in Washington, and you can contact either. These offices are staffed to listen to you and investigate your complaints about the government or its many programs.

The same is true at the state level. You have a congressman or senator who represent you in your state capitol and you should contact them with any problems you encounter dealing with state government programs or bureaucrats. If you have trouble locating the phone number or address of your state or federal elected official, contact your local library and they will get you the information.

THE NAME OF THE GAME IS FAILURE

The road to success is paved with aspirations and littered with failure. Thomas Edison failed more than 1,000 different times to light up the world before he got that first light bulb to work. Henry Ford, the auto entrepreneur, made the Model T the first mass-produced car because he failed with Models A through S. Think about it.

I had two businesses that failed before I got my first success. One of my businesses was a software company back in the 1970s. I must have been the only person in the world with a software company that failed in the 1970s. But it didn't stop me.

You are never going to get anywhere unless you embrace failure as a necessary part of the process. If you only choose those things that have already succeeded, you'll spend life in front of the TV doing nothing but arguing with the news commentators or complaining about the programs. If you're only going to attempt things you already know will succeed, your life is going to be predictable and boring. You're going to stop growing, and stop moving forward.

The fact is that very few people can say with certainty what will lead you to success. One successful person may know what led THEM to succeed, but they cannot tell YOU what will lead YOU to success. We are all different and have to try things our own way. You may be able to learn some tips about what not to do and what doesn't work, sometimes, but it is next to impossible to learn, from anyone else, exactly what will work for you.

We each have a unique set of skills and experiences and live in a unique environment. Sure it would be wonderful to meet some guru to reveal the secret of life, or the one little thing you can do to get what you want, but believe me, I can't do that for you and neither can anyone else. Because of my experience I may be able to give you dozens or even hundreds of things that potentially might work. But there is never a magic bullet that you can use over and over again to hit the jackpot.

If you are looking for just one thing you should know to get the money you need, it's simply this: Just keep trying.

I've learned that this is the key to accomplishment. It's a lesson we learn early, but tend to forget as we grow older. Have you ever seen a little one-year-old try to walk for the first time? My boy would hold on to the edge of the coffee table in the living room and try to step away, letting go of the table. He would then fall right down on his butt. But from there he would crawl back to the coffee table and pick himself up by holding on to the table and try again. And again he'd try to walk and BOOM, fall on his butt again.

There's a lesson in this. Think what would have happened if the kid stopped trying to walk because HE FAILED. He's 21 years old now and I'd be pushing him around in a wheel chair if he didn't continue to fall and fail until he got it right. It took him days and dozens and dozens of falls before he was able to walk. But he did it.

Learning how to get money from government programs is the same. Learning how to succeed takes the same amount of failure, but what keeps us coming back for more failure is the desire to succeed.

If you are resolute and dedicated, steadfastly seeking the things you really want out of life, you will have the desire to learn from your failures.

HURRY UP AND FAIL

The sooner you fail, the sooner you get rid of those voices in your head warning you about failure. Think of these voices as demons trying to keep you from succeeding. I used to be petrified of failure. The fear used to rule me. As a young man I believed that if I failed at something everyone would know it. People would point at me while I walked down the street and say things like, "Hey look. There goes Lesko. What a failure."

But after I had a couple of failures I quickly realized that no one really cared. Not even my own family. Everyone is so caught up in his or her own life, they really don't have time to think about your failures. Or else they love you for who you are, not what you are.

...So who cares if you apply for the money and don't get any?

...Who cares if you don't know what you are talking about when you call an office looking for help?

...Who cares if you fill out the application wrong and have to do it over and over again? That's right, no one.

Richard Nixon was thrown out of the White House and died a hero. Can you imagine calling your mother to tell that her that you're resigning as president of the United States to avoid being thrown out of the White House? The ex-mayor of Washington, D.C., Marion Barry, was caught on film doing cocaine in a hotel room with a prostitute. He went to prison, served his sentence, and was elected mayor again. No matter what your goals, your failures will never be that bad.

No one is following you around with a clipboard judging your every move, recording your thoughts and actions. No one is going to make you account for every misstep along the way, and neither should you. The only thing that matters is eventually getting the help you need. And you're not likely to get it until you learn the system, and by failing a few times. It's actually good for you.

Failure has even become a badge of honor and courage in our country. All the dotcom people wear their failures like medals on their chest. Our country forgives the most dismal failures as long as the individual continues to strive

Matthew Lesko
Author, Entrepreneur

$$$ Pay Your Living Expenses

Sometimes you just need a little help getting through to the end of the month. Whether you need help with your heating or phone bill, or help with transportation and medical issues, resources are available. The trick is knowing who to call. What we have done is pulled together information on programs and services across the country. Some are available to anyone, whereas others are only for a specific target group or residents of a particular town. This may give you ideas of who in your area may offer grants or other forms of assistance to those in need. Many of these groups and organizations are small and have limited funds, so they asked not to be included in a major publication for fear of being inundated with requests for funds. But they do exist and they do provide help, so call around and ASK. You will be surprised by what you hear. There are also organizations to help with issues such as:

- Free child care
- Money to fix your car
- Money for adoptions
- Private school tuition for your kids
- Child support help
- Money for heating, phone or food bills
- Free hospitalization and medications
- Discounts for seniors
- Dental and vision care assistance
- Free mammograms and immunizations

We have touched the tip of the iceberg. Read on and see what else is out there waiting for you to call.

Money for Cars, Bus Fare, Auto Repair, Insurance, and Drivers Ed.

The following are examples of what just some of the states are offering in transportation assistance for those who have serious transportation needs. Transportation is a growing concern in the workforce and programs are being added and changed every day. Be sure to contact your state transportation agency for the latest benefits your state has to offer.

The following are examples of what just some of the states are offering in transportation assistance for those who have serious transportation needs. Transportation is a growing concern in the workforce and programs are being added and changed every day. Be sure to contact your state transportation agency for the latest benefits your state has to offer. For a listing of the websites of all state departments of transportation, see {www.fhwa.dot.gov/webstate.htm}.

- Alaska: $85 a month towards transportation; {www.dot.state.ak.us/}
- Arizona: $5 a day towards transportation; {www.dot.state.az.us/}
- Arkansas: $200 for car repairs; {www.ahtd.state.ar.us/}
- Colorado: Free cars and 3 months of insurance; {www.dot.state.co.us/}
- Delaware: 30 free transit ride tickets with a new job; {www.deldot.net/public.ejs}
- Florida: Money for gas, repairs and insurance; {www11.myflorida.com/publicinformationoffice/}
- Illinois: $60 a month for gas or $88 a month to take the bus; {http://dot.state.il.us}
- Kansas: $30 a month for gas and money for car repairs; {www.ink.org/public/kdot/}
- Kentucky: $60 a month for gas and $300 to get a drivers license, pay for auto registration, taxes or repairs, and $900 to move to another city to get a job; {www.kytc.state.ky.us/}
- Louisiana: $100 a year for auto repairs; {www.dotd.state.la.us/}
- Massachusetts: $150 a month towards transportation; {www.state.ma.us/eotc/}
- Michigan: Money for auto repairs and insurance; {www.michigan.gov/mdot/}
- Mississippi provides door to door service; {www.mdot.state.ms.us/}
- Nebraska: Money for insurance, auto repairs; $2,000 to buy a car; 3 months of auto insurance, $500 for taxes, licensing, etc.; {www.dor.state.ne.us/}
- New Hampshire: $130 a month for transportation; $240 a year for auto repairs; and money to take drivers education; {www.state.nh.us/dot/}
- New Jersey: $500 for car repairs; {www.state.nj.us/transportation/}
- New York: $500 for car repairs; {www.dot.state.ny.us/}
- Oklahoma: Money for auto repairs and insurance; {www.okladot.state.ok.us/}
- Pennsylvania: $200 for auto repairs; {www.dot.state.pa.us/}
- South Dakota: Money for auto repairs; {www.sddot.com/}
- Vermont: $200 for auto repairs; {www.aot.state.vt.us/}
- Washington: $546 a month for transportation; {www.wsdot.wa.gov/}
- Wisconsin: $1600 interest free to buy a car or repay with community service; {www.dot.state.wi.us/}

Pay for Taxi Service to Work, School or Day Care

One county in Oregon has a program that picks up you and your child, taking your child to day care and you to work. It doesn't charge you anything, and doesn't even ask your income. North Carolina has programs where counties are given vans to transport people back and forth to work, with lower fees charged to those in welfare-to-work programs. Mississippi has a program that will pick you up at your house, almost anywhere in the state and take you back and forth to work if you are working to get off welfare.

Some communities, like Fairfax County in Virginia, maintain a database that helps locate the necessary transportation for work and day care needs. And Kentucky operates an 800 hotline that tries to solve any work-related transportation need, and soon they will have a separate hotline for each county. Do these people want you to get to work, or what?

To start looking for programs like this in your area, contact your local congressman's office or your local social service agency. They won't know about all the programs but can probably give you some starting places. You should also find out about local vanpool and rideshare programs. Your local chamber of commerce or library should have this kind of information for you.

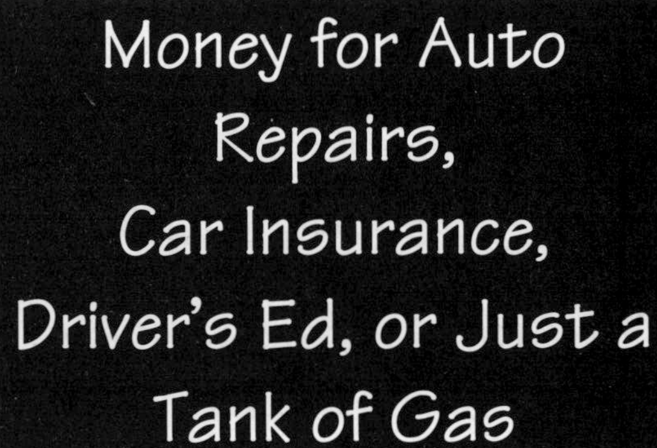

Money for Auto Repairs,
Car Insurance,
Driver's Ed, or Just a Tank of Gas

Whatever it takes to keep you on the road! There are federal programs as well as state programs to help people with limited incomes keep their vehicles on the road so that they can get back and forth to work, focusing on those trying to get off welfare.

Some states will even give you money for driver's education or to pay for a driver's license. The issue, like the programs for free cars, is to **help people make it to work**. Illinois and Kentucky offer $60 a month for gas money. New York and New Jersey give

people up to $500 for car repairs. Pennsylvania and Vermont only give $200 for car repairs. But Washington State provides people up to $546 a month for their transportation.

Limousines anyone? These programs are organized like a patchwork quilt in most areas involving federal, state, county and non-profit organizations.

To start looking for programs like this in your area, contact your local congressman's office or your local Social Services. They won't know about all the programs but can probably give you some starting places. Most branches of the Goodwill Industries have a Wheels to Work program. Other programs can be found by typing in the keywords "Wheels to Work" in an Internet search engine.

Here is just a *SAMPLING* of the Wheels to Work programs that we found:

Good Wheels
Goodwill Industries of Central Arizona
417 North 16th Street
Phoenix, AZ 85006
602-254-2222, ext. 142
Email: {dcrews@goodwillaz.org}
{www.goodwillaz.org/goodwheels.html}

Wheels to Work Program
Rockingham Community Action

7 Junkins Ave.
Portsmouth, NH 03801
603-431-2911
Client Access: 800-556-9300
Email: {w2@rcaction.org}
{www.geocities.com/ w2work/}

Wabash Valley Goodwill Industries, Inc.
2702 South 3rd Street
P.O. Box 2720
Terre Haute, IN 47802
812-235-1827
Fax: 812-235-1397
Email: {office@wvgoodwill.org}
{http://wvgoodwill.org/wtw1.htm}

Goodwill Industries of N. Carolina
1235 S. Eugene St.
Greensboro, NC 27406-2393
336-275-9801
Fax: 336-274-1352
Email: {kcaughron@goodwill-cnc.org}
{www.triadgoodwill.org/programs.htm#WheelstoWork}

Wheels to Work
Forsyth County Department of Social Services
P.O. Box 999
Winston-Salem, NC 27102
910-727-2175

Cooperative Ministry
Art Collier
P.O. Box 1705
Columbia, SC 29202
803-799-3853
{www.triadgoodwill.org/programs.htm#WheelstoWork}

New Leaf Services
3696 Greentree Farms Dr.
Decatur, GA 30034
404-289-9293

Cars for Work
Good Will and Crisis Assistance Ministry
2122 Freedom Dr.
Charlotte, NC 28266
704-332-0291

Wheels to Work
Resource Conservation & Development Council
240 Oak St., Suite 101
Lawrenceville, GA 30245
770-339-6071

Free Bus Passes

Detroit's **Suburban Mobility Authority for Regional Transportation (SMART)** has a program called "Get a Job/Get a Ride" that gives a month's worth of free rides to anyone in the Detroit area who gets a job.

The only requirement is that you started a new job within the last 30 days. You can be making $100,000 a year and they'll still give you the free passes. New Jersey will give a free one-month pass to those on low income that get a job or are going to training.

Check with your local Chamber of Commerce, Transit Authority, or your state Department of Transportation.

Get $65 a Month for Commuting to Work

Your employer can give you $65 a month to help pay for bus, train, ferry, or vanpool commuting expense and neither you nor the employer has to pay taxes on this money. Contact your local transit authority for more details on the program called *Tax Free Qualified Transportation Fringe Benefits*, or contact: Commuter Check Services Corporation, 401 S. Van Brunt Street, Suite 403, Englewood, NJ 07631; 201-833-9700; Fax: 201-833-8704; {www.commutercheck.com}.

Free Seminars on Buying a Car

You can't just go on color alone! You need to become savvy as to what options to look for and how to negotiate with the dealer. Do you really need rust proofing? What is the difference between the invoice and the sticker price? How can I find out what the dealer paid for the car?

Don't be intimidated by salesmanship. The dealer wants your money, so they don't want you to leave without signing on the bottom line. Many different organizations and groups offer classes on how to buy a car. Contact your county cooperative extension service, your local adult education department, or women's organizations in your area to see what they may have to offer.

Free Seminars on How to Fix Up a Car

What do you do if you are driving on a freeway and you get a flat tire? How often should you change the oil and can you do it yourself? How do you jump a car? It is better to plan ahead for emergencies, but where do you go for help?

Many different organizations and groups offer classes on how to fix a car. Begin by contacting your local car insurance company, automobile road service company, or department of motor vehicles. I have even seen classes being offered by automobile dealerships. Once you are there, maybe they can sell you a new car as well.

Other places to check include your county Cooperative Extension Service, your local adult education department, or women's organizations in your area. You can save yourself worry, stress, and money if you are prepared and knowledgeable regarding your car.

Free Car Repairs

June Rapp of Massachusetts took her family van into a dealer to have it fixed and they wanted to charge her over $1000 to make the repairs. She called the U.S. Department of Transportation and found out that her problem was part of a manufacturer recall. Recalls have to be fixed for free and the repair shop didn't know that. To find out about recalls for any car, contact:

- **Auto Safety Hotline**, US Dept. of Transportation, NEF-11.2HL, 400 Seventh St., SW, Washington, DC 20590; 888-327-4236; {www.nhtsa.dot.gov/cars/problems/recalls/recall_links.cfm}
- The **Consumer Report** people have a searchable database for car recall information. Contact Consumers Union, 101 Truman Ave., Yonkers, NY 10703; 914-378-2000; {consumerreports.org}

Discounts on Buses, Trains and Subways

If you are a senior citizen, you can usually ride most forms of transportation for about half-price. Amtrak and Greyhound offer discounts of 10-15% for the senior set. Children even get to take advantage of discount programs, with the youngest group often getting a free ride. Check out these websites: {www.amtrak.com}; {www.greyhound.com}.

Don't forget to ask about a variety of reduced fare programs, including student and military discounts. Often job training programs will compensate you for your

travel, so before you begin training, inquire about support services such as transportation and child care.

Get Free Taxi Rides for Grandma to go to the Doctor

Many seniors have to give up driving their cars, perhaps because of the cost or illness. But then how do they get to the doctor, the bank or the store? Many rely upon their friends and children to solve their transportation needs, but there are times when you need to come up with another alternative.

The Eldercare Locator provides access to an extensive network of organizations serving older people at state and local community levels. This service can connect you to information sources for a variety of services including transportation.

For more information, contact Eldercare Locator, National Association of Area Agencies on Aging, 1112 16th St., NW, Washington, DC 20024; 800-677-1116 between 9 a.m. and 8 p.m. EST; {www.aoa.gov}.

$170/Mo for Parking Money

Your employer can give you $65 a month to pay for going to work in a bus, van or metro, or give you $170 a month for parking. You get the money tax free, and the employer gets to take a tax deduction. Everybody wins!

It's called the *Qualified Transportation Fringe Benefit* or *Transit Benefit Program.* Get a copy of IRS Publication 535, *Business Expenses* and show your boss the section entitled "Qualified Transportation Fringe". The publication is available from your local IRS office or from 800-TAX-FORM or from their web site at {www.irs.gov}.

Free Rides to Pick Up a Sick Child at School

Suppose your child is sick at school and needs you in the middle of the day, but you don't have a way to get there because you go to work most days by some other way than using your car. Don't panic. You can probably get a free ride, taxi, or free rental car from the local *"Guaranteed Ride Home Program."*

You can also use the service for most family emergencies if your normal ride falls through, or if you have to work late unexpectedly. Call your local carpool or vanpool service to see if they have a similar program. Most of these programs require that you pre-register, but it is always best to plan ahead for emergencies anyway.

If you do a computer search using the terms (including the quotes) "guaranteed ride home program," you will find a listing of many of the programs offered. You can also contact your state Department of Transportation for starting places.

Free Child Safety Seats

It's easy to spend $100 on a child's car seat, so look for the deals. There are hospitals that give out free child safety seats as you leave with your new baby, with no questions asked and no income requirements. Local police and fire departments inspect child safety seats to see that they are in proper order and properly installed, and sometimes provide free seats to those whose current equipment is not considered safe. Local organizations, like the Easter Seals Society were part of a federal program that gives out millions of dollars worth of free seats because of a settlement the U.S. Department of Transportation made with General Motors. Other groups will lend you a seat for as little as $5. The state of Minnesota alone has over 225 such programs.

To find a program near you, contact your local police or fire department. Or contact your state information operator listed in the

Appendix and ask them for your state office for Highway Safety or Traffic Safety. These national organizations may also be able to give you a local source:

- *National SAFEKIDS Campaign*, 1301 Pennsylvania Ave., NW, Suite 1000, Washington, DC 20004; 202-626-0600; fax 202-393-2072; {www.safekids.org}
- *National Highway Traffic Safety Administration*, U.S. Department of Transportation, 400 Seventh St., SW, Washington, DC 20590; 800-424-9393; {www.nhtsa.dot.gov}

Cheap Air Fare to See Sick Relatives

Not free, but at least you don't have to pay full price. When a family member is very ill or has died, families have to make last minute airline reservations. Obviously you lose out on the 21-day advance purchase rates, but almost all airlines offer *bereavement* or *compassion* fares for domestic travel.

Generally the fares are available to close family members, and the discount on the full-fare rate varies from airline to airline. Many require that you provide the name of the deceased and the name, address and phone number of the funeral home handling arrangements. In the case of a medical emergency, the name and address of the affected family member and the name, address and phone number of the attending physician or hospital are required. Contact the airline of your choice to learn more about the "Bereavement/Compassion Fares." Full fare rate varies from airline to airline, but you could save up to 50%.

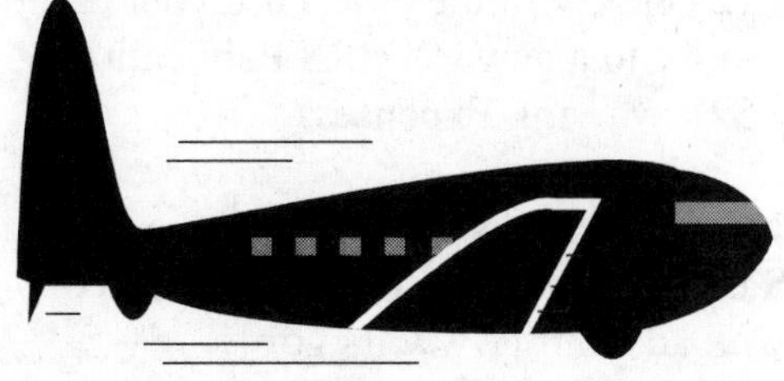

Free Cars and Air Fare to Go on Vacation

Not quite as easy as it sounds, but there are programs out there to help people move their cars. Most of the cars need to be driven across the country and in exchange, many car moving companies offer free gas and airline travel home.

This is not to say that you can take your family on a minivan vacation across the country. Certain rules and restrictions apply. But I have known many a college kid that has gotten to drive across the U.S. for free.

Obviously, you do not get to pick your make and model, and you need to be flexible as to the departure time and destination, but this is one way to see America. Contact local moving companies to see what they have to offer. There is even a website for those interested in having their cars moved at {www.movecars.com}, and they may be able to provide you with information.

Air courier services operate the same way, but you are required to have a valid passport. Most air freight services don't do enough business to send a plane overseas each day. As a courier, you carry a package checked as baggage to an overseas destination. There have been no incidences of contraband problems, and customs is familiar with this service. You deliver the package to a company representative in the customs section of the airport, then you are on your own. In exchange, you get to fly to exotic ports for FREE or cheap. Children are not allowed to accompany couriers. Contact companies listed in the air courier section of your phone book, do a web search using the terms "air courier service," or contact the Air Courier Association at 800-282-1202; or online at {www.aircourier.org}.

Free Taxi To Take Your Child to a Doctor's Appointment

The Federal Transit Administration provides over $50 million a year to over 1,000 local organizations to provide free non-emergency transportation for people who are old or have a disability. But the groups who get this federal money can also provide free transportation services to moms who are in a jam.

The regulations state that the vehicles can also be used to "serve the transportation needs of the general public on an incidental basis." You may have to do some educating to get a local group to give you a ride. Tell them to see Circular FTA C9070, 1D, for Section 5310 Program, Chapter V, Program Management, paragraph 3b. It's available from the U.S. Federal Transit Administration or on the web at {www.fta.dot.gov/library/policy/circ9070/chapter5.html}.

To find groups in your area who receive these FTA Section 5310 Grants for Elderly and Persons With Disabilities, contact your state department of transportation or the U.S. Federal Transit Administration, Office of Program Management, Office of Resource Management and State Programs, 400 7th St., SW, Washington, DC 20590; 202-366-4020; {www.fta.dot.gov}.

$200+ to Use Your Car

You can deduct:

- 34 1/2 cents per mile if you use your car for business (IRS Publication 463, Travel Entertainment, Gift, and Car Expenses)
- 14 cents per mile if you use your car during charity work (IRS Instructions for Schedule A, Itemized Deductions)
- 12 cents per mile if you use your car for medical care (IRS Instructions for Schedule A, Itemized Deductions)
- 12 cents per mile if you use your car to move to a new job (IRS Publication 521, Moving Expenses)

These publications are free from your local IRS office, by calling 1-800-829-3676 or download from {www.irs.gov}.

Discounts on Car Rentals

You never should pay full-price for car rentals and there are deals aplenty if you keep your eyes opened. AAA and AARP membership will save you a few bucks, as will many other membership programs. Car rental agencies also often offer discounts to senior citizens (check what age they consider "senior"). Many times, if you book your flight and car rental at the same time, you can get a discount rate, plus get miles added to your frequent flyer program. All you have to do is ask!

The free brochure, *Renting a Car*, outlines some points to consider and questions to ask when you reserve a rental car. You can learn how to choose a rental car company and understand the terms they use for insurance and charges. For your copy, contact Public Reference, Room 130, Federal Trade Commission, Washington, DC 20580; 202-326-2222, 877-FTC-HELP; or online at {www.ftc.gov}.

$15,000 to Pay for Child Care

In Connecticut your income can be $39,168 and you can get $640 a month for child care. Make $25,332 in Indiana and get $1,260 a month for infant care. Earn $38,244 in Alaska and receive $583 a month for child care.

The Child Care and Development Block Grant gives money to states to help families meet their child care needs. Parents may

choose from a variety of child care providers, including center-based, family child care and in-home care, care provided by relatives, and even sectarian child care providers. You can even get money to start a day care center! Income qualifications vary from state to state, and each state operates their programs slightly differently.

To find out how to take advantage of this program in your state and to learn the eligibility requirements, contact National Child Care Information Center, 243 Church St., NW, Vienna, VA 22180; 800-616-2242; http://nccic.org

Free Child Care When Training or Looking For a Job

Welfare reform, called ***Temporary Assistance for Needy Families (TANF),*** does more to help people not wind up on welfare. The new program includes free training, education, child care, and transportation assistance necessary to help you obtain employment.

Child care is an important part of the program. Eligibility requirements vary from state to state, so contact your TANF office nearest you to learn what options are available to you. For more information, contact Office of Family Assistance,

Administration for Children and Families, 370 L'Enfant Promenade, SW, Washington, DC 20447; 202-401-9215; {www.acf.dhhs.gov/programs/opa/facts/tanf .htm}.

Pay Only $9/wk for Child Care at Local Nonprofits

Local non-profits around the country get grants from the United Way or other institutions and offer free and sliding scale day care services. The United Way spends about a third of its funds, about $1 billion a year, on programs for children and families.

For example, the Community Partnerships for Children Program in Brockton, MA provides child care for a family of 2 with weekly income of $210 for only $9.00 a week, and families of 4 with income of $1,000 a week can get care for $114 a week per child. There are about 500 local United Way Information and Referral Services around the country that can point you to local groups that can help you solve your child care problems.

Look in the phone book for your local United Way agency, or contact United Way of America, 701 N. Fairfax Street, Alexandria, VA 22314-2045; 703-836-7100; 800-411-UWAY (8929); {www.unitedway.org}.

Free Child Care for AmeriCorp & Vista Workers

Over $10,000,000 a year is paid out to cover child care services for people working with AmeriCorps or VISTA. These programs allow you to tackle community problems on everything from disaster relief to tutoring. National Service jobs also provide a stipend, housing, and even college money; child care is a bonus.

Contact Corporation of National Service, 1201 New York Ave., NW, Washington, DC 20525; 202-606-5000; {www.nationalservice.org}.

Free Pre-School for Your Child

Head Start is one of those government programs that has proven to actually work. It's preschool that has a great student teacher ratio and all teachers are certified in early childhood development. It prepares the children with school readiness, and research shows that these children enter kindergarten with the skills necessary to succeed. Some Head Start programs are even home-based. There are income requirements for acceptance into the program, but the program does allow 10% of the students to have higher incomes. And 10% of the program needs to be offered to kids who have a disability.

To learn more about Head Start programs near you, contact your local board of education, the state Department of Social Services, or Administration for Children and Families, U.S. Department of Health and Human Services, Head Start Bureau, 330 C Street, SW, Washington, DC 20447; 202-205-8572; {www.acf.dhhs.gov/programs/hsb}.

Work for Companies That Offer Free/ Discount Child Care

You may be surprised at the number of daycare centers offering services right inside company office buildings. In fact the federal government may be in the lead as they have over 1,000 child care centers that are sponsored by various governmental agencies. Talk to other moms and dads on the playground, call human resources departments, and even check with your local chamber of commerce. All may be able to direct you to companies providing this benefit.

A directory of sites is available for $25 from the Work and Family Connection, 5197 Beachside Dr., Minnetonka, MN 55343; 800-487-7898; {www.workfamily.com}. Another resource is your local Child Care Resource and Referral Agency, who should be aware of programs in their area. To locate your local referral agency, contact Child Care Aware, 1319 F Street, NW, Suite 500, Washington, DC 20004; 800-424-2246, {www.childcareaware.org}.

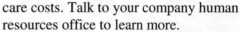

Besides child care centers, some employers offer a dependent care assistance plan that allows you to pay for child care out of pre-tax dollars. You get more care for your buck. Other employers offer direct subsidies to offset child care costs. Talk to your company human resources office to learn more.

Free Child Care For Teens With Disabilities

48 states provide a subsidy to parents who qualify for childcare for children ages 14 to 19 who are physically and/or mentally incapable of self-care. Each state sets their eligibility requirement and the amount of funds they have available for this type of care. To learn what your state has to offer, contact your state Child Care and Development Block Grant lead agency.

Money for Your Child Care Center

Child Care Works is a new partnership between the District of Columbia, eight area banks and three community organizations that make training, grants and loans available to licensed neighborhood day care providers to provide slots for 1,000 children. Maryland and Ohio provide special low-interest loans through their Department of Economic Development to fund child care centers. Even the Child Care and Development Block Grant provides money to develop child care centers and before and after school programs.

For more information, contact your state Department of Economic Development or your Child Care and Development Block Grant lead agency.

$2,500 to Help Pay for an Adoption

The National Adoption Foundation (NAF) is a national non-profit organization dedicated to providing financial support, information, and services for adoptive and prospective adoptive families. They recently announced the expansion of its programs to include home equity loans, as well as unsecured loans and grants for adoption expenses. A grant program to cover adoption expenses is also available on a limited basis for prospective adoptive parents.

Other sources of money for adoption include:

- Ask your employer for employee adoption assistance benefits. Approximately 65 percent of Fortune 500 companies now offer some kind of adoption benefit.
- Take advantage of the new adoption expense tax credit in advance by modifying your income tax withholding to reflect your tax savings when you file your return. This frees up cash for adoption expenses due now.

Contact: National Adoption Foundation, 1415 Flag Ave., So. , Minneapolis, MN 55426; 800-448-7061; 203-791-3811; Fax: 612-544-6698; Email: {info@nafadopt.org}; {www.nafadopt.org/default.asp}. To downloan an application: {www.nafadopt.org/pdf/adoption.pdf}.

$4,000 To Pay For Child Care

Remember that the Internal Revenue Service (IRS) offers some benefits for child care costs. IRS Publication 503, *Child and Dependent Care Expenses*, outlines the rules covering this benefit and describes how to figure the benefit if your employer covers some of the cost. You may claim up to $2,400 for the care of one child (or $4,800 for two or more).

For more information, contact the IRS Information Line at 800-829-1040; or {www.irs.gov}. In addition, 25 states and the District of Columbia offer some type of child care income tax benefit either in the form of credits or deductions. Contact your state Tax Revenue office to see what your state offers.

Free Credit Repair

It always seemed strange to me that if you're in debt enough to need help with credit repair, why in the world would you spend more money on a credit repair services? You can do it for free, yourself!

Spending money needlessly is what got you there in the first place. And more importantly, federal and state regulators have been warning consumers against using credit counseling companies. Companies, lawyers and others will charge you $300 to $1000 for something you can do for free.

Here are some of the free reports you can get from the Federal Trade Commission:

- ❑ ***Credit Repair: Self-Help May Be The Best***
- ❑ ***Knee Deep in Debt***
- ❑ ***How To Dispute Credit Reporting Errors***
- ❑ ***How To Deal With Credit Problems***
- ❑ ***How to Dispute Credit Report Errors***

For your copies, contact Public Reference, Room 130, Federal Trade Commission, Washington, DC 20580; 202-326-2222; 877-FTC-HELP; {www.ftc.gov}.

If you don't want to do it ALL yourself, you can ask for **FREE HELP**. The following non-profit and government organizations provide free, or low-fee credit counseling services. You can contact them to find the office nearest you. Some of these offices are

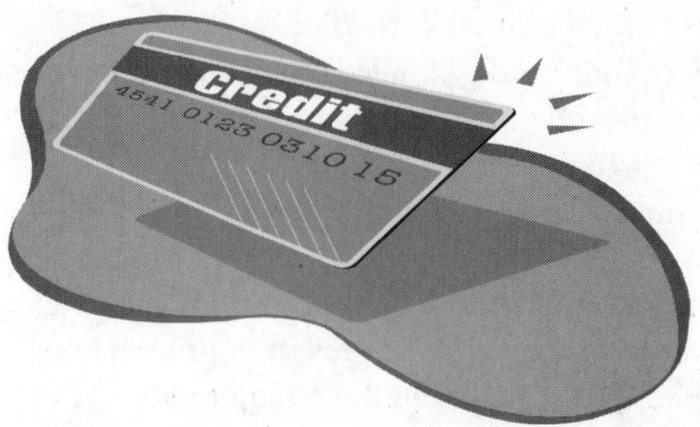

financed by the bank and credit card industry, who are biased toward having you pay all your bills without using the bankruptcy option. So be sure that they explain your bankruptcy options.

- ❑ ***National Foundation for Consumer Credit***, 8611 Second Avenue, Suite 100, Silver Spring, MD 20910; 800-388-2227; Spanish: 800-68AYUNDA; {www.nfcc.org}
- ❑ Free internet credit counseling services from the non-profit organization, ***Credit Counseling Center of America***, P.O. Box 830489, Richardson, TX 75083-0489; 800-493-2222; {www.cccamerica.org}
- ❑ ***County Cooperative Extension Service***: to find your local office, see the blue pages of your phone book.

Free Copies of Your Credit Report

You can get a free copy of your credit report if:

- you have been denied credit, insurance, or employment within the last 60 days
- you're unemployed and plan to look for a job within 60 days

- you're on welfare, or
- your report is inaccurate because of fraud.

Otherwise they can charge you up to $9 for a copy of your report. For copies of your report, contact the credit reporting agencies listed in the yellow pages of your telephone book, or contact the three major national credit bureaus:

Equifax
PO Box 740241, Atlanta, GA 30374; 800-685-1111; {www.equifax.com}

Experian (formerly TRW)
PO Box 949, Allen, TX 75013; 800-682-7654; {www.experian.com}

Trans Union
760 West Sproul Road, Springfield, PA 19064; 800-916-8800; {www.transunion.com}

If you have trouble getting satisfaction from a credit reporting agency contact: Consumer Response Center, Federal Trade Commission, CRC-240, Washington, DC 20580; 877-FTC-HELP; {www.ftc.gov}.

Get an Extra $9,500/yr to Live On

Struggling to pay bills and you are a senior or disabled? Supplemental Security Income (SSI) gives help to individuals or couples who are age 65 or older, or blind, or disabled. Assistance is also available for disabled and blind children. Benefits include money on a monthly basis and, depending on the state you live in, benefits and services such as, Medicaid, Medicare premiums, food stamps, and other social services.

To be eligible, certain requirements must be met. Applicants must be US citizens, but there are certain exceptions for non-citizens. Resources, cash and savings, cannot exceed $2,000 for individuals and $3,000 for couples. Monthly-unearned income must be below $545 for individuals and $817 for couples. Amounts are higher for people who have earned income. The amount of the SSI benefits varies depending on income, but the maximum benefit for an individual is $530 and $796 for a couple.

To meet the requirement of blind or disabled, one of the following must hold true:

- have corrected vision of 20/200 or less in the better eye;
- the field of vision is less than 20 degrees;
- a physical or mental impairment that keeps a person from performing any "substantial" work and is expected to last 12 months or result in death (A job that pays $780/month, $1,300 if blind, is generally considered substantial work);
- a child's impairment must result in "marked and severe functional limitations" and must be expected to last 12 months or result in death;

Resources that are considered include real estate, bank accounts, cash, and stocks and bonds. There are some things that are not considered to be in the category of resources. Some examples are:

- the home you live in and the land it is on;
- life insurance policies with a face value of $1,500 or less;
- your car usually does not count, depending on its use and value;
- up to $1,500 in burial funds for you and up to $1,500 in burial funds for your spouse may not count;
- burial plots for you and members of your immediate family; and
- if you are blind or have a disability, some items may not count if you plan to use them to work or earn extra income. If the applicant is attempting to sell property or another resource, they may be able to get SSI during the time they are trying to sell it.

Income is the money you have coming in, such as wages, Social Security benefits, and pensions. It also includes non-cash items received, like food, clothing, or shelter. If you are married, they look at the income of your spouse and things he or she owns. They look at the parent's income and the things they own if the applicant is less than 18 years old. For example, they do not count:

- the first $20 of most income received in a month;
- the first $65 a month earned from working and half of the amount over $65;
- food stamps;
- shelter received from private non-profit organizations; and
- most home energy assistance.

The basic amount of the monthly benefit is the same across the nation, but many states add money to that amount. Blind or disabled people who apply for SSI may be eligible for special services from their state. Some of those services are counseling, job training, and help in finding work. If you receive Medicare and have low-income and few resources, your Medicare premiums may be paid by your state. In some cases, other Medicare expenses such as deductibles and co-insurance will also be covered. For this information, contact your state or local welfare office or Medicaid agency.

The following states do not supplement Federal SSI payments: Arkansas, Georgia, Kansas, Mississippi, North Mariana Islands, Tennessee, and West Virginia. For the rest of the states, a separate application may need to be made for supplemental payments.

To apply for SSI and/or supplemental benefits, visit your local Social Security office, or call 800-772-1213 for an appointment with a Social Security representative who will help you apply. A list of each of the states Social Security offices, go to {http://s3abaca.ssa.gov/pro/fol/fol-home.html}.

$100 to Pay Your Heating Bill

The state of Michigan offers a home heating bill tax credit (that means you pay less in taxes) for people who are low income, receiving public assistance or unemployment.

Call your state department of taxation to learn about tax credits available to you. Michigan Department of Treasury, Lansing, MI 48956; 800-487-7000; {www.michigan.gov/treasury}.
To download a 12-page form: {www.michigan.gov/documents/mcr7f_2859_7.pdf}.

Free Voice Mail Services

If you are unemployed and the phone company cut off your phone, how does a potential employer get in touch with you? Free voice mail. You can get set up with your own personalized greeting, as well as get a security code and instructions on how you can retrieve your messages 24 hours a day. The program is available in over 27 cities and is growing.

See if you're eligible for your area by contacting Community Technology Institute, P.O. Box 61385, Seattle, WA 98121; 206-441-7872; Fax: 206-441-4784; {www.cvm.org}.

Free Tax Help For Seniors

It is nice to get special treatment every now and then, and tax time is no exception. The Tax Counseling for the Elderly program was designed to provide free taxpayer assistance to those ages 60 and above. The staff usually consists of retired individuals associated with nonprofit organizations that receive grants from the IRS to perform this service. Often they provide counseling in retirement homes, neighborhood sites or private houses of the homebound.

For information on the Tax Counseling for the Elderly program near you, contact your local IRS office, call the hotline at 800-829-1040; {www.irs.gov}.

$84 Towards Your Phone Bill

Link-Up and ***Lifeline*** are two government programs that offers up to $84 a year in discounts on your monthly bill and a 50% reduction for your hook-up service, or $30 which ever is less. These programs have income requirements that vary from state to state.

Ask your phone company about them or contact your state Utility Commissioner listed in the blue pages of your phone book or Federal Communications Commission, 445 12th St., SW, Washington, DC 20554; 888-CALL-FCC, 202-418-0190; {www.fcc.gov}.

$500 Extra for Seniors and Disabled

The state of Pennsylvania offers up to $500 for seniors and people with disabilities who pay property taxes or rent. If you live in Pennsylvania, contact Department of Aging, 555 Walnut St., 5th Floor, Harrisburg, PA 17101; 717-783-1549. If you live elsewhere, contact your state Office on Aging listed in the blue pages of your phone book, or your state Department of Revenue.

Free Gov't Benefits Check Up

The National Council on the Aging offers a service to seniors so that they may find available programs to help them pay for prescriptions, health care, utilities, and other related things. This free service is called Benefits CheckUp and it can be found at {www.benefitscheckup.org}.

At the site, a simple and confidential questionnaire is filled out, and then it will check over 1,000 programs to see if any are available based on the information given. This does not require a name, address, phone, or social security number. It only takes a few minutes to complete and may save you lots of money in the long run!

$400/wk When You're Out of Work

In Massachusetts, you can receive up to $402 a week for 30 weeks, and in special circumstances they will extend the benefits another 18 weeks. Mass lay-offs, base closings, trade agreements, and high unemployment in your state, all affect your ability to find and keep a job. If you are out of work, take advantage of unemployment insurance. This is the government's first line of defense against the ripple effects of unemployment.

All states are required to provide benefits up to 26 weeks and some extend them further. If your state has very high unemployment, you may be eligible for 13 additional weeks of compensation. If you lost your job because of an increase in imports, you may qualify to have your benefits extended up to an extra 52 weeks if you are in a job-retraining program.

Your weekly benefit amount depends upon your past wages within certain minimum and maximum limits that vary from state to state. Many states also will add additional funds depending upon the number of dependents. If you are denied benefits, learn about the appeal process, as your chances of winning are good. For more information, contact your state Unemployment Insurance office listed in the blue pages of your phone book.

Free Directory Assistance

Directory assistance can cost up to 95 cents per request and an additional 50 cents for the connection. To assist persons with visual, hearing, or other disabilities, local telephone companies offer directory and operator assistance exemptions. Simply request and complete a form from the local telephone company and have your physician complete the appropriate section. When you return the form to the phone company, you'll be eligible for the exemptions.

Contact the business office of your local telephone company.

$700 for Your Utility Bills

The legislature in Massachusetts passed a law giving discounts up to $700 on heating bills for families making up to $30,000, along with up to 40% discount on electric bills, $108 off telephone bills, and $100 off oil bills. It's in the Massachusetts Budget for FY 99 (Line Item 4403-2110). Also:

- **Mason County** in the state of Washington offers a utility bill discount of $12.00 a month for seniors making less than $18,000, and disabled people at 125% of poverty. Contact Public Utility District #3, 307 W. Cota St., Shelton, WA 98584; 800-424-5555; {www2.callatg.com}.
- **Phoenix, Arizona** offers discounts on utility bills, discounts on phone bills and even help paying utility deposits and heating repairs for low-income residents through the Arizona Public Service Energy Support Program, P.O. Box 6123-086Z, Phoenix, AZ 85008; 800-582-5706; {www.aps.com}.
- **Ameritech in Illinois** gives a 100% discount on connection charges and $5.25 off the monthly bill to low-income residents. To sign up, call Ameritech at 800-244-4444; {www.ameritech.com}.
- **Ohio** offers reduced or free phone hook up service and possibly $8.00 a month off your phone bill for low-income residents. Contact Public Utilities Commission, 180 E. Broad St., Columbus, OH 43215; 800-686-7826; {www.puco.ohio.gov/Consumer/PIC/assistance.html}.
- **Pennsylvania Bell Atlantic** offers free telephone hook up and $9.00 monthly discount to low-income residents through Lifeline and Universal Telephone Assistance Programs. To sign up, call 800-272-1006.

Contact your state's utilities office in the blue pages of your phone book to find out about special discounts on your gas, electric, cable or telephone in your state.

Government Supported Agencies Offer Free Money And Help When You Don't Know Where To Turn

If you need emergency money to pay a bill, or for housing, training, health care, or just additional support, these organizations can be of service and they are likely to have an office near you. Although these are private organizations, they do receive a portion of their funds from your favorite Uncle Sam.

1) Community Action Agencies

Nearly 1,000 agencies around the country received funds from the U.S. Government's Community Services Block Grants to offer education, counseling, employment, training, food packages, vouchers, weatherization and utility assistance, life skills, affordable housing, transportation, furnishings, recreation, emergency services, information and referral services. To locate an agency serving your area, contact: National Association Of Community Action Agencies. 1100 17th St., NW, Suite 500, Washington, DC 20036; 202-265-7546; Fax: 202-265-8850; Email: {info@communityactionpartnership.com}; {www.communityactionpartnership.com}.

2) Catholic Charities

Over 14,000 local organizations offer a variety of services for many different communities including: child care, elderly services, emergency financial services, emergency shelter, food pantries, housing assistance, job training, out-of-home care, parenting education, youth services, rental assistance, utility assistance, and health care. For an office near you, contact Catholic Charities USA, 1731 King Street #200, Alexandria, VA 22314; 703-549-1390; Fax: 703-549-1656; {www.catholiccharitiesusa.org}.

3) Salvation Army

Families in need can receive a wide range of services including: utility assistance, transitional housing, emergency food, furnishings, Section 8 tenant counseling, counseling, rent or mortgage assistance, and even clothing. Most services are for households who are below 150% of the poverty level (about $24,000 for family of 4). For an office near you, contact Salvation Army National Headquarters, 615 Slaters Lane, P.O. Box 269, Alexandria, VA 22313; 703-684-5500; Fax: 703-684-3478; {www.salvationarmy.org}.

Free Private Eye to Find Missing Children

Besides location and investigative services, as well as mediation services for families estranged by parental abduction, you can also get free kidnapping prevention programs and referral and support services. Contact Find-A-Child of America, Inc., P.O. Box 277, New Paltz, NY 12561; 800-I-AM-LOST; 914-255-1848; 800-A-WAY-OUT (for mediation and support); {www.childfindofamerica.org}.

$1,000 While You Wait For Gov't Money

General Public Assistance or just Public Assistance (it is known by many different names) is a welfare program offered in 42 states. This is a program of last resort for people either waiting to qualify for other government programs such as disability benefits, or who do not qualify for any programs, yet need money to live. The program eligibility and benefit levels vary

within and across state lines. In some states, this benefit is only available in certain areas. There are strict income and asset levels that you must meet to qualify.

In Kansas, General Assistance pays families $278 per month while they are waiting for other government money. In California, the benefit is $225. Contact your local welfare office, your state Department of Social Service, or your state Temporary Assistance to Needy Families office to see what your state offers and the eligibility requirements.

Dress For Success For Free

Looking for work and can't afford the right wardrobe? There are about 50 non-profit organizations around the country that provide women with two separate outfits for free. One can be used to go to an interview and the other can be used once you get the job. The following organization acts as a clearinghouse for similar opportunities around the country. Bottomless Closet, 445 North Wells, Chicago, IL 60610; 312-527-9664; Fax: 312-527-4305; {www.bottomlesscloset.org}.

Career Gear, 11 Pennsylvania Plaza, New York, NY 10001; 212-273-1194; Email: {info@careergear.org}; {www.careergear.org/}. This organization has locations in New York, Michigan, Ohio, Florida, Illinois, Minneapolis, and Washington, DC.

Dress for Success, 32 East 31st Street, 7th Floor, New York, NY 10016; 212-532-1922, ext. 23; Email: {newyork@dressforsuccess.org}; {www.dressforsuccess.org/}. This organization has locations in almost every state and internationally.

StyleWorks, 655 Fulton Street, #350, Brooklyn, NY 11217; 718-398-1264; {www.styleworks.org/}.

Suited For Change, 1712 I Street, NW, Suite B100, Washington, DC 20006-3750; 202-293-0351; {www.suitedforchange.org}.

10% Off Airline Tickets for Seniors

Every airline offers discounts to seniors amounting to usually 10%. What happens, though, is that some of the airlines' special offers may be exempt from the discount. It is best to see what the lowest available rate is and then inquire about the discount.

All the major airlines also offer coupon books for seniors that are four round-trip tickets good for wherever the airline flies. The price of the coupon books is around $540. In many instances, the airline only requires that one person meet the age requirement for a discount, so your companion can receive the lower rate as well.

10-50% Off Hotel Bills for Seniors

Almost all major hotel chains offer discounts from 10-30% off the cost of rooms. Some require that you belong to AARP or AAA, so it is best to call ahead and ask.

Three hotel chains, Ramada Inn {www.ramada.com}, Hilton {www.hilton.com} and Red Roof Inns {www.redroof.com} offer special deals to seniors who frequent their hotels. Ramada's Best Years Club charges $15 for a lifetime membership fee. The fee entitles you to 25% off regular two double bed room rates, plus you receive points redeemable for travel and prizes (800-672-6232; available at most Ramadas).

Hilton Senior HHonors program charges $50 ($40 annual renewal fee), and seniors receive up to 50% off rooms and 20% off hotel restaurants (800-492-3232). Red Roof has a lifetime Redicard for seniors that costs $10. The card gets you 10% off rooms, plus 3 $5 off coupons for lodging (800-843-7663).

50% Off Camping Bills For Seniors

Almost all states offer discounts to seniors at state parks. Entrance fees are usually waived for seniors, or states like Illinois offer 50% off camping fees. Eighteen states have no residency requirements to receive the discount, so if you are planning a cross country camping trip, contact the state Parks Department to find out about eligibility criteria.

For those wanting to camp in the National Forest, the Golden Age Passport is available to those 62 and over. For $10 you receive free lifetime admission to the parks, plus 50% off on camping and many other services. The Passport is available at all National Forests.

10-15% Off When You Travel Bills

All car rental chains offer senior discounts, but again AARP or AAA membership may be required. The amount of discount varies from location to location, but usually is 10%. You should call ahead to see if a discount is available. Some chains also require reservations 24 hours in advance.

For those that prefer to leave the driving to others, two other discount programs include AMTRAK and Greyhound. Amtrak offers 15% off any fare available to those 62 and older (800-USA-RAIL). Greyhound has an 8% discount for people 55 and over (800-231-2222).

10% Off Your Restaurant Bill

The Early Bird specials can happen all day once you hit a certain age. Many restaurant chains offer special deals for seniors. Most restaurant chains are independently owned and operated, but they usually follow the recommendations from the headquarters.

Places like Denny's, Bob Evan's, and International House of Pancakes frequently offer seniors a reduced price menu. Other chains, such as Applebee's, Kentucky Fried Chicken, and Wendy's, often give seniors a 10% discount on their meals. It never hurts to ask if a discount is offered.

Free Hunting and Fishing Licenses For Seniors

Practically every state has a special license rate for seniors. States such as Alabama, Alaska, Delaware, Georgia, Kansas, and others do not require that people age 65 and over to carry a fishing and hunting license. Other states offer seniors, on average, half off the cost of licenses. Inquire where you usually purchase these licenses to learn what age you need to be to receive the discount and the specific details.

10-100% Off Eye Glasses Bills for Seniors

Pearle Vision Centers offer 50% off either the lenses or frames when you purchase a complete set of glasses to people 50-59, 60% off to those 60-69, 70% to those 70-79, and so on until seniors reach 100 and they give them 100% off either the lenses or frames when they purchase a complete set of glasses. Lens Crafters and Eye Glass Factory also offer a 10% discount to seniors, and Sears Optical Centers give 15% off to AARP members. Now it makes seeing clearly less costly.

Discounts On Your Banking Bills

First Citizens Bank has **Senior Quest Accounts** where customers 60 and over receive unlimited check writing, no per check charge, interest bearing checking, no monthly service charge, free safe deposit box, no ATM fees, free cashier's checks, travelers' checks, and money orders. They even offer special rates on 6 and 12 month CD's, no annual fee credit card, free direct deposit and discount brokerage fees, with some of these services requiring a minimum balance. Not a bad deal. Other banks offer similar services, with most offering free checks, no minimum balance, and unlimited check writing.

$5,000 For Musicians and Singers to Pay Their Bills

Assistance is available to financial needy New York residents once prominent in opera and classical music through the Bagby Foundation for the Musical Arts, Inc. The Foundation also provides monetary support for coaching assistance to students desiring to make their professional opera debut.

Contact The Bagby Foundation for the Musical Arts, Inc., 501 5th Ave., Suite 1401, New York, NY 10017; 212-986-6094.

To sign up for this service, contact the customer service representative at your local telephone company.

Christian Scientists Get Free Money

The New Horizons Foundation provides financial assistance to residents of Los Angeles County, CA, who are over 65 years of age and active Christian Scientists. Contact: New Horizons Foundation, c/o Gifford & Dearing, 700 S. Flower St., Suite 1222, Los Angeles, CA 90017-4160; 213-626-4481.

Grants and camperships are available through the Sunnyside Foundation, Inc. to underprivileged Christian Science children under the age of 20 who regularly attend Sunday School and are Texas residents. Contact Sunnyside Foundation, Inc., 8222 Douglas Ave., Suite 501, Dallas, TX 75225-5936; 214-692-5686.

Extra Money For Pittsburgh-Area Jewish Families in Need

Financial assistance is offered to needy Jewish families residing in the Pittsburgh area through the Jewish Family Assistance Fund for living, personal, food and medical expenses. Contact Jewish Family Assistance Fund, 5743 Bartlett St., Pittsburgh, PA 15217-1515; 412-521-3237.

50% Off Your Phone Bill

Under the Federal Communication Commission's Link-Up America and Lifeline programs, low-income households seeking telephone service are given a 50% discount on local connection charges, and may be able to pay installment payments on the remaining charge. These programs are available in most states.

Extra Money For Indiana Presbyterians

The Frank L. and Laura L. Smock Foundation offers Presbyterian Indiana residents who are ailing, physically disabled, blind, needy or elderly medical and nursing care assistance.

Contact Frank L. and Laura L. Smock Foundation, c/o Norwest Bank Indiana, N.A., P.O. Box 960, Fort Wayne, IN 46801-6632; 219-461-6451.

$1,000 Extra for Seniors

1. The de Kay Foundation offers financial subsidies for living expenses to needy NY, NJ and CT residents with no assets. Applications must be submitted by social service agencies. Contact The de Kay Foundation, 1211 Avenue of the Americas, New York, NY 10036; Attn: Jean P. Wilhelm; 212-789-5255.

2. Monetary assistance is available for living expenses such as food and medicine through the Sarah A.W. Devens Trust to economically disadvantaged women over age 65 residing in MA. Contact Sarah A.W. Devens Trust, c/o Rice, Heard & Bigelow, Inc., 50 Congress St., Suite 1025, Boston, MA 02109; 617-557-7415.

3. Supplemental monthly income is available to elderly indigent residents of the Southeastern U.S. through the Alfred I. Dumont Foundation. Contact Alfred I. duPont Foundation, 1650 Prudential Dr., Suite 302, Jacksonville, FL 32207; 904-858-3123.

$2,000 For Music Teachers in Need

Emergency aid for medical needs is available to U.S. music teachers through the Presser Foundation. Assistance is primarily given to retired teachers. Contact Presser Foundation, 385 Lancaster Ave., #205, Haverford, PA 19041; 610-652-9030.

Extra Money For Masons

The Portland Area Acacia Fund provides relief assistance is to distressed Masons and their widows and orphans living in Oregon. Contact Portland Valley Acacia Fund, 709 SW 15th Ave., Portland, OR 97205; 503-228-9405

Money For Veterans

The Department of Veterans Affairs hotline can provide you with information on such programs as life insurance, comprehensive dental and medical care, nursing homes, home loan programs, burial services, and more.

Contact Department of Veterans Affairs, 810 Vermont Ave., NW, Washington, DC 20420; 800-827-1000; {www.va.gov}.

$2,000 For Being Mugged

Millions of people and their families are victimized by crime every year in the U.S. And to better address the growing belief that the law was better at protecting the rights of criminals than those of the victims, Congress enacted a law to establish a Crime Victims Fund to compensate innocent victims of violent crime. Part of the money is given to help compensate victims or their families for costs relating to such crimes as muggings, sexual crimes, and even murder.

One of the nice things about this money is that it does not come out of the pockets of taxpayers; rather it is collected from the criminals themselves through criminal fines, forfeited bail bonds, penalty fees, and forfeited literary profits. Each state gets a portion of this fund each year.

Part of the money from these funds is given out to victims as direct cash payments to help compensate for costs related to the violent crimes. Contact the office in your state if you find yourself the victim of a violent crime and need money to help pay for such related costs as medical bills, lost wages, and funeral expenses. For more information you may contact:

- Office for Victims of Crime Resource Center, National Criminal Justice Reference Service, P.O. Box 6000, Rockville, MD 20849; 800-627-6872 (8:30 am to 7 pm EST); {www.ncjrs.org}.
- Office for Victims of Crime, U.S. Department of Justice, 810 7th St., NW, Washington, DC 20530; 800-331-0075; {www.usdoj.gov/crimevictims.htm}

Alabama

Alabama Crime Victims Compensation Commission
RSA Union Building
100 North Union Street, Suite 736
P.O. Box 1548
Montgomery, AL 36102-1548
334-242-4007
Fax: 334-353-1401
www.agencies.state.al.us/crimevictims
Victim's Compensation provides monetary compensation for victims and victim's survivors for a variety of expenses. Receive up to $15,000 (as of May 1, 1998) with limitations on certain expenses. The award may cover the following: medical or psychiatric care, pay due to work loss, funeral expenses and rehabilitation of the victim.

Victim Assistance
Office of the Attorney General
Alabama State House
11 South Union Street, Third Floor
Montgomery, AL 36130
334-242-5811
Victim Hotline: 800-626-7676
Fax: 334-242-0712
www.ago.state.al.us/victim.cfm
Victim Assistance provides direct victim assistance as well as referrals to victim/witness programs that include help with crime counseling, victim's rights, advocacy and understanding the court process.

Alaska

Violent Crimes Compensation Board
P.O. Box 111200
Juneau, AK 99811
907-465-3040
Fax: 907-465-2379
www.dps.state.ak.us/vccb/htm

Victim's Compensation provides monetary compensation for victims and victim's survivors for a variety of expenses. The program may pay emergency victim compensation up to $1500 for immediate living expenses. The program also provides compensation for medical expenses, crime related counseling, lost wages, and funeral costs.

Victim Assistance
State Of Alaska Department Of Public Safety
Council on Domestic Violence and Sexual Assault
P.O. Box 111200
Juneau, AK 99811-1200
907-465-4356
Fax: 907-465-3627
www.dps.state.ak.us/cdvsa/index.htm
Victim's Compensation provides monetary compensation for victims and victim's survivors for a variety of expenses. The program provides planning and coordination of services to victims of domestic violence or sexual assault or to their families and to perpetrators of domestic violence and sexual assault and to provide for crisis intervention and prevention programs.

Arizona
Victim Compensation
Arizona Criminal Justice Commission
3737 North 7th Street, Suite 260
Phoenix, AZ 85024
602-230-0252
Fax: 602-728-0752
www.dps.state.az.us/azvictims
Victim's Compensation provides monetary compensation for victims and victim's survivors for a variety of expenses. The State of Arizona has a Crime Victim Compensation Program that offers financial help to victims of crime. Allowable expenses include medical expenses, mental health, loss of wages, and funeral expenses.

Victim Assistance
3737 North 7th Street, Suite 260
Phoenix, AZ 85014
602-230-0252
602-223-2465
Fax: 602-728-0752
www.acjc.state.az.us/rules.html
Victim Assistance provides direct victim assistance as well as referrals to victim/witness programs that include help with crime counseling, victim's rights, advocacy and understanding the court process. Victims may receive assistance with temporary shelter, petty cash, counseling and notification services.

Arkansas
Victim Compensation
323 Center Street, Suite 200
Little Rock, AR 72201
501-682-2007
501-682-1323
800-482-8982
Fax: 501-682-5313
www.ag.state.ar.us
Victim's Compensation provides monetary compensation for victims and victim's survivors for a variety of expenses. The program provides assistance to victims for medical and dental costs, wok loss, funeral expenses and crime scene cleanup.

Victim Justice and Assistance Grants Office
Suite 404, 1515 Building
1515 West Seventh Street
P.O. Box 3278
Little Rock, AR 72203
501-682-5153
Fax: 501-682-5155
www.state.ar.us/dfa/intergovernmental
Victim Assistance provides direct victim assistance as well as referrals to victim/witness programs that include help with crime counseling, victim's rights, advocacy and understanding the court process.

California
California Victim Compensation and Government Claims Board
Victim Compensation Program
P.O. Box 3036
Sacramento, CA 95812-3036
916-323-3432
Fax: 916-327-2933
www.boc.ca.gov
Victim's Compensation provides monetary compensation for victims and victim's survivors

for a variety of expenses. Victims may receive up to $70,000 per claim for victims to pay for medical/dental expenses, lost wages, funerals or job retraining.

Victim Assistance
Office of Criminal Justice Planning
1130 K Street, LL300
Sacramento, CA 95814
916-324-9100
Fax: 916-327-8711
www.ocjp.ca.gov/programs/prgms_brvw.htm
Victim Assistance provides direct victim assistance as well as referrals to victim/witness programs that include help with crime counseling, victim's rights, advocacy and understanding the court process. Victim assistant sites are located throughout the state.

Colorado

Victim Compensation
Department of Public Safety
Division of Criminal Justice
700 Kipling St., Suite 1000
Denver, CO 80215
303-239-4442
800-282-1080
Fax: 303-239-4411
www.cdpsweb.state.co.us/ovp/comp.htm
Victim's Compensation provides monetary compensation for victims and victim's survivors for a variety of expenses. Victims may receive up to $20,000 for out of pocket expenses not covered by insurance or other collateral resources, or up to $1,000 for emergency awards. The Department of Public Safety also administers the Victim Assistance program. Victim Assistance provides direct victim assistance as well as referrals to victim/witness programs that include help with crime counseling, victim's rights, advocacy and understanding the court process.

Connecticut

Victim Compensation
31 Cooke Street
Plainville, CT 06062
860-747-6070
800-822-8428 (in state)
Fax: 860-747-6428
www.jud.state.ct.us
Victim's Compensation provides monetary compensation for victims and victim's survivors for a variety of expenses. Compensation is provided in the form of reimbursement for all costs that are not covered by collateral sources. For survivors of homicide victims, up to $25,000 may be paid; for other crime victims up to $15,000 may be paid.

Delaware

Victim Compensation
240 N. James Street, Suite 203
Newport, DE 19804
302-995-8383
800-464-HELP
Fax: 302-995-8387
www.courts.state.de.us/vccb
Victim's Compensation provides monetary compensation for victims and victim's survivors for a variety of expenses. Financial help is available to assist victims and survivors of crime with payment of the following types of crime-related expenses: medical expenses, wage loss, counseling expenses, and other crime-related expenses.

Victim Assistance
Carvel State Office Building
820 North French Street
Wilmington, DE 19801
302-577-5030
302-577-8693
Fax: 302-577-3440
www.state.de.us/cjc/index.html
The Victims of Crime Act Formula (VOCA) Crime Victim Assistance Grant Program (authorized by the Victims of Crime Act of 1984) was established to support the provision of direct services to innocent victims of violent crime and to provide assistance.

District of Columbia

Victim Compensation
515 5th Street NW
Building A, Room 203
Washington, DC 20001
202-879-4216
Fax: 202-879-4230
www.dcbar.org/dcsc/victim.html

Victim's Compensation provides monetary compensation for victims and victim's survivors for a variety of expenses. Victims may receive up to $25,000 for compensation for medical expenses, counseling, lost wages and other victim expenses.

Victim Assistance
Metropolitan Police Department
John A. Wilson Building
1350 Pennsylvania Avenue, NW
Washington, DC 20004
202-727-6537
Fax: 202-727-1617
http://mpdc.dc.gov/serv/victims/victims.shtm
Victim Assistance provides direct victim assistance, as well as referrals to victim/witness programs that include help with crime counseling, victim's rights, advocacy and understanding the court process.

Florida
The Bureau of Victims' Compensation
Office of the Attorney General
The Capitol PL-01
Tallahassee, FL 32399-1050
850-414-3300
800-226-6667
Fax: 850-487-1595
legal.firn.edu/victims/compensation.html
Victim's Compensation provides monetary compensation for victims and victim's survivors for a variety of expenses. Injured crime victims may be eligible for financial assistance for medical care, lost income, mental health services, funeral expenses and other out-of-pocket expenses directly related to the injury.

Victim Assistance
Florida Attorney General
State of Florida
The Capitol
Tallahassee, FL 32399-1050
850-487-1963
Fax: 850-487-2564
legal.firn.edu/victims/index.html
Victim Assistance provides direct victim assistance, as well as referrals to victim/witness programs that include help with crime counseling, victim's rights, advocacy and understanding the court process.

Georgia
Victim Compensation
Criminal Justice Coordinating Council
503 Oak Place, Suite 540
Atlanta, GA 30349
404-559-4949
Fax: 404-559-4960
www.ganet.org/cjcc
Victim's Compensation provides monetary compensation for victims and victim's survivors for a variety of expenses. Victims may receive up to $10,000 for medical expenses, counseling, funeral costs and lost wages. The Criminal Justice Department also administers the Victim Assistance program. Victim Assistance provides direct victim assistance as well as referrals to victim/witness programs that include help with crime counseling, victim's rights, advocacy and understanding the court process.

Guam
Victim Witness Ayuda Services (VWAS)
Suite 202, C & A Professional Building
259 Martyr Street
Agana, GU 96910
9-1-671-475-3324, ext. 285
Fax: 9-1-671-472-2493
www.justice.gov.gu/dol/agpro1a.htm
The victim program provides information and referral, emotional support, transportation and other victim related needs.

Hawaii
Victim Compensation
333 Queen Street, #404
Honolulu, HI 96813
808-587-1143
Fax: 808-587-1146
www.ehawaiigov.org/psd/cvcc/html/
Victim's Compensation provides monetary compensation for victims and victim's survivors for a variety of expenses. Victims may receive up to $10,000 for medical expenses, counseling, lost wages, moving expenses, crime-scene cleanup and funeral costs.

Victim Assistance
Crime Prevention and Justice Assistance Division
Department of the Attorney General
235 South Beretania Street
Suite 401
Honolulu, HI 96813
808-586-1152
800-331-0075
Fax: 808-586-1373
www.cpja.ag.state.hi.us
Victim Assistance provides direct victim assistance as well as referrals to victim/witness programs that include help with crime counseling, victim's rights, advocacy and understanding the court process.

Idaho

Victim Compensation
P.O. Box 83720
Boise, ID 83720-0041
208-334-6080
Fax: 208-332-7559
www2.state.id.us/iic/crimevictims.htm
Victim's Compensation provides monetary compensation for victims and victim's survivors for a variety of expenses. The Crime Victims Compensation Program provides funds for expenses of up to $25,000 for medical expenses, counseling, wage loss, funeral costs and death benefits.

Victim Assistance
815 West Washington
Boise, ID 83702
208-334-5580
Fax: 208-332-7353
www2.state.id.us/crimevictim
Victim Assistance provides direct victim assistance as well as referrals to victim/witness programs that include help with crime counseling, victim's rights, advocacy and understanding the court process. The program also provides emergency shelter and crisis services for victims.

Illinois

Victim Compensation
Crime Victims Services Division
Office of the Illinois Attorney General
100 West Randolph St., 13th Floor
Chicago, IL 60601
312-814-2518
Fax: 312-814-5079
www.ag.state.il.us/crimevictims/crime.htm
Victim's Compensation provides monetary compensation for victims and victim's survivors for a variety of expenses. The Illinois Crime Victim Compensation Program can provide up to $27,000 worth of assistance for financial losses incurred due to violent crime.

Victim Assistance
Illinois Criminal Justice Information Authority
120 S. Riverside Plaza
Suite 1016
Chicago, IL 60606
312-793-8550
888-425-4248
Fax: 312-793-8422
www.icjia.state.il.us
Victim Assistance provides direct victim assistance as well as referrals to victim/witness programs that include help with crime counseling, victim's rights, advocacy and understanding the court process.

Indiana

Victim Assistance
Criminal Justice Institute
One North Capitol Avenue
Suite 1000
Indianapolis, IN 46204
317-232-1233
800-353-1484
Fax: 317-233-3912
www.state.in.us/cji
Victim's Compensation provides monetary compensation for victims and victim's survivors for a variety of expenses. The Victim Compensation Fund assists victims or their dependents with medical expenses, funeral expenses, lost wages and psychological counseling up to $15,000. The Criminal Justice Department also administers the Victim Assistance program. Victim Assistance provides direct victim assistance as well as referrals to victim/witness programs that include help with crime counseling, victim's rights, advocacy and understanding the court process.

Iowa
Crime Victim Assistance Division
Department of Justice
100 Court Ave., #100
Des Moines, IA 50319
800-373-5044
515-281-5044
Fax: 515-281-8199
www.state.ia.us/government/ag/cva.html
Victim's Compensation provides monetary compensation for victims and victim's survivors for a variety of expenses. The program will pay for up to $15,000 in medical expenses, $3,000 for counseling, $7,500 for funeral expenses and other benefits. The Department of Justice administers both the Victim Compensation and Victim Assistance programs. Victim Assistance provides direct victim assistance as well as referrals to victim/witness programs that include help with crime counseling, victim's rights, advocacy and understanding the court process.

Kansas
Crime Victim's Compensation Board
700 SW Jackson, Suite 400
Topeka, KS 66603-3756
785-296-2359
800-828-9745
Fax: 785-296-0652
www.ink.org/public/ksag/contents/crime/cvcbrochure.htm
Victim's Compensation provides monetary compensation for victims and victim's survivors for a variety of expenses. Victims may receive up to $25,000 in compensation and funeral expenses.

Victim Assistance
120 S.W. 10th Ave., 2nd Floor
Topeka, KS 66612-1597
785-296-2215
Fax: 785-296-6296
www.ink.org/public/ksag/contents/crime/kvaa.htm
Victim Assistance provides direct victim assistance as well as referrals to victim/witness programs that include help with crime counseling, victim's rights, advocacy and understanding the court process. The Kansas Organization for Victim Assistance's mission is to promote fair treatment of crime victims.

Kentucky
Crime Victims Compensation Board
130 Brighton Park Blvd.
Frankfort, KY 40601-3714
502-564-2290
800-469-2120
Fax: 502-573-4817
www.state.ky.us/agencies/cppr/cvcb
Victim's Compensation provides monetary compensation for victims and victim's survivors for a variety of expenses. Victims may receive up to $25,000 for medical expenses, counseling and burial services.

Victim Assistance
Victims Advocacy Division
Office of the Attorney General
1024 Capital Center Drive
Frankfort, KY 40601
502-696-5312
502-564-3251
Fax: 502-564-5244
www.law.state.ky.us/victims/rights.htm
Victim Assistance provides direct victim assistance as well as referrals to victim/witness programs that include help with crime counseling, victim's rights, advocacy and understanding the court process. The program provides information and support for victims and witnesses.

Louisiana
Victim Compensation
Crime Victims Reparations Board
Louisiana Commission on Law Enforcement
1885 Wooddale Blvd. Rm. 708
Baton Rouge, LA 70806
225-925-4437
888-6VICTIM
Fax: 225-925-1998
www.cole.state.la.us/cvr.htm
Victim's Compensation provides monetary compensation for victims and victim's survivors for a variety of expenses. Victims may receive up to $25,000 for medical costs, loss of earnings, counseling, childcare and funeral expenses.

Victim Assistance
Louisiana Commission on Law Enforcement
1885 Woodale Blvd., Room 1230
Baton Rouge, LA 70806
225-925-1757
www.cole.state.la.us/cva.htm
Victim Assistance provides direct victim assistance as well as referrals to victim/witness programs that include help with crime counseling, victim's rights, advocacy and understanding the court process.

Maine

Victims' Compensation Board
Department of the Attorney General
6 State House Station
Augusta, ME 04330-0006
207-624-7882
800-903-7882
Fax: 207-624-7730
www.state.me.us/ag/victim.htm
Victim's Compensation provides monetary compensation for victims and victim's survivors for a variety of expenses. Victims may receive up to $7,500 for medical expenses, counseling, lost wages and funeral costs. The Department of Attorney General also administers the Victim Assistance program. Victim Assistance provides direct victim assistance as well as referrals to victim/witness programs that include help with crime counseling, victim's rights, advocacy and understanding the court process.

Maryland

Victim Compensation
6776 Reisterstown Road, Suite 312
Baltimore, MD 21215-2341
410-585-3010
Fax: 410-764-3815
www.dpscs.state.md.us/cicb
Victim's Compensation provides monetary compensation for victims and victim's survivors for a variety of expenses. Victims may receive up to $45,000 for medical expenses, counseling, dependency and funeral expenses.

Victim Assistance
Department of Human Services
Saratoga State Center
311 Saratoga Street, 2nd Floor
Baltimore, MD 21201-3521
410-767-7565
Fax: 410-333-0256
www.dhr.state.md.us/victim
Victim Assistance provides direct victim assistance as well as referrals to victim/witness programs that include help with crime counseling, victim's rights, advocacy and understanding the court process. The program also provides victims a 24-hour hotline, shelter, counseling, and legal assistance.

Massachusetts

Victim Compensation
Office of Attorney General
One Ashburton Place
Boston, MA 02108-1698
617-727-2200
Fax: 617-367-3906
www.ago.state.ma.us/victim_svc
Victim's Compensation provides monetary compensation for victims and victim's survivors for a variety of expenses. The Victim Compensation Program uses funds obtained from criminal offenders to provide financial assistance, up to $25,000 per crime, to help victims pay for uninsured medical, dental, and counseling expenses, funeral and burial costs, and lost income. The Office of Attorney General also administers the Victim Assistance program. Victim Assistance provides direct victim assistance as well as referrals to victim/witness programs that include help with crime counseling, victim's rights, advocacy and understanding the court process.

Michigan

Victim Compensation
Crime Victims Services Commission
Sixth Floor, Lewis Cass Building
320 South Walnut Street
Lansing, MI 48913
517-334-9941
Fax: 517-241-2769
www.michigan.gov/mdch
Victim's Compensation provides monetary compensation for victims and victim's survivors for a variety of expenses. Victims may receive up to $15,000 for the un-reimbursable costs of medical expenses, counseling, loss of earnings or

support, and burial assistance to survivors. The Office of Crime Victim Services also administers the Victim Assistance program. Victim Assistance provides direct victim assistance as well as referrals to victim/witness programs that include help with crime counseling, victim's rights, advocacy and understanding the court process. The program's mission is to aid crime victims, help victims apply for compensation benefits, provide services at no charge to the victim and maintain confidentiality of client-counselor and research information.

Minnesota
Victim Compensation
Minnesota Crime Victims Reparation
245 E. 6th St., #705
St. Paul, MN 55101
651-282-6256
888-622-8799
Fax: 651-296-5787
www.dps.state.mn.us/mccvs/Reparations.htm
Victim's Compensation provides monetary compensation for victims and victim's survivors for a variety of expenses. Victims may receive reparations for medical expenses, counseling, childcare, lost wages, mileage and funeral expenses.

Victim Assistance
Minnesota Center for Crime Victim Services
NCL Tower, Suite 2300
445 Minnesota Street
St. Paul, MN 55101
651-282-6256
800-622-8799
Fax: 651-296-5787
www.dps.state.mn.us/mccvs
Victim Assistance provides direct victim assistance as well as referrals to victim/witness programs that include help with crime counseling, victim's rights, advocacy and understanding the court process.

Mississippi
Victim Compensation
Department of Finance and Administration
P.O. Box 267
Jackson, MS 39205
601-359-6766
800-829-6766
Fax: 601-359-3262
www.dfa.state.ms.us/cvcompx.html
Victim's Compensation provides monetary compensation for victims and victim's survivors for a variety of expenses. Victims may receive up to $10,000 for medical care, counseling, loss of wages, and funeral costs. The Department of Finance and Administration also administers the Victim Assistance program. Victim Assistance provides direct victim assistance as well as referrals to victim/witness programs that include help with crime counseling, victim's rights, advocacy and understanding the court process.

Missouri
Victim Compensation
P.O. Box 3001
Jefferson City, MO 65102-3001
573-526-6006
800-347-6881
Fax: 573-526-4940
www.dolir.state.mo.us/wc/dolir6f.htm
Victim's Compensation provides monetary compensation for victims and victim's survivors for a variety of expenses. Compensation includes medical costs, wage loss, psychological counseling, funeral expenses and support for dependent survivors to a maximum limit of $25,000.

Missouri Victim Assistance Network
P.O. Box 2232
Jefferson City, MO 65102
573-751-4905
Fax: 573-751-5399
mova.missouri.org
Victim Assistance provides direct victim assistance as well as referrals to victim/witness programs that include help with crime counseling, victim's rights, advocacy and understanding the court process.

Montana
Victim Compensation
Montana Department of Justice
Office of Victim Services and Restorative Justice
3075 North Montana Avenue
Helena, MT 59620
406-444-3653

800-498-6455
Fax: 406-444-4722
www.doj.state.mt.us/ago/victimservices/cvindex.htm
Victim's Compensation provides monetary compensation for victims and victim's survivors for a variety of expenses. Victims may receive up to $25,000 for loss of wages, counseling, medical expenses and funeral costs.

Victim Assistance
Montana Board of Crime Control
P.O. Box 201408
Helena, MT 59620-1408
406-444-3604
Fax: 406-444-4722
www.doj.state.mt.us/ago/victimservices/cvassist.htm
Victim Assistance provides direct victim assistance as well as referrals to victim/witness programs that include help with crime counseling, victim's rights, advocacy and understanding the court process.

Nebraska
Victim Compensation
Nebraska Crime Commission
301 Centennial Mall South
P.O. Box 94946
Lincoln, NE 68509-4946
402-471-2828
Fax: 402-471-2837
www.nol.org/home/crimecom/Administration/cvrbochure.htm
Victim's Compensation provides monetary compensation for victims and victim's survivors for a variety of expenses. Victims may receive up to $10,000 for medical expenses, loss of wages, counseling and funeral costs. The Crime Commission also administers the Victim Assistance program. Victim Assistance provides direct victim assistance as well as referrals to victim/witness programs that include help with crime counseling, victim's rights, advocacy and understanding the court process.

Nevada
Victim Compensation
Victims of Crime Program
Department of Administration
555 East Washington, Suite 3200
Las Vegas, NV 89101
702-486-2740
Fax: 702-486-2825
Email: Roy L. at rleo@govmail.state.nv.us
Victim's Compensation provides monetary compensation for victims and victim's survivors for a variety of expenses. Victims may receive up to $50,000 for medical expenses, counseling, lost wages, crime-scene cleanup and funeral costs.

New Hampshire
Victim Compensation
Department of Justice
33 Capitol Street
Concord, NH 03301-6397
603-271-1284
800-300-4500 (in state)
Fax: 603-271-2110
www.state.nh.us/nhdoj/victimwitness/victserviceindex.html
Victim's Compensation provides monetary compensation for victims and victim's survivors for a variety of expenses. Victims may receive up to $10,000 for medical and dental care, counseling, lost wages, relocation expenses and funeral costs. The Department of Justice also administers the Victim Assistance program. Victim Assistance provides direct victim assistance as well as referrals to victim/witness programs that include help with crime counseling, victim's rights, advocacy and understanding the court process.

New Jersey
Victim Compensation
50 Park Place
Newark, NJ 07102
800-242-0804 Emergency calls only
973-648-2107
Fax: 973-648-7031
www.state.nj.us/victims/VCCBDIR.HTM
Victim's Compensation provides monetary compensation for victims and victim's survivors for a variety of expenses. Victims may receive up to $25,000 for medical expenses, lost wages, transportation, emergency financial assistance, and funeral costs.

Victim Assistance
State Office of Victim-Witness Advocacy
NJ Division of Criminal Justice
P.O. Box 085
Trenton, NJ 08625
609-588-7900
Fax: 609-588-7890
www.state.nj.us/lps/dcj/victimwitness/home.htm
Victim Assistance provides direct victim assistance as well as referrals to victim/witness programs that include help with crime counseling, victim's rights, advocacy and understanding the court process.

New Mexico
New Mexico Crime Victims Reparation Commission
8100 Mountain Road, NE, Suite 106
Albuquerque, NM 87110
505-841-9432
800-306-6262
Fax: 505-841-9437
www.state.nm.us/cvrc
Victim's Compensation provides monetary compensation for victims and victim's survivors for a variety of expenses. The Commissions primary mission is to provide financial assistance to victims of violent crime in regard to expenses incurred as a result of being victimized. The Crime Victims Reparation Commission also administers the Victim Assistance program. Victim Assistance provides direct victim assistance as well as referrals to victim/witness programs that include help with crime counseling, victim's rights, advocacy and understanding the court process.

New York
Crime Victim Board
Victim Compensation Albany Office
845 Central Avenue
Albany, NY 12206
518-457-8727
800-247-8035
Fax: 518-457-8658

Victim Compensation Buffalo Office
65 Court Street
Buffalo, NY 14202
716-847-7992
800-247-8035
Fax: 716-847-7995

Victim Compensation Brooklyn Office
55 Hanson Place, 10th Floor
Brooklyn, NY 11217
800-247-8035
718-923-4325
www.cvb.state.ny.us
Victim's Compensation provides monetary compensation for victims and victim's survivors for a variety of expenses. Victims may receive up to $30,000 for lost wages, $2,000 for funeral costs, money for counseling, transportation and medical expenses.
The Crime Victim Board also administers the Victim Assistance program. Victim Assistance provides direct victim assistance as well as referrals to victim/witness programs that include help with crime counseling, victim's rights, advocacy and understanding the court process.

North Carolina
Division of Victims Compensation Services
4703 Mail Service Center
Raleigh, NC 27699-4703
919-733-7974
Fax: 919-715-4209
www.nccrimecontrol.org/vjs/cvcp0.htm
Victim's Compensation provides monetary compensation for victims and victim's survivors for a variety of expenses. Victims may receive up to $30,000 for medical expenses, lost wages and services (i.e. child care costs).

Victim Assistance
4708 Mail Service Center
Raleigh, NC 27699-4708
919-733-4564
Fax: 919-733-4625
www.gcc.state.nc.us
Victim Assistance provides direct victim assistance as well as referrals to victim/witness programs that include help with crime counseling, victim's rights, advocacy and understanding the court process.

North Dakota
Victim Compensation
Division of Parole and Probation

P.O. Box 5521
Bismarck, ND 58506-5521
701-328-6195
800-445-2322 (in-state)
Fax: 701-328-6651
www.state.nd.us/docr/field_services/victims.htm
Victim's Compensation provides monetary compensation for victims and victim's survivors for a variety of expenses. Victims may receive up to $25,000 for medical expenses, lost wages and funeral costs. The Division of Parole and Probation also administers the Victim Assistance program. Victim Assistance provides direct victim assistance as well as referrals to victim/witness programs that include help with crime counseling, victim's rights, advocacy and understanding the court process.

Northern Mariana Islands

Victim Assistance
9-1-670-664-4457
Fax: 9-1-670-664-4560
www.cjpa.gov.mp/programs.htm

Ohio

Ohio Victims of Crime Compensation Program
65 E. State St., Suite 800
Columbus, OH 43215
800-582-2877
614-466-5610
Fax: 614-995-5412
www.ag.state.oh.us/crimevic/cvcomps.htm
Victim's Compensation provides monetary compensation for victims and victim's survivors for a variety of expenses. Victims may receive benefits for medical expenses, attorney fees, crime-scene cleanup, counseling and funeral costs. The Ohio Victims of Crime Compensation Program also administers the Victim Assistance program. Victim Assistance provides direct victim assistance as well as referrals to victim/witness programs that include help with crime counseling, victim's rights, advocacy and understanding the court process.

Oklahoma

Crime Victims Compensation Board
Oklahoma District Attorneys Council
2200 N. Classen, Suite 1800
Oklahoma City, OK 73106
405-264-5006
800-745-6098
Fax: 405-264-5097
www.odawan.net
Victim's Compensation provides monetary compensation for victims and victim's survivors for a variety of expenses. Victims may receive up to $20,000 for medical expenses, rehabilitation, work loss, crime scene cleanup, and funeral costs. The Oklahoma District Attorneys Council also administers the Victim Assistance program. Victim Assistance provides direct victim assistance as well as referrals to victim/witness programs that include help with crime counseling, victim's rights, advocacy and understanding the court process.

Oregon

Victim Compensation
Department of Justice
1162 Court Street NE
Salem, OR 97301-4096
503-378-4400
503-378-5348
Fax: 503-378-5738
www.doj.state.or.us/CrimeV/comp.htm
Victim's Compensation provides monetary compensation for victims and victim's survivors for a variety of expenses. Victims may receive up to $20,000 for medical and/or counseling, up to $20,000 for lost wages, mileage reimbursement and up to $3,500 funeral costs. The Department of Justice also administers the Victim Assistance program. Victim Assistance provides direct victim assistance as well as referrals to victim/witness programs that include help with crime counseling, victim's rights, advocacy and understanding the court process.

Pennsylvania

Pennsylvania Commission on Crime and Delinquency
3101 North Front Street
Harrisburg, PA 17110
800-692-7292
717-787-2040
Fax: 717-783-7713
www.pccd.state.pa.us
Victim's Compensation provides monetary compensation for victims and victim's survivors

for a variety of expenses. Victims may receive reimbursement for medical expenses, counseling, lost wages, and funeral costs. The Pennsylvania Commission on Crime and Delinquency also administers the Victim Assistance program. Victim Assistance provides direct victim assistance as well as referrals to victim/witness programs that include help with crime counseling, victim's rights, advocacy and understanding the court process.

Puerto Rico
Office for Crime Victims Compensation
Department of Justice
P.O. Box 9020192
San Juan, PR 00902-0192
787-729-2055
Fax: 787-729-2593
Email: Lgozalez@justicia.prstar.net
Victim's Compensation provides monetary compensation for victims and victim's survivors for a variety of expenses. Victims may receive up to $3,000 for medical expenses, counseling, lost wages, and funeral costs.

Rhode Island
Victim Compensation
40 Fountain Street, 1st Floor
Providence, RI 02903
401-222-8590
Fax: 401-222-4577
www.state.ri.us/treas/vcfund.htm
Victim's Compensation provides monetary compensation for victims and victim's survivors for a variety of expenses. Victims may receive up to $25,000 for medical/dental expenses, counseling, lost wages, and funeral costs.

Victim Assistance
Rhode Island Justice Commission
One Capitol Hill
Providence, RI 02908
401-222-2620
Fax: 401-222-1294
www.rijustice.state.ri.us/voca
Victim Assistance provides direct victim assistance as well as referrals to victim/witness programs that include help with crime counseling, victim's rights, advocacy and understanding the court process.

South Carolina
State Office of Victim Assistance
1205 Pendleton Street
Edgar A. Brown Building, Room 401
Columbia, SC 29201
803-734-1930
800-220-5370 Victims only
Fax: 803-734-1708
www.govoepp.state.sc.us/sova/cvccomp.htm
Victim's Compensation provides monetary compensation for victims and victim's survivors for a variety of expenses. Victims may receive up to $25,000 medical expenses, counseling, lost wages, and funeral costs. The South Carolina of Victim Assistance also administers the Victim Assistance program. Victim Assistance provides direct victim assistance as well as referrals to victim/witness programs that include help with crime counseling, victim's rights, advocacy and understanding the court process.

South Dakota
Crime Victims' Compensation
Department of Social Services
700 Governors Drive
Pierre, SD 57501
605-773-6317
800-696-9476
Fax: 605-773-6834
www.state.sd.us/social/cvc/index.htm
Victim's Compensation provides monetary compensation for victims and victim's survivors for a variety of expenses. Victims may receive up to $15,000 for medical expenses, counseling, mileage, loss of wages and funeral costs. The South Dakota Department of Social Services also administers the Victim Assistance program. Victim Assistance provides direct victim assistance as well as referrals to victim/witness programs that include help with crime counseling, victim's rights, advocacy and understanding the court process. The program also provides victims with 24-hour hotline, transportation, shelter, and counseling.

Tennessee
State of Tennessee Treasury Department
Division of Claims Administration
9th Floor Andrew Jackson Building
Nashville, TN 37243-0243

615-741-2734
Fax: 615-532-4979
www.treasury.state.tn.us/injury.htm
Victim's Compensation provides monetary compensation for victims and victim's survivors for a variety of expenses. Victims may receive up to $18,000 for medical expenses, transportation, death benefits and pain and suffering.

Victim Assistance
Office of Criminal Justice Program
312 8th Avenue North
Suite 1200
William R Snodgrass Tennessee Tower
Nashville, TN 37243-1700
615-741-7662
Fax: 615-532-2989
www.state.tn.us/finance/rds/ocjp.htm
Victim Assistance provides direct victim assistance as well as referrals to victim/witness programs that include help with crime counseling, victim's rights, advocacy and understanding the court process.

Texas

Victim Compensation
Crime Victim Services Division - CVC Program
Office of the Attorney General
P.O. Box 12198
Austin, TX 78711-2548
512-936-1200
800-983-9933
Fax: 512-320-8270
www.oag.state.tx.us/victims/victims.htm
Victim's Compensation provides monetary compensation for victims and victim's survivors for a variety of expenses. Victims may receive up to $50,000 for medical expenses, counseling, loss of wages, crime scene cleanup, childcare, and attorney fees.

Victim Assistance
Criminal Justice Division
Office of the Governor
P.O. Box 12428
Austin, TX 78711
512-463-1919
Fax: 512-475-2042
www.governor.state.tx.us/criminaljustice/index.htm
Victim Assistance provides direct victim assistance as well as referrals to victim/witness programs that include help with crime counseling, victim's rights, advocacy and understanding the court process. The program provides shelter, counseling and a variety of assistance.

Utah

Office of Crime Victim Reparations
350 East 500 South, Suite 200
Salt Lake City, UT 84111
801-238-2367
800-621-7444
Fax: 801-533-4127
www.crimevictim.utah.gov/about.htm
Victim's Compensation provides monetary compensation for victims and victim's survivors for a variety of expenses. Victims may receive up to $25,000; $50,000 for medical expenses in homicide, attempted homicide, aggregated assault or drunk driving. Reimbursement is available for medical expenses, counseling, lost wages, relocation expenses, crime-scene cleanup, and attorney fees. The Utah Office of Crime Victim Reparation also administers the Victim Assistance program. Victim Assistance provides direct victim assistance as well as referrals to victim/witness programs that include help with crime counseling, victim's rights, advocacy and understanding the court process.

Vermont

Vermont Center for Crime Victim Services
Victims Compensation Program
103 South Main St.
Waterbury, VT 05671-2001
802-241-1250
800-750-1213 (in-state only)
Fax: 802-241-1253
www.ccvs.state.vt.us
Victim's Compensation provides monetary compensation for victims and victim's survivors for a variety of expenses. Victims may receive up to $10,000 for medical expenses, counseling, lost wages, moving expenses, crime scene cleanup and funeral costs. The Vermont Compensation Office also administers the Victim Assistance program. Victim Assistance provides direct victim assistance as well as referrals to

victim/witness programs that include help with crime counseling, victim's rights, advocacy and understanding the court process.

Virginia

Compensation Fund
Workers' Compensation Commission
11513 Allecingie Pkwy.
Richmond, VA 23235
804-378-3434
800-552-4007
Fax: 804-378-4390
www.vwc.state.va.us/cicf/cicf_start_page.htm
Victim's Compensation provides monetary compensation for victims and victim's survivors for a variety of expenses. Victims may receive up to $15,000 for medical expenses, counseling, lost wages, moving expenses, crime-scene clean-up, and funeral costs.

Victim Assistance
Victim Service Section
805 E Broad Street, 10th Floor
Richmond, VA 23219
804-786-4000
Fax: 804-786-7980
www.dcjs.state.va.us
Victim Assistance provides direct victim assistance as well as referrals to victim/witness programs that include help with crime counseling, victim's rights, advocacy and understanding the court process. .

Virgin Islands

Criminal Victims Compensation Commission
Department of Human Services
Knud Hanson Complex
Building A
1303 Hospital Ground
Charlotte Annalie, VI 00802
340-774-0930, ext. 4104
Fax: 340-774-3466
Email: crimevictims@islands.vi
Victim's Compensation provides monetary compensation for victims and victim's survivors for a variety of expenses. Victims may receive up to $25,000 for medical expenses, counseling, lost wages, travel, attorney fees, and funeral costs.

Washington

Crime Victim Compensation Program
Department of Labor and Industries
P.O. Box 44520
Olympia, WA 98504-4520
360-902-5355
800-762-3716
Fax: 360-902-5333
www.lni.wa.gov/insurance/cvc.htm
Victim's Compensation provides monetary compensation for victims and victim's survivors for a variety of expenses. Victims may receive up to $150,000 for medical expenses, counseling, lost wages and funeral costs.

Victim Assistance
DSHS/CA/Program and Policy
P.O. Box 47986, MS N17-3
Seattle, WA 98146-7986
206-923-4910
Fax: 206-923-4899
Email: Susan H. at hsus300@dshs.wa.gov
www1.dshs.wa.gov/ca/victimservices/index.html

West Virginia

Crime Victims Compensation Fund
West Virginia Court of Claims
1900 Kanawha Blvd., East, Room W-334
Charleston, WV 25305-0610
304-347-4850
800-642-8650 (in-state)
Fax: 304-347-4915
www.legis.state.wv.us/joint/court/victims/main.ht
ml
Victim's Compensation provides monetary compensation for victims and victim's survivors for a variety of expenses. Victims may receive up to $25,000 for medical expenses, counseling, lost wages, attorney fees and funeral costs.

Victim Assistance
State Capitol Complex, Building 4, Room 300
112 California Ave
Charleston, WV 25305
304-558-2036 ext. 29
304-558-8814
Fax: 304-558-0391
www.state.wv.us/wvdoc/victimservices.htm
Victim Assistance provides direct victim assistance as well as referrals to victim/witness

programs that include help with crime counseling, victim's rights, advocacy and understanding the court process.

Wisconsin
Office of Crime Victims Services
Department of Justice
P.O. Box 7951
Madison, WI 53707-7951
608-266-6470
800-446-6564
Fax: 608-264-6363
www.doj.state.wi.us/cvs/programs/cvc.asp
Victim's Compensation provides monetary compensation for victims and victim's survivors for a variety of expenses. Victims may receive up to $40,000 for medical expenses, counseling, lost wages, crime-scene cleanup, attorney fees and funeral costs.

The Wisconsin Department of Justice also administers the Victim Assistance program. Victim Assistance provides direct victim assistance as well as referrals to victim/witness programs that include help with crime counseling, victim's rights, advocacy and understanding the court process.

Wyoming
Division of Victim Services
Office of the Attorney General
2301 Central Ave.
Barrett Bldg., 4th Floor
Cheyenne, WY 82002
307-777-7200
Fax: 307-777-6683
www.vssi.state.wy.us
Victim's Compensation provides monetary compensation for victims and victim's survivors for a variety of expenses. Victims may receive up to $15,000 medical expenses, counseling, lost wages and funeral costs. The Wyoming Division of Victim Services also administers the Victim Assistance program. Victim Assistance provides direct victim assistance as well as referrals to victim/witness programs that include help with crime counseling, victim's rights, advocacy and understanding the court process.

Half Price Food For Volunteers

It's called the Self-Help and Resource Exchange (SHARE), and it distributes food at 50% discounts to 5,415 community-based organizations, which in turn give it to individuals. The only catch is that you have to volunteer your time in the community for at least 2 hours a month. You can coach little league or help fix up a playground. To find a SHARE affiliate near you, contact SHARE, 6950 Friars Road, San Diego, CA 92108; 888-742-7372; Fax: 618-686-5185; {www.worldshare.org}.

Free Meals At Day Care

Not only does the government offer free lunches for school children, but your younger children can also receive free meals at day care centers, family day care homes, and more. Child and Adult Care Food Program (CACFP) provides nutritious meals to 2.6 million children and 74,000 adults who receive day care outside of their home.

USDA's Child and Adult Care Food Program plays a vital role in improving the quality of day care and making it more affordable for many low-income families. CACFP reaches even further to provide meals to children residing in homeless shelters, and snacks and suppers to youths participating in eligible afterschool care programs.

CACFP reimburses participating centers and day care homes for their meal costs. It is administered at the Federal level by the Food and Nutrition Service (FNS), an agency of the U.S. Department of Agriculture. The State education or health department administers CACFP, in most States.

Child Care Centers. Public or private nonprofit child care centers, Head Start programs, and some for-profit centers which are licensed or approved to provide day care may serve meals and snacks to infants and children through CACFP. Afterschool care programs in low-income areas can participate in CACFP by providing free snacks to school-aged children and youths through age 18. Reimbursable suppers are also available to children in eligible afterschool care programs in seven States--Delaware, Illinois, Michigan, Missouri, New York, Oregon, and Pennsylvania.

Adult Day Care Centers. Public, private nonprofit, and some for-profit adult day care facilities which provide structured, comprehensive services to functionally impaired, nonresident adults may participate in CACFP.

Family Day Care Homes. CACFP provides reimbursement for meals and snacks served to small groups of children receiving nonresidential day care in licensed or approved private homes. A family or group day care home must sign an agreement with a sponsoring organization to participate in CACFP. The sponsoring organization organizes training, conducts monitoring, and helps with planning menus and filling out reimbursement forms.

Homeless Shelters. Emergency shelters which provide residential and food services to homeless families may participate in

Income Eligibility Guidelines July 1, 2002 - June 30, 2003
All States and Territories Except Alaska and Hawaii

Household Size	Federal Poverty Guidelines (100 Percent)			Reduced Price Meals (185 Percent)			Free Meals (130 Percent)		
No. of Household Members	Annual	Month	Week	Annual	Month	Week	Annual	Month	Week
1	8,860	739	171	16,391	1,366	316	11,518	960	222
2	11,940	995	230	22,089	1,841	425	15,522	1,294	299
3	15,020	1,252	289	27,787	2,316	535	19,526	1,628	376
4	18,100	1,509	349	33,485	2,791	644	23,530	1,961	453
5	21,180	1,765	408	39,183	3,266	754	27,534	2,295	530
6	24,260	2,022	467	44,881	3,741	864	31,538	2,629	607
7	27,340	2,279	526	50,579	4,215	973	35,542	2,962	684
8	30,420	2,535	585	56,277	4,690	1,083	39,546	3,296	761
For Each Additional Person, Add	+3,080	+257	+60	+5,698	+475	+110	+4,004	+334	+77

CACFP. Unlike most other CACFP facilities, a shelter does not have to be licensed to provide day care.

Children age 12 and younger are eligible to receive up to two meals and one snack, each day, at a day care home or center, through CACFP. Children who reside in homeless shelters may receive up to three reimbursable meals each day. Migrant children age 15 and younger, and persons with disabilities, regardless of their age, are also eligible for CACFP. Afterschool care snacks are available to children through age 18. Adult participants must be functionally impaired or age 60 or older, and enrolled in an adult care center where they may receive up to two meals and one snack, each day, through CACFP.

Contact your state program for specific information (see listings for School Lunch Program). Contact FNS Public Information, 3101 Park Center Drive, Room 914, Alexandria, VA 22302; 703-305-2286; {www.fns.usda.gov/cnd/care/cacfp/cacfphome.htm}. See table on page 68 for income eligibility guidelines.

Free Lunches For Students

The National School Lunch Program (NSLP) is a federally assisted meal program administered by the USDA, operating in public and nonprofit private schools and residential child care institutions. It provides nutritionally balanced, low-cost or free lunches to children each school day. The program was established under the National School Lunch Act, signed by President Harry Truman in 1946.

Any child at a participating school may purchase a meal through the National School Lunch Program. Children from families with incomes at or below 130 percent of the poverty level are eligible for free meals. Those with incomes between 130 percent and 185 percent of the poverty level are eligible for reduced-price meals, for which students can be charged no more than 40 cents. Currently, a family of four can receive free lunches with an income of $22,945; and reduced lunches with an income of $32,653. To apply, contact your local school or day care facility.

Contact USDA Food and Nutrition Service, 3101 Park Center Drive, Room 914, Alexandria, VA 22302; 703-305-2286; {www.fns.usda.gov/cnd/Lunch/}.

Free Snacks After School

The hours after school are a critical time when children and youth are most at-risk of engaging in delinquent behavior. An afterschool care program that serves snacks reimbursed through the U.S. Department of Agriculture (USDA) offers children and youth constructive activities and something to eat. It draws them into supervised afterschool care programs that are safe, fun and filled with learning opportunities.

Afterschool snacks fill the gap between the lunch they receive at school and supper, and helps ensure that children and youth receive the nutrition they need to learn, play and grow.

To be eligible to participate under the National School Lunch Program (NSLP), your school district must operate the NSLP and sponsor or operate an eligible afterschool care program. Also, your afterschool care program must provide children with regularly scheduled activities in an organized, structured and supervised environment; and include educational or enrichment activities. There are no federal licensing requirements to participate in the NSLP's afterschool snack service; however, afterschool care programs are required to meet any State or local licensing requirements. If there are no State or local licensing requirements, programs must meet State or local health and safety requirements.

If your afterschool care program is "area eligible" (i.e., located in a school or in a school attendance area in which at least 50% of the enrolled children qualify for free or reduced price meals), then all snacks will be reimbursed at the free rate, regardless of an individual student's eligibility. If your afterschool care program is not area eligible, snacks will be reimbursed at the free, reduced price or paid rate depending on each individual child's eligibility.

State Agencies Administering the Child Nutrition Programs

Alabama
NSLP, CACFP, SFSP
Child Nutrition Programs
Alabama Department of Education
Gordon Persons Building
50 North Ripley St., Room 5301
Montgomery, AL 36130-2101
334-242-1988
Fax: 334-242-2475
http://cnp.alsde.edu/

Alaska
NSLP, CACFP, SFSP
Child Nutrition Programs
Alaska Department of Education & Early Development
801 West 10th Street
Suite 200
Juneau, AK 99801-1894
907-465-8708
Fax: 907-465-8910
www.educ.state.ak.us/tls/schoolhealth/ nutrition.html

Arizona
NSLP, CACFP, SFSP
Student Services
State Department of Education
1535 West Jefferson Avenue
Phoenix, AZ 85007
602-542-8709
Fax: 602-542-3818
www.ade.state.az.us/health-safety/cnp/

Arkansas
NSLP (Public)
Child Nutrition Section
Department of Education
Executive Building Suite 404
2020 West 3rd Street
Little Rock, AR 72205-4465
501-324-9502
Fax: 501-324-9595
http://cnn.k12.ar.us/

NSLP (Private), CACFP, SFSP
Special Nutrition Programs
Division of Child Care and Early Childhood Education
Department of Human Services
P.O. Box 1437, Slot 705
Little Rock, AR 72203-1437
501-682-8869
Fax: 501-682-2334
www.state.ar.us/childcare/usda.html

California
NSLP, CACFP, SFSP
Nutrition Services Division
State Department of Education
560 J Street Room 270
Sacramento, CA 95814-2342
916-323-7311
800-952-5609
Fax: 916-327-0503
www.cde.ca.gov/nsd/

Colorado
NSLP (Public), SFSP
Child Nutrition/Transportation Unit
Colorado Department of Education
201 East Colfax Avenue
Room 209
Denver, CO 80203-1799
303-866-6661
Fax: 303-866-6663
www.cde.state.co.us/index_nutrition.htm

NSLP (Private)
MPRO USDA FNS SNP
1244 Speer Boulevard, Suite 903
Denver, CO 80204-3585

303-844-0354
Fax: 303-844-2234

CACFP
Colorado Department of Public Health and Environment
FCHSD-CAC-A4
4300 Cherry Creek Drive South
Denver, CO 80222-1530
303-692-2330
Fax: 303-756-9926
www.cdphe.state.co.us/ps/ns/cacfp/ cacfphom.asp

Connecticut
NSLP, CACFP, SFSP
Child Nutrition Programs
Department of Education
25 Industrial Park Road
Middletown, CT 06457-1543
860-807-2070
Fax: 860-807-2084
www.state.ct.us/sde/

Delaware
NSLP (Public), CACFP, SFSP
School Support Services
Child Nutrition Programs
Department of Education
Townsend Building
Federal and Lockerman Streets
Post Office Box 1402
Dover, DE 19903-1402
302-739-4676
Fax: 302-739-6397
www.doe.state.de.us/

NSLP (Private)
MARO USDA FNS SNP
Mercer Corporate Park
300 Corporate Boulevard
Robbinsville, NJ 08691-1598
609-259-5050
Fax: 609-259-5242

District of Columbia
NSLP, CACFP, SFSP
Special Nutrition and Commodity Programs
State Education Office
441 4th Street NW
Suite 350N
Washington D. C. 20001
202-727-6436
Fax: 202-727-2019
www.k12.dc.us/dcps/home.html

Florida
NSLP, SFSP
Florida Department of Education
325 W. Gaines St., Room #804
Tallahassee, FL 32399-0400
850-488-7256
Fax: 850-921-8824
http://fnm.doe.state.fl.us/

CACFP (Child)
Bureau of Child Nutrition Programs
Florida Department of Health
4052 Bald Cypress Way
Bin A17
Tallahassee, FL 32399-0700
850-245-4323
Fax: 850-414-1622
www.doh.state.fl.us/ccfp/

Georgia
NSLP (School)
Georgia School and Community Nutrition Programs
Georgia Department of Education
1662 Twin Towers East
Atlanta, GA 30334
404-657-9443
Fax: 404-657-9188
www.doe.k12.ga.us/nutrition/scnp.html

NSLP (Residential Institution)
SERO USDA FNS SNP
61 Forsyth Street, SW
Room 8T36
Atlanta, GA 30303
404-562-7099
Fax: 404-562-1807

CACFP, SFSP
Office of School Readiness
10 Park Place South
Suite 200
Atlanta, GA 30303-2927
404-656-5957
Fax: 404-651-7429
www.osr.state.ga.us/osrhome.html

Guam
NSLP, CACFP
Food Services Section
Guam Department of Education
Post Office Box DE
Agana, Guam 96932
671-475-6407
Fax: 671-477-5394

Hawaii
NSLP, CACFP, SFSP
School Food Services Business Division
Department of Education
1106 Koko Head Avenue
Honolulu, HI 96816
808-733-8400
Fax: 808-732-4293

Idaho
NSLP, CACFP, SFSP
Child Nutrition Programs
Department of Education
Len B. Jordan Office Building
650 West State Street
Post Office Box 83720
Boise, ID 83720-0027
208-332-6820
Fax: 208-332-6833
www.sde.state.id.us/child/

Illinois
NSLP, CACFP (Child), SFSP
Nutrition Programs & Education Services
Illinois State Board of Education
100 North First Street
Springfield, IL 62777-0001
217-782-2491
Fax: 217-524-6124
www.isbe.state.il.us/nutrition/

Indiana
NSLP, CACFP, SFSP
Division of School and Community
Nutrition Programs
Indiana Department of Education
State House Room 229
Indianapolis, IN 46204-2798
317-232-0850
Fax: 317-232-0855
http://ideanet.doe.state.in.us/food/

Iowa
NSLP, CACFP, SFSP
Bureau of Food and Nutrition
Department of Education
Grimes State Office Building

Des Moines, IA 50319-0146
515-281-4757
Fax: 515-281-6548
www.state.ia.us/educate/ecese/fn/

Kansas
NSLP, CACFP, SFSP
Kansas State Board of Education
Nutrition Services
120 East 10th Street
Topeka, KS 66612-1182
785-296-2276
Fax: 785-296-1413
www.kn-eat.org/HomePage/kneathome.htm

Kentucky
NSLP, CACFP, SFSP
Division of School and Community Nutrition
State Department of Education
1024 Capital Center Drive
Frankfort, KY 40601
502-573-4390
Fax: 502-573-6775
www.kde.state.ky.us/odss/nutrition/

Louisiana
NSLP, CACFP, SFSP
Food and Nutrition Services
Louisiana Department of Education
655 North Fifth Street
Post Office Box 94064
Baton Rouge, LA 70804-9064
225-342-3720
Fax: 225-342-3305
www.doe.state.la.us/DOE/asps/home.asp?I=DNA

Maine
NSLP, SFSP
Department of Education
23 State House Station
Augusta, ME 04333
207-624-6845
Fax: 207-624-6841
www.state.me.us/education/sfs/homepage.htm

CACFP
Child and Adult Care Food Program
Division of Contracted Community Services
Department of Human Services
State House, Station 11
221 State Street
Augusta, ME 04333
207-287-5060
Fax: 207-287-5031

Maryland
NSLP, CACFP, SFSP
School and Community Nutrition Programs
State Department of Education
200 W. Baltimore St., 3rd Floor
Baltimore, MD 21201-2595
410-767-0199
Fax: 410-333-2635
www.msde.state.md.us/programs/foodandnutrition/

Massachusetts
NSLP, CACFP, SFSP
Nutrition Programs and Services
Department of Education
350 Main Street
Malden, MA 02148-5023
781-338-6479
Fax: 781-338-3399
www.doe.mass.edu/cnp/

Michigan
NSLP, CACFP
School Management Services
Michigan Department of Education
Post Office Box 30008
Lansing, MI 48909
517-373-8642
Fax: 517-373-4022
www.state.mi.us/mde/off/oss/index.htm#FoodNutrition

SFSP
Summer Program Unit
MWRO USDA FNS SNP
77 West Jackson Boulevard, 20th Floor
Chicago, IL 60604-3507
312-353-3089
Fax: 312-353-4108

Minnesota
NSLP, CACFP, SFSP
Food and Nutrition Services
Department of Children, Families & Learning
1500 Highway 36 West
Roseville, MN 55113-4266
651-582-8526
800-366-8922
Fax: 651-582-8500
https://fns.state.mn.us/

Mississippi
NSLP, CACFP, SFSP
Bureau of Child Nutrition
State Department of Education
500 Greymont Avenue, Suite F
Post Office Box 771
Jackson, MS 39205-0771
601-354-7015
Fax: 601-354-7595
www.cn.mde.k12.ms.us/

Missouri
NSLP (School)
School Food Services
Department of Elementary and Secondary Education
400 Dix Road
Post Office Box 480
Jefferson City, MO 65102-0480
573-751-3526
Fax: 573-526-3897
www.dese.state.mo.us/divadm/food/

NSLP (Residential Institution)
MPRO USDA FNS SNP
1244 Speer Boulevard, Suite 903
Denver, CO 80204
303-844-0355
Fax: 303-844-2234

CACFP, SFSP
Bureau of Community Food and Nutrition Assistance
Missouri Department of Health and Senior Services
505 Hobbs (Lower Level)
Post Office Box 570
Jefferson City, MO 65109-0570
573-751-6269
800-733-6251
Fax: 573-526-3679

Montana
NSLP, SFSP
Division of School Food Services
Office of Public Instruction
1230 11th Avenue
Post Office Box 202501

Helena, MT 59620-2501
406-444-2501
Fax: 406-444-2955
www.metnet.state.mt.us/SchoolFood/ HTM/SchoolFood.shtml

Montana CACFP
Children's Services
Department of Public Health & Human Services
Post Office Box 8005
Helena, MT 59604
406-444-1828
Fax: 406-444-5956
www.dphhs.state.mt.us/ccrd/food.htm

Nebraska

NSLP, CACFP, SFSP
Child Nutrition Programs
State Department of Education
301 Centennial Mall South
Lincoln, NE 68509-4987
402-471-3566
Fax: 402-471-4407
www.nde.state.ne.us/NS/

Nevada

NSLP, CACFP, SFSP
Health and Safety Programs
Nevada Dept. of Education
700 East Fifth Street
Carson City, NV 89701-5096
775-687-9154
Fax: 775-687-9199
www.nde.state.nv.us/hlthsaf/index.html

New Hampshire

NSLP, CACFP, SFSP
Bureau of Nutrition Programs & Services
New Hampshire Department of Education
101 Pleasant Street
Concord, NH 03301
603-271-3860
Fax: 603-271-1953
www.ed.state.nh.us/FoodandNutrition/ foodnut.htm

New Jersey

NSLP, CACFP, SFSP
Bureau of Child Nutrition Programs
State Department of Agriculture
33 West State Street
Post Office Box 334
Trenton, NJ 08625-0334
609-984-0692
Fax: 609-984-0878
www.state.nj.us/agriculture/markets/ childnutrition.htm

New Mexico

NSLP
Student Nutrition Programs Unit
New Mexico Department of Education
120 South Federal Place
Room 207
Santa Fe, NM 87501-2786
505-827-1821
Fax: 505-827-1815
http://sde.state.nm.us/divisions/sipds/index.html

CACFP, SFSP
Family Nutrition Bureau
New Mexico Children Youth & Families Department
1422 Paseo De Peralta, Building 2
Post Office Box 5160
Santa Fe, NM 87502-5160
505-827-9961
Fax: 505-827-9957

New York

NSLP, SFSP (School)
Child Nutrition Program Administration
Room 55
State Education Building
Albany, NY 12234-0055
518-473-2185
Fax: 518-473-0018
http://cn.nysed.gov/pre_login/plsql/ cn_portal$.startup

SFSP (Private Institution)
Operations Chief
Food and Nutrition, USDA
201 Varick Street, Room #609
New York, NY 10014
212-620-6307
Fax: 212-620-6948

CACFP
Child & Adult Food Program
New York State Department of Health
Riverview Center
150 Broadway, 6th Floor West
Albany, NY 12204-2719
518-473-8781
800-942-3858
Fax: 518-402-7252
www.health.state.ny.us/nysdoh/nutrition/cacfp/pages/homepg.htm

North Carolina

NSLP
Child Nutrition Services Section
State Department of Public Instruction
North Carolina Education Building
301 North Wilmington Street
Raleigh, NC 27601-2825
919-807-3506
Fax: 919-807-3516

CACFP, SFSP
Nutrition Services Branch
Health & Human Services Department
1914 Mail Service Center
Raleigh, NC 27699-1914
919-715-1923
Fax: 919-733-1384
www.nutritionnc.com/snp/

North Dakota

NSLP, CACFP, SFSP
Child Nutrition & Food Distribution
State Department of Public Instruction
600 East Blvd Avenue
State Capitol
Bismarck, ND 58505-0440
701-328-2294
Fax: 701-328-2461
www.dpi.state.nd.us/child/index.shtm

Ohio

NSLP, CACFP, SFSP
School Food Services Division
State Department of Education
25 South Front Street, 3rd Floor
Columbus, OH 43215-4183
614-466-2945
800-808-MEAL
Fax: 614-752-7613

www.ode.state.oh.us/food_service/CNS_Services/cns_programs.asp

Oklahoma
NSLP (Public School), CACFP, SFSP
Child Nutrition Section
Oklahoma Department of Education
2500 North Lincoln Boulevard
Room 310
Oklahoma City, OK 73105-4599
405-521-3327
Fax: 405-521-2239
http://sde.state.ok.us/pro/nut.html

NSLP (Private School)
Commodity Distribution Unit
Department of Human Services
Post Office Box 25352
Oklahoma City, OK 73105-4599
405-521-6079
Fax: 405-521-6949

Oregon
NSLP, CACFP, SFSP
Child Nutrition & Food Distribution
State Department of Education
Public Services Building
255 Capitol Street NE
Salem, OR 97310-0203
503-378-3600
Fax: 503-378-5258
www.ode.state.or.us/nutrition/index.htm

Pennsylvania
NSLP, CACFP, SFSP
Child Nutrition Programs
Department of Education
333 Market Street 4th Floor
Harrisburg, PA 17126-0333
717-787-7698
Fax: 717-783-6566
www.pde.state.pa.us/food_nutrition/ site/default.asp

Puerto Rico
NSLP, CACFP, SFSP
Food & Nutrition Services
Department of Education
Post Office Box 190759
San Juan, PR 00919-0759
787-754-0790
Fax: 787-753-8155

Rhode Island
NSLP, CACFP, SFSP
Office of Integrated Social Services
Rhode Island Department of Education
Shepard Building
255 Westminster St., Room 600
Providence, RI 02903-3400
401-222-4600 ext 2364
Fax: 401-222-4979
www.ridoe.net/funding/grants/queries3/ nutrition.idc

South Carolina
NSLP
Office of School Food Services
State Department of Education
Rutledge Building Room 201
1429 Senate Street
Columbia, SC 29201
803-734-8195
Fax: 803-734-8061
www.myscschools.com/Offices/SFSN/pages/

CACFP, SFSP
Family Nutrition Programs
State Department of Social Services
Landmark Building II, Suite 300
3700 Forest Drive
Post Office Box 1520
Columbia, SC 29201-1520
803-737-9238
Fax: 803-734-9515
www.healthyhelpings.org/

South Dakota
NSLP, CACFP, SFSP
Child and Adult Nutrition Services
Department of Education and Cultural Affairs
700 Governors Drive
Pierre, SD 57501-2291
605-773-3413
Fax: 605-773-6846
www.state.sd.us/deca/desr/cans/

Tennessee
NSLP (Public School)
School Nutrition Programs
6th Floor Gateway Plaza
710 James Robertson Parkway
Nashville, TN 37243-0389
615-532-4714
Fax: 615-532-7937
www.state.tn.us/education/nutrition.htm

NSLP (Private School)
Commodity Distribution Division
Department of Agriculture
Melrose Station
Post Office Box 40627
Nashville, TN 37204
615-837-5530
Fax: 615-837-5014

CACFP, SFSP
Adult and Community Programs
Department of Human Services
Citizens Plaza Bldg. 15th Floor
400 Deadrick Street
Nashville, TN 37248-9500
615-313-4749
Fax: 615-532-9956

Texas
NSLP (Public School)
Child Nutrition Programs
Texas Education Agency
William B Travis Building
1701 North Congress Avenue
Austin, TX 78701-1494
512-997-6550
Fax: 512-475-3795
www.tea.state.tx.us/CNP/

NSLP (Private School), CACFP, SFSP
Office of Family Services
Special Nutrition Programs (Y-904)
Texas Dept. of Human Services
1106 Clayton Lane, Suite 325E
Post Office Box 149030
Austin, TX 78714-9030
512-420-2506
Fax: 512-371-1595
www.dhs.state.tx.us/programs/snp/index.html

Utah
NSLP, CACFP, SFSP
Child Nutrition Programs
Utah State Office of Education

250 East 500 South Street
Salt Lake City, UT 84111-3284
801-538-7513
Fax: 801-538-7883
www.usoe.k12.ut.us/cnp/index.htm

Vermont
NSLP, CACFP, SFSP
Child Nutrition Programs
State Department of Education
120 State Street
Montpelier, VT 05620
802-828-5154
Fax: 802-828-0573
www.state.vt.us/educ/nutrition/

Virgin Islands
NSLP, CACFP, SFSP
Child Nutrition Programs
Department of Education
44-46 Kongens Gade
Charlotte Amalie
St Thomas, U.S. Virgin Islands
00802
340-774-9373
Fax: 340-774-9705

Virginia
NSLP (Public School)
School Nutrition Programs
State Department of Education
101 North 14th Street
Post Office Box 2120
Richmond, VA 23218-2120
804-225-2074
Fax: 804-786-3117
www.pen.k12.va.us/VDOE/Finance/ Nutrition/

NSLP (Private School), CACFP, SFSP
MARO, USDA, FNS, SNP
Mercer Corporate Park
300 Corporate Boulevard
Robbinsville, NJ 08691-1598

609-259-5050
Fax: 609-259-5128

Washington
NSLP, CACFP, SFSP
Office of Superintendent of Public Instruction
Old Capitol Building
600 South Washington Street
Post Office Box 47200
Olympia, WA 98504-7200
360-753-3580
Fax: 360-664-9397
www.k12.wa.us/ChildNutrition/

West Virginia
NSLP, CACFP, SFSP
Office of Child Nutrition
Department of Education
Building 6 Room B-248
1900 Kanawha Boulevard East
Charleston, WV 25305-0330
304-558-2708
Fax: 304-558-1149

Wisconsin
NSLP, CACFP, SFSP
Food and Nutrition Services
Department of Public Instruction
125 South Webster Street
Post Office Box 7841
Madison, WI 53707-7841
NSLP 608-267-9121
CACFP/SFSP 608-267-9123
Fax: 608-267-0363
www.dpi.state.wi.us/dpi/dfm/fns/ hb3_105.html

Wyoming
NSLP, CACFP, SFSP
Child Nutrition Programs
Wyoming Department of Education
Hathaway Building, 2nd Floor
2300 Capitol Avenue
Cheyenne, WY 82002-0050
307-777-6262
Fax: 307-777-6234
www.k12.wy.us/hsandn/index.html

$800 To Pay For Food

You don't get the cash, but you do get it in the form of Food Stamps. The Food Stamp Program was designed to help low-income families buy the food they need to stay healthy and productive. The amount of Food Stamps you get each month is determined by the number of people in your family and by the household income. The average benefit is about $71 dollars a month, but a 4-person household could get up to $408 a month. There are obviously income requirements you must meet. In Ohio only 58% of those eligible take advantage of this program

To apply for the Program, look in the blue pages of your telephone book under "Food Stamps," "Social Services," or "Public Assistance." You can also find more

information by contacting U.S. Department of Agriculture, Food and Nutrition Service, 3101 Park Ctr. Dr., Park Office Center Bldg., Alexandria, VA 22302; 703-305-2276; {www.fns.usda.gov/fsp}.

$700 Food Money for Women & Children

Uncle Sam wants women and kids to have a healthy food. The Women, Infant and Children (WIC) Program's mission is to safeguard the health of low-income women, infants, and children up to age 5 who are at nutritional risk by providing nutritious foods to supplement diets, information on healthy eating, and referrals to health care. WIC is not an entitlement program as Congress does not set aside funds to allow every eligible individual to participate in the program. WIC is a Federal grant program for which Congress authorizes a specific amount of funds each year for the program. A family of four can make up to $33,485 and still qualify!

WIC foods include iron-fortified infant formula and infant cereal, iron-fortified adult cereal, vitamin C-rich fruit and/or vegetable juice, eggs, milk, cheese, peanut butter, dried beans or peas, tuna fish and carrots.

In addition to the regular WIC program, a majority of the states have chosen to operate the WIC Farmers' Market Nutrition Program (FMNP), established in 1992, it provides additional coupons to WIC participants that they can use to purchase fresh fruits and vegetables at participating farmers' markets.

The Food and Nutrition Service (FNS) is a Federal agency of the U.S. Department of Agriculture, responsible for administering the WIC Program at the national and regional levels.

WIC at FNS Headquarters:
Supplemental Food Programs Division
Food and Nutrition Service - USDA
3101 Park Center Drive
Alexandria, VA 22302
703-305-2746
Fax: 703-305-2196
www.fns.usda.gov/fns/

Northeast Regional Office - FNS - USDA
Supplemental Food Programs
10 Causeway Street, Room 501
Boston, MA 02222-1066
617-565-6440
Fax: 617-565-6472
Serving: Connecticut, Maine, Massachusetts, New Hampshire, New York, Rhode Island, Vermont

Mid-Atlantic Region - FNS - USDA
Supplemental Food Programs
Mercer Corporate Park
300 Corporate Boulevard
Robbinsville, NJ 08691 - 1598
609-259-5100
Fax: 609-259-5179
Serving: Delaware, District of Columbia, Maryland, New Jersey, Pennsylvania, Puerto Rico, Virginia, Virgin Islands, West Virginia

Southeast Region - FNS - USDA
Supplemental Food Programs
61 Forsyth Street, SW
Room 8T36
Atlanta, GA 30303
404-562-7100
Fax: 404-527-4519
Serving: Alabama, Florida, Georgia, Kentucky, Mississippi, North Carolina, South Carolina, Tennessee

Midwest Region - FNS - USDA
Supplemental Food Programs
77 West Jackson Blvd., 20th Floor
Chicago, IL 60604-3507
312-886-6625
Fax: 312-353-1706
Serving: Illinois, Indiana, Michigan, Minnesota, Ohio, Wisconsin

Southwest Region - FNS - USDA
Supplemental Food Programs
1100 Commerce Street
Room 5-C-30

Dallas, TX 75242
214-290-9812
Fax: 214-767-9599
Serving: Arkansas, Louisiana, New Mexico, Oklahoma, Texas

Mountain Plains Region - FNS - USDA
Supplemental Food Programs
1244 Speer Boulevard
Suite 903
Denver, CO 80204
303-844-0331
Fax: 303-844-6203
Serving: Colorado, Iowa, Kansas, Missouri, Montana, Nebraska, North Dakota, South Dakota, Utah, Wyoming

Western Region - FNS - USDA
Supplemental Food Programs
550 Kearny Street
Suite 400
San Francisco, CA 94108-2518
415-705-1313/1335
Fax: 415-705-1029
Serving: Alaska, American Samoa, Arizona, California, Guam, Hawaii, Idaho, Nevada, Oregon, Washington

Alabama
Division of WIC
Bureau of Family Health Services
Alabama Department of Public Health
RSA Tower, Suite 1300
P.O. Box 303017
Montgomery, AL 36130-3017
334-206-5673
Toll-free in-state: 1-800-654-1385
Fax: 334-206-2914
Email: wblackmon@adph.state.al.us
www.adph.org/wic/

Alaska
Maternal, Child, and Family Health
Division of Public Health
Nutrition Services - WIC
P.O. Box 110612
Juneau, AK 99811-0612
907-465-3100
Toll-free in-state: 1-800-478-2221
TDD: 907-586-4265
Fax: 907-465-3416
Email: Nancy_Rody@health.state.ak.us
http://health.hss.state.ak.us/dph/mcfh/WIC/ default.htm

American Samoa
Department of Human and Social Services
American Samoa Government
P.O. Box 997534
Pago Pago, AS 96799
011-684-633-2609
Fax: 011-684-633-7449
Email: ulealofi.dhss@samoatelco.com

Arizona
Office of Nutrition Services
Department of Health Services
State Health Building
2927 North 35th Ave.
Suite 400
Phoenix, AZ 85017
602-542-1886
Toll-free in-state: 1-800-252-5WIC
1-800-252-5942
Fax: 602-542-1890/1804
Email: mtate@hs.state.az.us
www.hs.state.az.us/cfhs/ons/wic.htm

Arizona Inter-Tribal Council of Arizona, Inc.
El Encanto Building
2214 N. Central Ave., Suite 100
Phoenix, AZ 85004
602-258-4822
Fax: 602-258-4825
Email: karen.sell@itcaonline.com

Arkansas
Arkansas Department of Health
Freeway Medical Building
Suite 810
5800 W. 10th Street
Little Rock, AR 72204
501-661-2473
Toll-free in-state: 1-800-235-0002
Fax: 501-661-2004
Email: mheird@healthyarkansas.com

California
WIC Supplemental Nutrition Branch
Department of Health Services
3901 Lennane Drive
Sacramento, CA 95834
916-928-8806
Toll-free in-state: 1-888-WICWORKS or 1-888-942-9675
Fax: 916-928-0706
Email: pbramson@dhs.ca.gov
www.wicworks.ca.gov/

Cherokee Indians, Eastern Band of
WIC Coordinator
Eastern Band of Cherokee Indians
P.O. Box 1145
Cherokee, NC 28719
828-497-7297
Toll-free: 1-800-248-6967
Fax: 828-497-4470
Email: tbryant@nc-cherokee.com

Cherokee Nation of Oklahoma
P.O. Box 948
Tahlequah, OK 74465
918-456-0671 ext. 2291
Fax: 918-458-7672
Email: brenda.carter@mail.ihs.gov

Cheyenne River Sioux Tribe
P.O. Box 590
Eagle Butte, SD 57625-0590
605-964-3947
Fax: 605-964-3949

Chickasaw Nation
P.O. Box 1548
Ada, OK 74820-1548
580-436-2603
Toll-free: 1-888-436-7255
Fax: 580-436-7225
Email: chickwic@chickasaw.com

Choctaw Indians, Mississippi Band
WIC Program
Mississippi Band of Choctaw Indians
P.O. Box 6010
Philadelphia, MS 39350
601-650-1845
Fax: 601-650-1860
www.choctaw.org/index/government/ ge/ge.html

Choctaw Nation Of Oklahoma
P.O. Drawer 1210
Durant, OK 74702-1210
580-924-8280 ext. 2201
Fax: 580-924-4831
Email: kimw@redriverok.com

Citizen Potawatomi Nation
1601 South Gordon Cooper Drive
Shawnee, OK 74801
405-273-3216
Toll-free: 1-800-880-9880
Fax: 405-273-4660
Email:
sschneider@potawatomi.org

Colorado
Nutrition Services
Colorado Department of Health
FCHSD-NS-A4
4300 Cherry Creek Drive, South
Denver, CO 80246-1530
303-692-2400
Toll-free in-state: 1-800-688-7777
Fax: 303-756-9926
Email:
William.Eden@state.co.us
www.cdphe.state.co.us/ps/ns/wic/wichom.asp

Connecticut
State WIC Program
Department of Public Health
410 Capitol Avenue MS #11WIC
P.O. Box 340308
Hartford, CT 06134-0308
860-509-8084
Fax: 860-509-8391
Toll-free in-state: 1-800-741-2142
Email:
Barbara.Walsh@po.state.ct.us

Delaware
Delaware Health and Social Services
Division of Public Health
WIC Program
Blue Hen Corporate Center
655 Bay Road, Suite 4-B
Dover, DE 19901
302-739-4614 or 3671
Toll-free in-state: 1-800-222-2189
Fax: 302-739-3970
Email: bwetherbee@state.de.us

District Of Columbia
WIC State Agency
2100 Martin Luther King Jr. Avenue, SE, Suite 409
Washington, DC 20020
202-645-5662
Toll-free: 1-800-345-1WIC or 1-800-345-1942
Fax: 202-645-0516
Email:
ampeterson@dchealth.com
www.dchealth.com/wic/welcome.htm

Eight Northern Indian Pueblos Council
Eight Northern Indian Pueblos Council
P.O. Box 969
San Juan Pueblo, NM 87566
505-455-3144
Fax: 505-455-3055
Email:
enipcwic@newmexico.com

Five Sandoval Indian Pueblos
1043 Highway 313
Bernalillo, NM 87004
505-867-3351
Fax: 505-867-3514

Florida
Bureau of WIC and Nutrition Services
Florida Department of Health
Bin #A-16, HSFW
4052 Bald Cypress Way
Tallahassee, FL 32399-1726
850-245-4202
Toll-free in-state: 1-800-342-3556
Fax: 850-922-3936
Email:
Debbie_Eibeck@doh.state.fl.us
www9.myflorida.com/family/wic/default.html

Georgia
State WIC Office
Division of Public Health
Georgia Department of Human Resources
Two Peachtree Street, NW, 10th Floor, Suite 476
Atlanta, GA 30303
404-657-2900
Toll-free in-state: 1-800-228-9173
Fax: 404-657-2910
Email:
AlPeterson@gdph.state.ga.us
www.ph.dhr.state.ga.us/programs/ wic/index.shtml

Guam
Nutrition Health Services/Guam WIC Program
Department of Public Health & Social Services
Government of Guam
P.O. Box 2816
Hagatna, GU 96932
671-475-0287
Fax: 671-477-7945
Email: cmorris@mail.gov.gu
www.admin.gov.gu/pubhealth/index.html

Hawaii
WIC Services Branch
Department of Health
235 South Beretania Street, Suite 701
Honolulu, HI 96813
808-586-8175
Toll-free in-state: 1-888-820-6425
TDD: 808-586-8175
Fax: 808-586-8189
Email:
lchock@mail.health.state.hi.us
http://mano.icsd.hawaii.gov/doh/resource/family/wic/index.html

Idaho
Idaho WIC Program
Department of Health and Welfare
P.O. Box 83720
Boise, ID 83720-0036
208-334-5951
Toll-free in-state: 1-800-926-2588
TDD: 208-332-7205
Fax: 208-332-7362
Email: mckiek@idhw.state.id.us
www2.state.id.us/dhw/wic/index.htm

Illinois
Bureau of Family Nutrition
Office of Family Health
Illinois Department of Human Services
535 West Jefferson Street
Springfield, IL 62702
217-782-2166
Toll-free in-state: 1-800-323-4769
Fax: 217-785-5247
Email: dhshp53@dhs.state.il.us
www.state.il.us/agency/dhs/wicnp.html

Indiana
WIC Program
Indiana State Department of Health
2 North Meridian St., Suite 700
Indianapolis, IN 46204
317-233-5578
Fax: 317-233-5609
Email: cmoles@isdh.state.in.us

Indian Township Passamaquoddy Reservation
WIC Program Director
Indian Township Health Center
One Newell Drive
P.O. Box 97
Indian Township, ME 04668-0097
207-796-2321
Fax: 207-796-2422

Iowa
Bureau of Nutrition and WIC
Iowa Department of Public Health
Lucas State Office Building
Des Moines, IA 50319-0075
515-281-3713
Toll-free in-state: 1-800-532-1579
Fax: 515-281-4913
Email: jsolberg@idph.state.ia.us
http://idph.state.ia.us/fch/n-wic.htm

Kansas
Nutrition and WIC Services
Kansas Department of Health & Environment
Charles Curtis Office Building
1000 SW Jackson, Suite 220
Topeka, KS 66612-1274
785-296-1320
Fax: 785-296-1326
Toll-free in-state: 1-800-332-6262
Email: dthomaso@kdhe.state.ks.us
www.kdhe.state.ks.us/nws-wic/index.htm

Kentucky
Nutrition Services Branch
Division of Maternal and Child Health
Kentucky Department of Public Health
Cabinet for Health Services
275 East Main Street
Frankfort, KY 40621
502-564-3827
Toll-free in-state: 1-800-462-6122
Fax: 502-564-8389
Email: mailto:Fran.Hawkins@mail.state.ky.us
http://publichealth.state.ky.us/wic-program.htm

Louisiana
Louisiana Department of Health and Hospitals
Nutrition Services
P.O. Box 60630
New Orleans, LA 70160
504-568-5065
Fax: 504-568-3065
Email: pmccandl@dhhmail.dhh.state.la.us
www.oph.dhh.state.la.us/nutrition/ wic/index.htm

Maine
Maine WIC Nutrition Program
Division of Maternal & Family Health
Department of Human Services
11 SHS
Key Bank Plaza, 8th Floor
Augusta, ME 04333
207-287-3991
Toll-free in-state: 1-800-437-9300
Fax: 207-287-3993
Email: reinhold.bansmer@state.me.us

Maryland
WIC Administration
Maryland Department of Health and Mental Hygiene
201 West Preston Street
P.O. Box 13528
Baltimore, MD 21203-3528
410-767-5242
Fax: 410-333-5243
Toll-free in-state: 1-800-242-4WIC or
1-800-242-4942
TTY 1-800-735-2258
Email: knolhoffk@dhmh.state.md.us
http://mdwic.org

Massachusetts
Massachusetts WIC Program
Massachusetts Department of Public Health
250 Washington St., 6th Floor
Boston, MA 02108-4619
617-624-6100
Toll-free in-state: 1-800-WIC-1007 or
1-800-942-1007
Fax: 617-624-6179
Email: mailto:mary.kassler@state.ma.us
www.state.ma.us/dph/wic.htm

Michigan
WIC Division
Michigan Department of Community Health
2150 Apollo Drive
P.O. Box 30195
Lansing, MI 48906
517-335-8951
Fax: 517-335-8835

Toll-free in-state: 1-800-942-1636
Email: CarrA@state.mi.us
www.mdch.state.mi.us/dch/clcf/wic.asp

Minnesota
Minnesota Department of Health
85 East Seventh Place
P.O. Box 64882
St. Paul, MN 55164-0882
651-215-8957
Fax: 651-215-8951
Toll-free in-state: 1-800-WIC-4030 or 1-800-942-4030
Email:
mailto:betsy.clarke@health.state.mn.us
www.health.state.mn.us/divs/fh/wic/wic.htm

Mississippi
WIC Program, Bureau of Health Services
State Department of Health
570 East Woodrow Wilson
Jackson, MS 39216
601-576-7100
Toll-free in-state: 1-800-721-7222
Fax: 601-354-6290
Email:
cjordan@msdh.state.ms.us

Missouri
Missouri Dept. of Health and Senior Services
920 Wildwood
P.O. Box 570
Jefferson City, MO 65102-0570
573-751-6204
Fax: 573-526-1470
Toll-free for participants searching for clinics/services: 1-800-TEL-LINK (800-835-5465)
Toll-free State office: 1-800-392-8209
Email: warrev@dhss.state.mo.us

Montana
Department of Public Health and Human Services
Cogswell Building
(1400 Broadway Avenue - UPS Delivery Only)
Helena, MT 59620-2951
406-444-5533
Toll-free in-state: 1-800-433-4298
Fax: 406-444-0239
Email: ggray@state.mt.us
www.dphhs.state.mt.us/hpsd/index.htm

Muscogee Creek Nation
Muscogee Creek Nation
1801 East 4th
P.O. Box 2158
Okmulgee, OK 74447-3901
918-758-2722
Fax: 918-758-4949
Email: joy.flud@mail.ihs.gov

Navajo Nation
Navajo Nation WIC Program
Navajo Division of Health
P.O. Box 1390
Window Rock, AZ 86515
520-871-6698
Fax: 520-871-6251
Email: aking@nndoh.nn.ihs.gov

Nebraska
Family Health Division
Nebraska Dept. of Health & Human Services
P.O. Box 95044
301 Centennial Mall South
Lincoln, NE 68509-5044
402-471-2781
Toll-free in-state: 1-800-942-1171
Fax: 402-471-7049
Email:
peggy.trouba@hhss.state.ne.us

Nevada
Nevada WIC Program
Health Division
505 East King Street
Room 204
Carson City, NV 89701-4799
775-684-5942
Toll-free in-state: 1-800-8-NEV-WIC or
1-800-863-8942
Fax: 775-684-4246
Email:
dschrauth@nshd.state.nv.us
http://health2k.state.nv.us/wic/index.htm

Nevada, Inter-tribal Council
Inter-Tribal Council of Nevada
680 Greenbrae Drive, Suite 265
Sparks, NV 89431
775-355-0600
Fax: 775-355-0648
Email: wic@itcn.org
www.itcn.org

New Hampshire
Bureau of WIC Nutrition Services
Office of Community & Public Health
6 Hazen Drive
Concord, NH 03301
603-271-4546
Fax: 603-271-4779
Toll-free in-state: 1-800-WIC-4321
or 1-800-942-4321
Email:
wicprogram@dhhs.state.nh.us

New Jersey
New Jersey State WIC Program
Department of Health
CN 364
Trenton, NJ 08625-0364
609-292-9560
Fax: 609-292-3580 or 9288
Toll-free in-state: 1-800-328-3838
Email: jmalloy@doh.state.nj.us
www.state.nj.us/health/fhs/wichome.htm

New Mexico
New Mexico Department of Health, Family, Food and Nutrition
2040 South Pacheco Street
Santa Fe, NM 87505
505-476-8801
Fax: 505-476-8512
Email: janep@doh.state.nm.us
http://home.sprynet.com/~jtpierce/wic.htm

New York
Bureau of Supplemental Food Programs
Division of Nutrition
New York State Dept. of Health
150 Broadway, Floor 6, West
Albany, NY 12204-2719

518-402-7093
Toll-free in-state: 1-800-522-5006
Fax: 518-402-7348
Email:
NYSWIC@health.state.ny.us

North Carolina
Nutrition Services Branch
NC Division of Public Health
Department of Health and Human Services
1914 Mail Service Center
Raleigh, NC 27699-1914
919-733-2973
Toll-free in-state: 1-800-FOR BABY or
1-800-367-2229
Fax: 919-733-1384
Email:
Alice.Lenihan@ncmail.net
www.nutritionnc.com/wic/

North Dakota
Maternal and Child Health
North Dakota State Department of Health
600 E. Boulevard Ave.
Bismarck, ND 58505-0200
701-328-2493
Fax: 701-328-1412
Toll-free in-state: 1-800-472-2286
Email: cpearce@state.nd.us
www.health.state.nd.us/ndhd/prevent/mch/wic/

North Dakota, Three Affiliated Tribes
Three Affiliated Tribes
Fort Berthold Reservation
HC-3, Box 2
New Town, ND 58763
701-627-4777
Fax: 701-627-3805
Email:
wic_tat@newton.ndak.net

Northern Arapahoe
Northern Arapahoe WIC Program
P.O. Box 136
St. Stephens, WY 82524
307-857-2722
Fax: 307-856-9314
Email:
wicdirector@wyoming.com

Ohio
Bureau of Women, Infants & Children
Ohio Department of Health
246 North High Street
P.O. Box 118
Columbus, OH 43216-0118
614-644-8006
Toll-free in-state: 1-800-755-GROW or
1-800-755-4769
Fax: 614-728-2881
Email:
lprohs@gw.odh.state.oh.us
or OHWIC@gw.odh.state.oh.us

Oklahoma
Oklahoma State Department of Health
WIC Services
2520 Villa Prom Street
Oklahoma City, OK 73107-2419
405-271-4676
Toll-free in-state: 1-888-655-2942
Fax: 405-271-5763
Email: tomf@health.state.ok.us
www.health.state.ok.us/program/wic

Oklahoma, Inter-Tribal Council
Inter-Tribal Council, Inc.
P.O. Box 1308
Miami, OK 74355
918-542-4486
Fax: 918-540-2500
Email:
shirlyebass@datalinkok.com

Omaha/Santee Sioux
Omaha/Santee Sioux WIC Program
Rural Route 1, Box 9 C
Macy, NE 68039
402-349-5042
Email: omasoo@huntel.net

Oregon
Oregon WIC Program
Oregon Health Division
Suite 865
800 Northeast Oregon Street
Portland, OR 97232-2162
503-731-4022
Toll-free in-state: 1-800-SAFENET or
1-800-723-3638
TDD: 1-800-SAFENET
Fax: 503-731-3477
Email: debra.j.huls@state.or.us
www.ohd.hr.state.or.us/wic/welcome.htm

Osage Tribal Council
Osage Tribal Council
1301 Grandview
Pawhuska, OK 74056
918-287-1015
Fax: 918-287-1050
Email: wic@mmind.net

Otoe-Missouria Tribe
WIC Program
8151 Highway 177
Red Rock, OK 74651-0348
580-723-4411 or 12
Toll-free: 1-800-228-7942
Fax: 580-723-4273

Pennsylvania
Pennsylvania Department of Health
Division of WIC
Health and Welfare Building, Room 604
P.O. Box 90
Harrisburg, PA 17108-0090
717-783-1289
Toll-free in-state: 1-800-WIC WINS or
1-800-942-9467
Fax: 717-705-0462
Email: Fmaisano@state.pa.us
www.health.state.pa.us/php/wic

Pleasant Point Passamaquoddy Reservation
WIC Program Director
Pleasant Point Health Center
P.O. Box 351/Back Road
Perry, ME 04667
207-853-0644
Fax: 207-853-2347

Pueblo Of Isleta
Pueblo of Isleta
P.O. Box 670

Isleta, NM 87022-0340
505-869-2662
Fax: 505-869-8309
Email: islwic@nm.net

Pueblo Of San Felipe
P. O. Box A
San Felipe, NM 87001
505-867-2466
Fax: 505-867-3383

Pueblo Of Zuni
P.O. Box 339
Zuni, NM 87327
505-782-2929
Fax: 505-782-4498
Email: rubywolf@nm.net

Puerto Rico
WIC Program
Puerto Rico Department of Health
PO Box 25220
Rio Piedras, PR 00928-5220
787-766-2805
Fax: 787-751-5229

Rhode Island
WIC Program
Department of Health
Cannon Building
3 Capitol Hill, Room 303
Providence, RI 02908-5097
401-222-3940
Toll-free in-state: 1-800-942-7434
TDD: 1-800-745-5555
Fax: 401-222-1442
Email: beckyb@doh.state.ri.us
www.health.state.ri.us/

Rosebud Sioux Tribe
P.O. Box 99
Rosebud, SD 57570-0099
605-747-2617
Fax: 605-747-2612
Email: rswicp@gwtc.net

Santo Domingo Tribe
P.O. Box 370
Santo Domingo Pueblo, NM 87052
505-465-1321
Fax: 505-465-2688
Email: sdwic@nm.net

Seneca Nation
WIC Program Coordinator
1510 Route 438
Irving, NY 14081
716-532-0167 ext. 117
Fax: 716-532-0110

Shoshone
Shoshone WIC Program
P.O. Box 999
Fort Washakie, WY 82514
307-332-6733
Fax: 307-332-4196

South Carolina
Division of Preventive and Personal Health
South Carolina Department of Health and Environmental Control
Mills/Jarrett Complex
P.O. Box 101106
1751 Calhoun Street
Columbia, SC 29201-2911
803-898-0743
Toll-free in-state: 1-800 868-0404
Fax: 803-898-0383
www.scdhec.net/hs/mch/wic/index.htm
Email: walkerbw@columb60.dhec.state.sc.us

South Dakota
Nutrition Services Program Director
Division of Health Services
South Dakota Department of Health
615 East 4th Capitol
Pierre, SD 57501-5070
605-773-3737
Toll-free in-state: 1-800-738-2301
Fax: 605-773-5509
Email: annis.stuart@state.sd.us
www.state.sd.us/doh/Famhlth/wic.htm

Standing Rock Sioux Tribe
P.O. Box D
Fort Yates, ND 58538-0437
701-854-7263
Fax: 701-854-7122
Email: wicsrock@westriv.com

Tennessee
Supplemental Food Programs
Nutrition Services Section
Tennessee Department of Health
Cordell Hull Building, 5th Floor
425 Fifth Avenue, North
Nashville, TN 37247-4501
615-741-7218
Toll-free in-state: 1-800-342-5942
Fax: 615-532-7189
Email: jseals@mail.tn.us
www2.state.tn.us/health/wic/index.htm

Texas
Bureau of Nutrition Services
Texas Department of Health
1100 West 49th Street
Austin, TX 78756-3199
512-458-7444
Toll-free in-state: 1-800-WIC-FOR-U or
1-800-942-3678
Fax: 512-458-7446
Email: mike.montgomery@tdh.state.tx.us
www.tdh.state.tx.us/wichd/

Three Affiliated Tribes
Fort Berthold Reservation
HC-3, Box 2
New Town, ND 58763
701-627-4777
Fax: 701-627-3805
Email: dbaker@mhanation.com

Utah
Division of Family Health Services
Utah State Department of Health
288 North 1460 West
P.O. Box 141013
Salt Lake City, UT 84114-1013
801-538-6960
Fax: 801-538-6729
Toll-free in-state: 1-877-WIC-KIDS or
1-877-942-5437
Email: KCondra@doh.state.ut.us
www.health.utah.gov/wic/

Ute Mountain Ute Tribe
P.O. Box 11
Towaoc, CO 81334
970-565-3751 ext. 652

Fax: 970-565-5648
Email: lbrown@utemountain.org

Vermont
Vermont WIC Program
Division of Community Public Health
Department of Health
P.O. Box 70
108 Cherry Street
Burlington, VT 05402-0070
802-863-7333
Fax: 802-863-7229
Toll-free in-state: 1-800-464-4343, ext. 7333
Email: dbister@vdh.state.vt.us
www.state.vt.us/health/_cph/nutrition/wic.htm

Virginia
Division of Chronic Disease Prevention and Nutrition
Department of Health
1500 E. Main St., Room 132
Richmond, VA 23219
804-786-5420
Toll-free in-state: 1-888-WIC FOOD or
1-888-942-3663
TDD: 1-800-828-1120
Fax: 804-371-6162
Email: dseward@vdh.state.va.us
www.vahealth.org/wic

Virgin Islands
Virgin Islands WIC Program
Department of Health
Charles Harwood Complex
3500 Estate Richmond
Christiansted, VI 00821
340-773-9157 (St. Croix)
Fax: 340-773-6495
340-776-1770 (St. Thomas)
Fax: 340-774-5820

Washington
WIC Program
Office of Community Wellness and Prevention
P.O. Box 47886
Olympia, WA 98504-7886
360-236-3688
Toll-free in-state: 1-800-841-1410
TDD: 1-800-833-6388
Fax: 360-586-3890
Email: kim.wallace@doh.wa.gov

Wichita, Caddo, and Delaware Tribes
WCD Enterprises, Inc.
P.O. Box 247
Anadarko, OK 73005
405-247-2533
Toll-free: 1-800-492-3942
Fax: 405-247-5277
Email: wcdwic@tanet.net

West Virginia
West Virginia WIC Program
350 Capitol Street
Room 519
Charleston, WV 25301-3717
304-558-0030
Toll-free in-state: 1-888-WV-FAMILY
Or 1-888-983-2645
Fax: 304-558-1541
Email: DFerris@wvdhhr.org
www.wvdhhr.org/ons

Winnebago
Winnebago WIC Program
Box 666
Winnebago, NE 68071
402-878-2499
Fax: 402-878-2544
Email: winnwic@huntel.net

Wisconsin
Wisconsin WIC Program
Wisconsin Department of Health and Family Services
1 W. Wilson Street
P.O. Box 2659
Madison, WI 53701-2659
608-266-9824
Fax: 608-266-3125
Toll-free in-state: 1-800-722-2295
Email: herriph@dhfs.state.wi.us
www.dhfs.state.wi.us/wic

Wyoming
Division of Public Health
Department of Health
456 Hathaway Building
Cheyenne, WY 82002-0050
307-777-7494
Fax: 307-777-5643
Toll-free in-state: 1-800-994-4769
Email:
jmoran@missc.state.wy.us
http://wdhfs.state.wy.us/WDH/wic.htm

Free Food for Seniors

The Nutrition Services Incentive Program (NSIP) is the new name for the United States Department of Agriculture (USDA) cash or commodity program, known as the Nutrition Program for the Elderly (NPE). The program will continue to be funded through an appropriation to USDA and administered by the Food and Nutrition Services (FNS) of the USDA.

While there is no means test for participation in this program, services are targeted to older people with the greatest economic or social need, with special attention given to low-income minorities. In addition to focusing on low-income and other older persons at risk of losing their independence, the following individuals may receive service including:

- a spouse of any age;
- disabled persons under age 60 who reside in housing facilities occupied primarily by the elderly where congregate meals are served;
- disabled persons who reside at home and accompany older persons to meals; and
- nutrition service volunteers.

Since American Indians, Alaskan Natives, and Native Hawaiians tend to have lower life expectancies and higher rates of illness at younger ages, Tribal Organizations are given the option of setting the age at which older people can participate in the program.

Contact your state or local Administration on Aging.

National Administration on Aging
Administration on Aging
330 Independence Avenue, SW
Washington, DC 20201
202-619-7501
www.aoa.gov/

Eldercare Locator
800-677-1116
www.eldercare.gov/

USDA Food and Nutrition Service
3101 Park Center Drive
Alexandria, VA 22302
703-305-2060
www.fns.usda.gov/fdd/programs/nsip/nsiphome.htm

Rich Kids Pay 2 Cents for Pint of Milk

The Special Milk Program (SMP) provides milk to children in schools and childcare institutions that do not participate in other Federal child nutrition meal service programs. The program reimburses schools for the milk they serve.

Schools in the National School Lunch or School Breakfast Programs may also participate in the Special Milk Program to provide milk to children in half-day pre-kindergarten and kindergarten programs where children do not have access to the school meal programs.

Any child at a participating school, kindergarten program or eligible camp can get milk through the Special Milk Program. Children may buy milk or receive it free, depending on the school's choice of program options.

When local school officials offer free milk under the program, any child from a family that meets income guidelines for free meals is eligible. Each child's family must apply annually for free milk eligibility. In 2000, nearly 7,000 schools and residential childcare institutions participated, along with 1,100 summer camps and 500 non-residential childcare institutions.

For more information, contact your local school or the USDA Food and Nutrition Service.

USDA Food and Nutrition Service
3101 Park Center Drive, Room 914
Alexandria, VA 22302.
703-305-2286
www.fns.usda.gov/cnd/Milk/

The Food Distribution Program on Indian Reservations (FDPIR) is a Federal program that provides commodity foods to low-income households, including the elderly, living on Indian reservations, and to Native American families residing in designated areas near reservations. Many Native Americans participate in the FDPIR as an alternative to the Food Stamp Program usually because they do not have easy access to food stores.

The program is administered at the Federal level by the Food and Nutrition Service (FNS), an agency of the U.S. Department of Agriculture. FDPIR is administered locally by either Indian Tribal Organizations (ITOs) or an agency of a State government. Currently, there are approximately 235 tribes receiving benefits under the FDPIR through 96 ITOs and 6 State agencies. USDA purchases and ships commodities to the ITOs and State agencies based on their orders from a list of available foods. These administering agencies store and distribute the food, determine applicant eligibility, and provide nutrition education to recipients. USDA provides the administering agencies with funds for program administrative costs.

Households are certified based on income and resource standards set by the Federal government, and must be recertified at least every 12 months. Households **may not** participate in FDPIR and the Food Stamp Program in the same month. Each month, participating households receive a food package. Participants may select from a food package containing over 70 products to help them maintain a nutritionally balanced diet. The food package includes:

- frozen ground beef and chicken; canned meats, poultry and fish
- canned fruits and vegetables; canned soups; and spaghetti sauce
- macaroni and cheese; pastas; cereals; rice; and other grains
- cheese; egg mix; and nonfat dry and evaporated milk
- flour; cornmeal; bakery mix; and crackers
- low-fat refried beans; dried beans; and dehydrated potatoes
- canned juices and dried fruit
- peanuts and peanut butter
- corn syrup; vegetable oil; and shortening

Participants on many reservations can choose fresh produce instead of canned fruits and vegetables. Contact the office in your area for more information.

Food and Nutrition Services Headquarters
Food and Nutrition Service - USDA
Food Distribution Division
3101 Park Center Drive
Alexandria, VA 22302
703-305-2888
Fax: 703-305-2420
www.fns.usda.gov/fdd/programs/fdpir/fdpirhome.htm

Arizona

Colorado River Indian Tribes
Route 1, Box 23-B
Parker, AZ 85344
520-669-1283
Fax: 520-669-5675
Tribes Served: Colorado River Indian Tribes Reservation

Gila River Indian Community
P.O. Box 7
Sacaton, AZ 85247
520-562-9233
Fax: 520-562-3573
Tribes served: Ak-Chin and Gila River Reservations

White Mountain Apache Tribe
P.O. Box 2019
White River, AZ 85941
520-338-4964
Fax: 520-338-4330
Tribes Served: Fort Apache Reservation

The Navajo Nation
P.O. Box 1390
Window Rock, AZ 86515-1390
520-871-6538
Fax: 520-871-6435
Tribes Served: The Navaho Nation

Tohono O'Odham Nation (Papago)
P.O. Box 185
Sells, AZ 85634
520-383-6275
Fax: 520-383-6250
Tribes Served: Tohono O'Odham, San Xavier, San Lucy, Florence Village

Quechan Indian Tribe
P.O. Box 1899
Yuma, AZ 85366-1899
760-572-0740
Fax: 760-572-5066
Tribe Served: Fort Yuma Reservation

San Carlos Apache Tribe
P.O. Box 0
San Carlos, AZ 85550
520-475-2302
Fax: 520-475-2303
Tribes Served: San Carlos Apache and Tonto Apache Reservations

California

Fort Mojave Indian Tribe
500 Merriman Avenue
Needles, CA 92363
760-629-4591
Fax: 760-629-2468
Tribes Served: Fort Mojave Reservation

Hoopa Valley Tribe
P.O. Box 498
Hoopa, CA 95546
530-625-4646
Fax: 530-625-4717
Tribes Served: Karuk Tribe, Trinidad Rancheria, Table Mountain Rancheria, Quartz Valley, Rohnerville Rancheria, Redding Rancheria, Greenville Rancheria, Resighini Rancheria, Smith River Rancheria, Elk Valley Rancheria

Riverside/San Bernardino County Indian Health
11555 1/2 Potrero Road
Banning, CA 92220
909-849-4761
Fax: 909-845-8259
Tribes Served: Morongo, Agua Caliente Band, Cahuilla Reservation, San Manuel, Santa Rosa, Rancheria, Soboba Band, Torres Martinez Reservation

Sherwood Valley Band of Pomo Indians
3907 N. State Street, Bldg. #5
Ukiah, CA 95482
707-485-7632
Fax: 707-485-1347
Tribes Served: Big Valley, Cortina Rancheria, Coyote Valley, Elem Nation, Grindestone Rancheria, Guidiville Reservation, Hopland Reservation, Laytonville Rancheria, Manchester-Point,Arena Rancheria, Middletown Rancheria, Pinoleville Rancheria, Potter Valley, Rancheria, Redwood Valley Rancheria, Robinson Rancheria, Round Valley Reservation, Sherwood Valley Rancheria, Scotts Valley Rancheria, Upper Lake Rancheria, Colusa Rancheria, Stewart Point

Southern California Tribal Chairman's Association
P.O. Box 1326
Valley Center, CA 92082
760-749-5608
Fax: 760-749-7700
Tribes Served: Barona Reservation, Campo Reservation, Inaja Band of Mission Indians, Jamul Indian Village, La Jolla Reservation, Los Coyotes, Manzanita, Mesa Grande, Pala, Pauma Yuima Reservation, Pechanga Reservation, Temecula Band of Luiseno Mission Indians, Rincon Band, San Pasqual Band, Santa Ysabel Band, Sycuan Rancheria, Viejas

Tule River Tribe
P.O. Box 589
Porterville, CA 93258

559-781-3128
Fax: 559-781-9192
Tribes Served: Tule River Reservation, North Fork Rancheria, Big Sandy Rancheria, Cold Springs Rancheria, Santa Rosa Reservation, Santa Ynez Reservation, Picayune, Tuolumne, Rancheria

Yurok Tribe
P.O. Box 1087
Crescent City, CA 95531
707-464-1852
Fax: 707-464-5492
Tribes Served: Yurok Tribe

Colorado

Ute Mountain Tribe of Indians
General Delivery
Attn: Troy Ralstin
General Delivery
Towaoc, CO 81334
970-565-3751 ext. 316
Fax: 970-564-5341
Tribes Served: Ute Mountain Tribe

Emergency Family Services
Food Distribution Service
Southern Ute Indian Tribe
Southern Ute Tribal Affairs Building
P.O. Box 737
Ignacio, CO 81137
970-563-0285
Fax: 970-563-0312
Tribes Served: Southern Ute Indian Tribe

Idaho

Food Distribution Program
Coeur D'Alene Tribe of Idaho
P.O. Box 408
Plummer, ID 83851
208-686-1771
Fax: 208-686-6501
Tribes Served: Coeur D'Alene and Kootenai Reservations

Food Distribution Program
The Nez Perce Tribe of Idaho
P.O. Box 365
Lapwai, ID 83540
208-843-7306
Fax: 208-843-7401
Tribes Served: Nez Perce Reservation

Commodity Distribution Program
The Shoshone-Bannock Tribes
P.O. Box 306
Fort Hall, ID 83203
208-478-3918
Fax: 208-478-3917
Tribes Served: Fort Hall Reservation

Kansas

Food Distribution Program
United Tribes of Kansas and Southeast Nebraska, Inc.
3301 Thrasher Road
White Cloud, KS 66094
785-595-3291
Fax: 785-595-6667
Tribes Served: Iowa and Sac & Fox Reservations

Food Distribution Program
Kickapoo Tribe in Kansas
885 112th Drive, Box 800
Horton, KS 66439
785-486-2687
Fax: 785-486-2687
Tribes Served: Kickapoo Tribe

Food Distribution Program
Prairie Band of Potawatomi Indians
14880 K. Road
Mayetta, KS 66509
785-966-2718
Fax: 785-966-2529
Tribes Served: Prairie Band of Potawatomi Indians

Michigan

Food Distribution Program
Sault Ste. Marie Tribe of Chippewa Indians
3601 Mackinaw Road
Sault Ste. Marie, MI 49783
906-635-6076
Fax: 906-635-3658
Tribes Served: Sault Ste. Marie Tribe of Chippewa

Food Distribution Program
Bay Mills Indian Community
Route 1, Box 306
Brimley, MI 49715
906-248-3241
Fax: 906-248-5765
Tribes Served: Bay Mills Indian Community

Commodity Food Program
Keeweenaw Bay Indian Community
Route 1, Box 470
Keeweenaw Bay, MI 49946
906-524-7340
Fax: 906-524-7349
Tribes Served: Keweenaw Bay Indian Community

Food Distribution Program
Pokagon Band of Potawatomi Indians
52366 M 51 North
Dowagiac, MI 49047
888-281-1111
Tribes Served: Pokagon Potawatomi and Huron Potawatomi

Food Distribution Program
Little Traverse Bay Band of Odawa Indians
1345 US 31 North
P.O. Box 246
Petosky, MI 49770
231-348-5951
Fax: 231-348-8217
Tribes Served: Little Traverse Bay Band of Odawa Indians

Commodity Program
Little River Band of Ottawa Indians
1726 US 31 North
Manistee, MI 49660
231-723-1556
Fax: 231-723-8020
Tribes Served: Little River Band of Ottawa Indians

Minnesota

Food Distribution Program
Bois Forte Reservation Business Committee
P.O. Box 16
Nett Lake, MN 55772
218-757-3504
Fax: 218-757-3636
Tribes Served: Bois Forte Reservation

Food Distribution Program
Fond Du Lac Reservation
Business Committee
1720 Big Lake Road
Cloquet, MN 55720
218-878-4635 or 4644
Fax: 218-879-4146
Tribes Served: Fond Du Lac Reservation

Food Distribution Program
Grand Portage Indian Reservation
P.O. Box 326
Grand Portage, MN 55605
218-475-2480
Fax: 218-475-2284
Tribes Served: Grand Portage Indian Reservation

Food Distribution Program
Leech Lake Reservation
Business Committee
Route 3, Box 100
Cass Lake, MN 56633
218-335-2676
Fax: 218-335-2152
Tribes Served: Leech Lake Reservation

Food Distribution Program
Mille Lacs Band of Chippewa Indians
HC67, Box 194
Onamia, MN 56359
320-532-7494
Fax: 320-532-4354
Tribes Served: Mille Lacs Band of Chippewa Indians

Food Distribution Program
Red Lake Band of Chippewa Indians
P.O. Box 253
Redby, MN 56670
218-679-3720 or 3730
Fax: 218-679-2185
Tribes Served: Red Lake Band of Chippewa Indians

Food Distribution Program
White Earth RTC
HCO 3, Box 111
Star Route
Mahnomen, MN 56577
218-935-2233
Fax: 218-935-2235
Tribes Served: White Earth Band of Chippewa

Mississippi

Food Distribution Program
Mississippi Band of Choctaw Indians
P.O. Box 6010
Choctaw Branch
Philadelphia, MS 39350
601-650-1730
Tribes Served: Mississippi Band of Choctaw Indians

Montana

Food Distribution Section
Montana Department of Public Health & Human Services
Inter-Governmental Human Services Bureau
1400 Carter Drive
P.O. Box 202956
Helena, MT 59620-2956
406-447-4262
Fax: 406-447-4287

Food Distribution Program
Assiniboine and Sioux Tribes
P.O. Box 1027
Poplar, MT 59255
406-768-5321
Tribes Served: Fort Peck Reservation

Food Distribution Program
Blackfeet Nation
P.O. Box 3003
Browning, MT 59417
406-338-7340
Tribes Served: Blackfeet Reservation

Food Distribution Program
Chippewa-Cree Tribe
Rocky Boy Route, Box 544
Box Elder, MT 59521
406-395-4315
Tribes Served: Rocky Boy's Reservation

Food Distribution Program
Confederated Salish and Kootenai Tribes of the Flathead Nation
P.O. Box 329
St. Ignatius, MT 59865
406-745-4115
Tribes Served: Flathead Reservation

Food Distribution Program
Crow Tribe/District VII Human Resources
409 Crook Avenue
Hardin, MT 59034
406-665-2523
Tribes Served: Crow Reservation

Food Distribution Program
Gros Ventre and Assiniboine Tribes
RR1, Box 2728
Harlem, MT 59526
406-353-2205
Tribes Served: Fort Belknap Reservation

Northern Cheyenne Tribe
P.O. Box 128
Lame Deer, MT 59043
406-477-8278
Tribes Served: Northern Cheyenne Reservation

Nebraska

Food Distribution Program
Omaha Tribe of Nebraska/Iowa
P.O. Box 338
Macy, NE 68039
402-349-5406 or 5408
Fax: 402-349-5416
Tribes Served: Omaha Tribe of Nebraska/Iowa

Food Distribution Program
Santee Sioux Tribe of Nebraska
52950 Highway 12, Suite 1
Niobrara, NE 68760-7074
402-857-3511
Fax: 402-857-3530
Tribes Served: Santee Sioux Tribe of Nebraska

Computer Technician
Food Distribution Program
Winnebago Tribe of Nebraska
P.O. Box 720
Winnebago, NE 68071
402-878-2799
Fax: 402-878-2877

Tribes Served: Winnebago Tribe of Nebraska

Nevada

Food Distribution Program
2250 Barnett Way
Reno, NV 89512
775-688-1160
Fax: 775-688-1503
Tribes Served: Dresslerville Colony, Duckwater Reservation, Battle Mountain (Te-Moak) Indian Colony, Goshute Reservation, Fort McDermitt Reservation, Pyramid Lake, South Fork Reservation, Wells Colony, Elko Colony, Ely Indian Colony

Food Distribution Program
Shoshone Paiute Tribal Council
P.O. Box 219
Owyhee, NV 89832
775-757-3131
Fax: 775-757-3132
Tribes Served: Duck Valley Reservation

Commodity Food Program
Yerington Paiute Tribe
171 Campbell Lane
Yerington, NV 89447
775-463-4396
Fax: 775-463-4396
Tribes Served: Bridgeport Indian Colony, Benton Reservation, Bishop Reservation, Big Pine Paiute (Shoshone Tribe), Fort Independence Reservation, Fallon Colony and Reservation, Yomba Colony, Carson Colony, Woodfords Colony, Lovelock Colony, Reno-Sparks Colony, Walker River Reservation, Death Valley Timbisha Tribe

New Mexico

Food Distribution Program
Pueblo of Acoma Tribal Council
P.O. Box 449
Acoma, NM 87034
505-552-9489
Fax: 505-552-6536
Tribes Served: Acoma Pueblo and Laguna Pueblo

Food Distribution Program
Eight Northern Indian Pueblos Council
P.O. Box 969
San Juan Pueblo, NM 87566
505-455-2288
Fax: 505-455-3828
Tribes Served: Nambe Pueblo, Tesuque Pueblo, Picuris Pueblo, Pojoaque Pueblo, San Ildefonso Pueblo, San Juan Pueblo, Taos Pueblo, Santa Clara Pueblo

Food Distribution Program
Five Sandoval Indian Pueblos, Inc.
5901-B Office Blvd., NE
Albuquerque, NM 87109
505-345-0831
Fax: 505-344-7532
Tribes Served: Santo Domingo, Cochiti Pueblo, Zia Pueblo, Jemez Pueblo, Sandia Pueblo, Santa Ana Pueblo, San Felipe, Isleta

Food Distribution Program
Pueblo of Zuni
P.O. Box 339
Zuni Pueblo, NM 87327
505-782-4463
Fax: 505-782-2767
Tribes Served: Zuni Pueblo

New York

Food Distribution Program
St. Regis Mohawk Health Services
Community Building
Hogansburg, NY 13655
518-358-2272
Fax: 518-358-3203
Tribes Served: St. Regis Mohawk

Food Distribution Programs
The Seneca Nation of Indians
1490 Route 438
Irving, NY 14081
716-532-1028
Fax: 716-532-1226 or 9132
Tribes Served: Seneca Nation

North Carolina

Food Distribution Division
North Carolina Department of Agriculture
PO Box 659
Butner, NC 27509
910-575-4490

Food Distribution Office
Cherokee Tribe of North Carolina
P.O. Box 1123
Cherokee, NC 28719
704-497-9751
Tribes Served: Cherokee Tribe of North Carolina

North Dakota

Food Distribution Programs
Standing Rock Sioux Tribe
c/o Tribal Office Box D
Fort Yates, ND 58538
701-854-7238
Fax: 701-854-3422
Tribes Served: Standing Rock Sioux Tribe

Child Nutrition and Food Distribution Programs
State Department of Public Instruction
State Capitol Building
Bismarck, ND 58505
701-328-2732
Fax: 701-328-2461

Food Distribution Program
Fort Totten Agency
P.O. Box 414
Fort Totten, ND 58335
701-766-4684
Tribes Served: Spirit Lake Sioux Nation

Three Affiliated Tribes
Tribal Administration Building
New Town, ND 58763
701-627-4292
Tribes Served: Fort Berthold Reservation

Food Distribution Program
Trenton Indian Service Area
P.O. Box 210
Trenton, ND 58853
701-572-1130
Tribes Served: Trenton Indian Service Area

Food Distribution Program
Turtle Mountain Band of Chippewa Indians
Turtle Mountain Agency
P.O. Box 900
Belcourt, ND 58316
701-477-3857
Tribes Served: Turtle Mountain Band of Chippewa Indians

Oklahoma

Food Distribution Program
Apache Tribe of OK
P.O. Box 1220
Anadarko, OK 73005
405-247-5883
Fax: 405-247-5883
Tribes Served: Apache Tribe

Food Distribution Program
Cherokee Nation of OK
P.O. Box 948
Tahlequah, OK 74465
918-456-0671 ext. 2362 or 2914
Fax: 918-458-6281
Tribes Served: Cherokee Nation

Food Distribution Program
Cheyenne and Arapaho Tribes of Oklahoma
P.O. Box 59
Watonga, OK 73772
580-623-7815
Fax: 580-623-7813
Tribes Served: Cheyenne-Arapaho Reservation

Food Distribution Program
Chickasaw Nation of OK
P.O. Box 1548
Ada, OK 74820
580-436-2603
Fax: 580-436-7225
Tribes Served: Chickasaw Nation of OK

Food Distribution Program
Choctaw Nation of OK
P.O. Box 1210
Durant, OK 74702-1210
580-924-8280
Fax: 580-924-7773
Tribes Served: Choctaw Nation of OK

Food Distribution Program
Comanche Tribe of OK
P.O. Box 908
Lawton, OK 73501
580-492-3777
Fax: 580-492-3744
Tribes Served: Comanche Tribe of OK

Food Distribution Program
Inter-Tribal Council, Inc.
P.O. Box 1308
Miami, OK 74355
918-542-3443
Fax: 918-542-5529
Tribes Served: Miami, Eastern Shawnee, Ottawa, Peoria, Seneca-Cayoga, Modoc

Food Distribution Program
Kiowa Tribe of OK
P.O. Box 369
Carnegie, OK 73015
580-654-2618
Fax: 580-654-1354
Tribes Served: Kiowa Tribe of OK

Food Distribution Program
Muscogee (Creek) Nation
P.O. Box 580
Okmulgee, OK 74447
918-756-3467
Fax: 918-758-0849
Tribes Served: Muscogee (Creek) Nation

Food Distribution Program
Osage Tribe of OK
P.O. Box 426
Hominy, OK 74035
918-885-6886
Fax: 918-885-6889
Tribes Served: Osage Tribe of OK

Food Distribution Program
Pawnee Tribe of OK
P.O. Box 470
Pawnee, OK 74058
918-762-2541
Fax: 918-762-4509
Tribes Served: Pawnee Tribe of OK

Food Distribution Program
Ponca Tribe of OK
20 White Eagle Drive
Ponca City, OK 74601
580-762-3437
Fax: 580-762-4121
Tribes Served: Ponca Reservation

Food Distribution Program
Sac and Fox Nation of OK
Route 2, Box 246
Stroud, OK 74079
918-968-3526
Fax: 918-986-4837
Tribes Served: Sac and Fox Nation

Food Distribution Program
Seminole Nation of OK
P.O. Box 111
Seminole, OK 74818-0111
405-382-3900
Fax: 405-382-3305
Tribes Served: Seminole Nation of OK

Food Distribution Program
Wichita and Affiliated Tribes
P.O. Box 729
Anadarko, OK 73005
405-247-9677
Fax: 405-247-9262
Tribe Served: Wichita Tribe

Oregon

Food Distribution Program
Burns Paiute Tribe
HC-71 100 Pasigo Street
Burns, OR 97720
541-573-7312
Fax: 541-573-4217
Tribes Served: Burns Paiute Reservation

Food Distribution Program
The Klamath Tribe
2200 South 6th Street
Klamath, OR 97601
541-883-7166
Fax: 541-883-6505
Tribes Served: Klamath Reservation

Food Distribution Program
Siletz Confederated Indian Tribes
P.O. Box 549
Siletz, OR 97380
541-444-8211 ext. 431
Fax: 541-444-2307
Tribes Served: Siletz and Grande Ronde Reservations

Warm Springs Confederated Tribes
4217-A Holiday Street, P.O. Box C
Warm Springs, OR 97761
541-553-3579
Fax: 541-553-2279
Tribes Served: Confederated Tribes of Warm Springs

OR Housing and Community Services
1600 State Street
Salem, OR 97310
503-986-2122
Fax: 503-986-2020

Food Distribution Program
Confederated Tribes of the Umatilla Indian Reservation
P.O. Box 638
Pendleton, OR 97801
503-986-2000
Tribes Served: Confederated Tribes of the Umatilla Indian Reservation

South Dakota

Child and Adult Nutrition Services
Division of Education
700 Governors Drive
Pierre, SD 57501
605-773-4769
Fax: 605-773-6846

Commodity Distribution Office
Crow Creek Sioux Tribe
P.O. Box 50
Fort Thompson, SD 57339
605-245-2221
Tribes Served: Crow Creek Sioux Tribe

Commodity Distribution Office
Lower Brule Sioux Tribe
P.O. Box 187
Lower Brule, SD 57548
605-473-5372
Tribes Served: Lower Brule Sioux Tribe

Commodity Distribution Office
Sisseton-Wahpeton Sioux Tribe
Agency Village, SD 57262
605-698-3762
Tribes Served: Sisseton-Wahpeton Sioux Tribe

Food Distribution Program
Cheyenne River Sioux Tribe
P.O. Box 590
Eagle Butte, SD 57625
605-964-3326 or 2931
Fax: 605-964-2932
Tribes Served: Cheyenne River Sioux Tribe

Food Distribution Program
Flandreau Santee Sioux Tribe
P.O. Box 283
Flandreau, SD 57028
605-997-2402
Fax: 605-997-2403
Tribes Served: Flandreau Santee Sioux Tribe

Commodity Distribution Program
Rosebud Sioux Tribe
P.O. Box 84
Mission, SD 57555
605-856-4558
Fax: 605-856-4283
Tribes Served: Rosebud Sioux Tribe

Commodity Distribution Office
Oglala Sioux Tribe
P.O. Box 278
Pine Ridge, SD 57770
605-867-5511
Fax: 605-867-5318
Tribes Served: Oglala Sioux Tribe

Food Distribution Program
Yankton Sioux Tribe
P.O. Box 235
Wagner, SD 57380
605-384-5549
Fax: 605-384-5987
Tribes Served: Yankton Sioux Tribe

Utah

Food Distribution Program
Ute Tribe
P.O. Box 280
Fort Duchesne, UT 84026
435-722-3674
Fax: 435-722-3675
Tribes Served: Ute Tribe

Washington

Food Distribution Program
Colville Confederated Tribes
P.O. Box 150
Nespelem, WA 99155
509-634-2766
Fax: 509-634-2795
Tribes Served: Colville Confederated Tribes

Commodity Food Program
The Yakama Indian Nation
P.O. Box 151
Toppenish, WA 98948
509-865-5121 ext. 4536
Fax: 509-865-7723
Tribes Served: Yakama Indian Nation

Food Distribution Program
Makah Indian Tribe
P.O. Box 115
Neah Bay, WA 98357
360-645-2154
Fax: 360-645-2154
Tribes Served: Makah Indian Tribe

Commodity Food Program
Lummi Indian Tribe
2590 Lummi View Drive
Bellingham, WA 98226
360-758-3066
Fax: 360-758-3068
Tribes Served: Lummi Indian Tribe

Food Distribution Program
Quileute Indian Tribe
P.O. Box 219
La Push, WA 98350
360-374-2147
Fax: 360-374-6311
Tribes Served: Quileute and Hoh Reservations

Food Distribution Program
Quinault Indian Nation
P.O. Box 189
Taholah, WA 98587
360-276-8211 ext. 336
Fax: 360-276-4191
Tribes Served: Quinault Indian Nation

Food Distribution Program
Small Tribes of Western Washington
3040 96th Street, South
Lakewood, WA 98499
253-589-7101 ext. 237
Fax: 253-589-7117
Tribes Served: Suquamish, Upper Skagit, Shoalwater Bay Tribe, Nooksack, Muckleshoot, Swinomish, Lower Elwha, Tulalip, Sauk-Suilattle, Stillaguamish, Puyallup, Jamestown Tribes, Samish Indian Tribe

Food Distribution Program
South Puget Inter-Tribal Planning Agency
4822 She-Na-Num Drive, S.E.
Olympia, WA 98513
360-459-9607
Fax: 360-438-9114
Tribes Served: Nisqually, Chehalis, Skokomish, Squaxin Island, Port Gamble/S'Klallam

Food Distribution Program
Spokane Tribe of Indians
P.O. Box 100
Wellpinit, WA 99040
509-258-7145
Fax: 509-258-7001
Tribes Served: Spokane and Kalispel Reservations

Wisconsin

Food Distribution Program
Bad River Band of Lake Superior Tribe of Chippewa Indians
P.O. Box 28
Odanah, WI 54861
715-682-7897
Fax: 715-682-7892
Tribes Served: Bad River Band of Lake Superior Tribe of Chippewa Indians

Food Distribution Program
Lac Courte Oreilles Tribal Governing Board
13394 W. Trepania Road
Bldg. #1
Hayward, WI 54843
715-634-3677
Fax: 715-634-4797
Tribes Served: Lac Courte Oreilles Tribe

Food Distribution Program
Lac Du Flambeau Band of Lake Superior Chippewa Indians
P.O. Box 305
Lac du Flambeau, WI 54538
715-588-9604
Fax: 715-588-7930
Tribes Served: Lac Du Flambeau Band of Lake Superior Chippewa Indians

Food Distribution Program
Menominee Indian Tribe of Wisconsin
P.O. Box 910
Keshena, WI 54135
715-799-5132
Fax: 715-799-4325
Tribes Served: Menominee Indian Tribe of Wisconsin

Food Distribution Program
Oneida Tribe of Indians of Wisconsin
7360 Water Circle Place
Oneida, WI 54115
414-869-1041
Fax: 414-869-1668
Tribes Served: Oneida Tribe of Indians of Wisconsin

Food Distribution Program
Red Cliff Band of Lake Superior Chippewa Indians
P.O. Box 529
Bayfield, WI 54814
715-779-3740
Fax: 715-779-3704
Tribes Served: Red Cliff Band of Lake Superior Chippewa Indians

Food Distribution Program
Sokaogon (Mole Lake) Chippewa Community
Route 1, Box 625
Crandon, WI 54520
715-478-3404
Fax: 715-478-7515
Tribes Served: Sokaogon (Mole Lake) Chippewa Community

Food Distribution Program
St. Croix Tribal Council
P.O. Box 287
Hertel, WI 54845
715-349-7368
Fax: 715-349-5768
Tribes Served: St. Croix Tribe

Food Distribution Program
Stockbridge-Munsee Community
N8476 Moh He Con Nuck Road
Bowler, WI 54416
715-793-4941
Fax: 715-793-1307
Tribes Served: Stockbridge-Munsee Community

Food Distribution Program
Ho Chunk Nation
P.O. Box 202
Black River Falls, WI 54615
715-284-7461
Fax: 715-284-5620
Tribes Served: Ho Chunk Nation (Winnebago)

Wyoming

Food Distribution Program
Arapaho Tribe
98 Gas Hill Road
P.O. Box 953
Riverton, WY 82501
307-856-9661
Fax: 307-856-6569
Tribes Served: Arapaho Tribe

Food Distribution Program
Eastern Shoshone Tribe
15451 U.S. Highway 287
P.O. Box 520
Fort Washakie, WY 82514
307-332-3087
Fax: 307-332-6008
Tribes Served: Eastern Shoshone Tribe

Free Extra Food

When the government has extra food, it passes it along to those in need. The Commodity Supplemental Food Program (CSFP) works to improve the health of low-income pregnant and breastfeeding women, other new mothers up to one year postpartum, infants, children up to age six, and elderly people at least 60 years of age by supplementing their diets with nutritious USDA commodity foods. It provides food and administrative funds to States to supplement the diets of these groups.

The population served by CSFP is similar to that served by USDA's Women, Infants and Children (WIC), but CSFP also serves elderly people, and provides food rather than the food vouchers that WIC participants receive. Eligible people cannot participate in both programs at the same time.

To be eligible, women, infants, children, and the elderly must reside in a state or Indian reservation that participates in CSFP. While elderly persons must have income at or below 130 percent of the Federal Poverty Income Guidelines (currently $15,522 for a family of two), women, infants and children must meet income eligibility requirements established by the state (typically 185 percent of the guidelines).

CSFP food packages do not provide a complete diet, but rather are good sources of the nutrients typically lacking in the diets of the target population. Food packages include a variety of foods, such as infant formula and cereal, non-fat dry and evaporated milk, juice, farina, oats, ready-to-eat cereal, rice, pasta, egg mix, peanut butter, dry beans or peas, canned meat or poultry or tuna, cheese, and canned fruits and vegetables.

CSFP is administered at the Federal level by the Food and Nutrition Service (FNS), an agency of the U.S. Department of Agriculture. Contact your state program for more information.

Headquarters
Food and Nutrition Service - USDA
Food Distribution Division
3101 Park Center Drive, Room 504
Alexandria, VA 22302
703-305-2888
Fax: 703-305-2420
www.fns.usda.gov/fdd/programs/csfp/csfphome.htm

Arizona
Department of Health Services
Office of Nutrition Services
1740 W. Adams St., Room 208
Phoenix, AZ 85007
602-542-1886

California
State Department of Education
560 J Street, Room 270
Sacramento, CA 95814
916-324-9880

Colorado
Food Distribution Programs
Colorado Department of Human Services
1575 Sherman St., 3rd Floor
Denver, CO 80203-1714
303-866-2652

District Of Columbia
Commodity Supplemental Food Program
Department of Human Services
2100 Martin Luther King Ave., SE, Room 400
Washington, D.C. 20020
202-645-5518

Illinois
Illinois Dept. of Human Services
Commodity Supplemental Food Program
535 West Jefferson Street
Springfield, IL 62761
217-782-2166

Iowa
Food Distribution
Iowa Dept. of Human Services
Hoover State Office Building
Des Moines, IA 50319
515-281-5410

Kansas
WIC/CSFP Director
Kansas Department of Health and Environmental Nutrition and WIC Services
900 S.W. Jackson St., 10th Floor
Topeka, KS 66612-1290
785-296-1324

Kentucky
Division of Food Distribution
Kentucky Department of Agriculture
100 Fair Oaks Lane, Suite 502
Frankfort, KY 40601-1136
502-564-4387

Louisiana
Nutrition Section
Louisiana Office of Public Health
P.O. Box 60630
New Orleans, LA 70160
504-568-7709

Michigan
Food Distribution and Fiscal Report
Michigan Dept. of Education
P.O. Box 30008
Lansing, MI 48909
517-373-4265

Minnesota
Minnesota Dept. of Health
85 E. Seventh Place, Suite 400
P.O. Box 64882
St. Paul, MN 55164-0882
651-281-9922

Red Lake
CSFP Program
Red Lake Band of Chippewa Indians
P.O. Box 253
Redby, MN 56670
ITO-RL
218-679-3720 or 3730

Mississippi
Mississippi Dept. of Health
3000 Old Canton Rd., Suite 300
P.O. Box 1700
Jackson, MS 39215-1700
601-987-6730

Missouri
Missouri Department of Health and Human Services
Bureau of Community Food and Nutrition Assistance
Division of Nutritional Health and Senior Services
P.O. Box 570
Jefferson City, MO 65102-0570
573-751-6400
800-733-6251

Montana
Food Distribution Section
Department of Public Health and Human Services
Inter-Gov. Human Services Bureau
1400 Carter Drive
Helena, MT 59620
406-447-4262

Nebraska
Nebraska Dept. of Health and Human Services
Division of Family Health
301 Centennial Mall South
P.O. Box 95044
Lincoln, NE 68509-5044
402-471-0189

New Hampshire
WIC Nutrition Services Bureau
NH Department of Health & Human Services
6 Hazen Drive
Concord, NH 03301-6527
603-271-4546

New Mexico
New Mexico Dept. of Health
525 Camino de los Marquez
Santa Fe, NM 87501
505-476-8490

New York
New York State Dept. of Health
Food and Nutrition Program (CSFP)
Division of Nutrition
11 University Place, 2nd Floor
Albany, NY 12203-3399
518-458-6838

North Carolina
Food Distribution Division
North Carolina Department of Agriculture
P.O. Box 725
Butner, NC 27509-0725
919-575-4490

North Dakota
Department of Public Instruction
600 E. Boulevard Ave.
Dept. 201
Bismarck, ND 58505-0440
701-328-2294

Ohio
TEFAP/CSFP Coordinator
Ohio Department of Job and Family Services
145 South Front Street
Columbus, OH 43215-4156
614-644-6919

Oregon
OPUS and Food Program Coordinator
Oregon Housing and Community Development
PO Box 14508
Salem, OR 97309-0409
503-986-2065
Fax: 503-986-2006

Pennsylvania
State Department of Agriculture
Bureau of Food Distribution
2301 North Cameron Street
Harrisburg, PA 17110-9408
717-772-2853

South Dakota
Food Distribution Supervisor
Child and Adult Nutrition Services
Department of Education and Cultural Affairs
800 Governors Drive
Pierre, SD 57501-2294
605-773-4769

Oglala Sioux
Commodity Distribution Program
Oglala Sioux Tribe
P.O. Box 278
Pine Ridge, SD 57770
605-867-5304

Tennessee
Tennessee Department of Health
Cordell Hull Bldg., 5th Floor
425 5th Avenue North
Nashville, TN 37247
615-741-7218

Texas
Special Nutrition Programs
TEFAP and CSFP Coordinator
Texas Department of Human Services
P.O. Box 149030
MC Y-904
Austin, TX 78714-9030
512-467-5847

Vermont
Department of Aging and Disability
103 South Main Street
Waterbury, VT 05671
802-241-2401
Fax: 802-241-2325

Washington
Program Manager
Washington Department of General Administration
Surplus Programs
2301 C Street SW
Auburn, WA 98001-7410
253-333-4909

Wisconsin
WIC/CSFP Director
Wisconsin Department of Health and Family Services
1 W. Wilson St.
P.O. Box 2659
Madison, WI 53701

Free Emergency Food

The Emergency Food Assistance Program (TEFAP) is a Federal program that helps supplement the diets of low-income needy people, including elderly people, by providing them with emergency food and nutrition assistance at no cost.

Under TEFAP, commodity foods are made available by the U.S. Department of Agriculture to States. States provide the food to local agencies that they have selected, usually food banks, which in turn, distribute the food to soup kitchens and food pantries that directly serve the public. TEFAP is administered at the Federal level by the Department of Agriculture's Food and Nutrition Services. State agencies receive the food and supervise overall distribution.

Who is eligible to get food?

- Public or private nonprofit organizations that provide food and nutrition assistance to the needy through the distribution of food for home use or the preparation of meals. See below:

- Households that meet State eligibility criteria. Each State sets criteria for determining what households are eligible to receive food for home consumption. Income standards may, at the State's discretion, be met through participation in other existing Federal, State, or local food, health, or welfare programs for which eligibility is based on income.

State agencies work out details of administration and distribution. They select local organizations that either directly distribute to households or serve meals, or distribute to other local organizations that perform these functions.

What types of food are available?
The types of commodity foods USDA purchases for TEFAP distribution vary depending on the preferences of States and

agricultural market conditions. More than 40 products were made available for Fiscal Year 2001, including: canned and dried fruits, canned vegetables, meat/poultry/fish, pasta, peanut butter and others.

Contact your state-administering agency for more information.

FNS Headquarters
Food and Nutrition Service - USDA
Food Distribution Division
3101 Park Center Drive
Alexandria, VA 22302
703-305-2888
Fax: 703-305-2420
www.fns.usda.gov/fdd/programs/tefap/tefaphome.htm

Alabama
Food Distribution Program
Department of Education
5306 Gordon Persons Bldg.
P.O. Box 302101
Montgomery, AL 26130-2101
334-242-8240
Fax: 334-242-2475
Email:
Dcooper@Sednet.Alsde.Edu

Alaska
USDA Commodity Program
Department of Education &
Early Development
801 West 10th Street, Suite 200
Juneau, AK 99801-1894
907-465-8710
Fax: 907-465-8638
Email:
Molly_Wheeler@eed.state.ak.us

Arizona
Hunger Relief Programs
Community Services
Administration
Dept. of Economic Security
P.O. Box 6123, Site Code 086Z
Phoenix, AZ 85005
602-542-9949
Fax: 602-542-6655

Arkansas
Arkansas Department of Human
Services
P.O. Box 5071
No. Little Rock, AR 72119-5071
501-371-1401
Fax: 501-371-1410
Email:
don.griffin@mail.state.ar.us

California
CA Dept. of Social Services
Emergency Food Assistance
Program
744 "P" Street MS 19-51
Sacramento, CA 94814
916-229-3338
Fax: 916-229-3342
Email: GJGrayson@aol.com

Colorado
Department of Human Services
1575 Sherman Street 3rd Floor
Denver, CO 80203
303-866-5105
Fax: 303-866-5098
Email: allison.hill@state.co.us

Connecticut
Department of Social Services
Capital Programs Division
25 Sigourney Street
Hartford, CT 06106-5033
860-424-5881
Fax: 860-424-4952
Email:
mary.plaskonka@po.state.ct.us

Delaware
Commodity Program
Dept. of Administrative Services
Division of Purchasing
P.O. Box 299
Delaware City, DE 19706-0299
302-834-4513
Fax: 302-836-7642
Email: cbiddle@state.de.us

District Of Columbia
Special Nutrition and
Commodities
State Education Office
441 4th Street, NW, Suite 350N
Washington, DC 20001-2714
202-727-6436
Fax: 202- 727-2834
Email: Sharon.Bland@dc.gov

Florida
Chief of Food Distribution
Department of Agriculture and
Consumer Services
Mayo Bldg.2nd Fl, M39
Tallahassee, FL 32399-0800
850-487-6694
Fax: 850- 488-6961
Email: vantreg@doacs.state.fl.us

Georgia
Food Distribution Administrator
Department of Education
1658 Twin Towers East
Atlanta, GA 30334
404-656-2470
Fax: 404-656-5697
Email: efreeman@doe.k12.ga.us

Guam
Food Services Administration
Department of Education
Government of Guam
P.O. Box DE
Agana, GU 96910
9-011-671-475-6400
Fax: 9-011-671-477-5394

Hawaii
Office of Community Services
Department of Labor and
Industrial Relations
830 Punchbowl St., Room 420
Honolulu, HI 96813
808-586-8675
Fax: 808-586-8685

Idaho
Division of Welfare
State of Idaho
450 West State Street, 6th Floor
P.O. Box 83720
Boise, ID 83720-0036
208-334-5734
Fax: 208-332-7343
Email: stokesl@idhw.state.id.us

Illinois
Office of Homeless Services and Supportive Housing
Division of Transitional Services
300 Iles Park, 1st Floor
Springfield, IL 62761
217-782-1317
Fax: 217-524-5829
Email: dhsd6067@dhs.state.il.us

Indiana
Division of Family & Children
Housing and Community Service
402 West Washington
PO Box 6116
Indianapolis, IN 46206
317-232-6997
Fax: 317-232-7079
Email:
mmcgraw@fssa.state.in.us

Iowa
Iowa Department of Human Services
Division of Financial, Health & Work Support
Bureau of Financial & Work Support
5th Floor, Hoover State Office Building
Des Moines, IA 50319-0114
515-281-5410
Fax: 515-281-7791
Email: kjones4@dhs.state.ia.us

Kansas
Food Distribution Manager
Department of Social and Rehab. Services
Income Maintenance/EPS, Food Distribution Unit
915 SW Harrison
DSOB, 681-W
Topeka, KS 66612
785-368-8126
Fax: 785-296-6960
Email: rjh@srskansas.org

Kentucky
Department of Agriculture
107 Corporate Drive
Frankfort, KY 40601
502-573-0282
Fax: 502 573-0304

Louisiana
Department of Agriculture & Forestry
P.O. Box 4194
Baton Rouge, LA 70821-4194
225-922-1255
Fax: 225-925-6012
Email:
Mike_S@LDAF.STATE.LA.US

Maine
Maine Department of Agriculture
Food and Rural Service
State House Station 28
Augusta, ME 04333
207-287-7513
Fax: 207-624-5017 *or* 207-287-7548
Email: randy.mraz@state.me.us

Maryland
Department of Human Resources
Emergency Food Assistance
311 W. Saratoga St., Room 239
Baltimore, MD 21201
410-767-7015
Fax: 410-333-0256
Email:
kwilborn@dhr.state.md.us

Massachusetts
Department of Education
350 Main Street
Malden, MA 02148
781-388-6473
Fax: 781-388-3399
Email: mherlihy@doe.mass.edu

Michigan
Office of School Support Services
Michigan Dept. of Education
PO Box 30008
Lansing, MI 48909
517-373-4265
Fax: 517-373-4022
Email: rhodesk@state.mi.us

Minnesota
Minnesota Department of Children, Families and Learning
Office of Economic Opportunity
1500 Highway 36 West
Roseville, MN 55113-4266
651-582-8396
Fax: 651-582-8521
Email: ty.morris@state.mn.us

Mississippi
Mississippi Department of Human Services
P.O. Box 352
Jackson, MS 39205
601-359-4812
Fax: 601-359-4435

Missouri
Food Distribution Programs
Division of Family Services
Department of Social Services
P.O. Box 310
Jefferson City, MO 65102-0310
573-751-4328
Fax: 573-526-4413
Email: ghilch@midamerica.net

Montana
Food Distribution Section
Department of Public Health and Human Services
Inter-Government Human Services Bureau
1400 Carter Drive
Helena, MT 59620
406-447-4262
Fax: 406- 447-4287

Nebraska
Food Distribution Program
Department of Health and Human Services
P.O. Box 95044
Lincoln, NE 68509-5044
402-471-9291
Fax: 402-471-9455
Email:
Julia.West@hhss.state.ne.us

Nevada
Nevada Purchasing Division
2250 Barnett Way
Reno, NV 89512

775-688-1160
Fax: 775-688-1503
Email:
dmeizel@govmail.state.nv.us

New Hampshire
Federal Supplies Manager
New Hampshire Distributing Agency
12 Hills Avenue
Concord, NH 03301-4899
603-271-2602
Fax: 603-271-6475
Email:
material@nhsa.state.nh.us

New Jersey
Food Distribution Programs
Department of Agriculture
P.O. Box 330
Trenton, NJ 08625
609-292-5068
Fax: 609-984-5367
Email: agmrita@ag.state.nj.us

New Mexico
Human Services Department
Community Development and Commodities Bureau
P.O. Box 26507
Albuquerque, NM 87125-6507
505-841-2602
Fax: 505-841-2691
Email:
dora.fresquez@state.nm.us

New York
Division of Donated Foods
Office of General Services
Corning Tower Bldg. 40th Floor
Empire State Plaza
Albany, NY 12242
518-474-5122
Fax: 518-486-5660
Email:
ernest.berger@ogs.state.ny.us

North Carolina
Food Distribution Division
Department of Agriculture & Consumer Services
P.O. Box 659
Butner, NC 27509-0659
919-575-4490
Fax: 919-575-4143
Email: gary.gay@ncmail.net

North Dakota
Department of Public Instruction
600 East Boulevard Avenue
Dept. 201
Bismarck, ND 58505-0440
701-328-2732
Fax: 701-328-2461
Email: jdasovick@state.nd.us

Ohio
Office of Family Stability
Ohio Department of Job & Family Services
145 South Front Street
Columbus, OH 43215-4156
614-644-6919
Fax: 614-644-9974
Email: barcuj@odjfs.state.oh.us

Oklahoma
Department of Human Services
P.O. Box 53160
Oklahoma City, OK 73152-3160
405-521-3581
Fax: 405-521-6949
Email: paula.price@okdhs.org

Oregon
Oregon Housing and Community Services Department
1600 State Street
Salem, OR 97310
503-986-2065
Fax: 503-986-2006

Oregon Food Bank
7900 N.E. 33rd Drive
Portland, OR 97211
503-282-0555, ext. 264
Fax: 503-282-4090

Pennsylvania
Department of Agriculture
Bureau of Food Distribution
2301 North Cameron Street
Harrisburg, PA 17110-9408
717-787-2940
Fax: 717-787-2387
Email: BShutt@state.pa.us

Puerto Rico
Department of the Family
P.O. Box 80000
San Juan, PR 00910-0800
787-722-7423
Fax: 787-725-1938

Rhode Island
Department of Human Services
Contract Management Section
600 New London Avenue
Cranston, RI 02920
401-462-6865
Fax: 401-462-2975
Email
gdunphy@gw.dhs.state.ri.us

South Carolina
Food Service Operations
Department of Social Services
P.O. Box 1520
Columbia, SC 29202-1520
803-898-9279
Fax: 803-734-9515
Email: lyoung@dss.state.sc.us

South Dakota
Child & Adult Nutrition Services
Department of Education and Cultural Affairs
700 Governors Drive
Pierre, SD 57501-2291
605-773-4769
Fax: 605-773-6846
Email: mark.mattke@state.sd.us

Tennessee
Department of Agriculture
Division of Commodity Distribution
Ellington Agriculture Center
Box 40627, Melrose Station
Nashville, TN 37204
615-837-5166
Fax: 615-837-5014

Texas
Texas Department of Human Services
Special Nutrition Programs
P.O. Box 149030 MCY906
Austin, TX 78714-9030
512-420-2432
Fax: 512-371-9684

Utah
State Office of Education
Child Nutrition Programs
250 East 500 South
Salt Lake City, UT 84111
801-538-7687
Fax: 801-538-7585

Email:
Wgaddis@USOE.k12.ut.us

Vermont
Office of Economic Opportunity
Donated Food Section
103 South Main Street
Waterbury, VT 05671-1801
802-241-2580
Fax: 802-241-1225

Virginia
Department of Agriculture and Consumer Services
Food Distribution Program
P.O. Box 1163
Suite 809
Richmond, VA 23218-1163
804-786-0665
Fax: 804-371-7788

Virgin Islands
Special Nutrition Programs
Department of Education
No. 44-46 Kongens Gade
St. Thomas, US VI00802
340-774-9373
Fax: 340-774-9705
Email:
specialnutrition@yahoo.com

Washington
General Administration
Office of State Procurement
Surplus Programs
2301 C Street SW
Auburn, WA 98001
253-333-4909
Fax: 253-333-4915
Email: kmcquad@ga.wa.gov

West Virginia
West Virginia Department of Agriculture
Donated Food Program
908 Bullitt Street
Charleston, WV 25301
304-558-0573
Fax: 304-558-2105
Email: dcarter@ag.state.wv.us

Wisconsin
Division of Economic Support
Department of Health & Family Services
One West Wilson Street
P.O. Box 8916
Madison, WI 53708
608-266-3362
Fax: 608-267-2069
Email:
buechva@dhfs.state.wi.us

Wyoming
Wyoming Department of Family Services
Hathaway Building, Room 347
2300 Capitol Avenue
Cheyenne, WY 82002-0490
307-777-6083
Fax: 307-777-7747
Email: egardn@state.wy.us

Free Food for Kids in the Summer

The Summer Food Service Program (SFSP) was created to ensure that children in lower-income areas can continue to receive nutritious meals during long school vacations, when they do not have access to school lunch or breakfast. Children who aren't hungry learn better, act better, and feel better. The Summer Food Service Program helps children get the nutrition they need to learn, play, and grow throughout the summer months when they are out of school. In some counties, only 13% of the children who get a free lunch during the school year take advantage of this program during the summer.

Schools, public agencies, and private nonprofit organizations may sponsor the program. Your state education department can tell you where and how to apply. The Food and Nutrition Service, an agency of the U.S. Department of Agriculture, administers SFSP at the Federal level. State education agencies administer the program in most States. Sponsors provide free meals to a group of children at a central site, such as a school or a community center.

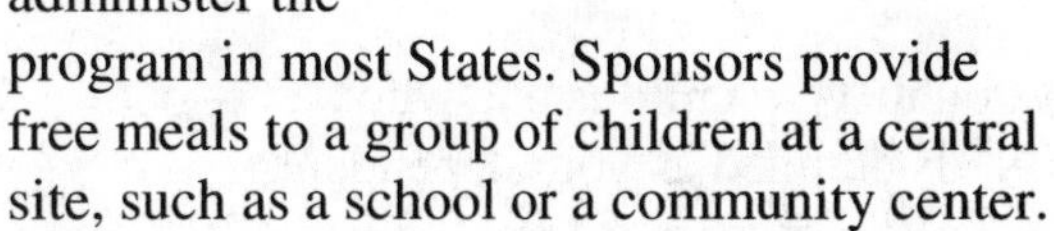

Open sites operate in low-income areas where at least half of the children come from families with incomes at or below 185 percent of the Federal poverty level, making them eligible for free and reduced-price school meals. Meals are served free to any child at the open site.

To learn more about SFSP in your State, contact your administrating agency (see listings for School Lunch Program). You may also contact:

USDA Food and Nutrition Service
3101 Park Center Drive, Room 914
Alexandria, Virginia 22302.
703-305-2286
www.fns.usda.gov/cnd/Summer/

Get $600 For Each Child

Kids cost a lot of money. They need food, clothing, shelter, music lessons, and soccer shoes. The child tax credit is a credit on your taxes up to $600 for each of your children. This will increase in stages up to $1,000 in 2010. To be able to take this credit you must meet certain requirements. The credit is limited to people with an income below a certain modified adjusted gross income level. The phase out begins with the following income levels:

- Married filing jointly $110,000
- Head of Household/Qualifying Widow or Widower $75,000
- Married filing separate $55,000

A qualifying child is one who:

- Is claimed as your dependent,
- Was under age 17 at the end of the tax year,
- Is your son, daughter, adopted child, descendant of a child, stepchild or eligible foster child, and
- Is a US citizen or resident.

The child tax credit is also limited by the total amount of your income tax. If there is no tax to reduce, the credit cannot be claimed. However, if the amount of the child tax credit is more than your taxes, it is possible to claim an "additional" child tax credit for as much as 10% of your earned income greater than $10,000. Also, if you have three or more qualifying children, you may be able to claim an additional child tax credit up to the amount of Social Security you paid during the year, less any earned income credit you receive. For this, you would need to file Form 8812 in addition to your other tax return. Still, the total of both credits still cannot be more than $600 per child. The child tax credit is in addition to the child and dependent care credit and the earned income credit.

The instructions and worksheet needed to figure this credit are included in the 1040 or 1040A tax return packets. If you are claiming an adoption credit, mortgage interest credit, or District of Columbia first time homebuyers credit, you must use Publication 972 from the IRS to figure your child tax credit. You can download that publication and Form 8812, referred to above, from the IRS website at www.irs.gov} To receive them by Fax-On-Demand, call 703-368-9694 or call 800-TAX-FORM (829-3676) to have them sent by mail or go to {www.irs.gov}.

$4,008 For You and Your Family

The Earned Income Tax Credit (EITC), also known as the Earned Income Credit (EIC) is a Federal income tax credit for low-income working individuals and families. It was originally approved by Congress to help ease the burden of social security taxes and provide an incentive to work. The EITC reduces the amount of taxes owed. If the credit exceeds the amount of taxes owed, it is possible to get a refund check. The amount of the EITC depends on the size and income of the family.

In order to claim the Earned Income Tax Credit:

- Your filing status cannot be "Married filing separately".
- You must be a US citizen or resident alien all year.
- You cannot file Form 2555 or Form 2555-EZ (Foreign Earned Income).
- Your investment income cannot exceed $2,450.
- You must have earned income.

If you have a qualifying child

- Your child must meet the relationship, age, and residency test.
- Your qualifying child must not be the qualifying child of another person with a higher modified adjusted gross income (AGI).
- You cannot be a qualifying child of another person.

If you do not have a qualifying child

- You must be at least 25 but under 65.
- You cannot be the dependent of another person.

- You cannot be the qualifying child of another person.
- You must have lived in the US more than half of the year.

Figuring and Claiming the EIC

Your earned income must be less than:

- $32,121 if you have more than one qualifying child,
- $28,281 if you have one qualifying child, or
- $10,710 if you do not have any qualifying children.

What Qualifies As Earned Income

Taxable Earned Income

1) Wages, Salaries, and Tips,
2) Net earnings from self-employment,
3) Gross income received as a statutory employee,
4) Union strike benefits, and
5) Taxable long-term disability benefits received before minimum retirement age.

What Does Not Qualify As Earned Income

1) Interest and dividends,
2) pensions and annuities,
3) social security and railroad retirement benefits (including disability benefits),
4) alimony and child support,
5) welfare benefits,

6) workers' compensation benefits,
7) unemployment compensation (insurance),
8) nontaxable foster care payments, and
9) veterans' benefits, including VA rehabilitation payments.

You can download that publication and Form W-5, referred to above, from the IRS website at {www.irs.gov}. To receive them by Fax-On-Demand, call 703-368-9694 or call 800-TAX-FORM (829-3676) to have them sent by mail or go to {www.irs.gov}.

$900+/Mo For 5 Years

Formerly known as AFDC, Temporary Assistance for Needy Families (TANF) replaced the JOBS and AFDC programs in July of 1997. It was established to help the States run a program to aid needy families with children, or expecting children, and provides parents with job preparation, work, and support services so that they may be able to leave the program and become self-sufficient. The States also provide other services under TANF that establish paternity and establish, modify, or enforce child support payments for children that are provided assistance. Its purpose is to provide assistance for needy families so that children can be cared for in their homes (or the homes of relatives) and to promote job preparation and work. It also looks to promote marriage; prevent and reduce out-of-wedlock pregnancies; and encourage 2-parent families.

Participants in the TANF program must work as soon as they are "job ready", or no later than 2 years after the date they started to receive assistance (there are a few exceptions). For single parents, participation must be in the form of a 30-hour work week. Two parent families must work a 35-50 hour work week, depending on their circumstances. If the work requirements are not met, families may get a reduction or termination of benefits. However, single parents that have a child under 6 years cannot be penalized for not meeting the work requirement if they cannot find child care. Single parents with a child under one year may be exempted from the work requirements. In West Virginia, you can get $100 bonus per month if you are married!

Initially, an assessment of a recipient's skills takes place. They may then develop a personal responsibility plan to show what education, training, and job placement services are needed for that person to become a member of the workforce.

In order for unmarried minor parents to receive assistance, they must participate in educational and training activities, and live with a responsible adult in an adult supervised location. States must help find adult supervised homes for teens that cannot live at home.

Work Activities
The following are to be considered as employment toward a state's participation level:

- unsubsidized or subsidized employment, on-the-job training, work experience, community service, job search, vocational training, job skills training related to work, or education directly related to work;
- satisfactory secondary school attendance; and
- providing child care services to individuals that are participating in community service.

Five Year Time Limit
There are limits for those adults that have been receiving federally-assisted funding for 5 years total. Families with an adult that have reached the limit, or less at a state's option, cannot receive cash assistance under the TANF program. However, states do have some discretion in allowing assistance after the 5-year limit. It may be extended beyond 60 months to up to 20% of a state's caseload. Also, they can use state-only funds, or they can use Social Service Block Grants to provide services to those families beyond the time limit.

To learn more on how to apply for this program, contact your local welfare office, social services office, or contact the Temporary Assistance for Needy Families Office listed in the Appendix.

Free Books on Tape

You used to love reading, but since your eyes have started to get bad, you've all but given up enjoying a good book anymore. Before you give up altogether, listen to this: The National Library Service (NLS) maintains a large collection of books, magazines, journals, and music materials in Braille, large type, and recorded formats for individuals who cannot read or use standard printed materials because of temporary or permanent visual loss or physical limitations.

Reading materials and necessary playback equipment for books on record and cassette are distributed through a national network of cooperating libraries. Books in the collection are selected on the basis of their appeal to a wide range of interests. Bestsellers, biographies, fiction, and how-to books are in great demand.

Contact your local library to find out what they have available to you, or you may contact handicapped Readers Reference Section, National Library Service for the Blind and physically Handicapped, Library of Congress, Washington, DC 20542; 202-707-5100; 800-424-8567; {www.loc.gov/nls}.

Take a Free Vacation

Never liked staying on the sidelines? Well then, dig in. "Passport In Time" help you open a window on the past by allowing you to join activities such as archaeological excavation, site mapping, drafting, laboratory and art work, collecting oral histories, restoration, and much more.

Projects vary in length and there is no registration cost or fee. You may even receive a small stipend to offset your living expenses. For information on upcoming opportunities, contact Passport In Time Clearinghouse, P.O. Box 31315, Tucson, AZ 85751; 800-281-9176; {www.passportintime.com}.

Free Concert or Theater Tickets

Many music and theater groups offer special programs to older adults in the form of discounted tickets, free concerts, transportation, afternoon teas, and/or daytime events. Contact your state arts group, state Department of Aging or local senior citizens groups to see what is available in your area.

Ca$h for Sharing What You Know

Retired Senior Volunteer Program offers maximum flexibility and choice to its volunteers. RSVP matches the personal interests and skills of older Americans with opportunities to help solve community problems. RSVP volunteers choose how and where they want to serve - from a few to over 40 hours a week. RSVP makes it easy for older adults to find the types of volunteer service opportunities that appeal to them.

RSVP volunteers provide hundreds of community services. They tutor children in reading and math, help to build houses, help get children immunized, model parenting skills to teen parents, participate in neighborhood watch programs, plan community gardens, deliver meals, offer disaster relief to victims of natural disasters, and help community organizations operate more efficiently.

Volunteers receive supplemental insurance while on duty, and receive on-the-job training. For more information contact National Senior Service Corps, 1201 New York Ave., NW, Washington, DC 20525; 800-424-8867; {www.seniorcorps.org}.

$3,000 While Helping Others

Foster Grandparents devote their volunteer service to one population: children with special or exceptional needs. Across the country, Foster Grandparents are offering emotional support to child victims of abuse and neglect, tutoring children who lag behind in reading, mentoring troubled teenagers and young mothers, and caring for premature infants and children with physical disabilities and severe illnesses.

If you meet certain income guidelines and are 60 or older, you may be eligible for this program. You will receive a modest tax free stipend to offset the cost of volunteering,

and are reimbursed for transportation, some meals, an annual physical and accident and liability insurance. For more information contact National Senior Service Corps, 1201 New York Ave., NW, Washington, DC 20525; 800-424-8867; {www.seniorcorps.org}.

Cash for Helping Fellow Seniors

Senior Companions reach out to adults, who need extra assistance to live independently in their own homes or communities. Senior Companions assist their adult clients with in basic but essential ways: they provide companionship and friendship to isolated frail seniors, assist with simple chores, provide transportation, and add richness to their clients' lives. Senior Companions serve frail older adults and their caregivers, adults with disabilities, and those with terminal illnesses.

If you meet certain income guidelines and are 60 or older, you may be eligible for this program. You will receive a modest tax free stipend to offset the cost of volunteering, and are reimbursed for transportation, some meals, an annual physical and accident and liability insurance. For more information contact National Senior Service Corps, 1201 New York Ave., NW, Washington, DC 20525; 800-424-8867; {www.seniorcorps.org}.

55+ Go To College Free

You are never too old to learn. Believe it or not, more than 350 colleges and universities all across the country have special programs for seniors (starting at age 55) who are interested in going back to school. This often means free or low-cost tuition, discounts on fees and books, and even special deals on housing. So why not go to college with your grandchildren? Anyone interested should contact the school they wish to attend to find out how to apply for a discount or waiver. Some limitations and restrictions may apply.

Money to Pay Employees At Your Non-Profit

Do you need people to work for your non-profit, but don't have the budget? There are several agencies within the Federal government which provides staffing for a variety agencies.

To register your organization for workers paid by the government, contact the Corporation for National and Community Service. They have several programs such as AmeriCorps and the Senior Corps that train and pay for volunteers to serve in a variety of public service agencies. In partnership with non-profit groups, faith-based organizations, schools, and other public agencies, participants in these programs tutor children, build and renovate homes, provide immunizations and health screenings, clean up and preserve the environment, serve on neighborhood crime-prevention patrols, and respond to disasters.

For more information on how to get your program listed, contact Corporation for National and Community Service, 1201 New York Ave., NW, Washington, DC 20525; 202-606-5000; 877-USACORPS; {www.nationalservice.org}.

Money To Pay For Your Kid's Bills

The Masonic Angel Fund is a special charity designed for children and sponsored by local Masonic Lodges across the country. Funds can be used to fill a wide variety of children's needs, such as a new winter coat, a pair of classes or shoes, and can even fund scholarships for music or arts instruction. If professional services are needed, for example a doctor or a dentist, the local Lodge may be able to rely on one of their members to donate their services.

Referrals for all these services are done through the school system, which helps build a good relationship between the schools and the Masonic Lodge. The goal of the Angel Fund is to provide a quick response to fill a need that would otherwise go unmet. Currently the Fund is available in 40 Lodges, but the goal is to have it spread to all the Masonic Lodges.

For more information on the Fund contact The Masonic Angel Fund, P.O. Box 1389, Orleans, MA 02653; 508-255-8812; {www. masonicangelfoundation.org/goal.htm}.

Free Fans

Fan Care is a great program sponsored by Virginia Power. If you are a resident of Virginia and 60 or older, you may be eligible for a free fan to help you make it safely through the hot summer. Fans are distributed through the local Area Agencies on Aging.

To learn about eligibility requirements, contact Fan Care, Department for the Aging, 1600 Forest Ave., Suite 102, Richmond, VA 23229; 800-552-3402; 804-662-9333. For those outside of Virginia, contact your state Department of Aging or your state utility commission, both listed in the Appendix to see what they have to offer.

Free Take Out Meals for Seniors

People 60 and over who are homebound because of illness, incapacity, or disability or who are otherwise isolated can receive hot meals delivered to their home. The program is funded in every state by the Older Americans Act.

Contact your local area agency on aging or your state Department on Aging to learn who you need to contact in your area. You can also contact the Eldercare Locator hotline at 800-677-1116 for more assistance.

Free Passports for Families of Vets

It's hard to believe that a passport can cost up to $60, but did you know that you can get it free of charge if you are a member of a family visiting an overseas grave site of a veteran? So when you are planning your next trip to Paris, keep dear Uncle Harry in Normandy in mind. Eligibility for these free passports includes widows, parents, children, sisters, brother, and guardians of the deceased who are buried or commemorated in permanent American military cemeteries on foreign soil.

For additional information, write to the American Battle Monuments Commission, 2300 Clarendon Blvd., Arlington, VA 22201; 703-696-6902; {www.abmc.gov}.

Money & Help for Those Who Served

We want to thank those who spent time serving and protecting our country. The U.S. Department of Veterans Affairs hotline can provide you with information on such programs as life insurance, comprehensive dental and medical care, nursing homes, home loan programs, burial services, and more. In addition each state offers some additional benefits which could be free license plates, free or reduced hunting and fishing licenses, and more.

To learn more contact U.S. Department of Veterans Affairs, 810 Vermont Ave., NW, Washington, DC 20420; 800-827-1000; {www.va.gov}. For a link to each state's veteran services, check out {www.nasdva.com/}.

Free Money For Members of Armed Services and Vets to Pay Bills

The American Red Cross helps those in need in a variety of ways. If they have been sent to serve with the U.S. military, then members of the armed services and their families can contact the Red Cross for help in cases of emergency. Services they can provide include communicating with family members, emergency financial assistance, counseling and more.

You may contact the American Red Cross Emergency Services, 8111 Gatehouse Rd., Falls Church, VA 22042; 877-272-7337; {www.redcross.org/services/afes}.

$400/wk When You Are Out of Work

If you have been laid off or downsized from your job through no fault of your own, then help is available to you. Unemployment compensation is the government's first line of defense against the ripple effects of unemployment. By cash payments made directly to laid off workers, the program ensures that at least a significant portion of the necessities of life, such as food, shelter, and clothing, can be met while a search for work takes place.

The Federal-State Unemployment Insurance Program provides unemployment benefits to eligible workers who are unemployed through no fault of their own (as determined under State law), and meet other eligibility requirements. There are several other unemployment programs for federal workers, extended benefits for high times of unemployment, disaster unemployment and more. Check to see if you qualify for any additional benefits above and beyond the Unemployment Insurance Program.

- Unemployment insurance payments (benefits) are intended to provide temporary financial assistance to unemployed workers who meet the requirements of State law.
- Each State administers a separate unemployment insurance program within guidelines established by Federal law.
- Eligibility for unemployment insurance, benefit amounts and the length of time benefits are available are determined by the State law under which unemployment insurance claims are established.

Eligibility

- You must meet the State requirements for wages earned or time worked during an established (one year) period of time referred to as a "base period". (In most States, this is usually the first four out of the last five completed calendar quarters prior to the time that your claim is filed.)
- You must be determined to be unemployed through no fault of your own, and meet other eligibility requirements of State law.

Filing a Claim

- You should contact your State Unemployment Insurance agency as soon as possible after becoming unemployed. In some States, you can now file a claim by telephone.
- It generally takes two to three weeks after you file your claim to receive your first benefit check. Some States require a one-week waiting period; therefore, the second week claimed is the first week of payment, if you are otherwise eligible.
- When you file the claim, you will be asked certain questions, such as addresses and dates about your former employment. To make sure your claim is not delayed, be sure to give complete and correct information.

Continued Eligibility

- You must file weekly or biweekly claims, and respond to questions concerning your continued eligibility. You must report any earnings from work you had during the week(s). You must also report any job offers or refusal of work during the week. These claims are usually filed by mail or telephone; the State will provide filing instructions.

- When directed, you must report to your local Unemployment Insurance Claims Office or One-Stop/Employment Service Office on the day and at the time you are scheduled to do so. If you fail to report as scheduled for any interview, benefits may be denied.
- You must continue to meet the eligibility requirements stated in the previous section.

Benefits

- In general, benefits are based on a percentage of an individual's earnings over a recent 52-week period - up to a State maximum amount.
- Benefits can be paid for a maximum of 26 weeks in most States.
- Additional weeks of benefits may be available during times of high unemployment (see Extended Benefits). Some States provide additional benefits for specific purposes.
- Benefits are subject to Federal income taxes and must be reported on your Federal income tax return. You may elect to have the tax withheld by the State Unemployment Insurance agency.

Temporary Extended Unemployment Compensation Program

Temporary Emergency Unemployment Compensation (TEUC) provides extra weeks of federally funded unemployment benefits to unemployed workers throughout the country who have received all regular unemployment benefits available to them.

Eligibility

Unemployed workers who had a claim for regular state benefits that ended during or after the week including March 15, 2001, may be eligible. State workforce agencies will be notifying these workers about how to file claims for TEUC if they are currently unemployed. People who want to find out if they are eligible should check with their state workforce agency.

Benefits

The program began in every state the week beginning March 10, 2002, and those who qualify could receive benefits for that week as early as the week beginning March 17. However, it takes some time for state agencies to get administrative processes in place to handle TEUC claims and determine eligibility, and it may take several weeks for payments to be made in all states. Benefits to eligible workers will be paid only through the last week of December 2002. Check to see if this program continues.

Each weekly payment will equal the amount payable for the unemployed worker's most recent claim for regular state benefits.

TEUC is a two-tiered program:

- TEUC Up to 13 weeks of TEUC are available to eligible unemployed workers in all states.
- TEUC-X In states where an "Extended Benefit" period is in effect when an individual exhausts the first tier of

TEUC, up to 13 additional weeks of benefits will be available.

Extended Benefits Program

Extended Benefits are available to workers who have exhausted regular unemployment insurance benefits during periods of high unemployment. The basic Extended Benefits program provides up to 13 additional weeks of benefits when a State is experiencing high unemployment. Some States have also enacted a voluntary program to pay up to 7 additional weeks (20 weeks maximum) of Extended Benefits during periods of extremely high unemployment.

Eligibility
Extended Benefits may start after an individual exhausts other unemployment insurance benefits (not including Disaster Unemployment Assistance or Trade Readjustment Allowances). Not everyone who qualified for regular benefits qualifies for Extended Benefits. The State agency will advise you of your eligibility for Extended Benefits.

Benefits
The weekly benefit amount of Extended Benefits is the same as the individual received for regular unemployment compensation. The total amount of Extended Benefits that an individual could receive may be fewer than 13 weeks (or fewer than 20 weeks).

Filing A Claim
When a State begins an Extended Benefit period; it notifies those who have received all of their regular benefits that they may be eligible for Extended Benefits. If your State's unemployment is high, you should contact the State Unemployment Insurance agency to ask whether Extended Benefits are available.

Unemployment Compensation for Federal Employees Program

Eligibility
The Unemployment Compensation for Federal Employees program provides benefits for eligible unemployed former civilian Federal employees. The program is administered by States as agents of the Federal government. This program is operated under the same terms and conditions that apply to regular State Unemployment Insurance (see State Unemployment Insurance). In general, the law of the State in which your last official duty station in Federal civilian service was located will be the State law that determines eligibility for unemployment insurance benefits.

There is no payroll deduction from a Federal employee's wages for unemployment insurance protection. Benefits are paid for by the various Federal agencies.

Benefits
The law of the State (under which the claim is filed) determines benefit amounts, number of weeks benefits can be paid, and other eligibility conditions.

Filing a Claim
You should contact your State Unemployment Insurance agency as soon as possible after becoming unemployed. In some States, you can now file a claim by telephone.

Unemployment Compensation for Ex-service Members Program

Eligibility
The Unemployment Compensation for Ex-service members program provides benefits for eligible ex-military personnel. The program is administered by the States as agents of the Federal government. If you were on active duty with a branch of the U.S. military, you may be entitled to benefits based on that service. You must have been separated under honorable conditions. There is no payroll deduction from the service member's wages for unemployment insurance protection. The various branches of the military pay for benefits.

Benefits
The law of the State (under which the claim is filed) determines benefit amounts, number of weeks benefits can be paid, and other eligibility conditions.

Filing A Claim
You should contact your State Unemployment Insurance agency as soon as possible after separation. You should have a copy of your separation papers (DD Form-214) available. In some States, you can now file a claim by telephone.

Disaster Unemployment Assistance Program

Disaster Unemployment Assistance provides financial assistance to individuals whose employment or self-employment has been lost or interrupted as a direct result of a major disaster declared by the President of the United States. Before an individual can be determined eligible for Disaster Unemployment Assistance, it must be established that the individual is not eligible for regular unemployment insurance benefits (under any state or federal law). The program is administered by states as agents of the federal government.

Eligibility
Disaster Unemployment Assistance is available to unemployed U.S. nationals and qualified aliens who worked or were self-employed if they:

- worked or were self-employed in or were scheduled to begin work or self-employment in an area declared as a federal disaster area.
- can no longer work or perform services because of physical damage or destruction to the place of employment as a direct result of a disaster.

- establish that the work or self-employment they can no longer perform was their primary source of income.
- do not qualify for regular unemployment insurance benefits from any state.
- Cannot perform work or self-employment because of an injury or because they were incapacitated as a direct result of the disaster.
- became the breadwinner or major support of a household because of the death of the head of the household.
- Cannot work or perform self-employment due to closure of a facility by the federal government.
- lose a majority of income or revenue because the employer or self-employed business was damaged, destroyed, or closed by the federal government.
- Suffering a monetary loss due to damage of property or crops does not automatically entitle an individual to Disaster Unemployment Assistance.

Benefits
Disaster Unemployment Assistance is available to individuals for weeks of unemployment beginning after the date the major disaster began and for up to 26 weeks after the major disaster was declared by the President, as long as their unemployment continues to be a result of the major disaster.

The maximum weekly benefit amount is determined under the provisions of the state law for unemployment insurance in the state where the disaster occurred.

Filing a Claim
Claims should be filed in accordance with the state's instructions published in announcements about the availability of Disaster Unemployment Assistance, or contact the State Unemployment Insurance agency.

For Those Who Lost Their Jobs Because Of Trade Act

Trade Readjustment Allowances (TRA) are income support to persons who have exhausted Unemployment compensation and whose jobs were affected by foreign imports.

The Federal Trade Act provides special benefits under the Trade Adjustment Assistance (TAA) program to those who were laid off or had hours reduced because their employer was adversely affected by increased imports from other countries. The North American Free Trade Agreement (NAFTA) provides special benefits under the NAFTA Transitional Adjustment Assistance (NAFTA-TAA) program to those who were laid off or had hours reduced because their employer was adversely affected by increased imports from Mexico or Canada or because their employer shifted production to either of these countries. These benefits include paid training for a new job, and financial help in making a job search in other areas or relocation to an area where jobs are more plentiful. Those who qualify may be entitled to weekly TRA after their unemployment compensation is exhausted.

Contact the State Unemployment Insurance agency or One-Stop Employment Service office and ask for information about filing a Petition for Trade Adjustment Assistance or a Petition for NAFTA Transitional Adjustment Assistance. The Petition for Trade Adjustment Assistance must be filed with the U.S. Department of Labor (DOL). If DOL approves and certifies the petition, the affected workers will be entitled to file a claim under the TAA or NAFTA-TAA program.

Self-Employment Assistance Program

Self-Employment Assistance offers dislocated workers the opportunity for early re-employment. The program is designed to encourage and enable unemployed workers to create their own jobs by starting their own small businesses. Under these programs, States can pay a self-employed allowance, instead of regular unemployment insurance benefits, to help unemployed workers while they are establishing businesses and becoming self-employed. Participants receive weekly allowances while they are getting their businesses off the ground.

This is a voluntary program for States and, to date, fewer than10 States have established and currently operate Self Employment Assistance programs.

Eligibility
Generally in order to receive these benefits, an individual must first be eligible to receive regular unemployment insurance under the State law. Individuals who have been permanently laid off from their previous jobs and are identified (through a States' profiling system) as likely to exhaust regular unemployment benefits are eligible to participate in the program. Individuals may be eligible even if they are engaged full-time in self-employment activities — including entrepreneurial training, business counseling, and technical assistance.

Benefits
Self-employment allowances are the same weekly amounts as the worker's regular unemployment insurance benefits. Participants work full-time on starting their business instead of looking for wage and salary jobs.

Filing A Claim
You should contact the State Unemployment Insurance agency as soon as possible after becoming unemployed. At the time you file your claim you should ask whether a Self Employment Assistance program operates in your State.

For information at the federal level contact:
U.S. Department of Labor
Employment & Training Administration
200 Constitution Avenue, NW
Washington, DC 20210
202-693-2700

To contact your State Unemployment Insurance agency online go to: {www.workforcesecurity.doleta.gov/map.asp}

Free Money For Kids To Go To 79 Camps

The Salvation Army is concerned about the happiness of children, so they operate many children's homes and nurseries. In additions there are 239 camps children can attend as well as over 400 clubs. The Salvation Army wants to offer children a healthy alternative, so they can live their lives to the fullest.

To learn more about the services offered contact the Salvation Army Office near you, or Salvation Army National Headquarters, 615 Slaters Lane, P.O. Box 269, Alexandria, VA 22313; 703-684-5500; {www.salvationarmy.org}.

Free Help Finding Lost Loved Ones

When a loved one disappears, those left behind struggle and often spends thousands trying to locate their missing person. The Salvation Army received over 35,000 requests for assistance, and was able to trace over 10,000 missing persons.

To learn more about the services offered contact the Salvation Army Office near you, or Salvation Army National Headquarters, 615 Slaters Lane, P.O. Box 269, Alexandria, VA 22313; 703-684-5500; {www.salvationarmy.org}.

Free Summer Camp For Kids With Parents In Prison

Angle Tree camping serves over 10,000 children each summer in week-long Christian camps. Supported by funds from the local churches and the Prison Fellowship, local children of prisoners are identified and given a week's vacation in the outdoors. In addition, Angel Tree provides gifts at Christmas time to children in need.

For more information contact Angel Tree, P.O. Box 1550, Merrifield, VA 22116; 800-55-ANGEL; {www.angeltree.org}.

Pay Your Bills While You Become An Entrepreneur

It is a dream for many people to own their own business, but often money is a concern. There are different programs to help you pay your bills while you start your business or go through microenterprise training.

This applies even if you are receiving Temporary Assistance for Needy Families (TANF), as TANF funds can be used to support you while are being trained or starting your business. Contact your state TANF office to see what programs are available in your area. You can also learn about other microenterprise programs by contacting your state economic development office.

For other resources and to locate programs in your area, contact:

- Center for Law and Social Policy, 1015 15th St., NW, Suite 400, Washington, DC 20005; 202-906-8000; {www.clsp.org}. See Microenterprise Development and Self-Employment for TANF Recipients in the publications section.
- The Aspen Institute, One Dupont Circle, NW, Suite 700, Washington, DC 20036; 202-736-1071; {http://fieldus.org/directory}.
- Association for Enterprise Opportunity, 1601 N. Kent St., Suite 101, Arlington, VA 22209; 703-841-7760; {www.microenterpriseworks.org}.

Money To Put In Your Savings Account

Triple your savings by taking advantage of Individual Development Accounts. These accounts are currently available in 350 communities with more in development.

Designed to help low-income people save for a down payment, college, or a small business, funds matched with one dollar from the government and one dollar from private funds. Currently over 10,000 people participate in IDA programs across the country. A short course on money management is usually required before you can start your savings plan.

To learn more about the program or to see what may be available in your community, contact Corporation for Enterprise Development, 777 N. Capitol St., NE, Suite 800, Washington, DC 20002; 202-408-9788; {www.idanetwork.org}.

372 Sources To Pay Emergency Expenses

Not sure where to turn or what resources exist for you? Bravekids.org has put together a resource directory that lists over 372 sources for financial and other types of assistance for those with disabled children or adults or low-income families in need of help. It could be anything from paying your utility bill to respite care or medical expenses.

No need to feel like help does not exist. Check out {www.bravekids.org}.

Financial Benefits For Caregivers

The Alexandria Division of Social Services offers financial benefits for caregivers of children and adolescents with disabilities. Check your local, city, county or state for financial benefits for which you may qualify if you care for someone who is disabled.

Services Available From Veterinary Teaching Hospitals

Veterinary teaching hospitals can be an excellent place to take your pet, and most of them will take new patients directly or as referrals from other veterinarians. But as research and teaching institutions, they have access to a lot more resources than your average veterinary hospital. Many of these hospitals provide services like:

Free Services and Drugs for People Who Can't Pay

* available in Illinois, Georgia, Texas, Virginia and Wisconsin.

Free Medical Treatment for Strays in Need Brought in by Non-owners

* Auburn University calls their program the "Good Samaritan Program"

Free Answers to Questions Over the Telephone

* available in Alabama, California, Colorado, Georgia, Illinois, Iowa, Kansas, Louisiana, Massachusetts (for Vets only), Michigan (for Vets only), Minnesota, Mississippi, Missouri, new York, North Carolina (for Vets only), Ohio, Oklahoma, Oregon, Tennessee, Texas, Virginia (for Vets only), and Washington

Free and Discount Treatment for Companion Animals and Assistance Dogs

* available in Minnesota, Louisiana, Massachusetts, Minnesota, Mississippi, Oklahoma, Pennsylvania, Wisconsin, and Tennessee

Discounts for Seniors

* Oklahoma gives a 10% discount for people over 62

Treatment for Exotic Pets and Wildlife

* available in Colorado, Georgia, Kansas, Michigan, and Oklahoma

Some also have very unique services like pet loss support hotlines, free newsletters, or the Llama Research program in Ohio. Programs are constantly changing, so contact the hospital nearest you to see what kinds of services they currently offer for your pet.

Alabama

Auburn University
Department of Large Animal Surgery and Medicine
McAdory Hall
Auburn University
Auburn, AL 36849
334-844-4490
www.vetmed.auburn.edu/lac

Department of Small Animal Surgery and Medicine
Hoerlein Hall
Auburn University
Auburn, AL 36849
334-844-4690
www.vetmed.auburn.edu/sac

Tuskegee University
College of Veterinary Medicine, Nursing and Allied Health
Tuskegee, AL 36088
334-727-8173
http://vetmed.tusk.edu

California
Veterinary Medical Teaching Hospital
University of California
One Shields Avenue
Davis, CA 95616-8747
530-752-1393- small animals
530-752-0290- large animals
www.vmth.ucdavis.edu

Colorado
Veterinary Teaching Hospital
Colorado State University
300 W. Drake Rd.
Fort Collins, CO 80523
970-491-4477- small animals
970-491-4471- large animals
www.vth.colostate.edu/vth

Florida
University of Florida
College of Veterinary Medicine
Veterinary Teaching Hospital
2015 SW 16th Ave.
Gainesville, FL 32610
352-392-4700 ext. 4000
Large Animal Hospital
352-392-4700 ext. 4700
Small Animal Hospital
www.vetmed.ufl.edu/vmth/index.htm

Georgia
College of Veterinary Medicine
Veterinary Medical Teaching Hospital
The University of Georgia
Athens, GA 30602
Small Animal: 706-542-2895; 800-542-9294
Large Animal: 706-542-3223
www.vet.uga.edu/testbed/Service/TeachingHospital/teachinghospital.html

Illinois
Department of Veterinary Clinical Medicine
College of Veterinary Medicine
University of Illinois
Large Animal Clinic
1102 W. Hazelwood Dr.
Urbana, IL 61802
217-333-2000

Small Animal Clinic
1008 W. Hazelwood Dr.
Urbana, IL 61802
217-333-5300
Appointment Hotline: 217-265-5163
www.cvm.uiuc.edu/vth

Indiana
Purdue University
School of Veterinary Medicine
Teaching Hospital
Lynn Hall
West Lafayette, IN 47907
765-494-1107- small animals
765-494-8548- large animals
www.vet.purdue.edu/hospital.html

Iowa
Iowa State University
College of Veterinary Medicine
Veterinary Teaching Hospital
Ames, IA 50011
Wildlife Care Clinic
Pet Loss Support Helpline: 888-478-7574
515-294-4900- small animals
515-294-1500- large animals
www.vetmed.iastate.edu/services/vth

Kansas
Kansas State University
College of Veterinary Medicine
Manhattan, KS 66502
785-532-5690- small animals
785-532-5700- large animals
www.vet.ksu.edu/depts/VMTH.index.htm

Louisiana
Louisiana State University
School of Veterinary Medicine
Baton Rouge, LA 70803
225-578-9500- large animals
225-578-9600- small animals
www.vetmed.lsu.edu

Massachusetts
Tufts University
School of Veterinary Medicine
Clinical and Diagnostic Services
200 Westboro Rd.
North Grafton, MA 01536
508-839-5395 ext. 84696- small animals
508-839-5395 Ext.4840- large animals
www.tufts.edu/vet/clinical/index.html

Michigan
College of Veterinary Medicine
Veterinary Teaching Hospital
G100 Veterinary Medical Center
East Lansing, MI 48824-1316
517-353-9710- large animals
517-353-5420- small animals
www.cvm.msu.edu/services/Vth.htm

Minnesota
The University of Minnesota
College of Veterinary Medicine
1365 Gortner Ave.
St. Paul, MN 55108
612-625-6700- large animals
612-625-1919- small animals
www.cvm.umn.edu

Mississippi
Mississippi State University
College of Veterinary Medicine
Animal Health Center
P.O. Box 9825
Mississippi State, MS 39762
662-325-3432
www.cvm.msstate.edu

Missouri
University of Missouri
College of Veterinary Medicine
Veterinary Teaching Medical Hospital
Clydesdale Hall
379 East Campus Drive
Columbia, MO 65211
573-882-7821- small animal
573-882-6857- large animal
573-882-3513- equine clinic
www.vmth.missouri.edu

New York
Veterinary Medical Teaching Hospital
Box 20 CVM
College of Veterinary Medicine
Cornell University
Ithaca, NY 14853
607-253-3060- companion animal hospital
607-253-3100- equine/farm animals
607-253-3140- ambulatory and production animal medicine service (will travel to farms)
Pet Loss Support Hotline-607-253-3932
www.vet.cornell.edu/hospital

North Carolina
North Carolina State University
College of Veterinary Medicine
Veterinary Teaching Hospital
4700 Hillsborough St.
Raleigh, NC 27606
919-513-6500
www.cvm.ncsu.edu/vth

Ohio
The Ohio State University
College of Veterinary Medicine
Columbus, OH 43210
614-292-3551- small animals
614-292-6661- large animals
www.vet.ohio-state.edu

Oklahoma
Oklahoma State University
College of Veterinary Medicine
Boren Veterinary Medical Teaching Hospital
Stillwater, OK 74078
405-744-6731- small animals
405-744-6656- large animals
www.cvm.okstate.edu/Depts/VTH/vth.htm

Oregon
Oregon State University
College of Veterinary Medicine
Veterinary Teaching Hospital
Corvallis, OR 97331
541-737-2858- large animals only
www.vet.orst.edu

Pennsylvania
Veterinary Hospital of the University of Pennsylvania
3850 Spruce Street
Philadelphia, PA 19104
215-898-4680- small animals

George D. Widener Hospital for Large Animals
New Bolton Center
382 West Street Road
Kennett Square, PA 19348
610-444-5800 ext. 2525
www.vet.upenn.edu/HospitalsandServices

Tennessee
University of Tennessee
College of Veterinary Medicine
Veterinary Teaching Hospital
Knoxville, TN 37996
865-974-VETS(8387)- small animals
865-974-5701- large animals
www.vet.utk.edu

Texas
Texas A&M University
College of Veterinary Medicine
Veterinary Teaching Hospital
College Station, TX 77843
979-845-3541- large animals
979-845-2351- small animals
www.cvm.tamu.edu/departments.htm

Virginia
Virginia Tech and University of Maryland
Virginia-Maryland Regional
College of Veterinary Medicine

Phase III Duckpond Drive
Blacksburg, VA 24061
540-231-4621-large & small
www.vetmed.vt.edu

Equine Medical Center
17690 Old Waterford Road at Morven Park
Leesburg, VA 20177
703-771-6800

Washington
Washington State University
College of Veterinary Medicine
Veterinary Teaching Hospital
Pullman, WA 99164
509-335-0751- small animal
509-335-0741- agricultural animals
509-335-0718- equine
www.vetmed.wsu.edu/depts-vth/hospital.html

Wisconsin
The University of Wisconsin- Madison
School of Veterinary Medicine
Veterinary Medical Teaching Hospital
2015 Linden Dr.
Madison, WI 53706
608-263-7600
800-DVM-VMTH
http://vmthpub.vetmed.wisc.edu

$$$ Pay Your Health Care Bills

$600 to Pay for Health Insurance

Don't have enough money to pay for Medicare Part B premiums? Qualified Medicare Beneficiary is one of the Medicare Savings Programs made available to help people pay for Medicare coverage. This State program pays for part or all of Medicare Part B (medical insurance) premiums and it could pay for deductibles and coinsurance. It is for those that have limited income and resources. More than half of the people that can use one of these programs do not ever apply. Savings for Medicare beneficiaries can be up to $600 a year!

For individuals, their monthly income must be less than $1,275, and for couples, less than $1,714. Things that are considered resources include checking or saving accounts, stocks, or bonds. It does not include a home, a car, burial plots, burial expenses up to $1,500, or $1,500 worth of life insurance. To be eligible, resources for an individual must not exceed $4,000, and for couples, the amount must be $6,000 or less.

Even if you are not sure you qualify, call a medical assistance office (Medicaid, Social Services, Human Services, Medical Assistance, or Community Services) to review your case. Or you can call Medicare at 800-MEDICARE (633-4227). To view a list of State Medicaid offices, go to {www.hcfa.gov/medicaid/mcontact.htm}.

Free Plastic Surgery For Children

Austin Smiles provides free reconstructive plastic surgery, mainly to repair cleft lip and palate, to the children around Austin, Texas. They do about 75 surgeries a year. Austin Plastic Surgery Foundation, P.O. Box 26694, Austin, TX 78755-0694; 512-451-9300; Fax: 512-451-9312; {www.austinsmiles.org}. To see if similar services are available anywhere near you contact Cleft Palate Foundation, 104 S. Estes Dr., Suite 204, Chapel Hill, NC 27514; 800-24-CLEFT; 919-933-9044; {www.cleftline.org}.

Discounts On Dental and Vision Care

If you live near a university that has a dental or optometry school, then you may be in luck. Many of these schools offer reduced fee services for dental care or vision screening. You will receive treatment from students, but they will be supervised by some of the best people in the field.

These schools also often conduct research studies, so you if you qualify, you may be able to receive treatment for free. My eleven-year-old daughter gets glasses, contacts, plus free contact solution for three years, because she is part of a study on nearsightedness in children. Not a bad deal!

To locate schools near you, you can contact American Dental Education Association, 1625 Massachusetts Ave., NW, Suite 600, Washington, DC 20036-2212; 202-667-9433; Fax: 202-667-0642; {www.adea.org}. You can also contact American Optometric Association, 243 N. Lindbergh Blvd., St. Louis, MO 63141; 314-991-4100; {www.aoanet.org}.

Grants Up To $2,500 and Loans To Finance Adoptions

The National Adoption Foundation helps arrange loans and provides limited grants for parents to cover expenses before and after adoption. They also provide information on sources of other financial help like the 325 Fortune 500 companies who offer an average cash reimbursement of $4,000 for their employees who adopt, or the new adoption expense tax credit that is available from the IRS. Contact: National Adoption Foundation, 100 Mill Plain Rd, Danbury, CT 06811; 203-791-3811; {www.nafadopt.org}.

The following organizations also provide free publications, referral services and advice on adoption and searching for birth relatives:

- **National Adoption Information Clearinghouse**, 330 C Street, SW, Washington, DC 20447; 888-251-0075; 703-352-3488; Fax: 703-385-3206; {www.calib.com/naic}.
- **National Adoption Center**, 1500 Walnut St, Suite 701, Philadelphia, PA, 19102; Answer Line: 215-735-9988, 800-TO-ADOPT; {www.adopt.org}.
- **National Council For Adoption**, 1930 17th Street, NW, Washington, DC 20009-6207; 202-328-1200; Fax: 202-332-0935; {www.ncfa-usa.org}.

Camp WheezeAway Is Free For Kids With Asthma

Every year, about 100 kids with asthma, between 8 and 12 years of age, can go to summer camp for free in Jackson Cap, Alabama. For information on how to apply, contact American Lung Association of Alabama, 3125 Independence Dr., Suite 325, Birmingham, AL 35209; 205-933-8821; Fax: 205-930-1717; {www.alabamalung.org}.

For more information on other camps for children with asthma, or other questions concerning asthma, contact The American Lung Association, 1740 Broadway, New York, NY 10019; 212-315-8700; 800-LUNG-USA; {www.lungusa.org}.

Free Flu Shots

Who should get flu shots? The U.S. Center for Disease Control recommends it for

- adults at or over 50 years
- residents of nursing home
- persons at or over 6 months of age with chronic cardiovascular or pulmonary disorders, including asthma
- persons at or over 6 months of age with chronic metabolic diseases (including diabetes), renal dysfunction, hemoglobinopathies, immunosuppressive or immunodeficiency disorders
- women in their 2nd or 3rd trimester of pregnancy during flu season
- persons 6 months to 18 years receiving aspirin therapy
- groups, including household members and care givers who can infect high risk persons

Almost anyone can get free or low cost ($10-$15) flu shots from their county health office or other community sources. Some doctors, like Dr. Donald McGee in New Hampshire {www.drmcgee.com}, offer free shots in their office. Medicare Part B also pays for flu shots.

Contact your county office of public health listed in your telephone book or your state Department of Health. If you have trouble finding a local low cost source, or would like more information on the flu vaccine contact the National Immunization Information Hotline at 800-232-2522 (English); 800-232-0233 (Spanish); {www.cdc.gov/nip}.

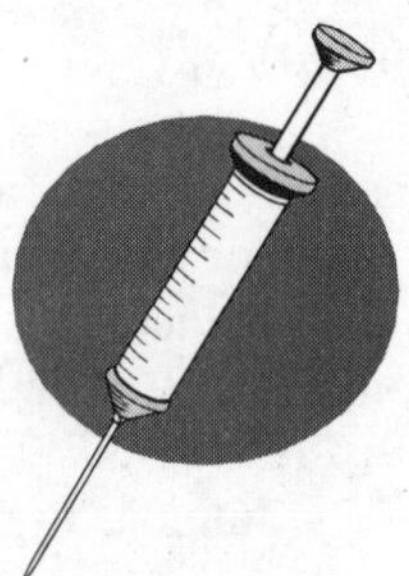

Kids Get Free Expert Care At 22 Hospitals

Children suffering from orthopedic injuries, diseases of the bones, joint and muscles, or burns can get free treatment from one of the 22 Shriners Hospitals. The requirements for admission are that the child is under the age of 18, and there is a reasonable possibility the condition can be helped.

For more information, contact Shriners Hospitals, 2900 Rocky Point Dr., Tampa, FL 33607-1460; 800-237-5055 (in Canada 800-361-7256); {www.shrinershq.org}.

Free Speech Therapy For Toddlers

It doesn't matter how much money you earn. You can have your child tested to see if any speech problems are developing and even get free speech therapy. It's part of the U.S. Individuals with Disabilities Education Act (IDEA) to make sure that children in need receive special education beginning on their third birthday, and in some states, like Virginia, it starts at age 2.

The program is run through your local school district, so check with them first, or your state Department of Education. You can also contact Office of Special Education Programs, Office of Special Education and

Rehabilitative Services, U.S. Department of Education, 400 Maryland Ave., SW, Washington, DC 20202; 202-205-5507; {www.ed.gov/offices/OSERS/OSEP}.

$1,300 Worth Of Dental Care For Seniors and Disabled

The National Foundation of Dentistry for the Handicapped started the Donated Dental Services program to help disabled and elderly persons who are low-income by matching them with volunteer dentists. Homeless and mentally ill people are also helped.

Volunteer dentists agree to treat one or two people each year with dental problems, and dental laboratories that make dentures, crowns, and bridges also donate services. The program now serves over 500 people each year with each patient receiving an average of $1,300 worth of services. In some areas of the country, Dental House Call projects have been started where dentists will come to homes or centers to provide dental care.

To learn where services are located in your area, contact National Foundation of Dentistry for the Handicapped, 1800 15th St., Suite 100, Denver, CO 80202; 303-534-5360, Fax: 303-534-5290.

Grants Assist with Eye Treatment, Eye Surgery and Low Vision Equipment

The Pearle Vision Foundation offers grants to U.S. residents for low vision equipment. Funding is also available to non-profit organizations for vision-care assistance.

Contact Pearle Vision Foundation, 2534 Royal Lane, Dallas, TX 75229; 972-277-6191.

Sightless Get Free Seeing Eye Dogs, Training, Travel and Air Fare

Pilot Dogs gives its trained animals to the blind at absolutely no charge. They also include four weeks of training in using the dog and will pay for room and board, all equipment, and round trip transportation. Other groups provide similar services:

- ***Pilot Dogs, Inc.***, 625 West Town Street, Columbus, OH 43215; 614-221-6367; fax: 614-221-1577; {www.pilotdogs.org}.

- ***Guide Dog Foundation for the Blind, Inc***, 371 East Jericho Tpke., Smithtown, NY 11787-2976; 800-548-4337; 631-265-2121; Fax: 631-361-5192; {www.guidedog.org}.

Free Help — At Your Home, — Every Day — For The First 3 Weeks After Childbirth

The Healthy Families America Project operates 400 programs in 47 states. It helps new mothers cope with the pressures of being a new parent by offering volunteer home visitors who come to your home for the first three weeks after birth. They are trained to show you how to deal with the physical, emotional and financial strains of a new baby. First time mothers and older mothers are among those considered for the program.

To see if there is a program in your area and if you qualify, contact Prevent Child Abuse America, 200 S. Michigan Ave., 17th Floor, Chicago, IL 60604; 312-663-3520; Fax: 312-939-8962; {www.preventchildabuse.org}.

Free Wheelchairs

Easter Seals, the American Cancer Society and other helpful organizations provide free wheelchairs and other medical related equipment, like walkers, commodes, bathtub rails, bathtub chairs, crutches, transfer

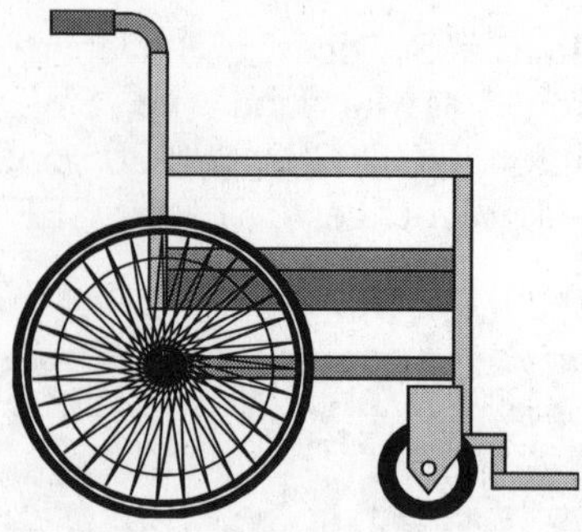

benches, electric wheelchairs and scooters, on a short- or long-term basis. Some programs require deposits that are completely refundable.

Check with your local office of Easter Seals and the American Cancer Society. You can also contact your state Department of Health.

- ***American Cancer Society, Inc***., 1599 Clifton Road, NE, Atlanta, GA 30329-4251; 800-ACS-2345; {www.cancer.org}.
- ***Easter Seals***, 230 West Monroe Street, Suite 1800, Chicago, IL 60606; 800-221-6827; 312-726-6200; fax: 312-726-1494; {www.easterseals.org}.

Alcohol and Drug Abuse Counseling & Treatment

Georgia provides outpatient counseling services, short-term residential programs, and even school student assistance programs. Florida provides substance abuse treatment programs through a partnership with 102 public and private not-for-profit community providers. Delaware contracts with private organizations around the state to provide screening, outpatient counseling, and detoxification, as well as short term and long term treatment. Contact your state Department of Health to see what your state has to offer.

There are also nonprofit organizations who, by themselves, offer free treatment to people, like the Center for Drug-Free Living in Orlando, Florida (P.O. Box 538350, Orlando, FL 32853-8350; 407-245-0012; Fax: 407-245-0011; {www.cfdfl.com}). If your state can't help you get the information or treatment you need, one or both of the following hotlines should be able to help:

- ***National Drug and Treatment Routing Service***, Center for Substance Abuse Treatment, National Institute on Alcohol Abuse and Alcoholism (NIAAA), 6000 Executive Blvd, Willco Bldg., Bethesda, MD 20892-7003; 800-662-HELP; {www.niaaa.nih.gov}.
- ***The National Clearinghouse for Alcohol and Drug Information***, 11426-28 Rockville Pike, Suite 200, Rockville, MD 20852; 800-729-6686 24 hours a day; 800-487-4889 TDD; {www.health.org}.

Make Over $40,000 And Get Free Health Care For Your Kids

Over 4.7 million children are eligible for this program and are not enrolled. Almost every state now has a Children's Health Insurance Program (CHIPS) which extends medical coverage to many children who may not be covered. A family of four living in Connecticut can make up to $42,535 and still qualify to get free health care for the kids. A family of four making $54,300 can join a health care program for their children and pay only $30 per month.

Benefits vary from state to state, but most of the programs cover doctor visits, prescriptions, hospitalization, dental care, vision care, immunizations, and more. Eligibility requirements also vary from state to state, but generally, children must be under the age of 18, a U.S. citizen or a legal alien, a resident of the state in which they are applying, uninsured and not qualified for Medicaid, and meet family income requirements.

Call 1-877-KIDS-NOW for more information about the Children's Health Insurance Program in your state, or check out the Insure Kids Now website at {www.insurekidsnow.gov}.

Alabama
All Kids
Alabama Department of Public Health
Children's Health Insurance Program
201 Monroe Street Suite 250
Montgomery, AL 36104
P.O. Box 303017
Montgomery, AL 36130-3017
334-206-5568
877-774-9521
888-373-KIDS (Toll Free)
www.adph.org/allkids
All Kids is a free or low-fee health insurance program for children under the age of 19. It provides quality medical care including preventative, dental and eye care. It does not cover children residing in an institution, but there is no exclusion for pre-existing conditions. The income limit for a family of four is $36,200. Applications are available on the ALL KIDS website.

Alaska
Denali KidCare
P.O. Box 240047
Anchorage, AK 99524-0047
907-269-6529

888-318-8890 (outstate)
www.hss.state.ak.us/dma/DenaliKidCare
Children up to age 18, and pregnant women are eligible for Denali Kidcare. A family of four can make up to $41,140 and still qualify. Benefits include medical, dental, vision, speech, physical and mental health therapy, hospitalization, prescriptions, and more. A printable application is available online.

Arizona
Kids Care
920 E. Madison, MD 500
Phoenix, AZ 85034
602-417-5437
877-764-5437
www.kidscare.state.az.us
Children age 18 and younger, who qualify for Kids Care, can get medical, dental, and vision services combined in one simple plan. A family of four's annual income must not be greater than $35,300 for children to be eligible. There is no interview and you can download an application or request one by phone.

Arkansas
Arkids First
Arkansas Department of Human Services
Donaghey Plaza West, slot 3440
P.O. Box 1437
Little Rock, AR 72203-1437
501-682-8650
888-474-8275 (toll free)
www.arkidsfirst.com/home.htm
Arkids First is available to children 18 and younger who do not have employer sponsored or group health insurance and have not had insurance for six months. The income requirement for a family of four is $35,300. You can print an application and mail it to your local Department of Human services office, or call and application information will be sent to you.

California
Healthy Families Program
P.O. Box 138005
Sacramento, CA 95813-8005
800-880-5305
916-324-4695
Fax: 916-324-4878
www.healthyfamilies.ca.gov
The Healthy Families Program provides comprehensive insurance coverage for children up to the age of 19, though parents or caretakers may be eligible also. Maximum income for a family of four to qualify is $45,252. You must call the program office to request an application.

Colorado
Child Health Plan Plus
700 South Ash, Suite B105
Glendale, CO 80246
800-359-1991
Fax: 303-692-1901
www.cchp.org
Health and Dental care are provided by the Child Health Plan Plus. Eligible children must be 18 or younger and living in a financially qualified family. Income must not exceed $2790/month or $33,480annually for a family of four. Call for more information or to receive an application.

Connecticut
Husky Plan
P.O. Box 280747
East Hartford, CT 06108
877-284-8759
800-842-4524 TDD/TYY
www.huskyhealth.com
Children under the age of 19, pregnant women, and parents and relative caregivers are all covered under the Husky Plan. This program has 3 parts. Husky Part A provides traditional Medicaid coverage. Husky Part B covers qualified children in higher income families. Husky Plus is a new coverage option for children who have intensive physical or behavioral health needs. Income guidelines vary greatly from plan to plan. Call 1-877-CT-HUSKY for more information and to apply, or print an application on line and mail it.

Delaware
Delaware Healthy Children Program
P.O. Box 950
New Castle, DE 19720-9914
800-996-9969
www.state.de.us/dhss/dss/healthychildren.html
The Delaware Healthy Children Program provides an extensive list of services for a single low monthly rate and no co-payments. Services include check ups as well as lab work, x-rays,

drug/alcohol abuse treatment and much more. There is no exclusion for preexisting conditions, and the income limit for a family of four is $36,200. You may print an application online and send the completed application in the mail, or call for more information or to get help with the application.

District of Columbia
DC Healthy Families
645 H Street NE
Washington, DC 20002
202-698-4200
800-MOM-BABY
877-6PARENT TDD/TTY
www.dchealth.com/dchf/svcdchfapp.htm
DC Healthy Families has 6 health Plans to choose from. These plans provide extensive coverage for qualified parents, pregnant women, and children under the age of 19. You can download an application online or pick one up at your local library, Giant, Safeway, or CVS. The income limit for a family of four is $35,000.

Florida
Florida Kid Care
P.O. Box 980
Tallahassee, FL 32302-0980
888-540-5437
877-316-8748 TTY
www.floridakidcare.org
Florida Kid Care covers many services including doctor visits, shots, surgery, dental, vision, and hearing. NO Kid Care program excludes children because of pre-existing health conditions. An annual income of $36,200 for a family of four determines eligibility. Print the one page application and mail it in, or call toll free for a form to be sent to you.

Georgia
Peachcare for Kids
Georgia Department of Community Health
2 Peachtree St. NW
Atlanta, GA 30303
877-GA-PEACH (toll free)
www.peachcare.org/dehome.asp
Peachcare for Kids provides free or low cost health insurance for children 18 and under. The income guideline for a family of four is $42,000. Benefits include sick visits, shots and check ups, dental, vision, hospitalization and emergency room services. Applications can be completed and submitted online.

Hawaii
Hawaii Quest
Department of Human Services
1390 Miller Street
Honolulu, HI 96813
808-692-8080
www.state.hi.us/dhs
To be eligible for Hawaii Quest, you cannot be certified blind or disabled, be over the age of 65, or reside in a public institution. The Quest program has income and asset limits. Call for more information or to apply.

Idaho
CHIP
Idaho Department of Health and Welfare
450 W. State St.
Boise, ID 83720-0036
800-926-2588
208-332-7205 TDD
www.idahochild.org
The Children's Health Insurance Program (CHIP) provides insurance to working and non-working families. Children under 19 are eligible if their family meets the income requirement, $26,472 for a family of four. Benefits include medical, dental, mental, vision, pharmacy, and hearing. Applications are available online.

Illinois
Kidcare
100 W. Randolph
10th Floor, Suite 300
Chicago, IL 60601
866-4-OUR-KID
877-204-1012 TTY
312-793-7369
www.kidcareillinois.com
Kidcare provides insurance coverage for children through age 18 and women who are pregnant, and also provides help in paying premiums of employer or private health insurance plans. Income requirements vary by Kidcare plan and are based on family size. Applications are available online, can be requested by email, or you can call to have one sent to you.

Indiana
Hoosier Healthwise
P.O. Box 1484
Indianapolis, IN 46206
800-889-9949
www.healthcareforhoosiers.com
Hoosier Healthwise is a health care program for low-income families, children and pregnant women. It has 3 Benefit packages which cover a wide range of services. You can apply in person or by mail. Applications are available online, by calling and requesting one, and at Healthwise enrollment centers.

Iowa
Healthy and Well Kids in Iowa (HAWK-I)
P.O. Box 71336
Des Moines, IA 50325-9958
800-257-8563
888-422-2319
515-457-8051 TDD
www.hawk-i.org
No family will have to pay more than $20 a month for full insurance coverage under the HAWK-I Program. Maximum income for a family of four is $36,200. Benefits include hospice care, nursing care, durable medical equipment, and home health care. Applications can be downloaded on the website.

Kansas
HealthWave
P.O. Box 3599
Topeka, KS 66601
800-792-4884
800-792-4292 TTY
www.kansashealthwave.org
HealthWave covers children from birth to age 19. Some of the services provided are prenatal care and delivery, substance abuse, medical, dental, immunizations, and prescriptions. The income guideline for a family of four is $36,200. Call for an application or to apply.

Kentucky
Kentucky Children's Health Insurance Program
P.O. Box 1704
Louisville, KY 40201-9814
877-KCHIP-18
877-KCHIP-19 TTY
800-662-5397 Espanol
http://chs.state.ky.us/kchip
Children from birth through age 18 from low-income families are eligible for CHIP. The annual income limit for a family of four is $36,200. Application to the program is made through a face to face interview at the local Department for Community Based Services Office in the county where the child lives. To make an appointment contact your local DCBS office.

Louisiana
LaChip
Louisiana Department of Health and Hospitals
1201 Capitol Access
P.O. Box 629
Baton Rouge, LA 70821-0629
877-2LA-CHIP
800-220-5404 TTY
Fax: 877-523-2987
www.dhh.state.la.us/MEDICAID/LACHIP/index.htm
LaChip provides health benefits for eligible children from birth up to age 19 using special income amounts ($35,000 annually for a family of four) and fewer requirements than other programs. Children keep their health coverage for one full year regardless of changes in income or circumstances. There are no enrollment fees, premiums, co-pays, or deductibles. Applications are available on the website. You can bring, mail, or fax your application to any local Medicaid office or to a Medicaid Application Center.

Maine
Maine Care
Department of Human Services
11 State House Station
222 State St.
Augusta, ME 04333-0011
877-KIDSNOW
800-965-7476 TDD
www.state.me.us/dhs/bfi/cubcareb.htm
Maine Care is a comprehensive medical plan that includes transportation for medical appointments, family planning services, ambulance, and Chiropractic services to name a few. Children under 18 and pregnant women are covered under the plan; parents may be eligible also. To get an application call your local DHS

Office to request one, email a request, or print a copy online.

Maryland

Maryland Children's Health Program
Maryland Department of Health and Mental Hygiene
201 W. Preston St.
Baltimore, MD 21201
800 456-8900
800-735-2258 TDD
www.dhmh.state.md.us/mma/mchp
The Maryland Children's Health Program provides full health benefits for children 18 and under, and pregnant women of any age who meet the income guideline of $35,300. Applications are available on-line, or from the Health Department, Department of Social Services, WIC Centers, and local hospitals and schools. Applications may be mailed in or dropped off at you're the Health Department.

Massachusetts

MassHealth
Division of Medical Assistance
600 Washington St.
Boston, MA 02111
888-665-9993
888-665-9997 TTY
www.state.ma.us/dma/masshealthinfo/applmemb_IDX.htm
MassHealth pays for health care for certain low and medium income people who are under age 65, not living in nursing homes or other long term care facilities. This includes families and children under the age of 19, pregnant women, disabled people and people who are HIV positive. The program offers health care benefits directly or by paying part or all of your health insurance premiums. Applications can be downloaded from the website or requested by calling a MassHealth Enrollment Center.

Michigan

MIChild
6th Floor Lewis Cass Building
320 South Walnut St.
Lansing, MI 48913
888-988-6300
888-263-5897 TTY
www.mdch.state.mi.us/msa/MDCH_MSA/miindex.htm
MIChild is a health insurance program for uninsured children of working families. Children under the age of 19 and pregnant women are eligible. Benefits include medical, dental, vision, and prenatal care. A full list of services is provided when coverage begins. The annual income guideline is $33, 600. Applications are available on-line.

Minnesota

Minnesota CARE
Minnesota Department of Human Services
444 Lafayette Road North
St. Paul, MN 55155
651-297-3862
800-657-3672 outstate
800-627-3529 TTY
www.dhs.state.mn.us/hlthcare/default.htm
Minnesota Care is a subsidized health care program for people who live in Minnesota and do not have access to health insurance. There are no health condition barriers, but applicants must meet income and program guidelines to qualify. Enrollees pay a monthly premium for their health coverage. The premium is based on income and family size. Coverage includes medical care, dental, mental health and substance abuse services and prescription drugs. Applications are available on the website.

Mississippi

Children's Health Insurance Program
Mississippi Department of Human Services
750 North State Street
Jackson, MS 39202
877-KIDS-NOW
601-359-4500
www.mschip.com
Chip provides uninsured children below age 19, whose annual family income is less than $35,300, with access to a comprehensive set of health services including physician, occupational and physical rehab, nursing, dental, hearing and vision services. To apply for the Chip program, visit your local Department of Human Services Office. Rural health centers, community health centers, county health departments, Head Start Centers, and some hospitals can also help you apply.

Missouri
MC+ for Kids
State of Missouri Department of Social Services
221 West High Street
P.O. Box 1527
Jefferson City, MO 65102-1527
www.dss.state.mo.us/mcplus/index.htm
To qualify for MC+ for Kids, children must be under the age of 19, have been uninsured for at least 6 months, and have an annual family income of less than $52,956. Eligible children will receive all medically necessary services. You can print on the website, call the toll free number, or visit your local Division of Family Services Office to get an application.

Montana
Montana CHIP
P.O. Box 202951
Helena, MT 59620-2951
877-KidsNow
406-444-6971
www.dphhs.state.mt.us/hpsd/pubheal/chip/index.htm
Chip is a low-cost, private health insurance plan for qualified Montana children through the age of 18. Financial eligibility is based on a family's adjusted gross income, $27,150 for a family of four. There are no asset or resource tests. Parents are in charge of the health care their children receive. Applications are available by mail, on the website, and in all Montana communities at County Health Departments and Health Care Facilities. The average time on the waiting list is 2-3 months.

Nebraska
Kids Connection
Nebraska Children's Health Insurance Program
P.O. Box 94926
Lincoln, NE 68509-4926
877-NEB-KIDS
www.hhs.state.ne.us/med/kidsconx.htm
Kids Connection is an extension of the Medicaid program in Nebraska. Its purpose is to provide health care to low-income uninsured children all across the state. There are no premiums or co-payments for children with Kids Connection coverage. The family of four annual income guideline is $33,480. To apply, you can print the mail-in application available on the website, call the toll-free number to request one, or go to your local Health and Human Services Office.

Nevada
Nevada Check Up
1100 East Williams Street, Suite 116
Carson City, NV 89701
775-684-3777
775-684-8792
800-360-6044
www.nevadacheckup.state.nv.us
Health care services are provides mainly by HMOs. Some of the services covered are well baby/well child, Home Health, shots, hearing aids, laboratory services, prescriptions, and x-rays. Applicants must be 18 or younger, have had no insurance for at least 6 months, and meet the income requirements. The guideline for a family of four is $35,300 annually. Nevada Check Up requires quarterly premiums. There is no retroactive coverage, and coverage is effective the 1st day of the month following enrollment approval.

New Hampshire
NH Healthy Kids
25 Hall Street, suite 303
Concord, NH 03301-3477
877-464-2447
www.nhhealthykids.com
The philosophy of Healthy Kids is to promote healthy lifestyles, encourage preventative health and dental care, treat illness early and manage chronic health conditions. Premiums are based on family size and income. Pregnant women are covered under the plan also. There is no exception for pre-existing conditions. A single application is used for all Healthy Kids Plans. It can be printed from the website and mailed in or you can apply in person at any district Human Services office in the state.

New Jersey
NJ Family Care
P.O. Box 4818
Trenton, NJ 08650-8955
800-701-0710
800-701-0720 TTY
www.njfamilycare.org
Family Care provides affordable health coverage and quality care for eligible uninsured children,

parents, and pregnant women. There are several different plans to fit every family's needs. A printable application is available on the website, or you may call the toll free number to have one mailed to you.

New Mexico
New Mexico Kids
Human Services Department
Medical Assistance Division
P.O. Box 2348
Santa Fe, NM 87504-2348
888-997-2583
505-827-3185
www.state.nm.us/hsd/mad/OtherDocs/NewMexiKids.htm
New Mexico Kids is no cost or low cost health coverage, depending on household income, for children under 19 years old. Preventative services such as Tot to Teen Health checks and shots do not require a co-payment. New Mexico Kids benefits include regular check ups, doctor visits, dental care, hospital care, prescriptions, glasses and hearing and vision exams. Other services may be covered if they are medically necessary. You can apply for New Mexico Kids at most clinics, hospitals, schools, and primary care providers, or at your local Income Support Division Office. Apply in person and health coverage begins immediately for qualified applicants.

New York
Child Health Plus
NYS Health Department
Box 2000
Albany, NY 12220
800-698-KIDS
877-898-5849 TTY
Fax: 518-486-2361
www.health.state.ny.us/nysdoh/chplus/index.htm
Child Health Plus covers diagnosis and treatment of illness and injury, prescription and non-prescription drugs if ordered, emergency care, and more. Children must be under the age of 19 and meet income requirements to qualify for one of the Child Health Plus health care plans. Call the toll free number for an application or more information. Printable applications are available on the website.

North Carolina
North Carolina Healthchoice for Children
2501 Mail Service Center
1985 Umstead Drive
Raleigh, NC 27699
800-367-2229
919-857-4011
Fax: 919-733-6608
www.dhhs.state.nc.us/dma/cpcont.htm
Families who make too much money to qualify for Medicaid, but not enough to afford health insurance on their own are able to get free or reduced cost comprehensive health care for their children. NC Health Choice for Children provides the same coverage that is provided for the children of state employees and teachers, plus vision, hearing, and dental benefits. The plan is open to qualified children up to age 19 on a first come first served basis. Enrollment is limited by the amount of funding available. Applications are available on the website. Completed applications can be mailed or taken to your county social services department.

North Dakota
Healthy Steps
Department 325
600 E. Boulevard Avenue
Bismarck, ND 58505-9985
800-755-2604
www.state.nd.us/childrenshealth
Healthy Steps is for children, 18 or younger, who meet income qualifications and who need health coverage. The income guideline for a family of four is $25,340. Some of the benefits provided by Healthy Steps are inpatient and outpatient services, mental health and substance abuse treatment, prescriptions, routine preventative services, dental, vision and prenatal care. Coverage is for a 12-month period and begins the first day of the month following the month in which eligibility is determined. Applications are available on the website, or at local county social services offices.

Ohio
Healthy Start
Ohio Department of Job and Family Services
30 E. Broad St. 32nd Floor
Columbus, OH 43215-3414
614-466-6282

Fax: 614-466-2815
614-752-3951 TDD
800-324-8680 Toll free Hotline
www.state.oh.us/odjfs/ohp/bcps/hshf/index.stm
Children up to age 19 and pregnant women can get free and low cost comprehensive health insurance coverage through Healthy Start. Coverage is guaranteed for 12 months regardless of changes in income. Coverage includes doctor visits, immunizations prescriptions, dental, mental health, vision, and hospital care. Applications are available from the Ohio Health Plans website or your local Office of Job and Family Services. Call the hotline for more information or assistance in filling out the form.

Oklahoma
SCHIP
Oklahoma Health Care Authority
4545 N. Lincoln Blvd. Suite 124
Oklahoma City, OK 73105
405-522-7300
www.ohca.state.ok.us
To be eligible for the State Children's Health Insurance program, children must have no creditable insurance, have family income below guidelines ($33,485 for a family of four), be under the age of 18, and not be eligible for Medicaid.

Oregon
Children's Health Insurance Program
500 Summer St. NE
Salem, OR 97301-1077
800-987-7767
503-945-5772
www.omap.hr.state.or.us/chip
The Oregon Department of Human Services administers the Children's Health Insurance Program. For more information, contact the office nearest you.

Pennsylvania
Children's Health Insurance Program
1300 Strawberry Square
Harrisburg, PA 17120
800-986-KIDS
Fax: 717-705-1643
www.insurance.state.pa.us/html/chip.html
To be eligible for CHIP in Pennsylvania, children must be a U.S. citizen or lawful alien, be uninsured, under the age of 19, and be a resident of PA for at least 30 days. Benefits include rehabilitation therapy, diagnostic testing, routine check ups, emergency care, maternity care, and up to 90 days hospitalization in any year. To apply for CHIP, call 1-800-986-KIDS.

Rhode Island
Rite Care
Center for Child and Family Health
600 New London Avenue
Cranston, RI 02920
401-462-1300
800-745-5555 TDD
Rite Care is Rhode Island's health insurance program that provides eligible uninsured pregnant women, parents, and children up to age 19 with comprehensive healthcare. Eligibility is based on family income and family size. Assets are not considered when determining eligibility. Families receive most of their medical care through one of three participating health plans: Neighborhood Health Plan of Rhode Island, United Healthcare of New England, and Blue ChiP. You can apply by mail or at your local Department of Human Services Office. Call for more information or to get a mail in application.

South Carolina
Partners for Healthy children
Department of Health and Human Services
P.O. Box 8206
Columbia, SC 29202-8206
803-898-2834
Fax: 803-898-4513
www.dhhs.state.sc.us/FAQ/children.htm
Qualifying for Partners for Healthy Children is based on the number of people in your family and your household income. Children must be 18 or younger to qualify. Applications are available online or by calling Partners for Healthy Children at 1-888-549-0820.

South Dakota
CHIP
Kneip Building
700 Governors Drive
Pierre, SD 57501-2291
800-305-3064
www.state.sd.us/doh/doh.html

The Children's Health Insurance Program (CHIP) provides free health insurance to eligible children. CHIP covers doctor appointments, hospital stays, dental and vision services, prescription drugs, mental health care and other medical services. Qualifying income for a family of four is $36,204. Children who already have private health insurance may also be eligible for CHIP paying deductibles, co-payments, and other medical services not covered by their private policy. An application can be printed on the website. Once completed it should be returned to the Department of Social Services Office serving your county.

Tennessee
Bureau of TennCare
729 Church Street
Nashville, TN 37247-6501
800-669-1851
www.state.tn.us/health/tenncare
TennCare coverage includes inpatient/outpatient services, lab and x-ray services, dental, vision, home health care, prescriptions, medical supplies, and dialysis to name a few. The income guideline for a family of four is $19,020. Call for an application, go to your local Department of Health Office, or visit the Bureau of TennCare in Nashville.

Texas
Tex-Care CHIP
P.O. box 13247
Austin, TX 78711-3247
512-424-6536
Fax: 512-424-6665
800-647-6558 toll free
www.texcarepartnership.com
To qualify for CHIP, a child must be a Texas resident and a U.S. citizen (the citizenship of the parents does not affect the child's eligibility), under age 19, meet family income requirements, and be uninsured for at least 90 days. CHIP covers hospital care, surgery, x-rays, therapy, prescriptions, eye exams and glasses, dental care, regular check ups and vaccinations. Children who enroll in CHIP receive 12 months of continuous coverage. Families must re-enroll their children once a year. Call the toll free number to apply over the phone.

Utah
UTAH CHIP
Department of Health
P.O. Box 144102
Salt Lake City, UT 84114-4102
801-538-9004
866-772-1261 toll free
www.utahchip.org
If you cannot afford health insurance and earn too much for Medicaid, your children under age 18 may qualify for CHIP. CHIP takes into consideration the number of people in your family and your family's current income. Currently, the income guideline for a family of four is $36,200. CHIP offers a comprehensive benefit package that covers most standard services including hospital and doctor charges. CHIP stresses preventative care. There are no co-pays required for any preventative services, and no exemptions for per-existing conditions. You must apply during an open enrollment period.

Vermont
Dr. Dynasaur
Health Access Member Services
Agency of Human Services
5 Burlington Square
Burlington, VT 05401
800-250-8427 toll free
www.dsw.state.vt.us/districts/ovha/ovha10.htm
Dr. Dynasaur provides health care for children under 18 and pregnant women. You may qualify even if you have a job, other health insurance and resources. Depending on your family's income you may have to pay a premium of up to $50.00/month. The Dr. Dynasaur benefits include doctor visits and check ups, dental, vision, hospitalization, shots, prescriptions and more. To apply, call the toll free number or write to the Agency of Human Services.

Virginia
Healthy Child Care
1500 E. Main St. Room 104
Richmond, VA 23219
866-87FAMIS
888-221 1590 TDD
www.vahealth.org/healthychildcareva/index.htm
Healthy Child Care is for children under age 18 who live in Virginia, do not have insurance and have been uninsured for at least 6 months, are

not eligible for Medicaid, and meet income guidelines. The income guideline for a family of four is $36,200. Covered services include doctor visits, well baby check ups, vaccinations, tests and x-rays, emergency care, vision and dental. An application is available on the website.

Washington

Healthy Kids Now
421 W. Riverside Suite 400
Spokane, WA 99201
877-543-7669
www.hipspokane.org.hkn.index.htm
Healthy Kids Now covers kids and teens under19. Premiums are billed monthly, $10 for each child with a maximum of $30 for 3 or more children. American Indians and Alaska Natives do not pay premiums. Benefits include full medical, dental and vision coverage. To apply, download the application on the website, complete it, and mail it.

West Virginia

West Virginia Chip
State Capitol Complex
Bldg. 3 room213
1900 Kanawha Blvd. East
Charleston, WV 25305
877-982-2447
304-558-2732
www.wvchip.org
WV Chip is a free or low-cost health care plan for children from birth up to age 19. Covered services include preventative care, well child visits, shots, prescriptions, hospital visits, dental, vision, and mental health services. The income guideline for a family of four is $36,200. An application is available on the website, or call to have an application filled out and mailed to you for your signature and proof of income.

Wisconsin

Badger Care
One West Wilson St. Room265
P.O. Box 309
Madison, WI 53701-0309
800-362-3002
www.dhfs.state.wi.us/badgercare/index.htm
Badger Care is Wisconsin's statewide program that provides health care coverage for uninsured working families. It is a comprehensive program that covers both illness and preventative services. To be eligible you must be a child under age 19 or a parent of a child age 19 or younger living with you. If you were recently covered by insurance there is a 3-month waiting period except with good cause. To apply, call or contact your county human or social services department.

Wyoming

Wyoming KidCare
2424 Pioneer Avenue, Suite 100
Cheyenne, WY 82002
888-996-8786
http://kidcare.state.wy.us
Wyoming Kid Care Plans A and B offer a complete set of health benefits. To be eligible children must be under age 19, U.S. citizen or eligible immigrant, a Wyoming resident, have no insurance, and not reside in a public institution. The entire application process can be done by mail. If you think you might be eligible, call and have an application sent to you or download it from the website.

Free Care Even If You Don't Qualify

You or your child may still be able to get free health care from local government programs even if you don't qualify. Many local health offices have the authority to stretch the rules if they see fit. Others have set up special arrangements with the local medical society for people who don't qualify for their programs. These offices can direct you to local nonprofit organizations or groups that can give you the care you need at the price you can afford.

Contact your county office of public health listed in your telephone book or your state Department of Health. If you cannot get satisfaction from these offices, contact your local office of your state or federal elected official.

Free Mammograms / Free Tests For Breast and Cervical Cancer

An estimated 2 million American women will be diagnosed with breast or cervical cancer in the next decade, and half a million will lose their lives from these diseases. Screening could prevent up to 30% of these deaths for women over 40.

The government's Center for Disease Control will spend about $174 million a year to maintain a state-by-state program to establish greater access to screening and follow-up services. Each state runs their program a little differently. Most states have the following requirements:

- ➔ women starting 40 or 50 years old,
- ➔ are underinsured or have no insurance
- ➔ have income below a certain level (usually $35,000 for a family of 4)

Some states can adjust eligibility requirements for special cases. States vary in the array of services covered but they normally include:

- ➔ breast and cervical cancer screening
- ➔ mammograms
- ➔ treatment if diagnosed with cancer
- ➔ breast reconstruction or prosthesis

States that don't have direct funds for treatment often make arrangements with other facilities to provide treatment for free. If your screening has been done elsewhere, you can still receive free treatment under this program. Men diagnosed with breast cancer can also receive free treatment.

Contact your county office of public health listed in your telephone book or your state Department of Health. You can also contact the main office of this program at Division of Cancer Prevention and Control, National Center for Chronic Disease Prevention and Health Promotion, Center for Disease Control and Prevention, 4770 Buford Highway, NE, MS K-64, Atlanta, GA 30341, 770-488-4751; 888-842-6355; Fax: 770-488-4760; {www.cdc.gov/nccdphp/dcpc/nbccedp/index.htm}.

More Free Mammograms

Not all insurance companies pay for mammograms, and not every woman is eligible for the government's program described earlier. The following organizations can help you identify free and low cost mammograms in your area.

1) ***The American Cancer Society***: contact your local office the national office at 800-ACS-2345.
2) ***YMCA's Encore Plus Program***: contact your local office or the national office at 800-95-EPLUS
3) ***National Cancer Institute***: 800-4-CANCER

4) ***State Office of Breast and Cervical Cancer***: contact your state Department of Health
5) ***October is National Breast Cancer Awareness Month***: many mammogram facilities offer their services at special fees during this period. Call and see what kind of deal you can get.
6) ***Medicare coverage of mammograms***: call 800-MEDICARE.

For a free copy of *How To Get A Low Cost Mammogram*, contact National Alliance of Breast Cancer Organizations, (NABCO) 9 East 37th Street, 10th Floor, New York, NY 10016; 888-80-NABCO; {www.nabco.org}. This publication is also available online at {www.nabco.org/index.php/13/40/index.php /214}.

Free Hospital Care

Don't have money for your gall bladder surgery? What about that hospital visit you had two months ago? You might not have to pay a cent. Call the Hill-Burton Hotline.

Under this program, certain hospitals and other health care facilities provide free or low-cost medical care to patients who cannot afford to pay. You may qualify even if your income is up to double the Poverty Income Guidelines. That's $36,200 for a family of four! You can apply before or after you receive care, and even after the bill has been sent to a collection agency.

Call the Hotline to find out if you meet the eligibility requirements and to request a list of local hospitals who are participating. For more information, contact Hill-Burton Hotline, Health Resources and Services Administration, U.S. Department of Health and Human Services, Parklawn Building, 5600 Fishers Lane, Rockville, MD 20857; 800-638-0742; 800-492-0359 (in MD); {www.hrsa.gov/osp/dfcr/about/aboutdiv. htm}.

Free Food At School For Your Kids

A 1998 Tufts University study states: "Children who participate in the U.S. Department of Agriculture's School Breakfast Program were shown to have significantly higher standardized achievement test scores than eligible non-participants. Children getting school breakfasts also had significantly reduced absence and tardiness rates."

Your child can get a free breakfast at one of the 72,000 participating schools at one income level ($23,530 for a family of four) and at a reduced fee at another level ($33,485 for a family of four).Families who pay full price still get a bargain. Over 7.7 million kids participate and 6.4 million get it for free or at a reduced rate. Lunch is also available under the U.S. Department of Agriculture's National School Lunch program at 97,700 schools serving 27 million children. The same general requirements apply to both programs.

Ask your school if they participate, or contact your local School Food Service Authority in your school system. If all this fails, contact your state Department of Education. Check out the Food and Nutrition Services web page at {www.fns.usda.gov/fns}.

Rich Kids Pay 2 Cents For Half-Pint of Milk

Milk at this price is available to students, no matter what the family income, at over 8,000 schools, 1,400 summer camps, and 500 non-residential child care institutions. The program is called the U.S. Department of Agriculture's **Special Milk Program** and is available to institutions that do not use the School Breakfast Program or the National School Lunch program.

Ask your school if they participate, or contact your local School Food Service Authority in your school system. If all this fails, contact your state Department of Education. If you cannot get satisfaction from these offices, contact your local office of your state or federal elected official.

Low Cost Immunizations for Travelers

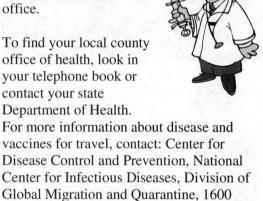

In order to prevent contracting diseases like yellow fever, cholera or Japanese encephalitis when traveling in other countries, the government's Center for Disease Control recommends that certain vaccines would eliminate your risk of infection. Some local Public Health offices offer these vaccines at a fraction of what you would pay at a doctor's office.

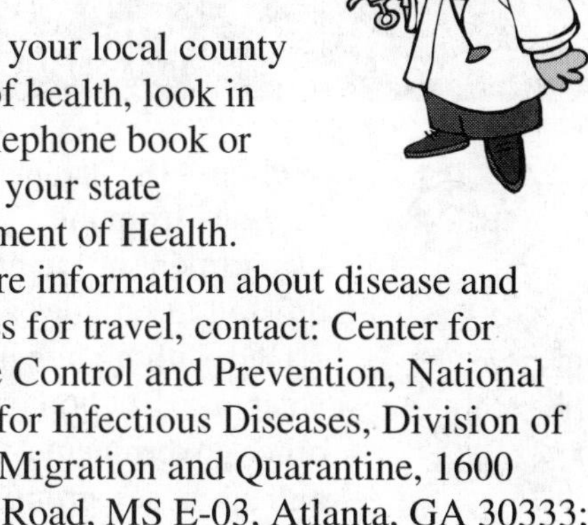

To find your local county office of health, look in your telephone book or contact your state Department of Health.
For more information about disease and vaccines for travel, contact: Center for Disease Control and Prevention, National Center for Infectious Diseases, Division of Global Migration and Quarantine, 1600 Clifton Road, MS E-03, Atlanta, GA 30333; 877-394-8747; 404-639-3534; {www.cdc.gov/travel/index.htm}.

National Immunization Information Hotline

This hotline tells you where you can go locally to get Free Immunization shots for your kids or flu shots for yourself. Immunizations for children can run as much as $335 per child. This program is run by the U.S. Government's Center for Disease Control, which can answer almost any question you have about shots over the telephone or send you free publications.

In most areas of the country, immunizations are available FREE for children. Adult services may be free or very low cost. Call 800-232-2522 (English); 800-232-0233 (Spanish); {www.cdc.gov/nip}.

How To Fight Your Doctor, Hospital, Or Insurance Company — Call The Marines

Well, not the actual Marines from the Department of Defense, dressed in fatigues and armed with high tech weapons. But you can call other government offices and advocacy groups that will do your fighting for you or give you the needed weapons to do your own fighting.

Before you call a lawyer, call these free offices first:

- ***State Insurance Commissioner***: will help you learn your legal rights regarding insurance.
- ***State Medical Boards***: will review your complaint (including billing issues) and help resolve disputes.
- ***State HMO boards***: will review your complaint (including billing issues) and help resolve disputes.
- ***The Center for Patient Advocacy***, 1350 Beverly Road, Suite 108, McLean, VA 22101; 800-846-7444; {www.patientadvocacy.org}: provides free advice and publications on how to fight the system, also does advocacy work for patients rights on Capitol Hill)
- ***Center for Medicare Advocacy, Inc***, P.O. Box 350, Willimantic, CT 06226; 800-262-4414 (toll free in Connecticut); 860-456-7790; 202-216-0028 (Washington, D.C. office) {www.medicareadvocacy.org}. Attorneys, paralegals, and technical assistants provide free legal help for elderly and disabled who are unfairly denied Medicare coverage in the state of Connecticut. Legal help and other services are also available to residents outside of Connecticut for a fee.
- ***American Self Help Clearinghouse***, Mental Help Net, 570 Metro Place, Dublin, OH 43017; 508-881-0488; {www.mentalhelp.net/selfhelp}: makes referrals to self-help organizations world wide and helps people interested in starting their own self help group.
- ***National Self-Help Clearinghouse***, Graduate School and University Center of the City University of New York, 365 5th Ave., Suite 3300, New York, NY 10016; 212-817-1822; {www.selfhelpweb.org}: makes referrals to self-help groups nationwide.

Fund Helps Foster Independence of Physically Disabled

Individuals with physical disabilities residing in Oregon may be eligible to receive financial assistance through the Blanche Fisher Foundation. The fund assists with the expense of hearing aids, eyeglasses, wheelchairs, ramps, tuition and skills training.

Contact Blanche Fisher Foundation, 1509 SW Sunset Blvd., Suite 1-B, Portland, OR 97201-2676; 503-819-8205; Fax: 503-246-4941; {www.bff.org}.

30% of All Families Eligible For Free Health Services — Others Pay Sliding Scale

Many services provided by county governments are free and persons who don't qualify for free services are charged on a sliding scale based on income. A typical fee chart is the one below from Denton, Texas. The data is based on 2002 Federal Poverty Rates from the Bureau of the Census. Denton also states that ***NO ONE WILL BE REFUSED SERVICES FOR INABILITY TO PAY***, which is typical for most counties. **REMEMBER**, if you don't qualify for free services, everyone qualifies for services on a sliding scale.

Estimated Income Limits For Free Service

Service	Single Person	Family of 2	Family of 4
Food Vouchers and Nutritional Info (185% of poverty AND a medical or nutritional need)	$16,391	$22,089	$33,485
Prenatal Care During Pregnancy (200% of poverty)	$17,720	$23,880	$36,200
Child Medical Care (200% of poverty)	$17,720	$23,880	$36,200
Adult Health Care (150% of poverty)	$13,290	$17,910	$27,150
Dental Care (150% of poverty)	$13,290	$17,910	$27,150
HIV Counseling & Testing	No limits, $10.00 donation requested		
Sexually Transmitted Disease Clinic	No limits, $10.00 donation requested		
Tuberculosis	No limits, $4.00 for testing		
Overseas Vaccinations	No limits, $5.00 to $105.00		
Immunizations	No limits, up to $30 per family, no one refused		
Substance Abuse Screening & Referral	No limits, some fees vary based on patient income according to poverty guidelines or program requirements		

Estimate of Families Living At Poverty Levels

% Of Poverty Level	Number of Families	% of Total Families
100%	12,594,000	12.3%
150%	21,055,000	20.0%
185%	28,174,000	27.4%
200%	30,078,000	29.3%

(Poverty Data from Census Report P60-198 1996 ----One Person = $7,995,
Two Persons = $ 10,233, Four Persons = $16,063,
Household Income Data from Census Current Population Reports, P60-200)
(Poverty Data 7/1/98 USDA {www.usda.gov/fcs/cnp/ieg98-99.htm}
1=$8,050, 2=$10,850, 3=13,650, 4=16,450, 5=19,250, 6=22,050, 7=24,850, 8=27,650

Grants and Fundraising Help For Transplant Patients

Organizations like The National Foundation for Transplants and National Transplant Assistance Fund assist patients, their families, and friends in raising significant amounts of money for the patient's transplant care when there is no public or private insurance that will cover all the costs. They also provide grants to help pay for medications required after a transplant, or money for transplant-related emergencies, and one-time assistance grants of $1,000.

Other transplant related non-profits, like the Liver Foundation's Liver Transplant Fund, provide services and help for patients and families to raise money for an organ transplant.

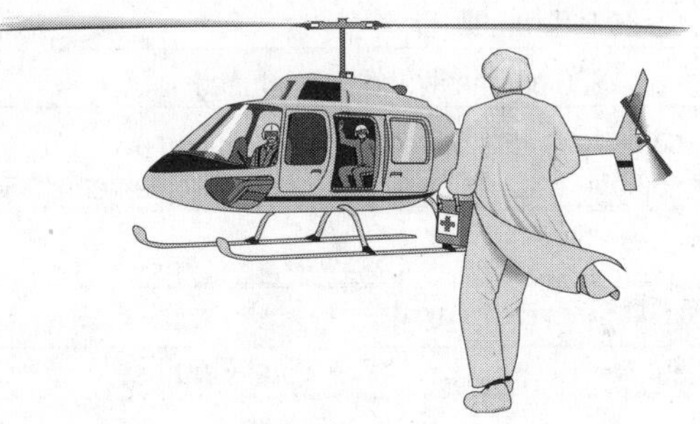

- ***National Foundation for Transplants***, 1102 Brookfield, Suite 200, Memphis, TN 38119; 800-489-3836, 901-684-1697, Fax: 910-684-3863; {www.transplants.org}.
- ***National Transplant Assistance Fund***, 3475 West Chester Pike, Suite 230, Newtown Square, PA 19073; 800-642-8399; 610-353-9684; Fax: 610-353-1616; {www.transplantfund.org}.
- ***American Liver Foundation***, 75 Maiden Lane, Suite 603, New York, NY 10038; 800-GO LIVER; 212-668-1000; Fax: 212-483-8179; {www.liverfoundation.org}.

Cancer Patients Receive Help with Expenses

Limited financial assistance is available through Cancer Care, Inc. to cancer patients and their families who are residents of NY, NJ and CT for home care, child care and transportation expenses.

Contact Cancer Care, Inc., 275 7th Ave., 22nd Floor, New York, NY 10001; 800-813-HOPE; 212-712-8080; Fax: 212-712-8495; {www.cancercare.org}.

Medical, Dental and Educational Expense Assistance to Children of Emergency Medical Technicians

Medical and dental assistance is available to children under the age of 18 through the Eagles Memorial Foundation, Inc. Assistance is provided for doctor, dentist and hospital bills, eyeglasses, drugs, and medical and dental devices. Educational Assistance not to exceed $6000/yr. or $30,000/4 yrs. is available through the

Eagles Memorial Foundation, Inc. to individuals over the age of 18. These benefits are offered to children of members of the Fraternal Order of Eagles and the Ladies Auxiliary who die from injuries or diseases incurred while in military service; while serving as a volunteer law enforcement officer, volunteer firefighter, or volunteer emergency medical service (EMS) officer; or in the commission of their daily employment.

Contact Eagles Memorial Foundation, Inc., 4710 14th St. W., Bradenton, FL 34207; 941-775-1976; Fax: 941-758-4042; {www.foe.com/memorial}.

Free Transportation To Medical Appointments For Your Mom

Mom has to get to a doctor's visit in the middle of the day and you can't take her. Or you have a disability that may cause you to miss an appointment if someone else doesn't drive. You may be able to get free transportation and escort services provided by either your local health office or local office on aging. Some communities even provide very low cost door-to-door services for seniors to go anywhere.

If you can't find your local area agency on aging or public health office in your telephone book, contact your state Department of Aging or Health. If that fails, contact the Eldercare Locator Hotline at 1-800-677-1116. They are available to help anyone identify services for seniors.

Working People With Disabilities Can Get Cheap Health Insurance

A change to the Balanced Budget Act of 1997 passed by Congress allows states to offer Medicaid to individuals who are working and who have a disability. Prior to this, states could only offer Medicaid to people with disabilities who were NOT working. The income limits goes up to $45,250 (for a family of four), and the state can charge premiums on an income-related sliding scale.

Contact your state Department of Health to identify your Medicaid office. You can contact the local office of your congressman or senator for more information on the law. You can also check out the website of the Bazelon Center for Mental Health Law at {www.bazelon.org}.

Free Health Insurance Counseling

Free one-on-one counseling is available to seniors and, in most areas, people with disabilities, to answer questions like:

- How much insurance is too much?
- If something sounds like fraud, where can I go for help?
- What's the best Medigap insurance plan?
- Do I qualify for government health benefits?
- Should I buy long-term care insurance?

The program is called **Health Insurance Counseling and Advocacy Program (HICAP)** and is sponsored by the Centers for Medicare & Medicaid Services (formerly U.S. Health Care Financing Administration). In most states, it is usually run by the state Department on Aging or the State Insurance Commissioner's office. If that fails, contact the Eldercare Locator hotline at 1-800-677-1116. They can give you the local number.

Low Cost Home Health Care

Montgomery County in Maryland provides home health care free or on a sliding scale, depending on income, through the local public health office. You don't have to be a senior to qualify.

A survey by the Center for Disease Control reports that about half of all local public health agencies provide similar services. To see what is available in your area, contact your county office of health listed in your telephone book or your state Department of Health. If you cannot get satisfaction from these offices, contact your local office of your state or federal elected official.

For similar services for seniors, contact your local area agency on aging or your state Department on Aging. If that fails, contact the Eldercare Locator hotline at 1-800-677-1116. They are available to help anyone identify services for seniors.

Free Health Insurance

Health insurance can be quite confusing, but you may qualify for help and not even realize it. Medicaid helps people with low income and resources pay for medical bills, doctor visits, and even prescription drugs. Federal and State governments fund it jointly. This program covers approximately 36 million individuals including children, the aged, blind and/or disabled, and those who are eligible for federally assisted income maintenance payments. Services include:

- inpatient hospital
- outpatient
- physician services
- medical and surgical dental services
- family planning
- laboratory services
- prenatal care

People that get SSI benefits are automatically eligible for Medicaid benefits in most states. Income and resource guidelines must be met for an individual, couple, or family to qualify. Income includes money received each month from Social Security, employment, or other

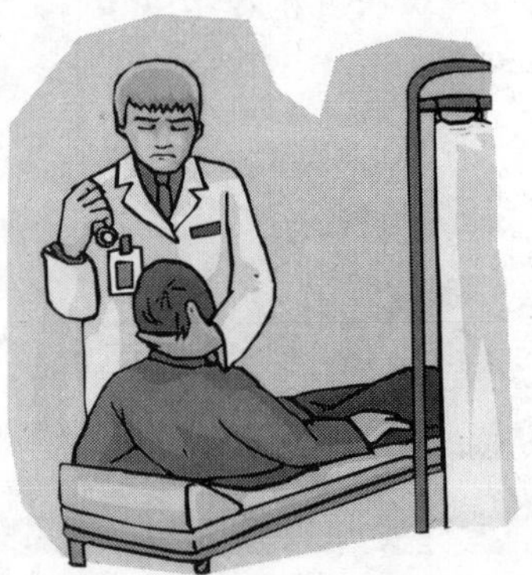

sources. The value of items owned, such as cash and savings, are resources. Some resources, such as the family home and one car, are not used to determine Medicaid eligibility. Individuals must be US citizens, with some exceptions for some non-citizens, to qualify. Medicaid does not provide medical assistance for all poor persons. Except for emergency services for certain persons, even the poorest of people must be in one of the groups described below. Medicaid benefits cover basic health services. Some services not covered by Medicare, such as medicine, nursing home care, eye exams, glasses, transportation for medical care, and other medical services, may also be paid for under the Medicaid program.

Each State establishes their own eligibility standards; determines the type, amount, duration and scope of services; sets the rate of payment for services; and administers their own program. Consequently, the Medicaid program varies considerably from State to State. States may use more liberal income and resources methods in determining eligibility for certain groups.

Eligibility

Each state must provide Medicaid coverage for most individuals who receive federally assisted income maintenance payments and also for related groups not receiving cash payments. Examples of the mandatory Medicaid eligibility groups are:

- Low income families with children who meet certain eligibility requirements in the State's TANF plan;
- Supplemental Security Income recipients.
- Infants born to Medicaid eligible pregnant women. Medicaid eligibility must continue through the first year of the infant's life so long as it remains in the mother's household and she remains eligible, or would be eligible if she were still pregnant;
- Children under age 6 and pregnant women whose family income is at or below 133% of the Federal poverty level. Certain States may have established a higher minimum mandatory income level.
- Once eligible, pregnant women remain so through the end of the calendar month 60 days after the end of the pregnancy, regardless of any change in the family income;
- Recipients of adoption assistance and foster care under Title IV-E of the Social Security Act;
- Certain Medicare beneficiaries; and
- Special protected groups who may keep Medicaid for a period of time. Examples are: persons that lose SSI payments because of earnings from work or increased Social Security payments; and families who are provided 6 to 12 months of Medicaid coverage following loss of eligibility because of an increase in child or spousal support.

States may also provide Medicaid coverage for other "category needy" groups. These are optional groups and share qualifications of the mandatory groups described above. However, the eligibility criteria is broader. Matching Federal funds are also given for these groups. Examples of them are:

- infants up to age one and pregnant women not covered under the mandatory rules whose family income is below 185% of the Federal poverty level, or some other percentage set by the State;
- optional targeted low income children;
- certain aged, blind or disabled adults who have incomes above those requiring mandatory coverage, but below the Federal poverty level;

- children under age 21 who meet income and resources requirements for TANF, but who are otherwise not eligible for TANF;
- institutionalized people with income and resource below specified limits;
- people who would be eligible if they were institutionalized, but are receiving care under home and community based services waivers;
- recipients of State supplementary payments; and
- TB-infected individuals who would be financially eligible for Medicaid at the SSI level (only for TB-related ambulatory services and TB drugs);
- low income, uninsured women screened and diagnosed with breast or cervical cancer at a Center's for Disease Control and Prevention's Breast and Cervical Cancer Early Detection Program. State's can also opt to have a "medically needy" program.

People with low income and limited resources that receive Medicare, may get help paying for out-of-pocket medical expenses from their State Medicaid program. Different benefits are available to those "dual eligibles." For individuals eligible for full Medicaid coverage, the program supplements Medicare coverage by providing services and supplies that are available under their State's Medicaid program. Services that are covered by both programs are first paid by Medicare and the difference paid by Medicaid, up to the State's payment limit. Medicaid also covers additional services such as nursing facility care beyond the 100-day limit covered by Medicare, prescription drugs, eyeglasses and hearing aids.

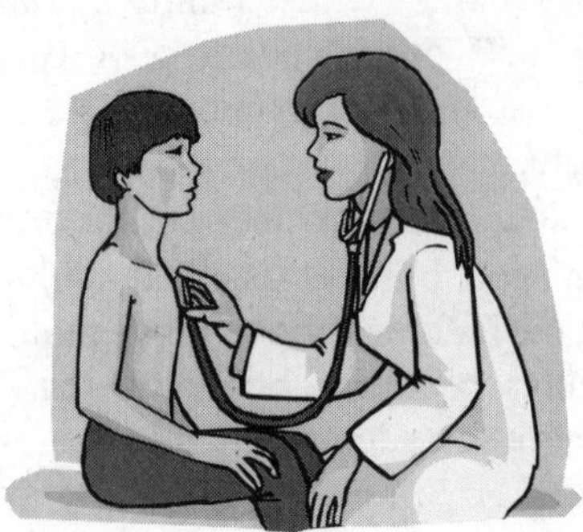

For a list of each State's Medicaid toll-free phone number, go to {http://cms.hhs.gov/medicaid/ tollfree.asp}. To view the Federal poverty limits, go to {http://cms.hhs.gov/medicaid/eligibility/ default.asp}.

For more information, or to find information on each State's Medicaid program, check out the Centers for Medicare and Medicaid Services (CMS) (formerly the Health Care Financing Administration) {http://cms.hhs.gov}. You can contact the lead agency at CMS, 7500 Security Boulevard, Baltimore, MD 21244-1850; 410-786-3000.

$$$$$ Money To Buy A Van, A Talking Computer Or Rubber Door Knob Grips

People with disabilities now have a place to turn to learn everything they need to know about how the latest in technology can improve their lives. It can be a specially equipped van, a talking computer, a special kitchen or eating aid, or adaptive toys for children. Or it may be a student with learning disabilities who needs special help getting through school.

A project funded by the U.S. Department of Education, called Technical Assistance

Project has established an office in each state that can provide:

- ▲ ***Information Services***: will help you identify the special products that are available to help you cope with your disability.
- ▲ ***Equipment Loan Program***: allows people to borrow new technology devices for a number of weeks before they purchase them.
- ▲ ***Recycling Program***: matches up people with needs for products with people who want to sell or donate products.
- ▲ ***Funding Information***: collects information on the various sources of funding for this equipment from public and private sources.
- ▲ ***Loans***: many states are offering special loans to help people purchase the necessary equipment; Ohio offers low-interest loans up to $10,000, North Carolina has loans up to $15,000, and California offers loan guarantees up to $35,000.

Contact your state information operator listed in the Appendix and ask for your state Office of Social Services or Vocational Rehabilitation. They should be aware of your state Assistance Technology Office. If you have trouble locating your state office, you can contact the office that coordinates all state activities: Rehabilitation Engineering and Assertive Technology Society of North America, (RESNA), 1700 North Moore Street, Suite 1540, Arlington, VA 22209-1903; 703-524-6686; Fax: 703-524-6630; TTY: 703-524-6639; {www.resna.org}.

Free Take Out Taxi For Seniors

People 60 and over who are homebound because of illness, incapacity, or disability, or who are otherwise isolated can receive hot meals delivered to their home. The program is funded in every state by the Older Americans Act.

Contact your local area agency on aging or your state Department on Aging. If that fails, contact the Eldercare Locator hotline at 1-800-677-1116. They are available to help anyone identify services for seniors.

Easter Seals in Arizona Offers Free Computers to People With Disabilities

Washington State chapter has a free loan program, and the chapters in Missouri offer computer classes. Contact yourlocal Easter Seals Society to see what they may offer in the way of computers and computer skills for people with disabilities. If you can't find your local office, contact: Easter Seals, 230 West Monroe Street, Suite 1800, Chicago, IL 60606; 800-221-6827; 312-726-6200; Fax: 312-726-1494; {www.easter-seals.com}.

Free Hepatitis B Shots To Children

Oswego County Health Department offers free shots for children 18 and younger. The same with Buena-Vista County in Iowa, but people 19 and over are charged $31.75 for the shot. However, you won't be turned away if you cannot pay.

Hepatitis can cause serious liver disease, cancer and even death. About 1 in 20 people in U.S. have been infected, and over 5,000 a year die. To find out about services in your area, contact the county office of health listed in your telephone book or your state Department of Health.

Free & Low Cost Dental Care for Kids, Seniors, and Certain Incomes

Many of the local health offices provide dental services to children and to income-eligible adults on a sliding fee scale. Contact your county office of health listed in your telephone book or your state Department of Health.

Many states have special free or discount services just for seniors. Contact your local Area Agency on Aging or your state Department on Aging. If that fails, contact the Eldercare Locator Hotline at 1-800-677-1116.

Free Care By the Best Doctors In The World

Bob Dole knew where to go when he had his cancer surgery — The National Institutes of Health (NIH). Each year, over 80,000 patients receive free medical care by some of the best doctors in the world. Medical research professionals receive millions of dollars each year to study the latest causes, cures, and treatments to various diseases or illnesses. If your health condition is being studied somewhere, you may qualify for what is called a "clinical trial" and get the treatment for free.

There are several ways to find out about ongoing clinical trials across the nation. Your first call should be to the National Institutes of Health Clinical Center. NIH is the federal government's focal point for health research. The Clinical Center is a 325-bed hospital that has facilities and services to support research at NIH. Your doctor can call the Patient Referral Line to find out if your diagnosis is being studied and to be put in contact with the primary investigator who can then tell if you meet the requirements for the study.

You can also search their website for your diagnosis and qualifying information, or search the newly established website {clinicaltrials.gov}, which contains information on approximately 6,300 clinical studies sponsored by NIH, other federal agencies, and the pharmaceutical industry. In addition, each Institute at NIH also funds research that is conducted by universities, research institutions, and others.

To learn about those studies, contact the Institute that handles your diagnosis. Or conduct a CRISP (Computer Retrieval of Information on Scientific Projects) search, which is a database of research projects and programs supported by the U.S. Department of Health and Human Services.

- **Patient Recruitment and Public Liaison Office**, Warren Grant Magnuson Clinical Center, National Institutes of Health, Bethesda, Maryland 20892-2655; 800-411-1222; Fax: 301-480-9793; {www.cc.nih.gov}.
- **National Institutes of Health**, Bethesda, MD 20892; 301-496-4000; {www.nih.gov}.
- **CRISP**, Office of Reports and Analysis, Division of Extramural Outreach and Information Resources, 6701 Rockledge Drive, Rockledge 2, MSC 7910, Bethesda, MD 20892-7910; 301-435-0656; Fax: 301-480-2845; {www-commons.cit.nih.gov/crisp/}.

Service Organizations Provide Free Care

Need help with child care, elderly services, substance abuse treatment? What about youth programs or disaster assistance? Many large service organizations have local offices that provide all this and more. Services vary depending upon the needs of the community, but before you fight your battles alone, contact these main offices to find out about local programs:

- ***Catholic Charities USA***, 1731 King St., #200, Alexandria, VA 23314; 703-549-1390; Fax: 703-549-1656; {www.catholiccharitiesusa.org}.
- ***Salvation Army***, 615 Slaters Lane, P.O. Box 269, Alexandria, VA 22313; 703-684-5500; 800-SAL-ARMY; Fax: 703-684-3478; {www.salvationarmyusa.org}.
- ***United Way of America***, 701 N. Fairfax St., Alexandria, VA 22314; 800-411-UWAY; 703-836-7112; {www.unitedway.org}.

Are You Eligible for Free Health Care?

Health insurance can be quite confusing. What exactly do you qualify for?

Medicare is a health insurance program, generally for people age 65 or older who are receiving *Social Security* retirement benefits. You can also receive Medicare if you are under 65 and receive Social Security or Railroad Retirement Board disability benefits for 24 months, or if you are a kidney dialysis or kidney transplant patient.

Medicaid is a federal program administered by each state, so eligibility and benefits vary from state to state. The program is administered by a state welfare agency, and it provides health insurance to people with low income and limited assets.

To determine your eligibility, contact your state Office of Social Services. For Medicare eligibility, contact Medicare Hotline, Centers for Medicare & Medicaid Services (formerly U.S. Health Care Financing Administration), 7500 Security Blvd., Baltimore, MD 21244-1850; 800-MEDICARE; {www.medicare.gov}.

Toll-Free Medicaid Numbers

Alabama
800-362-1504;
TDD: 800-253-0799

Alaska
Medicaid Hotline: 800-211-7470

Arizona
800-654-8713 (AZ)
800-523-0231 (out of state but not nationwide)
TDD: 800-334-5140

Arkansas
800-482-8988

California
888-747-1222
Medi-Cal Mental Health Ombudsman Services: 800-896-4042
Medi-Cal Managed Care: 800-430-4263
TTY: 800-896-2512;

Colorado
800-221-3943;
TDD: 800-659-2656
TDD/Voice: 800-659-3656

Connecticut
800-842-1508

Delaware
800-372-2022;
TDD: 800-924-3958

District of Columbia
Maternal Child Health: 800-666-2229 (Transportation/Counseling)
Healthy DC Kids: 800-666-2229

Florida
888-419-3456;
Kidcare TTY: 877-316-8748

Georgia
800-282-4536

Hawaii
Oahu: 800-587-3540 (recipients)
Maui, Molokai & Lanai: 800-894-5755

Idaho
800-685-3757

Illinois
800-252-8635 (IL)
800-843-6154 (out of state)
TTY: 800-447-6404

Indiana
800-889-9949 (IN)

Iowa
800-338-8366

Kansas
800-766-9012 (KS)

Kentucky
800-635-2570;
TTY: 800-775-0296

Louisiana
888-342-6207 (recipients eligibility-LA)

Maine
Client Eligibility:
800-452-4694 (ME)
TTY: 880-423-4331 (ME);

Maryland
800-332-6347 (Recorded Message-MD)
Recipient Services: 800-492-5231 (MD)

Massachusetts
800-841-2900 (MA);
TTY: 888-665-9997

Michigan
800-292-2500

Minnesota
800-657-3739;
TTY: 800-366-8930

Mississippi
800-421-2408 (MS)

Missouri
Recipient Services: 800-392-2161
Eligibility: 800-392-1261

Montana
Medicaid Provider Hotline: 800-480-6823

Nebraska
Medicaid Eligibility System: 800-642-6092
Medicaid Inquiry Lines: 877-255-3092 (payment claims)

Nevada
800-992-0900 (NV)

New Hampshire
800-852-3345;
TDD: 800-735-2964
CHIP: 877-464-2447

New Jersey
800-356-1561
Medicaid Dental Bureau Hotline: 800-782-0181
TTY: 800-201-0720

New Mexico
800-432-6217
Medicaid Managed Care: 888-997-2583
Medicaid Managed Care Enrollment: 888-532-8093
TDD: 800-609-4833

New York
800-206-8125
Office of Temporary and Disability Services: 800-342-3009
CHIP: 800-698-4543

North Carolina
800-367-2229 (NC);
TTY: 800-976-1922

North Dakota
800-755-2604;
TDD: 800-366-6888

Ohio
800-324-8680;
TDD: 800-292-3572
Home and Community Based Services: 800-324-8680

Oklahoma
Claims: 800-522-0310

To Enroll in Medicaid
Eligibility: 888-521-2778
CHIP:800-987-7767

Oregon
Provider Services:800-336-6016
TTY/TDD: 800-375-2863

Pennsylvania
800-842-2020;
TDD: 800-451-4886

Rhode Island
401-462-1300 (no toll-free number)

South Carolina
888-549-0820

South Dakota
800-452-7691
Medicare Savings Information: 877-999-5612

Tennessee
800-669-1851;
TDD: 800-772-7647

Texas
800-964-2777
Medicaid Eligibility: 888-834-7406
CHIP: 800-647-6558

Utah
800-662-9651
(UT,CO,WY,AZ,NV, & ID)
CHIP: 888-222-2542

Vermont
Eligibility: 800-250-8427 (VT)
TTY: 888-834-7898

Virginia
Eligibility Hotline: 800-884-9730

Washington
Automatic Enrollment System: 800-562-3022
Eligibility Questions: 800-865-7801
CHIP: 877-543-7669

West Virginia
Client Services: 800-642-8589
Medicaid Eligibility: 800-688-5810
CHIP: 888-983-2645

Wisconsin
Medicaid Recipient Services and Badge Care Hotline: 800-362-3002
Medicaid Recipient Hotline: 800-888-7989

Wyoming
Eligibility Information: 888-996-8678

Free Eye Care

If you or someone you love needs eye care, but cannot afford it, the following organizations can help:

- For those 65 and older: *National Eye Care Project*, American Academy of Ophthalmology (AAO), P.O Box 429098, San Francisco, CA 94142; 415-561-8500; 800-222-3937; Fax: 415-561-8567; {www.aao.org} or {www.medem.com}.
- For low-income families and children, applications are accepted on a first come-first serve basis in January with treatment following later in the year: *VISION USA*, American Optometric Association, 243 North Lindbergh Blvd., St. Louis, MO 63141; 314-991-4100; 800-766-4466; Fax: 314-991-4101; {www.aoanet.org}.
- *Lions Clubs International*, 300 22nd St., Oak Brook, IL 60523-8842; 630-571-5466; {www.lionsclubs.org}.
- *EyeCare America - Glaucoma Project*, American Academy of Ophthalmology (AAO), P.O Box 429098, San Francisco, CA 94142; 415-561-8500; 800-391-EYES; Fax: 415-561-8567; {www.aao.org} or {www.medem.com}.

Eye Care Helpline

The ***National Eye Care Project Helpline*** puts callers in touch with local ophthalmologists who have volunteered to provide medical eye care at no out-of-pocket expense. Individuals must be 65 or older and not have had access to an ophthalmologist within the past three years. The emphasis of this program is to help disadvantaged people.

For more information, contact National Eye Care Project Helpline, American Academy of Ophthalmology, P.O. Box 429098, San Francisco, CA 94142-9098; 800-222-3937 (8 a.m.- 4 p.m. PST); Fax: 415-561-8567; {www.aao.org} or {www.medem.com}.

Grants Assist with Eye Treatment, Eye Surgery and Low Vision Equipment

The Pearle Vision Foundation offers grants to U.S. residents for low vision equipment. Funding is also available to non-profit organizations for vision-care assistance. Contact Pearle Vision Foundation, 2465 Joe Field Rd., Dallas, TX 75229 or P.O. Box 227175, Dallas, TX 75222; 972-277-6191; Fax: 972-277-6422.

Free Help For Cancer Families

Local chapters of the American Cancer Society sponsor a wide range of services for cancer patients and their families, including self-help groups, transportation programs, and lodging assistance for those who must travel far for treatment.

To find your local chapter or for more information on cancer detection, prevention and treatment, contact American Cancer Society, 1599 Clifton Rd., NE, Atlanta, GA 30329-4251; 800-ACS-2345; {www.cancer.org}.

Financial Assistance for Ill and Indigent Registered Nurses

Nurses House, Inc. offers short-term financial assistance to ill and indigent U.S. Registered Nurses to help meet basic living expenses. Costs of medical and educational expenses are not funded. Contact Nurses House, Inc., 2113 Western Ave., Suite 2, Guilderland, NY 12084-9559; 518-456-7858; Fax: 518-452-3760; {www.nurseshouse.org}.

Foundation Assists Individuals with Spinal Cord Injuries

The William Heiser Foundation for the Cure of Spinal Cord Injuries, Inc. provides general welfare assistance to individuals with spinal cord injuries residing in the Wantagh, New York area. Contact: William Heiser Foundation for the Cure of Spinal Cord Injuries, 3280 Sunrise Highway, Suite 65, Wantagh, NY 11793; 516-826-9747; {members.aol.com/cure4sci/index.htm}.

Money For New Hearing Aids

You can get information on different types of hearing loss, lists of hearing professionals, and information on locating financial assistance for assistive hearing devices by calling The Better Hearing Institute, 515 King St., Suite 420, Alexandria, VA 22314, P.O. Box 1840, Washington, DC 20013; 800-EAR-WELL; 703-684-3391; Fax: 703-684-6048; {www.betterhearing.org}.

Money To Pay Your Shrink Bills

Many people are suffering needlessly because they think they cannot afford to see a mental health professional. It is estimated that over 38 million people think that they cannot afford the high cost of mental health care. Before all hope is lost, here is a listing of options to pursue:

- Private Health Insurance- Most health insurance policies, also cover mental health care cost. Contact your insurance company to see what your plan has to offer.
- Community Mental Health Centers- often offer services for free or on a sliding fee scale.
- Religious Organizations- Many churches, synagogues, and other religious agencies offer pastoral counseling.
- If you have Medicare or Medicaid, mental health services are covered.

For more information contact the following organizations:

- National Mental Health Services, Knowledge Exchange Network, P.O. Box 42490, Washington, DC 20015; 800-789-2647; {www.mentalhealth.org}.
- American Association of Pastoral Counselors, 9504-A Lee Highway, Fairfax. VA 22031; 703-385-6967; {www.aapc.org}.
- American Self-Help Clearinghouse, Saint Clares Hospital, 100 E. Hanover Ave., Cedar Knolls, NJ 07927; 973-326-8853; {www.mentalhelp.net/selfhelp}.
- National Alliance for the Mentally Ill, Colonial Place Three, 2107 Wilson Blvd., Suite 300, Arlington, VA 22201; 800-9506264; {www.nami.org}.
- National Empowerment Center, 599 Canal St., Lawrence, MA 01840; 800-769-3728; {www.power2u.org}.
- National Mental Health Consumers Self-Help Clearinghouse, 1211 Chestnut St., Suite 1207, Philadelphia, PA 19107; 800-553-4539; {www.mhselfhelp.org}.

Discounts On Bicycle Helmets

The Department of Health in Mesa County Colorado offers discounts on bicycle helmets for children in the county. Check with your local office of health to see if there are any programs like this in your area.

If not, you can start one with a free *Toolkit for Helmet Promotion Programs* from Bicycle Helmet Safety Institute, 4611 Seventh Street South, Arlington, VA 22204-1419; 703-486-0100; Fax 703-486-0100; {www.helmets.org}. This organization will also send you a free copy of *A Consumer's Guide to Bicycle Helmets.*

Money To Pay For Dental Bills

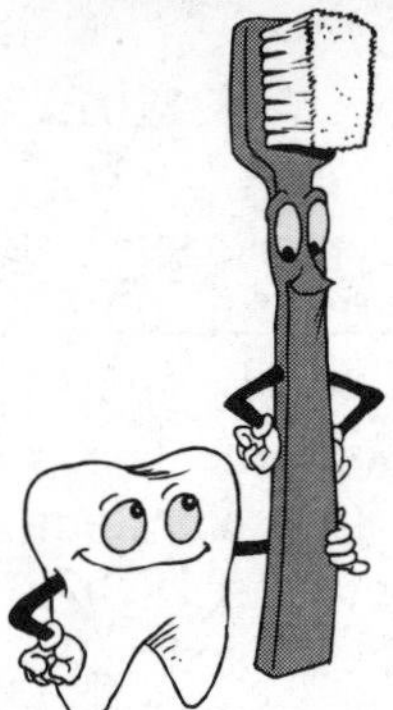

Dental care can be expensive, and therefore cost-prohibitive to many families. But many organizations are stepping in to fill the gaps.

In Colorado, Denver's Kinds In Need Of Dentistry program (KIND) offers free or discounted care by dentists, hygienists, and dental students either in clinics or their mobile dental van (KIND, 2465 S. Downing, Suite 207, Denver, CO 80210; 303-733-3710; {www.kindsmiles.org}).

Quantum Foundation in Florida has developed an orthodontic program for low-income residents which reduces the price for braces in half. Even the Scioto County Community Action Organization in Ohio is opening a Center for Dental Wellness for low income children and their families.

Contact your local dental society or community action agency to see what may be available in your area.

Free Contraceptives

Well there is not going to be a big "Free Condoms Come and Get'em" sign, but the federal government does provide family planning services under the Title X program. The program supports a network of approximately 4,600 clinics and provides reproductive health services to almost 4.5 million people each year. Services are delivered through a network of community-based clinics that include State and local health departments, hospitals, university health centers, Planned Parenthood affiliates, independent clinics and public and non-profit agencies.

These clinics provide contraceptive services, devices or drugs at little or no cost. In addition, these clinics offer infertility services, pregnancy tests, test and treatment for sexually transmitted diseases, and more. Publications are available on a variety of topics, and include titles such as *What You Should Know About The Male Condom, What You Should Know About The Pill*, and *What You Should Know About Abstinence*.

To locate a clinic near you or for more information contact Office of Population Affairs Clearinghouse, P.O. Box 30686, Bethesda, MD 20824; 301-654-6190; {http://opa.osophs.dhhs.gov}.

Free Health Care For Seniors And The Disabled

Over 16,000 seniors live in centers operated by the Salvation Army, as 1,600 disabled adults. The Salvation Army also operates hospitals and clinics throughout the world to provide healthcare for those in need. They even provide homes for those recently discharged from the hospital and need more recovery time.

To learn more about the services offered contact the Salvation Army Office near you, or Salvation Army National Headquarters, 615 Slaters Lane, P.O. Box 269, Alexandria, VA 22313; 703-684-5500; {www.salvationarmy.org}.

Free Healthcare For Native Americans

The Indian Health Service provides healthcare services to over 1.5 million Native Americans and Alaskan Natives free of charge. Services include hospital, medical and dental care and environment health and sanitation services, as well as outpatient services and the services of mobile clinics and public health nurses, and preventive care, including immunizations. All this for FREE!

Benefits are provided through 153 service units, 49 hospitals, 13 tribal hospitals, 219 health centers, and over 300 smaller health stations. The website provides links to local area offices and facilities. To receive these services you must be a member of a federally recognized tribe.

For more information on how to apply for benefits or the location of services, contact Indian health Service, 801 Thompson Ave., Suite 400, Rockville, MD 20852; 301-443-3024; {www.his.gov}.

Free Money To Pay Your Alcohol Rehab Bills

Treat of alcohol abuse can costs you thousands of dollars. The Salvation Army has 152 homes and centers for the treatment of those suffering from alcoholism, as well as many other drug rehabilitation programs.

To learn more about the services offered contact the Salvation Army Office near you,

or Salvation Army National Headquarters, 615 Slaters Lane, P.O. Box 269, Alexandria, VA 22313; 703-684-5500; {www.salvationarmy.org}.

Abortions Starting At $250

Some of the 900 Planned Parenthood clinics offer abortions during the first 11 weeks of pregnancy starting at $250 for those not covered by health insurance. In some cases they even have special funds to help women pay for services.

To investigate what your local clinic offers, call 1-800-230-PLAN. You can also contact Planned Parenthood Federation of America, 810 Seventh Avenue, New York, NY 10019; 212-261-4647; Fax: 212-261-4560; {www.plannedparenthood.org}.

There is another consumer hotline that can also handle your abortion related questions: Contact The National Abortion Federation, 1755 Massachusetts Ave., NW, Washington, DC 20036; 800-772-9100 or in Canada 800-424-2282, weekdays from 9:00 to 7:00 EST; {www.prochoice.org/index.html}.

372 Sources To Pay Emergency Expenses

Not sure where to turn or what resources exist for you? Bravekids.org has put together a resource directory that lists over 372 sources for financial and other types of assistance for those with disabled children or adults or low-income families in need of help. It could be anything from paying your utility bill to respite care or medical expenses.

No need to feel like help does not exist. Check out {www.bravekids.org}.

Free Health Care For Moms and Kids

Are you pregnant or the parent of young children? Do you have a child with special needs? Free maternal and child health services available include prenatal care, well-child care, dental services, immunizations, family planning, vision and hearing screenings, and much more. The federal government provides block grants,

called Title V, to each state to provide maternal and child (including teens) health care services. Each state has some latitude as to how they spend the money, but 30% must go to providing services for children with special health care needs, and 30% for children and adolescents. The Maternal and Child Health Division of your state Department of Health is responsible for administering the funds. The states are required by Title V to start establishing 800 numbers to provide information regarding services available in the state (see state by state listing later in this chapter).

Federal law requires that all states provide Medicaid to pregnant women and children through the age of six whose income does not exceed 133% of the poverty line. Federal poverty thresholds in 2002 were $8,860 for one person, $11,940 for two, $15,020 for three, and $18,100 for four people. The government is going to raise the age level for Medicaid benefits one year at a time until all children are covered to age eighteen. Many states have additional benefits for children and programs for children with special needs. The following states have extended Medicaid coverage:

- Minnesota: covers everyone with income below 225% of the federal poverty line, or about $50,000 for a family of four.
- Vermont: all children under eighteen with family incomes below 300% of the federal poverty line, or about $54,000 for a family of four.

Financial Benefits For Caregivers

The Alexandria Division of Social Services offers financial benefits for caregivers of children and adolescents with disabilities. Check your local, city, county or state for financial benefits for which you may qualify if you care for someone who is disabled.

- Washington: all children to age eighteen with family incomes 100% of federal poverty line, or about $15,020 for a family of four.
- Wisconsin: children one to six with family incomes below 185% of federal poverty line, or about $22,940 for a family of four.
- Maine: all children to age 18 with family incomes below 125% of poverty line, or about $9,500 for a family of four.
- 23 states have extended coverage for all pregnant women whose incomes are 100% of poverty line, or about $13,950.
- Several states, such as Ohio and West Virginia, have established special programs for children with special health care needs.

There are several ways to find out more about the programs available in your state. You can call the local department of health (found in the blue pages in your phone book), or the state Department of Health and the Maternal and Child Health Hotlines (listed below). Each year states enact new legislation to help provide health care for those in need. Your state representative can keep you updated regarding new legislation. To find out more about the programs available in your state, contact your state Maternal and Child Health Hotline (see listing below).

Alabama
Bureau of Family Health Services
Maternal and Infant Care
201 Monroe St.
Montgomery, AL 36130
334-206-5661
Maternal & Child Health Hotline
800-478-2221
This hotline can refer people to local maternal and infant health centers.

Alaska
Division of Public Assistance
Department of Health and Social Services
P.O. Box 110640
Juneau, AK 99811-0640
907-465-3347
Maternal & Child Health Hotline
800-654-1385

Arizona
Department of Health Services
Community and Family Health Services
1740 W. Adams St.
Phoenix, AZ 85007
602-542-1223
Maternal & Child Health Hotlines
800-773-2421 (Northern)
800-552-5252 (Central)
800-852-6616 (Southern)

Arkansas
Section of Maternal and Child Health
Arkansas State Department of Health
4815 W. Markham
Little Rock, AR 72205
501-661-2199
Maternal & Child Health Hotline 800-235-0002

California
Maternal and Child Health
State Department of Health
714 P. St., Room 740
Sacramento, CA 95814
916-657-1347
Maternal & Child Health Hotline
800-BABY-999 (222-9999)

Colorado
Family Health Services
Colorado Department of Public Health
4300 Cherry Creek Dr. S.
Denver, CO 80246
303-692-2302
Maternal & Child Health Hotline
800-688-7777

Connecticut
Connecticut Department of Public Health
Family Health Division
410 Capitol Ave., MS#11FHS
P.O. Box 340308
Hartford, CT 06134

860 509-8066
Maternal & Child Health Hotline
800-505-2000

Delaware
Division of Public Health
Health and Social Services Dept.
P.O. Box 637
Dover, DE 19903
302-739-4785
Maternal & Child Health Hotline
800-464-HELP (Kent and Sussex Counties)
302-877-3000 (New Castle County)
The Helpline can refer you to local health services, as well as provide you with other state services and information.

District of Columbia
Office of Maternal And Child Health
Commission of Public Health
800 9th St., SW
Washington, DC 20024
202-645-5620
Maternal & Child Health Hotline
800-MOM-BABY

Florida
Maternal and Child Health
Health and Rehabilitative Services Department
2020 Capitol Circle, SE
Tallahassee, FL 32399
850-487-1321
Maternal & Child Health Hotline
800-451-BABY

Georgia
Family Health Services Section
Division of Public Health
Department of Human Resources
2 Peachtree St., SW, 8th Floor
Atlanta, GA 30303
404-657-2850
Maternal & Child Health Hotline
800-822-2539

Hawaii
Family Health Services Division
State of Hawaii
Department of Health
741-A Sunset Ave.
Honolulu, HI 96816
808-733-9022

Idaho
Bureau of Maternal and Child Health
Idaho Department of Health and Welfare
450 W. State St.
Boise, ID 83720
208-334-0670
Maternal & Child Health Hotline
800-926-2588

Illinois
Department of Public Health
535 W. Jefferson St.
Springfield, IL 62761
217-782-2596
Maternal & Child Health Hotline
800-545-2200

Indiana
Division of Maternal and Child Health
Indiana State Department of Health
2 Meridian Street
Indianapolis, IN 46204
317-233-1240
Maternal & Child Health Hotline
800-433-0746

Iowa
Family and Community Health
Department of Public Health
Lucas State Office Bldg.
Des Moines, IA 50319
515-281-3126
Maternal & Child Health Hotline
800-926-2588

Kansas
Kansas Department of Health & Environment
Bureau of Children, Youth, and Families
900 SW Jackson, Suite 1052
Topeka, KS 66612
785-296-1310
Maternal & Child Health Hotline
800-332-6262

Kentucky
Division of Maternal and Child Health
Department of Health Services
State Dept. of Human Resources
275 East Main St.
Frankfort, KY 40621
502-564-4830
Maternal & Child Health Hotline
800-462-6122

Louisiana
Department of Health and Hospitals
325 Loyola Ave.
New Orleans, LA 70112
504-568-5073
Maternal & Child Health Hotline
800-251-BABY

Maine
Division of Maternal and Child Health
Department of Human Services
151 Capitol St.
State House- Station 11
Augusta, ME 04333
207-287-5396
Maternal & Child Health Hotline
800-698-3624

Maryland
Department of Health and Mental Hygiene
201 W. Preston St., 5th Fl.
Baltimore, MD 21201-2399
410-767-6721
Maternal & Child Health Hotline
800-456-8900

Massachusetts
Bureau of Family & Community Health
Massachusetts Department of Public Health
250 W. Washington
Boston, MA 02108
617-624-6090
Maternal & Child Health Hotline
800-531-MOMS

Michigan
Bureau of Child & Family Services
Division of Family & Community Health
3423 N Martin Luther King Jr. Blvd.
P.O. Box 30195
Lansing, MI 48909
517-335-9371
Maternal & Child Health Hotline
800-26-BIRTH

Minnesota
Department of Health
717 SE Delaware St.
Minneapolis, MN 55440
612-676-5167
Maternal & Child Health Hotline
800-728-5420

Mississippi
Department of Health
2423 N. State St.
Jackson, MS 39215
601-576-7463
Maternal & Child Health Hotline
800-721-7222

Missouri
Division of Child and Family Health Care
Department of Health
P.O. Box 570
Jefferson City, MO 65102
573-526-5520
Maternal & Child Health Hotline
800-835-5465 (TELL-LINK)

Montana
Health Services and Medical Facilities Division
Dept. of Health and Environmental Sciences
Cogswell Building
1400 Broadway
Helena, MT 59620-0901
406-444-4743
Maternal & Child Health Hotline
800-421-MOMS

Nebraska
Maternal and Child Health
State Department of Health
301 Centennial Mall South
P.O. Box 95044
Lincoln, NE 68509
402-471-0196
Maternal & Child Health Hotline
800-862-1889

Nevada
Family Health Services
Nevada Health Division
Kinkhead Building
State Department of Human Resources
505 East King St., Room 205
Carson City, NV 89710
775-687-4885
Maternal & Child Health Hotline
800-992-0900, ext. 4885

New Hampshire
Office of Health Management
Bureau of Family and Community Health

6 Hazen Dr.
Concord, NH 03301
603-271-4516
Maternal & Child Health Hotline
800-852-3345, ext. 4517

New Jersey
Maternal and Infant Health
New Jersey Dept. of Health
CN364
363 W. State St.
Trenton, NJ 08625-0364
609-984-1384
Maternal & Child Health Hotline
800-328-3838

New Mexico
Department Of Health
1190 St. Francis Dr.
Santa Fe, NM 87502
505-827-2642
Maternal & Child Health Hotline
800-890-4692

New York
Growing Up Healthy
New York State Dept. of Health
8th Floor, Room 789
Empire State Plaza
Albany, NY 12237
518-474-2084
Maternal & Child Health Hotline
800-522-5006

North Carolina
Division of Women's and Children's Health
Department of Health and Human Services
P.O. Box 29597
325 N. Salisbury St.
Raleigh, NC 27626
919-715-3813
Maternal & Child Health Hotline
800-FOR-BABY

North Dakota
Division of Maternal and Child Health
State Dept. of Health and Consolidated Labs
600 E Boulevard Ave.
State Capitol Building
Bismarck, ND 58505
701-328-4532
Maternal & Child Health Hotline
800-472-2286

Ohio
Bureau of Child and Family Health Services
Ohio Department of Health
246 N. High St.
Columbus, OH 43266
614-644-7848
Maternal & Child Health Hotline
800-755-GROW

Oklahoma
Maternal and Child Health
Department of Health
1000 NE 10th St.
Department of Health
Oklahoma City, OK 73112
405-271-4477
Maternal & Child Health Hotline
800-42-OASIS

Oregon
Oregon State Health Division
Center for Child and Family Health
800 Northeast Oregon St.
Portland, OH 97232
503-731-4398
Maternal & Child Health Hotline
800-SAFE-NET

Pennsylvania
Pennsylvania Department of Health
Bureau of Family Health
P.O. Box 90, Room 733
Health and Welfare Building
Harrisburg, PA 17108
717-787-7192
Maternal & Child Health Hotline
800-692-7295 (general)
800-986-BABY (prenatal)
800-986-KIDS (child health)

Rhode Island
Division of Family Health
Rhode Island Department of Health
3 Capitol Hill, Room 302
Providence, RI 02908
401-222-4655
Maternal & Child Health Hotline
800-942-7434

South Carolina
South Carolina Department of Health
1st Nine Care Line- MH
Robert Mills Complex
Box 101106
Columbia, SC 29211
803-898-0871
Maternal & Child Health Hotline
800-868-0404

South Dakota
Health Services
Department of Health
Anderson Bldg.
615 W. 4th St.
Pierre, SD 57501
(605) 773-5610
Maternal & Child Health Hotline
800-529-5000

Tennessee
Maternal and Child Health Section
Tennessee Department of Health
Tennessee Tower Bldg
425 5th Ave. N, 5th Floor
Nashville, TN 37247-4701
615-741-0323
Maternal & Child Health Hotline
800-428-BABY (2229)

Texas
Maternal and Child Health
Texas Department of Health
1100 West 49th St.
Austin, TX 78756
512-458-7321
Maternal & Child Health Hotline
800-4-Baby Love (422-2956)

Utah
Maternal & Infant Health
P.O. Box 142001
Salt Lake City, UT 84114
801-538-6869
Maternal & Child Health Hotline
800-826-9662

Vermont
Medical Services
Vermont Department of Health
P.O. Box 70
Burlington, VT 05402
802-863-7347
Maternal & Child Health Hotline
800-464-4343

Virginia
Department of Health
1500 E Main, Room 136
Richmond, VA 23219
804-371-0478
Maternal & Child Health Hotline
800-421-7376

Washington
Department of Health
P.O. Box 47830
Olympia, WA 98504-7830
360-236-3721
Maternal & Child Health Hotline
800-322-2588

West Virginia
Division of Maternal and Child Health
State Department of Health
1411 Virginia St., E
Charleston, WV 25301
304-558-5388
Maternal & Child Health Hotline
800-642-8522 (women's services)
800-642-9704 (children's services)

Wisconsin
Division of Health
Health and Family Services Department
1414 E. Washington
Madison, WI 53703
608-266-2684
Maternal & Child Health Hotline
800-722-2295
800-441-4576 (children with special health needs)

Wyoming
Division of Public Health
Department of Health
Hathaway Bldg.
Cheyenne, WY 82002
307-777-7942
Maternal & Child Health Hotline
800-994-GROW

Free Medications From Drug Companies

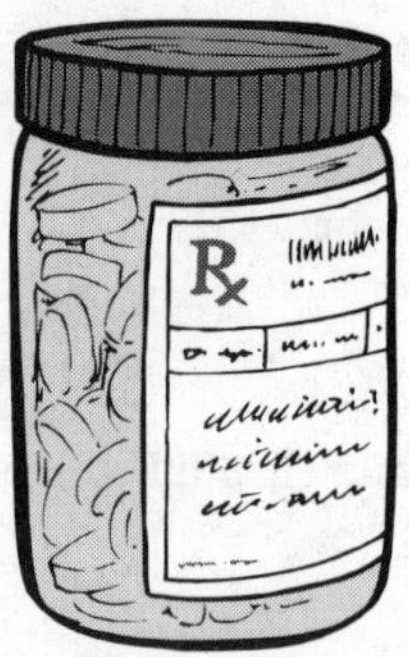

Leave it to the government to know where you can get free Halcion, AZT, Valium or Motrin but not make any effort to tell you about it. The U.S. Senate's Special Committee on Aging recently published a report on how certain eligible groups, including the elderly and the poor, can actually get their much needed prescription drugs free of charge directly from the companies that manufacture them. Here's what the committee discovered:

Taking prescription medications is often a matter of life and death for millions of Americans, yet many just can't afford the drugs they need simply because they're too expensive. Many are forced to choose between paying for food or their medications, especially the elderly. The relative lack of prescription drug insurance has been compounded by prescription cost increases that can actually surpass the rate of inflation by four times.

Though not widely known, drug companies have programs that offer many prescription drugs free of charge to poor and other vulnerable groups that cannot afford them. However, these free drug programs are being used by only a small number of people that could truly benefit from them. And to add to this, the programs often require long waiting times for qualified patients to receive their free medications from drug manufacturers.

The Pharmaceutical Research and Manufacturer's Association (PMA) has established a Directory of Prescription Drug Indigent Programs, which lists up-to-date information on individual manufacturers' patient programs. Although the directory does not always identify the drugs manufactured, it still should be your first call. Contact: Pharmaceutical Manufacturer's Association, 800-PMA-INFO, {www.phrma.org}.

The following pages contain an alphabetical list of all drugs currently covered under Prescription Drug Indigent Programs, as well as the manufacturer that supplies them. We have also included some helpful tips and questions you should ask when contacting the programs:

1) If a drug is not listed in the directory, it still may be provided by the company. You should call the manufacturer directly to check.
2) Ask about the eligibility requirements. Some companies require that you have a limited income or no insurance coverage, while others require only that you get a doctor's referral.
3) Ask about the enrollment process. Many drug companies require a phone call or letter from your doctor.
4) If your doctor refuses to call or does not believe the program will work, contact the drug companies yourself and find out about the application process. You will still need a doctor to fill the application, but you can at least get the forms, and then

encourage your doctor to complete them. If your doctor still refuses, maybe you can find another doctor who will.

Find out how you will receive the prescription drugs, and how you can get refills. Most companies send the medications directly to your doctor. There have been some problems with delays in receiving the drugs, so check to see what the company's shipping schedule is, and what you or your doctor should do if there is a problem.

A to Z Drug Listing

In this Section you'll find a comprehensive A to Z listing of all the drugs that are available to certain qualified groups free of charge directly from the manufacturers.

Each company determines the eligibility criteria for its program. Often, determination is based on the patient's income level and lack of insurance.

Unless specified below, manufacturers require a phone call or written statement from your doctor's office requesting the medication.

First, find the drug you need and the corresponding manufacturer. Next, look up the address and telephone number of the appropriate drug manufacturer from the Directory of Pharmaceutical Manufacturers, which follows the A to Z drug listing.

Your doctor will need to contact the drug company to find out about how to receive the drug free of charge. Remember, although they want your doctor to call, if your doctor refuses, make the call yourself. After they enroll you in the program, the drug manufacturer will send the medication directly to your doctor who will pass it along to you.

Important Note: More drugs are constantly being added to this list. If you do not find your drug listed here, contact the manufacturer of the drug to see if your drug is included in this program.

Alphabetical Listing of Drugs

Drug	Manufacturer
A —	
Accrupril	Parke-Davis
Aci-Jel	Ortho
Actigall	Ciba-Geigy
Actimmune	Genentech
Activase	Genentech
Adriamycin PFS	Adria
Adrucil	Adria
Aldactazide	Searle
Aldactone	Searle
Aldomet	Merck
ALT/S	Hoechst-Roussel
Altace	Hoechst-Roussel
Alupent	Boehringer
Amoxil	SmithKline Beecham
Anafranil	Ciba-Geigy
Anaprox	Syntex
Ansaid	Upjohn
Antivert	Pfizer
Anturane	Ciba-Geigy

Drug	Manufacturer
Anusol HC	Parke-Davis
Apresazide	Ciba-Geigy
Apresoline	Ciba-Geigy
Aralen	Sanofi Winthrop
Aredia	Ciba-Geigy
Artane	Lederle
Asacol	Procter & Gamble
Atrovent	Boehringer
Axid	Eli Lilly
Augmentin	SmithKline Beecham
Axid	Eli Lilly
AZT (Retrovir)	Burroughs-Wellcome
Azulfidine	Pharmacia
Azulfidine En-Tab	Pharmacia

B —

Drug	Manufacturer
Bactrim	Hoffman-LaRoche
Bactrim DS	Hoffman-LaRoche
Bactroban	SmithKline Beecham
Beconase	Glaxo
Beconase AQ	Glaxo
Berelan	Lederle
Betagen	Allergan
Betaseron	Berlex
Betaspace	Berlex
BICNU	Bristol-Myers
Blenoxance	Bristol-Myers
Bleph-10	Allergan
Blephamide	Allergan
Botox	Allergan
Breonesin	Sanofi Winthrop
Brethaire	Ciba-Geigy
Brethine	Ciba-Geigy
Bronkometer	Sanofi Winthrop
Bucladin-S	ICI
BuSpar	Bristol-Myers

C —

Drug	Manufacturer
Calan	Searle
Calan SR	Searle
Capoten	Bristol-Myers
Capozide	Bristol-Myers
Carafate	Marion Merrell Dow
Cardene	Syntex
Cardizem	Marion Merrell Dow
Cardizem CD	Marion Merrell Dow
Cardizem SR	Marion Merrell Dow
Cardura	Pfizer
Cataflam	Ciba-Geigy
Catapres	Boehringer
Ceclor	Eli Lilly
CEENU	Bristol-Myers
Ceftin	Glaxo
Cefzil	Bristol-Myers
Ceredase	Genzyme
Cipro	Miles
Claforan	Hoechst-Roussel
Cleocin	Upjohn
Clinoril	Merck
Clozaril	Sandoz
Cogentin	Merck
Cognex	Parke-Davis
Compazine	SmithKline Beecham
Cordarone	Wyeth-Ayerst
Corgard	Bristol-Myers
Corzide	Bristol-Myers
Coumadin	DuPont Merck
Cyclospasmol	Wyeth-Ayerst
Cytadren	Ciba-Geigy
Cytotec	Searle
Cytovene	Syntex
Cytoxan	Bristol-Myers

D —

Drug	Manufacturer
Dalmane	Hoffman-LaRoche
Danocrine	Sanofi Winthrop
Dantrium	Norwich-Eaton
Desferal	Ciba-Geigy
Desyrel	Bristol-Myers
Diabeta	Hoechst-Roussel
Diabinese	Pfizer
Diamox	Lederle
Didronel	Procter & Gamble
Dienestrol	Ortho
Diflucan	Pfizer
Dilantin	Parke-Davis
Dipentum	Pharmacia
Diprolene	Schering

Drug	Manufacturer
Diprosone	Schering
Dolobid	Merck
Drisdol	Sanofi Winthrop
Duragesic	Janssen
Duricef	Bristol-Myers
Dyazide	SmithKline Beecham
Dymelor	Eli Lilly
DynaCirc	Sandoz

E —

Drug	Manufacturer
E-Mycin	Upjohn
Efudex (Fluorouracil Injection)	Hoffman-LaRoche
Eldepryl	Sandoz
Emcyt	Pharmacia
Eminase	SmithKline Beecham
Entex	Procter & Gamble
Epifrin	Allergan
Epogen	Amgen
Ergamisol	Janssen
Erycette	Ortho
Esidrix	Ciba-Geigy
Esimil	Ciba-Geigy
Estrace	Bristol-Myers
Estraderm	Ciba-Geigy
Eulexin	Schering
Extel	Procter & Gamble

F —

Drug	Manufacturer
Famvir	SmithKline Beecham
Feldene	Pfizer
Flexeril	Merck
Floxin	Ortho
Fludara	Berlex
FML	Allergan
Folex	Adria
Folex PFS	Adria
Foscavir	Astra USA
Fulvicin	Schering

G —

Drug	Manufacturer
Gantrisin	Hoffman-LaRoche
Gantanol	Hoffman-LaRoche
Gastrocrom	Fisons
Glucotrol	Pfizer
Grifulvin Suppositories	Ortho

H —

Drug	Manufacturer
Habitrol	Ciba-Geigy
Halcion	Upjohn
Haldol	McNeil
Hismanal	Janssen
Hivid	Hoffman-LaRoche
HMS	Allergan
Humulin	Eli Lilly
Hydraea	Immunex
Hytakerol	Sanofi Winthrop

I —

Drug	Manufacturer
Idamycin	Adria
Ifex	Bristol-Myers
Iletin	Eli Lilly
Imodium	Janssen
IMOGAM Rabies	Connaught
IMOVAX Rabies	Connaught
Imuran	Burroughs-Wellcome
Indocin	Merck
Insulin Products	Eli Lilly
Interferon-A Recombinant	Hoffman-LaRoche
Intron-A	Schering
Ismelin	Ciba-Geigy
Isoptin	Knoll
Isordil	Wyeth-Ayerst
Isuprel	Sanofi Winthrop

K —

Drug	Manufacturer
K-Lyte	Bristol-Myers
Keflex	Eli Lilly
Kerlone	Searle
Kinesed	ICI
Klonopin	Hoffman-LaRoche
Klotrix	Bristol-Myers
Kytril	SmithKline Beecham

Drug	Manufacturer
L —	
Lamprene	Ciba-Geigy
Lanoxin	Burroughs-Wellcome
Lasix	Hoechst-Roussel
Lescol	Sandoz
Leucovorin Calcium	Lederle
Leukine	Immunex
Leustatin	Ortho-Biotech
Librium	Hoffman-LaRoche
Lidex	Syntex
Limbritol	Hoffman-LaRoche
Lincocin	Upjohn
Lindane Lotion/ Shampoo	Reed and Carnrick
Lioresal	Ciba-Geigy
Lithobid	Ciba-Geigy
Lodosyn	DuPont Merck
Loniten	Upjohn
Lo/ Ovral	Wyeth-Ayerst
Lopid	Parke-Davis
Lopressor	Ciba-Geigy
Lopressor/HCT	Ciba-Geigy
Loprox	Hoechst-Roussel
Lorelco	Marion Merrell Dow
Lotensin	Ciba-Geigy
Lotensin HCT	Ciba-Geigy
Lotrimin	Schering
Lotrisone	Schering
Loxapine	Lederle
Ludiomil	Ciba-Geigy
Lyophilized Cytoxan	Bristol-Myers
Lysodren	Bristol-Myers
M —	
Macrobid	Procter & Gamble
Macrodantin	Procter & Gamble
Marax	Pfizer
Marinol Capsules	Roxane
Maxaquin	Searle
Maxzide	Lederle
Meclan	Ortho
Medrol	Upjohn
Megace	Bristol-Myers

Drug	Manufacturer
Mepron	Burroughs-Wellcome
Mesnex	Bristol-Myers
Metrodin	Ares-Serono
Mevacor	Merck
Micronase	Upjohn
Minipress	Pfizer
Minizide	Pfizer
Minocin	Lederle
Monistat	Ortho
Monistat Derm	Ortho
Monopril	Bristol-Myers
Motrin	Upjohn
Mutamycin	Bristol-Myers
Myambutol	Lederle
Mycobutin	Pharmacia
Mycostatin	Bristol-Myers
Mytelase	Sanofi Winthrop
N —	
Naphcon-A	Allergan
Naprosyn	Syntex
Nasalide	Syntex
Natalins	Bristol-Myers
Natalins RX	Bristol-Myers
Navane	Pfizer
NebuPent	Fujisawa USA
NegGram	Sanofi Winthrop
Neosar	Adria
Neupogen	Amgen
Neurontin	Parke-Davis
Nicorette	Marion Merrell Dow
Nimotop	Miles
Nitrodisc	Searle
Nitrostat	Parke-Davis
Nizoral Tablets	Janssen
Nolvadex	Zeneca
Nordette	Wyeth-Ayerst
Normodyne	Schering
Norpace	Searle
Norpace CR	Searle
Noroxin	Merck
Norplant System	Wyeth-Ayerst
Norspace	Searle
Nutropin	Genentech

Drug	Manufacturer
O —	
Oculinium	Allergan
Ocusert	ALZA
Optimine	Schering
Oramorph SR Tablets	Roxane
Orinase	Upjohn
Ortho-Dienestrol	Ortho
Orudis	Wyeth-Ayerst
Ovcon	Bristol-Myers
P —	
Pancrease	McNeil
Parafon Forte DSC	McNeil
Paraplatin	Bristol-Myers
Parlodel	Sandoz
Pavabid	Marion Merrell Dow
PBZ	Ciba-Geigy
Pepcid	Merck
Periactin	Merck
Persa-Gel	Ortho
Persa-Gel W	Ortho
Persantine	Boehringer
Phenergan	Wyeth-Ayerst
PhisoHex	Sanofi Winthrop
Pilagan	Allergan
Plaquenil	Sanofi Winthrop
Platinol	Bristol-Myers
Plendil	Merck
Ponstel	Parke-Davis
Pravochol	Bristol-Myers
Premarin	Wyeth-Ayerst
Prilosec	Merck
Primaquine	Sanofi Winthrop
Prinivil	Merck
Procan	Parke-Davis
Procan SR	Parke-Davis
Procardia	Pfizer
Procardia YL	Pfizer
Procrit	Ortho-Biotech
Progestasert	ALZA
Prograf capsules	Fujisawa USA
Prokine	Hoechst-Roussel
Pronestyl SR	Bristol-Myers

Drug	Manufacturer
Propine	Allergan
Propulsid	Janssen
Proscar	Merck
Prostat	Ortho
Protropin	Genentech
Proventil	Schering
Provera	Upjohn
Prozac	Eli Lilly
Pyridium	Parke-Davis
Q —	
Questran	Bristol-Myers
Quinamm	Marion Merrell Dow
Quinaglute Dura-Tabs	Berlex
R —	
Regitine	Ciba-Geigy
Relafen	SmithKline Beecham
Rheumatrex	Lederle
Ridaura	SmithKline Beecham
Rifadin	Marion Merrell Dow
Rifamate	Marion Merrell Dow
Rifater	Marion Merrell Dow
Rimactane	Ciba-Geigy
Risperdal	Janssen
Rocaltrol	Hoffman-LaRoche
Rocephin Injectable	Hoffman-LaRoche
Roxanol	Roxane
Rubex	Immunex
Rythmol	Knoll
S —	
Sandimmune	Sandoz
Sandoglobulin	Sandoz
Sandostatin	Sandoz
Santyl	Knoll
Sectral	Wyeth-Ayerst
Seldane	Marion Merrell Dow
Seldane D	Marion Merrell Dow
Septra	Burroughs-Wellcome
Septra DS	Burroughs-Wellcome
Ser-Ap-Es	Ciba-Geigy
Sinemet	DuPont Merck
Sinemet Cr	DuPont Merck

Drug	Manufacturer
Sinequan	Pfizer
Slow-K	Ciba-Geigy
Sorbitrate	Zeneca
Spectazole	Ortho
Sporanox Capsules	Janssen
Sublingual	Parke-Davis
Sultrin	Ortho
Survanta	Abbott
Symmetrel	DuPont Merck
Synalar	Syntex
Synemol	Syntex
Synthroid	Boots
Sy Trexan	DuPont Merck

T —

Drug	Manufacturer
Tagamet	SmithKline Beecham
Tarabine	Adria
Tegretol	Ciba-Geigy
TEN-K	Ciba-Geigy
Tenormin	Zeneca
Tenoretic	Zeneca
Terazol	Ortho
Testoderm	ALZA
TheraCys	Connaught
Ticlid	Syntex
Timolol	Merck
Timoptic	Merck
Tenuate	Marion Merrell Dow
Tofranil	Ciba-Geigy
Tofranil-PM	Ciba-Geigy
Tolectin	McNeil
Tolinase	Upjohn
Topicort	Hoechst-Roussel
Toradol	Syntex
Trancopal	Sanofi Winthrop
Trandate	Glaxo
Transderm-Scop	Ciba-Geigy
Transdermal-Nitro	Ciba-Geigy
Trental	Hoechst-Roussel
Trexan	DuPont Merck
Tridesilon Cream	Miles
Trinalin	Schering
Triostat	SmithKline Beecham
Triphasil	Wyeth-Ayerst

V —

Drug	Manufacturer
Vagistat	Bristol-Myers
Valium	Hoffman-LaRoche
Vancenase	Schering
Vascor	McNeil
Vasodilan	Bristol-Myers
Vasoretic	Merck
Vasotec	Merck
Ventoli	Glaxo
VePesid	Bristol-Myers
Verelan	Lederle
Vermox	Janssen
Vibramycin	Pfizer
Videx	Bristol-Myers
Vincasar	Adria
Vincasar PFS	Adria
Vistaril	Pfizer
Voltaren	Ciba-Geigy

W —

Drug	Manufacturer
Wellcovorin	Burroughs-Wellcome
Winstrol	Sanofi Winthrop
Wytensin	Wyeth-Ayerst

X —

Drug	Manufacturer
Xanax	Upjohn

Z —

Drug	Manufacturer
Zantac	Glaxo
Zarontin	Parke-Davis
Zestoretic	Zeneca
Zestril	Zeneca
Zithromax	Pfizer
Zoladex	Zeneca
Zoloft	Pfizer
Zostrix	Knoll
Zovirax	Burroughs-Wellcome
Zyloprim	Burroughs-Wellcome

Directory of Pharmaceutical Manufacturer Patient Assistance Programs

NOTE: Most manufacturers require requests for assistance to be initiated by a physician's office.

ABBOTT LABORATORIES/ROSS LABORATORIES

Abbott Laboratories
Uninsured Patient Program
200 Abbott Park Rd.
D31C, J23
Abbott Park, IL 60064-6163 — 800-222-6885 (option 1)
www.abbott.com

ALZA PHARMACEUTICALS

Indigent Patient Assistance Program
ALZA Pharmaceuticals
1250 Bayhill Dr., Suite 300
San Bruno, CA 94066 — 800-577-3788

Products Covered by the Program
Testoderm, Ocusert, Progestasert

Other Program Information
The physician must request an Indigent Patient Application Kit from ALZA Pharmaceuticals. Due to state laws prohibiting sampling of controlled substances, the Indigent Program for Testoderm CIII is not available in New York, Ohio, Kentucky, Kansas and Georgia.

AMGEN, INC.

Name of Program
Safety Net Program for Epogen — 800-272-9376
www.amgen.com/patient/

Product Covered by the Program
Epogen (For patients on dialysis only)

Name of Program
Safety Net Program for Neupogen — 800-272-9376
www.amgen.com/patient/

Product Covered by the Program
Neupogen

Other Product Information
Providers apply on behalf of the patient. Any administering physician, hospital, home health company or retail pharmacy may sponsor a patient by applying to the program on his or her behalf. The program is based on a 12-month patient year rather than a calendar year.

BOEHRINGER INGLEHEIM PHARMACEUTICALS, INC.

Patient Assistance Program
Boehringer Ingelheim Pharmaceuticals, Inc.
c/o ESI/SDS
P.O. Box 66555
St. Louis, MO 63166-6773 — 800-556-8317

BRISTOL-MYERS SQUIBB COMPANY

Bristol-Myers Squibb
Patient Assistance Program
P.O. Box 4500 — 800-332-2056
Princeton, NJ 08543-4500 — Fax: 609-897-6859

Products Covered by the Program
Many Bristol-Myers Squibb Pharmaceutical Products.

Eligibility
Application forms are supplied by the company to physicians.

DU PONT PHARMACEUTICAL CO.

Du Pont Pharmaceuticals Company
Patient Assistance Program
Chestnut Run Plaza
Hickory Run Building
974 Centre Rd.
Wilmington, DE 19805 — 800-474-2762

GENENTECH, INC.

Genentech Assistance Program
Genentech, Inc.
Mail Stop #13
P.O. Box 2586 — 800-879-4747
S. San Francisco, CA 94083-2586 — Fax: 650-225-1366

Products Covered by the Program
Actimmune (interferon gamma-1b); Activase (alteplase recombinant); Protropin (somatrem for injection); Nutropin (somatropin for injection)

GENZYME CORPORATION

Ceredase/Cerezyme Access Program
Wytske Kingma, M.D.
Medical Affairs
Genzyme Corporation
1 Kendall Square
Cambridge, MA 01239 800-745-4447, ext. 17808
www.genzymetherapeutics.com/cerezyme/support/pap.htm

IMMUNEX CORPORATION

Patient Assistance Program 800-321-4669
Fax: 800-944-3184

Products Covered by the Program

All currently marketed Immunex Corporation prescription products.

JANSSEN PHARMACEUTICA

Janssen Patient Assistance Program
1800 Robert Fulton Drive
Reston, VA 20191 800-652-6227

KNOLL PHARMACEUTICAL COMPANY

Knoll Indigent Patient Program
Knoll Pharmaceutical Company
3000 Continental Drive, North
Mount Olive, NJ 07828-1234 800-524-2474

Products Covered by the Program

Isoptin (verapamil); Rythmol (propafenone); Santyl (collagenase)

ELI LILLY AND COMPANY

Lilly Cares
Program Administrator
P.O. Box 23099
Centreville, VA 20120 800-545-6962

Products Covered by the Program

Most all Lilly prescription products and insulins (except controlled substances).

MERCK & CO., INC.

Merck Patient Assistance Program 800-994-2111

Products Covered by the Program
Many Merck products.

Other Product Information
Up to a three-month supply of the prescribed medications will be sent directly to the physician for distribution to the patient. Any subsequent request for the same patient require the same procedure.

ORTHO BIOTECH INC.

Financial Assistance Program (FAP) For PROCRIT (Epoetin alfa) and LEUSTATIN (cladribine) Injection/Ortho Biotech

Procritline
1250 Bayhill Dr., Suite 300 — 800-553-3851
San Bruno, CA 94066 — Fax: 800-683-7855

Products Covered by the Program
Procrit (Epoetin alfa), for non-dialysis use; Leustatin (cladribine) Injection.

Other Program Information
Patient eligibility application forms are available from Ortho Biotech Product Specialists or by accessing the 800 number (800-553-3851). This call can help determine if a patient is eligible to enroll in the program.

PFIZER INC

Pfizer Prescription Assistance
P.O. Box 230970
Centreville, VA 20120 — 800-646-4455

Products Covered by the Program
All Pfizer outpatient products, except Diflucan and Zithromax are covered by this program. (Diflucan is covered under the Diflucan Patient Assistance Program).

Name of Program
Sharing the Care
Pfizer Inc.
235 E. 42nd St., 13th Floor
New York, NY 10017 — 800-984-1500

Products Covered by the Program
Pfizer single-source products.

The program, a joint effort of Pfizer, the National Governors' Association and the National Association of Community Health Centers, works solely through community, migrant and homeless health centers certified by the federal government as meeting criteria of Section 329,

339, or 340 of the Public Health Service Act. Center must have an in-house pharmacy to participate. To be eligible, patient must be a patient of a participating health center and must be uninsured, not eligible for government entitlement programs that cover pharmaceuticals, and at or below federal poverty line.

Other Product Information
Product is dispensed at health center pharmacy.

Name of Program
Arkansas Health Care Access Program

Physician Requests should be directed to:
Ms. Pat Keller
Program Director
Arkansas Health Care Access Foundation
P.O. Box 56248 — 800-950-8233
Little Rock, AR 72215 — 501-221-3033

Products Covered by the Program
All Pfizer products are covered.

Eligibility
Must be an Arkansas resident to qualify. Eligible individuals are certified by the Arkansas Local County Department of Human Services as being Arkansas residents below the federal poverty guidelines, who do not have health insurance benefits and do not qualify for any government entitlement programs. No co-payment or cost-sharing is required from the patient. Physician must waive his or her fee for the initial visit. This program does not apply to individuals during hospital inpatient stays.

Other Program Information
Physicians should contact the Arkansas Health Care Access Foundation for further information.

Name of Program
Kentucky Health Care Access Program

Physician Requests should be directed to:
Mr. J. Scott Judy
Executive Vice President
Health Kentucky, Inc. — 800-633-8100
12700 Shelbyville Road — 502-254-4214
Louisville, KY 40243 — Fax: 502-254-5117

Products Covered by the Program
All Pfizer products are covered.

Eligibility
Must be a Kentucky resident to qualify. Eligible individuals are certified by the Kentucky Cabinet for Human Resources as Kentuckians below the federal poverty guidelines, who do not have health insurance benefits and do not qualify for any government entitlement programs. No co-payment or cost-sharing is required from the patient. Physician must waive his or her fee for the initial visit. This program does not apply to individuals during hospital inpatient stays.

Other Program Information
Physicians should contact the Kentucky Health Care Access Foundation for further information.

Name of Program
Commun-I-Care

Physicians Requests should be directed to:
Mr. Ken Trogdon, Director
Commun-I-Care
P.O. Box 12054 — 800-763-0059
Columbia, SC 29211 — 803-933-9183

Products Covered By the Program
All Pfizer products are covered.

Eligibility
Eligible individuals must be South Carolina residents. Individuals are certified by Commun-I-Care as below the federal poverty line and not covered by any government entitlement programs. No copayment or cost-sharing is required from the patient. Physician must waive his or her fee.

Other Program Information
Physicians should contact Commun-I-Care for further information.

PHARMACIA INC.

Rx MAP Prescription Medication Assistance Program
P.O. Box 29043
Phoenix, AZ 85038 — 800-242-7014
www.patientsinneed.com

PROCTOR & GAMBLE PHARMACEUTICALS, INC.

Proctor & Gamble Pharmaceuticals, Inc.
c/o Express Scripts
P.O. Box 6553
St. Louis, MO 63166-6553 — 800-830-9049

Products Covered by the Program
Asacol, Dantrium Capsules, Didronel, Entex, Macrodantin, Macrobid

Other Product Information
The quantity of product supplied depends on diagnosis and need, but generally one month's supply is provided for a chronic medication. Refills require a new prescription and application from the physician. The prescription medication is sent directly to the physician, who provides it to the patient.

ROCHE LABORATORIES (A Division of Hoffman-La Roche Inc.)

Roche Medical Needs Programs
Roche Laboratories
340 Kingsland St.
Nutley, NJ 07110 800-285-4484

Products Covered by Program
Total product line.

Eligibility
Physicians make the determination. Those eligible are private practice outpatients who are considered to be medically indigent and who are not eligible to receive Roche drugs through another third-party drug reimbursement program.

Other Program Information
Roche Medical Needs Program forms are required and can be obtained from the Professional Services Department. Physician's signature and DEA number are required on application. Repeat requests require additional applications.

ROXANE LABORATORIES, INC

Patient Assistance Program
1101 King St., Suite 600
Alexandria, VA 22314 800-556-8317

Boehringer Ingelheim Pharmaceuticals, Inc.
c/o ESI/SDS
St. Louis, MO 63166-6773

Products Covered by the Program
Marinol (dronabinol) Capsules 2.5 mg in the Prescription Pre-Pac bottle of 60's only; Oramorph SR (morphine sulfate sustained release) Tablets 30 mg, 60 mg, and 100 mg; Roxanol (morphine sulfate concentrated oral solution) 20 mg/mL and 120 mL bottles; Roxanol 100 (morphine sulfate concentrated oral solution) 100 mg/5mL and 240 mL bottles.

Eligibility
Product will be provided free of charge to patients through their physician or pharmacist, provided the patient is uninsured and the patients' total annual income does not exceed $25,000 without dependents, or is less than $40,000 with dependents.

Other Program Information
Physicians should call the toll-free number to discuss their patient's eligibility with a program representative.

SANOFI-SYNTHELABO, INC.

Sanofi-Synthelabo, Inc.
Needy Patient Program
c/o Product Information Department
90 Park Avenue
New York, NY 10016 800-446-6267

Products Covered by the Program
Aralen; Breonesin; Bronkometer; Danocrine; Drisdol; Hytakerol; Isuprel; Mytelase: NegGram: PhisoHex; Primaquine; Plaquenil; Trancopal

SCHERING LABORATORIES/KEY PHARMACEUTICALS

Name of Program
Commitment to Care

Physician Requests Should be Directed to:
For Intron A/Eulexin 800-521-7157
www.sgp.com/patient.html

For Other Products
Schering Laboratories/Key Pharmaceuticals
Patient Assistance Program
P.O. Box 52122
Phoenix, AZ 85072 800-656-9485
www.sgp.com/patient.html

Products Covered by the Program
All products.

Eligibility
Patient eligibility is determined on a case-by-case basis based upon economic and insurance criteria. The company does not require indigent patients to participate in copayments or costsharing. Eligibility criteria are currently being evaluated and may be subject to change.

Other Program Information
Physician and patient complete an application form. Application is reviewed on a case-by-case basis. Repeat requests require a new application form to be completed.

SERONO LABORATORIES, INC.

Serono Connections for Growth — 800-582-7989

Sero Care
100 Longwater Circle — 800-714-2437
Norwell, MA 02061 — Fax: 800-214-8698

SIGMA-TAU PHARMACEUTICALS

Carnitor Drug Assistance Program Administrator
National Organization for Rare Diseases
P.O. Box 8923
New Fairfield, CT 06812 — 800-999-NORD

SOLVAY PHARMACEUTICALS, INC./ UNIMED PHARMACEUTICALS, INC.

Patient Assistance Program
Solvay Pharmaceuticals, Inc./
Unimed Pharmaceuticals, Inc.
c/o Express Scripts Specialty Distribution Services
P.O. Box 66550
St. Louis, MD 63166-6550 — 800-256-8918

Eligibility
Eligibility is determined on a case-by-case basis in consultation with each prescribing physician and is based on a patient's inability to pay, lack of insurance, and ineligibility for Medicaid. Patient must be a resident of the U.S.

Other Product Information
Physicians apply on behalf of the patient by submitting a written request on a request form. Blank request forms can be obtained by writing to Solvay Pharmaceuticals, Inc. or by calling the Patient Assistance Program Message Center at (800) 788-9277.

3M PHARMACEUTICALS ASSISTANCE PROGRAM

Indigent Patient Pharmaceutical Program
Medical Services Department
275-2E-13, 3M Center
P.O. Box 33275 — 800-328-0255
St. Paul, MN 55144-1000 — Fax: 651-733-6068

Products Covered by the Program
Most drug products sold by 3M Pharmaceuticals in the U.S.

Eligibility
Patients whose financial and insurance circumstances prevent them from obtaining 3M Pharmaceuticals drug products considered to be necessary by their physician. Consideration is on a case-by-case basis.

WYETH-AYERST LABORATORIES

Name of Program
Norplant Foundation
P.O. Box 25223
Alexandria, VA 22314 703-706-5933

Products Covered by the Program
The Norplant (levonorgestrel implants) five-year contraceptive system.

Eligibility
Determined on a case-by-case basis and limited to individuals who cannot afford the product and who are ineligible for coverage under private and public sector programs.

Name of Program
Wyeth-Ayers Laboratories Patient Assistance Program
John E. James
Professional Services IPP
31 Morehall Road
Frazer, PA 19355

Products Covered by the Program
Various products (not including schedule II, III, or IV products)

Eligibility
Limited to individuals, on a case-by-case basis, who have been identified by their physicians as "indigent."

Discount Drug Programs

Help can be just a phone call away. Several states have special drug programs that give huge discounts to seniors who are ineligible for Medicaid and who don't have private insurance. For example, seniors in New Jersey can get their prescriptions for only $5, and in Maine they can get them for as little as $2.

Often all it takes is a phone call and filling out a simple form. You will have to meet income eligibility, but you can make upwards of $23,000 a year and still be eligible in New York, for example. If your state is not listed below, contact your state Department of Aging, but also check out the free drug programs sponsored by the drug manufacturers themselves. You will find a detailed description of this program on page 167.

California

Eligibility Requirements

- Have a Medicare card

Cost

- You can take your Medicare card to any pharmacy that fills Medi-Cal (California's Medicaid) prescriptions. You will be charged the Medi-Cal rate plus a 15 cent processing fee.

Connecticut

Conn PACE
P.O. Box 5011
Hartford, CT 06102 800-423-5026

Eligibility Requirements

- You must be 65 years old or older.
- You must have lived in Connecticut for six months.
- Your income cannot exceed $15,100 if you are single, and $18,000 if you are married. (As of April, 2002, maximum income for individuals is $20,000; for couples $27,100).
- You may not have an insurance plan that pays for all or a portion of each prescription, a deductible insurance plan that includes prescriptions, or Medicaid.

Cost

- You pay a $25 one time registration fee.
- You pay $12 for each prescription.
- You must get generic drugs whenever possible, unless you are willing to pay the difference in price.

Delaware

Nemours Health Clinic
915 N. Dupont Blvd.

Milford, DE 19963 — 302-424-5420
www.nemours.org — 800-292-9538

Eligibility Requirements
- You must be a Delaware resident.
- You must be U.S. citizen.
- You must be 65 or older.
- Income requirements for single $12,500; for married $17,125.

Cost
- You must pay 20% of the prescription drug cost.

Delaware Prescription Drug Assistance Program
EDS DPAP
P.O. Box 950 — 302-577-4900
New Castle, DE 19720 — 800-996-9969, ext. 17
www.state.de.us/dhss/dss/prescription.html

Eligibility Requirements
- You must be resident of Delaware
- You must be at lest 65 years old or qualify for Social Security Disability
- Your income cannot exceed 200% of the Federal Poverty Level ($1,432 per month per person)
- You are not eligible if you qualify for Nemours Program

Cost
- You pay $5 or 25% of the cost of the prescription, whichever is greater.

Florida

Florida Medicare Prescription Assistance Program
Pharmaceutical Expense Assistance Program
Agency for Healthcare Administration — 888-419-3456
www.fdhs.state.fl.us

Eligibility
- If you are a Medicare card holder, you may go to any Medicaid participating pharmacy to have your prescriptions filled. The cost is 9% below the average wholesale price, plus a $4.50 filling charge.
- The Pharmaceutical Expense Assistance Program is for those age 65 and over and Florida residents. If you qualify for Medicare and partial Medicaid through your income, you can receive an $80 per month prescription benefit and pay a 10% co-pay for your drugs. You can learn more about this program through your local Medicaid office.

Illinois

Pharmaceutical Assistance Program
Illinois Department of Revenue
P.O. Box 19021
Springfield, IL 62794 800-624-2459
www.revenue.state.il.us/circuitbreaker/

Eligibility Requirements

- You must be 65 years of age or older, or over 16 and totally disabled, or a widow or widower who turned 63 before spouse's death.
- You must be a resident of Illinois.
- Your income must be less than $21,218 for individuals; $28,480 for couples.
- You must file a Circuit Breaker claim form.

Cost

- Pharmaceutical Assistance card will cost either $5 or $25, depending upon your income.
- You must choose the generic brand when available, unless you are willing to pay the difference in price.

Indiana

Hoosier Prescription Drug Program
P.O. Box 6224
Indianapolis, IN 46206 866-267-4679 (toll-free)
www.IN.gov/HoosierRx

Eligibility Requirements

- You must be 65 years or older
- You must have been in Indiana resident for at least 90 days
- You do not have prescription drug insurance
- Your income must be $967 or less a month if you are single; and $13,07 per month or less if you are married.
- You can pick up application forms at your local pharmacy, Area Agency on Aging, Social Security office, of Office of Family and Children.

Cost

- The Hoosier Rx program provides refunds for prescription drugs. You receive a refund of half of your prescription drug costs up to $500-$1,000 per year depending upon your monthly income.

Kansas

Kansas Department of Aging
New England Bldg.
503 S. Kansas 785-296-4986
Topeka, KS 66603 800-432-3535
www.k4s.org/dkoa/pharmacy.htm

Eligibility Requirements

- Kansas legislature passed a short-term Senior Pharmacy Assistance Program which provide reimbursement for part of a senior's prescription medication costs. There is some question regarding whether the program will continue to be funded. Contact your local Area Agency on Aging or the Kansas Department of Aging to learn if the program has been funded.

Maine

Elderly Low-Cost Drug Program
Maine Revenue Services
P.O. Box 9116 — 888-600-2466
Augusta, ME 04332 — 207-626-8475

Eligibility requirements

- You must be a Maine resident.
- You may not be receiving SSI payments.
- You must be at least 62 years old or part of a household where one person is 62 years old.
- Your income may not exceed $15,244 if you live alone; $20,461 if you are married or have dependents.

Cost

- Each drug will cost $2 or 20% of the price allowed by the Department of Human Services, whichever is greater.

Maryland

Maryland Pharmacy Assistance Program
P.O. Box 386 — 410-767-5397
Baltimore, MD 21203-0386 — 800-492-1974

Eligibility

- For anyone in the state who cannot afford their medications. Income requirements vary, so it is best to call. For a single person, income cannot exceed $10,000; for married couples, $10,850.

Cost

- You pay $5 copay.

Massachusetts

Prescription Advantage Plan
P.O. Box 15153
Worchester, MA 01615 — 800-AGE-INFO
www.800ageinfo.com

Eligibility Requirements

- You must be 65 years or old or have a qualified disability
- You must be a Massachusetts resident

Cost

- Monthly premium for the plan varies for $0-$82 per month depending upon your income. The co-payment also varies for $5-$25 depending upon income.
- After you pay $2,000 or 10% of your gross annual household income (whichever is less) toward your Prescription Advantage deductible and co-payments, the entire cost of your prescription drugs, including the co-payments are covered for the remainder of the year.

Michigan

Elder Prescription Insurance Coverage
P.O. Box 30676 517-373-8230
Lansing, MI 48909 866-747-5844

Eligibility Requirements

- You must be Michigan resident
- You must be age 65 or older
- Your annual income must be at or below 200% of the federal poverty level.
- You may not be receiving prescription drug benefits through any other insurance.

Cost

- Modest co-pay depending upon income.
- Michigan has an Emergency Pharmaceutical Program for Seniors (MEPPS) that provides up to three months of prescription drug payment to seniors whose monthly income is $1,044 for a single person and $1,406 for married couple.

Minnesota

Minnesota's Senior Drug Program
Department of Human Services
444 Lafayette Rd., N 651-297-3933
St Paul, MN 55155 800-333-2433
www.dhs.state.mn.us/hlthcare/asstprog/srdrug.htm

Eligibility Requirements

- Must be age 65 or older
- Must be a Minnesota resident for six months
- Have income at or below 120% of federal poverty guidelines (currently $844 a month for one person and $1,126 a month for a married couple)
- Have liquid assets of $4,00 or less for one; $6,00 or less for married couple
- Be eligible for one of the Medical Assistance programs (Medicaid), which help Medicare beneficiaries pay their Medicare premiums, such as Qualified Medicare Beneficiary (QMB) or Service Limited Medicare Beneficiary (SLMB).

Cost

- The Senior Drug Program pays for necessary prescription drugs after enrollees pay the first $35 monthly deductible. If no medications are purchased that month, there is no $35 cost. For more information contact your local county human services agency.

Nevada

Senior Rx
P.O. Box 21230
Carson City, NV 89721 800-243-3638
www.nevadaseniorrx.com

Eligibility Requirements

- Age 62 and older
- Nevada resident for at least one year
- Not eligible for full Medicaid with prescription benefits
- Household income not over $21,500

Cost

- You pay a copy of $10 per drug. Senior Rx provides up to $5,000 in benefits per year.

New Hampshire

Division of Elderly and Adult Services
Department of Health and Human Services
129 Pleasant St.
Concord, NH 03301 800-351-1888
www.dhhs.state.nh.us

Eligibility Requirements

- Age 65 or older
- New Hampshire resident
- No income requirement
- This is a two year trial program

Costs

- No enrollment fee
- You receive discounts on medications. Discounts vary based on pharmacy and medication, but could reach up to 40% for generic and up to 15% for brand name.

New Jersey

Pharmaceutical Assistance to the Aged and Disabled (PAAD)
Special Benefit Programs
CN 715 800-792-9745
Trenton, NJ 08625 609-588-7049

Eligibility

- You must be a New Jersey resident.
- Your income must be less than $19,238 if you are single, or less than $23,589 if you are married. Income can be $10,000 higher and you could qualify for Senior Gold.
- You must be at least 65 years of age, or receiving Social Security Disability.
- Drugs purchased outside the state of New Jersey are not covered, nor any pharmaceutical product whose manufacturer has not agreed to provide rebates to the state of New Jersey.

Cost

- You pay $5 for each covered prescription. PAAD collects payments made on your behalf from any other assistance program, insurance, or retirement benefits which may cover prescription drugs.
- Senior Gold members have a $15 copay plus ½ of the remainder of the cost of the drug.

New York

Elderly Pharmaceutical Insurance Coverage EPIC
P.O. Box 15018
Albany, NY 12212 — 800-332-3742
www.health.state.ny.us/nysdoh/epic/faq.htm — 518-452-6828

Eligibility Requirements

- You must be 65 or older.
- You must reside in New York State.
- Your income must not exceed $35,000 if you are single; or $50,000 if you are married.
- You are not eligible if you receive Medicaid benefits.

Cost

- You pay between $3-$20 per prescription depending upon the prescription cost.
- There are two plans for EPIC. You can pay an annual fee depending upon your income to qualify right away. The annual fee ranges from $8 to over $300, which can be paid in installments. The EPIC Deductible plan is that you pay no fee, but you pay full price for your prescriptions until you spend the deductible amount. The deductible amount also varies by income and starts at $530.

North Carolina

Prescription Drug Assistance Program
Department of Health and Human Services
Division of Public Health
1339 St. Mary's Street
1916 Mail Service Center — 800-662-7030
Raleigh, NC 27699 — 919-733-4534

Eligibility Requirements

- Age 65 and older

- Income less the 150% of the federal poverty level
- Not eligible for full Medicaid benefits
- Diagnosed with cardiovascular disease and/or diabetes

Cost

- You pay $6 co-pay for prescription

Pennsylvania

PACE Card
(Pennsylvania Pharmaceutical Assistance
Contract For The Elderly)
Pennsylvania Department of Aging
555 Walnut St., 5th Floor
Harrisburg, PA 17101 717-787-7313
800-225-7223

Eligibility Requirements

- You must be 65 or older.
- Your income cannot exceed $14,000 if you are single; $17,200 for married couples.
- You must also live in the state for at least 90 days.

Cost

- You pay a $6.00 co-payment for each prescription. You may not purchase drugs out of state.
- PACE limits drug amounts to no more than a 30-day supply or 100 pills. There are no vacation supplies allowed.

Rhode Island

Rhode Island Pharmaceutical Assistance to the Elderly (RIPAE)
Rhode Island Department of Elderly Affairs
160 Pine St. 800-322-2880
Providence, RI 02903 401-222-2858

Eligibility Requirements

- You must be a Rhode Island resident.
- You must be 65 years old.
- Your income must not exceed $16,490 if you are single; $20,613 if you are married.
- You can not have any other prescription drug coverage.

Cost

- Members pay 40% of the cost of prescription drugs used to treat certain illnesses.
- For incomes for single $20,700 and married $25,875, you pay 70%. For incomes for single $36,225 and married $41,400, you pay 85%.

South Carolina

SILVERRxCARD
ACS PBMS
P.O. Box 502569
Atlanta, GA 31150 — 877-239-5277 (toll-free)
www.silverxcard.com
www.dhhs.state.sc.us

Eligibility Requirements

- Open enrollment in month of October
  - Applications are available at local government offices, pharmacies, libraries, senior centers and Council on Aging offices.
- Must be 65 or older
- Resident of South Carolina for past six months
- Have no other prescription drug coverage
- Have income of $14,612 or less if single or $19,678 or less if married.

Costs

- You must pay $500 deductible before the plan begins to pay benefits
- Once you meet your deductible, you pay $10 co-pay on generic drugs at $21 co-pay on Brand drug.

Vermont

VScript Program
Department of Social Welfare
Medicaid Division
103 South Main St. — 802-241-2880
Waterbury, VT 05676 — 800-529-4060

Eligibility Requirements

- You must be a resident of Vermont.
- You must be at least 65.
- You may not have income in excess of 175% of the federal poverty guidelines. For singles, $15,036; for couples, $20,328. Vscript Expanded has income requirements of $19,332 for singles and $26,124 for couples. The Vhap Program has income of $12,888 for singles and $17,424 for couples. The Vscript and Vscript Expanded are for maintenance prescriptions only. The Vhap program is for both short-term and long-term prescriptions.
- You may not be in a health insurance plan that pays for all or a portion of the applicant's prescription drugs.

Cost

- There will be a co-payment requirement of $1-4 for Vscript and Vhap. Vscript Expanded copay is 41% of the cost of the drug..

Wyoming

Department of Family Services
2300 Capitol Ave.
Cheyenne, WY 82002 888-996-8678

Eligibility Requirements

- No age requirements
- Do not need to be a citizen
- Must have income no more than 100% of Federal poverty guidelines
- Limited to three prescriptions a month

Cost

- $25 co-pay per prescription
- No enrollment fee
- Apply at any field office for the Department of Family Services

$$$ Pay Your House And Apartment Bills

Free Money For Closing Costs and a Down Payment

Houston has a program that offers $4,000 in down-payment and closing costs through their First-Time Homebuyers Program.

Iowa offers up to $2,750 in grants for a down-payment. You can be earning up to $65,000 a year and still be eligible for the money in their Down Payment/Closing Cost Grant Program.

Many cities, like Minneapolis, will offer interest free loans, called Equity Participation Loans, for up to 10% of the cost of the home. You pay back the money when you sell the house.

Programs vary from state to state and city to city. Contact your city government, your county government, and your local community development office to learn about local programs. If you have trouble locating your local community development office, the following organizations may be able to help:

- ❑ National Association of Housing and Redevelopment Officials, 630 Eye St, NW, Washington, DC 20001; 202-289-3500; 877-866-2476, Fax: 202-289-8181; {www.nahro.org}
- ❑ Information Center, Office of Community Planning and Development, P.O. Box 7189, Gaithersburg, MD 20898; 800-998-9999, Fax: 301-519-5027; {www.comcon.org}
- ❑ Also be sure to contact your state housing office listed in the Appendix.

Free Housing Books

- *A Consumer's Guide to Mortgage Settlement Costs*
- *Home Mortgages: Understanding the Process*
- *A Consumer's Guide to Mortgage Refinancings*
- *Consumer Handbook on Adjustable Rate Mortgages*

For your copies, contact Board of Governors of the Federal Reserve System, Publications Services, MS-127, Washington, DC 20551; 202-452-3245; {www.federalreserve.gov/}.

WOW!...The Government Will Pay My Mortgage"

You'd never have thought to ask, would you?

There are now programs that will make your mortgage payments for you when you get into financial trouble. For example, Pennsylvania law, 35 P.S. § 1680.401 et seq., states it will provide "*mortgage assistance payments to homeowners who are in danger of losing their homes through foreclosure and through no fault of their own and who have a reasonable prospect of resuming mortgage payments within the prescribed time frame.*" Pennsylvania calls it the ***"Homeowners' Emergency Mortgage Assistance Program."***

One of the best ways to find out if there are programs like this in your area is to contact the local HUD approved Housing Counseling agencies. To find your closest agency, contact your state housing office listed in the Appendix, the Housing Counseling Center locator at 1-888-466-3487; {www.hud.gov/hsgcoun.html}, or Housing Counseling Clearinghouse, P.O. Box 9057, Gaithersburg, MD 20898; 800-217-6970; Fax: 301-519-6655.

If your local agency doesn't have money to pay your mortgage, they will certainly help you work out other arrangements with your mortgage company.

Free Mortgage Publications

The Federal Trade Commission understands this, so they have compiled several brochures to get you started. Some of the titles include *Home Financing Primer*, *Mortgage Servicing*, *Mortgage Discrimination*, and more.

To receive your copies, contact Public Reference, Room 130, Federal Trade Commission, Washington, DC 20580; 202-326-2222; 877-FTC-HELP; {www.ftc.gov}.

Make Money Going To Housing Classes

A HUD-approved housing counseling agency in Philadelphia offers $1,000 in settlement costs to certain people who attend pre-purchase house counseling sessions. A counseling agency in Boston offers new home buyers access to special low down-payment mortgages if they attend pre-housing classes.

There are over 350 HUD-approved counseling agencies that offer free classes and help in housing related issues including:

- The Best Way To Buy And Finance A Home
- Is A Reverse Mortgage For You?
- Foreclosure and Eviction Options
- The Best Way To Finance A Home Fix-Up

These non-profit agencies are trained and approved by the U.S. Department of Housing and Urban Development (HUD).

To find your closest agency, contact your State housing office listed in the Appendix, the Housing Counseling Center locator at 1-888-466-3487; {www.hud.gov/hsgcoun.html}, or Housing Counseling Clearinghouse, P.O. Box 9057, Gaithersburg, MD 20898; 800-217-6970, Fax: 301-519-6655.

"Get The Lead Out" And Get Your House Or Apartment Painted For Free

If you are living in a house or apartment that was built before 1978, you, or even your landlord, may be eligible for grant money and other assistance to make sure that you do not suffer the effects of lead poisoning from lead-based paint.

Chips or dust from this type of paint can be highly dangerous to humans, especially children. The U.S. Department of Housing and Urban Development spends over $60 million a year helping home owners and apartment owners eliminate the problems that may be caused by lead paint.

Contact your state department of housing listed in the Appendix to see if your state has money for lead paint removal.

How Lead Paint Can Affect Your Kids

Houses and apartments built before 1978 may contain lead contaminated surface dust and paint chips, which, if consumed by children, can result in reduced intelligence, behavioral problems, learning disabilities, and even permanent brain damage.

Government sponsored programs can help you inspect your home for lead paint and even get a blood test for your children for potential problems. To find out more about these programs or the effects of lead-based paint, contact the following:

☞ *National Lead Information Center*, EPA, 1200 Pennsylvania Ave., NW, Mail Code: 7404, Washington, DC

20460; 800-424-LEAD; {www.epa.gov/lead/nlic.htm}.

☞ *Office of Lead Hazard Control*, U.S. Department of Housing and Urban Development, 451 7th Street, SW, Room B-133, Washington, DC 20410; 202-708-1112; Fax: 202-708-1455; {www.hud.gov/offices/lead}.

Home Repair Programs

Here are a few *HOME REPAIR* programs we found that were available at the time we were doing research. Things change, but make sure to contact local agencies to see what may be available to you!

City of Sunnyvale
Housing Division
P.O. Box 3707
Sunnyvale, CA 94088
408-730-7250
www.ci.sunnyvale.ca.us/community-dev/housing/ index.htm

Tacoma Community Redevelopment Authority
747 Market St., Room 1036
Tacoma, WA 98402
253-591-5238
www.cityoftacoma.org

Community Development
City of Canton
218 Cleveland Ave., SW
Canton, OH 44702
330-489-3040
www.canton-ohio.com/canton/homerep.html

Minneapolis Community Development Agency
Crown Roller Mill
105 Fifth Ave. S, Suite 200
Minneapolis, MN 55401
612-673-5095
www.mcda.org

Los Angeles Housing Department
111 N. Hope St., Lobby Level
Los Angeles, CA 90012
213-369-9175; 800-994-4444
www.cityofla.org/LAHD

Department of Housing and Community Development
300 W. Washington St.
P.O. Box 3136
Greensboro, NC 27402
336-373-2349
www.ci.greensboro.nc.us/HCD/

Metropolitan Development and Housing Agency
701 S. 6th St.
Nashville, TN 37202
615-252-8590
www.nashville.org/mdha

Department of Community Development
Neighborhood Conservation Services Division
602 E. 1st St.
Des Moines, IA 50309
515-283-4787
www.ci.des-moines.ia.us/departments/cd/

Low-Income Weatherization Program
Housing Authority and Community Services Agency
177 Day Island Rd.
Eugene, OR 97401
541-682-3755
www.hacsa.org

$4,000 Grant To Paint Your Home

That's what Canton, Ohio offers to very low-income residents — grants to paint their house or put on new siding. They feel that an investment like this improves the value of all the properties in the area.

Sunnyvale, California offers some of their residents $400 in grant money to paint their homes. And if you're over 60 or have a disability, you can get a $1,200 grant.

See if your city or state offers a program like this.

Cut Your Rent By 50%

Studies show that people with less income pay a higher portion of their salary on housing than people in higher income categories. It is not unusual for a single mom to pay 70% of her salary in rent.

The government has a program called Section 8 Rental Assistance Program that offers vouchers and direct payments to landlords. This will, in turn, cut your rent down to only 30% of your income.

Of course, there are income requirements for this program. For example, in Arlington Country, VA, a one-person household with an income of $23,000 qualifies for the program. Arlington County also has housing grant rental assistance for low-income elderly, disabled, and working families with children. Some of these programs have waiting lists, but it could be worth the wait.

To apply for these federal programs, contact your state housing authority listed in the appendix, your local housing authority, or a community services agency. If you have trouble getting the help you need, you can contact Information Center, Office of Community Planning and Development, P.O. Box 7189, Gaithersburg, MD 20898; 800-998-9999, Fax: 301-519-5027; {www.comcon.org}.

Free Money To Fix Up Your Home

States, cities, and counties, as well as local community development agencies are providing grants, loans, and even supplies and technical assistance for homeowners who want to fix up the inside or outside of their homes. Many of these have income requirements you must meet. Others offer forgivable loans if you stay in the house a certain number of years. Here are some examples of what communities are offering to their residents:

☞ *Sunnyvale, CA*: $2,000 grant for disabled homeowners to fix up anything through the Home Access Grant Program.

☞ *Houston, TX*: loans and grants for major repairs through their Housing Assistance Program for the Elderly and Disabled.

☞ *Tacoma, WA*: Up to $3,500 loan at 0% interest with no monthly payments through the Major Home Repair Program.

☞ *Minneapolis, MN*: $15,000, no interest, and no payments until you sell in their Deferred Rehabilitation Loans.

☞ *Baton Rouge, LA*: $20,000 grant to fix up your home through the Housing Rehabilitation Grant Program.

☞ *Los Angeles, CA*: Free help with roofing, plumbing, electrical and heating work, painting, deadbolt locks, smoke alarms, screens, windows, and yard maintenance for seniors or disabled persons through the Handy Worker Program.

☞ *Michigan*: $1,000 to $10,000 at zero interest, to be paid back when you sell your home through the Rehabilitation Assistance Program.

☞ *Nashville, TN*: $18,000 at 3% to fix up your home.

☞ *Lane County, OR*: offers grants for weatherization assistance for weatherstripping, storm doors and windows, and insulation.

☞ *Des Moines, IA*: offers emergency repair loans.

☞ *Greensboro, NC*: has low interest loans for people with incomes over $30,000 and $8,500 grants for people with incomes up to $20,000.

Programs vary from state to state and city to city. Contact your city government, your county government, and your local community development office to learn about local programs.

If you have trouble locating your local community development office, the following organizations may be able to help:

- ❑ National Association of Housing and Redevelopment Officials, 630 Eye St., NW, Washington, DC 20001; 202-289-3500, 877-866-2476, Fax: 202-289-8181; {www.nahro.org}
- ❑ Information Center, Office of Community Planning and Development, P.O. Box 7189, Gaithersburg, MD 20898; 800-998-9999, Fax: 301-519-5027; {www.comcon.org}
- ❑ Also be sure to contact your state housing office listed in the Appendix.

Your Rich Uncle Will Cosign A Loan To Buy or Fix Up a Home

Both the U.S. Department of Housing and Urban Development (HUD) and the Rural Housing Service of the U.S. Department of

$ & Help To Fix-Up A Home For A Senior

The Home Modification Action Project at:

http://www.usc.edu/go/hmap/index.html

Agriculture offer loan guarantees to lending agencies around the county. A loan-guarantee assures the lending agency that the government will pay for the loan if you can't.

In addition, the Rural Housing Service has a direct loan program that provides loans to lower income families to buy, build, repair, renovate, or relocate their home. This is called the Section 502 Program.

To investigate the programs available in your area, contact your local HUD office listed in the blue pages of your telephone book, or U.S. Department of Housing and Urban Development (HUD), 451 7th Street, SW, Washington, DC 20410; 202-708-1112, 800-245-2691; {www.hud.gov}.

To find your local Rural Housing Service, look in the blue pages of your telephone book, or contact Single Family Housing Programs, USDA Rural Housing Service, Room 5037, South Building, 14th St. and Independence Ave., SW, Washington, DC 20250; 202-720-4323; {www.rurdev.usda.gov/}.

In addition, you may contact your state housing office located the Appendix.

Money For Seniors And Those With A Disability To Buy or Fix Up A Home

The city of Houston offers $5,000 fix up money for the disabled and elderly in their Emergency Repair Program. Minneapolis offers home repair grants of $10,000 to people with disabilities who have incomes under $18,000. Nebraska has a special low interest loan program to help people with disabilities buy a home.

The Rural Housing Service of the U.S. Department of Agriculture offers special grants through their Section 504 program of up to $7,500 if you're over 62, and need to fix up your home. Programs vary from state to state and city to city, and obviously, many have eligibility requirements.

Contact your city government, your county government and your local community development office to learn about local programs. If you have trouble locating your local community development office, contact *National Association of Housing and Redevelopment Officials*, 630 Eye St., NW, Washington, DC 20001; 202-289-3500, 877-866-2476, Fax: 202-289-8181; {www.nahro.org}, or *Information Center, Office of Community Planning and Development*, P.O. Box 7189, Gaithersburg, MD 20898; 800-998-9999, Fax: 301-519-5027; {www.comcon.org}.

To find your local *Rural Housing Service*, look in the blue pages of your telephone book, or contact Single Family Housing Programs, USDA Rural Housing Service, Room

5037, South Building, 14th St. and Independence Ave., SW, Washington, DC 20250; 202-720-4323; {www.rurdev.usda.gov/}. In addition, you may contact your state housing office listed in the Appendix.

Money To Buy Or Fix Up a Mobile Home

The city of Sunnyvale, Ca will lend you up to $7,500 at 0-5% interest for a mobile home. New York State offers loans to help you buy a mobile home park or the land your mobile home sits on through their ***Manufactured Home Cooperative Fund Program.*** And the U.S. Department of Agriculture has what is called ***Section 504 funds*** that allow loans of up to $20,000 to fix a mobile home or to move it from one site to another.

Here is how to contact the major programs for manufactured (mobile) homes.

VA-Guaranteed Manufactured Home Loan

Contact your local office of the Department of Veterans Affairs, or U.S. Department of Veterans Affairs, 1120 Vermont Avenue, Washington, DC 20420; 800-827-1000; {www.va.gov/about_va/programs.htm}.

FHA Insured Title I Manufactured Home Loan

Contact your local office of Housing and Urban Development listed in the blue pages of your telephone book, or your state housing office listed in the Appendix, or the Housing Counseling Clearinghouse, P.O. Box 10423, McLean, VA 22102; 800-217-6970; {www.hud.gov}

Section 504 Rural Housing Loans and Grants

To find your local Rural Housing Service, look in the blue pages of your telephone book, or contact Single Family Housing Programs, USDA Rural Housing Service, Room 5037, South Building, 14th St. and Independence Ave., SW, Washington, DC 20250; 202-720-4323; {www.rurdev.usda.gov/}.

HUD-man Goes After The Mobile Home Salesman

If your mobile home is not all that was promised, call HUD. The U.S. Department of Housing and Urban Development regulates the construction of mobile homes and investigates complaints about their performance.

$83,000 / YR Income and The Government Considers You Needy?

Many of the government housing programs, especially the grant and low interest programs, may have income requirements. But don't let a good salary stop you from investigating the opportunities. The first time home buyer program in Illinois has income requirements that go up to $83,000.

Contact: Manufactured Housing and Standards, Office of Consumer and Regulatory Affairs, U.S. Department of Housing and Urban Development, 451 7th St., SW, Room 9152, Washington, DC 20410; 800-927-2891, 202-708-1112, Fax: 202-708-4231; Email: {jerrold_h_mayer@hud.gov}; {www.hud.gov/fha/sfh/mhs/mhshome.html}

Money For Buying a Condo Or Co-op

In 1999 the U.S. Department of Housing and Urban Development will finance about $9 billion for people to buy condominiums. This is almost double the amount financed in 1997. The program is called *Mortgage Insurance — Purchase of Units in Condominiums (234c).* They also have a special program for units in co-op buildings called *Mortgage Insurance — Single Family Cooperative Housing (203n).*

Contact your local office of Housing and Urban Development listed in the blue pages of your telephone book, or your state housing office listed in the Appendix, or the Housing Counseling Clearinghouse, P.O. Box 10423, McLean, VA 22102; 800-217-6970; {www.hud.gov}.

Lead Poisoning and Your Children

This publication is free along with three fact sheets, and a list of state and local contacts for additional information. Specific lead questions can be answered by an information specialist at 800-424-LEAD.

For more information, contact National Lead Information Center, EPA, 1200 Pennsylvania Ave., NW, Washington, DC 20460; 800-424-LEAD; {www.epa.gov/lead/nlic.htm}.

Free Houses

Well, maybe they're not free, but they can cost you as little as a few hundred dollars a month. And maybe they're not in good shape, but many of the programs will also offer you a low interest loan to fix up the house.

Some states refer to the program as an ***Urban Homesteading Act***. The idea of the program is that the government gets you a home for next to nothing and you agree to live there for a certain number of years.

Minnesota has a program. Baltimore had a very active program for many years. Davenport, Iowa purchases homes, completely rehabs them, and then offers the houses in a lottery each May. You must get

a mortgage, but your monthly payments are under $400 a month for a completely rebuilt house!

There are some states, like Alaska, that still offer wilderness land for homesteading. Because the houses are so cheap, there is usually a lottery for eligible buyers. Contact your city government, your county government and your local community development office to learn about local programs.

If you have trouble finding your local community development agency, the following organizations may be able to help:

✦ National Association of Housing and Redevelopment Officials, 630 Eye St., NW, Washington, DC 20001; 202-289-3500, 877-866-2476, Fax: 202-289-8181; {www.nahro.org}

✦ Information Center, Office of Community Planning and Development, P.O. Box 7189, Gaithersburg, MD 20898; 800-998-9999; Fax: 301-519-5027; {www.comcon.org}

✦ You can also contact your state housing office located in the Appendix.

Free Legal Help For Renters and Home Buyers

It's illegal for landlords, realtors, bankers and others to discriminate against you because of your race, religion, sex, family status, or handicap. Landlords also have rules to follow in dealing with you as a

tenant. With the proper free help you can find out how to:

- Stop paying the rent if your toilet doesn't work.
- Get the government to sue your landlord for discriminating against your child.
- Break a lease and not pay a penalty.
- Get your eviction stopped.
- Force a bank to give you a loan for a new home.
- Get your landlord to widen your doorways to fit your wheelchair.
- Get a third party to fight your landlord for you.

To file a complaint or to learn more about your rights in dealing with landlords and people in the housing industry, contact any of the following:

Your state housing office

Your state Attorney General's office in the Appendix

Fair Housing and Equal Opportunity, U.S. Department of Housing and Urban Development, Room 5204, 451 Seventh St, SW, Washington, DC 20410; 800-669-9777; {www.hud.gov/complaints/housediscrim.cfm}.

National Fair Housing Advocate Online, Tennessee Fair Housing Council, 719 Thompson Lane, Suite 324, Nashville, TN 37206; 800-254-2166; {www.fairhousing.com}.

Use Your Sweat as a Down Payment and Get a No-Interest Loan

One of the biggest providers of this type of program is the non-profit organization called **Habitat for Humanity**. You've probably seen them in the news with Ex-President Jimmy Carter helping them build houses. They have even received government money to help support their program.

The typical arrangement is for people with incomes between $9,000 and $30,000. You and your family work an average of 300 to 500 hours building your home or other people's homes, and in return you get a home with no down-payment and a very low mortgage payment.

Because people provide free labor to build the home, you only pay about $60,000 for a $100,000 home, and you get the money interest free. A typical bank loan can cost you over $700 per month, but through this program you pay only about $200 a month.

Other local or national organizations may run similar programs in your area, with or without government financing. To find programs in your area, you can contact:

- ⇨ Habitat for Humanity International, 121 Habitat Street, Americus, GA 31709; 229-924-6935; {www.habitat. org}. To find a local affiliate, call 229-924-6935, ext. 2551 or ext. 2552
- ⇨ Information Center, Office of Community Planning and Development, P.O. Box 7189, Gaithersburg, MD 20898; 800-998-9999, Fax: 301-519-5027; {www.comcon.org}.

Staying Clear Of Deadly Radon Gases

Nowadays when you buy a home, you often have a radon level reading taken, but what do the numbers mean?

The ***National Radon Information Hotline*** has a free brochure that explains what radon is, how to test for it, and more.

There is also a Radon FIX-IT Program operated by the Consumer Research Council, a nonprofit consumer organization that provides free guidance and encouragement to consumers who are trying to fix their homes that have elevated radon levels. The Program operates from noon to 8 p.m. EST and has information on reducing elevated radon levels, referrals to experts, and names of contractors who are qualified to help.

For more information, contact National Radon Information Hotline at 800-767-7236 (SOS-RADON) and the Radon Fix-It Program at 800-644-6999; or Indoor Air Quality Information Clearinghouse, IAQ Info, P.O. Box 37133, Washington, DC 20013; 800-438-4318; {www.epa.gov/iaq/iaqinfo.html}.

Is Your Drinking Water Safe?

According to the National Consumer Water Survey, 75% of those surveyed have concerns about the quality of the water they drink. Many people are purchasing bottled water or water purification devices for drinking water, but is it a wise use of your money?

The ***Safe Drinking Water Hotline*** can answer any question or concern you may have regarding drinking water, and can provide you with publications such as: *Is Your Drinking Water Safe?, Home Water Testing, Home Water Treatment Units, Bottled Water* fact sheet, and more. Contact Safe Drinking Water Hotline, U.S. Environmental Protection Agency, 401 M St., SW, Washington, DC 20460; 800-426-4791; {www.epa.gov/OGWDW}.

Volunteers Will Fix Up Your (Or Your Mom's) Home For Free

Many service organizations have begun to organize community service days, where the town is beautified along with certain homes in need of repair.

Christmas in April is a national organization with over 185 affiliates that gather together volunteers to help rehabilitate the homes of low-income homeowners. The work is done for free with the goal being to provide a safe and secure home for those in need.

An example of a program in the Dallas area is the Volunteer Home Repair and Weatherization Program. This program provides home repairs that improve the health, safety, and energy efficiency of a home for low-income homeowners.

Contact your city government, your county government and your local community development office to learn about local programs.

- In the Dallas area, contact Volunteer Home Repair and Weatherization Program, Center for Housing Resources, 3103 Greenwood, Dallas, TX 75204; 214-828-4390, Fax: 214-828-4412; {www.chrdallas.org}

How To Save Up To $650/Year On Fuel Bills

The average family spends close to $1300 a year on their home's utility bills, and a large portion of that energy is wasted. By using a few inexpensive energy efficient measures, you can reduce your energy bills by 10% to 50%.

With the publication, *Energy Savers: Tips on Saving Energy and Money at Home*, you can go step by step through your home to learn energy saving tips. Topics covered include insulation/ weatherization, water heating, lighting, appliances, and more. There is even a major appliance shopping guide that explains the energy labels on appliances and shows you how to choose the best one for you.

The Energy Efficiency and Renewable Energy Clearinghouse can answer your questions on all these topics and has publications and easy to understand fact sheets. Contact the Energy Efficiency and Renewable and Energy Clearinghouse, Mail Stop EE-1, Washington, DC 20585; 800-363-3732, 202-586-9220; {www.eren.doe.gov}.

Who Qualifies As A First Time Homebuyer?

Most government programs define a first time homebuyer as someone who has not owned a home during the past 3 years or who is legally separated or divorced.

Get Money For Down Payments And Closing Costs Here

The following are examples of financial assistance programs offered by states, cities and counties at the time we were doing our initial research for this book. Be aware that these programs are constantly changing and all have some form of eligibility requirements, but don't let that stop you! New ones are added and old ones may be discarded.

To be sure that you are aware of all the programs available in your area, contact your state office on housing (listed in the Appendix), your city housing office, your county housing office, as well as any local community development offices that may be in your area. If you need help locating your community development office, the following may be of assistance: National Association of Housing and Redevelopment Officials, 630 Eye St., NW, Washington, DC 20001; 202-289-3500, 877-866-2476; Fax: 202-289-8181: {www.nahro.org}.

- *Houston*: $3,500 to help with a down payment and closing costs in the First-Time Homebuyers Program.
- *Iowa*: 5% of your mortgage in grant money for a down payment and closing costs through Down Payment/ Closing Cost Grant Program.
- *Minneapolis, MN*: $3,000 at 0% interest due when you sell the home
- *Michigan*: $5,000 at 0% interest and no monthly payments

- *Baton Rouge, LA*: $10,000 at 0% interest and no payments for 20 years through Home Buyers Assistance Program.
- *Georgia*: $5,000 for a down payment at 0% interest through Own HOME Program.
- *Hawaii*: $15,000 loans at 3% for down payments, but you only pay interest for the first 5 years in the Down Payment Loan Program.
- *Kansas*: You only need $500 and Kansas will assist with down payment, closing costs, and legal fees in First Time Homebuyers Downpayment Assistance Program.
- *Maine*: Buy a house with only $750, and finance your down payment at 0% through Down Home Program.
- *La Miranda, CA*: 10% loan for down payment for first time homebuyers in the Down Payment Assistance Program.
- *Tacoma, WA*: A $5,000 loan for your down payment and settlement costs in Down Payment Assistance Program.
- *Indianapolis, IN*: Put 1% down and your closing costs go into a 2nd mortgage in Good Neighbor II Loan Program.
- *Los Angeles, CA*: 2% forgivable loan for closing costs money, plus $35,000 loan for repairs with no payments for 30 years or until the house is sold through Home WORKS! Program.
- *New York State*: 0% down payment in Low Down Payment, Conventional Rate Program.
- *Walnut Creek, CA*: Get a second mortgage for half of the closing costs and 2% of down payment with nothing due until you sell or refinance.

- *Washington County, OR*: $19,300 loan with no interest and no payment for the first 5 years in First-Time Home Buyer Program.
- *Michigan*: Move into a $60,000 home with only $600 in your pocket in the Down Payment Assistance Program.
- *New Hampshire*: $5,000 low interest loan for closing costs through HELP Program.
- *Nashville, TN*: Nashville Housing Fund provides down payments, closing costs and low interest loans for first time home buyers.
- *Tucson, AZ*: $3,000 loan for down payment and they will pay all closing costs with the Tucson Metropolitan Ministry.
- *Oregon*: $500 to $6,000 grant for closing costs, down payment, or minor repairs in their First-Time Homebuyer Program.
- *Missouri*: Move into a home with only $750 through Down Payment Assistance for Homebuyers.
- *Canton, OH*: Renters can apply for $5,000 loan for first time home buyers that's forgiven after 5 years through the Down Payment Assistance Program.
- *South Carolina*: Loans for SINGLE PARENTS for a down payment and closing costs in their Single Parent Program.

How To Keep Your Air Clean Of Asbestos, Carbon Monoxide, and Second Hand Smoke

You don't need to hire some high priced consultants to find how to keep the air in your home clean of pollution and other toxic substances. The Indoor Air Quality Information Clearinghouse is the expert on all forms of indoor air pollution. They have publications and information on second hand smoke, asbestos, carbon monoxide, air cleaners, and more. You can contact them at Indoor Air Quality Information Clearinghouse, IAQ Info, P.O. Box 37133, Washington, DC 20013; 800-438-4318; {www.epa.gov/iaq/iaqinfo.html}.

Free Nutrition Counseling and Classes

Nutrition counseling, menu planning, cooking instruction and comparison shopping is available from your local County Cooperative Extension Service. Group instruction is free of charge, but persons requesting individual lessons are asked to pay for the lesson materials.

They also help neighborhoods establish and maintain community gardens, which provide fresh vegetables to area residents. To find an office near you, look in the blue pages of your local telephone book under county government for County Cooperative Extension Service, or contact the state lead office listed in the Appendix.

Government Foreclosed Homes At Bargain Prices

No, they are not giving away the kitchen sink, but you may be able to find some good deals nonetheless. The government sells foreclosed homes all across the country, and even in your neighborhood. You don't need to know someone to get in on these deals. All are sold through real estate agents.

Contact your agent, ask about government repossessed homes and they can do a search for you. These are not just HUD homes, but also those from the VA, Fannie Mae, IRS, Federal Deposit Insurance Corporation, and more.

Free Home Owner Calculators at {www.homepath.com/cgi-bin/ WebObjects-4/HomePathWOF. Woa/wa/calculator}

- How Much Is Your Monthly Payment?
- How Much House Can You Afford?
- What Monthly Payment Is Needed for a House with a Specific Sales Price?
- How Much House Can You Afford with a Specific Monthly Payment?

I want to be able to say that they give you these houses at 50% off, but I can't. Most want fair market value, but the government does not want to carry the real estate taxes for all these houses either. You can make a deal that works out best for everyone.

For more information, contact HUD USER, P.O. Box 6091, Rockville, MD 20850; 800-245-2691; {www.huduser.org} (Note: this website has links to all the major government home sale programs); U.S. Department of Veterans Affairs, 810 Vermont Ave., NW, Washington, DC 20420; 800-827-1000; {www.va.gov}.

Money To Pay Your Heating Bill

Storm windows, insulation, and even weatherstripping, can help reduce your fuel bill. Families can receive assistance to weatherize their homes and apartments at no charge if you meet certain income guidelines.

States allocate dollars to nonprofit agencies for purchasing and installing energy-related repairs, with the average grant being $2,000 per year. The elderly and families with children get first dibs. Contact your State Energy Office or the Weatherization Assistance Programs Branch, EE44, U.S. Department of Energy, 1000 Independence Ave., SW, Washington, DC 20585; 800-DIAL-DOE, 202-586-4074; {www.eren.doe.gov/EE/buildings-state.html}.

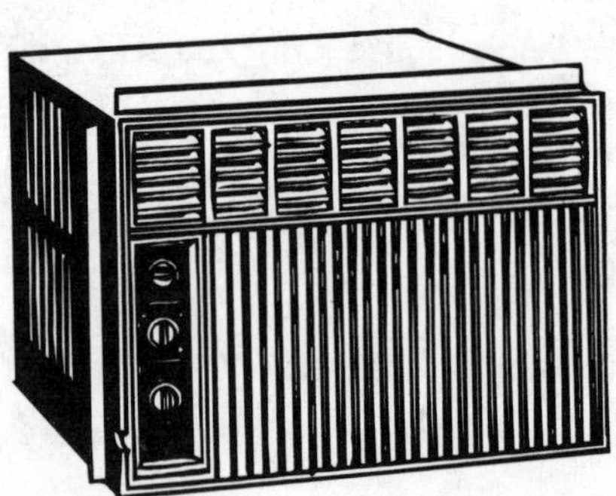

Free Housing Experts

The HUD website includes text of over 20 helpful guides, such as: *How To Buy a Home*, *How to Get A Mortgage*, and *Hud-approved Lenders*, as well as listings of government homes for sale. These are not just HUD homes, but also those from the Department of Veteran Affairs, General Services Administration, and more. Although the houses are not steals, you can find some great deals. For housing information, call HUD USER, P.O. Box 6091, Rockville, MD 20850; 800-245-2691; {www.huduser.org}.

$2,000 Grants or 2% Interest Loan To Fix Up Your Home

A family of 4 can be making close to $30,000 year and still be eligible for a 2% interest loan from local Community Action Agency. Some agencies also offer grants or are aware of other local organizations that provide grants. There are about 1,000 of them around the country to help neighborhoods.

To find an agency near you, contact National Association of Community Action

Agencies, 1100 17th St., NW, Suite 500, Washington, DC 20036, 202-265-7546; Fax: 202-265-8850; {www.nacaa.org}.

Free Weatherization, Fuel Bills, and Rent for Incomes Up to $50,000

If you are within a certain income and need help paying your heating bills, need money to make your house more energy efficient, or need funds for urgent repairs, call your local Community Action Agency. There are about 1,000 of them around the country to help neighborhoods. They will also come out and check if your home or apartment needs to be more energy efficient.

To find an agency near you, contact National Association of Community Action Agencies, 1100 17th St., NW, Suite 500, Washington, DC 20036; 202-265-7546; Fax: 202-265-8850; {www.nacaa.org}.

Also, your local utility can provide you with or refer you to other programs in your area to analyze your energy usage, recommend energy saving measures, provide fuel and utility assistance to retain or restore service, establish payment discounts based on income and usage, or establish affordable payment plans if you are in arrears. Contact your local utility company to take advantage of these services.

Free Furniture

The Community Action Agency in Albany, New York offers free furniture for those with a need because of fire or other hardship reasons. Other agencies offer free furniture if you are moving into a Community Action Agency's affordable housing or housing units operated by the agency. See if your local agency offers free furniture. There are about 1,000 of them around the country to help neighborhoods.

To find an agency near you, contact National Association of Community Action Agencies, 1100 17th St., NW, Suite 500, Washington, DC 20036; 202-265-7546; Fax: 202-265-8850; {www.nacaa.org}.

50% Discount On a New Heating System

The California Energy Commission offers residences and small businesses up to 50% of the cost of a new heating or air conditioning system if it meets their standards for “emerging renewable technologies,” like solar heating, but more.

Their program is called Emerging Renewables Buy-Down Program.

To learn more, contact California Energy Commission, Energy Call Center, 1516 Ninth St., MS-29, Sacramento, CA 95814; 800-555-7794; {www.consumerenergycenter.org}. Check with your state utility commission in the Appendix to see if your state offers similar programs.

New Home Help

Here's a listing of programs we found that were available at the time we were doing research. Don't forget to contact state and local housing agencies to see what may be available for you.

Nashville Housing Fund
P.O. Box 846
Nashville, TN 37202
615-252-8400
www.nashville.gov/mdha/index.htm

Washington County
Department of Housing Services
111 NE Lincoln St., Suite 200-L
Hillsboro, OR 97124
503-846-4794
www.co.washington.or.us/deptmts/hse_serv/housmain.htm

Indianapolis Neighborhood Housing Partnership
3550 N. Washington Blvd.
Indianapolis, IN 46205
317-925-1400
www.inhp.org

Department of Community Affairs
60 Executive Parks
Atlanta, GA 30329
800-651-0597
404-679-4940
www.dca.state.ga.us

State of New York Mortgage Agency
641 Lexington Ave.
New York, NY 10022
800-382-HOME
212-688-4000
www.nyhomes.org/sony/sonyma.html

Housing Hotline
Division of Housing
Kansas Dept. of Commerce and Housing
1000 SW Jackson St., Suite 100
Topeka, KS 66612-1354
785-296-3481
www.kansascommerce.com

Homes For Houston
P.O. Box 1562
Houston, TX 77251
713-868-8300
www.ci.houston.tx.us/departme/housing/

Iowa Finance Authority
100 E. Grand Ave., Suite 250
Des Moines, IA 50309
515-242-4990
800-432-7230
www.ifahome.com/home_buyer.htm

MN Housing Finance Agency
400 Sibley St., Suite 300
St. Paul, MN 55101
800-657-3769
651-296-7608
www.mhfa.state.mn.us

Missouri Housing Development Commission
3435 Broadway
Kansas City, MO 64111
816-759-6600
www.mhdc.com

Office of Community Development
P.O. Box 1471
Baton Rouge, LA 70802
225-389-3039
www.ci.baton-rouge.la.us/dept/ocd/Housing/housing.htm

New Hampshire Housing Finance Authority
32 Constitution Dr.
P.O. Box 5087
Bedford, NH 03110
800-640-7239
www.nhhfa.org

Oregon Housing and Community Services Department
1600 State St.
Salem, OR 97301
503-986-2000
www.hcs.state.or.us

Maine State Housing Authority
353 Water St.
Augusta, ME 04330
207-626-4600
800-452-4668
www.mainehousing.org

Community Development Dept.
1666 N. Main St.
Walnut Creek, CA 94596
925-943-5800
www.ci.walnut-creek.ca.us

South Carolina State Housing Finance and Development Authority
919 Bluff Rd.
Columbia, SC 29201
803-734-2207
www.sha.state.sc.us

Housing and Community Development
677 Queen St., Suite 300
Honolulu, HI 96813
808-587-0567
www.hcdch.state.hi.us/

$2,500 to Pay Your Insulation Bills

Storm windows, insulation, and even weatherstripping can help reduce your heating and cooling bills. The U.S. Department of Energy offers the Weatherization Assistance program.

As many as 20-30 million people are eligible for this program; everyone from homeowners to renters, from those who live in single or multi-family housing to those who lie in mobile homes. Each state varies on who is eligible for these services, but typically a family of four can make $24,000 and still qualify. Preference is given to persons over 60, those with disabilities and families with children. If you receive

Supplemental Security Income to Temporary Assistance to Needy Families, you are automatically eligible.

You must apply through your state weatherization agency. States allocate dollars to nonprofit agencies for purchasing and installing energy-related repairs, with an energy audit being the first step to determine what is necessary. The average grant is $2,500.

For more information on eligibility and where to apply in your state, contact Weatherization Assistance Programs Branch, EE44, U.S. Department of Energy, 1000 Independence Ave., SW, Washington, DC 20585; 800-DOE-3732; {www.eren.doe.gov/buildings/home_weatherizing.html}.

Alabama
Program Manager
Alabama Department of Economic and Community Affairs
401 Adams Avenue
P.O. Box 5690
Montgomery, AL 36103-5690
334-242-5365
Fax: 334-353-4311
www.adeca.state.al.us/

Alaska
Weatherization Program Manager
Alaska Housing Finance Corporation
P.O. Box 101020
Anchorage, AK 99510-1020
907-330-8192
Fax: 907-338-1747
www.ahfc.state.ak.us/

Arizona
Arizona Department of Commerce
3800 North Central Ave.
Suite 1500
Phoenix, AZ 85012
602-280-8115
Fax: 602-280-1445
www.commerce.state.az.us/

Division of County Operations
Office of Community Services
P.O. Box 1437, Slot# 1330
Little Rock, AR 72203-1437
501-682-8722
Fax: 501-682-6736

California
Department of Community Services and Development
700 North 10th Street
Sacramento, CA 95814-0338
916-341-4376
Fax: 916-319-5129
www.csd.ca.gov/

Colorado
Governor's Office of Energy Management and Conservation
225 E. 16th Avenue, Suite 650
Denver, CO 80203
303-894-2383
Fax: 303-894-2388
www.state.co.us/oemc/

Connecticut
Energy Services Program Supervisor
Department of Social Services
25 Sigourney Street, 10th Floor
Hartford, CT 06106-5033
860-424-5889
Fax: 860-424-4952
www.dss.state.ct.us/svcs/energy.htm

District of Columbia
District of Columbia Energy Office
2000 14th St., NW
Suite 300 East
Washington, DC 20009
202-673-6700
Fax: 202-673-6725
www.dcenergy.org

Delaware
Division of State Service Centers
Delaware Office of Community Service
1401 North Dupont Highway
New Castle, DE 19720
302-577-4965, ext. 232
Fax: 302-577-4973
www.state.de.us/dhss/dssc/dsschome.htm

Florida
Florida Energy Office
Dept. of Community Affairs
2555 Shumard Oak Boulevard
Tallahassee, FL 32399-2100
850-488-7541
Fax: 850-488-2488
http://dlis.dos.state.fl.us/fgils/agencies/energy.html

Georgia
Division of Energy Resources
Georgia Environmental Facilities Authority
100 Peachtree St., NW
Suite 2090
Atlanta, GA 30303
404-656-3826
Fax: 404-656-7970
www.gefa.org/energy_program.html

Hawaii
Office of Community Services
Department of Labor and Industrial Relations
830 Punchbowl Street
Room 420
Honolulu, HI 96813
808-586-8675
Fax: 808-586-8685
http://dlir.state.hi.us/

Idaho
Bureau of Benefit Program Operations
Department of Health and Welfare
P.O. Box 83720
Boise, ID 83720-0036
208-334-5753
Fax: 208-332-7343
www2.state.id.us/dhw/

Illinois
Division of Economic Opportunity
Department of Commerce and Community Affairs
620 East Adams Street, 4th Floor
Springfield, IL 62701
217-785-6135
Fax: 217-524-5904
www.commerce.state.il.us/

Indiana
Division of Family and Children
Housing and Community
Services Section
P.O. Box 6116
Indianapolis, IN 46206-6116
317-232-1997
Fax: 317-232-7079
www.state.in.us/fssa/families/

Iowa
Division of Community Action
Agencies
Department of Human Rights
Lucas State Office Building
Des Moines, IA 50319
515-242-6314
Fax: 515-242-6119
www.state.ia.us/government/dhr/

Kansas
Department of Commerce and
Housing
700 Southwest Harrison Street,
Suite 1300
Topeka, KS 66603-3712
785-296-2262
Fax: 785-296-8985
http://kdoch.state.ks.us/Program
App/index.jsp

Kentucky
Cabinet for Families and
Children
Department of Community
Based Services
275 East Main Street, 3W-B
Frankfort, KY 40621
502-564-3703
Fax: 502-564-6907
http://cfc.state.ky.us/

Louisiana
Louisiana Housing Finance
Agency
Energy Assistance Section
200 Lafayette, Suite 102
Baton Rouge, LA 70801
225-342-1320 ext. 304
Fax: 225-342-1310
www.lhfa.state.la.us/

Maine
Energy and Housing Services
Maine State Housing Authority
353 Water Street
Augusta, ME 04339-4633
207-626-4601
Fax: 207-624-5780
www.mainehousing.org

Maryland
Maryland Department of
Housing and Community
Development
100 Community Place
Crownsville, MD 21032-2023
410-514-7244
Fax: 410-514-7291
www.dhcd.state.md.us/

Massachusetts
Bureau of Energy Programs
Department of Housing and
Community Development
One Congress Street, 10th Floor
Boston, MA 02114
617-727-7004 ext. 533
Fax: 617-727-4259
www.state.ma.us/dhcd/addrbook
/default.htm

Michigan
Family Independence Agency
P.O. Box 30037
Grand Tower, Suite 1313
Lansing, MI 48909
517-335-5857
Fax: 517-335-5042
www.mfia.state.mi.us/

Minnesota
Energy Division Department of
Commerce
85 7th Place East, Suite 500
St. Paul, MN 55101-2198
651-284-3265
Fax: 651-297-7891
www.commerce.state.mn.us/

Mississippi
Weatherization Program
Manager
Mississippi Department of
Human Services
750 North State Street
Jackson, MS 39202
601-359-4772
Fax: 601-359-4370
www.mdhs.state.ms.us/

Missouri
Division of Energy
Dept. of Natural Resources
P.O. Box 176
Jefferson City, MO 65102-0176
573-751-7657
Fax: 573-751-6860
www.dnr.state.mo.us

Montana
Department of Public Health and
Human Services
P.O. Box 4210
Helena, MT 59601
406-447-4267
Fax: 406-447-4287
www.dphhs.state.mt.us/

Nebraska
Nebraska Energy Office
P.O. Box 95085
Lincoln, NE 68509-5085
402-471-3347
Fax: 402-471-3064
www.nol.org/home/NEO/

Nevada
Housing Division
1802 N. Carson St., Suite 154
Carson City, NV 89701
775-687-4258 x226
Fax: 775-687-4040
http://nvhousing.state.nv.us/

New Hampshire
Governor's Office of Energy and
Community Services
57 Regional Drive
Concord, NH 03301
603-271-6813
Fax: 603-271-2615
www.state.nh.us/governor/energ
ycomm/

New Jersey
New Jersey Department of
Community Affairs
P.O. Box 806
101 South Broad Street
Trenton, NJ 08625-0806
609-984-3301
Fax: 609-292-9798
www.state.nj.us/dca/

New Mexico
New Mexico Mortgage Finance
Authority
344 Fourth Street, SW
Albuquerque, NM 87102
505-843-6880

Fax: 505-243-3289
www.nmmfa.org/

New York
Energy Services Bureau
New York State Division of Housing and Community Renewal
38-40 State Street
Albany, NY 12207
518-473-3845
Fax: 518-474-9907
www.dhcr.state.ny.us

North Carolina
North Carolina Department of Health and Human Services
1110 Navaho Drive, Suite 106
Raleigh, NC 27609
919-981-5270
Fax: 919-981-5296
www.dhhs.state.nc.us/

North Dakota
ND Department of Commerce
Division of Community Services
400 East Broadway, Suite 50
P.O. Box 2057
Bismarck, ND 58502-2057
701-328-4140
Fax: 701-328-2308
www.state.nd.us/dcs/

Ohio
Office of Energy Efficiency
Ohio Department of Development
77 South High Street, Floor 26
Columbus, OH 43215-6108
614-466-8434
Fax: 614-466-1864
www.odod.state.oh.us/cdd/oee/default.htm

Oklahoma
Division of Community Affairs and Development
Oklahoma Department of Commerce
P.O. Box 26980
Oklahoma City, OK 73126-0980
405-815-5339
Fax: 405-815-5344
www.odoc.state.ok.us

Oregon
Oregon Housing and Community Services
123 Northeast 3rd St., Suite 470
Portland, OR 97232
503-963-2283
Fax: 503-230-8863
www.hcs.state.or.us/

Pennsylvania
Pennsylvania Department of Community and Economic Development
Forum Building, Room 352
Harrisburg, PA 17120
717-720-7439
www.inventpa.com

Rhode Island
Central Services Division
Rhode Island State Energy Office
One Capitol Hill
Providence, RI 02908-5890
401-222-3370
Fax: 401-222-1260
www.doa.state.ri.us

South Carolina
Office of the Governor
1205 Pendleton Street
Columbia, SC 29201
803-734-9861
Fax: 803-734-0356
www.state.sc.us/energy/

South Dakota
Office of Energy Assistance
Department of Social Services
206 West Missouri Avenue
Pierre, SD 57501-4517
605-773-4131
Fax: 605-773-6657
www.state.sd.us/social/ENERGY/

Tennessee
Tennessee Department of Human Services
Citizens Plaza Building
400 Deaderick Street, 14th Floor
Nashville, TN 37248-9500
615-313-4764
Fax: 615-532-9956
www.state.tn.us/humanserv/

Texas
Community Affairs Division
Texas Department of Housing and Community Affairs
P.O. Box 13941
Austin, TX 78711-3941
512-475-3864
Fax: 512-475-3935
www.tdhca.state.tx.us/

Utah
Division of Community Development
Utah Office of Energy Services
324 South State Street, Suite 500
Salt Lake City, UT 84111
801-538-8657
Fax: 801-538-8888
www.nr.utah.gov/energy/home.htm

Vermont
Vermont Office of Economic Opportunity Agency of Human Services
103 South Main Street
Waterbury, VT 05671-1801
802-241-2452
Fax: 802-241-2325
www.ahs.state.vt.us/oeo/

Virginia
Virginia Department of Housing and Community Development
501 North Second Street
Richmond, VA 23219-1321
804-371-7112
Fax: 804-371-7091
www.dhcd.state.va.us/

Washington
Office of Community Development
P.O. Box 48350
Olympia, WA 98504-8350
360-725-2948
Fax: 360-586-5880
www.cted.wa.gov/

West Virginia
Office of Economic Opportunity
950 Kanawha Boulevard, East
Charleston, WV 25301
304-558-8660
Fax: 304-558-4210
www.wvdo.org/

Wisconsin
Residential Efficiency Bureau
Department of Administration
Division of Energy
P.O. Box 8944
Madison, WI 53708-8944
608-266-7601
Fax: 608-264-6688
www.doa.state.wi.us/depb/weatherization/index.asp

Wyoming
Wyoming Department of Family Services
2300 Capitol Avenue, 3rd Floor
Cheyenne, WY 82002-0490
307-777-6346
Fax: 307-777-7747
http://dfsweb.state.wy.us/

$2,800 To Pay Your Heating Bill

Even if you are not approved for the U.S. Department of Energy's Weatherization Assistance Program, you might still be eligible for short-term assistance on your utility bill for the Low-Income Home Energy Assistance Program (LIHEAP). Funded by the U.S. Department of Health and Human Services, LIHEAP serves low-income families by offering heating and cooling subsidies, energy crisis intervention to assist in weather-related and fuel supply shortages and household energy-related emergencies, such as utility shutoffs. The amount of money and eligibility for this program varies from state to state, so you need to contact your state LIHEAP coordinator to learn how to apply.

Contact Office of Community Services, Division of Energy Assistance, Administration for Children and Families, U.S. Department of Health and Human Services, 370 L'Enfant Promenade, SW, 5th Floor West, Washington, DC 20447; 202-401-9351; toll-free 888-294-8662; {www.acf.dhhs.gov/programs/liheap}.

State Contacts

Alabama
Energy Section Supervisor
Alabama Department of Economic and Community Affairs
Community Services Division
P.O. Box 5690
Montgomery, AL 36103-5690
334-242-5365
Fax: 334-353-4311

Alaska
Energy Assistance Coordinator
Department of Health and Social Services
Division of Public Assistance
400 W. Willoughby Ave.
Room 301
Juneau, AK 99801-1700
907-465-3066
Fax: 907-465-3319
www.hss.state.ak.us/dpa/programs/hap.html
Public Inquiries: 1-800-470-3058

Arizona
Project Specialist
Community Services Administration
Arizona D of Economic Security
1789 W. Jefferson
Site Code 086z
P.O. Box 6123
Phoenix, AZ 85007
602-542-6600
Fax: 602-364-1756
www.de.state.az.us/links/csa_web/index.asp
Public Inquiries: 1-800-582-5706

Arkansas
Manager, Home Energy Assistance Program
Office of Community Services
Department of Human Services
P.O. Box 1437/Slot 1330
Little Rock, AR 72203-1437
501-682-8726
Fax: 501-682-6736
www.state.ar.us/dhs/dco/ocs/index.htm#haap
Public Inquiries: 1-800-432-0043

California
Chief Deputy Director
Department of Community Services and Development
700 North 10th St., Room 258
Sacramento, CA 95814
916-323-8694

Fax: 916-327-3153
www.csd.ca.gov/LIHEAP.htm
Public Inquiries: 1-800-433-4327

Colorado
Director, LIHEAP
Office of Self Sufficiency
Department of Human Services
1575 Sherman Street, 3rd Floor
Denver, CO 80203
303-866-5968
Fax: 303-866-5488
www.cdhs.state.co.us/oss/FAP/LEAP/LEAP.htm
Public Inquiries: 1-800-782-0721 or 303-866-5970

Connecticut
Program Supervisor
Energy Services Unit
Dept. Of Social Services
25 Sigourney Street, 10th Floor
Hartford, CT 06106
860-424-5889
Fax: 860-424-4952
www.dss.state.ct.us/svcs/energy.htm
Public Inquiries: 1-800-842-1132

Delaware
Management Analyst
Department of Health and Social Services
Division of State Service Centers
1901 N. Dupont Hwy.
New Castle, DE 19720
302-577-4965, ext. 231
Fax: 302-577-4973
1-800-464-HELP (4357)
New Castle County: 654-9295
Kent County: 674-1782
Sussex County: 856-6310
Public Inquiries: 1-800-464-HELP (4357)

District of Columbia
LIHEAP Director
Citizens Energy Resources Division
District of Columbia Energy Office
2000 14th St. N.W.
Washington, D.C. 20001
202-673-6727
Fax: 202-673-6725
www.dcenergy.org/programs/fuel.htm#LIHEAP
Public Inquiries: 202-673-6750 or 6700

Florida
Planning Manager
Community Assistance Section
Bureau of Community Assistance
Division of Housing and Community Development
Department of Community Affairs
2555 Shumard Oak Boulevard
Tallahassee, FL 32399-2100
850-922-1834
Fax: 850-488-2488
www.dca.state.fl.us/fhcd/programs/liheap
Public Inquiries: 850-488-7541

Georgia
Unit Chief
Community Services Section
Division of Family and Children Services
4 Department of Human Resources
Two Peachtree Street, N.W., Suite 19-268
Atlanta, GA 30303-3180
404-463-2016
Fax: 404-657-4480
www.state.ga.us/departments/dhr/energy.html
Public Inquiries: 1-800-869-1150

Hawaii
LIHEAP Coordinator
Department of Human Services
Benefit, Employment and Support Division (LIHEAP)
820 Mililani Street, Suite 606
Honolulu, HI 96813
808-586-5734
Fax: 808-586-5744
Public Inquiries: 1-808-586-5740

Idaho
Grants Unit Manager
Bureau of Benefit Program Operations
Idaho Department of Health and Welfare
P.O. Box 83720
Boise, ID 83720-0036
208-334-5753
Fax: 208-332-7343
Public Inquiries: 208-334-5730

Illinois
Chief, Office of Human Services
Dept. Of Commerce & Community Affairs
620 East Adams Street - CIPS-4
Springfield, IL 62701
www.commerce.state.il.us/resource_efficiency/Energy/LIHEAP.htm
Public Inquiries: 1-800-252-8643 or 217-785-6135

Indiana
Programs Specialist
Division of Children & Families
Indiana Family and Social Services Administration
P.O. Box 6116
Indianapolis, IN 46206-6116
317-232-7015
Fax: 317-232-7079
www.IN.gov/fssa/families/housing/eas.html
Public Inquiries: 1-800-622-4973

Iowa
Chief, Bureau of Energy Assistance
Division of Community Action Agencies
Department of Human Rights
Lucas State Office Building
Des Moines, IA 50319
515-281-0859
Fax: 515-242-6119
www.state.ia.us/government/dhr/caa/LIHEAP.html
Public Inquiries: 515-281-4204

Kansas
Energy Assistance Program Administrator
Economic Employment Support Services, DSRS
Docking State Office Bldg, 6th Floor
915 S.W. Harrison St.
Topeka, KS 66612-1505
785-296-3340
Fax: 785-296-0146

www.srskansas.org/ees/lieap.ht
m
Public Inquiries: 1-800-432-0043

Kentucky
Manager
Energy Assistance Branch, DMD
Cabinet for Families and Children
275 East Main Street, 2nd Floor
Frankfort, KY 40621
502-564-7536
Fax: 502-564-0328
http://cfc.state.ky.us/help/liheap.asp
Public Inquiries: 1-800-456-3452

Louisiana
Ms. Lawand Johnson, Program Manager
Louisiana Housing Finance Agency
Energy Assistance Section
200 Lafayette Street, Suite 102
Baton Rouge, LA 70801
225-342-1320, Ext. 304
Fax: 225-342-1339
www.lhfa.state.la.us/
Public Inquiries: 225-342-2288

Maine
LIHEAP Coordinator
Energy and Housing Services
Maine State Housing Authority
353 Water Street
Augusta, ME 04330
207-624-5708
Fax: 207-624-5780
www.bundlemeup.org/grants.ht
m
Public Inquiries: 1-800-452-4668

Maryland
Director, Home Energy Programs
Department of Human Resources
311 West Saratoga Street
Baltimore, MD 21202
410-767-7062
Fax: 410-333-0079
www.dhr.state.md.us/meap
Public Inquiries: 1-800-352-1446

Massachusetts
Director, Bureau of Energy Programs
Department of Housing and Community Development
One Congress Street, Suite 1001
Boston, MA 02114
617-727-7004, Ext. 533
Fax: 617-727-4259
www.state.ma.us/dhcd/compone
nts/dns/ htoha.htm
Winter Heating Helpline Website:
www.state.ma.us/winterheating/
Public Inquiries: 1-800-632-8175

Michigan
Director, Family Support Services
Michigan Family Independence Agency
235 S. Grand Avenue
Lansing, MI 48909
Fax: 517-241-8053
www.mfia.state.mi.us/1997fact.h
tm#a6-6
Public Inquiries: 1-800-292-5650

Minnesota
Energy Assistance Programs
Energy Division
Minnesota Department of Commerce
85 7th Place East, Suite 500
St. Paul, MN 55101-2198
651- 284-3275
Fax: 651-284-3277
www.commerce.state.mn.us/pag
es/Energy/mainassistance.htm

Mississippi
Branch Director
Division of Community Services
Mississippi Dept. Of Human Services
750 N. State Street
Jackson, MS 39202-4772
601 359-4766
Fax: 601-359-4370
www.mdhs.state.ms.us/cs_info.h
tml

Missouri
SS Manager, Energy Assistance
Division of Family Services
Department of Social Services
P.O. Box 88
Jefferson City, MO 65103
573-751-0472
Fax: 573-526-5592
www.dss.state.mo.us/dfs/liheap.
htm
Public Inquiries: 1-800-392-1261

Montana
Intergovernmental Human Services Bureau
Dept. of Public Health and Human Services
1400 Carter Drive
Helena, MT 59620
406-447-4260
Fax: 406-447-4287
Public Inquiries: 1-800-332-2272

Nebraska
Program and Planning Specialist
Program Assistance Unit
Department of Health and Human Services
301 Centennial Mall South, 4th Floor
P.O. Box 95026
Lincoln, NE 68509
402-471-9262
Fax: 402-471-9597
www.hhs.state.ne.us/fia/energy.h
tm
Public Inquiries: 1-800-430-3244

Nevada
Acting LIHEA Program Manager
Nevada Department of Human Resources
State Welfare Division
559 S. Saliman Rd., #101
Carson City, NV 89701-5040
775-687-6919
Fax: 775-687-1272
http://welfare.state.nv.us/benefit/
lihea.htm
Public Inquiries: 1-800-992-0900 (ext. 4420]

New Hampshire
Fuel Assistance Program Manager
Governor's Office of Energy and Community Services
57 Regional Drive
Concord, NH 03301-8519
603-271-8317
Fax: 603-271-2615
www.state.nh.us/governor/energycomm/assist.html

New Jersey
Coordinator
Home Energy Assistance Program
DHS, Division of Family Development
6 Quakerbridge Plaza,CN 716
Trenton, NJ 08625
609-588-2478
Fax: 609-588-3369
www.state.nj.us/humanservices/dfd/liheap.html
Public Inquiries: 1-800-510-3102

New Mexico
LIHEAP Program Manager
Income Support Division
Community Development & Commodities Bureau
New Mexico Human Services Department
5301 Central NE, Suite 1520
Albuquerque, NM 87108
505-841-6535 (Albuquerque Area)
1-800-283-4465 (Statewide)
Fax: 505-841-6522

New York
LIHEAP Coordinator
Division of Temporary Assistance
Office of Temporary and Disability Assistance
New York State Dept. of Family Assistance
40 North Pearl Street
Albany, NY 12243-0001
518-473-0332
Fax: 518-474-9347
Web Site:
www.otda.state.ny.us/otda/heap/default.htm
Public Inquiries: 1-800-342-3009

North Carolina
LIHEAP Coordinator
Division of Social Services
Department of Health and Human Services
325 North Salisbury Street
Raleigh, NC 27603-5905
919-733-7831
Fax: 919-733-0645
Web Site:
www.dhhs.state.nc.us/dss
Public Inquiries: 1-800-662-7030 (CARE LINE)

North Dakota
Assistant Director of Energy & Nutrition
Department of Human Services
State Capitol Building, Judicial Wing
600 E. Boulevard, Dept. 325
Bismarck, ND 58505-0250
701-328-4882
Fax: 701-328-1060
Web Site:
http://lnotes.state.nd.us/dhs/dhsweb.nsf/90c397dc8e2f73ad8625664300610449/7588ac9457b25c5886256a9c004dc544?Opendocument&Highlight=0,energy Opendocument&Highlight=0,energy
Public Inquiries: 701-328-2065

Ohio
Chief, OCS/HEAP
Ohio Dept. of Development
77 South High, 25th Floor
Columbus, OH 43216
614-644-6858
Fax: 614-728-6832
Web Site:
www.odod.state.oh.us/cdd/ocs/heap.htm
Public Inquiries: 1-800-282-0880 (TDD: 1-800-686-1557)

Oklahoma
Program Supervisor
Division of Family Support Services
Department of Human Services
P.O. Box 25352
Oklahoma City, OK 73125
405-521-4488
Fax: 405-521-4158
Email:
Melvin.Phillips@okdhs.org

Oregon
LIHEAP Program Manager
Oregon Department of Housing and Community Services
1600 State Street
Salem, OR 97310
503-986-2094
Fax: 503-986-2006
www.hcs.state.or.us/community_resources/energy_wx/index.html
Public Inquiries: 1-800-453-5511

Pennsylvania
Director
Division of Federal Programs
Department of Public Welfare
P.O. Box 2675
Harrisburg, PA 17105
717-772-7906
Fax: 717-772-6451
www.dpw.state.pa.us/oim/oimliheap.asp
Public Inquiries: 1-800-692-7462

Rhode Island
Program Manager
Dept. Of Administration
Division Of Central Services
State Energy Office
One Capitol Hill
Providence, RI 02908-5850
401-222-6920, ext. 112
Fax: 401-222-1260
Public Inquiries: 1-800-253-4328
or 401-222-6920

South Carolina
Program Manager for Energy
Division of Economic Opportunity
Suite 342, 1205 Pendleton Street
Columbia, SC 29201
803-734-9861

South Dakota
Administrator, Office of Energy Assistance
Department of Social Services

206 W. Missouri Avenue
Pierre, SD 57501-4517
605-773-4131/3668
Fax: 605-773-6657
www.state.sd.us/social/ENERGY/
Public Inquiries: 1-800-233-8503

Tennessee
Program Specialist
Department of Human Services
Citizens Plaza Building
400 Deaderick Street
Nashville, TN 37248
615-313-4764

Texas
Program Manager
Energy Assistance Section
Texas Dept. of Housing and Community Affairs
P.O. Box 13941
Austin, TX 78711-3941
512-475-3864
Fax: 512-475-3935
www.tdhca.state.tx.us/ea.htm
Public Inquiries: 1-877-399-8939

Utah
Program Manager, HEAT & SNAPS
Department of Community & Economic Development
324 South State, Suite 500
Salt Lake City, UT 84111
801-538-8644
Fax: 801-538-8888
www.dced.state.ut.us/community/heat.html
Public Inquiries: 1-877-488-3233

Vermont
Fuel Assistance Program Chief
Office of Home Heating Fuel Assistance
Department of Prevention, Assistance, Transition, and Health Access
103 South Main Street
Waterbury, VT 05676
802-241-2994
Fax: 802-241-1394
www.dsw.state.vt.us/districts/fuel/index.htm
Public Inquiries: 1-800-479-6151 or 1-802-241-1165

Virginia
Energy & Emergency Assistance Unit
Division of Benefit Programs
Virginia Department of Social Services
Theater Row Building
730 E. Broad Street, 7th Floor
Richmond, VA 23219-1849
804-692-1751
Fax: 804-225-2196
www.dss.state.va.us/benefit/energyasst.html
Public Inquiries: 1-800-552-3431 or 1-800-230-6977

Washington
LIHEAP (EPA/ECIP) Coordinator
Washington Department of Community, Trade and Economic Development
906 Columbia Street, S.W.
P.O. Box 48300
Olympia, WA 98504-8300
360-725-2854
Fax: 360-586-0489
www.liheapwa.org
Public Inquiries: 360-725-2854

West Virginia
LIHEAP Coordinator
Office of Family Support
West Virginia Department of Health and Human Resources
350 Capitol Street, Room B-18
Charleston, WV 25301-3704
304-558-8290
Fax: 304-558-2059
Public Inquiries: 304-558-8290

Wisconsin
Director, Energy Services
Wisconsin Department of Administration
P.O. Box 8944
Madison, WI 53708-8944
608-267-7601
Fax: 608-264-6688
www.doa.state.wi.us/depb/boe/index.asp
Public Inquiries: 608-267-3680

Wyoming
Program Manager
Department Of Family Services
Room #388 Hathaway Building
2300 Capitol Avenue
Cheyenne, WY 82002-0490
307-777-6346
Fax: 307-777-7747
http://dfsweb.state.wy.us/fieldop/briefing5a.htm
Public Inquiries: 1-800-246-4221

States Will Pay Your Property Taxes

Or pay part of the amount. Almost all states have some type of property or homestead tax exemption for the elderly and disabled, and often those with low incomes or veterans. How the program operates varies from state to state, with some states offering a reduced tax rate off of a percentage of the home's value. Other states offer a property tax deferral program for the elderly, where the state would pay the homeowner's property taxes. This would be considered a loan, and the equity would be the value of the home. The loan would be repaid when the home was sold or the homeowner dies. Contact your state or county tax office to see what your area offers.

State Tax Agencies

Alabama
Alabama Department of Revenue
50 N. Ripley
Montgomery, AL 36132-7123
334-242-1170
www.ador.state.al.us/advalorem/index.html
Alabama Homestead Exemption provides property tax exemption for citizens over 65 years of age on homes on less than 160 acres of land. Permanent & totally disabled citizens may also apply for the homestead exemption. Certain income levels also apply.

Alaska
Alaska State Office Building
333 Willoughby Ave., 11th Floor
P.O. Box 110400
Juneau, AK 99811-0400
907-465-2300
Fax: 907-465-2389
www.revenue.state.ak.us/
Alaska has a Permanent Fund Dividend Program. You must meet certain requirements such as residency to apply. Contact the state office for more information.

Arizona
Arizona Department of Revenue
1600 W. Monroe
Phoenix, AZ 85007
602-542 3572
Fax: 602-542-3867
www.revenue.state.az.us/

Arkansas
Office of Excise Tax Administration
P. O. Box 8054
Room 234, Ledbetter Bldg.
Little Rock, AR 72203
501-682-7106
Fax: 501-682-7900
www.state.ar.us/dfa/
Arkansas provides for a reduction in the amount of real property taxes assessed on the homestead of each taxpayer beginning with the 2000 assessment year. To claim this credit you must contact your local County Collector.

California
California Franchise Tax Board
P.O. Box 942840
Sacramento, CA 94240-0040
800-852-5711
www.ftb.ca.gov/geninfo/hra/index.html
California provides a Homeowner Assistance Program that allows a once-a-year payment from the State of California to qualified individuals based on part of the property taxes assessed and paid on their homes. You may be eligible if you were 62 years of age or older, blind, or disabled, owned and lived in your own home, and had a limited income. There is also a Renter Assistance Program.

Colorado
Colorado Division of Property Taxation
222 S. 6th, #410
Grand Junction, CO 81501
303-866-2371
www.dola.state.co.us/PropertyTax/
The Colorado Department of Local Affairs, Division of Property Taxation Department administers the Senior Homestead Exemption Program. To qualify residents must be 65 years of age or older, a 10 year owner of the residence and they must currently occupy the residence. Fifty percent of the first $200,000 value of the property is exempt from taxes. The state will pay the exempted property tax.

Connecticut
Department of Policy and Management
450 Capitol Avenue
Hartford, CT 06106-1308

860-418-6200
Fax: 860-418-6487
www.drs.state.ct.us/pubs/IP's/2001/ip01-12.html
There are property tax and rental exemptions for the elderly and disabled.

Delaware
Delaware Division of Revenue
820 N. French Street
Wilmington, DE 19801
302-323-2600
Fax: 302-577-8202
www.state.de.us/revenue/index.htm
Delaware provide property tax and school tax exemption to the disabled and elderly residents 65 years and older with certain income limitations.

District of Columbia
Office of Tax and Revenue
Real Property Tax Administration
941 North Capitol Street, NE, 4th Floor
Washington, DC 20002
202-727-4TAX
http://cfo.dc.gov/services/tax/property/credits.shtm
The District of Columbia provides for a variety of property tax relief including: homestead deductions, property tax deferral, senior citizen and low-income exemptions.

Florida
Tax Information Services
Florida Department Of Revenue
1379 Blountstown Hwy.
Tallahassee, FL 32304-2716
800-352-3671
850-488-6800
www.state.fl.us/dor/property/exemptions.html
Every person who has legal or equitable title to real property in the State of Florida and who resides on the property may be eligible for a homestead exemption. Check to see if you qualify to reduce your property taxes. There are additional exemptions for elderly and disabled homeowners.

Georgia
Georgia Department of Revenue
Property Tax Division offices
4245 International Parkway, Suite A
Hapeville, Georgia 30354-3918
404-968-0707
Fax: 404-968-0778
www2.state.ga.us/departments/dor/ptd/adm/taxguide/exempt/homestead2.html
There are several types of homeowner tax relief. The homestead exemption exempts a portion of the value of the home from property tax. The basic homestead exemption is not age or income dependent and varies from county to county. Other larger exemptions are age and income dependent. Contact the office or web site for your specific situation.

Hawaii
Hawaii Department of Taxation
P.O. Box 259
Honolulu, Hawaii 96809-0259
808-587-4242
Fax: 808-587-1488
www.state.hi.us/tax/tax.html

Idaho
Idaho State Tax Commission
PO Box 36
Boise, ID 83722-0410
208-334-7500
800-972-7660
www2.state.id.us/tax/index.html
Idaho provides a "Circuit Breaker" program that gives property tax relief to the elderly, disabled, and veterans with a qualifying income. This program is administered at a local level.

Illinois
Illinois Department of Revenue
Willard Ice Building
101 West Jefferson Street
Springfield, IL 62702
217-782-3336
www.revenue.state.il.us/LocalGovernment/PropertyTax/general.htm
Illinois provides for a number of tax relief provisions. Homeowners 65 year and older with total household income of less than $25,000 may qualify for tax relief. Veteran also may be eligible for property tax exemption up to $58,000 of the value of the assessed value.

Indiana
Indiana Department of Revenue
Department of Local Government Finance
100 N. Senate Ave, N-1058
Indianapolis, IN 46204
317-233-8285
www.in.gov/dlgf/
Indiana has property tax deductions for the elderly and the disabled; each has different requirements. Indiana also has a homestead credit and standard deduction, which all homeowners are eligible to receive. All of these are filed in the office of the county auditor where the property is located.

Iowa
Iowa Department of Revenue and Finance
Taxpayer Services
P.O. Box 10457

Des Moines, IA 50306-0457
515-281-4040
www.state.ia.us/tax/index.html
To be eligible for property tax reduction Iowa residents must meet certain income levels and be 65 years old or totally disabled and 18 years of age or older.

Kansas
Kansas Department of Revenue
Docking State Office Building
915 SW Harrison St.
Topeka, KS 66625-0001
785-368-8222
Fax: 785-291-3614
www.ksrevenue.org/pvd/main.html
There are currently no homestead property exemptions in Kansas.

Kentucky
Kentucky Revenue Cabinet
200 Fair Oaks Lane
Frankfort, KY 40620
502-564-4581
http://revenue.state.ky.us/property_info.htm
The homestead exemption in Kentucky is for homeowners who are at least 65 years of age.

Louisiana
Louisiana Tax Commission
P. O. Box 66788
Baton Rouge, LA 70896-6788
504-925-7830
Fax: 504-925-7827
http://leap.ulm.edu/LaGin/rtdepar/ltaxcomm.htm
Louisiana's homestead program provides property tax exemptions for homeowners 65 years and older.

Maine
Maine Property Tax Division
14 Edison Drive
Augusta, ME 04332
207-287-2011
Fax: 207-287-6396
www.state.me.us/revenue/propertytax/homepage.html
Maine provides a property tax or rent refund if you meet residency and income qualifications. They also provide a program for the disabled and elderly.

Maryland
Maryland State Department of Assessments and Taxation
301 W. Preston St.
Baltimore, MD 21201
410-767-1184
www.dat.state.md.us/sdatweb/homestead.html
The State of Maryland has developed a program that allows credits against the homeowner's or renter's property tax bill if the property taxes exceed a fixed percentage of the person's gross income. In other words, it sets a limit on the amount of property taxes any homeowner must pay based upon his or her income. There are many tax exemptions for the disabled, veterans, elderly, and charitable property. Check with the Maryland State Department of Assessments and Taxation for details on your specific situation.

Massachusetts
Massachusetts Department of Revenue
51 Sleeper Street
Boston, MA 02205
617-626-2201
www.dor.state.ma.us/help/taxtalk/105.htm
The credit for real estate taxes paid for persons Age 65 and Older, also known as the "Circuit Breaker" allows certain senior citizens in Massachusetts to claim a credit on their state income tax returns for the real estate taxes paid on their Massachusetts residential property.

Michigan
Michigan Department of Treasury
Lansing, MI 48922
517-373-3200
800-487-7000
www.michigan.gov/treasury/
Michigan has several options for homestead tax reduction. Contact your state and local agencies to determine your level of savings.

Minnesota
Minnesota Department of Revenue
Mail Station 5510
St. Paul, MN 55146-5510
651-296-3781
www.taxes.state.mn.us/proptax/factshts/prop.html
Minnesota has a Senior Citizens Property Tax Deferral program which is a low interest loan from the state, not a tax forgiveness program. The deferred tax is paid by the state to your county. Interest will be charged on this loan. Michigan also has a Special Agricultural Homestead program for qualifying farms.

Mississippi
Mississippi State Tax Commission
P.O. Box 1033
Jackson, MS 39215-1033
601-923-7000
www.mstc.state.ms.us/taxareas/property/rules/homerul s.htm

Mississippi has two kinds of homestead exemptions: regular and special. Each program has its own criteria for qualification.

Missouri
Missouri Department of Revenue
Harry S Truman State Office Building
301 West High Street
Jefferson City, MO 65101
573-751-5337
http://dor.state.mo.us/tax/ptcinfo.htm
Missouri has a property tax exemption that is determined by income. Check with your tax office or the web site to see if you qualify.

Montana
Montana Department of Revenue
P.O. Box 5805
Helena, MT. 59604-5805
406-444-6900
Montana has property exemption programs for veterans, disabled persons, the elderly and low-income families.

Nebraska
Nebraska Department of Revenue
301 Centennial Mall South
P.O. Box 94818
Lincoln, NE 68509-4818
402-471-5729
www.revenue.state.ne.us/
Nebraska has property exemption for persons over 65, certain disabled individuals and certain disabled veterans and their widows.

Nevada
Nevada Department of Taxation
1550 E. College Parkway, Suite 115
Carson City NV 89706
775-687-4892
Fax: 775-687-5981
http://tax.state.nv.us/
Homesteads are handled on a county level and apply to all taxpayers. Contact Nevada Department on Aging for Senior Citizens Property Tax Assistance Act.

New Hampshire
Department of Revenue Administration
45 Chenell Drive
PO Box 457
Concord, NH 03302-0457
603-271-2191
Fax: 603-271-6121
www.state.nh.us/revenue/property_tax/index.htm
New Hampshire has a Property Tax Hardship Relief Program to help families pay their property taxes.

New Jersey
New Jersey Division of Taxation
Office of Information and Publications
PO Box 281
Trenton, NJ 08695-0281
609-292-6400
www.state.nj.us/treasury/taxation/
New Jersey has property exemption programs for the disabled, the elderly and low- income families.

New Mexico
New Mexico Taxation And Revenue Department:
1100 S. St. Francis Dr.
P.O. Box 630
Santa Fe, NM 87504-0630
505-827-0870
Fax: 505-827-0782
www.state.nm.us/tax/
New Mexico provides a Property Tax Rebate for citizens age 65 and older.

New York
New York State Tax Department
Taxpayer Assistance Bureau
W. A. Harriman Campus
Albany, NY 12227
800-225-5829
www.tax.state.ny.us/
New York States Real Property Tax Credit is available to low-income families and residents 65 years old and older. Most taxpayers receive relief through exemptions to their property assessments for school tax purposes. The exemptions vary depending on the age of the taxpayer, income, and the county where the property is located.

North Carolina
North Carolina Property Tax Division
P.O. Box 871
Raleigh, NC 27602
919-733-7711
Fax: 919-733-1821
www.dor.state.nc.us/practitioner/property/index.html
North Carolina has property tax exemptions for elderly and disability persons and disabled veterans.

North Dakota
Office of State Tax Commissioner
State Capitol
600 E. Boulevard Avenue
Bismarck, ND 58505-0599
www.state.nd.us/taxdpt/forms/property.html
North Dakota provides property tax credits for homeowners and renters who are disabled or 65 years old or older.

Ohio
Ohio Department of Taxation
30 E. Broad Street, 22nd Floor
Columbus, OH 43215
888-644-6778
Fax: 614-466-6401
www.state.oh.us/tax/
Ohio's Homestead tax relief is granted to qualified elderly and disabled homeowners.

Oklahoma
Oklahoma Tax Commission
Post Office Box 26850
Oklahoma City, OK 73126-0850
405-521-3178
www.oktax.state.ok.us/
Oklahoma offers a homestead exemption for homeowners. A taxpayer who is at least 65 years old, or who is totally disabled, and whose gross household income from all sources does not exceed the current income levels may apply for a homestead exemption that reduces the assessed value of a taxpayer's actual residence.

Oregon
Oregon Department of Revenue
955 Center Street NE
Salem, OR 97301-2555
503-378-4988
www.dor.state.or.us/
Oregon offers property tax deferral programs for disabled and senior citizens age 62 and older. There is also a tax exemption for veterans.

Pennsylvania
Pennsylvania Dept Of Revenue
Property Tax Or Rent Rebate Program
Dept 280503
Harrisburg, PA 17128-0503
717-787-8201
www.revenue.state.pa.us/revenue/cwp/browse.asp
The Property Tax or Rent Rebate Program provides residents 65 years of age or older, widows or widowers 50 years of age or older and the permanently disabled 18 years of age or older meeting income eligibility requirements, rebates of paid property tax or rent.

Rhode Island
One Capitol Hill
Providence, RI 02908
401-222-2909
401-274-3676
www.tax.state.ri.us/
Rhode Island provides Property assistance for low-income families. This program is administered through the local government agencies.

South Carolina
South Carolina Department of Revenue
Post Office Box 125
Columbia, SC 29214
803-898-5480
www.sctax.org/
South Carolina provides a homestead exemption to residents who are 65 years of age, who are totally disabled or who are totally blind.

South Dakota
South Dakota Department of Revenue
445 East Capitol Avenue
Pierre, SD 57501
800-TAX-9188
605-773-3311
Fax: 605-773-5129
www.state.sd.us/revenue/spcltax.htm
To receive a property tax refund on your home, you must meet the residence, age or disability and income requirements.

Tennessee
Tennessee Comptroller of the Treasury
Property Tax Relief Program
1600 James K. Polk Building
505 Deaderick Street
Nashville, TN 37243-0278
615-747-8858
www.comptroller.state.tn.us/pa/patxr.htm
Tennessee provides tax relief for residence 65 years and older, totally disabled residence and veterans.

Texas
Comptroller of Public Accounts
111 E. 17th Street
Austin, TX 78774
512-305-9999
www.cpa.state.tx.us/taxinfo/proptax/proptax.html
Texas provides for several types of exemptions. All residence may receive a homestead exemption for their home's value for school taxes. Additional exemptions are available for disabled, veterans and homeowners 65 and older.

Utah
Utah Tax Commission
210 North 1950 West
Salt Lake City, UT 84134
801-297-3600
801-297-3699
www.tax.ex.state.ut.us/property/index.html
Utah provides abatement and deferral programs for veterans, disabled and low-income residence age 65 or older.

Vermont
Vermont Department of Taxes
109 State Street
Montpelier, VT 05609-1401
www.state.vt.us/tax/index.htm
Vermont provides a School Property Tax adjustment that is based on family income.

Virginia
Virginia Department of Taxation
Office of Customer Services
Post Office Box 1115
Richmond, VA 23218-1115
804-367-8031
www.tax.state.va.us/

Washington
Washington Department of Revenue
2101 4th Ave
Suite 1400
Seattle, WA 98121-2300
206-956-3002
Fax: 425-956-3037
Any homeowner or mobile home owner is eligible if they use their home as their principal residence, have a limited income, and will be age 61 by December 31st or is a disabled person of any age.

West Virginia
West Virginia Property Tax Division
P.O. Box 2389
Charleston, WV 25328-2389
304-558-3940
www.state.wv.us/taxdiv/
West Virginia provides a Homestead program for veterans, disabled homeowners and elderly 65 years and older.

Wisconsin
Wisconsin Department of Revenue
P.O. Box 34
Madison, WI 53786-0001
608-266-1657
Fax: 608-267-8964
www.dor.state.wi.us/

Wyoming
Wyoming Department of Revenue
Herschler Bldg, 2nd Floor West
122 West 25th Street
Cheyenne, WY 82002-0110
307-777-7961
http://revenue.state.wy.us/revframe.htm
Wyoming provides for property tax relief for veterans and other residence.

$328 a Month Towards Rent

In some parts of the country, a family of four can make up to $61,700 and still qualify for this program! The U.S. Department of Housing and Urban Development (HUD) offers a variety of rental assistance under the Section 8 Program. Public housing was established to provide decent and safe rental housing for eligible low-income families, the elderly, and persons with disabilities. Public housing comes in all sizes and types, from scattered single family houses to high-rise apartments for elderly families. There are approximately 1.3 million households living in public housing units, managed by some 3,300 housing agencies.

In addition to public housing, there are many different voucher programs designed to assist very low-income families, the elderly, and the disabled to afford decent, safe, and sanitary housing in the private market. Participants are often able to find their own housing, including single-family homes, townhouses and apartments. The Vouchers are administered locally by public housing agencies (PHAs). A family that is issued a housing voucher is responsible for finding a suitable housing unit of the family's choice where the owner agrees to rent under the program. A housing subsidy is paid to the landlord directly by the PHA on behalf of the participating family. The family then pays the difference between the actual rent charged by the landlord and the amount subsidized by the program. Under certain circumstances, if authorized by the PHA, a family may use its voucher to purchase a modest home. A voucher holder must pay 30% of its monthly adjusted gross income for rent and utilities.

Some voucher options include:

- Housing Choice Vouchers—allows very low-income families to choose and lease or purchase safe, decent, and affordable privately-owned rental housing.
- Conversion Vouchers—assists PHAs with the relocation or replacement housing needs that result from the demolition, disposition, or mandatory conversion of public housing units.
- Family Unification Vouchers—made available to families for whom the lack of adequate housing is a primary factor in the separation, or threat of imminent separation of children from their families or in the prevention of reunifying the children with their families.
- Homeownership Vouchers—assist first-time homeowners with their monthly homeownership expenses. The home must pass an initial housing quality standards t conducted by the PHA and an independent home inspection before the PHA may approve the purchase by the family.
- Mainstream Program Vouchers—enable families having a person with disabilities to lease affordable private housing of their choice. Vouchers also assist persons with disabilities who often face difficulties in locating suitable and accessible housing on the private market.
- Welfare to Work Vouchers—extra housing choice vouchers were awarded for this program to help families who have a critical need for housing in order to obtain or retain viable employment. Housing authorities are to work with others to ensure assistance is combined with job training, childcare, and other services families need.

WHO IS ELIGIBLE?

Section 8 rental assistance is limited to low-income families and individuals. A housing agency determines your eligibility based on: 1) annual gross income; 2) whether you qualify as elderly, a person with a disability, or as a family; and 3) U.S. citizenship or eligible immigration status. If you are eligible, the housing agency will check your references to make sure you and your family will be good tenants. Housing agencies will deny admission to any applicant whose habits and practices may be expected to have a detrimental effect on other tenants or on the project's environment.

Housing Agencies use **income limits** developed by HUD. HUD sets the lower income limits at 80% and very low income limits at 50% of the median income for the county or metropolitan area in which you choose to live. **Income limits** vary from area to area so you may be eligible at one housing agency but not at another. The Housing Agency serving your community can provide you with the income levels for your area and family size, or you can also find the income limits on the internet.

HOW DO I APPLY?

If you are interested in applying for public housing or the voucher programs, contact your housing agency, which can be found by contacting your city or county government, or you may contact your state U.S. Department of Housing and Urban Development (HUD). Not all Public Housing Agencies offer all vouchers, and there is often a waiting list. Once you get a voucher, you are frequently allowed to use the voucher outside the jurisdiction of the Public Housing Agency. If you are interested in applying for rental assistance, contact the local public housing agency or HUD office near you; {www.hud.gov}.

Contact the resource center through their toll-free number at 1-800-955-2232 from 9:00 a.m. to 6:00 p.m., Eastern Standard Time (EST) daily Monday through Friday.

U.S. Department of Housing and Urban Development
451 7th Street S.W.
Washington, DC 20410
Telephone: (202) 708-1112
TTY: (202) 708-1455
www.hud.gov

HUD State Offices

National Office
U.S. Department of Housing and Urban Development
451 7th Street, S.W.
Washington, DC 20410
202-708-1112
www.hud.gov

Alabama
HUD - Birmingham Office
950 22nd St N, Suite 900
Birmingham, AL 35203-2617
205-731-2630

Alaska
HUD Anchorage Office
949 East 36th Avenue, Suite 401
Anchorage, AK 99508-4399
907-271-4170
Fax: 907-271-3778
www.hud.gov/local/anc/index.html

Arizona
HUD Phoenix Office
400 North Fifth St., Suite 1600
Phoenix, AZ 85004-2361
602-379-4434
Fax: 602-379-3985

Tucson Area Office
HUD Tucson Office
160 North Stone Ave., Suite 100
Tucson, AZ 85701-1467
520-670-6000
Fax: 520-670-6207

Arkansas
HUD Little Rock Office
425 West Capitol Avenue #900
Little Rock, AR 72201-3488
501-324-5401
Fax: 501-324-6142
www.hud.gov/local/lrk/index.html

California
HUD - San Francisco Office
450 Golden Gate Avenue
San Francisco, CA 94102-3448
415-436-6560
Fax: 415-436-6446

Fresno Area Office
HUD - Fresno Office
2135 Fresno Street, Suite 100
Fresno, CA 93721-1718
559-487-5032
Fax: 559-487-5191
www.hud.gov/local/lrk/index.html

Los Angeles Area Office
HUD Los Angeles Office
611 W. Sixth Street, Suite 800
Los Angeles, CA 90017
213-894-8007
Fax: 213-894-8110
www.hud.gov/local/los/index.html

Sacramento Area Office
HUD Sacramento Office
925 L Street
Sacramento, CA 95814
916-498-5220
Fax: 916-498-5262
www.hud.gov/local/sac/index.html

San Diego Area Office
HUD San Diego Office
Symphony Towers
750 B Street, Suite 1600
San Diego, CA 92101-8131
619-557-5310
Fax: 619-557-5312
www.hud.gov/local/sdg/index.html

Santa Ana Area Office
HUD Santa Ana Office
1600 N. Broadway, Suite 100
Santa Ana, CA 92706-3927
714-796-5577
Fax: 714-796-1285
www.hud.gov/local/sna/index.html

Caribbean Office
HUD Caribbean Office
171 Carlos E. Chardon Avenue

San Juan, PR 00918-0903
787-766-5201
Fax: 787-766-5995

Colorado
HUD Denver Office
633 17th Street, 14th Floor
Denver, CO 80202-3607
303-672-5440
Fax: 303-672-5004
www.hud.gov/local/den/index.ht
ml

Connecticut
HUD - Hartford Office
One Corporate Center
Hartford, CT 06103-3220
860-240-4844
Fax: 860-240-4850
www.hud.gov/local/har/index.ht
ml

Delaware
HUD - Wilmington Office
920 King Street, Suite 404
Wilmington, DE 19801-3016
302-573-6300
Fax: 302-573-6259
www.hud.gov/local/wil/index.ht
ml

District of Columbia
HUD Washington, DC Office
820 First Street NE Suite 300
Washington, DC 20002-4205
202-275-9200
Fax: 202-275-9212
www.hud.gov/local/was/index.ht
ml

Florida
HUD Florida State Office
909 SE First Avenue
Miami, FL 33131
305-536-5678
Fax: 305-536-5765
www.hud.gov/local/fso/index.ht
ml

Jacksonville Area Office
HUD - Jacksonville Office
301 West Bay Street, Suite 2200
Jacksonville, FL 32202-5121
904-232-2627
Fax: 904-232-3759
www.hud.gov/local/jkv/index.ht
ml

Orlando Area Office
HUD - Orlando Office
3751 Maguire Blvd., Room 270
Orlando, FL 32803-3032
407-648-6441
Fax: 407-648-6310
www.hud.gov/local/orl/index.ht
ml

Tampa Area Office
HUD Tampa Office
500 Zack Street, Suite 402
Tampa, FL 33602
813-228-2026
Fax: 813-228-2431
www.hud.gov/local/tam/index.ht
ml

Georgia
40 Marietta Street - Five Points
Plaza
Atlanta, GA 30303-2806
404-331-4111
Fax: 404-730-2392
www.hud.gov/local/atl/index.ht
ml

Hawaii
HUD Honolulu Office
500 Ala Moana Blvd. Suite3A
Honolulu, HI 96813-4918
808-522-8175
Fax: 808-522-8194
www.hud.gov/local/hon/index.ht
ml

Idaho
HUD Boise Office
Plaza IV, Suite 220
800 Park Boulevard
Boise, ID 83712-7743
208-334-1990
Fax: 208-334-9648
www.hud.gov/local/boi/index.ht
ml

Illinois
Ralph Metcalfe Federal Building
77 West Jackson Boulevard
Chicago, IL 60604-3507
312-353-5680
Fax: 312-886-2729
www.hud.gov/local/chi/index.ht
ml

Springfield Area Office
HUD - Springfield Office
320 West Washington 7th Floor
Springfield, IL 62707
217-492-4120
Fax: 217-492-4154
www.hud.gov/local/chi/index.ht
ml

Indiana
HUD Indianapolis Office
151 N. Delaware St., Suite 1200
Indianapolis, IN 46204-2526
317-226-6303
Fax: 317-226-6317
www.hud.gov/local/ind/index.ht
ml

Iowa
HUD Des Moines Office
210 Walnut Street, Room 239
Des Moines, IA 50309-2155
515-284-4573
Fax: 515-284-4743
www.hud.gov/local/des/index.ht
ml

Kansas
HUD Kansas City Office
400 State Avenue, Room 200
Kansas City, KS 66101-2406
913-551-5462
Fax: 913-551-5469
www.hud.gov/local/kan/index.ht
ml

Kentucky
HUD - Louisville Office
601 West Broadway
Louisville, KY 40202
502-582-5251
Fax: 502-582-6074
www.hud.gov/local/lou/index.ht
ml

Louisiana
HUD New Orleans Office
Hale Boggs Bldg.
501 Magazine Street, 9th Floor
New Orleans, LA 70130-3099
504-589-7201
Fax: 504-589-6619
www.hud.gov/local/nor/index.ht
ml

Shreveport Area Office
HUD Shreveport Office
401 Edwards Street, Room. 1510
Shreveport, LA 71101-3289

318-676-3440
Fax: 318-676-3407
www.hud.gov/local/shr/index.ht
ml

Maine
HUD - Bangor Office
202 Harlow Street
Chase Bldg. Suite 101
Bangor, ME 04402-1384
207-945-0468
Fax: 207-945-0533
www.hud.gov/local/ban/index.ht
ml

Maryland
HUD Baltimore Office
5th Floor, 10 South Howard St.
Baltimore, MD 21201-2505
410-962-2520
Fax: 410-962-1849
www.hud.gov/local/bal/index.ht
ml

Massachusetts
HUD - Boston Office
10 Causeway Street, Room 301
Boston, MA 02222-1092
617-994-8200
Fax: 617-565-6558
www.hud.gov/local/bos/index.ht
ml

Michigan
HUD Detroit Office
477 Michigan Avenue
Detroit, MI 48226-2592
313-226-7900
Fax: 313-226-5611
www.hud.gov/local/det/index.ht
ml

Flint Area Office
HUD Flint Office
1101 S. Saginaw St.
Flint, MI 48502-1953
810-766-5110
Fax: 810-766-5122
www.hud.gov/local/fli/index.ht
ml

Grand Rapids Area Office
HUD Grand Rapids Office
Trade Center Building
50 Louis Street, N.W.
Grand Rapids, MI 49503-2633
616-456-2100
Fax: 616-456-2114
www.hud.gov/local/gra/index.ht
ml

Minnesota
HUD Minneapolis Office
220 Second Street, South
Minneapolis, MN 55401-2195
612-370-3000
Fax: 612-370-3220
www.hud.gov/local/min/index.ht
ml

Mississippi
HUD Jackson Office
McCoy Federal Building
100 W. Capitol St., Room 910
Jackson, MS 39269-1096
601-965-4700
Fax: 601-965-4773
www.hud.gov/local/jac/index.ht
ml

Missouri
HUD St. Louis Office
1222 Spruce Street #3207
St. Louis, MO 63103-2836
314-539-6560
Fax: 314-539-6384
www.hud.gov/local/stl/index.ht
ml

Montana
HUD Helena Office
7 W 6th Ave
Helena, MT 59601
406-449-5050
Fax: 406-449-5052
www.hud.gov/local/hel/index.ht
ml

Nebraska
HUD Omaha Office
10909 Mill Valley Road
Suite 100
Omaha, NE 68154-3955
402-492-3103
Fax: 402-492-3150
www.hud.gov/local/oma/index.h
tml

Nevada
HUD Las Vegas Office
333 N. Rancho Drive - Atrium
Bldg. Suite 700
Las Vegas, NV 89106-3714
702-388-6208/6500
Fax: 702-388-6244
www.hud.gov/local/veg/index.ht
ml

Reno Area Office
HUD Reno Office
3702 S. Virginia Street
Reno, NV 89502-6581
775-784-5356
Fax: 775-784-5066
www.hud.gov/local/ren/index.ht
ml

New Hampshire
HUD - Manchester Office
Norris Cotton Federal Bldg.
275 Chestnut Street
Manchester, NH 03103-2487
603-666-7682
Fax: 603-666-7667
www.hud.gov/local/man/index.h
tml

New Jersey
HUD - Newark Office
13th Floor, One Newark Center
Newark, NJ 07102-5260
973-622-7619
Fax: 973-645-2323
www.hud.gov/local/njn/index.ht
ml

Camden Area Office
HUD - Camden Office
Hudson Bldg. 2nd Floor
800 Hudson Square
Camden, NJ 08102-1156
856-757-5081
Fax: 856-757-5373
www.hud.gov/local/cam/index.h
tml

New Mexico
HUD Albuquerque Office
625 Silver Ave. SW, Suite 100
Albuquerque, NM 87102
505-346-6463
Fax: 505-346-6704

New York
HUD - New York Office
26 Federal Plaza - Suite 3541
New York, NY 10278-0068
212-264-1161
Fax: 212-264-3068
www.hud.gov/local/nyn/index.ht
ml

Albany Area Office
HUD - Albany Office
52 Corporate Circle
Albany, NY 12203-5121
518-464-4200
Fax: 518-464-4300
www.hud.gov/local/aly/index.ht
ml

Buffalo Area Office
HUD - Buffalo Office
Lafayette Court, 5th Floor
465 Main Street
Buffalo, NY 14203-1780
716-551-5733
Fax: 716-551-5752
www.hud.gov/local/buf/index.ht
ml

Syracuse, Storefront Office
128 Jefferson Street
Syracuse, NY 13202
315-477-0616
Fax: 315-477-0196

North Carolina
HUD Greensboro Office
Koger Building
2306 West Meadowview Road
Greensboro, NC 27401-3707
336-547-4001
Fax: 336-547-4138
www.hud.gov/local/gre/index.ht
ml

North Dakota
HUD - Fargo Office
657 2nd Avenue North
Room 366
Fargo, ND 58108
701-239-5040
Fax: 701-239-5249
www.hud.gov/local/far/index.ht
ml

Ohio
HUD Columbus Office
200 North High Street
Columbus, OH 43215-2499
614-469-2540
Fax: 614-469-2432
www.hud.gov/local/clb/index.ht
ml

Cincinnati Area Office
HUD Cincinnati Office
15 E. Seventh Street
Cincinnati, OH 45202-2401
513-684-3451
Fax: 513-684-6224
www.hud.gov/local/cin/index.ht
ml

Cleveland Area Office
HUD Cleveland Office
1350 Euclid Avenue, Suite 500
Cleveland, OH 44115-1815
216-522-4058
Fax: 216-522-4067
www.hud.gov/local/cle/index.ht
ml

Oklahoma
HUD Oklahoma City Office
500 W. Main Street, Suite 400
Oklahoma City, OK 73102-2233
405-553-7500
Fax: 405-553-7588
www.hud.gov/local/okl/index.ht
ml

Tulsa Area Office
HUD Tulsa Office
1516 South Boston Avenue
Suite 100
Tulsa, OK 74119-4030
918-581-7496
Fax: 918-581-7440
www.hud.gov/local/tul/index.ht
ml

Oregon
HUD Portland Office
400 SW 6th Avenue #700
Portland, OR 97204-1632
503-326-2561
Fax: 503-326-2568
www.hud.gov/local/por/index.ht
ml

Pennsylvania
HUD Philadelphia Office
The Wanamaker Building
100 Penn Square, East
Philadelphia, PA 19107-3380
215-656-0600
Fax: 215-656-3445
www.hud.gov/local/phi/index.ht
ml

Pittsburgh Area Office
HUD Pittsburgh Office
339 Sixth Avenue - Sixth Floor
Pittsburgh, PA 15222-2515
412-644-5945
Fax: 412-644-4240
www.hud.gov/local/pit/index.ht
ml

San Juan/ US Virgin Islands
171 Carlos Chardon Ave.
Suite 301
San Juan, PR 00918-0903
787-766-5400
www.hud.gov/local/car/index.ht
ml

Rhode Island
HUD - Providence Office
10 Weybosset Street Sixth Floor
Providence, RI 02903-2808
401-528-5352
Fax: 401-528-5097
www.hud.gov/local/prv/index.ht
ml

South Carolina
HUD Columbia Office
1835 Assembly Street
Columbia, SC 29201-2480
803-765-5592
Fax: 803-253-3040
www.hud.gov/local/col/index.ht
ml

South Dakota
HUD - Sioux Falls Office
2400 West 49th St., Room. I-201
Sioux Falls, SD 57105-6558
605-330-4223
Fax: 605-330-4428
www.hud.gov/local/six/index.ht
ml

Tennessee
HUD - Nashville Office
235 Cumberland Bend
Suite 200
Nashville, TN 37228-1803
615-736-5213
Fax: 615-736-2018
www.hud.gov/local/nas/index.ht
ml

Knoxville Area Office
HUD - Knoxville Office
710 Locust Street, SW
Knoxville, TN 37902-2526
423-545-4384
Fax: 423-545-4569

www.hud.gov/local/knx/index.html

Memphis Area Office
HUD - Memphis Office
200 Jefferson Ave., Suite 1200
Memphis, TN 38103-2335
901-544-3367
Fax: 901-544-3697
www.hud.gov/local/mem/index.html

Texas
HUD Ft. Worth Office
801 Cherry Street
PO Box 2905
Ft. Worth, TX 76113-2905
817-978-5980
Fax: 817-978-5567
www.hud.gov/local/ftw/index.html

Dallas Area Office
HUD Dallas Office
525 Griffin Street, Room 860
Dallas, TX 75202-5007
214-767-8300
Fax: 214-767-8973
www.hud.gov/local/dal/index.html

Houston Area Office
HUD Houston Office
2211 Norfolk #200
Houston, TX 77098-4096
713-313-2274
Fax: 713-313-2319
www.hud.gov/local/hou/index.html

Lubbock Area Office
HUD Lubbock Office
1205 Texas Ave., Room. 5111
Lubbock, TX 79401-4093
806-472-7265
Fax: 806-472-7275
www.hud.gov/local/lub/index.html

San Antonio Area Office
HUD San Antonio Office
800 Dolorosa
San Antonio, TX 78207-4563
210-475-6806
Fax: 210-472-6804
www.hud.gov/local/san/index.html

Utah
HUD Salt Lake City Office
257 East, 200 South, Room. 550
Salt Lake City, UT 84111-2072
801-524-6071
Fax: 801-524-3439
www.hud.gov/local/sla/index.html

Vermont
HUD - Burlington Office
159 Bank Street, 2nd Floor
Burlington, VT 05401
802-951-6290
Fax: 802-951-6298
www.hud.gov/local/bur/index.html

Virginia
HUD Richmond Office
600 East Broad Street
Richmond, VA 23219-4920
804-771-2100
Fax: 804-771-2090
www.hud.gov/local/ric/index.html

Washington
HUD Seattle Office
909 First Avenue, Suite 200
Seattle, WA 98104-1000
206-220-5101
Fax: 206-220-5108
www.hud.gov/local/sea/seahome.html

Spokane Area Office
HUD Spokane Office
US Courthouse Bldg.
920 W. Riverside, Suite 588
Spokane, WA 99201-1010
509-353-0674
Fax: 509-353-0682

West Virginia
HUD - Charleston Office
405 Capitol Street
Suite 708
Charleston, WV 25301-1795
304-347-7000
Fax: 304-347-7050
www.hud.gov/local/cha/index.html

Wisconsin
HUD Milwaukee Office
310 West Wisconsin Avenue
Room 1380
Milwaukee, WI 53203-2289
414-297-3214
Fax: 414-297-3947
www.hud.gov/local/mil/index.html

Wyoming
HUD - Wyoming Office
100 East B Street
Room 1010
Casper, WY 82601-1969
307-261-6251
Fax: 307-261-6245
www.hud.gov/local/cas/index.html

Having Trouble Getting the House or Apartment you Want?

Federal law prohibits housing discrimination based on your race, color, national origin, religion, sex, family status, or disability. If you have been trying to buy or rent a home or apartment and you believe your rights have been violated, you can file a fair housing complaint. There are several ways to file a complaint; you can file a complaint online at {www.hud.gov/complaints/housediscrim.cfm}; you can call 1-800-669-9777 toll free; or you can print out a form online, complete it, and drop it off at your local HUD office or mail it to the Office of Fair Housing and Equal Opportunity.

Office of Fair Housing and Equal Opportunity
Department of Housing and Urban Development
Room 5204
451 Seventh St. SW
Washington, DC 20410-2000
www.hud.gov/offices/fheo/index.cfm

You can also file a complaint in writing. Your letter should include the following information:

- Your name and address
- The name and address of the person your complaint is about
- The address of the house or apartment you were trying to rent or buy
- The date when this incident occurred
- A short description of what happened

Then mail it to the Fair Housing Hub closest to you.

Alabama
Fair Housing Hub
U.S. Department of Housing and Urban Development
Five Points Marietta Plaza
40 Marietta Street, 16th Floor
Atlanta, GA 30303-2806
404-331-5140
1-800-440-8091
TTY: 404-730-2654

Alaska
Fair Housing Hub
U.S. Department of Housing and Urban Development
Seattle Federal Office Building
909 First Avenue, Room 205
Seattle, WA 98104-1000
206-220-5170
1-800-877-0246
TTY: 206-220-5185

Arizona
Fair Housing Hub
U.S. Department of Housing and Urban Development
Phillip Burton Federal Building and U.S. Courthouse
450 Golden Gate Ave., 9th Floor
P.O. Box 36003
San Francisco, CA 94102-3448
415-436-8400
1-800-347-3739
TTY: 415-436-6594

Arkansas
Fair Housing Hub
U.S. Department of Housing and Urban Development
801 Cherry Street, 27th Floor
P.O. Box 2905
Fort Worth, TX 76113-2905
817-978-5900
1-800-669-9777
TTY: 817-978-5595

California
Fair Housing Hub
U.S. Department of Housing and Urban Development
Phillip Burton Federal Building and U.S. Courthouse
450 Golden Gate Ave., 9th Floor
P.O. Box 36003
San Francisco, CA 94102-3448
415-436-8400
1-800-347-3739
TTY: 415-436-6594

Caribbean
Fair Housing Hub
U.S. Department of Housing and Urban Development
Five Points Marietta Plaza
40 Marietta Street, 16th Floor
Atlanta, GA 30303-2806
404-331-5140
1-800-440-8091
TTY: 404-730-2654

Colorado
Fair Housing Hub
U.S. Department of Housing and Urban Development
633 17th Street, 13th Floor
Denver, CO 80202-3690
303-672-5437
1-800-877-7353
TTY: 303-672-5248

Connecticut
Fair Housing Hub
U.S. Department of Housing and Urban Development
Thomas P. O'Neill, Jr. Federal Building
10 Causeway Street, Room 321
Boston, MA 02222-1092
617-994-8300
1-800-827-5005
TTY: 617-565-5453

Delaware
Fair Housing Hub
U.S. Department of Housing and Urban Development
The Wanamaker Building
100 Penn Square East
12th Floor
Philadelphia, PA 19107-3380
215-656-0663 ext.3260
1-888-799-2085
TTY: 215-656-3450

District of Columbia
Fair Housing Hub
U.S. Department of Housing and Urban Development
The Wanamaker Building
100 Penn Square East
12th Floor
Philadelphia, PA 19107-3380
215-656-0663 ext.3260
1-888-799-2085
TTY: 215-656-3450

Florida
Fair Housing Hub
U.S. Department of Housing and Urban Development
Five Points Marietta Plaza
40 Marietta Street, 16th Floor
Atlanta, GA 30303-2806
404-331-5140
1-800-440-8091
TTY: 404-730-2654

Georgia
Fair Housing Hub
U.S. Department of Housing and Urban Development
Five Points Marietta Plaza
40 Marietta Street, 16th Floor
Atlanta, GA 30303-2806
404-331-5140
1-800-440-8091
TTY: 404-730-2654

Hawaii
Fair Housing Hub
U.S. Department of Housing and Urban Development
Phillip Burton Federal Building and U.S. Courthouse
450 Golden Gate Ave., 9th Floor
P.O. Box 36003
San Francisco, CA 94102-3448
415-436-8400
1-800-347-3739
TTY: 415-436-6594

Idaho
Fair Housing Hub
U.S. Department of Housing and Urban Development
Seattle Federal Office Building
909 First Avenue, Room 205
Seattle, WA 98104-1000
206-220-5170
1-800-877-0246
TTY: 206-220-5185

Illinois
Fair Housing Hub
U.S. Department of Housing and Urban Development
Ralph H. Metcalfe Federal Building
77 West Jackson Boulevard
Room 2101
Chicago, IL 60604-3507
312-353-7776 ext. 2453
1-800-765-9372
TTY: 312-353-7143

Indiana
Fair Housing Hub
U.S. Department of Housing and Urban Development
Ralph H. Metcalfe Federal Building
77 West Jackson Boulevard
Room 2101
Chicago, IL 60604-3507
312-353-7776 ext. 2453
1-800-765-9372
TTY: 312-353-7143

Iowa
Fair Housing Hub
U.S. Department of Housing and Urban Development
Gateway Tower II
400 State Avenue, Room 200
Kansas City, KS 66101-2406
913-551-6958
1-800-743-5323
TTY: 913-551-6972

Kansas
Fair Housing Hub
U.S. Department of Housing and Urban Development
Gateway Tower II
400 State Avenue, Room 200
Kansas City, KS 66101-2406
913-551-6958
1-800-743-5323
TTY: 913-551-6972

Kentucky
Fair Housing Hub
U.S. Department of Housing and Urban Development
Five Points Marietta Plaza
40 Marietta Street, 16th Floor
Atlanta, GA 30303-2806
404-331-5140
1-800-440-8091
TTY: 404-730-2654

Louisiana
Fair Housing Hub
U.S. Department of Housing and Urban Development
801 Cherry Street, 27th Floor
P.O. Box 2905
Fort Worth, TX 76113-2905
817-978-5900
1-800-669-9777
TTY: 817-978-5595

Maine
Fair Housing Hub
U.S. Department of Housing and Urban Development
Thomas P. O'Neill, Jr. Federal Building
10 Causeway Street, Room 321
Boston, MA 02222-1092
617-994-8300
1-800-827-5005
TTY: 617-565-5453

Maryland
Fair Housing Hub
U.S. Department of Housing and Urban Development
The Wanamaker Building
100 Penn Square East
12th Floor
Philadelphia, PA 19107-3380

215-656-0663 ext.3260
1-888-799-2085
TTY: 215-656-3450

Massachusetts
Fair Housing Hub
U.S. Department of Housing and Urban Development
Thomas P. O'Neill, Jr. Federal Building
10 Causeway Street, Room 321
Boston, MA 02222-1092
617-994-8300
1-800-827-5005
TTY: 617-565-5453

Michigan
Fair Housing Hub
U.S. Department of Housing and Urban Development
Ralph H. Metcalfe Federal Building
77 West Jackson Boulevard
Room 2101
Chicago, IL 60604-3507
312-353-7776 ext. 2453
1-800-765-9372
TTY: 312-353-7143

Minnesota
Fair Housing Hub
U.S. Department of Housing and Urban Development
Ralph H. Metcalfe Federal Building
77 West Jackson Boulevard
Room 2101
Chicago, IL 60604-3507
312-353-7776 ext. 2453
1-800-765-9372
TTY: 312-353-7143

Mississippi
Fair Housing Hub
U.S. Department of Housing and Urban Development
Five Points Marietta Plaza
40 Marietta Street, 16th Floor
Atlanta, GA 30303-2806
404-331-5140
1-800-440-8091
TTY: 404-730-2654

Missouri
Fair Housing Hub
U.S. Department of Housing and Urban Development
Gateway Tower II
400 State Avenue, Room 200
Kansas City, KS 66101-2406
913-551-6958
1-800-743-5323
TTY: 913-551-6972

Montana
Fair Housing Hub
U.S. Department of Housing and Urban Development
633 17th Street, 13th Floor
Denver, CO 80202-3690
303-672-5437
1-800-877-7353
TTY: 303-672-5248

Nebraska
Fair Housing Hub
U.S. Department of Housing and Urban Development
Gateway Tower II
400 State Avenue, Room 200
Kansas City, KS 66101-2406
913-551-6958
1-800-743-5323
TTY: 913-551-6972

Nevada
Fair Housing Hub
U.S. Department of Housing and Urban Development
Phillip Burton Federal Building and U.S. Courthouse
450 Golden Gate Ave., 9th Floor
P.O. Box 36003
San Francisco, CA 94102-3448
415-436-8400
1-800-347-3739
TTY: 415-436-6594

New Hampshire
Fair Housing Hub
U.S. Department of Housing and Urban Development
Thomas P. O'Neill, Jr. Federal Building
10 Causeway Street, Room 321
Boston, MA 02222-1092
617-994-8300
1-800-827-5005
TTY: 617-565-5453

New Jersey
Fair Housing Hub
U.S. Department of Housing and Urban Development
26 Federal Plaza, Room 3532
New York, NY 10278-0068
212-264-9610
1-800-496-4294
TTY: 212-264-0927

New Mexico
Fair Housing Hub
U.S. Department of Housing and Urban Development
801 Cherry Street, 27th Floor
P.O. Box 2905
Fort Worth, TX 76113-2905
817-978-5900
1-800-669-9777
TTY: 817-978-5595

New York
Fair Housing Hub
U.S. Department of Housing and Urban Development
26 Federal Plaza, Room 3532
New York, NY 10278-0068
212-264-9610
1-800-496-4294
TTY: 212-264-0927

North Carolina
Fair Housing Hub
U.S. Department of Housing and Urban Development
Five Points Marietta Plaza
40 Marietta Street, 16th Floor
Atlanta, GA 30303-2806
404-331-5140
1-800-440-8091
TTY: 404-730-2654

North Dakota
Fair Housing Hub
U.S. Department of Housing and Urban Development
633 17th Street, 13th Floor
Denver, CO 80202-3690
303-672-5437
1-800-877-7353
TTY: 303-672-5248

Ohio
Fair Housing Hub
U.S. Department of Housing and Urban Development
Ralph H. Metcalfe Federal Building
77 West Jackson Boulevard
Room 2101
Chicago, IL 60604-3507
312-353-7776 ext. 2453

1-800-765-9372
TTY: 312-353-7143

Oklahoma
Fair Housing Hub
U.S. Department of Housing and Urban Development
801 Cherry Street, 27th Floor
P.O. Box 2905
Fort Worth, TX 76113-2905
817-978-5900
1-800-669-9777
TTY: 817-978-5595

Oregon
Fair Housing Hub
U.S. Department of Housing and Urban Development
Seattle Federal Office Building
909 First Avenue, Room 205
Seattle, WA 98104-1000
206-220-5170
1-800-877-0246
TTY: 206-220-5185

Pennsylvania
Fair Housing Hub
U.S. Department of Housing and Urban Development
The Wanamaker Building
100 Penn Square East
12th Floor
Philadelphia, PA 19107-3380
215-656-0663 ext.3260
1-888-799-2085
TTY: 215-656-3450

Rhode Island
Fair Housing Hub
U.S. Department of Housing and Urban Development
Thomas P. O'Neill, Jr.
Federal Building
10 Causeway Street, Room 321
Boston, MA 02222-1092
617-994-8300
1-800-827-5005
TTY: 617-565-5453

South Carolina
Fair Housing Hub
U.S. Department of Housing and Urban Development
Five Points Marietta Plaza
40 Marietta Street, 16th Floor
Atlanta, GA 30303-2806
404-331-5140
1-800-440-8091
TTY: 404-730-2654

South Dakota
Fair Housing Hub
U.S. Department of Housing and Urban Development
633 17th Street, 13th Floor
Denver, CO 80202-3690
303-672-5437
1-800-877-7353
TTY: 303-672-5248

Tennessee
Fair Housing Hub
U.S. Department of Housing and Urban Development
Five Points Marietta Plaza
40 Marietta Street, 16th Floor
Atlanta, GA 30303-2806
404-331-5140
1-800-440-8091
TTY: 404-730-2654

Texas
Fair Housing Hub
U.S. Department of Housing and Urban Development
801 Cherry Street, 27th Floor
P.O. Box 2905
Fort Worth, TX 76113-2905
817-978-5900
1-800-669-9777
TTY: 817-978-5595

Utah
Fair Housing Hub
U.S. Department of Housing and Urban Development
633 17th Street, 13th Floor
Denver, CO 80202-3690
303-672-5437
1-800-877-7353
TTY: 303-672-5248

Vermont
Fair Housing Hub
U.S. Department of Housing and Urban Development
Thomas P. O'Neill, Jr.
Federal Building
10 Causeway Street, Room 321
Boston, MA 02222-1092
617-994-8300
1-800-827-5005
TTY: 617-565-5453

Virginia
Fair Housing Hub
U.S. Department of Housing and Urban Development
The Wanamaker Building
100 Penn Square East
12th Floor
Philadelphia, PA 19107-3380
215-656-0663 ext.3260
1-888-799-2085
TTY: 215-656-3450

Washington
Fair Housing Hub
U.S. Department of Housing and Urban Development
Seattle Federal Office Building
909 First Avenue, Room 205
Seattle, WA 98104-1000
206-220-5170
1-800-877-0246
TTY: 206-220-5185

West Virginia
Fair Housing Hub
U.S. Department of Housing and Urban Development
The Wanamaker Building
100 Penn Square East
12th Floor
Philadelphia, PA 19107-3380
215-656-0663 ext.3260
1-888-799-2085
TTY: 215-656-3450

Wisconsin
Fair Housing Hub
U.S. Department of Housing and Urban Development
Ralph H. Metcalfe Federal Building
77 West Jackson Boulevard
Room 2101
Chicago, IL 60604-3507
312-353-7776 ext. 2453
1-800-765-9372
TTY: 312-353-7143

Wyoming
Fair Housing Hub
U.S. Department of Housing and Urban Development
633 17th Street, 13th Floor
Denver, CO 80202-3690
303-672-5437
1-800-877-7353
TTY: 303-672-5248

Federal Law May Save You Hundreds of Dollars Each Year

Private Mortgage Insurance (PMI) is a monthly premium that you are required to pay if you put less than a 20% down payment on a home. It protects the lender if you default on the loan. The Homeowners Protection Act of 1998 establishes rules for automatic termination and borrowers cancellation of PMI on home mortgages. PMI can end up costing you thousands of dollars during a loan. Check your annual escrow account statement or call your lender to find out exactly what it costs you each year. This act is applicable for certain mortgages signed on or after July 29, 1999 for the purchase, initial construction, or refinance of a single-family home. It does not apply to government-insured FHA or VA loans or to loans with lender-paid PMI.

With a few exceptions, for those mortgages meeting the date feature, the PMI must be terminated automatically when you reach 22% equity in your home. Your PMI can also be canceled, with a few exceptions, when you request its removal when you reach 20% equity in your home.

The exceptions are as follows:

- if your loan is high risk,
- if you have not been current in your payments within the year prior to the time for termination or cancellation, and
- if you have other liens on your property.

If any of those are present, your PMI may continue.

Other provisions in the Homeowners Protection Act are:

- New borrowers must be informed at closing and once a year about PMI terminations and cancellation.
- Mortgage servicers must provide a telephone number to call for information about termination and cancellation of PMI.
- Even those with loans signed before July 29, 1999, or loans with lender paid PMI, must be notified of termination or cancellation rights they may otherwise have under those loans.

If your mortgage was signed before July 29, 1999, you can still request the removal of the PMI once you exceed 20% equity in your home. However, federal law does not require the lender or mortgage servicer to cancel the insurance in that situation.

Some states may also have laws concerning the removal or cancellation of PMI even if the mortgage was signed before the July 29, 1999 date. Be sure to check with your lender or mortgage servicer or call Fannie Mae or Freddie Mac for information.

To receive information from the Federal Trade Commission on the removal of PMI, contact Federal Trade Commission, Public Reference, Washington, DC 20580; 877-FTC-HELP (382-4357); {www.ftc.gov}.

House Rich, But Cash Poor

A Reverse Mortgage is a type of home equity loan that allows you to convert some of the equity in your home into cash while you retain ownership. This works like a traditional mortgage, but in reverse. So, instead of making a house payment each month, you receive a payment from your lender. Depending on the type of Reverse Mortgage and the lender, you can take the money in a lump sum, in monthly advances, through a line-of-credit, or a combination of the three. Most Reverse Mortgages do not require any repayment of principal, interest, or servicing fees, for as long as you live in your home. These loans are called rising-debt loans for that reason. The money you get from this type of loan can normally be used for any reason, including paying housing expenses like taxes, insurance, fuel, and maintenance costs.

You do not need income to qualify, but you must own your home. The value of your home, your age and life expectancy, the loan's interest rate, and the lenders policy determines the maximum loan amount limit. That can range from 50% to 75% of your home's fair market value. Generally, the older you are, the more money you can get; and the more your house is worth, the more money you can get. However, you must be at least 62 years old to apply for a Reverse Mortgage. You will keep the title to your home and you are still responsible for the taxes, repairs, and maintenance. Depending on the plan you choose, the Reverse Mortgage becomes due with interest either when you permanently move, sell your home, die, or reach the end of the loan term. After your death, your heirs must pay off the loan. The debt is usually repaid by

refinancing the loan into a forward mortgage (if the heirs are eligible) or by using the proceeds of the sale of the home.

Eligible properties are single family one-unit dwellings. Some lenders will allow 2 to 4 unit owner-occupied dwellings, condominiums, planned unit developments, and manufactured homes. However, mobile homes and cooperative are not normally eligible properties. A Reverse Mortgage generally must be first mortgages which means there cannot be any other debt against your house. If there is, you can either pay off that debt first, or pay it off with the Reverse Mortgage money.

Major Types Of Reverse Mortgages

These types of loans differ in where they are available; who can get them; what types of loan advances they provide; how much cash they will likely provide; how much they will likely cost; who offers them; and who backs them.

A) ***The FHA-insured plan has several payment options.***
   1) You can receive monthly loan advances for a fixed term or for as long as you live in the home,
   2) a line of credit, or
   3) monthly loan advances plus a line of credit.

The loan is not due as long as you live in your home.

Some of the costs associated with this loan are, closing costs, a mortgage insurance premium, and sometimes a monthly servicing fee. Interest is charged at an adjustable rate on your loan balance. The change in interest rates does not affect the monthly payment, but the rate at which the loan balance grows.

This type of Reverse Mortgage allows changes in payment options at a small cost. It also protects you by ensuring that the payments continue even if your lender defaults.

The balance of the credit line grows larger every month until all of the funds are withdrawn. This is because the unused portion of the credit line grows at the same rate that you are charged on your loan balance.

The down side is that FHA-insured Reverse Mortgages may provide smaller loan advances than other lender-insured plans. This type of loan is offered by banks, mortgage companies, and other private sector lenders.

B) ***Lender-insured Reverse Mortgages offer two types of payment options:***
   1) monthly loan advances, or
   2) monthly loan advances plus a line of credit.

These are available to you as long as you live in your home at either a fixed or adjustable interest rate.

This type of Reverse Mortgage may have a larger loan advance than those with an FHA-insured plan. They may also allow you to mortgage less than the full value of your home, which will preserve some equity for you or your heirs. But they may involve greater costs than FHA-insured loans or uninsured loans.

Additional loan costs can include a mortgage premium, at a fixed or variable rate, and other fees. Those higher costs mean that your loan balance will grow more quickly, leaving you with less equity over time.

Some lender-insured plans include an annuity that continues to make monthly payments even if you sell your home. The security of those payments are dependent upon the company's financial strength, so it is important to check their financial rating. Annuity payments may be taxable and affect eligibility for Supplemental Security Income and Medicaid. Reverse annuity mortgages can also include additional charges based on any increase in the value of your home during the term of the loan. These loans are offered by banks, mortgage companies, and other private sector lenders.

It may be to your benefit to choose a lender that offers both of these types of Reverse Mortgages. That way you could get a side-by-side comparison of the costs of each, how much money you could get from each, and what would be the equity that is left in your home at the end of the loan.

C) ***Single-purpose reverse mortgages are usually offered by state and local governments.*** The lump sum advances can only be used for a specific purpose. Some can be only for home improvements or repairs; others for the payment of property taxes or special assessments. Connecticut has a program that can only be used to pay for long term care services. This is the least expensive type of Reverse Mortgage. Because of the restrictions, they do not offer as much money as other types Reverse Mortgages. It is not available in all areas and may not be available to homeowners with high income.

D) ***Uninsured Reverse Mortgages are only available now in parts of Arizona, California,*** Massachusetts, and Minnesota. It differs greatly from the previous programs. It offers monthly advances for a fixed term that you determine when you take out the loan. The balance is due at the end of that term. Interest is normally set at a fixed rate and a mortgage insurance premium is not needed.

There are some important factors to consider before choosing this type of Reverse Mortgage. You should think about the amount of money you need monthly; how many years you may need it; how you will repay the loan when it is due; and how much remaining equity you will need after paying off the loan.

If you need a substantial amount of money for just a short time, this type of Reverse Mortgage can offer greater monthly payments than other plans. It is important though to have a source of repayment when the loan comes due. If not, you may have to sell your home.

While the value of your home is part of the equation in a Reverse Mortgage, each home is subject to a maximum mortgage limit. If your home's worth exceeds the county's median home value, the amount of your loan will be limited by that value. The ranges for 2002 are $144,336 in most non-metro areas to $261,609 in a majority of urban areas. These values change yearly and there is currently discussion on a single national limit. You can look up your county limit at https://entp.hud.gov/idapp/html/hicostlook.cfm.

The following are common features of all Reverse Mortgages

- Reverse Mortgages are rising-debt loans. The interest is added to the principal loan balance each month, because it is not paid on a current basis. Because of this, the total amount of interest you owe, increases significantly with time.
- All 3 plans charge origination fees and closing costs. Insured plans also charge insurance premiums and some will add mortgage servicing charges. Your lender may allow you to finance those costs instead of paying cash. However, doing so will add more to your loan amount.
- Reverse Mortgages use up all or some of the equity in your home.
- Generally, you can request a loan advance at closing that is substantially larger than the rest of your payments.
- Your legal obligation to pay back the loan is limited by the value of your home at the time the loan is repaid. This cap, called a "non-recourse" limit, means you can never owe more than your home is worth at the end of the loan term.
- Reverse Mortgage loan advances are not taxable. They do not affect your Social Security or Medicare benefits. If you get Supplemental Security Income, it is not affected by your Reverse Mortgage payments as long as you spend the SSI benefits within the month it is received. This also applies to Medicaid benefits in

most states. To be sure, check with a benefit specialist.

- Loans can be for a fixed rate or adjustable rate.
- Interest on the loan is not deductible on your income taxes until you pay off all or part of your Reverse Mortgage debt.

There are some safeguards with a Reverse Mortgage. The Federal Truth in Lending Act is one of the best protections to have. It requires lenders to inform you about the plan's terms and costs. Make sure you understand those before signing the loan papers. Among other information, the Annual Percentage Rate (APR) and payment terms must be disclosed. On plans with adjustable rates, they must inform you of specific information on the variable rate feature. For those plans with credit lines, you must be made aware of any charges to open and use the account, such as appraisal, credit report or attorney's fees. Also, the non-recourse limit mentioned above, means that the lender cannot come after yours or you heirs income or other assets in order to pay back a loan with that cap.

Lenders can require repayment at any time if you:

- fail to pay property taxes;
- fail to maintain and repair your home; or
- fail to keep your home insured.
- you declare bankruptcy;
- you donate or abandon your home;

Because of the costs and complexity of a Reverse Mortgage, other options should be considered before taking the step to obtain a loan. You should check to see if you could be eligible for Supplemental Security Income, Medicaid, or Qualified Medical Benefits; or consider selling your home and moving; or check out state or local plans that could help you pay taxes and make repairs as alternatives first.

If you would like a current list of lenders that participate in the FHA-insured program, sponsored by the Department of Housing and Urban Development (HUD), or additional information on reverse mortgages, write to:

AARP Home Equity Information Center
601 E Street, NW
Washington, DC 20049
or visit their website at,
{www.aarp.com}.

For additional information, send a self-addressed stamped envelope to :

National Center for Home Equity Conversion
7373-147 Street West, Suite 115
Apple Valley, MN 55124

You can also contact the Federal Trade Commission (FTC) for information about Reverse Mortgages. Contact Federal Trade Commission, Public Reference, Washington, DC 20580; 877-FTC-HELP (382-4357); {www.ftc.gov}.

Short-Term Rent Money

Many city and states offer short-term rent assistance for those in danger of losing their homes or who need help with the security deposit. This is usually only for assistance lasting one to six months.

Often an unexpected car repair or hospitalization, can send a family into a financial crisis situation, so rental assistance programs were begun to help address this need, hoping to stabilize a family. Who qualifies for these programs varies from place to place and where this money is located can also be a challenge. The first

place you should check is with your local Social Services Department, local housing programs, or with the welfare office.

Although the following list is not by all means comprehensive, it is designed to give you some ideas of the programs that do exist. Contact your local authorities to see what may be available to you in your area.

Arizona
Arizona Department of Commerce
Housing Trust Fund
3800 N. Central Ave, Suite 1500
Phoenix, AZ 85012
602-280-1458

California
California Department of Mental Health
1600 9th St., Room 151
Sacramento, CA 95814
916-653-0261

Connecticut
Connecticut Department of Social Services
Family Services Division
25 Sigourney St.
Hartford, CT 06106
860-424-5031

Delaware
West End Neighborhood House
710 N. Lincoln St.
Wilmington, DE 19805
302-658-4171

Lutheran Community Services
1304 N. Rodney St.
Wilmington, DE 19806
302-654-8886

District of Columbia
Community Partnership for Prevention of Homelessness
801 Pennsylvania Ave., SE
Suite 360
Washington, DC 20003
202-543-5298
www.community-partnership.org

Florida
Department of Community Development
695 E. University Blvd.,
Melbourne, FL 32901
321-674-5734
(for Melbourne only)

Department of Community Development
4401 Emerson St., Suite 1
Jacksonville, FL 32207
904-398-4424
(for Jacksonville only)

Georgia
Georgia Department of Community Affairs
60 Executive Park South, NE
Atlanta, GA 30329
404-327-6870
www.dca.state.ga.us

Illinois
Department of Human Services
100 S. Grand Ave.
Springfield, IL 62762
217-782-1317

Department of Housing
Chicago Low Income Housing Trust Fund
318 S. Michigan Ave.
Chicago, IL 60604
312-747-6172

Louisiana
Department of Social Services
Office of Community Services
755 3rd St.
Baton Rouge, LA 70802
225-342-2763
www.dss.state.la.us/offocs

Maine
Department of Human Services
221 State St.
Augusta, ME 04333
207-287-1921

Maryland
Department of Housing and Community Development
100 Community Place
Crownsville, MD 21032
410-514-7494

Minnesota
Minnesota Office of Economic Opportunity
Department of Children, Families and Learning
1500 Highway 36 West
Roseville, MN 55113
651-582-8399

Missouri
Missouri Housing Development Commission
Housing Trust Fund
3435 Broadway
Kansas City, MO 64111
816-759-6600
www.mhdc.com

Nevada
Nevada Department of Business and Industry
Housing Trust Fund
1802 North Carson St., Suite 154
Carson City, NV 89701
775-687-4258
www.state.nv.us/bi/hd

New Hampshire
Department of Health and Human Services
129 Pleasant St.

Concord, NH 03301
603-271-5043
www.dhhs.state.nh.us

New Jersey
Department of Human Services
P.O. Box 700
Trenton, NJ 08625
800-792-9773

North Carolina
Department of Health and Human Services
325 North Salisbury Ave.
Raleigh, NC 2703
919-733-7831

Ohio
Department of Development
Housing Trust Fund
77 South High St.
P.O. Box 1001
Columbus, OH 43215
614-752-8096
www.odod.state.oh.us

Oregon
Department of Housing and Community Services
1600 State St.
Salem, OR 97301
503-986-2101
www.hcs.state.or.us

Rhode Island
Rhode Island Housing and Mortgage Finance Corporation
44 Washington St.
Providence, RI 02903
401-457-1285

Virginia
Department of Housing and Community Development
501 North Second St.
Richmond, VA 23219
804-371-7113
www.dhcd.vipnet.org

Washington
Department of Community, Trade and Economic Development
906 Columbia St., SW
P.O. Box 48350
Olympia, WA 98504
360-753-1928

Emergency Rent Money

Need rent money in a hurry or you could lose your house or apartment? Close to half the states offer some type of emergency assistance to help prevent homelessness. These programs sometimes focus on exclusively on families or those of very low-income. Who operates these programs also varies from place to place. The first place you should check is with your local Social Services Department, local housing programs, or with the welfare office.

Although the following list is not by all means comprehensive, it is designed to give you some ideas of the programs that do exist. Contact your local authorities to see what may be available to you in your area.

Arizona
Arizona Department of Commerce
Housing Trust Fund
3800 North Central Ave.
Suite 1500
Phoenix, AZ 85012
602-280-1458

California
California Department of Housing and Community Development
1800 3rd St., Room 390-A
Sacramento, CA 95814
916-323-3176

Connecticut
Connecticut Department of Social Services
Family Services Division
25 Sigourney St.
Hartford, CT 06106
860-424-5031

Department of Economic and Community Development
505 Hudson St.
Hartford, CT 06106
860-270-8171
www.ct.state.us/ecd

Delaware
West End Neighborhood House
710 N. Lincoln St.
Wilmington, DE 19805
302-658-4171

District of Columbia
Community Partnership for Prevention of Homelessness
801 Pennsylvania Ave., SE,
Suite 360
Washington, DC 20003
202-543-5298
www.community-partnership.org

Georgia
Georgia Department of Community Affairs
60 Executive Park
Atlanta, GA 30329
404-327-6870
www.dca.state.ga.us

Illinois
Department of Human Services
100 S. Grand Ave.
Springfield, IL 62762
217-782-1317

Iowa
Iowa Finance Authority
100 E. Grand Ave., Suite 250
Des Moines, IA 50309
515-242-4990

Maine
Department of Human Services
21 State St.
Augusta, ME 04333
207-287-1921

Michigan
Family Independence Center
235 South Grand, Suite 1305
Lansing, MI 48909
517-335-3588

Minnesota
Minnesota Office of Economic Opportunity
Department of children, Families and Learning
1500 Highway 36 West
Roseville, MN 55113
651-582-8399

Missouri
Missouri Housing Development Commission
Housing Trust Fund
3435 Broadway
Kansas City, MO 64111
816-759-6600

Nevada
Nevada Department of Business and Industry
Housing Trust Fund
1802 North Carson St., Suite 154
Carson City, NV 89701
775-687-4258
www.state.nv.us/bi/hd

New Hampshire
Housing Finance Authority
P.O. Box 5087
Manchester, NH 03108
603-472-8623 ext. 235
www.nhhfa.org

North Dakota
North Dakota Housing Finance Agency
P.O. Box 1535
Bismarck, ND 58502
701-328-8056
www.ndhfa.state.nd.us

Rhode Island
Rhode Island Housing and Mortgage Finance Corp.
44 Washington St.
Providence, RI 02903
401-457-1285

Virginia
Department of Housing and Community Development
501 North Second St.
Richmond, VA 23219
804-371-7113
www.dhcd.vipnet.org

Washington
Department of Community, Trade and Economic Development
906 Columbia St., SW
Olympia, WA 98504
360-753-1928

$7,000 for a Bathroom/Kitchen

Money is available to help those in rural areas install basic services to make their homes more habitable. Grant funds may be used to connect service lines to a residence, pay utility hook-up fees, install plumbing and related fixtures, i.e. a bathroom sink, bathtub or shower, commode, kitchen sink, water heater, outside spigot, or bathroom, if lacking.

These grants are available to households who own and occupy the dwelling, and are available only in Arizona, California, New Mexico, and Texas. This program is called Individual Water and Waste Grants.

For more information contact your state, area or local Rural Development office or contact Single Family Housing, Direct Loan Division, U.S. Department of Agriculture, Washington, DC 20250; 202-720-1474; {www.rurdev.usda.gov}.

$200,000 to Help Your Farm Workers

The Farm Labor Housing Loan and Grant program provides capital financing for the development of housing for domestic farm laborers. 1% loans and grants are provided to buy, build, improve, or repair housing for farm laborers, including persons whose income is earned in aquaculture (fish and oyster farms) and those engaged in on-farm processing.

Funds can be used to purchase a site or a leasehold interest in a site; to construct housing, day care facilities, or community rooms; to pay fees to purchase durable household furnishings; and to pay construction loan interest. Loans are for 33 years at 1% interest, except as noted above. Grants may cover up to 90% of development costs. The balance may be a Farm Labor Housing Program loan. Funds may also be used to build, buy, improve, or repair labor housing and to provide related facilities.

For more information on the Farm Housing Loans and Grants Program contact your state, area or local Rural Development office or contact Multi-Family Housing, U.S. Department of Agriculture, Washington, DC 20250; 202-720-1604; {www.rurdev.usda.gov}.

$7,000 to Fix Up Your Home

The Housing Preservation Grants program provides funds to repair or rehabilitate individual housing, rental properties, or co-ops owned and/or occupied by very low- and low-income rural persons. Housing Preservation Grant assistance is available from grantees to assist very-low and low-income homeowners to repair and rehabilitate their homes.

Assistance is also available to rental property owners to repair and rehabilitate their units providing they agree to make such units available to very-low and low-income families. Financial assistance provided by the grantee may be in the form of a grant, loan, interest reduction on commercial loans, or other comparable assistance. Those assisted must own very low- or low-income housing, either as homeowners, landlords, or members of a cooperative.

For more information on Rural Housing Preservation Grants contact your state, area or local Rural Development office or contact Multi-Family Housing, U.S. Department of Agriculture, Washington, DC 20250; 202-720-1600; {www.rurdev.usda.gov}.

Disaster Housing Assistance

Was your home in the country hurt by a natural disaster? The Rural Housing Service assists homeowners to meet emergency needs resulting from a natural disaster. Money is only available to the extent that funds are not provided by the Federal Emergency Management Agency (FEMA).

Applicants must own and occupy the home in a rural area. Loan recipients must have sufficient income to repay the loan. Grant recipients must be 62 years of age or older and be unable to repay a loan for that part of the assistance received as a grant. The applicant's income for a loan may not exceed the very low-income limit.

For more information contact your state, area or local Rural Development office or contact Single Family Housing, U.S. Department of Agriculture, Washington, DC 20250; 202-720-1474; {www.rurdev.usda.gov}.

Free Money For Your Downpayment

Here is a program that will give you 5% of the downpayment costs for your new home. This program is open to everyone, not just first time home buyers, and the homes can be valued at up to $300,700!

Funds for this program do not need to be repaid and come from funds raised through the AmeriDream Charity. You must purchase a home from a builder or seller who has enrolled their home in the program. Over 4,500 people become homeowners each month through the AmeriCream Downpayment Gift Program.

To learn more contact AmeriDream Charity, 18310 Montgomery Village Ave., Suite 300, Gaithersburg, MD 20879; 301-977-9133; toll-free 866-263-7437; {www.ameridream.org}.

$2,700 A Year For Rent

Can't afford rent or want to help those with limited incomes? Rural Rental Assistance Payments help people with very low and low incomes, the elderly, and persons with disabilities if they are unable to pay the basic monthly rent.

Tenants in Rural Housing contribute 30% of their adjusted income, and the Rural Housing Service pays the rest of the rental rate. Prospective tenants can contact their local rural housing office to see what apartments participate in this program. Landlords can contact the local Rural Housing office to learn how they can qualify to participate in this program.

For more information contact your state, area or local Rural Development office or contact Multi-Family Housing, U.S. Department of Agriculture, Washington, DC 20250; 202-720-1600; {www.rurdev.usda.gov}.

$20,000 at 1%

That is the amount of money you can get to repair your rural home through the Section 504 Rural Housing Repair and Loan program. These low interest long-term loans helped over 4,000 homeowners used this money to fix up their homes. This program is limited to very low income homeowners.

For more information contact your state, area or local Rural Development office or contact Single Family Housing, U.S. Department of Agriculture, Washington, DC 20250; 202-720-1474; {www.rurdev.usda.gov}.

Country Living Loans

Want to buy a home in the country, but don't think you can afford it? Think again. Rural Housing Service provides financing for individuals and families who cannot obtain credit from other sources to purchase homes in rural areas.

Applications are received at USDA offices. Funds may be used to purchase suitable existing homes, new site build homes, approved modular units, and new manufactured units from an approved dealer/contractor. Funds may also be used to repair or remodel homes, or to make the home accessible and usable for persons who are developmentally disabled.

Loans may be made for up to 100% of the appraised value of the site and the home. Maximum repayment period is 33 years, or under certain conditions, 38 years. Down payment is not required if your net assets do not exceed $7,500. Certain fees must be paid and you cannot currently own a home.

Applicants for direct loans from RHS must have very low or low incomes. Very low income is defined as below 50 percent of the area median income (AMI); low income is between 50 and 80 percent of AMI; moderate income is 80 to 100 percent of AMI. Form required: Uniform Residential Loan Application. (Section 502 Direct Loan Program -10.410 Very Low to Moderate Income Housing Loans).

For more information contact your state, area or local Rural Development office or contact Single Family Housing, Direct Loan Division, U.S. Department of Agriculture, Washington, DC 20250; 202-720-1474; {www.rurdev.usda.gov}.

Need Help Getting A Loan?

Through USDA's Guaranteed Rural Housing Loan Program, Low and Moderate Income people can qualify for mortgages even without a down-payment. Loans may be for up to 100% of appraised value. Mortgages are 30-year fixed rate.

Guaranteed loans can be made on either new or existing homes. Homes must be located in rural areas (USDA can determine eligible areas). Home buyers make application with participating lenders. Applicants for loans may have an income of up to 115% of the median income for the area. Form required: Uniform Residential Loan Application. Bank determines what other forms you will need. (Section 502 Guaranteed Loan Program- 10.410 Very Low to Moderate Income Guaranteed Housing Loans).

Approved lenders under the Single Family Housing Guaranteed Loan program include:

- Any State housing agency;
- Lenders approved by:
  - HUD for submission of applications for Federal Housing Mortgage Insurance or as an issuer of Ginnie Mae mortgage backed securities;
  - the U.S. Veterans Administration as a qualified mortgagee;

  - Fannie Mae for participation in family mortgage loans;
  - Freddie Mac for participation in family mortgage loans;
- Any FCS (Farm Credit System) institution with direct lending authority;
- Any lender participating in other USDA Rural Development and/or Consolidated Farm Service Agency guaranteed loan programs.

For more information contact your state, area or local Rural Development office or contact Single Family Housing, Direct Loan Division, U.S. Department of Agriculture, Washington, DC 20250; 202-720-1474; {www.rurdev.usda.gov}.

Want To Help Build Your Country Home?

Here is a chance for you to put in some sweat equity and build the home of your dreams. The Section 502 Mutual Self-Help Housing Loan program is used primarily to help very low- and low-income households construct their own homes.

The program is targeted to families who are unable to buy clean, safe housing through conventional methods. Families participating in a mutual self-help project perform approximately 65 percent of the construction labor on each other's homes under qualified supervision. The savings from the reduction in labor costs allows otherwise ineligible families to own their homes. If families cannot meet their mortgage payments during the construction phase, the funds for these payments can be included in the loan.

Maximum repayment period is 33 years, or under certain conditions, 38 years. Applicants for direct loans from RHS must have very low or low incomes. Very low income is defined as below 50 percent of the area median income (AMI); low income is between 50 and 80 percent of AMI; moderate income is 80 to 100 percent of AMI. Form required: Uniform Residential Loan Application. (Section 502 Mutual Self-Help Loan Program- 10.410 Very Low to Moderate Income Housing Loans).

For more information contact your state, area or local Rural Development office or contact Single Family Housing, Direct Loan Division, U.S. Department of Agriculture, Washington, DC 20250; 202-720-1474; {www.rurdev.usda.gov}.

Money For Conserving the Water and Soil During an Emergency

Farmers often face natural disasters, like floods, hurricanes, or droughts. The Emergency Conservation Program provides assistance to rehabilitate eligible farmlands.

These funds are made available without regard to a Presidential emergency disaster designation. To be eligible, the applicant must have suffered a natural disaster that if untreated would impair or endanger the land. Money can be used for debris removal, fence restoration, grading and shaping of farmland, water conservation, and more. (10.054 - Emergency Conservation Program).

For more information contact your state or local Rural Development office or contact U.S. Department of Agriculture, Farm Service Agency, Stop 0513, 1400 Independence Ave., SW, Washington, DC 20250; 202-720-6221; {www.fsa.usda.gov}.

Loans to Help Your Country Property Recover From an Emergency

Disasters can strike at any time. The Farm Service Agency provides emergency loans to help producers recover from production and physical losses due to drought, flooding and other natural disasters. Emergency loan funds may be used to restore or replace essential property, pay all or part of production costs associated with the disaster year, pay essential family living expenses, refinance certain debts, and more. Farmers and ranchers must have suffered at least a 30% loss of crop production or a physical loss to livestock, livestock products, real estate, or chattel property. (10.404 - Emergency Loans).

For more information contact your state or local Rural Development office or contact U.S. Department of Agriculture, Farm Service Agency, Stop 0520, 1400 Independence Ave., SW, Washington, DC 20250; 202-720-1632; {www.fsa.usda.gov}.

Money To Improve Your Water and Soil

The Conservation Reserve Program encourages farmers to plant long-term resource-conserving covers to improve soil, water, and wildlife resources. This is a voluntary program that offers annual rental payments, incentive payments, and annual maintenance payments for certain activities, and cost-share assistance to establish approved cover on eligible cropland. In addition, the program encourages restoration of wetlands by offering a one-time incentive payment, and other conservation practices are also eligible. (10.069 - Conservation Reserve Program).

For more information contact your state or local Rural Development office or contact U.S. Department of Agriculture, Farm Service Agency, Stop 0513, 1400 Independence Ave., SW, Washington, DC 20250; 202-720-6221; {www.fsa.usda.gov}.

Money For Farmers and Ranchers to Improve Water and Soil

Many farmers face serious threats to soil, water, and related natural resources. The Environmental Quality Incentives Program provides technical, financial, and educational assistance to address these concerns in an environmentally beneficial and cost-effective manner.

The program works primarily in priority areas where significant natural resource programs exist. All activities must be carried out according to a conservation plan. These plans are site-specific for each farm or ranch. The program offers incentive payments and cost sharing for these plans. (10.912- Environmental Quality Incentives Program).

For more information contact your state or local Rural Development office or contact Deputy Chief for Natural Resources, Conservation Programs, Natural Resources Conservation Service, U.S. Department of Agriculture, P.O. Box 2890, Washington, DC 20013; 202-720-1868; {www.nrcs.usda.gov}.

Money To Fix Up An Abandoned Coal Mine

Approximately 1.1 million acres exists of abandoned coal-mined land and are need of reclaiming. Money is available to protect people and the environment from the adverse effects of past coal mining practices, and to promote the development of soil and water resources of unreclaimed mined lands. (10.910 - Rural Abandoned Mine program).

For more information contact your state or local Rural Development office or contact Deputy Chief for Natural Resources, conservation programs, Natural Resources Conservation Service, U.S. Department of Agriculture, P.O. Box 2890, Washington, DC 20013; 202-720-1873; {www.nrcs.usda.gov}.

Rural Rental Housing Loans

Rural Rental Housing Loans are direct, competitive mortgage loans made to provide affordable multifamily rental housing for very low-, low-, and moderate-income families; the elderly; and persons with disabilities. This is primarily a direct mortgage program, but its funds may also be used to buy and improve land and to provide necessary facilities such as water and waste disposal systems.

In new Section 515 projects, 95 percent of tenants must have very low incomes. In existing projects 75 percent of new tenants must have very low incomes. Very low-, low-, and moderate-income families; the elderly; and persons with disabilities are eligible for tenancy of Section 515-financed housing. Very low income is defined as below 50 percent of the area median income (AMI); low income is between 50 and 80 percent of AMI; moderate income is capped at $5,500 above the low-income limit.

Those living in substandard housing are given first priority for tenancy. When rental assistance is used top priority is given to very low-income households. The program is adaptable for participation by a wide variety of owners. Loans can be made to individuals, trusts, associations, partnerships, limited partnerships, State or local public agencies, consumer cooperatives, and profit or nonprofit corporations. (10.415 Rural Rental Housing Loans).

For more information contact your state, area or local Rural Development office or contact Multi-Family Housing, U.S. Department of Agriculture, Washington, DC 20250; 202-720-1600; {www.rurdev.usda.gov}.

Get A Loan Guarantee To Build Apartments

The Rural Housing Service guarantees loans under the Rural Rental Housing Guaranteed loan program for development of multi-family housing facilities in rural areas of the United States. Loan guarantees are provided for the construction, acquisition, or rehabilitation of rural multi-family housing.

Occupants must be very- low-, low- or moderate-income households, elderly, handicapped, or disabled persons with income not in excess of 115% of the area median income. Very low income is defined as below 50 percent of the area median income (AMI); low income is between 50 and 80 percent of AMI; moderate income is capped at $5,500 above the low-income limit.

The average rent of all units is 30% of 100% of the median income of the surrounding area (adjusted for family size). The terms of the loans guaranteed may be up to 40 years, and the loans must be fully amortized. Rates of the loans guaranteed must be fixed, as negotiated between lender and borrower, within the RHS maximum established under the Notice of Fund Availability (NOFA). The rate is based on the 30-year Treasury Bond rate on the day prior to date of loan closing. Maximum rent is 30 percent of 115 percent of median income, and average rent of all units is 30 percent of 100 percent of the median income adjusted for family size.

The program is limited to rural areas. Generally, communities are eligible if they have populations of not more than 10,000, nor more than 20,000 if there is a serious lack of mortgage credit. An applicant must be: A citizen of the United States or a legally admitted alien for permanent residence in the United States; a nonprofit organization such as a local government,

community development group or American Indian tribe, band, group, or nation (including Alaskan Indians, Aleuts, Eskimos, and any Alaskan native village); or a for-profit corporation. Eligible lenders are those currently approved and considered eligible by the Federal National Mortgage Association, the Federal Home Loan Mortgage Corporation, the Federal Home Loan Bank members, or the Department of Housing and Urban Development for guaranteed programs supporting multifamily housing. State Housing Finance Agencies may also be considered eligible lenders. Other lenders have the opportunity to enter into a correspondent bank relationship with approved lenders in order to participate in the program. (10.438 Section 538 Guaranteed Rural Rental Housing Program).

For more information contact your state, area or local Rural Development office or contact Multi-Family Housing, U.S. Department of Agriculture, Washington, DC 20250; 202-720-1604; {www.rurdev.usda.gov}.

Rural Development Offices

National Office

Rural Housing Service National Office
U.S. Department of Agriculture
Room 5037, South Building
14th Street and Independence Avenue, S.W.
Washington, DC 20250
202-720-4323
www.rurdev.usda.gov/rhs/

National Centralized Servicing Center
1520 Market Street
St. Louis, Missouri 63103
800-414-1226

Alabama

State Office
Alabama USDA Rural Development Office
Suite 601, Sterling Centre
4121 Carmichael Road
Montgomery, AL 36106-3683
334-279-3400
Fax: 334-279-3403
TDD/TTY: 334-279-3495

Area Offices
Contact the Area Office, listed below, serving your county for information on community facilities, business and industry, cooperatives, rural utilities, and/or multi-family housing programs.

AREA 1
USDA Rural Development
4890 University Square
Suite 3-G
P.O. Box 5267
Huntsville, AL 35814-5267
256-544-5795
Fax: 256-544-2158
Serving: Calhoun, Cherokee, Clay, Cleburne, Colbert, DeKalb, Etowah, Franklin, Jackson, Lauderdale, Lawrence, Limestone, Madison, Marshall, Morgan, Randolph, St. Clair, and Talladega Counties

AREA 2
USDA Rural Development
205 W. Adams Street
P.O. Box 2026
Dothan, AL 36302
334-793-7819
Fax: 334-793-2744
Serving: Autauga, Barbour, Bullock, Chambers, Coffee, Coosa, Dale, Elmore, Geneva, Houston, Henry, Lee, Macon, Montgomery, Pike, Russell, and Tallapoosa Counties

AREA 3
USDA Rural Development
3831-B Palisades Drive
Tuscaloosa, AL 35405
205-553-1733, Ext. 5
Fax: 205-553-5100
Serving: Bibb, Blount, Chilton, Cullman, Fayette, Greene, Hale, Jefferson, Lamar, Marion, Pickens, Shelby, Sumter, Tuscaloosa, Walker, and Winston Counties

AREA 4
USDA Rural Development
213 East 1st Street
P.O. Box 517
Bay Minette, AL 36507
251-937-7350
Fax: 251-937-4984
Serving: Baldwin, Butler, Choctaw, Clarke, Conecuh, Covington, Crenshaw, Dallas, Escambia, Lowndes, Marengo, Mobile, Monroe, Perry, Washington, and Wilcox Counties

Local Offices
Contact the Local Office serving your county for information on our single family housing programs.

USDA Rural Development
1504-B Hwy 31 S.
Bay Minette, AL 36507
251-937-3297, Ext. 4
Serving: Baldwin, Mobile, Washington, and Counties

USDA Rural Development
1413-C Hillyer
Robinson Industrial Pkwy
Anniston, AL 36201
256-831-3067

Serving: Calhoun Cherokee Cleburne Etowah, and Counties

USDA Rural Development
733 Logan Road
Clanton, AL 35045
205-755-5101, Ext. 4
Serving: Chilton, Bibb, and Shelby Counties

USDA Rural Development
117 Neil Morris Road, Suite C
P.O. Box 646
Tuscumbia, AL 35674
256-383-4323, Ext. 4
Serving: Colbert, Franklin, Lauderdale and, Lawrence Counties.

USDA Rural Development
376 Southern Bypass
Andalusia, AL 36420
334-222-6528, Ext. 4
Serving: Covington, Butler, Conecuh, Crenshaw, and Escambia Counties.

USDA Rural Development
205 4th Avenue NE, Suite 103
Cullman, AL 35055
256-734-6471, Ext. 4
Serving: Cullman, Blount, Jefferson, Walker, and Winston Counties.

USDA Rural Development
1702 Hwy 123 South, Suite H
Ozark, AL 36360
334-774-4926
Serving: Dale, Coffee, Geneva, and Pike Counties

USDA Rural Development
200 Main St. West, Suite 105
P.O. Box 1607
Rainsville, AL 35986
256-638-7423
Serving: DeKalb, Jackson, and Marshall Counties.

USDA Rural Development
105 Gossom Switch Rd., Suite A
Wetumpka, AL 36092
334-567-2264, Ext. 4
Serving: Elmore, Autauga, Coosa, Montgomery, and Tallapoosa Counties.

USDA Rural Development
1849 Ross Clark Circle, Suite 1
Dothan, AL 36301-5331
334-793-2310, Ext. 4
Serving: Houston, Barbour, and Henry Counties.

USDA Rural Development
145 Columbus Avenue
P.O. Box 737
Vernon, AL 35592
205-695-7622, Ext. 4
Serving: Lamar, Fayette, Marion, and Pickens Counties.

USDA Rural Development
600 South 7th Street, Suite 1
Opelika, AL 36801
334-745-7638
Serving: Lee, Bullock, Chambers, Macon, and Russell Counties.

USDA Rural Development
819 Cook Ave., N.W., Suite 150
Huntsville, AL 35801-5983
256-532-1677, Ext. 4
Serving: Madison, Limestone, and Morgan Counties.

USDA Rural Development
334 Agricultural Drive
Hwy 21 South
Monroeville, AL 36460
251-743-2587, Ext. 4
Serving: Monroe, Choctaw, and Clarke Counties.

USDA Rural Development
127 N. East Street
Room 204, Fed Bldg
Talladega, AL 35160
256-362-8210, Ext. 4
Serving: Talladega, Clay, Randolph, and St. Clair Counties.

USDA Rural Development
3831-C Palisades Dr.
Tuscaloosa, AL 35405
205-553-1733, Ext. 4
Serving: Tuscaloosa, Greene, Hale, and Sumter Counties.

USDA Rural Development
Three Camden Bypass
P.O. Box 130
Camden, AL 36726
334-682-4116, Ext. 4
Serving: Wilcox, Dallas, Lowndes, Marengo, and Perry Counties.

Alaska

Rural Development State Office
800 West Evergreen
Suite 201
Palmer, AK 99645
907-761-7705
Fax: 907-761-7783

Bethel Area Office
311 Willow Building 3
PO Box 1869
Bethel, AK 99559
907-543-3858
Fax: 907-543-3855
Serving Bethel, Bristol Bay, and Wade Hampton Counties

Dillingham Area Office
Kangiiqutaq Building
123 Main St
PO Box 1370
Dillingham, AK 99576
907-842-3921
Fax: 907-842-3922
Serving Dillingham County

Fairbanks Service Center
590 University Ave
Fairbanks, AK 99709-3661
907-479-4362
Fax: 907-479-6998
Serving North Slope, Denali, Fairbanks North Star, Nome, Northwest Arctic, Southeast Fairbanks, Valdez-Cordova, and Yukon-Koyukuk Counties

Kenai Area Office
110 Trading Bay Road
Suite 160
Kenai AK 99611
907-283-8732
Fax: 907-283-9667
Serving Aleutians East, Aleutians West, Kenai Peninsula, Kodiak Island, Lake and Peninsula Counties

Nome Area Office
240 Front St, Room 106
PO Box 1569

Nome, AK 99762
907-443-6022

Sitka Area Office
204 Siganaka Way
Sitka AK 99835
907-747-4324
Fax: 907-747-4325
Serving Haines, Juneau, Ketchikan Gateway, Prince Of Wales-Outerketchikan, Sitka, Skagway-Hoonah-Angoon, Wrangell-Petersburg, and Yakutat Counties

American Samoa, Hawaii and Western Pacific

See also Hawaii

American Samoa Local Office
USDA Rural Development
Pago Plaza, Suite 203
P.O. Box 2447
Pago Pago, AS 96799-2447
011-684-633-1131
Fax: 011-684-633-4329

USDA Rural Development
Rural Housing Program State Office
3003 N. Central Avenue Suite 900
Phoenix, AZ 85012-2906
602-280-8755
Fax: 602-280-8879

Phoenix Area Office
Rural Development Manager
3003 N. Central Ave., Suite 900
Phoenix, AZ 85012-2906
602-280-8737
Fax: 602-280-8753

Casa Grande Local Office
115 East First Street, Suite A
Casa Grande, AZ 85222
520-836-1960, Ext. 4
Fax: 520-836-1297

Flagstaff Sub-Office
1585 South Plaza Way
Suite 120
Flagstaff, AZ 86001
928-774-2401, Ext. 5
Fax: 928-774-2780

Kingman Local Office
101 E. Beale St., Suite B
Kingman, AZ 86401
928-753-6181, 6182 Ext. 4
Fax: 928-753-3254

Holbrook Local Office
51 West Vista, Suite 5
Holbrook, AZ 86025
928-524-2771, 2887 Ext. 4
Fax: 928-524-6609

Nogales Local Office
2585 N. Grand Avenue, Suite 5
Nogales, AZ 85621
520-281-0221, 2498
Fax: 520-281-1460

Phoenix Local Office
3150 N. 35th Avenue, Suite 6
Phoenix, AZ 85017
602-353-0378 Ext. 4
Fax: 602-353-0906

Prescott Valley Local Office
8841 Florentine, Suite B
Prescott Valley, AZ 86314
928-759-9301 Ext. 3
Fax: 928-759-9284

St. Michaels Local Office
St. Michaels Professional Plaza - Hwy 264
P.O. Box 859
St. Michaels, AZ 86511
928-871-5038, Ext. 4
Fax: 928-871-4530

Safford Local Office
305 E. 4th Street
Safford, AZ 85546
928-428-0635 Ext. 4
Fax: 928-428-4284

Tucson Local Office
4650 N. Highway Drive, Suite 1
Tucson, AZ 85705
520-887-4505 Ext. 4
Fax: 520-888-1467

Willcox Local Office
658 North Bisbee Avenue
Willcox, AZ 85643
520-384-3529 Ext. 4
Fax: 520-384-2735

Yuma Local Office
2450 S. 4th Avenue, Suite 401
Yuma, AZ 85364
928-344-8902, Ext. 4
Fax: 928-341-1499

Arkansas

USDA Service Center State Office
700 West Capitol, Room 3416
Little Rock, AR 72201-3225
501-301-3200
Fax: 501-301-3278

Batesville Service Center
490 E. College St.
Fed Bldg., Room 226A
Batesville, AR 72501
870-793-4164
Fax: 870-793-3175
Serving Cleburne, Independence, Jackson, and Sharp Counties

Bentonville Service Center
101 NE 3rd St
Bentonville, AR 72712-5390
479-273-2622
Fax: 479-273-3721
Serving Benton, Madison, and Washington Counties

Camden Service Center
351 W Washington St., Suite 218
Camden, AR 71701-3901
870-836-2089
Fax: 870-836-8041
Serving Calhoun, Columbia, Dallas, Ouachita, and Union Counties

Clarendon Service Center
605 Madison St
Clarendon, AR 72029-2824
870-747-3431
Fax: 870-474-3617
Serving Arkansas, Monroe, Phillips, and Prairie Counties

Conway Service Center
1111 Main St., Suite 221
Conway, AR 72032-5449
501-327-6509
Fax: 501-450-7748
Serving Conway, Faulkner, Perry, and Van Buren Counties

Forrest City Service Center
107 W Cook St.
Forrest City, AR 72335-2730

870-633-3055
Fax: 870-630-0241
Serving Crittenden, Cross, Lee, and St Francis Counties

Fort Smith Service Center
3913 Brooken Hill Dr.
Fort Smith, AR 72908-9289
479-646-8300
Fax: 479-646-2691
Serving Crawford, Franklin, Logan, Scott, and Sebastian Counties

Harrison Service Center
402 N Walnut St., Suite 127
Harrison, AR 72601-3621
870-741-8600
Fax: 870-741-2613
Serving Boone, Carroll, Marion, Newton, and Searcy Counties

Hope Service Center
2510 N Hervey St.
Hope, AR 71801-8419
870-777-8800
Fax: 870-777-3284
Serving Hempstead, Lafayette, Little River, Miller, and Nevada Counties

Jonesboro Area Office
1306 Stone St
Jonesboro, AR 72401-4522
870-972-4720
Fax: 870-972-4762
Serving Craighead, Mississippi, and Poinsett Counties

Malvern Service Center
220 Olive St., Suite 3
Malvern, AR 72104-3728
501-337-7381
Fax: 501-332-4185
Serving Clark, Garland, Hot Spring, and Saline Counties

Melbourne Service Center
1107 Hwy 69 E
Melbourne, AR 72556
870-368-4413
Fax: 870-368-5505
Serving Baxter, Fulton, Izard, and Stone Counties

Monticello Service Center
419 W Gaines St
Monticello, AR 71655-4723
870-367-8400
Fax: 870-367-5816
Serving Ashley, Bradley, Chicot, Desha, and Drew Counties

Nashville Service Center
121 W Sypert St
Nashville, AR 71852-2431
870-845-4121
Fax: 870-845-2177
Serving Howard, Montgomery, Pike, Polk, and Sevier Counties

Pine Bluff Service Center
100 E 8th Ave., Room 2603
Pine Bluff, AR 71601-5073
870-534-3200
Fax: 870-535-0236
Serving Cleveland, Grant, Jefferson, and Lincoln Counties

Russellville Service Center
420 N Hampton Ave
Russellville, AR 72802-8240
501-968-3497
Fax: 501-968-5933
Serving Johnson, Pope, and Yell Counties

Searcy Service Center
505 S Elm St
Searcy, AR 72143-6604
501-268-5866
Fax: 501-268-7153
Serving Lonoke, Pulaski, White, and Woodruff Counties

Walnut Ridge Service Center
1100 W Main St
Walnut Ridge, AR 72476-1006
870-886-7791
Fax: 870-886-7552
Serving Clay, Greene, Lawrence, and Randolph Counties

California

USDA Rural Development State Office
430 G Street, #4169
Davis, CA 95616-4169
530-792-5800, ext 1
Fax: 530-792-5838

Region 1
Serving Butte, Clousa, Glenn, Lassen, Modoc, Plumas, Shasta, Siskiyou, Sutter, Tehama, Trinity, Yolo and Yuba Counties.

Alturas Local Office
808 W. 12th St.
Alturas, CA 96101
530-233-4615

Oroville Local Office
150-D Chuck Yeager Way
Oroville, CA 95965
530-533-4401 ext. 4

Red Bluff Local Office
2 Sutter St., Suite. B
Red Bluff, CA 96080
530-527-1013 ext. 4

Redding Local Office
3179 Bechelli Ln., Suite. 109
Redding, CA 96002
530-246-5244 ext. 4

Willows Local Office
132 N. Enright Ave., Suite. C
Willows, CA 95988
530-934-4614 ext. 4

Yreka Local Office
215 Executive Ct., Suite. B
Yreka, CA 96097
530-842-6123 ext. 4

Yuba City Local Office
1521-D Butte House Rd.
Yuba City, CA 95993
530-673-4347 ext. 4

Region 2
USDA Rural Development
777 Sonoma Avenue E Street Annex
Santa Rosa, CA 95404
Serving Alameda, Alpine, Amador, Calaveras, Contra Costa, Del Norte, El Dorado, Lake, Marin, Mendocino, Mono, Monterey, Napa, Nevada, Placer, Sacramento, San Benito, San Francisco, San Joaquin, San Mateo, Santa Clara, Santa Cruz, Sierra, Solano, and Sonoma Counties.

Auburn Local Office
251 Auburn Ravine Rd., Ste. 103

Auburn, CA 95603
530-885-7081 ext. 4

Elk Grove Local Office
9701 Dino Dr., Ste. 170
Elk Grove, CA 95624
916-714-1104 ext. 4

Eureka Local Office
5630 South Broadway
Eureka, CA 95503
707-442-6058 ext. 4

Salinas Local Office
744 LaGuardia St., Ste. A
Salinas, CA 93905
831-424-1036 ext. 4

Santa Rosa Local Office
777 Sonoma Avenue
E Street Annex
Santa Rosa, CA 95404-4731
707-526-6797

Stockton Local Office
1222 Monaco Ct., Ste. 19
Stockton, CA 95207
209-946-6455 ext. 4

Ukiah Local Office
405 S. Orchard Ave.
Ukiah, CA 95482
707-462-2916 ext. 4

Region 3
USDA Rural Development
4625 W. Jennifer #126
Fresno CA 93631
Serving Fresno, Inyo, Los Angeles, Madera, Merced, Riverside (W), San Bernardino, Stanislaus, Tuolumne Counties.

Fresno Local Office
4625 W. Jennifer
Fresno, CA 93722
559-276-7494 ext. 4

Indio Local Office
82-901 Bliss Ave.
Indio, CA 92201
760-347-7658

Merced Local Office
2135 W. Wardrobe Ave Suite A
Merced, CA 95349
209-723-3714 ext. 4

Modesto Local Office
3800 Cornucopia Way Suite E
Modesto, CA 95358
209-491-9320 ext. 4

Victorville Local Office
17330 Bear Valley Road, Suite 106
Victorville, CA 92392
760-843-6882

Region 4
Serving Imperial, Kern. Kings, Orange, Riverside (E), San Diego, San Luis, Obispo, Santa Barbara, Tulare, and Ventura Counties.

Bakersfield Local Office
1601 New Stine Rd., Ste. 280
Bakersfield, CA 93309
661-861-4221 ext. 4

El Centro Local Office
177 N. Imperial Ave.
El Centro, CA 92243
760-352-4418

Hanford Local Office
680 Campus Dr., Ste. D
Hanford, CA 93230
559-584-9209 ext. 4

Moreno Valley Local Office
22690 Cactus Ave., Ste. 280
Moreno Valley, CA 92553
909-656-6800

Santa Maria Local Office
920 E. Stowell Rd.
Santa Maria, CA 93454
805-928-9269 ext. 4

Visalia Local Office
3530 W. Orchard Ct.
Visalia, CA 93277
559-734-8732, ext. 4

Colorado

Rural Development State Office
Lakewood State Office
655 Parfet Street, Room E-100
Lakewood, CO 80215
720-544-2903
800-659-3656
TTY 720-544-2976

Alamosa Rural Development Local Office
2205 State Street
Alamosa, CO 81101
719-589-5661 ext. 4
Fax: 719-589-0515

Burlington Rural Development Local Office
111 So.14th Street, Suite #2
Burlington, CO 80807
719-346-7699 ext. 4
Fax: 719-346-5523

Canon City Rural Development Local Office
248 Dozier Avenue
Canon City, CO 81212
719-275-4465 ext. 4
Fax: 719-275-3019

Cortez Rural Development Local Office
628 W. 5th Street
Cortez, CO 81321
970-565-8416 ext. 4
Fax: 970-565-8797

Craig Rural Development Local Office
356 Ranney Street
Craig, CO 81625
970-824-3476 ext. 4
Fax: 970-824-7055

Fort Morgan Rural Development Local Office
220 State Street
Fort Morgan, CO 80701
970-867-9419 ext. 4
Fax: 970-867-9410

Grand Junction Rural Development Local Office
2754 Compass Drive, Suite #185
Grand Junction, CO 81506
970-242-4511 ext. 4
Fax: 970-241-2782

Greeley Rural Development Local Office
4302 W. 9th Street Road
Greeley, CO 80634
970-356-8097 ext. 4
Fax: 970-351-0392

Hugo Rural Development Local Office
318 5th Street
P.O. Box 218
Hugo, CO 80821
719-743-2408 ext. 4
Fax: 719-743-2701

Lamar Rural Development Local Office
3501 So. Main, #C
Lamar, CO 81052
719-336-3437 ext. 4
Fax: 719-336-7958

Montrose Rural Development Local Office
102 Par Place, #1
Montrose, CO 81401
970-249-8407 ext. 4
Fax: 970-249-5718

Rocky Ford Rural Development Local Office
202 South 10th
Rocky Ford, CO 81067
719-254-7616 ext. 4
Fax: 719-254-4541

Trinidad Rural Development Local Office
422 East 1st
Trinidad, CO 81082
719-846-3681 ext. 4
Fax: 719-846-0525

Wray Rural Development Local Office
247 N. Clay, Suite 2
P.O. Box 405
Wray, CO 80758
970-332-3107 ext. 4
Fax: 970-332-9801

Connecticut

(Southern New England)
Rural Development State Office
451 West Street, Suite 2
Amherst MA 01002-2999
413-253-4300
Fax: 413-253-4347

Norwich Service Center
Serving Eastern Connecticut
238 West Town Street
Norwich, CT 06360
860-859-5218 Ext. 3004
Fax: 860-859-5223
Serving Windham and New London Counties.

Windsor Service Center
Serving Western and Central Connecticut
627 River Street
Windsor, CT 06790
860-688-7725 Ext. 4
Fax: 860-688-7979
Serving Tolland, Middlesex, Hartford, Litchfield, New Haven, and Fairfield Counties.

Delaware

Delaware USDA Rural Development
4607 South DuPont Highway
Post Office Box 400
Camden, DE 19934
302-697-4300
Fax: 302-697-4390

Frederick Area Office
USDA Rural Development
92 Thomas Johnson Drive
Suite 110
Frederick, MD 21702
301-694-7522, Ext. 5
Fax: 301-694-5840

Dover Local Office
USDA Rural Development
3500 South DuPont Highway
Dover, DE 19901
302-697-2600 Ext 4
Fax: 302-697-8259
Serving Kent and New Castle Counties.

Georgetown Local Office
USDA Rural Development
Agricultural Service Center
408-A North DuPont Highway
Georgetown, DE 19947
302-856-3990 Ext 4
Fax: 302-856-4381
Serving Sussex County.

Florida/Virgin Islands

USDA Rural Development State Office
4440 N.W. 25th Place
Gainesville, FL 32606
352-338-3402
Fax: 352-338-3405

Area 1
Crestview Area Office
932 N. Ferdon Blvd., Suite B
Crestview, FL 32536
850-682-2416
Serving Bay, Escambia, Holmes, Okaloosa, Santa Rosa, Walton and Washington Counties.

Milton Local Office
USDA, Agriculture Center
6275 Dogwood Drive
Milton, FL 32570
850-623-2441
Fax: 850-623-8012
Serving Escambia and Santa Rosa Counties.

Defuniak Springs Local Office
732 N. Ninth Street, Suite A
DeFuniak Springs, FL 32433
850-892-3712
Fax: 850-892-6002
Serving Okaloosa and Walton Counties.

Chipley Local Office
1424 Jackson Ave., Suite B
Chipley, FL 32428
850-638-1982
Fax: 850-638-9325
Serving Bay, Holmes and Washington Counties.

Area 2
Marianna Area Office
2741 Pennsylvania Ave., Suite 5
Marianna, FL 32448
850-526-2610
Serving Calhoun, Columbia, Franklin, Gadsden, Gulf, Hamilton, Jackson, Jefferson, Lafayette, Leon, Liberty, Madison, Suwannee, Taylor and Wakulla Counties.

Marianna Local Office
2741 Pennsylvania Ave., Suite 7
Marianna, FL 32448-4014
850-526-2610
Fax: 850-526-7534
Serving Calhoun, Gulf, Jackson and Liberty Counties.

Quincy Local Office
2138 W. Jefferson St.
Quincy, FL 32351

850-627-6365
Fax: 850-627-7297
Serving Franklin, Gadsden, Leon and Wakulla Counties.

Live Oak Local Office
10094 US 129 South
Live Oak, FL 32060
904-362-2681
Fax: 904-362-3375
Serving Columbia, Hamilton, Jefferson, Lafayette, Madison, Suwannee and Taylor Counties.

Area 3
Ocala Area Office
2303 N.E. Jacksonville Road, Suite 400
Ocala, FL 34470
352-732-7534
Serving Alachua, Baker, Bradford, Citrus, Clay, Dixie, Duval, Flagler, Gilchrist, Levy, Marion, Nassau, Putnam, Seminole, St. Johns, Union and Volusia Counties.

Baldwin Local Office
260 U.S. 301 North
Baldwin, FL 32234
904-266-0088
Fax: 904-266-4858
Serving Baker, Bradford, Clay, Duval, Nassau, St. Johns and Union Counties.

Deland Local Office
1342-A South Woodland Blvd.
DeLand, FL 32720
904-734-2535
Fax: 904-736-9339
Serving Flagler, Putnam, Seminole and Volusia Counties.

Ocala Local Office
2303 N.E. Jacksonville Road, Ste. 300
Ocala, FL 34470
352-732-7534
Fax: 352-732-9728
Serving Alachua, Citrus, Dixie, Gilchrist, Levy and Marion Counties.

Area 4
Tavares Area Office
32245 David Walker Drive
Tavares, FL 32778
352-742-7005
Serving Brevard, DeSoto, Hardee, Hernando, Hillsborough, Lake, Manatee, Orange, Osceola, Pasco, Pinellas, Polk and Sumter Counties. Also serves St. Croix, St. Thomas & St. John, Virgin Islands

Bartow Local Office
1700 Hwy. 17 S., Suite 3
Bartow, FL 33830-6633
863-533-2051
Fax: 863-533-1884
Serving Desoto, Hardee and Polk Counties.

Plant City Local Office
201 S. Collins Street, Suite 200
Plant City, FL 33566
813-752-1474
Fax: 813-754-7297
Serving Hillsborough, Manatee, Pinellas and Pasco Counties.

Tavares Local Office
32235 David Walker Drive
Tavares, FL 32778
352-742-7005
Fax: 352-343-6275
Serving Brevard, Hernando, Lake, Orange, Osceola and Sumter Counties.

Area 5
West Palm Beach Area Office
750 S. Military Trail, Suite J
West Palm Beach, FL 33415
561-683-2285
Serving Broward, Charlotte, Collier, Dade, Glades, Hendry, Highlands, Indian River, Lee, Martin, Monroe, Okeechobee, Palm Beach, Sarasota and St. Lucie Counties.

North Fort Myers Local Office
3434 Hancock Bridge Pkwy., Suite 209-A
N. Ft. Myers, FL 33903-7005
941-997-7331
Fax: 941-997-7557
Serving Charlotte, Collier, Hendry, Lee and Sarasota Counties.

Okeechobee Local Office
454 N.W. Hwy. 98
Okeechobee, FL 34972
863-763-3345
Fax: 863-763-6407
Serving Glades, Highlands and Okeechobee Counties.

West Palm Beach Local Office
750 S. Military Trail, Suite H
West Palm Beach, FL 33415
561-683-2285
Fax: 561-683-6249
Serving Broward, Dade, Indian River, Martin, Monroe, Palm Beach and St. Lucie Counties.

Georgia

USDA Rural Development State Office
Stephens Federal Building
335 East Hancock Avenue
Athens, GA 30601-2768
706-546-2162
Fax: 706-546-2152

Area I
Cartersville Area Office
Suite A, 12 Felton Place
Cartersville North Business Center
Cartersville, GA 30120
770-386-3393
Fax: 770-387-0429
Serving Bartow, Butts, Carroll, Catoosa, Chatooga, Cherokee, Clayton, Cobb, Coweta, Dade, DeKalb, Douglas, Fannin, Fayette, Floyd, Fulton, Gilmer, Gordon, Haralson, Heard, Henry, Meriwether, Murray, Paulding, Pickens, Polk, Rockdale, Troup, Walker, and Whitfield Counties.

Area II
Athens Area Office
355 East Hancock Avenue
Stephens Federal Building
Room 259 Box 1
Athens, GA 30601
706-546-2471
Fax: 706-546-3273
Serving Banks, Barrow, Clarke, Dawson, Elbert, Forsyth, Franklin, Greene, Gwinnett, Habersham, Hall, Hart, Jackson,

Lumpkin, Madison, Morgan, Newton, Oconee, Oglethorpe, Rabun, Stephens, Towns, Union, Walton, and White Counties.

Area III
Macon Area Office
915 Hill Park, Suite 100
Macon, GA 31201
912-752-8121
Fax: 912-752-3452
Serving Bibb, Bleckley, Chattahoochee, Clay, Crawford, Dodge, Harris, Houston, Jasper, Jones, Lamar, Laurens, Lee, Macon, Marion, Monroe, Muscogee, Peach, Pike, Pulaski, Quitman, Randolph, Schley, Spalding, Stewart, Sumter,Talbot, Taylor, Terrell, Twiggs, Upson, Webster, and Wilkinson Counties.

Area IV
Waynesboro Area Office
501 W. Sixth St.
P.O. Box 829
Waynesboro, GA 30830
706-554-7001
Fax: 706-554-4539
Serving Baldwin, Burke, Columbia, Emmanuel, Glascock, Hancock, Jefferson, Jenkins, Johnson, Lincoln, McDuffie, Putnam, Richmond, Screven, Taliaferro, Truetlen, Warren, Washington, and Wilkes Counties.

Area V
Tifton Area Office
Tift County Admin. Bldg.
114 West 12th St., Suite F
Tifton, GA 31794
912-382-0273
Fax: 912-382-2823
Serving Baker, Ben Hill, Berrien, Brooks, Calhoun, Clinch, Colquitt, Cook, Crisp, Decatur, Dooly, Dougherty, Early, Echols, Grady, Irwin, Lanier, Lowndes, Miller, Mitchell, Seminole, Thomas, Tift, Turner, Wilcox, and Worth Counties.

Area VI
Baxley Area Office
605 S. Main St. Building E
P.O. Box 30
Baxley, GA 31513
Phone 912-3657-3603
Fax: 912-367-0503
Serving Appling, Atkinson, Bacon, Brantley, Bryan, Camden, Candler, Charlton, Chatham, Clinch, Coffee, Effingham, Evans, Glynn, Jeff Davis, Liberty, Long, McIntosh, Montgomery, Pierce, Screven, Tatnall, Telfair, Toombs, Ware, Wayne, and Wheeler Counties.

Georgia Local Field Offices
Barnesville Local Field Office
118 Academy Drive
Barnesville, GA 30204
770-358-2280
Fax: 770-358-6788
Serving Lamar, Jasper, Jones, Monroe, Pike, Spalding, and Upson Counties.

Blackshear Local Field Office
707 Hendry Street
Blackshear, GA 31516
912-449-5577
Fax: 912-449-1024
Serving Appling, Bacon, Brantley, Camden, Charlton, Clinch, Glynn, Pierce, Ware, and Wayne Counties.

Byron Local Field Office
102 Church Street
P.O. Box 849
Byron, GA 31008-0849
912-956-6495
Fax: 912-956-6473
Serving Bibb, Chatahoochee, Crawford, Harris, Houston, Macon, Marion, Muscogee, Peach, Schley, Talbot, and Taylor Counties.

Camilla Local Field Office
30 W. Broad Street
P.O. Box 232
Camilla, GA 31730
912-336-0371
Fax: 912-336-1867
Serving Baker, Dougherty, Grady, Mitchell, and Thomas Counties.

Clarkesville Local Field Office
555 Monroe Street
P.O. Box 1240
Clarkesville, GA 30523
706-754-6239
Fax: 706-754-9821
Serving Banks, Habersham, Rabun, Stephens, Towns, Union, and White Counties.

Cochran Local Field Office
Professional Building
Peacock Street
P.O. Box 428
Cochran, GA 31014
912-934-6392
Fax: 912-934-9211
Serving Bleckley, Dodge, Laurens, Pulaski, Twiggs, and Wilkinson Counties.

Dawson Local Field Office
955 Forrester Drive
P.O. Box 311
Dawson, GA 31742
912-995-5819
Fax: 912-995-8414
Serving Clay, Lee, Quitman, Randolph, Stewart, Sumter,Terrell, and Webster Counties.

Douglas Local Field Office
711 E. Ward Street
P.O. Box 1344
Douglas, GA 31533
912-384-4811
Fax: 912-384-5446
Serving Atkinson, Coffee, Jeff Davis, Montgomery, Telfair, and Wheeler Counties.

Gainesville Local Field Office
734 E. Crescent Drive
Suite 100
Gainesville, GA 30501
770-536-0547
Fax: 770-536-6076
Serving Barrow, Dawson, Forsyth, Gwinnett, Hall, Jackson, Lumpkin, Union, and White Counties.

Hartwell Local Field Office
88 Market Street
P.O. Box 308
Hartwell, GA 30643
706-376-3954
Fax: 706-856-3350
Serving Clarke, Elbert, Franklin, Hart, Madison, and Oglethorpe Counties.

Jasper Local Field Office
35 West Church Street, Suite 119
Jasper, GA 30143
706-692-6417
Fax: 706-692-9344
Serving Cherokee, Cobb, Fannin, Gilmer, Gordon, Murray, and Pickens Counties.

LaFayette Local Field Office
208-A North Duke Street
LaFayette, GA 30728
Phone 706-638-2189
Fax: 760-638-2371
Serving Catoosa, Chattooga, Dade, Walker, and Whitfield Counties.

McDonough Local Field Office
333 Phillips Drive, Suite C
McDonough, GA 30253
770-957-1228
Fax: 770-957-3191
Serving Butts, Clayton, DeKalb, Henry, and Rockdale Counties.

Monroe Local Field Office
129 North Midland Avenue
Monroe, GA 30655
770-267-1413
Fax: 770-267-1341
Serving Greene, Morgan, Newton, Oconee, Walton Counties.

Newnan Local Field Office
580 Bullsboro Drive
Suite C
Newnan, GA 30263
770-253-2555
Fax: 770-253-7032
Serving Carroll, Coweta, Douglas, Fayette, Fulton, Heard, Meriwether, and Troup Counties.

Ocilla Local Field Office
Agricultural Building
1st Cherry Street
P.O. Box 86
Ocilla, GA 31774
912-468-9461
Fax: 912-468-9561
Serving Ben Hill, Crisp, Dooly, Irwin, Tift, Turner, Wilcox, and Worth Counties.

Rome Local Field Office
1401 Dean Street, Suite M
Rome, GA 30161
706-291-5705
Fax: 706-291-5623
Serving Bartow, Floyd, Haralson, Paulding, and Polk Counties.

Statesboro Local Field Office
52 North Main Street
Federal Building, Room 204
Statesboro, GA 30458
912-764-9841
Fax: 912-489-5947
Serving Bulloch, Bryan, Candler, Chatham, Effingham, Evans, Liberty, Long, McIntosh, Screven, Tatnall, and Toombs Counties.

Tennille Local Field Office
114 Smith Street
Tennille, GA 31089
912-552-0901
Fax: 912-553-0372
Serving Baldwin, Hancock, Johnson, Putnam, and Washington Counties.

Thomson Local Field Office
226 Bob Kirk Road, NW
Thomson, GA 30824
706-595-7643
Fax: 706-595-5025
Serving Columbia, Glascock, Lincoln, McDuffie, Taliaferro, Warren, and Wilkes Counties.

Valdosta Local Field Office
Federal Building, Room 108M
401 N. Patterson
Valdosta, GA 31601
912-244-9828
Fax: 912-249-9924
Serving Berrien, Brooks, Clinch, Colquitt, Cook, Echols, Lanier, and Lowndes Counties.

Waynesboro Local Field Office
Burke Co, Office Park
West 6th Street, Room 108
P.O. Box 689
Waynesboro, GA 30830
706-554-4486
Fax: 706-554-4408
Serving Burke, Emmanuel, Jefferson, Jenkins, Richmond, Screven, and Truetlen Counties.

Hawaii, American Samoa, Western Pacific

Rural Development Area Office
Room 311, Federal Building
154 Waianuenue Avenue
Hilo, HI 96720
808-933-8380
Fax: 808-933-8327

Area I - Hawaii/American Samoa
Hilo Local Office
USDA Rural Development
Room 327, Federal Building
154 Waianuenue Avenue
Hilo, HI 96720-2486
808-933-8330
Fax: 808-933-8336

Oahu Local Office
USDA Rural Development
99-193 Aiea Heights Drive, Suite 156
Aiea, HI 96701-3911
808-483-8600/option 4
Fax: 808-483-8605

Kauai Local Office
USDA Rural Development
4334 Rice Street, Room 106
Lihue, HI 96766-1365
808-245-9014/option 4
Fax: 808-246-0277

Maui Local Office
USDA Rural Development
Millyard Plaza
210 Imi Kala St., Suite 206
Wailuku, HI 96793-1274
808-244-3100/option 4
Fax: 808-242-7005

Kealakekua (Kona) Local Office
USDA Rural Development
Ashikawa Building
P.O. Box 756
Kealakekua, HI 96750-0756
808-322-9351
Fax: 808-322-2565

Molokai Local Office
USDA Rural Development
Kahua Ctr, Unit 4
Kaunakakai Place
P.O. Box 527
Kaunakakai, HI 96748-0527
808-553-5321
Fax: 808-553-3739

American Samoa Local Office
USDA Rural Development
Pago Plaza, Suite 203
P.O. Box 2447
Pago Pago, AS 96799-2447
011-684-633-1131
Fax: 011-684-633-4329

Area II-WESTERN PACIFIC
Rural Development Area Office
First Hawaiian Bank Bldg.
400 Route 8, Ste. 303
Hagatna, Guam 96910
671-472-7361
Fax: 671-472-7366

Barrigada Local Office
USDA Rural Development
494 West Route 8, Suite 103
Hagatna, GU 96910
671-735-2102
Fax: 671-735-2108

Palau Local Office
USDA Rural Development
Pierantozzi Bldg. II
Lebuu Rd, Dngeronger
P.O. Box 430
Koror, Palau, PW 96940
011-680-488-2499
Fax: 011-680-488-1373

Pohnpei Local Office
USDA Rural Development
Jem's Building
P.O. Box 396
Pohnpei, FM 96941
011-691-320-2581
Fax: 011-691-320-2662

Saipan Local Office
USDA Rural Development
D.Y. Building
P.O. Box 500370
Saipan, MP 96950
670-236-0875
Fax: 670-236-0876

Chuuk Local Office
USDA Rural Development
Inek Building
P.O. Box 430
Chuuk, FM 96942
011-691-330-2658
Fax: 011-691-330-4658

Yap Local Office
USDA Rural Development
Waab Commercial Center
P.O. Box 98
Yap, FM 96943
011-691-350-2191
Fax: 011-691-350-2250

Kosrae Local Office
USDA Rural Development
Skilling Building
P.O. Box 421
Tofol, Kosrae, FM 96944
011-691-370-3198
Fax: 011-691-370-2079

Majuro Local Office
USDA, Rural Development
Mako Building
P.O. Box 764
Majuro, MH 96960
011-692-625-3846
Fax: 011-692-625-3995

Idaho

Idaho State Office
USDA Rural Development
9173 West Barnes, Ste A 1
Boise, ID 83709
208-378-5600
Fax: 208-378-5643

Idaho Area Offices
Blackfoot Area Office
725 Jensen Grove Drive, Suite 1
Blackfoot, ID 83221
208-785-5840
Fax: 208-785-6561
Serving Bannock, Bear Lake, Bingham, Bonneville, Butte, Caribou, Clark, Custer, Franklin, Fremont, Jefferson, Lemhi, Madison, Oneida, Power, and Teton Counties.

Caldwell Area Office
2208 East Chicago, Ste C
Caldwell, ID 83605
208-459-0761
Fax: 208-459-0762
Serving Ada, Adams, Boise, Canyon, Elmore, Gem, Owyhee, Payette, Valley, and Washington Counties.

Coeur d' Alene Area Office
7830 Meadowlark Way, Ste. C3
Coeur d'Alene, ID 83815
208-762-4939
Fax: 208-762-9799
Serving Benewah, Bonner, Boundary, Clearwater, Idaho, Kootenai, Latah, Lewis, Nez Perce, and Shoshone Counties.

Twin Falls Area Office
1441 Fillmore, Suite C
Twin Falls, ID 83301
208-733-5380
Fax: 208-734-0428
Serving Blaine, Camas, Cassia, Gooding, Jerome, Lincoln, Minidoka, and Twin Falls Counties.

Idaho Outreach Offices
Blackfoot Outreach Office
725 Jensen Grove Drive, Suite 1
Blackfoot, ID 83221
208-785-6600
Fax: 208-785-5847
Serving Bannock, Bingham, Bonneville, Butte, Custer, Oneida, and Power Counties.

Caldwell Outreach Office
2208 East Chicago, Ste C
Caldwell, ID 83605
208-454-8691
Fax: 208-454-8053
Serving Ada, Boise, Canyon, Gem, and W. Owyhee Counties.

Coeur d' Alene Outreach Office
7830 Meadowlark Way, Ste. C3
Coeur d'Alene, ID 83815
208-667-0833
Fax: 208-667-5693

Serving Benewah, Bonner, Boundary Kootenai, and Shoshone Counties.

Grangeville Outreach Office
Route 1, Box 2 (Highway 95 North)
Grangeville, ID 83530-1201
208-983-2330
Fax: 208-983-0519
Serving Idaho, and Lewis Counties.

Lewistown Outreach Office
3113 E. Main St.
Lewiston, ID 83501
208-746-9621
Fax: 208-798-3164
Serving Clearwater, Latah, and Nez Perce Counties.

Mountain Home Outreach Office
795 South Haskett
Mountain Home, ID 83647-3140
208-587-9791
Fax: 208-587-6630
Serving Elmore, and E. Owyhee Counties.

Rexburg Outreach Office
265 East 4th North
Rexburg, ID 83440-0459
208-356-7248
Fax: 208-356-7240
Serving Clark, Fremont, Jefferson, Lemhi, Madison, and Teton Counties.

Rupert Outreach Office
98-B South 200 West
Rupert, ID 83350-9603
208-436-0116
Fax: 208-436-3098
Serving Cassia, and Minidoka Counties.

Soda Springs Outreach Office
390 East Hooper, No. 3
Soda Springs, ID 83276
208-547-4926
Fax: 208-547-4801
Serving Bear Lake, Caribou, Franklin, and SE Bonneville Counties.

Twin Falls Outreach Office
1441 Fillmore, Suite C
Twin Falls, ID 83301
208-733-5380
Fax: 208-734-0428
Serving Blaine, Camas, Gooding, Jerome, Lincoln, and Twin Falls Counties.

Weiser Outreach Office
845 East 9th
Weiser, ID 83672-2356
208-549-4280
Fax: 208-549-4229
Serving Adams, Payette, Valley, and Washington Counties.

Illinois

USDA Rural Development State Office
2118 West Park Court, Suite A
Champaign, IL 61821
217-403-6202
Fax: 217-403-6243

Area Office

Northeast Illinois
Morris Area Office
1802 N. Division, Suite 218
Morris, IL 60450
815-942-9390
Fax: 815-942-9394

Northwest Illinois
Princeton Area Office
312 E. Backbone Road, Ste B
Princeton, IL 61356
815-875-8732
Fax: 815-872-1175

East Central Illinois
Champaign Area Office
2118 West Park Court, Suite B
Champaign, IL 61821
217-403-6236
Fax: 217-403-6237

Southeast Central Illinois
Effingham Area Office
USDA Building
2301 Hoffman Drive
Effingham, IL 62401
217-347-7107
Fax: 217-342-9855

Southwest Central Illinois
Jacksonville Area Office
1904 West Lafayette
Jacksonville, IL 62650
217-243-1535
Fax: 217-245-4875

Southern Illinois
Harrisburg Area Office
230 W. Poplar
Harrisburg, IL 62946
618-252-8371
Fax: 618-252-8024

Southwest Illinois
Nashville Area Office
256 South Mill Street
Nashville, IL 62263
618-327-8822
Fax: 618-327-8774

Local Offices

Carthage Local Office
110 Buchanan Street
Route 136 West
Carthage, IL 62321
217-357-2188
Fax: 217-357-3412
Serving Hancock, and McDonough Counties.

Champaign Local Office
2110 West Park Court, Suite B
Champaign, IL 61821
217-398-5201
Fax: 217-398-5200
Serving Champaign, Douglas, Edgar, Iroquois, Macon, Piatt, and Vermilion Counties.

Charleston Local Office
990A W. State Street
Charleston, IL 61920
217-345-3901
Fax: 217-345-9669
Serving Coles, Clark, Cumberland, Montgomery, Moultrie, and Shelby Counties.

Edwardsville Local Office
7205 Marine Road, Suite A
Edwardsville, IL 62025
618-656-7300
Fax: 618-656-9144
Serving Madison, Bond, Clinton, Monroe, and St. Clair Counties.

Effingham Local Office
2301 Hoffman Drive
Effingham, IL 62401
217-347-7107

Fax: 217-342-9855
Serving Effingham, Crawford, Fayette, and Jasper Counties.

Galesburg Local Office
233 South Soangetaha Road
Galesburg, IL 61401
309-342-5138
Fax: 309-342-2259
Serving Knox, Fulton, Henderson, Peoria, and Warren Counties.

Harrisburg Local Office
809 S. Commercial
Harrisburg, IL 62946
618-252-8621
Fax: 618-252-2295
Serving Saline, Gallatin, Hamilton, Hardin, Pope, and White Counties.

Jacksonville Local Office
1904 West Lafayette
Jacksonville, IL 62650
217-243-1535
Fax: 217-245-0371
Serving Morgan, Calhoun, Cass, Christian, Greene, Jersey, Macoupin, Sangamon, and Scott Counties.

Lincoln Local Office
1650 Fifth Street
Lincoln, IL 62656
217-735-5508
Fax: 217-732-9916
Serving Logan, DeWitt, Hancock, Mason, McDonough, Menard, and Tazewell Counties.

Mt. Vernon Local Office
109 Shiloh Drive
Mt. Vernon, IL 62864
618-244-0773
Fax: 618-244-5942
Serving Jefferson, Marion, and Washington Counties.

Murphysboro Local Office
1213 North 14th
Murphysboro, IL 62966
618-684-3471
Fax: 618-684-3980
Serving Jackson, Franklin, Perry, and Randolph Counties.

Olney Local Office
821B South West Street
Olney, IL 62450
618-392-7141
Fax: 618-392-4325
Serving Richland, Clay, Edwards, Lawrence, Wabash, and Wayne Counties.

Ottawa Local Office
Rural Route 2
1691 N. 31st. Road
Ottawa, IL 61350
815-433-0551
Fax: 815-433-0665
Serving LaSalle, Boone, Cook, DeKalb, DuPage, Grundy, Kane, Kankakee, Kendall, Lake, McHenry, and Will Counties.

Princeton Local Office
312 E. Backbone Rd. Suite B
Princeton, IL 61356
815-875-8732
Fax: 815-872-1175
Serving Bureau, Carroll, Henry, Jo Daviess, Lee, Marshall, Mercer, Ogle, Putnam, Rock

Pontiac Local Office
P.O. Box 80
Route 116 West
Pontiac, IL 61764
815-844-6127
Fax: 815-844-6344
Serving Livingston, Ford, McLean, and Woodford Counties.

Quincy Local Office
338 South 36th Street
Quincy, IL 62301
217-224-9307
Fax: 217-224-4969
Serving Adams, Brown, Pike, and Schuyler Counties.

Tamms Local Office
505 Front Street
R.R. #1. Box 19
Tamms, IL 62988
618-747-2305
Fax: 618-747-9210
Serving Alexander, Massac, Johnson, Pulaski, Union, and Williamson Counties.

Indiana

State Office
Indiana USDA Rural Development
5975 Lakeside Boulevard
Indianapolis, IN 46278
317-290-3100 (extension 400)
Fax: 317-290-3095

AREA 1

Columbia Rural Development Area Office
1919 East Business 30
P.O. Box 699
Columbia City, IN 46725
219-248-8924
Fax: 219-248-2778

Area I Local Offices - Albion, Decatur, Plymouth, LaPorte, Lafayette

Albion Rural Development Local Office
104 East Park Drive
Albion, IN 46701
219-636-7682
Fax: 219-636-2525
Serving DeKalb, LaGrange, Noble, Steuben, and Whitley Counties

Decatur Rural Development Local Office
210 E. Monroe
Decatur, IN 46733
219-724-4124
Fax: 219-728-2988
Serving Adams, Allen, Jay, Huntington, Wabash, and Wells Counties

Lafayette Rural Development Local Office
188 Professional Court
Lafayette, IN 47905
765-448-1805
Fax: 765-449-4451
Serving Benton, Cass, Carroll, Howard, Miami, Newton, Tippecanoe, and White Counties

Laporte Rural Development Local Office
100 Legacy Plaza W.
LaPorte, IN 46350
219-324-6303
Fax: 219-324-8317

Serving Jasper, Lake, LaPorte, Porter, and St. Joseph Counties

The Plymouth Rural Development Local Office
2903 Gary Drive
Plymouth, IN 46563
219-936-9872
Fax: 219-936-5715
Serving Elkhart, Fulton, Kosciusko, Marshall, Pulaski, and Starke Counties

AREA II
North Vernon Rural Development Area Office
Highway 7 North
P.O. Box 116
North Vernon, IN 47265
812-346-3411
Fax: 812-346-8154

Area II Offices - Anderson, Scottsburg, Shelbyville, Versailles, Winchester and Muncie
Muncie Sub-Office
2908 N. Granville Ave.
P.O. Box 1889
Muncie, IN 47308
317-747-5531
Fax: 317-747-5506

Anderson Rural Development Local Office
1917 E. University Blvd.
Suite B
Anderson, IN 46011
765-644-4249
Fax: 765-640-9029
Serving Blackford, Delaware, Grant, Hancock, Madison, and Tipton Counties.

Scottsburg Rural Development Local Office
656 S. Boatman Rd., Suite 1
Scottsburg, IN 47170
812-752-2269
Fax: 812-752-7066
Serving Clark, Floyd, and Scott Counties.

Shelbyville Rural Development Local Office
1110 Amos Road, A
Shelbyville, IN 46176
317-392-1394
Fax: 317-392-0739
Serving Bartholomew, Decatur, Johnson, Rush and Shelby Counties

Versailles Rural Development Local Office
P.O. Box 716
1981 S. Industrial Park, Suite 4
Versailles, IN 47042
812-689-6410
Fax: 812-689-3141
Serving services Dearborn, Franklin, Jefferson, Jennings, Ohio, Ripley, and Switzerland Counties.

Winchester Rural Development Local Office
975 E. Washington Street, Suite 3
Winchester, IN 47394
765-584-4505
Fax: 765-584-1939
Serving Fayette, Henry, Randolph, Union, and Wayne Counties.

AREA III
Bloomfield Rural Development Area Office
30 W. Indiana Avenue
P.O. Box 191
Bloomfield, IN 47424
812-384-4634
Fax: 812-384-8131

Area III Offices - Bedford, Bloomington, Boonville, Covington, Jasper,Lebanon, Sullivan
Bedford Rural Development Local Office
1919 Steven Avenue
Bedford, IN 47421
812-279-8117
Fax: 812-279-0472
Serving Harrison, Jackson, Lawrence, and Washington Counties.

Bloomington Rural Development Local Office
1931 Liberty
Bloomington, IN 47403
812-334-4318
Fax: 812-334-4279
Serving Brown, Monroe, Morgan, and Owen Counties.

Boonville Rural Development Local Office
P.O. Box 442
1124 S. 8th Street
Boonville, IN 47601
812-897-2840
Fax: 812-897-2859
Serving Gibson, Perry, Posey, Spencer, Vandenburgh, and Warrick Counties.

Covington Rural Development Local Office
P.O. Box 191
US 136 E. USDA Bldg.
Covington, IN 47932
765-793-3651
Fax: 765-793-7252
Serving Fountain, Montgomery, Parke, Putnam, Vermillion, and Warren Counties.

Jasper Rural Development Local Office
1484 Executive Blvd.
Jasper IN 47547
812-482-1171
Fax: 812-482-9427
Serving Fountain, Montgomery, Parke, Putnam, Vermillion, and Warren Counties.

Lebanon Rural Development Local Office
801 West Pearl Street
Lebanon, IN 46052
765-482-6355
Fax: 765-482-9478
Serving Boone, Clinton, Hamilton, Hendricks, and Marion Counties.

Sullivan Rural Development Local Office
2326 N. Section St.
Sullivan, IN 47882
812-268-5157
Fax: 812-268-0232
Serving Clay, Greene, Knox, Sullivan, and Vigo Counties.

Iowa
Indiana USDA Rural Development State Office

210 Walnut Street, Room 873
Des Moines, IA 50309-2196
515-284-4663
Fax: 515-284-4821

Area 1
Storm Lake Area Office
1619 North Lake
P.O. Box 1107
Storm Lake, IA 50588-1107
712-732-1851
Fax: 712-732-6059
Serving Buena Vista, Cherokee, Clay, Dickinson, Emmet, Ida, Lyon, O'Brien, Osceola, Palo Alto, Plymouth, Sac, Sioux and Woodbury Counties.

Storm Lake Local Office
1619 North Lake
P.O. Box 1107
Storm Lake, IA 50588-1107
712-732-1851
Fax: 712-732-6059
Buena Vista, Ida and Sac Counties.

LeMars Local Office
1100 B 12th Street SW
P.O. Box 809
LeMars, IA 51031-0809
712-546-5149
Fax: 712-546-5187
Serving Cherokee, Lyon, O'Brien, Plymouth, Sioux and Woodbury Counties.

Spencer Local Office
P.O. Box 1418
Spencer, IA 51301-1418
712-262-3173
Fax: 712-262-7127
Serving Clay and Palo Alto Counties.

Spirit Lake Local Office
2414 17th Street
P.O. Box H
Spirit Lake, IA 51360-9407
712-336-3782
Fax: 712-336-4278
Serving Dickenson, Emmet and Osceola Counties.

Area 2
Humboldt Area Office
1301 6th Ave. North, Suite 1
Humboldt, IA 50548-1150
515-332-4411
Fax: 515-332-4113
Serving Calhoun, Cerro Gordo, Franklin, Hamilton, Hancock, Hardin, Humboldt, Kossuth, Pocahontas, Webster, Winnebago, Worth and Wright Counties.

Humboldt Local Office
1301 6th Ave. North
Suite 1
Humboldt, IA 50548-1150
515-332-4411
Fax: 515-332-4113
Serving Calhoun, Humboldt, Kosuth, Pocahontas, Webster and Wright Counties.

Garner Local Office
192 State Street
Garner, IA 50438-1227
641-923-2853
Fax: 641-923-3660
Serving Cerro Gordo, Hancock, Winnebago and Worth Counties.

Iowa Falls Local Office
840 Brooks Road
Iowa Falls, IA 50126-8008
641-648-5181
Fax 641-648-4630
Serving Franklin, Hamilton and Hardin Counties.

Area 3
New Hampton Area Office
420 West Milwaukee
New Hampton, IA 50659-0430
641-394-3183
Fax: 641-394-3769
Serving Allamakee, Black Hawk, Bremer, Buchanan, Butler, Chickasaw, Clayton, Delaware, Fayette, Floyd, Grundy, Howard, Mitchell and Winneshiek Counties.

New Hampton Local Office
420 West Milwaukee
New Hampton, IA 50659-0430
641-394-3183
Fax: 641-394-3769
Serving Chickasaw, Floyd, Howard and Mitchell Counties.

Waverly Local Office
2504 East Bremer Avenue
Waverly, IA 50677-0179
319-352-1715
Fax: 319-352-5846
Serving Black Hawk, Bremer, Buchanan, Butler and Grundy Counties.

West Union Local Office
120 N. Industrial Parkway
West Union, IA 52175-1612
563-422-3839
Fax: 563-422-6018
Serving Alamakee, Clayton, Delaware, Fayette and Winneshiek Counties.

Area 4
Tipton Area Office
205 W. South Street
Tipton, IA 52772-0466
563-886-6006
Fax: 563-886-6023
Serving Benton, Cedar, Clinton, Dubuque, Iowa, Jackson, Johnson, Jones, Linn, Louisa, Muscatine, Poweshiek, Scott, Tama and Washington Counties.

Iowa City Local Office
238 Stevens Drive
Iowa City, IA 52240-4353
319-354-1074
Fax: 319-351-2997
Serving Benton, Cedar, Iowa, Johnson, Linn, Louisa, Muscatine, Poweshiek, Tama and Washington Counties.

Maquoketa Local Office
603 E. Platt
Maquoketa, IA 52060-2416
563-652-3237
Fax: 563-652-4889
Serving Clinton, Dubuque, Jackson, Jones and Scott Counties.

Area 5
Albia Area Office
1709 South B Street
Albia, IA 52531
641-932-3031
Fax 641-932-3370
Serving Appanoose, Davis, Des Moines, Henry, Jefferson,

Keokuk, Lee, Lucas, Mahaska, Monroe, Van Buren, Wapello and Wayne Counties.

Albia Local Office
1709 South B Street
Albia, IA 52531
641-932-3031
Fax: 641-932-3370
Serving Appanoose, Lucas, Monroe and Wayne Counties.

Fairfield Local Office
605 South 23rd Street
Fairfield, IA 52556-4212
641-472-6556
Fax: 641-472-1430
Serving Davis, Jefferson, Mahaska, Keokuk, Van Buren and Wapello Counties.

Fort Madison Local Office
1035 Avenue H
P.O. Box 401
Fort Madison, IA 52627-0401
319-372-4378
Fax: 319-372-9443
Serving Des Moines, Henry and Lee Counties.

Area 6
Indianola Area Office
909 East 2nd Avenue
Suite C
Indianola, IA 50125-2812
515-961-5365
Fax: 515-961-3509
Serving Boone, Clarke, Dallas, Decatur, Greene, Jasper, Madison, Marion, Marshall, Polk, Ringgold, Story, Union and Warren Counties.

Indianola Local Office
909 East 2nd. Ave., Suite D
Indianola, IA 50125-2812
515-961-7473
Fax: 515-961-3509
Serving Clarke, Decatur, Madison, Marion, Ringgold, Union and Warren Counties.

Ankeny Local Office
1513 N. Ankeny Blvd
Ankeny, IA 50021-1793
515-964-4770
Fax: 515-964-8613
Serving Boone, Dallas, Greene, Jasper, Marshall, Polk and Jasper Counties.

Area 7
Atlantic Area Office
511 West 7th Street
P.O. Box 405
Atlantic, IA 50022-0405
712-243-2107
Fax: 712-243-1565
Serving Adair, Adams, Audubon, Carroll, Cass, Crawford, Fremont, Guthrie, Harrison, Mills, Monona, Montgomery, Page, Pottawattamie, Shelby and Taylor Counties.

Atlantic Local Office
511 West 7th Street
P.O. Box 405
Atlantic, IA 50022-0405
712-243-2107
Fax: 712-243-1565
Serving Adair, Adams, Audubon, Carroll, Cass, Guthrie, Montgomery, Page, and Taylor Counties.

Logan Local Office
721 North 2nd Avenue
Logan, IA 51546-1042
712-644-2993
Fax: 712-644-3247
Serving Crawford, Fremont, Harrison, Mills, Monona, Pottawattamie and Shelby Counties.

Kansas

USDA - Rural Development
State Office
1303 First American Place, Suite 100
Topeka, KS 66604
785-271-2700
Fax: 785-271-2708

Altamonte Local Office
115 West 4th Street
Altamonte, KS 67330
620-784-5431
Fax: 620-784-5900
Serving Chautauqua, Cherokee, Crowford, Elk, Labette and Montgomery Counties.

Colby Local Office
915 East Walnut
Colby, KS 67701
785-462-7671
Fax: 785-462-9726
Serving Cheyenne, Rawlins, Decatur, Norton, Sherman, Thomas, Sheridan, Wallace, Logan, Gove, Greeley, Wichita, Scott and Lane Counties.

El Dorado Local Office
2503 Enterprise, Ste. C
El Dorado, KS 67042
316-321-5818
Fax: 316-321-4958
Serving Butler, Chase, Cowley, Greenwood, Harvey, Marion, Sedgwick and Sumner Counties.

Garden City Local Office
2106 East Spruce
Garden City, KS 67846
620-275-0211
Fax: 620-275-4903
Serving Clark, Finney, Ford, Grant, Gray, Hamilton, Haskell, Hodgeman, Kearney, Meade, Morton, Seward, Stanton and Stevens Counties.

Hays Local Office
2715 Canterbury Drive
Hays, KS 67601
785-628-3081
Fax: 785-625-6065
Serving Barton, Ellis, Graham, Jewell, Mitchell, Ness, Osborne, Pawnee, Phillips, Rooks, Rush, Russell, Smith and Trego Counties.

Iola Local Office
202 West Miller Road
Iola, KS 66749
620-365-2901
Fax: 620-365-5785
Serving Allen, Anderson, Bourbon, Coffey, Neosho, Wilson and Woodson Counties.

Lawrence Local Office
3010 Four Wheel Drive, Unit C
Lawrence, KS 66046
785-843-4260
Fax: 785-841-1087

Serving Atchison, Brown, Doniphan, Douglas, Franklin, Jackson, Jefferson, Leavenworth, Nemaha, Osage and Shawnee Counties.

Lyons Local Office
1480 Highway 56, Suite 103
Lyons, KS 67554
620-257-5184
Fax: 620-257-5653
Serving Barber, Comanche, Edwards, Ellsworth, Harper, Kingman, Kiowa, Lincoln, McPherson, Pratt, Reno, Rice, Saline, and Stafford Counties.

Manhattan Local Office
2615 Farm Bureau Road
Manhattan, KS 66502
785-776-7582
Fax: 785-539-2733
Serving Clay, Cloud, Dickinson, Geary, Lyon, Marshall, Morris, Ottawa, Pottawatomie, Riley, Republic, Sabaunsee and Washington Counties.

Paola Local Office
100 North Angela
Paola, KS 66071
(913) 294-3751
Fax: (913) 294-3386
Serving Johnson, Linn, Miami and Wyandotte Counties.

Kentucky

USDA Rural Development State Office
771 Corporate Drive, Suite 200
Lexington, KY 40503
859-224-7300
Fax: 859-224-7425

Area Offices

Western Kentucky Area Office
320B Traylor Street
Princeton, KY 42445
270-365-6530 Ext.5
Fax: 270-365-7842

South Central Kentucky Area Office
205 Burkesville Street
Columbia, KY 42728
270-384-4759-Ext.4
Fax: 270-384-6351

Central Kentucky Area Office
90 Howard Drive, #3
Shelbyville, KY 40065
502-633-0891-Ext 4
Fax: 502-633-0552

Northeastern Kentucky Area Office
220 West First Street
Morehead, KY 40351
606-784-6447-Ext.4
Fax: 606-784-2076

Southeastern Kentucky Area Office
95 South Laurel Road
Suite A
London, KY 40741
606-864-2172-Ext.5
Fax: 606-878-7717

Local Offices

Bardstown Local Office
974 Bloomfield Road
Bardstown, KY 40004
502-348-3024
Fax: 502-349-1136
Serving Nelson, Bullitt, Jefferson, Spencer, Washington, Marion, and Taylor Counties.

Bowling Green Local Office
975 Lovers Lane
Bowling Green, KY 42103
270-832-1111 Ext 4
Fax: 270-796-9228
Serving Warren, Simpson, Allen, Edmonson, and Butler Counties.

Elizabethtown Local Office
587 Westport Road
Elizabethtown, KY 42701
270-769-1555
Fax: 270-765-2634
Serving Hardin, Grayson, Breckinridge, Meade, and LaRue Counties.

Elkton Local Office
101 Elk Fork Road
Elkton, KY 42220
270-265-5638 Ext.4
Fax: 270-265-2068
Serving Todd, Logan, Christian, Hopkins, Caldwell, Lyon, and Trigg Counties.

Flemingsburg Local Office
Flemming Agricultural Building
Flemingsburg, KY 41041
Highway 11 South
Route 2 Box 27A
606-845-2851 Ext.4
Fax: 606-845-0764
Serving Fleming, Bath, Rowan, Lewis, Mason, Robertson, Bracken, Pendleton, Campbell, and Nicholas Counties.

Glasgow Local Office
108C Reynolds Road
Glasgow, KY 42141
270-678-2636
Fax: 270-678-1706
Serving Barren, Hart, Green, Metcalfe, Adair, Cumberland, Clinton, and Monroe Counties.

Grayson Local Office
526 East Main Street
Grayson, KY 41143
606-474-5185
Fax: 606-474-2047
Serving Carter, Greenup, Boyd, Lawrence, and Elliott Counties.

Hazard Local Office
625 Memorial Drive
Hazard, KY 41701
606-439-1378
Fax: 606-436-6357
Serving Perry, Letcher, Harlan, and Leslie Counties.

London Local Office
95 South Laurel Road, Suite B
London, KY 40741
606-864-2172-Ext.4
Fax: 606-878-7717
Serving Laurel, Clay, Knox, Bell, and Whitley Counties.

New Castle Local Office
1125 Campbellsburg Road
New Castle, KY 40050
502-845-4700
Fax: 502-845-2005
Serving Henry, Franklin, Shelby, Oldham, Trimble, and Carrol Counties.

Nicholasville Local Office
800A South Main Street
Nicholasville, KY 40356

859-887-2461 Ext.4
Fax: 859-887-5517
Serving Jessamine, Woodford, Anderson, Mercer, and Boyle Counties.

Owensboro Local Office
3032 Alvery Park Drive West, Suite 3
Owensboro, KY 42303
270-683-0927
Fax: 270-926-7808
Serving Daviess, Hancock, Ohio, McLean, Webster, Union, Henderson, Muhlenburg, and Crittenden Counties.

Paducah Local Office
2715 Olivet Church Road
Paducah, KY 42001
270-554-7265 Ext.4
Fax: 270-554-5702
Serving McCracken, Graves, Fulton, Hickman, Carlisle, Ballard, Calloway, Marshall, and Livingston Counties.

Prestonburg Local Office
214 South Central Avenue, Suite 103
Prestonburg, KY 41653
606-886-9545 Ext.4
Fax: 606-886-3971
Serving Floyd, Knott, Pike, Johnson, and Martin Counties.

Richmond Local Office
2150 Lexington Road, Suite C
Richmond, KY 40475
859-624-1982 Ext.4
Fax: 859-624-5719
Serving Madison, Garrard, Estill, Rockcastle, and Jackson Counties.

Somerset Local Office
100 Parkway Drive
Somerset, KY 42503
606-678-4842 Ext.4
Fax: 606-677-9582
Serving Pulaski, Lincoln, Cassey, Russell, Wayne, and McCreary Counties.

West Liberty Local Office
955 Prestonburg Street, Suite 1
West Liberty, KY 41472
606-743-3193
Fax: 606-743-3174
Serving Morgan, Magoffin, Breathitt, Owsley, Lee, Wolfe, and Menifee Counties.

Williamstown Local Office
486 Helton Street
Williamstown, KY 41097
606-824-7171
Fax: 606-824-3172
Serving Grant, Boone, Kenton, Owen, Gallatin, Scott, and Harrison Counties.

Winchester Local Office
30 Taylor Avenue
Winchester, KY 40391
859-744-5561 Ext 4
Fax: 859-744-9714
Serving Clark, Fayette, Bourbon, Montgomery, and Powell Counties.

Louisiana

USDA, Rural Development
Louisiana State Office
3727 Government Street
Alexandria, LA 71302
318-473-7921
Fax: 318-473-7963

Area Offices

Monroe Area Office
2410 Old Sterlington Road, Suite C
Monroe, LA 71203
318-343-4467 Ext. 4
Fax: 318-343-5776.
Serving Caldwell, Catahoula, Claiborne, Concordia, East Carroll, Franklin, Jackson, LaSalle, Lincoln, Madison, Morehouse, Ouachita, Richland, Tensas, Union, and West Carroll Parishes.

Natchitoches Area Office
6949 LA Hwy 1-Bypass, Suite 103
Natchitoches LA, 71457
318-352-7100 Ext. 4
Fax: 318-354-1682.
Serving Avoyelles, Bienville, Bossier, Caddo, DeSoto, Grant, Natchitoches, Rapides, Red River, Sabine, Vernon, Webster, and Winn Parishes.

Lafayette Area Office
Whitney National Bank
905 Jefferson Street, Suite 320
Lafayette LA 70501
337-262-6601, Ext. 4
Fax: 337-262-6823
Serving Acadia, Allen, Beauregard, Calcasieu, Cameron, Evangeline, Iberia, Jefferson Davis, Lafayette, St. Landry, St. Martin, St. Mary, and Vermilion Parishes.

Amite Area Office
805 West Oak Street, Room 3
Amite LA, 70422
985-748-8751 Ext. 4
Fax: 985-748-4940
Serving Ascension, Assumption, East Baton Rouge, East Feliciana, Iberville, Jefferson, Lafourche, Livingston, Orleans, Plaquemines, Pointe Coupee, St. John the Baptist, St. Bernard, St. Charles, St. Helena, St. James, St. Tammany, Tangipahoa, Terrebonne, Washington,West Baton Rouge, and West Feliciana Parishes.

Local

Acadia Parish - Crowley Part-time Office
1708 N. Parkerson Avenue
Crowley LA, 70526
337-783-2061 Ext. 4
Serving Acadia Parish.

Avoyelles Parish - Marksville Part-time Office
313 North Monroe Street
Marksville LA 71351
318-253-9235 Ext. 4
Serving Avoyelles Parish.

Caddo Parish - Shreveport Sub Office
1402 Hawn Avenue
Shreveport, LA 71107
318-676-3461 Ext. 4
Fax: 318-676-3336
Serving Caddo, Bossier, and Desoto Parishes.

Catahoula Parish - Jonesville Sub Office
3545 Fourth Street
Jonesville, LA 71343
318-339-4239 Ext. 4
Fax: 318-339-4824
Serving Catahoula, Concordia, and LaSalle Parishes.

Concordia Parish - Ferriday Part-time Office
8331 Highway 84 West
Ferriday, LA 71334
318-757-4870 Ext. 4
Serving Concordia Parish.

Desoto Parish - Mansfield Part-time Office
R.C. Bridges Building
211 Washington
Mansfield, LA 71052
318-872-4814 Ext. 4
Serving Desoto Parish.

East Carroll Parish - Lake Providence Part-time Office
406 Lake Street, Suite B
Lake Providence, LA 71254
318-559-2188 Ext. 4
Serving East Carroll Parish.

Evangeline Parish - Ville Platte Part-time Office
205 Court Street
Ville Platte, LA 70586
337-363-6603 Ext. 4.
Serving Evangeline and Allen Parishes.

Franklin Parish - Winnsboro Part-time Office
616 Riser Road
Winnsboro, LA 71295
318-435-9424 Ext. 4
Serving Franklin Parish.

Jefferson Davis Parish - Jennings Part-time Office
2003 Port Drive
Jennings, LA 70546
318-824-0263 Ext. 4
Serving Jefferson Davis Parish.

Lafayette Parish - Lafayette Sub Office
Whitney National Bank, Suite 320
905 Jefferson Street
Lafayette, LA 70501
337-262-6602 Ext. 4
Fax: 318-262-6823
Serving Lafayette and Vermillion Parishes.

Lafourche Parish - Thibodaux Sub Office
204 E. Bayou Road
Thibodaux, LA, 70301
985-447-6311, Ext. 4
Fax: 985-447-2793
Serving Lafourche, Assumption, St. James, and Terrebonne Parishes.

Lincoln Parish - Ruston Sub Office
1803 Trade Drive
P.O. Box 1990
Ruston, LA 71273-1990
318-255-2826 Ext. 4
Fax: 318-255-8063
Serving Lincoln, Claiborne, Jackson, and Union Parishes.

Livingston Parish - Denham Springs Sub Office
2191 Tower Street
Denham Springs, LA 70726
225-667-9528 Ext. 4
Fax: 225-791-8874
Serving Livingston, East Baton Rouge, East Feliciana, and West Feliciana Parishes

Madison Parish - Tallulah Local Office
1900 Crothers Drive
P.O. Box 1228
Tallulah, LA 71284
318-574-4158 Ext. 4
Fax: 318-574-5453
Serving Madison, Franklin, and Tensas Parishes.

Morehouse Parish - Bastrop Part-time Office
9602 Marlatt Street
Bastrop, LA 71220-9758
318-281-1561 Ext. 4
Serving Morehouse Parish.

Natchitoches Parish - Natchitoches Sub Office
6949 LA Hwy 1 Bypass
Suite 103
Natchitoches, LA 71457
318-352-7100 Ext. 4
Fax: 318-354-1682
Serving Natchitoches and Vernon Parishes.

Ouachita Parish - Monroe Sub Office
2410 Old Sterlington Road, Suite C
Monroe, LA 71203
318-343-4467 Ext. 4
Fax: 318-343-5776
Serving Ouachita, Caldwell, and Richland Parishes.

Plaquemines Parish - Belle Chasse Part-time Office
805 West Oak Street, Room 3
Amite, LA 70422
985-748-8751 Ext. 4
Fax: 985-748-4940
Serving Plaquemines, Jefferson, Orleans, St. Bernard, St. Charles, and St. John Parishes.

Pointe Coupee Parish - New Roads Part-time Office
180 East Main Street
New Roads, LA 70760
225-618-8524 Ext. 4
Serving Point Coupee Parish.

Rapides Parish - Alexandria Local Office
3732 Government Street, Building C
Alexandria, LA 71302
318-473-7710 Ext. 4
Fax: 318-473-7628
Serving Rapides and Avoyelles Parishes.

Red River Parish - Coushatta Part-time Office
1311 Ringgold Avenue
Coushatta, LA 71019
318-932-4231 Ext. 4
Serving Red River Parish.

Richland Parish - Rayville Part-time Office
141 Industrial Loop
Rayville, LA 71269
318-728-2081 Ext. 114
Serving Richland Parish.

St. Landry Parish - Opelousas Sub Office
111 N. Main Street, Suite A
Opelousas, LA 70570
337-948-3091 Ext. 4
Fax: 337-948-8241
Serving St. Landry, Evangeline, and Allen Parishes.

St. Martin Parish - St. Martin Part-time Office
Whitney National Bank
905 Jefferson Street, Suite 320
Lafayette, LA 70501
337-262-6602 Ext. 4
Fax: 337-262-6823
Serving St. Martin, St. Mary, and Iberia Parishes.

St. Mary Parish - Franklin Part-time Office
500 Main Street
Franklin, LA 70538-6144
337-828-4100 Ext. 104
Serving St. Mary Parish.

Tangipahoa Parish - Amite Sub Office
805 West Oak Street, Room 3
Amite, LA 70422
985-748-8751 Ext. 4
Serving Tangipahoa and St. Helena Parish.

Tensas Parish - St. Joseph Part-time Office
1301 Plank Road
St. Joseph, LA 71366
318-766-3502 Ext. 4
Serving Tensas Parish.

Vernon Parish - Leesville Part-time Office
1100 S. Third Street, Suite C
Leesville, LA 71449
337-239-0057 Ext. 4
Serving Vernon Parish.

Washington Parish - Franklinton Sub Office
1111 Washington Street
Franklinton, LA 70438
985-839-5686 Ext. 4
Fax: 985-839-9935
Serving Washington and St. Tammany Parishes.

Webster Parish - Minden Sub Office
216 B. Broadway
Minden, LA 71055
318-377-1871 Ext. 4
Fax: 318-377-2221
Serving Webster, Bienville, and Red River Parishes.

West Baton Rouge Parish - Addis Local Office
7747 Highway 1 South
Addis, LA 70710
225-687-2184 Ext. 4
Fax: 225-687-3412
Serving West Baton Rouge, Ascension, Iberville, and Point Coupee Parishes.

West Carroll Parish - Oak Grove Sub Office
206 S. Constitution Avenue
P.O. Box 200
Oak Grove, LA 71263
318-428-9303 Ext. 4,
Fax: 318-428-2822
Serving West Carroll, East Carroll, and Morehouse Parishes.

Maine

State Office
USDA Rural Development
967 Illinois Avenue
P.O. Box 405
Bangor, ME 04402-0405
207-990-9100
Fax: 207-990-9165

Area Offices

Presque Isle Area Office
99 Fort Fairfield Road
Preque Isle, ME 04769-5015
207-764-4155/4157
Fax: 207-762-2246
Serving Aroostook, a Portion of Northern Penobscot, and Washington Counties

Bangor Area Office
28 Gilman Plaza, Suite 3
Bangor, ME 04401-3550
207-990-3676
Fax: 207-990-5092
Serving Hancock, Knox, Lincoln, Penobscot, Piscataquis, Somerset, and Waldo Counties

Lewistown Area Office
254 Goddard Road
P.O. Box 1938
Lewistown, ME 04241-1938
207-753-9400
Fax: 207-784-1335
Serving Androscoggin, Cumberland, Franklin, Kennebec, Oxford, Sagadahoc, and York Counties

Maryland

Maryland USDA Rural Development
4607 South DuPont Highway
Post Office Box 400
Camden, DE 19934
302-697-4300
Fax: 302-697-4390

Frederick Area Office
USDA Rural Development
92 Thomas Johnson Drive
Suite 220
Frederick, MD 21702
301-694-7522, Ext 5
Fax: 301-694-5840

Mountain Lake Park Local Office
USDA/Rural Development
1916 Maryland Highway
Suite D
Mt. Lake Park, MD 21550
301-334-6970
Fax: 301-334-6952
Serving Allegany and Garrett Counties

Hagerstown Local Office
USDA/Rural Development
1260 Maryland Avenue, Suite 105
Hagerstown, MD 21740
301-797-0500 Ext. 4
Fax: 301-739-4775
Serving Carroll, Frederick, Howard, Montgomery, Baltimore, and Washington Counties

Prince Frederick Local Office
USDA/Rural Development
65 Duke Street, Suite 110
Prince Frederick, MD 20678
410-535-1521 Ext. 4
Fax: 410-535-0591

Serving Anne Arundel, Calvert, Charles, District of Columbia, Prince George's and St. Mary's Counties

Elkton Local Office
USDA/Rural Development
Upper Chesapeake Corporate Center
105 Chesapeake Blvd,. Suite B4
Elkton, MD 21921
410-398-4411 Ext. 4
Fax: 410-392-6530
Serving Cecil, Harford and Kent Counties

Denton Local Office
USDA/Rural Development
640 Legion Road, Suite 1
Denton, MD 21629
410-479-1202 Ext. 4
Fax: 410-479-2069
Serving Caroline, Dorchester, Talbot and Queen Anne Counties

Snow Hill Local Office
USDA/Rural Development
304 Commerce Street, Suite B
Snow Hill, MD 21863
410-632-0616 Ext. 4
Fax: 410-632-2732
Serving Worcester, Somerset and Wicomico Counties:

Massachusetts (Southern New England)

Rural Development State Office
451 West Street, Suite 2
Amherst MA 01002-2999
413-253-4300
Fax: 413-253-4347

Northampton Service Center
243 King Street, Room 24
Northampton, MA 01060
413-585-1000 Ext. 4
Fax: 413-586-8648
Serving Western Massachusetts Berkshire, Franklin, Hampshire, and Hampden Counties

Holden Service Center
52 Boyden Road
Holden, MA 01520
508-829-4477 Ext. 4
Fax: 508-829-3721
Serving Central Massachusetts and North Shore Worcester, Middlesex, Suffolk, and Essex Counties

West Wareham Service Center
15 Cranberry Highway
West Wareham MA, 02576
508-295-5151 Ext. 3
Fax: 508-291-2368
Serving South Eastern Massachusetts, Cape Cod and the Islands Bristol, Norfolk, Plymouth, Dukes, Nantucket and Barnstable Counties

Michigan

East Lansing, State Office
3001 Coolidge Road, Suite 200
East Lansing, MI 48823
517-324-5210
Fax: 517-324-5225

Gladstone Area Office
2003 Minneapolis
P.O. Box 231
Gladstone, MI 49837
906-428-1060, ext. 6
Fax: 906-428-1086

Caro Area Office
1975 Cleaver Road
P.O. Box 291
Caro, MI 48723
989-673-7588, ext. 6
Fax: 989-673-1848

Grand Rapids Area Office
3260 Eagle Park Drive, Suite 107
Grand Rapids, MI 49525
616-942-4111, ext. 6
Fax: 616-949-6042

Sault Ste. Marie Local Office
2769 Ashmum & M-129
Sault Ste. Marie, MI 49783
906-632-9611, ext. 4
Fax: 906-632-0341
Serving Alger, Baraga, Chippewa, Delta, Dickinson, Gogebic, Houghton, Iron, Keweenaw, Luce, Mackinac, Marquette, Menominee, Ontonagon, and Schoolcraft Counties.

Cadillac Local Office
7192 E. 34 Road
Cadillac, MI 49601
231-775-7681, ext. 4
Fax: 231-775-0938

Baldwin Local Office
1101 E. Washington
P.O. Box 220
Baldwin, MI 49304
231-745-8364
Fax: 231-745-8493
Serving Lake County.

West Branch Local Office
240 W. Wright Street
West Branch, MI 48661
517-345-5470, ext. 4
Fax: 517-345-4010
Serving Alcona, Alpena, Arenac, Clare, Crawford, Gladwin, Iosco, Montmorency, Ogemaw, Oscoda, Ostego, Presque Isle and Roscommon Counties.

Grand Rapids Local Office
3260 Eagle Park Dr, Suite 109
Grand Rapids, MI 49525
616-942-4111, ext. 4
Fax: 616-949-6042
Kent, Montcalm, Gratiot, Ionia, Clinton, Mecosta, Muskegon, Newago, Oceana, Ottawa and Isabella.

Flint Local Office
1525 North Elms Rd.
Flint, MI 48532
810-230-8766, ext. 4
Fax: 810-230-2404
Serving Bay, Genesee, Huron, Midland, Lapeer, Saginaw, St. Clair, Sanilac, Shiawassee and Tuscola Counties.

Howell Local Office
3469 E. Grand River
Howell, MI 48843
517-548-1550, ext. 4
Fax: 517-548-0533
Hillsdale Ingham Jackson Lenawee Livingston, Macomb Monroe, Oakland, Washtenaw Wayne

Berrien Springs Local Office
3334 Edgewood Rd.

P.O. Box 129
Berrien Springs, MI 49103
616-471-9111, ext. 4
Fax: 616-471-3773
Allegan, Barry, Berrien, Branch, Calhoun, Cass, Eaton, Kalamazoo, St. Joseph and Van Buren Counties

Howell Guaranteed Housing Office
3469 East Grand River
Howell, MI 48843
517-548-1550, ext. 6
Fax: 517-548-0533

Traverse City Guaranteed Housing Office
1501 Cass St., Suite A
Traverse City, MI 49684
231-941-0951, ext. 6
Fax: 231-929-7890

Minnesota

Rural Development State Office
410 Farm Credit Service Building
375 Jackson Street
St. Paul, MN 55101-1853
651-602-7800
Fax: 651-602-7824

Willmar Field Service Center
Willmar Service Center
1005 High Avenue
P.O. Box 1013
Willmar, MN 56201
320-235-5612 Option #4
Fax: 320-235-0984
Serving Becker, Beltrami, Blue Earth, Big Stone, Brown, Cass, Chippewa, Clay, Clearwater, Cottonwood, Douglas, Faribault, Grant, Hubbard, Jackson, Kandiyohi, Kittson, LacQuiParle, Lake of the Woods, Lincoln, Lyon, Mahnomen, Marshall, Martin, McLeod, Meeker, Murray, Nicollet, Nobles, Norman, Ottertail, Pennington, Pipestone, Polk, Pope, Red Lake, Redwood, Renville, Rock, Roseau, Sibley, Stevens, Swift, Todd, Traverse, Wadena, Watonwan, Wilkin, and Yellow Medicine Counties

North Branch Area Office
38694-12 Tanger Drive
North Branch, MN 55056
651-674-7051 Option #4
Fax: 651-674-8016
Serving Aitkin, Anoka, Benton, Carlton, Carver, Cook, Chisago, Crow Wing, Dakota, Dodge, Fillmore, Freeborn, Goodhue, Houston, Isanti, Itasca, Kanabec, Lake, LeSeuer, Mille Lacs, Morrison, Mower, Olmsted, Pine, Rice, Scott, Sherburne, St. Louis, Stearns, Steele, Wabasha, Waseca, Winona, and Wright Counties.

Northwest Region
Detroit Lakes Service Center
809 8th Street SE
Detroit Lakes, MN 56501
218-847-9392
Fax: 218-847-8910
Serving Becker, Mahnomen, Hubbard, Normal and Clay Counties.

Bemidji Service Center
3217 Bemidji Avenue
North Bemidji, MN 56601
218-751-1942
Fax: 218-751-9531
Serving Beltrami, Lake of the Woods, and Clearwater Counties

Thief River Falls Service Center
201 Sherwood Avenue South
P.O. Box 16
Thief River Falls, MN 56701
218-681-2843
Fax: 218-681-4732
Serving Pennington, Marshall, Red Lake, Roseau, Kittson, and Polk Counties.

Northeast Region
Brainerd Service Center
512 NE C. Street
Brainerd, MN 56401
218-829-5965
Fax: 218-829-8764
Serving Aitkin, Crow Wing, Morrison, and Cass Counties.

Duluth Service Center
4850 Miller Trunk Highway, Suite 1B
Duluth, MN 55811
218-720-5330
Fax: 218-720-3129
Serving S. St. Louis, Carlton, Cook, Lake, Aitkin, and Pine Counties.

Virginia Field Service Center
230 1st Street South, Suite 104
Virginia, MN 55792
218-741-3929
Fax: 218-741-9407
Serving Itasca, N. St. Louis, and Koochiching Counties.

West Central Region
Willmar Field Service Center
1005 High Avenue
P.O. box 1013
Willmar, MN 56201
320-235-5612
Fax: 320-235-0984
Serving Kandiyohi, Meeker, Renville, Big Stone, Swift, and Chippewa Counties.

Alexandria Service Center
900 Robert Street NE, Suite 103
Alexandria, MN 56308
320-763-3191
Fax: 320-762-5502
Serving Douglas, Pope, Grant, Traverse, Stevens, Wilkin, Todd, Otter Trail, and Wadena Counties.

East Central Region
Cambridge Field Service Center
380 South Garfield Street
Cambridge, MN 55008
763-689-3354
Fax: 763-689-2309
Serving Anoka, Chisago, Isanti, Kanabec, and Washington Counties.

Buffalo Service Center
306 B. Brighton Avenue
Southeast Buffalo, MN 55313
763-682-1151
Fax: 763-682-2903
Serving Wright, Ramsey, Hennepin, Carver, Sibley, McLeod, and Nicollet Counties.

Waite Park Service Center
110 South 2nd Street, Suite 120

Waite Park, MN 56387
320-255-9111
Fax: 320-255-1455
Serving Stearns, Sherburne, Benton, Mille Lacs, and Morrison Counties.

Southwest Region
Worthington Service Center
1567 North McMillian
Worthington, MN 56187
507-372-7784
Fax: 507-372-7751
Serving Nobles, Jackson, Rock, Cottonwood, Murray, Pipestone, Watonwan, and Martin Counties.

Marshall Service Center
1424 East College Drive, Suite 500
Marshall, MN 56258
507-532-3234
Fax: 507-532-7479
Serving Lyon, Brown, Lac qui Parle, Redwood, Lincoln, and Yellow Medicine Counties.

Southeast Region
Faribault Service Center
1810 30th Street, NW, #3
Faribault, MN 55021
507-332-7418 Option #4 (phone)
Fax: 507-332-9892
Serving Rice, Goodhue, Scott, Dakota, Steele, LeSueur, Wabasha, and Waseca Counties.

Austin Service Center
101 21st Street SE
Austin, MN 55912
507-437-8247, Option #4 (phone)
Fax: 507-437-8567
Serving Mower, Dodge, Winona, Blue Earth, Freeborn, Fillmore, Faribault, Houston, and Olmsted Counties.

Mississippi

USDA Rural Development State Office
100 West Capitol St., Suite 831
Federal Building
Jackson, MS 39269
601-965-4318
Fax: 601-965-5384

Brookhaven Area Office
1395 Johnny Johnson Drive.
Brookhaven, MS 39601
601-833-9321
Fax: 601-835-2437
Serving Adams, Amite, Claiborne, Copiah, Franklin, Hinds, Jefferson, Jefferson Davis, Lawrence, Lincoln, Pike, Warren and Wilkinson Counties.

Newton Area Office
100 North Main Street
Newton, MS 39345
601-683-6175
Fax: 601-683-7205
Serving Rankin, Simpson, Leake, Scott, Newton, Lauderdale, Jasper, Smith, Clarke, Jones, Wayne and Covington Counties.

Grenada Area Office
75 Kirk Avenue
Grenada, MS 38901
662-226-4724
Fax: 662-227-1018
Serving Attala, Carroll, Grenada, Leflore, Montgomery, Yalobusha, Calhoun, Chickasaw, Lafayette, Union and Pontotoc Counties.

Greenville Area Office
3038 East Reed Road
Greenville, MS 38704
662-335-4862
Fax: 662-378-9638
Serving Bolivar, Sunflower, Humphreys, Sharkey, Issaquena, Holmes,
Yazoo, Madison and Washington Counties.

Batesville Area Office
103 Woodland Rd. Suite 1
Batesville, MS 38606
662-578-7008
Fax: 662-578-0670
Serving Desoto, Coahoma, Tunica, Quitman, Tallahatchie, Panola, and Tate Counties.

Booneville Area Office
109 North Road
Booneville, MS 38829
662-728-8104
Fax: 662-728-3120
Serving Marshall, Tippah, Benton, Alcorn, Tishomingo, Prentiss, Lee and Ittawamba Counties.

Hattiesburg Area Office
132 Mayfair Road, Suite C
Hattiesburg, MS 39402
601-261-3293
Fax: 601-261-3254
Serving Marion, Walthall, Lamar, Forrest, Perry, Stone, George, Greene, Jackson, Hancock, Harrison and Pearl River Counties.

Starkville Area Office
505 Russell Street
Starkville, MS 39659
662-323-8031
Fax: 662-323-7648
Serving Monroe, Choctaw, Webster, Clay, Oktibbeha, Lowndes, Noxubee, Winston, Neshoba, and Kemper Counties.

Adams County Local Office
339-A Liberty Road
Natchez, MS 39120
601-442-1791
Fax: 601-446-6655
Serving Adams and Franklin Counties

Alcorn County Local Office
3301 Mullins Drive
Corinth, MS 38834
662-287-7223
Fax: 662-286-8068
Serving Alcorn and Tishomingo Counties

Amite County Local Office
442 Hwy 24
Centreville, MS 39631
601-645-5025
Fax: 601-645-6540
Serving Amite and Wilkinson counties

Attala County Local Office
502 Veterans Memorial Drive
Kosciusko, MS 39090
662-290-0702
Fax: 662-289-4241

Bolivar County Local Office
406 N. Martin Luther King
Cleveland, MS 38732
662-846-1448
Fax: 662-843-1688

Calhoun County Local Office
413 South Main Street
Calhoun City, MS 38916
662-628-8732
Fax: 662-628-8804
Serving Calhoun and Chickasaw Counties

Choctaw County Local Office
163 Highway 15 South
Ackerman, MS 39735
662-285-3238
Fax: 662-285-3166

Clarke County Local Office
109 East Donald Street
Quitman, MS 39355
601-776-9009
Fax: 601-776-5156

Clay County Local Office
515-A Highway 45 North
West Point, MS 39773
662-494-6344
Fax: 662-494-7480

Coahoma County Local Office
2655 North State Street
Clarksdale, MS 38614
662-776-9009
Fax: 662-627-5598
Serving Coahoma and Tunica Counties

Copiah County Local Office
1012 Carroll Drive
Hazlehurst, MS 39083
601-894-1118
Fax: 601-894-5588

Covington County Local Office
3193 Hwy 49
Collins, MS 39428
601-765-6311
Fax: 601-765-6497

Desoto County Local Office
Hwy 51 South 3260
Hernando, MS 39632
662-429-8687
Fax: 662-429-4882

Forrest County Local Office
701 North Main Street, Suite 311
Hattiesburg, MS 39401
601-583-4371
Fax: 601-583-3806
Serving Forrest, Perry and Stone Counties

George County Local Office
111 Ventura Drive
Lucedale, MS 39452
601-766-3962
Fax: 601-947-2911
Serving George, Greene and Jackson Counties

Grenada County Local Office
782-B E. Govan
Grenada, MS 38901
662-226-4151
Fax: 662-226-7271
Serving Grenada, Montgomery and Yalobusha Counties

Harrison County Local Office
2909 13th Street, Room 214
One Government Plaza
Gulfport, MS 39501
228-831-0881
Fax: 228-831-5578
Serving Harrison and Hancock Counties

Hinds County Local Office
322 New Market Drive
Jackson, MS 39209
601-965-5682
Fax: 601-965-4199
Serving Hinds and Warren Counties

Holmes County Local Office
Highway 12 West
Lexington, MS 39095
662-834-4688
Fax: 662-834-3196

Humphreys County Local Office
304 West Jackson Street
Belzoni, MS 39038
601-247-8732
Fax: 601-247-2368
Serving Humphreys, Issaquena and Sharkey Counties

Jasper County Local Office
3rd & 8th Street
Bay Springs, MS 38422
601-764-2025
Fax: 601-764-2186
Serving Jasper and Smith Counties

Jefferson County Local Office
415-B Gilcrest Street
Fayette, MS 39069
601-786-3412
Fax: 601-786-9955
Serving Jefferson and Claiborne Counties

Jefferson Davis County Local Office
2700 Highway 13
Prentiss, MS 39474
601-792-8601
Fax: 601-792-4595

Jones County Local Office
2011 Highway 15 North
Laurel, MS 39440
601-425-4622
Fax: 601-425-9289
Serving Jones and Wayne Counties

Kemper County Local Office
101 Hooper Avenue
Dekalb, MS 39238
601-743-9588
Fax: 601-743-9070

Lafayette County Local Office
2606 West Oxford Loop
Oxford, MS 38655
662-234-8701
Fax: 662-234-6575
Serving Lafayette and Union Counties

Lamar County Local Office
175 Shelby Speights
Purvis, MS 39475
601-794-5600
Fax: 601-794-8355

Lauderdale County Local Office
2412 7th Street
Meridian, MS 39302
601-483-4100
Fax: 601-693-5379

Lawrence County Local Office
214 Main Street

Monticello, MS 39654
601-587-0885
Fax: 601-587-0430

Leake County Local Office
407 Valley Street
Carthage, MS 39051
601-298-9101
Fax: 601-267-4571

Lee County Local Office
3098 Cliff Gookin Blvd.
Tupelo, MS 38803
662-680-9991
Fax: 662-844-6043
Serving Lee and Itawamba Counties

Leflore County Local Office
517 Brentwood Ave.
Greenwood, MS 38930
662-455-1199
Fax: 662-455-5887
Serving Leflore and Carroll Counties

Lincoln County Local Office
212 South First St.
Brookhaven, MS 39601
601-833-9322
Fax: 601-835-0930

Lowdnes County Local Office
1551 2nd Avenue North
Columbus, MS 39701
662-328-5921
Fax: 662-241-5944
Serving Lowndes and Noxubee Counties

Madison County Local Office
175-B Commercial Parkway
Canton, MS 39046
601-859-4272
Fax: 601-859-7091

Marion County Local Office
1010 Main Street, Suite 6
Columbia, MS 39429
601-731-5400
Fax: 601-736-0784
Serving Marion and Walthall Counties

Marshall County Local Office
250-C Whaley Drive
Holly Springs, MS 38635
662-252-1286
Fax: 662-252-7862

Monroe County Local Office
517 Hwy. 45 North
Aberdeen, MS 39730
662-369-0044
Fax: 662-369-3005

Neshoba County Local Office
511 East Lawn Drive
Philadelphia, MS 39350
601-656-8783
Fax: 601-656-3710

Oktibbeha County Local Office
706 Taylor Street,
Starkville, MS 39759
662-320-4009,
Fax: 662-323-7146

Panola County Local Office
510 Hwy. 51 South,
Batesville, MS 38606
662-578-8045,
Fax: 662-563-3337
Serving Panola and Tate Counties

Pearl River County Local Office
1222 South Main Street
Poplarville, MS 39470
601-795-4409
Fax: 601-795-6644

Pike County Local Office
101 North Cherry Street
Magnolia, MS 39652
601-783-2241
Fax: 601-783-6947

Pontotoc County Local Office
186 Hwy. 15 Bypass
Pontotoc, MS 38863
662-489-3563
Fax: 662-489-2802

Prentiss County Local Office
611 West Church Street
Booneville, MS 38829
662-728-9003
Fax: 662-728-9654

Rankin County Local Office
206-A East Government Street
Brandon, MS 39042
601-824–4601
Fax: 601-825-9662
Serving Rankin and Simpson Counties

Scott County Local Office
1099 Hwy. 35 South
Forest, MS 39074
601-469-3464
Fax: 601-469-1713
Serving Scott and Newton Counties

Sunflower County Local Office
214 North Martin Luther King
Indianola, MS 38751
662-887-9799
Fax: 662-887-5430

Tallahatchie County Local Office
309 West Cypress Street
Charleston, MS 38921
662-647-8857
Fax: 662-647-5673
Serving Tallahatchie and Quitman Counties

Tippah County Local Office
733-A South Line Street
Ripley, MS 38663
662-837-4464
Fax: 662-837-8336
Serving Tippah and Benton Counties

Washington County Local Office
3038 East Reed Road Suite 3
Greenville, MS 38701
662-332-5491
Fax: 662-335-6040

Winston County Local Office
218 South Columbus Avenue
Louisville, MS 39339
662-773-2207
Fax: 662-773-8731

Yazoo County Local Office
711 Jackson Avenue
Yazoo City, MS 39194
662-746-8358
Fax: 662-746-8496

Missouri

USDA Rural Development State Office

601 Business Loop 70 West
Parkade Center, Suite 235
Columbia, MO 65203
573-876-0976
Fax: 573-876-0977

St. Joseph Area Office- Area 1
USDA Service Center
3915 Oakland Avenue
St. Joseph, MO 64506-4929
816-364-3767, ext. 5
Fax: 816-364-0562

Kirksville Area Office- Area 2
USDA Service Center
2410 South Franklin Street
Kirksville, MO 63501-6503
660-665-3274, ext. 4
Fax: 660-665-0266

Clinton Area Office- Area 3
USDA Service Center
1306 North Second Street
Clinton, MO 64735
660-885-5567 ext. 5
Fax: 660-885-6260

Farmington Area Office- Area 4
USDA Service Center
812 Progress Drive
Farmington, MO 63640
573-756-6413, ext. 4
Fax: 573-756-8037

Springfield Area Office- Area 5
USDA Service Center
688 State Highway B, Suite 400
Springfield, MO 65802
417-831-5246, ext. 5
Fax: 417-863-0256

Houston Area Office- Area 6
USDA Service Center
6726 South Highway 63, Suite B
Houston, MO 65483
417-967-4525
Fax: 417-967-4879

Dexter Area Office- Area 7
USDA Service Center
18450 Ridgeview Lane
Dexter, MO 63841
573-624-5939, ext. 4
Fax: 573-624-6964

Area 1 Local Offices
Chillicothe Local Office
1100 Morton Parkway
Chillicothe, MO 64601-3723
660-646-6222
Fax: 660-646-4894
Serving Daviess, Grundy, Harrison, Linn, Livingston, Mercer, Putnam and Sullivan Counties

Marysville Local Office
206 E. South Hills Drive, Suite 103
Maryville, MO 64468-6504
660-582-7421
Fax: 660-582-8366
Serving Atchison, Gentry, Holt, Nodaway and Worth Counties

Richmond Local Office
500 Wollard Blvd.
Richmond, MO 64085
816-776-2266
Fax: 816-776-6902
Serving Caldwell, Carroll, Clay and Ray Counties

St. Joseph Local Office
3915 Oakland Avenue
St. Joseph, MO 64506-4929
816-364-2328
Fax: 816-364-0562
Serving Andrew, Buchanan, Clinton, DeKalb and Platte Counties

Area 2 Local Offices
Columbia Local Office
1715 W. Worley Street, Suite D
Columbia, MO 65203
573-446-9091
Fax: 573-446-0177
Serving Boone, Cooper and Howard Counties

Kirksville Local Office
2410 South Franklin Street
Kirksville, MO 63501-6503
660-665-3274 ext. 4
Fax: 660-665-0266
Serving Adair, Knox, Macon, Schuyler and Scotland Counties

Mexico Local Office
4617 South Clark
Mexico, MO 65265
573-581-4177
Fax: 573-581-7283
Serving Audrain, Callaway and Montgomery Counties

Moberly Local Office
Route 3, Box 135
Moberly, MO 65270
660-263-7400
Fax: 660-263-3725
Serving Chariton, Monroe, Randolph and Shelby Counties

London Local Office
17623 Highway 19
New London, MO 63459
573-985-7211
Fax: 573-985-3928
Serving Clark, Lewis, Marion and Ralls Counties

Troy Local Office
114 Frenchman Bluff Road
Troy, MO 63379
636-528-7046
Fax: 636-528-9582
Serving Lincoln, Pike and Warren Counties

Area 3 Local Offices
Butler Local Office
625 W. Nursery Box A
Butler, MO 64730
660-679-6114
Fax: 660-679-6207
Serving Bates, Cass and Vernon Counties

Clinton Local Office
1306 North 2nd Street
Clinton, MO 64735
660-885-5567
Fax: 660-885-6812
Serving Cedar, Henry, Johnson and St. Clair Counties

Eldon Local Office
405 W. 4th Street
Eldon, MO 65026
573-392-5667
Fax: 573-392-4052
Serving Camden, Miller and Morgan Counties

Higginsville Local Office
120 West 19th Street
Higginsville, MO 64037
660-584-8732
Fax: 660-584-2191

Serving Jackson and Lafayette Counties

Sedalia Local Office
1407 W. 32nd Street
Sedalia, MO 65301
660-826-3339
Fax: 660-826-7982
Serving Benton, Hickory, Pettis and Saline Counties

Area 4 Local Offices
Farmington Local Office
812 Progress Drive
Farmington, MO 63640
573-756-6413
Fax: 573-756-8037
Serving Iron, Madison, St. Francois and Ste Genevieve Counties

Hillsboro Local Office
10820 State Route 21, Ste. 112
Hillsboro, MO 63050
636-789-3551
Fax: 636-789-2175
Serving Jefferson, St. Louis and Washington Counties

Jackson Local Office
480 West Jackson Trails
Jackson, MO 63755-2665
573-243-1467
Fax: 573-243-8843
Serving Bollinger, Cape Girardeau and Perry Counties

Area 5 Local Offices
Carthage Local Office
416 East Airport Drive
Carthage, MO 64836
417-358-8196
Fax: 417-358-5792
Serving Barton, Daade, Jasper and Lawrence Counties

Neosho Local Office
1900 S Business Hwy 71
Neosho, MO 64850
417-451-1007, Ext. 4
Fax: 417-451-9244
Serving Barry, McDonald and Newton Counties

Ozark Local Office
1786 S. 16th Avenue, Suite 103
Ozark, MO 65721
417-581-3905
Fax: 417-485-3863
Serving Christian, Stone and Taney Counties

Springfield Local Office
688 S. State Highway B, Suite 400
Springfield, MO 65802
417-831-5246
Fax: 417-863-0256
Serving Dallas, Greene and Polk Counties

Area 6 Local Offices
Houston Local Office
6726 S. Hwy. 63, Suite B
Houston, MO 65843
417-967-3321
Fax: 417-967-4059
Serving Dent, Shannon and Texas Counties

Jefferson City Local Office
1911 Boggs Creed Road
Jefferson City, MO 65101
573-893-8504
Fax: 573-893-7238
Serving Cole, Moniteau and Osage Counties

Lebanon Local Office
1242 Deadra Drive
Lebanon, MO 65536
417-532-5741
Fax: 417-533-3689
Serving Laclede, Webster and Wright Counties

Rolla Local Office
1050 Highway 72
Rolla, MO 65402
573-364-1479
Fax: 573-364-7936
Serving Crawford, Maries, Phelps and Pulaski Counties

Union Local Office
1004 Vondera, Suite 3
Union, MO 63084-3122
636-583-2121
Fax: 636-583-6936
Serving Franklin, Gasconade and St. Charles Counties

West Plains Local Office
111 Walnut Street
West Plains, MO 65775
417-256-7117
Fax: 417-256-5564
Serving Douglas, Howell, Oregon and Ozark Counties

Area 5 Local Offices
Charleston Local Office
831 South Hwy 105
Charleston, MO 63834
573-649-9947
Fax: 573-649-9950
Serving Mississippi and New Madrid Counties

Dexter Local Office
18450 Ridgeview Lane
Dexter, MO 63841
573-624-5939
Fax: 573-624-6964
Serving Scott and Stoddard Counties

Kennett Local Office
704 North Bypass
Kennett, MO 63857
573-888-6664
Fax: 573-888-6736
Serving Dunklin and Pemiscot Counties

Poplar Bluff Local Office
4327 Highway 67 N
Poplar Bluff, MO 63901
573-785-9679
Fax: 573-686-0187
Serving Butler, Carter, Reynolds, Ripley and Wayne Counties

Montana

USDA Rural Development State Office
P.O. Box 850
Bozeman, MT 59771
406-585-2580
Fax: 406-585-2565

Billings Local Office
1629 Avenue D
Billings, MT 59102
406-657-6297, ext. 4
Fax: 406-657-6294
Serving Big Horn, Carbon, Carter, Custer, Fallon, Golden Valley, Mussellshell, Powder River, Rosebud, Stillwater,

Treasure, Yellowstone, Crow and Northern Cheyenne Indian Reservations.

Bozeman Local Office
900 Technology Blvd, Suite B
Bozeman, MT 59718
406-585-2530
Fax: 406-585-2565
Serving Gallatin, Meagher, Park, Sweet Grass, and Wheatland

Choteau Local Office
1102 Main Avenue NW
P.O. Box 316
Choteau, MT 59422
406-466-5351, ext. 4
Fax: 406-466-5328
Serving Glacier, Lewis & Clark (No of Hwy 200), Pondera, Powell (No. of Hwy 200, including Helmville), Teton, Toole and Blackfeet Indian Reservation

Glasgow Local Office
54062 Highway 2 West
Glasgow, MT 59230
406-228-4321, ext. 4
Fax: 406-228-8101
Serving Blaine, Daniels, Dawson, Garfield, McCone, Phillips, Prairie, Richland, Roosevelt, Sheridan, Valley, Wibaux, Fort Belknap and Fort Peck Indian Reservations.

Great Falls Local Office
12 3rd Street, NW, 2nd Floor
Great Falls, MT 59404
406-761-4077, ext. 4
Fax: 406-452-3806
Serving Cascade, Chouteau, Fergus, Hill, Judith Basin, Liberty, Petroleum, and Rocky Boys Indian Reservation

Helena Local Office
790 Colleen Street
Helena, MT 59601
406-449-5000, ext. 4
Fax: 406-449-5039
Serving Beaverhead, Broadwater, Deer Lodge, Jefferson, Lewis and Clark (So. of Hwy 200), Madison, Powell (So. of Hwy 200 but not Helmville) and Silver Bow

Kalispell Local Office
30 Lower Valley Road
Kalispell, MT 59901
406-752-4242, ext. 4
Fax: 406-752-4879
Serving Flathead, Lake, Lincoln and Flathead Indian Reservation

Missoula Local Office
5115 Hwy 93 South
Missoula, MT 59804
406-251-4826, ext. 4
Fax: 406-251-6268
Serving Granite, Mineral, Missoula, Ravalli, and Sanders

Nebraska

USDA Rural Development State Office
Federal Building Room 152
100 Centennial Mall North
Lincoln, NE 68508.
402-437-5551
Fax: 402-437-5408

Area 1
West/West Central Nebraska
Kearney Area Office
4009 North 6th Avenue
P.O. Box 730
Kearney, NE 68848-0730
308-237-3118, Ext. 4
Fax: 308-236-6290

Hastings Branch Office of Kearney Office
2727 West 2nd Street, Suite 108
Hastings, NE 68901-4608
402-463-6771, Ext. 4
Fax: 402-462-6771

Lexington Branch Office of Kearney Office
721 E. Pacific Street
P.O. Box 0
Lexington, NE 68850
308-324-6314, Ext. 4
Fax: 308-324-7232
The Kearney Area Office, along with the Hastings and Lexington Branch Offices, services the following Nebraska counties: Adams, Blaine, Buffalo, Clay, Custer, Dawson, Franklin, Furnas, Garfield, Gosper, Hall, Hamilton, Harlan, Howard, Kearney, Loup, Merrick, Nuckolls, Phelps, Sherman, Valley, and Webster.

North Platte Field Office
1202 S. Cottonwood
P.O. Box 2009
North Platte, NE 69103
308-534-2360, Ext. 4
Fax: 308-534-8645

Mccook Branch Office of North Platte Office
1400 W. 5th Street, Suite 4
McCook, NE 69001
308-345-4163, Ext. 4
Fax: 308-345-3642

Valentine Branch Office of North Platte Office
518 W. Hwy 20, Suite 2
P.O. Box 607
Valentine, NE 69201
402-376-1712, Ext. 4
Fax: 402-376-3515
The North Platte Field Office, along with the McCook and Valentine Branch Offices, services the following counties: Arthur, Brown, Chase, Cherry, Dundy, Frontier, Grant, Hayes, Hitchcock, Hooker, Keith, Keya Paha, Lincoln, Logan, McPherson, Perkins, Red Willow, Rock, and Thomas.

Scottsbluff Field Office
818 Ferdinand Plaza, Suite B
Scottsbluff, NE 69361-4401
308-632-2195, Ext. 4
Fax: 308-635-2787

Chadron Branch Office of Scottsbluff Office
1020 West 6th
Chadron, NE 69337-2909
308-432-4616, Ext. 4
Fax: 308-432-5117

Sidney Branch Office of Scottsbluff Office
2244 Jackson, Box 365
Sidney, NE 69162

308-254-4507, Ext. 4
Fax: 308-254-0545
The Scottsbluff Field Office, along with the Chadron and Sidney Branch Offices, services the following counties: Banner, Box Butte, Cheyenne, Dawes, Deuel, Garden, Kimball, Morrill, Scotts Bluff, Sheridan, and Sioux.

Area 2
Southeast Nebraska
Beatrice Area Office
201 N. 25th Street
Beatrice, NE 68310
402-223-3125, Ext. 4
Fax: 402-228-0535
The Beatrice Area Office services the following counties: Gage, Jefferson, Johnson, Nemaha, Pawnee, Richardson, Saline, and Thayer.

Lincoln Field Office
6030 S. 58th Street
Suite B
P.O. Box 6549
Lincoln, NE 68516
402-423-9683, Ext. 4
Fax: 402-423-7614
The Lincoln Field Office services the following counties: Butler, Cass, Fillmore, Lancaster, Otoe, Polk, Saunders, Seward, and York.

Area 3
Northeast Nebraska
Norfolk Area Office
1909 Vicki Lane, Suite 103
Norfolk, NE 68701
402-371-5350
Fax: 402-371-8930

Bloomfield Branch Office of Norfolk Office
111 N. Washington St.
Bloomfield, NE 68718
402-373-4914, Ext. 4
Fax: 402-373-2621

O'Neill Branch Office of Norfolk Office
107-B E. Hwy 20
P.O. Box 630
O'Neill, NE 68763
402-336-3796, Ext. 4
Fax: 402-336-1735

Wayne Branch Office of Norfolk Office
709 Providence Road
P.O. Box 200
Wayne, NE 68787
402-375-2453, Ext. 4
Fax: 402-375-4419
The Norfolk Area Office, along with the Bloomfield, O'Neill, and Wayne Branch Offices, services the following counties: Antelope, Boyd, Cedar, Dakota, Dixon, Holt, Knox, Madison, Pierce, Stanton, Thurston, Wayne, and Wheeler.

Columbus Field Office
3100 23rd Street
US 30 Center
Columbus, NE 68601
402-564-0506, Ext. 4
Fax: 402-564-6348
The Columbus Field Office services the following counties: Boone, Colfax, Greeley, Nance, and Platte

Omaha Field Office
8901 South 154th Street
Suite 2
Omaha, NE 68138-3621
402-891-0430
Fax: 402-891-0529

Fremont Branch Office of Omaha Office
1740 W. 23rd Street
Fremont, NE 68025-6607
402-721-8455, Ext. 4
Fax: 402-721-5268
The Omaha Field Office, along with the Fremont Branch Office, services the following counties: Burt, Cuming, Dodge, Douglas, Sarpy, and Washington.

Nevada

USDA Rural Development State Office
1390 S. Curry Street
Carson City, NV 89703
775-887-1222
Fax: 775-885-0841

Elko Field Office
2002 Idaho Street
Elko, NV 89801
775-738-8468
Fax: 775-738-7229

Fallon Field Office
111 Sheckler Road
Fallon, NV 89406
775-423-7541
Fax: 775-423-0784

Las Vegas Field Office
5820 S. Pecos Rd.
Bldg. A, Suite 400
Las Vegas, NV 89120
702-262-9047
Fax: 702-262-9969

Winnemucca Field Office
1200 Winnemucca Blvd E.
Winnemucca, NV 89445
775-623-4461
Fax: 775-623-0647

New Hampshire

USDA Rural Development State Office
Suite 218, Box 317
10 Ferry Street
Concord, NH 03301-5004
603-223-6035
Fax: 603-223-6061

Berlin Area Office
15 Mount Forist
Berlin, NH 03570
603-752-1328
Fax: 603-752-1354
Serving Coos and Carroll Counties

Concord Service Center
10 Ferry St.
Ste 212, Box 22
Concord, NH 03301-5081
603-223-6003
Fax: 603-223-6030
Serving Merrimack, Belknap & Hillsborough Counties

Epping Area Office
241 Calef Highway
Telly's Plaza
Epping, NH 03042
603-679-4650 ext 20
Fax: 603-679-4658

Serving Strafford, Rockingham Counties

Walpole Area Office
R1, Route 12, Box 315
Walpole, NH 03608-9744
603-756-3230 ext. 18
Fax: 603-756-2978
Serving Cheshire and Sullivan Counties

Woodsville Area Office
250 Swiftwater Road, Suite 4
Woodsville, NH 03785
603-747-2777
Fax: 603-747-3477
Serving Grafton County

New Jersey

Rural Development State Office
5th Floor North, Suite 500
8000 Midlantic Drive
Mt. Laurel, NJ 08054
856-787-7700
Fax: 856-787-7783

Hackettstown Local Office
Building 1, Hackettstown Commerce Park
101 Bilby Road
Hackettstown, NJ 07840
908-852-2576, Extension 4
Fax: 908-852-4666
Serving Bergen, Essex, Hudson, Hunterdon, Morris, Passaic, Somerset, Sussex, Union, and Warren Counties.

Hainesport Local Office
1289 Route 38, Suite 200
Hainesport, NJ 08036
609-267-1639, Extension 4
Fax: 609-261-3007
Serving Burlington, Mercer, and Middlesex Counties.

Toms River Local Office
776J Commons Way
Toms River, NJ 08755
732-349-1067
Fax: 732-505-8572
Serving Monmouth and Ocean Counties.

Vineland Local Office
1317 South Main Road
Building 3
Vineland, NJ 08360
856-205-1225, Extension 4
Fax: 856-205-0691
Serving Atlantic, Cape May, and Cumberland Counties.

Woodstown Local Office
Suite 2, 51 Cheney Road
Woodstown, NJ 08098
856-769-1127, Extension 398
Fax: 856-769-0718
Serving Camden, Gloucester, and Salem Counties.

New Mexico

USDA Rural Housing State Office
6200 Jefferson NE, Room 255
Albuquerque, NM 87109
505-761-4944
Fax: 505-761-4976

Aztec Local Office
San Juan and McKinley
1427 West Aztec, Suite 1
Aztec, NM 87410-1977
505-334-3090
Fax: 505-334-8659
Serving San Juan and McKinley Counties

Carlsbad Local Office
114 South Halagueno Room 108
Carlsbad, NM 88220-5738
505-887-6669 Ext. 202
Fax: 505-887-5700
Serving Eddy and Lea Counties

Deming Local Office
405 East Florida
Deming, NM 88030-5235
505-546-9692
Fax: 505-546-0038
Serving Luna & Hidalgo Counties

Espanola Local Office
424 Suite 1 South
Espanola, NM 87532
505-758-3701
Fax: 505-758-7650
Serving Taos, Rio Arriba, Northern Santa Fe & Northern Counties

Estancia Local Office
521 5th St
Estancia, NM 87016
505-384-2272
Fax: 505-384-3043
Serving Torrance & Southern Santa Fe Counties

Gallup Local Office
1658 South 2nd
Gallup, NM 87301
505-722-4357, Ext.4
Fax: 505-722-0847
Serving McKinley County

Las Cruces State Office
2507 N. Telshor, Suite 3
Las Cruces, NM 88011-8236
505-522-8775 Ext.4
Fax: 505-521-3905
Serving Dona Ana & Otero Counties

Los Lunas Local Office
267 Courthouse Rd
Los Lunas, NM 87031-6811
505-865-4643
Fax: 505-866-0662
Serving Valencia, Bernalillo, Cibola & Southern Sandoval Counties

Las Vegas Local Office
242 Mills Avenue
Las Vegas, NM 87701
505-425-3594
Fax: 505-425-1430
Serving San Miguel, Mora, Guadalupe, De Baca & Quay Counties

Raton Local Office
245 Park Avenue
Raton, NM 87740
505-445-9571
Fax: 505-445-4066
Serving Colfax, Harding and Union Counties

Roswell Local Office
1011 S Atkinson Ave
Roswell, NM 88203
505-622-8745
Fax: 505-623-0570
Serving Chaves, Curry, Lincoln, and Roosevelt Counties

Silver City Local Office
2610 N Silver Street

Silver City, NM 88061
505-546-9291
Fax: 505-546-0038
Serving Grant and Catron Counties.

Socorro Local Office
101 Elm Street
Socorro, NM 87777
505-835-5555
Fax: 505-835-5556
Serving Socorro and Sierra Counties

New York

Syracuse State Office
441 S Salina St
Syracuse, NY 13202-2405
315-477-6518
Fax: 315-477-6550

Batavia Service Center
29 Liberty St
Batavia, NY 14020-3247
585-343-9167
Fax: 585-344-4662
Serving Genesee, Monroe, Niagara, Orleans, and Wyoming Counties

Bath Service Center
415 W Morris St
Bath, NY 14810-1038
607-776-7398
Fax: 607-776-7487
Serving Allegany, Livingston, and Steuben Counties

Binghamton Service Center
1163 Upper Front St
Binghamton, NY 13905-1117
607-723-1384
Fax: 607-723-1015
Serving Broome, Chenango, Cortland, Delaware, and Tioga Counties

Canandaigua Service Center
3037 County Road 10
Canandaigua, NY 14424-8303
585-394-5970
Fax: 585-394-8224
Serving Ontario, Wayne, and Yates Counties

Canton Service Center
Route 2-3 Commerce Lane
Canton, NY 13617
315-386-2401
Fax: 315-386-1608
Serving St Lawrence County

Ellicottville Service Center
8 Martha St
Ellicottville, NY 14731-9714
716-699-2375
Fax: 716-699-5357
Serving Cattaraugus, Chautauqua, and Erie Counties

Greenwich Service Center
2530 State Route 40
Greenwich, NY 12834-2300
518-692-9940
Fax: 518-692-2203
Serving Columbia, Hamilton, Rensselaer, Saratoga, Warren, and Washington Counties

Ithaca Service Center
903 Hanshaw Rd
Ithaca, NY 14850-1530
607-257-2737
Fax: 607-257-5592
Serving Chemung, Schuyler, Seneca, and Tompkins Counties

Johnstown Service Center
113 Hales Mills Rd
Johnstown, NY 12095-3741
518-762-0077
Fax: 518-762-7020
Serving Albany, Fulton, Montgomery, Otsego, Schenectady, and Schoharie Counties

Lafayette Service Center
2571 Us Route 11
La Fayette, NY 13084-3353
315-677-3552
Fax: 315-677-0072
Serving Cayuga, and Oswego Counties

Marcy Service Center
9025 State Route 49
Marcy, NY 13403-2301
315-736-3316
Fax: 315-768-2739
Serving Herkimer, Madison, and Oneida Counties

Middletown Service Center
225 Dolson Ave
Middletown, NY 10940-6569
845-343-1872
Fax: 845-343-2630
Serving Bronx, Dutchess, Greene, Kings, New York, Orange, Putnam, Queens, Richmond, Rockland, Sullivan and Ulster Counties

Plattsburgh Service Center
6064 State Route 22
Plattsburgh, NY 12901-6263
518-561-4616
Fax: 518-563-4540
Serving Clinton, Essex, Franklin, and Westchester Counties

Riverhead Service Center
209 E Main St
Riverhead, NY 11901-2456
631-727-5666
Fax: 631-727-4408
Serving Nassau, and Suffolk Counties

Watertown Service Center
21168 State Route 232
Watertown, NY 13601-5377
315-782-7289
Fax: 315-788-2454
Serving Jefferson, and Lewis Counties

North Carolina

USDA Rural Development State Office
4405 Bland Road
Raleigh, NC 27609
919-873-2000
Fax: 919-873-2075

Waynesville Area Office
589 Racoon Road, Suite 202
Waynesville, NC 28786
828-452-0319
Fax: 828-452-1644
Serving Buncombe, Cherokee, Clay, Cleveland, Gaston, Graham, Haywood, Henderson, Jackson, Lincoln, Macon, Madison, McDowell, Mitchell, Polk, Rutherford, Swain, Transylvania and Yancey Counties.

Jefferson Area Office
134 Government Circle, Suite 201

Jefferson, NC 28640
336-246-2885
Fax: 910-246-9173
Serving Alleghany, Alexander, Ashe, Avery, Burke, Caldwell, Catawba, Forsyth, Iredell, Stokes, Surry, Watauga, Wilkes, and Yadkin Counties.

Elizabethtown Area Office
450 Smith Circle, Rm 137
Elizabethtown, NC 28337
910-862-3179
Fax: 910-862-4670
Serving Bladen, Brunswick, Columbus, Hoke, New Hanover, Pender, Robeson, and Scotland Counties.

Albemarle Area Office
26032-F Newt Road, Box 10
Albemarle, NC 28001
704-982-5114
Fax: 704-983-7921
Serving Alamance, Anson, Cabarrus, Caswell, Davidson, Davie, Guilford, Mecklenburg, Montgomery, Moore, Randolph, Richmond, Rockingham, Rowan, Stanley and Union Counties.

Henderson Area Office
945-B W. Andrews Avenue
Henderson, NC 27536
252-438-3141
Fax: 252-438-3647
Serving Durham, Edgecombe, Franklin, Granville, Halifax, Nash, Northampton, Orange, Person, Vance, and Warren Counties.

Williamston Area Office 104
Kehukee Park Road
Williamston, NC 27892
252-792-7603
Fax: 252-809-0561
Serving Beaufort, Bertie, Camden, Chowan, Currituck, Dare, Gates, Hertford, Hyde, Martin, Northampton, Pasquotank, Perquimans, Tyrell, and Washington Counties.

Garner Area Office
Hartwell Plaza
1027 Hwy 70 East, Suite 219
Garner, NC 27529
919-779-7164
Fax: 919-779-9068
Serving Chatham, Cumberland, Durham, Harnett, Johnston, Lee, Pitt, Wake and Wilson Counties.

Kinston Area Office 1308 Hwy
258 North
PO Box 6189
Kinston, NC 28501
252-526-9799
Fax: 252-526-9607
Serving Carteret, Craven, Duplin, Greene, Jones, Lenoir, Onslow, Pamlico, Sampson and Wayne Counties.

North Dakota

USDA Rural Development State Office
Federal Building, Room 208
220 East Rosser Ave.
P.O. Box 1737
Bismarck, ND 58502
701-530-2037
Fax: 701-530-2108

Dickinson Area Office
2493 4th Ave West, Room B
Dickinson ND 58601-2623
701-225-9168
Toll Free in ND: 1-800-688-2251, Ext. 4
Fax: 701-225-1353

Minot Area Office
2001 6th St SE
Minot ND 58701-6700
701-852-1754
Toll Free in ND: 1-800-765-9476, Ext. 4
Fax: 701-839-8317

Devils Lake Area Office
502 Highway 2 West, Suite 5
Devils Lake ND 58301-0280
701-662-8634
Toll Free in ND: 1-800-688-2279, Ext. 4
Fax: 701-662-1227

Valley City Area Office
575 10th St SW, #4
Valley City, ND 58072-3906
701-845-5150
Toll Free in ND: 1-800-688-2293, Ext. 4
Fax: 701-845-5605

Bismarck Local Office - Single Family Housing Serving Office
1511 East Interstate Ave
Bismarck ND 58501-0560
701-250-4367
Toll free in ND: 1-800-688-2297, Ext. 4
Fax: 701-250-4363

Park River Local Office - Single Family Housing Serving Office
RR 1 Box 52, Suite 3
503 Park St West
Park River ND 58270-9701
701-284-7118
Toll free in ND: 1-800-688-2307, Ext. 4
Fax: 701-284-7238

Williston Local Office - Single Family Housing Serving Office
1106 2nd St West
Williston, ND 58801-5804
701-572-4597
Toll Free in ND: 1-800-688-2308, Ext. 4
Fax: 701-572-0482

Ohio

USDA Rural Development
Federal Building, Room 507
200 North High Street
Columbus, Ohio 43215
614-255-2500

Findlay Area Office
7868 C.R. 140, Suite D
Findlay, OH 45840
419-422-0242
Fax: 419-422-5423

Hillsboro Area Office
514 Harry Sauner Road, Suite 3
Hillsboro, OH 45133
937-393-1921
Fax: 937-393-1656

Wooster Area Office
5200 Cleveland Road, Suite A
Wooster, OH 44691
330-345-6791
Fax: 330-345-9206

Marietta Area Office
Route 9, Box 286A
Marietta, OH 45750
740-373-7113
Fax: 740-373-4838

Oklahoma

USDA Rural Development State Office
100 USDA, Suite 108
Stillwater, OK 74074
405-742-1000
Fax: 405-742-1005

Atoka Area Office
Rt.4, Box 1118
Atoka, OK 74525
580-889-6668

Hobart Area Office
806 W. 11th St.
Hobart, OK 73651
580-726-5625

Stillwater Area Office
2600 S. Main, Ste. B
Stillwater, OK 74074
405-624-0144

Woodward Area Office
4900 Oklahoma Ave.
Suite 310
Woodward, OK 73801
580-256-3375

Area 1 Serving Northwest Oklahoma
Enid Local Office
1216 West Willow, Suite B
Enid, OK 73703
580-237-4323
Fax: 580-233-4608
Serving Canadian, Garfield, Grant, Kay, Kingfisher, Logan Noble and Oklahoma Counties.

Woodward Local Office
4900 Oklahoma Ave.
Suite 110
Woodward, OK 73801-3713
580-256-6038
Fax: 580-254-5236
Serving Alfalfa, Blaine, Beaver, Cimarron, Dewey, Ellis, Harper, Major, Texas, Woods, and Woodward Counties.

Area 2 Serving Northeast Oklahoma
Chandler Local Office
210 North Sandy Lane, Suite B
Chandler, OK 74834-9003
405-258-1043
Fax: 405-258-1237
Serving Creek, Lincoln, Okfuskee, Pawnee, Payne, Pottawatomie, and Seminole Counties.

Muskogee Local Office
3001 Azalea Park Drive, Suite 3
Muskogee, OK 74401
918-686-0669
Fax: 918-686-0648
Serving Adair, Cherokee, Muskogee, Okmulgee, Sequoyah, Tulsa and Wagoner Counties

Vinita Local Office
P.O. Box 593
235 West Hope
Vinita, OK 74301
918-256-7863
Fax: 918-256-2407
Serving Craig, Delaware, Mayes, Nowata, Osage, Ottawa, Rogers, and Washington Counties

Area 3 Serving Southwest Oklahoma
Altus Local Office
3100 North Main, Suite B
Altus, OK 73521-1305
580-482-1714
Fax: 580-482-6243
Serving Comanche, Cotton, Greer, Harmon, Jackson, Kiowa, and Tillman Counties

Cordell Local Office 1505 N. Glenn English
Cordell, OK 73632
580-832-3393
Fax: 580-832-2434
Serving Beckham, Caddo, Custer, Grady, Roger Mills, and Washita Counties

Pauls Valley Local Office
P.O. Box 648
105 North Meridian
Pauls Valley, OK 73075
405-238-7561
Fax: 405-238-3279
Serving Carter, Cleveland, Garvin, Jefferson, Love, McClain, Stephens and Murray Counties

Area 4 Serving Southeast Oklahoma
Ada Local Office
1312 Cradduck Road
Ada, OK 74820
580-332-3070
Fax: 580-332-4256
Serving Bryan, Coal, Hughes, Johnston, Pontotoc and Marshall Counties

Antlers Local Office
P.O. Box 357
508 Highway 271 North
Antlers, OK 74523
580-298-3339
Fax: 580-298-3480
Serving Atoka, Choctaw, McCurtain and Pushmataha Counties

McAlester Local Office
P.O. Box 490
Federal Building, Room 303
McAlester, OK 74502
918-423-7602
Fax: 918-423-2745
Serving McIntosh, Haskell, LeFlore, Latimer and Pittsburg Counties

Oregon

USDA Rural Development State Office
101 SW Main, Suite 1410
Portland, OR 97204-3222
503-414-3300
Fax: 503-414-3392

Eugene Area Office
1600 Valley River Dr., Ste 230
Eugene, OR 97401-2129
541-465-6443, Ext. 4
Fax: 541-465-6483
Serving Benton, Lane, and Linn Counties

Medford Area Office
573 Parsons Drive Suite 103
Medford, OR 97501-1103
541-776-4270, Ext. 4

Fax: 541-776-4295
Serving Jackson, Josephine, Klamath, and Lake Counties

Pendleton Area Office
1229 SE 3rd St., Ste. A
Pendleton, OR 97801-4198
541-278-8049, Ext. 4
Fax: 541-278-8048
Serving Baker, Gilliam, Grant, Malheur, Morrow, Umatilla, Union, and Wallowa Counties

Redmond Area Office
625 S.E. Salmon Ave., Ste. 5
Redmond, OR 97756
541-923-4358 Ext. 4
Fax: 541-923-4713
Serving Crook, Deschutes, Harney, Hood River, Jefferson, Sherman, Wasco, and Wheeler Counties

Roseburg Area Office
251 NE Garden Valley Blvd., #M
Roseburg, OR 97470-1498
541-673-0136 Ext. 4
Fax: 541-672-3818
Serving Coos, Curry, Douglas, Lindie and Champ Counties

Salem Area Office
381 Development
67 Wolverine Way
Bldg. F, Ste. 19
Salem, OR 97305-1372
503-399-5741, Ext. 4
Fax: 503-399-5799
Serving Clackamas, Clatsop, Columbia, Lincoln, Marion, Multnomah, Polk, Tillamook, Washington, and Yamhill Counties

Pennsylvania

USDA Rural Development State Office
Suite 330
One Credit Union Place
Harrisburg, PA 17110-2996
717-237-2186
Fax: 717-237-2193

Multi-Family Housing Area Offices
Butler Area Office
602 Evans City Road, Suite 101
Butler, PA 16001-8701
724-482-4800, ext. 4
Fax: 724-482-4826
Serving Allegheny, Armstrong, Beaver, Butler, Cambria, Fayette, Greene, Indiana, Somerset, Washington, Westmoreland Counties

Crawford Area Office
14699 N. Main Street, Extension
Meadville, PA 16335-9441
814-336-6155
Fax: 814-337-0294
Serving Cameron, Clarion, Clearfield, Crawford, Elk, Erie, Forest, Jefferson, Lawrence, McKean, Mercer, Potter, Venango, Warren Counties

Juniata Area Office
R. D. #3, Box 301
Mifflintown, PA 17059-9621
717-436-8953, ext. 4
Fax: 717-436-9128
Serving Adams, Bedford, Blair, Cumberland, Franklin, Fulton, Huntingdon, Juniata, Mifflin, Perry, York Counties

Lehigh Area Office
2211 Mack Blvd.
Allentown, PA 18103-5623
610-791-9810, ext. 4
Fax: 610-791-9820
Serving Berks, Bucks, Carbon, Chester, Dauphin, Delaware (CF only), Lackawanna, Lancaster, Lebanon, Lehigh, Luzerne, Monroe, Montgomery, Northampton, Philadelphia, Pike, Schuylkill, Wayne Counties

Lycoming Area Office
542 County Farm Road
Suite 205
Montoursville, PA 17754-9685
570-433-3008
Fax: 570-433-3013
Serving Bradford, Centre, Clinton, Columbia, Lycoming, Montour, Northumberland, Snyder, Sullivan, Susquehanna, Tioga, Union, Wyoming Counties

Single Family Housing Area Offices
Butler Area Office
602 Evans City Road, Suite 101
Butler, PA 16001-8701
724-482-4800, ext. 4
Fax: 724-482-4826
Serving Allegheny, Armstrong, Beaver, Butler, Crawford, Erie, Fayette, Forest, Greene, Indiana, Lawrence, Mercer, Washington, Westmoreland and Venango Counties

Clinton Area Office
216 Spring Run Road
Room 103
Mill Hall, PA 17751-9543
570-726-3196, ext. 203
Fax: 570-726-0064
Serving Bradford, Cameron, Centre, Clarion, Clearfield, Clinton, Elk, Jefferson, Lycoming, McKean, Montour, Northumberland, Potter, Snyder, Sullivan, Tioga, Union and Warren Counties

Lehigh Area Office
2211 Mack Blvd.
Allentown, PA 18103-5623
610-791-9810, ext. 4
Fax 610-791-9820
Serving Berks, Bucks, Carbon, Chester, Columbia, Dauphin, Delaware, Lackawanna, Lancaster, Lebanon, Lehigh, Luzerne, Monroe, Montgomery, Northampton, Philadelphia, Pike, Schuylkill, Susquehanna, Wayne and Wyoming Counties

York Area Office
124 Pleasant Acres Road
York, PA 17402-9899
717-755-2966, ext. 4
Fax: 717-840-1302
Serving Adams, Bedford, Blair, Cambria, Cumberland, Franklin, Fulton, Huntingdon, Juniata, Mifflin, Perry, Somerset and York Counties

Puerto Rico

USDA Rural Development State Office
IBM Building

654 Munoz Rivera Avenue,
Suite 601
San Juan, PR 00918
787-766-5095
Fax: 787-766-5844

Rhode Island

Southern New England
Rural Development State Office
451 West Street, Suite 2
Amherst MA 01002-2999
413-253-4300
Fax: 413-253-4347

Warwick Service Center
60 Quaker Lane, Suite 44
Warwick, RI 02886
Serving all of Rhode Island
Bristol, Kent, Newport,
Providence and Washington
Counties

South Carolina

USDA Rural Development State
Office
Strom Thurmond Federal
Building
1835 Assembly Street, Room
1007
Columbia, SC, 29201
803-765-5163
Fax: 803-765-5633

Aiken Area Office
Aiken County Agriculture
Building
1555 E. Richland Ave.
Room 100
Aiken, SC 29801
803-649-4221
Fax: 803-642-0732
Serving Aiken, Lexington and
Edgefield counties, plus offices
of Bamberg, Greenwood and
Orangeburg

Bamberg Local Office
3828 Main Highway
P.O. Box 503
Bamberg, SC 29003
803-245-4311
Fax: 803-245-0054
Serving Allendale, Bamberg,
and Barnwell Counties

Greenwood Local Office
115 Enterprise Court, Suite A
Greenwood, SC 29649
864-229-3004
Fax: 864-229-2845
Serving Abbeville, Greenwood,
and McCormick Counties

Orangeburg Office
1550 Henley Street, Room 100
Orangeburg, SC 29115
803-534-2409
Fax: 803-536-5827
Serving Orangeburg, Calhoun,
and Richland Counties

Colleton Area Office
531 Robertson Blvd., Suite D
Walterboro, SC 29488
843-549-1822
Fax: 843-549-6001
Serving Colleton, Beaufort,
Hampton, and Jasper counties,
plus offices of Charleston and
Williamsburg

Charleston Local Office
4045 Bridgeview Drive
Charleston, SC 29405
843-727-4160
Fax: 843-727-4541
Serving Charleston, Berkeley,
and Dorchester Counties

Williamsburg Local Office
502 Martin Luther King Hwy.
P.O. Box 769
Kingstree, SC 29556-0769
843-354-9613
Fax: 843-354-5463
Serving Williamsburg,
Clarendon, and Georgetown
Counties

Florence Area Office
McMillan Federal Building
401 West Evans St.
Room 110-A
P.O. Drawer 2468
Florence, SC 29503-2468
843-669-9686
Fax: 843-669-2563
Serving Darlington, Florence,
and Marion counties, plus
offices of Horry, Marlboro and
Sumter

Horry Local Office
1949 Industrial Park Road
Conway, SC 29526
843-365-8732
Fax: 843-365-6660
Serving Horry county

Marlboro Local Office
USDA Service Center
210 Throop Street
Bennettsville, SC 29512-4616
843-479-4341
Fax: 843-479-8386
Serving Marlboro, Dillon, and
Chesterfield Counties

Sumter Local Office
Federal Building
101 South Main Street
Suite 103
Sumter, SC 29150-5253
803-775-8732
Fax: 803-775-5712
Serving Sumter, Lee, and
Kershaw counties

Spartanburg Area Office
105 Corporate Drive
Suite G
Spartanburg, SC 29303
864-814-2471
Fax: 864-814-2904
Serving Spartanburg, Greenville,
Union and Cherokee Counties)

Anderson Local Office
1521 N. Pearman Dairy Road
Anderson, SC 29625
864-224-2126
Fax: 864-224-8914
Serving Anderson, Pickens, and
Oconee Counties

Chester Local Office
744 A Wilson Street
Chester, SC 29706
803-581-1906
Fax: 803-581-0852
Serving Chester, Fairfield,
Lancaster, and York Counties

Newberry Local Office
719 Kendall Road
P.O. Box 99
Newberry, SC 29108
803-276-1978
Fax: 803-276-7887
Serving Newberry, Laurens, and
Saluda Counties

South Dakota

USDA Rural Development State Office
200 4th Street SW
Federal Building, Room 210
Huron, SD 57350
605-352-1100
Fax: 605-352-1146

Area I (Northeast) Office
810 10th Avenue SE, Suite 2
Watertown, SD 57201-5256
605-886-8202
Fax: 605-882-3268

Aberdeen Local Office
1707 4th Avenue, SE, Suite 100
Aberdeen, SD 57401
605-226-3360
Fax: 605-225-7829
Serving Brown, Campbell, Day, Edmunds, Marshall, McPherson, Roberts, and Walworth Counties.

Huron Local Office
1386 Lincoln Avenue, SW
Suite C
Huron, SD 57350
605-352-2998
Fax: 605-353-1476
ServingBeadle, Faulk, Hand, and Spink Counties.

Watertown Local Office
810 10th Avenue, SE, Suite 2
Watertown, SD 57201-5256
605-886-8202
Fax: 605-882-3268
Serving Brookings, Clark, Codington, Deuel, Grant, Hamlin, and Kingsbury Counties.

Area II (Southeast) Office
2408 Benson Road
Sioux Falls, SD 57104
605-330-4515
Fax: 605-330-4595

Mitchell Local Office
1820 North Kimball, Suite C
Mitchell, SD 57301-1114
605-996-1564
Fax: 605-996-0130
Serving Aurora, Brule, Buffalo, Davison, Douglas, Hanson, Hutchinson, Jerauld, and Sanborn Counties.

Sioux Falls Local Office
2408 Benson Road
Sioux Falls, SD 57104
605-330-4515
Fax: 605-330-4595
Serving Lake, Lincoln, McCook, Miner, Minnehaha, Moody and Turner Counties.

Vermillion Local Office
121 West Kidder Street
Suite 104
Vermillion, SD 57069-3033
605-624-7060
Fax: 605-624-4365
Serving Clay and Union.

Yankton Local Office
2914 Broadway
Yankton, SD 57078
605-665-2662
Fax: 605-668-9729
Serving Bon Homme, Charles Mix, and Yankton Counties.

Area III (West) Office
1530 Samco Road, Suite 2
Rapid City, SD 57702-8007
605-342-0301
Fax: 605-341-0583

Pierre Local Office
316 South Coteau, Suite 102
Pierre, SD 57501-3109
605-224-8870
Fax: 605-224-1803
Serving Corson, Dewey, Gregory, Hughes, Hyde, Jones, Lyman, Potter, Stanley, Sully, Tripp, and Ziebach Counties.

Rapid City Local Office
1530 Samco Road, Suite 2
Rapid City, SD 57702-8007
605-342-0301
Fax: 605-341-0583
Serving Bennett, Custer, Fall River, Haakon, Jackson, Mellette, Pennington, Shannon, and Todd Counties.

Sturgis Local Office
2202 West Main Street
Sturgis, SD 57785-0730
605-347-4952
Fax: 605-347-3016
Serving Butte, Harding, Lawrence, Meade, and Perkins Counties.

Tennessee

USDA Rural Development State Office
3322 West End Avenue
Suite 300
Nashville, TN 37203
615-783-1300
Toll Free: 800-342-3149
Fax: 615-783-1301

Greeneville Area Office
214 N. College St., Suite 300
P.O. Box 307
Greeneville, TN 37744-0307
423-638-4771 ext. 4
Fax: 423-639-0956
Serving Carter, Greene, Hancock, Hawkins, Johnson, Sullivan, Unicoi, and Washington Counties.

Knoxville Area Office
4730 New Harvest Lane
Suite 300,
Knoxville, TN 37918-7000
865-523-3338 ext. 4
Fax: 865-525-7622
Serving Anderson, Blount, Campbell, Claiborne, Cocke, Grainger, Hamble, Jefferson, Knox, Loudon, Monroe, Morgan, Roane, Scott, Sevier, and Union Counties

Chattanooga Area Office
25 Cherokee Blvd., Suite A
P.O. Box 4941
Chattanooga, TN 37405
423-756-2239 ext.100
Fax: 423-756-9278
Serving Bledsoe, Bradley, Grundy, Hamilton, McMinn, Marion, Meigs, Polk, Rhea, and Sequatchie Counties.

Cookeville Area Office
Fountain Court, Suite K,
390 South Lowe Avenue
P.O. Box 555
Cookeville, TN 38503
931-528-6539

Fax: 931-528-1976
Serving Cannon, Clay, Cumberland, DeKalb, Fentress, Jackson, Macon, Overton, Pickett, Putnam, Smith, Van Buren, Warren, White Counties.

Nashville Area Office
3322 West End Avenue, Suite 302
Nashville, TN 37203-6835
615-783-1359
Fax: 615-783-1340
Serving Cheatham, Davidson, Dickson, Houston, Humphries, Montgomery, Robertson, Rutherford, Stewart, Sumner, Trousdale, Williamson, and Wilson Counties.

Lawrenceburg Area Office
237 Waterloo Street
P.O. Box 1046,
Lawrenceburg, TN 38464
931-762-6913 ext.4
Fax: 931-762-4193
Serving Bedford, Coffee, Franklin, Giles, Hickman, Lawrence, Lewis, Lincoln, Marshall, Maury, Moore, Perry and Wayne Counties.

Jackson Area Office
West Towne Commons,
85G Stonebrook Place
Jackson, TN 38305
901-668-2091 ext. 100
Fax: 901-668-6911
Serving Chester, Decatur, Hardeman, Hardin, Haywood, Henderson, McNairy, and Madison Counties.

Covington Area Office
2043 Highway 51 South,
Covington, TN 38019
901-475-3350 ext. 203
Fax: 901-475-3356
Serving Fayette, Lauderdale, Shelby, Tipton Counties.

Union City Area Office
1216 Stad Avenue, Suite 3,
Union City, TN 38281
901-885-6480 ext. 203
Fax: 901-885-5487
Serving Benton, Carroll, Crockett, Dyer, Gibson, Henry, Lake, Obion, and Weakley Counties.

Texas

Texas USDA Rural Development State Office
101 South Main Street, Suite 102
Temple, TX 76501
254-742-9700
Fax: 254-742-9709

Area #1 Rural Development Manager
6113 - 43rd Street, Suite B
Lubbock, TX 79407
806-785-5644
Fax: 806-785-5974
Serving Andrews, Armstrong, Bailey, Borden, Briscoe, Carson, Castro, Childress, Cochran, Collingsworth, Cottle, Crosby, Culberson, Dallam, Dawson, Deaf Smith, Dickens, Donley, El Paso, Floyd, Gaines, Garza, Gray, Hale, Hall, Hansford, Hartley, Hemphill, Hockley, Howard, Hudspeth, Hutchinson, King, Lamb, Lipscomb, Lubbock, Lynn, Martin, Moore, Motley, Ochiltree, Oldham, Parmer, Potter, Randall, Roberts, Sherman, Swisher, Terry, Wheeler, and Yoakum Counties

Amarillo Local Office Potter County
6565 Amarillo Boulevard West
Suite C
Amarillo, TX 79106
806-468-8600
Fax: 806-468-7248
Serving Armstrong, Briscoe, Carson, Castro, Childress, Collingsworth, Dallam, Deaf Smith, Donley, Gray, Hall, Hansford, Hartley, Hemphill, Hutchinson, Lipscomb, Moore, Ochiltree, Oldham, Parmer, Potter, Randall, Roberts, Sherman, Swisher, and Wheeler Counties

El Paso Local Office El Paso County
11930 Vista del Sol, Suite C
El Paso, TX 79936
915-855-1229
Fax: 915-857-3647
Serving Culberson, El Paso, and Hudspeth Counties

Lubbock Local Office (50-52)
Lubbock County
6113 - 43rd Street
Suite B
Lubbock, TX 79407
806-785-5644
Fax: 806-785-5974
Serving Andrews, Bailey, Borden, Cochran, Cottle, Crosby, Dawson, Dickens, Floyd, Gaines, Garza, Hale, Hockley, Howard, King, Lamb, Lubbock, Lynn, Martin, Motley, Terry, and Yoakum Counties

Area #2 Rural Development Manager
2608 Highway 377 South
Suite A
Brownwood, TX 76801
915-643-1585
Fax: 915-646-8630
Serving Archer, Baylor, Brewster, Brown, Callahan, Coke, Coleman, Comanche, Concho, Crane, Crockett, Eastland, Ector, Fisher, Foard, Glasscock, Hamilton, Hardeman, Haskell, Irion, Jeff Davis, Jones, Kent, Knox, Loving, McCulloch, Midland, Mills, Mitchell, Nolan, Pecos, Presidio, Reagan, Reeves, Runnels, San Saba, Scurry, Shackelford, Stephens, Sterling, Stonewall, Taylor, Terrell, Throckmorton, Tom Green, Upton, Ward, Wichita, Wilbarger, Winkler, and Young Counties

Abilene Local Office Taylor County
4400 Buffalo Gap Road
Suite 4150
Abilene, TX 79606
915-690-6162
Fax: 915-695-0528
Serving Archer, Baylor, Callahan, Fisher, Foard, Hardeman, Haskell, Jones, Kent, Knox, Mitchell, Nolan, Scurry,

Shackelford, Stephens, Stonewall, Taylor, Throckmorton, Wichita, Wilbarger, and Young Counties

Brownwood Local Office Brown County
2608 Highway 377 South
Suite A
Brownwood, TX 76801
915-643-1585
Fax: 915-646-8630
Serving Brown, Coke, Coleman, Comanche, Concho, Eastland, Hamilton, Irion, McCulloch, Mills, Runnels, San Saba, Sterling, and Tom Green Counties

Fort Stockton Local Office Pecos County
2306 West Dickinson Blvd.
Suite 2
Fort Stockton, TX 79735
915-336-7585
Fax: 915-336-9620
Serving Brewster, Crane, Crockett, Ector, Glasscock, Jeff Davis, Loving, Midland, Pecos, Presidio, Reagan, Reeves, Terrell, Upton, Ward, and Winkler Counties

Area #3 Rural Development Manager
1406-E North McDonald Road
McKinney, TX 75071
972-542-0081
Fax: 972-542-4028
Serving Clay, Collin, Cooke, Dallas, Denton, Ellis, Erath, Fannin, Grayson, Hood, Hunt, Jack, Johnson, Montague, Palo Pinto, Parker, Rockwall, Somervell, Tarrant, and Wise Counties

Cleburne Local Office Johnson County
105-C Poindexter Street
Cleburne, TX 76033-4400
817-641-4481
Fax: 817-641-7629
Serving Ellis, Erath, Hood, Johnson, Somervell, and Tarrant Counties

Decatur Local Office Wise County
1604 West Business 380
Suite A
Decatur, TX 76234
940-627-3531
Fax: 940-627-5228
Serving Clay, Cooke, Jack, Montague, Palo Pinto, Parker, and Wise Counties

McKinney Local Office Collin County
1406-E North McDonald Road
McKinney, TX 75071
972-542-0081
Fax: 972-542-4028
Serving Collin, Dallas, Denton, Fannin, Grayson, Hunt, and Rockwall Counties

Area #4 Rural Development Manager
1305 South Main, Suite 103
Henderson, TX 75654
903-657-8221
Fax: 903-657-2571
Serving Bowie, Camp, Cass, Cherokee, Delta, Franklin, Gregg, Harrison, Henderson, Hopkins, Kaufman, Lamar, Marion, Morris, Panola, Rains, Red River, Rusk, Smith, Titus, Upshur, Van Zandt, and Wood Counties

Canton Local Office Van Zandt County
700 Trade Days Boulevard, Suite 3
Canton, TX 75103
903-567-6051
Fax: 903-567-4894
Serving Henderson, Kaufman, Rains, Smith, and Van Zandt Counties

Henderson Local Office Rusk County
1305 South Main, Suite 103
Henderson, TX 75654
903-657-8221
Fax: 903-657-2571
Serving Cherokee, Gregg, Harrison, Marion, Panola, Rusk, Upshur, and Wood Counties

Mount Pleasant Local Office Titus County
1809 Ferguson Road, Suite E
Mount Pleasant, TX 75456-1328
903-572-5411
Fax: 903-572-5411
Serving Bowie, Camp, Cass, Delta, Franklin, Hopkins, Lamar, Morris, Red River, and Titus Counties

Area #5 Rural Development Manager
1502 Highway 77 North
Hillsboro, TX 76645
254-582-7328
Fax: 254-582-7622
Serving Anderson, Bell, Bosque, Brazos, Burnet, Coryell, Falls, Freestone, Grimes, Hill, Lampasas, Limestone, McLennan, Milam, Navarro, Robertson, Travis, Waller, and Williamson Counties

Bryan Local Office Brazos County
3833 South Texas Avenue, Suite 117
Bryan, TX 77802
979-846-0548
Fax: 979-691-8967
Serving Brazos, Grimes, Robertson, and Waller Counties

Georgetown Local Office Williamson County
Post Office Box 58
505 West University Drive, Suite G
Georgetown, TX 78627-0058
512-863-6502
Fax: 512-869-0579
Serving Burnet, Milam, Travis, and Williamson Counties

Groesbeck Local Office Limestone County
Post Office Box 410
1213 East Yeagua
Groesbeck, TX 76642-0410
254-729-2310
Fax: 254-729-3459
Serving Anderson, Falls, Freestone, Limestone, and Navarro Counties

Hillsboro Local Office Hill County
1502 Highway 77 North
Hillsboro, TX 76645
254-582-7328
Fax: 254-582-7622
Serving Bell, Bosque, Coryell, Hill, Lampasas, and McLennan Counties

Area #6 Rural Development Manager
2 Financial Plaza, Suite 745
Huntsville, TX 77340
936-291-1901
Fax: 936-294-0533
Serving Angelina, Brazoria, Chambers, Fort Bend, Galveston, Hardin, Harris, Houston, Jasper, Jefferson, Leon, Liberty, Madison, Montgomery, Nacogdoches, Newton, Orange, Polk, Sabine, San Augustine, San Jacinto, Shelby, Trinity, Tyler, and Walker Counties

Angleton Local Office Brazoria County
209 East Mulberry, Suite 500
Angleton, TX 77515-4650
979-849-5251
Fax: 979-849-7190
Serving Brazoria, Fort Bend, and Galveston Counties

Huntsville Local Office Walker County
2 Financial Plaza, Suite 745
Huntsville, TX 77340
936-291-1901
Fax: 936-294-0533
Serving Chambers, Harris, Leon, Liberty, Madison, Montgomery, San Jacinto, and Walker Counties

Jasper Local Office Jasper County
714 West Gibson, Suite 1
Jasper, TX 75951
409-384-5779
Fax: 409-384-7079
Serving Hardin, Jasper, Jefferson, Newton, Orange, Polk, and Tyler Counties

Lufkin Local Office Angelina County
1520 East Denman, Suite 104
Lufkin, TX 75901-5817
936-639-8661
Fax: 936-634-8140
Serving Angelina, Houston, Nacogdoches, Sabine, San Augustine, Shelby, and Trinity Counties

Area #7 Rural Development Manager
3251 North Highway 123 Bypass
Seguin, TX 78155-6115
830-372-1043
Fax: 830-372-0020
Serving Atascosa, Austin, Bandera, Bastrop, Bexar, Blanco, Burleson, Caldwell, Colorado, Comal, Fayette, Gillespie, Gonzales, Guadalupe, Hays, Karnes, Kendall, Kerr, Kimble, Lee, Llano, Mason, Medina, Menard, Schleicher, Sutton, Washington, and Wilson Counties

Bastrop Local Office Bastrop County
Post Office Box 576
208 Old Austin Hwy
Bastrop, TX 78602
512-321-3428
Fax: 512-321-4177
Serving Austin, Bastrop, Burleson, Colorado, Fayette, Lee, and Washington Counties

Fredericksburg Local Office Gillespie County
1906 North Llano, Room 102
Fredericksburg, TX 78624
830-997-8902
Fax: 830-997-0837
Serving Bandera, Blanco, Gillespie, Kendall, Kerr, Kimble, Llano, Mason, Medina, Menard, Schleicher, and Sutton Counties

Seguin Local Office Guadalupe County
3251 North Highway 123 Bypass
Seguin, TX 78155-6115
830-372-1043
Fax: 830-372-0020
Serving Atascosa, Bexar, Caldwell, Comal, Gonzales, Guadalupe, Hays, Karnes, and Wilson Counties

Area #8 Rural Development Manager
2287 North Texas Blvd., Suite 1
Alice, TX 78332
361-668-0453
Fax: 361-668-3947
Serving Aransas, Bee, Brooks, Calhoun, DeWitt, Dimmit, Duval, Edwards, Frio, Goliad, Jackson, Jim Hogg, Jim Wells, Kenedy, Kinney, Kleberg, La Salle, Lavaca, Live Oak, Matagorda, Maverick, McMullen, Nueces, Real, Refugio, San Patricio, Uvalde, Val Verde, Victoria, Wharton, and Zavala Counties

Alice Local Office Jim Wells County
2287 North Texas Boulevard, Suite 1
Alice, TX 78332
361-668-0453
Fax: 361-668-3947
Serving Aransas, Bee, Duval, Frio, Jim Wells, Kenedy, Kleberg, La Salle, Live Oak, McMullen, Nueces, Refugio, and San Patricio Counties

Edna Local Office Jackson County
700 North Wells, Room 101
Edna, TX 77957
361-782-7151
Fax: 361-782-3680
Serving Calhoun, DeWitt, Goliad, Jackson, Lavaca, Matagorda, Victoria, and Wharton Counties

Hebbronville Local Office Jim Hogg County
1700 North Smith Street, Suite A
Hebbronville, TX 78361
361-527-3253
Fax: 361-527-5547
Serving Brooks and Jim Hogg Counties

Uvalde Local Office Uvalde County
101 Weeping Willow
Uvalde, TX 78801
830-278-9503
Fax: 830-278-9503
Serving Dimmit, Edwards, Kinney, Maverick, Real, Uvalde, Val Verde, and Zavala Counties

Area #9 Rural Development Manager
4400 East Highway 83
Rio Grande City, TX 78582
956-487-5576
Fax: 956-487-7882
Serving Cameron, Hidalgo, Starr, Webb, Willacy, and Zapata Counties

Edinburg Local Office Hidalgo County
2514 South I Road, Suite 4
Edinburg, TX 78539
956-383-4928
Fax: 956-383-6088
Serving Hidalgo County

Rio Grande City Local Office Starr County
4400 East Highway 83
Rio Grande City, TX 78582
956-487-5576
Fax: 956-487-7882
Serving Starr, Webb, and Zapata Counties

San Benito Local Office Cameron County
2315 West Expressway 83, Room 102
San Benito, TX 78586
956-399-1551
Fax: 956-399-9468
Serving Cameron and Willacy Counties

Utah

USDA Rural Development State Office
Wallace F. Bennett Federal Bldg
Room 4311, 125 South State Street
P.O. Box 11350
Salt Lake City, UT 84147-0350
801-524-4321
Fax: 801-524-4406

Richfield Area Office
340 North 600 East
Richfield, UT 84701-0218
435-896-8250 ext.22
Fax: 435-896-6566

Ogden Area Office
2871 South Commerce Way
Ogden, UT 84401-3277
801-629-0566 ext. 11
Fax: 801-629-0574

Richfield Area Office
340 North 600 East
Richfield, UT 84701-0218
435-896-8250 ext.23
Fax: 435-896-6566

Cedar City Local Office
2390 West Highway 56, Suite 13
Cedar City, UT 84720-4133
435-586-7274 ext. 27
Fax: 435-586-0649
Serving Iron, Beaver, Garfield

Manti Local Office
50 South Main St.
Manti, UT 84642-1349
435-835-4111 ext. 12
Fax: 435-835-4113
Serving Sanpete, Millard, Juab Counties

Monticello Local Office
32 South 100 East
P.O. Box 10
Monticello, UT 84535-0010
435-587-2473 ext.10
Fax: 435-587-2104
Serving San Juan, Grand (East) on a North-South line, West of Townships 16 S - 26 S, Range 20E (52-10)

Price Local Office
350 North 4th East
Price, UT 84501-2571
435-637-4354 ext. 12
Fax: 435-637-1237
Serving Carbon, Emery, Grand (West) on a North-South line, East of Townships 16 S - 26 S, Range 20E)

Provo Local Office
BOR Building
302 East 1860 South
Provo, UT 84606-7317
801-377-5580 ext. 12
Fax: 801-356-1237
Serving Utah, Salt Lake, Wasatch, Summit, Tooele Counties

Richfield Local Office
340 North 600 East
Richfield, UT 84701-0218
435-896-8258 ext. 19
Fax: 435-896-4819
Serving Sevier, Wayne, Piute Counties

St. George Local Office
Federal Building, 196 East Tabernacle, Room 34
St. George, UT 84770-3474
435-628-0461 ext.14
Fax: 435-673-0312
Serving Washington; Kane; Coconino, Arizona; Mohave, Arizona Counties

Tremonton Local Office
91 South 100 East
Tremonton, UT 84337-1605
435-257-5404 ext.25
Fax: 435-257-1930
Serving Box Elder, Cache, Rich, Weber, Davis, Morgan Counties

Vernal Local Office
80 North 500 West
Vernal, UT 84078-2094
435-789-1338 ext. 19
Fax: 435-789-4160
Serving Daggett, Uintah, Duchesne Counties

Vermont

Montpelier Office Staff
3rd Floor, City Center
89 Main Street
Montpelier, VT 05602
802-828-6010
Fax: 802-828-6076

Brattleboro Area Office
28 Vernon Street, Suite 3
Brattleboro, VT 05301
802-257-7878 ext 102
Fax: 802-254-3307
Serving Windham & Windsor Counties

Montpelier Area Office
3rd Floor, City Center
89 Main Street
Montpelier, VT 05602
802-828-6004
Fax: 802-828-6076
Serving Washington, Orange & Lamoille Counties

Rutland Area Office
170 South Main Street at Trolley Square
Rutland, VT 05701
802-775-8957 ext 4
Fax: 802-773-4177
Serving Addison, Rutland & Bennington Counties

St. Johnsbury Area Office
1153 Main Street, Suite 3
St. Johnsbury, VT 05819
802-748-8646 ext 102
Fax: 802-748-1621
Serving Caledonia, Essex & Orleans Counties

St. Albans Area Office
27 Fisher Pond Road, Suite 8
St. Albans, VT 05478
802-524-6503 ext 102
Fax: 802-524-4575
Serving Franklin, Chittenden & Grand Isle Counties

Virginia

USDA Rural Development State Office
Culpeper Building, Suite 238
1606 Santa Rosa Road
Richmond, VA 23229
804-287-1552
Fax: 804-287-1718

Harrisonburg Area Office
1934 Deyerle Avenue, Suite D
Harrisonburg, VA 22801
540-433-9126
Fax: 540-432-1707
Serving Albemarle, Fluvanna, Greene, Louisa, Nelson, Culpeper, Fauquier, Orange, Madison, Rappahannock, Spotsylvania, Arlington, Caroline, Falls Church, Fairfax, Fredericksburg, King George, Loudoun, Manassas, Prince William, Stafford, Frederick, Clarke, Page, Shenandoah, Warren, Winchester, Augusta, Bath, Buena Vista, Harrisonburg, Highland, Lexington, Rockbridge, Rockingham, Staunton, and Waynesboro Counties

Lebanon Area Office
383 Highland Drive Suite 5
Lebanon, VA 24266
276-889-4650
Fax: 276-889-2105
Serving Russell, Tazewell, Dickenson, Buchanan, Lee, Scott, and Wise, and the City of Norton Counties.

Lynchburg Area Office
20311-A Timberlake Rd.
P.O. Box 4337
Lynchburg, VA 24502
434-239-3473
Fax: 434-239-3735
Serving Mecklenburg, Halifax, Brunswick, Prince Edward, Amelia, Cumberland, Nottoway, Lunenburg, Charlotte, Buckingham, Campbell, Amherst, Appomattox, Bedford, Lynchburg City, Franklin, Danville, Henry, Martinsville, Pittsylvania, Patrick and the cities of Lynchburg, Martinsville, Danville and Bedford Counties

Suffolk Area Office
1548 Holland Road
Suffolk, VA 23434
757-539-9265
Fax: 757-925-4750
Serving Accomack, Northampton, Dinwiddie, Charles City, Chesterfield, Colonial Heights, Emporia, Goochland, Greensville, Hanover, Henrico, Hopewell, New Kent, Petersburg, Prince George, Sussex, Surry, Powhatan, Isle of Wight, Chesapeake City, Franklin, Hampton, Suffolk, James City, Newport News Poquoson, Southampton, VA Beach City, Williamsburg, York, Essex, Gloucester, King & Queen, Lancaster, Mathews, Richmond, Middlesex, King William, Northumberland, and Westmoreland Counties

Wytheville Area Office
100 USDA Drive
Wytheville, VA 24382
276-228-3513
Fax: 276-228-2049
Montgomery, Alleghany, Botetourt, Clifton Forge, Covington, Craig, Floyd, Giles, Pulaski, Radford, Roanoke, Salem, Wythe, Bland, Bristol, Carroll, Galax, Grayson, Smyth, and Washington Counties

Accomac Local Office
22545 Center Parkway
Accomac, VA 23301
757-787-3181
Fax: 757-787-8142
Serving Accomack and Northampton Counties

Boydton Local Office
1028 Madison Street
Boydton, VA 23917
434-738-0300
Fax: 434-738-0201
Serving Halifax, Mecklenburg and Brunswick Counties

Charlottesville Local Office
695 Berkmar Ct.
Suite 3
Charlottesville, VA 22901
434-975-0047 Ext. 4
Fax: 434-975-0223
Serving Albemarle, Fluvanna, Greene, Louisa, and Nelson Counties

Christiansburg Local Office
75 Hampton Blvd
Christiansburg, VA 24073
540-382-0267
Fax: 540-381-5604
Serving Montgomery, Alleghany, Botetourt, Clifton Forge, Covington, Craig Floyd, Giles, Pulaski, Roanoke and Salem Counties

Culpeper Local Office
351 Lakeside Avenue
Culpeper, VA 22701
540-825-4200
Fax: 540-825-1655
Serving Culpeper, Fauquier, Orange, Madison, and Rappahannock Counties

Dinwiddie Local Office
P.O. Box 279
13915 Boydton Plank Rd.
Dinwiddie, VA 23841
804-469-3311
Fax: 804-469-5962
Serving Dinwiddie, Charles City, Chesterfield, Emporia, Goochland, Greensville, Hanover, Henrico, New Kent, Prince George, Sussex, Surry, and Powhatan Counties

Farmville Local Office
100 C. Dominion Drive
Farmville, VA 23901
434-392-4906
Fax: 434-392-4577
Serving Prince Edward, Amelia, Cumberland, Nottoway, and Lunenburg, Charlotte, Buckingham Counties

Fredericksburg Local Office
4805 Carr Drive
Jackson Sq. Office Park
Fredericksburg, VA 22408
540-899-9492
Fax: 540-889-2014
Serving Spotsylvania, Arlington, Caroline, Falls Church, Fairfax,Fredericksburg, King George, Loudoun, Manassas, Prince William, 55-12 Stafford Counties

Gate City Local Office
95 US Hwy 23 S., Suite 1
Gate City, VA 24251
540-386-3951
Fax: 540-386-9051
Serving Scott, Wise, Lee, and Norton Counties

Lebanon Local Office
383 Highland Drive, Suite 5
Lebanon, VA 24266
276-889-4650
Fax: 276-889-2105
Serving Russell, Buchanan, Dickenson, and Tazewell Counties

Lynchburg Local Office
20311-A Timberlake Rd.
P.O. BOX 4337
Lynchburg, VA 24502
434-239-3473
Fax: 434-239-3735
Serving Campbell, Amherst, Appomattox, Bedford, and Lynchburg City Counties

Rocky Mount Local Office
1297 State Street
Rocky Mount, VA 24151
540-483-5341
Fax: 540-483-0006
Serving Franklin, Henry, Pittsylvania, Patrick and cities of Martinsville and Danville Counties

Smithfield Local Office
203 Wimbledon Lane
Smithfield, VA 23430-1853
757-357-7004
Fax: 757-357-7798
Serving Isle of Wight, Chesapeake City, Franklin, Hampton, Suffolk, James City, Newport News, Poquoson, Southampton, VA Beach City, Williamsburg, and York Counties

Stephens City Local Office
130 Carriebrook Drive
Stephens City, VA 22655
540-868-1130
Fax: 540-868-1135
Serving Frederick, Clarke, Page, Shenandoah, Warren, and Winchester Counties

Tappahannock Local Office
772 Richmond Beach Road
Rappahannock Office Bldg.
P.O. Box 700
Tappahannock, VA 22560
804-443-4304
Fax: 804-443-1375
Serving Essex, Gloucester, King & Queen, Lancaster, Mathews, Richmond, Middlesex, King William, Northumberland, and Westmoreland Counties

Verona Local Office
PO Box 70
70 Dick Huff Lane
Verona, VA 24482
540-248-6218
Fax: 540-248-0691
Serving Augusta, Bath, Buena Vista, Harrisonburg, Highland, Lexington, Rockbridge, Rockingham, Staunton, and Waynesboro Counties

Wytheville Local Office
100 USDA Drive
Wytheville, VA 24383
276-228-3513
Fax: 276-228-2049
Serving Wythe, Bland, Bristol, Carroll, Galax, Grayson, Smyth, and Washington Counties

Washington

USDA Rural Development State Office
1835 Black Lake Blvd. SW, Suite B
Olympia, WA 98501-5715
360-704-7740
Fax: 360-704-7742

Multi-Family Housing Program Division
1011 East Main, Suite 306
Puyallup, WA 98372
253-845-9272
Fax: 253-845-9106
Serving Skagit, Snohomish, Whatcom Island, San Juan, Skagit, and King Counties

Olympia Area Office
1835 Black Lake Blvd. SW, Suite B
Olympia, WA 98512-5715
360-704-7768
Serving Clallam, Jefferson, Kitsap, Mason, Pierce Clark, Cowlitz, Grays Harbor, Lewis, Mason, Pacific, Pierce, Skamania, Thurston Counties

Yakima Area Office
1606 Perry Street, Suite E
Yakima, WA 98902-5769

509-454-5743 ext. 136
Serving Adams, Franklin, Kittitas, Whitman, Yakima, S. Grant Asotin, Benton, Columbia, Franklin, Klickitat, Walla Walla, Yakima Counties

Brush Prairie Local Office
11104 NE 149th Street, Suite C-300
Brush Prairie, WA 98606-9558
360-883-1987 ext. 4
Fax: 360-885-2284
Serving Clark, Cowlitz, Lewis, Pacific, Skamania and Wahkiakum Counties

Mt. Vernon Local Office
2021 E. College Way, Suite 216
Mt. Vernon, WA 98273-3610
360-428-4322 ext. 4
Fax: 360-424-6172
Serving Island, San Juan, Skagit, Snohomish and Whatcom Counties

Port Angeles Local Office
111 E. Third Street, Suite 2C
Port Angeles, WA 98362-3020
360-452-8994 ext. 4
Fax: 360-452-5088
Serving Clallam, Grays Harbor, Jefferson, Kitsap and Mason Counties

Puyallup Local Office
1011 East Main, Suite 106
Puyallup, WA 98372-3796
253-845-0553 ext. 4
Fax: 253-770-2274
Serving King, Pierce and Thurston Counties

Spokane Local Office
1908 N. Dale Lane
Spokane, WA 99212
509-924-7350 ext. 4
Fax: 509-924-7787
Serving Asotin, Ferry, Lincoln, Pend O'reille, Stevens, Spokane and Whitman Counties

Wenatchee Local Office
Room 314, Federal Building
301 Yakima Street
Wenatchee, WA 98801-2998
509-664-0242
Fax: 509-664-0250
Serving Chelan, Douglas, N. Grant and Okanogan Counties

Yakima Local Office
1606 Perry Street, Suite D
Yakima, WA 98902-5769
509-454-5740
Fax: 509-454-5682
Serving Adams, Benton, Columbia, Franklin, S. Grant, Garfield, Kittitas, Klickitat, Walla Walla and Yakima Counties

West Virginia

USDA Rural Development State Office
75 High Street, Room 320, Federal Building
Morgantown, WV 26505
304-284-4860
Fax: 304-284-4893

Parkersburg Area Office
425 Federal Building, Room 2052
Parkersburg, WV 26102
304-420-6664
Fax: 304-420-6876

Elkin Area Office
401 Davis Avenue
Elkins, WV 26241
304-636-2158
Fax: 304-636-5902

Beckley Area Office
481 Ragland Road
Beckley, WV 25801
304-252-8644
Fax: 304-252-5809

Beckley Community Development Office
471 Ragland Road
Beckley WV 25801
304-252-4343
Fax: 304-252-5809

Cross Lanes Community Development Office
418 Goff Mountain Road
Room 103
Cross Lanes, WV 25313
304-776-5298
Fax: 304-776-5326

Elkins Community Development Office
Forest Svc. Bldg, Room 109
200 Sycamore St., Elkins, WV 26241
304-636-6785
Fax: 304-636-1568

Fairmont Community Development Office
7009 Mt. Park Dr.
Fairmont, WV 26554
304-366-2921
Fax: 304-363-7027

Huntington Community Development Office
2631 Fifth St. Rd.
Huntington, WV 25701
304-697-6033
Fax: 304-697-4164

Lewisburg Community Development Office
717 N. Jefferson St.
Lewisburg, WV 24901
304-645-7422
Fax: 304-647-9627

Logan Community Development Office
513 Dingess St.
Logan, WV 25601
304-752-8427
Fax: 304-752-7657

Martinsburg Community Development Office
1450-4 Edwin Miller Blvd.
Martinsburg, WV 25401
304-263-7547
Fax: 304-267-9172

Morgantown Community Development Office
201 Scott Ave., Vista Del-Rio
Morgantown, WV 26505
304-291-4116
Fax: 304-291-4139

Mt. Clare Community Development Office
Rt. 2, Box 204C
Stonewood, WV 26408
304-624-6453
Fax: 304-524-5976

Parkersburg Community
Development Office
Rt. 5 Box 1000
Mill Run Road
Parkersburg, WV 26102
304-422-9070
Fax: 304-422-9079

Pineville Community
Development Office
P.O. Bldg., Second Floor
Pineville, WV 24874
304-732-8855
Fax: 304-732-9140

Princeton Community
Development Office
114 Gott Road
Princeton, WV 24740
304-487-1402
Fax: 304-425-0695

Ripley Community Development
Office
530 Freedom Road
Ripley, WV 25271
304-372-3441
Fax: 304-372-6856

Romney Community
Development Office
500 East Main St.
Heritage Hill Complex
Romney, WV 26757
304-822-3891
Fax: 304-822-3728

Sistersville Community
Development Office
10 Pleasantview Lane
Sistersville, WV 26175
304-758-2351
Fax: 304-758-4303

Summersville Community
Development Office
Rt. 39 & Water St.
Federal Bldg.
Summersville, WV 26651
304-872-4966
Fax: 304-872-4715

Weston Community
Development Office
1 Gateway Center
Weston, WV 26452
304-269-8431
Fax: 304-269-7583

Wheeling Community
Development Office
RD #4 Box 297
Wheeling, WV 26003
304-242-0576
Fax: 304-242-7039

Wisconsin

Altoona Local Office
227 1st Street West
P.O. Box 158 Altoona, WI
54720-0158
715-839-5081
Fax: 715-839-1822
Serving Buffalo, Chippewa,
Dunn, Eau Claire, Pepin
Counties

Ashland Local Office
2014 3rd Street West
Ashland, WI 54806
715-682-9117
Fax: 715-682-0320
Serving Ashland, Bayfield, Iron,
Price, Walworth Counties

Barron Local Office
330 E LaSalle Avenue, Rm 100
Barron, WI 45812
715-537-5645
Fax: 715-537-6836
Serving Baron, Brown, Door,
Florence, Forest, Kewaunee,
Langglade, Marinette,
Menominee, Ononto, Oneida,
Outagamie, Polk, Shawano,
Vilas Counties

Black River Falls Local Office
311 County A
Black River Falls, WI 54615
715-284-4515
Fax: 715-284-9686
Serving Jackson, Juneau,
Monroe, Trempelaeau Counties

Dodgeville Local Office
138 S Iowa St
Dodgeville, WI 53533
608-935-2791 Ext. 4
Fax: 608-935-9713
Serving Dane, Grant, Green,
Iowa, Lafayette Counties

Elkhorn Local Office
225 O'Connor Dr.
Elkhorn, WI 53121
414-723-3216
Fax: 414-723-3292
Serving Kenosha, Racine, Rock,
Rusk Counties

Fond du Lac Local Office
485 S Military Rd
Fond du Lac, WI 54935
920-907-2976
Fax: 920-907-2983
Serving Calumet, Fon du Lac,
Manitowoc, Sheboygan,
Winnebago Counties

Medford Local Office
925 Donald St., Rm 104
Medford, WI 54451
715-748-3355
Fax: 715-748-9766
Serving Clark, Lincoln,
Marathon, Taylor Counties

Portage Local Office
2912 Red Fox Run
Portage, WI 53901
608-742-5361
Fax: 608-742-0194
Serving Adams, Columbia,
Green Lake, Marquette, Sauk
Counties

Spooner Local Office
206 Vine Street
Spooner, WI 54801
715-635-8228
Fax: 715-635-6816
Serving Burnett, Douglas,
Pierce, Sawyer, St Croix,
Washburn Counties

Stevens Point Local Office
1462 Strongs Ave
Stevens Point, WI 54481
715-346-1313
Fax: 715-343-6222
Serving Portage, Waupaca,
Waushara, Wood Counties

Viroqua Local Office
220 Airport Road
Viroqua, WI 54665
608-637-2183
Fax: 608-637-3146

Serving Crawford, La Crosse, Richland, Vernon Counties

West Bend Local Office
333 E Washington Street
Suite 3000
West Bend, WI 53095
262-335-6850
Fax: 262-335-6852
Serving Dodge, Jefferson, Milwaukee, Ozaukee, Washington, Waukesha Counties

Wyoming

USDA Rural Development State Office
100 E. B Street
Room 1005
Casper, WY 82601
307-261-6300
Fax: 307-261-6327

Northwest Area Office
208 Shiloh Road
Worland, WY 82401-2914
307-347-2456 ext. 5
Fax: 307-347-2802
Serving Big Horn, Hot Springs, Park, and Washakie Counties

Central Area Office
201 East Washington Avenue
P.O. Box 1607
Riverton, WY 82501-1607
307-856-5383
Fax: 307-856-4426
Serving Carbon, Fremont, and Natrona Counties

Southwest Area Office
625 Washington St., Room B
P.O. Box 190
Afton, WY 83110-0190
307-886-9001
Fax: 307-886-3744
Serving Lincoln, Sublette, Sweetwater, Teton, and Uinta Counties

Northeast Area Office
1949 Sugarland Drive, Suite 118
Sheridan, WY 82801-5749
307-672-5820 ext. 4
Fax: 307-672-0052
Serving Campbell, Crook, Johnson, Sheridan, and Weston Counties

Southeast Area Office
1441 East "M" Street, Suite A
Torrington, WY 82240-3521
307-532-2125
Fax: 307-532-5783
Serving Albany, Converse, Goshen, Laramie, Niobrara, and Platte Counties

Rent Money and Money To Buy A Home

Who needs affordable housing? More families than you think need help finding and paying for affordable housing. In general, under the HOME Investment Partnerships Program, HUD allocates funds to eligible State and local governments to strengthen public-private partnerships and to expand the supply of decent, safe, sanitary, and affordable housing. Participating jurisdictions may use HOME funds to help renters, new homebuyers or existing homeowners, with primary attention for very low-income and low-income families. Since 1990, almost 400,000 affordable housing units have been acquired, constructed or rehabilitated, and nearly 72,000 tenants have received direct rental assistance.

The HOME program is implemented through State and local governments called participating jurisdictions. Participating jurisdictions may be States or units of general local government. HOME participating jurisdictions have a great deal of flexibility in designing and managing their HOME programs. HUD's Office of Affordable Housing Programs Office administers the HOME program.

HUD Office of Affordable Housing
Office of Community Planning and Development
451 7th Street, SW
Washington, DC 20410

202-708-2470
TTY: 800-877-8339
www.hud.gov/offices/cpd/affordablehousing/programs/home

To find which jurisdictions implement state or local HOME programs in your area and how these programs work, check the listings for your state.

HOME Program—HUD

State of Alabama

Ms. Barbara Wallace,
HOME/Tax Credit Coordinator
Housing Finance Authority
P.O. Box 230909
Montgomery, AL 36123
334-244-9200
Fax: 334-244-9214

Cities

City of Birmingham
Mr. Ronnie D. White, Program Director
Department of Community Development
710 20th St., N., Room 700
Birmingham, AL 35203-2216
205-254-2312
Fax: 205-254-2628

City of Huntsville
Mr. Bill Taylor, Housing Specialist
Division of Community Development
120 E. Holmes Ave.
Huntsville, AL 35804
256-427-5400
Fax: 256-427-5431

City of Mobile
Mr. Steve Kohrman, Director
Mobile Housing Board
P.O. Box 1345
Mobile, AL 36633-1345
334-476-4165
Fax: 334-470-0582

City of Montgomery
Mr. George Stathopoulos, Chief
Department of Community Development
P.O. Box 1111
Montgomery, AL 36101
334-241-2997
Fax: 334-241-4432

City of Tuscaloosa
Ms. Evelyn Young, Associate Director
Department of Community Planning and Development
P.O. Box 2089
Tuscaloosa, AL 35401
205-349-0160
Fax: 205-349-0135

Counties

County of Jefferson
Mr. Robert Newbill, Supervisor
Department of Planning and Community Development
805 22nd St., N.
Birmingham, AL 35203-2303
205-325-5761
Fax: 205-325-5095

State of Alaska

Ms. Carma Edith Reed, Planner
Alaska Housing Finance Corp.
P.O. Box 101020
Anchorage, AK 99510-1020
907-330-8275
Fax: 907-338-2585

Municipalities

Municipality of Anchorage
Ms. Lynn Taylor, Manager
Division of Housing and Community Development
P.O. Box 196650
Anchorage, AK 99519-6650
907-343-4881
Fax: 907-343-6831

American Samoa Government

Mr. Ali'imau H. Scanlan, Director
Department of Commerce
American Samoa Government
Pago Pago, AS 96799
684-633-5155
Fax: 684-633-4195

State of Arizona

Ms. Carol Ditmore, HOME Coordinator
Department of Commerce
3800 N. Central Ave., Suite 1500
Phoenix, AZ 85012-1908
602-280-1365
Fax: 602-280-1470

Cities

City of Phoenix
Ms. Elizabeth DeMichael, Manager
Department of Housing
251 W. Washington St., Fourth Floor
Phoenix, AZ 85034-2218
602-262-4785
Fax: 602-534-1214

City of Tucson
Ms. Nancy Magelli, Project Coordinator
City of Tucson
Department of Community Services/Technical Services
P.O. Box 27210
Tucson, AZ 85726-7210
520-791-4132
Fax: 520-791-5648

Counties

County of Maricopa
Ms. Isabel McDougall, Director
Department of Community Development
3003 N. Central Ave.
Suite 1040
Phoenix, AZ 85012
602-240-2210
Fax: 602-240-6960

Consortia

Maricopa County Consortium
Mr. Jim Prante, HOME Coordinator

Department of Community Development
3003 N. Central Ave.
Suite 1040
Phoenix, AZ 85012-2906
602-240-2210
Fax: 602-240-6960

State of Arkansas

Mr. Don Jackson, HOME Program Manager
Arkansas Development Finance Authority
P.O. Box 8023
Little Rock, AR 72203-8023
501-682-5900
Fax: 501-682-5859

Cities

City of Ft. Smith
Mr. Matt Jennings, Director
Department of Economic and Community Development
P.O. Box 1908
Ft. Smith, AR 72902-1908
501-784-2209
Fax: 501-784-2462

City of Little Rock
Ms. Lisa Spigner, Housing Manager
Housing and Neighborhood Programs
500 W. Markham St.
Little Rock, AR 72201
501-371-6825
Fax: 501-399-3461

City of North Little Rock
Ms. Mary Bowman, Director
Community Development Agency
P.O. Box 5868
North Little Rock, AR 72119
501-340-5342
Fax: 501-340-5345

City of Pine Bluff
Mr. Donald R. Sampson, Director
Department of Community Development
200 E. Eighth Ave.
City Hall, Room 103
Pine Bluff, AR 71601
870-543-1820
Fax: 870-543-1821

State of California

Mr. Wayne Walker, Section Chief
State of California
Department of Housing and Community Development
P.O. Box 952054
Sacramento, CA 94254-2054
916-445-4782
Fax: 916-322-1560

Cities

City of Alhambra
Mr. Stanley Smalewitz, Housing Manager
Division of Housing
111 S. First St.
Alhambra, CA 91801-3702
626-570-5037
Fax: 626-458-4201

City of Anaheim
Ms. Bertha Chavoya, Housing Manager
Department of Community Development
201 S. Anaheim Blvd., Second Floor
Anaheim, CA 92805
714-765-4340
Fax: 714-765-4331

City of Bakersfield
Ms. Trisha Richter
HOME Coordinator
Department of Economic and Community Development
515 Truxtun Ave.
Bakersfield, CA 93301
661-326-3765
Fax: 661-328-1548

City of Baldwin Park
Mr. Tad Mimura, Housing Manager
Department of Community Development
4141 N. Maine Ave.
Baldwin Park, CA 91706
626-869-7500
Fax: 626-337-2965

City of Bellflower
Ms. Margo Wheeler, Director
Department of Community Development
16600 Civic Center Dr.
Bellflower, CA 90706
562-804-1424
Fax: 562-925-8660

City of Berkeley
Ms. Teri Piccolo, Planner
Department of Planning
2201 Dwight Way
Berkeley, CA 94704
510-644-6001
Fax: 510-644-8678

City of Burbank
Mr. Duane Solomon, HOME Coordinator
Department of Redevelopment and Housing
275 E. Olive Ave.
Burbank, CA 91502
818-238-5108
Fax: 818-238-5174

City of Chico
Mr. Dennis McLaughlin, Officer
P.O. Box 3420
Chico, CA 95927
530-895-4862
Fax: 530-895-4825

City of Chula Vista
Mr. Juan Arroyo, HOME Manager
Department of Community Development
276 Fourth Ave.
Chula Vista, CA 91910-2631
619-585-5722
Fax: 619-585-5698

City of Compton
Ms. Arlene W. Williams, Director
Department of Economic and Resource Development
205 S. Willowbrook Ave.
Compton, CA 90220
310-605-5580
Fax: 310-761-1419

City of Costa Mesa
Mrs. Muriel Ullman, Manager
City of Costa Mesa
Department of Redevelopment and Housing
P.O. Box 1200
Costa Mesa, CA 92628-1200

714-754-5635
Fax: 714-754-5330

City of Davis
Ms. Jerilyn Cochran, Grants Coordinator
Department of Community Services
23 Russell Blvd.
Davis, CA 95616-3837
530-757-5691
Fax: 530-757-6628

City of Downey
Mr. Edward G. Velasco, Housing Manager
Department of Community Development
7850 Quill Dr.
Apollo Neighborhood Center
Suite C
Downey, CA 90242
562-904-7167
Fax: 562-869-2810

City of El Cajon
Mr. James S. Griffin, Director
Department of Community Development
200 E. Main St.
El Cajon, CA 92020
619-441-1741
Fax: 619-441-1743

City of El Monte
Ms. Martha Murillo, Housing Director
Department of Community Development
11333 Valley Blvd.
El Monte, CA 91731-3293
626-580-2070
Fax: 626-580-2293

City of Escondido
Ms. Susan Wurtzel, Housing Manager
Division of Housing
201 N. Broadway
Escondido, CA 92025
760-839-4518
Fax: 760-839-4313

City of Fontana
Mr. Steven Pasarow, Project Specialist
Department of Community Development
8434 Wheeler St.
Fontana, CA 92335
909-350-6625
Fax: 909-350-6616

City of Fresno
Ms. Yvonne Quiring, Director
Department of Housing and Neighborhood Development
2600 Fresno St., Room 3076
Fresno, CA 93721-3605
559-498-1282
Fax: 559-488-1078

City of Fullerton
Ms. Linda R. Morad, Coordinator
Division of Development Services
303 W. Commonwealth Ave.
Fullerton, CA 92832-1710
714-738-6878
Fax: 714-738-3110

City of Garden Grove
Ms. Allison Moore, Specialist
Department of Economic Development
11222 Acacia Pkwy.
Garden Grove, CA 92840-5310
714-741-5140
Fax: 714-741-5136

City of Glendale
Ms. Beth Stochl, HOME Coordinator
Department of Community Development
141 N. Glendale Ave., Suite 202
Glendale, CA 91206
818-548-2060
Fax: 818-548-3724

City of Hawthorne
Ms. Mari Guerrero, CDBG/HOME Coordinator
4455 W. 126th St.
Hawthorne, CA 90250-4482
310-970-7103
Fax: 310-970-7473

City of Huntington Beach
Mr. Steve Holty
Department of Economic Development
2000 Main St., Fifth Floor
Huntington Beach, CA 92648-2702
714-536-5542
Fax: 714-375-5087

City of Huntington Park
Mr. Clarence P. Williams, CDBG/Coordinator
Department of Community Development
6550 Miles Ave., Suite 145
Huntington Park, CA 90255-4302
323-584-6266
Fax: 323-588-4578

City of Inglewood
Ms. Pamela Thigpen, Grants Manager
Department of Business and Economic Development
One W. Manchester Blvd.
Suite 700
Inglewood, CA 90301-1750
310-412-8800
Fax: 310-412-5188

City of Long Beach
Mr. David D. Lewis, Officer
333 W. Ocean Blvd., Second Floor
Long Beach, CA 90802
562-570-6879
Fax: 562-570-5921

City of Los Angeles
Mr. Walter Clark, Community and Housing Program Manager
Department of Housing
111 N. Hope St.
Seventh Floor, Room 722
Los Angeles, CA 90012
213-367-9128
Fax: 213-367-9242

City of Lynwood
Mr. Donyea Adams, HOME Coordinator
Department of Community Development
11330 Bullis Rd.
Lynwood, CA 90262
310-603-0220
Fax: 310-639-6957

City of Merced
Mr. Lee Pevsner, Director
Department of Housing and Transportation

678 W. 18th St.
Merced, CA 95340
209-385-6863
Fax: 209-725-8775

City of Modesto
Mr. Miguel Galvez, Associate Planner
Division of Housing and Neighborhoods
1010 10th St., Room 4300
Modesto, CA 95354-0825
209-571-5506
Fax: 209-544-3982

City of Montebello
Ms. Patty Castreye, Administrator
Department of Economic Development
1600 W. Beverly Blvd.
Montebello, CA 90640
323-887-1390
Fax: 323-887-1401

City of Monterey Park
Mr. Roger Grody, Coordinator
Department of Economic Development
320 W. Newmark Ave.
Monterey Park, CA 91754
626-307-1385
Fax: 626-307-1467

City of Moreno Valley
Ms. Mary Lanier, Manager
Department of Community and Economic Development
14177 Frederick St.
Moreno Valley, CA 92553
909-413-3453
Fax: 909-413-2210

City of Mountain View
Ms. Adriana Garefalos, Planner
Department of Community Development
P.O. Box 7540
Mountain View, CA 94039
650-903-6306
Fax: 650-903-6474

City of National City
Mr. Paul Desrochers, Executive Director
Department of Community Development
140 E 12th St., Suite B
National City, CA 91950-3312
619-336-4250
Fax: 619-336-4286

City of Norwalk
Mr. Jesus Santeze, Specialist
Department of Housing and Community Development
12700 Norwalk Blvd.
City Hall
Norwalk, CA 90650
562-929-5951
Fax: 562-929-5780

City of Oakland
Mr. Jeff Levin, Program Manager
Community and Economic Development Agency
250 Frank H. Ogawa Plaza, Fifth Floor
Oakland, CA 94612
510-238-3502
Fax: 510-238-2226

City of Oceanside
Ms. Margarie Pierce, Assistant Director
Department of Housing
300 N. Coast Hwy.
Oceanside, CA 92054-2824
760-966-4187
Fax: 760-966-4177

City of Ontario
Mr. Douglas Ford, Director
Department of Revitalization
316 E. E St.
Ontario, CA 91764
909-395-2006
Fax: 909-395-2288

City of Orange
Ms. Mary Ellen Laster, CDBG and Housing Rehab Manager
Department of Economic Development
230 E. Chapman Ave.
Orange, CA 92866
714-288-2580
Fax: 714-288-2598

City of Oxnard
Mr. Ernest Whitaker, Housing Manager
Department of Housing
555 S. A St.
Oxnard, CA 93030
805-385-7400
Fax: 805-385-7416

City of Paramount
Mr. Jose Gomez, Director
Department of Finance
16400 Colorado Ave.
Paramount, CA 90723-5050
562-220-2200
Fax: 562-529-8497

City of Pasadena
Ms. Stella J. Lucero, HOME Coordinator
Department of Housing and Development
100 N. Garfield Ave., Suite 101
Pasadena, CA 91109
626-744-8300
Fax: 626-744-8340

City of Pomona
Mr. Cleve Jackson, HOME Coordinator
P.O. Box 660
Pomona, CA 91769-0660
909-620-3761
Fax: 909-620-4567

City of Redding
Mr. Don Meek, Supervisor
Office of Community Development
777 Cypress Ave.
Redding, CA 96001-2718
530-225-4121
Fax: 530-225-4126

City of Redwood City
Mrs. Debbi Jones-Thomas, Housing Coordinator
Department of Housing Services
P.O. Box 391
Redwood City, CA 94064-0391
650-780-7290
Fax: 650-780-0128

City of Richmond
Ms. Harriette Langston, Manager
Redevelopment Agency
330 25th St., Second Floor
Richmond, CA 94804
510-307-8147
Fax: 510-307-8149

City of Riverside
Ms. Tranda Drumwright, Manager
Department of Housing and Community Development
3900 Main St., Suite 500
Riverside, CA 92522-3717
909-826-5608

City of Rosemead
Ms. Lisa Baker, Grants Coordinator
Department of Community Development
8838 E. Valley Blvd.
Rosemead, CA 91770
626-569-2100
Fax: 626-307-9218

City of Sacramento
Ms. Vicky Cook, Manager
Sacramento Housing and Redevelopment Agency
630 I St.
Sacramento, CA 95814-1834
916-440-1368
Fax: 916-498-1655

City of Salinas
Ms. Barbara Batyi, Community Development Administrative Supervisor
Department of Community Improvement
200 Lincoln Ave.
Salinas, CA 93901
831-758-7206
Fax: 831-758-7215

City of San Bernardino
Ms. Peggy Eaeheco, Director
Economic Development Agency
201 N. East St., Third Floor
San Bernardino, CA 92401-1507
909-663-1044
Fax: 909-888-9413

City of San Diego
Mr. Joseph Correia, Manager
Housing Commission
1625 Newton Ave.
San Diego, CA 92113-1038
619-231-9400
Fax: 619-702-2189

City of San Francisco
Ms. Marcia Rosen, Administrator
Department of Community Development
25 Van Ness Ave., Suite 600
San Francisco, CA 94102
415-252-3177
Fax: 415-252-3140

City of San Jose
Mr. Alex Sanchez, Director
Department of Housing
Four N. Second St., Suite 1350
San Jose, CA 95113
408-277-4747
Fax: 408-277-3197

City of San Mateo
Mr. Robert R. Muehlbauer, Manager
Division of Housing and Economic Development
330 W. 20th Ave.
San Mateo, CA 94403-1338
650-522-7222
Fax: 650-522-7201

City of Santa Ana
Ms. Patricia Whitaker, Housing Manager
Community Development Agency
P.O. Box 1988
Santa Ana, CA 92702-1988
714-667-2224
Fax: 714-667-2225

City of Santa Barbara
Mr. Steven Faulstich, Supervisor
Department of Community Development
630 Garden St.
Santa Barbara, CA 93102-1990
805-564-5461
Fax: 805-564-5477

City of Santa Clara
Mr. Jeffrey Pedersen, Manager
Division of Community Services
1500 Warburton Ave.
Santa Clara, CA 95050
408-615-2490
Fax: 408-248-3381

City of Santa Cruz
Mr. Eugene Arner, Manager
Department of Housing and Community Development
809 Center St., Room 206
Santa Cruz, CA 95060-3826
831-420-6253
Fax: 831-420-6458

City of Santa Monica
Mr. Robert T. Moncrief, Manager
Division of Housing and Redevelopment
1685 Main St., Room 212
Santa Monica, CA 90401
310-458-8702
Fax: 310-458-3380

City of Santa Rosa
Mr. David Gouin, Manager
Department of Housing and Redevelopment
P.O. Box 1806
Santa Rosa, CA 95402-1806
707-543-3316
Fax: 707-543-3317

City of South Gate
Ms. Kathy Johnston, HOME Coordinator
Department of Community Development
8650 California Ave.
South Gate, CA 90280
323-563-9531
Fax: 323-567-0725

City of Stockton
Mr. Robert Bressani, Supervisor
Department of Housing and Redevelopment
305 N. El Dorado St.
Suite 200
Stockton, CA 95202
209-937-8278
Fax: 209-937-8822

City of Sunnyvale
Ms. Marilyn Roaf, Specialist
Department of Community Development
P.O. Box 3707
Sunnyvale, CA 94088-3707
408-730-7442
Fax: 408-728-0711

City of Torrance
Ms. Donna R. Richardson, Housing Administrator
3031 Torrance Blvd.
Torrance, CA 90503

310-618-5840
Fax: 310-618-2429

City of Vallejo
Mr. Gary Truelsen, Manager
Department of Community Development
P.O. Box 1432
Vallejo, CA 94590
707-648-4393
Fax: 707-648-5249

City of Visalia
Ms. Mary-Alice Avila, Project Manager
315 E. Acequia Ave.
Visalia, CA 93291
559-738-3414
Fax: 559-730-7031

City of Westminster
Ms. Gerry Gehres, Analyst
Department of Community Development
8200 Westminster Blvd.
Westminster, CA 92683
714-898-3311
Fax: 714-898-8251

City of Whittier
Mrs. Anne O'Donnel-Ivarra, Manager
13230 Penn St.
Whittier, CA 90602-1772
562-464-3380
Fax: 562-464-3509

Counties
County of Alameda
Ms. Linda Gardner
Housing Director
224 W. Winton Ave., Room 108
Hayward, CA 94544-1215
510-670-5404
Fax: 510-670-6378

County of Contra Costa
Ms. Kathleen Hamm, Program Manager
Department of Community Development
651 Pine St.
Fourth Floor, N. Wing
Martinez, CA 94553-0095
925-335-1253
Fax: 925-335-1265

County of Fresno
Mr. Jerry Rutz, Analyst
2220 Tulare St., Eighth Floor
Fresno, CA 93721-2104
559-262-4277
Fax: 559-488-3316

County of Kern
Mr. Mark A. Smith, Program Manager
Department of Community Development
2700 M St., Suite 250
Bakersfield, CA 93301-2370
661-862-5050
Fax: 661-862-5052

County of Los Angeles
Mr. Greg Kawczynski, HOME Coordinator
Community Development Corp.
Two Coral Cir., Bldg. A
Monterey Park, CA 91755
323-838-7761
Fax: 323-890-8586

County of Orange
Ms. Pam Leaning, Assistant Director
Department of Housing and Community Development
1770 N. Broadway
Santa Ana, CA 92706-2642
714-480-2899
Fax: 714-480-2803

County of Marin
Mr. Roy Bateman, Coordinator
Community Development Agency
3501 Civic Center Dr.
Room 308
San Rafael, CA 94903-4157
415-499-6698
Fax: 415-499-7880

County of Riverside
Ms. Susan Wamsley, Assistant Director
Economic Development Agency
3525 14th St.
Riverside, CA 92501-3813
909-955-8916
Fax: 909-955-6686

County of Sacramento
Ms. Vicky Cook, Program Manager
Housing and Redevelopment Agency
630 I St.
Sacramento, CA 95814-1834
916-440-1368
Fax: 916-498-1655

County of San Joaquin
Mr. Jonathan M. Moore, Deputy Director
Department of Community Development
1810 E. Hazelton Ave.
Stockton, CA 95205
209-468-3065
Fax: 209-468-3163

County of San Luis Obispo
Mr. Dana C. Lilley, Planner
Department of Planning and Building
County Government Center
San Luis Obispo, CA 93408
805-781-5715
Fax: 805-781-5624

County of San Mateo
Mr. Tom Roberts, Director
Office of Housing
262 Harbor Blvd., Bldg. A
Belmont, CA 94002
650-802-5050
Fax: 650-802-5049

County of Santa Clara
Mr. Charles Chew
Program Manager
County of Santa Clara
Department of Housing and Community Development
1735 N. First St., Suite 265
San Jose, CA 95112-4511
408-441-0261
Fax: 408-441-0365

County of Santa Barbara
Ms. Susan Ruby, Manager
Department of Planning and Development
P.O. Box 2219
Santa Barbara, CA 93120-2219
805-568-3521
Fax: 805-568-2289

County of Sonoma
Mr. Charles D. McGowan, Specialist

Community Development
Commission
1440 Guernville Rd.
Santa Rosa, CA 95403-4107
707-524-7500
Fax: 707-524-7557

County of Ventura
Ms. Loretta McCarty
HOME Coordinator
800 S. Victoria Ave.
Chief Administrative Office,
L#1940
Ventura, CA 93009-1940
805-654-2876
Fax: 805-654-5106

Consortia
County of San Bernardino Consortium
Ms. Julie Hemphel, Deputy
Director
Department of Housing and
Economic Development
290 N. D St., Sixth Floor
San Bernardino, CA 92415-0040
909-388-0800
Fax: 909-388-0820

County of San Diego Consortium
Ms. April York, Temporary
Coordinator
Department of Housing and
Community Development
3989 Ruffin Rd.
San Diego, CA 92123-1815
858-694-8724
Fax: 858-694-4871

State of Colorado

Mr. Pat Coyle, HOME Program
Manager
Division of Housing
1313 Sherman St., Suite 518
Denver, CO 80203
303-866-2033
Fax: 303-866-4077

Cities
City of Aurora
Mr. Michael G. Hilliard,
Manager
Department of Community
Development
9801 E. Colfax Ave.
Aurora, CO 80010-2109
303-360-0053
Fax: 303-361-2989

City of Boulder
Mrs. Jan Oldham
Grants Administrator
Department of Housing and
Human Services
P.O. Box 791
Boulder, CO 80306-0791
303-441-3157
Fax: 303-441-4368

City of Colorado Springs
Ms. Valerie Jordan, Manager
Department of Community
Redevelopment
P.O. Box 1575
Colorado Springs, CO 80901-
1575
719-385-5336
Fax: 719-578-6543

City of and County of Denver
Ms. Laurie Baker, Program
Specialist
Community Development
Agency
7111 E. 56th Ave.
Commerce City, CO 80022-1859
720-913-1540
Fax: 720-913-1800

City of Ft. Collins
Ms. Julie Smith, HOME
Administrator
Department of Planning
P.O. Box 580
Ft. Collins, CO 80522-0580
970-221-6595
Fax: 970-224-6111

City of Greeley
Ms. Terry McKellar,
Community Development
Specialist
Department of Community
Development
1100 Tenth St., Suite 201
Greeley, CO 80631-3808
970-350-9781
Fax: 970-350-9895

City of Lakewood
Mr. Steven Gundel
HOME Coordinator
Department of Housing
480 S. Allison Pkwy.
Lakewood, CO 80226
303-987-7599
Fax: 303-987-7821

Counties
County of Adams
Mr. Jim Rose, Office Manager
Office of Community Outreach
7111 E. 56th Ave.
Commerce City, CO 80022-2236
303-286-4175
Fax: 303-286-4166

County of Arapahoe
Mr. James M. Taylor, Director
Department of Housing and
Community Development
2009 W. Littleton Blvd.
Littleton, CO 80120
303-738-8060
Fax: 303-738-8069

County and City of Denver
Ms. Laurie Baker, Program
Specialist
Community Development
Agency
7111 E. 56th Ave.
Commerce City, CO 80022-1859
720-913-1540
Fax: 720-913-1800

County of Jefferson
Ms. Rebecca McLean, Program
Manager
Office of Community
Development
730 Simms St., Suite 300
Golden, CO 80401
303-271-4609
Fax: 303-271-4021
Consorita

City of Pueblo Consortium
Mr. Tony Berumen, Director
Department of Housing and
Community Development
P.O. Box 1427
Pueblo, CO 81002-1427
719-584-0830
Fax: 719-584-0831

State of Connecticut

Mr. Elliot Stone, HOME
Program Manager
Department of Economic and
Community Development

505 Hudson St.
Hartford, CT 06106
860-270-8168
Fax: 860-270-8055

Cities
City of Bridgeport
Mr. Les Gulyos, Manager
Department of Housing
45 Lyon Ter.
City Hall
Bridgeport, CT 06604
203-576-8143
Fax: 203-576-7135

City of Hartford
Mr. Jon Labelle, Project Manager
Department of Housing and Community Development
Ten Prospect St., Third Floor
Hartford, CT 06103-2814
860-522-4888
Fax: 860-722-6630

City of New Britain
Mr. Kenneth A. Malinowski, Director
Department of Municipal Development
27 W. Main St., Suite 311
New Britain, CT 06051-4241
860-826-3330
Fax: 860-826-2682

City of New Haven
Ms. Regina Winters, Interim Director
Office of Housing and Neighborhood Development
165 Church St.
New Haven, CT 06510
203-946-7090
Fax: 203-946-4899

City of Stamford
Mr. Timothy R. Beeble, Director
Office of Community Development
P.O. Box 10152
Stamford, CT 06904-2152
203-977-4864
Fax: 203-977-4775

City of Waterbury
Ms. Mary Welz-Schlosky, Manager
Office of Community Development
236 Grand St.
Chase Municipal Bldg., Room 222
Waterbury, CT 06702-1042
203-757-9621
Fax: 203-596-7977

State of Delaware

Mr. Jim M. Loescher, Manager
Delaware State Housing Authority
18 The Green
Dover, DE 19901-3612
302-577-5001
Fax: 302-739-1118

Cities
City of Wilmington
Ms. Jane C.W. Vincent, Director
Department of Real Estate and Housing
800 French St.
Louis L. Redding City-County Bldg., Seventh Floor
Wilmington, DE 19801-3537
302-571-4057
Fax: 302-573-5588

Counties
County of New Castle
Ms. Charlotte Gilbert
Community Services Coordinator
Department of Community Development and Housing
800 N. French St.
Louis L. Redding City-County Bldg.
Wilmington, DE 19801-3590
302-395-5600
Fax: 302-395-5592

District of Columbia

Ms. Gail Lyle, HOME Program Manager
Department of Housing and Community Development
801 N. Capitol St., N.W.
Washington, DC 20002
202-442-7200
Fax: 202-535-1955

State of Florida

Ms. Joyce Martinez
HOME Rental Administrator
State of Florida Housing and Finance Corp.
227 N. Brounough St.
Suite 5000
Tallahassee, FL 32301-5026
850-488-4197
Fax: 850-488-9809

Cities
City of Clearwater
Mr. Michael Holmes, Manager
Department of Planning and Development Services
P.O. Box 4748
Clearwater, FL 33758-4748
727-562-4032
Fax: 727-562-4037

City of Daytona Beach
Ms. Jennifer Thomas, Deputy Director
Department of Community Development
P.O. Box 2451
Daytona Beach, FL 32115-2451
904-258-3175
Fax: 904-947-3020

City of Ft. Lauderdale
Ms. Margarette Hayes, Coordinator
Department of Economic Development
101 N.E. Third Ave.
Suite 200
Ft. Lauderdale, FL 33301-1965
954-468-1526
Fax: 954-468-1529

City of Gainesville
Mr. James A. Hencin, Manager
Block Grant Program
P.O. Box 490
Gainesville, FL 32602-0490
352-334-5031
Fax: 352-334-3166

City of Hialeah
Mr. Frederick H. Marinelli, Director
Department of Grants and Human Services
P.O. Box 110040
Hialeah, FL 33011-0040
305-883-8042
Fax: 305-883-5817

City of Hollywood
Ms. Jeannette M. Smith, Director
Division of Housing and Community Development
P.O. Box 229045
Hollywood, FL 33022-9045
954-921-3271
Fax: 954-921-3365

City of Jacksonville/County of Duval
Ms. Janet Hamer, Chief
City of Jacksonville/County of Duval
Division of Housing Services
128 E. Forsythe St., Suite 500
Jacksonville, FL 32202-4011
904-630-7000
Fax: 904-630-3605

City of Lakeland
Ms. Nancy Bennett, Coordinator
Department of Community Development
228 S. Massachusetts Ave.
Lakeland City Hall
Lakeland, FL 33801
863-603-6317
Fax: 863-603-6323

City of Miami/County of Dade
Mr. Rickert Glasgow, Director
City of Miami/County of Dade
Division of Community Development
140 W. Flagler St., Suite 1000
Miami, FL 33130-1519
305-375-3418
Fax: 305-372-6304

City of Miami
Ms. Gwendolyn Warren, Director
Department of Community Development
444 S.W. Second Ave.
Second Floor
Miami, FL 33130
305-416-2088
Fax: 305-416-2090

City of Miami Beach
Mr. Miguell DelCampillo, Housing Director
Division of Housing
1700 Convention Center Dr.
Miami Beach, FL 34102-1819
305-673-7260
Fax: 305-673-7772

City of Orlando
Ms. Lelia Allen, Bureau Chief
Department of Housing and Community Development
400 S. Orange Ave., Sixth Floor
Orlando, FL 32801
407-246-2708
Fax: 407-246-2895

City of Pompano Beach
Mr. L. James Hudson, Director
Department of Housing and Urban Improvement
P.O. Drawer 1300
Pompano Beach, FL 33061
954-786-4659
Fax: 954-786-4666

City of St. Petersburg
Ms. Stephane Lampe, Coordinator
Department of Housing and Neighborhood Improvement
P.O. Box 2842
St. Petersburg, FL 33701-2842
727-892-5563
Fax: 727-892-5397

City of Tallahassee
Ms. Martha Bentley, Supervisor
Department of Neighborhood and Community Services
300 S. Adams St., B27
Tallahassee, FL 32301-1731
850-891-6540
Fax: 850-891-6597

City of Tampa
Mr. David Snyder, Assistant Manager
Community Redevelopment Agency
2105 N. Nebraska Ave.
Tampa, FL 33602-3616
813-274-7989
Fax: 813-274-7927

City of Hillsborough
Mr. Kevin McConnell, Director
Department of Community Improvement
P.O. Box 1110
Tampa, FL 33619-4488
813-744-5557
Fax: 813-744-5777

City of West Palm Beach
Mr. Jerry Kelly, Community Development Specialist
City of West Palm Beach
Department of Economic and Community Development
P.O. Box 3366
West Palm Beach, FL 33402-3366
561-835-7300
Fax: 561-835-7348

Counties

County of Brevard
Ms. Rosa Reich, Planner
Department of Human Services
2725 Judge Fran Jamieson Way, Bldg. B, Suite 106
Viera, FL 32940
321-633-2076
Fax: 321-633-2170

County of Broward
Ms. Sue Fejes, Assistant Director
Division of Community Development
201 S. Andrews Ave., Second Floor
Ft. Lauderdale, FL 33301-1801
954-765-4910
Fax: 954-765-4919

County of Dade/City of Miami
Mr. Rickert Glasgow, Director
Division of Community Development
140 W. Flagler St., Suite 1000
Miami, FL 33130-1519
305-375-3418
Fax: 305-372-6304

County of Duval/City of Jacksonville
Ms. Janet Hamer, Chief
Division of Housing Services
128 E. Forsythe St., Suite 500
Jacksonville, FL 32202-4011
904-630-7000
Fax: 904-630-3605

County of Lee
Mr. Dennis Simon, Principal Planner

Department of Human Services
P.O. Box 398
Ft. Myers, FL 33902-0398
941-656-7930
Fax: 941-656-7960

County of Palm Beach
Mr. John R. Batey
HOME Coordinator
Department of Housing and Community Development
3323 Belvedere Rd., Bldg. 501
West Palm Beach, FL 33406
561-233-3635
Fax: 561-233-3651

County of Pasco
Ms. Dianne W. Morris, Manager
Department of Community Development
7530 Little Rd.
West Pasco Government Center
Suite 340
New Port Richey, FL 34654
727-847-8970
Fax: 727-847-8021

County of Pinellas
Mr. Larry Yancey
Department of Community Development
600 Cleveland St., Suite 800
Clearwater, FL 33755
727-464-8210
Fax: 727-464-8254

County of Polk
Ms. Nancy Sutton, Housing Coordinator
Department of Housing and Neighborhood Development
P.O. Box 9005
Bartow, FL 33831-9005
941-534-5244
Fax: 941-534-0349

County of Orange
Mr. Frantz Dutes, Assistant Manager
Department of Housing and Community Development
525 E. South St.
Orlando, FL 32801-2817
407-836-4240
Fax: 407-836-4205

County of Volusia
Mr. John V. Angiulli, Manager
Continuum of Care
123 W. Indiana Ave.
De Land, FL 32720-4611
904-943-7039
Fax: 904-943-7011

Consorita
Escambia County Consortium
Mr. Randy Wilkerson, Executive Director
Neighborhood Enterprise Foundation, Inc.
P.O. Box 18178
Pensacola, FL 32523-8178
850-458-0466
Fax: 850-458-0464

Sarasota Consortium
Mr. Donald D. Hadsell, Director
Department of Community Development
P.O. Box 1058
Sarasota, FL 34230-1058
941-316-1070
Fax: 941-316-1078

State of Georgia
Mr. Kevin Mac, Director
Dept. of Community Affairs
60 Executive Park, S., N.E.
Atlanta, GA 30329-2231
706-821-1797

Cities
City of Albany
Mr. Rudolph Goddard, Director
Department of Community and Economic Development
230 S. Jackson St., Suite 315
Albany, GA 31701-2887
912-430-5283
Fax: 912-430-2737

City of Athens/Clarke County
Ms. Julie Brunner
Administrator
Department of Human and Economic Development
P.O. Box 1868
Athens, GA 30603-1868
706-613-3155
Fax: 706-613-3158

City of Atlanta
Mr. Philip Smith, Director
Department of Planning, Development and Neighborhood Conservation
68 Mitchell St., S.W., Suite 1200
Atlanta, GA 30303-3520
404-330-6390
Fax: 404-658-7384

City of Augusta/County of Richmond
Ms. Franciene Parham, Administrator
Department of Community Development
One Tenth St., Suite 430
Augusta, GA 30911
706-821-1797
Fax: 706-821-1784

City of Columbus/County of Muscogee
Mr. Greg Clark, Chief
Division of Economic Development
P.O. Box 1340
Columbus, GA 31902-1340
706-653-4487
Fax: 706-653-4486

City of Macon
Mr. Chester Wheeler, Director
Department of Economic and Community Development
439 Cotton Ave.
Southern Trust Bldg.
Macon, GA 31201
912-751-7190
Fax: 912-751-7390

City of Savannah
Ms. Victoria Bertolozzi, Analyst
Neighborhood Planning and Community Development/Bureau of Public Development
P.O. Box 1027
Savannah, GA 31402-1027
912-651-6520
Fax: 912-651-6525

Counties
County of Clarke/City of Athens
Ms. Julie Brunner, Administrator
Department of Human and Economic Development
P.O. Box 1868
Athens, GA 30603-1868
706-613-3155
Fax: 706-613-3158

County of Clayton
Mr. Craig Goebeh, Director
Housing and Community Development Program
136 South Main Street, Suite B
Jonesboro, GA 30236
770-210-5210
Fax: 770-210-5215

County of Cobb
Mr. W. Lance Crawford, Director
Community Development Program
127 Church St.
The Brumby Bldg. at Marietta Station
Suite 270
Marietta, GA 30060
770-528-4630
Fax: 770-528-4613

County of DeKalb
Mr. Rick Herman, Director
Department of Community Development
1807 Candler Rd.
Decatur, GA 30032-4162
404-286-3353
Fax: 404-286-3337

County of Gwinnett
Ms. Virginia McKinny
Community Development Block Grants
P.O. Box 1750
Laurenceville, GA 30046-1750
770-822-5190
Fax: 770-822-5193

County of Muscogee/City of Columbus
Mr. Greg Clark, Chief
Division of Economic Development
P.O. Box 1340
Columbus, GA 31902-1340
706-653-4487
Fax: 706-653-4486

County of Richmond/City of Augusta
Ms. Franciene Parham, Administrator
Department of Community Development
One Tenth St., Suite 430
Augusta, GA 30911
706-821-1797
Fax: 706-821-1784

Consortia

County of Fulton Consortium
Mr. Melvin Richardshon, Assistant Director
Office of Environment and Community Development
141 Pryor Street, SW
Suite 5001
Atlanta, GA 30303
404-730-8066
Fax: 404-730-8112

Guam

Housing and Urban Renewal Authority
Ms. Taling M. Taitano, Executive Director
117 Bien Venida Ave.
Sinajana, GU 96926
671-477-9851
Fax: 671-472-7565

State of Hawaii

Ms. Sharyn Miyashiro
Acting Executive Director
Department of Business Economic Development and Tourism
677 Queen St., Suite 300
Honolulu, HI 96813
808-587-0641
Fax: 808-587-0600

Cities/Counties

City and County of Honolulu
Ms. Jean Tangi, Acting Coordinator
Department of the Budget
530 S. King St., Room 208
Honolulu, HI 96813-3018
808-523-4375
Fax: 808-527-6968

State of Idaho

Mr. Earl Cook, Grants Manager
Idaho Housing and Finance Association
P.O. Box 7899
Boise, ID 83707-1899
208-331-4712
Fax: 208-331-4808

Cities

City of Boise
Mr. Jim Fackrell, Director
Division of Housing and Community Development
1025 S. Capitol Blvd.
Boise, ID 83706
208-384-4158
Fax: 208-384-4195

State of Illinois

Ms. Mary Somrak-Arey
HOME Program Director
Illinois Housing Development Authority
401 N. Michigan Ave., Suite 900
Chicago, IL 60611-4255
312-836-5364
Fax: 312-832-2176

Cities

City of Chicago
Mr. Nancy Pomes, Deputy Commissioner
Division of Compliance and Monitoring
318 S. Michigan Ave.
Chicago, IL 60604-4200
312-747-2608
Fax: 312-747-5023

City of Decatur
Reginald Fluker, Manager
Department of Neighborhood Services
One Gary K. Anderson Plaza
Decatur, IL 62523-1196
217-424-2778
Fax: 217-424-2728

City of East St. Louis
Ms. Chris Anderson, HOME Coordinator
CDBG Operations Corp.
301 River Park Dr., Third Floor
E. St. Louis, IL 62201-1201
618-482-6635
Fax: 618-271-8194

City of Evanston
Ms. Roberta Schur, Planner
Division of Planning
2100 Ridge Ave., Room 3900
Evanston, IL 60201
847-866-2928
Fax: 847-448-8120

City of Joliet
Mr. Robert Listner, Director
Division of Neighborhood Services
150 W. Jefferson St.
Joliet, IL 60432
815-724-4090
Fax: 815-724-4118

City of Peoria
Ms. Pat S. Landes, Assistant Director
Department of Development
456 Fulton St., Suite 402
Peoria, IL 61602-1217
309-494-8605
Fax: 309-494-8680

City of Rockford
Ms. Vicki Manson, Neighborhood Development Coordinator
Department of Community Development
425 E. State St.
Rockford, IL 61104-1014
815-987-5690
Fax: 815-967-6933

City of Springfield
Mr. Jan Sorenson, Grants Coordinator
Office of Economic Development
231 S. Sixth St.
Springfield, IL 62701-1502
217-789-2377
Fax: 217-789-2380

City of Urbana
Mr. Michael J. Loschen
Grants Coordinator
Department of Community Development Services
400 S. Vine St.
Urbana, IL 61801
217-384-2335
Fax: 217-384-2367

Counties

County of DuPage
Mr. Phil Smith, Administrator
Department of Human Services
421 N. County Farm Rd.
Wheaton, IL 60187
630-682-7543
Fax: 630-682-7179

County of Lake
Mr. Vern Witkowski, Community Development Administrator
Department of Planning, Building and Development
18 N. County St., Sixth Floor
Waukegan, IL 60085-4356
847-360-6495
Fax: 847-360-6734

County of Madison
Ms. Dorothy Hummel
HOME Program Coordinator
Department of Community Development
130 Hillsboro Ave.
Edwardsville, IL 62025-1955
618-692-6200
Fax: 618-692-7022

County of McHenry
Mr. John W. Labaj, Deputy Director
Department of Planning and Development
2200 N. Seminary Ave.
Annex Bldg. A
Woodstock, IL 60098
815-338-2040
Fax: 815-337-3720

County of Will
Mr. Ron Pullman, Director
Department of Community Development
100 Manhattan Rd.
Farm Bureau Bldg.
Joliet, IL 60433-4060
815-727-2332
Fax: 815-727-2341

Consortia

Cook County Consortium
Mr. Ted Sucharski, HOME Program Coordinator
Department of Planning and Development
69 W. Washington Blvd.
Suite 2900
Chicago, IL 60602-1304
312-603-1066
Fax: 312-603-9970

St. Clair County Consortium
Mr. David Van Toll, HOME Program Coordinator
Division of Community Development
19 Public Sq., Suite 200
Belleville, IL 62220-1624
618-277-6790
Fax: 618-236-1190

State of Indiana

Ms. Sheryl Sharpe
Community Development Manager
Housing Finance Authority
115 W. Washington St.
Suite 1350, South Tower
Indianapolis, IN 46204-3413
317-232-7777
Fax: 317-232-7778

Cities

City of Anderson
Mr. Ron Harris, Deputy Director
Department of Community Development
P.O. Box 2100
Anderson, IN 46018
765-648-6097
Fax: 765-648-5914

City of Bloomington
Ms. Doris Sims, Executive Director
Department of Redevelopment
P.O. Box 100
Bloomington, IN 47402
812-349-3401
Fax: 812-349-3582

City of East Chicago
Mr. John D. Artis, Director
Department of Redevelopment and Housing Authority
P.O. Box 498
East Chicago, IN 46312-0498
219-397-9974
Fax: 219-397-4249

City of Evansville
Ms. Brenda Taylor, Community Development Specialist
Department of Metropolitan Development
One N.W. Martin Luther King, Jr. Blvd.
306 Civic Center Complex
Evansville, IN 47708-1831
812-436-7823
Fax: 812-436-7809

City of Ft. Wayne
Mr. Brian White, Community Development Administrator
Department of Community and Economic Development
One E. Main St.
City-County Bldg., Room 910
Ft. Wayne, IN 46802
219-427-2158
Fax: 219-427-1115

City of Gary
Ms. Letty Almodovar, Director
Department of Planning and Community Development
475 Broadway
Third Floor, Suite 318
Gary, IN 46402-1239
219-881-5075
Fax: 219-881-5085

City of Hammond
Ms. Katrina Burns, Loan Officer
Department of Community Development
649 Conkey St.
Hammond, IN 46324-3027
219-853-6371
Fax: 219-853-6334

City of Indianapolis
Mr. Jim Kaufman, Grants Manager
Department of Metropolitan Development/HOME Program
200 E. Washington St.
City County Bldg.
Suite 1841
Indianapolis, IN 46204
317-327-5866
Fax: 317-327-5908

City of Lafayette
Ms. Aimee Dibble, Director
Department of Community and Redevelopment
20 N. Sixth St.
Lafayette, IN 47901-1412
765-476-4510
Fax: 765-476-4513

City of Muncie
Mr. Jerry L. Thornburg, Director
Department of Community Development
300 N. High St.
Muncie, IN 47305
765-747-4825
Fax: 765-747-4898

City of South Bend
Ms. Elizabeth Leonard, Director
Department of Community and Economic Development
227 W. Jefferson Blvd.
County-City Bldg., Suite 1200
South Bend, IN 46601
219-235-9330
Fax: 219-235-9021

City of Terre Haute
Mr. Mike Kass, Administrator
Department of Redevelopment
17 Harding Ave.
City Hall, Room 301
Terre Haute, IN 47807
812-232-0018
Fax: 812-235-3652

Counties
County of Lake
Ms. Alverna Hooks, Deputy Director
Department of Community Development
2293 N. Main St.
Crown Point, IN 46307-1885
219-755-3232
Fax: 219-736-5925

State of Iowa

Ms. Anna Woolson, Team Leader
Department of Economic Development
200 E. Grand Ave.
Des Moines, IA 50309-1827
515-242-4825
Fax: 515-242-4809

Cities
City of Cedar Rapids
Mr. Dan Schmelzinger, Director
Department of Housing, Building, and Zoning
1201 Sixth St., S.W.
Cedar Rapids, IA 52404-1256
319-286-5836
Fax: 319-286-5870

City of Davenport
Mr. Gregg Hoover, Director
Department of Community and Economic Development
226 W. Fourth St.
Davenport, IA 52801-1308
319-326-7766
Fax: 319-328-6714

City of Des Moines
Mr. Bob Schulte, Director
Department of Housing and Community Services
602 E. First St.
Des Moines, IA 50309-1881
515-237-1384
Fax: 515-237-1687

City of Iowa City
Mr. Steven Nasby, Community Development Coordinator
Department of Planning and Community Development
410 E. Washington St.
Iowa City, IA 52240
319-356-5230
Fax: 319-356-5009

City of Sioux City
Mr. Russell Kock, Administrator
Department of Community Development
P.O. Box 447
Sioux City, IA 51102
712-279-6283
Fax: 712-279-6196

City of Waterloo
Mr. Richard W. Earles, Director
Department of Community Development
620 Mulberry St.
Suite 202
Waterloo, IA 50703
319-291-4429
Fax: 319-291-4431

State of Kansas

Ms. Barbara Cowdin, HOME Program Director
Division of Housing
700 S.W. Harrison St.
Suite 1300
Topeka, KS 66603-3755
785-296-4819
Fax: 785-296-8985

Cities
City of Kansas City
Mr. Brian Z. White, Program Coordinator

Department of Housing and
Community Development
701 N. Seventh St.
Kansas City, KS 66101-3064
913-573-5100
Fax: 913-573-5115

City of Lawrence
Ms. Margene Swarts,
Community Development
Manager
Department of Housing and
Neighborhood Development
Six E. Sixth St.
Lawrence, KS 66044
785-832-3100
Fax: 785-832-3405

City of Topeka
Mr. Mark Stock, CDBG
Program Manager
Department of Housing and
Neighborhood Development
2010 S.E. California Ave.
Topeka, KS 66607
785-368-3711
Fax: 785-368-2546

City of Wichita
Mr. Mark Stanberry, HOME
Coordinator
Department of Human Services
332 N. Riverview St.
Wichita, KS 67203
316-268-4685
Fax: 316-268-4291

Counties
*County of Sedgwick/ Central
Plains HOME Consortium*
Mr. Bradley Snapp, Coordinator
Department of Community
Development
1540 N. Broadway
Suite 203
Wichita, KS 67214
316-383-7433
Fax: 316-383-8271

Consortia
Johnson County Consortium
Ms. Mary Scott, Director
Department of Housing
9305 W. 74th St.
Merriam, KS 66204
913-432-2174
Fax: 913-722-3296

*Central Plains HOME
Consortium/County of Sedgwick*
Mr. Bradley Snapp, Coordinator
Department of Community
Development
1540 N. Broadway, Suite 203
Wichita, KS 67214
316-383-7433
Fax: 316-383-8271

State of Kentucky
Mr. Rob Ellis, CPD Director
Kentucky Housing Corp.
1231 Louisville Rd.
Frankfort, KY 40601-6156
502-564-7630
Fax: 502-564-6445

Cities
City of Covington
Mr. Howard Hodge, Director
Department of Housing and
Community Development
638 Madison Ave.
Covington, KY 41011-2422
606-292-2188
Fax: 606-292-2139

*City of Lexington/County of
Fayette*
Ms. Paula King
HOME Coordinator
City of Lexington/County of
Fayette
Division of Housing and
Community Development
200 E. Main St.
Sixth Floor
Lexington, KY 40507
606-258-3070
Fax: 606-258-3081

City of Louisville
Ms. Barbara Ferrell,
Administrator
Department of Housing and
Urban Development
745 W. Main St., Suite 300
Louisville, KY 40202-2675
502-574-4397
Fax: 502-574-4199

City of Owensboro
Mr. Keith Free, Associate
Director
Metropolitan Planning
Commission
P.O. Box 732
Owensboro, KY 42302-9003
270-687-8656
Fax: 270-687-8664

Counties
*County of Fayette/City of
Lexington*
Ms. Paula King
HOME Coordinator
City of Lexington/County of
Fayette
Division of Housing and
Community Development
200 E. Main St., Sixth Floor
Lexington, KY 40507
606-258-3070
Fax: 606-258-3081

County of Jefferson
Ms. Brenda White, Director
Division of Community
Development
810 Barret Ave., Sixth Floor
Louisville, KY 40204-1700
502-574-6550
Fax: 502-574-6912

State of Louisiana
Ms. Debra Washington, Program
Manager
Housing Finance Agency
200 Lafayette St., Suite 300
Baton Rouge, LA 70801
225-342-1320
Fax: 225-342-1310

Cities
City of Alexandria
Ms. Brenda Ray, Director
Department of Community
Development
P.O. Box 71
Alexandria, LA 71309-0071
318-449-5072
Fax: 318-449-5031

City of Baton Rouge
Mr. Al Gensler, Director
Department of Community
Development
P.O. Box 1471
Baton Rouge, LA 70821-1471
225-389-3039
Fax: 225-389-3939

City of Houma/Parish of Terrebonne
Ms. Melanie VanBuren
HOME Program Manager
Department of Housing and Human Services
P.O. Box 6097
Houma, LA 70361
985-873-6892
Fax: 985-873-6880

City of Lafayette
Mr. Joe Bourg, Manager
Governmental and Business Relations Division
P.O. Box 4017-C
Lafayette, LA 70502-4017
337-291-8411
Fax: 337-291-8415

City of Lake Charles
Mr. Mark Tizano, Planner
Department of Planning and Economic Development
P.O. Box 900
Lake Charles, LA 70602-0900
337-491-1440
Fax: 337-491-1437

City of Monroe
Dr. James Tarver, Interim Director
Division of Community Development
P.O. Box 123
Monroe, LA 71201-0123
318-329-2256
Fax: 318-329-2845

City of New Orleans
Mr. John Roussell, Deputy Director
Division of Housing and Neighborhood Development
1340 Poydras St., Tenth Floor
New Orleans, LA 70112
504-299-4800
Fax: 504-299-4951

City of Shreveport
Mr. Larry Ferdinand, Director
Department of Community Development
P.O. Box 31109
Shreveport, LA 71130-1109
318-673-5900
Fax: 318-673-5903

Parishes
Parish of Jefferson
Mr. Kim Thompson, Manager
Department of Community Development Programs
1221 Elmwood Park Blvd.
Suite 605
Harahan, LA 70123-2337
504-736-6262
Fax: 504-736-6425

Parish of Terrebonne/City of Houma
Ms. Melanie VanBuren
HOME Program Manager
Department of Housing and Human Services
P.O. Box 6097
Houma, LA 70361
985-873-6892
Fax: 985-873-6880

State of Maine

Mr. Michael Martin
State of Maine Housing Authority
353 Water St.
Augusta, ME 4338
207-626-4615
Fax: 207-626-4692

Cities
City of Portland
Mr. Roger Bondeson, Manager
Department of Housing and Neighborhood Service
389 Congress St., Room 313
Portland, ME 04101-3509
207-874-8711
Fax: 207-756-8990

Northern Mariana Islands

Northern Mariana Islands Housing Corp.
Ms. Mary Lou S. Ada, Executive Director
Commonwealth Development Authority
P.O. Box 502149
Saipan, MP 96950-2149
670-234-7145
Fax: 670-234-7144

State of Maryland

Ms. Vicky Semour
HOME Program Manager
State of Maryland
Department of Housing and Community Development
100 Community Place
Crownsville, MD 21032-2025
410-514-7440
Fax: 410-987-4097

Cities
City of Baltimore
Mr. James R. Majors, Chief
Department of Housing and Community Development
417 E. Fayette St., Suite 1036
Baltimore, MD 21202-3431
410-396-5590
Fax: 410-625-0830

Counties
County of Anne Arundel
Ms. Kathleen M. Koch, Executive Director
County of Anne Arundel
Arundel Community Development Services, Inc.
2660 Riva Rd., Suite 210
Annapolis, MD 21401
410-222-7600
Fax: 410-222-7619

County of Baltimore
Mr. Kevin M. Roddy, Grants Administrator
Office of Community Conservation
One Investment Place, Suite 800
Towson, MD 21204
410-887-6055
Fax: 410-887-5696

County of Montgomery
Ms. Luann W. Korona, Section Chief
Department of Housing and Community Affairs
100 Maryland Ave., Fourth Floor
Rockville, MD 20850
240-777-3600
Fax: 240-777-3653

County of Prince Georges
Mr. James M. Lyons, Manager
Department of Housing and Community Development
9400 Peppercorn Place
Suite 120
Largo, MD 20774

301-883-5570
Fax: 301-925-4147

State of Massachusetts

Ms. JoAnn McGuirk
HOME Program Director
State of Massachusetts
Department of Housing and Community Development
One Congress St., Tenth Floor
Boston, MA 2114
617-727-7824
Fax: 617-727-0532

Cities

City of Boston
Ms. Charlotte Golar Richie, Director
Department of Neighborhood Development
26 Court St.
Boston, MA 2108
617-635-0500
Fax: 617-635-0561

City of Brockton
Mr. Steven C. Cruz, Executive Director
Redevelopment Authority
140 School St.
Brockton, MA 02302-3114
508-587-6085
Fax: 508-584-2362

City of Cambridge
Ms. Elsa Campbell, Manager
Department of Community Development
57 Inman St.
Cambridge, MA 2139
617-349-4634
Fax: 617-349-4669

City of Fall River
Mr. Thomas McCloskey, Executive Director
Community Development Agency
P.O. Box 1711
Fall River, MA 02720-2107
508-679-0131
Fax: 508-679-0752

City of Fitchburg
Mr. David Streb, Coordinator
718 Main St.
Fitchburg, MA 01420-3182
978-345-1018
Fax: 978-342-0161

City of Holyoke
Mr. William H. Murphy, Administrator
Office of Community Development
20 Korean Veterans Plaza
City Hall Annex, Room 400
Holyoke, MA 01040-5036
413-534-2230
Fax: 413-534-2231

City of Lawrence
Mr. William Luster, Director
Department of Community Development
225 Essex St., Third Floor
Lawrence, MA 1840
978-794-5891
Fax: 978-683-4894

City of Lowell
Mr. Jay Matthew Coggins, Director
Division of Planning and Development
50 Arcand Dr.
JFK Civic Center
Lowell, MA 1852
978-970-4252
Fax: 978-970-4262

City of Lynn
Mr. Charles J. Gaeta, Executive Director
Lynn Housing Authority
Ten Church St.
Lynn, MA 1902
781-477-2800
Fax: 781-592-6296

City of Malden
Mr. Peter Garbaiti, HOME Coordinator
Malden Redevelopment Authority
200 Pleasant St., Room 621
Malden, MA 02148-4802
781-324-5720
Fax: 781-322-3734

City of New Bedford
Mr. Patrick Sullivan, Director
Department of Community Development
608 Pleasant St.
New Bedford, MA 02740-6113
508-979-1500
Fax: 508-979-1575

City of Newton
Mr. Stephen D. Gartrell, Director
Department of Community Development
1000 Commonwealth Ave.
Newton Center
Newton, MA 2159
617-552-7135
Fax: 617-965-6620

City of Peabody/North Shore HOME Consortium
Mr. Kevin J. Hurley, HOME Coordinator
Department of Community Development
24 Lowell St.
City Hall
Peabody, MA 01960-5440
978-532-5000 Ext. 327
Fax: 978-531-9908

City of Quincy
Mr. Angelito Santos, Principal Planner
Department of Planning and Community Development
1305 Hancock St.
Quincy, MA 2169
617-376-1362
Fax: 617-376-1097

City of Somerville
Mr. Stephen M. Post, Executive Director
Office of Housing and Community Development
93 Highland Ave.
Somerville, MA 02143-1740
617-625-6000
Fax: 617-625-0722

City of Springfield
Ms. Kathleen Lindenburg
Housing Director
Department of Community Development
81 State St.
Springfield, MA 01103-1699
413-787-6500
Fax: 413-787-6515

City of Worcester
Mr. Stephen O'Neil, Director
Office of Planning and
Community Development
418 Main St., Suite 400
Worcester, MA 1608
508-799-1400
Fax: 508-799-1406

Consortia
Barnstable County Consortium
Mr. Edward Allard, Specialist
Cape Cod Commission
3225 Main St.
Barnstable, MA 2630
508-362-3828
Fax: 508-362-3136

North Shore HOME Consortium/City of Peabody
Mr. Kevin J. Hurley, HOME
Coordinator
Department of Community
Development
24 Lowell St.
City Hall
Peabody, MA 01960-5440
978-532-5000 Ext. 327
Fax: 978-531-9908

State of Michigan

Mr. Bill Parker, Coordinator
State of Michigan
Housing Development Authority
P.O. Box 30044
Lansing, MI 48909-7544
517-373-1462
Fax: 517-335-4797

Cities
City of Ann Arbor
Mr. Larry Friedman
Department of Community
Development
P.O. Box 8647
Ann Arbor, MI 48107-8647
734-994-2589
Fax: 734-994-2915

City of Battle Creek
Mr. Tim Parks, Coordinator
Department of Planning and
Community Development
P.O. Box 1717
Battle Creek, MI 49016-1717
616-966-3315
Fax: 616-966-3659

City of Bay City
Ms. Debbie Kiesel, Acting
Director
Department of Redevelopment
and Housing Services
301 Washington Ave.
Bay City, MI 48708
517-894-8153
Fax: 517-894-8220

City of Detroit
Ms. Leah Vest, Executive
Manager
Department of Planning and
Development
65 Cadillac Tower
Suite 1900
Detroit, MI 48226
313-224-3461
Fax: 313-224-9149

City of Flint
Ms. Karen Morris
Department of Community and
Economic Development
1101 S. Saginaw St.
Flint, MI 48502
810-766-7436
Fax: 810-766-7351

City of Grand Rapids
Mr. Thomas S. Syrek, Director
Department of Housing and
Community Development
300 Monroe Ave., N.W.
City Hall, Room 460
Grand Rapids, MI 49503-2206
616-456-3445
Fax: 616-456-4619

City of Jackson
Mr. Michael Sims, Assistant
Director
Department of Community
Development
161 W. Michigan Ave.
Jackson, MI 49201
517-768-4060
Fax: 517-768-5832

City of Kalamazoo
Ms. Peg Giem
Department of Community
Development
241 W. South St.
Kalamazoo, MI 49007-4796
616-337-8225

City of Lansing
Mr. Dennis Lysakowski
Division of Development
316 N. Capitol Ave.
Suite D-2
Lansing, MI 48933-1234
517-483-4051
Fax: 517-483-6036

City of Muskegon
Mr. Will Griffin, Director
Department of Community and
Neighborhood Services
P.O. Box 536
Muskegon, MI 49443
231-724-6963
Fax: 231-726-2501

City of Pontiac
Ms. Ruth Steed, HOME Program
Administrator
Department of Community
Development
51000 Woodward Ave.
Pontiac, MI 48342-5015
248-857-5670
Fax: 248-857-5744

City of Port Huron
Ms. Mary Wrocklage
Department of Planning and
Community Development
100 McMorran Blvd.
Port Huron, MI 48060
810-984-9736
Fax: 810-982-7872

City of Saginaw
Mr. Robert Brown, Director
Department of Rehabilitation
and Block Grant Services
1315 S. Washington Ave
Room 210
Saginaw, MI 48601-2513
517-759-1530
Fax: 517-759-1756

City of Warren
Ms. Rosemary Furlong, Program
Coordinator
Department of Community
Development
29500 Van Dyke Ave.
Warren, MI 48093-6726
810-574-4687
Fax: 810-574-4685

City of Westland
Mr. James Gilbert, Director
Department of Community Development
32715 Dorsey Rd.
Westland, MI 48185
734-595-0288
Fax: 734-595-1680

Counties
County of Genesee
Ms. Christine Keisling
Metropolitan Planning Commission
1101 Beach St., Room 223
Flint, MI 48502
810-766-6549
Fax: 810-257-3185

County of Macomb
Mr. James Baumgartner, Director
Department of Planning and Economic Development
One S. Main St., Seventh Floor
Mt. Clemens, MI 48043
810-469-5285
Fax: 810-469-6787

County of Oakland
Ms. Karry Reith, Manager
Department of Community Development
1200 N. Telegraph Rd.
Executive Office Bldg. 112, Department 414
Pontiac, MI 48341-1043
248-858-0493
Fax: 248-858-5311

County of Wayne
Mr. James Constan, Program Manager
Division of Community Development
600 Randolph St.
Wayne County Bldg.
Detroit, MI 48226
313-224-6655
Fax: 313-224-7450

State of Minnesota
Mr. Jim Cegla
Federal Programs and Policy Director
Minnesota Housing Finance Agency
400 Sibley St., Suite 300
St. Paul, MN 55101-1941
800-657-3701
Fax: 651-296-8139

Cities
City of Duluth
Mr. Keith Hamre, Manager
Division of Community Development and Housing
411 W. First St.
City Hall, Room 407
Duluth, MN 55802-1100
218-723-3357
Fax: 218-723-3400

City of Minneapolis
Mr. Ken Brunsvold, Director
Office of Grants and Special Projects
350 S. Fifth St.
City Hall, Room 200
Minneapolis, MN 55415
612-673-2348
Fax: 612-673-3724

City of St. Paul
Mr. Ron Ross, Manager
Department of Planning and Economic Development
25 Fourth St., W., 14th Floor
St. Paul, MN 55102-1634
651-266-6692
Fax: 651-228-3220

Counties
County of Dakota
Ms. Stephanie Newburg, HOME Coordinator
Housing and Redevelopment Authority
2496 145th St.
Rosemount, MN 55068
651-423-8117
Fax: 651-423-8180

County of Hennepin
Mr. Rod Waara, Director
Office of Planning and Development
10709 Wayzata Blvd., Suite 260
Hopkins, MN 55305
612-541-7080
Fax: 612-541-7090

Consortia
St. Louis County Consortium
Ms. Nancy Larson
Department of Community Development
227 W. First St.
Missabe Bldg., Room 901
Duluth, MN 55802-1202
218-749-9741
Fax: 218-725-5029

State of Mississippi
Ms. Deborah Franklin
Grants Management Manager
State of Mississippi
Division of Community Services
P.O. Box 24628
Jackson, MS 39225-4628
601-949-2250
Fax: 601-949-2230

Cities
City of Hattiesburg
Mr. Joe Strahan, Senior Planner/Housing Coordinator
Department of Planning and Community Development
200 Forest Street, City Hall
Hattiesburg, MS 39401
601-545-4598
Fax: 601-545-4592

City of Jackson
Mr. Leo Stevens, Director
Division of Development Assistance
P.O. Box 17
Jackson, MS 39205-0017
601-960-2155
Fax: 601-960-2403

State of Missouri
Ms. Angela Campbell, Administrator
Housing Development Commission
3435 Broadway
Kansas City, MO 64111
816-759-6660
Fax: 816-759-6828

Cities
City of Columbia
Mr. John Fleck, Planner
Department of Planning and Development
P.O. Box N
Columbia, MO 65205
573-874-7244
Fax: 573-874-7546

City of Independence
Mr. Herb Webb
HOME Coordinator
Department of Community Development
P.O. Box 1019
Independence, MO 64051
816-325-7425
Fax: 816-325-7400

City of Kansas City
Mr. John Tangeman, Director
City of Kansas City
Department of Housing and Community Development
414 E. 12th St.
City Hall, 11th Floor
Kansas City, MO 64106
816-513-3000
Fax: 816-513-3011

City of Springfield
Mr. R. Charles Marinec, Grants Administrator
Department of Planning and Development
840 Boonville Ave.
Springfield, MO 65802
417-864-1038
Fax: 417-864-1881

City of St. Joseph
Mr. Gerald McCush
HOME Coordinator
Department of Community Development
1100 Frederick Ave.
City Hall, Room 405
St. Joseph, MO 64501
816-271-4646
Fax: 816-271-5365

City of St. Louis
Ms. Jill Claybour, HOME Coordinator
City of St. Louis
Community Development Agency
1015 Locust, Suite 1140
St. Louis, MO 63101
314-622-3400
Fax: 314-622-3413

Counties
County of St. Louis
Mr. Phil Minden, Housing Manager
Office of Community Development
121 S. Meramec Ave.
St. Louis, MO 63105
314-615-8337
Fax: 314-889-3420

State of Montana

Ms. Connie Oustad
HOME Program Manager
Department of Commerce
P.O. Box 200545
Helena, MT 59620-0545
406-444-0092
Fax: 406-444-9774

Cities
City of Billings
Mr. John Walsh, Director
Department of Community Development
P.O. Box 1178
Billings, MT 59103
406-657-8281
Fax: 406-657-8252

City of Great Falls
Ms. Kim Johnson, CDBG/HOME Administrator
Department of Community Development
P.O. Box 5021
Great Falls, MT 59403-5021
406-455-8407
Fax: 406-454-3181

State of Nebraska

Ms. Lara Huskey
Housing Coordinator
Office of Economic Development
P.O. Box 94666
Lincoln, NE 68509-4666
402-471-3759
Fax: 402-471-3778

Cities
City of Lincoln
Mr. Steve Werthmann, Manager
Department of Urban Development
129 N. Tenth St., Room 110
Lincoln, NE 68508
402-441-7864
Fax: 402-441-8711

City of Omaha
Mr. Mike Saklar, Director
Department of Planning
1819 Farnam St., Suite 1111
Omaha, NE 68183-1100
402-444-5150
Fax: 402-444-6140

State of Nevada

Ms. Debbie Parra
Officer Department of Commerce
1802 N. Carson St., Suite 154
Carson City, NV 89701-1215
775-687-4258
Fax: 775-687-4040

Cities
City of Reno
Ms. Linda Johnson, Housing Administrator
Department of Community Development
P.O. Box 1900
Reno, NV 89505-1900
775-334-2305
Fax: 775-334-2343

Counties
County of Clark
Mr. Michael J. Pawlak, Administrator
Division of Community Resources Management
P.O. Box 551212
Las Vegas, NV 89155-1212
702-455-5025
Fax: 702-455-5038

County of Lyon
Ms. Denise Cox
Public Information Contact
County of Lyon
Western Nevada Development District
31 S. Main St.
Yerington, NV 89447
775-883-7333

State of New Hampshire

Mr. William Ray
Planner New Hampshire Housing Finance Authority
Division of Planning and Development
P.O. Box 5087
Manchester, NH 03108-5087
603-472-8623
Fax: 603-471-1043

Cities

City of Manchester
Mr. Samuel Maranto, City Planner
One City Hall Plaza
Manchester, NH 03101-2018
603-624-6530
Fax: 603-624-6529

State of New Jersey

Ms. Sheri Malnak, Administrator
State of New Jersey
Division of Housing and Community Resources
P.O. Box 806
Trenton, NJ 08625-0806
609-984-8453
Fax: 609-984-8454

Cities

City of Atlantic City
Mr. Michael P. Toland, CDBG Director
Department of Planning and Development
1301 Bacharach Blvd.
Room 505, City Hall
Atlantic City, NJ 8401
609-347-5330
Fax: 609-347-5317

City of Camden
Mr. Louis Pastoriza, Clerk
Bureau of Grants Management
P.O. Box 95120
Camden, NJ 08101-5120
856-757-7000

City of East Orange
Ms. Lancie Marchan, Manager
Department of Policy, Planning, and Development
44 City Hall Plaza
East Orange, NJ 07019-4104
973-266-5138
Fax: 973-674-2180

City of Elizabeth
Ms. Stephanie Welch, Secretary
Department of Community Development
50 Winfield Scott Plaza
Elizabeth, NJ 07201-2408
908-352-8450
Fax: 908-352-2275

City of Irvington
Ms. Tonique Griffin, Public Information Contact
Office of Community Development and Planning
Civic Sq.
Municipal Bldg., Room 102
Irvington, NJ 07111-4518
973-399-6658
Fax: 973-399-0827

City of Jersey City
Ms. Elenor O'Malley, Manager
Office of Grants Management
30 Montgomery St., Room 404
Jersey City, NJ 7302
201-547-6910
Fax: 201-547-5104

City of New Brunswick
Ms. Carole Small-Lyons, HOME Coordinator
Department of Planning, Community and Economic Development
390 George St.
New Brunswick, NJ 8901
732-745-5050
Fax: 732-545-2390

City of Newark
Mr. Basil Franklin, Director
Department of Economic Development
920 Broad St., Suite 218
Newark, NJ 07102-2609
973-733-3682
Fax: 973-733-3769

City of Passaic
Ms. Sonya Dasilva, Assistant Director
Department of Community Development
330 Passaic St.
Passaic, NJ 07055-5815
973-365-5641
Fax: 973-365-5552

City of Paterson
Ms. Anna-Lisa Dopirak, Director
Department of Community Development
125 Ellison St., Second Floor
Paterson, NJ 07505-1310
973-279-5980
Fax: 973-278-2981

City of Perth Amboy
Mr. Michael W. Keller, Director
Office of Economic and Community Development
One Olive St., Second Floor
Perth Amboy, NJ 08861-4517
732-442-4000
Fax: 732-442-9274

City of Trenton
Ms. Rhonda Coe, Director
Department of Housing and Development
319 E. State St., Third Floor
Trenton, NJ 08608-1809
609-989-3598
Fax: 609-989-4243

City of Vineland
Mr. Joseph Bullock
Community Development Director
Department of Administration
P.O. Box 5108
Vineland, NJ 8360
856-794-4000
Fax: 856-794-6163

Counties

County of Atlantic
Mr. Stephen Lingle, Director
Department of Community Development/Improvement Authority
201 Shore Rd.
Stillwater Bldg.
Northfield, NJ 8225
609-345-5838
Fax: 609-645-5931

County of Bergen
Ms. Lynn Bartlett-DeLuise, HOME Coordinator
Department of Community Development
25 E. Salem St., Room 601
Hackensack, NJ 07601-7021
201-646-3458
Fax: 201-487-0945

County of Burlington
Mr. Robert Schmidt, Public Information Contact
Department of Economic Development

795 Woodlane Rd.
Mount Holly, NJ 08060-1317
609-265-5072
Fax: 609-265-5500

County of Camden
Ms. Beth Pugh, Analyst
P.O. Box 100
Blackwood, NJ 08012-0100
856-374-6335
Fax: 856-374-6348

County of Essex
Ms. Maggie Benz, Coordinator
Division of Housing and Community Development
50 S. Clinton St.
Fourth Floor, Suite 4300
East Orange, NJ 7018
973-395-8450
Fax: 973-395-8437

County of Gloucester
Ms. Diane Kirwan-Patterson, Division Head
Office of Government Services
P.O. Box 337
Woodbury, NJ 08096-7337
856-384-6955
Fax: 856-384-6938

County of Hudson
Mr. Kathy Jacobs, Director
Division of Community Planning
583 Newark Ave.
Jersey City, NJ 07306-2301
201-795-6186
Fax: 201-795-1903

County of Monmouth
Ms. Virginia A. Edwards, Director
Community Development Program
One E. Main St.
Hall of Records Annex
Freehold, NJ 07728-1255
732-431-7490
Fax: 732-308-2995

County of Ocean
Mr. Tony Agliata, Community Development Director
Department of Planning
129 Hooper Ave.
Toms River, NJ 08753-7605
732-929-2054
Fax: 732-244-8396

County of Somerset
Ms. Rosalee Yurasko, Director
County of Somerset
Office of Community Development
P.O. Box 3000
Somerville, NJ 08876-1262
908-231-7039
Fax: 908-707-4127

County of Union
Mr. President Carlisle, Housing Coordinator
Division of Community Development
Elizabethtown Plaza
Union County Administration Bldg.
Elizabeth, NJ 7207
908-527-4227
Fax: 908-527-4901

Consortia
Hudson County Consortium
Ms. Kathy A. Jacob, HOME Coordinator
Division of Community Planning
583 Newark Ave.
Second Floor
Jersey City, NJ 07306-2301
201-795-6186
Fax: 201-795-1903

Mercer County Consortium
Mr. Keith Rick Johnson, Aid
Department of Housing and Community Development
P.O. Box 8068
Trenton, NJ 08650-0068
609-989-6959
Fax: 609-989-0306

County of Middlesex Consortium
Mr. John A. Sully, Executive Director
Department of Housing and Community Development
JFK Sq.
County Administration Bldg.
New Brunswick, NJ 8901
732-745-3519
Fax: 732-745-4117

Morris County Consortium
Ms. Helen Wolfmeyer, HOME Coordinator
Division of Community Development
P.O. Box 900
Morristown, NJ 07963-0900
973-285-6060
Fax: 973-285-6031

State of New Mexico

Ms. Terri Sais
Public Information Contact
State of New Mexico
Mortgage Finance Authority
P.O. Box 2047
Albuquerque, NM 87102-4147
505-843-6880
Fax: 505-243-3289

Cities
City of Albuquerque
Ms. Marti Luick, Manager
Department of Family and Community Services
P.O. Box 1293
Albuquerque, NM 87106-1293
505-768-2871
Fax: 505-768-3204

City of Las Cruces
Mr. Don Fahrenkrog, Director
Department of Neighborhood Development
575 S. Alameda Blvd., Room 231
Las Cruces, NM 88005
505-528-3105
Fax: 505-528-3102

State of New York

Public Information Office
38-40 State St.
Albany, NY 12207
518-473-2526

Cities
City of Albany
Ms. Patricia Hourigan, Public Information Contact
Department of Housing and Community Development
200 Henry Johnson Blvd., Second
Albany, NY 12210-2867
518-434-5240
Fax: 518-434-5242

City of Islip
Ms. Carole Carroll, Director
Community Development
Agency
15 Shore Ln.
Bay Shore, NY 11706
631-665-1185
Fax: 631-665-0036

City of Binghamton
Mr. Paul Nelson, Director
Office of Community
Development
38 Hawley St.
City Hall, Governmental Plaza,
Fourth Floor
Binghamton, NY 13901-3793
607-772-7028
Fax: 607-772-0508

City of Buffalo
Ms. Dawn Sanders, Director
Department of Neighborhood
Services
65 Niagra Sq., Room 313
Buffalo, NY 14202
716-851-4182
Fax: 716-851-4242

City of Elmira
Ms. Cheryl Schneider, HOME
Coordinator
Department of Business and
Housing Development
317 E. Church St.
City Hall Armory Annex
Elmira, NY 14901
607-737-5607
Fax: 607-737-5696

City of Babylon/Long Island
Housing Partnership
Ms. Patricia Bourne, Director
Town of Babylon/Long Island
Housing Partnership
Department of Community and
Economic Development
180 Oser Ave.
Hauppauge, NY 11788
631-434-9277
Fax: 631-434-9311

City of Jamestown
Ms. Jan Kurth, Grants
Coordinator
Community Development
Office/Urban Renewal Agency
200 E. Third St.
Municipal Bldg., Third Floor
Jamestown, NY 14701
716-483-7656
Fax: 716-483-7772

City of Mount Vernon
Ms. Carmen Sylvester, Director
Department of Planning and
Community Development
One Roosevelt Sq.
City Hall, Second Floor
Mount Vernon, NY 10550
914-699-7230
Fax: 914-699-1435

City of New Rochelle
Ms. Christine Magrin
Administrator
City of New Rochelle
Department of Development
515 North Ave.
City Hall
New Rochelle, NY 10801-3405
914-654-2184
Fax: 914-632-3626

City of New York City
Mr. Ted Gallagher, Planner
City of New York City
Department of Housing
Preservation and Development
100 Gold St.
New York, NY 10038
212-863-8061
Fax: 212-863-8067

City of Niagara Falls
Mr. Robert Antonucci, HOME
Coordinator
Office of Community
Development
P.O. Box 69
Niagara Falls, NY 14302
716-286-8800
Fax: 716-286-8809

City of Rochester
Mr. Robert M. Barrows,
Assistant Director
Department of Community
Development
30 Church St., Room 028B
Rochester, NY 14614-1290
716-428-6150
Fax: 716-428-6229

City of Schenectady/Troy/
Colonie Consortium
Mr. Terrance Connelly, Deputy
Director
Department of Planning and
Economic Development
105 Jay St.
City Hall, Room 1
Schenectady, NY 12305
518-382-5147
Fax: 518-382-5275

City of Syracuse
Mr. James Laurenzo
Economic Development Chief
Department of Community and
Economic Development
201 E. Washington Str.
Room 612
Syracuse, NY 13202
315-448-8110
Fax: 315-448-8036

Mr. Paul Driscoll
Senior Urban Planner
Department of Community
Development
201 E. Washington St.
Room 612
Syracuse, NY 13202
315-448-8726
Fax: 315-448-8720

Ms. Linda Delaney
Investor Housing Specialist
Department of Community
Development
201 E. Washington St.
Room 612
Syracuse, NY 13202-1410
315-448-8713
Fax: 315-448-8705

City of Utica
Ms. Lori Calabrese, Housing
Director
Office of Community
Development
One Kennedy Plaza
Utica, NY 13502-4236
315-792-0181
Fax: 315-797-6607

City of Watertown
Mr. Kevin Jordan
Public Information Contact

Development Authority of the
North Country
317 Washington St.
Watertown, NY 13601
315-785-2593

City of Yonkers
Mr. J. Stephen Whetstone, Commissioner
Bureau of Community Development
87 Nepperhan Ave., Suite 315
Yonkers, NY 10701-3892
914-377-6650
Fax: 914-377-6672
Counties

County of Erie
Mr. Tom Dearing, Coordinator
Department of Environment and Planning
95 Franklin St., Room 1016
Buffalo, NY 14202
716-858-7256
Fax: 716-858-7248

County of Nassau
Mr. Donald J. Campbell, Commissioner
Office of Housing and Intergovernmental Affairs
250 Fulton Ave., Sixth Floor
Hempstead, NY 11550-3901
516-572-0880
Fax: 516-572-0889

Development Authority of the North County
Mr. Kevin Jordan, Public Information Contact
317 Washington St.
Watertown, NY 13601
315-785-2593

County of Orange
Mr. John Ebert, HOME Coordinator
Department of Community Development
223 Main St.
Goshen, NY 10924-2124
914-291-2424
Fax: 914-291-2430

County of Rockland
Mr. Michael Dolan, Director
Office of Community Development
151 S. Main St., Suite 212
New City, NY 10956-3516
914-638-5646
Fax: 914-638-5157

County of Suffolk
Mr. Joseph T. Sanseverino, Director
Department of Community Development
P.O. Box 6100
Hauppauge, NY 11788-0099
631-853-5705
Fax: 631-853-5688

County of Westchester
Mr. William C. Brady, HOME Coordinator
Department of Housing and Community Development
148 Martine Ave.
County Office Bldg., Room 414
White Plains, NY 10601
914-285-4271
Fax: 914-285-9093

Consortia
Amherst Consortium
Ms. Susan Davida, Assistant Planner
5583 Main St.
Williamsville, NY 14221-5409
716-631-7082
Fax: 716-631-7153

Colonie Consortium/City of Schenectady/Troy
Mr. Terrance Connelly, Deputy Director
Department of Planning and Economic Development
105 Jay St.
City Hall, Room 1
Schenectady, NY 12305
518-382-5147
Fax: 518-382-5275

Dutchess County Consortium
Ms. Anne Saylor, Specialist
27 High St.
Poughkeepsie, NY 12601-1935
914-486-3600
Fax: 914-486-3610

Monroe County Consortium
Ms. Sandra H. Mindel, Specialist
Division of Community Development
50 W. Main St., Suite 8100
Rochester, NY 14614-1225
716-428-2185
Fax: 716-428-5336

Onondaga County Consortium
Ms. Linda DeFichy, Administrator
Department of Community Development
421 Montgomery St.
1100 Civic Center
Syracuse, NY 13202
315-435-3558
Fax: 315-435-3794

State of North Carolina

Mr. Bill Dowse, Director
Housing Finance State Agency
P.O. Box 28066
Raleigh, NC 27611-8066
919-877-5622
Fax: 919-877-5701

Cities
City of Asheville
Mr. Sherman Fearing, Analyst
Division of Community Development
P.O. Box 7148
Asheville, NC 28802-7148
828-259-5721
Fax: 828-259-5428

City of Charlotte
Mr. Stanley D. Watkins, City Manager
Department of Neighborhood Development
600 E. Trade St., Suite 200
Charlotte, NC 28202
704-336-3380
Fax: 704-336-2904

City of Concord
Mr. Steve Osborne, Community Development Code Enforcement Manager
Department of Community and Economic Development
P.O. Box 308
Concord, NC 28026
704-786-6161
Fax: 704-795-0983

City of Durham
Ms. Ava Hinton, HOME Coordinator

Department of Housing and
Economic Development
101 City Hall Plaza
Durham, NC 27701-3329
919-560-4570
Fax: 919-560-4090

City of Fayetteville
Mr. Michael E. McNair, HOME Coordinator
P.O. Box 635
Fayetteville, NC 28302-0635
910-433-1590
Fax: 910-433-1592

City of Goldsboro
Ms. Linda Bullock, Coordinator
Department of Community Development
P.O. Drawer A
Goldsboro, NC 27533
919-580-4317
Fax: 919-580-4315

City of Greenville
Ms. Alice Faye Brewington, HOME Coordinator
Department of Planning and Community Development
P.O. Box 7207
Greenville, NC 27835
252-329-4509
Fax: 252-329-4424

City of Lenoir/Hickory County Consortium
Mr. Rick Oxford, Community Development Administrator
Western Piedmont Council of Governments
P.O. Box 9026
Hickory, NC 28603-9026
828-322-9191
Fax: 828-322-5991

City of High Point
Ms. Paulette Anderson, Community Development Administrator
Department of Community Development and Housing
P.O. Box 230
High Point, NC 27261-0230
336-883-3349
Fax: 336-883-3355

City of Raleigh
Ms. Eileen B. Breazeale, Director
Department of Community Development
P.O. Box 590
Raleigh, NC 27602-0590
919-857-4330
Fax: 919-857-4359

City of Rocky Mount
Ms. Vanessa McCleary, Administrator
Department of Planning and Development
P.O. Box 1180
Rocky Mount, NC 27802-1180
252-972-1101
Fax: 252-972-1590

City of Wilmington
Ms. Elizabeth Roheaugh
Interim Director
Department of Housing and Neighborhood Development
P.O. Box 1810
Wilmington, NC 28402-1810
910-341-7836
Fax: 910-341-7802

Counties

County of Cumberland
Ms. Thanena Wilson, Director
Department of Community Development
P.O. Box 1829
Fayetteville, NC 28302-1829
910-323-6111
Fax: 910-323-6114

County of Orange
Ms. Tara L. Fikes, Director
Department of Housing and Community Development
P.O. Box 8181
Hillsborough, NC 27278
919-245-2490
Fax: 919-644-3056

County of Wake
Mr. David Cristeal, Director
Division of Housing and Community Revitalization
P.O. Box 550
Raleigh, NC 27602
919-856-5689
Fax: 919-856-5594

Consortia

Gastonia Consortium
Ms. Annie Thombs
Administrator
Department of Community Development
P.O. Box 1748
Gastonia, NC 28053-1748
704-866-6752
Fax: 704-864-9732

City of Greensboro Consortium
Ms. Linda Wilson, Manager
Department of Housing and Community Development
P.O. Box 3136
Greensboro, NC 27402-3136
336-373-2349
Fax: 336-373-2153

Hickory County Consortium/City of Lenoir
Mr. Rick Oxford, Community Development Administrator
Western Piedmont Council of Governments
P.O. Box 9026
Hickory, NC 28603-9026
828-322-9191
Fax: 828-322-5991

Surry County Consortium
Mr. Dennis Thompson, County Manager
Office of the County Manager
P.O. Box 706
Dobson, NC 27017-0706
336-401-8201
Fax: 336-401-8217

Winston-Salem Consortium
Dr. Monica R. Lett, Director
Department of Housing and Neighborhood Development
P.O. Box 2511
Winston-Salem, NC 27101-2511
336-727-8597
Fax: 336-727-2878

State of North Dakota

Mr. Mike Spletto, Program Manager
Division of Community Services
600 E. Boulevard Ave.
Bismarck, ND 58505-0660
701-328-2094
Fax: 701-328-2308

State of Ohio

Mr. Les Warner
HOME Coordinator
Office of Housing and
Community Partnerships
P.O. Box 1001
Columbus, OH 43216-1001
614-466-2285
Fax: 614-752-4575

Cities

City of Akron
Mr. Warren R. Walfish,
Manager
Department of Planning and
Urban Development
161 S. High St., Room 201
Akron, OH 44308-1626
330-375-2618
Fax: 330-375-2434

City of Canton
Mr. William E. McGeorge,
Director
Department of Planning and
Community Development
P.O. Box 24218
Canton, OH 44701-4218
330-489-3258
Fax: 330-580-2070

City of Cincinnati
Mrs. Connie Roesch, HOME
Coordinator
Department of Neighborhood
Services
801 Plum St.
Cincinnati, OH 45202-1927
513-352-3735
Fax: 513-352-6113

City of Cleveland
Ms. Bobbie Peery, HOME
Coordinator
City of Cleveland
Department of Community
Development
601 Lakeside Ave., Room 302
Cleveland, OH 44114
216-664-4218
Fax: 216-420-7960

City of Columbus
Ms. Gail Gregory, Deputy
Director
Department of Trade and
Development
50 W. Gay St., Third Floor
Columbus, OH 43215-9040
614-645-6767
Fax: 614-645-6295

City of Dayton
Mr. David B. Sutton, Specialist
Department of Community
Development
101 W. Third St.
Dayton, OH 45401-1814
937-333-3870
Fax: 937-333-4281

City of East Cleveland
Mr. William Ellington, Director
Department of Community
Development
13601 Euclid Ave.
East Cleveland, OH 44112
216-681-2388
Fax: 216-681-2085

City of Hamilton
Ms. Carla Tipton
HOME/IDIS Coordinator
Department of Planning
20 High St., Suite 207
Hamilton, OH 45011
513-868-5886
Fax: 513-867-7364

City of Lima
Mr. Richard Friensen, Public
Information Contact
Department of Community
Development
50 Town Sq.
Municipal Bldg.
Lima, OH 45801-4900
419-221-5147
Fax: 419-221-5214

City of Lorain
Mr. Sanford A. Prudoff, Director
Department of Community
Development
200 W. Erie Ave., Fifth Floor
Lorain, OH 44052-1606
440-246-2020
Fax: 440-245-9428

City of Mansfield
Ms. Cynthia Baker, Manager
Department of Community
Development
30 N. Diamond St.
Mansfield, OH 44902
419-755-9795
Fax: 419-755-9465

City of Springfield
Ms. Selena Singletary, Director
Department of Planning and
Development
76 E. High St.
Springfield, OH 45502-1214
937-324-7380
Fax: 937-328-3489

City of Toledo
Ms. Debra L. Younger, Director
Department of Neighborhoods
One Government Center
Suite 1800
Toledo, OH 43604
419-245-1400
Fax: 419-245-1413

City of Youngstown
Ms. Mary June Tartan
HOME Coordinator
Community Development
Agency
Nine W. Front St., Room 205
Youngstown, OH 44503
330-744-0854
Fax: 330-744-7522

Counties

County of Cuyahoga
Mr. Paul Herdeg, Manager
Department of Development
112 Hamilton Ave., Fourth Floor
Cleveland, OH 44114
216-443-7260
Fax: 216-443-7258

County of Franklin/Mid Ohio RPC
Ms. Tonya Sims
HOME Ownership Project
Director
Department of Community
Development
285 E. Main St.
Columbus, OH 43215
614-233-4181
Fax: 614-228-1904

County of Hamilton
Ms. Susan Walsh, Deputy
Director
Department of Community
Development

138 E. Court St., Room 507
Cincinnati, OH 45202
513-946-4802
Fax: 513-946-4919

County of Lake
Ms. Marianne Norman, Director
Planning Commission
125 E. Erie St.
Painesville, OH 44077
440-350-2339
Fax: 440-350-2740

County of Montgomery
Ms. Roberta E. Longfellow, Housing Administrator
Department of Development and Building Regulations
451 W. Third St., Tenth Floor
Dayton, OH 45422
937-225-4631
Fax: 937-496-6629

County of Stark
Ms. Beth Pearson, Chief
Regional Planning Commission
201 Third St., N.E., Suite 201
Canton, OH 44702-2298
330-451-7395
Fax: 330-438-0990

County of Summit
Ms. Donna Marcinek, Housing Coordinator
Department of Development
175 S. Main St., Suite 207
Akron, OH 44308
330-643-2561
Fax: 330-643-2886

Consortia
County of Butler Consortium
Ms. Donna Everson
Administrator
Division of Community Development
130 High Street, Sixth Floor
Hamilton, OH 45011
513-785-5391
Fax: 513-785-5723

Warren City Consortium
Mr. Alexander Bobersky, Acting Director
Department of Community Development
418 S. Main Ave.
Warren, OH 44481
330-841-2595
Fax: 330-841-2643

State of Oklahoma

Mr. Byron DeBruler, State Contact
Oklahoma Housing Finance Agency
P.O. Box 26720
Oklahoma City, OK 73126-0720
405-419-8137
Fax: 405-879-8820

Cities
City of Lawton
Mr. Jim Phillips, HOME Coordinator
Department of Planning and Community Development
206 S.W. Third St.
Lawton, OK 73501
580-581-3347
Fax: 580-581-3346

City of Norman
Ms. Linda Price, Manager
Department of Planning
P.O. Box 370
Norman, OK 73070-0370
405-366-5439
Fax: 405-366-5379

City of Oklahoma City
Mr. Curtis Williams
Department of Neighborhood and Community Planning
420 W. Main St., Suite 920
Oklahoma City, OK 73102
405-297-2846
Fax: 405-297-3798

City of Tulsa
Mr. Roy Marshall, HOME Coordinator
Department of Urban Development
110 S. Hartford Ave., Suite 200
Tulsa, OK 74120-1816
918-596-2600
Fax: 918-699-3570

Consortia
Tulsa County Consortium
Ms. Claudia Ellingsworth Brierre, Planner
Department of Community Development
201 W. Fifth St., Suite 600
Tulsa, OK 74103
918-579-9431
Fax: 918-583-1024

State of Oregon

Ms. Betty Markey
HOME Program Manager
Department of Housing and Community Services
1600 State St.
Salem, OR 97301-4246
503-986-2116
Fax: 503-986-2020

Cities
City of Salem
Mr. Maurice Anderson, Coordinator
Department of Community Development
555 Liberty St., S.E., Room 305
Salem, OR 97301
503-588-6173
Fax: 503-588-6005

Counties
County of Clackamas
Ms. Evelyn Harris
HOME Project Manager
Department of Community Development
112 11th St.
Oregon City, OR 97045-1021
503-655-8591
Fax: 503-655-8563

County of Washington
Mr. Todd Adkins, Specialist
Department of Housing Services
111 N.E. Lincoln St., Suite 200L
Hillsboro, OR 97123-3082
503-846-4797
Fax: 503-693-4795

Consortia
City of Eugene Consortium
Ms. Linda L. Dawson, Manager
Department of Planning and Development
99 W. Tenth Ave., Suite 240
Eugene, OR 97401-3038
541-682-5071
Fax: 541-682-5572

City of Portland Consortium
Ms. Martha McLennan, Director
Bureau of Housing and Community Development
421 S.W. Sixth Ave.
Suite 1100-A
Portland, OR 97204
503-823-2386
Fax: 503-823-2387

State of Pennsylvania

Mr. Scott Dunwoody
HOME Coordinator
Department of Community and Economic Development
Commonwealth Ave.
502 Forum Bldg.
Harrisburg, PA 17120
717-468-3065
Fax: 717-234-4560

Cities

City of Allentown
Ms. Heidi Baer, Coordinator
Department of Community Development
435 Hamilton St.
Allentown, PA 18101
610-437-7761
Fax: 610-437-8781

City of Altoona
Mr. Carl Fisher, Manager
Department of Planning and Community Development
1117 Ninth Ave.
Altoona, PA 16602
814-949-2470
Fax: 814-949-0372

City of Bethlehem
Mr. Tony Hanna, Director
Department of Community and Economic Development
Ten E. Church St.
Bethlehem, PA 18018-6025
610-865-7085
Fax: 610-865-7330

City of Chester
Mr. David N. Sciocchetti, Acting Executive Director
Economic Development Authority
P.O. Box 407
Chester, PA 19016-0407
610-447-7850
Fax: 610-447-7856

City of Erie
Mr. David Deter, Manager
Department of Planning and Development
626 State St.
Municipal Bldg.
Room 404
Erie, PA 16501
814-870-1270
Fax: 814-870-1443

City of Harrisburg
Ms. Angela Smith, HOME Coordinator
Department of Building and Housing Development
Ten N. Second St.
Martin Luther King Jr. Government Ctr., Suite 206
Harrisburg, PA 17101-1677
717-255-6480
Fax: 717-255-6421

City of Johnstown
Mr. Ronald Andrews, Coordinator
Department of Community and Economic Development
Main and Market Sts.
City Hall, Room 205
Johnstown, PA 15901
814-533-2056
Fax: 814-533-2111

City of Lancaster
Mr. Thomas A. Fields, Director
Department of Housing and Community Development
P.O. Box 1599
Lancaster, PA 17608-1599
717-291-4730
Fax: 717-291-4713

City of Philadelphia
Mr. John Kromer, Housing Director
Office of Housing and Community Development
1234 Market St., 17th Floor
Philadelphia, PA 19107
215-686-9721
Fax: 215-686-9801

Urban Redevelopment Authority of Pittsburgh
Division of Housing
200 Ross St., Tenth Floor
Pittsburgh, PA 15219-2069
412-255-6666
Fax: 412-255-6645

City of Reading
Mr. Eric Galosi, Director
Department of Community Development
815 Washington St., Room 306
Reading, PA 19601-3690
610-655-6211
Fax: 610-373-2858

City of Scranton
Mr. Thomas J. Kane, HOME Coordinator
Office of Economic and Community Development
340 N. Washington Ave., Third Floor
Scranton, PA 18503
570-348-4168
Fax: 570-348-4293

Borough of State College
Ms. Lu B. Hoover
118 S. Fraser St.
State College, PA 16801-3899
814-234-7109
Fax: 814-231-3082

Redevelopment Authority of Washington County
Mr. Richard Galway, Specialist
Department of Community Development
100 W. Beau St.
Courthouse Square Bldg., Room 603
Washington, PA 15301
724-228-6875
Fax: 724-228-6829

City of Wilkes-Barre
Mr. Frank Eick, Housing Director
Office of Community Development
40 E. Market St.
City Hall
Wilkes-Barre, PA 18711
570-208-4129
Fax: 570-208-4136

City of Williamsport
Ms. Mary Rucinski, Assistant Director
Office of Economic and Community Development
245 W. Fourth St.
City Hall
Williamsport, PA 17701
570-327-7511
Fax: 570-327-7509

City of York
Ms. Leigh Smith, Assistant
Division of Community Affairs
One Mark Way
York, PA 17401-1231
717-849-2264
Fax: 717-849-2329

Counties

County of Allegheny
Ms. Laura Richeson-Zinski
Housing Manager
Department of Economic Development
425 Sixth Ave., Suite 800
Pittsburgh, PA 15219
412-350-1000
Fax: 412-350-1050

County of Beaver
Mr. Robert Dyson, Director
Office of Community Development
699 Fifth St.
Beaver, PA 15009-1927
724-775-4711
Fax: 724-775-4117

County of Berks
Mr. Kenneth L. Pick, Director
Department of Community Development
633 Court St., 14th Floor
Reading, PA 19601-3584
610-478-6325
Fax: 610-478-6326

County of Bucks
Mr. Gerard Pescatore
Department of Community Development
1260 Almshouse Rd.
Neshaminy Manor Center
Doylestown, PA 18901
215-345-3842
Fax: 215-345-3865

County of Chester
Ms. Dolores Colligan
Office of Housing and Community Development
P.O. Box 2747
West Chester, PA 19380-2747
610-344-6772
Fax: 610-344-5748

County of Delaware
Ms. Carol Murdock Catania, Housing Coordinator
Office of Housing and Community Development
600 N. Jackson St., Room 101
Media, PA 19063-2561
610-891-5425
Fax: 610-566-0532

County of Lancaster
Mr. David Brazina, HOME Coordinator
Housing and Redevelopment Authority
29 E. King St., Suite 316
Lancaster, PA 17602-2852
717-394-0793
Fax: 717-394-7635

County of Luzerne
Ms. Sandra Russell, Assistant Director
Department of Community Development
54 W. Union St.
Wilkes-Barre, PA 18701-1410
570-824-7214
Fax: 570-829-2910

County of Montgomery
Ms. Ivy Torres, Assistant Director
Office of Housing and Community Development
P.O. Box 311
Norristown, PA 19404-0311
610-278-3540
Fax: 610-278-3636

County of Westmoreland
Ms. Kathy Fetsko, HOME Coordinator
Department of Planning and Development
Two N. Main St.
Courthouse Square,Suite 601
Greensburg, PA 15601-1603
724-830-3616
Fax: 724-830-3611

County of York
Mr. M. Chris Rafferty, Community Development Coordinator
Planning Commission
100 W. Market St.
County Government Center
York, PA 17401-1231
717-771-9870
Fax: 717-771-9511

Commonwealth of Puerto Rico

Ms. Maria Nagron, Director
Department of Housing
Avenida Barbosa Num. 606
Apartado 21365
Rio Piedras, PR 928
787-274-2121
Fax: 787-763-0008

Cities

Municipio de Aguadilla
Ms. Daisy Caceres, HOME Coordinator
Department of Federal Programs
P.O. Box 1008
Aguadilla, PR 605
787-891-3965
Fax: 787-891-3930

Municipio de Arecibo
Mr. Jaime Adames Cruz, HOME Coordinator
P.O. Box 1086
Arecibo, PR 00613-1086
787-881-3946
Fax: 787-817-5881

Municipio de Bayamon
Mr. Angel Martinez, HOME Coordinator
P.O. Box 2988
Bayamon, PR 960
787-269-3980
Fax: 787-786-1032

Municipio de Caguas
Ms. Carmen Berrios, HOME Coordinator
Department of Housing
P.O. Box 7889
Caguas, PR 726

787-744-8833
Fax: 787-745-2250

Municipio de Carolina
Mr. Juan A. Cancel, Executive Director
CADEN
P.O. Box 8
Carolina, PR 00986-0008
787-762-8686
Fax: 787-257-1008

Municipio de Guaynabo
Mr. Orlando Perez Delgado, HOME Coordinator
Department of Housing
P.O. Box 7885
Guaynabo, PR 00970-7885
787-287-3334
Fax: 787-731-4160

Municipio de Mayaguez
Mr. Israel Alvares, HOME Coordinator
Division of Housing
P.O. Box 447
Mayaguez, PR 00681-0447
787-834-1460
Fax: 787-833-0805

Municipio de Ponce
Mr. Miguel Mercado, Executive Director
Department of Housing and Federal Programs
P.O. Box 331709
Ponce, PR 00733-1709
787-840-9200
Fax: 787-841-0140

Municipio de San Juan
Ms. Eliana Echegoyen, Executive Director
Department of Housing
P.O. Box 36-2138
San Juan, PR 00936-2138
787-722-8088
Fax: 787-725-7715

Municipio de Toa Baja
Ms. Norma Santiago, Director
Office of Planning and Community Development
P.O. Box 51983
Toa Baja, PR 00950-1983
787-261-0244
Fax: 787-261-7930

State of Rhode Island

Ms. Susan Bodington, Assistant Director
Rhode Island Housing and Mortgage Finance Corp.
44 Washington St.
Providence, RI 2903
401-457-1286
Fax: 401-457-1140

Cities

City of Pawtucket
Mr. Edward G. Soares, HOME Program Manager
Department of Planning and Redevelopment
175 Main St.
Pawtucket, RI 02860-4119
401-724-5200
Fax: 401-726-6237

City of Providence
Mr. Arthur Hanson, HOME Director
Department of Planning and Development
400 Westminster St.
Providence, RI 02903-3215
401-351-4300
Fax: 401-351-9533

City of Woonsocket
Ms. Rita Cicchitelli
Department of Planning and Development
169 Main St.
Woonsocket, RI 02895-4379
401-767-9228
Fax: 401-766-9312

State of South Carolina

Ms. Valerie M. Williams, Director
Housing Finance and Development Authority
919 Bluff Rd.
Columbia, SC 29201
803-734-2000
Fax: 803-253-6884

Cities

City of Charlseston
Ms. Patricia W. Crawford, Director
Department of Housing and Community Development
75 Calhoun St.
Third Floor, Division 616
Charleston, SC 29401-3506
843-724-3766
Fax: 843-724-7354

City of Columbia
Mr. Richard J. Semon, Director
Department of Community Development
P.O. Box 147
Columbia, SC 29217-0147
803-733-8315
Fax: 803-988-8014

City of Greenville
Mr. Thurman Norris, Administrator
Department of Community Development and Relations
P.O. Box 2207
Greenville, SC 29602
864-467-4570
Fax: 864-467-5735

Greenville County Redevelopment Authority
Ms. Gwendolyn Kennedy, Executive Director
301 University Ridge
Suite 2500
Greenville, SC 29601
864-242-9801
Fax: 864-232-9946

City of Spartanburg
Mr. Ed Memmot, Director
Department of Community Development
P.O. Box 1749
Spartanburg, SC 29304
864-596-3560
Fax: 864-596-2680

Counties

County of Charleston
Ms. Henrietta Canty Woodward, Director
Department of Community Development
Two Courthouse Sq.
O.T. Wallace Office Bldg.
Sixth Floor
Charleston, SC 29401
843-958-3560
Fax: 843-720-2209

Consortia

Santee-Lynches HOME Consortium
Mr. James T. Darby, Executive Director
Regional Council of Governments
P.O. Drawer 1837
Sumter, SC 29151
803-775-7381
Fax: 803-773-9903

State of South Dakota

Housing Development Authority
Mr. Ron Wagner, Manager
Office of Planning and Housing Development
P.O. Box 1237
Pierre, SD 57501-1237
605-773-5897
Fax: 605-773-5154

Cities

City of Sioux Falls
Mr. Randy Bartunek, Director
Department of Community Development
224 W. Ninth St.
Sioux Falls, SD 57104-6407
605-367-7125
Fax: 605-367-8798

State of Tennessee

Ms. Jane Boles, Director
Housing Development Agency
404 James Robertson Pkwy., Suite 1114
Nashville, TN 37219-1505
615-741-3007
Fax: 615-532-5069

Cities

City of Chattanooga
Ms. Sandra Gober, Director
Office of Economic and Community Development
100 E. 11th St., Room 101
Chattanooga, TN 37402
423-757-5133
Fax: 423-757-4851

City of Clarksville/County of Montgomery
Mr. Ron Tedford, Director
Office of Community Development
329 Main St.
Clarksville, TN 37040
931-645-7448
Fax: 931-645-7481

Jackson Housing Authority
Mr. David Ralston, Director
Office of Community Development
125 Preston St.
Jackson, TN 38301
901-422-1671
Fax: 901-425-4617

City of Knoxville
Ms. Diana Gerard Lobertini, Manager
Department of Community Development
P.O. Box 1631
Knoxville, TN 37901-1631
865-215-2120
Fax: 865-215-2554

City of Memphis
Mr. Carl Reynolds, Administrative Director
Department of Community Development
701 N. Main St.
Memphis, TN 38107-2311
901-576-7300
Fax: 901-576-6555

City of Nashville/County of Davidson
Mr. Paul Johnson, Assistant Director
Metropolitan Development and Housing Agency
P.O. Box 846
Nashville, TN 37202-0846
615-252-8508
Fax: 615-252-8559

Counties

County of Davidson/City of Nashville
Mr. Paul Johnson, Assistant Director
Metropolitan Development and Housing Agency
P.O. Box 846
Nashville, TN 37202-0846
615-252-8508
Fax: 615-252-8559

County of Knox
Mr. Bill Niemeyer, Director
Development Corporation of Knox County
601 W. Summit Hill Dr., Suite 200A
Knoxville, TN 37902-2011
865-546-5887
Fax: 865-546-6170

County of Montgomery/City of Clarksville
Mr. Ron Tedford, Director
Office of Community Development
329 Main St.
Clarksville, TN 37040
931-645-7448
Fax: 931-645-7481

County of Shelby
Mr. Jim Vasquez, Administrator
Department of Housing
1075 Mullins Station Rd.
Memphis, TN 38134
901-387-5700
Fax: 901-387-5708

State of Texas

Ms. Jeannie Arellano
HOME Program Manager
Department of Housing and Community Affairs
P.O. Box 13941
Austin, TX 78711-3941
512-475-3109
Fax: 512-475-3287

Cities

City of Abilene
Mr. Kelly Cheek, Specialist
Office of Community and Economic Development
P.O. Box 60
Abilene, TX 79604-0060
915-676-6383
Fax: 915-676-6242

City of Amarillo
Ms. Vicki Covey, HOME Coordinator
Department of Community Services
P.O. Box 1971
Amarillo, TX 79186-1971
806-378-3098
Fax: 806-378-9389

City of Arlington
Ms. Charmaine Pruitt, HOME Coordinator
Department of Neighborhood Services
P.O. Box 231
Arlington, TX 76011-0231
817-276-6730
Fax: 817-861-8097

City of Austin
Mr. Paul Hilgers, Director
Department of Housing and Conservation
505 Barton Springs Road, Suite 600
Austin, TX 78704
512-499-3100
Fax: 512-499-3112

City of Beaumont
Mr. Richard Chappell, Director
Department of Community Development
P.O. Box 3827
Beaumont, TX 77704-3827
409-880-3763
Fax: 409-880-3125

City of Brownsville
Mr. Ben Medina, Community Development Coordinator
Department of Planning and Community Development
P.O. Box 911
Brownsville, TX 78522-0911
956-548-6150
Fax: 956-548-6144

City of Bryan
Ms. Alsie Bond, Administrator
Department of Community Development
P.O. Box 1000
Bryan, TX 77801-1000
409-779-5175
Fax: 409-779-5184

City of College Station
Mr. Randy J. Brumley
HOME Coordinator
Department of Community Development
P.O. Box 9960
College Station, TX 77840-9960
409-764-3778
Fax: 409-764-3785

City of Corpus Christi
Mr. Norbert Hart, Director
Community Improvement Corp.
P.O. Box 9277
Corpus Christi, TX 78469-9277
361-880-3010
Fax: 361-880-3011

City of Dallas
Ms. Mary Kay Vaughn, Director
Department of Community Development
1500 Marilla St.
Six Delta N.
Dallas, TX 75201
214-670-5988
Fax: 214-670-0156

City of Denton
Ms. Barbara Ross, Community Development Coordinator
Division of Community Development
100 W. Oak St., Suite 208
Denton, TX 76201
940-349-7235
Fax: 940-383-2445

City of El Paso
Mr. Robert Soto, Administrator
Department of Community and Human Development
Two Civic Center Plaza, Ninth Floor
El Paso, TX 79901-1196
915-541-4639
Fax: 915-541-4370

City of Ft. Worth
Ms. Gloria Eurotas, Assistant Director
Department of Housing
1000 Throckmorton St.
City Hall Annex
Ft. Worth, TX 76102-6383
817-871-7540
Fax: 817-871-7328

City of Galveston
Mr. Sterling W. Patrick, Director
Department of Community Development
P.O. Box 779
Galveston, TX 77550-0779
409-766-2101
Fax: 409-762-7079

City of Garland
Ms. Renee Ramey, Director
Division of Neighborhood Services
P.O. Box 469002
Garland, TX 75046-9002
972-205-3321
Fax: 972-205-3303

City of Grand Prairie
Ms. Sherie L. Goin, Community Development Manager
Department of Housing and Community Development
P.O. Box 534045
Grand Prairie, TX 75053-4045
972-237-8166
Fax: 972-237-8187

City of Harlingen
Mrs. Diana R. Serna, Coordinator
Department of Community Development
P.O. Box 2207
Harlingen, TX 78551-2207
956-427-8735
Fax: 956-430-6691

City of Houston
Ms. Paulette Wagner, Grants Manager
Department of Housing and Community Development
P.O. Box 1562
Houston, TX 77251-1562
713-868-8300
Fax: 713-865-4113

City of Irving
Ms. Barbara Vanderloop, Manager
Department of Community Development
P.O. Box 152288
Irving, TX 75015-2288
972-721-4800
Fax: 972-721-4813

City of Killeen
Ms. Cinda Hayward, HOME Coordinator
Division of Community and Economic Development
P.O. Box 1329
Killeen, TX 76540-1329

254-501-7840
Fax: 254-526-3594

City of Laredo
Mr. Erasmo Villarreal, Director
Department of Community Development
P.O. Box 1276
Laredo, TX 78040-1276
956-795-2675
Fax: 956-795-2689

City of Longview
Ms. Linda H. Strotheide, Specialist
Department of Housing and Community Development
P.O. Box 1952
Longview, TX 75606-1952
903-237-1235
Fax: 903-237-1254

City of Lubbock
Ms. Nancy J. Haney, Manager
Department of Housing and Community Development
P.O. Box 2000
Lubbock, TX 79457-2000
806-775-2300
Fax: 806-775-3281

City of McAllen
Mr. Richard Montesdeoca, Program Director
Department of Community Development
P.O. Box 220
McAllen, TX 78505-0220
956-687-7238
Fax: 956-972-7253

City of Odessa
Mr. Michael Marrero, Program Manager
Department of Community Development
P.O. Box 4398
Odessa, TX 79760-4398
915-335-4820
Fax: 915-335-4817

City of Pasadena
Mr. Miles Arena, Administrator
Department of Planning
1211 Southmore Avenue
Room 208
Pasadena, TX 77506-0672
713-475-7243
Fax: 713-477-1072

City of Port Arthur
Ms. Vivian Ballou, Administrator
Department of Community Development
P.O. Box 1089
Port Arthur, TX 77640-1089
409-983-8259
Fax: 409-983-8120

City of San Angelo
Ms. Teresa Special, HOME Coordinator
City of San Angelo
Department of Community Development
P.O. Box 1751
San Angelo, TX 76902-1751
915-657-4294
Fax: 915-658-6561

City of San Antonio
Ms. Ivy Taylor, Coordinator
Department of Housing and Community Development
419 S. Main St., Suite 200
San Antonio, TX 78204
210-207-6614
Fax: 210-886-0006

City of Tyler
Ms. Donna Beddingfield, HOME Coordinator
Department of Neighborhood Services
P.O. Box 2039
Tyler, TX 75702-2039
903-531-1303
Fax: 903-531-1155

City of Waco
Ms. Dedri Brown, Community Development Administrator
Planning and Community Development Services
P.O. Box 2570
Waco, TX 76702-2570
254-750-5650
Fax: 254-750-1605

City of Wichita Falls
Mr. Michael Uriniack, HOME Coordinator
Department of Housing and Community Development
P.O. Box 1431
Wichita Falls, TX 76307-1431
940-761-7475
Fax: 940-761-8877

Counties

County of Bexar
Mr. Jesse Flores, HOME Coordinator
Department of Housing and Human Services
233 N. Pecos St., Suite 590
San Antonio, TX 78207
210-335-3708
Fax: 210-335-6788

County of Brazoria
Mr. David Lewis, CDBG Administrator
Government Service Agency
9500 Forest Ln., Suite 408
Dallas, TX 75243
800-775-2633
Fax: 214-342-1896

County of Dallas
Mr. Rick Lossberg, Director
Department of Housing and Community Development
411 Elm St.
Third Floor
Dallas, TX 75202-3301
214-653-7601
Fax: 214-653-6517

County of Ft. Bend
Ms. Marilynn Kindell, Director
Department of Community Development
301 Jackson St., Suite 740
Richmond, TX 77469
281-341-4410
Fax: 281-341-3762

County of Harris
Mr. Bruce A. Austin, Director
Community Development Agency
2727 El Camino St.
Houston, TX 77054
713-747-0132
Fax: 713-747-4274

County of Hidalgo
Mr. Anthony Covacevick, Director
Urban County Program

100 E. Cano St., Second Floor
Edinburg, TX 78539-1356
956-318-2619
Fax: 956-383-5971

County of Tarrant
Ms. Patricia Ward, Director
Department of Community Development
1509-B S. University Dr.
Suite 276
Ft. Worth, TX 76107-6568
817-338-9129
Fax: 817-338-9136

State of Utah

Ms. Lauren Rayner, HOME Coordinator
Division of Community Development
324 S. State St., Suite 500
Salt Lake City, UT 84111-2388
801-538-8650
Fax: 801-538-8888

Cities

City of Ogden
Mr. Aaron Wolfe-Bertling, Manager
Neighborhood and Community Development Agency
2484 Washington Blvd.
Suite 211
Ogden, UT 84401
801-629-8940
Fax: 801-629-8902

City of Salt Lake City
Ms. Anita J. Short, Community Development Planner
Division of Capital Planning and Programming
451 S. State St., Room 406
Salt Lake City, UT 84111
801-535-7115
Fax: 801-535-6131

Counties

County of Salt Lake
Mr. Lynn J. Feveryear, Manager
Department of Housing and Community Development
2001 S. State St.
Suite N2100
County Government Center
Salt Lake City, UT 84190-0001
801-468-3246
Fax: 801-468-3684

Consortia

Utah Valley Consortium
Ms. Geo Drake, HOME Administrator
Provo Redevelopment Agency
55 N. University Ave., Suite 215
Provo, UT 84601
801-852-6164
Fax: 801-375-1469

State of Vermont

Mr. David Weinstein, Director
Department of Housing and Community Affairs
P.O. Drawer 20
Montpelier, VT 05620-0501
802-828-3250
Fax: 802-828-2928

State of Virginia

Ms. Charlene Sinclair, Financial Officer
Department of Housing and Community Development
501 N. Second St.
Jackson Center
Richmond, VA 23219-1321
804-371-7101
Fax: 804-371-7091

Cities

City of Alexandria
Mr. Bob Muderig, Public Information Contact
Office of Housing
P.O. Box 178
Alexandria, VA 22314
703-838-4990
Fax: 703-706-3904

City of Charlottesville
Mr. William Warner, Program Manager
Thomas Jefferson Planning District Commission
P.O. Box 1505
Charlottesville, VA 22902
804-979-7310
Fax: 804-979-1597

City of Chesapeake
Ms. Elizabeth Allen, Loan Officer
Redevelopment and Housing Authority
P.O. Box 1304
Chesapeake, VA 23320
757-523-0401
Fax: 757-523-1601

City of Danville
Mr. Lars Laubinger
Public Information Contact
Department of Community Development
P.O. Box 3300
Danville, VA 24543
804-799-5260
Fax: 804-797-8919

City of Hampton
Ms. Joan Kennedy, Director
Office of Neighborhood Services
22 Lincoln St.
Hampton, VA 23669
757-727-6460
Fax: 757-727-6074

City of Lynchburg
Mr. Keith Wright, Coordinator
Department of Community Planning and Development
P.O. Box 60
Lynchburg, VA 24505-0060
804-847-1671
Fax: 804-845-7630

City of Newport News
Ms. Phyllis Hardy
Public Information Contact
Redevelopment and Housing Authority
P.O. Box 77
Newport News, VA 23607-0077
757-247-9701
Fax: 757-247-6535

City of Norfolk
Mr. David Young, Community Development Director
Redevelopment and Housing Authority
P.O. Box 968
Norfolk, VA 23501-0968
757-623-1111
Fax: 757-626-1607

City of Portsmouth
Mr. Bob Creecy, Director
Portsmouth Environmental Services
801 Crawford St.
Portsmouth, VA 23704

757-393-8641
Fax: 757-393-5475

City of Richmond
Mr. David Ingross, Grants Administrator
Department of Planning and Community Development
900 E. Broad St., Room 501
Richmond, VA 23219
804-646-6365
Fax: 804-646-6358

City of Roanoke
Mr. Frank Baretta, HOME/CDBG Coordinator
Office of Grants Monitoring
541 Luck Ave., S.W., Suite 221
Roanoke, VA 24016
540-853-6003
Fax: 540-853-1252

City of Suffolk
Ms. Cynthia D. Rohes, Assistant City Manager
Department of Management Services
P.O. Box 1858
Suffolk, VA 23439-1858
757-923-2085
Fax: 757-923-2091

City of Virginia Beach
Ms. Sharon Prescott, Administrator
Department of Housing Development
2424 Courthouse Dr.
Municipal Center, Bldg. 18A
Virginia Beach, VA 23456-9083
757-426-5803
Fax: 757-426-5766

Counties

County of Arlington
Mr. Ken Aughenbaug, Team Leader
Department of Economic Development
2100 Clarendon Blvd., Suite 709
Arlington, VA 22201
703-228-3772
Fax: 703-228-3834

County of Chesterfield
Mr. Thomas Taylor, Director
Department of Community Development
P.O. Box 40
Chesterfield, VA 23832
804-768-6056
Fax: 804-748-7549

County of Fairfax
Ms. Heather Davis, Public Information Contact
Department of Housing and Community Development
3700 Pender Dr., Suite 300
Fairfax, VA 22030-7444
703-246-5103
Fax: 703-246-5115

County of Henrico
Mr. Eric Leabough, Public Information Contact
Department of Planning
P.O. Box 27032
Richmond, VA 23273
804-261-8248
Fax: 804-261-8256

County of Prince William
Ms. Mary Lively, Supervisor
Office of Housing and Community Development
15941 Cardinal Dr., Suite 112
Woodbridge, VA 22191
703-792-7530
Fax: 703-792-4978

U.S. Virgin Islands

Ms. Janine Hector, Director
Housing Finance Authority
210-3A Altona
Frostco Bldg.
Saint Thomas, VI 802
340-772-3180
Fax: 340-775-7913

State of Washington

Mr. Doug Hunter
HOME Development Project Manager
Department of County Development
P.O. Box 48300
Olympia, WA 98504-8300
360-753-4930
Fax: 360-586-5880

Cities

City of Bellevue
Mr. Dan Stroh, Director
King County Consortium/Planning Division
P.O. Box 90012
Bellevue, WA 98009-9012
425-452-5255
Fax: 425-452-2814

City of Bellingham
Mr. David M. Cahill, Manager
Community Development Division
210 Lottie St.
Bellingham, WA 98225-4009
360-676-6880
Fax: 360-738-7306

City of Bremerton
Ms. Deborah Peavler-Stewart, Administrative Analyst
Department of Community Development
286 Fourth St.
Bremerton, WA 98337
360-478-7996
Fax: 360-478-5278

City of Seattle
Mr. Richard Hooper, Director
Department of Human Services
618 Second Ave., Eighth Floor
Seattle, WA 98104-2232
206-684-0338
Fax: 206-233-7117

City of Spokane
Ms. Melora Sharts, Administrator
Department of Community and Economic Development
808 W. Spokane Falls Blvd., Room 650
Spokane, WA 99201-3339
509-625-6325
Fax: 509-625-6315

City of Tacoma
Mr. Ray Spadafore, Auditor
747 Market St.
Suite 1036
Tacoma, WA 98402-3794
253-591-5222
Fax: 253-591-5050

City of Yakima
Ms. Fran Eads, Specialist
112 S. Eighth St.
Yakima, WA 98901
509-575-6101
Fax: 509-575-6176

Counties
County of Clark
Mr. Pete C. Munroe,
CDBG/HOME Program
Manager
Department of Community
Services
P.O. Box 5000
Vancouver, WA 98666-5000
360-397-2130
Fax: 360-397-6128

County of Kitsap
Ms. Shirley Christensen,
Administrator
Department of Community
Development
614 Division St.
Port Orchard, WA 98366
360-337-7285
Fax: 360-337-4609

County of Pierce
Mr. Gary Aden, Administrative
Program Manager
Department of Community
Service
8815 S. Tacoma Way
Suite 202
Tacoma, WA 98499-4588
253-798-7038
Fax: 253-798-3999

County of Spokane
Mr. Tim Crowley, Specialist
721 N. Jefferson, Suite 200
Spokane, WA 99260-0190
509-477-4488
Fax: 509-477-2561

Consortia
King County Consortium
Ms. Linda Peterson, Manager
Housing and Community
Development Program
700 Fifth Ave., 37th Floor
Seattle, WA 98104-5037
206-296-8672
Fax: 206-296-0229

Longview Consortium
Ms. Julie Hourcle, Assistant
Planner
Department of Community and
Economic Development
P.O. Box 128
Longview, WA 98632-0128
360-577-3329
Fax: 360-577-4018

Tri-Cities HOME Consortium
Ms. Josie Woods, Specialist
P.O. Box 190
Richland, WA 99352
509-942-7595
Fax: 509-942-7764

State of West Virginia

Housing Development Fund
Mr. Carl R. Moore, Director
Department of Operations and
Program Development
814 Virginia St., E., Third Floor
Charleston, WV 25301
304-345-6475
Fax: 304-340-9943

Cities
City of Charleston
Ms. Zora Rogers, HOME
Supervisor
Mayor's Office of Economic and
Community Development
P.O. Box 2749
Charleston, WV 25330
304-348-8035
Fax: 304-348-0704

City of Charleston-Kanawha
County Consortium
Ms. Beth Cade, Assistant
Director
Mayor's Office Economic and
Community Development
P.O. Box 2749
Charleston, WV 25301
304-348-8035
Fax: 304-348-0704

City of Parkersburg
Mr. Steve Brodsky, Director
Department of Development
P.O. Box 1627
Parkersburg, WV 26102
304-424-8542
Fax: 304-424-8464

City of Wheeling
Mr. Gary A. Lange, Community
Development Specialist
Department of Community
Development
1500 Chapline St.
City-County Bldg.
Wheeling, WV 26003
304-234-3701
Fax: 304-234-3605

Consortia
Cabell County Consortium
Mr. Bill Toney, Program
Director
Office of Development and
Planning
P.O. Box 1659
Huntington, WV 25717
304-696-4458
Fax: 304-696-4465

*City of Charleston-Kanawha
County Consortium*
Ms. Beth Cade, Assistant
Director
Mayor's Office Economic and
Community Development
P.O. Box 2749
Charleston, WV 25301
304-348-8035
Fax: 304-348-0704

State of Wisconsin

Ms. Mary Francis Fay-Troudt
HOME Program Manager
Division of Housing
P.O. Box 8944
Madison, WI 53708-8944
608-266-0288
Fax: 608-267-6917

Cities
City of Eau Claire
Ms. Carol Doyle, Executive
Director
Division of Housing
203 S. Farwell St.
Eau Claire, WI 54701
715-839-4943
Fax: 715-839-4939

City of Green Bay
Ms. Lori DeNault, Coordinator
Department of Community
Development
100 N. Jefferson St., Suite 608
Green Bay, WI 54301
920-448-3400
Fax: 920-448-3426

City of Kenosha
Mr. Jim Schultz, Director
Department of Neighborhood
Services and Inspections

625 52nd St., Room 100
Kenosha, WI 53140
262-653-4263
Fax: 262-653-4254

City of LaCrosse
Mr. John Florine, Community Development Administrator
Department of City Planning
400 La Crosse St.
La Crosse, WI 54601
608-789-7512
Fax: 608-789-7318

City of Madison
Mr. Hickory R. Hurie, Community Development Grants Supervisor
Department of Planning and Development
P.O. Box 2985
Madison, WI 53701
608-267-0740
Fax: 608-261-9661

City of Milwaukee
Mr. Skip Seager, President
Neighborhood Improvement Development Corp.
841 N. Broadway
Milwaukee, WI 53202-3515
414-286-5618
Fax: 414-286-8667

City of Racine
Mr. Richard A. Linsmeier, Director
Department of Planning
730 Washington Ave.
Racine, WI 53403
262-636-9151
Fax: 262-636-9298

Counties
County of Waukesha
Mr. Glen Lewinski, CDBG Coordinator
Department of Community Development
1320 Pewaukee Rd.
Waukesha, WI 53188
262-548-7921
Fax: 262-896-8510

Consortia
Milwaukee County Consortium
Mr. Gary Bottoni, HOME Coordinator
Department of Housing and Community Development
907 N. Tenth St.
Courthouse Annex, Room 310
Milwaukee, WI 53223-1442
414-278-4880
Fax: 414-223-8196

State of Wyoming

Ms. Cheryl Gillum, Director
Community Development Authority
P.O. Box 634
Casper, WY 82602
307-265-0603
Fax: 307-266-5414

Pay Your Mortgage, Downpayment, or Closing Costs

Trouble in the house? HUD may be able to help. Layoffs and threatened unemployment causes many homeowners to worry about making their mortgage payments. HUD provides a list of HUD-approved housing counseling agencies! HUD funds housing counseling agencies throughout the country that can give you advice on buying a home, renting, defaults, foreclosures, credit issues, reverse mortgages and working with lenders. Some even offer money to pay your mortgage payments till you get back on your feet. Just contact the agency nearest to you or call 1-888-466-3487. Homeowners with problems that could result in default of their mortgage or foreclosure on their property need to contact a HUD-approved housing counseling agency immediately.

The Housing Counseling Clearinghouse (HCC) operates a toll-free, 24-hour a day automated voice response system that provides homeowners and homebuyers referrals to local housing counseling agencies toll-free at 1-800-569-4287.

The Housing Counseling Clearinghouse
P.O. Box 10423
McLean, VA 22102
888-466-3487 (toll-free)
TDD: 703-734-1444
Fax: 703-734-7929
www.hud.gov/offices/hsg/sfh/hcc/hccprof14.cfm

For those homeowners with FHA mortgages, another resource also exists. The goal of HUD's National Servicing Center is to help FHA homeowners by working with lenders to find creative solutions to avoid foreclosure.

Department of Housing and Urban Development
National Servicing Center
500 W. Main Street, Suite 400
Oklahoma City, OK 73102
888-297-8685 (toll-free)

HUD Approved Housing Counseling Agencies

(Agencies with a ** have not been individually HUD approved, but are affiliates of one of the HUD funded National Intermediaries.)

Alabama

COMMUNITY SERVICES OF CALHOUN COUNTIES
1702 Noble Street, Suite 112
Anniston, AL 36202
256-231-1798
Fax: 256-241-2965
Email: eftcsccc@aol.com
Type of Counseling:
Default/Foreclosure Counseling, Prepurchase Counseling, Rental Counseling, HECM Counseling

CONSUMER CREDIT COUNSELING SERVICE OF WEST FLORIDA/POARCH CREEK INDIAN RESERVATION
5811 Jack Springs Road
Atmore, AL 36502
334-368-9136
Fax: 850-432-5078
Type of Counseling:
Prepurchase Counseling, Rental Counseling, Default/Foreclosure Counseling, HECM Counseling

ALABAMA COUNCIL ON HUMAN RELATIONS, INCORPORATED
319 W Glenn Ave
Auburn, AL 368310409
334-821-8336
Fax: 334-826-6397
Type of Counseling:
HECM Counseling, Default/Foreclosure Counseling, Rental Counseling, Prepurchase Counseling

AUBURN HOUSING AUTHORITY
931 Booker St
Auburn, AL 36832-2902
334-821-2262
Fax: 334-821-2264
Type of Counseling:
HECM Counseling, Default/Foreclosure Counseling, Rental Counseling, Prepurchase Counseling

JEFFERSON COUNTY COMMITTEE FOR ECONOMIC OPPORTUNITY
300 Eighth Avenue, West
Birmingham, AL 352043039
205-327-7500
Fax: 205-326-4179
Type of Counseling:
Prepurchase Counseling, Default/Foreclosure Counseling, HECM Counseling, Rental Counseling

BIRMINGHAM URBAN LEAGUE, INCORPORATED
1229 3rd Avenue North
Birmingham, AL 35202-1269
205-326-0162
Fax: 205-521-6951
Email: burbanleag@aol.com
Type of Counseling:
HECM Counseling, Default/Foreclosure Counseling, Rental Counseling, Prepurchase Counseling

JEFFERSON COUNTY HOUSING AUTHORITY
3700 Industrial Parkway
Birmingham, AL 35217
205-849-0123
Fax: 205-849-0137
Type of Counseling:
HECM Counseling, Default/Foreclosure Counseling, Rental Counseling, Prepurchase Counseling

**BIRMINGHAM NEIGHBORHOOD HOUSING SERVICES
1200 Tuscaloosa Ave SW
Birmingham, AL 35203-
205-328-4292
Fax: 205-328-1057
Type of Counseling:
Prepurchase Counseling, HECM Counseling
Affiliate of: NEIGHBORHOOD REINVESTMENT CORPORATION

**CONSUMER CREDIT COUNSELING SERVICES, DIVISION OF UNITED FAMILY SERVICES
2000 First Avenue North, Suite 600
Birmingham, AL 35203-4117
205-251-1572
Fax: 205-251-1574
Type of Counseling:
Prepurchase Counseling, Default/Foreclosure Counseling, HECM Counseling, Rental Counseling
Affiliate of: NATIONAL FOUNDATION FOR CONSUMER CREDIT, INCORPORATED

**LEGAL SERVICES OF METRO BIRMINGHAM, INCORPORATED
1820 McFarland
Birmingham, AL 35202
205-328-3540
Fax: 205-328-3548
Email: kenc@lsmbi.com

Type of Counseling:
Prepurchase Counseling,
Default/Foreclosure Counseling,
Rental Counseling, HECM
Counseling
Affiliate of: WEST TENNESSEE
LEGAL SERVICES,
INCORPORATED

HOUSING AUTHORITY OF
BIRMINGHAM DISTRICT
1826 3rd Ave S
Birmingham, AL 35233-1905
205-521-0686
Fax: 205-521-7789
Type of Counseling:
Default/Foreclosure Counseling,
Rental Counseling, Prepurchase
Counseling

COMMUNITY ACTION AND
COMMUNITY DEVELOPMENT
AGENCY OF NORTH ALABAMA,
INCORPORATED
207 Commerce Circle SW
Decatur, AL 35601
256-355-7843
Fax: 256-355-7953
Email: mail@cacdana.org
Type of Counseling:
HECM Counseling,
Default/Foreclosure Counseling,
Rental Counseling, Prepurchase
Counseling

**LEGAL SERVICES OF NORTH
CENTRAL ALABAMA,
INCORPORATED
17 Vine Street NW
Decatur, AL 35602-
256-350-3551
Fax: 256-350-6722
Type of Counseling:
Prepurchase Counseling,
Default/Foreclosure Counseling,
Rental Counseling, HECM
Counseling
Affiliate of: WEST TENNESSEE
LEGAL SERVICES,
INCORPORATED

**LEGAL SERVICES
CORPORATION OF ALABAMA,
INCORPORATED
119 South Foster Street Suite 101
Dothan, AL 36301-
334-793-2882
Toll-Free:
TTY/TDD:
Fax: 334-793-7932
Type of Counseling:
Prepurchase Counseling,
Default/Foreclosure Counseling,
Rental Counseling, HECM
Counseling
Affiliate of: WEST TENNESSEE
LEGAL SERVICES,
INCORPORATED

HUMAN RESOURCE
DEVELOPMENT CORPORATION
100 George Wallace Dr
Enterprise, AL 36331
334-678-0084
Fax: 334-393-0048
Type of Counseling:
HECM Counseling,
Default/Foreclosure Counseling,
Rental Counseling, Prepurchase
Counseling

COMMUNITY ACTION AGENCY
OF NORTHWEST ALABAMA,
INCORPORATED
745 Thompson St
Florence, AL 35630
256-766-4330
Fax: 256-766-4367
Type of Counseling:
HECM Counseling,
Default/Foreclosure Counseling,
Rental Counseling, Prepurchase
Counseling

**LEGAL SERVICES
CORPORATION OF ALABAMA,
INCORPORATED
412 S. Court Street
Florence, AL 35631-
256-767-2020
Fax: 256-767-2212
Type of Counseling:
Prepurchase Counseling,
Default/Foreclosure Counseling,
Rental Counseling, HECM
Counseling
Affiliate of: WEST TENNESSEE
LEGAL SERVICES,
INCORPORATED

**LEGAL SERVICES
CORPORATION OF ALABAMA,
INCORPORATED
802 Chestnut Street
Gadsden, AL 35901-
256-543-2435
Fax: 256-543-2438
Type of Counseling:
Prepurchase Counseling,
Default/Foreclosure Counseling,
Rental Counseling, HECM
Counseling
Affiliate of: WEST TENNESSEE
LEGAL SERVICES,
INCORPORATED

WIL-LOW NON-PROFIT
HOUSING CORPORATION,
INCORPORATED
200 A Commerce Street
Hayneville, AL 36040
334-548-2191
Fax: 334-548-2576
Email: willowa@htcnet.net
Type of Counseling:
Default/Foreclosure Counseling,
Rental Counseling

COMMUNITY ACTION AGENCY
- HUNTSVILLE, MADISON,
LIMESTONE
3516 Stringfield Rd NW
Huntsville, AL 35810-1758
256-851-9800
Fax: 256-851-9803
Type of Counseling:
HECM Counseling,
Default/Foreclosure Counseling,
Rental Counseling, Prepurchase
Counseling

**LEGAL SERVICES OF NORTH
CENTRAL ALABAMA,
INCORPORATED
2000-C Vemon Drive
Huntsville, AL 35804
256-536-9645
Fax: 256-536-1544
Email: tkeith00@lsnca.org
Type of Counseling:
Prepurchase Counseling,
Default/Foreclosure Counseling,
Rental Counseling, HECM
Counseling
Affiliate of: WEST TENNESSEE
LEGAL SERVICES,
INCORPORATED

CONSUMER CREDIT
COUNSELING SERVICE OF
JACKSON
P.O. Box 1432
Jackson, AL 36545
251-246-9898
Toll-Free: 888-880-1413
Fax: 251-246-9898
Email: dunaway@mobilecan.org
Type of Counseling:
Prepurchase Counseling,
Default/Foreclosure Counseling,
HECM Counseling, Rental
Counseling
Affiliate of: NATIONAL
FOUNDATION FOR CONSUMER
CREDIT, INCORPORATED

MOBILE HOUSING BOARD
HOUSING COUNSELING
SERVICES
151 S Clairborne St

Mobile, AL 36633-1345
334-434-2202
Fax: 334-434-2220
Type of Counseling:
HECM Counseling,
Default/Foreclosure Counseling,
Rental Counseling, Prepurchase
Counseling

CONSUMER CREDIT
COUNSELING SERVICE OF
MONTROSE
P.O. Box 91068
Mobile, AL 36609-
251-990-8499
Fax: 251-666-6854
Type of Counseling:
Prepurchase Counseling,
Default/Foreclosure Counseling,
HECM Counseling

CONSUMER CREDIT
COUNSELING SERVICE OF
MOBILE
705 Oak Circle Drive East
Mobile, AL 36609
251-602-0011
Toll-Free: 888-880-1416
Fax: 251-666-6850
Email: dunaway@mobilecan.org
Type of Counseling:
Prepurchase Counseling,
Default/Foreclosure Counseling,
HECM Counseling
Affiliate of: NATIONAL
FOUNDATION FOR CONSUMER
CREDIT, INCORPORATED

**LEGAL SERVICES
CORPORATION OF ALABAMA,
INCORPORATED
103 Dauphin Street, Suite 601
Mobile, AL 36602-
334-433-1032
Fax: 334-433-2488
Type of Counseling:
Prepurchase Counseling,
Default/Foreclosure Counseling,
Rental Counseling, HECM
Counseling
Affiliate of: WEST TENNESSEE
LEGAL SERVICES,
INCORPORATED

CONSUMER CREDIT
COUNSELING SERVICE OF
WEST FLORIDA
4365 Midwest Drive Suite 5
Mobile, AL 36609-
251-460-4600
Toll-Free: 800-343-3317
Fax: 251-460-9090
Type of Counseling:
Prepurchase Counseling, Rental
Counseling, Default/Foreclosure
Counseling, HECM Counseling

CONSUMER CREDIT
COUNSELING SERVICE OF
ALABAMA, INCORPORATED
777 S Lawrence St Ste 101
Montgomery, AL 36104-5075
334-265-8545
Toll-Free: 800-662-6119
Fax: 334-265-5926
Website: www.budgethelp.com
Type of Counseling:
HECM Counseling,
Default/Foreclosure Counseling,
Rental Counseling, Prepurchase
Counseling
Affiliate of: NATIONAL
FOUNDATION FOR CONSUMER
CREDIT, INCORPORATED

HOUSING AUTHORITY OF THE
CITY OF MONTGOMERY
1020 Bell St
Montgomery, AL 36104-3006
334-206-7200
Fax: 334-206-7222
Type of Counseling:
Default/Foreclosure Counseling,
Rental Counseling, Prepurchase
Counseling

**LEGAL SERVICES
CORPORATION OF ALABAMA
207 Montgomery St.
500 Bell Bldg.
Montgomery, AL 36104
334-264-1471
Fax: 334-264-1474
Email: mwaters@compumise.com
Type of Counseling:
Prepurchase Counseling,
Default/Foreclosure Counseling,
Rental Counseling, HECM
Counseling
Affiliate of: WEST TENNESSEE
LEGAL SERVICES,
INCORPORATED

**LEGAL SERVICES
CORPORATION OF ALABAMA,
INCORPORATED
207 Montgomery Street, Suite 500
Montgomery, AL 36104-
334-264-1471
Fax: 334-264-1474
Type of Counseling:
Prepurchase Counseling,
Default/Foreclosure Counseling,
Rental Counseling, HECM
Counseling

Affiliate of: WEST TENNESSEE
LEGAL SERVICES,
INCORPORATED

CONSUMER CREDIT
COUNSELING SERVICE OF
MONTROSE
22787 U. S. Highway 98
Building B-2
Montrose, AL 36559-
251-990-8499
Toll-Free: 888-880-1412
Fax: 251-990-8406
Email: dunaway@mobilecan.org
Type of Counseling:
Rental Counseling, Prepurchase
Counseling, Default/Foreclosure
Counseling, HECM Counseling
Affiliate of: NATIONAL
FOUNDATION FOR CONSUMER
CREDIT, INCORPORATED

DALLAS-SELMA COMMUNITY
ACTION AND COMMUNITY
DEVELOPMENT
713 Jeff Davis Ave
Selma, AL 367020988
334-875-2450
Fax: 334-872-3590
Type of Counseling:
HECM Counseling,
Default/Foreclosure Counseling,
Rental Counseling, Prepurchase
Counseling

**LEGAL SERVICES
CORPORATION OF ALABAMA,
INCORPORATED
1114 Church Street
Selma, AL 36702-
334-875-3770
Fax: 334-875-3773
Type of Counseling:
Prepurchase Counseling,
Default/Foreclosure Counseling,
Rental Counseling, HECM
Counseling
Affiliate of: WEST TENNESSEE
LEGAL SERVICES,
INCORPORATED

ORGANIZED COMMUNITY
ACTION PROGRAM
507 North Three Notch Street
Troy, AL 36081-0908
334-566-1712
Fax: 334-566-7417
Type of Counseling:
HECM Counseling,
Default/Foreclosure Counseling,
Rental Counseling, Prepurchase
Counseling

CITY OF TUSCALOOSA COMMUNITY PLANNING AND DEVELOPMENT DEPARTMENT
1802 41st Avenue/Westgate office
Tuscaloosa, AL 35401
205-349-0175
Fax: 205-349-0397
Type of Counseling:
HECM Counseling, Default/Foreclosure Counseling, Rental Counseling, Prepurchase Counseling

COMMUNITY SERVICE PROGRAMS OF WEST ALABAMA, INCORPORATED
601 17th St
Tuscaloosa, AL 35401-4807
205-752-5429
Fax: 205-758-7229
Type of Counseling:
Default/Foreclosure Counseling, Rental Counseling, Prepurchase Counseling, HECM Counseling

**LEGAL SERVICES CORPORATION OF ALABAMA, INCORPORATED
131 McFarland Blvd E.
Tuscaloosa, AL 35402-
205-758-7503
Fax: 205-758-6041
Type of Counseling:
Prepurchase Counseling, Default/Foreclosure Counseling, Rental Counseling, HECM Counseling
Affiliate of: WEST TENNESSEE LEGAL SERVICES, INCORPORATED

Alaska

CONSUMER CREDIT COUNSELING SERVICE (CCCS) OF ALASKA
208 E 4th Ave
Anchorage, AK 99501-2508
907-279-6501
Toll-Free: 800-478-6501
Fax: 907-276-6083
Email: jjones@cccsofak.com
Type of Counseling:
Default/Foreclosure Counseling, Rental Counseling, Prepurchase Counseling, HECM Counseling

**ANCHORAGE NEIGHBORHOOD HOUSING SERVICES, INCORPORATED
480 West Tudor Road
Anchorage, AK 99503-
907-677-8490
Fax: 907-677-8450
Email: cparker@alaska.net
Type of Counseling:
Default/Foreclosure Counseling, Rental Counseling, Prepurchase Counseling
Affiliate of: NEIGHBORHOOD REINVESTMENT CORPORATION

**FAIRBANKS NEIGHBORHOOD HOUSING SERVICES, INCORPORATED
1616 South Cushman St Ste 201
Fairbanks, AK 99707
907-451-7230
Fax: 907-451-7236
Email: fnhs@ptialaska.net
Type of Counseling:
Prepurchase Counseling
Affiliate of: NEIGHBORHOOD REINVESTMENT CORPORATION

Arizona

SOUTHEASTERN ARIZONA GOVERNMENTS ORGANIZATION
118 Arizona St
Bisbee, AZ 85603-1800
520-432-5301
Fax: 520-432-5858
Type of Counseling:
HECM Counseling, Default/Foreclosure Counseling, Rental Counseling, Prepurchase Counseling

COMMUNITY SERVICES OF ARIZONA
670 N Arizona Ave Ste 23
Chandler, AZ 85225
480-899-8717
Toll-Free: 800-471-8247
Fax: 480-786-4173
Type of Counseling:
Prepurchase Counseling, HECM Counseling
Affiliate of: THE HOUSING PARTNERSHIP NETWORK

**HOUSING FOR MESA, INCORPORATED
251 W. Main Street
Mesa, AZ 85211-4457
480-649-1335
Fax: 480-649-1020
Email: hfm@uswest.net
Type of Counseling:
Prepurchase Counseling
Affiliate of: NATIONAL COUNCIL OF LA RAZA

CHICANOS POR LA LACAUSA, INC
1242 E Washington St Ste 103
Phoenix, AZ 85034-1149
602-253-0838
Fax: 602-253-4203
Type of Counseling:
Default/Foreclosure Counseling, Prepurchase Counseling
Affiliate of: NATIONAL COUNCIL OF LA RAZA

CITY OF PHOENIX NEIGHBORHOOD IMPROVEMENT AND HOUSING SERVICES
200 W Washington St 4th Fl
Phoenix, AZ 85003-1611
602-534-4446
Fax: 602-534-1555
Type of Counseling:
Rental Counseling

**NEIGHBORHOOD HOUSING SERVICES OF PHOENIX, INCORPORATED
320 E McDowell Rd Ste 120
Phoenix, AZ 85004-4514
602-258-1659
Fax: 602-258-1666
Email: ritac@dancris.com
Affiliate of: NEIGHBORHOOD REINVESTMENT CORPORATION

ADMINISTRATION OF RESOURCES AND CHOICES
1366 East Thomas Road, Suite 108
Phoenix, AZ 85014-
602-241-6169
Toll-Free: 888-264-2258
TTY/TDD: 602-241-6110
Fax: 602-230-9132
Email: kwhitearc@earthlink.net
Type of Counseling:
Prepurchase Counseling, Default/Foreclosure Counseling, HECM Counseling

**ACORN HOUSING CORPORATION
1018 W Roosevelt St
Phoenix, AZ 85007-2107
602-253-7501
Fax: 602-258-7143
Type of Counseling:
HECM Counseling, Default/Foreclosure Counseling, Rental Counseling, Prepurchase Counseling
Affiliate of: ACORN HOUSING CORPORATION

LABOR'S COMMUNITY SERVICE AGENCY
5818 N 7th St Ste 100
Phoenix, AZ 85014-5810
602-263-5741
Fax: 602-263-0815
Type of Counseling:
Default/Foreclosure Counseling

**ARIZONA FEDERATION OF HOUSING COUNSELING
2502 N. 22nd Avenue
Phoenix, AZ 85009-1926
602-257-1715
Fax: 602-254-6080
Type of Counseling:
Default/Foreclosure Counseling, Rental Counseling, Prepurchase Counseling
Affiliate of: HOUSING OPPORTUNITIES, INCORPORATED

COMMUNITY HOUSING RESOURCES OF ARIZONA
500 E Thomas Rd Ste 300
Phoenix, AZ 85012-3207
602-631-9780
Fax: 602-631-9757
Email: chr1@aol.com
Type of Counseling:
Default/Foreclosure Counseling, Prepurchase Counseling
Affiliate of: NATIONAL COUNCIL OF LA RAZA

**HOUSING AMERICA CORPORATION
130 North State Avenue
Somerton, AZ 85350
520-627-4221
Fax: 520-627-4213
Email: nogalesm@juno.com
Type of Counseling:
Prepurchase Counseling
Affiliate of: NATIONAL COUNCIL OF LA RAZA

ADMINISTRATION OF RESOURCES AND CHOICES
P.O. Box 86802
Tucson, AZ 85754-
520-327-8250
TTY/TDD: 520-623-9577
Fax: 520-327-2665
Email: kwhitearc@earthlink.net
Type of Counseling:
Prepurchase Counseling, Default/Foreclosure Counseling, HECM Counseling

FAMILY HOUSING RESOURCES
3777 E. Broadway, Ste. 100
Tucson, AZ 85716
520-318-0993
Toll-Free: 800-622-7462
Fax: 520-323-3788
Email: cpoor@quest.net
Type of Counseling: Prepurchase Counseling

**CHICANOS POR LA CAUSA-TUCSON
200 N. Stone
Tucson, AZ 85701
520-882-0018
Fax: 520-884-9007
Email: edcplc@azstarnet.com
Type of Counseling:
Prepurchase Counseling, Default/Foreclosure Counseling, Rental Counseling
Affiliate of: NATIONAL COUNCIL OF LA RAZA

**TUCSON URBAN LEAGUE INCORPORATED
2305 South Park Avenue
Tucson, AZ 85713-
520-620-1988
Fax: 520-620-1987
Email: bcrobinsonbc@netscape.net
Type of Counseling:
Prepurchase Counseling, Default/Foreclosure Counseling, HECM Counseling, Rental Counseling
Affiliate of: NATIONAL URBAN LEAGUE

Arkansas

CONSUMER DEBT COUNSELING
555 St. Louis Street
Batesville, AR 72501
870-793-7807
Toll-Free: 877-786-3328
Fax: 314-647-1359
Type of Counseling:
Default/Foreclosure Counseling

CONSUMER DEBT COUNSELING
422 W. Main Street
Blytheville, AR 72315
870-763-2227
Toll-Free: 877-786-3328
Fax: 314-647-1359
Type of Counseling:
Default/Foreclosure Counseling

FAMILY SERVICE AGENCY/CONSUMER CREDIT COUNSELING SERVICE
740 S. Salem Road Suite 104
Conway, AR 72032
501-450-9399
Fax: 501-450-3036
Email: wcohns@fsainc
Website: www.helpingfamilies.org
Type of Counseling:
Prepurchase Counseling, Rental Counseling, Default/Foreclosure Counseling, HECM Counseling

ARKANSAS RIVER VALLEY AREA COUNCIL, INCORPORATED
613 North 5th Street
Dardanells, AR 72834-0808
501-229-4861
Fax: 501-229-4863
Type of Counseling: HECM Counseling, Default/Foreclosure Counseling, Rental Counseling, Prepurchase Counseling

FAMILY SERVICE AGENCY CONSUMER CREDIT COUNSELING SERVICE
1301-B So. Waldron Road
Fort Smith, AR 72903-
501-450-9399
Fax: 501-450-3036
Email: wcohns@fsainc.org
Type of Counseling:
Prepurchase Counseling, Default/Foreclosure Counseling, HECM Counseling, Rental Counseling

CRAWFORD-SEBASTIAN COMMUNITY DEVELOPMENT COUNCIL, INCORPORATED
4831 Armour St.
Fort Smith, AR 72914
501-785-2303
Fax: 501-785-2341
Type of Counseling:
HECM Counseling, Default/Foreclosure Counseling, Rental Counseling, Prepurchase Counseling

EAST ARKANSAS LEGAL SERVICES
402 Franklin St
Helena, AR 72342-3206
870-338-9834
Fax: 870-338-9837
Type of Counseling:
HECM Counseling, Default/Foreclosure Counseling, Prepurchase Counseling

FAMILY SERVICE AGENCY CONSUMER CREDIT COUNSELING SERVICE
1401 Malvern Avenue, Suite 100
Hot Springs, AR 71913
501-321-1238

Fax: 501-624-5636
Email: wcohns@fsainc.org
Type of Counseling:
Prepurchase Counseling, Default/Foreclosure Counseling, HECM Counseling, Rental Counseling

CONSUMER DEBT COUNSELING
2218 East Race Street
Jonesboro, AR 724017217
870-932-8277
Toll-Free: 877-786-3328
Fax: 314-647-1359
Type of Counseling:
Default/Foreclosure Counseling

CROWLEY'S RIDGE DEVELOPMENT COUNCIL, INCORPORATED
249 S Main St
Jonesboro, AR 72403-1497
870-935-8610
Fax: 870-935-0291
Type of Counseling:
HECM Counseling, Default/Foreclosure Counseling, Rental Counseling, Prepurchase Counseling

FAMILY SERVICE AGENCY CONSUMER CREDIT COUNSELING SERVICE
4504 Burrow Dr
Little Rock, AR 72231-6615
501-753-0202
Fax: 501-812-4309
Email: wcohns@fsainc.org
Type of Counseling:
HECM Counseling, Default/Foreclosure Counseling, Prepurchase Counseling, Rental Counseling

FAMILY SERVICE AGENCY/CONSUMER CREDIT COUNSELING SERVICE
300 S. Rodney Parham, Suite 6
Little Rock, AR 72205
501-219-2208
Fax: 501-219-2214
Email: lracccs@helpingfamilies.org
website: www.helping families.org
Type of Counseling:
Prepurchase Counseling, Default/Foreclosure Counseling, HECM Counseling, Rental Counseling

IN AFFORDABLE HOUSING, INCORPORATED
1200 John Barrow Rd # 109
Little Rock, AR 72205-6523
501-221-2203
Fax: 501-221-2279
Type of Counseling:
Default/Foreclosure Counseling, Prepurchase Counseling

**ARGENTA COMMUNITY DEVELOPMENT CORPORATION
401 Main Street, Suite 200
North Little Rock, AR 72114
501-372-6936
Fax: 501-374-0496
Type of Counseling:
Prepurchase Counseling, Default/Foreclosure Counseling, Rental Counseling
Affiliate of: NEIGHBORHOOD REINVESTMENT CORPORATION

FAMILY SERVICE AGENCY/CONSUMER CREDIT COUNSELING SERVICE
121 West 6th Ave. Suite 7C
Pine Bluff, AR 71601
870-536-6003
Fax: 870-535-4741
Email: wcohns@fsainc.org
Type of Counseling:
Prepurchase Counseling, Rental Counseling, Default/Foreclosure Counseling, HECM Counseling

UNIVERSAL HOUSING DEVELOPMENT
301 E 3rd St
Russellville, AR 72811-5109
501-968-5001
Fax: 501-968-5002
Type of Counseling:
Default/Foreclosure Counseling, Rental Counseling, Prepurchase Counseling

FAMILY SERVICE AGENCY CONSUMER CREDIT COUNSELING SERVICE
5204 S Thompson Ste C
Springdale, AR 72764
501-751-4575
Fax: 501-751-7114
Email: wcohns@fsainc.org
Type of Counseling:
Default/Foreclosure Counseling, Rental Counseling, Prepurchase Counseling, HECM Counseling

LEGAL AID OF ARKANSAS
2126 E. Broadway
West Memphis, AR 723033201
870-732-6370
Fax: 870-732-6373
Type of Counseling:
Default/Foreclosure Counseling, Rental Counseling, Prepurchase Counseling

CONSUMER DEBT COUNSELING
310 Mid-Continent Plaza, Suite 320
West Memphis, AR 723011748
870-735-2022
Toll-Free: 877-786-3328
Fax: 314-647-1359
Type of Counseling:
Default/Foreclosure Counseling

California

ANAHEIM HOUSING AUTHORITY
201 S. Anaheim Blvd. 2nd Floor
Anaheim, CA 92085-
714-765-4340
Fax: 714-765-4654
Type of Counseling: Prepurchase Counseling, Default/Foreclosure Counseling, Rental Counseling

**NEIGHBORHOOD HOUSING SERVICES OF ORANGE COUNTY
198 West Lincoln Ave., 2nd floor
Anaheim, CA 92805
714-490-1250
Fax: 714-490-1263
Type of Counseling: Prepurchase Counseling
Affiliate of: NEIGHBORHOOD REINVESTMENT CORPORATION

CONSUMER CREDIT COUNSELING SERVICE OF ORANGE COUNTY
2450 E. Lincoln
Anaheim, CA 92809-4272
714-547-2227
Fax: 714-245-1690
Email: gbengoch@cccsoc.org
Website: www.cccsoc.org/
Type of Counseling:
Default/Foreclosure Counseling, Rental Counseling, Prepurchase Counseling

CONSUMER CREDIT COUNSELING SERVICES OF EAST BAY
3700 Delta Fair Boulevard #202
Antioch, CA 94509-
510-729-6966
Toll-Free: 888-788-8528
Fax: 510-729-6961
Website: www.cccsebay.org
Type of Counseling: Prepurchase Counseling, Default/Foreclosure Counseling, Rental Counseling

CONSUMER CREDIT COUNSELING SERVICE OF KERN AND TULARE COUNTIES
5300 Lennox Ave Ste 200
Bakersfield, CA 93309-1662
661-324-9628
Toll-Free: 800-272-2482
Fax: 661-324-0750
Email: nancyjohnson cccsbakersfield@att.net
Type of Counseling:
HECM Counseling,
Default/Foreclosure Counseling,
Prepurchase Counseling

SPRINGBOARD-BARSTOW
170 North Yucca (SBCCCU)
Barstow, CA 92311
800 -947-3752
Fax: 909-781-8027
Type of Counseling:
Default/Foreclosure Counseling,
Prepurchase Counseling

SPRINGBOARD-BEAUMONT
499 E 6th St
Beaumont, CA 92223-2215
800-947-3752-
Fax: 909-781-8027
Type of Counseling: HECM Counseling, Default/Foreclosure Counseling, Rental Counseling, Prepurchase Counseling

CONSUMER CREDIT COUNSELING SERVICES OF LOS ANGELES
6510 Atlantic Ave.
Bell, CA 90201-
800-750-2227
Toll-Free: 800-750-2227
Fax: 213-890-9589
Type of Counseling: Prepurchase Counseling, Default/Foreclosure Counseling, HECM Counseling, Rental Counseling

CONSUMER CREDIT COUNSELING SERVICES OF EAST BAY
2326 Fourth Street #2
Berkeley, CA 94710-
510-729-6966
Toll-Free: 888-788-8528
Fax: 510-729-6961
Website: www.cccsebay.org
Type of Counseling: Prepurchase Counseling, Default/Foreclosure Counseling, Rental Counseling

SPRINGBOARD-BISHOP
362 North Main St, 2nd Floor
Bishop, CA 93514
800-947-3752
Fax: 909-781-1003
Email: www.credit.org
Type of Counseling: Prepurchase Counseling, Rental Counseling, Default/Foreclosure Counseling, HECM Counseling

CONSUMER CREDIT COUNSELING SERVICE OF ORANGE COUNTY
695 Madison Way
Brea, CA 92821-5732
714-547-2227
Fax: 714-245-1690
Email: gbengoch@cccsoc.org
Website: www.cccsoc.org
Type of Counseling: Prepurchase Counseling, Default/Foreclosure Counseling, HECM Counseling, Rental Counseling

CONSUMER CREDIT COUNSELING SERVICE OF VENTURA COUNTY INCORPORATED
80 N Wood Rd Ste 312
Camarillo, CA 93010
800-540-2227
Toll-Free: 800-540-2227
Fax: 805-383-7721
Type of Counseling:
HECM Counseling,
Default/Foreclosure Counseling,
Rental Counseling, Prepurchase Counseling
Affiliate of: NATIONAL FOUNDATION FOR CONSUMER CREDIT, INCORPORATED

SPRINGBOARD-CANOGA PARK
22048 Sherman Way, Suite 212
Canoga Park, CA 91303-
800-947-3752
Type of Counseling: Prepurchase Counseling, Default/Foreclosure Counseling

HOUSING AUTHORITY OF THE COUNTY OF SANTA CRUZ
2160 41st Ave
Capitola, CA 95010-2060
831-464-0170
Fax: 831-475-3861
Type of Counseling:
Default/Foreclosure Counseling,
HECM Counseling

CONSUMER CREDIT COUNSELING SERVICE OF VENTURA COUNTY, INCORPORATED
4140 Jade Street
Capitola, CA 95010-
831-476-7733
Fax: 831-462-6606
Type of Counseling:
Default/Foreclosure Counseling,
Prepurchase Counseling, Rental Counseling
Affiliate of: NATIONAL FOUNDATION FOR CONSUMER CREDIT, INCORPORATED

CONSUMER CREDIT COUNSELING SERVICE OF LOS ANGELES
11829 South St Ste 101
Cerritos, CA 90703-6825
323-890-9500
Toll-Free: 800-750-2227
Fax: 323-890-9590
Type of Counseling: HECM Counseling, Default/Foreclosure Counseling, Rental Counseling, Prepurchase Counseling

COMMUNITY HOUSING AND CREDIT COUNSELING CENTER
1001 Willow Street
Chico, CA 95928
530-891-4124
Toll-Free: 888-423-6333
Fax: 530-891-8547
Email: srodriguez@chiphousing.org
Type of Counseling: Prepurchase Counseling, Rental Counseling, Default/Foreclosure Counseling

CONSUMER CREDIT COUNSELING SERVICE OF KERN AND TULARE COUNTIES
610 Blandy-NAWS Family Service Center
China Lake, CA 93555
661-324-9628
Toll-Free: 800-272-2482
Fax: 661-324-0750
Email: nancyjohnson cccsbakersfield@att.net
Type of Counseling:
HECM Counseling,
Default/Foreclosure Counseling,
Prepurchase Counseling

SPRINGBOARD-CHINO
12150 Ramona Ave. Suite 12B
Chino, CA 91710
800-947-3752
Fax: 909-781-8027
Type of Counseling:
HECM Counseling, Prepurchase Counseling, Default/Foreclosure Counseling

CONSUMER CREDIT COUNSELORS OF SAN DIEGO AND IMPERIAL COUNTY
660 Bay Blvd Ste 114

Chula Vista, CA 91910-5200
619-498-0600
Fax: 619-498-0642
Type of Counseling: HECM Counseling, Default/Foreclosure Counseling, Rental Counseling, Prepurchase Counseling

SPRINGBOARD-CHULA VISTA
229 "F" Street, Suite F
Chula Vista, CA 91910
800-947-3752
Type of Counseling: Prepurchase Counseling, Default/Foreclosure Counseling, HECM Counseling

SPRINGBOARD-CITY OF COMMERCE
8900 Southeastern Avenue
City of Commerce, CA 90040
800-947-3752
Type of Counseling: Prepurchase Counseling, Default/Foreclosure Counseling

CONSUMER CREDIT COUNSELING SERVICE OF LOS ANGELES
500 Citadel Dr Ste 300
Commerce, CA 90040
213-890-9511
Toll-Free: 800-750-2227
Fax: 323-869-5196
Email: cccsla.org.com
Type of Counseling: HECM Counseling, Default/Foreclosure Counseling, Rental Counseling, Prepurchase Counseling

CONSUMER CREDIT COUNSELING SERVICE OF LOS ANGELES
600 Citadel Dr Ste 400
Commerce, CA 90040
323-890-9500
Toll-Free: 800-750-2227
Fax: 323-890-9590
Type of Counseling: HECM Counseling, Default/Foreclosure Counseling, Rental Counseling, Prepurchase Counseling

CONSUMER CREDIT COUNSELING SERVICES OF EAST BAY
1070 Concord Avenue #170
Concord, CA 94510-
510-729-6966
Toll-Free: 888-788-8528
Fax: 510-729-6961
Website: www.cccsebay.org
Type of Counseling: Prepurchase Counseling, Default/Foreclosure Counseling, Rental Counseling

SPRINGBOARD-CORONA
370 W Grand Blvd Ste 104
Corona, CA 91720-2174
800-947-3752
Fax: 909-781-8027
Type of Counseling: Default/Foreclosure Counseling, Prepurchase Counseling

CONSUMER CREDIT COUNSELING SERVICE OF ORANGE COUNTY
2701 S. Harbor Boulevard, E-6
Costa Mesa, CA 92626-
714-547-2227
Fax: 714-245-1680
Email: gbengoch@cccsoc.org
Type of Counseling: Prepurchase Counseling, Default/Foreclosure Counseling, HECM Counseling, Rental Counseling

CONSUMER CREDIT COUNSELING SERVICE OF LOS ANGELES
6167 Bristol Pkwy Ste 340
Culver City, CA 90230
323-890-9500
Toll-Free: 800-750-2227
Fax: 323-890-9590
Type of Counseling: HECM Counseling, Default/Foreclosure Counseling, Prepurchase Counseling

CONSUMER CREDIT COUNSELING SERVICE OF SAN FRANCISCO, DALY CITY
2171 Junipero Serra Blvd., Ste. 300
Daly City, CA 94015
800-777-7526
Toll-Free: 800-777-7526
Fax: 415-788-7817
Type of Counseling: Prepurchase Counseling, Default/Foreclosure Counseling, Rental Counseling, HECM Counseling

SPRINGBOARD-DOWNEY
8444 Florence Ave
Downey, CA 90241-
800-947-3752
Type of Counseling: Prepurchase Counseling, Default/Foreclosure Counseling

CONSUMER CREDIT COUNSELING SERVICES OF EAST BAY
6500 Dublin Court #213
Dublin, CA 94568
510-729-6966
Toll-Free: 888-788-8528
Fax: 510-729-6961
Website: www.cccsebay.org
Type of Counseling: Default/Foreclosure Counseling, Prepurchase Counseling, Rental Counseling

SPRINGBOARD-EL CAJON
1150 Broadway, Suite 230
El Cajon, CA 92021-
800-947-3752
Type of Counseling: Prepurchase Counseling, Default/Foreclosure Counseling

CONSUMER CREDIT COUNSELORS OF SAN DIEGO AND IMPERIAL COUNTY
700 North Johnson Ave Ste G
El Cajon, CA 92020
619-447-5700
Fax: 619-447-0519
Type of Counseling: HECM Counseling, Default/Foreclosure Counseling, Rental Counseling, Prepurchase Counseling

CONSUMER CREDIT COUNSELORS OF SAN DIEGO AND IMPERIAL COUNTY
370 Aurora St Ste A & B
El Centro, CA 92243
760-337-2300
Fax: 760-233-8196
Type of Counseling: HECM Counseling, Default/Foreclosure Counseling, Rental Counseling, Prepurchase Counseling

SPRINGBOARD- ESCONDIDO
139 East Third Ave. Suite 108
Escondido, CA 92025-
800-947-3752
Type of Counseling: Prepurchase Counseling, Default/Foreclosure Counseling

PACIFIC COMMUNITY SERVICES FAIRFIELD
934 Missouri St., Ste. D
Fairfield, CA 94533
925-439-1056
Toll-Free: 800-914-6874
Type of Counseling: Prepurchase Counseling, Default/Foreclosure Counseling, Rental Counseling

CONSUMER CREDIT COUNSELING SERVICES OF EAST BAY
609 Jefferson Street, G2
Fairfield, CA 94533-
510-729-6966
Toll-Free: 888-788-8528
Fax: 510-729-6961

Website: www.cccsebay.org
Type of Counseling: Prepurchase Counseling, Default/Foreclosure Counseling, Rental Counseling

SPRINGBOARD- FOUNTANA
8275 Sierra Ave,Suite 106
Fountana, CA 92335
800-947-3752
Fax: 909-781-8027
Type of Counseling: Prepurchase Counseling, Default/Foreclosure Counseling

CONSUMER CREDIT COUNSELING SERVICES OF EAST BAY
3100 Mowry Avenue #403A
Fremont, CA 94538-
510-729-6966
Toll-Free: 888-788-8528
Fax: 510-729-6961
Website: www.cccsebay.org
Type of Counseling: Prepurchase Counseling, Default/Foreclosure Counseling, Rental Counseling

CONSUMER CREDIT COUNSELING SERVICE OF CENTRAL VALLEY
4969 E McKinley Ave Ste 107
Fresno, CA 93727-1968
559-454-1700
Toll-Free: 800-773-9009
Fax: 559-454-1405
Type of Counseling: HECM Counseling, Default/Foreclosure Counseling, Rental Counseling, Prepurchase Counseling

CONSUMER CREDIT COUNSELING SERVICE OF MID COUNTIES FRESNO
4270 N. Blackstone, Ste. 312
Fresno, CA 93726
559-650-7658
Fax: 559-650-7657
Type of Counseling: Prepurchase Counseling, Default/Foreclosure Counseling, Rental Counseling, HECM Counseling

CONSUMER CREDIT COUNSELING SERVICES OF CENTRAL VALLEY
3170 N. Chestnut Avenue, Suite 101
Fresno, CA 93703-
559-454-5090
Fax: 559-454-0672
Type of Counseling: Prepurchase Counseling, Default/Foreclosure Counseling, HECM Counseling, Rental Counseling

SPRINGBOARD- FORT IRWIN
Fort Irwin Military Base
Ft. Irwin, CA 92310
800-947-3752
Fax: 909-781-9896
Type of Counseling: Default/Foreclosure Counseling, Prepurchase Counseling

SPRINGBOARD- FULLERTON
801 E. Chapman Ave., Suite 213
Fullerton, CA 92831-
800-947-3752
Type of Counseling: Prepurchase Counseling, Default/Foreclosure Counseling

CONSUMER CREDIT COUNSELING SERVICE OF ORANGE COUNTY
2501 E Chapman Ave Ste 100
Fullerton, CA 92631
714-547-2227
Fax: 714-245-1680
Email: gbengoch@cccsoc.org
Website: www.cccsoc.org
Type of Counseling: Default/Foreclosure Counseling, Prepurchase Counseling, HECM Counseling

CONSUMER CREDIT COUNSELING SERVICE OF VENTURA COUNTY, INCORPORATED
8339 Church Street, Suite 106
Gilroy, CA 95020-
408-842-1927
Fax: 408-842-0035
Type of Counseling: Default/Foreclosure Counseling, Prepurchase Counseling, Rental Counseling
Affiliate of: NATIONAL FOUNDATION FOR CONSUMER CREDIT, INCORPORATED

PROJECT SENTINEL
7365 Monterey Rd., Ste. D1
Gilroy, CA 95020
408-842-7740
Toll-Free: 800-468-7464
Fax: 408-842-8054
Type of Counseling: Rental Counseling, Prepurchase Counseling

CONSUMER CREDIT COUNSELING SERVICE OF LOS ANGELES
112 West Broadway, Suite 212
Glendale, CA 91204
323-890-9500
Toll-Free: 800-750-2227
Fax: 323-890-9590
Type of Counseling: HECM Counseling, Default/Foreclosure Counseling, Rental Counseling, Prepurchase Counseling

CONSUMER CREDIT COUNSELING SERVICE OF LOS ANGELES
16800 Devonshire Ste 301
Granada Hills, CA 91344
323-890-9500
Toll-Free: 800-750-2227
Fax: 323-890-9590
Type of Counseling: HECM Counseling, Default/Foreclosure Counseling, Rental Counseling, Prepurchase Counseling

CATHOLIC CHARITIES
221 Turner Street
Guasti, CA 91743
909-390-2424
Fax: 909-390-2433
Type of Counseling: Rental Counseling

CONSUMER CREDIT COUNSELING SERVICES OF CENTRAL VALLEY
598 W. Grangeville Blvd. Suite 102
Hanford, CA 93230-
559-454-1700
Fax: 559-454-1405
Type of Counseling: Prepurchase Counseling, Default/Foreclosure Counseling, HECM Counseling, Rental Counseling

EDEN COUNCIL FOR HOPE AND OPPORTUNITY/ECHO HOUSING
770 A St
Hayward, CA 94541-3956
510-581-9380
Fax: 510-537-4793
Type of Counseling: Prepurchase Counseling, Default/Foreclosure Counseling, HECM Counseling, Rental Counseling

SPRINGBOARD- HEMET
1700 E Florida Ave
Hemet, CA 92544-4679
800-947-3752
Fax: 909-781-8027
Type of Counseling: HECM Counseling, Default/Foreclosure Counseling, Prepurchase Counseling

CONSUMER CREDIT COUNSELING SERVICE OF ORANGE COUNTY
8907 Warner Avenue Ste 215

Huntington Beach, CA 92647
714-547-2227
Fax: 714-245-1690
Type of Counseling: HECM Counseling, Default/Foreclosure Counseling, Rental Counseling, Prepurchase Counseling

SPRINGBOARD- INDIO
81730 Highway 111, Unit #3
Indio, CA 92201-3937
800-947-3752
Fax: 909-781-8027
Type of Counseling: HECM Counseling, Default/Foreclosure Counseling, Rental Counseling, Prepurchase Counseling

CATHOLIC CHARITIES
45149 Smurr St
Indio, CA 92201
760-347-1188
Fax: 760-347-8388
Type of Counseling: Rental Counseling

**INGLEWOOD NEIGHBORHOOD HOUSING SERVICES, INCORPORATED
335 E Manchester Blvd
Inglewood, CA 90301
310-674-3756
Fax: 310-674-6915
Email: Nwinglewood@earthlink.net
Type of Counseling: Prepurchase Counseling, Default/Foreclosure Counseling
Affiliate of: NEIGHBORHOOD REINVESTMENT CORPORATION

CONSUMER CREDIT COUNSELING SERVICES OF CENTRAL VALLEY
Null
Kingsburg, CA 93631
559-454-1700
Fax: 559-454-1405
Type of Counseling: Prepurchase Counseling, Default/Foreclosure Counseling, HECM Counseling, Rental Counseling

EDEN COUNCIL FOR HOPE AND OPPORTUNITY/ECHO HOUSING
3311 Pacific Ave
Livermore, CA 94705
925-449-7340
Fax: 925-449-0704
Type of Counseling: Default/Foreclosure Counseling, Rental Counseling, Prepurchase Counseling, HECM Counseling

CONSUMER CREDIT COUNSELING SERVICES OF VENTURA COUNTY, INCORPORATED LOMPOC
1320 N. H St.
Lompoc, CA 93436
800-540-2227
Toll-Free: 800-540-2227
Fax: 805-383-7722
Type of Counseling: Prepurchase Counseling, Default/Foreclosure Counseling, Rental Counseling, HECM Counseling

HOUSING AUTHORITY OF THE COUNTY OF SANTA BARBARA
815 W Ocean Ave
Lompoc, CA 93436-6526
805-736-3423
Fax: 805-735-7672
Type of Counseling: HECM Counseling, Default/Foreclosure Counseling, Rental Counseling, Prepurchase Counseling

CONSUMER CREDIT COUNSELING SERVICE OF LOS ANGELES
2501 Cherry Ave Ste 260
Long Beach, CA 90806-2034
323-890-9500
Toll-Free: 800-750-2227
Fax: 323-890-9590
Type of Counseling: HECM Counseling, Default/Foreclosure Counseling, Rental Counseling, Prepurchase Counseling

CONSUMER CREDIT COUNSELING SERVICE OF LOS ANGELES
500 Citadel Drive Suite 300
Los Angeles, CA 90040-
323-890-9500
Toll-Free: 800-750-2227
Fax: 323-890-9590
Type of Counseling: HECM Counseling, Default/Foreclosure Counseling, Prepurchase Counseling, Rental Counseling

CONSUMER CREDIT COUNSELING SERVICES OF LOS ANGELES
4929 Wilshire Blvd. #400
Los Angeles, CA 90010-
800-750-2227
Toll-Free: 800-750-2227
Fax: 213-890-9589
Type of Counseling: Prepurchase Counseling, Default/Foreclosure Counseling, HECM Counseling, Rental Counseling

**ACORN HOUSING CORPORATION
3655 South Grand Street Suite 250
Los Angeles, CA 90007-
213-748-1345
Fax: 213-747-4221
Type of Counseling: Default/Foreclosure Counseling, Prepurchase Counseling
Affiliate of: ACORN HOUSING CORPORATION

SPRINGBOARD- LOS ANGELES
1605 W. Olympic Blvd. Ste. 9023
Los Angeles, CA 90015
800-947-3752
Type of Counseling: Prepurchase Counseling, Default/Foreclosure Counseling

CONSUMER CREDIT COUNSELING SERVICE OF LOS ANGELES
4060 S Figueroa St
Los Angeles, CA 90037-2042
323-890-9500
Toll-Free: 800-750-2227
Fax: 323-890-9590
Type of Counseling: HECM Counseling, Default/Foreclosure Counseling, Rental Counseling, Prepurchase Counseling

**LOS ANGELES NEIGHBORHOOD HOUSING SERVICES, INCORPORATED
3111 S Flower St
Los Angeles, CA 90007-3727
213-749-7797
Fax: 213-749-3325
Email: lorig@lanhs.corpusa.com
Type of Counseling: Default/Foreclosure Counseling, Prepurchase Counseling
Affiliate of: NEIGHBORHOOD REINVESTMENT CORPORATION

CONSUMER CREDIT COUNSELING SERVICES OF CENTRAL VALLEY
800 E. Yosemite
Madera, CA 93638-
559-454-1700
Fax: 559-454-1405
Type of Counseling: Prepurchase Counseling, Default/Foreclosure Counseling, HECM Counseling, Rental Counseling

CONSUMER CREDIT COUNSELING SERVICE OF MID COUNTIES MERCED

885 W. 18th St.
Merced, CA 95340
209-723-9982
Fax: 209-723-4315
Type of Counseling:
Prepurchase Counseling,
Default/Foreclosure Counseling,
Rental Counseling, HECM
Counseling

PROJECT SENTINEL
79 S. Main Street
Milpitas, CA 95035-
408-946-6582
Fax: 650-321-4173
Type of Counseling:
Prepurchase Counseling,
Default/Foreclosure Counseling,
HECM Counseling, Rental
Counseling

CONSUMER CREDIT
COUNSELING SERVICE OF
ORANGE COUNTY
28570 Marguerite Parkway, Ste 213
Mission Viejo, CA 92692-
714-547-2227
Fax: 714-245-1690
Email: gbengoch@cccsoc.org
Website: www.cccsoc.org
Type of Counseling: HECM
Counseling, Default/Foreclosure
Counseling, Rental Counseling,
Prepurchase Counseling

STANISLAUS COUNTY
AFFORDABLE HOUSING
CORPORATION
201 East Rumble Road, Suite E
Modesto, CA 95350
209-574-1155
Fax: 209-574-0586
Type of Counseling: HECM
Counseling, Default/Foreclosure
Counseling, Rental Counseling,
Prepurchase Counseling

CONSUMER CREDIT
COUNSELING SERVICE OF MID
COUNTIES MODESTO
1800 Tully Rd., Ste. A-1
Modesto, CA 95350
209-522-1261
Fax: 209-522-5845
Type of Counseling: Prepurchase
Counseling, Default/Foreclosure
Counseling, Rental Counseling,
HECM Counseling

COMMUNITY HOUSING AND
SHELTER SERVICES
936 McHenry Avenue Room 230
Modesto, CA 95354
209-574-1149
Fax: 209-575-9818
Type of Counseling:
Default/Foreclosure Counseling,
Rental Counseling, Prepurchase
Counseling

**NEIGHBORHOOD
PARTNERSHIP OF MONTCLAIR
9916 Central Ave
Montclair, CA 91763
909-624-9110
Fax: 909-624-9263
Email: margaret@npnhs.com
Type of Counseling:
Default/Foreclosure Counseling,
Prepurchase Counseling
Affiliate of: NEIGHBORHOOD
REINVESTMENT
CORPORATION

SPRINGBOARD- MONTCLAIR
4959 Palo Verde St Ste 100C
Montclair, CA 91763-2330
909-781-0114
Toll-Free: 800-947-3752
Fax: 909-781-8027
Type of Counseling:
HECM Counseling,
Default/Foreclosure Counseling,
Prepurchase Counseling

CONSUMER CREDIT
COUNSELING SERVICE OF
VENTURA COUNTY,
INCORPORATED
801 Lighthouse Avenue, suite 106
Monterey, CA 93940-
831-643-0531
Fax: 831-643-0532
Type of Counseling:
Default/Foreclosure Counseling,
Rental Counseling, Prepurchase
Counseling, HECM Counseling
Affiliate of: NATIONAL
FOUNDATION FOR CONSUMER
CREDIT, INCORPORATED

CATHOLIC CHARITIES
23-700 Sunnymead Blvd
Moreno Valley, CA 92556
909-485-2125
Fax: 909-485-2188
Type of Counseling: Rental
Counseling

SPRINGBOARD- MORENO
VALLEY
23800 Sunnymead Blvd Suite F
Moreno Valley, CA 92553
800-947-3752
Fax: 909-781-8027
Type of Counseling:
HECM Counseling,
Default/Foreclosure Counseling,
Prepurchase Counseling

CONSUMER CREDIT
COUNSELING SERVICE OF
SACRAMENTO VALLEY -
NORTH HIGHLANDS
4636 Watt Ave.
North Highlands, CA 95660
916-379-3600
Toll-Free: 800-736-2227
Fax: 916-379-0636
Type of Counseling:
Prepurchase Counseling,
Default/Foreclosure Counseling,
HECM Counseling

**ACORN HOUSING
CORPORATION
3205 Farnam Ave
Oakland, CA 94601
510-436-6532
Fax: 510-436-6395
Type of Counseling:
Default/Foreclosure Counseling,
Prepurchase Counseling
Affiliate of: ACORN HOUSING
CORPORATION

CONSUMER CREDIT
COUNSELING SERVICES OF
EAST BAY
587 15th Street
Oakland, CA 94612
510-729-6966
Toll-Free: 888-788-8528
Fax: 510-729-6961
Website: www.cccsebay.org
Type of Counseling:
Prepurchase Counseling,
Default/Foreclosure Counseling,
Rental Counseling

**SPANISH SPEAKING UNITY
COUNCIL
1900 Fruitvale Avenue, Suite 2-A
Oakland, CA 94601
510-535-6941
Fax: 510-534-7771
Email: wleone@unitycouncil.org
Type of Counseling: Prepurchase
Counseling
Affiliate of: NATIONAL COUNCIL
OF LA RAZA

**HOME BUYER ASSISTANCE
CENTER
1611 Telegraph Ave. #620
Oakland, CA 94612
510-832-6925
Fax: 510-832-1335
Website: www.hbac.org

Type of Counseling: Prepurchase Counseling
Affiliate of: THE HOUSING PARTNERSHIP NETWORK

CONSUMER CREDIT COUNSELING SERVICES OF EAST BAY
333 Hegenberger Rd Ste 710
Oakland, CA 94621-1462
510-729-6969
Toll-Free: 888-788-8528
Fax: 510-729-6961
Email: ljd8421@aol.com
Website: www.cccsebay.org
Type of Counseling: Default/Foreclosure Counseling, Prepurchase Counseling, Rental Counseling

EDEN COUNCIL FOR HOPE AND OPPORTUNITY/ECHO HOUSING
1305 Franklin St Ste 305
Oakland, CA 94612-3213
510-271-7931
Fax: 510-763-3736
Type of Counseling: Prepurchase Counseling, Default/Foreclosure Counseling, HECM Counseling, Rental Counseling

**CATHOLIC CHARITIES OF THE EAST BAY
433 Jefferson Street
Oakland, CA 94607
510-768-3100
Type of Counseling: Prepurchase Counseling, Default/Foreclosure Counseling, HECM Counseling, Rental Counseling
Affiliate of: CATHOLIC CHARITIES USA

EDEN COUNCIL FOR HOPE AND OPPORTUNITY/ECHO HOUSING
4768 Lucchesi Court
Oakley, CA 94561
925-679-8023
Fax: 925-625-4189
Type of Counseling: HECM Counseling

CONSUMER CREDIT COUNSELORS OF SAN DIEGO AND IMPERIAL COUNTY
2741 Vista Way Ste 205
Oceanside, CA 92054-6372
760-757-2227
Fax: 760-757-9600
Type of Counseling: HECM Counseling, Default/Foreclosure Counseling, Rental Counseling, Prepurchase Counseling

INLAND FAIR HOUSING MEDIATION BOARD
1005 N Begonia Ave
Ontario, CA 91762
909-984-2254
Toll-Free: 800-321-0911
Fax: 909-460-0274
Type of Counseling: HECM Counseling, Default/Foreclosure Counseling, Rental Counseling, Prepurchase Counseling

CONSUMER CREDIT COUNSELING SERVICE OF SACRAMENTO VALLEY - ORANGEVALE
6000 Main Ave.
Orangevale, CA 95662
916-379-3600
Toll-Free: 800-736-2227
Fax: 916-379-0636
Type of Counseling: Prepurchase Counseling, Default/Foreclosure Counseling, HECM Counseling

CONSUMER CREDIT COUNSELING SERVICE OF VENTURA COUNTY, INCORPORATED OXNARD
750 W. Gonzales Rd., Ste.
Oxnard, CA
800-540-2227
Toll-Free: 800-540-2227
Fax: 805-383-7722
Type of Counseling: Prepurchase Counseling, Default/Foreclosure Counseling, Rental Counseling, HECM Counseling

SPRINGBOARD- PALM SPRINGS
1001 South Palm Canyon Ste 103
Palm Springs, CA 92262
800-947-3752
Fax: 909-781-8027
Type of Counseling: HECM Counseling, Default/Foreclosure Counseling, Rental Counseling, Prepurchase Counseling

CONSUMER CREDIT COUNSELING SERVICE OF LOS ANGELES
1605 E Palmdale Blvd Ste E
Palmdale, CA 93550
661-265-8142
Toll-Free: 800-750-2227
Fax: 661-265-8508
Type of Counseling: HECM Counseling, Default/Foreclosure Counseling, Rental Counseling, Prepurchase Counseling

PROJECT SENTINEL
430 Sherman Avenue Suite 308
Palo Alto, CA 94306
650-321-6291
Fax: 650-321-4173
Type of Counseling: Default/Foreclosure Counseling, Prepurchase Counseling, Rental Counseling, HECM Counseling

CONSUMER CREDIT COUNSELING SERVICE OF VENTURA COUNTY, INCORPORATED
480 Lytton Ave.
Palo Alto, CA 74301
650-329-9674
Fax: 650-322-2302
Type of Counseling: Default/Foreclosure Counseling, Prepurchase Counseling, Rental Counseling
Affiliate of: NATIONAL FOUNDATION FOR CONSUMER CREDIT, INCORPORATED

CONSUMER CREDIT COUNSELING SERVICE OF LOS ANGELES
505 E. Colorado Blvd
Pasadena, CA 91101-
323-890-9500
Toll-Free: 800-750-2227
Fax: 323-890-9590
Type of Counseling: HECM Counseling, Default/Foreclosure Counseling, Rental Counseling, Prepurchase Counseling

CONSUMER CREDIT COUNSELING SERVICE OF VENTURA COUNTY, INCORPORATED PASO ROBLES
Null
Paso Robles, CA 93446
800-540-2227
Toll-Free: 800-540-2227
Fax: 805-383-7722
Type of Counseling: Prepurchase Counseling, Default/Foreclosure Counseling, Rental Counseling, HECM Counseling

PACIFIC COMMUNITY SERVICES
329 Railroad Ave
Pittsburg, CA 94565-2245
925-439-1056
Fax: 925-439-0831

Type of Counseling: Rental Counseling, Default/Foreclosure Counseling, Prepurchase Counseling

CONSUMER CREDIT COUNSELING SERVICE OF LOS ANGELES
281 S.Thomas Street Suite 505
Pomona, CA 91766
909-622-7203
Toll-Free: 800-750-2227
Fax: 909-622-5625
Email: fharris@cccsla.org
Type of Counseling: HECM Counseling, Default/Foreclosure Counseling, Rental Counseling, Prepurchase Counseling

SPRINGBOARD- RANCHO CUCAMONGA
9267 Haven Avenue, Suite 101
Rancho Cucamonga, CA 91730-
800-947-3752
Fax: 909-328-7742
Type of Counseling: Default/Foreclosure Counseling, Prepurchase Counseling

CONSUMER CREDIT COUNSELING SERVICE OF SACRAMENTO VALLEY - REDDING
3609 Bechelli Lane, Ste. I
Redding, CA 96002
916-379-3600
Toll-Free: 8007362227
Fax: 9163790636
Type of Counseling: Prepurchase Counseling, Default/Foreclosure Counseling, HECM Counseling

**RICHMOND NEIGHBORHOOD HOUSING SERVICES, INCORPORATED
500 S 15th St
Richmond, CA 94804-3709
510-237-6459
Fax: 510-237-3317
Email: rnhs-ca@ix.netcom.com
Type of Counseling: Prepurchase Counseling, Default/Foreclosure Counseling
Affiliate of: NEIGHBORHOOD REINVESTMENT CORPORATION

CONSUMER CREDIT COUNSELING SERVICES OF EAST BAY
700 Barrett Avenue
Richmond, CA 94801-
510-729-6966
Toll-Free: 888-788-8528
Fax: 510-729-6961
Website: www.cccsebay.org
Type of Counseling: Prepurchase Counseling, Default/Foreclosure Counseling, Rental Counseling

**VOLUNTEER CENTER OF RIVERSIDE COUNTY
2060 University Avenue
Riverside, CA 92517
909-686-4402
Fax: 909-686-7417
Type of Counseling: Rental Counseling
Affiliate of: HOUSING OPPORTUNITIES, INCORPORATED

SPRINGBOARD NON PROFIT CONSUMER CREDIT MANAGEMENT
6370 Magnolia Ave Ste 200
Riverside, CA 92517-2149
909-781-0114
Toll-Free: 800-947-3752
Fax: 909-781-9896
Email: springboard@credit.org
Website: www.credit.org
Type of Counseling: Default/Foreclosure Counseling, Rental Counseling, Prepurchase Counseling

CONSUMER CREDIT COUNSELING SERVICE OF SACRAMENTO VALLEY
8795 Folsom Boulevard, Suite 250
Sacramento, CA 95826
916-379-3600
Toll-Free: 800-736-2227
Fax: 916-379-0626
Website: www.cccssacto.org
Type of Counseling: HECM Counseling, Default/Foreclosure Counseling, Prepurchase Counseling

**ACORN HOUSING CORPORATION
4921 San Francisco Blvd.
Sacramento, CA 95820
916-451-9659
Fax: 916-455-1797
Type of Counseling: Prepurchase Counseling, Default/Foreclosure Counseling
Affiliate of: ACORN HOUSING CORPORATION

CONSUMER CREDIT COUNSELING SERVICE OF SACRAMENTO VALLEY - DOWNTOWN
800 H St.
Sacramento, CA 95814
916-379-3600
Toll-Free: 800-736-2227
Fax: 916-379-0636
Type of Counseling: Prepurchase Counseling, Default/Foreclosure Counseling, HECM Counseling

SACRAMENTO NEIGHBORHOOD HOUSING SERVICES HOMEOWNERSHIP CENTER
3447 5th Avenue
Sacramento, CA 95817-
916-452-5361
Fax: 916-431-3209
Type of Counseling: Prepurchase Counseling, Default/Foreclosure Counseling, Rental Counseling

CONSUMER CREDIT COUNSELING SERVICE OF VENTURA COUNTY, INCORPORATED
601 E Romie Lane
Suite 9
Salinas, CA 93901-4229
831-751-9517
Fax: 831-751-9521
Type of Counseling: Default/Foreclosure Counseling, Rental Counseling, Prepurchase Counseling, HECM Counseling

**NEIGHBORHOOD HOUSING SERVICES OF THE INLAND EMPIRE, INCORPORATED
1390 North D ST
San Bernardino, CA 92405
909-884-6891
Fax: 909-884-6893
Email: dawkins@nhsie.org
Type of Counseling: HECM Counseling, Default/Foreclosure Counseling, Rental Counseling, Prepurchase Counseling
Affiliate of: NEIGHBORHOOD REINVESTMENT CORPORATION

SPRINGBOARD- SAN BERNARDINO
1814 Commerce Center West
Suite B
San Bernardino, CA 92408
800 947-3752
Fax: 909-781-8027
Type of Counseling: Prepurchase Counseling, Rental Counseling, Default/Foreclosure Counseling, HECM Counseling

SPRINGBOARD- SAN BERNARDINO
1814 Commerce Center West
Suite B
San Bernardino, CA 92408-
800-947-3752
Toll-Free: 800-947-3752
Fax: 909-890-4071
Type of Counseling: Default/Foreclosure Counseling, Rental Counseling, Prepurchase Counseling

SPRINGBOARD- SAN BERNARDINO
7285 Boulder Ave.
San Bernardino, CA 92402
800 947 3752
Fax: 909-781-8027
Type of Counseling: HECM Counseling, Prepurchase Counseling, Default/Foreclosure Counseling, Rental Counseling

**SAN DIEGO URBAN LEAGUE
720 Gateway Center Drive
San Diego, CA 92102-
619-263-3115
Fax: 619-263-3660
Email: michelle@sdul.org
Type of Counseling: Prepurchase Counseling, Default/Foreclosure Counseling, HECM Counseling, Rental Counseling
Affiliate of: NATIONAL URBAN LEAGUE

**SAN DIEGO NEIGHBORHOOD HOUSING SERVICES, INCORPORATED
4336 54th St., Ste B
San Diego, CA 92115
619-229-2370
Fax: 619-229-2375
Type of Counseling: Prepurchase Counseling
Affiliate of: NEIGHBORHOOD REINVESTMENT CORPORATION

CONSUMER CREDIT COUNSELORS OF SAN DIEGO AND IMPERIAL COUNTY
1550 Hotel Cir N Ste 110
San Diego, CA 92108-2901
888-298-2227
Fax: 619-542-1328
Type of Counseling: HECM Counseling, Default/Foreclosure Counseling, Rental Counseling, Prepurchase Counseling

SAN DIEGO HOME LOAN COUNSELING AND EDUCATION CENTER
3180 University Avenue Suite 430
San Diego, CA 92104
619-624-2330
Fax: 619-624-0314
Type of Counseling: Default/Foreclosure Counseling, Prepurchase Counseling

UNION OF PAN ASIAN COMMUNITIES
3288 El Cahon Boulevard, #3
San Diego, CA 92104
619-280-5197
Fax: 619-235-9002
Type of Counseling: Default/Foreclosure Counseling, Prepurchase Counseling

SPRINGBOARD- SAN DIEGO
8998 El Cajon Boulevard
San Diego, CA 92115
800-947-3752
Type of Counseling: Prepurchase Counseling, Default/Foreclosure Counseling

SPRINGBOARD- SAN DIEGO
7710 Balboa Avenue, Suite 218-F
San Diego, CA 92111
800-947-3752
Type of Counseling: Prepurchase Counseling, Default/Foreclosure Counseling

CONSUMER CREDIT COUNSELORS OF SAN DIEGO AND IMPERIAL COUNTY
15373 Innovation Dr Ste 115
San Diego, CA 92128-3413
888-298-2227
Fax: 858-276-0296
Type of Counseling: HECM Counseling, Default/Foreclosure Counseling, Rental Counseling, Prepurchase Counseling

SPRINGBOARD- SAN DIEGO
2550 Fifth Ave, Suite 169
San Diego, CA 92103
800-947-3752
Type of Counseling: Prepurchase Counseling, Default/Foreclosure Counseling

UNION OF PAN ASIAN COMMUNITIES
1031 25th Street
San Diego, CA 92102
619-232-6454
Fax: 619-235-9002
Type of Counseling: Default/Foreclosure Counseling, Prepurchase Counseling

NEIGHBORHOOD HOUSE ASSOCIATION
841 S 41st St
San Diego, CA 92113-1801
619-263-7761
Fax: 619-263-6398
Email: ebrown@neighborhoodhouse.org
Type of Counseling: HECM Counseling, Default/Foreclosure Counseling, Rental Counseling, Prepurchase Counseling

CONSUMER CREDIT COUNSELING SERVICES
1406 A Valencia St
San Francisco, CA 94110
800-777-7526
Toll-Free: 800-777-7526
Fax: 415-788-7817
Type of Counseling: Default/Foreclosure Counseling, Rental Counseling, Prepurchase Counseling, HECM Counseling

CONSUMER CREDIT COUNSELING SERVICES OF SAN FRANCISCO
150 Post Street, 5th floor
San Francisco, CA 94108-
800-777-7526
Toll-Free: 800-777-7526
Fax: 415-788-7817
Type of Counseling: HECM Counseling, Default/Foreclosure Counseling, Rental Counseling, Prepurchase Counseling
Affiliate of: NATIONAL FOUNDATION FOR CONSUMER CREDIT, INCORPORATED

PROJECT SENTINEL
25 Van Ness Avenue #800
San Francisco, CA
415-468-7464
Fax: 650-321-4173
Type of Counseling: Prepurchase Counseling, Default/Foreclosure Counseling, HECM Counseling, Rental Counseling

SAN FRANCISCO HOUSING DEVELOPMENT CORPORATION
5266 Third St.
San Francisco, CA 94124
415-822-1022
Fax: 415-822-1077
Type of Counseling: Default/Foreclosure Counseling,

Prepurchase Counseling, Rental Counseling

CONSUMER CREDIT COUNSELING SERVICE OF VENTURA COUNTY, INCORPORATED
2150 Alum Rock
San Jose, CA 95116-
408-923-3914
Fax: 408-251-0218
Type of Counseling: Default/Foreclosure Counseling, Prepurchase Counseling, Rental Counseling
Affiliate of: NATIONAL FOUNDATION FOR CONSUMER CREDIT, INCORPORATED

PROJECT SENTINEL
111W. St. John Street Suite 302
San Jose, CA
408-287-2943
Fax: 650-321-4173
Type of Counseling:Prepurchase Counseling, Default/Foreclosure Counseling, HECM Counseling, Rental Counseling

CONSUMER CREDIT COUNSELING SERVICE OF VENTURA COUNTY, INCORPORATED SAN LUIS OBISPO
3220 S. Higuera, Ste. 232
San Luis Obispo, CA 93401
800-540-2227
Toll-Free: 800-540-2227
Fax: 805-383-7722
Type of Counseling: Prepurchase Counseling, Default/Foreclosure Counseling, Rental Counseling, HECM Counseling

CONSUMER CREDIT COUNSELING SERVICE OF SAN FRANCISCO, SAN MATEO
520 El Camino Real, Ste. 310
San Mateo, CA 94402
800-777-7526
Toll-Free: 800-777-7526
Fax: 415-788-7817
Type of Counseling: Prepurchase Counseling, Default/Foreclosure Counseling, Rental Counseling, HECM Counseling

HUMAN INVESTMENT PROJECT, INCORPORATED
364 S Railroad Ave
San Mateo, CA 94401-4024
650-341-5679
Fax: 650-348-0284
Type of Counseling: HECM Counseling

CONSUMER CREDIT COUNSELING SERVICE OF EAST BAY, INCORPORATED
13925 San Pablo Ave Ste 110
San Pablo, CA 94806-3675
510-729-6966
Fax: 510-729-6961
Type of Counseling: HECM Counseling, Default/Foreclosure Counseling, Rental Counseling, Prepurchase Counseling

CONSUMER CREDIT COUNSELING SERVICES OF SAN FRANCISCO, SAN RAFAEL
950 Northgate Ave., Ste. 204
San Rafael, CA 94903
800-777-7526
Toll-Free: 800-777-7526
Fax: 415-788-7817
Type of Counseling: Prepurchase Counseling, Default/Foreclosure Counseling, Rental Counseling, HECM Counseling

CONSUMER CREDIT COUNSELING SERVICE OF ORANGE COUNTY
2115 N Broadway
Santa Ana, CA 92706-2613
714-547-2227
Fax: 714-245-1690
Type of Counseling: HECM Counseling, Default/Foreclosure Counseling, Rental Counseling, Prepurchase Counseling

CONSUMER CREDIT COUNSELING SERVICE OF ORANGE COUNTY
1920 Old Tustin Ave
Santa Ana, CA 92705
714-247-2227
Fax: 714-245-1680
Email: gbengoch@cccsoc.org
Type of Counseling: HECM Counseling, Default/Foreclosure Counseling, Rental Counseling, Prepurchase Counseling

FAIR HOUSING COUNCIL OF ORANGE COUNTY
201 S. Broadway
Santa Ana, CA 92701-5633
714-569-0825
Toll-Free: 800-698-3247
Fax: 714-835-0281
Type of Counseling: HECM Counseling, Default/Foreclosure Counseling, Rental Counseling, Prepurchase Counseling

CATHOLIC CHARITIES OF ORANGE COUNTY
1506 Brookhollow Dr Ste 112
Santa Ana, CA 92705-5405
714-957-4671
Fax: 714-957-4612
Type of Counseling: Default/Foreclosure Counseling, Rental Counseling, Prepurchase Counseling

CATHOLIC CHARITIES OF ORANGE COUNTY, INCORPORATED
3631 W Warner Ave
Santa Ana, CA 92704-5216
714-668-1130
Fax: 714-957-2523
Type of Counseling: Rental Counseling

CONSUMER CREDIT COUNSELING SERVICES OF VENTURA COUNTY, INCORPORATED SANTA BARBARA
5276 Hollister Ave., Ste. 405
Santa Barbara, CA 93105
800-540-2227
Toll-Free: 800-540-2227
Fax: 805-383-7722
Type of Counseling: Prepurchase Counseling, Default/Foreclosure Counseling, Rental Counseling, HECM Counseling

CONSUMER CREDIT COUNSELING SERVICE OF VENTURA COUNTY, INCORPORATED
1825 de La Cruz Blvd Ste 204
Santa Clara, CA 95050-3012
408-988-7881
Toll-Free: 800-969-7526
Fax: 408-988-0911
Website: www.cccssc.org
Type of Counseling: Rental Counseling, Prepurchase Counseling, HECM Counseling, Default/Foreclosure Counseling
Affiliate of: NATIONAL FOUNDATION FOR CONSUMER CREDIT, INCORPORATED

CONSUMER CREDIT COUNSELING SERVICES OF VENTURA COUNTY, INCORPORATED SANTA MARIA
1203 S. Broadway St.
Santa Maria, CA 93454

800-540-2227
Toll-Free: 800-540-2227
Fax: 805-383-7722
Type of Counseling: Prepurchase Counseling, Default/Foreclosure Counseling, Rental Counseling, HECM Counseling

CONSUMER CREDIT COUNSELING SERVICE OF LOS ANGELES
2444 Wilshire Blvd Ste 501
Santa Monica, CA 90403-5808
323-890-9500
Toll-Free: 800-750-2227
Fax: 323-890-9590
Type of Counseling: HECM Counseling, Default/Foreclosure Counseling, Rental Counseling, Prepurchase Counseling

**CATHOLIC CHARITIES, DIOCESE OF SANTA ROSA
PO Box 4900
Santa Rosa, CA 95402-4900
707-528-8712
Fax: 707-575-4910
Type of Counseling: Prepurchase Counseling, Default/Foreclosure Counseling, Rental Counseling, HECM Counseling
Affiliate of: CATHOLIC CHARITIES USA

CONSUMER CREDIT COUNSELING SERVICE OF SAN FRANCISCO, SANTA ROSA
85 Brookwood Ave., Ste. 14
Santa Rosa, CA 95404
800-777-7526
Toll-Free: 800-777-7526
Fax: 415-788-7817
Type of Counseling: Prepurchase Counseling, Default/Foreclosure Counseling, Rental Counseling, HECM Counseling

**CABRILLO ECONOMIC DEVELOPMENT CORPORATION
11011 Azahar Street
Saticoy, CA 93004
805-659-3791
Fax: 805-659-3195
Email: cdc@rain.org
Type of Counseling: Prepurchase Counseling
Affiliate of: NATIONAL COUNCIL OF LA RAZA

CONSUMER CREDIT COUNSELING SERVICE OF LOS ANGELES
25129 The Old Road Ste 200
Stevenson Ranch, CA 91381
323-890-9500
Toll-Free: 800-750-2227
Fax: 323-890-9590
Type of Counseling: HECM Counseling, Default/Foreclosure Counseling, Rental Counseling, Prepurchase Counseling

CONSUMER CREDIT COUNSELING SERVICE OF MID-COUNTY
2575 Grand Canal Blvd., Ste 100
Stockton, CA 95207
209-956-1170
Fax: 209-956-1178
Type of Counseling: HECM Counseling, Default/Foreclosure Counseling, Prepurchase Counseling, Rental Counseling

PROJECT SENTINEL
1055 Sunnyvale Saratoga Rd Ste 3
Sunnyvale, CA 94087-2539
888-331-3332
Toll-Free: 888-321-3332
Fax: 408-720-0810
Type of Counseling: Default/Foreclosure Counseling, Rental Counseling

CONSUMER CREDIT COUNSELING SERVICE OF LOS ANGELES
18401 Burbank Blvd Ste 127
Tarzana, CA 91356-2803
323-890-9500
Toll-Free: 800-750-2227
Fax: 323-890-9590
Type of Counseling: HECM Counseling, Default/Foreclosure Counseling, Rental Counseling, Prepurchase Counseling

SPRINGBOARD- TEMECULA
27715 Jefferson Ave Ste 113 E
Temecula, CA 92590-2660
800-947 3752
Fax: 909-781-8027
Type of Counseling: Default/Foreclosure Counseling, Rental Counseling

CONSUMER CREDIT COUNSELING SERVICE OF VENTURA COUNTY, INCORPORATED THOUSAND OAKS
80 E. Hillcrest Dr., Ste. 102
Thousand Oaks, CA 91360
800-540-2227
Toll-Free: 800-540-2227
Fax: 805-383-7722
Type of Counseling: Prepurchase Counseling, Default/Foreclosure Counseling, Rental Counseling, HECM Counseling

CONSUMER CREDIT COUNSELING SERVICE OF LOS ANGELES
3848 Carson St Ste E103
Torrance, CA 90503-6701
323-890-9500
Toll-Free: 800-750-2227
Fax: 323-890-9500
Type of Counseling: HECM Counseling, Default/Foreclosure Counseling, Rental Counseling, Prepurchase Counseling

SPRINGBOARD- TWENTY-NINE PALMS
29 Palms Military Base
Twenty-Nine Palms, CA 92278
909-781-0114
Fax: 909-781-9896
Type of Counseling: Default/Foreclosure Counseling, Rental Counseling, Prepurchase Counseling

CONSUMER CREDIT COUNSELING SERVICE OF SACRAMENTO VALLEY - VACAVILLE
11 Cemon St.
Vacaville, CA 95688
916-379-3600
Toll-Free: 8007362227
Fax: 9163790636
Type of Counseling: Prepurchase Counseling, Default/Foreclosure Counseling, HECM Counseling

CITY OF VACAVILLE OFFICE OF HOUSING AND REDEVELOPMENT
40 Eldridge Ave #1-5
Vacaville, CA 95688-6800
707-449-5675
Fax: 707-449-6242
Email: jdias@ci.vacaville.ca.us
Type of Counseling: HECM Counseling, Default/Foreclosure Counseling, Rental Counseling, Prepurchase Counseling

**VALLEJO NEIGHBORHOOD HOUSING SERVICES, INCORPORATED
610 Lemon St
Vallejo, CA 94590-7276
707-552-4663

Fax: 707-643-2143
Email: reneew@fmcompserve.com
Type of Counseling:
HECM Counseling,
Default/Foreclosure Counseling,
Prepurchase Counseling, Rental
Counseling
Affiliate of: NEIGHBORHOOD
REINVESTMENT
CORPORATION

CONSUMER CREDIT
COUNSELING SERVICES OF
EAST BAY
515 Broadway Street, D3
Vallejo, CA 94590-
510-729-6966
Toll-Free: 888-788-8528
Fax: 510-729-6961
Website: www.cccsebay.org
Type of Counseling: Prepurchase
Counseling, Default/Foreclosure
Counseling, Rental Counseling

CONSUMER CREDIT
COUNSELING SERVICE OF
VENTURA COUNTY,
INCORPORATED VENTURA
1915 E. Main St.
Ventura, CA 93001
800-540-2227
Toll-Free: 800-540-2227
Fax: 805-383-7722
Type of Counseling:
Prepurchase Counseling,
Default/Foreclosure Counseling,
Rental Counseling, HECM
Counseling

SPRINGBOARD- VICTORVILLE
14298 Saint Andrews Dr
Suite 1
Victorville, CA 92392-4367
909-781-0114
Toll-Free: 800-947-3752
Fax: 909-781-9896
Type of Counseling:
Default/Foreclosure Counseling

CONSUMER CREDIT
COUNSELING SERVICE OF
KERN AND TULARE COUNTIES
718 W Center Ave Ste C
Visalia, CA 93291-6016
559-732-2227
Toll-Free: 800-272-2482
Fax: 661-324-0750
Email: nancyjohnson
cccsbakersfield@att.net
Type of Counseling:
HECM Counseling,
Default/Foreclosure Counseling,
Prepurchase Counseling

**SELF HELP ENTERPRISES
8445 W. Elowin Court
Visalia, CA 93279-
559-651-1000
Fax: 559-651-3634
Email: tomc@selfhelpenterprises.org
Type of Counseling: Prepurchase
Counseling
Affiliate of: NATIONAL COUNCIL
OF LA RAZA

CONSUMER CREDIT
COUNSELING SERVICE OF
VENTURA COUNTY,
INCORPORATED
406 Main Street, Room 319
Watsonville, CA 95077-
831-728-5160
Fax: 831-728-5195
Type of Counseling:
Default/Foreclosure Counseling,
Prepurchase Counseling, Rental
Counseling
Affiliate of: NATIONAL
FOUNDATION FOR CONSUMER
CREDIT, INCORPORATED

CONSUMER CREDIT
COUNSELING SERVICE OF LOS
ANGELES
1700 West Cameron Ste 108
West Covina, CA 91790-2707
323-890-9500
Toll-Free: 800-750-2227
Fax: 323-890-9500
Type of Counseling:
HECM Counseling,
Default/Foreclosure Counseling,
Rental Counseling, Prepurchase
Counseling

SPRINGBOARD- WEST COVINA
100 N. Barranca Ave.
7th Fl., Ste 17
West Covina, CA 91791-1600
800-947-3752
Type of Counseling:
Prepurchase Counseling,
Default/Foreclosure Counseling

CONSUMER CREDIT
COUNSELING SERVICE OF
SACRAMENTO VALLEY -
WOODLAND
266 W. Main St.
Woodland, CA 95695
916-379-3600
Toll-Free: 800-736-2227
Fax: 916-379-0636
Type of Counseling:
Prepurchase Counseling,
Default/Foreclosure Counseling,
HECM Counseling

CONSUMER CREDIT
COUNSELING SERVICES OF
SOUTHERN OREGON
999 Main St., #D
Yreka, CA 96097
530-841-1516
Fax: 530-841-1516
Type of Counseling: Prepurchase
Counseling, Rental Counseling

Colorado

CITY OF AURORA COMMUNITY
DEVELOPMENT DIVISION
9801 E. Colfax Ave.
Aurora, CO 80010
303-739-7900
Fax: 303-361-2989
Type of Counseling:
Prepurchase Counseling, Rental
Counseling, Default/Foreclosure
Counseling, HECM Counseling

BOULDER COUNTY HOUSING
AUTHORITY
3482 North Broadway
Boulder, CO 80306-0471
303-441-3929
Fax: 303-441-1537
Email: njcho@co.boulder.co.us
Type of Counseling: HECM
Counseling, Default/Foreclosure
Counseling, Rental Counseling,
Prepurchase Counseling

**CONSUMER CREDIT
COUNSELING SERVICE OF
GREATER DENVER,
INCORPORATED
5350 Manhattan Circle, #231
Boulder, CO 80303
303-632-2100
Toll-Free: 800-224-9885
Fax: 303-543-9814
Type of Counseling:
Default/Foreclosure Counseling,
Prepurchase Counseling, Rental
Counseling

SUMMIT HOUSING AUTHORITY
106 North Ridge
Breckenridge, CO 80424
970-453-3555
Fax: 970-453-3554
Website:
www.co.summit.co.us/housing/
Type of Counseling: Prepurchase
Counseling

CONSUMER CREDIT
COUNSELING SERVICE OF
SOUTHERN COLORADO
1233 Lake Plaza Dr Ste A
Colorado Springs, CO 80906-3555

719-576-0909
Toll-Free: 888-258-0685
Fax: 719-576-3756
Email: cccs@codenet.net
Type of Counseling:
HECM Counseling,
Default/Foreclosure Counseling,
Rental Counseling, Prepurchase
Counseling
Affiliate of: NATIONAL
FOUNDATION FOR CONSUMER
CREDIT, INCORPORATED

ADAMS COUNTY HOUSING
AUTHORITY
7190 Colorado Blvd 6th Fl
Commerce City, CO 80022-1812
303-227-2075
Fax: 303-227-2098
Type of Counseling: HECM
Counseling, Default/Foreclosure
Counseling, Rental Counseling,
Prepurchase Counseling

**CONSUMER CREDIT
COUNSELING SERVICE OF
GREATER DENVER,
INCOPRORATED
928 E. Main
Cortez, CO 81321
303-632-2100
Toll-Free: 800-224-9885
Fax: 218-726-1251
Type of Counseling:
Default/Foreclosure Counseling,
Prepurchase Counseling, Rental
Counseling

**CONSUMER CREDIT
COUNSELING SERVICE OF
GREATER DENVER,
INCORPORATED
1740 Broadway
Denver, CO 80202
303-632-2100
Toll-Free: 800-224-9885
Fax: 303-863-5865
Type of Counseling:
Default/Foreclosure Counseling,
Prepurchase Counseling, Rental
Counseling

**NEWSED COMMUNITY
DEVELOPMENT CORPORATION
1029 Santa Fe Drive
Denver, CO 80204
303-534-8342
Fax: 303-534-7418
Email: laura@newsed.org
Type of Counseling: Prepurchase
Counseling
Affiliate of: NATIONAL COUNCIL
OF LA RAZA

**ACORN HOUSING
CORPORATION
1760 High St
Denver, CO 80205
303-388-1989
Fax: 303-393-1451
Type of Counseling:
Prepurchase Counseling,
Default/Foreclosure Counseling
Affiliate of: ACORN HOUSING
CORPORATION

**DEL NORTE NEIGHBORHOOD
DEVELOPMENT CORPORATION
2926 Zuni Street, #202
Denver, CO 80211
303-477-4774
Fax: 303-433-0924
Email: delnortndc@aol.com
Type of Counseling: Prepurchase
Counseling
Affiliate of: NATIONAL COUNCIL
OF LA RAZA

**CONSUMER CREDIT
COUNSELING SERVICE OF
GREATER DENVER,
INCORPORATED
10375 East Harvard Ave #300
Denver, CO 80231
303-632-2100
Toll-Free: 800-224-9885
Fax: 303-632-2013
Type of Counseling:
Default/Foreclosure Counseling,
Rental Counseling, Prepurchase
Counseling
Affiliate of: NATIONAL
FOUNDATION FOR CONSUMER
CREDIT, INCORPORATED

**CONSUMER CREDIT
COUNSELING SERVICE OF
GREATER DENVER,
INCORPORATED
5353 W. Dartmouth, Suite 305
Denver, CO 80227
303-632-2100
Toll-Free: 800-224-9885
Fax: 303-969-9137
Type of Counseling:
Default/Foreclosure Counseling,
Rental Counseling, Prepurchase
Counseling

BROTHERS REDEVELOPMENT,
INCORPORATED
2250 Eaton St
Denver, CO 80214-1210
303-202-6340
Fax: 303-274-1314
Email: meganb@briathome.org
Website: www.briathome.org
Type of Counseling:
HECM Counseling,
Default/Foreclosure Counseling,
Rental Counseling, Prepurchase
Counseling

**ROCKY MOUNTAIN MUTUAL
HOUSING ASSOCIATION,
INCORPORATED
1550 Park Avenue
Denver, CO 80218-
303-863-8651
Fax: 303-866-0850
Type of Counseling: Prepurchase
Counseling
Affiliate of: THE HOUSING
PARTNERSHIP NETWORK

**SOUTHWEST IMPROVEMENT
COUNCIL
1000 South Lowell Blvd.
Denver, CO 80219
303-934-8057
Fax: 303-934-0035
Email: lizswic@hotmail.com
Type of Counseling: Prepurchase
Counseling
Affiliate of: NATIONAL COUNCIL
OF LA RAZA

NORTHEAST DENVER HOUSING
CENTER
1735 Gaylord St
Denver, CO 80206-1208
303-377-3334
Fax: 303-377-3327
Type of Counseling:
HECM Counseling,
Default/Foreclosure Counseling,
Rental Counseling, Prepurchase
Counseling

SOUTHWEST COMMUNITY
RESOURCES
295 Girard St
Durango, CO 81303-
970-259-1086
Fax: 970-259-2037
Type of Counseling:
HECM Counseling,
Default/Foreclosure Counseling,
Rental Counseling, Prepurchase
Counseling

CONSUMER CREDIT
COUNSELING SERVICE OF
NORTHERN COLORADO AND
SOUTHEAST WYOMING
1247 Riverside Avenue
Fort Collins, CO 80524-3258
970-229-0695
Toll-Free: 800-424-2227
Fax: 970-229-0721
Website: www.cccsnc.org
Type of Counseling:

HECM Counseling,
Default/Foreclosure Counseling,
Rental Counseling, Prepurchase
Counseling
Affiliate of: NATIONAL
FOUNDATION FOR CONSUMER
CREDIT, INCORPORATED

NEIGHBOR TO NEIGHBOR
424 Pine St Ste 203
Fort Collins, CO 80524
970-484-7498
Fax: 970-407-7045
Type of Counseling:
HECM Counseling,
Default/Foreclosure Counseling,
Rental Counseling, Prepurchase
Counseling

TRI-COUNTY HOUSING,
INCORPORATED
34385 Highway 167
Fowler, CO 81039-5460
719-263-5460
Fax: 719-261-5168
Type of Counseling: Prepurchase
Counseling

**CONSUMER CREDIT
COUNSELING SERVICE OF
GREATER DENVER,
INCORPORATED
901 Grand Avenue
Glenwood Springs, CO 81602
303-632-2100
Toll-Free: 800-224-9885
Fax: 218-726-1251
Type of Counseling:
Default/Foreclosure Counseling,
Prepurchase Counseling, Rental
Counseling

GRAND JUNCTION HOUSING
AUTHORITY
1011 North 10th Street
Grand Junction, CO 81501
970-245-0388
Fax: 970-254-8347
Type of Counseling:
Default/Foreclosure Counseling,
Prepurchase Counseling

**CONSUMER CREDIT
COUNSELING OF GREATER
DENVER, INCORPORATED
2764 Compassor, Suite 217-5
Grand Junction, CO 81506
303-632-2100
Toll-Free: 800-224-9885
Fax: 303-243-6005
Type of Counseling:
Default/Foreclosure Counseling,
Prepurchase Counseling, Rental
Counseling

CONSUMER CREDIT
COUNSELING SERVICE
NORTHERN COLORADO AND
SOUTHEAST WYOMING
1228 8th St Ste 101
Greeley, CO 80631
970-229-0695
Fax: 970-229-0721
Website: www.cccsnc.org
Type of Counseling:
HECM Counseling,
Default/Foreclosure Counseling,
Rental Counseling, Prepurchase
Counseling
Affiliate of: NATIONAL
FOUNDATION FOR CONSUMER
CREDIT, INCORPORATED

CONSUMER CREDIT
COUNSELING SERVICE
NORTHERN COLORADO AND
SOUTHEAST WYOMING
2919 W. 17th Avenue
Longmont, CO 80503-
800-424-2227
Toll-Free: 800-424-2227
Fax: 970-229-0721
Website: www.cccsnc.org
Type of Counseling:
HECM Counseling,
Default/Foreclosure Counseling,
Rental Counseling, Prepurchase
Counseling

NEIGHBOR TO NEIGHBOR
565 North Cleveland Avenue
Loveland, CO 80537-4801
970-663-4163
Fax: 970-663-2860
Type of Counseling:
HECM Counseling,
Default/Foreclosure Counseling,
Rental Counseling, Prepurchase
Counseling

CONSUMER CREDIT
COUNSELING SERVICE N
COLORADO AND SOUTHEAST
WYOMING
315 E 7th St
Loveland, CO 80537-4801
970-229-0695
Fax: 970-229-0721
Website: www.cccsnc.org
Type of Counseling:
HECM Counseling,
Default/Foreclosure Counseling,
Rental Counseling, Prepurchase
Counseling

**NEIGHBORHOOD HOUSING
SERVICES OF PUEBLO,
INCORPORATED
825 N Greenwood Ave
Pueblo, CO 81003-2925
719-544-8078
Fax: 719-544-0271
Email: nhs5@ix.netcom.com
Type of Counseling:
Prepurchase Counseling,
Default/Foreclosure Counseling
Affiliate of: NEIGHBORHOOD
REINVESTMENT
CORPORATION

CONSUMER CREDIT
COUNSELING SERVICE OF
SOUTHERN COLORADO
200 West 1st Street, Suite 302
Pueblo, CO 81003
719-542-6620
Fax: 719-542-7057
Type of Counseling:
HECM Counseling,
Default/Foreclosure Counseling,
Rental Counseling, Prepurchase
Counseling

CATHOLIC CHARITIES OF THE
DIOCESE OF PUEBLO,
INCORPORATED
429 W. 10th Street, Suite 101
Pueblo, CO 81003
800-303-4690
Toll-Free: 800-303-4690
Fax: 719-544-4215
Type of Counseling:
HECM Counseling,
Default/Foreclosure Counseling,
Rental Counseling, Prepurchase
Counseling
Affiliate of: CATHOLIC
CHARITIES USA

CONSUMER CREDIT
COUNSELING SERVICE
NORTHERN COLORADO AND
SOUTHEAST WYOMING
508 S. 10th Avenue
Sterling, CO 80751-
800-424-2227
Toll-Free: 800-424-2227
Fax: 970-229-0721
Website: www.cccsnc.org
Type of Counseling:
HECM Counseling,
Default/Foreclosure Counseling,
Rental Counseling, Prepurchase
Counseling

**CONSUMER CREDIT
COUNSELING SERVICE OF
GREATER DENVER,
INCORPORATED
9101 Harlan
Westminister, CO 80030
303-632-2100
Toll-Free: 800-224-9885

Fax: 303-426-9029
Type of Counseling:
Default/Foreclosure Counseling, Prepurchase Counseling, Rental Counseling

COLORADO RURAL HOUSING DEVELOPMENT CORPORATION
3621 West 73rd Avenue, Suite C
Westminster, CO 80030
303-428-1448
Fax: 303-428-1989
Type of Counseling: Prepurchase Counseling

Connecticut

BRIDGEPORT NEIGHBORHOOD TRUST
177 State St, 5th Floor
Bridgeport, CT 06604-4806
203-332-7977
Fax: 203-579-2338
Type of Counseling:
Rental Counseling, Prepurchase Counseling, Default/Foreclosure Counseling

**ACORN HOUSING CORPORATION
2310 Main St. 3rd Fl.
Bridgeport, CT 06606
203-366-4180
Fax: 203-366-0020
Type of Counseling:
Prepurchase Counseling, Default/Foreclosure Counseling
Affiliate of: ACORN HOUSING CORPORATION

CONSUMER CREDIT COUNSELING SERVICE OF CONNECTICUT
40 Old Ridgebury Rd Ste. 105
Danbury, CT 06810
800-450-2808
Toll-Free: 800-450-2808
Fax: 203-798-2725
Type of Counseling:
HECM Counseling, Default/Foreclosure Counseling, Prepurchase Counseling

CONSUMER CREDIT COUNSELING SERVICE OF CONNECTICUT, INCORPORATED
111 Founders Plz Ste 1400
East Hartford, CT 06108-3212
800-450-2808
Fax: 860-282-2001
Type of Counseling:
Prepurchase Counseling, Rental Counseling, Default/Foreclosure Counseling, HECM Counseling

URBAN LEAGUE OF GREATER HARTFORD
1229 Albany Ave, 3rd floor
Hartford, CT 06112-2156
860-527-0147 x1421
Fax: 860-520-1159
Type of Counseling:
Prepurchase Counseling, Default/Foreclosure Counseling, Rental Counseling, HECM Counseling
Affiliate of: NATIONAL URBAN LEAGUE

**CO-OPPORTUNITY
117 Murphy Rd
Hartford, CT 06114
860-236-3617
Fax: 860-808-1757
Email: jerryd@co-opportunity.org
Type of Counseling: Prepurchase Counseling, Default/Foreclosure Counseling
Affiliate of: CITIZENS' HOUSING AND PLANNING ASSOCIATION, INCORPORATED

**HOUSING EDUCATION RESOURCE CENTER
901 Wethersfield Ave.
Hartford, CT 06114
860-296-4242
Fax: 860-296-1317
Email: herc@hartnet.org
Type of Counseling:
Prepurchase Counseling, Rental Counseling
Affiliate of: CITIZENS' HOUSING AND PLANNING ASSOCIATION, INCORPORATED

HARTFORD AREAS RALLY TOGETHER
227 Lawrence Street
Hartford, CT 06106
860-525-3449
Fax: 860-525-7759
Type of Counseling: Prepurchase Counseling
Affiliate of: CITIZENS' HOUSING AND PLANNING ASSOCIATION, INCORPORATED

**CO-OP INITIATIVES
999 Asylum Ave. Suite 506
Hartford, CT 06105
860-724-4940
Fax: 860-724-7102
Email:
TNADEAU@COOPINIT.ORG
Type of Counseling:
Prepurchase Counseling
Affiliate of: CITIZENS' HOUSING AND PLANNING ASSOCIATION, INCORPORATED

CONSUMER CREDIT COUNSELING SERVICE OF CONNECTICUT
185 Plains Rd
Suite W201
Milford, CT 06460-2474
800-450-2808
Fax: 203-882-3429
Type of Counseling:
HECM Counseling, Default/Foreclosure Counseling, Rental Counseling, Prepurchase Counseling

NEIGHBORHOOD HOUSING SERVICES OF NEW BRITAIN, INCORPORATED
223 Broad St
New Britain, CT 06053-4107
860-224-2433
Fax: 860-225-6131
Type of Counseling:
Default/Foreclosure Counseling, Rental Counseling, Prepurchase Counseling

**NEIGHBORHOOD HOUSING SERVICES OF NEW HAVEN, INCORPORATED
333 Sherman Ave
New Haven, CT 06511-3107
203-562-0598
Fax: 203-772-2876
Email: paley2@ix.netcom.com
Type of Counseling:
Prepurchase Counseling, Default/Foreclosure Counseling
Affiliate of: NEIGHBORHOOD REINVESTMENT CORPORATION

**ACORN HOUSING CORPORATION
215 Grand Avenue
New Haven, CT 06513
203-789-8671
Type of Counseling:
Prepurchase Counseling, Default/Foreclosure Counseling
Affiliate of: ACORN HOUSING CORPORATION

HILL DEVELOPMENT CORPORATION OF NEW HAVEN
649 Howard Avenue
New Haven, CT 06519-1506
203-776-3759
Fax: 203-785-1321

Type of Counseling:
Prepurchase Counseling,
Default/Foreclosure Counseling,
Rental Counseling

**SHILOH DEVELOPMENT CORP.
3 Garvin Street
New London, CT 06320
860-443-9647
Fax: 860-447-8812
Type of Counseling:
Prepurchase Counseling
Affiliate of: CONGRESS OF NATIONAL BLACK CHURCHES, INCORPORATED

**NEIGHBORHOOD HOUSING SERVICES OF NORWALK, INCORPORATED
23 Leonard St
Norwalk, CT 068502074
203-852-1717
Fax: 203-852-0879
Email: nhsnwlk@ix.netcom.com
Type of Counseling:
Default/Foreclosure Counseling,
Rental Counseling, Prepurchase Counseling
Affiliate of: NEIGHBORHOOD REINVESTMENT CORPORATION

**CATHOLIC CHARITIES
1020 Market Street
Norwich, CT 06360
860-889-8346
Type of Counseling:
Prepurchase Counseling, Rental Counseling, Default/Foreclosure Counseling
Affiliate of: CATHOLIC CHARITIES USA

CONNECTICUT HOUSING FINANCE AGENCY
999 West Street
Rocky Hill, CT 06067
860-721-9501
Fax: 860-571-4367
Type of Counseling:
Prepurchase Counseling,
Default/Foreclosure Counseling,
HECM Counseling

**NEIGHBORHOOD HOUSING SERVICE OF WATERBURY, INCORPORATED
139 Prospect St
Waterbury, CT 06710-2318
203-753-1896
Fax: 203-757-6496
Email: wbynhs@ix.netcom.com
Prepurchase Counseling,
Default/Foreclosure Counseling
Affiliate of: NEIGHBORHOOD REINVESTMENT CORPORATION

Delaware

NATIONAL COUNCIL ON AGRICULTURAL LIFE AND LABOR RESEARCH, INCORPORATED
20 E Division St
Dover, DE 199031092
302-678-9400
Fax: 302-678-9058
Type of Counseling: Prepurchase Counseling

FIRST STATE COMMUNITY ACTION AGENCY, INCORPORATED
308 N Railroad Ave
Georgetown, DE 19947-1252
302-856-7761
Toll-Free: 800-372-2240
Fax: 302-856-2599
Type of Counseling:
HECM Counseling,
Default/Foreclosure Counseling,
Rental Counseling, Prepurchase Counseling

DELAWARE STATE HOUSING AUTHORITY
Carvel StateOffice Building
Wilmington, DE 19801
302-577-5001
Fax: 302-577-5021
Type of Counseling: Prepurchase Counseling

YOUNG WOMEN'S CHRISTIAN ASSOCIATION, CENTERS FOR HOMEOWNERSHIP
233 King St
Wilmington, DE 19801-2521
302-888-7790
Fax: 302-658-7547
Type of Counseling:
Prepurchase Counseling,
Default/Foreclosure Counseling

NEIGHBORHOOD HOUSE, INCORPORATED
1218 B St
Wilmington, DE 19801-5844
302-652-3928
Fax: 302-652-3983
Email: karenqbrady@msn.com
Type of Counseling:
HECM Counseling,
Default/Foreclosure Counseling,
Rental Counseling, Prepurchase Counseling

COMMUNITY HOUSING, INCORPORATED
613 N Washington St
Wilmington, DE 19801-2135
302-652-3991
Fax: 302-652-3945
Type of Counseling:
HECM Counseling,
Default/Foreclosure Counseling,
Rental Counseling, Prepurchase Counseling

INTERFAITH HOUSING DELAWARE, INCORPORATED
2 S. Augustine Street Ste B
Wilmington, DE 19804
302-995-7428
Fax: 302-225-4770
Email: ckarnai@ihd.sbs.dca.net
Type of Counseling:
Rental Counseling, Prepurchase Counseling, HECM Counseling
Affiliate of: HOUSING OPPORTUNITIES, INCORPORATED

HOUSING OPPORTUNITIES OF NORTHERN DELAWARE
100 W. 10th Street, Ste 1004
Wilmington, DE 19501
302-429-0974
Fax: 302-429-0795
Type of Counseling:
Prepurchase Counseling,
Default/Foreclosure Counseling,
HECM Counseling, Rental Counseling

District Of Columbia

NEIGHBORHOOD REINVESTMENT CORPORATION
1325 G St NW
Washington, DC 20005-3104
202-220-2300
Fax: 202-376-2600

NEAR NORTHEAST COMMUNITY IMPROVEMENT CORPORATION
1326 Florida Ave NE
Washington, DC 20002-7108
202-399-6900
Fax: 202-399-6942
Email: WyHodgesl@aol.com
Type of Counseling:
HECM Counseling,
Default/Foreclosure Counseling,
Rental Counseling, Prepurchase Counseling

PEOPLES INVOLVEMENT CORPORATION
2146 Georgia Ave NW
Washington, DC 20001-3029
202-797-3900
Fax: 202-332-7891

UNIVERSITY LEGAL SERVICES
300 I St NE Ste 202
Washington, DC 20002-4389
202-547-4747
Fax: 202-547-2083
Type of Counseling:
HECM Counseling, Default/Foreclosure Counseling, Rental Counseling, Prepurchase Counseling

DISTRICT OF COLUMBIA HOUSING FINANCE AGENCY
815 Florida Ave.Suite 209,NW
Washington, DC 20001
202-777-1600
Fax: 202-986-6705
Type of Counseling:
Prepurchase Counseling

MARSHALL HEIGHTS COMMUNITY DEVELOPMENT ORGANIZATION, INCORPORATED
3939 Benning Road, NE
Washington, DC 20019-2662
202-396-1200
Fax: 202-396-4106
Type of Counseling:
HECM Counseling, Default/Foreclosure Counseling, Rental Counseling, Prepurchase Counseling

GREATER WASHINGTON URBAN LEAGUE
3501 14th St NW
Washington, DC 20010
202-265-8200
Fax: 202-328-3064
Email: jex6@aol.com
Type of Counseling:
Default/Foreclosure Counseling, Prepurchase Counseling, Rental Counseling, HECM Counseling
Affiliate of: NATIONAL URBAN LEAGUE

HOUSING COUNSELING SERVICES, INCORPORATED
2430 Ontario Rd NW
Washington, DC 20009-2705
202-667-7006
Fax: 202-462-5305
Type of Counseling:
HECM Counseling, Default/Foreclosure Counseling, Rental Counseling, Prepurchase Counseling

CONSUMER CREDIT COUNSELING SERVICE OF GREATER WASHINGTON
1275 K St NW
Washington, DC 20005-4006
202-682-1500
Fax: 202-682-1505
Type of Counseling:
HECM Counseling, Default/Foreclosure Counseling, Rental Counseling, Prepurchase Counseling

UNIVERSITY LEGAL SERVICES
3220 Pennsylvania Avenue SE
Suite 4
Washington, DC 20020
202-645-7175
Fax: 202-654-7178
Type of Counseling:
HECM Counseling, Default/Foreclosure Counseling, Rental Counseling, Prepurchase Counseling

NATIONAL COUNCIL OF LA RAZA
1111 19th Street NW Ste 1000
Washington, DC 20036
202-785-1670
Fax: 202-776-1792

HOMEFREE - U S A
318 Riggs Rd NE
Washington, DC 20011-2534
202-526-2000
Fax: 202-526-4072
Type of Counseling:
HECM Counseling, Default/Foreclosure Counseling, Prepurchase Counseling

**ACORN HOUSING CORPORATION
739 8th St SE
Washington, DC 20003-2802
202-547-9295
Fax: 202-546-2483
Type of Counseling:
Prepurchase Counseling, Default/Foreclosure Counseling
Affiliate of: ACORN HOUSING CORPORATION

**CATHOLIC CHARITIES OF THE ARCHDIOCESE OF WASHINGTON, D C
1438 Rhode Island Ave NE
Washington, DC 20018-3709
202-526-4100 ext.206
Fax: 202-526-1829
Type of Counseling:
Prepurchase Counseling, Default/Foreclosure Counseling, Rental Counseling, HECM Counseling
Affiliate of: CATHOLIC CHARITIES USA

CONGRESS OF NATIONAL BLACK CHURCHES, INCORPORATED
2000 L Street NW Suite 225
Washington, DC 20036-4962
202-296-5637
Fax: 202-296-4939
Type of Counseling: Prepurchase Counseling

**LYDIA'S HOUSE
4101 Martin Luther King Jr. Avenue SW
Washington, DC 20032
202-563-7629
Fax: 202-563-7621
Type of Counseling:
Prepurchase Counseling, Default/Foreclosure Counseling, Rental Counseling
Affiliate of: CONGRESS OF NATIONAL BLACK CHURCHES, INCORPORATED

LATINO ECONOMIC DEVELOPMENT CORPORATION
2316 18th Street NW
Washington, DC 20009
202-588-5102
Fax: 202-588-5204
Type of Counseling:
Prepurchase Counseling, Rental Counseling

Florida

HOMES IN PARTNERSHIP, INCORPORATED
235 E 5th St
Apopka, FL 32703-5315
407-886-2451
Fax: 407-886-5304
Type of Counseling: Prepurchase Counseling

CONSUMER CREDIT COUNSELING SERVICE OF WEST FLORIDA/ COUNTY COURTHOUSE
425 E. Central Ave. Rm 321
Blountstown, FL 32424
850-674-2678
Fax: 850-432-5078
Type of Counseling:

Prepurchase Counseling, Rental Counseling, Default/Foreclosure Counseling, HECM Counseling

CONSUMER CREDIT COUNSELING SERVICES
9045 La Fontana Blvd
Suite C6-B
Boca Raton, FL 33434-5633
800-330-2227
Fax: 561-470-1390
Email: derrick@cccsinc.com
Website: www.cccsinc.com
Type of Counseling:
HECM Counseling, Default/Foreclosure Counseling, Rental Counseling, Prepurchase Counseling

CONSUMER CREDIT COUNSELING SERVICE OF THE FLORIDA GULF
4910 14th St W
Suite 104
Bradenton, FL 34207-2482
941-746-4476
Toll-Free: 800-741-7040
Fax: 813-755-6944
Email: LPICHCCCS@aol.com
Website: www.cccsfl.org
Type of Counseling:
HECM Counseling, Default/Foreclosure Counseling, Rental Counseling, Prepurchase Counseling

MANATEE OPPORTUNITY COUNCIL, INCORPORATED
236 9th Ave W
Bradenton, FL 34205-8833
941-708-8440
Fax: 941-708-8445
Email: mocsandy@aol.com
Type of Counseling:
HECM Counseling, Default/Foreclosure Counseling, Rental Counseling, Prepurchase Counseling

CONSUMER CREDIT COUNSELING SERVICE OF THE FLORIDA GULF
407 N. Parsons, Suite 104A
Brandon, FL 33510-
813-289-8923
Fax: 813-289-6452
Email: LPICHCCCS@aol.com
Website: www.cccsfl.org
Type of Counseling:
HECM Counseling, Default/Foreclosure Counseling, Rental Counseling, Prepurchase Counseling

CONSUMER CREDIT COUNSELING SERVICE OF THE FLORIDA GULF
1 East Jefferson Street
Brooksville, FL 34605-3460
352-754-9675
Fax: 352-754-5545
Email: LPICHCCCS@aol.com
Website: www.cccsfl.org
Type of Counseling:
HECM Counseling, Default/Foreclosure Counseling, Rental Counseling, Prepurchase Counseling

CONSUMER CREDIT COUNSELING SERVICE OF THE FLORIDA GULF
2503 Del Prado Blvd.
Cape Coral, FL 33990
914-278-3121
Fax: 941-772-7112
Email: LPICHCCCS@aol.com
Website: www.cccsfl.org
Type of Counseling:
HECM Counseling, Default/Foreclosure Counseling, Rental Counseling, Prepurchase Counseling

**UNIVERSAL TRUTH COMMUNITY DEVELOPMENT CORPORATION
21310 NW 37th Ave.
Carol City, FL 33056
305-624-4991
Fax: 305-628-2008
Type of Counseling:
Prepurchase Counseling, Default/Foreclosure Counseling
Affiliate of: CONGRESS OF NATIONAL BLACK CHURCHES, INCORPORATED

**CLEARWATER NEIGHBORHOOD HOUSING SERVICES, INCORPORATED
608 N Garden Ave
Clearwater, FL 33755
727-442-4155
Fax: 727-446-4911
Email: clwnhs@ix.netcom.com
Type of Counseling:
Prepurchase Counseling, Default/Foreclosure Counseling
Affiliate of: NEIGHBORHOOD REINVESTMENT CORPORATION

THE HOMEBUYER'S CLUB
2139 NE Coachman Road
Clearwater, FL 33765
727-446-6222
Fax: 727-446-8727
Website: www.tampabaycdc.org
Type of Counseling:
Prepurchase Counseling, Default/Foreclosure Counseling

CONSUMER CREDIT COUNSELING SERVICE OF WEST FLORIDA
648-B North Wilson
Crestview, FL 32536
850-689-0177
Fax: 850-432-5078
Type of Counseling:
Prepurchase Counseling, Rental Counseling, Default/Foreclosure Counseling, HECM Counseling

CENTRAL FLORIDA COMMUNITY DEVELOPMENT CORPORATION
847 Orange Avenue
Daytona Beach, FL 32114
386-258-7520
Fax: 386-238-3428
Type of Counseling:
Prepurchase Counseling, Rental Counseling

MID-FLORIDA HOUSING COUNSELING PARTNERSHIP, INCORPORATED
330 North Street
Daytona Beach, FL 32114
386-252-7200
Toll-Free: 800-644-6125
Fax: 386-239-7119
Email: MFHP330@aol.com
Type of Counseling:
Default/Foreclosure Counseling, Prepurchase Counseling, Rental Counseling

CONSUMER CREDIT COUNSELING SERVICE OF CENTRAL FLORIDA
1176 Pelican Bay Drive
Daytona Beach, FL 32119
386-761-5361
Toll-Free: 800-388-2227
Fax: 386-756-6705
Email: counselor@cccscfl.com
Type of Counseling:
Prepurchase Counseling, HECM Counseling, Default/Foreclosure Counseling, Rental Counseling

CONSUMER CREDIT COUNSELING SERVICE OF WEST FLORIDA
11-B East Nelson
DeFuniak Springs, FL 32433
850-892-5234
Fax: 850-432-5078
Type of Counseling:

Prepurchase Counseling, Rental Counseling, Default/Foreclosure Counseling, HECM Counseling

URBAN LEAGUE SOUTH COUNTY OFFICE
301 SW 14th Ave
Delray Beach, FL 33444-1455
561-265-3318
Fax: 561-265-3318
Type of Counseling:
HECM Counseling, Default/Foreclosure Counseling, Rental Counseling, Prepurchase Counseling

CONSUMER CREDIT COUNSELING SERVICE OF WEST FLORIDA/EGLIN AIR FORCE BASE
502 W. Van Matre Ave. Suite 1
Eglin Air Force Base, FL 32542
850-678-7726
Fax: 850-432-5078
Type of Counseling:
Prepurchase Counseling, Rental Counseling, Default/Foreclosure Counseling, HECM Counseling

CREDIT COUNSELORS OF NORTH AMERICA
3317 NW 10 Terrace #408
Fort Lauderdale, FL 33309
800-330-1616
Toll-Free: 800-330-1616
Fax: 954-563-3052
Type of Counseling:
Default/Foreclosure Counseling, Prepurchase Counseling, Rental Counseling

**NEW VISIONS COMMUNITY DEVELOPMENT CORPORATION
1214 NE Fourth Avenue
Fort Lauderdale, FL 33304
954-768-0920
Fax: 954-768-0964
Type of Counseling:
Prepurchase Counseling, Default/Foreclosure Counseling
Affiliate of: CONGRESS OF NATIONAL BLACK CHURCHES, INCORPORATED

CONSUMER CREDIT COUNSELING SERVICE OF THE FLORIDA GULF
12811 Kenwood Lane, Suite 111
Fort Myers, FL 33907
941-278-3121
Fax: 941-278-9097
Email: LPICHCCCS@aol.com
Website: www.cccsfl.org
Type of Counseling:
HECM Counseling, Default/Foreclosure Counseling, Rental Counseling, Prepurchase Counseling

CONSUMER CREDIT COUNSELING SERVICES OF WEST FLORIDA
244 Racetrack Rd NE
Fort Walton Beach, FL 32547-1866
850-314-9888
Fax: 850-314-9891
Type of Counseling:
HECM Counseling, Default/Foreclosure Counseling, Prepurchase Counseling

CONSUMER CREDIT COUNSELING SERVICE OF MID-FLORIDA, INCORPORATED
1227 NW 16th Ave
Gainesville, FL 32601-4023
352-867-1865
Fax: 352-867-8490
Type of Counseling:
HECM Counseling, Default/Foreclosure Counseling, Rental Counseling, Prepurchase Counseling

CITY OF GAINESVILLE HOUSING AND ECON0MIC DEVELOPMENT
200 E University Ave Rm. 341
Gainesville, FL 32602-0490
352-334-5026
Fax: 352-334-2272
Type of Counseling:
HECM Counseling, Default/Foreclosure Counseling, Rental Counseling, Prepurchase Counseling

**NEIGHBORHOOD HOUSING AND DEVELOPMENT CORPORATION OF GREATER GAINESVILLE
633 NW 8th Ave
Gainesville, FL 32601
352-380-9119
Fax: 352-380-9170
Email: dlherk@aol.com
Type of Counseling:
Prepurchase Counseling, Default/Foreclosure Counseling
Affiliate of: NEIGHBORHOOD REINVESTMENT CORPORATION

GOULDS COMMUNITY DEVELOPMENT CORPORATION
11293 S. W. 216th St.
Goulds, FL 33170
305-278-6950
Fax: 305-278-1519
Type of Counseling:
Prepurchase Counseling, Rental Counseling

CONSUMER CREDIT COUNSELING SERVICES
1800 W 49th St Ste 303
Hialeah, FL 33012-2900
954-828-0585
Toll-Free: 800-928-2227
Fax: 305-828-1030
Type of Counseling:
HECM Counseling, Default/Foreclosure Counseling, Rental Counseling, Prepurchase Counseling

BROWARD COUNTY HOUSING AUTHORITY
7481 NW 33rd St
Hollywood, FL 33024-2376
954-432-6506
Fax: 954-484-5650
Type of Counseling:
HECM Counseling, Default/Foreclosure Counseling, Rental Counseling, Prepurchase Counseling

BROWARD COUNTY HOUSING AUTHORITY
3100 N 24th Ave #8
Hollywood, FL 33020-1401
954-921-2702
Fax: 954-920-6573
Type of Counseling:
HECM Counseling, Default/Foreclosure Counseling, Rental Counseling, Prepurchase Counseling

CONSUMER CREDIT COUNSELING SERVICE OF JACKSONVILLE
1639 Atlantic Blvd
Jacksonville, FL 32207-3346
904-396-4846
Fax: 904-398-6649
Type of Counseling:
HECM Counseling, Default/Foreclosure Counseling, Rental Counseling, Prepurchase Counseling
Affiliate of: NATIONAL FOUNDATION FOR CONSUMER CREDIT, INCORPORATED

**OAKLAND TRACE COMMUNITY DEVELOPMENT CORPORATION
1025 Jessie Street
Jacksonville, FL 32206
904-354-0776

Toll-Free:
TTY/TDD:
Fax: 904-354-0630
Type of Counseling:
Prepurchase Counseling
Affiliate of: CONGRESS OF NATIONAL BLACK CHURCHES, INCORPORATED

CONSUMER CREDIT COUNSELING SERVICE OF FAMILY COUNSELING
C Avenue Naval Air Station
Jacksonville, FL 32207
904-396-4846
Fax: 904-398-6649
Type of Counseling:
HECM Counseling, Default/Foreclosure Counseling, Rental Counseling, Prepurchase Counseling

JACKSONVILLE URBAN LEAGUE
903 W. Union St
Jacksonville, FL 32204-1161
904-356-8336
Fax: 904-356-8369
Type of Counseling:
HECM Counseling, Default/Foreclosure Counseling, Rental Counseling, Prepurchase Counseling

**JACKSONVILLE HOUSING PARTNERSHIP
4401 Emerson St. Suite 1
Jacksonville, FL 322074954
904-398-4424
Fax: 904-398-0828
Type of Counseling:
Default/Foreclosure Counseling, Prepurchase Counseling
Affiliate of: THE HOUSING PARTNERSHIP NETWORK

CATHOLIC CHARITIES BUREAU, INCORPORATED
134 E Church St Ste 2
Jacksonville, FL 32202-3130
904-354-4846
Fax: 904-354-4718
Type of Counseling:
Prepurchase Counseling, HECM Counseling, Default/Foreclosure Counseling, Rental Counseling
Affiliate of: CATHOLIC CHARITIES USA

CONSUMER CREDIT COUNSELING SERVICE OF FAMILY COUNSELING
1316 3rd St N
Jacksonville Beach, FL 32250-7348
904-246-6539
Fax: 904-398-6649
Type of Counseling:
HECM Counseling, Default/Foreclosure Counseling, Rental Counseling, Prepurchase Counseling

CONSUMER CREDIT COUNSELING SERVICE OF SOUTH FLORIDA, INCORPORATED
1010 Kennedy Dr
Key West, FL 33040-4019
800-928-2227
Fax: 305-892-1667
Type of Counseling:
HECM Counseling, Default/Foreclosure Counseling, Prepurchase Counseling

CONSUMER CREDIT COUNSELING SERVICE OF CENTRAL FLORIDA
1935 E Edgewood Dr
Lakeland, FL 33803-3473
941-687-2515
Fax: 941-683-9793
Type of Counseling:
HECM Counseling, Default/Foreclosure Counseling, Rental Counseling, Prepurchase Counseling

BROWARD COUNTY HOUSING AUTHORITY
1773 North State Road 7
Lauderhill, FL 33313
954-739-1114
Fax: 954-484-5650
Email: bchabm@mail.state.fl.us
Website: www.bchafl.org
Type of Counseling:
HECM Counseling, Default/Foreclosure Counseling, Rental Counseling, Prepurchase Counseling

CONSUMER CREDIT COUNSELING SERVICE OF CENTRAL FLORIDA
1211 North Boulevard West
Leesburg, FL 34748-3959
352-326-9004
Fax: 352-326-1916
Type of Counseling:
HECM Counseling, Default/Foreclosure Counseling, Rental Counseling, Prepurchase Counseling

CONSUMER CREDIT COUNSELING SERVICE OF WEST FLORIDA
2878 Green St. Suite 209
Marianna, FL 32446
850-526-1221
Fax: 850-432-5078
Type of Counseling:
Prepurchase Counseling, Rental Counseling, Default/Foreclosure Counseling, HECM Counseling

COMMUNITY HOUSING INITIATIVE
3033 College Wood Drive
Melbourne, FL 32934
321-253-0053
Fax: 321-253-1575
Type of Counseling:
Default/Foreclosure Counseling, Prepurchase Counseling

CONSUMER CREDIT COUNSELING SERVICE OF BREVARD
507 N Harbor City Blvd
Melbourne, FL 32935-6837
321-259-1070
Fax: 321-259-5202
Email: cccsjulie@aol.com
Type of Counseling:
HECM Counseling, Default/Foreclosure Counseling, Rental Counseling, Prepurchase Counseling

ACORN HOUSING CORPORATION HOUSING COUNSELING OFFICES - MIAMI
6025 NW 6 Court
Miami, FL
305-756-7166
Fax: 305-756-7765
Type of Counseling:
Prepurchase Counseling, Rental Counseling, Default/Foreclosure Counseling

CONSUMER CREDIT COUNSELING SERVICES
16201 SW 95th Ave Ste 210
Miami, FL 33157-3459
305-233-2480
Fax: 305-893-4466
Type of Counseling:
HECM Counseling, Default/Foreclosure Counseling, Rental Counseling, Prepurchase Counseling

**MIAMI-DADE NEIGHBORHOOD HOUSING SERVICES, INCORPORATED
7100 Biscayne Blvd, 2nd Floor
Miami, FL 33137
305-751-5511
Fax: 305-751-2228

Type of Counseling:
Default/Foreclosure Counseling,
Prepurchase Counseling
Affiliate of: NEIGHBORHOOD
REINVESTMENT
CORPORATION

WEST PERRINE COMMUNITY
DEVELOPMENT CORPORATION,
INCORPORATED
17747 Homestead Ave
Miami, FL 33157-5341
305-252-0129
Fax: 305-235-5809
Type of Counseling:
Default/Foreclosure Counseling,
Rental Counseling, Prepurchase
Counseling

WEST PERRINE HOUSING
OPPORTUNITY CENTER
17623 Homestead Ave
Miami, FL 33157-5340
305-233-2997
Fax: 305-233-4165
Type of Counseling:
Default/Foreclosure Counseling,
Prepurchase Counseling

**ACORN HOUSING
CORPORATION
3510 Biscayne Blvd, Suite 201
Miami, FL 33137-4143
305-438-9061
Fax: 305-438-9064
Type of Counseling:
Prepurchase Counseling
Affiliate of: ACORN HOUSING
CORPORATION

**GREATER MIAMI
NEIGHBORHOODS
300 NW 12th Ave
Miami, FL 33128
305-324-5505
Fax: 305-324-5506
Type of Counseling:
Prepurchase Counseling, Rental
Counseling, Default/Foreclosure
Counseling, HECM Counseling
Affiliate of: THE HOUSING
PARTNERSHIP NETWORK

MIAMI BEACH COMMUNITY
DEVELOPMENT CORP
945 Pennsylvania Avenue 2nd Floor
Miami Beach, FL 33139
305-538-0090
Fax: 305-538-2863
Type of Counseling:
Default/Foreclosure Counseling,
Prepurchase Counseling, HECM
Counseling, Rental Counseling

HOMES IN PARTNERSHIP,
INCORPORATED
75 Lucerne Drive
Mount Dora, FL 32757-
352-383-7300
Fax: 407-886-5304
Type of Counseling:
Prepurchase Counseling

CONSUMER CREDIT
COUNSELING SERVICE OF
CENTRAL FLORIDA
2400 Tamiami Trail, North
Suite 402
Naples, FL 34112-4883
941-775-6688
Fax: 941-430-1153
Type of Counseling:
HECM Counseling,
Default/Foreclosure Counseling,
Rental Counseling, Prepurchase
Counseling
Affiliate of: NATIONAL
FOUNDATION FOR CONSUMER
CREDIT, INCORPORATED

CONSUMER CREDIT
COUNSELING SERVICE OF
SOUTH FLORIDA,
INCORPORATED
11645 Biscayne Blvd, Suite 205
North Miami, FL 33181-3155
305-893-5225
Toll-Free: 800-928-2227
Fax: 305-892-1667
Email: MARCIA@cccs-sfl.com
Type of Counseling:
HECM Counseling,
Default/Foreclosure Counseling,
Prepurchase Counseling

CONSUMER CREDIT
COUNSELING SERVICE OF MID-
FLORIDA, INCORPORATED
1539 NE 22nd Ave
Ocala, FL 34478
352-867-1865
Fax: 352-867-8490
Type of Counseling:
HECM Counseling,
Default/Foreclosure Counseling,
Rental Counseling, Prepurchase
Counseling

OCALA HOUSING AUTHORITY
233 SW 3rd Street
Ocala, FL 344782468
352-369-2636
Fax: 352-369-2642
Type of Counseling:
Prepurchase Counseling, Rental
Counseling, Default/Foreclosure
Counseling

CONSUMER CREDIT
COUNSELING SERVICES
205 N Parrot Ave Barnett Bank
Okeechobee, FL 34972
800-330-2227
Fax: 561-434-2540
Type of Counseling:
HECM Counseling,
Default/Foreclosure Counseling,
Rental Counseling, Prepurchase
Counseling

CONSUMER CREDIT
COUNSELING SERVICE OF
CENTRAL FLORIDA
815 S Volusia Ave Ste1
Orange City, FL 32763-6568
407-895-8886
Fax: 407-895-3807
Type of Counseling:
HECM Counseling,
Default/Foreclosure Counseling,
Rental Counseling, Prepurchase
Counseling

CONSUMER CREDIT
COUNSELING SERVICE OF
FAMILY COUNSELING
1409 Kingsley Ave
Bld 4 Ste B
Orange Park, FL 32073-4537
904-269-6679
Fax: 904-269-4111
Type of Counseling:
HECM Counseling,
Default/Foreclosure Counseling,
Rental Counseling, Prepurchase
Counseling

METROPOLITAN ORLANDO
URBAN LEAGUE,
INCORPORATED
2512 W Colonial Dr
Orlando, FL 32804-8009
407-841-7654
Fax: 407-841-9114
Type of Counseling:
HECM Counseling,
Default/Foreclosure Counseling,
Rental Counseling, Prepurchase
Counseling
Affiliate of: NATIONAL URBAN
LEAGUE

CONSUMER CREDIT
COUNSELING SERVICE OF
CENTRAL FLORIDA
6220 S Orange Blossom Trl Ste 145
Orlando, FL 32809-4630
407-895-8886
Fax: 407-895-3807
Type of Counseling:
HECM Counseling,
Default/Foreclosure Counseling,

Rental Counseling, Prepurchase Counseling

PALMETTO CATHOLIC CHARITIES HOUSING COUNSELING
506 26th St W
Palmetto, FL 34221
941-721-0924
Fax: 941-722-1063
Type of Counseling:
Rental Counseling, Prepurchase Counseling
Affiliate of: CATHOLIC CHARITIES USA

CONSUMER CREDIT COUNSELING SERVICE OF WEST FLORIDA/TYNDALL AIR FORCE BASE
721 Suwannee Rd.
Panama City, FL 32403
850-283-4205
Fax: 850-432-5078
Type of Counseling:
Prepurchase Counseling, Rental Counseling, Default/Foreclosure Counseling, HECM Counseling

CONSUMER CREDIT COUNSELING SERVICES OF WEST FLORIDA/Bonifay/Chipley
121 W 23rd St
Panama City, FL 32405-4504
850-784-6301
Fax: 850-784-2980
Type of Counseling:
HECM Counseling, Default/Foreclosure Counseling, Prepurchase Counseling

**SOUTH MISSISSIPPI LEGAL SERVICES CORPORATION
P.O. Box 1654
Pascagoula, FL 39568-1654
228-769-7817
Fax: 228-769-7477
Type of Counseling:
Prepurchase Counseling, Default/Foreclosure Counseling, Rental Counseling, HECM Counseling
Affiliate of: WEST TENNESSEE LEGAL SERVICES, INCORPORATED

CONSUMER CREDIT COUNSELING SERVICE OF WEST FLORIDA/Whiting Field Naval Air Station
14 S Palafox Pl
Pensacola, FL 32501
850-434-0268
Toll-Free: 800-343-3317
Fax: 850-432-5078
Website: www.cccs-wfla.com
Type of Counseling:
HECM Counseling, Default/Foreclosure Counseling, Prepurchase Counseling, Rental Counseling

COMMUNITY EQUITY INVESTMENTS, INCORPORATED
302 North Barcelona St
Pensacola, FL 32501
850-595-6234
Fax: 850-595-6264
Type of Counseling:
Prepurchase Counseling

CONSUMER CREDIT COUNSELING SERVICE OF WEST FLORIDA
Pensacola Naval Air Station FSC Bldg. 625
Pensacola, FL 32508
850-452-5101
Fax: 850-432-5078
Type of Counseling:
Prepurchase Counseling, Rental Counseling, Default/Foreclosure Counseling, HECM Counseling

BROWARD COUNTY HOUSING AUTHORITY
3801 NE 8th Ave
Pompano Beach, FL 33064-4364
954-941-0664
Fax: 954-484-5650
Type of Counseling:
HECM Counseling, Default/Foreclosure Counseling, Rental Counseling, Prepurchase Counseling

CONSUMER CREDIT COUNSELING SERVICES
9466 S US Highway 1
Port Saint Lucie, FL 34952-5001
800-330-2227
Fax: 561-398-3479
Email: derric@cccsinc.com
Website: www.cccsinc.com
Type of Counseling:
HECM Counseling, Default/Foreclosure Counseling, Rental Counseling, Prepurchase Counseling

CONSUMER CREDIT COUNSELING SERVICE OF WEST FLORIDA
305 Fifth Street
Port St. Joe, FL 32456
850-784-6301
Fax: 850-432-5078
Type of Counseling:
Prepurchase Counseling, Rental Counseling, Default/Foreclosure Counseling, HECM Counseling

CONSUMER CREDIT COUNSELING SERVICE OF BREVARD
220 Coral Sands Dr
Rockledge, FL 32955-2702
321-259-1070
Fax: 321-259-5202
Type of Counseling:
HECM Counseling, Default/Foreclosure Counseling, Rental Counseling, Prepurchase Counseling

THE CENTER FOR AFFORDABLE HOUSING INCORPORATED
203 E. 3rd Street, Suite 201
Sanford, FL 32771-
407-323-3268
Fax: 407-323-3800
Type of Counseling:
Prepurchase Counseling, Default/Foreclosure Counseling

CONSUMER CREDIT COUNSELING SERVICE OF THE FLORIDA GULF
1750 17th Street, Unot D
Sarasota, FL 34234-
941-316-9600
Fax: 941-951-7788
Email: LPICHCCCS@aol.com
Website: www.cccsfl.org
Type of Counseling:
HECM Counseling, Default/Foreclosure Counseling, Rental Counseling, Prepurchase Counseling

CONSUMER CREDIT COUNSELING SERVICE SARASOTA-EAST
5899 Whitfield Ave NW Suite 100
Mail Code 0327
Sarasota, FL 34243
941-316-9600
Toll-Free: 800-741-7040
Fax: 813-289-6452
Type of Counseling:
Prepurchase Counseling, Rental Counseling, Default/Foreclosure Counseling, HECM Counseling

CONSUMER CREDIT COUNSELING SERVICE OF CENTRAL FLORIDA
228 N Ridgewood Dr 2nd Fl
Sebring, FL 33870
941-385-3485

Fax: 941-382-5425
Type of Counseling:
HECM Counseling,
Default/Foreclosure Counseling,
Rental Counseling, Prepurchase
Counseling

CONSUMER CREDIT
COUNSELING SERVICE OF
FAMILY COUNSELING
SERVICES
2535 US 1 South
St. Augustine, FL 32086
904-396-4846
Fax: 904-398-6649
Type of Counseling:
HECM Counseling,
Default/Foreclosure Counseling,
Rental Counseling, Prepurchase
Counseling

**CATHOLIC CHARITIES OF
SAINT PETERSBURG
6533 9th Avenue
North Suite 1E
St. Petersburg, FL 33710
727-893-1313
Fax: 727-893-1307
Email: scanlancch@aol.com
Type of Counseling:
Default/Foreclosure Counseling,
Prepurchase Counseling, Rental
Counseling, HECM Counseling
Affiliate of: CATHOLIC
CHARITIES USA

**SAINT PETERSBURG
NEIGHBORHOOD HOUSING
SERVICES, INCORPORATED
1640 Martin Luther King St S
St. Petersburg, FL 33701
727-821-6897
Fax: 727-821-7457
Type of Counseling:
Prepurchase Counseling,
Default/Foreclosure Counseling
Affiliate of: NEIGHBORHOOD
REINVESTMENT
CORPORATION

**MOUNT ZION HUMAN
SERVICES COMMUNITY
DEVELOPMENT CORPORATION
945-20th Street South
St. Petersburg, FL 33712
727-894-4311
Fax: 727-823-8002
Type of Counseling:
Prepurchase Counseling,
Default/Foreclosure Counseling
Affiliate of: CONGRESS OF
NATIONAL BLACK CHURCHES,
INCORPORATED

CONSUMER CREDIT
COUNSELING SERVICE OF
WEST FLORIDA
1311 Executive Center Dr. Suite 222
Tallahassee, FL 32301
850-402-0378
Fax: 850-432-5078
Type of Counseling:
Prepurchase Counseling, Rental
Counseling, Default/Foreclosure
Counseling, HECM Counseling

TALLAHASSEE URBAN
LEAGUE
923 Old Bainbridge Road
Tallahassee, FL 323036042
850-222-6111
Fax: 850-561-8390
Type of Counseling:
Prepurchase Counseling

FLORIDA HOUSING FINANCE
CORPORTATION
227 N. Bronough Street Suite 5000
Tallahassee, FL 32301
850-488-4197
Fax: 850-488-9809
Type of Counseling:
Prepurchase Counseling

TALLAHASSEE LENDERS
CONSORTIUM
1114 East Tennessee St
Tallahassee, FL 32308
850-222-6609
Fax: 850-222-6687
Email: tucc22095@aol.com
Type of Counseling:
HECM Counseling,
Default/Foreclosure Counseling,
Prepurchase Counseling, Rental
Counseling

CONSUMER CREDIT
COUNSELING SERVICE OF
CENTRAL FLORIDA
1648 Metropolitan Cir Ste 2
Tallahassee, FL 32308-3740
850-878-0975
Fax: 850-878-2716
Type of Counseling:
HECM Counseling,
Default/Foreclosure Counseling,
Rental Counseling, Prepurchase
Counseling

CONSUMER CREDIT
COUNSELING SERVICE OF THE
FLORIDA GULF
5201 W Kennedy Blvd Ste 110
Tampa, FL 33609-1845
813-289-8923
Fax: 813-289-6452
Email: LPICHCCCS@aol.com
Website: www.cccsfl.org
Type of Counseling:
HECM Counseling,
Default/Foreclosure Counseling,
Rental Counseling, Prepurchase
Counseling

CITY OF TAMPA COMMUNITY
REDEVELOPMENT AGENCY
2105 N Nebraska Ave
Tampa, FL 33602-2529
813-274-7954
Fax: 813-274-7927
Type of Counseling:
Prepurchase Counseling

CONSUMER CREDIT
COUNSELING SERVICE OF
BREVARD
725 S Deleon Ave
Titusville, FL 32780-4115
321-636-9210
Fax: 321-259-5202
Type of Counseling:
HECM Counseling,
Default/Foreclosure Counseling,
Rental Counseling, Prepurchase
Counseling

CONSUMER CREDIT
COUNSELING SERVICE OF THE
FLORIDA GULF
3700 South Tamiami Trail
Venice, FL 34285
941-493-3180
Toll-Free: 800-741-7040
Fax: 941-488-9483
Email: LPICHCCCS@aol.com
Website: www.cccsfl.org
Type of Counseling:
Prepurchase Counseling, Rental
Counseling, Default/Foreclosure
Counseling, HECM Counseling

CONSUMER CREDIT
COUNSELING SERVICE OF
BREVARD
2046 14th Ave
Vero Beach, FL 32960-3430
561-562-6512
Fax: 407-259-5202
Email: cccsjulie@aol.com
Type of Counseling:
HECM Counseling,
Default/Foreclosure Counseling,
Rental Counseling, Prepurchase
Counseling

URBAN LEAGUE OF PALM
BEACH COUNTY,
INCORPORATED
1700 N Austrian Ave
West Palm Beach, FL 33407
561-833-1461

Fax: 561-833-6050
Email: ulwest@aol.com
Type of Counseling:
HECM Counseling,
Default/Foreclosure Counseling,
Rental Counseling, Prepurchase
Counseling
Affiliate of: NATIONAL URBAN
LEAGUE

CONSUMER CREDIT
COUNSELING SERVICE OF
GREATER ATLANTA, INC
2330 S Congress Ave
Suite 1A
West Palm Beach, FL 33406-7666
561-434-2544
Toll-Free: 800-330-2227
Fax: 561-434-2540
Email: derrick@cccsinc.com
Website: www.cccsinc.com
Type of Counseling:
HECM Counseling,
Default/Foreclosure Counseling,
Rental Counseling, Prepurchase
Counseling

**WEST PALM BEACH
HOUSING PARTNERSHIP
4016 Broadway Ave.
West Palm Beach, FL 33407
561-841-3500
Fax: 561-841-3555
Type of Counseling:
HECM Counseling,
Default/Foreclosure Counseling,
Rental Counseling, Prepurchase
Counseling
Affiliate of: NEIGHBORHOOD
REINVESTMENT
CORPORATION

CONSUMER CREDIT
COUNSELING SERVICES OF
SOUTH FLORIDA
2101 N Andrews Ave Ste 405
Wilton Manors, FL 33311-3940
800-928-2227
Fax: 954-561-4084
Type of Counseling:
HECM Counseling,
Default/Foreclosure Counseling,
Prepurchase Counseling

THE AGRICULTURE AND
LABOR PROGRAM,
INCORPORATED
7301 Lynchburg Rd
Winter Haven, FL 33885
863-956-3491
Toll-Free: 800-330-3491
Fax: 863-956-5560
Type of Counseling:
Default/Foreclosure Counseling,
Rental Counseling, Prepurchase
Counseling

HANDS HOUSING AND
NEIGHBORHOOD
DEVELOPMENT SERVICES OF
CENTRAL FLORIDA
INCORPORATED
990 N Bennett Ave.
Suite 200
Winter Park, FL 32789
407-740-0805
Fax: 407-740-8576
Type of Counseling:
Default/Foreclosure Counseling,
Rental Counseling, Prepurchase
Counseling

Georgia

CITY OF ALBANY COMMUNITY
AND ECONOMIC
DEVELOPMENT
230 South Jackson St
Suite 315
Albany, GA 31701
229-430-5283
Toll-Free: 800-251-2910
Fax: 229-430-2737
Type of Counseling:
Default/Foreclosure Counseling,
Rental Counseling, Prepurchase
Counseling

**GEORGIA LEGAL SERVICES
PROGRAM
111 West Oglethorpe Boulevard
Albany, GA 31701-
912-430-4261
Fax: 912-430-4344
Type of Counseling:
Prepurchase Counseling,
Default/Foreclosure Counseling,
Rental Counseling, HECM
Counseling
Affiliate of: WEST TENNESSEE
LEGAL SERVICES,
INCORPORATED

ATHENS-CLARKE COUNTY
UNIFIED GOVERNMENT
HUMAN AND ECONOMIC
DEVELOPMENT
375 Satula Ave.
Athens, GA 30601-2746
706-613-3155
Fax: 706-613-3158
Type of Counseling:
HECM Counseling,
Default/Foreclosure Counseling,
Rental Counseling, Prepurchase
Counseling

EAST ATHENS DEVELOPMENT
CORPORATION,
INCORPORATED
410 McKinley drive, Suite 101
Athens, GA 30601-
706-208-0048
Fax: 706-208-0015
Type of Counseling:
Prepurchase Counseling,
Default/Foreclosure Counseling,
Rental Counseling

HOUSING AND ECONOMIC
LEADERSHIP PARTNERS,
INCORPORATED
485 Huntington Road, Suite 200
Athens, GA 30606
706-549-5200
Fax: 706-549-5004
Type of Counseling:
HECM Counseling, Prepurchase
Counseling, Rental Counseling,
Default/Foreclosure Counseling

ATLANTA URBAN LEAGUE,
INCORPORATED
100 Edgewood Ave NE
Suite 600
Atlanta, GA 30303-3066
404-659-1150
Fax: 404-230-9950
Email: au1198@bellsouth.net
Type of Counseling:
Default/Foreclosure Counseling,
Rental Counseling, Prepurchase
Counseling
Affiliate of: NATIONAL URBAN
LEAGUE

CONSUMER CREDIT
COUNSELING OF GREATER
ATLANTA, INCORPORATED
100 Edgewood Ave NE
Suite 1500
Atlanta, GA 30303-3026
866-255-2227
Toll-Free: 866-255-2227
Fax: 404-653-8883
Email: jjordan@cccsatl.org
Type of Counseling:
Default/Foreclosure Counseling,
Rental Counseling, Prepurchase
Counseling, HECM Counseling

**ACORN HOUSING
CORPORATION HOUSING
COUNSELING OFFICES -
ATLANTA
250 Auburn Ave. Ste 304
Atlanta, GA 30303
404-525-0033
Fax: 404-525-2655
Type of Counseling:

Prepurchase Counseling, Rental Counseling, Default/Foreclosure Counseling
Affiliate of: ACORN HOUSING CORPORATION

LATIN AMERICAN ASSOCIATION
2750 Buford Highway
Atlanta, GA 30324
404-638-1800
Fax: 404-638-1806
Email: rconcepcion@latinamericanassoc.org
Type of Counseling:
Prepurchase Counseling, Default/Foreclosure Counseling

ATLANTA CENTER FOR HOME OWNERSHIP
228 Auburn Avenue
Atlanta, GA 30315
404-588-3700
Fax: 404-588-3733
Type of Counseling:
Prepurchase Counseling
Affiliate of: HOUSING OPPORTUNITIES, INCORPORATED

FULTON ATLANTA COMMUNITY ACTION AUTHORITY
1690 Chantilly Drive, N.E.
Atlanta, GA 30324-
404-320-0166
Fax: 404-810-0098
Type of Counseling:
Default/Foreclosure Counseling, Rental Counseling, Prepurchase Counseling

GEORGIA HOUSING AND FINANCE AUTHORITY
60 Exec Park South, NE
Atlanta, GA 30340
404-679-0670
Fax: 404-679-4844
Email: tchilds@dca.state.ga.us
Type of Counseling:
Rental Counseling, Prepurchase Counseling

**CHRISTIAN FAMILY WORSHIP CENTER
1401 Hosea L. Williams Dr., SE
Atlanta, GA 30317-1703
404-584-7429
Fax: 404-222-9444
Type of Counseling:
Prepurchase Counseling, Rental Counseling
Affiliate of: CONGRESS OF NATIONAL BLACK CHURCHES, INCORPORATED

ATLANTA CENTER FOR HOMEOWNERSHIP
818 Pollard Boulevard
Atlanta, GA 30315
404-588-3700
Fax: 404-588-3733
Type of Counseling:
Prepurchase Counseling

**GEORGIA LEGAL SERVICES PROGRAM
1100 Spring St. NW, Ste. 200-A
Atlanta, GA 303092848
404-206-5378
Fax: 404-206-5346
Email: sreif@glsp.org
Type of Counseling:
Prepurchase Counseling, Default/Foreclosure Counseling, Rental Counseling, HECM Counseling
Affiliate of: WEST TENNESSEE LEGAL SERVICES, INCORPORATED

DEKALB/FULTON HOUSING COUNSELING CENTER
233 Mitchell St SW Ste 100
Atlanta, GA 30303-3300
404-659-6744
Fax: 404-659-6739
Type of Counseling:
HECM Counseling, Default/Foreclosure Counseling, Rental Counseling, Prepurchase Counseling

CONSUMER CREDIT COUNSELING SERVICE OF THE CENTRAL SAVANNAH RIVER AREA
1341 Druid Park Ave.
Augusta, GA 30904
706-736-2090
Fax: 706-736-0637
Type of Counseling:
Prepurchase Counseling, Default/Foreclosure Counseling, Rental Counseling

**GEORGIA LEGAL SERVICES PROGRAM
811 Telfair Street Suite 202
Augusta, GA 30901-
706-721-2327
Fax: 706-721-4897
Type of Counseling:
Prepurchase Counseling, Default/Foreclosure Counseling, Rental Counseling, HECM Counseling
Affiliate of: WEST TENNESSEE LEGAL SERVICES, INCORPORATED

**GEORGIA LEGAL SERVICES PROGRAM
1311 Union Street
Brunswick, GA 31520-7226
912-264-7301
Fax: 912-262-2312
Type of Counseling:
Prepurchase Counseling, Default/Foreclosure Counseling, Rental Counseling, HECM Counseling
Affiliate of: WEST TENNESSEE LEGAL SERVICES, INCORPORATED

**GEORGIA LEGAL SERVICES PROGRAM
1214 First Avenue
Columbus, GA 31902-
706-649-7493
Fax: 706-649-7519
Type of Counseling:
Prepurchase Counseling, Default/Foreclosure Counseling, Rental Counseling, HECM Counseling
Affiliate of: WEST TENNESSEE LEGAL SERVICES, INCORPORATED

METRO COLUMBUS URBAN LEAGUE, INCORPORATED
802 1st Ave
Columbus, GA 31901-2702
706-323-3687
Fax: 706-596-2144
Type of Counseling:
Default/Foreclosure Counseling, Prepurchase Counseling

**GEORGIA LEGAL SERVICES PROGRAM
107 King Street
Dalton, GA 30722-2204
706-272-2359
Fax: 706-272-2259
Type of Counseling:
Prepurchase Counseling, Default/Foreclosure Counseling, Rental Counseling, HECM Counseling
Affiliate of: WEST TENNESSEE LEGAL SERVICES, INCORPORATED

**GREEN FOREST COMMUNITY DEVELOPMENT CORPORATION
3299 Rainbow Drive

Decatur, GA 30034
404-284-7799
Fax: 404-284-8727
Type of Counseling:
Prepurchase Counseling, Default/Foreclosure Counseling
Affiliate of: HOUSING OPPORTUNITIES, INCORPORATED

CONSUMER CREDIT COUNSELING SERVICE OF GREATER ATLANTA
5304 Panola Industrial Blvd. Suite N
Decatur, GA 30035-
866-255-2227
Toll-Free: 866-255-2227
Fax: 404-653-8883
Email: jjordan@cccsatl.org
Type of Counseling:
Prepurchase Counseling, Default/Foreclosure Counseling, HECM Counseling, Rental Counseling

THE HOUSING AUTHORITY OF THE CITY OF DECATUR, GEORGIA
325 Swanton Way
Decatur, GA
404-377-0425
Fax: 404-378-7249
Type of Counseling:
Rental Counseling, Prepurchase Counseling, Default/Foreclosure Counseling

DEKALB/FULTON HOUSING COUNSELING CENTER
4151 Memorial Dr Suite 107E
Decatur, GA 30032-1504
404-508-0922
Fax: 404-508-0967
Type of Counseling:
HECM Counseling, Default/Foreclosure Counseling, Rental Counseling, Prepurchase Counseling

HEART OF GEORGIA COMMUNITY ACTION COUNCIL
213 Pine Street
Eastman, GA 31203
478-374-4301
Fax: 478-374-7648
Type of Counseling:
Default/Foreclosure Counseling

CONSUMER CREDIT COUNSELING SERVICE OF GREATER ATLANTA
140 Carnegie Place Suite 106
Fayetteville, GA 30214-
866-255-2227
Toll-Free: 866-255-2227
Fax: 404-653-8883
Email: jjordan@cccsatl.org
Prepurchase Counseling, Default/Foreclosure Counseling, HECM Counseling, Rental Counseling

**GEORGIA LEGAL SERVICES PROGRAM
1276 Jesse Jewel Parkway
Gainesville, GA 30503-
404-535-5717
Fax: 404-531-6011
Type of Counseling:
Prepurchase Counseling, Default/Foreclosure Counseling, Rental Counseling, HECM Counseling
Affiliate of: WEST TENNESSEE LEGAL SERVICES, INCORPORATED

GAINESVILLE-HALL COUNTY NEIGHBORHOOD REVITALIZATION
924 Athens Street
Gainesville, GA 30503
770-297-1800
Fax: 770-297-1097
Type of Counseling:
Prepurchase Counseling, Default/Foreclosure Counseling

CONSUMER CREDIT COUNSELING SERVICE OF FAMILY COUNSELING
1063 Tennessee Ave Bldg. 1051
Kings Bay, GA 31547
912-673-4512
Fax: 912-673-2031
Email:
qlharvem@subasekb.navy.mil
Type of Counseling:
HECM Counseling, Default/Foreclosure Counseling, Rental Counseling, Prepurchase Counseling

LATIN AMERICAN ASSOCIATION
134 S. Clayton Street, Suite 32
Lawrenceville, GA 30045
770-339-4335
Fax: 770-339-9154
Type of Counseling:
Default/Foreclosure Counseling, Prepurchase Counseling

CONSUMER CREDIT COUNSELING SERVICE OF MIDDLE GEORGIA, INCORPORATED
277 M.L.K. Jr. W Ste 202
Macon, GA 31201
478-745-6197
Fax: 478-745-6270
Email: counselor@cccsmacon.org
Type of Counseling:
Default/Foreclosure Counseling, Rental Counseling, Prepurchase Counseling

**GEORGIA LEGAL SERVICES PROGRAM
111 Third Street, Suite 230
Macon, GA 31202-1507
912-751-6261
Fax: 912-751-6581
Type of Counseling:
Prepurchase Counseling, Default/Foreclosure Counseling, Rental Counseling, HECM Counseling
Affiliate of: WEST TENNESSEE LEGAL SERVICES, INCORPORATED

CONSUMER CREDIT COUNSELING SERVICE OF GREATER ATLANTA
1341 Canton Road Suite F
Marietta, GA 30066-
866-255-2227
Toll-Free: 866-255-2227
Fax: 404-653-8883
Email: jjordan@cccsatl.org
Type of Counseling:
Prepurchase Counseling, Default/Foreclosure Counseling, HECM Counseling, Rental Counseling

LATIN AMERICAN ASSOCIATION
48 Henderson Street
Marietta, GA 30064
770-420-6556
Fax: 678-354-0500
Type of Counseling:
Default/Foreclosure Counseling, Prepurchase Counseling

COBB HOUSING, INCORPORATED
700 Sandy Plains Rd Ste B8
Marietta, GA 30062-6370
770-429-4400
Fax: 770-429-4405
Type of Counseling:
Default/Foreclosure Counseling, Rental Counseling, Prepurchase Counseling

CONSUMER CREDIT COUNSELING SERVICE OF GREATER ATLANTA
6000 Live Oak Parkway Suite 113

Norcross, GA 30093-
866-255-2227
Toll-Free: 866-255-2227
Fax: 404-653-8883
Email: jjordan@cccsatl.org
Type of Counseling:
Prepurchase Counseling, Default/Foreclosure Counseling, HECM Counseling, Rental Counseling

GWINNETT HOUSING RESOURCE PARTNERSHIP, INCORPORATED
3453 Holcomb Bridge Rd Ste 140
Norcross, GA 30092
770-448-0702
Fax: 770-448-6958
Type of Counseling:
HECM Counseling, Default/Foreclosure Counseling, Rental Counseling, Prepurchase Counseling

APPALACHIAN HOUSING COUNSELING AGENCY
800 Avenue B
Rome, GA 30162-
706-378-9917
Fax: 706-290-0042
Type of Counseling:
Prepurchase Counseling, Rental Counseling, Default/Foreclosure Counseling, HECM Counseling

NATIONAL ASSOCIATION OF HOUSING COUNSELORS AND AGENCIES
PO Box 5607
Savannah, GA 31414-5607
912-236-9670
Fax: 912-238-2977
Type of Counseling:
HECM Counseling, Default/Foreclosure Counseling, Rental Counseling, Prepurchase Counseling

ECONOMIC OPPORTUNITY AUTHORITY FOR SAVANNAH-CHATHAM COUNTY AREA, INCORPORATED
618 W Anderson St
Savannah, GA 31404
912-238-2960
Fax: 912-238-2977
Type of Counseling:
Default/Foreclosure Counseling, Rental Counseling, Prepurchase Counseling

**GEORGIA LEGAL SERVICES PROGRAM
10 Whittaker Street 2nd Floor
Savannah, GA 31401
912-651-2180
Fax: 912-651-3300
Type of Counseling:
Prepurchase Counseling, Default/Foreclosure Counseling, Rental Counseling, HECM Counseling
Affiliate of: WEST TENNESSEE LEGAL SERVICES, INCORPORATED

CONSUMER CREDIT COUNSELING SERVICE OF WEST FLORIDA
Chamber of Commerce Building
St. Mary's, GA 31558
912-673-1526
Fax: 850-432-5078
Type of Counseling:Prepurchase Counseling, Rental Counseling, Default/Foreclosure Counseling, HECM Counseling

**GEORGIA LEGAL SERVICES PROGRAM
150 South Ridge Avenue
Tifton, GA 31794-
912-386-3566
Fax: 912-386-3880
Type of Counseling:
Prepurchase Counseling, Default/Foreclosure Counseling, Rental Counseling, HECM Counseling
Affiliate of: WEST TENNESSEE LEGAL SERVICES, INCORPORATED

**GEORGIA LEGAL SERVICES PROGRAM
114 N. Toombs Street
Valdosta, GA 31601
912-333-5252
Fax: 912-333-5236
Type of Counseling:
Prepurchase Counseling, Default/Foreclosure Counseling, Rental Counseling, HECM Counseling
Affiliate of: WEST TENNESSEE LEGAL SERVICES, INCORPORATED

CONSUMER CREDIT COUNSELING SERVICE OF MIDDLE GEORGIA, INCORPORATED
511 N. Houston Road
Suite C-1
Warner Robins, GA 31093-
912-745-6197
Fax: 912-745-6270
Email: counselor@cccsmacon.org
Type of Counseling:
Prepurchase Counseling

MIDDLE GEORGIA COMMUNITY ACTION AGENCY, INCORPORATED
708 Elberta Rd
Warner Robins, GA 31093-1734
478-922-4464
Toll-Free: 800-422-9053
Fax: 478-329-0959
Type of Counseling:
Prepurchase Counseling

-GEORGIA LEGAL SERVICES PROGRAM
1057 Grove Avenue
Waycross, GA 31501-
912-285-6181
Fax: 912-285-6187
Type of Counseling:
Prepurchase Counseling, Default/Foreclosure Counseling, Rental Counseling, HECM Counseling
Affiliate of: WEST TENNESSEE LEGAL SERVICES, INCORPORATED

CONSUMER CREDIT COUNSELING SERVICE OF FAMILY COUNSELING
505 Haines Ave
Waycross, GA 31501-2266
912-284-2261
Fax: 912-284-2284
Type of Counseling:
HECM Counseling, Default/Foreclosure Counseling, Rental Counseling, Prepurchase Counseling

Hawaii

LEGAL AID SOCIETY OF HAWAII
305 Wailuku Dr
Hilo, HI 96720-2448
808-536-4302
Fax: 808-527-8088
Type of Counseling:
Default/Foreclosure Counseling, Rental Counseling, Prepurchase Counseling

LEGAL AID SOCIETY OF HAWAII
924 Bethel Street
Honolulu, HI 96813
808-536-4302
Fax: 808-527-8088
Type of Counseling:
HECM Counseling, Default/Foreclosure Counseling,

Rental Counseling, Prepurchase Counseling

CATHOLIC CHARITIES COMMUNITY AND IMMIGRANT SERVICES
712 North School Street
Honolulu, HI 96817
808-528-5233
Fax: 808-531-1970
Email: dmilazzolevy@catholiccharitieshawaii.org
Type of Counseling:
Rental Counseling, Prepurchase Counseling, Default/Foreclosure Counseling, HECM Counseling
Affiliate of: CATHOLIC CHARITIES USA

HALE MAHAOLU HOMEOWNERSHIP/HOUSING COUNSELING
200 Hina Ave
Kahului, HI 96732-1821
808-872-4114
Fax: 808-872-4120
Email: hmahaolu@maui.net
Type of Counseling:
HECM Counseling, Default/Foreclosure Counseling, Rental Counseling, Prepurchase Counseling

LEGAL AID SOCIETY OF HAWAII
47-200 Waihee Rd Ste 104
Kaneohe, HI 96744-4947
808-536-4302
Fax: 808-527-8088
Type of Counseling:
Rental Counseling, HECM Counseling, Prepurchase Counseling

LEGAL AID SOCIETY OF HAWAII
19-23 Ala Malama St
Kaunakakai, HI 96748
808-536-4302
Toll-Free: 800-499-4302
Fax: 808-527-8088
Type of Counseling:
Default/Foreclosure Counseling, Rental Counseling

LEGAL AID SOCIETY OF HAWAII
3-3359 Kuhio Hwy
Lihue, HI 96766
808-536-4302
Fax: 808-499-4302
Type of Counseling:
Default/Foreclosure Counseling, Rental Counseling

LEGAL AID SOCIETY OF HAWAII
85-555 Farrington Hwy Ste A
Waianae, HI 96792-2354
808-536-4302
Fax: 808-527-8088
Type of Counseling:
Default/Foreclosure Counseling, Rental Counseling

LEGAL AID SOCIETY OF HAWAII
2287 Main St
Wailuku, HI 96793-1655
808-436-4302
Fax: 808-527-8088
Type of Counseling:
Default/Foreclosure Counseling, Rental Counseling

Idaho

IDAHO HOUSING AND FINANCE ASSOCIATION
565 West Myrtle
Boise, ID 83702
208-331-4847
Fax: 208-331-4801
Type of Counseling:
Prepurchase Counseling

CALDWELL BOARD OF REALTORS
PO Box 1516
Caldwell, ID 836051516
208-463-2727
Fax: 208-453-8875
Type of Counseling:
Prepurchase Counseling

ST VINCENT DE PAUL
108 East Walnut
Coeur d' Alene, ID 83814
208-664-3095
Fax: 208-664-3095
Type of Counseling:
Prepurchase Counseling

**IDAHO FALLS ASSOCIATION OF REALTORS
1388 Cambridge
Idaho Falls, ID 83401
208-523-1477
Fax: 208-522-7867
Type of Counseling:
Prepurchase Counseling

COMMUNITY ACTION AGENCY
124 New Sixth Street
Lewiston, ID 83501
208-746-3351
Fax: 208-746-5456
Email: s.smith@caanid.org
Type of Counseling:
HECM Counseling, Default/Foreclosure Counseling, Rental Counseling, Prepurchase Counseling

NAMPA NEIGHBORHOOD HOUSING SERVICES
704 11th Avenue North
Nampa, ID 83687
208-467-7336
Fax: 208-463-9136
Type of Counseling:
Prepurchase Counseling

**COLLEGE OF SOUTHERN IDAHO COMMUNITY EDUCATION CENTER
315 Falls Ave
Twin Falls, ID 83301
208-733-9554
Fax: 208-736-3014
Type of Counseling:
Prepurchase Counseling

Illinois

MADISON COUNTY URBAN LEAGUE
210 William St
Alton, IL 62002-6146
618-463-1906
Fax: 618-463-9021
Email: sjh95@aol.com
Type of Counseling:
HECM Counseling, Default/Foreclosure Counseling, Rental Counseling, Prepurchase Counseling
Affiliate of: NATIONAL URBAN LEAGUE

CONSUMER CREDIT COUNSELING SERVICE- SAINT LOUIS
1623 Washington Ave., Suite 200
Alton, IL 620023933
618-463-1660
Toll-Free: 800-966-3328
Fax: 314-647-1359
Email: sueash@dellepro.com
Type of Counseling:
Default/Foreclosure Counseling

**JOSEPH CORPORATION
32 South Broadway Avenue
Aurora, IL 60507
630-906-9400
Fax: 630-906-9406
Type of Counseling:
Prepurchase Counseling, Default/Foreclosure Counseling
Affiliate of: HOUSING OPPORTUNITIES, INCORPORATED

NEIGHBORS UNITED FOR PROGRESS
19 Public Square, Suite 300
Belleville, IL 62220
618-234-9165
Fax: 618-234-9217
Type of Counseling:
Prepurchase Counseling, Default/Foreclosure Counseling

MID CENTRAL COMMUNITY ACTION
923 E Grove St
Bloomington, IL 61701-4201
309-829-0691
Fax: 309-828-8811
Type of Counseling:
Default/Foreclosure Counseling, Rental Counseling, Prepurchase Counseling

NEIGHBORS UNITED FOR PROGRESS
5701 Bond Avenue
Centreville, IL 62207
618-274-4206
Fax: 618-234-9217
Type of Counseling:
Prepurchase Counseling

CONSUMER CREDIT COUNSELING
201 W. Springfield Avenue
Suite 702
Champaign, IL 61820-
217-425-0654
Toll-Free: 800-959-2227
Fax: 217-425-4793
Email: cris@cccsillinois.org
Type of Counseling:
HECM Counseling, Prepurchase Counseling, Default/Foreclosure Counseling, Rental Counseling

URBAN LEAGUE OF CHAMPAIGN COUNTY
17 Taylor Street
Champaign, IL 61820
217-356-6018
Fax: 217-356-1310
Email: tparson@prarienet.org
Type of Counseling:
Prepurchase Counseling, Default/Foreclosure Counseling
Affiliate of: NATIONAL URBAN LEAGUE

**ACORN HOUSING CORPORATION
650 S. Clark Street #301
Chicago, IL 60605
312-939-1611
Fax: 312-939-4239
Type of Counseling:
Default/Foreclosure Counseling, Prepurchase Counseling
Affiliate of: ACORN HOUSING CORPORATION

CONSUMER CREDIT COUNSELING SERVICE OF GREATER CHICAGO
150 N Wacker Dr Ste 1400
Chicago, IL 606061607
312-849-2227
Toll-Free: 888-527-3328
Fax: 312-849-2135
Website: www.cccsgrchicago.org
Type of Counseling:
Rental Counseling, Prepurchase Counseling, HECM Counseling
Affiliate of: NATIONAL FOUNDATION FOR CONSUMER CREDIT, INCORPORATED

**RESURRECTION PROJECT
1818 S. Paulina
Chicago, IL 60608
312-666-1323
Toll-Free:
TTY/TDD:
Fax: 312-942-1123
Email:
maricruz_poncedeleon@yahoo.com
Website:
Type of Counseling:
Prepurchase Counseling, Default/Foreclosure Counseling, Rental Counseling, HECM Counseling
Affiliate of: NATIONAL COUNCIL OF LA RAZA

LATIN UNITED COMMUNTIY HOUSING ASSOCIATION
3541 West North Avenue
Chicago, IL 60647
773-276-5338
Toll-Free: 800-217-6970
Fax: 773-276-5358
Email: jmartens@lucha.org
Type of Counseling:
Prepurchase Counseling, Rental Counseling, Default/Foreclosure Counseling

SPANISH COALITION FOR HOUSING
4035 W North Ave
Chicago, IL 60639
773-342-7575
Fax: 773-342-8528
Type of Counseling:
HECM Counseling, Default/Foreclosure Counseling, Rental Counseling, Prepurchase Counseling

CHICAGO ROSELAND COALITION FOR COMMUNITY CONTROL
11015 S Michigan Ave
Chicago, IL 60628-4308
773-264-3500
Fax: 773-264-9634
Email: crcc@cnt.org
Type of Counseling:
HECM Counseling, Default/Foreclosure Counseling, Prepurchase Counseling

COMMUNITY AND ECONOMIC DEVELOPMENT ASSOCIATION - CEDA
208 S La Salle St Ste 1900
Chicago, IL 60604-1104
312-795-8961
Fax: 312-795-1034
Type of Counseling:
HECM Counseling, Default/Foreclosure Counseling, Rental Counseling, Prepurchase Counseling

CHICAGO URBAN LEAGUE DEVELOPMENT CORPORATION
4510 S Michigan Ave
Chicago, IL 60653-3898
773-451-3606
Fax: 773-285-0879
Email: Sstanley@cul-chicago.org
Type of Counseling:
HECM Counseling, Default/Foreclosure Counseling, Rental Counseling, Prepurchase Counseling
Affiliate of: NATIONAL URBAN LEAGUE

CHICAGO COMMONS HOUSING RESOURCE CENTER
6247c South Halsted Street
Chicago, IL 60621
773-783-2472
Fax: 773-783-0667
Email: CommonsHRC@aol.com
Type of Counseling:
Prepurchase Counseling, Default/Foreclosure Counseling, Rental Counseling

ILLINOIS HOUSING DEVELOPMENT AUTHORITY
401 North Michigan Ave. Suite 900
Chicago, IL 60611
312-836-5200
Fax: 312-832-2170

LEADERSHIP COUNCIL FOR METROPOLITAN OPEN COMMUNITIES
111 Wesr Jackson Blvd, 12 th Floor

Chicago, IL 60604-
312-341-5678
Fax: 312-341-1958
Type of Counseling:
Prepurchase Counseling, Rental Counseling

ROGERS PARK COMMUNITY COUNCIL
1530 West Morse Avenue
Chicago, IL 60626
773-338-7722
Fax: 773-338-7774
Type of Counseling:
HECM Counseling, Default/Foreclosure Counseling, Prepurchase Counseling

AGENCY METROPOLITAN PROGRAM SERVICES
3210 West Arthington Street
Chicago, IL 60624
773-533-0242
Fax: 773-533-0243
Type of Counseling:
Prepurchase Counseling, Rental Counseling

LOGAN SQUARE NEIGHBORHOOD ASSOCIATION
3321 Wrightwood Avenue
Chicago, IL 60647
773-384-4370
Fax: 773-384-0624
Type of Counseling:
HECM Counseling, Default/Foreclosure Counseling, Rental Counseling, Prepurchase Counseling

LEGAL ASSISTANCE FOUNDATION OF METROPOLITAN CHICAGO
111 West Jackson Ste 300
Chicago, IL 60604
312-341-1070
Fax: 312-341-1041
Type of Counseling:
HECM Counseling, Prepurchase Counseling, Default/Foreclosure Counseling, Rental Counseling

CITY OF CHICAGO DEPARTMENT OF HOUSING
318 S Michigan Ave
Chicago, IL 60604-4208
312-747-2858
Fax: 312-747-1670
Type of Counseling:
HECM Counseling, Default/Foreclosure Counseling, Rental Counseling, Prepurchase Counseling

CHICAGO HEIGHTS COMMUNITY SERVICE CENTER - CEDA
1203 W End Ave
Chicago Heights, IL 60411-2746
708-754-4575
Fax: 708-754-4595
Type of Counseling:
HECM Counseling, Default/Foreclosure Counseling, Rental Counseling, Prepurchase Counseling

CEDA NEAR WEST
5142 West 25th Street
Cicero, IL 60804-
708-222-3824
Fax: 708-222-0026
Type of Counseling:
HECM Counseling, Default/Foreclosure Counseling, Rental Counseling, Prepurchase Counseling

CONSUMER CREDIT COUNSELING
220 N Vermilion St
Danville, IL 61832-
217-425-0654
Toll-Free: 800-959-2227
Fax: 217-425-4793
Email: cris@cccsillinois.org
Type of Counseling:
HECM Counseling, Default/Foreclosure Counseling, Rental Counseling, Prepurchase Counseling
Affiliate of: NATIONAL FOUNDATION FOR CONSUMER CREDIT, INCORPORATED

CONSUMER CREDIT COUNSELING SERVICE OF EAST CENTRAL ILLINOIS
222 E. North Street
Decatur, IL 62523
217-425-0654
Toll-Free: 800-959-2227
Fax: 217-425-4793
Email: cris@cccsillinois.org
Type of Counseling:
HECM Counseling, Default/Foreclosure Counseling, Rental Counseling, Prepurchase Counseling
Affiliate of: NATIONAL FOUNDATION FOR CONSUMER CREDIT, INCORPORATED

COMMUNITY DEVELOPMENT BLOCK GRANT OPERATIONS CORPORATION
301 River Park Dr. 3rd Floor
East St Louis, IL 62201-3022
618-482-6635
Fax: 618-271-8194
Type of Counseling:
Rental Counseling, Default/Foreclosure Counseling

CEFS EFFINGHAM OUTREACH OFFICE
202 N Banker Street
Effiingham, IL 62401-
217-347-7514
Fax: 217-347-5331
Email: outreach@effengham.net
Type of Counseling:
HECM Counseling, Default/Foreclosure Counseling, Rental Counseling, Prepurchase Counseling

CONSUMER CREDIT COUNSELING SERVICE- SAINT LOUIS
1901 South 4th Street, Suite 201, Lincoln Land Building
Effingham, IL 62401
217-342-6761
Toll-Free: 800-966-3328
Fax: 314-647-1359
Type of Counseling:
Default/Foreclosure Counseling

EFFINGHAM ECONOMIC OPPORTUNITY CORPORATION
204 W Washington Ave
Effingham, IL 62401-2357
217-347-7514
Fax: 217-347-5331
Type of Counseling:
HECM Counseling, Default/Foreclosure Counseling, Rental Counseling, Prepurchase Counseling

CEFS ECONOMIC OPPORTUNITY CORPORATION
1805 S Banker St
Effingham, IL 62401-3482
217-342-2193
Fax: 217-342-4701
Type of Counseling:
HECM Counseling, Default/Foreclosure Counseling, Rental Counseling, Prepurchase Counseling

LEADERSHIP COUNCIL FOR METROPOLITAN OPEN COMMUNITIES NORTHWEST SUBURBAN HOUSING CENTER
25 Turner Avenue Suite 204
Elk Grove Village, IL 60007-
847-290-0148
Fax: 847-290-0451
Type of Counseling:

Prepurchase Counseling, Rental Counseling

COMMUNITY AND ECONOMIC DEVELOPMENT ASSOCIATION NEIGHBORS AT WORK
1229 Emerson St
Evanston, IL 60201-3524
847-328-5166
Fax: 847-328-9262
Type of Counseling:
HECM Counseling, Default/Foreclosure Counseling, Rental Counseling, Prepurchase Counseling

LEADERSHIP COUNCIL FOR METROPOLITAN OPEN COMMUNITIES
9730 S. Western Avenue, Suite 828
Evergreen Park, IL 60305
708-636-2811
Fax: 708-636-9360
Type of Counseling:
Prepurchase Counseling, Rental Counseling

CONSUMER CREDIT COUNSELING SERVICE OF GREATER CHICAGO-EVERGREEN PARK
3317 W. 95th Street
Suite 3
Evergreen Park, IL 60805-
888-527-3328
Fax: 312-849-2135
Email: jgarcia@cccsgrchicago.org
Type of Counseling:
Prepurchase Counseling, HECM Counseling, Rental Counseling

CONSUMER CREDIT COUNSELING SERVICE -SAINT LOUIS
10314 Lincoln Trail
Suite 100
Fairview Heights, IL 622081801
618-394-1137
Toll-Free: 800-966-3328
Fax: 314-647-1359
Type of Counseling:
Default/Foreclosure Counseling

CLAY ECONOMIC OPPORTUNITY CORPORATION
832 W North Ave
Flora, IL 62839-1219
618-662-4024
Fax: 618-662-2721
Type of Counseling:
HECM Counseling, Default/Foreclosure Counseling, Rental Counseling, Prepurchase Counseling

CEFS CLAY COUNTY OUTREACH OFFICE
832B West North
Flora, IL 62839-
618-662-4024
Fax: 618-662-2721
Email: ccefs@wabash.net
Type of Counseling:
HECM Counseling, Default/Foreclosure Counseling, Rental Counseling, Prepurchase Counseling

FORD HEIGHTS COMMUNITY SERVICE CENTER - CEDA
1647 Cottage Grove Ave
Ford Heights, IL 60411-3899
708-758-2510
Fax: 708-758-0825
Type of Counseling:
HECM Counseling, Default/Foreclosure Counseling, Rental Counseling, Prepurchase Counseling

CONSUMER CREDIT COUNSELING SERVICES OF CENTRAL ILLINOIS, INCORPORATED
180 s. Soangetaha Road, Knox Agricultural Center Building
Galesburg, IL 61401-
309-676-2941
Toll-Free: 888-671-2227
Fax: 309-676-6143
Email: cris@cccsillinois.org
Type of Counseling:
Rental Counseling, Prepurchase Counseling, Default/Foreclosure Counseling, HECM Counseling

HOUSING AUTHORITY OF THE COUNTY LAKE ILLINOIS
33928 North Route 45
Grayslake, IL 60030
847-223-1170
TTY/TDD: 847-223-1270
Fax: 847-223-1174
Type of Counseling:
HECM Counseling, Default/Foreclosure Counseling, Rental Counseling, Prepurchase Counseling

AFFORDABLE HOUSING CORPORATION OF LAKE COUNTY
3701 W. Grand Avenue, Suite H
Gurnee, IL 60031
847-263-7478
Fax: 847-263-9381
Type of Counseling:
Prepurchase Counseling, Default/Foreclosure Counseling

Affiliate of: HOUSING OPPORTUNITIES, INCORPORATED

COMMUNITY AND ECONOMIC SEVELOPMENT ASSOCIATION CENTER OF COMMUNITY ACTION
53 E 154th St
Harvey, IL 60426-3645
708-339-3610
Fax: 708-331-4539
Type of Counseling:
HECM Counseling, Default/Foreclosure Counseling, Rental Counseling, Prepurchase Counseling

SOUTH SUBURBAN HOUSING CENTER
18220 Harwood Avenue, Suite 1
Homewood, IL 60430
708-957-4874
Fax: 708-957-4761
Type of Counseling:
Prepurchase Counseling, Rental Counseling

WILL COUNTY CENTER FOR COMMUNITY CONCERNS
309 N. Scott Street
Joliet, IL 60432-
815-722-0722
Fax: 815-722-6344
Type of Counseling:
HECM Counseling, Default/Foreclosure Counseling, Rental Counseling, Prepurchase Counseling

**KANKAKEE NEIGHBORHOOD HOUSING SERVICES, INCORPORATED
512 S Chicago Ave
Kankakee, IL 60901-0831
815-939-9700
Fax: 815-939-3730
Email: knhs@colint.com
Type of Counseling:
HECM Counseling, Default/Foreclosure Counseling, Prepurchase Counseling
Affiliate of: NEIGHBORHOOD REINVESTMENT CORPORATION

CEFS MONTGOMERY CORPORATION OUTREACH OFFICE
311 S. State .
Litchfield, IL 62056-
217-324-2367
Fax: 217-324-2241
Email: montcefs@mcleodusa.net

Type of Counseling:
HECM Counseling,
Default/Foreclosure Counseling,
Rental Counseling, Prepurchase
Counseling

CONSUMER CREDIT
COUNSELING SERVICE- SAINT
LOUIS
1616 West Main Street, Suite 200
Marion, IL 62959-1144
618-997-1880
Toll-Free: 800-966-3328
Fax: 314-647-1359
Type of Counseling:
Default/Foreclosure Counseling

CONSUMER CREDIT
COUNSELING SERVICE- SAINT
LOUIS
613 Lake Land Blvd.
Mattoon, IL 61938
217-235-3570
Toll-Free: 800-966-3328
Fax: 314-647-1359
Type of Counseling:
Default/Foreclosure Counseling

PROVISO-LEYDEN COUNCIL
FOR COMMUNITY ACTION -
CEDA
411 Madison St
Maywood, IL 60153-1939
708-450-3500
Fax: 708-449-2699
Type of Counseling:
HECM Counseling,
Default/Foreclosure Counseling,
Rental Counseling, Prepurchase
Counseling

CEDA NORTHWEST SELF-HELP
CENTER, INCORPORATED
1300 W Northwest Hwy
Mount Prospect, IL 60056-2217
847-392-2332
Fax: 847-392-2427
Type of Counseling:
HECM Counseling,
Default/Foreclosure Counseling,
Rental Counseling, Prepurchase
Counseling

CONSUMER CREDIT
COUNSELING SERVICE- SAINT
LOUIS
123 S. 10TH Street, Suite 205
Mt. Vernon, IL 62864
618-241-9102
Toll-Free: 800-966-3328
Fax: 314-647-1359
Type of Counseling:
Default/Foreclosure Counseling

CONSUMER CREDIT
COUNSELING SERVICE OF
GREATER CHICAGO-OAK PARK
1515 N Harlem Ave Ste 205
Oak Park, IL 60302-1205
888-527-3328
Fax: 312-849-2135
Type of Counseling:
HECM Counseling, Rental
Counseling, Prepurchase Counseling

PANA ECONOMIC
OPPORTUNITY CORPORATION
Raymond and Route 16
Pana, IL 62557
217-562-2311
Fax: 217-342-4701
Type of Counseling:
HECM Counseling,
Default/Foreclosure Counseling,
Rental Counseling, Prepurchase
Counseling

CEFS CHRISTIAN COUNTY
OUTREACH OFFICE
2295 Illinois Street, Route 16
Pana, IL 62557
217-562-2311
Fax: 217-824-5018
Email: chcefs@mcleodusa.net
Type of Counseling:
HECM Counseling,
Default/Foreclosure Counseling,
Rental Counseling, Prepurchase
Counseling

CONSUMER CREDIT
COUNSELING SERVICES OF
CENTRAL ILLINOIS,
INCORPORATED
110 N. 5th Street, Suite 210
Pekin, IL 61554
309-676-2941
Toll-Free: 888-671-2227
Fax: 309-676-6143
Email: cris@cccsillinois.org
Type of Counseling:
Rental Counseling, Prepurchase
Counseling, Default/Foreclosure
Counseling, HECM Counseling

CONSUMER CREDIT
COUNSELING SERVICES OF
CENTRAL ILLINOIS,
INCORPORATED
719 Main Street
Peoria, IL 61602
309-676-2941
Toll-Free: 888-671-2227
Fax: 309-676-6143
Email: cris@cccsillinois.org
Type of Counseling:
Prepurchase Counseling,
Default/Foreclosure Counseling,
HECM Counseling, Rental
Counseling
Affiliate of: NATIONAL
FOUNDATION FOR CONSUMER
CREDIT, INCORPORATED

CONSUMER CREDIT
COUNSELING SERVICES OF
CENTRAL ILLINOIS,
INCORPORATED
Backbone Road East, Options EAP
Princeton, IL 61356-
309-676-2941
Toll-Free: 888-671-2227
Fax: 309-676-6143
Email: cris@cccsillinois.org
Type of Counseling:
Rental Counseling, Prepurchase
Counseling, Default/Foreclosure
Counseling, HECM Counseling

CONSUMER CREDIT
COUNSELING SERVICE - SAINT
LOUIS
1890 Maine Street
Quincy, IL 623014231
217-222-0621
Toll-Free: 800-966-3328
Fax: 314-647-1359
Type of Counseling:
Default/Foreclosure Counseling

SOUTHEAST CEDA
3518 W 139th St
Robbins, IL 60472-2002
708-371-1522
Fax: 708-371-1247
Type of Counseling:
HECM Counseling,
Default/Foreclosure Counseling,
Rental Counseling, Prepurchase
Counseling

**ROCK ISLAND ECONOMIC
GROWTH CORPORATION
120 16 1/2 Street
Rock Island, IL 61201
309-788-6311
Fax: 309-788-6323
Type of Counseling:
Prepurchase Counseling
Affiliate of: HOUSING
OPPORTUNITIES,
INCORPORATED

CONSUMER CREDIT
COUNSELING SERVICE OF
GREATER CHICAGO-
ROCKFORD
810 E State St Ste 306
Rockford, IL 61104-1001
888-527-3328
Fax: 312-849-2135
Email: jgarcia@cccsgrchicago.org

Type of Counseling:
HECM Counseling, Rental Counseling, Prepurchase Counseling

ROCKFORD AREA AFFORDABLE HOUSING COALITION
205 N. Church St.
Rockford, IL 611051354
815-962-2011
Fax: 815-964-0144
Type of Counseling:
Prepurchase Counseling, Default/Foreclosure Counseling, Rental Counseling
Affiliate of: HOUSING OPPORTUNITIES, INCORPORATED

COMMUNITY SERVICE COUNCIL OF NORTHERN WILL COUNTY
719 Parkwood Ave
Romeoville, IL 60446-1134
815-886-5000
Fax: 815-886-6700
Type of Counseling:
HECM Counseling, Default/Foreclosure Counseling, Prepurchase Counseling

CONSUMER CREDIT COUNSELING SERVICE OF GREATER CHICAGO-SCHAUMBURG
1320 Tower Rd Suite 150
Schaumburg, IL 60173
888-527-3328
Fax: 847-519-7095
Email: jgarcia@cccsgrchicago.org
Type of Counseling:
HECM Counseling, Rental Counseling, Prepurchase Counseling

CEFS SHELBY COUNTY OUTREACH OFFICE
Route 16 Main Street
Shelbyville, IL 62565
217-774-4541
Fax: 217-774-3532
Email: shelbycocefs@ mcleodusa.net
Type of Counseling:
HECM Counseling, Default/Foreclosure Counseling, Rental Counseling, Prepurchase Counseling

SHELBY ECONOMIC OPPORTUNITY CORPORATION
County Courthouse
Shelbyville, IL 62565
217-774-4541
Fax: 217-774-3532
Type of Counseling:
HECM Counseling, Default/Foreclosure Counseling, Rental Counseling, Prepurchase Counseling

CEFS MOULTRIE COUNTY OUTREACH OFFICE
114 E Harrison Street
Sillivan, IL 61951-
217-728-7721
Fax: 217-728-2923
Email: cefsoutreach@one-eleven.net
Type of Counseling:
HECM Counseling, Default/Foreclosure Counseling, Rental Counseling, Prepurchase Counseling

**SPRINGFIELD URBAN LEAGUE
100 North 11th Street
Springfield, IL 62798-
217-789-0830
Fax: 217-789-9838
Email: kadavis59@hotmail.com
Type of Counseling:
Prepurchase Counseling, Default/Foreclosure Counseling, HECM Counseling, Rental Counseling
Affiliate of: NATIONAL URBAN LEAGUE

CONSUMER CREDIT COUNSELING SERVICE- SAINT LOUIS
3111 Normandy Road
Springfield, IL 62703
217-585-2227
Toll-Free: 800-966-3328
Fax: 314-647-1359
Type of Counseling:
Default/Foreclosure Counseling

THE SPRINGFIELD PROJECT HOPE, INCORPORATED
1507 East Cook Street
Springfield, IL 62708
217-206-7690
Fax: 217-522-6442
Type of Counseling:
Prepurchase Counseling, Default/Foreclosure Counseling, Rental Counseling

SPRINGFIELD DEPARTMENT OF COMMUNITY RELATIONS
800 E Monroe St
Suite 108
Springfield, IL 62701-1900
217-789-2271
Fax: 217-789-2268
Type of Counseling:
Default/Foreclosure Counseling, Rental Counseling, Prepurchase Counseling

MOULTRIE ECONOMIC OPPORTUNITY CORPORATION
County Courthouse
Sullivan, IL 61951
217-728-7721
Fax: 217-728-4743
Type of Counseling:
HECM Counseling, Default/Foreclosure Counseling, Rental Counseling, Prepurchase Counseling

SOUTHWEST DEVELOPMENT ASSOCIATION - CEDA
5818 S Archer Rd
Summit Argo, IL 60501-1410
708-458-2736
Fax: 708-458-5242
Type of Counseling:
HECM Counseling, Default/Foreclosure Counseling, Rental Counseling, Prepurchase Counseling

MONTGOMERY ECONOMIC OPPORTUNITY CORPORATION
South Rt. 127
Taylor Springs, IL 62089
217-532-5971
Fax: 217-532-3551
Type of Counseling:
HECM Counseling, Default/Foreclosure Counseling, Rental Counseling, Prepurchase Counseling

CEFS MONTGOMERY CORPORATION OUTREACH OFFICE
S. Route 127, Box 128
Taylor Springs, IL 62089-
217-532-5971
Fax: 217-532-2367
Email: montcefs@mcleodusa.net
Type of Counseling:
HECM Counseling, Default/Foreclosure Counseling, Rental Counseling, Prepurchase Counseling

CEFS CHRISTIAN COUNTY OUTREACH OFFICE
311 S. Main Street
Taylorville, IL 62568-
217-824-4712
Fax: 217-824-5018
Email: chcefs@mcleodusa.net
Type of Counseling:
HECM Counseling, Default/Foreclosure Counseling,

Rental Counseling, Prepurchase Counseling

CHRISTIAN ECONOMIC OPPORTUNITY CORPORATION
124 S Main
Taylorville, IL 62568
217-824-4712
Fax: 217-824-5018
Type of Counseling:
HECM Counseling, Default/Foreclosure Counseling, Rental Counseling, Prepurchase Counseling

CONSUMER CREDIT COUNSELING SERVICE OF GREATER CHICAGO-TINLEY PARK
16860 Oak Park Ave Ste 102
Tinley Park, IL 60477-2761
888-527-3328
Fax: 312-849-2135
Email: jgarcia@cccsgrchicago.org
Type of Counseling:
HECM Counseling, Rental Counseling, Prepurchase Counseling

CEFS FAYETTE COUNTY OUTREACH OFFICE
517 W. Gattatin Street
Vandalia, IL 62471-
618-283-2631
Fax: 618-283-2715
Email: cefs@swetland.net
Type of Counseling:
HECM Counseling, Default/Foreclosure Counseling, Rental Counseling, Prepurchase Counseling

FAYETTE ECONOMIC OPPORTUNITY CORPORATION
517 West Gallatin St
Vandalia, IL 62471-0044
618-283-2631
Fax: 618-283-2715
Type of Counseling:
HECM Counseling, Default/Foreclosure Counseling, Rental Counseling, Prepurchase Counseling

LAKE COUNTY COMMUNITY ACTION PROJECT
102-6 S Sheridan Rd
Waukegan, IL 60085-5610
847-249-4330
Fax: 847-249-4393
Type of Counseling:
HECM Counseling, Default/Foreclosure Counseling, Rental Counseling, Prepurchase Counseling

POSITIVE SYSTEMATIC TRANSFORMATIONS, INCORPORATED
1528 Washington St
Waukegan, IL 60085-5347
847-625-8629
Fax: 847-625-8631
Type of Counseling:
Rental Counseling, Prepurchase Counseling

CATHOLIC CHARITIES OF THE ARCHDIOCESE OF CHICAGO
671 S Lewis Ave
Waukegan, IL 60085
847-782-4160
Fax: 847-249-0116
Type of Counseling:
HECM Counseling, Default/Foreclosure Counseling, Rental Counseling, Prepurchase Counseling
Affiliate of: CATHOLIC CHARITIES USA

LEADERSHIP COUNCIL FOR METROPOLITAN OPEN COMMUNITIES NEARWEST SUBURBAN HOUSING CENTER
9999 W. Roosevelt Road, Suite 203
Westchester, IL 60154-
708-450-0070
Fax: 708-450-0082
Type of Counseling:
Rental Counseling, Prepurchase Counseling

DU PAGE HOMEOWNERSHIP CENTER
1333 N Main St
Wheaton, IL 60187-3579
630-260-2500
Fax: 630-260-2505
Type of Counseling:
Default/Foreclosure Counseling, Prepurchase Counseling

CONSUMER CREDIT COUNSELING SERVICE OF GREATER CHICAGO-WHEELING
212 S Milwaukee Ave Ste D
Wheeling, IL 60090-5080
888-527-3328
Fax: 312-849-2135
Type of Counseling:
HECM Counseling, Default/Foreclosure Counseling, Rental Counseling, Prepurchase Counseling

INTERFAITH HOUSING DEVELOPMENT CORPORATION
620 Lincoln Avenue
Winnetka, IL 600935722
847-501-3278
Fax: 847-501-5722
Type of Counseling:
Prepurchase Counseling, Rental Counseling

**CONSUMER CREDIT COUNSELING SERVICE OF MCHENRY COUNTY, INCORPORATED
400 Russel Ct Ste A
Woodstock, IL 60098-2640
815-338-5757
Fax: 815-338-9646
Type of Counseling:
HECM Counseling, Default/Foreclosure Counseling, Rental Counseling, Prepurchase Counseling
Affiliate of: NATIONAL FOUNDATION FOR CONSUMER CREDIT, INCORPORATED

Indiana

ANDERSON HOUSING AUTHORITY
528 West 11th St
Anderson, IN 46016-1228
765-641-2620
Fax: 765-641-2629
Type of Counseling:
HECM Counseling, Default/Foreclosure Counseling, Rental Counseling, Prepurchase Counseling

**CONSUMER CREDIT COUNSELING SERVICE OF CENTRAL INDIANA
931 Meridian Plaza, Ste 704
Anderson, IN 46016
317-266-1300
Toll-Free: 888-711-7227
TTY/TDD: 317-266-1324
Fax: 317-266-1315
Email: mwright@cccsmidwest.org
Website: www.cccsmidwest.org
Type of Counseling:
Prepurchase Counseling, Default/Foreclosure Counseling, HECM Counseling, Rental Counseling
Affiliate of: NATIONAL FOUNDATION FOR CONSUMER CREDIT, INCORPORATED

KNOX COUNTY HOUSING AUTHORITY
Tilly Estates Office
Bicknell, IN 47512
812-882-0220
Fax: 812-735-2004

Type of Counseling:
Rental Counseling

CITY OF BLOOMINGTON HOUSING AND NEIGHBORHOOD DEVLOPMENT
401 N Morton St
Bloomington, IN 47404-3729
812-349-3576
Fax: 812-349-3582
Email: hand@city.bloomington.in.us
Type of Counseling:
HECM Counseling, Default/Foreclosure Counseling, Rental Counseling, Prepurchase Counseling

**CONSUMER CREDIT COUNSELING SERVICE OF CENTRAL INDIANA
205 N. College, Suite 014
Bloomington, IN 47404
812-333-6083
Toll-Free: 888-711-7227
TTY/TDD: 317-266-1324
Fax: 317-266-1315
Email: mwright@cccsmidwest.org
Website: www.cccsmidwest.org
Type of Counseling:
Default/Foreclosure Counseling, Rental Counseling, Prepurchase Counseling, HECM Counseling
Affiliate of: NATIONAL FOUNDATION FOR CONSUMER CREDIT, INCORPORATED

**CONSUMER CREDIT COUNSELING SERVICE OF CENTRAL INDIANA
551 First Street
Columbus, IN 47201
812-372-1015
Toll-Free: 888-711-7227
TTY/TDD: 317-266-1324
Fax: 317-266-1315
Email: mwright@cccsmidwest.org
Website: www.cccsmidwest.org
Type of Counseling:
Default/Foreclosure Counseling, Rental Counseling, Prepurchase Counseling, HECM Counseling
Affiliate of: NATIONAL FOUNDATION FOR CONSUMER CREDIT, INCORPORATED

**CONSUMER CREDIT COUNSELING SERVICE OF CENTRAL INDIANA
Fayette Senior Center, 477 Grand Avenue
Connersville, IN 47331
888-711-7227
Toll-Free: 888-711-7227
TTY/TDD: 317-266-1324
Fax: 317-266-1315
Email: mwright@cccsmidwest.org
Website: www.cccsmidwest.org
Type of Counseling:
Default/Foreclosure Counseling, Rental Counseling, Prepurchase Counseling, HECM Counseling
Affiliate of: NATIONAL FOUNDATION FOR CONSUMER CREDIT, INCORPORATED

LAKE COUNTY COMMUNITY ECONOMIC DEPARTMENT
2293 N Main St
Crown Point, IN 46307-1885
219-755-3232
Fax: 219-736-5925
Type of Counseling:
HECM Counseling, Default/Foreclosure Counseling, Rental Counseling, Prepurchase Counseling

**CONSUMER CREDIT COUNSELING SERVICE OF CENTRAL INDIANA
1500 E. Main Street
Danville, IN 46112
888-711-7227
Toll-Free: 888-711-7227
TTY/TDD: 317-266-1324
Fax: 317-266-1315
Email: mwright@cccsmidwest.org
Website: www.cccsmidwest.org
Type of Counseling:
Default/Foreclosure Counseling, Rental Counseling, Prepurchase Counseling, HECM Counseling
Affiliate of: NATIONAL FOUNDATION FOR CONSUMER CREDIT, INCORPORATED

ELKHART HOUSING AUTHORITY
1396 Benham Ave
Elkhart, IN 46516-3341
219-295-0065
Fax: 219-293-6878
Type of Counseling:
HECM Counseling, Default/Foreclosure Counseling, Rental Counseling, Prepurchase Counseling

**CONSUMER CREDIT COUNSELING SERVICE OF NORTHERN INDIANA
3422 S Main St
Elkhart, IN 46517-3124
574-293-0075
Toll-Free: 800-794-6559
Fax: 574-293-0365
Type of Counseling:
Default/Foreclosure Counseling, Rental Counseling, Prepurchase Counseling, HECM Counseling
Affiliate of: NATIONAL FOUNDATION FOR CONSUMER CREDIT, INCORPORATED

CONSUMER CREDIT COUNSELING OF THE TRI-STATE. INCORPORATED
715 First Ave, 3rd Floor
Evansville, IN 47710
812-422-1108
Toll-Free: 800-451-6293
Fax: 812-424-9050
Type of Counseling:
HECM Counseling, Default/Foreclosure Counseling, Rental Counseling, Prepurchase Counseling
Affiliate of: NATIONAL FOUNDATION FOR CONSUMER CREDIT, INCORPORATED

HOPE OF EVANSVILLE, INCORPORATED
608 Cherry St
Evansville, IN 47713
812-423-3169
Fax: 812-424-2848
Email: hope@sigecom.net
Type of Counseling:
HECM Counseling, Default/Foreclosure Counseling, Rental Counseling, Prepurchase Counseling

FORT WAYNE URBAN LEAGUE, INCORPORATED
227eAST Washington Blvd.
Fort Wayne, IN 46802-
260-424-6326
Fax: 260-422-1626
Type of Counseling:
Prepurchase Counseling, Default/Foreclosure Counseling, Rental Counseling

**CONSUMER CREDIT COUNSELING SERVICE OF NORTHEASTERN INDIANA
4105 W Jefferson Blvd
Fort Wayne, IN 46858
219-432-8200
Toll-Free: 800-432-0420
Fax: 219-432-7415
Type of Counseling:
Prepurchase Counseling, Default/Foreclosure Counseling, HECM Counseling, Rental Counseling
Affiliate of: NATIONAL FOUNDATION FOR CONSUMER CREDIT, INCORPORATED

FORT WAYNE HOUSING AUTHORITY
2013 S Anthony Blvd
Ft. Wayne, IN 46869-3489
219-449-7800
Fax: 219-449-7133
Email: mmorris@fwha.org
Type of Counseling:
HECM Counseling, Default/Foreclosure Counseling, Prepurchase Counseling

**CATHOLIC CHARITIES GARY, INDIANA
520 El Camino Real
Suite 204
Gary, IN 46402-
650-696-1255
Type of Counseling:
Prepurchase Counseling, Default/Foreclosure Counseling, Rental Counseling
Affiliate of: CATHOLIC CHARITIES USA

URBAN LEAGUE OF NORTHWEST INDIANA, INCORPORATED
3101 Broadway
Gary, IN 46409-1006
219-887-9621
Fax: 219-887-0020
Type of Counseling:
HECM Counseling, Default/Foreclosure Counseling, Rental Counseling, Prepurchase Counseling

CONSUMER CREDIT COUNSELING SERVICE
3637 Grant St
Gary, IN 46408-1423
219-980-4800
Fax: 219-980-5012
Email: CCCSofNWIN@aol.com
Type of Counseling:
HECM Counseling, Default/Foreclosure Counseling, Rental Counseling, Prepurchase Counseling

**CONSUMER CREDIT COUNSELING SERVICE OF CENTRAL INDIANA
98 E. North St.
Greenfield, IN 46140
888-711-7227
Toll-Free: 888-711-7227
TTY/TDD: 317-266-1324
Fax: 317-266-1315
Email: mwright@cccsmidwest.org
Website: www.cccsmidwest.org
Type of Counseling:
Default/Foreclosure Counseling, Rental Counseling, Prepurchase Counseling, HECM Counseling
Affiliate of: NATIONAL FOUNDATION FOR CONSUMER CREDIT, INCORPORATED

**CONSUMER CREDIT COUNSELING SERVICE OF CENTRAL INDIANA
1025 Freeland Rd.
Greensburg, IN 47240
812-662-6458
Toll-Free: 888-711-7227
TTY/TDD: 317-266-1324
Fax: 317-266-1315
Email: mwright@cccsmidwest.org
Website: www.cccsmidwest.org
Type of Counseling:
Default/Foreclosure Counseling, Rental Counseling, Prepurchase Counseling, HECM Counseling
Affiliate of: NATIONAL FOUNDATION FOR CONSUMER CREDIT, INCORPORATED

**CONSUMER CREDIT COUNSELING SERVICE OF CENTRAL INDIANA
500 S. Polk, Suite 18
Greenwood, IN 46142
317-865-4979
Toll-Free: 888-711-7227
TTY/TDD: 317-266-1324
Fax: 317-266-1315
Email: mwright@cccsmidwest.org
Website: www.cccsmidwest.org
Type of Counseling:
Default/Foreclosure Counseling, Rental Counseling, Prepurchase Counseling, HECM Counseling
Affiliate of: NATIONAL FOUNDATION FOR CONSUMER CREDIT, INCORPORATED

HAMMOND HOUSING AUTHORITY
4923 Hohman Avenue
Hammond, IN 46320
219-937-8660
Fax: 219-937-8670
Type of Counseling:
HECM Counseling, Default/Foreclosure Counseling, Rental Counseling, Prepurchase Counseling

HAMMOND HOUSING AUTHORITY
7329 Columbia Circle West
Hammond, IN 46324-2831
219-989-3265
Fax: 219-989-3275
Type of Counseling:
Default/Foreclosure Counseling, Rental Counseling, Prepurchase Counseling

**INDIANAPOLIS NEIGHBORHOOD HOUSING PARTNERSHIP, INCORPORATED
3550 N Washington Blvd
Indianapolis, IN 46205-3719
317-925-1400
Fax: 317-610-4678
Type of Counseling:
Default/Foreclosure Counseling, Prepurchase Counseling
Affiliate of: THE HOUSING PARTNERSHIP NETWORK

COMMUNITY ACTION OF GREATER INDIANAPOLIS, INCORPORATED
2445 N Meridian St
Indianapolis, IN 46208-5731
317-924-4397
Fax: 317-396-1528
Type of Counseling:
Default/Foreclosure Counseling, Prepurchase Counseling

INDIANAPOLIS URBAN LEAGUE
777 Indiana Ave.
Indianapolis, IN 46202
317-693-7603
Fax: 317-693-7611
Type of Counseling:
Prepurchase Counseling, Rental Counseling

**CONSUMER CREDIT COUNSELING SERVICE OF CENTRAL INDIANA
615 N Alabama St Ste 134
Indianapolis, IN 46204-1431
317-266-1300
Toll-Free: 888-711-7227
TTY/TDD: 317-266-1324
Fax: 317-266-1315
Email: mwright@cccsmidwest.org
Website: www.cccsmidwest.org
Type of Counseling:
Default/Foreclosure Counseling, Rental Counseling, Prepurchase Counseling, HECM Counseling
Affiliate of: NATIONAL FOUNDATION FOR CONSUMER CREDIT, INCORPORATED

**FAMILY SERVICE ASSOCIATION OF CENTRAL INDIANA INCORPORATED
615 North Alabama Suite 220
Indianapolis, IN 46204-
317-634-6341
Fax: 317-464-9575

Type of Counseling:
Default/Foreclosure Counseling, Rental Counseling, Prepurchase Counseling
Affiliate of: HOUSING OPPORTUNITIES, INCORPORATED

MARTIN LUTHER KING CENTER
40 West 40th Street
Indianapolis, IN 46208
317-923-4581
Fax: 317-923-4583
Type of Counseling:
Prepurchase Counseling, Rental Counseling, Default/Foreclosure Counseling, HECM Counseling

**LAFAYETTE NEIGHBORHOOD HOUSING SERVICES, INCORPORATED
1119 Ferry St
Lafayette, IN 47902-0252
765-423-1284
Fax: 765-742-2874
Type of Counseling:
Default/Foreclosure Counseling, Prepurchase Counseling
Affiliate of: NEIGHBORHOOD REINVESTMENT CORPORATION

**CONSUMER CREDIT COUNSELING SERVICE OF CENTRAL INDIANA
327 N. Lebanon St.
Suite 103
Lebanon, IN 46052
765-482-6396
Toll-Free: 888-711-7227
TTY/TDD: 317-266-1324
Fax: 317-266-1315
Email: mwright@cccsmidwest.org
Website: www.cccsmidwest.org
Type of Counseling:
Default/Foreclosure Counseling, Rental Counseling, Prepurchase Counseling, HECM Counseling
Affiliate of: NATIONAL FOUNDATION FOR CONSUMER CREDIT, INCORPORATED

AFFORDABLE HOUSING CORPORATION OF MARION INDIANA, INCORPORATED
601 S. Adams Street
Marion, IN
765-664-5194
Fax: 765-668-3045
Type of Counseling:
Prepurchase Counseling, Rental Counseling

THE GREATER MICHIGAN CITY COMMUNITY DEVELOPMENT CORP
1709 East Michigan Blvd
Michigan City, IN 46360
219-873-1207
Fax: 219-873-1208
Type of Counseling:
Prepurchase Counseling, Rental Counseling

HOOSIER UPLANDS ECONOMIC DEVELOPMENT CORPORATION
521 W Main St
Mitchell, IN 47446-1410
812-849-4447
Toll-Free: 800-827-2219
Fax: 812-849-0627
Type of Counseling:
Rental Counseling

MUNCIE HOMEOWNERSHIP AND DEVELOPMENT CENTER/URBAN ENTERPRISE ASSOCIATION, INCORPORATED
407 S Walnut St
Muncie, IN 47308
765-282-6656
Fax: 765-282-8391
Type of Counseling:
HECM Counseling, Default/Foreclosure Counseling, Rental Counseling, Prepurchase Counseling

**CONSUMER CREDIT COUNSELING SERVICE OF CENTRAL INDIANA
2803 N. Oakwood
Muncie, IN 47304
765-284-7154
Toll-Free: 888-711-7227
TTY/TDD: 317-266-1324
Fax: 317-266-1315
Email: mwright@cccsmidwest.org
Website: www.cccsmidwest.org
Type of Counseling:
Default/Foreclosure Counseling, Rental Counseling, Prepurchase Counseling, HECM Counseling
Affiliate of: NATIONAL FOUNDATION FOR CONSUMER CREDIT, INCORPORATED

CRAIG STANLEY AGENCY
133 Edgemont Drive
New Albany, IN 47150
812-949-9997
Fax: 812-948-4603
Type of Counseling:
HECM Counseling, Default/Foreclosure Counseling, Rental Counseling, Prepurchase Counseling

**CONSUMER CREDIT COUNSELING SERVICE OF CENTRAL INDIANA
100 S. Main Street
New Castle, IN 47388-
765-533-6390
Toll-Free: 888-711-7227
TTY/TDD: 317-266-1324
Fax: 317-266-1315
Email: mwright@cccsmidwest.org
Website: www.cccsmidwest.org
Type of Counseling:
Default/Foreclosure Counseling, Rental Counseling, Prepurchase Counseling, HECM Counseling
Affiliate of: NATIONAL FOUNDATION FOR CONSUMER CREDIT, INCORPORATED

**CONSUMER CREDIT COUNSELING SERVICE OF CENTRAL INDIANA
942 N. 10th Street
Noblesville, IN 46060
317-776-3480
Toll-Free: 888-711-7227
TTY/TDD: 317-266-1324
Fax: 317-266-1315
Email: mwright@cccsmidwest.org
Website: www.cccsmidwest.org
Type of Counseling:
Default/Foreclosure Counseling, Rental Counseling, Prepurchase Counseling, HECM Counseling
Affiliate of: NATIONAL FOUNDATION FOR CONSUMER CREDIT, INCORPORATED

**CONSUMER CREDIT COUNSELING SERVICE OF CENTRAL INDIANA
50 Hancock Street, Suite 5
Seymour, IN 47274
812-523-3760
Toll-Free: 888-711-7227
TTY/TDD: 317-266-1324
Fax: 317-266-1315
Email: mwright@cccsmidwest.org
Website: www.cccsmidwest.org
Type of Counseling:
Default/Foreclosure Counseling, Rental Counseling, Prepurchase Counseling, HECM Counseling
Affiliate of: NATIONAL FOUNDATION FOR CONSUMER CREDIT, INCORPORATED

**CONSUMER CREDIT COUNSELING SERVICE OF NORTHERN INDIANA
1635 N. Ironwood Drive
South Bend, IN 46553
574-273-2121
Toll-Free: 800-794-6559

Fax: 574-273-9478
Type of Counseling:
Default/Foreclosure Counseling, Rental Counseling, Prepurchase Counseling, HECM Counseling
Affiliate of: NATIONAL FOUNDATION FOR CONSUMER CREDIT, INCORPORATED

HOUSING ASSISTANCE OFFICE, INCORPORATED
1138 Lincoln Way E
South Bend, IN 46601-3728
219-233-9305
Fax: 219-282-3429
Type of Counseling:
HECM Counseling, Rental Counseling, Prepurchase Counseling

REAL SERVICES OF SAINT JOSEPH COUNTY, INCORPORATED AREA 2 AGENCY ON AGING
1151 S Michigan St
South Bend, IN 46634
219-284-2644
Toll-Free: 800-552-7928
Fax: 219-284-2691
Type of Counseling: HECM Counseling

HOUSING AUTHORITY OF THE CITY OF SOUTH BEND
501 S Scott St
South Bend, IN 46601-2766
219-235-9346
Fax: 219-235-9440
Type of Counseling:
HECM Counseling, Default/Foreclosure Counseling, Rental Counseling, Prepurchase Counseling

HOUSING DEVELOPMENT CORPORATION OF SAINT JOSEPH COUNTY
1200 County-City Building
South Bend, IN 46601
219-235-9475
Fax: 219-235-9697
Type of Counseling:
Default/Foreclosure Counseling, Prepurchase Counseling, Rental Counseling, HECM Counseling

LINCOLN HILLS DEVELOPMENT CORPORATION
302 Main St
Tell City, IN 47586-0336
812-547-3435
Fax: 812-547-3466
Email: sharon@LHDC.Dubois.net
Type of Counseling:
Prepurchase Counseling

**CONSUMER CREDIT COUNSELING SERVICE OF CENTRAL INDIANA
2901 Ohio Boulevard
Suite 139
Terre Haute, IN 47803
812-232-1803
Toll-Free: 888-711-7227
TTY/TDD: 317-266-1324
Fax: 317-266-1315
Email: mwright@cccsmidwest.org
Website: www.cccsmidwest.org
Type of Counseling:
Default/Foreclosure Counseling, Rental Counseling, Prepurchase Counseling, HECM Counseling
Affiliate of: NATIONAL FOUNDATION FOR CONSUMER CREDIT, INCORPORATED

HOUSING OPPORTUNITES, INCORPORATED
2801 Evans Avenue
Valparaiso, IN 46383-
219-464-9621
Fax: 219-464-9635
Type of Counseling:
Rental Counseling, Prepurchase Counseling, Default/Foreclosure Counseling

SWITZERLAND COUNTY COMMUNITY HOUSING DEVELOPMENT ORGANIZATION
317 Ferry Street
Vevay, IN 47043
812-427-2533
Fax: 812-427-9173
Type of Counseling:
Prepurchase Counseling, Rental Counseling

Iowa

IOWA STATE UNIVERSITY-FINANCIAL COUNSELING CLINIC
Palmer HDFS Building #1331
Ames, IA 50011-4380
515-294-8644
Fax: 515-294-5464
Type of Counseling:
Default/Foreclosure Counseling, Prepurchase Counseling, Rental Counseling, HECM Counseling

CONSUMER CREDIT COUNSELING SERVICES OF AMES
2546 Lincolnway, Suite 110
Ames, IA 50010
515-296-1968
Toll-Free: 866-723-7468
Fax: 515-296-1968
Type of Counseling:
Prepurchase Counseling, Default/Foreclosure Counseling, Rental Counseling, HECM Counseling

FAMILY HOUSING ADVISORY SERVICES, INCORPORATED
500 West Broadway
Suite 403
Council Bluffs, IA 51503
712-322-4436
Fax: 402-934-7928
Type of Counseling:
Default/Foreclosure Counseling, Prepurchase Counseling, Rental Counseling, HECM Counseling

**MISSISSIPPI VALLEY NEIGHBORHOOD HOUSING SERVICES
131 W. 3rd Street
Davenport, IA 528072114
563-324-1556
Fax: 563-324-3540
Type of Counseling:
Prepurchase Counseling, Default/Foreclosure Counseling
Affiliate of: NEIGHBORHOOD REINVESTMENT CORPORATION

UNITED NEIGHBORS INCORPORATED
808 Harrison St.
Davenport, IA 52803
319-322-7363
Type of Counseling:
Prepurchase Counseling, Default/Foreclosure Counseling

CITIZENS FOR COMMUNITY IMPROVEMENT
2005 Forest Avenue
Des Moines, IA 50311
515-255-0800
Fax: 515-255-1314
Type of Counseling:
Default/Foreclosure Counseling, Prepurchase Counseling

SERVICES FOR HOMEOWNERS PROGRAM
602 E 1st St
Des Moines, IA 503091812
515-283-4787
Fax: 515-237-1687
Type of Counseling:
HECM Counseling, Default/Foreclosure Counseling, Rental Counseling, Prepurchase Counseling

NEIGHBORHOOD HOUSING SERVICES OF DES MOINES
1153 24th Street
Des Moines, IA 50311
515-277-6647
Fax: 515-277-6681
Email: nhsdm@aol.com
Type of Counseling:
Default/Foreclosure Counseling, Prepurchase Counseling
Affiliate of: NEIGHBORHOOD REINVESTMENT CORPORATION

CONSUMER CREDIT COUNSELING SERVICES OF DUBUQUE
2255 JF Kennedy Rd.
Dubuque, IA 52001
563-582-2885
Toll-Free: 866-720-9049
Fax: 563-582-4504
Type of Counseling:
Prepurchase Counseling, Default/Foreclosure Counseling, Rental Counseling, HECM Counseling

HAWKEYE AREA COMMUNITY ACTION PROGRAM, INCORPORATED
1515 Hawkeye Dr.
Hiawatha, IA 52233
319-393-7811
Fax: 319-739-1533
Email: jwhite@hacap.org
Type of Counseling:
HECM Counseling, Default/Foreclosure Counseling, Rental Counseling, Prepurchase Counseling

CONSUMER CREDIT COUNSELING SERVICES OF MARSHALLTOWN
24 East Main St.
Marshalltown, IA 50158
641-752-6161
Toll-Free: 866-720-9048
Fax: 641-754-6970
Type of Counseling:
Prepurchase Counseling, Default/Foreclosure Counseling, Rental Counseling, HECM Counseling

CONSUMER CREDIT COUNSELING SERVICES OF MASON CITY
520 S. Pierce Suite 202
Mason City, IA 50401
641-421-7619
Toll-Free: 866-720-9050
Fax: 515-421-7738
Type of Counseling:
HECM Counseling, Default/Foreclosure Counseling, Rental Counseling, Prepurchase Counseling

THE CENTER FOR ASSISTANCE, INFORMATION AND DIRECTION
715 Douglas St
Sioux City, IA 51101-1208
877-580-5526
Toll-Free: 877-580-5526
Fax: 712-255-1352
Type of Counseling:
HECM Counseling, Default/Foreclosure Counseling, Rental Counseling, Prepurchase Counseling

LA CASA LATINA
206 6th Street
Sioux City, IA 51101-1208
712-252-4259
Fax: 712-252-5655
Email: cccs@willinet.net
Website: www.cccsofsiouxland.com
Type of Counseling:
Prepurchase Counseling, Default/Foreclosure Counseling, Rental Counseling, HECM Counseling

CONSUMER CREDIT COUNSELING SERVICE OF GREATER SIOUXLAND
705 Douglas Street, Suite 350
Sioux City, IA 51101-1018
712-252-5666
Toll-Free: 800-509-5601
Fax: 712-252-1621
Email: cccs@willienet.net
Website: www.cccsofsiouxland.com
Type of Counseling:
HECM Counseling, Default/Foreclosure Counseling, Rental Counseling, Prepurchase Counseling

CONSUMER CREDIT COUNSELING SERVICE OF GREATER SIOUXLAND
515 Grand
Spencer, IA 51301-3913
800-509-5601
Toll-Free: 800-509-5601
Fax: 712-252-1621
Email: cccs@willienet.net
Website: www.cccsofsiouxland.com
Type of Counseling:
Prepurchase Counseling, Default/Foreclosure Counseling, Rental Counseling, HECM Counseling

CONSUMER CREDIT COUNSELING SERVICE OF NORTHEASTERN IOWA, INCORPORATED
1003 W 4th St
Waterloo, IA 50702-2803
319-234-0661
Toll-Free: 800-714-4388
Fax: 319-234-7533
Type of Counseling:
HECM Counseling, Default/Foreclosure Counseling, Rental Counseling, Prepurchase Counseling
Affiliate of: NATIONAL FOUNDATION FOR CONSUMER CREDIT, INCORPORATED

FAMILY MANAGEMENT CREDIT COUNSELORS, INCORPORATED
1409 W 4th St
Waterloo, IA 50702-2907
319-234-6695
Fax: 319-236-6626
Type of Counseling:
Default/Foreclosure Counseling, Rental Counseling, Prepurchase Counseling, HECM Counseling

Kansas

21ST CENTURY HOMESTEAD, INCORPORATED
600 S. Houston Street
Altamont, KS 67330
620-784-2177
Fax: 620-784-2665
Type of Counseling:
HECM Counseling, Default/Foreclosure Counseling, Rental Counseling, Prepurchase Counseling

HOUSING AND CREDIT COUNSELING INCORPORATED
417 Commercial, Ste. 7
Emporia, KS 66801
620-342-7766
Toll-Free: 800-383-0217
TTY/TDD:
Fax: 785-234-0237
Type of Counseling:
Prepurchase Counseling, Default/Foreclosure Counseling, Rental Counseling

CONSUMER CREDIT COUNSELING SERVICE, INCORPORATED
1608 Belmont Place
Garden City, KS 67846-
800-279-2227
Toll-Free: 800-279-2227

Fax: 785-827-8280
Email: cccs@salhelp.org
Website: www.salhelp.org/cccs
Type of Counseling:
Prepurchase Counseling,
Default/Foreclosure Counseling,
HECM Counseling, Rental
Counseling

CONSUMER CREDIT
COUNSELING SERVICE,
INCORPORATED
1200 N. Main, Room 414
Hays, KS 67601
785-827-6731
Toll-Free: 800-279-2227
Fax: 785-827-8280
Email: cccs@salhelp.org
Website: www.salhelp.org/cccs
Type of Counseling:
HECM Counseling,
Default/Foreclosure Counseling,
Rental Counseling, Prepurchase
Counseling

NORTHEAST KANSAS
COMMUNITY ACTION
PROGRAM, INCORPORATED
1260 220th Rd
Hiawatha, KS 66434-0380
785-742-2222
Fax: 785-742-2164
Type of Counseling:
HECM Counseling,
Default/Foreclosure Counseling,
Rental Counseling, Prepurchase
Counseling

CONSUMER CREDIT
COUNSELING SERVICE,
INCORPORATED
Quest Building, 1 E 9th Suite 201
Hutchinson, KS 67501-
800-279-2227
Toll-Free: 800-279-2227
Fax: 785-827-8280
Email: cccs@salhelp.org
Website: www.salhelp.org/cccs
Type of Counseling:
Prepurchase Counseling,
Default/Foreclosure Counseling,
HECM Counseling, Rental
Counseling

ECONOMIC OPPORTUNITY
FOUNDATION
1542 Minnesota Ave
Kansas City, KS 66102-4312
913-371-7800
Fax: 913-371-0457
Type of Counseling:
Default/Foreclosure Counseling,
Rental Counseling

CONSUMER CREDIT
COUNSELING SERVICE OF
GREATER KANSAS CITY
1314 N 38th St
Kansas City, KS 66102-2231
816-753-0535
Fax: 816-753-3374
Type of Counseling:
Default/Foreclosure Counseling,
Prepurchase Counseling

**EL CENTRO, INCORPORATED
1333 South 27th Street
Kansas City, KS 66106
913-677-0100
Fax: 913-362-8250
Email: mimio8@aol.com
Type of Counseling:
Prepurchase Counseling,
Default/Foreclosure Counseling
Affiliate of: NATIONAL COUNCIL
OF LA RAZA

CITY VISION MINISTRIES,
INCORPORATED
1321 North 7th Street
Kansas City, KS 66101
913-371-5200
Fax: 913-371-2555
Type of Counseling: Prepurchase
Counseling

HOUSING AND CREDIT
COUNSELING INCORPORATED
2518 Ridge Court, Ste. 207
Lawrence, KS 66046
785-749-4224
Toll-Free: 800-383-0217
Fax: 785-234-0237
Type of Counseling:
Prepurchase Counseling,
Default/Foreclosure Counseling,
Rental Counseling, HECM
Counseling

CONSUMER CREDIT
COUNSELING SERVICE OF
GREATER KANSAS CITY
2830 S 4th St
Leavenworth, KS 66048-4519
816-753-0535
Fax: 816-753-3374
Type of Counseling:
Default/Foreclosure Counseling,
Prepurchase Counseling

HOUSING AND CREDIT
COUNSELING INCORPORATED
513 Leavenworth, Ste. C
Manhattan, KS 66502
785-539-6666
Toll-Free: 800-383-0217
Fax: 785-234-0237
Type of Counseling:
Prepurchase Counseling,
Default/Foreclosure Counseling,
Rental Counseling, HECM
Counseling

HOUSING INFORMATION
CENTER
333 East Poplar, Suite D
Olathe, KS 66061-
913-829-4584
Fax: 816-931-0722
Type of Counseling:
Prepurchase Counseling, Rental
Counseling

CONSUMER CREDIT
COUNSELING SERVICE OF
GREATER KANSAS CITY
11111 West 9th Street Suite 1200
Overland Park, KS 66214
816-753-0535
Fax: 816-753-3374
Type of Counseling:
Default/Foreclosure Counseling,
Prepurchase Counseling

CONSUMER CREDIT
COUNSELING SERVICE,
INCORPORATED
1201 W Walnut St
Salina, KS 67402-0843
785-827-6731
Toll-Free: 800-279-2227
Fax: 785-827-8280
Email: cccs@salhelp.org
Website: www.salhelp.org/cccs
Type of Counseling:
HECM Counseling,
Default/Foreclosure Counseling,
Rental Counseling, Prepurchase
Counseling

HOUSING AND CREDIT
COUNSELING, INCORPORATED
1195 SW Buchanan St
Suite 101
Topeka, KS 66604-1183
800-383-0217
Toll-Free: 800-383-0217
Fax: 785-234-0237
Type of Counseling:
HECM Counseling,
Default/Foreclosure Counseling,
Rental Counseling, Prepurchase
Counseling

KANSAS DEPARTMENT OF
COMMERCE AND HOUSING
700 SW Harrison, Suite 1300
Topeka, KS 66603-3712
785-296-5865
Fax: 785-296-8985
Type of Counseling:

Prepurchase Counseling, Rental Counseling, Default/Foreclosure Counseling

CONSUMER CREDIT COUNSELING SERVICE, INCORPORATED
1515 E Lewis St
Wichita, KS 67211-1836
316-265-2000
Fax: 316-265-8507
Website: www.salhelp.org/cccs
Type of Counseling:
HECM Counseling, Default/Foreclosure Counseling, Rental Counseling, Prepurchase Counseling

URBAN LEAGUE OF WICHITA, INCORPORATED
1802 E 13th St N
Wichita, KS 67214-1704
316-262-2463
Fax: 316-262-8841
Type of Counseling:
HECM Counseling, Default/Foreclosure Counseling, Prepurchase Counseling

MENNONITE HOUSING REHABILITATION SERVICES, INCORPORATED
2145 North Topeka
Wichita, KS 67214-1140
316-942-4848
Fax: 316-942-0190
Type of Counseling:
Default/Foreclosure Counseling, Rental Counseling, Prepurchase Counseling

Kentucky

**NORTHERN KENTUCKY LEGAL AID SOCIETY, INCORPORATED
1312 Highway Drive
Ashland, KY 41105-
606-329-1321
Fax: 606-325-0615
Type of Counseling:
Prepurchase Counseling, Default/Foreclosure Counseling, Rental Counseling, HECM Counseling
Affiliate of: WEST TENNESSEE LEGAL SERVICES, INCORPORATED

KENTUCKY LEGAL AID
520 E. Main Street
Bowling Green, KY 42102-1776
270-782-1924
Toll-Free: 800-782-1924
Fax: 270-782-1993
Email: ctls@ctls.bowlinggreen.net
Website: www.ctls.bowlinggreen.net
Type of Counseling:
Rental Counseling, Default/Foreclosure Counseling, Prepurchase Counseling, HECM Counseling
Affiliate of: WEST TENNESSEE LEGAL SERVICES, INCORPORATED

HOUSING AND COMMUNITY DEVELOPMENT DEPARTMENT CITY OF BOWLING GREEN
1017 College Street
Bowling Green, KY 42102-0430
270-393-3630
Fax: 270-393-3168
Type of Counseling:
Prepurchase Counseling

CAMPBELLSVILLE HOUSING AND REDEVELOPMENT AUTHORITY
400 Ingram Ave
Campbellsville, KY 42718-1627
270-465-3576
Fax: 270-465-2444
Type of Counseling:
Default/Foreclosure Counseling, Rental Counseling, Prepurchase Counseling, HECM Counseling

KENTUCKY LEGAL AID
120 E 1st St
Campbellsville, KY 42719-0059
270-789-2366
Fax: 270-465-2368
Type of Counseling:
Rental Counseling, Default/Foreclosure Counseling, Prepurchase Counseling, HECM Counseling

**APPALACHIAN RESEARCH AND DEFENSE FUND OF KENTUCKY, INCORPORATED
p. o. Box 460
Columbia, KY 42728-0460
502-384-5907
Fax: 502-384-4707
Type of Counseling:
Default/Foreclosure Counseling, Prepurchase Counseling, HECM Counseling, Rental Counseling
Affiliate of: WEST TENNESSEE LEGAL SERVICES, INCORPORATED

**NORTHERN KENTUCKY LEGAL AID SOCIETY, INCORPORATED
302 Greenup Street
Covington, KY 41011
859-431-8200
Fax: 859-431-3009
Email: blcnklas@hotmail.com
Type of Counseling:
Prepurchase Counseling, Default/Foreclosure Counseling, Rental Counseling, HECM Counseling
Affiliate of: WEST TENNESSEE LEGAL SERVICES, INCORPORATED

NORTHERN KENTUCKY COMMUNITY CENTER
824 Greenup St
Covington, KY 41011-3210
859-431-5700
Fax: 859-392-2672
Type of Counseling:
HECM Counseling, Default/Foreclosure Counseling, Rental Counseling, Prepurchase Counseling

**CATHOLIC SOCIAL SERVICES OF NORTHERN KENTUCKY
3629 Church Street
Covington, KY 41015
859-581-8974
Fax: 859-581-9595
Type of Counseling:
Prepurchase Counseling, HECM Counseling, Rental Counseling
Affiliate of: CATHOLIC CHARITIES USA

KENTUCKY HOUSING CORPORATION
1231 Louisville Road
Frankfort, KY 40601
502-564-7630
Fax: 502-564-7664
Email: mcrawfor@ mail.kentuckyhousing .org
Type of Counseling:
Default/Foreclosure Counseling, Prepurchase Counseling

**APPALACHIAN RESEARCH AND DEFENSE FUND OF KENTUCKY, INCORPORATED
108 S. Main Street Suite 202
Harlan, KY 40831-2100
606-573-6301
Fax: 606-573-6301
Type of Counseling:
Default/Foreclosure Counseling, Prepurchase Counseling, HECM Counseling, Rental Counseling
Affiliate of: WEST TENNESSEE LEGAL SERVICES, INCORPORATED

**APPALACHIAN RESEARCH AND DEFENSE FUND OF KENTUCKY, INCORPORATED
P.O. Box 7220
Hazard, KY 41702-7220
606-439-2315
Fax: 606-439-4364
Type of Counseling:
Default/Foreclosure Counseling, Prepurchase Counseling, HECM Counseling, Rental Counseling
Affiliate of: WEST TENNESSEE LEGAL SERVICES, INCORPORATED

CONSUMER CREDIT COUNSELING SERVICE OF THE TRI-STATE, INCORPORATED
435 First Street
Henderson, KY 42420
812-422-1108
Toll-Free: 800-451-6293
Fax: 812-424-9050
Type of Counseling:
HECM Counseling, Prepurchase Counseling, Default/Foreclosure Counseling, Rental Counseling

PENNYRILE ALLIED COMMUNITY SERVICES, INCORPORATED
1100 S Liberty St
Hopkinsville, KY 42241-0582
270-885-4959
Fax: 270-885-6078
Type of Counseling:
Default/Foreclosure Counseling, Rental Counseling, Prepurchase Counseling

**APPALACHIAN RESEARCH AND DEFENSE FUND OF KENTUCKY, INCORPORATED
P.O. Box 725
Jackson, KY 41339-0725
606-666-4941
Fax: 606-666-9815
Type of Counseling:
Default/Foreclosure Counseling, Prepurchase Counseling, HECM Counseling, Rental Counseling
Affiliate of: WEST TENNESSEE LEGAL SERVICES, INCORPORATED

TENANT SERVICES AND HOUSING COUNSELING, INCORPORATED
136 N Martin Luther King Blvd
Lexington, KY 40507-1526
859-258-3960
Fax: 859-258-3968
Type of Counseling:
HECM Counseling, Default/Foreclosure Counseling, Rental Counseling, Prepurchase Counseling

REALTOR-COMMUNITY HOUSING FOUNDATION
2250 Regency Rd
Lexington, KY 40503-2302
859-276-2693
Fax: 859-277-0286
Type of Counseling:
Default/Foreclosure Counseling, Prepurchase Counseling

LOUISVILLE URBAN LEAGUE
1535 W Broadway
Louisville, KY 40203-3515
502-585-4622
Fax: 502-568-4663
Email: KDUNLAP@lul.org
Type of Counseling:
HECM Counseling, Default/Foreclosure Counseling, Rental Counseling, Prepurchase Counseling

HOME OWNERSHIP PARTNERS
NIA Center- 2900 West Broadway, Suite 310
Louisville, KY 40202
502-585-5451
Fax: 502-585-5568
Type of Counseling:
HECM Counseling, Default/Foreclosure Counseling, Prepurchase Counseling, Rental Counseling

THE HOUSING PARTNERSHIP/ HOME OWNERSHIP PARTNERS
333 Guthrie Green, Suite 404
Louisville, KY 40202
502-585-5451
Fax: 502-585-5568
Type of Counseling:
HECM Counseling, Default/Foreclosure Counseling, Prepurchase Counseling, Rental Counseling
Affiliate of: THE HOUSING PARTNERSHIP NETWORK

CONSUMER CREDIT COUNSELING
510 East Chestnut Street
Louisville, KY 40201
502-458-8840
Toll-Free: 800-278-9219
Fax: 502-458-9361
Email: cccservices.com
Type of Counseling:
HECM Counseling, Default/Foreclosure Counseling, Rental Counseling, Prepurchase Counseling

CONSUMER CREDIT COUNSELING SERVICE OF THE TRI STATE
1002 1/2 Main St
Madisonville, KY 42431
800-451-6293
Fax: 812-424-9050
Type of Counseling:
HECM Counseling, Default/Foreclosure Counseling, Rental Counseling, Prepurchase Counseling

**APPALACHIAN RESEARCH AND DEFENSE FUND OF KENTUCKY, INCORPORATED
P.O. Box 613
Manchester, KY 40962-0613
606-598-6188
Fax: 606-886-3704
Type of Counseling:
Default/Foreclosure Counseling, Prepurchase Counseling, HECM Counseling, Rental Counseling
Affiliate of: WEST TENNESSEE LEGAL SERVICES, INCORPORATED

PURCHASE AREA HOUSING CORPORATION
1002 Medical Dr
Mayfield, KY 42066-0588
270-247-7171
Fax: 270-251-6110
Type of Counseling:
Default/Foreclosure Counseling, Rental Counseling, Prepurchase Counseling

**NORTHERN KENTUCKY LEGAL AID
320 E. Main Street
Morehead, KY 403511040
606-784-8921
Toll-Free: 800-274-5863
Fax: 606-783-1342
Email: blcnklas@hotmail.com
Type of Counseling:
Prepurchase Counseling, Default/Foreclosure Counseling, Rental Counseling, HECM Counseling
Affiliate of: WEST TENNESSEE LEGAL SERVICES, INCORPORATED

CONSUMER CREDIT COUNSELING SERVICE- SAINT LOUIS
The Village 1406 North 12th Street. Suite D

Murray, KY 42071-
270-753-4200
Toll-Free: 800-966-3328
Fax: 314-647-1359
Type of Counseling:
Default/Foreclosure Counseling

BRIGHTON CENTER, INCORPORATED
741 Central Ave
Newport, KY 410721222
859-431-5649
Fax: 859-491-8702
Type of Counseling:
HECM Counseling, Default/Foreclosure Counseling, Rental Counseling, Prepurchase Counseling

CONSUMER CREDIT COUNSELING SERVICE OF THE TRI STATE
920 Frederica St Ste 213
Owensboro, KY 42301-3050
800-451-6293
Fax: 812-424-9050
Type of Counseling:
HECM Counseling, Default/Foreclosure Counseling, Rental Counseling, Prepurchase Counseling

CONSUMER CREDIT COUNSELING SERVICE- SAINT LOUIS
546 Lone Oak Rd, Suite 1
Paducah, KY 42003-4538
270-443-7917
Toll-Free: 800-966-3328
Fax: 314-647-1359
Type of Counseling:
Default/Foreclosure Counseling

**APPALACHIAN RESEARCH AND DEFENSE FUND OF KENTUCKY, INCORPORATED
410 Third Street
Pikeville, KY 41501-1249
606-432-2181
Fax: 606-432-2183
Type of Counseling:
Default/Foreclosure Counseling, Prepurchase Counseling, HECM Counseling, Rental Counseling
Affiliate of: WEST TENNESSEE LEGAL SERVICES, INCORPORATED

**APPALACHIAN RESEARCH AND DEFENSE FUND OF KENTUCKY, INCORPORATED
28 North Front Street
Prestonsburg, KY 416531221
606-886-3876
Fax: 606-886-3704
Email: ardfpres@se-tel.com
Type of Counseling:
Default/Foreclosure Counseling, Prepurchase Counseling, HECM Counseling, Rental Counseling
Affiliate of: WEST TENNESSEE LEGAL SERVICES, INCORPORATED

Louisiana

CENLA COMMUNITY ACTION COMMITTEE, INCORPORATED
230 Bolton Ave
Alexandria, LA 71301-7126
318-487-5878
Fax: 318-487-5858
Type of Counseling:
HECM Counseling, Default/Foreclosure Counseling, Rental Counseling, Prepurchase Counseling

CONSUMER CREDIT COUNSELING
3915 Independence Blvd
Alexandria, LA 71303-3551
225-923-2227
Toll-Free: 800-364-5595
Fax: 225-926-7912
Type of Counseling:
HECM Counseling, Default/Foreclosure Counseling, Rental Counseling, Prepurchase Counseling

JEFFERSON COMMUNITY ACTION PROGRAM
4008 U.S. Highway 90
Avondale, LA 70092
504-349-5414
Fax: 504-349-5417
Type of Counseling:
Prepurchase Counseling, Default/Foreclosure Counseling, HECM Counseling, Rental Counseling

CONSUMER CREDIT COUNSELING SERVICES - BATON ROUGE
615 Chevelle Ct.
Baton Rouge, LA 70896-6478
225-923-2227
Toll-Free: 800-364-5595
Fax: 225-926-7912
Email: info@cccs-la.com
Website: www.cccs-la.com
Type of Counseling:
HECM Counseling, Default/Foreclosure Counseling, Rental Counseling, Prepurchase Counseling
Affiliate of: NATIONAL FOUNDATION FOR CONSUMER CREDIT, INCORPORATED

SAINT JAMES PARISH DEPARTMENT OF HUMAN RESOURCES
5153 Canatelle Street
Convent, LA 70723-0087
225-562-2300
Fax: 225-562-2425
Type of Counseling:
Prepurchase Counseling, Default/Foreclosure Counseling, Rental Counseling

CONSUMER CREDIT COUNSELING OF GREATER NEW ORLEANS, INCORPORATED
1 Courtano Dr.
Covington, LA 70433
504-893-0650
Fax: 504-641-4159
Type of Counseling:
HECM Counseling, Default/Foreclosure Counseling, Rental Counseling, Prepurchase Counseling

**SEVENTH DISTRICT PAVILLION
225 North Avenue C
Crowley, LA 70527
318-788-3103
Fax: 318-783-0278
Type of Counseling:
Prepurchase Counseling, Rental Counseling, Default/Foreclosure Counseling
Affiliate of: CONGRESS OF NATIONAL BLACK CHURCHES, INCORPORATED

ASSIST AGENCY
125 West 3rd Street
Crowley, LA 705271404
337-783-7490
Fax: 337-783-9353
Type of Counseling:
Default/Foreclosure Counseling, Prepurchase Counseling

SAINT MARY COMMUNITY ACTION AGENCY, INCORPORATED
1407 Barrow St
Franklin, LA 70538-3514
337-828-5703
Fax: 337-828-5754
Type of Counseling:
HECM Counseling, Default/Foreclosure Counseling,

Rental Counseling, Prepurchase Counseling

CONSUMER CREDIT COUNSELING
401 Whitney Ave Ste 301
Gretna, LA 70056-2558
504-366-8952
Fax: 504-367-5360
Type of Counseling:
HECM Counseling, Default/Foreclosure Counseling, Rental Counseling, Prepurchase Counseling

JEFFERSON COMMUNITY ACTION PROGRAM
1501 Estalote Street
Harvey, LA
504-227-1221
Fax: 504-227-1229
Type of Counseling:
Prepurchase Counseling, Default/Foreclosure Counseling, HECM Counseling, Rental Counseling

JEFFERSON HOUSING FOUNDATION
2418 Westbank Expressway
Harvey, LA 70058
504-368-5809
Fax: 504-368-5816
Type of Counseling:
Default/Foreclosure Counseling, Rental Counseling, Prepurchase Counseling

**CATHOLIC SOCIAL SERVICE
1220 Aycock Street
Houma, LA 70361
985-876-0490
Fax: 985-876-7751
Type of Counseling:
Default/Foreclosure Counseling, Prepurchase Counseling, Rental Counseling, HECM Counseling
Affiliate of: CATHOLIC CHARITIES USA

CONSUMER CREDIT COUNSELING
1340 W Tunnel Blvd Ste 500
Houma, LA 70360-2801
504-876-2225
Fax: 504-876-2182
Type of Counseling:
HECM Counseling, Default/Foreclosure Counseling, Rental Counseling, Prepurchase Counseling

JEFFERSON COMMUNITY ACTION PROGRAM
1221 Elmwood Park Blvd Ste 402
Jefferson, LA 70123
504-736-6158
Fax: 504-736-7093
Type of Counseling:
HECM Counseling, Default/Foreclosure Counseling, Rental Counseling, Prepurchase Counseling

JEFFERSON COMMUNITY ACTION PROGRAM
1121 Causeway Blvd
Jefferson, LA 70121-1925
504-838-4277
Fax: 504-838-1179
Type of Counseling:
HECM Counseling, Default/Foreclosure Counseling, Rental Counseling, Prepurchase Counseling

CONSUMER CREDIT COUNSELING
3701 Williams Blvd Ste 310
Kenner, LA 70065-3070
504-443-1015
Fax: 504-443-1527
Type of Counseling:
HECM Counseling, Default/Foreclosure Counseling, Rental Counseling, Prepurchase Counseling

PEOPLE'S ORGANIZATION FOR SOCIAL EQUALITY, INCORPORATED
625 Veterans Boulevard
Kenner, LA 70062
504-468-2063
Fax: 504-468-3469
Type of Counseling:
Default/Foreclosure Counseling, Prepurchase Counseling, Rental Counseling

CONSUMER CREDIT COUNSELING SERVICES
117 Liberty Ave.
Lafayette, LA 70508-6821
225-923-2227
Toll-Free: 800-364-5595
Fax: 225-926-7912
Type of Counseling:
HECM Counseling, Default/Foreclosure Counseling, Rental Counseling, Prepurchase Counseling

SAINT MARTIN, IBERIA, LAFAYETTE COMMUNITY ACTION AGENCY, INCORPORATED
501 Saint John St
Lafayette, LA 70501-5709
337-234-3272
Fax: 337-234-3274
Email: smilecaa@netconnect.net
Type of Counseling:
HECM Counseling, Default/Foreclosure Counseling, Rental Counseling, Prepurchase Counseling

LAFAYETTE CONSOLIDATED GOVERNMENT
1017 Mudd Avenue
Lafayette, LA 70501
337-291-8447
Fax: 337-291-5459
Type of Counseling:
Prepurchase Counseling, Rental Counseling, Default/Foreclosure Counseling, HECM Counseling

NEIGHBORHOOD COUNSELING SERVICES
Jessie L. Taylor Center
1017 Mudd Ave.
Lafayette, LA 70501
337-291-8447
Fax: 337-291-5459
Type of Counseling:
HECM Counseling, Default/Foreclosure Counseling, Rental Counseling, Prepurchase Counseling

CONSUMER CREDIT COUNSELING SERVICES
2021 Oak Park Blvd
Lake Charles, LA 70601-7827
225-923-2227
Toll-Free: 800-364-5595
Fax: 225-926-7912
Type of Counseling:
HECM Counseling, Default/Foreclosure Counseling, Rental Counseling, Prepurchase Counseling

MARRERO-MULTI SERVICE CENTER
2001 Lincolnshire Dr
Marrero, LA 70072-4617
504-349-5458
Fax: 504-349-5495
Type of Counseling:
HECM Counseling, Default/Foreclosure Counseling, Rental Counseling, Prepurchase Counseling

DOROTHY B. WATSON MEMORIAL CENTER
1300 S Myrtle St
Metairie, LA 70003-5928
504-736-6480

Fax: 504-731-4480
Type of Counseling:
Prepurchase Counseling,
Default/Foreclosure Counseling,
Rental Counseling, HECM
Counseling

OUACHITA MULTI-PURPOSE
COMMUNITY ACTION AGENCY
315 Plum St
Monroe, LA 71210-3086
318-322-7151
Fax: 318-387-0449
Type of Counseling:
HECM Counseling,
Default/Foreclosure Counseling,
Rental Counseling, Prepurchase
Counseling

CONSUMER CREDIT
COUNSELING AGENCY
2912 Evangeline Street
Monroe, LA 71201
225-923-2227
Toll-Free: 800-364-5595
Fax: 225-926-7912
Type of Counseling:
HECM Counseling,
Default/Foreclosure Counseling,
Rental Counseling, Prepurchase
Counseling

NORTH LOUISIANA LEGAL
ASSISTANCE CORPORATION
200 Washington Street
Monroe, LA 71201
318-323-8851
Toll-Free: 800-256-1262
Fax: 318-323-8856
Email: nnls@nnls.org
Type of Counseling:
Prepurchase Counseling,
Default/Foreclosure Counseling,
Rental Counseling

CONSUMER CREDIT
COUNSELING SERVICES
Offshore Oil Cntr Ste 108 6502
Highway 90 E
Morgan City, LA 70380
504-385-2055
Fax: 504-876-2182
Type of Counseling:
HECM Counseling,
Default/Foreclosure Counseling,
Rental Counseling, Prepurchase
Counseling

FAMILY RESOURCES OF NEW
ORLEANS
1418 N. Claiborne Avenue, Suite 1
New Orleans, LA 70116
504-947-1555
Fax: 504-947-1575
Type of Counseling:
Default/Foreclosure Counseling,
Rental Counseling, Prepurchase
Counseling

DESIRE COMMUNITY HOUSING
CORPORATION
2709 Piety Street
New Orleans, LA 70126
504-944-6425
Fax: 504-949-8646
Type of Counseling:
HECM Counseling,
Default/Foreclosure Counseling,
Rental Counseling, Prepurchase
Counseling

CONSUMER CREDIT
COUNSELING SERVICES OF
NEW ORLEANS EAST
6800 Plaza Dr
Suite 150
New Orleans, LA 70127
504-241-9760
Fax: 504-241-4245
Type of Counseling:
HECM Counseling,
Default/Foreclosure Counseling,
Rental Counseling, Prepurchase
Counseling

**LIVING WATER BAPTIST
CHURCH
2114 Elysian Fields Ave.
New Orleans, LA 70117
504-944-1795
Fax: 504-944-1212
Type of Counseling:
Prepurchase Counseling,
Default/Foreclosure Counseling
Affiliate of: CONGRESS OF
NATIONAL BLACK CHURCHES,
INCORPORATED

CONSUMER CREDIT
COUNSELING SERVICE OF
GREATER NEW ORLEANS,
INCORPORATED
1539 Jackson Ave
Suite 501
New Orleans, LA 70130-5858
504-529-2396
Toll-Free: 888-818-2275
Fax: 504-598-6366
Website: www.cccsno.org
Type of Counseling:
HECM Counseling,
Default/Foreclosure Counseling,
Rental Counseling, Prepurchase
Counseling
Affiliate of: NATIONAL
FOUNDATION FOR CONSUMER
CREDIT, INCORPORATED

**NEIGHBORHOOD HOUSING
SERVICE OF NEW ORLEANS,
INCORPORATED
4700 Freret St
New Orleans, LA 70115
504-899-5900
Fax: 504-899-6190
Email: nhsno@worldnet.att.net
Type of Counseling:
Prepurchase Counseling, Rental
Counseling, HECM Counseling,
Default/Foreclosure Counseling
Affiliate of: NEIGHBORHOOD
REINVESTMENT
CORPORATION

**ACORN HOUSING
CORPORATION
1024 Elysian Fields Ave
New Orleans, LA 70117-8402
504-943-7513
Fax: 504-943-3842
Type of Counseling:
Rental Counseling, Prepurchase
Counseling, Default/Foreclosure
Counseling
Affiliate of: ACORN HOUSING
CORPORATION

**NEW ORLEANS
NEIGHBORHOOD
DEVELOPMENT FOUNDATION
3801 Canal Street Suite 329
New Orleans, LA 70119
504-488-0155
Fax: 504-488-2275
Type of Counseling:
HECM Counseling,
Default/Foreclosure Counseling,
Rental Counseling, Prepurchase
Counseling
Affiliate of: THE HOUSING
PARTNERSHIP NETWORK

CENTRAL CITY HOUSING
DEVELOPMENT
2020 Jackson Ave
New Orleans, LA 70113-1475
504-522-4273
Fax: 504-522-7948
Type of Counseling:
HECM Counseling,
Default/Foreclosure Counseling,
Rental Counseling, Prepurchase
Counseling

SAINT LANDRY COMMUNITY
ACTION AGENCY
1065 Hwy. 749, suite E
Opelousas, LA 70589
337-948-3651
Fax: 337-948-4153
Type of Counseling:

HECM Counseling,
Default/Foreclosure Counseling,
Rental Counseling, Prepurchase
Counseling

CONSUMER CREDIT
COUNSELING AGENCY
8575 Business Park Dr.
Shreveport, LA 71105-5655
225-923-2227
Toll-Free: 800-364-5595
Fax: 225-726-7912
Type of Counseling:
HECM Counseling,
Default/Foreclosure Counseling,
Rental Counseling, Prepurchase
Counseling

QUEENSBOROUGH
NEIGHBORHOOD ASSOCIATION
2805 Missouri Avenue
Shreveport, LA 71109-
318-631-6573
Fax: 318-635-8100
Type of Counseling: Prepurchase
Counseling

CADDO COMMUNITY ACTION
AGENCY
4055 Saint Vincent Ave
Shreveport, LA 71108-2542
318-861-4808
Fax: 318-861-4958
Type of Counseling:
HECM Counseling,
Default/Foreclosure Counseling,
Rental Counseling, Prepurchase
Counseling

NEW SHREVEPORT
COMMUNITY HOUSING
DEVELOPMENT
ORGANIZATION,
INCORPORATED
2210 Line Avenue, Suite 201
Shreveport, LA 71104
318-425-5540
Fax: 318-425-5549
Type of Counseling:
Prepurchase Counseling, Rental
Counseling

CONSUMER CREDIT
COUNSELING
1338 Gause Blvd
Suite 202
Slidell, LA 70458-3040
504-641-4158
Fax: 504-641-4159
Type of Counseling:
HECM Counseling,
Default/Foreclosure Counseling,
Rental Counseling, Prepurchase
Counseling

Maine

MAINE STATE HOUSING
AUTHORITY
353 Water Street
Augusta, ME 04330
207-626-4600
Toll-Free: 800-452-4668
TTY/TDD: 800-452-4603
Fax: 207-626-4678
Type of Counseling:
Prepurchase Counseling,
Default/Foreclosure Counseling

PINE TREE LEGAL SERVICES,
INCORPORATED
39 Green St
Augusta, ME 04330-7436
207-622-4731
TTY/TDD: 207-623-7770
Fax: 207-623-7774
Website: www.ptla.org
Type of Counseling:
HECM Counseling, Rental
Counseling, Prepurchase Counseling

SENIOR SPECTRUM
One Weston Court.
Augusta, ME 04338-2589
800-639-1553
Fax: 207-622-7857
Email: dashby@seniorspectrum.com
Type of Counseling:
HECM Counseling

PENQUIS COMMUNITY ACTION
PROGRAM
262 Harlow St.
Bangor, ME 04401-
207-973-3500
Fax: 207-973-3699
Email: laverill@penquiscap.org
Website: www.penquiscap.org
Type of Counseling:
Prepurchase Counseling,
Default/Foreclosure Counseling

**PENQUIS COMMUNITY
ACTION PROGRAM
PO BOX 1162
Bangor, ME 04402
207-973-3500
Fax: 207-973-3699
Email: laverhill@penquiscap.org
Type of Counseling:
Prepurchase Counseling,
Default/Foreclosure Counseling
Affiliate of: CITIZENS' HOUSING
AND PLANNING ASSOCIATION,
INCORPORATED

PINE TREE LEGAL SERVICES,
INCORPORATED
61 Main St Rm. 41
Bangor, ME 04401
207-942-8241
TTY/TDD: 207-942-1060
Fax: 207-942-8323
Website: www.ptla.org
Type of Counseling:
HECM Counseling, Rental
Counseling, Prepurchase Counseling

COASTAL ECONOMIC
DEVELOPMENT CORPORATION
39 Andrews Rd
Bath, ME 04530-2105
207-442-7963
Fax: 207-443-7447
Type of Counseling: Rental
Counseling

PINE TREE LEGAL SERVICES,
INCORPORATED
145 Lisbon Street
Lewiston, ME 04042
207-784-1558
TTY/TDD: 207-828-2308
Fax: 207-828-2300
Website: www.ptla.org
Type of Counseling:
HECM Counseling, Rental
Counseling, Prepurchase Counseling

PINE TREE LEGAL SERVICES,
INCORPORATED
1 School Street
Machias, ME
207-255-8656
TTY/TDD: 207-255-6179
Fax: 207-255-8657
Website: www.ptla.org
Type of Counseling:
Prepurchase Counseling, Rental
Counseling, HECM Counseling

SOUTHERN MAINE AREA
AGENCY ON AGING
307 Cumberland Ave
Portland, ME 04104
207-775-6503
Toll-Free: 800-427-7411
TTY/TDD: 207-775-6503
Fax: 207-775-7319
Email: sdavis@smaaa.org
Type of Counseling: HECM
Counseling

**PEOPLES REGIONAL
OPPORTUNITY PROGRAM
510 Cumberland Avenue
Portland, ME 04101
207-874-1140
Fax: 207-874-1155
Type of Counseling:
Prepurchase Counseling

Affiliate of: CITIZENS' HOUSING AND PLANNING ASSOCIATION, INCORPORATED

PINE TREE LEGAL SERVICES, INCORPORATED
88 Federal St
Portland, ME 04112
207-774-8211
TTY/TDD: 207-828-2308
Fax: 207-828-2300
Website: www.ptla.org
Type of Counseling:
HECM Counseling, Rental Counseling, Prepurchase Counseling

PINE TREE LEGAL SERVICES, INCORPORATED
373 Main St
Presque Isle, ME 04769-2811
207-764-4349
TTY/TDD: 207-764-2453
Fax: 207-764-2455
Website: www.ptla.org
Type of Counseling:
HECM Counseling, Rental Counseling, Prepurchase Counseling

SOUTHERN MAINE AREA AGENCY ON AGING
Kimball Center
Saco, ME 04072
207-775-6503
Fax: 207-775-7319
Type of Counseling:
HECM Counseling

YORK COUNTY COMMUNITY ACTION AGENCY
11 Cottage St
Sanford, ME 04073
207-324-5762
Fax: 207-490-5025
Type of Counseling:
Prepurchase Counseling, Default/Foreclosure Counseling, Rental Counseling, HECM Counseling
Affiliate of: CITIZENS' HOUSING AND PLANNING ASSOCIATION, INCORPORATED

**KENNEBEC VALLEY COMMUNITY ACTION PROGRAM
Mary Street; RR1 Box 4747
Skowhegan, ME 04976
207-873-2122
Fax: 207-474-6614
Type of Counseling:
Prepurchase Counseling
Affiliate of: NEIGHBORHOOD REINVESTMENT CORPORATION

**COMMUNITY CONCEPTS, INC.
PO Box 278
South Paris, ME 04281
207-743-7716
Fax: 207-743-6513
Type of Counseling:
Prepurchase Counseling
Affiliate of: CITIZENS' HOUSING AND PLANNING ASSOCIATION, INCORPORATED

CONSUMER CREDIT COUNSELING SERVICE OF MAINE, INCORPORATED
111 Westcott Rd
South Portland, ME 04106
207-773-1411
Toll-Free: 800-539-2227
Fax: 207-773-1824
Email: cccs@ccsme.org
Website: www.cccsme.org
Type of Counseling:
HECM Counseling, Default/Foreclosure Counseling, Rental Counseling, Prepurchase Counseling

COASTAL ENTERPRISES, INCORPORATED
36 Water Street
Wiscasset, ME 04578-0268
207-882-7552
Fax: 207-882-4457
Email: els@ceimaine.org
Type of Counseling:
HECM Counseling, Default/Foreclosure Counseling, Rental Counseling, Prepurchase Counseling

Maryland

ANNE ARUNDEL COUNTY ECONOMIC OPPORTUNITY COMMITTEE, INCORPORATED
251 West St
Annapolis, MD 21401-3427
410-626-1941
Fax: 410-626-1920
Email: incoi@aol.com
Type of Counseling:
HECM Counseling, Default/Foreclosure Counseling, Rental Counseling, Prepurchase Counseling

ANNE ARUNDEL DEPARTMENT OF AGING
2666 Riva Rd Ste 400
Annapolis, MD 21401-0675
410-222-4464
Toll-Free: 800-492-2499
Fax: 410-222-4346
Type of Counseling:
HECM Counseling

ARUNDEL COMMUNITY DEVELOPMENT SERVICE INC
2660 Riva Road Suite 210
Annapolis, MD 21401-
410-222-7600
Fax: 410-222-7619
Type of Counseling:
Prepurchase Counseling, Default/Foreclosure Counseling

COMMUNITY ORGANIZED TO IMPROVE LIFE
9-11 S Carrollton Ave
Baltimore, MD 21223-2626
410-752-8500
Fax: 410-332-1804
Type of Counseling:
HECM Counseling, Default/Foreclosure Counseling, Rental Counseling, Prepurchase Counseling

ASSOCIATED CATHOLIC CHARITIES, INCORPORATED
4367 Hollins Ferry Rd suite 3-D
Baltimore, MD 21227
410-354-6811
Fax: 410-659-0750
Type of Counseling:
Rental Counseling, Prepurchase Counseling

**NEIGHBORHOOD HOUSING SERVICES OF BALTIMORE, INCORPORATED
244 North Patterson Park Ave
Baltimore, MD 21231
410-327-1200
Fax: 410-675-1855
Email: nhsbalto@ix.netcom.com
Type of Counseling:
Default/Foreclosure Counseling, Prepurchase Counseling
Affiliate of: NEIGHBORHOOD REINVESTMENT CORPORATION

**ACORN HOUSING CORPORATION
825 Park Ave.
Baltimore, MD 21218
410-752-4213
Fax: 410-685-3521
Type of Counseling:
Prepurchase Counseling, Default/Foreclosure Counseling
Affiliate of: ACORN HOUSING CORPORATION

HARBEL HOUSING PARTERSHIP

5807 Harford Rd.
Baltimore, MD 21214
410-444-9152
Fax: 410-444-9181
Type of Counseling:
Prepurchase Counseling

DRUID HEIGHTS COMMUNITY DEVELOPMENT CORPORATION
1821 McCullough Street
Baltimore, MD 21217
410-523-1350
Fax: 410-523-1374
Email: dheights@smart.net
Type of Counseling:
HECM Counseling, Default/Foreclosure Counseling, Rental Counseling, Prepurchase Counseling

MIDDLE EAST COMMUNITY DEVELOPMENT
730 N Collington Ave
Baltimore, MD 21205-2311
410-675-0900
Fax: 410-327-8204
Type of Counseling:
HECM Counseling, Default/Foreclosure Counseling, Rental Counseling, Prepurchase Counseling

THE DEVELOPMENT CORPORATION OF NORTHWEST BALTIMORE
3521 W. Belvedere Avenue
Baltimore, MD 21215-
410-578-7190
Fax: 410-578-7193
Type of Counseling:
Prepurchase Counseling, Default/Foreclosure Counseling, HECM Counseling

BEA GADDY FAMILY CENTERS, INC.
140 N Collington Ave
Baltimore, MD 21231-1635
410-563-2749
Fax: 410-675-5830
Type of Counseling:
HECM Counseling, Rental Counseling, Prepurchase Counseling

BALTIMORE URBAN LEAGUE
512 Orchard St
Baltimore, MD 21201-1947
410-523-8150
Fax: 410-523-4022
Email: twjordan@hotmail.com
Type of Counseling:
HECM Counseling, Default/Foreclosure Counseling, Rental Counseling, Prepurchase Counseling
Affiliate of: NATIONAL URBAN LEAGUE

HOMEOWNERSHIP AND REHABILITATION SERVICES DIVISION
417 E Fayette St Rm 1125
Baltimore, MD 21202-3431
410-396-3124
Fax: 410-545-6912
Type of Counseling:
HECM Counseling, Default/Foreclosure Counseling, Rental Counseling, Prepurchase Counseling

SAINT AMBROSE HOUSING AID CENTER
321 E 25th St
Baltimore, MD 21218-5303
410-235-5770
Fax: 410-366-8795
Type of Counseling:
HECM Counseling, Default/Foreclosure Counseling, Rental Counseling, Prepurchase Counseling

HARLEM PARK REVITALIZATION CORPORATION
1017 Edmondson Ave
Baltimore, MD 21223-1325
410-728-5086
Fax: 410-728-4186
Email: hprcorp@worldnet.att.net
Type of Counseling:
HECM Counseling, Default/Foreclosure Counseling, Rental Counseling, Prepurchase Counseling

TRI-CHURCHES HOUSING, INCORPORATED
815 Scott St
Baltimore, MD 21230-2509
410-385-1463
Fax: 410-752-4643
Type of Counseling:
Prepurchase Counseling

SOUTHEAST DEVELOPMENT, INCORPORATED
10 S Wolfe St
Baltimore, MD 21231-1912
410-327-1626
Fax: 410-276-5807
Type of Counseling:
HECM Counseling, Default/Foreclosure Counseling, Rental Counseling, Prepurchase Counseling

**PAYNE MEMORIAL OUTREACH CENTER
1505 Eutaw Place
Baltimore, MD 21217
410-462-3800
Fax: 410-462-3810
Type of Counseling:
Prepurchase Counseling
Affiliate of: CONGRESS OF NATIONAL BLACK CHURCHES, INCORPORATED

COMMUNITY ASSISTANCE NETWORK
7701 Dunmanway
Baltimore, MD 21222-5437
410-285-4674
Fax: 410-285-6707
Type of Counseling:
HECM Counseling, Default/Foreclosure Counseling, Rental Counseling, Prepurchase Counseling

GOVANS ECONOMIC MANAGEMENT SENATE, INCORPORATED
4324 York Road, Ste 203
Baltimore, MD 21212
410-433-3400
Fax: 410-433-7140
Email: GEMS4234@YAHOO.COM
Type of Counseling:
HECM Counseling, Default/Foreclosure Counseling, Rental Counseling, Prepurchase Counseling

EASTERN BALTIMORE AREA CHAMBER OF COMMERCE
7835 Eastern Ave Ste 302
Baltimore, MD 21224
410-282-9100
Fax: 410-284-9864
Email: rruddle@ebacc.org
Type of Counseling:
HECM Counseling, Default/Foreclosure Counseling, Rental Counseling, Prepurchase Counseling

HARFORD COUNTY HOUSING AGENCY
15 S Main Street Ste 106
Bel Air, MD 21014
410-638-3045
Fax: 410-893-9816
Type of Counseling:
HECM Counseling, Default/Foreclosure Counseling, Prepurchase Counseling, Rental Counseling

HOME PARTNERSHIP, INCORPORATED
1221 B Brass Mill Road
Belcamp, MD 21017
410-297-6700
Fax: 410-297-6613
Type of Counseling:
HECM Counseling, Default/Foreclosure Counseling, Rental Counseling, Prepurchase Counseling

DORCHESTER COMMUNITY DEVELOPMENT CORPORATION
435 High St
Cambridge, MD 21613-0549
410-228-3600
Fax: 410-228-4531
Type of Counseling:
HECM Counseling, Default/Foreclosure Counseling, Rental Counseling, Prepurchase Counseling

MARYLAND DEPARTMENT OF HOUSING AND COMMUNITY DEVELOPMENT
100 Community Place
Crownsville, MD 21032
410-514-7530
Fax: 410-987-4136

**CUMBERLAND NEIGHBORHOOD HOUSING SERVICES, INCORPORATED
400 N Mechanic St
Cumberland, MD 21502
301-722-6958
Fax: 301-722-6966
Type of Counseling:
Prepurchase Counseling
Affiliate of: NEIGHBORHOOD REINVESTMENT CORPORATION

AFFORDABLE HOUSING ALLIANCE
4785 Dorsey Hall Drive
Ellicott, MD 21042
410-995-5815
Fax: 301-596-5817
Email: wrossr106@aol.com
Type of Counseling:
HECM Counseling, Default/Foreclosure Counseling, Rental Counseling, Prepurchase Counseling

HOUSING AUTHORITY -CITY OF FREDERICK
209 Madison Street
Frederick, MD 21701
301-662-8173
Fax: 301-663-1464
Type of Counseling:
Default/Foreclosure Counseling, Rental Counseling, Prepurchase Counseling

FREDERICK COMMUNITY ACTION AGENCY
100 S Market St
Frederick, MD 21701-5527
301-694-1506
Fax: 301-662-9079
Type of Counseling:
HECM Counseling, Default/Foreclosure Counseling, Rental Counseling, Prepurchase Counseling

CONSUMER CREDIT COUNSELING SERVICE OF GREATER WASHINGTON
10 N. Jefferson St Suite 403
Frederick, MD 21701-4802
301-695-0369
Fax: 301-695-4878
Type of Counseling:
HECM Counseling, Default/Foreclosure Counseling, Rental Counseling, Prepurchase Counseling

MARYLAND RURAL DEVELOPMENT CORPORATION
101 Cedar Ave
Greensboro, MD 21639-0739
410-479-3566
Fax: 410-479-3710
Email: dothouse@dmv.com
Type of Counseling:
Rental Counseling, Prepurchase Counseling, Default/Foreclosure Counseling

WASHINGTON COUNTY CAP
101 Summit Ave.
Hagerstown, MD 21740-
301-797-4161
Fax: 301-791-9062
Type of Counseling:
Prepurchase Counseling, Default/Foreclosure Counseling, Rental Counseling

CONSUMER CREDIT COUNSELING SERVICE OF GREATER WASHINGTON
44 N Potomac St Ste 101
Hagerstown, MD 21740-4855
301-416-8284
Fax: 301-791-1641
Type of Counseling:
HECM Counseling, Default/Foreclosure Counseling, Rental Counseling, Prepurchase Counseling

SOUTHERN MARYLAND TRI-COUNTY COMMUNITY ACTION COMMITTEE, INCORPORATED
8383 Leonardtown Rd.
Hughesville, MD 20637
301-274-4474
Fax: 301-274-0637
Type of Counseling:
HECM Counseling, Prepurchase Counseling, Default/Foreclosure Counseling, Rental Counseling

HOUSING INITIATIVES PARTNERSHIP, INCORPORATED
4310 Gallatin Street
Hyattsville, MD 20781-
301-699-3835
Fax: 301-699-8184
Type of Counseling:
Prepurchase Counseling, Default/Foreclosure Counseling, Rental Counseling

GREATER WASHINGTON URBAN LEAGUE
5012 Rhode Island Ave
Hyattsville, MD 20781
301-985-3519
Fax: 301-985-3523
Type of Counseling:
Default/Foreclosure Counseling, Prepurchase Counseling

HOUSING OPPORTUNITIES COMMISSION OF MONTGOMERY COUNTY
10400 Detrick Ave
Kensington, MD 20895-2440
301-933-9750
Fax: 301-929-4336
Type of Counseling:
Prepurchase Counseling, Rental Counseling

GARRETT COUNTY COMMUNITY ACTION COMMITTEE, INCORPORATED
104E E Center St
Oakland, MD 21550-1328
301-334-9431
Fax: 301-334-8555
Type of Counseling:
Default/Foreclosure Counseling, Rental Counseling, Prepurchase Counseling

COMMUNITY ASSISTANCE NETWORK
8737-B Liberty Rd
Randallstown, MD 21133-4708
410-887-0600
Fax: 410-887-0713
Type of Counseling:

Default/Foreclosure Counseling, Rental Counseling, Prepurchase Counseling

CONSUMER CREDIT COUNSELING SERVICE OF GREATER WASHINGTON
5515 Security Ln Ste 525
Rockville, MD 20852
301-231-5833
Fax: 301-881-3670
Type of Counseling:
HECM Counseling, Default/Foreclosure Counseling, Rental Counseling, Prepurchase Counseling

CONSUMER CREDIT COUNSELING SERVICE OF GREATER WASHINGTON
15848 Crabbs Branch Way
Rockville, MD 20855-2635
301-590-1010
Toll-Free: 800-747-4222
Fax: 301-948-7498
Email: hdrivon@cccswdc.org
Type of Counseling:
HECM Counseling, Default/Foreclosure Counseling, Rental Counseling, Prepurchase Counseling

MAC INCORPORATED - AREA AGENCY ON AGING
1504 Riverside Dr
Salisbury, MD 21801-6740
410-742-0505
Fax: 410-742-0525
Type of Counseling:
HECM Counseling

**SALISBURY NEIGHBORHOOD HOUSING SERVICES, INCORPORATED
513 Camden Ave
Salisbury, MD 21801
410-543-4626
Fax: 410-543-9204
Type of Counseling:
Default/Foreclosure Counseling, Prepurchase Counseling
Affiliate of: NEIGHBORHOOD REINVESTMENT CORPORATION

SHORE UP
520 Snow Hill Rd
Salisbury, MD 218030430
410-749-1142
Fax: 410-742-9191
Email: tchase@shoreup.org
Type of Counseling:
HECM Counseling, Default/Foreclosure Counseling, Rental Counseling, Prepurchase Counseling

NATIONAL FOUNDATION FOR CONSUMER CREDIT, INCORPORATED
8611 2nd Ave Ste 100
Silver Spring, MD 20910-3372
301-589-5600
Fax: 301-495-5623

SPANISH SPEAKING COMMUNITY OF MARYLAND, INCORPORATED
8519 Piney Branch Rd
Silver Spring, MD 20901-3919
301-587-7217
Fax: 301-589-1397
Type of Counseling:
Rental Counseling

ROOTS OF MANKIND CORPORATION
Park Place Professional Center, 5835 Allentown Road
Suitland, MD 20746-
301-899-6800
Toll-Free: 866-490-6800
Fax: 301-899-8444
Website:
www.romkind.org/index.htm
Type of Counseling:
Prepurchase Counseling, Rental Counseling, Default/Foreclosure Counseling

CARROLL COUNTY BUREAU OF HOUSING AND COMMUNITY DEVELOPMENT
10 Distillery Drive Ste 101
Westminster, MD 21157
410-386-3600
Toll-Free: 888-302-8978
TTY/TDD: 410-848-9747
Fax: 410-876-5255
Type of Counseling:
Default/Foreclosure Counseling, Rental Counseling, HECM Counseling

Massachusetts

**ALLSTON BRIGHTON COMMUNITY DEVELOPMENT CORPORATION
15 North Beacon Street
Allston, MA 02134
617-787-3874
Fax: 617-787-0425
Email:
MHN@ALLSTONBRIGHTONCDC.ORG
Type of Counseling:
Prepurchase Counseling
Affiliate of: CITIZENS' HOUSING AND PLANNING ASSOCIATION, INCORPORATED

HOMEOWNER OPTIONS FOR MASSACHUSETTS ELDERS
30 Winter S 7th Floor
Boston, MA 02108-4720
617-451-0680
Fax: 617-451-5838
Type of Counseling:
HECM Counseling, Default/Foreclosure Counseling, Prepurchase Counseling
Affiliate of: HOUSING OPPORTUNITIES, INCORPORATED

CONSUMER CREDIT COUNSELING SERVICES OF MASSACHUSETTS
8 Winter St 10th floor
Boston, MA 02108-4705
617-426-6644
Toll-Free: 800-282-6196
Fax: 617-960-1492
Website: www.cccsma.org
Type of Counseling:
HECM Counseling, Default/Foreclosure Counseling, Rental Counseling, Prepurchase Counseling

CITIZENS' HOUSING AND PLANNING ASSOCIATION, INCORPORATED
18 Tremont Street, Suite 401
Boston, MA 02108
617-742-0820
Fax: 617-742-3953
Website: www.chapa.org
Affiliate of: CITIZENS' HOUSING AND PLANNING ASSOCIATION, INCORPORATED

GREATER BOSTON LEGAL SERVICES
197 Friend St
Boston, MA 02114-1802
617-371-1234
Fax: 617-371-1222
Type of Counseling: Rental Counseling

THE HOUSING PARTNERSHIP NETWORK
160 State Street, 5th Fl
Boston, MA 02109
617-720-1999
Fax: 617-720-3939
Email: turner@nahp.net

MASSACHUSETTS HOUSING FINANCE AGENCY

One Beacon Street
Boston, MA 02108
617-854-1000
Fax: 617-854-1029
Type of Counseling: Prepurchase Counseling

**METROPOLITAN BOSTON HOUSING PARTNERSHIP, INCORPORATED
569 Columbus Ave
Boston, MA 02118-1180
617-425-6767
Fax: 617-437-9311
Type of Counseling:
Rental Counseling, Prepurchase Counseling, Default/Foreclosure Counseling
Affiliate of: THE HOUSING PARTNERSHIP NETWORK

**ACORN HOUSING CORPORATION
13 1/2 Perkins St.
Brockton, MA 02302
508-580-4111
Fax: 508-580-0278
Type of Counseling:
Prepurchase Counseling, Default/Foreclosure Counseling
Affiliate of: ACORN HOUSING CORPORATION

**FAMILY SERVICE OF NORFOLK COUNTY
18 Norfolk Street
Dedham, MA 02026
781-326-0400
Fax: 781-326-1141
Type of Counseling:
Prepurchase Counseling, Rental Counseling, Default/Foreclosure Counseling
Affiliate of: HOUSING OPPORTUNITIES, INCORPORATED

**ACORN HOUSING CORPORATION
1453 Dorchester Ave
Dorchester, MA 02122-1338
617-436-6161
Fax: 617-436-4878
Type of Counseling:
Prepurchase Counseling, Default/Foreclosure Counseling
Affiliate of: ACORN HOUSING CORPORATION

**MASSACHUSETTS AFFORDABLE HOUSING ALLIANCE
1803 Dorchester Ave.
Dorchester, MA 02124
617-265-8995
Fax: 617-265-7503
Email:
FHAGINS@MAHAHOME.ORG
Type of Counseling:
Prepurchase Counseling
Affiliate of: CITIZENS' HOUSING AND PLANNING ASSOCIATION, INCORPORATED

**NEIGHBORHOOD OF AFFORDABLE HOUSING
22 Paris St
East Boston, MA 02128
617-567-5882
Fax: 617-567-7563
Email: NOAH22@ix.netcom.com
Type of Counseling:
Default/Foreclosure Counseling, Rental Counseling, Prepurchase Counseling
Affiliate of: NEIGHBORHOOD REINVESTMENT CORPORATION

**CATHOLIC SOCIAL SERVICES
783 Slade St
Fall River, MA 02724-2509
508-674-4682
Fax: 508-675-2224
Type of Counseling:
Rental Counseling, Prepurchase Counseling, Default/Foreclosure Counseling, HECM Counseling
Affiliate of: CATHOLIC CHARITIES USA

**TWIN CITIES COMMUNITY DEVELOPMENT CORPORATION
195 Kimball Street
Fitchburg, MA 01420
978-342-9561
Fax: 978-345-7905
Email: twincdc@ix.netcom.com
Type of Counseling:
Prepurchase Counseling, Rental Counseling
Affiliate of: NEIGHBORHOOD REINVESTMENT CORPORATION

CATHOLIC CHARITIES NORTH
11-15 Parker St
Gloucester, MA 01930-3017
978-740-6923
Fax: 978-745-1863
Type of Counseling:
Default/Foreclosure Counseling, Rental Counseling, Prepurchase Counseling

**HOUSING ASSISTANCE CORPORATION
460 West Main Street
Hyannis, MA 02601
508-771-5400
Fax: 508-775-7434
Website: www.haconcapecod.org
Type of Counseling:
Default/Foreclosure Counseling, Rental Counseling, Prepurchase Counseling, HECM Counseling
Affiliate of: THE HOUSING PARTNERSHIP NETWORK

LEGAL SERVICES OF CAPE COD AND ISLANDS, INCORPORATED
460 W Main St
Hyannis, MA 02601-3653
508-428-8161
Toll-Free: 800-742-4107
Fax: 508-790-3955
Type of Counseling:
HECM Counseling, Default/Foreclosure Counseling, Rental Counseling, Prepurchase Counseling

**ECUMENICAL SOCIAL ACTION COMMITTEE, INCORPORATED
3134 Washington St
Jamaica Plain, MA 02130
617-524-2555
Fax: 617-524-2315
Type of Counseling:
Default/Foreclosure Counseling
Affiliate of: HOUSING OPPORTUNITIES, INCORPORATED

**CITY LIFE/ VIDA URBANA
3353 Washington Street
Jamaica Plain, MA 02130
617-524-3541
Fax: 617-524-3555
Type of Counseling:
Prepurchase Counseling, Rental Counseling
Affiliate of: HOUSING OPPORTUNITIES, INCORPORATED

MERRIMACK VALLEY HOUSING PARTNERSHIP
10 Kirk Street
Lowell, MA 01852
978-459-8490
Fax: 978-459-0194
Email: MVHP1@aol.com
Type of Counseling:
Rental Counseling, Prepurchase Counseling
Affiliate of: CITIZENS' HOUSING AND PLANNING ASSOCIATION, INCORPORATED

**COMMUNITY TEAMWORK, INC.
167 Dutton Street
Lowell, MA 01852
978-459-0551
Fax: 978-453-9128
Email:
CBCAUREGARD@COMTEAM.ORG
Type of Counseling:
Prepurchase Counseling, Default/Foreclosure Counseling
Affiliate of: CITIZENS' HOUSING AND PLANNING ASSOCIATION, INCORPORATED

**COALITION FOR A BETTER ACRE
450 Merrimack Street
Lowell, MA 01854
508-452-7523
Fax: 508-452-4923
Type of Counseling:
Prepurchase Counseling
Affiliate of: NEIGHBORHOOD REINVESTMENT CORPORATION

HOUSING ALLOWANCE PROJECT, INCORPORATED
20 Hampton Ave Suite 185
Northampton, MA 01060
413-584-8495
Toll-Free: 800-851-8495
Fax: 413-586-3571
Type of Counseling:
HECM Counseling, Default/Foreclosure Counseling, Rental Counseling, Prepurchase Counseling

BERKSHIRE HOUSING DEVELOPMENT CORPORATION
74 North St
Pittsfield, MA 01201-5116
413-499-1630
Fax: 413-445-7633
Email:
dblacklo@bershirehousing.com
Type of Counseling:
Prepurchase Counseling

PLYMOUTH REDEVELOPMENT AUTHORITY
11 Lincoln Street
Plymouth, MA 02360
508-830-4115
Fax: 508-830-4116
Type of Counseling:
Prepurchase Counseling, Default/Foreclosure Counseling, HECM Counseling, Rental Counseling

QUINCY COMMUNITY ACTION PROGRAMS, INCORPORATED
1509 Hancock St
Quincy, MA 02169-5200
617-479-8181
Fax: 617-479-7228
Email: Agardner@QCAP.org
Type of Counseling:
HECM Counseling, Default/Foreclosure Counseling, Rental Counseling, Prepurchase Counseling

**URBAN EDGE HOUSING CORPORATION
2010 Columbus Ave
Roxbury, MA 02119
617-522-5515
Fax: 617-522-5584
Type of Counseling:
Prepurchase Counseling, Default/Foreclosure Counseling
Affiliate of: NEIGHBORHOOD REINVESTMENT CORPORATION

**ACORN HOUSING CORPORATION
1655 Main Street #204
Springfield, MA 01103
413-736-7713
Fax: 413-736-7715
Type of Counseling:
Default/Foreclosure Counseling, Prepurchase Counseling, Rental Counseling
Affiliate of: ACORN HOUSING CORPORATION

HAMPDEN HAMPSHIRE HOUSING PARTNERSHIP
322 Main St
Springfield, MA 01105
800-332-9667
Toll-Free: 800-332-9667
Fax: 413-731-8723
Type of Counseling:
HECM Counseling, Default/Foreclosure Counseling, Rental Counseling, Prepurchase Counseling
Affiliate of: THE HOUSING PARTNERSHIP NETWORK

COMMUNITY SERVICE NETWORK, INCORPORATED
52 Broadway
Stoneham, MA 02180-1003
781-438-1977
Fax: 781-438-6037
Type of Counseling:
Prepurchase Counseling, Default/Foreclosure Counseling, HECM Counseling, Rental Counseling

PRO-HOME INCORPORATED
PO Box 2793
Taunton, MA 02780
508-821-1092
Fax: 508-821-1091
Type of Counseling:
Prepurchase Counseling, Default/Foreclosure Counseling, Rental Counseling, HECM Counseling

**RURAL DEVELOPMENT INCORPORATED
42 Canal Road
Turners Falls, MA 01376-
413-863-9781
Fax: 413-863-8160
Affiliate of: HOUSING OPPORTUNITIES, INCORPORATED

HOUSING ALLOWANCE PROJECT, INCORPORATED
79 Broad St
Westfield, MA 01085-2925
413-568-7200
Fax: 413-785-1251
Type of Counseling:
HECM Counseling, Default/Foreclosure Counseling, Rental Counseling, Prepurchase Counseling

RURAL HOUSING IMPROVEMENT, INCORPORATED
218 Central St
Winchendon, MA 01475-1633
978-297-5300
Fax: 978-2972606
Type of Counseling:
Rental Counseling

Michigan

GREENPATH DEBT SOLUTIONS
7445 Allen Rd Rm. 260
Allen Park, MI 48101-1963
800-547-5005
Toll-Free: 800-547-5005
Fax: 313-381-3158
Type of Counseling:
HECM Counseling, Default/Foreclosure Counseling, Rental Counseling, Prepurchase Counseling
Affiliate of: NATIONAL FOUNDATION FOR CONSUMER CREDIT, INCORPORATED

WASHTENAW HOMEBUYERS PROGRAM
2301 Platt Road
Ann Arbor, MI 48104
734-975-0559
Fax: 734-975-1665
Type of Counseling:
Prepurchase Counseling, Default/Foreclosure Counseling

GREENPATH DEBT SOLUTIONS
3840 Packard Rd Ste. 270
Ann Arbor, MI 48108
734-477-0700
Fax: 734-477-0706
Type of Counseling:
HECM Counseling, Default/Foreclosure Counseling, Rental Counseling, Prepurchase Counseling
Affiliate of: NATIONAL FOUNDATION FOR CONSUMER CREDIT, INCORPORATED

GREENPATH DEBT SOLUTIONS
131 Columbia Ave E Ste 204
Battle Creek, MI 49015-3761
616-963-4575
Fax: 616-963-6123
Type of Counseling:
HECM Counseling, Default/Foreclosure Counseling, Rental Counseling, Prepurchase Counseling

**NEIGHBORHOODS INCORPORATED OF BATTLE CREEK
47 N Washington Avenue
Battle Creek, MI 49017
616-968-1113
Fax: 616-963-7022
Type of Counseling:
Default/Foreclosure Counseling, Prepurchase Counseling, Rental Counseling
Affiliate of: NEIGHBORHOOD REINVESTMENT CORPORATION

SOUTHWEST CMMUNITY ACTION AGENCY
185 E. Main, 2nd. Floor
Benton Harbor, MI 49022-
616-925-9077
Fax: 616-925-9271
Type of Counseling:
Prepurchase Counseling

GREENPATH DEBT SOLUTIONS
2525 Telegraph Road, Suite 306
Bloomfield Hills, MI 48302-0289
248-332-5273
Fax: 248-332-5537
Type of Counseling:
Prepurchase Counseling, Default/Foreclosure Counseling, HECM Counseling, Rental Counseling
Affiliate of: NATIONAL FOUNDATION FOR CONSUMER CREDIT, INCORPORATED

GREENPATH DEBT SOLUTIONS
211 North First Street, Suite 300
Brighton, MI 48116-1297
810-227-0200
Fax: 810-227-0474
Type of Counseling:
Prepurchase Counseling, Default/Foreclosure Counseling, HECM Counseling, Rental Counseling
Affiliate of: NATIONAL FOUNDATION FOR CONSUMER CREDIT, INCORPORATED

NORTHWEST MICHIGAN HUMAN SERVICES AGENCY, INCORPORATED
1640 Marty Paul St
Cadillac, MI 49601-9608
616-775-9781
Fax: 616-775-1448
Type of Counseling:
HECM Counseling, Default/Foreclosure Counseling, Rental Counseling, Prepurchase Counseling

HUMAN DEVELOPMENT COMMISSION
429 Montague Ave
Caro, MI 48723-1921
989-673-4121
Fax: 989-673-2031
Type of Counseling:
HECM Counseling, Default/Foreclosure Counseling, Rental Counseling, Prepurchase Counseling

DETROIT NON-PROFIT HOUSING CORPORATION
2990 West Grand Blvd., Suite 200
Detroit, MI
313-972-1111
Fax: 313-972-1125
Email: detroitnon@aol.com
Type of Counseling:
Default/Foreclosure Counseling, Rental Counseling, Prepurchase Counseling, HECM Counseling

PEOPLE UNITED AS ONE
660 Martin Luther King Blvd.
Detroit, MI 48201-
313-993-9077
Fax: 313-993-6502
Type of Counseling:
Prepurchase Counseling, Rental Counseling, HECM Counseling, Default/Foreclosure Counseling

**ACORN HOUSING CORPORATION
1249 Washington Blvd Ste 1301
Detroit, MI 48226-1822
313-963-1841
Fax: 313-963-6905
Type of Counseling:
Prepurchase Counseling, Default/Foreclosure Counseling
Affiliate of: ACORN HOUSING CORPORATION

PHOENIX NON-PROFIT, INCORPORATED
1640 Porter St
Detroit, MI 48216-1936
313-964-4207
Fax: 313-964-3861
Email: FatMarv@AOL.COM
Type of Counseling:
Default/Foreclosure Counseling, Prepurchase Counseling

U SNAP BAC
11101 Morang Dr
Detroit, MI 48224-1702
313-640-1100
Fax: 313-640-1112
Type of Counseling:
Default/Foreclosure Counseling, Rental Counseling, Prepurchase Counseling

GREENPATH DEBT SOLUTIONS
3011 W Grand Blvd Ste 561 Fisher Bldg
Detroit, MI 48202
313-872-2401
Fax: 313-872-3041
Type of Counseling:
HECM Counseling, Default/Foreclosure Counseling, Rental Counseling, Prepurchase Counseling

NEIGHBORHOOD SERVICE ORGANIZATION
18829 McNichols
Detroit, MI 48221-
313-537-5268
Fax: 313-537-5358
Type of Counseling:
Prepurchase Counseling, Default/Foreclosure Counseling

DETROIT NEIGHBORHOOD HOUSING SERVICES
3839 Woodward Avenue

Detroit, MI 482012009
313-833-1943
Type of Counseling:
HECM Counseling,
Default/Foreclosure Counseling,
Rental Counseling, Prepurchase
Counseling

MICHIGAN STATE UNIVERSITY
EXTENSION SERVICES
108 Agricultural Hall
East Lansing, MI 48224-
517-432-7686
Fax: 517-353-4846
Website: www.msue.msu.edu/home/
Type of Counseling:
Prepurchase Counseling,
Default/Foreclosure Counseling,
HECM Counseling, Rental
Counseling

GREENPATH DEBT SOLUTIONS
38505 Country Club Dr Ste 210
Farmington Hills, MI 483313429
248-553-5400
Toll-Free: 800-547-5005
Fax: 248-553-2224
Type of Counseling:
HECM Counseling,
Default/Foreclosure Counseling,
Prepurchase Counseling
Affiliate of: NATIONAL
FOUNDATION FOR CONSUMER
CREDIT, INCORPORATED

URBAN LEAGUE OF FLINT
5005 Cloverlawn Dr
Flint, MI 48504-2067
810-789-7611
Fax: 810-787-4518
Email: ulflint@aol.com
Type of Counseling:
Default/Foreclosure Counseling,
Prepurchase Counseling, HECM
Counseling, Rental Counseling
Affiliate of: NATIONAL URBAN
LEAGUE

**METRO HOUSING
PARTNERSHIP, INCORPORATED
503 S Saginaw St, Suite 519
Flint, MI 48502
810-767-4622
Fax: 810-767-4664
Type of
Counseling:Default/Foreclosure
Counseling, Prepurchase Counseling,
HECM Counseling
Affiliate of: THE HOUSING
PARTNERSHIP NETWORK

GREENPATH DEBT SOLUTIONS
2222 South Linden Rd Ste I
Flint, MI 48532
810-230-1077
Fax: 810-230-7508
Type of Counseling:
HECM Counseling,
Default/Foreclosure Counseling,
Rental Counseling, Prepurchase
Counseling
Affiliate of: NATIONAL
FOUNDATION FOR CONSUMER
CREDIT, INCORPORATED

MICHIGAN HOUSING
COUNSELORS
G1173 N Ballenger Hwy Ste 100
Flint, MI 48504-4462
810-235-4649
Fax: 810-235-4649
Type of Counseling:
HECM Counseling,
Default/Foreclosure Counseling,
Rental Counseling, Prepurchase
Counseling

MISSION OF PEACE
Windmill Place, 877 East Fifth Ave.
Flint, MI 48503
810-232-0104
Toll-Free: 877-334-0104
Fax: 810-235-6878
Type of Counseling:
Prepurchase Counseling, Rental
Counseling, Default/Foreclosure
Counseling, HECM Counseling
Affiliate of: CONGRESS OF
NATIONAL BLACK CHURCHES,
INCORPORATED

GREENPATH DEBT SOLUTIONS
3051 Commerce Dr Ste 3
Fort Gratiot, MI 48059-3820
810-385-8562
Fax: 810-385-8569
Type of Counseling:
HECM Counseling,
Default/Foreclosure Counseling,
Rental Counseling, Prepurchase
Counseling
Affiliate of: NATIONAL
FOUNDATION FOR CONSUMER
CREDIT, INCORPORATED

GREENPATH DEBT SOLUTIONS
810 South Otsego Avenue, Suite 105
Gaylord, MI 49735-1780
989-732-2260
Fax: 989-732-1054
Type of Counseling:
Prepurchase Counseling,
Default/Foreclosure Counseling,
HECM Counseling, Rental
Counseling
Affiliate of: NATIONAL
FOUNDATION FOR CONSUMER
CREDIT, INCORPORATED

GARFIELD DEVELOPMENT
CORPORATION
1725 S Division Ave
Grand Rapids, MI 49507-1603
616-248-3235
Fax: 616-248-3445
Email: gdc@iserv.net
Type of Counseling:
Prepurchase Counseling

GREENPATH DEBT SOLUTIONS
2922 Fuller Ave NE Ste B203
Grand Rapids, MI 49505-3459
616-281-0013
Fax: 616-361-5573
Type of Counseling:
HECM Counseling,
Default/Foreclosure Counseling,
Rental Counseling, Prepurchase
Counseling
Affiliate of: NATIONAL
FOUNDATION FOR CONSUMER
CREDIT, INCORPORATED

GRAND RAPIDS URBAN
LEAGUE
745 Eastern Ave SE
Grand Rapids, MI 49503-5544
616-245-2207
Fax: 616-245-6510
Type of Counseling:
HECM Counseling,
Default/Foreclosure Counseling,
Rental Counseling, Prepurchase
Counseling

EIGHTCAP, INCORPORATED
904 Oak Dr-Turk Lake
Greenville, MI 48838
989-772-0110
Fax: 989-775-3907
Type of Counseling:
Default/Foreclosure Counseling,
Rental Counseling, Prepurchase
Counseling

GREENPATH DEBT SOLUTIONS
675 E 16th St Ste 220
Holland, MI 49423-3752
616-394-9003
Fax: 616-394-4308
Type of Counseling:
HECM Counseling,
Default/Foreclosure Counseling,
Rental Counseling, Prepurchase
Counseling
Affiliate of: NATIONAL
FOUNDATION FOR CONSUMER
CREDIT, INCORPORATED

GREENPATH DEBT SOLUTIONS
Plaza Central 415 Stephenson Ave
Iron Mountain, MI 49801
906-774-7565

Fax: 906-774-0461
Type of Counseling:
HECM Counseling,
Default/Foreclosure Counseling,
Rental Counseling, Prepurchase
Counseling

GREENPATH DEBT SOLUTIONS
127 East Ayer Street, East Side
Ironwood, MI 49938-2037
906-932-4169
Fax: 906-932-2635
Type of Counseling:
Prepurchase Counseling,
Default/Foreclosure Counseling,
HECM Counseling, Rental
Counseling
Affiliate of: NATIONAL
FOUNDATION FOR CONSUMER
CREDIT, INCORPORATED

GREENPATH DEBT SOLUTIONS
211 W Ganson St
Jackson, MI 49201-1241
517-788-9866
Fax: 517-788-9248
Type of Counseling:
HECM Counseling,
Default/Foreclosure Counseling,
Rental Counseling, Prepurchase
Counseling
Affiliate of: NATIONAL
FOUNDATION FOR CONSUMER
CREDIT, INCORPORATED

**KALAMAZOO
NEIGHBORHOOD HOUSING
SERVICES, INCORPORATED
814 S Westnedge Ave
Kalamazoo, MI 49008
616-385-2916
Fax: 616-385-9912
Type of Counseling:
Prepurchase Counseling,
Default/Foreclosure Counseling
Affiliate of: NEIGHBORHOOD
REINVESTMENT
CORPORATION

GREENPATH DEBT SOLUTIONS
2450 44th St SE Ste 204
Kentwood, MI 49512-9081
616-281-0013
Fax: 616-281-0293
Type of Counseling:
HECM Counseling,
Default/Foreclosure Counseling,
Prepurchase Counseling
Affiliate of: NATIONAL
FOUNDATION FOR CONSUMER
CREDIT, INCORPORATED

GREENPATH DEBT SOLUTIONS
612 S Creyts Rd Ste C
Lansing, MI 48917-9201
517-321-5836
Fax: 517-321-5863
Type of Counseling:
HECM Counseling,
Default/Foreclosure Counseling,
Rental Counseling, Prepurchase
Counseling

MICHIGAN STATE HOUSING
DEVELOPMENT AUTHORITY
735 E. Michigan Avenue
Lansing, MI 48909
517-373-6208
Fax: 517-241-4756
Type of Counseling:
Prepurchase Counseling,
Default/Foreclosure Counseling

FERRIS DEVELOPMENT
820 N. Capitol Avenue
Lansing, MI 48906-
517-485-9100
Fax: 517-485-0179
Email: tmunson@ferris.org
Type of Counseling:
Prepurchase Counseling,
Default/Foreclosure Counseling

GREENPATH DEBT SOLUTIONS
712 Chippewa Sq. Ste 103
Marquette, MI 49855-4827
906-228-5505
Fax: 906-228-5856
Type of Counseling:
HECM Counseling,
Default/Foreclosure Counseling,
Rental Counseling, Prepurchase
Counseling

GREENPATH DEBT SOLUTIONS
25 S Monroe St Rm 307
Monroe, MI 48161-2230
734-457-0370
Fax: 734-457-3856
Type of Counseling:
HECM Counseling,
Default/Foreclosure Counseling,
Rental Counseling, Prepurchase
Counseling
Affiliate of: NATIONAL
FOUNDATION FOR CONSUMER
CREDIT, INCORPORATED

GREENPATH DEBT SOLUTIONS
37060 Garfield Rd Ste T-4
Mount Clemens, MI 48036
810-263-1160
Fax: 810-263-0715
Type of Counseling:
HECM Counseling,
Default/Foreclosure Counseling,
Rental Counseling, Prepurchase
Counseling
Affiliate of: NATIONAL
FOUNDATION FOR CONSUMER
CREDIT, INCORPORATED

MICHIGAN HOUSING
COUNSELORS
237 Southbound Gratiot Ave
Mount Clemens, MI 48043-2410
810-468-4594
Fax: 810-468-0119
Type of Counseling:
HECM Counseling,
Default/Foreclosure Counseling,
Rental Counseling, Prepurchase
Counseling

GREENPATH DEBT SOLUTIONS
950 W Norton Ave Ste 210
Muskegon, MI 49441-4169
616-737-6404
Fax: 616-739-7510
Type of Counseling:
HECM Counseling,
Default/Foreclosure Counseling,
Rental Counseling, Prepurchase
Counseling
Affiliate of: NATIONAL
FOUNDATION FOR CONSUMER
CREDIT, INCORPORATED

NELSON NEIGHBORHOOD
IMPROVEMENT ASSOCIATION,
INCORPORATED
1330 5th St
Muskegon, MI 49441-2004
231-722-0529
Fax: 231-722-3201
Type of Counseling:
Default/Foreclosure Counseling,
Rental Counseling, Prepurchase
Counseling

NORTHWEST MICHIGAN
HUMAN SERVICES AGENCY,
INCORPORATED
441 Bay St
Petoskey, MI 49770-2408
616-347-9070
Fax: 616-347-3664
Type of Counseling:
Default/Foreclosure Counseling,
Rental Counseling

OAKLAND COUNTY - HOUSING
COUNSELING
1200 N Telegraph Rd
Bldg. 34, Rm 112
Pontiac, MI 48341-0435
248-858-5402
Fax: 248-858-5311
Email:
FrederiksenA@CO.Oakland.MI.US
Type of Counseling:

HECM Counseling,
Default/Foreclosure Counseling,
Rental Counseling, Prepurchase
Counseling

OAKLAND LIVINGSTON
HUMAN SERVICE AGENCY
196 Cesar Chavez Ave.
Pontiac, MI 48343-0598
248-209-2767
Fax: 248-209-2777
Type of Counseling:
Prepurchase Counseling,
Default/Foreclosure Counseling,
HECM Counseling, Rental
Counseling

PONTIAC NEIGHBORHOOD
HOUSING SERVICES
69 S Ardmore
Pontiac, MI 48342
248-335-5840
Fax: 248-335-2014
Type of Counseling:
Default/Foreclosure Counseling,
Rental Counseling, Prepurchase
Counseling

GREENPATH DEBT SOLUTIONS
576 Romence Rd Ste 220
Portage, MI 49024-3472
616-329-7153
Fax: 616-329-7498
Type of Counseling:
HECM Counseling,
Default/Foreclosure Counseling,
Rental Counseling, Prepurchase
Counseling
Affiliate of: NATIONAL
FOUNDATION FOR CONSUMER
CREDIT, INCORPORATED

MICHIGAN STATE UNIVERSITY
EXTENSION SERVICE
MONTMORENEY/PRESQUE ILSE
COUNTY BRANCH
151 E. Huron Avenue
Rogers City, MI 49779-0110
989-785-8013
Fax: 989-785-4183
Type of Counseling:
Prepurchase Counseling,
Default/Foreclosure Counseling,
HECM Counseling, Rental
Counseling

MICHIGAN STATE UNIVERSITY
EXTENSION SERVICES
One Tuscola Street
Saginaw, MI 48607-
989-758-2500
Fax: 989-758-2509
Type of Counseling:
Prepurchase Counseling,
Default/Foreclosure Counseling,
HECM Counseling, Rental
Counseling

**NEIGHBORHOOD RENEWAL
SERVICES OF SAGINAW,
INCORPORATED
427 Atwater
Saginaw, MI 48605
517-753-4900
Fax: 517-753-8545
Type of Counseling:
Default/Foreclosure Counseling,
Prepurchase Counseling
Affiliate of: NEIGHBORHOOD
REINVESTMENT
CORPORATION

SAGINAW COUNTY
COMMUNITY ACTION
COMMITTEE, INCORPORATED
2824 Perkins St
Saginaw, MI 48601-1505
989-753-7741
Fax: 989-753-2439
Type of Counseling:
HECM Counseling,
Default/Foreclosure Counseling,
Rental Counseling, Prepurchase
Counseling

GREENPATH DEBT SOLUTIONS
4600 Fashion Square Blvd Ste 110
Saginaw, MI 48604-2616
517-793-5623
Fax: 517-793-2898
Type of Counseling:
HECM Counseling,
Default/Foreclosure Counseling,
Rental Counseling, Prepurchase
Counseling
Affiliate of: NATIONAL
FOUNDATION FOR CONSUMER
CREDIT, INCORPORATED

GREENPATH DEBT SOLUTIONS
24725 W 12 Mile Rd Ste 240
Southfield, MI 48034-1801
248-352-5344
Fax: 248-352-9938
Type of Counseling:
Default/Foreclosure Counseling,
Rental Counseling, Prepurchase
Counseling
Affiliate of: NATIONAL
FOUNDATION FOR CONSUMER
CREDIT, INCORPORATED

NORTHWEST MICHIGAN
HUMAN SERVICES AGENCY,
INCORPORATED
3963 3 Mile Rd
Traverse City, MI 49686-9164
231-947-3780
Fax: 231-947-4935
Type of Counseling:
HECM Counseling,
Default/Foreclosure Counseling,
Rental Counseling, Prepurchase
Counseling

MICHIGAN STATE UNIVERSITY
EXTENSION SERVICE
BENZIE/GRAND
TRAVERSE/LEEIANAU COUNTY
BRANCH
Grand Traverse County Extension,
Suite A
Traverse City, MI 49684-2208
231-922-4821
Fax: 231-922-4633
Type of Counseling:
Prepurchase Counseling,
Default/Foreclosure Counseling,
HECM Counseling, Rental
Counseling

GREENPATH DEBT SOLUTIONS
812 South Garfield Avenue, Suite 7
Traverse City, MI 49686-3456
231-933-4980
Fax: 231-933-0975
Type of Counseling:
Prepurchase Counseling,
Default/Foreclosure Counseling,
HECM Counseling, Rental
Counseling
Affiliate of: NATIONAL
FOUNDATION FOR CONSUMER
CREDIT, INCORPORATED

GREENPATH DEBT SOLUTIONS
675 E Big Beaver Rd Rm 101
Troy, MI 48083-1418
248-689-2440
Fax: 248-689-6527
Type of Counseling:
HECM Counseling,
Default/Foreclosure Counseling,
Rental Counseling, Prepurchase
Counseling
Affiliate of: NATIONAL
FOUNDATION FOR CONSUMER
CREDIT, INCORPORATED

GREENPATH DEBT SOLUTIONS
38545 Ford Rd Ste 202
Westland, MI 48185-7901
734-326-4466
Fax: 734-326-3060
Type of Counseling:
HECM Counseling,
Default/Foreclosure Counseling,
Rental Counseling, Prepurchase
Counseling

Affiliate of: NATIONAL FOUNDATION FOR CONSUMER CREDIT, INCORPORATED

Minnesota

**CONSUMER CREDIT COUNSELING SERVICE OF DULUTH
2409 Forthun Roads
Baxter, MN 56425-
218-829-5000
Fax: 218-829-9726
Type of Counseling:
Default/Foreclosure Counseling, Prepurchase Counseling, Rental Counseling

LEGAL AID SERVICE OF NORTHEASTERN MINNESOTA BRAINERD LAKES OFFICE
1342 Highway 210 West
Baxter, MN 56425
218-829-1701
Fax: 218-829-4792
Type of Counseling:
Default/Foreclosure Counseling, Rental Counseling

**CONSUMER CREDIT COUNSELING OF DULUTH
403 4TH Street NW #120
Bemidji, MN 56601
218-751-1305
Fax: 218-751-0703
Type of Counseling:
Default/Foreclosure Counseling, Rental Counseling

ANOKA COUNTY COMMUNITY ACTION PROGRAM, INCORPORATED
1201 89th Ave NE Ste 345
Blaine, MN 55434-3373
763-783-4705
Fax: 763-783-4700
Type of Counseling:
Default/Foreclosure Counseling, Prepurchase Counseling, Rental Counseling, HECM Counseling

CARVER COUNTY HOUSING AND REDEVELOPMENT AUTHORITY
500 N Pine St Ste 300
Chaska, MN 55318-1953
952-448-7715
Fax: 952-448-6506
Type of Counseling:
Default/Foreclosure Counseling, Rental Counseling, Prepurchase Counseling

CONSUMER CREDIT COUNSELING SERVICE OF MINNESOTA
277 Coon Rapids Blvd NW
Ste 410 Rm. 16
Coon Rapids, MN 55433-5843
612-874-8164
Fax: 612-874-8465
Type of Counseling:
Default/Foreclosure Counseling, Rental Counseling, Prepurchase Counseling

**NEIGHBORHOOD HOUSING SERVICES OF DULUTH, INCORPORATED
2910 West 3rd Street
Duluth, MN 55806-
218-628-1057
Fax: 218-628-1060
Type of Counseling:
Default/Foreclosure Counseling, Prepurchase Counseling
Affiliate of: NEIGHBORHOOD REINVESTMENT CORPORATION

LAW OFFICES OF LEGAL AID SERVICE OF NORTHEASTERN MINNESOTA
302 Ordean Building, 424 West Superior St.
Duluth, MN 55802
218-726-4800
Fax: 218-726-4804
Type of Counseling:
Default/Foreclosure Counseling, Rental Counseling

**CONSUMER CREDIT COUNSELING SERVICE OF DULUTH/LUTHERAN SOCIAL SERVICES
424 West Superior Street
Duluth, MN 558020306
218-726-4767
Fax: 218-726-1251
Email: cedland@lss-dul.usa.com
Type of Counseling:
Prepurchase Counseling, Default/Foreclosure Counseling
Affiliate of: NATIONAL FOUNDATION FOR CONSUMER CREDIT, INCORPORATED

LEGAL AID SERVICE OF NORTHEASTERN MINNESOTA ITASCA OFFICE
204 1st Ave. Northwest, Suite 7
Grand Rapids, MN 55744
218-326-6695
Fax: 218-326-2298
Type of Counseling:
Rental Counseling, Default/Foreclosure Counseling

**CONSUMER CREDIT COUNSELING SERVICE OF DULUTH
501 Pokegama Avenue South
Grand Rapids, MN 55744
218-326-1269
Fax: 218-326-1147
Type of Counseling:
Default/Foreclosure Counseling, Prepurchase Counseling, Rental Counseling

**CONSUMER CREDIT COUNSELING OF DULUTH
301 e. Howard Street #106
Hibbing, MN 55746
218-262-3372
Fax: 213-362-7701
Type of Counseling:
Default/Foreclosure Counseling, Prepurchase Counseling, Rental Counseling

COMMUNITY ACTION FOR SUBURBAN HENNEPIN, INCORPORATED
33 10th Ave South, Ste 150
Hopkins, MN 55343-1303
952-933-9639
Fax: 952-933-8016
Email: mtimm@Cashenn.org
Type of Counseling:
HECM Counseling, Default/Foreclosure Counseling, Prepurchase Counseling

**CONSUMER CREDIT COUNSELING SERVICE OF DULUTH
710 South 2nd Street
Mankato, MN 56001
507-625-8021
Fax: 507-625-8998
Type of Counseling:
Default/Foreclosure Counseling, Prepurchase Counseling, Rental Counseling

SENIOR HOUSING, INCORPORATED
2021 E Hennepin Ave Ste 372
Minneapolis, MN 55413-
612-617-1925
Toll-Free: 888-399-4663
Fax: 612-617-1022
Type of Counseling:
HECM Counseling

PILOT CITY REGIONAL CENTER
1315 Penn Ave N
Minneapolis, MN 55411-3047

612-348-4752
Fax: 612-348-4434
Type of Counseling:
Default/Foreclosure Counseling, Rental Counseling, Prepurchase Counseling

CONSUMER CREDIT COUNSELING SERVICE OF MINNESOTA
10560 Wayzata Blvd Ste 11
Woodside Complex
Minnetonka, MN 55305-1524
651-874-8164
Fax: 651-439-4894
Type of Counseling:
Default/Foreclosure Counseling, Rental Counseling, Prepurchase Counseling

**THE VILLAGE FAMILY CENTER
715 N. 11th Street, Suite 302
Moorhead, MN 56560
218-291-1227
Fax: 218-233-7930
Type of Counseling:
HECM Counseling, Default/Foreclosure Counseling, Prepurchase Counseling, Rental Counseling

**CONSUMER CREDIT COUNSELING SERVICE OF DULUTH
602 East First Street
Park Rapids, MN 56470
218-732-4320
Type of Counseling:
Default/Foreclosure Counseling, Prepurchase Counseling, Rental Counseling

LEGAL AID SERVICE OF NORTHEASTERN MINNESOTA PINE CITY OFFICE
235 6th St.
Pine City, MN 55063
320-629-7166
Fax: 320-629-0185
Type of Counseling:
Rental Counseling, Default/Foreclosure Counseling

CATHOLIC CHARITIES/CARITAS FAMILY SERVICES
305 North 7th Avenue
Saint Cloud, MN 56303-3633
320-650-1660
Fax: 320-650-1672
Email: Bcorson@gw.stcdio.org
Type of Counseling:
HECM Counseling, Default/Foreclosure Counseling, Rental Counseling, Prepurchase Counseling
Affiliate of: CATHOLIC CHARITIES USA

TRI-COUNTY ACTION PROGRAMS, INCORPORATED
700 W Saint Germain St
Saint Cloud, MN 56301-3507
320-251-1612
Toll-Free: 888-765-5597
Fax: 320-251-6469
Email: caroleen.boeder@tricap.org
Type of Counseling:
Default/Foreclosure Counseling

**SOUTHWEST MINNESOTA HOUSING PARTNERSHIP
2401 Broadway Ave, Suite 204
Slayton, MN 56172-1142
507-836-8673
Fax: 507-836-8866
Email: swmhp@rconnect.com
Type of Counseling:
Prepurchase Counseling
Affiliate of: THE HOUSING PARTNERSHIP NETWORK

SOUTHERN MINNESOTA REGIONAL LEGAL SERVICES, INCORPORATED
46 E 4th St 300 Minnesota Bldg
St. Paul, MN 55101-1121
651-222-5863
Fax: 651-297-6457
Type of Counseling:
Default/Foreclosure Counseling, Rental Counseling, Prepurchase Counseling

SAINT PAUL HOUSING INFORMATION CENTER
25 4th St W Room 150 CHA
St. Paul, MN 55102-1634
651-266-6000
Fax: 651-298-5054
Type of Counseling:
Default/Foreclosure Counseling, Rental Counseling, Prepurchase Counseling

SAINT PAUL URBAN LEAGUE
401 Selby Ave
St. Paul, MN 55102-1724
651-224-5771
Fax: 651-224-8009
Type of Counseling:
Rental Counseling, Prepurchase Counseling, Default/Foreclosure Counseling

**ACORN HOUSING CORPORATION
Security Building 757 Raymond Avenue
St. Paul, MN 55114
651-203-0008
Fax: 651-642-0060
Type of Counseling:
Prepurchase Counseling, Rental Counseling, Default/Foreclosure Counseling
Affiliate of: ACORN HOUSING CORPORATION

MINNESOTA HOUSING FINANCE AGENCY
400 Sibley Street, Suite 300
St. Paul, MN 55101
651-296-7608
Fax: 651-296-8139
Type of Counseling:
Prepurchase Counseling, Rental Counseling, Default/Foreclosure Counseling

**HOME OWNERSHIP CENTER
1885 University Ave W
Suite 350
St. Paul, MN 55104-3403
651-659-9336
Fax: 651-659-9518
Email: hocenter@qwest.net
Website: www.hocmn.org
Type of Counseling:
Default/Foreclosure Counseling, Prepurchase Counseling
Affiliate of: THE HOUSING PARTNERSHIP NETWORK

**COMMUNITY NEIGHBORHOOD HOUSING SERVICES, INCORPORATED
35 W. Water St
St. Paul, MN 55107
651-292-8710
Fax: 651-292-0473
Type of Counseling:
Prepurchase Counseling
Affiliate of: NEIGHBORHOOD REINVESTMENT CORPORATION

FAMILY SERVICE, INCORPORATED SAINT PAUL
166 4th St E
Suite 200
St. Paul, MN 55101-1464
651-222-0311
Fax: 651-222-8920
Type of Counseling:
Default/Foreclosure Counseling, Rental Counseling, Prepurchase Counseling

**DAYTON'S BLUFF NEIGHBORHOOD HOUSING SERVICES, INCORPORATED
823 E 7th St
St. Paul, MN 55106
651-774-6995
Fax: 651-774-0445
Type of Counseling:
Prepurchase Counseling
Affiliate of: NEIGHBORHOOD REINVESTMENT CORPORATION

LEGAL AID SERVICE OF NORTHEASTERN MINNESOTA IRON RANGE OFFICE
Olcott Plaza
820 N. 9th St.
Suite 150
Virginia, MN 55792
218-749-3270
Fax: 218-749-0706
Type of Counseling:
Default/Foreclosure Counseling, Rental Counseling

**CONSUMER CREDIT COUNSELING SERVICE OF DULUTH
333 Litchfield Avenue SW
Wilmar, MN 56201
320-235-7916
Fax: 320-231-1619
Type of Counseling:
Default/Foreclosure Counseling, Prepurchase Counseling, Rental Counseling

Mississippi

**SOUTH MISSISSIPPI LEGAL SERVICES CORPORATION
202 Fountain Square Building Suite 203
Biloxi, MS 395331386
228-374-4160
Fax: 228-374-6045
Email: smlsc01@aol.com
Type of Counseling:
Prepurchase Counseling, Default/Foreclosure Counseling, Rental Counseling, HECM Counseling
Affiliate of: WEST TENNESSEE LEGAL SERVICES, INCORPORATED

NORTH MISSISSIPPI RURAL LEGAL SERVICES OF CLARKSDALE
606 DeSoto Avenue
Clarksdale, MS 38614
662-627-4184
Toll-Free: 800-388-3163
Fax: 662-624-4009
Email: watsa@nmrls.com
Website: www.nmrls.com
Type of Counseling:
Prepurchase Counseling, Rental Counseling, Default/Foreclosure Counseling
Affiliate of: WEST TENNESSEE LEGAL SERVICES, INCORPORATED

**NORTH MISSISSIPPI RURAL LEGAL SERVICES
606 Desoto Avenue
Clarksdale, MS 38614
601-627-4184
Fax: 601-624-4009
Type of Counseling:
Prepurchase Counseling, Default/Foreclosure Counseling, Rental Counseling, HECM Counseling
Affiliate of: WEST TENNESSEE LEGAL SERVICES, INCORPORATED

**NORTH MISSISSIPPI RURAL LEGAL SERVICES
301 Washington Street
Greenville, MS 38701
601-335-8203
Fax: 601-335-7500
Type of Counseling:
Prepurchase Counseling, Default/Foreclosure Counseling, Rental Counseling, HECM Counseling
Affiliate of: WEST TENNESSEE LEGAL SERVICES, INCORPORATED

NORTH MISSISSIPPI RURAL LEGAL SERVICES OF GREENVILLE
835 Main Street
Greenville, MS 38701
662-335-8203
Toll-Free: 800-545-1909
Fax: 662-335-7500
Email: watsa@nmrls.com
Website: www.nmrls.com
Type of Counseling:
Prepurchase Counseling, Rental Counseling, Default/Foreclosure Counseling
Affiliate of: WEST TENNESSEE LEGAL SERVICES, INCORPORATED

GULF COAST COMMUNITY ACTION AGENCY
500 24th St
Gulfport, MS 39507-1711
228-868-4250
Fax: 228-868-4163
Type of Counseling:
HECM Counseling, Default/Foreclosure Counseling, Rental Counseling, Prepurchase Counseling

**SOUTHEAST MISSISSIPPI LEGAL SERVICES CORPORATION
111 East Front Street
Hattiesburg, MS 39403
601-545-2950
Fax: 601-545-2935
Type of Counseling:
Prepurchase Counseling, Default/Foreclosure Counseling, Rental Counseling, HECM Counseling
Affiliate of: WEST TENNESSEE LEGAL SERVICES, INCORPORATED

HOUSING EDUCATION AND ECONOMIC DEVELOPMENT
3405 Medgar Evers Blvd
Jackson, MS 39213-6360
601-981-1960
Fax: 601-981-0258
Type of Counseling:
HECM Counseling, Default/Foreclosure Counseling, Rental Counseling, Prepurchase Counseling

DIVISION OF AGING AND ADULT SERVICES
750 N State St
Jackson, MS 39202-
601-359-4366
Fax: 601-359-9664
Email:
ELAnderson@MDHS.State.MS.US
Type of Counseling:
Prepurchase Counseling, Rental Counseling, Default/Foreclosure Counseling, HECM Counseling

URBAN LEAGUE OF GREATER JACKSON
2310 Highway 80 W
Bldg. 1, Ste.E
Jackson, MS 39204
601-714-4600
Fax: 601-714-4040
Email: jul@netdoor.com
Type of Counseling:
HECM Counseling, Default/Foreclosure Counseling, Rental Counseling, Prepurchase Counseling
Affiliate of: NATIONAL URBAN LEAGUE

JACKSON METRO HOUSING PARTNERSHIP, INCORPORATED
1217 N. West St
Jackson, MS 39202
601-969-1895
Fax: 601-969-5300
Type of Counseling:
Default/Foreclosure Counseling, Rental Counseling, Prepurchase Counseling, HECM Counseling
Affiliate of: THE HOUSING PARTNERSHIP NETWORK

**CENTRAL MISSISSIPPI LEGAL SERVICES
PO Box 951
Jackson, MS 392050951
601-948-6752
Fax: 601-948-6757
Email: hn6720@handsnet.org
Type of Counseling:
Prepurchase Counseling, Default/Foreclosure Counseling, Rental Counseling, HECM Counseling
Affiliate of: WEST TENNESSEE LEGAL SERVICES, INCORPORATED

MISSISSIPPI CHILDREN'S HOME SOCIETY AND FAMILY SERVICES ASSOCIATION
1900 North West St.
Jackson, MS 392021034
601-352-7784
Toll-Free: 800-388-6247
Fax: 601-968-0028
Type of Counseling:
Prepurchase Counseling, HECM Counseling, Default/Foreclosure Counseling, Rental Counseling

**SOUTHWEST MISSISSIPPI LEGAL SERVICES CORPORATION
221 Main Street
McComb, MS 39649
601-684-0578
Fax: 601-684-0575
Type of Counseling:
Prepurchase Counseling, Default/Foreclosure Counseling, Rental Counseling, HECM Counseling
Affiliate of: WEST TENNESSEE LEGAL SERVICES, INCORPORATED

**SOUTHEAST MISSISSIPPI LEGAL SERVICES
2305 5th St., 2nd Fl.
Meridian, MS 39302
601-693-5470
Fax: 601-693-5473
Type of Counseling:
Prepurchase Counseling, Default/Foreclosure Counseling, Rental Counseling, HECM Counseling
Affiliate of: WEST TENNESSEE LEGAL SERVICES, INCORPORATED

**SOUTHWEST MISSISSIPPI LEGAL SERVICES CORPORATION
261 D'Evereux Drive Unit 20
Natchez, MS 39121-0427
601-446-7590
Fax: 601-446-7592
Type of Counseling:
Prepurchase Counseling, Default/Foreclosure Counseling, Rental Counseling, HECM Counseling
Affiliate of: WEST TENNESSEE LEGAL SERVICES, INCORPORATED

NORTH MISSISSIPPI RURAL LEGAL SERVICES OF OXFORD
P.O. Box 928
Oxford, MS 38655
662-234-2918
Toll-Free: 800-559-5074
Fax: 662-234-2965
Email: watsa@nmrls.com
Website: www.nmrls.com
Type of Counseling:
Prepurchase Counseling, Rental Counseling, Default/Foreclosure Counseling
Affiliate of: WEST TENNESSEE LEGAL SERVICES, INCORPORATED

NORTH MISSISSIPPI RURAL LEGAL SERVICES - ADMINISTRATIVE OFFICE
2134 West Jackson Avenue
Oxford, MS 38655
662-234-8731
Toll-Free: 800-898-8731
Fax: 662-236-3263
Email: watsa@nmrls.com
Website: www.nmrls.com
Type of Counseling:
Prepurchase Counseling, Default/Foreclosure Counseling, Rental Counseling
Affiliate of: WEST TENNESSEE LEGAL SERVICES, INCORPORATED

**NORTH MISSISSIPPI RURAL LEGAL SERVICES
658 W. Main Street
Tupelo, MS 38802
601-842-3702
Fax: 601-840-8060
Type of Counseling:
Prepurchase Counseling, Default/Foreclosure Counseling, Rental Counseling, HECM Counseling
Affiliate of: WEST TENNESSEE LEGAL SERVICES, INCORPORATED

NORTH MISSISSIPPI RURAL LEGAL SERVICES OF TUPELO
658 West Main Street
Tupelo, MS 38802
662-842-3702
Toll-Free: 800-898-3702
Fax: 662-840-8060
Email: watsa@nmrls.com
Website: www.nmrls.com
Type of Counseling:
Prepurchase Counseling, Rental Counseling, Default/Foreclosure Counseling
Affiliate of: WEST TENNESSEE LEGAL SERVICES, INCORPORATED

**CENTRAL MISSISSIPPI LEGAL SERVICES CORPORATION
P.O.Box 52
Vicksburg, MS 39181-052
601-636-8322
Fax: 601-636-8405
Type of Counseling:
Prepurchase Counseling, Default/Foreclosure Counseling, Rental Counseling, HECM Counseling
Affiliate of: WEST TENNESSEE LEGAL SERVICES, INCORPORATED

SACRED HEART SOUTHERN MISSIONS HOUSING CORPORATION
6144 Highway 161 N
Walls, MS 38680-0365
662-781-1516
Fax: 662-781-3534
Type of Counseling:
Default/Foreclosure Counseling, Rental Counseling, Prepurchase Counseling, HECM Counseling

**NORTH MISSISSIPPI RURAL LEGAL SERVICES
221 Commerce Street
West Point, MS 39773
601-494-6122
Fax: 601-898-6122
Type of Counseling:
Prepurchase Counseling, Default/Foreclosure Counseling,

Rental Counseling, HECM Counseling
Affiliate of: WEST TENNESSEE LEGAL SERVICES, INCORPORATED

NORTH MISSISSIPPI RURAL LEGAL SERVICES OF WEST POINT
221 Commerce Street
West Point, MS 39773
662-494-6122
Toll-Free: 800-898-6122
Fax: 662-494-0670
Email: watsa@nmrls.com
Website: www.nmrls.com
Type of Counseling:
Prepurchase Counseling, Default/Foreclosure Counseling, Rental Counseling
Affiliate of: WEST TENNESSEE LEGAL SERVICES, INCORPORATED

Missouri

WEST CENTRAL MISSOURI RURAL COMMUNITY ACTION AGENCY
106 W 4th St
Appleton City, MO 64724
660-476-2184
Fax: 660-476-2259
Email: wchsghc@iland.net
Type of Counseling:
HECM Counseling, Default/Foreclosure Counseling, Rental Counseling, Prepurchase Counseling

CONSUMER CREDIT COUNSELING SERVICE - SAINT LOUIS
1699 Jeffco Boulevard
Arnold, MO 630102281
636-282-2227
Toll-Free: 800-966-3328
Fax: 314-647-1359
Type of Counseling:
Default/Foreclosure Counseling

NORTH EAST COMMUNITY ACTION CORPORATION
16 North Court Street
Bowling Green, MO 63334-0470
573-324-2231
Fax: 573-324-6335
Type of Counseling:
Default/Foreclosure Counseling, Prepurchase Counseling, Rental Counseling

CONSUMER CREDIT COUNSELING SERVICE- SAINT LOUIS
1301 N. Kingshighway, Suite A
Cape Girardeau, MO 63701-
573-334-7050
Toll-Free: 800-966-3328
Fax: 314-647-1359
Type of Counseling:
Default/Foreclosure Counseling

EDUCATION, TRAINING, RESEARCH, AND DEVELOPMENT, INC.
608 E. Cherry Street, Suite 103
Columbia, MO 65201
573-442-1122
Toll-Free: 877-355-3135
Fax: 573-443-2677
Type of Counseling:
Prepurchase Counseling

CONSUMER CREDIT COUNSELING OF MID-MISSOURI, INCORPORATED
1900 N Providence Ste 301
Columbia, MO 65202
573-449-5199
Toll-Free: 8007360535
Fax: 573-875-4953
Type of Counseling:
HECM Counseling, Default/Foreclosure Counseling, Rental Counseling, Prepurchase Counseling

CONSUMER DEBT COUNSELING
2401 Bernadette Drive, Suite 115
Columbia, MO 65203
573-234-1851
Toll-Free: 877-786-3328
Fax: 314-647-1359
Type of Counseling:
Default/Foreclosure Counseling

CONSUMER CREDIT COUNSELING SERVICE- SAINT LOUIS
400 N. Washington, Suite 118
Farmington, MO 63640
573-760-1510
Toll-Free: 800-966-3328
Fax: 314-647-1359
Type of Counseling:
Default/Foreclosure Counseling

CONSUMER CREDIT COUNSELING SERVICE- SAINT LOUIS
493 Rue St., Francois, Suite 6
Florissant, MO 63031
314-830-6464
Toll-Free: 800-966-3328
Fax: 314-647-1359
Type of Counseling:
Default/Foreclosure Counseling

CONSUMER CREDIT COUNSELING SERVICE - SAINT LOUIS
2801 St. Mary's Avenue (lower level)
Hannibal, MO 634014443
573-248-0059
Toll-Free: 800-966-3328
Fax: 314-647-1359
Type of Counseling:
Default/Foreclosure Counseling

COMMUNITY SERVICES LEAGUE
300 W Maple Ave
Independence, MO 64050-2818
816-254-4100
Fax: 816-252-9906
Type of Counseling:
HECM Counseling, Default/Foreclosure Counseling, Rental Counseling, Prepurchase Counseling

CONSUMER DEBT COUNSELING
1110 Missouri Blvd.
Jefferson City, MO 65109
573-556-5578
Toll-Free: 877-786-3328
Fax: 314-647-1359
Type of Counseling:
Default/Foreclosure Counseling

CONSUMER CREDIT COUNSELING SERVICE- SAINT LOUIS
1288 St. Cyr Road
Jennings, MO 63137
314-867-7049
Toll-Free: 800-966-3328
Fax: 314-647-1359
Type of Counseling:
Default/Foreclosure Counseling

CONSUMER CREDIT COUNSELING SERVICE OF GREATER KANSAS CITY
211 West Armour Blvd Ste 304
Kansas City, MO 64111
816-753-0535
Fax: 816-753-3374
Type of Counseling:
Default/Foreclosure Counseling, Prepurchase Counseling

HOUSING INFORMATION CENTER
3201 Southwest Trafficway
Kansas City, MO 64108-

816-759-4170
Fax: 816-931-0722
Type of Counseling:
Prepurchase Counseling,
Default/Foreclosure Counseling,
Rental Counseling

**ACORN HOUSING
CORPORATION
3931 Main St Fl 2
Kansas City, MO 64111-1916
816-931-3310
Fax: 816-931-5522
Type of Counseling:
Prepurchase Counseling
Affiliate of: ACORN HOUSING
CORPORATION

HOUSING INFORMATION
CENTER
3810 Paseo Blvd
Kansas City, MO 64109-2721
816-931-0443
Fax: 816-931-0722
Type of Counseling:
Default/Foreclosure Counseling,
Rental Counseling, Prepurchase
Counseling

MISSOURI VALLEY HUMAN
RESOURCE COMMUNITY
ACTION AGENCY
PO Box 550
Marshall, MO 65340-0550
660-886-7476
Fax: 660-886-5868
Type of Counseling:
HECM Counseling,
Default/Foreclosure Counseling,
Rental Counseling, Prepurchase
Counseling

CONSUMER CREDIT
COUNSELING SERVICE- SAINT
LOUIS
2300 West Osage, Suite 1
Pacific, MO 63069
636-257-8186
Toll-Free: 800-966-3328
Fax: 314-647-1359
Type of Counseling:
Default/Foreclosure Counseling

CONSUMER CREDIT
COUNSELING SERVICE- SAINT
LOUIS
3069A N. Westwood Blvd.
Poplar Bluff, MO 639012808
573-686-3323
Toll-Free: 800-966-3328
Fax: 314-647-1359
Type of Counseling:
Default/Foreclosure Counseling

**CATHOLIC CHARITIES-
KANSAS CITY/ST. JOSEPH
426 S. Jefferson, Suite 207
Springfield, MO 65806-
417-865-0050
Fax: 417-865-0070
Email: tonya@infac.com
Affiliate of: CATHOLIC
CHARITIES USA

SOUTHWEST MISSOURI OFFICE
ON AGING
1735 S. Fort
Springfield, MO 65807
417-862-0762
Toll-Free: 800-497-0822
Fax: 417-865-2683
Type of Counseling: HECM
Counseling

CONSUMER CREDIT
COUNSELING SERVICE –ST.
LOUIS
1600 Heritage Landing, Suite 211
St. Charles, MO 633038442
636-441-9107
Toll-Free: 800-966-3328
Fax: 314-647-1359
Type of Counseling:
Default/Foreclosure Counseling

ECONOMIC OPPORTUNITY
CORPORATION OF GREATER
SAINT JOSEPH
817 Monterey
St. Joseph, MO 64503
816-233-8281
Fax: 816-233-8262
Type of Counseling: Prepurchase
Counseling

**ACORN HOUSING
CORPORATION OF ST. LOUIS
4304 Manchester Ave
St. Louis, MO 63110-2138
314-531-6204
Fax: 314-531-4942
Type of Counseling:
Prepurchase Counseling,
Default/Foreclosure Counseling
Affiliate of: ACORN HOUSING
CORPORATION

**CATHOLIC COMMISSION ON
HOUSING
4140 Lindell Blvd
St. Louis, MO 63108-2998
314-371-4980
Fax: 314-371-0058
Type of Counseling:
Default/Foreclosure Counseling,
Prepurchase Counseling
Affiliate of: CATHOLIC
CHARITIES USA

**NEIGHBORHOOD HOUSING
SERVICES OF SAINT LOUIS,
INCORPORATED
4156 Manchester St
St. Louis, MO 63110-3847
314-533-0600
Fax: 314-533-0476
Type of Counseling:
Default/Foreclosure Counseling,
Prepurchase Counseling
Affiliate of: NEIGHBORHOOD
REINVESTMENT
CORPORATION

LEGAL SERVICES OF EASTERN
MISSOURI, INCORPORATED
4232 Forest Park Ave
St. Louis, MO 63108-2811
314-534-4200
Toll-Free: 800-444-0514
Fax: 314-534-1028
Type of Counseling:
Default/Foreclosure Counseling,
Rental Counseling, Prepurchase
Counseling

A J H HOUSING
INCORPORATED
4545 Gravois Ave
St. Louis, MO 63116
314-352-7248
Fax: 314-352-3444
Type of Counseling: Prepurchase
Counseling

URBAN LEAGUE OF
METROPOLITAN SAINT LOUIS
3701 Grandel Sq
St. Louis, MO 63108-3627
314-615-3600
Fax: 314-615-3611
Type of Counseling:
Default/Foreclosure Counseling,
Rental Counseling, Prepurchase
Counseling

BETTER FAMILY LIFE, INC.
1017 Olive, 6th Floor
St. Louis, MO 63101
314-241-8704
Fax: 314-241-1277
Type of Counseling:
Prepurchase Counseling, Rental
Counseling, Default/Foreclosure
Counseling

JUSTINE PETERSEN HOUSING
AND REINVESTMENT
CORPORATION
5031 Northrup
St. Louis, MO 63110
314-664-5051
Fax: 314-664-5364

Email:
sflanigan@justinepetersen.org
Type of Counseling:
Default/Foreclosure Counseling, Prepurchase Counseling, Rental Counseling

ST. LOUIS REINVESTMENT CORPORATION
55 Plaza Square, Suite 202
St. Louis, MO 63103
314-588-9334
Fax: 314-588-9354
Type of Counseling:
Default/Foreclosure Counseling, Prepurchase Counseling

CONSUMER CREDIT COUNSELING SERVICE
1300 Hampton Ave at West Park
St. Louis, MO 63139-8901
314-647-9004
Toll-Free: 800-966-3328
Fax: 314-647-1359
Type of Counseling:
Default/Foreclosure Counseling

HOUSING OPTIONS PROVIDED FOR THE ELDERLY
4265 Shaw Blvd
St. Louis, MO 63110-3526
314-776-0155
Fax: 314-776-0852
Type of Counseling: HECM Counseling

URBAN LEAGUE OF METROPOLITAN SAINT LOUIS
9860 Jennings Station Road
St. Louis, MO 63136-1413
314-388-9840
Fax: 314-389-9845
Type of Counseling:
Default/Foreclosure Counseling, Rental Counseling, Prepurchase Counseling

BETTER FAMILY LIFE, INC.
724 North Union Blvd., Suite 301
St. Louis, MO 63108
314-367-3440
Fax: 314-367-1414
Type of Counseling:
Prepurchase Counseling, Rental Counseling, Default/Foreclosure Counseling

Montana

DISTRICT 7 HUMAN RESOURCES DEVELOPMENT COUNCIL
7 N 31 St
Billings, MT 59103
406-247-4736
Toll-Free: 800-433-1411
Fax: 406-248-2943
Type of Counseling:
HECM Counseling, Default/Foreclosure Counseling, Rental Counseling, Prepurchase Counseling

**NEIGHBORHOOD HOUSING SERVICES OF GREAT FALLS, INCORPORATED
509 First Avenue, South
Great Falls, MT 59401
406-761-5861
Fax: 406-761-5852
Type of Counseling:
Prepurchase Counseling, Default/Foreclosure Counseling
Affiliate of: NEIGHBORHOOD REINVESTMENT CORPORATION

HELENA HOUSING AUTHORITY
812 Abbey St
Helena, MT 59601-7924
406-443-8211
Fax: 406-442-0574
Type of Counseling:
HECM Counseling, Default/Foreclosure Counseling, Rental Counseling, Prepurchase Counseling

NORTH WEST MONTANA HUMAN RESOURCES
214 Main St
Kalispell, MT 59904-1300
406-752-6565
Toll-Free: 800-344-5979
Fax: 406-752-6582
Type of Counseling:
HECM Counseling, Default/Foreclosure Counseling, Rental Counseling, Prepurchase Counseling

WOMEN'S OPPORTUNITY RESOURCE DEVELOPMENT, INCORPORATED
127 N Higgins Ave, Room 307
Missoula, MT 59802-4457
406-543-3550
Fax: 406-721-4584
Type of Counseling:
Default/Foreclosure Counseling, Rental Counseling, Prepurchase Counseling, HECM Counseling

Nebraska

HIGH PLAINS COMMUNITY DEVELOPMENT CORPORATION
130 E. 2nd Street
Chadron, NE 69337
308-432-4346
Fax: 308-432-4655
Type of Counseling:
Default/Foreclosure Counseling, Prepurchase Counseling, Rental Counseling

**CONSUMER CREDIT COUNSELING OF NEBRASKA
2121 North Webb Road, Suite 307
Grand Island, NE 68802
308-381-4551
Fax: 308-381-1434
Type of Counseling:
HECM Counseling, Default/Foreclosure Counseling, Prepurchase Counseling, Rental Counseling

**CONSUMER CREDIT COUNSELING SERVICE OF NEBRASKA
1001 S. 70th Street, Suite 200
Lincoln, NE 68505
402-484-7200
Fax: 402-484-7332
Type of Counseling:
HECM Counseling, Default/Foreclosure Counseling, Prepurchase Counseling, Rental Counseling

**NEIGHBORHOOD HOUSING SERVICES OF LINCOLN, INCORPORATED
2121 N 27th St
Lincoln, NE 68503
402-477-7181
Fax: 402-477-7406
Type of Counseling:
Prepurchase Counseling
Affiliate of: NEIGHBORHOOD REINVESTMENT CORPORATION

LINCOLN ACTION PROGRAM, INCORPORATED
210 O Street
Lincoln, NE 68508
402-416-6970
Fax: 402-471-4844
Type of Counseling:
HECM Counseling, Default/Foreclosure Counseling, Rental Counseling, Prepurchase Counseling

**CONSUMER CREDIT COUNSELING SERVICE OF NEBRASKA
125 S. 4th Street, Suite 213
Norfolk, NE 68701
402-371-4656

Fax: 402-371-7462
Type of Counseling:
HECM Counseling,
Default/Foreclosure Counseling,
Prepurchase Counseling, Rental
Counseling

NORTHERN PONCA HOUSING
AUTHORITY
1501 Michigan Ave.
Norfolk, NE 68701
402-379-8224
Fax: 402-379-8557
Type of Counseling:
Prepurchase Counseling,
Default/Foreclosure Counseling,
Rental Counseling

**CONSUMER CREDIT
COUNSELING SERVICE OF
NEBRASKA
509 East Fourth Street, Suite F
North Platte, NE 69103
308-532-9760
Fax: 308-532-9439
Type of Counseling:
HECM Counseling,
Default/Foreclosure Counseling,
Prepurchase Counseling, Rental
Counseling

FAMILY HOUSING ADVISORY
SERVICES, INCORPORATED
3605 Q Street
Omaha, NE 68107
402-546-1013
Fax: 402-734-8887
Email: fhc_is@fhasinc.org
Website: www.fhasinc.org
Type of Counseling: Rental
Counseling

**CONSUMER CREDIT
COUNSELING SERVICE OF
NEBRASKA
10843 Old Mill Rd Ste 401
Omaha, NE 68154
402-333-2227
Fax: 402-333-8443
Type of Counseling:
Default/Foreclosure Counseling,
Rental Counseling, HECM
Counseling, Prepurchase Counseling
Affiliate of: NATIONAL
FOUNDATION FOR CONSUMER
CREDIT, INCORPORATED

**MMMBC DEVELOPMENT
CORPORATION
3223 North 45th St.
Omaha, NE 681043711
402-457-7811
Fax: 402-457-7814
Type of Counseling:
Prepurchase Counseling
Affiliate of: CONGRESS OF
NATIONAL BLACK CHURCHES,
INCORPORATED

FAMILY HOUSING ADVISORY
SERVICES, INCORPORATED
2416 Lake St
Omaha, NE 68111-3831
402-934-7921
Fax: 402-934-7928
Email: fhc_is@fhasinc.org
Website: www.fhasinc.org
Type of Counseling:
HECM Counseling,
Default/Foreclosure Counseling,
Rental Counseling, Prepurchase
Counseling

FAMILY HOUSING ADVISORY
SERVICES, INCORPORATED
2505 N. 24th Street, Suite 219
Omaha, NE 68110
402-934-6675
Fax: 402-934-7928
Email: fhc_is@fhasinc.org
Website: www.fhasinc.org
Type of Counseling:
HECM Counseling,
Default/Foreclosure Counseling,
Rental Counseling, Prepurchase
Counseling

Nevada

CITIZENS FOR AFFORDABLE
HOMES, INCORPORATED
308 N Curry St Ste 210
Carson City, NV 89703
775-883-7101
Fax: 775-883-7115
Type of Counseling:
Default/Foreclosure Counseling,
Rental Counseling, Prepurchase
Counseling

CONSUMER CREDIT
COUNSELING SERVICE OF
NORTHERN NEVADA
625 Fairview Ste 123
Carson City, NV 89701
702-887-1442
Fax: 702-887-0407
Type of Counseling:
Default/Foreclosure Counseling,
Rental Counseling, Prepurchase
Counseling

CONSUMER CREDIT
COUNSELING SERVICE OF
NORTHERN NEVADA
368 7th St
Elko, NV 89801
775-753-4966
Fax: 775-753-4050
Type of Counseling:
Default/Foreclosure Counseling,
Rental Counseling, Prepurchase
Counseling

CONSUMER CREDIT
COUNSELING SERVICE OF SO.
NEVADA
2920 N. Green Valley Parkway
Henderson, NV 89014
702-364-0344
Fax: 702-364-0773
Email: cccsnv@aol.com
Website: www.cccsnevada.com
Type of Counseling:
HECM Counseling,
Default/Foreclosure Counseling,
Prepurchase Counseling, Rental
Counseling

CONSUMER CREDIT
COUNSELING OF SO. NEVADA
Nellis Air Force Base, NV
Las Vegas, NV 89119
702-364-0344
Fax: 702-364-0773
Email: cccsnv@aol.com
Website: www.cccsnevada.org
Type of Counseling:
HECM Counseling,
Default/Foreclosure Counseling,
Prepurchase Counseling, Rental
Counseling

**LIVING WORD AMEZ
5240 Ferrell Mountain Court
Las Vegas, NV 89031
702-631-0098
Fax: 702-631-0098
Type of Counseling:
Prepurchase Counseling
Affiliate of: CONGRESS OF
NATIONAL BLACK CHURCHES,
INCORPORATED

COMMUNITY DEVELOPMENT
PROGRAMS CENTER OF
NEVADA
2009 Alta Drive
Las Vegas, NV 89106
702-873-8882
Fax: 702-873-8942
Email:
dora_d_lagrande@hotmail.com
Type of Counseling: Prepurchase
Counseling

WOMEN'S DEVELOPMENT
CENTER
953 E Sahara Ave Ste 201
Las Vegas, NV 89104-3016
702-796-7770
Fax: 702-796-3007

Type of Counseling:
Rental Counseling, Prepurchase Counseling

ECONOMIC OPPORTUNITY BOARD OF CLARK COUNTY
3674 N Rancho Dr Ste 32
Las Vegas, NV 89130
702-647-7816
Fax: 702-647-3125
Type of Counseling:
Default/Foreclosure Counseling, HECM Counseling

CONSUMER CREDIT COUNSELING SERVICE OF SOUTHERN NEVADA
3650 S Decatur Blvd Ste 30
Las Vegas, NV 89103-5864
702-364-0344
Fax: 702-364-0773
Email: cccsnv@aol.com
Website: www.cccsnevada.com
Type of Counseling:
HECM Counseling, Default/Foreclosure Counseling, Rental Counseling, Prepurchase Counseling

CONSUMER CREDIT COUNSELING OF SO. NEVADA
2290 McDaniel
N. Las Vegas, NV 89030
702-364-0344
Fax: 702-364-0773
Email: cccsnv@aol.com
Website: www.cccsnevada.org
Type of Counseling:
HECM Counseling, Default/Foreclosure Counseling, Prepurchase Counseling, Rental Counseling

CONSUMER CREDIT COUNSELING OF SOUTH NEVADA
3100 Mill Street, Ste.111
Reno, NV 89502
775-337-6363
Fax: 775-337-6679
Email: cccsnv@aol.com
Website: www.cccsnevada.org
Type of Counseling:
HECM Counseling, Default/Foreclosure Counseling, Prepurchase Counseling, Rental Counseling

WASHOE LEGAL SERVICES
650 Tahoe St
Reno, NV 89509-1721
775-329-2727
Fax: 775-324-5509
Website:
www.washoelegalservices.org
Type of Counseling:
HECM Counseling, Default/Foreclosure Counseling, Rental Counseling, Prepurchase Counseling

WASHOE COUNTY SENIOR LAW PROJECT
1155 E Ninth St
Reno, NV 89512
775-328-2592
Fax: 775-328-6193
Type of Counseling:
HECM Counseling, Default/Foreclosure Counseling, Rental Counseling

CONSUMER CREDIT COUNSELING SERVICE OF NORTHERN NEVADA
575 E Plumb Lane, Suite 101
Reno, NV 89502-3540
775-322-6557
Toll-Free: 888-298-9622
Fax: 775-322-2059
Website: www.vrpr.com/fcs/
Type of Counseling:
Default/Foreclosure Counseling, Rental Counseling, Prepurchase Counseling

New Hampshire

TRI-COUNTY CAP
30 Exchange Street
Berlin, NH 03570-
603-536-1911
Toll-Free: 800-552-4617
Fax: 603-536-8222
Type of Counseling:
Prepurchase Counseling, Default/Foreclosure Counseling, Rental Counseling

NEW HAMPSHIRE HOUSING FINANCE AUTHORITY
P. O. Box 5087
Manchester, NH 03108
603-472-8623
Fax: 603-472-2663
Type of Counseling:
Prepurchase Counseling, HECM Counseling

**MANCHESTER NEIGHBORHOOD HOUSING SERVICES, INCORPORATED
969 Elm Street
Manchester, NH 03103
603-626-4663
Fax: 603-623-8011
Email: john@mnhs.net
Type of Counseling:
Prepurchase Counseling, Default/Foreclosure Counseling
Affiliate of: NEIGHBORHOOD REINVESTMENT CORPORATION

THE WAY HOME
214 Spruce Street
Manchester, NH 03103-
603-627-3491
Fax: 603-644-7949
Type of Counseling: Rental Counseling

NEIGHBORHOOD HOUSING SERVICES OF GREATER NASHUA, INCORPORATED
50 Tolles St
Nashua, NH 03060
603-882-2077
Fax: 603-881-9894
Email: fhnhs@ix.netcom.com
Type of Counseling:
Default/Foreclosure Counseling, Prepurchase Counseling

New Jersey

FAMILY SERVICE/CONSUMER CREDIT COUNSELING SERVICE
312 E White Horse Pike
Absecon, NJ 08201
800-473-2227
Toll-Free: 800-473-2227
Fax: 609-748-1498
Website: www.aclink.crg.fsa.htm
Type of Counseling:
HECM Counseling, Default/Foreclosure Counseling, Rental Counseling
Affiliate of: NATIONAL FOUNDATION FOR CONSUMER CREDIT, INCORPORATED

CHECK MATE INCORPORATED
550 Cookman Ave
Asbury Park, NJ 07712-7120
732-774-3100
Fax: 732-774-3220
Email: KEVIN@BEONLINE.COM
Type of Counseling:
Default/Foreclosure Counseling, Rental Counseling, Prepurchase Counseling

NEW JERSEY CITIZEN ACTION
1 Municipal Plaza
Asbury Park, NJ 07712
800-656-9637
Toll-Free: 800-656-9637
Fax: 732-714-5386
Email: jennifer@njcitizenaction.org
Website: www.njcitizenaction.org

Type of Counseling:
HECM Counseling,
Default/Foreclosure Counseling,
Rental Counseling, Prepurchase
Counseling

FAMILY SERVICE
ASSOCIATION/CONSUMER
CREDIT COUNSELING
SERVICES OF SOUTH JERSEY
1 S. New York Avenue
Atlantic City, NJ 08401
609-569-0239
Toll-Free: 800-473-2227
Fax: 609-569-1752
Type of Counseling:
Default/Foreclosure Counseling,
Prepurchase Counseling, Rental
Counseling
Affiliate of: NATIONAL
FOUNDATION FOR CONSUMER
CREDIT, INCORPORATED

ATLANTIC HUMAN
RESOURCES, INCORPORATED
1 S New York Ave Ste 303
Atlantic City, NJ 08401-8012
609-348-4131
Fax: 609-345-5750
Type of Counseling:
HECM Counseling,
Default/Foreclosure Counseling,
Rental Counseling, Prepurchase
Counseling

BAYONNE ECONOMIC
OPPORTUNITY FOUNDATION
555 Kennedy Blvd
Bayonne, NJ 07002-2627
201-437-7222
Fax: 201-437-2810
Type of Counseling:
Rental Counseling, Prepurchase
Counseling

FAMILY SERVICE
ASSOCIATION/CONSUMER
CREDIT COUNSELING
SERVICES OF SOUTH JERSEY
150 S. WHP
Hudson Savings Bank
Berlin, NJ
609-569-0239
Toll-Free: 800-473-2227
Fax: 609-569-1752
Type of Counseling:
Default/Foreclosure Counseling,
Prepurchase Counseling, Rental
Counseling
Affiliate of: NATIONAL
FOUNDATION FOR CONSUMER
CREDIT, INCORPORATED

JERSEY COUNSELING AND
HOUSING DEVELOPMENT,
INCORPORATED
29 S Black Horse Pike
Blackwood, NJ 08012-2952
856-227-3683
Fax: 856-228-0662
Type of Counseling:
HECM Counseling,
Default/Foreclosure Counseling,
Rental Counseling, Prepurchase
Counseling

TRI-COUNTY COMMUNITY
ACTION AGENCY
110 Cohansey St.
Bridgeton, NJ 08302
856-453-0803
Fax: 856-455-7288
Type of Counseling:
HECM Counseling, Prepurchase
Counseling, Default/Foreclosure
Counseling, Rental Counseling

CATHOLIC CHARITIES OF THE
DIOCESE OF METUCHEN
540-550 Route 22 East
Bridgewater, NJ 08807
908-722-1881
Fax: 908-704-0215
Type of Counseling:
Default/Foreclosure Counseling,
Rental Counseling, Prepurchase
Counseling

BURLINGTON COUNTY
COMMUNITY ACTION
PROGRAM
718 Rt. 130 S.
Burlington, NJ 08016
609-386-5800
Fax: 609-386-7380
Type of Counseling:
Prepurchase Counseling,
Default/Foreclosure Counseling,
Rental Counseling

JERSEY COUNSELING AND
HOUSING DEVELOPMENT,
INCORPORATED
1840 S Broadway
Camden, NJ 08104-1334
856-541-1000
Fax: 856-541-8836
Type of Counseling:
HECM Counseling,
Default/Foreclosure Counseling,
Rental Counseling, Prepurchase
Counseling

**NEIGHBORHOOD HOUSING
SERVICES OF CAMDEN,
INCORPORATED
601 Clinton St
Camden, NJ 08103-1415
856-541-0720
Fax: 856-541-8440
Type of Counseling:
Prepurchase Counseling,
Default/Foreclosure Counseling,
HECM Counseling, Rental
Counseling

NEW JERSEY CITIZEN ACTION
527 Cooper St
Camden, NJ 08102-1210
800-656-9637
Toll-Free: 800-656-9637
Fax: 732-714-5386
Email: Jennifer@njcitizenaction.org
Website: www.njcitizenaction.org
Type of Counseling:
HECM Counseling,
Default/Foreclosure Counseling,
Rental Counseling, Prepurchase
Counseling

**CENTER FOR FAMILY
SERVICES
584 Benson Street
Camden, NJ 08103
856-964-9508
Fax: 856-964-0242
Type of Counseling:
Prepurchase Counseling,
Default/Foreclosure Counseling,
Rental Counseling
Affiliate of: HOUSING
OPPORTUNITIES,
INCORPORATED

FAMILY SERVICES
ASSOCIATION/CONSUMER
CREDIT COUNSELING SERVICE
217 N. Main St.
Suite 201, 2nd floor
Cape May Court House, NJ 08210-2191
800-473-2227
Toll-Free: 800-473-2227
Fax: 609-569-1752
Type of Counseling:
HECM Counseling,
Default/Foreclosure Counseling,
Rental Counseling, Prepurchase
Counseling
Affiliate of: NATIONAL
FOUNDATION FOR CONSUMER
CREDIT, INCORPORATED

CONSUMER CREDIT
COUNSELING SERVICE OF NEW
JERSEY
185 Ridgedale Ave.
Cedar Knolls, NJ 07927
973-264-4324
Toll-Free: 888-726-3260
Fax: 973-267-0484

Website: www.cccsnj.com
Type of Counseling:
HECM Counseling,
Default/Foreclosure Counseling,
Prepurchase Counseling

NEW JERSEY CITIZEN ACTON
556 Haddon Ave
Collingswood, NJ 08108-1444
800-656-9637
Toll-Free: 800-656-9637
Fax: 732-714-5386
Email: Jennifer@njcitizenaction.org
Website: www.njcitizenaction.org
Type of Counseling:
HECM Counseling,
Default/Foreclosure Counseling,
Rental Counseling, Prepurchase Counseling

FAMILY SERVICE ASSOCIATION/CONSUMER CREDIT COUNSELING SERVICES OF SOUTH JERSEY
1675 Clemens Bridge Road
First Union Bank
Deptford, NJ 08096-
609-569-0239
Toll-Free: 800-473-2227
Fax: 609-569-1752
Type of Counseling:
Default/Foreclosure Counseling,
Prepurchase Counseling, Rental Counseling
Affiliate of: NATIONAL FOUNDATION FOR CONSUMER CREDIT, INCORPORATED

HOUSING PARTNERSHIP FOR MORRIS COUNTY
2 E. Blackwell St. Ste 29
Dover, NJ 07801
973-659-9222
Fax: 973-659-9220
Type of Counseling:
Prepurchase Counseling, Rental Counseling

**YES LORD COMMUNITY DEVELOPMENT CORPORATION
10 South Oraton Pkwy.
East Orange, NJ 07018
973-399-0416
Fax: 973-399-0416
Type of Counseling:
Prepurchase Counseling, Rental Counseling, Default/Foreclosure Counseling
Affiliate of: CONGRESS OF NATIONAL BLACK CHURCHES, INCORPORATED

FAMILY SERVICE ASSOCIATION/CONSUMER CREDIT COUNSELING SERVICES OF SOUTH JERSEY
3073 English Creek Avenue Ste 3
Egg Harbor TWP, NJ 08234-
609-569-0239
Toll-Free: 800-473-2227
Fax: 609-569-1752
Type of Counseling:
Default/Foreclosure Counseling,
Prepurchase Counseling, Rental Counseling
Affiliate of: NATIONAL FOUNDATION FOR CONSUMER CREDIT, INCORPORATED

COMMUNITY ACCESS UNLIMITED
80 West Grand Avenue
Elizabeth, NJ 07202
908-354-3040
Fax: 908-354-2665
Type of Counseling:
Prepurchase Counseling, Rental Counseling, HECM Counseling,
Default/Foreclosure Counseling

URBAN LEAGUE OF UNION COUNTY
288 N Broad St
Elizabeth, NJ 07208-3789
908-351-7200
Fax: 908-527-9881
Type of Counseling:
HECM Counseling,
Default/Foreclosure Counseling,
Rental Counseling, Prepurchase Counseling

URBAN LEAGUE FOR BERGEN COUNTY
106 W Palisade Ave
Englewood, NJ 07631-2619
201-568-4988
Fax: 201-568-3192
Type of Counseling:
HECM Counseling,
Default/Foreclosure Counseling,
Prepurchase Counseling

MONMOUTH COUNTY DIVISION OF SOCIAL SERVICES
Kozloski Road
Freehold, NJ 07728
732-845-2071
Fax: 732-577-6605
Type of Counseling:
HECM Counseling,
Default/Foreclosure Counseling,
Rental Counseling, Prepurchase Counseling

FAIR HOUSING COUNCIL OF NORTHERN NEW JERSEY
131 Main St, Suite 140
Hackensack, NJ 07601-7140
201-489-3552
Fax: 201-489-8472
Email: fhcnnj@bellatlantic.net
Type of Counseling:
Default/Foreclosure Counseling,
Rental Counseling, Prepurchase Counseling

COUNTY OF BERGEN, DEPARTMENT OF HUMAN SERVICES
21 Main St Rm 109W
Hackensack, NJ 07601-7021
201-336-7575
Fax: 201-336-7450
Type of Counseling:
HECM Counseling

NEW JERSEY CITIZEN ACTION
400 Main St
Hackensack, NJ 07601-5903
800-656-9637
Toll-Free: 800-656-9637
Fax: 732-714-5386
Email: jennifer@njcitizenaction.org
Website: www.njcitizenaction.org
Type of Counseling:
HECM Counseling,
Default/Foreclosure Counseling,
Rental Counseling, Prepurchase Counseling

CONSUMER CREDIT COUNSELING SERVICE OF NEW JERSEY
Airport 17 Office Center
377 Route 17 South Room 108
Hasbrouck Heights, NJ 07604
973-267-4324
Toll-Free: 888-726-3260
Fax: 973-267-0484
Type of Counseling:
HECM Counseling,
Default/Foreclosure Counseling,
Prepurchase Counseling

NEW JERSEY CITIZEN ACTION
85 Raritan Ave Ste 100
Highland Park, NJ 08904
800-656-9637
Toll-Free: 800-656-9637
Fax: 732-714-5386
Email: Jennifer@njcitizenaction.org
Website: www.njcitizenaction.org
Type of Counseling:
HECM Counseling,
Default/Foreclosure Counseling,
Rental Counseling, Prepurchase Counseling

NEW JERSEY CITIZEN ACTION
583 Newark Ave. 2nd Floor
Jersey City, NJ 07306-4551

800-656-9637
Toll-Free: 800-656-9637
Fax: 732-714-5386
Email: Jennifer@njcitizenaction.org
Website: www.njcitizenaction.org
Type of Counseling:
HECM Counseling,
Default/Foreclosure Counseling,
Rental Counseling, Prepurchase
Counseling

**ACORN HOUSING
CORPORATION
22 Journal Square, 3rd Fl.
Jersey City, NJ 07306-4307
201-222-7741
Fax: 201-222-1199
Type of Counseling:
Default/Foreclosure Counseling,
Rental Counseling, Prepurchase
Counseling
Affiliate of: ACORN HOUSING
CORPORATION

NEW JERSEY CITIZEN ACTION
213 Broadway
Long Branch, NJ 07740-7005
800-656-9637
Toll-Free: 800-656-9637
Fax: 732-714-5386
Email: Jennifer@njcitizenaction.org
Website: www.njcitizenaction.org
Type of Counseling:
HECM Counseling,
Default/Foreclosure Counseling,
Rental Counseling, Prepurchase
Counseling

CONSUMER CREDIT
COUNSELING SERVICE OF NEW
JERSEY
479 Route 17 North-Constantine Rd.
2nd Floor
Mahwah, NJ 07430
973-267-4324
Toll-Free: 888-726-3260
Fax: 973-267-0484
Type of Counseling:
Default/Foreclosure Counseling,
Prepurchase Counseling, HECM
Counseling

CONSUMER CREDIT AND
BUDGET COUNSELING
299 S. Shore Road, Route 9 South
Marmora, NJ 082230866
888-738-8233
Toll-Free: 888-738-8233
Type of Counseling:
HECM Counseling,
Default/Foreclosure Counseling,
Prepurchase Counseling, Rental
Counseling

AFFORDABLE HOMES OF
MILLVILLE ECUMENICAL
511 Buck Street
Millville, NJ 08332
856-293-0100
Fax: 856-293-0101
Email: ahomeinc@juno.com
Type of Counseling:
Prepurchase Counseling,
Default/Foreclosure Counseling

CONSUMER CREDIT
COUNSELING SERVICE OF NEW
JERSEY
484 Bloomfield Avenue
Montclair, NJ 07042
973-267-4324
Toll-Free: 888-726-3260
Fax: 973-267-0484
Type of Counseling:
Default/Foreclosure Counseling,
HECM Counseling, Prepurchase
Counseling

**FAMILY SERVICE LEAGUE,
INC
204 Claremont Avenue
Montclair, NJ 07042-
973-746-0800
Fax: 973-746-2822
Email:
dfann@familyserviceleague.org
Type of Counseling:
Rental Counseling
Affiliate of: HOUSING
OPPORTUNITIES,
INCORPORATED

MORRIS COUNTY FAIR
HOUSING COUNCIL
65 Spring St.
Morristown, NJ 07963-0773
973-538-2975
Fax: 973-292-9392
Type of Counseling:
HECM Counseling, Rental
Counseling, Prepurchase Counseling

SENIOR CITIZENS UNITED
COMMUNITY SERVICES
146 Black Horse Pike
Mount Ephraim, NJ 08059-2007
856-456-1121
Fax: 856-456-1076
Type of Counseling:
HECM Counseling

CONSUMER CREDIT
COUNSELING SERVICE OF NEW
JERSEY
374 Livingston Avenue
New Brunswick, NJ 08901
973-267-4324
Toll-Free: 888-726-3260
Fax: 973-267-0484
Type of Counseling:
Default/Foreclosure Counseling,
Prepurchase Counseling, HECM
Counseling

HOUSING COALITION OF
CENTRAL JERSEY
78 New St
New Brunswick, NJ 08901-2502
732-249-9700
Fax: 732-249-4121
Type of Counseling:
HECM Counseling, Rental
Counseling, Prepurchase Counseling,
Default/Foreclosure Counseling

NEW JERSEY CITIZEN ACTION
432 Lafayette St
Newark, NJ 07105-2704
800-656-9637
Toll-Free: 800-656-9637
Fax: 732-714-5386
Email: Jennifer@njcitizenaction.org
Website: www.njcitizenaction.org
Type of Counseling:
HECM Counseling,
Default/Foreclosure Counseling,
Rental Counseling, Prepurchase
Counseling

URBAN LEAGUE OF ESSEX
COUNTY
508 Central Ave
Newark, NJ 07107
973-624-9535
Fax: 973-624-1103
Type of Counseling:
HECM Counseling, Prepurchase
Counseling

NEW JERSEY CITIZEN ACTION
346 Mount Prospect Ave
Newark, NJ 07104-2106
800-656-9637
Toll-Free: 800-656-9637
Fax: 732-714-5386
Email: Jennifer@njcitizenaction.org
Website: www.njcitizenaction.org
Type of Counseling:
HECM Counseling,
Default/Foreclosure Counseling,
Rental Counseling, Prepurchase
Counseling

**CATHOLIC COMMUNITY
SERVICES- DOMUS
CORPORATION
494 Broad Street, 5th Fl.
Newark, NJ 07102
973-596-5117
Fax: 973-424-9596
Email:
catherinedaly@ccsnewark.org

Type of Counseling:
Default/Foreclosure Counseling, Prepurchase Counseling, Rental Counseling, HECM Counseling
Affiliate of: CATHOLIC CHARITIES USA

ST. JAMES COMMUNITY DEVELOPMENT CORPORATION
260 Broadway, Suite 300
Newark, NJ 07104
973-482-5700
Fax: 973-482-0176
Type of Counseling:
Prepurchase Counseling, Rental Counseling, Default/Foreclosure Counseling

MIDDLESEX COUNTY ECONOMIC OPPORTUNITIES CORPORATION
1215 Livingston Avenue
North Brunswick, NJ 08902
732-846-6600
Fax: 732-846-3728
Type of Counseling:
Prepurchase Counseling, Default/Foreclosure Counseling, Rental Counseling, HECM Counseling

ATLANTIC COUNTY INTERGENERATIONAL SERVICES
101 S Shore Rd Shoreview Bldg
Northfield, NJ 08225
609-645-7700
Fax: 609-645-5907
Type of Counseling:
HECM Counseling

NEW JERSEY CITIZEN ACTION
336 Oakwood Ave
Orange, NJ 07050-3223
800-656-9637
Toll-Free: 800-656-9637
Fax: 732-714-5386
Email: Jennifer@njcitizenaction.org
Website: www.njcitizenaction.org
Type of Counseling:
HECM Counseling, Default/Foreclosure Counseling, Rental Counseling, Prepurchase Counseling

**CHILDREN'S AID AND FAMILY SERVICES, INC
200 Robin Road
Paramus, NJ 07652
201-261-2800
Fax: 201-261-6013
Type of Counseling:
Rental Counseling

Affiliate of: HOUSING OPPORTUNITIES, INCORPORATED

NEW JERSEY CITIZEN ACTION
128 Market St.
Passaic, NJ 07055
800-656-9637
Toll-Free: 800-656-9637
Fax: 732-714-5386
Email: jennifer@njcitizenaction.org
Website: www.njcitizenaction.org
Type of Counseling:
HECM Counseling, Default/Foreclosure Counseling, Rental Counseling, Prepurchase Counseling

PATTERSON HOUSING AUTHORITY
60 Van Houten Street
Paterson, NJ 07505
973-345-5650
Fax: 973-977-9085
Type of Counseling:
Prepurchase Counseling

NEW JERSEY CITIZEN ACTION
90 Martin St
Paterson, NJ 07501-3622
800-656-9637
Toll-Free: 800-656-9637
Fax: 732-714-5386
Email: Jennifer@njcitizenaction.org
Website: www.njcitizenaction.org
Type of Counseling:
HECM Counseling, Default/Foreclosure Counseling, Rental Counseling, Prepurchase Counseling

PATERSON TASK FORCE FOR COMMUNITY ACTION, INCORPORATED
155 Ellison St
Paterson, NJ 07505-1304
973-279-2333
Fax: 973-279-2334
Type of Counseling:
HECM Counseling, Default/Foreclosure Counseling, Rental Counseling, Prepurchase Counseling

PATERSON COALITION FOR HOUSING, INCORPORATED
262 Main St, 5th floor
Paterson, NJ 07505-1704
973-684-5911
Fax: 973-684-7538
Type of Counseling:
Rental Counseling, Prepurchase Counseling, HECM Counseling, Default/Foreclosure Counseling

NEW JERSEY CITIZEN ACTION
280 McClellan St
Perth Amboy, NJ 08861-4320
800-656-9637
Toll-Free: 800-656-9637
Fax: 732-714-5386
Email: Jennifer@njcitizenaction.org
Website: www.njcitizenaction.org
Type of Counseling:
HECM Counseling, Default/Foreclosure Counseling, Rental Counseling, Prepurchase Counseling

NORTH WEST NEW JERSEY COMMUNITY ACTION PROGRAM
350 Marshall St.
Phillipsburg, NJ 08865
908-454-7000
Toll-Free: 888-454-4778
Fax: 908-454-3768
Type of Counseling:
HECM Counseling

NORTH STELTON ECONOMIC DEVELOPMENT CORPORATION
6 Ethel Road
Piscataway, NJ 088550756
732-287-6111
Fax: 732-287-0828
Type of Counseling:
Rental Counseling, Prepurchase Counseling, Default/Foreclosure Counseling, HECM Counseling

CITY OF PLAINFIELD DIVISION OF PLANNING AND COMMUNITY DEVELOPMENT
515 Watchung Ave
Plainfield, NJ 07060-1720
908-753-3377
Fax: 908-753-3500
Type of Counseling:
Prepurchase Counseling

NEW JERSEY CITIZEN ACTION
1613 Beaver Dam Road, Suite 1
Point Pleasant, NJ 08742
800-656-9637
Toll-Free: 800-656-9637
Fax: 732-714-5386
Email: jennifer@njcitizenaction.org
Website: www.njcitizenaction.org
Type of Counseling:
HECM Counseling, Default/Foreclosure Counseling, Rental Counseling, Prepurchase Counseling

CONSUMER CREDIT COUNSELING SERVICE OF NEW JERSEY
148 Prospect Street

Ridgewood, NJ 07450
973-267-4324
Toll-Free: 888-726-3260
Fax: 973-267-0484
Type of Counseling:
Default/Foreclosure Counseling, Prepurchase Counseling, HECM Counseling

CONSUMER CREDIT COUNSELING SERVICE OF NEW JERSEY
148 W. Main Street
Somerville, NJ 08876
973-267-4324
Toll-Free: 888-726-3260
Fax: 973-267-0484
Type of Counseling:
Default/Foreclosure Counseling, Prepurchase Counseling, HECM Counseling

SOMERSET COUNTY COALITION ON AFFORDABLE HOUSING
One W Main St 2nd Fl
Somerville, NJ 08876-2201
908-704-8901
Fax: 908-704-9235
Type of Counseling:
Prepurchase Counseling, HECM Counseling, Rental Counseling, Default/Foreclosure Counseling

NEW JERSEY HOUSING FINANCE AND MORTGAGE FINANCE AGENCY
63 Clinton Avenue
Trenton, NJ 08650
609-278-7400
Fax: 609-278-1754
Type of Counseling:
Prepurchase Counseling, Default/Foreclosure Counseling, Rental Counseling

**NEIGHBORHOOD HOUSING SERVICES OF TRENTON, INCORPORATED
1100 West State Street
Trenton, NJ 08618-
609-392-5494
Fax: 609-392-5615
Type of Counseling:
Default/Foreclosure Counseling, Prepurchase Counseling, HECM Counseling
Affiliate of: NEIGHBORHOOD REINVESTMENT CORPORATION

ISLES, INCORPORATED
10 Wood St
Trenton, NJ 08618-3921
609-393-5656
Fax: 609-393-2124
Type of Counseling:
Prepurchase Counseling

MERCER COUNTY HISPANIC ASSOCIATION
200 East State Street
Trenton, NJ 08607
609-392-2446
Fax: 609-695-7618
Type of Counseling:
Rental Counseling, Prepurchase Counseling, HECM Counseling, Default/Foreclosure Counseling

NEW JERSEY CITIZEN ACTION
130 Parkway Ave
Trenton, NJ 08618-3010
800-656-9637
Toll-Free: 800-656-9637
Fax: 732-714-5386
Email: Jennifer@njcitizenaction.org
Website: www.njcitizenaction.org
Type of Counseling:
HECM Counseling, Default/Foreclosure Counseling, Rental Counseling, Prepurchase Counseling

FAMILY SERVICE ASSOCIATION/CONSUMER CREDIT COUNSELING SERVICES OF SOUTH JERSEY
5581 Route 42, Plaza Office Center Unit #6
Turnersville, NJ 08012-
609-569-0239
Toll-Free: 800-473-2227
Fax: 609-569-1752
Type of Counseling:
Default/Foreclosure Counseling, Prepurchase Counseling, Rental Counseling
Affiliate of: NATIONAL FOUNDATION FOR CONSUMER CREDIT, INCORPORATED

FAMILY SERVICES ASSOCIATION/CONSUMER CREDIT COUNSELING SERVICE
744 E Landis Ave
Vineland, NJ 08360-8017
800-473-2227
Toll-Free: 800-473-2227
Fax: 609-569-1752
Type of Counseling:
HECM Counseling, Default/Foreclosure Counseling, Rental Counseling, Prepurchase Counseling
Affiliate of: NATIONAL FOUNDATION FOR CONSUMER CREDIT, INCORPORATED

GENESIS HOUSING CORPORATION
217 S Barber Ave
Woodbury, NJ 08096
856-848-8863
Fax: 856-848-1934
Type of Counseling:
Default/Foreclosure Counseling, Rental Counseling, Prepurchase Counseling

New Mexico

HOME-NEW MEXICO, INCORPORATED
2300 Menaul Blvd.
Albuquerque, NM 87107-
505-889-9486
Type of Counseling: Prepurchase Counseling

NEW MEXICO MORTGAGE FINANCE AUTHORITY
344 Fourth Street, SW
Albuquerque, NM 87102
505-843-6880
Fax: 505-243-3289
Type of Counseling: Prepurchase Counseling, Default/Foreclosure Counseling, Rental Counseling

**ACORN HOUSING CORPORATION
1202 Central Avenue N.W.
Albuquerque, NM 87102-3047
505-244-1086
Fax: 505-244-1088
Type of Counseling:
Prepurchase Counseling, Default/Foreclosure Counseling
Affiliate of: ACORN HOUSING CORPORATION

LEGAL AID SOCIETY OF ALBUQUERQUE. INCORPORATED
121 Tijeras NE, Suite 3100
Albuquerque, NM 87125-5486
505-243-7871
Fax: 505-842-9864
Type of Counseling:
Prepurchase Counseling, Default/Foreclosure Counseling, Rental Counseling

**NEIGHBORHOOD HOUSING SERVICES OF ALBUQUERQUE, INCORPORATED
1500 Lomas Blvd NW Ste. B
Albuquerque, NM 87194
505-243-5511
Fax: 505-242-2911
Email: albnhs@ix.netcom.com
Type of Counseling:

Default/Foreclosure Counseling,
Prepurchase Counseling
Affiliate of: NEIGHBORHOOD REINVESTMENT CORPORATION

CONSUMER CREDIT COUNSELING SERVICES SOUTHWEST
2727 San Pedro Dr NE Ste 117
Albuquerque, NM 87110-3364
505-880-1892
Fax: 505-880-1891
Type of Counseling:
HECM Counseling,
Default/Foreclosure Counseling,
Rental Counseling, Prepurchase Counseling

GREATER ALBUQUERQUE HOUSING PARTNERSHIP
7717 Zuni SE
Albuquerque, NM 87108
505-262-9697
Fax: 505-244-0137
Type of Counseling: Prepurchase Counseling

**UNITED SOUTH BROADWAY CORPORATION
2301 Yale Blvd S.E.
Albuquerque, NM 87102
505-764-8867
Fax: 505-764-9121
Type of Counseling:
Prepurchase Counseling,
Default/Foreclosure Counseling
Affiliate of: HOUSING OPPORTUNITIES, INCORPORATED

CONSUMER CREDIT COUNSELING SERVICE OF GREATER DALLAS, CLOVIS NEW MEXICO
1800 Sheffield Ste B
Clovis, NM 88101
800-538-2227
Fax: 505-769-3245
Type of Counseling:
HECM Counseling,
Default/Foreclosure Counseling,
Rental Counseling, Prepurchase Counseling

CONSUMER CREDIT COUNSELING SERVICE OF SOUTHWEST
3001 Northridge Dr Ste A
Farmington, NM 87401-2084
505-325-5431
Fax: 505-325-5191
Type of Counseling:
HECM Counseling,
Default/Foreclosure Counseling,
Rental Counseling, Prepurchase Counseling

CONSUMER CREDIT COUNSELING SERVICE OF GREATER FORT WORTH
726 E Michigan Dr Ste 138
Hobbs, NM 88240-3456
800-867-2227
Fax: 817-332-2247
Type of Counseling:
HECM Counseling,
Default/Foreclosure Counseling,
Rental Counseling, Prepurchase Counseling

CONSUMER CREDIT COUNSELING SERVICES SOUTHWEST
1065 S Main St Ste B12
Las Cruces, NM 88005-2956
505-527-2585
Fax: 505-527-1975
Type of Counseling:
HECM Counseling,
Default/Foreclosure Counseling,
Prepurchase Counseling

CONSUMER CREDIT COUNSELING SERVICES SOUTHWEST
228 S Saint Francis Dr Ste C2
Santa Fe, NM 87501-2453
505-984-8707
Fax: 505-984-8798
Type of Counseling:
HECM Counseling,
Default/Foreclosure Counseling,
Rental Counseling, Prepurchase Counseling

New York

**AFFORDABLE HOUSING PARTNERSHIP
175 Central Ave.
Albany, NY 12205
518-434-1730
Fax: 518-434-1767
Type of Counseling:
Prepurchase Counseling,
Default/Foreclosure Counseling
Affiliate of: THE HOUSING PARTNERSHIP NETWORK

CONSUMER CREDIT COUNSELING SERVICE OF CENTRAL NEW YORK, INCORPORATED
2 Computer Dr W
Albany, NY 12205-1622
518-482-2227
Toll-Free: 800-479-6026
Fax: 518-482-2296
Type of Counseling:
HECM Counseling,
Default/Foreclosure Counseling,
Rental Counseling, Prepurchase Counseling

UNITED TENANTS OF ALBANY, INCORPORATED
33 Clinton Ave
Albany, NY 12207-2221
518-436-8997
Fax: 518-436-0320
Type of Counseling:
HECM Counseling,
Default/Foreclosure Counseling,
Rental Counseling, Prepurchase Counseling

**CATHOLIC CHARITIES OF THE DIOCESE OF ALBANY
40 North Main Avenue
Albany, NY 19903
518-453-6605
Type of Counseling:
Prepurchase Counseling,
Default/Foreclosure Counseling,
HECM Counseling, Rental Counseling
Affiliate of: CATHOLIC CHARITIES USA

CAPITOL HILL IMPROVEMENT CORPORATION
148 Dove St
Albany, NY 12202-1329
518-462-9696
Fax: 518-462-9698
Email: mbesse@iname.com
Type of Counseling:
HECM Counseling,
Default/Foreclosure Counseling,
Prepurchase Counseling

CAYUGA COUNTY HOMESITE DEVELOPMENT CORPORATION
60 Clark St.
Auburn, NY 13021-3343
315-253-8451
Fax: 315-255-6114
Type of Counseling:
HECM Counseling,
Default/Foreclosure Counseling,
Rental Counseling, Prepurchase Counseling

CORNELL COOPERATIVE EXTENSION
50 W High St
Ballston Spa, NY 12020-1979
518-885-8995
Fax: 518-885-9078
Type of Counseling:

HECM Counseling, Prepurchase Counseling

BELLPORT, HAGERMAN, EAST PATCHOQUE ALLIANCE
1492 Montaugh Highway
Bellport, NY 11713
631-286-9236
Fax: 631-286-3948
Type of Counseling:
HECM Counseling, Default/Foreclosure Counseling, Rental Counseling, Prepurchase Counseling

TRI-COUNTY HOUSING COUNCIL
143 Hibbard Road
Big Flats, NY 14814
607-562-2477
Fax: 607-562-3856
Email: info@tricountyhousing.org
Type of Counseling:
Rental Counseling, Prepurchase Counseling, Default/Foreclosure Counseling, HECM Counseling

METRO-INTERFAITH SERVICES, INCORPORATED
21 New St.
Binghamton, NY 13903
607-723-0723
Fax: 607-722-8912
Email: metrohc@aol.com
Type of Counseling:
HECM Counseling, Default/Foreclosure Counseling, Rental Counseling, Prepurchase Counseling

CONSUMER CREDIT COUNSELING OF CENTRAL NEW YORK, INCORPORATED
49 Court St.
Binghamton, NY 13901
607-723-2984
Fax: 607-723-3007
Type of Counseling:
HECM Counseling, Default/Foreclosure Counseling, Rental Counseling, Prepurchase Counseling

LONG ISLAND HOUSING SERVICES
3900 Veterans Memorial Hwy
Suite 251
Bohemia, NY 11716
631-467-5111
Fax: 631-467-5131
Email: LongIslandHousingServices@yahoo.com
Type of Counseling:
HECM Counseling, Default/Foreclosure Counseling, Rental Counseling, Prepurchase Counseling

SOUTH BRONX ACTION GROUP, INCORPORATED
384 E 149th St Ste 220
Bronx, NY 10455-3908
718-993-5869
Fax: 718-993-7904
Type of Counseling: Rental Counseling

2 OR 3 GATHERED TOGETHER, INCORPORATED
5301 Avenue N
Brooklyn, NY 11234
718-436-1754
Fax: 718-854-3541
Type of Counseling: Rental Counseling, Prepurchase Counseling

CYPRESS HILLS LOCAL DEVELOPMENT CORPORATION
3214 Fulton St
Brooklyn, NY 11208-1908
718-647-8100
Fax: 718-647-2104
Type of Counseling:
HECM Counseling, Default/Foreclosure Counseling, Rental Counseling, Prepurchase Counseling

CARROLL GARDENS ASSOCIATION, INCORPORATED
201 Columbia St
Brooklyn, NY 11231-1402
718-243-9301
Fax: 718-243-9304
Type of Counseling:
Rental Counseling, Prepurchase Counseling

NEIGHBORS HELPING NEIGHBORS
443 39th Street, Suite 202
Brooklyn, NY 11232
718-686-7946
Fax: 718-686-7948
Email: info@nhnhome.org
Website: www.nhnhome.org
Type of Counseling:
HECM Counseling, Default/Foreclosure Counseling, Rental Counseling, Prepurchase Counseling

NEIGHBORHOOD HOUSING SERVICES
1 Hanson Place
Brooklyn, NY 11243-
718-230-7610
Fax: 718-230-0032
Type of Counseling:
HECM Counseling, Default/Foreclosure Counseling, Rental Counseling, Prepurchase Counseling

BROOKLYN NEIGHBORHOOD IMPROVEMENT ASSOCIATION
1482 Saint Johns Place Ste 1F
Brooklyn, NY 11213-3929
718-773-4116
Fax: 718-221-1711
Type of Counseling:
HECM Counseling, Default/Foreclosure Counseling, Rental Counseling

**ACORN HOUSING CORPORATION
88 3rd Ave -3rd Floor
Brooklyn, NY 11217
718-246-8080
Fax: 718-246-7939
Type of Counseling:
Prepurchase Counseling, Default/Foreclosure Counseling
Affiliate of: ACORN HOUSING CORPORATION

BUFFALO URBAN LEAGUE
13 East Genesee St
Buffalo, NY 14203-1405
716-854-7625
Fax: 716-854-8960
Email: jbaun@buffalourban.org
Type of Counseling:
HECM Counseling, Default/Foreclosure Counseling, Rental Counseling, Prepurchase Counseling
Affiliate of: NATIONAL URBAN LEAGUE

FILLMORE-LEROY AREA RESIDENTS
307 Leroy Ave
Buffalo, NY 14214-2520
716-838-6740
Fax: 716-838-6919
Type of Counseling:
Prepurchase Counseling, Rental Counseling
Affiliate of: HOUSING OPPORTUNITIES, INCORPORATED

**KENSINGTON-BAILEY NEIGHBORHOOD HOUSING SERVICES
995 Kensington Ave.
Buffalo, NY 14215
716-836-3600
Fax: 716-836-3686

Email: kbnhsivy@yahoo.com
Type of Counseling:
Prepurchase Counseling
Affiliate of: NEIGHBORHOOD REINVESTMENT CORPORATION

BELMONT SHELTER CORPORATION
1195 Main Street
Buffalo, NY 14209-
716-884-7791
Fax: 716-884-8026
Email: mriegel@belmontshelter.org
Type of Counseling:
Prepurchase Counseling, Rental Counseling, Default/Foreclosure Counseling, HECM Counseling

**WEST SIDE NEIGHBORHOOD HOUSING SERVICES, INCORPORATED
359 Connecticut St
Buffalo, NY 14213
716-885-2344
Fax: 716-885-2346
Type of Counseling:
Prepurchase Counseling, Default/Foreclosure Counseling
Affiliate of: NEIGHBORHOOD REINVESTMENT CORPORATION

ORANGE COUNTY RURAL DEVELOPMENT ADVISORY CORPORATION
Route 207 Professional Bldg
Campbell Hall, NY 10916
845-291-7300
Fax: 845-291-7322
Type of Counseling: HECM Counseling

BISHOP SHEEN ECUMENICAL HOUSING FOUNDATION
2520 Country Rd
Canandaigua, NY 14424
716-461-4263
Fax: 716-461-5177
Email: sheen@netacc.net
Type of Counseling:
HECM Counseling, Default/Foreclosure Counseling, Rental Counseling, Prepurchase Counseling

STONELEIGH HOUSING, INCORPORATED
120 East Center Street
Canastota, NY 13032
315-697-3737
Fax: 315-697-3700
Email: stonelie@twcny.rr.com
Type of Counseling:
HECM Counseling, Default/Foreclosure Counseling, Rental Counseling, Prepurchase Counseling

ST. LAWRENCE COUNTY HOUSING COUNCIL
19 Main Street
Canton, NY 13617
315-386-8576
Fax: 315-386-1564
Type of Counseling:
HECM Counseling, Default/Foreclosure Counseling, Prepurchase Counseling, Rental Counseling

PUTNAM COUNTY HOUSING CORPORATION
11 Seminary Hill Rd
Carmel, NY 10512
845-225-8493
Fax: 845-225-8532
Type of Counseling:
HECM Counseling, Default/Foreclosure Counseling, Rental Counseling, Prepurchase Counseling

CATSKILL MOUNTAIN HOUSING DEVELOPMENT CORPORATION
448 Main St
Catskill, NY 12414
518-943-6700
Fax: 518-943-0113
Email: cmh@mhonline.net
Type of Counseling:
HECM Counseling, Default/Foreclosure Counseling, Rental Counseling, Prepurchase Counseling

COMMUNITY DEVELOPMENT CORPORATION OF LONG ISLAND
2100 Middle Country Road Suite 300
Centereach, NY 11720
631-471-1215
Fax: 631-471-2167
Type of Counseling:
Default/Foreclosure Counseling, Prepurchase Counseling

ROCKLAND HOUSING ACTION COALITION
747 Chestnut Ridge Road, Suite 300
Chestnut Ridge, NY 10977-6224
845-352-3819
Fax: 845-352-2126
Type of Counseling:
Prepurchase Counseling, Default/Foreclosure Counseling

CORTLAND HOUSING ASSISTANCE COUNCIL, INCORPORATED
159 Main St
Cortland, NY 13045
607-753-8271
Fax: 607-756-6267
Type of Counseling:
HECM Counseling, Default/Foreclosure Counseling, Rental Counseling, Prepurchase Counseling

DELAWARE OPPORTUNITIES, INCORPORATED
47 Main St
Delhi, NY 137531124
607-746-2165
Fax: 607-746-6269
Email: houseoff@catskill.net
Type of Counseling:
Prepurchase Counseling, Rental Counseling, Default/Foreclosure Counseling, HECM Counseling

CHAUTAUQUA OPPORTUNITIES, INCORPORATED
17 W Courtney St
Dunkirk, NY 14048-2754
716-366-3333
Fax: 716-366-7366
Email: lesliefagan@hotmail.com
Type of Counseling:
HECM Counseling, Default/Foreclosure Counseling, Rental Counseling, Prepurchase Counseling

**VICTORY HOUSING DEVELOPMENT FUND
1415 Montauk Hwy.
East Patchogue, NY 11772
631-286-5525
Fax: 631-286-0325
Type of Counseling:
Prepurchase Counseling, Rental Counseling
Affiliate of: HOUSING OPPORTUNITIES, INCORPORATED

HOUSING ASSISTANCE PROGRAM OF ESSEX COUNTY, INCORPORATED
2 Church St
Elizabethtown, NY 12932
518-873-6888
Fax: 518-873-9102
Type of Counseling:
HECM Counseling, Default/Foreclosure Counseling, Rental Counseling, Prepurchase Counseling

**CATHOLIC CHARITIES ELMIRA NEW YORK THE SOUTHERN TIER
25 East Church Street
Elmira, NY 14901
607-734-9784
Type of Counseling:
Prepurchase Counseling, Default/Foreclosure Counseling, HECM Counseling, Rental Counseling
Affiliate of: CATHOLIC CHARITIES USA

MARGERT COMMUNITY CORPORATION
1931 Mott Avenue Room 412
Far Rockaway, NY 11691-4103
718-471-3724
Fax: 718-471-5342
Email: stephanielawes@nyct.net
Type of Counseling:
HECM Counseling, Default/Foreclosure Counseling, Prepurchase Counseling, Rental Counseling

ROCKAWAY DEVELOPMENT AND REVITALIZATION CORPORATION
1920 Mott Ave Ste 2
Far Rockaway, NY 11691-4102
718-471-6040
Fax: 718-327-4990
Type of Counseling:
HECM Counseling, Default/Foreclosure Counseling, Rental Counseling, Prepurchase Counseling

MARBLE CITY HOUSING CORPORATION
68 W Main St
Gouverneur, NY 13642-0430
315-287-0143
Fax: 315-287-2492
Type of Counseling:
Default/Foreclosure Counseling, Rental Counseling, Prepurchase Counseling

HOUSING HELP, INCORPORATED
91-101 Broadway, Suite 6
Greenlawn, NY 11740-
631-754-0373
Fax: 631-754-0821
Type of Counseling:
Rental Counseling, Prepurchase Counseling, Default/Foreclosure Counseling

NORTH FORK HOUSING ALLIANCE, INCORPORATED
110 South St
Greenport, NY 11944-1619
631-477-1070
Fax: 631-477-1769
Type of Counseling:
HECM Counseling, Default/Foreclosure Counseling, Rental Counseling, Prepurchase Counseling
Affiliate of: HOUSING OPPORTUNITIES, INCORPORATED

**LONG ISLAND HOUSING PARTNERSHIP, INCORPORATED
180 Osner Ave, Suite 800
Hauppauge, NY 11788-3709
631-435-4710
Fax: 631-435-4751
Type of Counseling:
Default/Foreclosure Counseling, Prepurchase Counseling, HECM Counseling
Affiliate of: THE HOUSING PARTNERSHIP NETWORK

HOUSING OPPORTUNITIES FOR GROWTH, ADVANCEMENT AND REVITILIZATION, INCORPORATED
12 Broadway
Haverstraw, NY 10927-1605
845-429-1100
Fax: 845-429-0193
Email: rivers4556@aol.com
Type of Counseling:
HECM Counseling, Default/Foreclosure Counseling, Prepurchase Counseling

FAMILY AND CHILDREN'S ASSOCIATION
336 Fulton Ave
Hempstead, NY 11550
516-485-5600
Fax: 516-538-2548
Type of Counseling:
HECM Counseling, Default/Foreclosure Counseling, Rental Counseling, Prepurchase Counseling

**HOUSING RESOURCES OF COLUMBIA COUNTY, INCORPORATED
605 State St
Hudson, NY 12534
518-822-0707
Fax: 518-822-0367
Email: margaret@housingresources.org
Website: www.housingresources.org
Type of Counseling:
HECM Counseling, Default/Foreclosure Counseling, Rental Counseling, Prepurchase Counseling
Affiliate of: NEIGHBORHOOD REINVESTMENT CORPORATION

TOWN OF HUNTINGTON HOUSING AUTHORITY
1 Lowndes Ave Ste A
Huntington Station, NY 11746-1261
516-427-6220
Fax: 516-427-6288
Type of Counseling:
Default/Foreclosure Counseling, Rental Counseling

HOST PROGRAM OF TOMPKINS COUNTY OFFICE FOR THE AGING
320 N Tioga St
Ithaca, NY 14850-4206
607-274-5482
Fax: 607-274-5495
Email: David_Stoyell@einstein.co.tompkins.NY.US
Type of Counseling: HECM Counseling

**ITHACA NEIGHBORHOOD HOUSING SERVICES, INCORPORATED
115 W Clinton St
Ithaca, NY 14850
607-277-4500
Fax: 607-277-4536
Email: pdm@claritycomm
Type of Counseling:
Rental Counseling, Prepurchase Counseling
Affiliate of: NEIGHBORHOOD REINVESTMENT CORPORATION

JAMAICA HOUSING IMPROVEMENT, INCORPORATED
161-10 Jamaica Ave Ste 601
Jamaica, NY 11432-6149
718-658-5050
Fax: 718-658-5065
Type of Counseling:
HECM Counseling, Default/Foreclosure Counseling, Rental Counseling, Prepurchase Counseling

COMMISSION ON HUMAN RIGHTS
89-31 161 St. 2nd Floor #210
Jamaica, NY 11432
718-657-9333
Fax: 718-262-8834

Type of Counseling:
HECM Counseling,
Default/Foreclosure Counseling

CHAUTAUQUA OPPORTUNITIES, INCORPORATED
610 W 3rd St
Jamestown, NY 14701-4705
716-661-9430
Fax: 716-661-9436
Type of Counseling:
HECM Counseling,
Default/Foreclosure Counseling,
Rental Counseling, Prepurchase Counseling

RURAL ULSTER PRESERVATION COMPANY
289 Fair St
Kingston, NY 12401
845-331-2140
Fax: 845-331-6217
Type of Counseling:
HECM Counseling,
Default/Foreclosure Counseling,
Prepurchase Counseling

COMMUNITY ACTION IN SELF HELP, INCORPORATED
48 Water St
Lyons, NY 14489-1244
315-946-6992
Fax: 315-946-3314
Type of Counseling:
Rental Counseling, Prepurchase Counseling

KIRYAS JOEL COMMUNITY HOUSING DEVELOPMENT ORGANIZATION, INCORPORATED
51 Forest Road, Suite 360
Monroe, NY 10950
845-782-7790
Fax: 845-783-7415
Type of Counseling:
Prepurchase Counseling,
Default/Foreclosure Counseling,
HECM Counseling, Rental Counseling

RURAL SULLIVAN COUNTY HOUSING OPPORTUNITIES, INCORPORATED
6 Pelton Street
Monticello, NY 12701-1128
845-794-0348
Fax: 845-794-3042
Type of Counseling:
HECM Counseling,
Default/Foreclosure Counseling,
Rental Counseling, Prepurchase Counseling

NEW ROCHELLE CAP
95 Lincoln Ave
New Rochelle, NY 10801-3912
914-636-3050
Fax: 914-633-0617
Type of Counseling:
Default/Foreclosure Counseling,
Rental Counseling, Prepurchase Counseling

OPEN HOUSING CENTER, INCORPORATED
45 John St. Rm 308
New York, NY 10038
212-231-7080
Fax: 212-231-7087
Type of Counseling:
Prepurchase Counseling

ASIAN AMERICANS FOR EQUALITY
129 Rivington St
New York, NY 10002-6103
212-477-2265
Fax: 212-477-2429
Type of Counseling:
HECM Counseling,
Default/Foreclosure Counseling,
Rental Counseling, Prepurchase Counseling

**NEW YORK MORTGAGE COALITION
305 Seventh Avenue, Suite 2001
New York, NY 10001
646-336-8609
Fax: 212-463-9606
Email: c.alleyne@worldnet.att.net
Type of Counseling:
Default/Foreclosure Counseling,
Prepurchase Counseling
Affiliate of: THE HOUSING PARTNERSHIP NETWORK

NATIONAL URBAN LEAGUE
120 Wall Street
New York, NY 10005
212-558-5453
Fax: 212-344-8948

NORTHERN MANHATTAN IMPROVEMENT CORPORATION
76 Wadsworth Ave
New York, NY 10033-7000
212-568-9166
Fax: 212-740-9646
Type of Counseling:
Rental Counseling

HARLEM COMMUNITY DEVELOPMENT CORPORATION
163 West 125th Street, 17th floor
New York, NY 10027
212-961-4100
Fax: 212-961-4143
Email:
dphillpotts@empire.state.ny.us
Type of Counseling:
Prepurchase Counseling,
Default/Foreclosure Counseling,
HECM Counseling, Rental Counseling

WEST HARLEM GROUP ASSISTANCE, INCORPORATED
1528 Amsterdam Avenue
New York City, NY 10031-
212-862-1399
Fax: 212-862-3281
Type of Counseling:
Prepurchase Counseling,
Default/Foreclosure Counseling,
HECM Counseling, Rental Counseling

COALITION FOR PEOPLE'S RIGHTS
13 Paddock Place
Newburgh, NY 12550
914-564-4259
Fax: 914-564-4259
Type of Counseling:
Default/Foreclosure Counseling,
Rental Counseling

CENTER CITY NEIGHBORHOOD DEVELOPMENT CORPORATION
1824 Main St
Niagara Falls, NY 14305-2661
716-282-3738
Fax: 716-282-9607
Email: mfrancisco@centercitynf.org
Type of Counseling:
Rental Counseling, Prepurchase Counseling, Default/Foreclosure Counseling

OPPORTUNITIES FOR CHENANGO, INCORPORATED
44 W Main St
Norwich, NY 13815-1613
607-334-7114
Fax: 607-336-6958
Type of Counseling:
HECM Counseling,
Default/Foreclosure Counseling,
Rental Counseling, Prepurchase Counseling

OSWEGO HOUSING DEVELOPMENT COUNCIL, INCORPORATED
2822 St. Rt. 29
Parish, NY 13131
315-625-4520
Fax: 315-625-7347
Type of Counseling:

HECM Counseling,
Default/Foreclosure Counseling,
Rental Counseling, Prepurchase
Counseling

ECONOMIC OPPORTUNITY
COUNCIL OF SUFFOLK INC.
475 E. Main Street, Suite 206
Patchogue, NY 11772
800-300-4362
Toll-Free: 800-300-4362
Fax: 631-289-2178
Type of Counseling:
Prepurchase Counseling, Rental
Counseling, Default/Foreclosure
Counseling, HECM Counseling

SHARP COMMITTEE,
INCORPORATED
98 Main St
Phoenicia, NY 12464
845-688-5777
Fax: 845-688-5007
Type of Counseling:
HECM Counseling,
Default/Foreclosure Counseling,
Rental Counseling, Prepurchase
Counseling

DUTCHESS COUNTY OFFICE
FOR THE AGING
27 High Street
Poughkeepsie, NY 12601
845-486-2555
Fax: 845-486-2571
Email: dc4@mhv.net
Type of Counseling: HECM
Counseling

NEW JERSEY CITIZEN ACTION
80 Elm St.
Rahway, NY 07065
800-656-9637
Toll-Free: 800-656-9637
Fax: 732-714-5386
Email: jennifer@njcitizenaction.org
Website: www.njcitizenaction.org
Type of Counseling:
HECM Counseling,
Default/Foreclosure Counseling,
Rental Counseling, Prepurchase
Counseling

HOUSING COUNCIL IN
MONROE COUNTY,
INCORPORATED
183 Main St E Ste 1100
Rochester, NY 14604
716-546-3700
Fax: 716-546-2946
Type of Counseling:
HECM Counseling,
Default/Foreclosure Counseling,
Rental Counseling, Prepurchase
Counseling

**RURAL OPPORTUNITIES,
INCORPORATED
400 East Ave
Rochester, NY 14607-1910
716-546-7180
Fax: 716-340-3337
Type of Counseling:
Prepurchase Counseling
Affiliate of: NEIGHBORHOOD
REINVESTMENT
CORPORATION

**NEIGHBORHOOD HOUSING
SERVICES OF ROCHESTER,
INCORPORATED
570 South Ave
Rochester, NY 14620-1345
716-325-4170
Fax: 716-325-2587
Type of Counseling:
Prepurchase Counseling
Affiliate of: NEIGHBORHOOD
REINVESTMENT
CORPORATION

BISHOP SHEEN ECUMENICAL
HOUSING FOUNDATION
935 East Ave Suite 300
Rochester, NY 14607-2216
716-461-4263
Fax: 716-461-5177
Email: sheen@netacc.net
Type of Counseling:
HECM Counseling,
Default/Foreclosure Counseling,
Rental Counseling, Prepurchase
Counseling

**CATHOLIC CHARITIES OF
THE DIOCESE OF ROCHESTER
NEW YORK
1150 Buffalo Road
Rochester, NY
716-328-3210
Type of Counseling:
Prepurchase Counseling,
Default/Foreclosure Counseling,
HECM Counseling, Rental
Counseling
Affiliate of: CATHOLIC
CHARITIES USA

ROOSEVELT ASSISTANCE
CORPORATION
455D Nassau Road
Roosevelt, NY 11575-
516-223-7077
Fax: 516-223-0863
Type of Counseling:
Prepurchase Counseling,
Default/Foreclosure Counseling,
HECM Counseling

CATTARAUGUS
PRESERVATION CORPORATION
25 Jefferson St
Salamanca, NY 14779
716-945-1041
Fax: 716-945-1301
Type of Counseling:
Default/Foreclosure Counseling,
Rental Counseling, Prepurchase
Counseling

BETTER NEIGHBORHOODS,
INCORPORATED
986 Albany St
Schenectady, NY 12307
518-372-6469
Fax: 518-372-6460
Type of Counseling:
HECM Counseling,
Default/Foreclosure Counseling,
Rental Counseling, Prepurchase
Counseling

WESTERN CATSKILLS
COMMUNITY REVITALIZATION
COUNCIL, INCORPORATED
125 Main Street, Box A
Stamford, NY 12167
607-652-2823
Fax: 607-652-2825
Type of Counseling:
Prepurchase Counseling, Rental
Counseling, Default/Foreclosure
Counseling

NORTHFIELD COMMUNITY
LOCAL DEVELOPMENT
CORPORATION
160 Heberton Ave.
Staten Island, NY 10302
718-442-7351
Fax: 718-981-3441
Type of Counseling:
Prepurchase Counseling, Rental
Counseling, Default/Foreclosure
Counseling

CONSUMER CREDIT
COUNSELING SERVICE OF
CENTRAL NEW YORK,
INCORPORATED
500 S Salina St Ste 600
Syracuse, NY 132023394
315-474-6026
Toll-Free: 800-479-6026
Fax: 315-479-8421
Website: www.cccscny.org
Type of Counseling:
HECM Counseling,
Default/Foreclosure Counseling,

Rental Counseling, Prepurchase Counseling
Affiliate of: NATIONAL FOUNDATION FOR CONSUMER CREDIT, INCORPORATED

NORTHEAST HAWLEY DEVELOPMENT ASSOCIATION, INCORPORATED
101 Gertrude St
Syracuse, NY 13203-2417
315-425-1032
Fax: 315-425-1089
Email: nehda@a-znet.com
Type of Counseling: Prepurchase Counseling

HOME HEADQUARTERS, INCORPORATED
124 E Jefferson St
Syracuse, NY 13202
315-474-1939
Fax: 315-474-0637
Email: homehq.org
Type of Counseling:
Prepurchase Counseling, Default/Foreclosure Counseling
Affiliate of: NEIGHBORHOOD REINVESTMENT CORPORATION

URBAN LEAGUE OF ONONDAGA COUNTY, INCORPORATED
1211 S. Salina Street
Syracuse, NY 13205-
315-472-6955
Fax: 315-472-6445
Email: urbanleaguesyr@hotmail.com
Type of Counseling:
HECM Counseling, Default/Foreclosure Counseling, Rental Counseling, Prepurchase Counseling

HOUSING ASSISTANCE CENTER OF NIAGARA FRONTIER, INCORPORATED
200 Niagara St
Tonawanda, NY 14150-1003
716-695-1807
Fax: 716-881-2378
Type of Counseling:
HECM Counseling, Default/Foreclosure Counseling, Rental Counseling, Prepurchase Counseling

RENSSELAER COUNTY HOUSING RESOURCES
415 River St, Third floor
Troy, NY 12180
518-272-8289
Fax: 518-272-1950
Type of Counseling:
HECM Counseling, Default/Foreclosure Counseling, Prepurchase Counseling, Rental Counseling

TROY REHABILITATION AND IMPROVEMENT PROGRAM, INCORPORATED
251 River Street
Troy, NY 12180-2834
518-690-0020
Fax: 518-690-0025
Email: tripinc@ix.netcom
Type of Counseling:
HECM Counseling, Default/Foreclosure Counseling, Prepurchase Counseling
Affiliate of: NEIGHBORHOOD REINVESTMENT CORPORATION

**UTICA NEIGHBORHOOD HOUSING SERVICES, NEIGHBORWORKS HOMEOWNERSHIP CENTER
1611 Genesee St.
Utica, NY 13501
315-724-4197
Toll-Free: 866-724-4197
Fax: 315-724-1415
Email: jforte@unhs.org
Website: www.thehomeownershipcenter.org
Type of Counseling:
Default/Foreclosure Counseling, Prepurchase Counseling, HECM Counseling
Affiliate of: NEIGHBORHOOD REINVESTMENT CORPORATION

CONSUMER CREDIT COUNSELING SERVICE OF CENTRAL NEW YORK
289 Genesee St
Utica, NY 13501-3804
315-797-5366
Fax: 315-797-9410
Type of Counseling:
HECM Counseling, Default/Foreclosure Counseling, Rental Counseling, Prepurchase Counseling

ALBANY COUNTY RURAL HOUSING ALLIANCE, INCORPORATED
24 Martin Road
Voorheesville, NY 12186
518-765-2425
Fax: 518-765-9014
Email: acrha@gateway.net
Website: www.timesunion.com/communities/acrha
Type of Counseling:
HECM Counseling, Default/Foreclosure Counseling, Rental Counseling, Prepurchase Counseling

WESTCHESTER RESIDENTIAL OPPORTUNITIES, INCORPORATED
470 Mamaroneck Ave,suite 410
White Plains, NY 10605-1830
914-428-4507
Fax: 914-428-9455
Email: toni@wroinc.org
Type of Counseling:
HECM Counseling, Default/Foreclosure Counseling, Rental Counseling, Prepurchase Counseling

WYANDANCH COMMUNITY DEVELOPMENT CORPORATION
30 William St VFW Bldg
Wyandanch, NY 11798-3326
631-643-4786
Fax: 631-253-0139
Type of Counseling:
HECM Counseling, Default/Foreclosure Counseling, Prepurchase Counseling, Rental Counseling

North Carolina

CONSUMER CREDIT COUNSELING CENTERS OF GREATER GREENSBORO IN ASHEBORO
135 Sunset Avenue
Asheboro, NC 27204-
336-373-8882
Fax: 336-387-9167
Type of Counseling:
Prepurchase Counseling, Default/Foreclosure Counseling, HECM Counseling, Rental Counseling
Affiliate of: NATIONAL FOUNDATION FOR CONSUMER CREDIT, INCORPORATED

AFFORDABLE HOUSING COALITION OF ASHEVILLE AND BUNCOMBE COUNTY
34 Wall Street, Suite 607
Asheville, NC 28801
828-259-9216
Fax: 828-259-9469
Type of Counseling:
Prepurchase Counseling, Default/Foreclosure Counseling, Rental Counseling

CONSUMER CREDIT COUNSELING OF WESTERN NORTH CAROLINA
50 S French Broad Ave Ste 227
Asheville, NC 288013217
828-255-5166
Toll-Free: 800-737-5485
Fax: 828-255-5129
Website: www.cccsofwnc.org
Type of Counseling:
HECM Counseling, Default/Foreclosure Counseling, Rental Counseling, Prepurchase Counseling

**NEIGHBORHOOD HOUSING SERVICES OF ASHEVILLE, NORTH CAROLINA
135 Cherry St
Asheville, NC 28801-2223
828-251-5054
Fax: 828-251-1323
Type of Counseling:
Prepurchase Counseling

NORTHWESTERN REGIONAL HOUSING AUTHORITY
869 Highway 105 Ext Ste 10
Boone, NC 28607-2510
828-264-6683
Fax: 828-264-0160
Type of Counseling:
Default/Foreclosure Counseling, Prepurchase Counseling, Rental Counseling, HECM Counseling

**CONSUMER CREDIT COUNSELING SERVICE OF GREATER GREENSBORO IN BURLINGTON
719 Hermitage Road
Burlington, NC 27215
336-373-8882
Fax: 336-387-9167
Type of Counseling:
HECM Counseling, Default/Foreclosure Counseling, Prepurchase Counseling, Rental Counseling
Affiliate of: NATIONAL FOUNDATION FOR CONSUMER CREDIT, INCORPORATED

NORTHEASTERN COMMUNITY DEVELOPMENT CORPORATION, INCORPORATED
154 Highway 158 East
Camden, NC 27921-0367
252-338-5466
Fax: 252-338-5639
Email: ncdc@net-change.com
Type of Counseling:
Prepurchase Counseling, Default/Foreclosure Counseling, Rental Counseling

SANDHILLS COMMUNITY ACTION PROGRAM, INCORPORATED
103 Saunders St
Carthage, NC 28327-0937
910-947-5675
Fax: 910-947-5514
Email:
kristanb@portlandhousingcenter.org
Type of Counseling:
HECM Counseling, Default/Foreclosure Counseling, Rental Counseling, Prepurchase Counseling

EMPOWERMENT INCORPORATED
109 North Grahm Street Suite 200
Chapel Hill, NC 27516
919-967-8779
Fax: 919-967-0710
Type of Counseling: Prepurchase Counseling

CONSUMER CREDIT COUNSELING AND HOUSING SERVICES/ UNITED FAMILY SERVICES
200 North Sharon Amity
Charlotte, NC 28211
704-332-4191
Fax: 704-362-3137
Email: agreene@UFSCLT.org
HECM Counseling, Prepurchase Counseling, Rental Counseling, Default/Foreclosure Counseling

CHARLOTTE-MECKLENBURG HOUSING PARTNERSHIP, INCORPORATED
1201 Greenwood Cliff Ste 300
Charlotte, NC 28204-2822
704-342-0933
TTY/TDD: 704-343-4692
Fax: 704-342-2745
Email: info@cmhp.org
Website: www.cmhp.org
Type of Counseling:
Prepurchase Counseling
Affiliate of: THE HOUSING PARTNERSHIP NETWORK

URBAN LEAGUE OF CENTRAL CAROLINAS, INCORPORATED
740 West 5th Street
Charlotte, NC 28202
704-373-2256
Fax: 704-373-2262
Email: cnuljerri@aol.com
Website: www.urbanleaguecc.org
Type of Counseling:
Prepurchase Counseling, Rental Counseling, Default/Foreclosure Counseling
Affiliate of: NATIONAL URBAN LEAGUE

CONSUMER CREDIT COUNSELING SERVICE
212 Le Phillip Ct Ste 106
Concord, NC 28025-2954
704-786-7918
Fax: 704-786-7709
Type of Counseling:
Default/Foreclosure Counseling

DURHAM AFFORDABLE HOUSING COALITION
331 W Main St Ste 408
Durham, NC 27701-3232
919-683-1185
Fax: 919-688-0082
Type of Counseling:
HECM Counseling, Default/Foreclosure Counseling, Prepurchase Counseling, Rental Counseling
Affiliate of: HOUSING OPPORTUNITIES, INCORPORATED

**CONSUMER CREDIT COUNSELING SERVICE OF DURHAM
413 East Chapel Hill Street
Durham, NC 27701-3221
919-688-3381
Toll-Free: 888-562-3732
Fax: 919-682-4021
Type of Counseling:
HECM Counseling, Default/Foreclosure Counseling, Prepurchase Counseling, Rental Counseling
Affiliate of: NATIONAL FOUNDATION FOR CONSUMER CREDIT, INCORPORATED

ELIZABETH CITY STATE UNIVERSITY
1704 Weeksville Rd.
Elizabeth City, NC 27909
252-335-3702
Fax: 252-335-3735
Type of Counseling:
Prepurchase Counseling, Rental Counseling, Default/Foreclosure Counseling

RIVER CITY COMMUNITY DEVELOPMENT CORPORATION
501 East Main St
Elizabeth City, NC 27909
252-331-2925

Fax: 252-331-1425
Type of Counseling:
Default/Foreclosure Counseling, Rental Counseling, Prepurchase Counseling

SANDHILLS COMMUNITY ACTION PROGRAM, INCORPORATED
122 Railroad St
Ellerbe, NC 28338-0389
910-652-6167
Fax: 910-947-5514
Type of Counseling:
HECM Counseling, Default/Foreclosure Counseling, Rental Counseling, Prepurchase Counseling

CUMBERLAND COUNTY COMMUNITY ACTION PROGRAM, INCORPORATED
PO Box 2009
Fayetteville, NC 28301
910-323-3192
Fax: 910-323-4990
Type of Counseling:
HECM Counseling, Default/Foreclosure Counseling, Rental Counseling, Prepurchase Counseling

CONSUMER CREDIT COUNSELING SERVICE
130 South Oakland Street
Gastonia, NC 28052
704-862-0702
Toll-Free: 888-213-8853
Fax: 704-862-0239
Type of Counseling:
HECM Counseling, Default/Foreclosure Counseling, Rental Counseling, Prepurchase Counseling
Affiliate of: NATIONAL FOUNDATION FOR CONSUMER CREDIT, INCORPORATED

CONSUMER CREDIT COUNSELING SERVICE OF GOLDSBORO
678 North Spence Avenue
Goldsboro, NC 27534
919-751-3868
Fax: 919-751-0382
Type of Counseling:
HECM Counseling, Default/Foreclosure Counseling, Rental Counseling, Prepurchase Counseling

HOMEKEEPING MORTGAGE DEFAULT COUNSELING, INCORPORATED
2808 Four Seasons Blvd.
Greensboro, NC 27406
336-299-3827
Fax: 336-299-3827
Type of Counseling:
Prepurchase Counseling, Default/Foreclosure Counseling, Rental Counseling

**CONSUMER CREDIT COUNSELING SERVICE OF GREATER GREENSBORO
315 E. Washington Street
Greensboro, NC 27401
336-373-8882
Fax: 336-387-9167
Type of Counseling:
Prepurchase Counseling, Default/Foreclosure Counseling, HECM Counseling, Rental Counseling
Affiliate of: NATIONAL FOUNDATION FOR CONSUMER CREDIT, INCORPORATED

ALBEMARLE COMMISSION
512 South Church St
Hertford, NC 27944
252-426-5753
Fax: 252-426-8482
Type of Counseling:
HECM Counseling

WESTERN PIEDMONT COUNCIL OF GOVERNMENTS
736 4th Street South-West
Hickory, NC 28602
828-322-9191
Fax: 828-322-5991
Type of Counseling:
HECM Counseling

**CONSUMER CREDIT COUNSELING SERVICE OF GREATER GREENSBORO IN HIGH POINT
1401 Long Street
High Point, NC 27262
336-373-8882
Fax: 336-387-9167
Type of Counseling:
Prepurchase Counseling, Default/Foreclosure Counseling, Rental Counseling
Affiliate of: NATIONAL FOUNDATION FOR CONSUMER CREDIT, INCORPORATED

HOUSING AUTHORITY OF THE CITY OF HIGH POINT
500E Russell Avenue
High Point, NC 272611779
336-878-2300
Fax: 336-887-9366
Type of Counseling:
Prepurchase Counseling, Rental Counseling, Default/Foreclosure Counseling

DAVIDSON COUNTY COMMUNITY ACTION INCORPORATED
701 S Salisbury St
Lexington, NC 27292
336-249-0234
Fax: 336-249-2078
Type of Counseling:
Prepurchase Counseling, Rental Counseling, Default/Foreclosure Counseling, HECM Counseling

**FAMILY SERVICE CREDIT COUNSELORS
235 East CenterStreet
Lexington, NC 27292
336-249-0237
Fax: 336-243-7685
Type of Counseling:
HECM Counseling, Default/Foreclosure Counseling, Prepurchase Counseling, Rental Counseling

COASTAL COMMUNITY DEVELOPMENT CORPORATION
1017 A Broad St
New Bern, NC 28563
252-636-0893
Fax: 252-636-1062
Type of Counseling:
HECM Counseling, Default/Foreclosure Counseling, Prepurchase Counseling

TWIN RIVERS OPPORTUNITIES, INC.
318 Craven St.
New Bern, NC 28563
252-637-3599
Fax: 252-637-7101
Type of Counseling:
Prepurchase Counseling, Rental Counseling

NORTH CAROLINA HOUSING FINANCE AGENCY
3508 Bush Street
Raleigh, NC 27609-8066
919-877-5700
Fax: 919-877-5701

**DOWNTOWN HOUSING IMPROVEMENT CORPORATION
113 S. Wilmington Street
Raleigh, NC 27601
919-832-4345
Fax: 919-832-2206
Website: www.dhic.org

Type of Counseling:
Prepurchase Counseling,
Default/Foreclosure Counseling,
Rental Counseling
Affiliate of: NEIGHBORHOOD REINVESTMENT CORPORATION

RESOURCES FOR SENIORS
1110 Navaho Dr. Ste 400
Raleigh, NC 27609-7318
919-872-7933
Fax: 919-872-9574
Type of Counseling: HECM Counseling

ISOTHERMAL PLANNING AND DEVELOPMENT COMMISSION
101 W Court St
Rutherfordton, NC 28139-2804
828-287-2281
Fax: 828-287-2735
Type of Counseling: HECM Counseling

JOHNSTON-LEE COMMUNITY ACTION, INCORPORATED
1102 Massey Street
Smithfield, NC 27577-0711
919-934-2145
Fax: 919-934-6231
Email: jlca.usa.net
Type of Counseling:
HECM Counseling,
Default/Foreclosure Counseling,
Rental Counseling, Prepurchase Counseling

CONSUMER CREDIT COUNSELING SERVICE OF THE CAROLINA FOOTHILLS, INCORPORATED
200 Ohio St
Spindale, NC 28160-0006
828-286-7062
Fax: 828-286-7064
Type of Counseling:
HECM Counseling,
Default/Foreclosure Counseling,
Rental Counseling, Prepurchase Counseling
Affiliate of: NATIONAL FOUNDATION FOR CONSUMER CREDIT, INCORPORATED

SANDHILLS COMMUNITY ACTION PROGRAM, INCORPORATED
217 S Main St Ste B
Troy, NC 27371-3200
910-576-9071
Fax: 910-947-5514
Type of Counseling:
HECM Counseling,
Default/Foreclosure Counseling,
Rental Counseling, Prepurchase Counseling

SANDHILLS COMMUNITY ACTION PROGRAM, INCORPORATED
208 Rutherford Street
Wadesboro, NC 28170-0065
704-694-5161
Fax: 910-947-5514
Type of Counseling:
HECM Counseling,
Default/Foreclosure Counseling,
Rental Counseling, Prepurchase Counseling

MID-EAST COMMISSION-AREA AGENCY ON AGING
1385 John Small Avenue
Washington, NC 27889-1787
252-974-1835
Fax: 252-948-1884
Type of Counseling: HECM Counseling

**CONSUMER CREDIT COUNSELING SERVICE OF GREATER GREENSBORO IN WENTWORTH
525 NC-65
Wentworth, NC 27320
336-373-8882
Fax: 336-387-9167
Type of Counseling:
HECM Counseling,
Default/Foreclosure Counseling,
Prepurchase Counseling, Rental Counseling
Affiliate of: NATIONAL FOUNDATION FOR CONSUMER CREDIT, INCORPORATED

WILMINGTON HOUSING FINACE AND DEVELOPMENT, INCORPORATED
310 North Fron Street
Wilmington, NC 28401
910-763-7775
Fax: 910-763-7705
Type of Counseling:
Prepurchase Counseling,
Default/Foreclosure Counseling,
Rental Counseling

**SCOTLAND NECK COMMUNITY OUTREACH CENTER
135 New Street
Williamston, NC 27892
252-826-0314
Type of Counseling:
Prepurchase Counseling
Affiliate of: CONGRESS OF NATIONAL BLACK CHURCHES, INCORPORATED

WILSON COMMUNITY IMPROVEMENT ASSOCIATION, INCORPORATED
504 E Green St
Wilson, NC 27893
252-243-4855
Fax: 252-243-2945
Type of Counseling:
HECM Counseling, Prepurchase Counseling

CONSUMER CREDIT COUNSELING SERVICE OF FORSYTH COUNTY
8064 North Point Boulevard, Suite 204
Winston Salem, NC 27106
336-896-1191
Fax: 336-896-0481
Type of Counseling:
HECM Counseling,
Default/Foreclosure Counseling,
Rental Counseling, Prepurchase Counseling

EAST WINSTON COMMUNITY DEVELOPMENT CORPORATION, INCORPORATED
1225 E Fifth St
Winston-Salem, NC 27101
336-723-1783
Fax: 336-761-8014
Type of Counseling:
Prepurchase Counseling,
Default/Foreclosure Counseling,
Rental Counseling, HECM Counseling

North Dakota

COMMUNITY ACTION PROGRAM REGION VII, INCORPORATED
2105 Lee Ave
Bismarck, ND 58504-6798
701-258-2240
Fax: 701-258-2245
Type of Counseling:
HECM Counseling,
Default/Foreclosure Counseling,
Rental Counseling, Prepurchase Counseling

INDUSTRIAL COMMISSION OF NORTH DAKOTA
North Dakota Housing Finance Agency
P.O. Box 1535
Bismarck, ND 58502
701-328-8080

Fax: 701-328-8090
Type of Counseling:
Rental Counseling,
Default/Foreclosure Counseling,
Prepurchase Counseling

COMMUNITY ACTION AND DEVELOPMENT PROGRAM
202 E Villard St
Dickinson, ND 58601-5247
701-227-0131
Fax: 701-227-4750
Email:
comact1@dickinson.ctctel.com
Type of Counseling:
Prepurchase Counseling, Rental Counseling, Default/Foreclosure Counseling, HECM Counseling

VILLAGE FAMILY SERVICE CENTER (CCCS)
1201 25th Street South
Fargo, ND 58106
701-451-4900
Toll-Free: 800-627-8220
Fax: 701-235-9693
Email: www.thefamilyvillage.org
Type of Counseling:
Prepurchase Counseling
Affiliate of: NATIONAL FOUNDATION FOR CONSUMER CREDIT, INCORPORATED

SOUTHEASTERN NORTH DAKOTA COMMUNITY ACTION AGENCY
3233 S University Dr
Fargo, ND 58104-6221
701-232-2452
Fax: 701-298-3115
Type of Counseling:
HECM Counseling,
Default/Foreclosure Counseling,
Rental Counseling, Prepurchase Counseling

VILLAGE FAMILY SERVICE CENTER (CCCS)
Riverview Center, 215 North 3rd Street #104
Grand Forks, ND 58203
701-746-4584
Fax: 701-746-1239
Email:
bflickinger@thevillagefamily.org
Website: www.thevillagefamily.org
Type of Counseling:
Prepurchase Counseling

RED RIVER VALLEY COMMUNITY ACTION
1013 N 5th St
Grand Forks, ND 58203-2442
701-746-5431
Fax: 701-746-0406
Type of Counseling:
HECM Counseling,
Default/Foreclosure Counseling,
Rental Counseling, Prepurchase Counseling

COMMUNITY ACTION OPPORTUNITIES, INCORPORATED
220 8th Ave. SE
Minot, ND 58701
701-839-7221
Toll-Free: 800-726-8645
Fax: 701-839-1747
Email: cao@minot.ndak.net
Type of Counseling:
Default/Foreclosure Counseling,
Rental Counseling, Prepurchase Counseling

Ohio

FAIR HOUSING CONTACT SERVICE
333 South Main Street, Suite 300
Akron, OH 44308
330-376-6191
Fax: 330-376-8391
Type of Counseling:
Prepurchase Counseling, Rental Counseling, HECM Counseling

CATHOLIC CHARITIES OF ASHTABULA COUNTY
4200 Park Avenue
Ashtabula, OH 44004
440-992-0300
Fax: 440-992-5974
Type of Counseling:
HECM Counseling,
Default/Foreclosure Counseling,
Rental Counseling, Prepurchase Counseling

CONSUMER CREDIT COUNSELING OF NORTHEAST OHIO, INCORPORATED
4274 Manhattan Ave
Brunswick, OH 44212-3523
216-771-0790
Fax: 216-781-8852
Type of Counseling:
HECM Counseling,
Default/Foreclosure Counseling,
Prepurchase Counseling

CATHOLIC COMMUNITY SERVICES OF STARK COUNTY, INCORPORATED
1500 Market Ave. N, Suite 3
Canton, OH 44714
330-454-2220
Fax: 330-454-2255

BETTER HOUSING LEAGUE OF GREATER CINCINNATI
2400 Reading Rd
Cincinnati, OH 452021429
513-721-6855
Fax: 513-721-8160
Type of Counseling:
HECM Counseling,
Default/Foreclosure Counseling,
Prepurchase Counseling

**HOME OWNERSHIP CENTER OF GREATER CINCINNATI, INCORPORATED
2820 Vernon Place
Cincinnati, OH 45219
513-961-2800
Fax: 513-961-8222
Type of Counseling:
Default/Foreclosure Counseling,
Prepurchase Counseling
Affiliate of: NEIGHBORHOOD REINVESTMENT CORPORATION

**NEIGHBORHOOD HOUSING SERVICES OF CLEVELAND, INCORPORATED
3210 Euclid Avenue
Cleveland, OH 44115
216-361-0516
Fax: 216-361-1252
Type of Counseling:
Prepurchase Counseling
Affiliate of: NEIGHBORHOOD REINVESTMENT CORPORATION

CONSUMER PROTECTION ASSOCIATION
3030 Euclid Ave Ste 105
Cleveland, OH 44115-2521
216-881-3434
Fax: 216-881-6524
Type of Counseling:
Default/Foreclosure Counseling,
Rental Counseling, Prepurchase Counseling

CLEVELAND HOUSING NETWORK, INCORPORATED
2999 Payne Ave Ste 306
Cleveland, OH 44114-4400
216-574-7100
Fax: 216-574-7130
Email: jciammai@chnnet.com
Website: www.chnnet.com
Type of Counseling:
Rental Counseling, Prepurchase Counseling
Affiliate of: THE HOUSING PARTNERSHIP NETWORK

CONSUMER CREDIT COUNSELING OF NORTHEAST OHIO, INCORPORATED
1228 Euclid Ave Ste 390
Cleveland, OH 44115-1831
216-781-8624
Fax: 216-781-8852
Type of Counseling:
HECM Counseling, Default/Foreclosure Counseling, Prepurchase Counseling
Affiliate of: NATIONAL FOUNDATION FOR CONSUMER CREDIT, INCORPORATED

NEAR WEST SIDE MULTI-SERVICE CORPORATION
4115 Bridge Ave
Cleveland, OH 44113-3304
216-631-5800
Fax: 216-631-4595
Email: maydugan@multiverse.com
Type of Counseling:
Prepurchase Counseling

LUTHERAN HOUSING CORPORATION-WEST SIDE OFFICE
1967 W 45th St
Cleveland, OH 44102-3449
216-651-0077
Fax: 216-651-0072
Type of Counseling:
HECM Counseling, Default/Foreclosure Counseling, Rental Counseling, Prepurchase Counseling

LUTHERAN HOUSING CORPORATION-LARCHMERE OFFICE
12114 Larchmere Blvd
Cleveland, OH 44120-1139
216-231-5815
Fax: 216-231-5845
Type of Counseling:
HECM Counseling, Default/Foreclosure Counseling, Rental Counseling, Prepurchase Counseling

CONSUMER CREDIT COUNSELING OF NORTHEAST OHIO, INCORPORATED
2490 Lee Blvd Ste 310 Maylee Bldg.
Cleveland Heights, OH 44118-1255
216-771-0790
Fax: 216-781-8852
Type of Counseling:
HECM Counseling, Default/Foreclosure Counseling, Prepurchase Counseling

**COLUMBUS NEIGHBORHOOD HOUSING SERVICES, INCORPORATED
604 E Rich St 3rd Fl
Columbus, OH 43215-5341
614-224-3603
Fax: 614-224-5946
Email: CNHS@ix.netcom.com
Type of Counseling:
Default/Foreclosure Counseling, Prepurchase Counseling
Affiliate of: NEIGHBORHOOD REINVESTMENT CORPORATION

CONSOC CONSULTANTS
3632 Indianola Avenue, Ste A
Columbus, OH 432143734
614-267-8970
Fax: 614-267-8976
Type of Counseling:
HECM Counseling, Default/Foreclosure Counseling, Rental Counseling, Prepurchase Counseling

CONSUMER CREDIT COUNSELING OF COLUMBUS
697 E Broad St
Columbus, OH 43215-3948
614-464-2227
Fax: 614-464-2124
Type of Counseling:
Prepurchase Counseling, Default/Foreclosure Counseling, HECM Counseling

MID-OHIO REGIONAL PLANNING COMMISSION
285 E Main St
Columbus, OH 43215-5272
614-233-4181
Fax: 614-228-1904
Email: morpc.org
Type of Counseling:
HECM Counseling, Rental Counseling, Prepurchase Counseling

HOMES ON THE HILL
12 South Terrace Avenue
Columbus, OH 43204
614-275-4663
Fax: 614-275-3060
Type of Counseling:
Default/Foreclosure Counseling, Rental Counseling, Prepurchase Counseling

COLUMBUS HOUSING PARTNERSHIP
562 East Main St.
Columbus, OH 43215-5312
614-221-8889
Fax: 614-221-8591
Type of Counseling:
Default/Foreclosure Counseling, Prepurchase Counseling, HECM Counseling
Affiliate of: THE HOUSING PARTNERSHIP NETWORK

FAMILY SOLUTIONS
2100 Front Street - Mall
Cuyahoga, OH 44221
330-928-1159
Fax: 330-928-2191
Type of Counseling:
Default/Foreclosure Counseling, Rental Counseling, Prepurchase Counseling

LUTHERAN SOCIAL SERVICES
3131 S Dixie Dr Suite 300
Dayton, OH 45439
937-643-5599
Toll-Free: 800-359-0831
Fax: 937-643-9970
Email: jclifton@lssma.org
Type of Counseling:
Default/Foreclosure Counseling, Prepurchase Counseling, HECM Counseling
Affiliate of: NATIONAL FOUNDATION FOR CONSUMER CREDIT, INCORPORATED

LUTHERAN HOUSING CORPORATION
13944 Euclid Ave Ste 208
East Cleveland, OH 44112-3832
216-651-0077
Fax: 216-651-0072
Type of Counseling:
HECM Counseling, Default/Foreclosure Counseling, Rental Counseling, Prepurchase Counseling

**HAMILTON NEIGHBORHOOD HOUSING SERVICES, INCORPORATED
100 S. Martin Luther King, Jr. Blvd.
Hamilton, OH 45011
513-737-9301
Toll-Free: 800-525-5420
Fax: 513-737-9304
Type of Counseling:
Default/Foreclosure Counseling, Prepurchase Counseling
Affiliate of: NEIGHBORHOOD REINVESTMENT CORPORATION

CONSUMER CREDIT COUNSELING OF NORTHEAST OHIO, INCORPORATED
763 Broadway Ste 202
Lorain, OH 44052-1857

216-771-0790
Fax: 216-781-8852
Type of Counseling:
HECM Counseling,
Default/Foreclosure Counseling,
Prepurchase Counseling

MARION-CRAWFORD
COMMUNITY ACTION
COMMISSION
1183 Bellefontaine Ave
Marion, OH 43302-7007
740-383-2154
Fax: 740-387-3407
Type of Counseling:
Default/Foreclosure Counseling,
Rental Counseling, Prepurchase
Counseling

MASSILLON URBAN LEAGUE
325 Third Street, SE
Massillon, OH 44646-
330-833-2804
Fax: 330-833-0126
Type of Counseling:
Default/Foreclosure Counseling,
Rental Counseling

CONSUMER CREDIT
COUNSELING OF NORTHEAST
OHIO, INCORPORATED
7519 Mentor Avenue Rm. A104
Mentor, OH 44060
216-771-0790
Fax: 216-781-8852
Type of Counseling:
HECM Counseling,
Default/Foreclosure Counseling,
Prepurchase Counseling

CONSUMER CREDIT
COUNSELING OF NORTHEAST
OHIO, INCORPORATED
5339 Ridge Rd Ste 201
Parma, OH 44129-1467
216-771-0790
Fax: 216-781-8852
Type of Counseling:
HECM Counseling,
Default/Foreclosure Counseling,
Prepurchase Counseling

PORTSMOUTH-INNER CITY
CORPORATION
1206 Waller St
Portsmouth, OH 45662-3524
740-354-6626
Fax: 740-353-2695
Type of Counseling:
HECM Counseling,
Default/Foreclosure Counseling,
Rental Counseling, Prepurchase
Counseling

**PORTAGE AREA
DEVELOPMENT CORPORATION
218 West Main Street
Ravenna, OH 44266
330-297-6400
Fax: 330-297-5305
Type of Counseling:
Prepurchase Counseling
Affiliate of: NEIGHBORHOOD
REINVESTMENT
CORPORATION

COMMUNITY ACTION
COMMISSION OF BELMONT
COUNTY, INCORPORATED
100 W. Main Street, Suite 209
Saint Clairsville, OH 43950-
740-695-5477
Fax: 740-695-5477
Email: cachousing@aol.com
Type of Counseling:
HECM Counseling, Prepurchase
Counseling, Default/Foreclosure
Counseling

JEFFERSON COUNTY
COMMUNITY ACTION COUNCIL
114 N. Fourth Street
Steubenville, OH 43952-
740-282-0971
Fax: 740-282-8631
Type of Counseling:
Prepurchase Counseling, HECM
Counseling, Rental Counseling

**NEIGHBORHOOD HOUSING
SERVICES OF TOLEDO,
INCORPORATED
704 Second St
Toledo, OH 43605
419-691-2900
Fax: 419-244-4035
Email: wfarnsel@toledolink.com
Type of Counseling:
Default/Foreclosure Counseling,
Prepurchase Counseling
Affiliate of: NEIGHBORHOOD
REINVESTMENT
CORPORATION

CATHOLIC CHARITIES,
DIOCESE OF TOLEDO, HOUSING
AND EMPLOYMENT SERVICES
One Stranahan Square, Suite 354
Toledo, OH 436041495
419-244-6711
Fax: 419-242-4220
Type of Counseling:
HECM Counseling,
Default/Foreclosure Counseling,
Rental Counseling, Prepurchase
Counseling
Affiliate of: CATHOLIC
CHARITIES USA

CONSUMER CREDIT
COUNSELING SERVICE-
COMMUNITY SOLUTIONS
ASSOCIATION
320 High Street NE
Warren, OH 44481-1222
330-394-9090
Fax: 330-394-5910
Type of Counseling:
Default/Foreclosure Counseling,
Rental Counseling, Prepurchase
Counseling
Affiliate of: NATIONAL
FOUNDATION FOR CONSUMER
CREDIT, INCORPORATED

**CATHOLIC COMMUNITY
SERVICES, INCORPORATED
175 Laird Ave NE 3rd Fl
Warren, OH 44482-1740
330-393-5254
Fax: 330-393-4050
Type of Counseling:
Rental Counseling, Prepurchase
Counseling, Default/Foreclosure
Counseling, HECM Counseling
Affiliate of: CATHOLIC
CHARITIES USA

COMMUNITY ACTION
COMMISSION OF FAYETTE
COUNTY
324 E Court St
Washington Court House, OH
43160-1402
740-335-7282
Fax: 740-335-6802
Type of Counseling:
HECM Counseling, Rental
Counseling, Prepurchase Counseling

JACKSON-VINTON
COMMUNITY ACTION,
INCORPORATED
14333 State Route 327
Wellston, OH 45692-9307
740-384-3722
Fax: 740-384-5815

FAMILY SERVICE AGENCY
CONSUMER CREDIT
COUNSELING
535 Marmion Ave
Youngstown, OH 44502-2323
330-782-9113
Fax: 330-782-1614
Type of Counseling:
HECM Counseling,
Default/Foreclosure Counseling,
Rental Counseling, Prepurchase
Counseling
Affiliate of: NATIONAL
FOUNDATION FOR CONSUMER
CREDIT, INCORPORATED

**CATHOLIC CHARITIES
HOUSING OPPORTUNITIES
225 Elm St
Youngstown, OH 44503-1005
330-744-8451
Fax: 330-742-6447
Type of Counseling:
Prepurchase Counseling,
Default/Foreclosure Counseling,
Rental Counseling, HECM
Counseling
Affiliate of: CATHOLIC
CHARITIES USA
YOUNGSTOWN AREA URBAN
LEAGUE
1350 5th Ave Ste 300
Youngstown, OH 44504-1728
330-744-4111
Fax: 330-744-1140
Type of Counseling:
HECM Counseling,
Default/Foreclosure Counseling,
Rental Counseling, Prepurchase
Counseling

UNIVERSAL CREDIT
COUNSELING SERVICES,
INCORPORATED
531 Market St
Zanesville, OH 43701-3610
740-450-2227
Toll-Free: 888-900-8227
Fax: 740-454-3933
Type of Counseling:
HECM Counseling,
Default/Foreclosure Counseling,
Rental Counseling, Prepurchase
Counseling

Oklahoma

CONSUMER CREDIT
COUNSELING SERVICE
Irving Center
704 North Oak, Room 7
Ada, OK 74820
800-364-2227
Toll-Free: 800-364-2227
Fax: 405-789-5052
Email: lhoover@cccsok.com
Type of Counseling:
Prepurchase Counseling, Rental
Counseling, Default/Foreclosure
Counseling, HECM Counseling

THE CHICKASAW NATION
601 W. 33rd St.
Ada, OK 74820
580-421-8800
Fax: 580-421-8879
Email: carolynB@Chickasaw.com
Type of Counseling:
Rental Counseling, Prepurchase
Counseling, Default/Foreclosure
Counseling

CONSUMER CREDIT
COUNSELING SERVICE
Midfirst Bank, 2511 North Main
Altus, OK 73521
800-364-2227
Toll-Free: 800-364-2227
Fax: 405-789-5052
Email: lhoover@cccsok.com
Type of Counseling:
Prepurchase Counseling, Rental
Counseling, Default/Foreclosure
Counseling, HECM Counseling

CONSUMER CREDIT
COUNSELING SERVICE OF
GREATER DALLAS/ARDMORE
OK
333 W. Main, Suite 150
Ardmore, OK 73402
800-944-3826
Toll-Free: 800-944-3826
Fax: 580-224-9196
Type of Counseling:
Prepurchase Counseling, Rental
Counseling, Default/Foreclosure
Counseling, HECM Counseling

CREDIT COUNSELING CENTERS
OF OKLAHOMA,
INCORPORATED
210 S. Keeler
Bartlesville, OK 74006-
918-336-7619
Toll-Free: 800-324-5611
Fax: 918-336-2722
Type of Counseling:
Prepurchase Counseling,
Default/Foreclosure Counseling,
HECM Counseling, Rental
Counseling
Affiliate of: NATIONAL
FOUNDATION FOR CONSUMER
CREDIT, INCORPORATED

CONSUMER CREDIT
COUNSELING SERVICE
3230 N Rockwell Ave
Bethany, OK 730081789
800-364-2227
Toll-Free: 800-364-2227
Fax: 405-789-5052
Email: lhoover@cccsok.com
Type of Counseling:
HECM Counseling,
Default/Foreclosure Counseling,
Rental Counseling, Prepurchase
Counseling

CREDIT COUNSELING CENTERS
OF OKLAHOMA,
INCORPORATED
828 N. Sycamore Ave.
Broken Arrow, OK 77012
918-259-0164
Toll-Free: 800-324-5611
Fax: 918-258-6237
Type of Counseling:
Prepurchase Counseling,
Default/Foreclosure Counseling,
HECM Counseling, Rental
Counseling
Affiliate of: NATIONAL
FOUNDATION FOR CONSUMER
CREDIT, INCORPORATED

CONSUMER CREDIT
COUNSELING SERVICE
Canadian Valley Technology Center,
1401N. Michigan
Chickasha, OK 73018
800-364-2227
Toll-Free: 800-364-2227
Fax: 405-789-5052
Email: lhoover@cccsok.com
Type of Counseling:
Prepurchase Counseling, Rental
Counseling, Default/Foreclosure
Counseling, HECM Counseling

CREDIT COUNSELING CENTERS
OF OKLAHOMA,
INCORPORATED
400 W. Will Rogers Blvd.
Claremore, OK 74017
918-343-3313
Toll-Free: 800-324-5611
Fax: 918-343-2712
Type of Counseling:
Prepurchase Counseling,
Default/Foreclosure Counseling,
HECM Counseling, Rental
Counseling
Affiliate of: NATIONAL
FOUNDATION FOR CONSUMER
CREDIT, INCORPORATED

CENTRAL OKLAHOMA
COMMUNITY ACTION ACENCY
122 N. Cleveland
Cushing, OK 74023
918-225-7469
Fax: 405-275-9442
Type of Counseling:
Prepurchase Counseling,
Default/Foreclosure Counseling,
HECM Counseling, Rental
Counseling

CONSUMER CREDIT
COUNSELING SERVICE
Del West Center, 3907 SE 29th St
Del City, OK 73115-2639

800-364-2227
Toll-Free: 800-364-2227
Fax: 405-789-5052
Email: lhoover@cccsok.com
Type of Counseling:
HECM Counseling,
Default/Foreclosure Counseling,
Rental Counseling, Prepurchase
Counseling

CONSUMER CREDIT
COUNSELING SERVICE
Local Oklahoma Bank, 2210 North
Hwy 81 Suite A
Duncan, OK 73533
800-364-2227
Toll-Free: 800-364-2227
Fax: 405-789-5052
Email: lhoover@cccsok.com
Type of Counseling:
Prepurchase Counseling, Rental
Counseling, Default/Foreclosure
Counseling, HECM Counseling

CONSUMER CREDIT
COUNSELING SERVICE
Broadway South Building
2 East 11th Street Suite 109
Edmond, OK 73034-3922
800-364-2227
Toll-Free: 800-364-2227
Fax: 405-789-5052
Email: lhoover@cccsok.com
Type of Counseling:
HECM Counseling,
Default/Foreclosure Counseling,
Rental Counseling, Prepurchase
Counseling

COMMUNITY DEVELOPMENT
SUPPORT ASSOCIATION
2615 E Randolph
Enid, OK 73701
580-242-6131
Fax: 580-234-3554
Type of Counseling:
HECM Counseling,
Default/Foreclosure Counseling,
Rental Counseling, Prepurchase
Counseling

CONSUMER CREDIT
COUNSELING SERVICE
317 West Cherokee Ste A
Enid, OK 73701
800-364-2227
Toll-Free: 800-364-2227
Fax: 405-789-5052
Email: lhoover@cccsok.com
Type of Counseling:
HECM Counseling,
Default/Foreclosure Counseling,
Rental Counseling, Prepurchase
Counseling

CONSUMER CREDIT
COUNSELING SERVICE
Army Community Service Building,
1651 Randolph Road
Ft. Sill, OK 73503
800-364-2227
Toll-Free: 800-364-2227
Fax: 405-789-5052
Email: lhoover@cccsok.com
Type of Counseling:
Prepurchase Counseling, Rental
Counseling, Default/Foreclosure
Counseling, HECM Counseling

CONSUMER CREDIT
COUNSELING SERVICE
First Capital Bank, 110 East
Cleveland
Guthrie, OK 73044
800-364-2227
Toll-Free: 800-364-2227
Fax: 405-789-5052
Email: lhoover@cccsok.com
Type of Counseling:
Prepurchase Counseling, Rental
Counseling, Default/Foreclosure
Counseling, HECM Counseling

CENTRAL OKLAHOMA
COMMUNITY ACTION ACENCY
109 Oklahoma
Guthrie, OK 73044
405-282-4332
Fax: 405-275-9442
Type of Counseling:
Prepurchase Counseling,
Default/Foreclosure Counseling,
HECM Counseling, Rental
Counseling

CONSUMER CREDIT
COUNSELING SERVICE OF
NORTH CENTRAL TEXAS,
HUGO, OK
502 E. Rosewood
Hugo, OK 74743
580-326-5434
Fax: 972-542-3623
Type of Counseling:
Prepurchase Counseling, Rental
Counseling, Default/Foreclosure
Counseling, HECM Counseling

CONSUMER CREDIT
COUNSELING SERVICES OF
NORTH CENTRAL
TEXAS/HUGO, OK
502 E Rosewood
Hugo, OK 74743
580-326-5434
Fax: 972-542-3623
Type of Counseling:
Prepurchase Counseling, Rental
Counseling, Default/Foreclosure
Counseling, HECM Counseling

**LITTLE DIXIE COMMUNITY
ACTION AGENCY
502 West Duke Street
Hugo, OK 74743
580-326-5434
Fax: 580-326-0556
Type of Counseling:
Prepurchase Counseling,
Default/Foreclosure Counseling,
HECM Counseling
Affiliate of: NEIGHBORHOOD
REINVESTMENT
CORPORATION

CHOCTAW HOUSING
AUTHORITY
1005 S. 5th Street
Hugo, OK 74743
580-326-7521
Fax: 580-326-7641
Type of Counseling:
Rental Counseling,
Default/Foreclosure Counseling

CONSUMER CREDIT
COUNSELING SERVICE
Bank First, 501 C Avenue Ste 308 C
Lawton, OK 735014325
800-364-2227
Toll-Free: 800-364-2227
Fax: 405-789-5052
Email: lhoover@cccsok.com
Type of Counseling:
HECM Counseling,
Default/Foreclosure Counseling,
Rental Counseling, Prepurchase
Counseling

HOUSING AUTHORITY OF THE
CITY OF LAWTON
609 SW F Avenue
Lawton, OK 73501
580-353-7392
Fax: 580-353-6111
Type of Counseling:
Prepurchase Counseling, Rental
Counseling, Default/Foreclosure
Counseling, HECM Counseling

CENTRAL OKLAHOMA
COMMUNITY ACTION ACENCY
131 S. Main
Lexington, OK 73051
405-527-5883
Fax: 405-275-9442
Type of Counseling:
Prepurchase Counseling,
Default/Foreclosure Counseling,
HECM Counseling, Rental
Counseling

CENTRAL OKLAHOMA
COMMUNITY ACTION ACENCY
410 W. Main Street
Maud, OK 74854
405-374-2222
Fax: 405-275-9442
Type of Counseling:
Prepurchase Counseling,
Default/Foreclosure Counseling,
HECM Counseling, Rental
Counseling

CREDIT COUNSELING CENTERS
OF OKLAHOMA,
INCORPORATED
100 North 5th
McAlester, OK 74501
918-423-2193
Toll-Free: 800-324-5611
Fax: 918-420-5901
Type of Counseling:
Prepurchase Counseling,
Default/Foreclosure Counseling,
HECM Counseling, Rental
Counseling
Affiliate of: NATIONAL
FOUNDATION FOR CONSUMER
CREDIT, INCORPORATED

CENTRAL OKLAHOMA
COMMUNITY ACTION ACENCY
2026 N. Broadway
Moore, OK 73160
405-799-5778
Fax: 405-275-9442
Type of Counseling:
Prepurchase Counseling,
Default/Foreclosure Counseling,
HECM Counseling, Rental
Counseling

CREDIT COUNSELING CENTERS
OF OKLAHOMA,
INCORPORATED
917 W. Broadwat
Muskogee, OK 74401
918-683-2778
Toll-Free: 800-324-5611
Fax: 918-683-5571
Type of Counseling:
Prepurchase Counseling,
Default/Foreclosure Counseling,
HECM Counseling, Rental
Counseling
Affiliate of: NATIONAL
FOUNDATION FOR CONSUMER
CREDIT, INCORPORATED

THE HOUSING AUTHORITY OF
THE CITY OF MUSKOGEE
220 North 40th Street
Muskogee, OK 74401
918-687-6301
Fax: 918-687-3249
Email: blake@mhastaff.org
Website: www.mhastaff.org
Type of Counseling:
Prepurchase Counseling, Rental
Counseling, Default/Foreclosure
Counseling

CONSUMER CREDIT
COUNSELING SERVICE
Midtown Plaza, 330 W Gray Ste 410
Norman, OK 73069-7111
800-364-2227
Toll-Free: 800-364-2227
Fax: 405-789-5052
Email: lhoover@cccsok.com
Type of Counseling:
HECM Counseling,
Default/Foreclosure Counseling,
Rental Counseling, Prepurchase
Counseling

HOUSING AUTHORITY OF THE
CITY OF NORMAN
700 N Berry Rd
Norman, OK 73069
405-329-0933
Fax: 405-329-2542
Type of Counseling:
HECM Counseling,
Default/Foreclosure Counseling,
Rental Counseling, Prepurchase
Counseling

CENTRAL OKLAHOMA
COMMUNITY ACTION ACENCY
1121E. Main
Norman, OK 73071
405-701-2120
Fax: 405-275-9442
Type of Counseling:
Prepurchase Counseling,
Default/Foreclosure Counseling,
HECM Counseling, Rental
Counseling

CONSUMER CREDIT
COUNSELING SERVICE
Western Tower Building, 5350
South Western, Suite 601
Oklahoma City, OK 73139-2740
800-364-2227
Toll-Free: 800-364-2227
Fax: 405-789-5052
Email: lhoover@cccsok.com
Type of Counseling:
HECM Counseling,
Default/Foreclosure Counseling,
Rental Counseling, Prepurchase
Counseling

OKLAHOMA HOUSING
FINANCE AGENCY
1140 Northwest 63rd, Suite 200
Oklahoma City, OK 73126-0720
405-848-1144
Fax: 405-840-1109
Type of Counseling:
Prepurchase Counseling, Rental
Counseling, Default/Foreclosure
Counseling

COMMUNITY ACTION AGENCY
OF OKLAHOMA CITY AND
OKLAHOMA/CANADIAN
COUNTIES
1900 NW 10th St
Oklahoma City, OK 73106-2428
405-232-0199
Fax: 405-232-9074
Type of Counseling:
HECM Counseling,
Default/Foreclosure Counseling,
Rental Counseling, Prepurchase
Counseling

CONSUMER CREDIT
COUNSELING
CLEARINGHOUSE
420 Southwest 10th
Oklahoma City, OK 73109
800-364-2227
Toll-Free: 800-364-2227
Fax: 405-789-5052
Email: lhoover@cccsok.com
Type of Counseling:
Prepurchase Counseling, Rental
Counseling, Default/Foreclosure
Counseling, HECM Counseling

**NEIGHBORHOOD HOUSING
SERVICES OF OKLAHOMA
CITY, INCORPORATED
1320 Classen Dr. Ste 200
Oklahoma City, OK 73103
405-231-4663
Fax: 405-231-5137
Email: nhsokc@ixnetcom.com
Type of Counseling:
Prepurchase Counseling,
Default/Foreclosure Counseling
Affiliate of: NEIGHBORHOOD
REINVESTMENT
CORPORATION

CONSUMER CREDIT
COUNSELING SERVICE
Urban League Building, 3017 North
Martin Luther King Blvd.
Oklahoma City, OK 73111
800-364-2227
Toll-Free: 800-364-2227
Fax: 405-789-5052
Email: lhoover@cccsok.com
Type of Counseling:
Prepurchase Counseling, Rental
Counseling, Default/Foreclosure
Counseling, HECM Counseling

**LATINO COMMUNITY
DEVELOPMENT AGENCY
420 SW 10th
Oklahoma City, OK 73109
405-236-0701
Fax: 405-236-0737
Email: LCDACHODO@juno.com
Type of Counseling:
Prepurchase Counseling
Affiliate of: NATIONAL COUNCIL OF LA RAZA

CONSUMER CREDIT
COUNSELING SERVICE
Macarthur Executive Building, 4614 North MacArthur Suite 232
Oklahoma City, OK 73122
800-364-2227
Toll-Free: 800-364-2227
Fax: 405-789-5052
Email: lhoover@cccsok.com
Type of Counseling:
Prepurchase Counseling, Rental Counseling, Default/Foreclosure Counseling, HECM Counseling

DEEP FORK COMMUNITY
ACTION FOUNDATION,
INCORPORATED
313 W 8th St
Okmulgee, OK 74447-5006
918-756-2826
Fax: 918-756-6829
Type of Counseling:
Rental Counseling, Prepurchase Counseling, HECM Counseling

CREDIT COUNSELING CENTERS
OF OKLAHOMA,
INCORPORATED
114 N. Grand, suite 212
Okmulgee, OK 74447
918-756-5170
Toll-Free: 800-324-5611
Fax: 918-756-5170
Type of Counseling:
Prepurchase Counseling, Default/Foreclosure Counseling, HECM Counseling, Rental Counseling
Affiliate of: NATIONAL FOUNDATION FOR CONSUMER CREDIT, INCORPORATED

CREDIT COUNSELING CENTERS
OF OKLAHOMA,
INCORPORATED
207 S. Cedar
Owasso, OK 74055
918-272-3226
Toll-Free: 800-324-5611
Fax: 918-274-0601
Type of Counseling:
Prepurchase Counseling, Default/Foreclosure Counseling, HECM Counseling, Rental Counseling
Affiliate of: NATIONAL FOUNDATION FOR CONSUMER CREDIT, INCORPORATED

CONSUMER CREDIT
COUNSELING SERVICE
Pioneer Technology Center, 2015 North Ash, Room D107
Ponca City, OK 74601
800-364-2227
Toll-Free: 800-364-2227
Fax: 405-789-5052
Email: lhoover@cccsok.com
Type of Counseling:
Prepurchase Counseling, Rental Counseling, Default/Foreclosure Counseling, HECM Counseling

CENTRAL OKLAHOMA
COMMUNITY ACTION ACENCY
807 Jim Thorpe Blvd.
Prague, OK 74864
405-587-4591
Fax: 405-275-9442
Type of Counseling:
Prepurchase Counseling, Default/Foreclosure Counseling, HECM Counseling, Rental Counseling

CREDIT COUNSELING CENTERS
OF OKLAHOMA,
INCORPORATED
210 E. Dewey
Sapulpa, OK 74066
918-224-8412
Toll-Free: 800-324-5611
Fax: 918-224-8759
Type of Counseling:
Prepurchase Counseling, Default/Foreclosure Counseling, HECM Counseling, Rental Counseling
Affiliate of: NATIONAL FOUNDATION FOR CONSUMER CREDIT, INCORPORATED

CENTRAL OKLAHOMA
COMMUNITY ACTION ACENCY
600 E. Strothers
Seminole, OK 74888
405-382-1800
Fax: 405-275-9442
Type of Counseling:
Prepurchase Counseling, Default/Foreclosure Counseling, HECM Counseling, Rental Counseling

CONSUMER CREDIT
COUNSELING SERVICE
Mid First Bank
330 N. Broadway
Shawnee, OK 74801
800-364-2227
Toll-Free: 800-364-2227
Fax: 405-789-5052
Email: lhoover@cccsok.com
Type of Counseling:
Prepurchase Counseling, Rental Counseling, Default/Foreclosure Counseling, HECM Counseling

CENTRAL OKLAHOMA
COMMUNITY ACTION ACENCY
132 N. Bell
Shawnee, OK 74801
405-878-9500
Fax: 405-275-9442
Type of Counseling:
Prepurchase Counseling, Default/Foreclosure Counseling, HECM Counseling, Rental Counseling

CENTRAL OKLAHOMA
COMMUNITY ACTION ACENCY
510 W. Benedict
Shawnee, OK 74801
405-214-4455
Fax: 405-275-9442
Type of Counseling:
Prepurchase Counseling, Default/Foreclosure Counseling, HECM Counseling, Rental Counseling

KI BOIS COMMUNITY ACTION
FOUNDATION, INCORPORATED
301 E Main
Stigler, OK 74462
918-967-9050
Fax: 918-967-9025
Type of Counseling:
Prepurchase Counseling, Rental Counseling, Default/Foreclosure Counseling

STILLWATER HOUSING
AUTHORITY
807 S Lowry
Stillwater, OK 74074
405-372-4906
Fax: 405-372-1416
Email: sha@ionet.net
Type of Counseling:
HECM Counseling, Default/Foreclosure Counseling, Rental Counseling, Prepurchase Counseling

CONSUMER CREDIT
COUNSELING SERVICE
Postal Plaza Building, 720 South
Husband, Suite 10
Stillwater, OK 74074
800-364-2227
Toll-Free: 800-364-2227
Fax: 405-789-5052
Email: lhoover@cccsok.com
Type of Counseling:
Prepurchase Counseling, Rental
Counseling, Default/Foreclosure
Counseling, HECM Counseling

CENTRAL OKLAHOMA
COMMUNITY ACTION ACENCY
619 W. 12
Stillwater, OK 74074
405-624-2533
Fax: 405-275-9442
Type of Counseling:
Prepurchase Counseling,
Default/Foreclosure Counseling,
HECM Counseling, Rental
Counseling

HOUSING AUTHORITY OF THE
CHEROKEE NATION
1500 Hensley Drive
Tahlequah, OK 74465-1007
918-456-5482
Fax: 918-458-5018
Type of Counseling:
Default/Foreclosure Counseling,
Rental Counseling, Prepurchase
Counseling

CONSUMER CREDIT
COUNSELING SERVICE
Building 420
Tinker AFB, OK 73145
800-364-2227
Toll-Free: 800-364-2227
Fax: 405-789-5052
Email: lhoover@cccsok.com
Type of Counseling:
Prepurchase Counseling, Rental
Counseling, Default/Foreclosure
Counseling, HECM Counseling

CREDIT COUNSELING CENTERS
OF OKLAHOMA,
INCORPORATED
4646 S Harvard Ave
Tulsa, OK 741590450
918-744-5611
Toll-Free: 800-324-5611
Fax: 918-744-0232
Website: www.cccsofok.com
Type of Counseling:
Prepurchase Counseling, Rental
Counseling, Default/Foreclosure
Counseling, HECM Counseling
Affiliate of: NATIONAL
FOUNDATION FOR CONSUMER
CREDIT, INCORPORATED

COMMUNITY ACTION PROJECT
OF TULSA
717 South Houston, Ste. 200
Tulsa, OK 74127
918-382-3200
Fax: 918-382-3213
Type of Counseling:
Prepurchase Counseling,
Default/Foreclosure Counseling
Affiliate of: NEIGHBORHOOD
REINVESTMENT
CORPORATION

CREDIT COUNSELING CENTERS
OF OKLAHOMA,
INCORPORATED
1 W. 36TH Street N
Tulsa, OK 74106
918-425-8289
Toll-Free: 800-324-5611
Fax: 918-428-7510
Type of Counseling:
Prepurchase Counseling,
Default/Foreclosure Counseling,
HECM Counseling, Rental
Counseling
Affiliate of: NATIONAL
FOUNDATION FOR CONSUMER
CREDIT, INCORPORATED

METROPOLITAN TULSA URBAN
LEAGUE
240 E Apache Street
Tulsa, OK 74106-3799
918-584-5221
Fax: 918-584-3620
Type of Counseling: Rental
Counseling

HOUSING PARTNERS OF
TULSA, INCORPORATED
415 E. Independence
Tulsa, OK 74106
918-581-5711
Fax: 918-582-0397
Type of Counseling:
Prepurchase Counseling, Rental
Counseling, Default/Foreclosure
Counseling, HECM Counseling

CONSUMER CREDIT
COUNSELING SERVICE
1st National Bank Building, 1100
East Main, 3rd Floor
Weatherford, OK 73096
800-364-2227
Toll-Free: 800-364-2227
Fax: 405-789-5052
Email: lhoover@cccsok.com
Type of Counseling:
Prepurchase Counseling, Rental
Counseling, Default/Foreclosure
Counseling, HECM Counseling

CENTRAL OKLAHOMA
COMMUNITY ACTION ACENCY
318 W. 4TH Street
Wewoka, OK 74884
405-257-3423
Fax: 405-275-9442
Type of Counseling:
Prepurchase Counseling,
Default/Foreclosure Counseling,
HECM Counseling, Rental
Counseling

Oregon

**CONSUMER CREDIT
COUNSELING SERVICE OF
LINN-BENTON
214 NW Hickory Street
Albany, OR 97321-0381
541-926-5843
Toll-Free: 888-225-0009
Fax: 541-926-6731
Type of Counseling:
HECM Counseling,
Default/Foreclosure Counseling,
Rental Counseling, Prepurchase
Counseling
Affiliate of: NATIONAL
FOUNDATION FOR CONSUMER
CREDIT, INCORPORATED

**CONSUMER CREDIT
COUNSELING SERVICE OF
COOS-CURRY, INCORPORATED
2110 Newmark Ave
Coos Bay, OR 97420-2957
541-888-7040
Fax: 541-888-7044
Type of Counseling:
HECM Counseling,
Default/Foreclosure Counseling,
Rental Counseling, Prepurchase
Counseling
Affiliate of: NATIONAL
FOUNDATION FOR CONSUMER
CREDIT, INCORPORATED

**CORVALLIS NEIGHBORHOOD
HOUSING SERVICES,
INCORPORATED
2797 NW 9th St
Corvallis, OR 97330
541-752-7220
Fax: 541-752-5037
Email: cnhs@proaxis.com
Type of Counseling:
Prepurchase Counseling
Affiliate of: NEIGHBORHOOD
REINVESTMENT
CORPORATION

CONSUMER CREDIT COUNSELING SERVICE OF LANE COUNTY, INCORPORATED
149 W 12th Ave Ste 100
Eugene, OR 97440
541-342-4459
Toll-Free: 888-830-7235
Fax: 541-342-5467
Email: cccslane@clipper.net
Website: www.creditdebthelp.com
Type of Counseling:
HECM Counseling, Default/Foreclosure Counseling, Rental Counseling, Prepurchase Counseling

CONSUMER CREDIT COUNSELING SERVICE OF OREGON-HILLSBORO
1050 SW Baseline Rd Ste A8
Hillsboro, OR 97123-3873
888-875-2227
Fax: 503-408-6820
Type of Counseling:
HECM Counseling, Default/Foreclosure Counseling, Rental Counseling, Prepurchase Counseling

OPEN DOOR COUNSELING CENTER
34420 SW Tualatin Valley Hwy
Hillsboro, OR 97123-5470
503-640-6689
Fax: 503-640-9374
Type of Counseling:
Default/Foreclosure Counseling, Prepurchase Counseling, HECM Counseling, Rental Counseling

CONSUMER CREDIT COUNSELING SERVICES OF SOUTHERN OREGON
740 Main St.
Klamath Falls, OR 97601
541-883-8118
Fax: 541-883-8118
Type of Counseling: Prepurchase Counseling, Rental Counseling

CONSUMER CREDIT COUNSELING SERVICES OF SOUTHERN OREGON
820 Crater Lake Ave., Ste. 202
Medford, OR 97504
541-779-2273
Fax: 5417796412
Type of Counseling:
Prepurchase Counseling, Rental Counseling
Affiliate of: NATIONAL FOUNDATION FOR CONSUMER CREDIT, INCORPORATED

ACCESS INCORPORATED
3630 Aviation Way
Medford, OR 97501
541-779-6691
Toll-Free: 800-452-2463
Fax: 541-779-8886
Type of Counseling:
HECM Counseling, Default/Foreclosure Counseling, Rental Counseling, Prepurchase Counseling

PORTLAND HOUSING CENTER
3233 NE Sandy Blvd.
Portland, OR 972322557
503-282-7744
Fax: 503-736-0101
Email: kburkert@teleport.com
Type of Counseling:
Default/Foreclosure Counseling, Rental Counseling, Prepurchase Counseling
Affiliate of: NEIGHBORHOOD REINVESTMENT CORPORATION

CENTRAL OREGON COMMUNITY ACTION AGENCY NETWORK
2303 SW First St
Redmond, OR 97756
541-548-2380
Fax: 541-548-6013
Type of Counseling:
Default/Foreclosure Counseling, Prepurchase Counseling, HECM Counseling

UMPQUA COMMUNITY ACTION NETWORK
2448 W Harvard Blvd
Roseburg, OR 97470
541-673-1789
Fax: 541-672-1983
Type of Counseling:
HECM Counseling, Default/Foreclosure Counseling, Rental Counseling, Prepurchase Counseling

Pennsylvania

HISPANIC AMERICAN ORGANIZATION
136 S. 4th Street
Allentown, PA 18102
610-435-5334
Fax: 610-435-2131
Type of Counseling:
Prepurchase Counseling

**ALLENTOWN NEIGHBORHOOD HOUSING SERVICES, INCORPORATED
239 N.10th Street
Allentown, PA 18102
610-437-4571
Fax: 610-437-9958
Email: Jjanisnhs@aol.com
Type of Counseling:
Default/Foreclosure Counseling, Prepurchase Counseling
Affiliate of: NEIGHBORHOOD REINVESTMENT CORPORATION

HOUSING OPPORTUNITIES OF BEAVER COUNTY, INCORPORATED
650 Corporation St Ste 207
Beaver, PA 15009
724-728-7511
Fax: 724-728-7202
Email: hobc@timesnet.net
Website: www.hobc123.org
Type of Counseling:
Default/Foreclosure Counseling, Prepurchase Counseling

BUTLER COUNTY HOUSING AUTHORITY
111 S. Cliff Street
Butler, PA 16003-1917
724-287-6797
Fax: 724-287-7906
Type of Counseling:
Prepurchase Counseling, Default/Foreclosure Counseling, HECM Counseling, Rental Counseling

CONSUMER CREDIT COUNSELING SERVICE OF NORTHEASTERN PENNSYLVANIA
1400 Abington Executive Park Suite #1
Clarks Summit, PA 18411
570-587-9163
Toll-Free: 800-922-9537
Fax: 570-587-9134
Email: cccsnepa@epix.net
Website:
www.websiteint.com/cccsnepa
Type of Counseling:
Prepurchase Counseling, Default/Foreclosure Counseling, HECM Counseling, Rental Counseling
Affiliate of: NATIONAL FOUNDATION FOR CONSUMER CREDIT, INCORPORATED

**SHILOH COMMUNITY SERVICES, INCORPORATED
548 Canal Street
Easton, PA 18042
610-252-5538

Fax: 610-252-0928
Type of Counseling:
Prepurchase Counseling, Rental Counseling, Default/Foreclosure Counseling, HECM Counseling
Affiliate of: CONGRESS OF NATIONAL BLACK CHURCHES, INCORPORATED

NORTHERN TIER COMMUNITY ACTION CORPORATION
135 W 4th St
Emporium, PA 15834-1123
814-486-1161
Fax: 814-486-0825
Type of Counseling: Rental Counseling, Prepurchase Counseling

**SAINT MARTIN CENTER
1701 Parade Street
Erie, PA 16503-1994
814-452-6113
Fax: 814-456-7310
Email: DPESCH1@AOL.COM
Type of Counseling:
Prepurchase Counseling, Rental Counseling, Default/Foreclosure Counseling, HECM Counseling
Affiliate of: CATHOLIC CHARITIES USA

GREATER ERIE COMMUNITY ACTION AGENCY
18 W 9th St
Erie, PA 16501-1343
814-459-4581
Fax: 814-456-0161
Email: rllgeac@erie.net
Type of Counseling:
HECM Counseling, Default/Foreclosure Counseling, Rental Counseling, Prepurchase Counseling

BOOKER T. WASHINGTON CENTER
1720 Holland St
Erie, PA 16503-1808
814-453-5744
Fax: 814-453-5749
Type of Counseling:
HECM Counseling, Default/Foreclosure Counseling, Rental Counseling, Prepurchase Counseling

BAYFRONT NATO, INCORPORATED
312 Chestnut St
Erie, PA 16507-1222
814-459-2761
Fax: 814-455-2743
Email: Bmlkcenter@aol.com
Type of Counseling:
Prepurchase Counseling, Rental Counseling, Default/Foreclosure Counseling

SHENANGO VALLEY URBAN LEAGUE
601 Indiana Ave
Farrell, PA 16121-1759
724-981-5310
Fax: 724-981-1544
Type of Counseling:
HECM Counseling, Default/Foreclosure Counseling, Rental Counseling, Prepurchase Counseling
Affiliate of: NATIONAL URBAN LEAGUE

CONSUMER CREDIT COUNSELING SERVICE OF WESTERN PENNSYLVANIA
2000 Linglestown Road
Suite 302
Harrisburg, PA 17110
717-541-1757
Toll-Free: 888-599-2227
Fax: 717-540-4670
Website: www.cccspa.org
Type of Counseling:
Default/Foreclosure Counseling, HECM Counseling, Prepurchase Counseling, Rental Counseling

URBAN LEAGUE OF METROPOLITAN HARRISBURG
2107 N 6th St
Harrisburg, PA 17110-2453
717-234-3253
Fax: 717-234-9459
Type of Counseling:
Default/Foreclosure Counseling, Prepurchase Counseling

FAIR HOUSING COUNCIL OF THE CAPITAL REGION, INCORPORATED
2100 North 6th Street
Harrisburg, PA 17110-2401
717-238-9540
Fax: 717-233-5001
Email: hfhc@pa.net
Type of Counseling:
HECM Counseling, Default/Foreclosure Counseling, Rental Counseling, Prepurchase Counseling

PENNSYLVANIA HOUSING FINANCE AGENCY
2101 North Front Street
Harrisburg, PA 17105-8029
717-780-3800
Toll-Free: 800-342-2397
Fax: 717-780-3905
Type of Counseling:
Default/Foreclosure Counseling

INDIANA COUNTY COMMUNITY ACTION PROGRAM, INCORPORATED
827 Water St
Indiana, PA 15701-1755
724-465-2657
Fax: 724-465-5118
Email: iccap@mail.microserve.net
Type of Counseling:
HECM Counseling, Default/Foreclosure Counseling, Rental Counseling, Prepurchase Counseling

ELK COUNTY HOUSING AUTHORITY
424 Water Street Ext
Johnsonburg, PA 15845-1547
814-965-2532
Fax: 814-965-5616
Type of Counseling:
Rental Counseling

ARMSTRONG COUNTY COMMUNITY ACTION AGENCY
124 Armsdale Road Suite 211
Kittanning, PA 16201-0028
724-548-3405
Fax: 724-548-3413
Type of Counseling: Rental Counseling

TABOR COMMUNITY SERVICES
439 E King St
Lancaster, PA 17602-3004
717-397-5182
Fax: 717-399-4127
Email: kmmcdivitt@tabornet.org
Type of Counseling:
Prepurchase Counseling, Default/Foreclosure Counseling, HECM Counseling, Rental Counseling

HOUSING OPPORTUNITIES, INCORPORATED
133 7th St
Mc Keesport, PA 15134
412-664-1590
Fax: 412-664-0873
Email: HOIMAIN@AOL.COM
Type of Counseling:
Default/Foreclosure Counseling, Prepurchase Counseling, HECM Counseling
Affiliate of: HOUSING OPPORTUNITIES, INCORPORATED

CENTER FOR FAMILY SERVICES, INCORPORATED

213 W Center St
Meadville, PA 16335-3406
814-337-8450
Fax: 814-337-8457
Type of Counseling:
HECM Counseling,
Default/Foreclosure Counseling,
Rental Counseling, Prepurchase Counseling

TREHAB CENTER OF NORTHEAST PENNSYLVANIA
10 Public Avenue
Montrose, PA 18801-0366
570-278-3338
Fax: 570-278-1889
Email: JCRONK@EPIX.NET
Type of Counseling:
HECM Counseling,
Default/Foreclosure Counseling,
Prepurchase Counseling

LAWRENCE COUNTY SOCIAL SERVICES, INCORPORATED
241 W. Grant Street
New Castle, PA 16103-0189
724-658-7258
Fax: 724-658-7664
Email: dhennon@lawcss.org
Type of Counseling:
HECM Counseling,
Default/Foreclosure Counseling,
Rental Counseling, Prepurchase Counseling

PHILADELPHIA COUNCIL FOR COMMUNITY ADVANCEMENT
100 N 17th St Ste 700
Philadelphia, PA 19103-2736
215-567-7803
Toll-Free: 800-930-4663
Fax: 215-963-9941
Email: philapcca@aol.com
Website:
www.nelsononline.com/pcca/
Type of Counseling: HECM Counseling, Prepurchase Counseling, Default/Foreclosure Counseling

HOUSING ASSOCIATION INFORMATION PROGRAM
658-60 N Watts St
Philadelphia, PA 19123-2422
215-978-0224
Fax: 215-765-7614
Type of Counseling:
Default/Foreclosure Counseling,
Rental Counseling, Prepurchase Counseling

TENANTS' ACTION GROUP OF PHILADELPHIA
21 S 12th St 12th Fl
Philadelphia, PA 19107-3614
215-575-0700
Fax: 215-575-0718
Type of Counseling:
Rental Counseling

PHILADELPHIA HOUSING DEVELOPMENT CORPORATION
1234 Market St 17th Fl
Philadelphia, PA 19107-3721
215-448-3137
Fax: 215-448-3133

NORTHWEST COUNSELING SERVICE
5001 N Broad St
Philadelphia, PA 19141-2217
215-324-7500
Fax: 215-324-8753
Type of Counseling:
HECM Counseling,
Default/Foreclosure Counseling,
Rental Counseling, Prepurchase Counseling

URBAN LEAGUE OF PHILADELPHIA
251-53 S 24th St
Philadelphia, PA 19103-5529
215-451-5005
Fax: 215-451-5006
Email: rwsulp@aol.com
Default/Foreclosure Counseling,
Prepurchase Counseling, Rental Counseling, HECM Counseling

NUEVA ESPERANZA, INCORPORATED
4261 N. 5th Street
Philadelphia, PA 19140
215-324-0746
Fax: 215-324-2542
Email: motero@nueva.org
Type of Counseling:
Prepurchase Counseling,
Default/Foreclosure Counseling

**THE REINVESTMENT FUND
718 Arch Street Suite 300 North
Philadelphia, PA 19106
215-925-1130
Fax: 215-717-4627
Type of Counseling:
Prepurchase Counseling,
Default/Foreclosure Counseling
Affiliate of: THE HOUSING PARTNERSHIP NETWORK

**ASOCIACION PUERTORIQUENOS EN MARCHA
600 West Diamond Street
Philadelphia, PA 19122
215-235-6070
Fax: 215-235-7335
Email: apmhc@philly.infi.net
Type of Counseling:
Prepurchase Counseling, Rental Counseling
Affiliate of: NATIONAL COUNCIL OF LA RAZA

GERMANTOWN SETTLEMENT
218 W. Chelten Avenue
Philadelphia, PA 19144
215-849-3104
Fax: 215-843-7264
Type of Counseling:
Default/Foreclosure Counseling,
Prepurchase Counseling, Rental Counseling
Affiliate of: HOUSING OPPORTUNITIES, INCORPORATED

**MOUNT AIRY, U S A
6639-41 Germantown Ave
Philadelphia, PA 19119
215-844-6021
Fax: 215-844-9167
Type of Counseling:
Rental Counseling,
Default/Foreclosure Counseling,
Prepurchase Counseling
Affiliate of: HOUSING OPPORTUNITIES, INCORPORATED

PHILADELPHIA NEIGHBORHOOD HOUSING SERVICES, INCORPORATED
511 North Broad St 4TH Floor
Philadelphia, PA 19123
215-988-9879
Fax: 215-988-1297
Type of Counseling:
Prepurchase Counseling,
Default/Foreclosure Counseling
Affiliate of: NEIGHBORHOOD REINVESTMENT CORPORATION

INTERCULTURAL FAMILY SERVICES, INCORPORATED
4225 Chestnut St
Philadelphia, PA 19104-3014
215-386-1298
Fax: 215-386-9348
Type of Counseling:
Rental Counseling, Prepurchase Counseling, Default/Foreclosure Counseling

NEW KENSINGTON COMMUNITY DEVELOPMENT CORPORATION
2513-15 Frankford Ave
Philadelphia, PA 19125-1708
215-427-0322

Fax: 215-427-1302
Email: newkenwlibertynet.org
Type of Counseling:
Default/Foreclosure Counseling,
Prepurchase Counseling
Affiliate of: HOUSING
OPPORTUNITIES,
INCORPORATED

CENTRO PEDRO CLAVER,
INCORPORATED
3565 N 7th St
Philadelphia, PA 19140-4401
215-227-7111
Fax: 215-227-7105
Email: centro@Libertynet.org
Type of Counseling:
Prepurchase Counseling,
Default/Foreclosure Counseling

**CONSUMER CREDIT
COUNSELING SERVICE OF
DELAWARE VALLEY
1515 Market St Ste 1325
Philadelphia, PA 19102
215-563-5665
Fax: 215-563-7020
Type of Counseling:
Default/Foreclosure Counseling,
Rental Counseling
Affiliate of: NATIONAL
FOUNDATION FOR CONSUMER
CREDIT, INCORPORATED

HOUSING CONSORTIUM FOR
DISABLED INDIVIDUALS
4701 Pine Street
Philadelphia, PA
215-528-5056
Fax: 215-528-5848
Type of Counseling:
Rental Counseling, Prepurchase
Counseling, Default/Foreclosure
Counseling

**PHILADELPHIA
DEVELOPMENT PARTNERSHIP
1334 Walnut St 7th Fl
Philadelphia, PA 19107
215-545-3100
Fax: 215-546-8055
Website: www.pdp-inc.org
Type of Counseling:
Prepurchase Counseling,
Default/Foreclosure Counseling,
Rental Counseling
Affiliate of: THE HOUSING
PARTNERSHIP NETWORK

UNEMPLOYMENT
INFORMATION CENTER
1201 Chestnut Street, #702
Philadelphia, PA 19107
215-848-0848
Fax: 215-557-6981
Type of Counseling:
Default/Foreclosure Counseling

ACORN HOUSING
CORPORATION
846 N Broad St 2nd floor
Philadelphia, PA 19130-2234
215-765-1221
Fax: 215-765-0045
Type of Counseling:
Default/Foreclosure Counseling,
Prepurchase Counseling
Affiliate of: ACORN HOUSING
CORPORATION

**DIVERSIFIED COMMUNITY
SERVICES
1210 South Broad Street
Philadelphia, PA 19146
215-336-3511
Fax: 215-551-4327
Type of Counseling:
Prepurchase Counseling,
Default/Foreclosure Counseling,
Rental Counseling
Affiliate of: HOUSING
OPPORTUNITIES,
INCORPORATED

ACTION HOUSING,
INCORPORATED
425 Sixth Ave Ste 950
Pittsburgh, PA 15219-1819
412-391-1956
Fax: 412-391-4512
Type of Counseling:
HECM Counseling,
Default/Foreclosure Counseling,
Rental Counseling, Prepurchase
Counseling
Affiliate of: THE HOUSING
PARTNERSHIP NETWORK

**OPERATION NEHEMIAH
235 Eastgate Drive
Pittsburgh, PA 152351413
412-704-1247
Fax: 412-244-3512
Type of Counseling:
Prepurchase Counseling
Affiliate of: CONGRESS OF
NATIONAL BLACK CHURCHES,
INCORPORATED

CENTER FOR INDEPENDENT
LIVING SW PA
7110 Penn Ave
Pittsburgh, PA 15208-2434
412-371-7700
Fax: 412-371-9430
Type of Counseling:
HECM Counseling,
Default/Foreclosure Counseling,
Rental Counseling, Prepurchase
Counseling

CONSUMER CREDIT
COUNSELING OF WESTERN
PENNSYLVANIA
2403 Sidney Street, Suite 40
Pittsburgh, PA 152222294
412-390-1300
Toll-Free: 888-599-2227
Fax: 412-390-1336
Website: www.cccspa.org
Type of Counseling:
HECM Counseling,
Default/Foreclosure Counseling,
Rental Counseling, Prepurchase
Counseling
Affiliate of: NATIONAL
FOUNDATION FOR CONSUMER
CREDIT, INCORPORATED

GARFIELD JUBILEE
ASSOCIATION, INCORPORATED
5138 Penn Ave
Pittsburgh, PA 15224-1616
412-665-5200
Fax: 412-665-5205
Email:
GARFIELD@HILLHOUSE.CKP.EDU
Type of Counseling:
HECM Counseling,
Default/Foreclosure Counseling,
Rental Counseling, Prepurchase
Counseling

NEIGHBORHOOD HOUSING
SERVICES, INCORPORATED
355 5th Ave. Suite 1022, Park
Building
Pittsburgh, PA 15222-2407
412-281-9773
Fax: 412-232-3615
Type of Counseling:
Prepurchase Counseling
Affiliate of: NEIGHBORHOOD
REINVESTMENT
CORPORATION

URBAN LEAGUE OF
PITTSBURGH
One Smithfield St 3rd Floor
Pittsburgh, PA 15222-2222
412-227-4802
Fax: 412-227-4870
Email: league@hillhouse.ckp.edu
Type of Counseling:
HECM Counseling,
Default/Foreclosure Counseling,
Rental Counseling, Prepurchase
Counseling
Affiliate of: NATIONAL URBAN
LEAGUE

**NAZARETH HOUSING SERVICES
285 Bellevue Road
Pittsburgh, PA 15229-2173
412-931-3510
Fax: 412-931-7255
Email: SRCINDY@JUNO.COM
Type of Counseling:
Prepurchase Counseling, Default/Foreclosure Counseling
Affiliate of: HOUSING OPPORTUNITIES, INCORPORATED

ELDER-ADO, INCORPORATED
320 Brownsville Rd
Pittsburgh, PA 15210-2249
412-381-6900
Fax: 412-381-3797
Type of Counseling:
HECM Counseling

SCHUYKILL COMMUNITY ACTION
225 N Centre St
Pottsville, PA 17901-2511
570-622-1995
Fax: 570-622-0429
Email: ECONOPP@PTD.NET
Type of Counseling:
Rental Counseling, Prepurchase Counseling, Default/Foreclosure Counseling, HECM Counseling

BERKS COMMUNITY ACTION AGENCY BUDGET COUNSELING CENTER
247 N 5th St
Reading, PA 19601-3303
610-375-7866
Fax: 610-375-7830
Type of Counseling:
HECM Counseling, Default/Foreclosure Counseling, Rental Counseling, Prepurchase Counseling

**NEIGHBORHOOD HOUSING SERVICES OF READING, INCORPORATED
383 Schuylkill Ave
Reading, PA 19601
610-372-8433
Fax: 610-374-2866
Type of Counseling:
Prepurchase Counseling, Default/Foreclosure Counseling
Affiliate of: NEIGHBORHOOD REINVESTMENT CORPORATION

UNITED NEIGHBORHOOD CENTERS OF LACKAWANNA COUNTY
410 Olive Street
Scranton, PA 18509
570-346-0759
Fax: 570-342-3972
Type of Counseling:
Default/Foreclosure Counseling, Rental Counseling, Prepurchase Counseling

**CATHOLIC SOCIAL SERVICES
400 Wyoming Avenue
Scranton, PA 18503
570-207-2291
Fax: 570-341-1293
Type of Counseling:
Default/Foreclosure Counseling, Prepurchase Counseling, Rental Counseling, HECM Counseling
Affiliate of: CATHOLIC CHARITIES USA

MERCER COUNTY COMMUNITY ACTION AGENCY
296 A St
Sharon, PA 16146-1241
724-342-6222
Fax: 724-342-6301
Type of Counseling:
Prepurchase Counseling, Default/Foreclosure Counseling, HECM Counseling
Affiliate of: HOUSING OPPORTUNITIES, INCORPORATED

TABLELAND SERVICES, INCORPORATED
535 E Main St
Somerset, PA 15501-2108
814-445-9628
Toll-Free: 800-452-0148
Fax: 814-443-3690
Type of Counseling:
HECM Counseling, Default/Foreclosure Counseling

PHOENIXVILLE HOMES
250 N. Main Street
Spring City, PA 19475
610-948-1797
Fax: 610-948-1765
Type of Counseling:
Prepurchase Counseling, Default/Foreclosure Counseling

KEYSTONE LEGAL SERVICES, INCORPORATED
2054 E College Ave
State College, PA 16801-7201
814-238-4958
Fax: 814-238-9504
Type of Counseling:
Default/Foreclosure Counseling, Prepurchase Counseling

FAYETTE COUNTY COMMUNITY ACTION AGENCY
140 North Beeson Avenue
Uniontown, PA 15401
724-437-6050
Fax: 724-437-4418
Type of Counseling:
HECM Counseling, Default/Foreclosure Counseling, Rental Counseling, Prepurchase Counseling

WARREN FOREST COUNTY ECONOMIC OPPORTUNITY COUNCIL
1209 Pennsylvania Ave W
Warren, PA 16365-1841
814-726-2400
Toll-Free: 800-231-1797
Fax: 814-723-0510
Type of Counseling:
Default/Foreclosure Counseling, Rental Counseling, Prepurchase Counseling, HECM Counseling

TRI-COUNTY PATRIOTS FOR INDEPENDENT LIVING
69 E Beau St
Washington, PA 15301-4711
724-223-5115
Fax: 724-223-5119
Type of Counseling:
HECM Counseling, Rental Counseling

COMMUNITY ACTION SOUTHWEST
315 E Hallam Ave
Washington, PA 15301-3407
724-225-9550
Fax: 724-228-9966
Type of Counseling:
HECM Counseling, Default/Foreclosure Counseling, Rental Counseling, Prepurchase Counseling

WASHINGTON COUNTY HOUSING AUTHORITY
100 Crumrine Tower, Franklin Street
Washington, PA 15301-6995
724-228-6060
Fax: 724-228-6089
Type of Counseling: Rental Counseling

WASHINGTON-GREENE COMMUNITY ACTION CORPORATION
22 W High St
Waynesburg, PA 15370-1324
724-852-2893
Fax: 724-627-7713
Type of Counseling:

Default/Foreclosure Counseling, Rental Counseling

CONSUMER CREDIT COUNSELING SERVICE OF LEHIGH VALLEY, INC
3671 Crescent Court East
Whitehall, PA 18052-0233
610-821-4011
Fax: 610-821-8932
Type of Counseling:
Default/Foreclosure Counseling, Prepurchase Counseling, HECM Counseling, Rental Counseling
Affiliate of: HOUSING OPPORTUNITIES, INCORPORATED

COMMISSION ON ECONOMIC OPPORTUNITY OF LUZERNE COUNTY
165 Amber Lane
Wilkes Barre, PA 18703-1127
570-826-0510
Fax: 570-829-1665
Type of Counseling:
Rental Counseling, Default/Foreclosure Counseling

BUCKS COUNTY HOUSING GROUP
2324 Second Street Pike Suite 17
Wrightstown, PA 18940
215-598-3566
Toll-Free: 866-866-0280
Fax: 215-598-1289
Email: rmilgram@bchg.org
Type of Counseling:
Prepurchase Counseling, Default/Foreclosure Counseling

HOUSING COUNCIL OF YORK
116 N George St
York, PA 17401-1106
717-854-1541
Fax: 717-845-7934
Type of Counseling:
HECM Counseling, Default/Foreclosure Counseling, Rental Counseling, Prepurchase Counseling

Puerto Rico

CONSUMER CREDIT COUNSELING SERVICE OF PUERTO RICO, INCORPORATED
Bayamon Shopping Center Office 6 2nd Fl
Bayamon, PR 00961
787-269-4100
Fax: 787-269-4153
Email: infor@cccspr.org
Website: www.cccspr.org
Type of Counseling:
Default/Foreclosure Counseling, Prepurchase Counseling, HECM Counseling

CONSUMER CREDIT COUNSELING SERVICE OF PUERTO RICO, INCORPORATED
Calle Nazario #1A
Caguas, PR 00725
787-703-0506
Fax: 787-703-0580
Email: info@cccspr.org
Website: www.cccspr.org
Type of Counseling:
Prepurchase Counseling, Default/Foreclosure Counseling, HECM Counseling

CONSUMER CREDIT COUNSELING SERVICE OF PUERTO RICO, INCORPORATED
Ave Fragoso 3 DS-5 Edif Tiri Villa Fontana
Carolina, PR 00983
787-269-4100
Fax: 787-769-1360
Email: info@cccs.org
Website: www.cccspr.org
Type of Counseling:
Default/Foreclosure Counseling, Prepurchase Counseling, HECM Counseling

CEIBA HOUSING AND ECONOMIC DEVELOPMENT CORPORATION
Ave Lauro Pinero 252 alto
Ceiba, PR 00735-0203
787-885-3020
Fax: 787-885-0716
Type of Counseling:
HECM Counseling, Default/Foreclosure Counseling, Rental Counseling, Prepurchase Counseling

CONSUMER CREDIT COUNSELING SERVICE OF PUERTO RICO, INCORPORATED
Calle Mendes Vigo #208
Managuez, PR 00680
787-265-0480
Fax: 787-265-0560
Email: info@cccspr.org
Website: www.cccspr.org
Type of Counseling:
Default/Foreclosure Counseling, Prepurchase Counseling, HECM Counseling

CONSUMER CREDIT COUNSELING SERVICE OF PUERTO RICO, INCORPORATED
4021Condominium Plaza Del Sur Ste #1 Calle Carlos Cartagena
Ponce, PR 00717
787-844-4550
Fax: 787-844-4540
Email: info@cccspr.org
Website: www.cccspr.org
Type of Counseling:
Default/Foreclosure Counseling, Prepurchase Counseling, HECM Counseling

CONSUMER CREDIT COUNSELING SERVICE OF PUERTO RICO, INCORPORATED
1603 Ponce De Leon Ave. Stop 23
Cobian's Plaza, Suite GM-09
Santurce, PR 00909
787-722-8835
Toll-Free: 800-717-2227
Fax: 787-724-4142
Email: info@cccspr.org
Website: www.cccspr.org
Type of Counseling:
HECM Counseling, Default/Foreclosure Counseling, Rental Counseling, Prepurchase Counseling

Rhode Island

**EAST BAY COMMUNITY DEVELOPMENT CORPORATION
150 Franklin Street
Bristol, RI 02809
401-253-2080
Fax: 401-253-6997
Type of Counseling:
Prepurchase Counseling
Affiliate of: CITIZENS' HOUSING AND PLANNING ASSOCIATION, INCORPORATED

**COMMUNITY HOUSING CORPORATION
25 West Independence Way
Kingston, RI 02881
401-782-4646
Fax: 401-783-6190
Email: act@netsence.net
Type of Counseling:
Prepurchase Counseling, Default/Foreclosure Counseling
Affiliate of: CITIZENS' HOUSING AND PLANNING ASSOCIATION, INCORPORATED

**CHURCH COMMUNITY HOUSING CORPORATION
50 Washington Square
Newport, RI 02840
401-846-5114
Fax: 401-849-7930
Type of Counseling:

Prepurchase Counseling
Affiliate of: CITIZENS' HOUSING AND PLANNING ASSOCIATION, INCORPORATED

BLACKSTONE VALLEY COMMUNITY ACTION PROGRAM, INCORPORATED
32 Goff Ave
Pawtucket, RI 02860-2928
401-723-4520
Fax: 401-723-3325
Type of Counseling:
Default/Foreclosure Counseling, Prepurchase Counseling
Affiliate of: CITIZENS' HOUSING AND PLANNING ASSOCIATION, INCORPORATED

**ACORN HOUSING CORPORATION
807 Broad St., Suite 220
Providence, RI 02907
401-780-0500
Fax: 401-780-0826
Email: riacorn@acorn.org
Type of Counseling:
Prepurchase Counseling, Rental Counseling, Default/Foreclosure Counseling, HECM Counseling
Affiliate of: ACORN HOUSING CORPORATION

**STOP WASTING ABANDONED PROPERTY
439 Pine Street
Providence, RI 02907
401-272-0526
Fax: 401-272-5653
Email: alcxnamzoff@hotmail.com
Type of Counseling:
Prepurchase Counseling
Affiliate of: CITIZENS' HOUSING AND PLANNING ASSOCIATION, INCORPORATED

**PROVIDENCE PRESERVATION SOCIETY REVOLVING FUND
24 Meeting Street
Providence, RI 02903
401-272-2760
Fax: 401-273-9190
Type of Counseling:
Prepurchase Counseling
Affiliate of: CITIZENS' HOUSING AND PLANNING ASSOCIATION, INCORPORATED

**HOUSING DEVELOPMENT CORPORATION OF THE NORTH END
481 Charles Street
Providence, RI 02904
401-351-3311
Fax: 401-351-4900
Email: hdcne@aol.com
Type of Counseling:
Prepurchase Counseling, Default/Foreclosure Counseling
Affiliate of: CITIZENS' HOUSING AND PLANNING ASSOCIATION, INCORPORATED

**ELMWOOD FOUNDATION
1 Trinity Square
Providence, RI 02907
401-273-2330
Fax: 401-274-3670
Type of Counseling:
Prepurchase Counseling
Affiliate of: CITIZENS' HOUSING AND PLANNING ASSOCIATION, INCORPORATED

**ALLEN MINISTRIES ENRICHING NEIGHBORHOODS (AMEN)
161 Bellevue Avenue.
Providence, RI 02907
401-831-0367
Fax: 401-861-9492
Type of Counseling:
Prepurchase Counseling, Rental Counseling
Affiliate of: CONGRESS OF NATIONAL BLACK CHURCHES, INCORPORATED

RHODE ISLAND HOUSING AND MORTGAGE FINANCE CORPORATION
44 Washington St
Providence, RI 02903-1721
401-751-5566
Fax: 401-243-0016
Type of Counseling: HECM Counseling

RHODE ISLAND DEPARTMENT OF ELDERLY AFFAIRS
160 Pine St
Providence, RI 02903-3708
401-222-2858
Fax: 401-222-1490
Type of Counseling:
HECM Counseling, Rental Counseling

URBAN LEAGUE OF RHODE ISLAND
246 Prairie Ave
Providence, RI 02905-2333
401-351-5000
Fax: 401-454-1946
Type of Counseling:
HECM Counseling, Default/Foreclosure Counseling, Rental Counseling, Prepurchase Counseling

**WEST ELMWOOD HOUSING DEVELOPMENT CORPORATION
392 Cranston St
Providence, RI 02907
401-453-3220
Fax: 401-453-3222
Email: scw@aol.com
Type of Counseling:
Default/Foreclosure Counseling, Prepurchase Counseling
Affiliate of: NEIGHBORHOOD REINVESTMENT CORPORATION

CONSUMER CREDIT COUNSELING SERVICE
535 Centerville Rd Ste 103
Warwick, RI 02886-4376
401-732-1800
Toll-Free: 800-781-2227
Fax: 401-732-0250
Website: www.creditcounseling.org
Type of Counseling:
Default/Foreclosure Counseling, Rental Counseling, Prepurchase Counseling, HECM Counseling
Affiliate of: NATIONAL FOUNDATION FOR CONSUMER CREDIT, INCORPORATED

South Carolina

SUNBELT HUMAN ADVANCEMENT RESOURCES, INCORPORATED - SHARE
400 E River St
Anderson, SC 29624-2448
864-224-7028
Fax: 864-226-8636
Type of Counseling:
HECM Counseling, Default/Foreclosure Counseling, Rental Counseling, Prepurchase Counseling

WATEREE COMMUNITY ACTIONS, INCORPORATED
637 Rutledge St
Camden, SC 29020-4237
803-432-3411
Fax: 803-432-3411
Type of Counseling:
Default/Foreclosure Counseling, Rental Counseling, Prepurchase Counseling

TRIDENT URBAN LEAGUE, INCORPORATED
656 King Street
Charleston, SC 294130249
843-965-4037

Fax: 843-965-4039
Type of Counseling:
Prepurchase Counseling

FAMILY SERVICES INCORPORATED
4925 Lacross St. Ste. 215
Charleston, SC 28406
843-744-1348
Toll-Free: 800-232-6489
Fax: 843-744-2886
Email:
dwalker@familyserviceschassc.com
Type of Counseling:
Prepurchase Counseling, Default/Foreclosure Counseling, Rental Counseling

CHESTERFIELD-MARLBORO ECONOMIC OPPORTUNITY COUNCIL, INCORPORATED
318-322 Front Street
Cheraw, SC 29520
843-320-9760
Fax: 843-320-9770
Type of Counseling:
Prepurchase Counseling, Default/Foreclosure Counseling, Rental Counseling

NATIONAL ASSOCIATION FOR THE ADVANCEMENT OF COLORED PEOPLE
1114 Blanding Street
Columbia, SC 29201
803-256-8771
Fax: 803-252-5999

PALMETTO LEGAL SERVICE
2109 Bull St
Columbia, SC 29201-2103
803-799-9668
Fax: 803-799-1781
Type of Counseling:
HECM Counseling, Default/Foreclosure Counseling, Rental Counseling, Prepurchase Counseling

SOUTH CAROLINA STATE HOUSING FINANCE AND DEVELOPMENT AUTHORITY
919 Bluff Road
Columbia, SC 29201
803-734-2000
Toll-Free: 800-476-0412
Fax: 803-734-2356
Type of Counseling:
Prepurchase Counseling, Default/Foreclosure Counseling

CONSUMER CREDIT COUNSELING SERVICE OF FAMILY SERVICE CENTER
1800 Main St
Columbia, SC 29201-2433
803-929-6666
Fax: 803-929-6665
Type of Counseling:
Default/Foreclosure Counseling, Rental Counseling, Prepurchase Counseling, HECM Counseling

WATEREE COMMUNITY ACTIONS, INCORPORATED
3220 Two Notch Rd
Columbia, SC 29202
803-786-4250
Fax: 803-786-4252
Type of Counseling:
Default/Foreclosure Counseling, Prepurchase Counseling

SUNBELT HUMAN ADVANCEMENT RESOURCES, INCORPORATED - SHARE
121 E First Avenue
Easley, SC 29641-1628
864-859-2989
Fax: 864-859-1401
Type of Counseling:
HECM Counseling, Default/Foreclosure Counseling, Rental Counseling, Prepurchase Counseling

**SAVANNAH GROVE HOUSING COUNSELING PROGRAM
2620 Alligator Road
Effingham, SC 29541
843-662-7851
Fax: 843-662-3140
Type of Counseling:
Prepurchase Counseling
Affiliate of: CONGRESS OF NATIONAL BLACK CHURCHES, INCORPORATED

CAROLINA REGIONAL LEGAL SERVICES CORPORATION
279 W Evans St
Florence, SC 29503
843-667-1896
Toll-Free: 800-304-9939
Fax: 843-664-2406
Email: crls@logicsouth.com
Type of Counseling:
Default/Foreclosure Counseling, Rental Counseling, HECM Counseling

SUNBELT HUMAN ADVANCEMENT RESOURCES, INCORPORATED
1200 Pendleton St
Greenville, SC 29611-4832
864-269-0700
Fax: 864-295-6151
Type of Counseling:
HECM Counseling, Default/Foreclosure Counseling, Rental Counseling, Prepurchase Counseling

URBAN LEAGUE OF THE UPSTATE, INCORPORATED
15 Regency Hill Dr
Greenville, SC 29607-1230
864-244-3862
Fax: 864-244-6134
Email: hbarksdale@aol.com
Type of Counseling:
Default/Foreclosure Counseling, Rental Counseling, Prepurchase Counseling, HECM Counseling
Affiliate of: NATIONAL URBAN LEAGUE

GREENVILLE COUNTY HUMAN RELATIONS COMMISSION
301 University Ridge, Suite 1600
Greenville, SC 296013660
864-467-7095
Fax: 864-467-5965
Type of Counseling:
Prepurchase Counseling, Default/Foreclosure Counseling, Rental Counseling, HECM Counseling

PALMETTO LEGAL SERVICES
426 S Lake Dr
Lexington, SC 29072-3414
803-359-4154
Fax: 803-359-9351
Type of Counseling:
HECM Counseling, Default/Foreclosure Counseling, Rental Counseling, Prepurchase Counseling

WATEREE COMMUNITY ACTIONS, INCORPORATED
3 W Boyce St
Manning, SC 29102-3205
803-435-4337
Fax: 803-435-4338
Type of Counseling:
Default/Foreclosure Counseling, Prepurchase Counseling

FAMILY SERVICES INCORPORATED
4925 Lacross Road Suite 215
North Charleston, SC 29406-
843-744-1348
Fax: 843-744-2886
Type of Counseling:
Prepurchase Counseling, Default/Foreclosure Counseling, Rental Counseling

TRIDENT UNITED WAY
6296 Rivers Ave
North Charleston, SC 29419
843-740-9000
Fax: 843-566-7193
Type of Counseling:
HECM Counseling,
Default/Foreclosure Counseling,
Rental Counseling, Prepurchase
Counseling

PALMETTO LEGAL SERVICES
1557 Carolina St NE
Orangeburg, SC 29115-4925
803-533-0116
Fax: 803-531-5102
Type of Counseling:
HECM Counseling,
Default/Foreclosure Counseling,
Rental Counseling, Prepurchase
Counseling

SUNBELT HUMAN
ADVANCEMENT RESOURCES,
INCORPORATED - SHARE
204 N Fairplay St
Seneca, SC 29678-3216
864-882-3495
Fax: 864-885-0634
Type of Counseling:
HECM Counseling,
Default/Foreclosure Counseling,
Rental Counseling, Prepurchase
Counseling

WATEREE COMMUNITY
ACTIONS, INCORPORATED
13 S Main St
Sumter, SC 29150-5244
803-775-4354
Fax: 803-773-9782
Type of Counseling:
HECM Counseling,
Default/Foreclosure Counseling,
Rental Counseling, Prepurchase
Counseling

PALMETTO LEGAL SERVICES
207A North Washington St
Sumter, SC 29151
803-773-1471
Fax: 803-773-8765
Type of Counseling:
HECM Counseling,
Default/Foreclosure Counseling,
Rental Counseling, Prepurchase
Counseling

South Dakota

NEIGHBORHOOD HOUSING
SERVICES OF THE BLACK
HILLS, INCORPORATED
817 1/2 Main Street
Deadwood, SD 57732
605-578-1401
Fax: 605-578-1405
Type of Counseling:
Default/Foreclosure Counseling,
Prepurchase Counseling, Rental
Counseling, HECM Counseling

SOUTH DAKOTA HOUSING
DEVELOPMENT AUTHORITY
221 South Central
Pierre, SD 57501-1237
605-773-3181
Toll-Free: 800-540-4241
TTY/TDD: 605-773-6107
Fax: 605-773-5154
Website: www.sdhda.org
Type of Counseling:
Rental Counseling,
Default/Foreclosure Counseling,
Prepurchase Counseling

OGLALA SIOUX TRIBE
PARTNERSHIP FOR HOUSING,
INCORPORATED
Old Ambulance Building
Pine Ridge, SD 57770
605-867-1555
Fax: 605-867-1522
Type of Counseling:
Default/Foreclosure Counseling,
Prepurchase Counseling, Rental
Counseling

CONSUMER CREDIT
COUNSELING SERVICE OF THE
BLACK HILLS, INCORPORATED
111 St. Joseph Street
Rapid City, SD 57701
605-348-4550
Toll-Free: 800-568-6613
Fax: 605-348-0107
Type of Counseling:
Default/Foreclosure Counseling,
Rental Counseling, Prepurchase
Counseling, HECM Counseling

BLACK HILLS LEGAL SERVICES
621 6th St Ste 202
Rapid City, SD 577091500
605-342-7171
Fax: 605-348-5874
Type of Counseling:
HECM Counseling,
Default/Foreclosure Counseling,
Rental Counseling, Prepurchase
Counseling

SIOUX EMPIRE HOUSING
PARTNERSHIP
200 North Phillips Avenue STE. 303
Sioux Falls, SD 57104
605-339-0942
Fax: 605-339-0201
Type of Counseling:
Prepurchase Counseling, Rental
Counseling

EAST RIVER LEGAL SERVICES
335 N Main Ave Ste 300
Sioux Falls, SD 57104-6004
605-336-9230
Fax: 605-336-6919
Type of Counseling:
HECM Counseling,
Default/Foreclosure Counseling,
Rental Counseling

CONSUMER CREDIT
COUNSELING SERVICE-
LUTHERN SOCIAL SERVICES
705 E 41st St Ste 100
Sioux Falls, SD 57105-6025
605-330-2700
Fax: 605-357-0150
Type of Counseling:
HECM Counseling,
Default/Foreclosure Counseling,
Rental Counseling, Prepurchase
Counseling
Affiliate of: NATIONAL
FOUNDATION FOR CONSUMER
CREDIT, INCORPORATED

Tennessee

CONSUMER CREDIT
COUNSELING SERVICE
Osborne Office Pk 6000 Bldg Ste
2300
Chattanooga, TN 37411
423-490-5620
Fax: 423-490-5624
Type of Counseling:
HECM Counseling,
Default/Foreclosure Counseling,
Rental Counseling, Prepurchase
Counseling

DEPARTMENT OF HUMAN
SERVICES CITY OF
CHATTANOOGA
501 W 12th St
Chattanooga, TN 37402-3852
423-757-5551
Fax: 423-757-4852
Type of Counseling:
HECM Counseling,
Default/Foreclosure Counseling,
Rental Counseling

**SOUTHEAST TENNESSEE
LEGAL SERVICES
414 McCallie Ave.
Chattanooga, TN 37402
423-756-4013
Fax: 423-265-4165

Email:
rfowler@setnlegalservices.org
Type of Counseling:
Prepurchase Counseling,
Default/Foreclosure Counseling,
Rental Counseling, HECM
Counseling
Affiliate of: WEST TENNESSEE
LEGAL SERVICES,
INCORPORATED

FAMILY AND CHILDREN'S
SERVICE OF CHATTANOOGA,
INCORPORATED
300 East 8th Street
Chattanooga, TN 37403
423-755-2822
Fax: 423-755-2897
Type of Counseling:
Prepurchase Counseling,
Default/Foreclosure Counseling,
Rental Counseling

**LEGAL AID SOCIETY OF
MIDDLE TENNESSEE AND THE
CUMBERLANDS
120 Franklin St.
Clarksville, TN 27040
931-552-6656
Fax: 931-552-9442
Email: pmack@lasmt.org
Type of Counseling:
Prepurchase Counseling,
Default/Foreclosure Counseling,
Rental Counseling, HECM
Counseling
Affiliate of: WEST TENNESSEE
LEGAL SERVICES,
INCORPORATED

CONSUMER DEBT
COUNSELING
1685 Ft. Campbell Blvd., Suite D
Clarksville, TN 370423513
Toll-Free: 800-966-3328
Fax: 314-647-1359
Type of Counseling:
Default/Foreclosure Counseling

**SOUTHEAST TENNESSEE
LEGAL SERVICES
85 Central Avenue NW
Cleveland, TN 37311
423-756-4013
Fax: 423-265-4164
Email:
rfowler@setnlegalservices.org
Type of Counseling:
Prepurchase Counseling,
Default/Foreclosure Counseling,
Rental Counseling, HECM
Counseling
Affiliate of: WEST TENNESSEE
LEGAL SERVICES,
INCORPORATED

**LEGAL AID OF SOCIETY OF
MIDDLE TENNESSEE
85 Central Avenue NW
Cleveland, TN 37311
931-552-6656
Fax: 931-552-9442
Type of Counseling:
HECM Counseling,
Default/Foreclosure Counseling,
Rental Counseling, Prepurchase
Counseling
Affiliate of: WEST TENNESSEE
LEGAL SERVICES,
INCORPORATED

**LEGAL SERVICES OF SOUTH
CENTRAL TENNESSEE
104 W. 7th Street
Columbia, TN 38402
931-381-5533
Fax: 931-381-5541
Email: pfrison@bellsouth.net
Type of Counseling:
Prepurchase Counseling,
Default/Foreclosure Counseling,
Rental Counseling, HECM
Counseling
Affiliate of: WEST TENNESSEE
LEGAL SERVICES,
INCORPORATED

**LEGAL AID SOCIETY OF
MIDDLE TENNESSEE AND THE
CUMBERLANDS
Null
Cookeville, TN 38503
931-528-7436
Fax: 931-528-9350
Type of Counseling:
Prepurchase Counseling,
Default/Foreclosure Counseling,
Rental Counseling, HECM
Counseling
Affiliate of: WEST TENNESSEE
LEGAL SERVICES,
INCORPORATED

WEST TENNESSEE LEGAL
SERVICES, INCORPORATED
208 s. Church St.
Dyersburg, TN 38024
901-285-8181
Fax: 901-285-8184
Type of Counseling:
HECM Counseling,
Default/Foreclosure Counseling,
Rental Counseling, Prepurchase
Counseling
Affiliate of: WEST TENNESSEE
LEGAL SERVICES,
INCORPORATED

**LEGAL AID OF SOCIETY OF
MIDDLE TENNESSEE
650 N. Water Avenue
Gallatin, TN 37066
615-451-1880
Fax: 615-451-1882
Type of Counseling:
HECM Counseling,
Default/Foreclosure Counseling,
Rental Counseling, Prepurchase
Counseling
Affiliate of: WEST TENNESSEE
LEGAL SERVICES,
INCORPORATED

WEST TENNESSEE LEGAL
SERVICES, INCORPORATED
113 W. Paris St.
Huntingdon, TN 38344
901-986-8975
Fax: 901-986-8977
Type of Counseling:
HECM Counseling,
Default/Foreclosure Counseling,
Rental Counseling, Prepurchase
Counseling
Affiliate of: WEST TENNESSEE
LEGAL SERVICES,
INCORPORATED

WEST TENNESSEE LEGAL
SERVICES, INCORPORATED
210 W Main St
Jackson, TN 38302-2066
731-285-8181
Email: wtlegal@usit.net
Type of Counseling:
HECM Counseling,
Default/Foreclosure Counseling,
Rental Counseling, Prepurchase
Counseling
Affiliate of: WEST TENNESSEE
LEGAL SERVICES,
INCORPORATED

CONSUMER CREDIT
COUNSELING SERVICE OF
GREATER KNOXVILLE,
INCORPORATED
2700 S Roan St Ste 212
Johnson City, TN 37601-7557
800-358-9231
Fax: 865-637-3637
Type of Counseling:
HECM Counseling,
Default/Foreclosure Counseling,
Rental Counseling, Prepurchase
Counseling

**AMERICAN CREDIT COUNSELORS, INCORPORATED
208 Sunset Drive, Suite 505
Johnson City, TN 37604
800 646-0042
Toll-Free: 800-646-0042
Fax: 540-366-7140
Type of Counseling:
HECM Counseling, Default/Foreclosure Counseling, Prepurchase Counseling, Rental Counseling

**CONSUMER CREDIT COUNSELING SERVICE OF SOUTHWESTERN VIRGINIA, INCORPORATED
2615 E. Center Street
Kingsport, TN 37664
800-926-0042
Toll-Free: 800-926-0042
Fax: 540-366-7140
Type of Counseling:
HECM Counseling, Default/Foreclosure Counseling, Prepurchase Counseling, Rental Counseling

CONSUMER CREDIT COUNSELING SERVICE OF EAST TENNESSEE
1011 N. Broadway
Knoxville, TN 37917
865-522-2661
Toll-Free: 800-358-9231
Fax: 865-637-3637
Email: cccser@usit.net
Type of Counseling:
HECM Counseling, Default/Foreclosure Counseling, Rental Counseling, Prepurchase Counseling

KNOXVILLE AREA URBAN LEAGUE
1514 E. Fifth Avenue
Knoxville, TN 37917
865-524-5511
Fax: 865-525-5154
Email: rgiles@kornet.org
Type of Counseling:
Default/Foreclosure Counseling, Rental Counseling, Prepurchase Counseling
Affiliate of: NATIONAL URBAN LEAGUE

KNOX HOUSING PARTNERSHIP, INCORPORATED
900 E Hill Avenue Suite 270
Knoxville, TN 37921-6362
865-637-1679
Fax: 865-637-9713
Type of Counseling:
Prepurchase Counseling, Default/Foreclosure Counseling
Affiliate of: NEIGHBORHOOD REINVESTMENT CORPORATION

MEMPHIS AREA LEGAL SERVICES
109 N Main 2nd Fl
Memphis, TN 38103
901-523-8822
Fax: 901-843-6789
Type of Counseling:
Prepurchase Counseling, Rental Counseling, Default/Foreclosure Counseling, HECM Counseling

VOLLINTINE EVERGREEN COMMUNITY ASSOCIATION
1680 Jackson Ave
Memphis, TN 38107-5044
901-276-1782
Fax: 901-276-1784
Type of Counseling:
HECM Counseling, Default/Foreclosure Counseling, Rental Counseling, Prepurchase Counseling

CONSUMER DEBT COUNSELING
1750 Madison Avenue, Suite 200
Memphis, TN 38104
901-276-2000
Toll-Free: 877-786-3328
Fax: 314-647-1359
Type of Counseling:
Default/Foreclosure Counseling

ASSOCIATED CATHOLIC CHARITIES, INCORPORATED
1325 Jefferson Ave
Memphis, TN 38104
901-722-4700
Fax: 901-722-4791
Email: clifton@cathchar.org
Type of Counseling:
Default/Foreclosure Counseling, Rental Counseling, Prepurchase Counseling, HECM Counseling
Affiliate of: CATHOLIC CHARITIES USA

**ACORN HOUSING CORPORATION HOUSING COUNSELING OFFICES - MEMPHIS
1254 Lamar Ave, # 304
Memphis, TN 38104
901-274-8080
Fax: 901-274-8305
Type of Counseling:
Prepurchase Counseling, Rental Counseling, Default/Foreclosure Counseling
Affiliate of: ACORN HOUSING CORPORATION

**LEGAL AID OF SOCIETY OF MIDDLE TENNESSEE
526 N. Walnut Street
Murfreesboro, TN 37130
615-890-0905
Fax: 615-890-5274
Type of Counseling:
HECM Counseling, Default/Foreclosure Counseling, Rental Counseling, Prepurchase Counseling
Affiliate of: WEST TENNESSEE LEGAL SERVICES, INCORPORATED

**VICTORY HOUSING COUNSELING CENTER
3447 Brickchurch Pike
Nashville, TN 37207
615-226-9556
Fax: 615-226-9987
Type of Counseling:
Prepurchase Counseling, Default/Foreclosure Counseling
Affiliate of: CONGRESS OF NATIONAL BLACK CHURCHES, INCORPORATED

RESIDENTIAL RESOURCES, INC.
961 Woodland Street
Nashville, TN 37206
615-650-9779
Fax: 615-650-1253
Type of Counseling:
Default/Foreclosure Counseling, Prepurchase Counseling, Rental Counseling

CONSUMER DEBT COUNSELING
2131 Murfreesboro Pike, Suite L2
Nashville, TN 37217
615-361-0710
Toll-Free: 877-786-3328
Fax: 314-647-1359
Type of Counseling:
Default/Foreclosure Counseling

WOODBINE COMMUNITY ORGANIZATION
222 Oriel Ave.
Nashville, TN 37210
615-860-3453
Fax: 615-833-9727
Type of Counseling:
Prepurchase Counseling, Default/Foreclosure Counseling

CITIZENS FOR AFFORDABLE HOUSING
1719 West End Ave Ste 322W
Nashville, TN 37203-5120
615-321-5626
Fax: 615-321-5640
Email: cfah@gobot.com
Website: www.cfahi.gobot.com
Type of Counseling:
Default/Foreclosure Counseling, Rental Counseling, Prepurchase Counseling

AFFORDABLE HOUSING RESOURCES
1011 Cherry Ave
Nashville, TN 37203
615-251-0025
Fax: 615-256-9836
Type of Counseling:
Default/Foreclosure Counseling, Prepurchase Counseling
Affiliate of: NEIGHBORHOOD REINVESTMENT CORPORATION

METROPOLITAN ACTION COMMISSION
1624 5th Ave N
Nashville, TN 37208-2243
615-862-8860
Fax: 615-862-8881
Type of Counseling:
Default/Foreclosure Counseling, Rental Counseling, Prepurchase Counseling

**LEGAL AID OF SOCIETY OF MIDDLE TENNESSEE
211 Union Street, Suite 800
Nashville, TN 37201
615-244-6610
Fax: 615-224-6186
Email: pmoct@lasmt.org
Type of Counseling:
HECM Counseling, Default/Foreclosure Counseling, Rental Counseling, Prepurchase Counseling
Affiliate of: WEST TENNESSEE LEGAL SERVICES, INCORPORATED

CONSUMER CREDIT COUNSELING SERVICE OF MIDDLE TENNESSEE, INCORPORATED
PO Box 160328
Nashville, TN 37216-0328
615-650-3116
Fax: 615-777-3414
Type of Counseling:
HECM Counseling, Default/Foreclosure Counseling, Rental Counseling, Prepurchase Counseling

HOUSING DEVELOPMENT CORPORATION OF THE CLINCH VALLEY
Nations Bank Building 795 W Main St., 2nd Floor
Oak Ridge, TN 37831
865-482-7345
Fax: 865-220-8645
Type of Counseling:
Default/Foreclosure Counseling, Prepurchase Counseling, Rental Counseling
Affiliate of: NEIGHBORHOOD REINVESTMENT CORPORATION

**LEGAL AID SOCIETY OF MIDDLE TENNESSEE AND THE CUMBERLANDS
PO Box 5209
Oak Ridge, TN 37831
865-483-8454
Toll-Free: 800-483-8457
Fax: 865-483-8905
Email: hn0517@handsnet.org
Type of Counseling:
Prepurchase Counseling, Default/Foreclosure Counseling, Rental Counseling, HECM Counseling
Affiliate of: WEST TENNESSEE LEGAL SERVICES, INCORPORATED

WEST TENNESSEE LEGAL SERVICES, INCORPORATED
141 N. Third Street
Selmer, TN 38375
901-645-7961
Fax: 901-645-7963
Type of Counseling:
HECM Counseling, Default/Foreclosure Counseling, Rental Counseling, Prepurchase Counseling
Affiliate of: WEST TENNESSEE LEGAL SERVICES, INCORPORATED

**LEGAL SERVICES OF SOUTH CENTRAL TENNESSEE
123 North Atlantic St.
Tullahoma, TN 37388
931-455-7000
Fax: 931-455-7003
Type of Counseling:
Prepurchase Counseling, Default/Foreclosure Counseling, Rental Counseling, HECM Counseling
Affiliate of: WEST TENNESSEE LEGAL SERVICES, INCORPORATED

Texas

CONSUMER CREDIT COUNSELING
241 Pine St Ste 101A
Abilene, TX 79601-5944
915-677-9323
Toll-Free: 800-527-0526
Fax: 915-673-0405
Type of Counseling:
Default/Foreclosure Counseling, Rental Counseling, Prepurchase Counseling

CONSUMER CREDIT COUNSELING SERVICE OF GREATER DALLAS, AMARILLO
6300 I 40 West, Suite 106
Amarillo, TX 79106
800-878-2227
Toll-Free: 800-878-2227
Fax: 806-356-0677
Type of Counseling:
Default/Foreclosure Counseling, Rental Counseling, Prepurchase Counseling, HECM Counseling

CATHOLIC FAMILY SERVICE, INCORPORATED
200 S Tyler St
Amarillo, TX 79101-1448
806-376-4571
Fax: 806-345-7911
Email: cfs@arn.net
Website:
www.catholicfamilyservice.org
Type of Counseling:
Default/Foreclosure Counseling, Rental Counseling, Prepurchase Counseling, HECM Counseling
Affiliate of: CATHOLIC CHARITIES USA

CONSUMER CREDIT COUNSELING SERVICE OF GREATER DALLAS, ARLINGTON
201 E Abram St, Ste 730
Arlington, TX 76010
817-461-2227
Fax: 817-460-0409
Type of Counseling:
Default/Foreclosure Counseling, Rental Counseling, Prepurchase Counseling, HECM Counseling

CONSUMER CREDIT COUNSELING SERVICE OF GREATER DALLAS/ ARLINGTON-SOUTH

5850 West I-20, Suite 110
Arlington, TX 76017
817-572-2467
Fax: 817-572-0752
Type of Counseling:
Prepurchase Counseling, Rental Counseling, Default/Foreclosure Counseling, HECM Counseling

LEGAL AID OF CENTRAL TEXAS
2201 Post Road Street #104
Austin, TX 78704
512-447-7707
Toll-Free: 800-369-9270
Fax: 512-447-3940
Type of Counseling:
Default/Foreclosure Counseling, Rental Counseling, Prepurchase Counseling

AUSTIN TENANTS' COUNCIL
1619 E. Cesar Chavez St.
Austin, TX 78702-4455
512-474-7007
Fax: 512-474-0197
Email: bruce@housing-rights.org
Type of Counseling: Rental Counseling

TEXAS DEPARTMENT OF HOUSING AND COMMUNITY AFFAIRS
507 Sabine, Suite 900
Austin, TX 78701
512-475-3800
Fax: 512-472-8526
Type of Counseling:
Rental Counseling, Prepurchase Counseling

CONSUMER CREDIT COUNSELING SERVICE OF GREATER FORT WORTH/BEDFORD
4001 Airport Freeway, Ste 500
Bedford, TX 76021
817-283-4111
Fax: 817-283-4045
Type of Counseling:
Rental Counseling, Default/Foreclosure Counseling, Prepurchase Counseling

CONSUMER CREDIT COUNSELING SERVICE OF GREATER FORT WORTH/BIG SPRING
1801 Virginia Ave. Suite 4
Big Spring, TX 79720
915-264-0321
Fax: 915-264-0321
Type of Counseling:
Default/Foreclosure Counseling, Rental Counseling, Prepurchase Counseling

COMMUNITY DEVELOPMENT CORPORATION OF BROWNSVILLE
901 East Levee Street
Brownsville, TX 78520-5804
956-541-4955
Fax: 956-982-1804
Type of Counseling:
Default/Foreclosure Counseling, Prepurchase Counseling

CONSUMER CREDIT COUNSELING SERVICE OF GREATER FORT WORTH/BROWNWOOD
300 N. Main, Suite C
Brownwood, TX 76801
915-643-3426
Fax: 915-643-3426
Type of Counseling:
Rental Counseling, Default/Foreclosure Counseling, Prepurchase Counseling

BRAZOS VALLEY AFFORDABLE HOUSING CORPORATION
1706 E. 29th St.
Bryan, TX 77805-4128
979-775-4244
Fax: 979-775-3466
Type of Counseling:
Prepurchase Counseling

CONSUMER CREDIT COUNSELING SERVICE OF GREATER FORT WORTH/BURLESON
1161 SW Wilshire, Ste. 116
Burleson, TX 76028
817-295-3828
Fax: 817-295-4012
Type of Counseling: Rental Counseling, Default/Foreclosure Counseling, Prepurchase Counseling

CONSUMER CREDIT COUNSELING SERVICE OF GREATER DALLAS/CARROLLTON
3630 N. Josey Lane French Quarter Executive Suite 20
Carrollton, TX 75007
972-242-6548
Fax: 972-570-5996
Type of Counseling:
Prepurchase Counseling, Rental Counseling, Default/Foreclosure Counseling

CONSUMER CREDIT COUNSELING SERVICE OF GREATER DALLAS/CEDAR HILL
630 N. Hwy 67, Suite B-4
Cedar Hill, TX 75104
972-291-4754
Fax: 972-228-2992
Type of Counseling:
Prepurchase Counseling, Rental Counseling, Default/Foreclosure Counseling

**CONSUMER CREDIT COUNSELING SERVICE OF SOUTH TEXAS
1706 South Padre Island Dr
Corpus Christi, TX 78416
361-854-4357
Toll-Free: 800-333-4357
Fax: 361-854-1334
Website: www.cccsstx.org
Type of Counseling:
Default/Foreclosure Counseling, Rental Counseling, Prepurchase Counseling, HECM Counseling
Affiliate of: NATIONAL FOUNDATION FOR CONSUMER CREDIT, INCORPORATED

CONSUMER CREDIT COUNSELING SERVICE OF GREATER DALLAS, CORSICANA
200 N 13th St Ste 208
Corsicana, TX 75110-4674
800-886-2227
Toll-Free: 800-886-2227
Fax: 903-872-8097
Type of Counseling:
Default/Foreclosure Counseling, Rental Counseling, Prepurchase Counseling, HECM Counseling

WEST DALLAS NEIGHBORHOOD DEVELOPMENT CORPORATION
2907 N. Hampton Rd.
Dallas, TX 75212
214-688-1596
Fax: 214-688-0499
Type of Counseling:
Prepurchase Counseling, Default/Foreclosure Counseling, Rental Counseling

CONSUMER CREDIT COUNSELING SERVICE OF GREATER DALLAS, NORTH DALLAS
14110 Dallas Pkwy Plaza I
Bldg Ste 280
Dallas, TX 75240
972-387-2227
Fax: 972-866-6761

Type of Counseling:
Default/Foreclosure Counseling, Rental Counseling, Prepurchase Counseling, HECM Counseling

CONSUMER CREDIT COUNSELING SERVICE OF GREATER DALLAS OF DALLAS
8737 King George Dr Ste 200
Dallas, TX 75235
800-783-5018
Toll-Free: 800-783-5018
Fax: 214-630-6805
Type of Counseling:
Default/Foreclosure Counseling, Rental Counseling, Prepurchase Counseling, HECM Counseling

DALLAS URBAN LEAGUE, INCORPORATED
4315 S. Lancaster Rd
Dallas, TX 75216
214-915-4600
Fax: 214-915-4601
Email: Clarene.Whitfi@dallasurbanleague.com
Type of Counseling:
Default/Foreclosure Counseling, Rental Counseling, Prepurchase Counseling

DALLAS COUNTY HOME LOAN COUNSELING CENTER
2377 N. Stemmons Freeway
Suite 724
Dallas, TX 752072710
214-819-6060
Fax: 214-819-6069
Type of Counseling:
Prepurchase Counseling, Default/Foreclosure Counseling, Rental Counseling, HECM Counseling

HOUSING COUNSELORS OF TEXAS, INCORPORATED
501 Wynnewood Village Shopping Center, #201
Dallas, TX 752241899
214-941-8222
Fax: 214-941-3598
Type of Counseling:
Default/Foreclosure Counseling, Prepurchase Counseling, Rental Counseling

DALLAS COUNTY COMMUNITY ACTION COMMITTEE, INCORPORATED
611 E. Jefferson
Dallas, TX 75203
214-941-8712
Fax: 214-827-6584
Type of Counseling:
Default/Foreclosure Counseling, Rental Counseling

CONSUMER CREDIT COUNSELING SERVICE OF GREATER DALLAS, ONE NORTHPARK
8950 N Central Expy Suite 122
Dallas, TX 75231
214-363-4357
Fax: 214-363-3538
Type of Counseling:
Default/Foreclosure Counseling, Rental Counseling, Prepurchase Counseling, HECM Counseling

**ACORN HOUSING CORPORATION
4415 San Jacinto St
Dallas, TX 75204-5087
214-823-9885
Fax: 214-823-0819
Type of Counseling:
Default/Foreclosure Counseling, Prepurchase Counseling
Affiliate of: ACORN HOUSING CORPORATION

**VECINOS UNIDOS
3603 N. Winnetka Ave.
Dallas, TX 75212
214-761-1086
Fax: 214-761-0838
Email: vecinosunidos@juno.com
Type of Counseling:
Prepurchase Counseling
Affiliate of: NATIONAL COUNCIL OF LA RAZA

CONSUMER CREDIT COUNSELING SERVICE OF GREATER DALLAS, OAK CLIFF
400 S Zang ST SUITE 1004
Dallas, TX 75208
214-943-2075
Fax: 214-943-4753
Type of Counseling:
Default/Foreclosure Counseling, Rental Counseling, Prepurchase Counseling, HECM Counseling

CONSUMER CREDIT COUNSELING SERVICE OF GREATER DALLAS
2710 North Stemmons Frwy North Tower, Suite 1000N
Dallas, TX 75207
800-249-2227
Fax: 214-638-4398
Type of Counseling:
Prepurchase Counseling, Rental Counseling, Default/Foreclosure Counseling, HECM Counseling

CONSUMER CREDIT COUNSELING SERVICE OF NORTH CENTRAL TEXAS, DECATUR
1411 S Hwy 51 Ste 7
Decatur, TX 76234
940-627-5235
Fax: 940-627-6981
Type of Counseling:
Default/Foreclosure Counseling, Rental Counseling, Prepurchase Counseling, HECM Counseling

CONSUMER CREDIT COUNSELING SERVICE OF NORTH CENTRAL TEXAS, DENISON
101 E. Main Street, Suite 125
Denison, TX 75020
903-463-3298
Fax: 903-463-3573
Type of Counseling:
Prepurchase Counseling, Rental Counseling, Default/Foreclosure Counseling, HECM Counseling

**HOPE, INCORPORATED
415 E. Sherman
Denton, TX 76206
940-380-0513
Fax: 940-382-0609
Email: hope-inc@juno.com
Type of Counseling:
Prepurchase Counseling, Rental Counseling, Default/Foreclosure Counseling
Affiliate of: HOUSING OPPORTUNITIES, INCORPORATED

CONSUMER CREDIT COUNSELING SERVICE OF NORTH CENTRAL TEXAS, DENTON
207 W Hickory St Ste 202
Denton, TX 76201-4156
940-382-0331
Fax: 940-387-0123
Type of Counseling:
Default/Foreclosure Counseling, Rental Counseling, Prepurchase Counseling, HECM Counseling

CONSUMER CREDIT COUNSELING SERVICE OF GREATER DALLAS, DESOTO, LANCASTER
1229 Pleasant Run Rd., Ste 214
DeSoto, TX 75115
972-224-4786
Fax: 972-228-2992
Type of Counseling:

Prepurchase Counseling, Rental Counseling, Default/Foreclosure Counseling, HECM Counseling

CONSUMER CREDIT COUNSELING SERVICE OF GREATER DALLAS/DUNCANVILLE
402 W. Wheatland Rd, Suite 116
Duncanville, TX 75137
972-709-1723
Fax: 972-709-8974
Type of Counseling:
Prepurchase Counseling, Rental Counseling, Default/Foreclosure Counseling, HECM Counseling

PROJECT BRAVO, INCORPORATED
4838 Montana Ave
El Paso, TX 79903
915-562-4100
Fax: 915-562-8952
Type of Counseling:
Default/Foreclosure Counseling, Rental Counseling, Prepurchase Counseling, HECM Counseling

GUADALUPE ECONOMIC SERVICES CORPORATION
221 N Kansas St Ste 1503
El Paso, TX 79901
915-577-0185
Fax: 915-577-0187
Type of Counseling:
Default/Foreclosure Counseling, Rental Counseling, Prepurchase Counseling

YWCA-CONSUMER CREDIT COUNSELING SERVICE
1600 N. Brown St
El Paso, TX 79902-4725
915-577-2530
Fax: 915-533-8132
Type of Counseling:
Default/Foreclosure Counseling, Prepurchase Counseling, HECM Counseling
Affiliate of: NATIONAL COUNCIL OF LA RAZA

YOUNG WOMENS CHRISTIAN ASSOCIATION EL PASO DEL NORTE REGION
1918 Texas Avenue
El Paso, TX 79901
915-533-2311
Fax: 915-774-5002
Type of Counseling:
Prepurchase Counseling, Default/Foreclosure Counseling, HECM Counseling
Affiliate of: NATIONAL COUNCIL OF LA RAZA

CONSUMER CREDIT COUNSELING SERVICE OF GREATER FORT WORTH/FORT HOOD
Bldg. 1 Rm 106
Family Support Center
Fort Hood, TX 76544
254-532-4808
Fax: 254-532-4808
Type of Counseling:
Default/Foreclosure Counseling, Rental Counseling, Prepurchase Counseling

CONSUMER CREDIT COUNSELING SERVICE OF GREATER FORT WORTH/FORT STOCKTON
1008 North Kansas # 9
Fort Stockton, TX 79735
915-336-3288
Fax: 915-550-8910
Type of Counseling:
Rental Counseling, Default/Foreclosure Counseling, Prepurchase Counseling

CITY OF FORT WORTH HOUSING DEPARTMENT
1000 Throckmorton St
Fort Worth, TX 76102
817-871-7540
Fax: 817-871-7328
Type of Counseling:
Default/Foreclosure Counseling, Rental Counseling, Prepurchase Counseling

CONSUMER CREDIT COUNSELING SERVICE OF GREATER FORT WORTH/EAST FORT WORTH
6737 Brentwood Stair Rd. Suite 130
Fort Worth, TX 76112
800-867-2227
Fax: 817-283-4018
Type of Counseling:
Rental Counseling, Default/Foreclosure Counseling, Prepurchase Counseling, HECM Counseling

HOUSING OPPORTUNITIES OF FORT WORTH
1305 W Magnolia Ave SUITE E
Fort Worth, TX 76104-4345
817-923-9192
Fax: 817-924-8252
Email: HOFW@SWBELL.NET
Type of Counseling:
Default/Foreclosure Counseling, Prepurchase Counseling, Rental Counseling, HECM Counseling
Affiliate of: HOUSING OPPORTUNITIES, INCORPORATED

CONSUMER CREDIT COUNSELING SERVICE OF GREATER FORT WORTH/NORTHSIDE
2100 N. Main St. # 224
Fort Worth, TX 76106
800-867-2227
Fax: 817-283-4018
Type of Counseling:
Rental Counseling, Default/Foreclosure Counseling, Prepurchase Counseling, HECM Counseling

CONSUMER CREDIT COUNSELING SERVICE OF GREATER FORT WORTH/SOUTHWEST
4900 Overton Ridge # 213B
Fort Worth, TX 76132
800-867-2227
Fax: 817-283-4018
Type of Counseling:
Rental Counseling, Default/Foreclosure Counseling, Prepurchase Counseling, HECM Counseling

**NEIGHBORHOOD HOUSING SERVICES OF FORT WORTH, INCORPORATED
2315 N Main St Ste 401
Fort Worth, TX 76106
817-624-9454
Fax: 817-624-0860
Email: nhsfw@swbell.net
Type of Counseling:
Prepurchase Counseling
Affiliate of: NEIGHBORHOOD REINVESTMENT CORPORATION

CONSUMER CREDIT COUNSELING SERVICE OF GREATER FORT WORTH
1320 South University, Suite 190
Fort Worth, TX 76107
817-732-2227
Toll-Free: 800-374-2227
Fax: 817-882-8623
Type of Counseling:
Prepurchase Counseling, Rental Counseling, Default/Foreclosure Counseling, HECM Counseling
Affiliate of: NATIONAL FOUNDATION FOR CONSUMER CREDIT, INCORPORATED

CONSUMER CREDIT COUNSELING SERVICE OF GREATER FORT WORTH/SOUTHEAST
2801 Miller Ave.
Fort Worth, TX 76104
800-867-2227
Fax: 817-283-4018
Type of Counseling:
Rental Counseling, Default/Foreclosure Counseling, Prepurchase Counseling, HECM Counseling

CONSUMER CREDIT COUNSELING SERVICE OF NORTH CENTRAL TEXAS, FRISCO
6817 Main Street
Frisco, TX 75034
972-377-2647
Fax: 972-542-3623
Type of Counseling:
Prepurchase Counseling, Rental Counseling, Default/Foreclosure Counseling, HECM Counseling

CONSUMER CREDIT COUNSELING SERVICE OF NORTH CENTRAL TEXAS, GAINESVILLE
715 E. California
Gainesville, TX 76240
940-668-1967
Fax: 960-665-4707
Type of Counseling:
Prepurchase Counseling, Rental Counseling, Default/Foreclosure Counseling, HECM Counseling

CONSUMER CREDIT COUNSELING SERVICE OF GREATER DALLAS, GARLAND
705 W Avenue B Ste 502
Garland, TX 75040-6229
888-843-2227
Toll-Free: 888-843-2227
Fax: 972-205-1029
Type of Counseling:
Default/Foreclosure Counseling, Rental Counseling, Prepurchase Counseling, HECM Counseling

CONSUMER CREDIT COUNSELING SERVICE OF GREATER DALLAS, GRAND PRAIRIE
801 W Freeway Ste 240
Grand Prairie, TX 75051
972-642-3100
Fax: 972-237-0610
Type of Counseling:
Default/Foreclosure Counseling, Rental Counseling, Prepurchase Counseling, HECM Counseling

CONSUMER CREDIT COUNSELING SERVICE OF NORTH CENTRAL TEXAS, GREENVILLE
2304 Stonewall, Suite 210
Greenville, TX 75401-5759
903-455-4311
Fax: 903-455-2594
Type of Counseling:
Default/Foreclosure Counseling, Rental Counseling, Prepurchase Counseling, HECM Counseling

TEJANO CENTER OF COMMUNITY CONCERNS
6901 Brownwood
Houston, TX 77020
713-673-1080
Fax: 713-673-1304
Type of Counseling:
Prepurchase Counseling, Rental Counseling

AVENUE COMMUNITY DEVELOPMENT CORPORATION
2505 Washington Street, Suite 400
Houston, TX 77007
713-864-8099
Fax: 713-864-0027
Type of Counseling: Prepurchase Counseling

CONSUMER CREDIT COUNSELING SERVICES OF THE GULF COAST AREA, INCORPORATED
4600 Gulf Freeway, Ste 500
Houston, TX 77023-3551
713-923-2227
Toll-Free: 800-873-2227
Fax: 713-394-3209
Type of Counseling:
Default/Foreclosure Counseling, Rental Counseling, Prepurchase Counseling

GULF COAST COMMUNITY SERVICE ASSOCIATION
5000 Gulf Frwy, Bldg 1
Houston, TX 77023-4634
713-393-4700
Fax: 713-393-4754
Type of Counseling:
Default/Foreclosure Counseling, Rental Counseling, Prepurchase Counseling, HECM Counseling

HOUSTON AREA URBAN LEAGUE
1301 Texas Ave.
Houston, TX 77002
713-393-8700
Fax: 713-393-8760
Email: philipi@haul.org
Website: www.haul.org
Type of Counseling:
Default/Foreclosure Counseling, Prepurchase Counseling, HECM Counseling, Rental Counseling
Affiliate of: NATIONAL URBAN LEAGUE

HOUSING OPPORTUNITIES OF HOUSTON INCORPORATED
2900 Woodridge Dr Ste 300
Houston, TX 77087
713-644-8488
Fax: 713-644-5054
Email: hoh@neosoft.com
Type of Counseling:
Default/Foreclosure Counseling, Prepurchase Counseling
Affiliate of: NATIONAL COUNCIL OF LA RAZA

**ACORN HOUSING CORPORATION
704 East 11 1/2 Street
Houston, TX 77008
713-863-9002
Fax: 713-863-1964
Type of Counseling:
Default/Foreclosure Counseling, Rental Counseling, Prepurchase Counseling
Affiliate of: ACORN HOUSING CORPORATION

**DOMINION COMMUNITY DEVELOPMENT CORPORATION
1102 Pinemont Dr.
Houston, TX 77018
713-957-2789
Fax: 713-957-3087
Type of Counseling:
Prepurchase Counseling, Default/Foreclosure Counseling, Rental Counseling, HECM Counseling
Affiliate of: CONGRESS OF NATIONAL BLACK CHURCHES, INCORPORATED

GREATER PARK PLACE COMMUNITY DEVELOPMENT CORPORATION
8130 Park Place Blvd.
Houston, TX 77207-2784
713-641-3462
Fax: 713-641-0847
Email: jgreen2281@aol.com
Type of Counseling:

Prepurchase Counseling,
Default/Foreclosure Counseling,
Rental Counseling

CREDIT COALITION
3300 Lyons Avenue, Number 203A
Houston, TX 77020-
713-224-7772
Fax: 713-224-7792
Type of Counseling:
Prepurchase Counseling, Rental Counseling, Default/Foreclosure Counseling

CONSUMER CREDIT COUNSELING - MID-CITIES
1500 Norwood Dr Bldg B
Suite 203
Hurst, TX 76054-3604
800-374-2227
Toll-Free: 800-374-2227
Fax: 817-377-0036
Type of Counseling:
Default/Foreclosure Counseling, Rental Counseling, Prepurchase Counseling

CONSUMER CREDIT COUNSELING SERVICE OF GREATER DALLAS, IRVING
4322 N. Belt Line Rd.
Suite B-207
Irving, TX 75038
972-255-0079
Fax: 972-570-5996
Type of Counseling:
Default/Foreclosure Counseling, Rental Counseling, Prepurchase Counseling, HECM Counseling

CONSUMER CREDIT COUNSELING SERVICE OF GREATER FORT WORTH/KILLEEN
1711 E. Central Texas Expwy # 302
Killeen, TX 76541
800-219-2227
Fax: 254-628-2457
Website:
Type of Counseling:
Rental Counseling,
Default/Foreclosure Counseling,
Prepurchase Counseling

KINGSVILLE AFFORDABLE HOUSING, INCORPORATED
1000 West Corral
Kingsville, TX 78363
361-592-6783
Fax: 361-595-1997
Type of Counseling:
Default/Foreclosure Counseling, Rental Counseling, Prepurchase Counseling

METRO AFFORDABLE HOUSING CORPORATION
2000 San Francisco Ave.
Laredo, TX 78040
956-722-4521
Fax: 956-722-6561
Type of Counseling:
Prepurchase Counseling,
Default/Foreclosure Counseling,
Rental Counseling

**LAREDO-WEBB NEIGHBORHOOD HOUSING SERVICES, INCORPORATED
216 Bob Bulloch Loop
Laredo, TX 78046
956-712-9100
Fax: 956-712-9102
Email: ldonhs@icsi.net
Type of Counseling:
Default/Foreclosure Counseling,
Prepurchase Counseling
Affiliate of: NEIGHBORHOOD REINVESTMENT CORPORATION

CONSUMER CREDIT COUNSELING SERVICE OF NORTH CENTRAL TEXAS, PARIS
2600 Lamar Ave Ste B
Leessburg, TX 75460
903-785-9888
Fax: 903-785-7296
Type of Counseling:
Default/Foreclosure Counseling, Rental Counseling, Prepurchase Counseling, HECM Counseling

CONSUMER CREDIT COUNSELING SERVICE OF GREATER FORT WORTH/LEVELLAND
1001 8th Street, # 2
Levelland, TX 79336
806-894-8511
Fax: 806-785-2250
Type of Counseling:
Rental Counseling,
Default/Foreclosure Counseling,
Prepurchase Counseling

CONSUMER CREDIT COUNSELING SERVICE OF NORTH CENTRAL TEXAS, LEWISVILLE
1165 S Stemmons Fwy Ste 263
Lewisville, TX 75067-5374
972-221-6798
Fax: 972-353-3118
Type of Counseling:
Default/Foreclosure Counseling, Rental Counseling, Prepurchase Counseling, HECM Counseling

CONSUMER CREDIT COUNSELING SERVICE OF GREATER DALLAS, LONGVIEW
1800 NW Loop 281 Ste 201
Longview, TX 75064
800-577-2227
Toll-Free: 800-577-2227
Fax: 903-295-3315
Type of Counseling:
Default/Foreclosure Counseling, Rental Counseling, Prepurchase Counseling, HECM Counseling

CONSUMER CREDIT COUNSELING SERVICE OF GREATER FORT WORTH/LUBBOCK
4010 82nd St. # 250
Lubbock, TX 79423
800-867-2227
Fax: 806-785-2250
Website: www.cccsfw.org
Type of Counseling:
Rental Counseling,
Default/Foreclosure Counseling,
Prepurchase Counseling

GUADALUPE ECONOMIC SERVICES CORPORATION
1416 1st St
Lubbock, TX 79401-1312
806-744-4416
Fax: 806-744-7940
Type of Counseling:
Default/Foreclosure Counseling,
Prepurchase Counseling

CONSUMER CREDIT COUNSELING SERVICE OF MANSFIELD
209 N Walnut Creek Dr Ste D
Mansfield, TX 76063-1791
817-732-2227
Fax: 817-377-0036
Type of Counseling:
Default/Foreclosure Counseling, Rental Counseling, Prepurchase Counseling

MARSHALL HOUSING AUTHORITY
1401 Poplar St
Marshall, TX 75671
903-938-0717
Fax: 903-938-0737
Type of Counseling:
Default/Foreclosure Counseling, Rental Counseling, Prepurchase Counseling

CONSUMER CREDIT COUNSELING SERVICE OF GREATER DALLAS, MARSHALL
101 E Austin St Ste 209

Marshall, TX 75670-3301
800-577-2227
Fax: 903-295-3315
Type of Counseling:
Default/Foreclosure Counseling, Rental Counseling, Prepurchase Counseling

**CONSUMER CREDIT COUNSELING SERVICE OF NORTH CENTRAL TEXAS
901 N. McDonald, Suite 600
McKinney, TX 75070-0299
800-856-0257
Toll-Free: 800-856-0257
Fax: 972-542-3623
Type of Counseling:
Default/Foreclosure Counseling, Rental Counseling, Prepurchase Counseling, HECM Counseling
Affiliate of: NATIONAL FOUNDATION FOR CONSUMER CREDIT, INCORPORATED

CONSUMER CREDIT COUNSELING SERVICE OF GREATER DALLAS, MESQUITE
3939 Highway 80 Ste 302
Mesquite, TX 75150
972-681-2227
Fax: 972-681-9895
Type of Counseling:
Prepurchase Counseling, Rental Counseling, Default/Foreclosure Counseling, HECM Counseling

**MIDLAND NEIGHBORHOOD HOUSING SERVICES, INCORPORATED
300 E. Indiana, Ste 1
Midland, TX 79701
915-687-6647
Fax: 915-684-8293
Email: mnhs@planetlink.net
Type of Counseling:
Default/Foreclosure Counseling, Prepurchase Counseling
Affiliate of: NEIGHBORHOOD REINVESTMENT CORPORATION

CONSUMER CREDIT COUNSELING SERVICE OF GREATER FORT WORTH/MIDLAND
2500 N. Big Spring St. # 290
Midland, TX 79705
915-570-9011
Toll-Free: 800-374-2227
Fax: 915-684-3720
Type of Counseling:
Rental Counseling, Default/Foreclosure Counseling, Prepurchase Counseling

CONSUMER CREDIT COUNSELING SERVICE OF GREATER FORT WORTH/MINERAL WELLS
116 SE First St.
Mineral Wells, TX 76067
940-325-2952
Fax: 817-599-0813
Type of Counseling:
Rental Counseling, Default/Foreclosure Counseling, Prepurchase Counseling

**AMIGOS DEL VALLE, INCORPORATED
116 N Conway Ave
Mission, TX 78572
956-581-9494
Fax: 956-581-2210
Email: chino@main.rgv.net
Type of Counseling:
Prepurchase Counseling
Affiliate of: NEIGHBORHOOD REINVESTMENT CORPORATION

CONSUMER CREDIT COUNSELING SERVICE OF NORTH CENTRAL TEXAS, MOUNT PLEASANT
1805 N. Jefferson St.
Mount Pleasant, TX 75456
903-577-9569
Fax: 903-575-0086
Type of Counseling:
Default/Foreclosure Counseling, Rental Counseling, Prepurchase Counseling, HECM Counseling

CONSUMER CREDIT COUNSELING SERVICE
2626 John Ben Shepperd Pkwy Bldg B Ste 103
Odessa, TX 79761-1956
800-374-2227
Toll-Free: 800-374-2227
Fax: 915-550-8910
Type of Counseling:
Default/Foreclosure Counseling, Rental Counseling, Prepurchase Counseling

CONSUMER CREDIT COUNSELING SERVICE OF GREATER DALLAS/PALESTINE
1006 N. Mallard
Palestine, TX 75801
800-396-2227
Fax: 903-872-8097
Type of Counseling:
Prepurchase Counseling, Rental Counseling, Default/Foreclosure Counseling

COLONIAS DE VALLE
1203 E Ferguson St
Pharr, TX 78577
956-787-9903
Fax: 956-782-1016
Type of Counseling:
Prepurchase Counseling, Rental Counseling

CONSUMER CREDIT COUNSELING SERVICE OF GREATER FORT WORTH/PLAINVIEW
1900 W. &th St. Rm 201
Plainview, TX 79072
806-296-6167
Fax: 806-785-2250
Type of Counseling:
Rental Counseling, Default/Foreclosure Counseling, Prepurchase Counseling

CONSUMER CREDIT COUNSELING SERVICE OF NORTH CENTRAL TEXAS, WEST PLANO
2301 Ohio Dr., Suite 295
Plano, TX 75093
972-985-2713
Fax: 972-519-9763
Type of Counseling:
Prepurchase Counseling, Rental Counseling, Default/Foreclosure Counseling, HECM Counseling

CONSUMER CREDIT COUNSELING SERVICE OF NORTH CENTRAL TEXAS, PLANO
101 E Park Blvd Ste 757
Plano, TX 75074-5477
972-881-2887
Fax: 972-424-4815
Type of Counseling:
Default/Foreclosure Counseling, Rental Counseling, Prepurchase Counseling, HECM Counseling

CONSUMER CREDIT COUNSELING SERVICE OF GREATER DALLAS, RICHARDSON
100 N Central Expy Ste 400
Richardson, TX 75080
972-437-6252
Fax: 972-234-0227
Type of Counseling:
Default/Foreclosure Counseling, Rental Counseling, Prepurchase Counseling, HECM Counseling

CONSUMER CREDIT COUNSELING, Telephone counseling

2235 Ridge Rd Ste 103
Rockwall, TX 75087-5142
214-638-2263
Fax: 214-638-4398
Type of Counseling:
Default/Foreclosure Counseling,
Rental Counseling, Prepurchase
Counseling

CONSUMER CREDIT
COUNSELING OF SAN ANGELO
3115 Loop 306 Ste 102
San Angelo, TX 76904-5983
915-942-9156
Fax: 817-377-0036
Type of Counseling:
Default/Foreclosure Counseling,
Rental Counseling, Prepurchase
Counseling

CONSUMER CREDIT
COUNSELING SERVICE OF
GREATER FORT
WORTH/GOODFELLOW AIR
FORCE BASE
225 Fort Lancaster
San Angelo, TX 76908
915-954-3893
Fax: 915-947-1237
Type of Counseling:
Rental Counseling,
Default/Foreclosure Counseling,
Prepurchase Counseling

AVENIDA GUADALUPE
ASSOCIATION
1327 Guadalupe St
San Antonio, TX 78207
210-223-3151
Fax: 210-223-4405
Website: www.agatx.org
Type of Counseling:
Prepurchase Counseling

**SAN ANTONIO HOUSING
TRUST FOUNDATION
118 Broadway St Ste 606
San Antonio, TX 78205-1945
210-735-2772
Fax: 210-735-2112
Website: www.sahousingtrust.org
Type of Counseling:
Prepurchase Counseling,
Default/Foreclosure Counseling,
Rental Counseling
Affiliate of: THE HOUSING
PARTNERSHIP NETWORK

OUR CASAS RESIDENT
COUNCIL, INCORPORATED
3006 Gaudalupe Street
San Antonio, TX 782075162
210-433-2787
Fax: 210-433-2789
Type of Counseling:
Prepurchase Counseling,
Default/Foreclosure Counseling,
Rental Counseling

SAN ANTONIO DEVELOPMENT
AGENCY
115 E Travis Ste 800
San Antonio, TX 78205
210-225-6833
Fax: 210-225-0233
Type of Counseling:
Default/Foreclosure Counseling,
Prepurchase Counseling

COMMUNITY ACTION DIVISION
CITY OF SAN ANTONIO
115 Plaza de Armas Ste 150
San Antonio, TX 78205
210-207-5910
Fax: 210-207-5914
Email: espencer@ci.sat.tx.us
Type of Counseling:
Default/Foreclosure Counseling,
Rental Counseling, Prepurchase
Counseling

**NEIGHBORHOOD HOUSING
SERVICES OF SAN ANTONIO,
INCORPORATED
851 Steves Ave
San Antonio, TX 78210-0339
210-533-6673
Fax: 210-533-0923
Type of Counseling:
Prepurchase Counseling
Affiliate of: NEIGHBORHOOD
REINVESTMENT
CORPORATION

CONSUMER CREDIT
COUNSELING SERVICE OF
NORTH CENTRAL TEXAS,
SHERMAN
200 N Travis St Ste 406
Sherman, TX 75090-0005
903-892-6927
Fax: 903-868-1367
Type of Counseling:
Default/Foreclosure Counseling,
Rental Counseling, Prepurchase
Counseling, HECM Counseling

CONSUMER CREDIT
COUNSELING SERVICE OF
GREATER FORT
WORTH/STEPHENVILLE
150 Harbin Dr. # 327
Stephenville, TX 76401
254-965-7454
Fax: 254-965-3841
Type of Counseling:
Rental Counseling,
Default/Foreclosure Counseling,
Prepurchase Counseling

CONSUMER CREDIT
COUNSELING SERVICE OF
NORTH CENTRAL TEXAS,
SULPHUR SPRINGS
521 Main Street, Suite 211
Sulphur Springs, TX 75480
903-439-1130
Fax: 903-438-0125
Type of Counseling:
Prepurchase Counseling, Rental
Counseling, Default/Foreclosure
Counseling, HECM Counseling

CONSUMER CREDIT
COUNSELING SERVICE OF
GREATER FORT
WORTH/SWEETWATER
119 E. 3rd St. # 303
Sweetwater, TX 79556
915-235-0222
Fax: 915-673-0405
Type of Counseling:
Rental Counseling,
Default/Foreclosure Counseling,
Prepurchase Counseling

CONSUMER CREDIT
COUNSELING SERVICE OF
GREATER FORT
WORTH/TEMPLE
1506 Paseo Del Plata # 100
Temple, TX 76502
254-771-1818
Fax: 254-771-0210
Type of Counseling:
Rental Counseling,
Default/Foreclosure Counseling,
Prepurchase Counseling

CONSUMER CREDIT
COUNSELING SERVICE OF
NORTH CENTRAL TEXAS,
TEXARKANA
4520 Summerhill Rd
Texarkana, TX 75503
903-792-1116
Fax: 903-792-1208
Type of Counseling:
Default/Foreclosure Counseling,
Rental Counseling, Prepurchase
Counseling, HECM Counseling

CONSUMER CREDIT
COUNSELING SERVICE OF
GREATER DALLAS, TYLER
1001 Loop 323 ESE Ste 250
Tyler, TX 75701
800-396-2227
Toll-Free: 800-396-2227
Fax: 903-581-6986

Type of Counseling:
Default/Foreclosure Counseling,
Rental Counseling, Prepurchase
Counseling, HECM Counseling

CONSUMER CREDIT
COUNSELING SERVICE OF
GREATER FORT WORTH/WACO
6801 Sanger Ave. Suite 202
Waco, TX 76710
254-772-8626
Fax: 254-772-4037
Type of Counseling:
Rental Counseling,
Default/Foreclosure Counseling,
Prepurchase Counseling

**NEIGHBORHOOD HOUSING
SERVICES OF WACO,
INCORPORATED
922 Franklin Avenue
Waco, TX 76701
254-752-1647
Fax: 254-752-6472
Email: egreen@swbell.net
Type of Counseling:
Prepurchase Counseling
Affiliate of: NEIGHBORHOOD
REINVESTMENT
CORPORATION

CONSUMER CREDIT
COUNSELING SERVICE OF
GREATER DALLAS,
WAXAHACHIE
820 Ferris Ave Ste 375
Waxahachie, TX 75165
888-397-2227
Toll-Free: 888-397-2227
Fax: 972-923-1269
Type of Counseling:
Default/Foreclosure Counseling,
Rental Counseling, Prepurchase
Counseling, HECM Counseling

CONSUMER CREDIT
COUNSELING SERVICE OF
GREATER FORT
WORTH/WEATHERFORD
200 Palo Pinto # 107
Weatherford, TX 76086
817-599-0813
Fax: 817-599-0813
Type of Counseling:
Rental Counseling,
Default/Foreclosure Counseling

CONSUMER CREDIT
COUNSELING SERVICE OF
GREATER DALLAS, WICHITA
FALLS
4245 Kemp St. Suite 502
Wichita Falls, TX 76308-2129
800-380-2227
Toll-Free: 800-380-2227
Fax: 940-692-3239
Type of Counseling:
Default/Foreclosure Counseling,
Rental Counseling, Prepurchase
Counseling, HECM Counseling

Utah

CEDAR CITY HOUSING
AUTHORITY
364 South 100 East
Cedar City, UT 84720
435-586-8462
Fax: 435-865-9397
Type of Counseling:
Prepurchase Counseling,
Default/Foreclosure Counseling,
Rental Counseling

UTAH STATE UNIVERSITY -
FAMILY LIFE CENTER
493 N 700 E
Logan, UT 84321-4231
435-797-7224
Toll-Free:
TTY/TDD:
Fax: 435-797-7432
Email: tawnee@cc.usu.edu
Website: www.usu.edu/flc
Type of Counseling:
HECM Counseling,
Default/Foreclosure Counseling,
Rental Counseling, Prepurchase
Counseling

YOUR COMMUNITY
CONNECTION
2261 Adams Ave
Ogden, UT 84401-1510
801-394-9456
Fax: 801-394-9456
Type of Counseling:
HECM Counseling,
Default/Foreclosure Counseling,
Rental Counseling, Prepurchase
Counseling

**NEIGHBORHOOD HOUSING
SERVICES OF PROVO
91 West 200 South
Provo, UT 84601-
801-375-5820
Fax: 801-375-5966
Type of Counseling:
Prepurchase Counseling,
Default/Foreclosure Counseling
Affiliate of: NEIGHBORHOOD
REINVESTMENT
CORPORATION

COMMUNITY ACTION
SERVICES
257 East Center
Provo, UT 84606
801-373-7634
Fax: 801-373-8228
Type of Counseling:
HECM Counseling,
Default/Foreclosure Counseling,
Rental Counseling, Prepurchase
Counseling

**SALT LAKE NEIGHBORHOOD
HOUSING SERVICES,
INCORPORATED
622 West 500 North
Salt Lake City, UT 84116-3417
801-539-1590
Fax: 801-539-1593
Website: www.slnhs.org
Type of Counseling:
Default/Foreclosure Counseling,
Prepurchase Counseling
Affiliate of: NEIGHBORHOOD
REINVESTMENT
CORPORATION

SALT LAKE COMMUNITY
ACTION PROGRAM
764 S 200 W
Salt Lake City, UT 84101-2710
801-359-2444
Fax: 801-355-1798
Type of Counseling:
HECM Counseling,
Default/Foreclosure Counseling,
Rental Counseling, Prepurchase
Counseling

Vermont

**CENTRAL VERMONT
COMMUNITY LAND TRUST
107 North Main Street
Barre, VT 05641
802-476-4493
Fax: 802-479-0020
Type of Counseling:
Prepurchase Counseling, Rental
Counseling
Affiliate of: NEIGHBORHOOD
REINVESTMENT
CORPORATION

**BRATTLEBORO AREA
COMMUNITY LAND TRUST
192 Canal Street
Brattleboro, VT 05301
802-254-4604
TTY/TDD: 802-254-4604
Fax: 802-254-4656
Email: esjohnson@bacl.org
Type of Counseling:
Prepurchase Counseling
Affiliate of: CITIZENS' HOUSING
AND PLANNING ASSOCIATION,
INCORPORATED

BURLINGTON COMMUNITY LAND TRUST
179 S Winooski Ave
Burlington, VT 05402-0523
802-660-0642
Fax: 802-660-0641
Email: admin@getahome.org
Type of Counseling:
Prepurchase Counseling,
Default/Foreclosure Counseling

CHAMPLAIN VALLEY OFFICE OF ECONOMIC OPPORTUNITY
191 North St
Burlington, VT 05402
802-660-3456
Fax: 802-660-3454
Email: bayder@together.net
Type of Counseling:
Prepurchase Counseling, Rental Counseling
Affiliate of: CITIZENS' HOUSING AND PLANNING ASSOCIATION, INCORPORATED

**GILMAN HOUSING TRUST
101 Main Street
Lyndonville, VT 05851
802-334-1241
Email: info@nekhome.com
Type of Counseling:
Prepurchase Counseling,
Default/Foreclosure Counseling,
HECM Counseling
Affiliate of: NEIGHBORHOOD REINVESTMENT CORPORATION

**LAMOILLE HOUSING PARTNERSHIP
109 Professional Drive, Suite 1
Morrisville, VT 05661
802-888-5714
Fax: 802-888-3082
Email: lucy@pshift.com
Type of Counseling:
Prepurchase Counseling
Affiliate of: CITIZENS' HOUSING AND PLANNING ASSOCIATION, INCORPORATED

**RANDOLPH AREA COMMUNITY DEVELOPMENT CORPORATION
PO Box 409
Randolph, VT 05060
802-728-4305
Fax: 802-728-4016
Email: RACDC@quest-net.com
Type of Counseling:
Prepurchase Counseling
Affiliate of: CITIZENS' HOUSING AND PLANNING ASSOCIATION, INCORPORATED

**RUTLAND COUNTY COMMUNITY LAND TRUST
128 Merchants Row, 6th floor
Rutland, VT 05701
802-775-3139
Toll-Free: 800-545-7989
Fax: 802-775-0434
Email: ekrcclt@sover.net
Type of Counseling:
Prepurchase Counseling
Affiliate of: CITIZENS' HOUSING AND PLANNING ASSOCIATION, INCORPORATED

**ROCKINGHAM COMMUNITY AREA LAND TRUST
23 Pleasant St.
Springfield, VT 05156
802-885-3220
Fax: 802-885-5811
Type of Counseling:
Prepurchase Counseling
Affiliate of: NEIGHBORHOOD REINVESTMENT CORPORATION

**LAKE CHAMPLAIN HOUSING DEVELOPMENT CORPORATION
2 Federal Street, Suite 101
St. Albans, VT 05478
802-527-2361
Fax: 802-527-2961
Email: lchdcsta@together.net
Type of Counseling:
Prepurchase Counseling,
Default/Foreclosure Counseling
Affiliate of: CITIZENS' HOUSING AND PLANNING ASSOCIATION, INCORPORATED

**RUTLAND WEST NEIGHBORHOOD HOUSING SERVICES
71 Marble Street
West Rutland, VT 05777
802-438-2303
Fax: 802-438-5338
Email: rwnhs@vermontel.com
Type of Counseling:
Default/Foreclosure Counseling,
Prepurchase Counseling
Affiliate of: NEIGHBORHOOD REINVESTMENT CORPORATION

Virginia

PEOPLE INCORPORATED
1173 W Main St
Abingdon, VA 24210-2428
540-623-9000
Fax: 540-628-2931
Type of Counseling:
HECM Counseling,
Default/Foreclosure Counseling,
Prepurchase Counseling

SENIOR CITIZENS EMPLOYMENT AND SERVICES, INCORPORATED
121 N Saint Asaph St
Alexandria, VA 22314-3109
703-836-4414
Fax: 703-836-1252

CONSUMER CREDIT COUNSELING SERVICE OF GREATER WASHINGTON
801 N Pitt St Ste 117
Alexandria, VA 22314-1765
703-836-8772
Fax: 703-548-7704
Type of Counseling: HECM Counseling

CATHOLIC CHARITIES USA
1731 King St Ste 200
Alexandria, VA 22314-2720
703-549-1390
Fax: 703-549-1656

ARLINGTON AGENCY ON AGING
1800 North Edison St.
Arlington, VA 22207-1955
703-228-5030
Fax: 703-228-5073
Type of Counseling: HECM Counseling

ARLINGTON HOUSING CORPORATION
2300 S 9th St S Ste 200
Arlington, VA 22204-2320
703-486-0626
Fax: 703-486-0653
Type of Counseling: Rental Counseling, Prepurchase Counseling

**CONSUMER CREDIT COUNSELING SERVICE OF SOUTHWESTERN VIRGINIA, INCORPORATED
506 Cumberland Street
Bristol, VA 24201
800-926-0042
Fax: 540-366-7140
Type of Counseling:
HECM Counseling,
Default/Foreclosure Counseling,
Prepurchase Counseling, Rental Counseling

PIEDMONT HOUSING ALLIANCE
515 Park Street
Charlottesville, VA 22902-

434-817-2436
Fax: 434-817-0664
Website: www.avenue.org/pha
Type of Counseling:
Prepurchase Counseling, Default/Foreclosure Counseling, Rental Counseling

MONTICELLO AREA COMMUNITY ACTION AGENCY
1025 Park St
Charlottesville, VA 22901-3934
804-295-3171
Fax: 804-296-0093
Type of Counseling:
HECM Counseling, Default/Foreclosure Counseling, Rental Counseling, Prepurchase Counseling

**CATHOLIC CHARITIES OF HAMPTON ROADS, INCORPORATED
3804 Poplar Hill Road, Suite A
Chesapeake, VA 23321
757-484-0703
Fax: 757-484-1096
Email: cchrcccs@aol.com
Type of Counseling:
HECM Counseling, Default/Foreclosure Counseling, Prepurchase Counseling, Rental Counseling
Affiliate of: CATHOLIC CHARITIES USA

**COMMUNITY HOUSING PARTNERS CORPORATION
930 Cambria Street NE
Christianburg, VA 24073
757-422-9664
Fax: 757-425-5826
Type of Counseling:
Prepurchase Counseling
Affiliate of: THE HOUSING PARTNERSHIP NETWORK

**CONSUMER CREDIT COUNSELING SERVICE OF SOUTHWESTERN VIRGINIA, INCORPORATED
Tudor Square, Ste. 10
211 Roanoke St.
Christiansburg, VA 24073
800-926-0042
Toll-Free: 800-926-0042
Fax: 540-366-7140
Type of Counseling:
HECM Counseling, Default/Foreclosure Counseling, Prepurchase Counseling, Rental Counseling

**CONSUMER CREDIT COUNSELING SERVICE OF SOUTHWESTERN VIRGINIA, INCORPORATED
First Union Bank Building Main Street
Covington, VA 24426
800-926-0042
Toll-Free: 800-926-0042
Fax: 540-366-7140
Type of Counseling:
HECM Counseling, Default/Foreclosure Counseling, Prepurchase Counseling, Rental Counseling

CONSUMER CREDIT COUNSELING SERVICE OF GREATER WASHINGTON
3927 Old Lee Hwy
Fairfax, VA 22030-2422
703-591-9020
Fax: 703-591-3927
Type of Counseling:
HECM Counseling, Default/Foreclosure Counseling, Prepurchase Counseling

OFFICE FOR WOMEN FAIRFAX COUNTY
1200 Government Center Pkwy
Fairfax, VA 22035
703-324-5730
Fax: 703-324-3959

**CATHOLIC CHARITIES OF HAMPTON ROADS, INCORPORATED
121 South Main Street
Franklin, VA 23851
757-562-6222
Fax: 757-562-3930
Type of Counseling:
Rental Counseling, Default/Foreclosure Counseling, Prepurchase Counseling
Affiliate of: CATHOLIC CHARITIES USA

TELAMON CORPORATION
111 Henry St
Gretna, VA 24557-0500
804-656-8357
Fax: 804-656-8356
Type of Counseling:
Default/Foreclosure Counseling, Rental Counseling, Prepurchase Counseling

HAMPTON REDEVELOPMENT AND HOUSING AUTHORITY
22 Lincoln St
Hampton, VA 23669-3522
757-727-1111
Fax: 757-727-1090
Email: hrha@aol.com
Type of Counseling:
Prepurchase Counseling, Default/Foreclosure Counseling, Rental Counseling

CENTER FOR CHILD AND FAMILY SERVICE/CONSUMER CREDIT COUNSELING SERVICE OF HAMPTON ROADS
2021 Cunningham Drive, Suite 400
Hampton, VA 23666-3375
757-826-2227
Fax: 757-838-8021

Type of Counseling:
HECM Counseling, Default/Foreclosure Counseling, Prepurchase Counseling
Affiliate of: NATIONAL FOUNDATION FOR CONSUMER CREDIT, INCORPORATED

CONSUMER CREDIT COUNSELING SERVICE OF GREATER WASHINGTON
604 South King Street, Suite 007
Leesburg, VA 20175
703-777-3787
Fax: 703-548-7704
Type of Counseling:
HECM Counseling, Prepurchase Counseling, Default/Foreclosure Counseling, Rental Counseling

**AMERICAN CREDIT COUNSELORS, INCORPORATED
Null
Lynchburg, VA 24502
800-646-0042
Toll-Free: 800-646-0042
Fax: 540-366-7140
Type of Counseling:
HECM Counseling, Default/Foreclosure Counseling, Prepurchase Counseling, Rental Counseling

LYNCHBURG COMMUNITY ACTION GROUP, INCORPORATED
1310 Church St
Lynchburg, VA 24504-4604
804-846-2778
Fax: 804-845-1547
Type of Counseling:
Default/Foreclosure Counseling, Rental Counseling, Prepurchase Counseling

SKYLINE COMMUNITY ACTION PROGRAM, INCORPORATED
Old Elementary School Route 687

Madison, VA 22727
540-948-2237
Fax: 540-948-2264
Type of Counseling:
HECM Counseling,
Default/Foreclosure Counseling,
Rental Counseling, Prepurchase
Counseling

CONSUMER CREDIT
COUNSELING SERVICE OF
GREATER WASHINGTON
10629 Crestwood Dr
Manassas, VA 20109-3433
703-690-4779
Fax: 703-335-1632
Type of Counseling:
HECM Counseling,
Default/Foreclosure Counseling,
Prepurchase Counseling

VIRGINIA COOPERATIVE
EXTENSION - PRINCE WILLIAM
OFFICE
8033 Ashton Ave Ste 105
Manassas, VA 20109-8202
703-792-6287
Fax: 703-792-4630
Email: mleon@pwcgov.org
Website:
www.pwcgov.org/vce/html/personal
_finance.html
Type of Counseling:
Prepurchase Counseling,
Default/Foreclosure Counseling,
Rental Counseling, HECM
Counseling

**CONSUMER CREDIT
COUNSELING SERVICE OF
SOUTHWESTERN VIRGINIA,
INCORPORATED
900 Starling Avenue
Martinsville, VA 24112
800-926-0042
Toll-Free: 800-926-0042
Fax: 540-366-7140
Type of Counseling:
HECM Counseling,
Default/Foreclosure Counseling,
Prepurchase Counseling, Rental
Counseling

NORTHHAMPTON HOUSING
TRUST, INCORPORATED
Lankford Highway Rt 13
Nassawadox, VA 23413-0814
757-442-4509
Fax: 757-442-7530
Email: veseehc@esva.net
Type of Counseling:
Default/Foreclosure Counseling,
Rental Counseling, Prepurchase
Counseling

VIRGINIA EASTERN SHORE
ECONOMIC EMPOWERMENT
AND HOUSING CORPORATION
UPS Address is 10340, Lankford
Highway Birdsnest VA
Nassawadox, VA 23413
757-442-4509
Fax: 757-442-7530
Type of Counseling:
HECM Counseling,
Default/Foreclosure Counseling,
Rental Counseling, Prepurchase
Counseling

CENTER FOR CHILD AND
FAMILY SERVICE/CONSUMER
CREDIT COUNSELING SERVICE
OF HAMPTON ROADS`
12891 Jefferson Avenue
Newport News, VA 23606
757-826-2227
Fax: 757-838-8021
Type of Counseling:
HECM Counseling,
Default/Foreclosure Counseling,
Prepurchase Counseling, Rental
Counseling

**CATHOLIC CHARITIES OF
HAMPTON ROADS,
INCORPORATED
12829 Jefferson Avenue, Ste. 101
Newport News, VA 23608
757-484-0703
Fax: 757-484-1096
Email: CCHRCCCS@aol.com
Type of Counseling:
HECM Counseling,
Default/Foreclosure Counseling,
Rental Counseling
Affiliate of: CATHOLIC
CHARITIES USA

NEWPORT NEWS OFFICE OF
HUMAN AFFAIRS
6060 Jefferson Ave
Newport News, VA 23607
757-245-3271
Fax: 757-244-8146
Email: pcdcohainc.org
Type of Counseling:
HECM Counseling,
Default/Foreclosure Counseling,
Rental Counseling, Prepurchase
Counseling

CENTER FOR CHILD AND
FAMILY SERVICE/CONSUMER
CREDIT COUNSELING OF
HAMPTON ROADS
Fort Eustis Building #601
Newport News, VA 23604
757-826-2227
Fax: 757-838-8021
Type of Counseling:
HECM Counseling,
Default/Foreclosure Counseling,
Prepurchase Counseling, Rental
Counseling

CONSUMER FINANCIAL
COUNSELING OF TIDEWATER,
DIVISION OF FAMILY
SERVICES OF TIDEWATER
INCORPORATED
222 W 19th St
Norfolk, VA 23517
757-625-2227
Fax: 757-640-8402
Type of Counseling:
HECM Counseling,
Default/Foreclosure Counseling,
Rental Counseling, Prepurchase
Counseling

**CATHOLIC CHARITIES OF
HAMPTON ROADS,
INCORPORATED
1301 Colonial Avenue
Norfolk, VA 23517
757-625-2568
Fax: 757-625-5684
Email: CCHRCCCS@aol.com
Type of Counseling:
Default/Foreclosure Counseling,
Prepurchase Counseling, Rental
Counseling, HECM Counseling
Affiliate of: CATHOLIC
CHARITIES USA

THE STOP ORGANIZATION
2551 Almeda Ave
Norfolk, VA 23513-2443
757-858-1360
Fax: 757-858-1389
Type of Counseling:
HECM Counseling,
Default/Foreclosure Counseling,
Rental Counseling, Prepurchase
Counseling

CRATER DISTRICT AREA
AGENCY ON AGING
23 Seyler Dr
Petersburg, VA 23805-9243
804-732-7020
Fax: 804-732-7232
Email: Cccrater@aol.com
Type of Counseling: HECM
Counseling

RESTON INTERFAITH,
INCORPORATED
11484 Washington Plaza W Ste 400
Reston, VA 20190
703-787-3100
Fax: 703-787-3046
Type of Counseling:
Rental Counseling

RICHMOND URBAN LEAGUE
101 E Clay Street
Richmond, VA 23219-1331
804-649-8407
Fax: 804-643-5724
Email: ulr@aol.com
Type of Counseling:
HECM Counseling,
Default/Foreclosure Counseling,
Rental Counseling, Prepurchase
Counseling
Affiliate of: NATIONAL URBAN
LEAGUE

HOUSING OPPORTUNITIES
MADE EQUAL, INCORPORATED
2201 W. Broad Street, Suite 200
Richmond, VA 23220
804-354-0641
Fax: 804-354-0690
Type of Counseling:
HECM Counseling,
Default/Foreclosure Counseling,
Rental Counseling, Prepurchase
Counseling

COMMONWEALTH OF
VIRGINIA DEPARTMENT FOR
THE AGING
1600 Forest Ave Ste 102
Richmond, VA 23229
804-662-9333
Fax: 804-662-9354
Type of Counseling: HECM
Counseling

CAPITAL AREA AGENCY ON
AGING
24 E Cary St
Richmond, VA 23219-3733
804-343-3025
Fax: 804-649-2258
Type of Counseling: HECM
Counseling

**RICHMOND NEIGHBORHOOD
HOUSING SERVICES,
INCORPORATED
2712 Chamberlayne Avenue
Richmond, VA 23222-2634
804-329-2500
Fax: 804-329-2100
Type of Counseling:
Default/Foreclosure Counseling,
Prepurchase Counseling
Affiliate of: NEIGHBORHOOD
REINVESTMENT
CORPORATION

SOUTHSIDE COMMUNITY
DEVELOPMENT AND HOUSING
CORPORATION
1624 Hull Street
Richmond, VA 23224
804-231-4449
Fax: 804-231-3959
Type of Counseling:
Prepurchase Counseling, Rental
Counseling, Default/Foreclosure
Counseling, HECM Counseling

**COMMONWEALTH
CATHOLIC CHARITIES
1512 Willow Lawn Dr.
Richmond, VA 23230
804-285-5900
Fax: 804-285-9130
Email: comcathric@aol.com
Type of Counseling:
Prepurchase Counseling,
Default/Foreclosure Counseling,
Rental Counseling
Affiliate of: CATHOLIC
CHARITIES USA

TOTAL ACTION AGAINST
POVERTY IN ROANOKE
VALLEY
510 11th St. NW
Roanoke, VA 24017
540-777-2777
Fax: 540-777-2778
Type of Counseling:
HECM Counseling,
Default/Foreclosure Counseling,
Rental Counseling, Prepurchase
Counseling

CITY OF ROANOKE
REDEVELOPMENT AND
HOUSING COUNSELING
AUTHORITY
2624 Salem Tpke NW
Roanoke, VA 24017-5334
540-342-4561
Fax: 540-983-9229
Type of Counseling:
HECM Counseling,
Default/Foreclosure Counseling,
Rental Counseling, Prepurchase
Counseling

AMERICAN CREDIT
COUNSELORS
7000 Peters Creek Rd
Roanoke, VA 24019
540-366-6926
Toll-Free: 800-926-0042
Fax: 540-366-7140
Type of Counseling:
Default/Foreclosure Counseling,
Prepurchase Counseling, Rental
Counseling, HECM Counseling

**CATHOLIC CHARITIES OF
HAMPTON ROADS,
INCORPORATED
4855 Princess Anne Road
Virginia Beach, VA 23462
757-484-0703
Fax: 757-484-1096
Email: CCHRCCCS@aol.com
Type of Counseling:
Default/Foreclosure Counseling,
Prepurchase Counseling, Rental
Counseling, HECM Counseling
Affiliate of: CATHOLIC
CHARITIES USA

**CATHOLIC CHARITIES OF
HAMPTON ROADS,
INCORPORATED
1315 Jamestown Road, Suite 202
Williamsburg, VA 23185
757-875-0060
Fax: 757-877-7883
Email: CCHRCCCS@aol.com
Type of Counseling:
Prepurchase Counseling,
Default/Foreclosure Counseling,
Rental Counseling, HECM
Counseling
Affiliate of: CATHOLIC
CHARITIES USA

CENTER FOR CHILD AND
FAMILY SERVICE/ CONSUMER
CREDIT COUNSELING SERVICE
OF HAMPTON ROADS
1031 Richmond Road
Williamsburg, VA 23186
757-826-2227
Fax: 757-838-8021
Type of Counseling:
HECM Counseling,
Default/Foreclosure Counseling,
Prepurchase Counseling, Rental
Counseling

CONSUMER CREDIT
COUNSELING SERVICE OF
GREATER WASHINGTON
2971 Valley Ave Ste 2
Winchester, VA 22601-2631
800-747-4222
Fax: 540-948-7498
Type of Counseling:
HECM Counseling,
Default/Foreclosure Counseling,
Prepurchase Counseling

CONSUMER CREDIT
COUNSELING SERVICE OF
GREATER WASHINGTON
12662 B Lake Ridge Dr
Woodbridge, VA 22192
703-494-1014
Fax: 703-494-1594
Type of Counseling:
HECM Counseling,
Default/Foreclosure Counseling,
Prepurchase Counseling

Washington

ABERDEEN NEIGHBORHOOD HOUSING SERVICES
710 E Market St
Aberdeen, WA 98520-3430
360-533-7828
Fax: 360-533-7851
Email: bmacfarlane@aberdeen-nhs.com
Website: www.aberdeen-nhs.com
Type of Counseling:
HECM Counseling, Default/Foreclosure Counseling, Rental Counseling, Prepurchase Counseling
Affiliate of: NEIGHBORHOOD REINVESTMENT CORPORATION

HOMESIGHT OF KING COUNTY
55 A. St
Auburn, WA 98001
206-723-4355
Toll-Free: 888-749-4663
Fax: 206-723-7137
Email:
Tenesha@HOMESIGHTWA.org
Website: www.homesightwa.org
Type of Counseling: Prepurchase Counseling
Affiliate of: HOUSING OPPORTUNITIES, INCORPORATED

CONSUMER CREDIT COUNSELING SERVICE OF KITSAP COUNTY
2817 Wheaton Way Ste 206
Bremerton, WA 98310
360-373-9138
Toll-Free: 800-244-1183
Fax: 253-582-5158
Type of Counseling:
HECM Counseling, Default/Foreclosure Counseling, Prepurchase Counseling

CONSUMER CREDIT COUNSELING SERVICE OF OLYMPIC SOUTH SOUND
2451 NE Kresky Road
Chehalis, WA 98532-2436
253-588-1858
Toll-Free: 800-244-1183
Fax: 253-582-5158
Type of Counseling:
HECM Counseling, Default/Foreclosure Counseling, Prepurchase Counseling

CONSUMER CREDIT COUNSELING SERVICE OF GRAYS HARBOR COUNTY
3001 Ingham Street
Hoquiam, WA 98550
253-588-1858
Toll-Free: 800-244-1183
Fax: 253-582-5158
Type of Counseling:
HECM Counseling, Default/Foreclosure Counseling, Prepurchase Counseling

**CONSUMER CREDIT COUNSELING SERVICES OF THE TRI-CITIES
401 N. Morain Street
Kennewick, WA 99336
509-737-1973
Toll-Free: 800-201-2181
Fax: 509-737-9722
Type of Counseling:
Prepurchase Counseling, Default/Foreclosure Counseling, HECM Counseling, Rental Counseling
Affiliate of: NATIONAL FOUNDATION FOR CONSUMER CREDIT, INCORPORATED

PIERCE COUNTY, DEPARTMENT OF COMMUNITY SERVICES, HOUSING PROGRAMS
8815 South Tacoma Way, Suite 211
Lakewood, WA 98499
253-798-7038
Toll-Free: 800-562-0336
Fax: 253-798-3999
Type of Counseling:
HECM Counseling, Default/Foreclosure Counseling, Rental Counseling, Prepurchase Counseling

HOMESIGHT SNOHOMISH COUNTY
22001- 66th Avenue West
Mountlake Terrace, WA 98043
206-723-4355
Toll-Free: 888-749-4663
Fax: 206-723-7137
Email:
tanesha@HOMESIGHTWA.ORG
Website: www.homesightwa.org
Type of Counseling: Prepurchase Counseling
Affiliate of: HOUSING OPPORTUNITIES, INCORPORATED

CONSUMER CREDIT COUNSELING SERVICE OF THURSTON COUNTY
409 Cluster Way, Suite E
Olympia, WA 98502
360-943-5740
Toll-Free: 800-244-1183
Fax: 253-582-5158
Type of Counseling:
HECM Counseling, Default/Foreclosure Counseling, Prepurchase Counseling

CONSUMER CREDIT COUNSELING SERVICE OF CLALLAM COUNTY
3430 Highway 101 E
Port Angeles, WA 98362-9068
253-588-1858
Toll-Free: 800-244-1183
Fax: 253-582-5158
Type of Counseling:
HECM Counseling, Default/Foreclosure Counseling, Prepurchase Counseling

CONSUMER CREDIT COUNSELING SERVICE OF KITSAP COUNTY
18943 Caldart Ave
Poulsbo, WA 98370
253-588-1858
Toll-Free: 800-244-1183
Fax: 253-582-5158
Type of Counseling:
HECM Counseling, Default/Foreclosure Counseling, Prepurchase Counseling

CONSUMER CREDIT COUNSELING SERVICE OF PACIFIC COUNTY
408 Second St
Raymond, WA 98577-1710
253-588-1858
Toll-Free: 800-244-1183
Fax: 253-582-5158
Type of Counseling:
HECM Counseling, Default/Foreclosure Counseling, Prepurchase Counseling

**ACORN HOUSING CORPORATION
5416 Rainier Avenue South
Seattle, WA 98118
206-723-5845
Fax: 206-723-8658
Type of Counseling:
Default/Foreclosure Counseling, Prepurchase Counseling, Rental Counseling, HECM Counseling
Affiliate of: ACORN HOUSING CORPORATION

WASHINGTON STATE HOUSING FINANCE COMMISSION
1000 2nd Avenue, Suite 2700
Seattle, WA 98104
206-464-7139

Fax: 206-587-5113
Type of Counseling: Prepurchase Counseling

HOMESIGHT
5117 Rainier Avenue South
Seattle, WA 98118
206-723-4355
Toll-Free: 888-749-4663
Fax: 206-760-4210
Email: tenesha@homesightwa.org
Website: www.homesightwa.org
Type of Counseling:
Prepurchase Counseling
Affiliate of: HOUSING OPPORTUNITIES, INCORPORATED

URBAN LEAGUE OF METROPOLITAN SEATTLE
105 14th Ave
Seattle, WA 98122-5558
206-461-3792
Fax: 206-461-8425
Type of Counseling:
Default/Foreclosure Counseling, Rental Counseling, Prepurchase Counseling, HECM Counseling

FREMONT PUBLIC ASSOCIATION
1501 N. 45th St
Seattle, WA 98103
206-694-6700
Fax: 206-694-6777
Email: krisb@fremontpublic.org
Website: www.fremontpublic.org
Type of Counseling:
Default/Foreclosure Counseling, Rental Counseling, Prepurchase Counseling, HECM Counseling

**NEW BIRTH COGIC
12643 Renton Avenue South
Seattle, WA 98108
206-772-6557
Fax: 206-772-4419
Type of Counseling: Prepurchase Counseling
Affiliate of: CONGRESS OF NATIONAL BLACK CHURCHES, INCORPORATED

CONSUMER CREDIT COUNSELING SERVICE OF OLYMPIC-SOUTH SOUND
428 Birch St RM 12A
Shelton, WA 98584-1700
253-588-1858
Toll-Free: 800-244-1183
Fax: 253-582-5158
Type of Counseling:
HECM Counseling,
Default/Foreclosure Counseling,
Prepurchase Counseling

**SPOKANE HOMEOWNERSHIP RESOURCE CENTER
55 West Mission St Ste # 103
Spokane, WA 99201
509-343-7472
Fax: 509-343-7474
Type of Counseling: Prepurchase Counseling

SPOKANE NEIGHBORHOOD ACTION PROGRAMS
500 S. Stone
Spokane, WA 99202-3937
509-456-7105
Fax: 509-456-7159
Type of Counseling:
HECM Counseling,
Default/Foreclosure Counseling,
Prepurchase Counseling

THE MARTIN LUTHER KING DEVELOPMENT ASSOCIATION
1023 Martin Luther King, Jr. Way
Tacoma, WA 98405
253-627-1099
Fax: 253-627-1187
Type of Counseling: Prepurchase Counseling

CONSUMER CREDIT COUNSELING SERVICE OF OLYMPIC SOUTH SOUND
11306 Bridgeport Way SW
Tacoma, WA 98499
253-588-1858
Toll-Free: 800-244-1183
Fax: 253-582-5158
Type of Counseling:
HECM Counseling,
Default/Foreclosure Counseling,
Prepurchase Counseling

CONSUMER CREDIT COUNSELING SERVICE OF OLYMPIC-SOUTH SOUND
11306 Bridgeport Way SW
Tacoma, WA 98499-3005
253-588-1858
Toll-Free: 800-244-1183
Fax: 253-582-5158
Website: www.cccs-nw.org
Type of Counseling:
HECM Counseling,
Default/Foreclosure Counseling,
Prepurchase Counseling

COMMUNITY HOUSING RESOURCE CENTER
3801-A Main Street
Vancouver, WA
360-690-4496
Fax: 360-694-6665
Type of Counseling:
HECM Counseling,
Default/Foreclosure Counseling,
Prepurchase Counseling

West Virginia

CONSUMER CREDIT COUNSELING OF SOUTHERN WEST VIRGINIA
735 S Kanawha St
Beckley, WV 25801-5626
800-869-7758
Fax: 304-255-2412
Type of Counseling:
HECM Counseling,
Default/Foreclosure Counseling,
Prepurchase Counseling

CONSUMER CREDIT COUNSELING SERVICE OF BLUEFIELD, INCORPORATED
Green Valley Retail Center
Bluefield, WV 24701-6282
304-325-5143
Toll-Free: 800-313-5097
Fax: 304-324-0375
Type of Counseling:
Prepurchase Counseling,
Default/Foreclosure Counseling,
HECM Counseling

**RELIGIOUS COALITION FOR COMMUMITY RENEWAL - JUBILEE HOUSING
1516 Washington Street East
Charleston, WV 25311
304-346-6398
Fax: 304-346-6417
Type of Counseling:
Prepurchase Counseling,
Default/Foreclosure Counseling,
HECM Counseling
Affiliate of: THE HOUSING PARTNERSHIP NETWORK

WEST VIRGINIA HOUSING DEVELOPMENT FUND
814 Virginia Street, East
Charleston, WV 25301
304-345-6475
Fax: 304-340-9941
Type of Counseling:
Prepurchase Counseling,
Default/Foreclosure Counseling,
Rental Counseling

CONSUMER CREDIT COUNSELING SERVICE OF THE KANAWHA VALLEY
8 Capitol St Ste 200
Charleston, WV 25301-2828

800-281-5969
Fax: 304-344-3871
Type of Counseling:
HECM Counseling,
Default/Foreclosure Counseling,
Rental Counseling, Prepurchase
Counseling

**COMMUNITY WORKS IN
WEST VIRGINIA
4710 Chimney Drive Suite 6
Charlestown, WV 25032-4148
304-965-2241
Fax: 304-965-2264
Email: housenwv@aol.com
Type of Counseling:
Default/Foreclosure Counseling,
Prepurchase Counseling
Affiliate of: NEIGHBORHOOD
REINVESTMENT
CORPORATION

CONSUMER CREDIT
COUNSELING SERVICE OF
NORTH CENTRAL WEST
VIRGINIA
115 S 4th St Ste 208
Clarksburg, WV 26302
304-623-0921
Toll-Free: 800-498-6681
Fax: 304-624-4089
Type of Counseling:
HECM Counseling,
Default/Foreclosure Counseling,
Rental Counseling, Prepurchase
Counseling
Affiliate of: NATIONAL
FOUNDATION FOR CONSUMER
CREDIT, INCORPORATED

KANAWHA INSTITUTE FOR
SOCIAL RESEARCH ACTION
124 Marshall Avenue
Dunbar, WV 25064
304-768-8924
Fax: 304-768-0376
Type of Counseling: Prepurchase
Counseling

CONSUMER CREDIT
COUNSELING SERVICE, A
DIVISION OF GOODWILL
INDUSTRIES
1102 Memorial Blvd.
Huntington, WV 25701
304-522-4321
Toll-Free: 888-534-4387
Fax: 304-525-7038
Type of Counseling:
HECM Counseling,
Default/Foreclosure Counseling,
Rental Counseling, Prepurchase
Counseling

CONSUMER CREDIT
COUNSELING SERVICE OF MID-
OHIO VALLEY
2715 Murdoch Ave Rm B4
Parkersburg, WV 26101-1059
304-485-3141
Toll-Free: 888-785-1997
Fax: 304-485-3286
Type of Counseling:
Prepurchase Counseling, HECM
Counseling, Default/Foreclosure
Counseling
Affiliate of: NATIONAL
FOUNDATION FOR CONSUMER
CREDIT, INCORPORATED

FAMILY SERVICE CREDIT
COUNSELING
51 11th St
Wheeling, WV 26003-2937
304-232-6733
Toll-Free: 800-220-3252
Fax: 304-233-7237
Type of Counseling:
HECM Counseling,
Default/Foreclosure Counseling,
Rental Counseling, Prepurchase
Counseling

Wisconsin

**NEIGHBORHOOD HOUSING
SERVICES OF BELOIT,
INCORPORATED
156 St. Lawrence Ave
Beloit, WI 53511
608-362-9051
Fax: 608-362-7226
Type of Counseling:
Default/Foreclosure Counseling,
Rental Counseling, Prepurchase
Counseling
Affiliate of: NEIGHBORHOOD
REINVESTMENT
CORPORATION

COMMUNITY ACTION,
INCORPORATED
1545 Hobbs Dr
Delavan, WI 53115-2027
262-728-8296
Toll-Free: 800-424-8297
Fax: 262-728-8294
Email: action@genevaonline.com
Type of Counseling:
Default/Foreclosure Counseling,
Rental Counseling, Prepurchase
Counseling

**NEIGHBORHOOD HOUSING
SERVICES OF GREEN BAY,
INCORPORATED
700 Cherry St
Green Bay, WI 54301
920-448-3075
Fax: 920-448-3078
Email: nhsbob@netnet.net
Type of Counseling:
Prepurchase Counseling,
Default/Foreclosure Counseling
Affiliate of: NEIGHBORHOOD
REINVESTMENT
CORPORATION

LEGAL SERVICES OF
NORTHEAST WISCONSIN,
INCORPORATED
201 West Walnut Street, Suite 203
Green Bay, WI 54303
920-432-4645
Toll-Free: 800-236-1127
Fax: 920-432-5078
Type of Counseling:
Default/Foreclosure Counseling,
Rental Counseling

COMMUNITY ACTION,
INCORPORATED
2300 Kellogg Ave
Janesville, WI 53546-5921
608-755-2470
Toll-Free: 800-424-8297
Fax: 608-755-2246
Email: action@genevaonline.com
Type of Counseling:
HECM Counseling,
Default/Foreclosure Counseling,
Rental Counseling, Prepurchase
Counseling

**NEIGHBORHOOD HOUSING
SERVICES OF KENOSHA,
INCORPORATED
1119 60th St.
Kenosha, WI 53140
262-652-6766
Fax: 262-652-8108
Type of Counseling:
Prepurchase Counseling,
Default/Foreclosure Counseling
Affiliate of: NEIGHBORHOOD
REINVESTMENT
CORPORATION

URBAN LEAGUE OF GREATER
MADISON, INCORPORATED
151 E. Gorham Street
Madison, WI 53703
608-251-8550
Fax: 608-251-0944
Type of Counseling:
Default/Foreclosure Counseling,
Prepurchase Counseling, Rental
Counseling

COMMUNITY DEVELOPMENT
AUTHORITY OF THE CITY OF
MADISON

Madison Municipal Bldg., Suite 318
215 Martin Luther King Jr. Blvd.
Madison, WI 53710
608-266-4675
TTY/TDD: 608-264-9290
Fax: 608-264-9291
Type of Counseling: Prepurchase Counseling, Rental Counseling

WISCONSIN HOUSING AND ECONMIC DEVELOPMENT AUTHORITY
201 W. Washington Ave, Suite 700
Madison, WI 53703-1728
608-266-7884
Fax: 608-267-1099
Type of Counseling:
Prepurchase Counseling, Rental Counseling, Default/Foreclosure Counseling

COALITION OF WISCONSIN AGING GROUPS, INCORPORATED
2850 Dairy Drive Ste. 100
Madison, WI 53718
608-224-0606
Fax: 608-224-0607
Email: carolmat@midplains.net
Type of Counseling: HECM Counseling

**THE WISCONSIN PARTNERSHIP FOR HOUSING DEVELOPMENT INCORPORATED
121 South Pinckney St. Suite 200
Madison, WI 53703
608-258-5560
Fax: 608-258-5565
Website: www.wphp.org
Type of Counseling:
HECM Counseling, Default/Foreclosure Counseling, Rental Counseling, Prepurchase Counseling
Affiliate of: THE HOUSING PARTNERSHIP NETWORK

TENANT RESOURCE CENTER
1202 Williamson St. Suite A
Madison, WI 5370
608-257-0006
Fax: 608-286-0804
Type of Counseling: Rental Counseling

**ACORN HOUSING CORPORATION
152 W. Wisconsin Ave #731
Milwaukee, WI 53203
414-273-1905
Fax: 414-276-8191
Type of Counseling:
Prepurchase Counseling, Default/Foreclosure Counseling
Affiliate of: ACORN HOUSING CORPORATION

HOUSING RESOURCES, INCORPORATED
4850 W. Fond du Lac Ave.
Milwaukee, WI 53216
414-272-3933
Fax: 414-272-3968
Type of Counseling: Prepurchase Counseling

SOUTH COMMUNITY ORGANIZATION
1635 South 8th Street
Milwaukee, WI 53204
414-643-7913
Fax: 414-643-5972
Type of Counseling:
Prepurchase Counseling, Default/Foreclosure Counseling, Rental Counseling

CAREER YOUTH DEVELOPMENT, INCORPORATED
2601 N. Martin Luther King Drive
Milwaukee, WI 53212
414-264-6888
Fax: 414-264-5622
Type of Counseling: Prepurchase Counseling, Rental Counseling

WALKER'S POINT DEVELOPMENT CORPORATION
914 S 5th St
Milwaukee, WI 53204-1711
414-645-9222
Fax: 414-645-9386
Type of Counseling:
Default/Foreclosure Counseling, Rental Counseling, Prepurchase Counseling

**NEIGHBORHOOD HOUSING SERVICES OF MILWAUKEE, INCORPORATED
635 North 35th Street
Milwaukee, WI 53208
414-344-3013
Fax: 414-344-3196
Type of Counseling: Prepurchase Counseling
Affiliate of: NEIGHBORHOOD REINVESTMENT CORPORATION

DANE COUNTY HOUSING AUTHORITY
2001 W Broadway, #1
Monona, WI 53713-3707
608-224-3636
Fax: 608-224-3632
Website:
Type of Counseling:
HECM Counseling, Default/Foreclosure Counseling, Rental Counseling, Prepurchase Counseling

THE RACINE/KENOSHA COMMUNITY ACTION AGENCY, INCORPORATED
2113 N. Wisconsin Street
Racine, WI 53402-
262-637-8377
Fax: 262-637-6419
Type of Counseling: Rental Counseling

**CONSUMER CREDIT OF RACINE
420 7th St
Racine, WI 53403-1222
262-634-2391
Fax: 262-635-7135
Type of Counseling:
Default/Foreclosure Counseling, Prepurchase Counseling
Affiliate of: NATIONAL FOUNDATION FOR CONSUMER CREDIT, INCORPORATED

NEIGHBORHOOD HOUSING SERVICES OF RICHLAND COUNTY, INCORPORATED
133 N Central Park Rm 220
Richland Center, WI 53581
608-647-4949
Fax: 608-647-8792
Email: nhsrcwi@ix.netcom.com
Type of Counseling:
Default/Foreclosure Counseling, Prepurchase Counseling
Affiliate of: NEIGHBORHOOD REINVESTMENT CORPORATION

**CATHOLIC CHARITIES BUREAU, INCORPORATED
1416 Cumming Ave
Superior, WI 54880-1720
888-831-8446
Toll-Free: 888-831-8446
Fax: 715-394-5951
Type of Counseling:
Default/Foreclosure Counseling, Prepurchase Counseling
Affiliate of: CATHOLIC CHARITIES USA

WAUKESHA COUNTY DEPARTMENT OF AGING
25042 West Northview Rd
Waukesha, WI 53188
262-548-7848

Fax: 262-896-8273
Type of Counseling: HECM Counseling, Rental Counseling

**CATHOLIC CHARITIES OF THE DIOCESE OF LA CROSSE, INC.
200 Washington Street
Wausau, WI 54403
715-849-3311
Toll-Free: 888-849-3311
Fax: 715-849-8414
Email: dhutchinson@catholiccharitselax.org
Type of Counseling: Prepurchase Counseling, Default/Foreclosure Counseling, Rental Counseling
Affiliate of: CATHOLIC CHARITIES USA

Wyoming

INTERFAITH OF NATRONA COUNTY, INCORPORATED
1514 East 12th Street, #303
Casper, WY 82601
307-235-8043
Fax: 307-235-8711
Type of Counseling: Rental Counseling

CONSUMER CREDIT COUNSELING SERVICE OF NORTHERN COLORADO AND SOUTHEAST WYOMING
2113 Warren Ave
Cheyenne, WY 82001-3739
800-424-2227
Fax: 970-229-0721
Website: www.cccsnc.org
Type of Counseling: HECM Counseling, Default/Foreclosure Counseling, Rental Counseling, Prepurchase Counseling

CONSUMER CREDIT COUNSELING SERVICE OF NORTHERN COLORADO AND SOUTHEAST WYOMING
221 E Ivinson Ave, 2nd Floor
Laramie, WY 82070-3038
800-424-2227
Toll-Free: 800-424-2227
Fax: 970-229-0721
Website: www.cccsnc.org
Type of Counseling:
HECM Counseling, Default/Foreclosure Counseling, Rental Counseling, Prepurchase Counseling

$$$ Pay Your Legal Bills

Free Lawyers for Millionaires

No matter what your income, you can get the most powerful organization in the world, *your government*, to fight for you to:

1) Establish paternity;
2) Set up a court order for child support;
3) Track down a missing parent and collect your child support; and even
4) Get the courts to adjust child support orders when circumstances change.

Actually I lied. There are a few states that may charge you up to $25.00. So the maximum you will pay is $25.00. So, why hire an attorney, who may or may not know the law, and will charge you up to $200 an hour, when you can call someone who wrote the law, whose duty is to enforce it for you, and who is free?

Contact your state Child Support Enforcement Office, or contact Office of Child Support Enforcement, U.S. Department of Health and Human Services, 370 L'Enfant Promenade, SW, Washington, DC 20447; 202-401-9383; {www.acf.dhhs.gov/programs/cse/}.

Rid Your Neighborhood of Troublemakers

Some states allow local community groups to get tenants or property owners thrown out of the neighborhood — under civil laws, not criminal laws — if they are involved with drugs or are a nuisance to the community. It's easier to enforce a civil law than a criminal law. Which is probably why O.J. Simpson lost his civil trial, but won his criminal trial.

The Community Law Center in Maryland provides free legal assistance to communities in Maryland to enforce these laws. Their services are free to non-profit community groups who seek to rid their neighborhood of troublemakers.

To find out if your community has similar services, contact your state Attorney General's office. The Community Law Center can be reached at 2500 Maryland Avenue, Baltimore, MD 21218; 410-366-0922; Fax: 410-366-7763; Email: {clawc@aol.com}.

Free Legal Help with Family, Consumer, Housing Income, Work, Children and Senior Issues

Legal Services Corporation is a collection of over 269 government supported local offices that provide free legal services in their area. Over 5000 attorneys and paralegals are available to individuals and families that are under certain income limits. The maximum income can be up to $30,000 for a family of four, or even more depending on certain financial obligations.

To find an office near you, contact your state information operator listed in the Appendix and ask for the Legal Services Office or contact: Legal Services Corporation, 750 First Street NE, 10th Floor, Washington, DC 20002; 202-336-8800; {www.lsc.gov}.

Free Legal Assistance for Domestic Violence Problems

Seven days a week, 24 hours a day, you can call the hotline and not only get access to sources that will solve your immediate problem, but also get information and sources in your area that can explain your legal options and get you through the legal process. Contact: National Domestic Violence Hotline, P.O. Box 161810, Austin, TX 78716; 800-799-SAFE; TTY: 800-787-3224; ndvh@ndvh.org; www.ndvh.org.

Help for Families Fighting Veterans Benefits

Through low cost publications, training courses and other services, for 25 years the **National Veterans Legal Services Program** has been helping veterans get their due. Current publications include: *VA Claims*, *Agent Orange*, and *Veterans Family Benefits*. Contact: National Veterans Legal Services Program, P.O. Box 753, Waldorf, MD 20604-0753; 301- 638-1327; 800-688-5VET; Fax 301-843-0159; {www.nvlsp.org}.

10,000 Lawyers that Work for Free

If your income is less than $32,000 (for a family of 4), it's worth checking out the pro bono legal services that are available in your state. And even if your income is more, it's worth checking because some of these services have flexible requirements depending upon your situation and the problem involved. Every year tens of thousands of lawyers volunteer their services to people who need help with almost any kind of problem.

For a listing of pro bono organizations in your state, contact your state bar association listed in your state capitol. The state information operator listed in the Appendix can provide you with a number, or you can contact: American Bar Association 750 N. Lake Shore Dr., Chicago, IL 60611; 312-988-5000; {www.abanet.org/legalservices/probono}.

Free Lawyers Will Fight for Your Rights

We've all heard of the ***American Civil Liberties Union (ACLU)***. They have over 300 offices around the country and handle close to 6,000 cases a year. The ACLU has more than 60 staff attorneys who collaborate with at least 2,000 volunteer attorneys in handling cases. They have appeared before the Supreme Court more than any other organization except the U.S. Department of Justice. If you feel that your civil liberties have been violated, they may take your case. The kinds of issues they are most currently active in include: woman's rights, reproductive freedom, workplace rights, AIDS, arts censorship, capital punishment, children's rights, education reform, lesbian and gay rights, immigrants' rights, national security, privacy and technology, prisoners' rights, and voting rights.

Contact the local ACLU office listed in your telephone directory or the main office website can provide you with a local

contact: ACLU - American Civil Liberties Union, 125 Broad Street, 18th Floor, New York, NY 10004-2400; {www.aclu.org/action/chapters.html}.

Free Legal Help with Sexual Harassment at Work or School

Free assistance to women and girls who are facing sex, or race discrimination, sexual harassment at work or at school, pregnancy, discrimination, or problems with family medical leave and other employment issues related specifically to women. The staff offers information and answers questions, and occasionally can draft "demand" letters, demanding that an employer or other person or organization stop doing something. In some circumstances, they can help you pursue internal grievance or administrative procedures, and in some precedent-setting cases, they will provide legal representation.

Contact: Equal Rights Advocates, 1663 Mission Street, Suite 550, San Francisco, CA 94103; 415-621-0672; Fax: 415-621-6744; Advice and Counseling Line: 800-839-4ERA; {www.equalrights.org}.

Free Legal Help for Breast Cancer Patients

If you are a breast cancer patient living in California, you maybe eligible to receive free legal assistance on issues such as:

- Debt collection problems with hospital and doctor bills.
- Barriers to access to diagnosis and treatment.
- Negotiations with insurance carriers for coverage and payment options.
- Housing discrimination.
- Employment discrimination.
- Temporary guardianships or modification of custody arrangements.

If you don't live in California, ask them if they are aware of similar services in your area. Contact: Breast Cancer Legal Project, California Women's Law Center, 3460 Wilshire Blvd., Suite 1102, Los Angeles, CA 90010; 213-637-9900; Fax: 213-637-9909; Email: {cwcl@cwcl.org}; {www.cwlc.org/BCLC. intro.html}.

Free Women's Law Centers

Rich or poor, women in **Maryland** can get free telephone help in filling out the forms to represent themselves in family court matters that are simple and uncontested. The hotline number is ***800-845-8550*** and it operates Tuesdays and Thursdays 9:30 am to 4:30 pm. Or women can call the hotline for information on family law issues, such as, how to obtain a separation, child custody, child support, and how to escape domestic violence. Contact: The Women's Law Center of Maryland, Inc., 305 West Chesapeake Ave., Towson, MD 21205; 410-321-8761; Email: {info-flc@ wlcmd.org}; {www.wlcmd.org}.

Women in the state of **Washington** can call a free legal ***Information and Referral line*** that is staffed with attorneys and paralegals to respond to questions about family law or employment. They also can receive legal rights publications including *Sexual Harassment in Employment and Education*; *Family Law in Washington State: Your Rights and Responsibilities*; and *Grandparents Raising Grandchildren; A Legal Guide for Washington State*. You can also attend free legal workshops, or receive help in filling out legal forms, and free legal consultations in domestic violence cases. Contact: Northwest Women's Law Center, 119 South Main St., Suite 410, Seattle WA 98104-2515; 206 682 9552; Fax: 206 682 9556; Legal Information and Referral: 206-621-7691; Email: {NWWLC@nwwlc.org}; {www.nwwlc.org}.

Free Legal Help for People with Disabilities

The disability laws not only cover people with disabilities that everyone can see. It's also for children who aren't getting the education they need from the local school, or for the cancer patient who feels discriminated against at work.

Free Legal Help to Fight Your Union At Work

If you feel your rights have been violated by compulsory unionism, or you simply have a question about your Right to Work, legal experts are available for free to help answer your questions. Contact: The National Right to Work Legal Defense Foundation, 8001 Braddock Rd., Springfield, VA 22160; 800-336-3600; {www.nrtw.org}.

A free hotline will help you learn about your rights, help you enforce them, and will even handle some high impact legal cases. Contact: Disability Rights Education and Defense Fund, Inc., 2212 Sixth Street, Berkeley, CA 94710; 510-644-2555 V/TTY; Fax: 510-841-8645; Email: {edf@dredf.org}; {www.dredf.org}.

Protecting Families with Children from Housing Discrimination

This book is written by one of the country's leading advocates for children's rights. It shows how to tell if families with children have been discriminated against in housing and what to do about it! A great guide for parents, as well as advocates who work with families. 1990 (ISBN: 0-938008-74-9. $4.75, plus $2.00 postage). Contact: Children's Defense Fund, CDF Publications, 25 E Street NW, Washington, DC 20001; 202-628-8787; Fax: 202-628-8333; {www.childrensdefense.org}.

Free Legal Help for Welfare Rights

Over 157 local organizations around the country fight for the rights of low-income people on welfare. These organizations can be a good place to turn to insure that you are getting the proper benefits, and for knowing your rights in dealing with the bureaucracy. You can contact your local social services agency to locate an office near you or the website for the Welfare Law Center that contains a directory of all the organizations. Contact: Welfare Law Center, 275 Seventh Ave., Suite 1205, New York, NY 10001; 212-633-6967; Email: {dirk@ welfarelaw.org}; {www.lincproject.org/lid/lid.html}.

Free Legal Help to Fight for Home Schooling Rights

The Home School Legal Defense Association (HSLDA) provides legal help for members on home schooling issues. Families receive legal consultation by letter and phone, and representation for negotiations with local officials, and court proceedings.

HSLDA also takes the offensive, filing actions to protect members against government intrusion and to establish legal precedent. On occasion, HSLDA will handle precedent-setting cases for non-members, as well. Contact: HSLDA, P.O. Box 3000, Purcellville, VA 20134; 540-338-5600; Fax: 540-338-2733; {www.hslda.org}.

Free Consulting in Sex Discrimination Law Suits

If, as a woman, you feel discriminated against in higher education, the Legal Advocacy Fund (LAF) of the American Association of University Women (AAUW) may be able to help by providing financial support for sex discrimination lawsuits. LAF organizes a network of volunteer attorneys and social scientists who consult with women on legal strategy, informational resources, and the strength of current or potential lawsuits.

To find out if you're eligible, please contact: AAUW Legal Advocacy Fund, Dept. LAF.INT., American Association of University of Women, 1111 16th St., NW, Washington, DC 20036; 800-326-AAUW; Fax: 202-872-1425; TDD: 202-785-7777; Email: {info@aauw.org}; {www.aauw.org}.

Free Legal Rights for Women's Issues

The National Organization for Women Legal Defense and Education Fund (NOW LDEF) has a hotline that provides free information and referrals on women's issues including reproductive rights, violence against women, economic justice, and gender equity in education. They also provide low-cost legal guides, some of which are available free on the Internet, on the following topics:

- *A Guide to Court Watching in Domestic Violence and Sexual Assault Cases*
- *Divorce and Separation*
- *Domestic Violence and Child Custody*
- *Employment Sexual Harassment & Discrimination* (Spanish)
- *Incest and Child Sexual Abuse*
- *Pregnancy & Parental Leave*
- *Sexual Harassment in Housing*
- *Sexual Harassment in the Schools*
- *Sexual Harassment in the Schools: A Blueprint for Action* (Spanish)
- *Stalking*
- *Violence Against Women*
- *How to Find a Lawyer* (free)

Contact: NOW LDEF, 395 Hudson Street, New York, NY 10014; 212-925-6635 (9:30 a.m. to 11:00 p.m. EST); Fax: 212-226-1066; email your question to {astrubel@ nowldef.org}; {www.nowldef.org}.

Legal Assistance for Overseas Teachers

Free legal aid is available for teachers employed in U.S. Department of Defense schools overseas and are members of the ***Federal Education Association (FEA)***. The FEA legal staff conducts arbitration and other legal actions to insure the rights and benefits of teachers. Contact: Federal Education Association, 1201 16th St. NW, Washington, DC 20036; 202-822-7850; Fax:

202-822-7867 (legal/ president); Email: {FEA_Legal/Pres@odedodea.edu} (legal office, president); {www.feaonline.org}.

Free Legal Help for Pregnant Teens Discriminated in Honors Society

Feminists for Life of America, along with the ACLU, got the a federal court to rule that two high school seniors, whose school denied them National Honor Society membership because they became pregnant and chose to give birth, must be admitted into the society. For free legal information on these kinds of issues, contact Feminists for Life of America, 733 15th St. NW, Suite 1100, Washington, DC 20005; 202-737-FFLA; {www.serve.com/fem4life/index.htm}.

Free Legal Help with Civil Liberties, Religious Freedom, and Parental Rights

The Rutherford Institute defends people who have been denied civil and human rights without charging them for such services. The issues they cover include civil liberties, religious freedom, parental rights, and sexual harassment. You may remember them from their involvement in the Paula Jones case. If you need legal help, contact The Rutherford Institute, Legal Department, P.O. Box 7482, Charlottesville, VA 22906; 804-978-3888; {www.rutherford.org}.

Free Help Collecting Child Support

An association of concerned parents helps others learn about their rights and the remedies available for collecting what is due to them. Some services are free, others are for those who join for only $20. They can show you that you don't need to use a professional collection agency, and they will even contact officials on your behalf.

Contact: Association for Children for Enforcement and Support (ACES), 260 Upton Ave., Toledo, OH 43006; 800-537-7072; Fax: 419-472-5943; {www.childsupport-aces.org}.

Free Legal Help for Gays and Those with HIV/AIDS

Lambda carries out carries out legal work on issues such as discrimination in employment, housing, public accommodations, and the military; HIV/AIDS-related discrimination and public policy issues; parenting and relationship issues; equal marriage rights; equal employment and domestic partnership benefits; "sodomy" law challenges; immigration issues; anti-gay initiatives; and free speech and equal protection rights. If you are seeking assistance with a legal matter, contact one of the offices listed below. They can guide you to a solution or help you directly:

National Headquarters Lambda
120 Wall Street, Suite 1500
New York, NY 10005-3904
212-809-8585
Fax: 212-809-0055

Western Regional Office
6030 Wilshire Boulevard
Los Angeles, CA 90036-3617
323-937-2728
Fax: 323-937-0601

Midwest Regional Office
11 East Adams, Suite 1008
Chicago, IL 60603-6303
312-663-4413
Fax: 312-663-4307

Southern Regional Office
1447 Peachtree Street, NE, Suite 1004
Atlanta, GA 30309-3027
404-897-1880
Fax: 404-897-1884

Lambda's website is {www.lambdalegal.org}.

Legal Help at a 75% Discount

The only things a paralegal can't do that a lawyer can, is give legal advice and represent you in court. That means they can file uncontested divorce papers, family court petitions, wills and probate, power of attorney, bankruptcy, incorporation. etc.

There are states where paralegals can represent clients in cases like those involving evictions or government agencies. And if you are seeking a legal opinion from an attorney, you may want to get a paralegal to research the law for you, so that you can make your own decisions.

Remember 50% of all lawyers lose their cases in court. So why pay $200 an hour for a lawyer, when you can get a lot of the same services done for less than $50 and hour. Paralegals are in the yellow pages and you can contact your state or local paralegal association by contacting the national association that can give you a local contact. For more information, contact National Federation of Paralegal Associations, P.O. Box 33108, Kansas City, MO 64114; 816-941-4000; Fax: 816-941-2752; {www.paralegals.org}.

Free Legal Latino Help

The Mexican American Legal Defense and Educational Fund (MALDEF) is a national nonprofit organization whose mission is to protect and promote the civil rights of the more than 29 million Latinos living in the United States in the areas of education, employment, political access, and more.

They take cases to court and provide other legal help for the Latino community.

Contact: MALDEF, 634 South Spring St., 11th Floor, Los Angeles, CA 90014; 213-629-2512; Fax: 213-629-0266; {www.maldef.org}.

Free Help with Housing Discrimination

Buying your first home is a very exciting time. But for many, house shopping is more than an eye opening experience. Some people are not shown houses in particular neighborhoods or are denied a home because of their sex, race, or living arrangement.

If you feel you have been treated unfairly, contact office of Fair Housing and Equal Opportunity, U.S. Department of Housing and Urban Development, 451 7th St., SW, Room 5100, Washington, DC 20410; 202-708-4252; 800-669-9777; {www.hud.gov}.

Fight Your Bank, Credit Card Company, etc.

Finding the right bank, savings and loan, or credit union means figuring out your own needs first. How much money can you keep on deposit and how many checks will you write? Examine your future loans and savings needs, as well as look at the convenience of the financial institution, its service charges, fees, and deposit and loan interest rates. You can contact one of the following offices to learn more. These offices will also help you if you think the bank is messing with your money.

National Banks (banks that have the word "National" in their names or the initials "N.A." after their names)
Comptroller of the Currency
U. S. Department of the Treasury
Customer Assistance Group
1301 McKinner St.
Suite 3710
Houston, TX 77010
800-613-6743
www.occ.treas.gov

FDIS-Insured Banks
Office of Consumer Affairs
Federal Deposit Insurance Corporation
550 17th St., NW
Room F-130
Washington, DC 20429
202-898-3542
800-934-3342
www.fdic.gov

Savings and Loans
Office of Thrift Supervision
U.S. Department of Treasury
1700 G St., NW
Washington, DC 20552
202-906-6237
800-842-6929
www.ots.treas.gov

State Banks

Contact your State Government Banking Commissioner located in your state capital (look in the blue pages of your phone book or contact your state capitol operator).

Discrimination Because you're a Women, Pregnant, Person of Color, etc.

There's no need to take harassment or bullying on the job. Here is your chance to fight back. If you believe you have been discriminated against by an employer, labor union, or employment agency when applying for a job or while on the job because of race, color, sex, religion, national origin, age, or disability, you may file a charge with the Equal Employment Opportunity Commission (EEOC).

For more information, contact Equal Employment Opportunity Commission, 1801 L St., NW, Washington, DC 20507; 800-669-4000; {www.eeoc.gov}.

Fight Lawyers, Accountants, Pharmacists, Doctors, Real Estate Agents and Other Professionals

Lawyer over-charging you? Do you feel you have been mistreated by your doctor?

These issues and more are handled by the agency or board that licenses that particular profession. Whether it is your accountant, real estate agent, doctor, dentist, or other professional, you can contact the licensing board directly to file a grievance. These boards will then help you to resolve the problem. To locate the correct board usually located in your state capital, contact your state operator.

Where to Get Help to Stop Sexual Harassment

Call **"9 to 5"** if you experience any of the following at work:

- Suggestive comments about your appearance
- Unwanted touching or other physical contact
- Unwanted sexual jokes or comments
- Sexual advances

Sexual harassment is not only offensive, it's against the law. It is illegal even if the harasser is not your boss, even if he is not threatening that you will lose your job if you don't go along. 9to5's **toll free job problem hotline** and trained job counselors give information and support to thousands of working women.

If you decide to pursue a legal remedy, contact your state discrimination agency or the federal Equal Employment Opportunity Commission (look in your phone book for the field office closest to you). The federal agency covers workplaces of 15 or more. State law covers workplaces with fewer employees.

Contact: 9to5, National Association of Working Women, 1430 West Peachtree St., Suite 610, Atlanta, GA 30309; 800-522-0925; {www.9to5.org}.

How an Abuser Can Discover Your Internet Activities

The ***American Bar Association's (ABA) Commission on Domestic Violence*** has issued a warning concerning possible threats to you if an abuser has access to your email account and thus may be able to read your incoming and outgoing mail. If you believe your account is secure, make sure you choose a password he or she will not be able to guess. If an abuser sends you threatening or harassing email messages, they may be printed and saved as evidence of this abuse. Additionally, the messages may constitute a federal offense.

For more information on this issue, contact your local United States Attorney's Office. For more information about what you can do, and the efforts of the ABA's Commission on Domestic Violence, please contact American Bar Association Commission on Domestic Violence, 740 15th Street, NW, 9th Floor, Washington, DC 20005-1022; 202-662-1737/1744; Fax: 202-662-1594, Email: {abacdv@abanet.org}; {www.abanet.org}.

Fight Retailers, Mail Order Companies, Auto Dealers, Contractors, etc.

You go to a store to get the best price on the gift for Uncle George, only to learn that the store is out of stock despite the product being advertised in the paper. Did the salesman try to get you to buy a higher priced item? You could be the victim of the old bait and switch scam. Is the paint peeling off of the new toy doll you bought your daughter? Problems dealing with your car dealership or car repair shop? (This is the number one complaint heard.) What about the contractor that has yet to finish the job?

There are ways to deal with all these problems and get them resolved to your satisfaction. You just need to pull in the big guns. The States' Attorney General's Offices have Consumer Protection Offices, and many also have separate offices that handle only car complaints. They will take your complaint and try to help you get the satisfaction you deserve. For other problems contact:

- ***Defective Products*** — contact Consumer Product Safety Commission,

5401 Westbard Ave., Washington, DC 20207; 800-638-2772; {www.cpsc.gov}.

- ***Contractor or Licensed Professional Problems*** — contact the state Licensing Board for the profession located in your state capitol. You can contact the state operator for assistance in finding the office.
- ***Mail Order Problems*** — contact the U.S. Postal Service, Public Affairs Branch, 475 L'Enfant Plaza, SW, Room 3140, Washington, DC 202060; 202-268-5400; {www.usps.gov}.
- ***Fraud Issues*** — contact Federal Trade Commission, Public Reference, CRC-2480, Washington, DC 20580; 202-382-4357, 877-FTC-HELP; {www.ftc.gov}.

Free Legal Help if Your Child is Suspended from School

"Zero Tolerance" and other school system disciplinary practices can place your child's education in jeopardy if you are not aware of your rights. Your first meeting with the principal on such matters can actually serve as a trial for your child's future.

The School House Legal Services of Baltimore, Maryland provides free attorneys and paralegals to represent Maryland families in these matters. Maryland has an income limit for representation that is about $30,000 for a family of four, but information about the process is free.

If you don't live in Maryland, contact your local Legal Services Office or your State Department of Education for more information and help. School House Legal Services can be reached at Maryland Disability Law Center, 1800 N. Charles St., Suite 202, Baltimore, MD 21201; 410-727-6352.

Free Help in Writing a Will

Estate planning is not something that people often relish doing, but it is extremely important. It is difficult enough when a loved one dies, but then to have to search through papers trying to find information about insurance, or investments is often too much. When children are involved, estate planning is essential. Who will take care of the children and how can you secure their financial future?

Your local Cooperative Extension Service often offers classes or publications on estate planning. The time to plan ahead is now. Look in the blue pages of your phone book for the nearest Cooperative Extension office, as they are in almost every county across the country.

Free Help Fighting an Electric Bill or Stopping a Turn Off

The state utility commissions can help you fight high gas or electric bills. Some will even come out and make sure that your meter is not over charging you. They don't have money to pay for your bills, but they can negotiate payment arrangements with the company for you or suggest non-profit organizations that may have emergency funds to help. For example Maryland suggests the Fuel Fund for Central Maryland or the Maryland Energy Assistance program. The office can also force the utility not to cut off your service because of medical emergencies or cold weather. Contact your state utility commission listed in the blue pages of your phone book for further assistance.

Free Legal Help to Fight Care Dealers and Repair Shops

When you can't get satisfaction from the manager or owner, then it is time to bring in the big guns:

- ✦ Your state attorney general's office is set up to handle automobile complaints. Sometimes all you have to do is send a letter to the attorney general with a copy to the business owner.
- ✦ Automotive Consumer Action Program (AUTOCAP) is a complaint handling system sponsored by the automobile industry for new or used car purchases from NEW car dealers only. To find a source in your area, contact: National Automobile Dealers Association, 8400 Westpark Drive, McLean, VA 22102; 703-821-7000; {www.nada.org/}
- ✦ Better Business Bureau (BBB) Auto Line is a FREE, out-of-court arbitration program, paid for by the business community to handle automobile complaints between consumers and most auto manufacturers. Contact your local Better Business Bureau or BBB Auto Line, Dispute Resolution Division, Council of Better Business Bureaus, Inc., 4200 Wilson Blvd, Suite 800, Arlington, VA 22202; 703-276-0100; {www.bbb.org/complaints/BBBautoLine.asp}

Money To Pay Your Legal Bills

Many lawyers around the country offer their services for free to those who cannot cover the costs of legal services. In addition, special Pro Bono projects are underway at the American Bar Association, including the Child Custody Project, Immigration Development Project and the Rural Pro Bono Delivery Initiative.

If you need legal services, you can contact your local bar association to see who is offering to do Pro Bono work or you can contact the American Bar Association, 740 15th St., NW, Washington, DC 20005; 202-662-1000; {www.abanet.org/legalservices/probono/home.html}. A directory of Pro Bono organizations is available on this website.

Lawyer's Referral Service

The ***American Bar Association's*** lawyer referral service is designed to assist you in finding the appropriate service-provider to help you solve your legal problem. There are two steps to this process: first, helping you determine whether you need to see a lawyer, and second, referring you to a lawyer who handles your type of case or to an appropriate community or governmental agency if that will be of more help to you. Lawyer referral can also provide you with information on procedures in the courts and legal system in your community.

When you contact lawyer referral, be prepared to briefly describe your situation so that the consultant can determine what kind of help you need. Lawyer Referral does not offer legal advice or free legal services. If you are referred to an attorney, you are entitled to a half-hour initial consultation at no charge, or for a nominal fee that goes to fund the lawyer referral service's operation. If additional legal services are required, you may choose to hire the lawyer.

It is important to discuss legal fees and costs with the lawyer. We strongly recommend that you and the lawyer sign a written fee agreement, so that there is no question about what services the lawyer will perform, and what those services will cost you.

Contact your state Bar Association listed in your state capitol or The American Bar Association, 750 N. Lake Shore Dr., Chicago, IL 60611; 312-988-5000; Email: {info@abanet.org}; {www.abanet.org}.

Emergency Shelter, Housing & Counseling for Violence Victims

If violence is ripping your life apart, you have nowhere to go, and you do not know how to reclaim your life, the YWCA, the nation's leading provider of shelter and services to women and their families can help you! In the United States, more than 650,000 people come to the YWCA each year for services and support overcome violence. For more information about the services offered in your state, contact your local YWCA.

The YWCA takes a holistic approach to helping women escape, recover from and prevent violence in their lives and the lives of their families. Many local YWCAs offer programs and services including emergency shelter for women and children, transitional housing, support to victims of rape and sexual assault, individual and group counseling, peer support, self-defense training, programs for batterers and legal advocacy.

Contact: YWCA of the U.S.A., Empire State Building, Suite 301, 350 Fifth Ave., New York, NY 10118; 212-273-7800; Fax: 212-465-2281; {www.ywca.org}. National Domestic Violence Hotline 800-799-SAFE; hearing impaired 800-787-3224.

When All Else Fails

People forget that they can turn to their representative or senators for help resolving a complaint. You vote these people into office, and most of them want to stay there. They know that if they can help you, then you and your family will vote for them in each and every election.

Their offices have case managers whose job is to cut the red-tape and push your case through quickly. Look in your phone book for their local office or you can call U.S. House of Representatives, Washington, DC 20515; 202-224-3121; {www.house.gov}; or U.S. Senate, Washington, DC 20510; 202-224-3121; {www.senate.gov}.

$$$ Pay Your College And Education Bills

So you know you need more education to get ahead, but you are not sure how to pay for it? Never fear, we are here! There are billions of dollars worth of money just waiting to help you achieve your dreams. You just need to know where to look. The following sections outline all the federal and state money programs for college, as well as scholarship search engines and hundreds of college scholarships offered by various organizations.

Uncle Sam wants you to go to college, so that is why he set up the Federal government's great website {www.students.gov}. Here you can find information on:

- preparing for college
- vocational schools
- study abroad
- distance education
- fellowships and internships
- student job programs
- scholarships, grants, and student loans
- state financial aid
- work-study
- and much more.

Now there is no reason you can't go to college. There is even help choosing a major!

Happy hunting!

Federal Money for College

Most people have heard of the federal government's largest money programs for students like the Pell Grant Program and the Guaranteed Student Loan program. But did you know that the federal government is the single largest source of money for students — whether they show financial need or not? It's true, but very few people are aware of the many grant programs in place and just waiting to give money to those students smart enough to find out about them. These little known programs provide students with:

- $15,000 to do graduate studies in housing related topics for the Department of Housing and Urban Development
- Money to finance a graduate degree in criminal justice from the Department of Justice
- $14,000 to get a graduate degree in foreign languages from the Department of Education
- $8,800 plus tuition and expenses to be a nurse from the Department of Health and Human Services

How To Apply

Requirements and application procedures vary widely from program to program. Some programs accept applications once a year, while others award money on a year round basis. Some programs require you to apply directly to the main funding office in Washington, DC, while other programs distribute the money to local organizations, which then distribute funds to individuals. Many of the programs give the money directly to the schools, and then the schools distribute it. For those, you need to request a listing of the schools that receive the funds.

All these federal programs are listed in the Catalog of Federal Domestic Assistance, which is available in most libraries. This catalogue lists all the government grant and loan programs available. The program name and number in parenthesis refer to this publication. You can search the catalog easily at {www.cfda.gov}.

Get Loans Directly From Your School
(Federal Direct Loan 84.268)

The Direct Loan Program was begun to provide loans directly to students through schools, rather than through private lenders. Borrowers complete an application, the Free Application for Federal Student Aid (FAFSA), for all Department student financial aid programs. Schools receive the funds and then disburse them to students.

There are four different direct loans: Federal Direct Stafford/Ford Loans are for students who demonstrate financial need; Federal Direct Unsubsidized Stafford/Ford Loans are for students regardless of financial need; Federal Direct PLUS Loans are for parents to pay for their children's education; and Federal Direct Consolidation Loans help combine one or more federal education loans into one loan. The amount one can borrow depends upon dependent/ independent status of student and year in school. There are several different repayment options including income contingent repayment plan. Interest rates for loans vary each year.

For your Free Application for Federal Student Aid, contact Federal Student Aid Information Center, P.O. Box 84, Washington, DC 20044; 800-433-3243. Contact: U.S. Department of Education, Direct Loan Payment Center, P.O. Box 746000, Atlanta, GA 30374; 800-557-7394; {www.ed.gov/DirectLoan/}.

$15,000 For Graduate Students To Study Overseas
(Educational Exchange - Graduate Students 19.400)

Graduate students who would like to spend a year studying overseas can apply for the Fulbright Program, where if accepted, they will receive round trip transportation, tuition, books, maintenance for one academic year in one country, and health insurance. Students apply through the Fulbright program adviser located at their college or university, or they can apply as an at-large applicant by contacting the New York office of the Institute of International Education. Money available: $14,500,000. The average award per student is $21,000, but awards can range anywhere from $1,200 to $35,000.

Contact Institute of International Education, 809 United Nations Plaza, New York, NY 10017; 212-883-8200, Fax: 212-984-5452; {www.iie.org}.

$4,000 Grants For Students Having Trouble Paying Tuition

(Federal Supplemental Education Opportunity Grants 84.007)

If you are working towards your first undergraduate baccalaureate degree and are having trouble paying the bills, you may qualify for money through the Federal Supplemental Educational Opportunity Grants (FSEOG) program. Grants are for undergraduate study and range from $100 to $4000 per academic year, with the student eligible to receive a FSEOG for the time it takes to complete their first degree.

Students should contact the Financial Aid office of the school they attend or plan to attend for information regarding application.

A student *Financial Aid Handbook* is available, as is a list of grantee institutions by contacting the Federal Student Aid Information Center, P.O. Box 84, Washington, DC 20044; 800-433-3243. Money available: $725,000,000. Estimated average award is $748.

Contact Student Financial Assistance Program, Office of the Assistant Secretary for Post-Secondary Education, U.S. Department of Education, 400 Maryland Ave., SW, Washington, DC 20202; 800-USA-LEARN, TTY: 800-437-0833, Fax: 202-401-0689; {www.ed.gov/offices/OSPAP}.

Money For a Foreign Language Degree

(National Resource Centers and Fellowships Program for Language and Area or Language and International Studies 84.015)

In this global world, foreign languages and international studies are becoming increasingly important. The Department of Education has funds to support centers which promote instruction in foreign language and international studies at colleges and universities. In addition, there are graduate fellowships to pursue this course of study in order to develop a pool of international experts to meet our nation's needs.

Funds for centers may be used for instructional costs of language and area and international studies programs, administration, lectures and conferences, library resources and staff, and travel. Grants for fellowships include tuition, fees, and a basic subsistence allowance. Students must apply to those institutions that received the money.

For a listing of institutions that received money, contact the office listed below. Students can contact these institutions directly. Money available: Grants: $27,500,000.

Contact Higher Education Programs, U.S. Department of Education, 1990 K Street, NW, Washington, DC 20006; 202-502-7700; {www.ed.gov/offices/OPE/HEP/iegps/flasf.html}

Travel Overseas For Your Doctorate Research
(International Overseas Doctoral Dissertation 84.022)

This program provides opportunities for graduate students to engage in full-time dissertation research abroad in modern foreign language and area studies with the exception of Western Europe. The program is designed to develop research knowledge and capability in world areas not widely included in American curricula. Money available: $4,150,000. Grants average $27,000.

For more information, contact Advanced Training and Research Team, International Education and Graduate Programs Service, Office of Postsecondary Education, U.S. Department of Education, 400 Maryland Ave., SW, Washington, DC 20202; 202-502-7632; {www.ed.gov/offices/OPE/Professionals}.

Money For Students And Teachers To Travel Overseas
(Fulbright-Hays Training Grants - Group Projects Abroad 84.021)

The program objective is to help educational institutions improve their programs in modern foreign language and area studies through overseas study/travel seminar group research, advanced foreign language training, and curriculum development. Funds are available to support overseas study/travel seminar group research and advanced foreign language training. Grant funds may be used for international travel, maintenance allowances, rental of instructional facilities in the country of study, and more. Money available: $4,000,000.

Contact Higher Education Programs, U.S. Department of Education, Office of PostSecondary Education, 1990 K Street, NW, 6th Floor, Washington, DC 20006; 202-502-7700; {www.ed.gov/offices/OPE/HEP/iegps/gpa.html}.

Loans To Go To School
(Federal Family Education Loans 84.032)

Guaranteed loans for educational expenses are available from eligible lenders such as banks, credit unions, savings and loan association, pension funds, insurance companies, and schools to vocational, undergraduate, and graduate students enrolled at eligible institutions. Loans can be used to pay the costs associated with obtaining a college education. The PLUS program is also available, which allows parents to borrow for their dependent student. More information is available by contacting the lending institution regarding the loans available and the application procedure. Money available: $35,000,000,000.

Contact Office of Student Financial Assistance, U.S. Department of Education, Washington, DC 20202; 800-4FED-AID; {www.ifap.ed.gov/}.

Money For Ph.D. Students To Do Research Overseas

(Fulbright-Hays Training Grants - Doctoral Dissertation Research Abroad 84.022)

Graduate students now have the opportunity to engage in full time dissertation research abroad in modern foreign language and area studies. This program is designed to develop research knowledge and capability in world areas not widely included in American curricula. The grant includes a basic stipend, round trip airfare, baggage allowance, tuition payments, local travel, and more. Candidates apply directly to the institutions at which they are enrolled. Money available: $4,150,000.

Contact Karla Ver Bryck Block, Advanced Training and Research Team, Center for International Education, Office of Assistant Secretary for Postsecondary Education, U.S. Department of Education, 400 Maryland Ave., SW, Washington, DC 20202, 202-502-7632, {www.ed.gov/offices/OPE/HEP/iegps/ddrap.html}

Work-Study Program Pays For School

(Federal Work-Study Program 84.033)

Part-time employment is available to students to help meet education expenses. This program pays an hourly wage to undergraduates. Graduate students may be paid by the hour or may receive a salary. There are Federal Work-Study jobs both on and off campus. Money can be used to help defray the costs of higher education.

Students should contact the educational institution they attend or plan to attend to find out about application procedures. A Student Financial Aid Handbook is available, as is a list of grantee institutions, by contacting Federal Student Aid Information Center, P.O. Box 84, Washington, DC 20044; 800-433-3243. Money available: $1,011,000,000. Average Award: $1,252.00.

Contact Division of Policy Development, Student Financial Assistance Programs, Office of Assistant Secretary for Postsecondary Education, 400 Maryland Ave., SW, Washington, DC 20202; 800-443-3243; {www.ed.gov/offices/OSFAP/Students}.

Get Help To Study
(TRIO Upward Bound 84.047)

This program generates skills and motivation necessary for success in education beyond high school among low income and potential first-generation college students and veterans. The goal of the program is to increase the academic performance and motivational levels of eligible enrollees so that they have a better chance of completing secondary school and successfully pursuing postsecondary educational programs.

Eligible students must have completed the eighth grade and be between the ages of 13 and 19, enrolled in high school, and need such services to achieve their goal of college. The program provides instruction in reading, writing, study skills, and mathematics. They can provide academic, financial, or personal counseling, tutorial services, information on student financial assistance, assistance with college and financial aid applications, and more.

Contact your local Upward Bound project to find out more about this program. For a listing of institutions that received money contact the office listed below. Money available: $264,000,000.

Contact Margaret Wingfield, Federal Trio Programs, College and University Preparation and Support Team, Office of

Post Secondary Education, U.S. Department of Education, 400 Maryland Ave., SW, Washington, DC 20202-5249; 202-502-7600; {www.ed.gov/offices/OPE/OHEP/trio}.

Low-Interest Student Loans
(Federal Perkins Loan Program 84.038)

Low-interest loans are available to eligible post-secondary students with demonstrated financial need to help meet educational expenses. Students can borrow money to meet the costs of school. These loans are for students with exceptional financial need. To apply, contact the Financial Aid office of the school you attend or plan to attend. A student Financial Aid Handbook is available, as well as a list of grantee institutions by contacting the Federal Student Aid Information Center, P.O. Box 84, Washington, DC 20044; 800-433-3242; TTY: 800-730-8913. Money available: $100,000,000.

Contact Division of Policy Development Student Financial Assistance Programs, Office of Assistant Secretary for

Postsecondary Education, U.S. Department of Education, 400 Maryland Ave., SW, Washington, DC 20202-5446; 800-433-3242; {www.ed.gov/offices/OSFAP/Students}.

$2,700 Grants To Go To School
(Federal Pell Grant Program 84.063)

Grants are available to students with financial need to help meet education expenses. Grants may not exceed $2,700 per year, and must be used for student's first bachelor's or other professional degree. Once an application is completed, the student's financial eligibility for assistance is calculated and the agency then notifies the student of eligibility. A Free Application for Federal Student Aid is available from the Federal Student Aid Information Center, P.O. Box 84, Washington, DC 20044; 800-433-3243. Money available: $8,756,000,000. Average award: $2057.

Contact Division of Policy Development, Office of Student Financial Assistance, U.S. Department of Education, 400 Maryland Ave., SW, Washington, DC 20202; 800-433-3243; {www.ed.gov/offices/OSFAP/Students/}.

Aid For Students Who Want To Help The Deaf
(Training Interpreters For Individuals Who Are Deaf and Individuals Who Are Deaf-Blind 84.160)

This program supports projects that train new interpreters and improve the skills of manual, oral, and cued speech interpreters already providing services to individuals who are deaf and individuals who are deaf-blind. Grants are awarded for training, classroom instruction, workshops, seminars, and field placements. Ten grants are awarded to colleges and universities that have ongoing sign language/oral interpreter training programs of proven merit.

Programs include training courses connected to degree programs in interpreting; short term practical training leading to interpreter certification; and workshops, seminars, and practices. Students must apply to those institutions that have received the program money. For a listing of institutions that received money contact the office listed below. Money available: $2,100,000.

Contact Mary Lovley, Office of Special Education and Rehabilitation Services, U.S. Department of Education, 400 Maryland Ave., SW, Washington, DC 20202; 202-205-9393; TTY: 202-401-3664; {www.ed.gov/offices/OSERS/RSA/PGMS/RT/scholrsp.html}.

Money For Students Interested In Helping People With Disabilities (Rehabilitation Training 84.129)

This program supports projects that provide new personnel and improve the skills of existing personnel trained in providing vocational rehabilitation services to individuals with disabilities in areas targeted as having personnel shortages.

Training grants are provided in fields directly related to the vocational and independent living rehabilitation of individuals with disabilities, such as rehabilitation counseling, independent living, rehabilitation medicine, physical and occupational therapy, speech-language, pathology and audiology, and more. Projects include residency scholarships in physical medicine and rehabilitation; teaching and graduate scholarships in rehabilitation counseling; and more.

Students must apply to those institutions that have received the program money. A catalogue of projects is available that provides address, phone number, contact person, and an abstract for each grant awarded. Money available: $25,000,000. Contact Tim Muzzio at Rehabilitation Services Administration, Office of Special Education and Rehabilitation Services, U.S. Department of Education, 400 Maryland Ave., Washington, DC 20202; 202-205-8926; {www.ed.gov/offices/OSERS/RSA/PGMS/RT/scholrsp.html}.

$25,400 Per Year For Graduate Study (Jacob K. Javits Fellowships 84.170)

This program provides fellowships to individuals of superior ability for graduate study in the fields within the arts, humanities, and social sciences. Money can be used to support a student while he or she attends an institution of higher education.

To apply for these fellowships contact the Federal Student Aid Information Center, P.O. Box 84, Washington, DC 20044; 800-4-FED-AID. Money available: $10,800,000. Contact Higher Education Programs, Office of Postsecondary Education, U.S. Department of Education, 1990 K Street, NW, 6th Floor, Washington, DC 20006; 202-502-7567; Carolyn Proctor, {www.ed.gov/offices/OPE/HEP/iegps/javits.html}.

$1,500 Per Year For College (Robert C. Byrd Honors Scholarships 84.185)

Scholarships are available to exceptionally able students who show promise of continued academic achievement. Scholarships for up to four years to study at any institution of higher education are available through grants to the states. The scholarships are awarded on the basis of merit and are renewable.

To apply for this grant award, interested applicants must contact their state educational agency, which administers this program. Money available: $41,001,000. U.S. Department of Education, Office of Student Financial Assistance, Office of the Assistant Secretary for Postsecondary Education, Division of Higher Education Incentive Programs, 400 Maryland Ave., SW, Washington, DC 20024; 202-502-7700; {www.ed.gov/offices/OPE/HEP/idues/byrd.html}. Contact Argelia Velez-Rodrigues, 202-502-7582.

Money For Graduate Study

(Graduate Assistance In Areas Of National Need 84.200)

Fellowships are available through graduate academic departments to graduate students of superior ability who demonstrate financial need and are able to enhance the capacity to teach and conduct research in areas of national need.

Designated academic areas change each year and are currently biology, chemistry, engineering, foreign languages, mathematics, and physics. Money can be used to support a student completing a graduate degree program. Students must apply to those institutions that have received the money. For a listing of institutions that received money contact the office listed below. Money available: $31,000,000. Contact International Education and Graduate Programs Service, Office of Postsecondary Education, U.S. Department of Education, 400 Maryland Ave., SW, Washington, DC 20202; 202-502-7700; {www.ed.gov/offices/OPE/HEP/iegps/gaann.html}. Contact: Brandy Silverman, 202-502-7886.

Grants for the Environment

(Training and Fellowships for the Environmental Protection Agency-66.607)

The funds for this program are to provide resources to allow for training and fellowships related to environmental issues. Money available $35,000,000. Grants range from $4,000 to $5,000,000. For more information, contact Environmental Protection Agency, Grants Administration Division, 3903R, 401 M St., SW, Washington, DC 20460; {www.epa.gov/epapages/epahome/intern.htm}.

Grants For Those Who Have Trouble Paying Tuition

(Ronald E. McNair Post Baccalaureate Achievement 84.217)

This program provides grants to institutions of higher education to prepare low income, first-generation college students and students underrepresented in graduate education for graduate study. Money can be used to pay the costs for research and other scholarly activities, summer internships, seminars, tutoring, academic counseling, and securing admission and financial assistance for graduate study.

Students must apply to those institutions that have received the money. For a listing of institutions that received money contact the office listed below. Money available: $36,856,000. Contact U.S. Department of Education, Federal Trio Programs, College and University Support Team, Office of Postsecondary Education, 400 Maryland Ave., SW, Washington, DC 20202; 202-502-7600; {www.ed.gov/offices/OPE/HEP/trio/mcnair.html}.

Money For Public Service Students

(Harry S. Truman Scholarship Program 85.001)

A special scholarship program for college juniors has been established to encourage students to pursue careers in public service. Money can be used to support a student completing his or her undergraduate and graduate studies.

A faculty representative is appointed for each school and is responsible for publicizing the scholarship program; soliciting recommendations on students with significant potential for leadership; conducting a competition on campus; and forwarding the institution's official nomination to the Truman Scholarship Review committee. For more information write to the Foundation listed above. Money available: $3,187,000. Contact Louis Blair, Executive Secretary Truman Scholarship Foundation, 712 Jackson Place, NW, Washington, DC 20006; 202-395-4831; {www.truman.gov}.

Money For Minority Students At Junior Colleges Who Are Energy Majors

(Minority Technical Education Program 81.082)

The program objective is to provide scholarship funding to financially needy minority honor students pursuing training in energy related technologies and to develop linkages with energy industries. Scholarship funds are available to defray costs of tuition, books, tools, transportation, and laboratory fees for minority students attending junior colleges and majoring in energy related field. The students must apply to those institutions that received the money. For a listing of those institutions contact the office listed below. Money available: $500,000.

Contact Office of Economic Impact and Diversity, U.S. Department of Energy, Ed-1, Forrestal Building, 5B-110, Washington, DC 20585; 202-586-8383; {www.hr.doe.gov/ed/OMEI/Omei.html}.

Part-Time Jobs In The Government
(Student Temporary Employment Program 27.003)

The program gives students 16 years of age and older an opportunity for part time temporary employment with federal agencies in order to allow them to continue their education without interruptions caused by financial pressures. The money can be used to pay expenses while attending school. Apply for this program through the youth division of the local office of the State Employment Service.

Look in the government section of your phone book to find an office near you, or contact the Main State Employment Service office for referral to a local office. Contact Employment Service, Office of Personnel Management, 1900 E St., NW, Washington, DC 20415; 202-606-0830; {www.usajobs.opm.gov}.

Internships For Graduate Students To Work AT 54 Government Agencies
(Presidential Management Intern Program 27.013)

The PMI Program is a two-year entry-level employment and career development program designed to attract to the federal civil service men and women with graduate degrees from diverse cultural and academic backgrounds. Interns will have demonstrated academic excellence, possess management and leadership potential, and have a commitment to and a clear interest in a public service career. Nominees for the PMI Program undergo a rigorous, competitive screening process.

Being selected as a PMI Finalist is a first step, but does not guarantee a job. Agencies designate positions for the PMIs and each establishes its own procedures for considering and hiring PMIs. Once hired by agencies, PMIs are encouraged to work with their agencies to establish an "individual development plan." PMIs participate in training conferences, seminars, and congressional briefings. Money can be used to pay for expenses.

An application form and more information can be requested by contacting the Career America Hotline at 912-757-3000. Contact U.S. Office of Personnel Management, Philadelphia Service Center, Federal Building, 600 Arch St., Philadelphia, PA 19106; 215-597-7136, 215-597-1920; {www.usajobs.opm.gov}.

Money For Nursing Students
(Nursing Student Loans 93.364)

The Nursing Student Loan program provides for long-term, low-interest loans to full-time and half-time financially needy students pursuing a course of study leading to a diploma, associate, baccalaureate or graduate degree in nursing. Federal funds for this program are allocated to accredited public or nonprofit nursing schools. These schools are responsible for selecting the recipients of loans and for determining the amount of assistance a student requires.

To apply for this loan, contact the student financial aid office at the school where you intend to apply for admission or where you are enrolled. Interest rate is 5%. Money available: $4,500,000. Contact Mary Farrington, Division of Health Careers, Diversity and Development, Bureau of Health Professions, Health Resources and Services Administration, Public Health Service, U.S. Department of Health and Human Services Administration, Parklawn Building, Room 8-34, 5600 Fishers Lane, Rockville, MD 20857; 301-443-4776; {http://bhpr.hrsa.gov/dsa/}.

Money for Health Profession Students

(Health Professions Student Loans 93.342)

The Health Professions Student Loan Program provides long-term, low interest rate loans to full-time financially needy students pursuing a degree in dentistry, optometry, pharmacy, pediatric medicine, or veterinary medicine. Under this program, funds are made available to schools for the establishment of revolving student loan funds.

To apply for this loan, contact the student financial aid office at the school where you intend to apply for admission or where you are enrolled. Loans can not exceed tuition. The interest rate is 5%. A Health Professions Student Loan Fact Sheet is available from the office listed above. Money available: $14,000,000.

Contact Mary Farrington, Division of Health Careers, Diversity and Development, Bureau of Health Professions, Health Resources and Services Administration, Public Health Service, U.S. Department of Health and Human Services Administration, Parklawn Building, Room 8-34, 5600 Fishers Lane, Rockville, MD 20857; 301-443-4776; {http://bhpr.hrsa.gov/dsa/}.

Loans For Disadvantaged Health Profession Students

(Loans for Disadvantaged Students 93.342)

Loans for Disadvantaged Students Program provides funding to eligible health professions schools for the purpose of providing long-term, low-interest loans to assist full-time, financially needy, disadvantaged students to pursue a career in allopathic or osteopathic medicine, dentistry, optometry, podiatry, pharmacy, or veterinary medicine. To apply for this loan, contact the student financial aid office at the school where you intend to apply for admission or where you are enrolled. *Loans For Disadvantaged Students Fact Sheet* is available from the office listed below. Money available: $14,000,000.

Contact Mary Farrington, Division of Health Careers, Diversity and Development, Bureau of Health Professions' Health Resources and Services Administration, Public Health Service, U.S. Department of Health and Human Services Administration, Parklawn Building, Room 8-34, 5600 Fishers Lane, Rockville, MD 20857; 301-443-4776; {http://bhpr.hrsa.gov/dsa/}.

Money For Primary Care Students

(Health Professions Student Loans, Including Primary Care Loans 93.342)

The Primary Care Loan Program provides long-term low interest rate loans to full-time financially needy students pursuing a degree in allopathic or osteopathic medicine. Under this program, funds are made to schools to establish revolving student loan funds. Students must agree to enter and complete residency training in primary care and to practice in primary care until the loan is paid in full.

To apply for this loan, contact the student financial aid office at the school where you intend to apply for admission or where you are enrolled. Loans cannot exceed tuition. Money available: $14,000,000. Contact Mary Farrington, Bureau of Health Professions, Health Resources and Services Administration, Public Health Service, U.S. Department of Health and Human Services Administration, Parklawn Building, Room 8-34, 5600 Fishers Lane, Rockville, MD 20857; 301-443-4776; {http://bhpr.hrsa.gov/dsa/}.

Money For Faculty Loan Repayments

(Disadvantaged Health Professions Faculty Loan Repayment Program 93.923)

The Faculty Loan Repayment Program provides a financial incentive for degree-trained health professionals from disadvantaged backgrounds to pursue an academic career. The health professional must agree to serve as a member of a faculty of a health professions school, providing teaching services for a minimum of two years, faculty for schools of medicine, nursing, osteopathic medicine, dentistry, pharmacy, pediatric medicine, optometry, veterinary medicine, public health, or a school that offers a graduate program in clinical psychology. The federal government, in turn, agrees to pay as much as $20,000 of the outstanding principal and interest on the individual's educational loans.

To participate in the program, an individual must be from a disadvantaged background, must not have been a member of a faculty of any school at any time during the 18 month period preceding the date on which the program application is received, must have a degree or be enrolled as a full-time student in the final year of training leading to a degree in one of the eligible disciplines, and must have entered into a contract with an eligible health professions school to serve as a full-time faculty member for a minimum of two years. Money available: $1,003,000.

Contact Mary Farrington, Division of Health Careers, Diversity and Development, Bureau of Health Professions, Health Resources and Services Administration, Public Health Service, U.S. Department of Health and Human Services Administration, Parklawn Building, Room 8-34, 5600 Fishers Lane, Rockville, MD 20857; 301-443-4776; 888-275-4772; {http://bhpr.hrsa.gov/DSA/flrp/index.htm}.

Scholarships For Disadvantaged Health Profession Students

(Scholarships For Health Profession Students From Disadvantaged Backgrounds 93.925)

The Scholarships For Disadvantaged Students program provides funds to eligible schools for the purpose of providing scholarships to full-time financially needy students from disadvantaged backgrounds enrolled in health professions and nursing programs. Under this program, funds are awarded to accredited schools of medicine, osteopathic medicine, dentistry, optometry, pharmacy, podiatric medicine, veterinary medicine, nursing (diploma, associate, baccalaureate, and graduate degree), public health, allied health (baccalaureate and graduate degree programs of dental hygiene, medical laboratory technology, occupational therapy, physical therapy, radiologic technology), and graduate programs in clinical psychology.

The schools are responsible for selecting recipients, making reasonable determinations of need and disadvantaged student status, and providing scholarships that cannot exceed the student's financial need. To apply for this scholarship, contact the student financial aid office at the school where you intend to apply for admission or where you are enrolled. Money available: $46,000,000.

Contact Mary Farrington, Bureau of Health Professions, Health Resources and Services Administration, Public Health Service, U.S. Department of Health and Human Services Administration, Parklawn Building, Room 8-34, 5600 Fishers Lane, Rockville, MD 20857; 301-443-4776; {http://bhpr.hrsa.gov/dsa/}.

Money For American Indians Who Want To Be Health Care Professionals

(Health Professions Recruitment Program For Indians 93.970)

The program objective is to increase the number of American Indians and Alaskan Natives who become health professionals and money has been set aside to help identify students interested in the field and to assist them in enrolling schools. Some of the projects funded include the recruitment of American Indians into health care programs, a variety of retention services once students have enrolled, and scholarship support.

Students should contact their school directly for assistance. Money available: $2,881,321. Contact Indian Health Service, Division of Health Professions Support, 801 Thompson Ave., Suite 120, Rockville, MD 20852; 301-443-4242; {www.ihs.gov}.

Health Professions Scholarships For American Indians
(Health Professions Pregraduate Scholarship Program for Indians 93.123)

The program objective is to provide scholarships to American Indians and Alaskan Natives for the purpose of completing pregraduate education leading to baccalaureate degree in the areas of pre-medicine or pre-dentistry. Money can be used to support a student while completing their degree.

Contact the Indian Health Service for application information. Money available: $2,004,879. Awards range from $18,913 to $27,217. Contact Indian Health Service, Scholarship Program, 801 Thompson Ave., Suite 120, Rockville, MD 20852; 301-443-6197; {www.ihs.gov}.

Money For American Indians Who Need Extra Studies For Health Care Program
(Health Professions Preparatory Scholarship Program for Indians 93.971)

The program objective is to make scholarships available to American Indians and Alaskan Natives who need to take some extra courses in order to qualify for enrollment or re-enrollment in a health profession school. Money can be used for up to two years of scholarship support, and the funds can cover tuition, stipends, and books.

Students must apply to the Indian Health Service Office for application information. Money available: $1,024,584. Grants range from $17,000 to $26,019. Contact Indian Health Service, Scholarship Program, 801 Thompson Ave., Suite 120, Rockville, MD 20852; 301-443-6197; {www.ihs.gov}.

Scholarships For Health Care Professionals
(Health Professions Scholarship Program 93.972)

This program objective is to provide scholarships to American Indians and Alaskan natives attending health professions schools and who are interested in serving other Indians. Upon completion, scholarship recipients are obligated to serve in the Indian Health Service one year for each year of scholarship support, with a minimum of two years.

The health professions needed are listed annually in the Federal Register. The money can be used to support a student completing a health profession degree. Money available: $8,469,000. Grants range from $24,128 to $38,222. Contact Indian Health Service, Scholarship Program, 801 Thompson Ave., Suite 120, Rockville, MD 20852; 301-443-6197; {www.ihs.gov}.

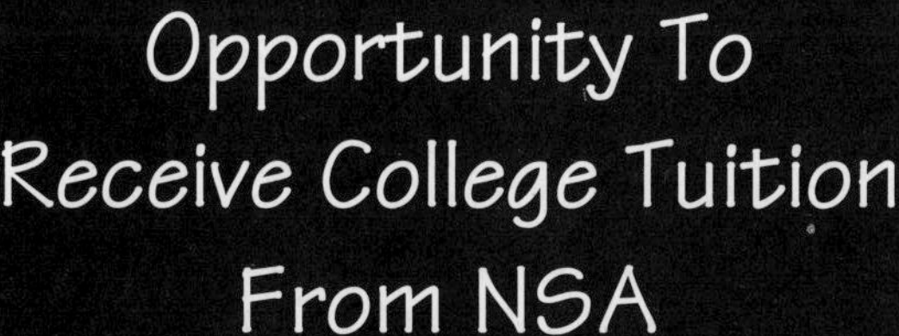

Opportunity To Receive College Tuition From NSA

(Mathematical Sciences Grants Program 12.901)

National Security Agency (NSA) will consider any student who meets the requirements below and who chooses a full-time college major in either computer science, electrical or computer engineering, languages or mathematics. Requirements consist of having a minimum SAT score of 1100 and a minimum composite ACT score of 25. Chosen students can receive college tuition, reimbursement for books, year-round salary, summer work and have a guaranteed job with the NSA after graduation.

Students must work for NSA for one and a half times their length of study, which is usually about five years. Money available: $2,600,000. Contact National Security Agency, Manager, Undergraduate Training Program, Attn: R51A, 9800 Savage Rd., Suite 6840, Ft. Meade, MD 20755-6840; 301-688-0400; {www.nsa.gov}.

Money For Dental Students For Advanced Residency Training

(Residency Training And Advanced Education in General Practice Of Dentistry 93.897)

The program objective is to assist schools of dentistry or dental training to institute residency training and advanced educational programs in the general practice of dentistry. The grant can be used to support personnel, residents or trainees who are in need of financial assistance, to purchase equipment, and for other expenses necessary to conduct the program. Money can be used to support a student while he or she completes a dental training program or residency. Students must apply to those institutions that have received the money.

For a listing of institutions that received money contact the office listed below.

Money available: $3,500,000. Contact Public Health and Dental Education Branch, Division of Public Health and Allied Health, Bureau of Health Professions, Health Resources and Services Administration, Public Health Service, U.S. Department of Health and Human Services, 5600 Fishers Lane, Room 8C-26, Rockville, MD 20857; 301-443-6880; {http://bhpr.hrsa.gov/dadphp/dadphp.htm}.

Health Careers Opportunity Program

(Health Careers Opportunity Program 93.822)

The Health Careers Opportunity Program provides assistance to individuals from disadvantaged backgrounds to obtain a health or allied health profession degree. Grants can be used to identify, recruit, and select individuals from minority and disadvantaged backgrounds for education and training in a health or allied health professions school; facilitate entry of eligible students into such schools; provide counseling or other services designed to assist such individuals in successfully completing their education and training; provide preliminary education for a period prior to entry into the regular course of health or allied health professions education, designed to assist students in successfully completing regular courses of education, or refer the appropriate individuals to institutions providing preliminary education; and provide disadvantaged students with information on financial aid resources.

For a listing of institutions that received money contact the office listed below. Money available: $34,795,000. Contact Division of Health Careers, Diversity and Development, Bureau of Health Professions, Health Resources and Services Administration, Public Health Services, U.S. Department of Health and Human Services, Room 8A-09, 5600 Fishers Lane, Rockville, MD 20857; 301-443-2100; {http://bhpr.hrsa.gov/dhpd/hcophome1.htm}.

Grants for Native Hawaiian Students

(Native Hawaiian Higher Education Program 84.316)

Grants are give to provide full or partial fellowship support for Native Hawaiian students enrolled at two or four year degree granting institutions of higher education. Awards are based on academic potential and financial need. Full or partial support will also be given to support Native Hawaiian students enrolled at post-baccalaureate degree granting institutions. Priority will be given to providing fellowship support for professions that are underrepresented in the Native Hawaiians community. Money available: $3,500,000.

For more information, contact Susana Easton, Higher Education Programs, Office of Postsecondary Education, Department of Education, 1990 K Street, NW, Washington, DC 20006; 202-502-7700; {www.ed.gov}.

Money For Nursing Students To Repay Their Loans

(Nursing Education Loan Repayment Agreements For Registered Nurses Entering Employment At Eligible Health Facilities 93.908)

As an incentive for registered nurses to enter into full time employment at health facilities with nursing shortages, this program assists in the repayment of their nursing education loans. The program is designed to increase the number of registered nurses serving designated nurse shortage areas. Nurses can use the money to pay off nursing student loans. An Applicant Information Bulletin For Registered Nurses is available at the address listed below. Money available: $15,000,000.

Contact Chief, Diversity and Basic Nurse Education Branch, Division of Nursing, Bureau of Health Professionals, Health Resources and Services Administration, 5600 Fishers Lane, Room 9-36, Rockville, MD 20857; 301-443-3232; 866-813-3753; {http://bphc.hrsa.gov/nursing/}.

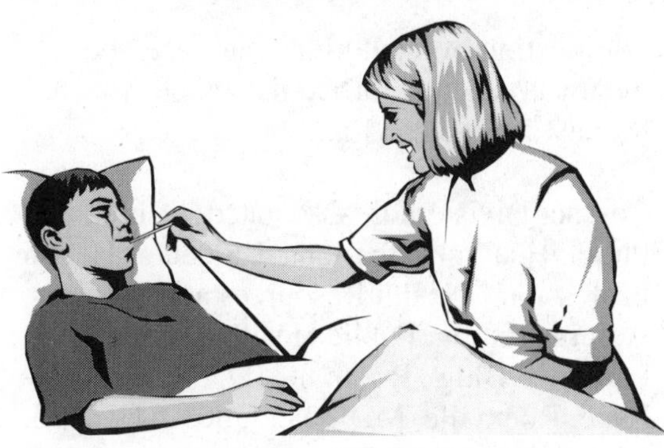

Scholarships For National Health Service Corps

(National Health Service Corps Scholarship Program 93.288)

The program objective is to provide service-conditioned scholarships to health professions students to assure an adequate supply of physicians, dentists, certified nurse midwives, certified nurse practitioners, and physician assistants in Health Professional Shortage Areas.

The scholarship pays for tuition and required fees, books, supplies, and equipment for the year, plus a monthly stipend to students ($1065 per month), and a single annual payment to cover the cost of all other reasonable educational expenses.

Each year of support incurs one year of service, with a two-year minimum service obligation required. Service sites are selected from those listed by the National Health Service Corps one year prior to service in federally designated Health Professional Shortage Areas. Money available: $39,600,000.

Contact National Health Service Corps Scholarships, Division of Scholarships and Loan Repayments, Bureau of Primary Health Care, Health Resources and Services Administration, Public Health Service, U.S. Department of Health and Human Services, 4350 East-West Hwy., 10th Floor, Bethesda, MD 20814; 301-594-4410; 800-638-0824; {www.bphc.hrsa.dhhs.gov/nhsc}.

Money To Train To Be A Professional Nurse

(Professional Nurse Traineeships 93.358)

The program objective is to prepare individuals who have completed basic nursing preparation as nurse educators, public health nurses, nurse midwives, and nurse practitioners, or as other clinical nursing specialists. Money can be used to support a student while they complete the professional nurse traineeships. Students must apply to those institutions that have received the program money. A fact sheet is available entitled *Program Guide for Professional Nurse Traineeship Program.*

For a listing of institutions that received money contact the office listed below. Money available: $18,547,184. Students may receive stipends up to $8,800 plus tuition and other expenses. Contact Division of Nursing, Bureau of Health Professions, Health Resources and Services Administration, Public Health Service, U.S. Department of Health and Human Services, 5600 Fishers Lane, Room 9-35, Rockville, MD 20857; 301-443-6333; {http://bhpr.hrsa.gov/}.

Money For Health Professionals Who Want To Be In Public Health

(Public Health Traineeships 93.964)

The program objective is to help support graduate students who are studying in the field of public health. Grants are given to colleges and universities offering graduate or specialized training in the public health field. Support is limited to the fields of biostatistics, epidemiology, environmental health, toxicology, public health nutrition, and maternal and child health.

Money can be used to support a student completing a public health degree, and includes a stipend, tuition, and fees, and a transportation allowance. Students must apply to those institutions that have received the money.

For a listing of institutions that received money contact the office listed below. Money available: $1,822,000.

Contact Division of Associated, Dental, and Public Health Professions, Bureau of Health Professions, Health Resources and Services Administration, Public Health Service, Parklawn Bldg., Room 8C-09, 5600 Fishers Lane, Rockville, MD 20857; 301-443-6896; {http://bhpr.hrsa.gov}.

Money For Job Safety and Health Training

(Occupational Safety and Health - Training Grants 93.263)

The program objective is to develop specialized professional and paraprofessional personnel in the occupational safety and health field with training in occupational medicine, occupational health nursing, industrial hygiene, and occupational safety. Money can be used to pay for long and short-term training and educational resource centers. Students must apply to those institutions that have received the money.

For a listing of institutions that received money contact the office listed below. Money available: $18,379,866. Contact National Institute for Occupational Safety and Health (NIOSH), Centers for Disease Control and Prevention, Public Health Service, U.S. Department of Health and Human Services, E-74, 1600 Clifton Rd., Atlanta, GA 30333; 404-498-2537; {www.cdc.gov/niosh}.

$30,000 To Study The Humanities

(Promotion of the Humanities - Fellowships and Stipends 45.160)

Fellowships and Summer Stipends provide support for scholars to undertake full-time independent research and writing in the humanities. Grants are available for 6 to 12 month fellowships and two months of summer study. Projects may contribute to scholarly knowledge or to the general public's understanding of the humanities. The proposed study or research may be completed during the grant period or it may be part of a longer project.

Contact the office listed below for application information. Money available: $7,000,000. Stipends are $5,000 for summer; $24,000 for 6-8 months; and $40,000 for 9-12 months. Contact Fellowships and Stipends, Division of Research and Education, National Endowment for the Humanities, 1100 Pennsylvania Ave., Room 318, Washington, DC 20506; 202-606-8200; {www.neh.gov}.

Money For Health Care Training In Rural Areas

(Interdisciplinary Training For Health Care For Rural Areas 93.192)

This program is designed to help fulfill the health care needs of people living in rural areas. Money is set aside to recruit and retain health care professionals in rural health care settings. Funds can be used for student stipends, postdoctoral fellowships, faculty training, and the purchase or rental of necessary transportation and telecommunication equipment. Money can be used to support health profession students while they complete their degree or training. Students must apply to those institutions that have received the money.

For a listing of institutions that received money contact the office listed below. Money available: $6,081,419. Contact

Division of Associated, Dental and Public Health Professions, Bureau of Health Professions, Health Resources and Services Administration, Room 8C-26, Parklawn Building, 5600 Fishers Lane, Rockville, MD 20857; 301-443-6867; {http://bhpr.hrsa.gov/interdisciplinary/rural.html}.

Grants For Pediatric Training

(Pediatric Residency in Primary Care 93.181)

Hospitals and schools of pediatric medicine can receive money to support residency programs for primary care pediatric practice. Funds can be used to cover the development and establishment of Pediatric Primary Care Residency programs and to provide resident stipends for those planning to specialize in pediatric primary care. Money can be used to support a resident while he or she completes his or her pediatric primary care residency. Students must apply to those institutions that have received the money.

For a listing of institutions that received money contact the office listed below. Money available: $770,000. Contact Division of Medicine, Bureau of Health Professions, Health Resources and Services Administration, Public Health Service, U.S. Department of Health and Human Services, Room 8C-26, Parklawn Building, 5600 Fishers Lane, Rockville, MD 20857; 301-443-6880; {http://bhpr.hrsa.gov}.

Money For Disadvantaged Students To Study Nursing

(Nursing Education Opportunities For Individuals From Disadvantaged Backgrounds 93.178)

Schools of nursing can receive financial assistance to meet the costs of projects that increase nursing education opportunities for individuals from disadvantaged backgrounds. Money can be used for counseling, preliminary education of students, and to support a student while completing a nursing degree. Students must apply to those institutions that have received the money.

For a listing of institutions that received money contact the office listed below. Money available: $6,173,000.

Contact Division of Nursing, Bureau of Health Professions, Health Resources and Services Administration, Public Health Services, U.S. Department of Health and Human Services, Room 8C-26, Parklawn Building, 5600 Fishers Lane, Rockville, MD 20857; 301-443-6880; {http://bhpr.hrsa.gov}.

Money To Repay Loans (National Health Service Corps Loan Repayment 93.162)

The National Health Service Corps provides for the repayment of educational loans for health professionals who agree to serve in a health manpower shortage area. Priority is given to primary care physicians, dentists, certified nurse midwives, certified nurse practitioners, and physicians' assistants. Money can be used to repay student loans. The amount of money available per professional is up to $25,000 a year during the first two years of practice and $35,000 for each year after that. Health professionals also receive a very competitive salary and benefits package. Money available: $49,820,000.

Contact National Health Service Corps Scholarships, Division of Scholarships and Loan Repayments, Bureau of Primary Health Care, Health Resources and Services Administration, Public Health Service, U.S. Department of Health and Human Services, 4350 East-West Hwy., 10th Floor, Bethesda, MD 20814; 301-594-4400; 800-435-6464; {www.nhsc.bhpr.hrsa.gov}.

Get Your Loans Paid Through Indian Health Service (Indian Health Service Loan Repayment Program 93.164)

To ensure that there are enough trained health professionals, the Indian Health Service provides for the repayment of loans to those professionals who agree to serve in an Indian Health Service Facility. Money can be used for the repayment of student loans. An application is available by contacting the office listed below. Money available: $16,923,500. The minimum period of participation is two years, and the maximum loan payment is $20,000 per year.

Contact Indian Health Service, Loan Repayment Program, 801 Thompson Ave., Suite 120, Rockville, MD 20852; 301-443-3369; {www.ihs.gov}.

Money For Minorities Pursuing a Health Professions Education (Programs of Excellence In Health Professions Education For Minorities 93.157)

The program helps health professions schools train minority health professionals. These funds can be used to recruit and retain faculty, improve the facilities and information resources, and improve student performance, student recruitment, and student research. Students must apply to those institutions that have received the money. For a listing of institutions that received money contact the office listed below. Money available: $32,637,370.

Contact Division of Disadvantaged Assistance, Bureau of Health Professions, Health Resources and Services Administration, Public Health Service, U.S. Department of Health and Human Services, Room 8A-09, Parklawn Building, 5600 Fishers Lane, Rockville, MD 20857; 301-443-2100; {http://bhpr.hrsa.gov/}.

Money To Train To Become A Nurse Anesthetist

(Nurse Anesthetist Traineeships 93.124)

Registered nurses can receive money to become nurse anesthetists through this program that provides funds for a maximum 18-month period of full-time study. Nurses must complete 12 months of study in a nurse anesthetist program. Money can be used to support a student while completing the training program. Students need to apply to those institutions that have received the money. For a listing of institutions that received money contact the office listed below. Student stipend is usually $8,800 plus tuition and other expenses. Money available: $3,036,158.

Contact Karen Breeden, Division of Nursing, Bureau of Health Professions, Health Resources and Services Administration, Public Health Service, U.S. Department of Health and Human Services, Room 9-36, 5600 Fishers Lane, Rockville, MD 20857; 301-443-5787; {http://bhpr.hrsa.gov}.

Money To Study Food

(Food and Agricultural Science National Needs Graduate Fellowship Grants 10.210)

The program awards grants to colleges and universities that have superior teaching and research competencies in the food and agricultural sciences. These grants are to be used to encourage outstanding students to pursue and complete a graduate degree in an area of the food and agricultural sciences for which there is a national need for development of scientific expertise.

Money can be used to support a student completing a graduate, masters, or doctorate degree. Students must apply to those institutions that received the money. For a listing of institutions that received money contact the office listed below. Money available: $2,873,280.

Contact Grants Program Manager, Office of Higher Education Programs, CSREES, U.S.

Department of Agriculture, Room 3912, South Building, Washington, DC 20250; 202-720-7854; {www.reeusda.gov/serd/hep/index.htm}.

Money To Study Community Planning and Development (Community Development Work-Study Program 14.512)

The Community Development Work-Study Program makes grants to institutions of higher education to provide assistance to economically disadvantaged and minority students. Students take part in community development work-study programs while they are enrolled full-time in graduate or undergraduate programs with that major. Grants are given to encourage minority and economically disadvantaged students to develop careers in community and economic development, community planning, and community management. Related fields include public administration, urban management, and urban planning.

Student assistance is in the form of work stipends, tuition support, and additional support to cover books and travel related to conferences and seminars. Students must apply to those institutions that received the money. For a listing of institutions that received money contact the office listed below. Money available: $3,000,000. Average grant per student is $30,000. Contact U.S. Department of Housing and Urban Development, Community Planning and Development, Office of University Partnerships, 451 7th St., SW, Room 8106, Washington, DC 20410; 202-708-3061, 800-245-2691; {www.hud.gov/progdesc/cdwsp.cfm}.

Money To Help Math Students and Summer Scientists (Independent Education and Science Projects and Programs 11.449)

This program objective is to increase the number of minority students enrolling in college and majoring in math, science and engineering. Another objective is to recruit scientists and engineers from the Boulder county area to serve as science/math tutors. Money can be used to help high school and middle school students who are part of the Math, Engineering, Science Achievement (MESA) Program in Colorado. It is also for students pursuing a course of study related to oceanic and atmospheric sciences and who are interested in a summer hands-on experience in a laboratory setting. Money can be used for transportation, housing and stipends for students during the summer months where students learn about the laboratories mission and perform hands-on assignments. Money available: $75,000.

Contact Tony Tafoya, NOAA/OAR, Building 20, 325 Broadway, Boulder, CO 80303; 303-497-6731; {www.noaa.gov}.

Money To Study Housing Issues

(Doctoral Dissertation Research Grant Program 14.516)

The program objective is to encourage doctoral candidates to engage in policy related housing and urban development research and to assist them in its timely completion. Money can used to support Ph.D candidates while they complete work towards their degree. Students must have a fully developed and approved dissertation proposal that addresses the purpose of this program. Students can request an application package from the address listed below or by calling HUD USER at 800-245-2691. Each student is eligible for up to $25,000 per year.

Contact Armand Carriere, Office of University Partnerships, U.S. Department of Housing and Urban Development, 451 7th St., SW, Room 8106, Washington, DC 20410; 202-708-3061; {www.huduser.org}.

Money For Members Of Indian Tribes To Go To College

(Indian Education-Higher Education Grant Program 15.114)

The program objective is to provide financial aid to eligible Indian students to enable them to attend accredited institutions of higher education. Members of an Indian tribe may be eligible for these grants to supplement the total financial aid package prepared by their college financial aid officer. Once you have been accepted by a college and have completed their financial aid application, you may request a grant application form from your tribal group. Money available: $25,267,060. The amount of assistance per student ranges from $300-$5000 per year.

Contact Bureau of Indian Affairs, Office of Indian Education Programs, Room MS-3512-MIB, U.S. Department of the Interior, 1849 C St., NW, Washington, DC 20240; 202-208-3478; {www.oiep.bia.edu}.

Money To Study The Break Up Of The USSR

(Russian, Eurasian, and East European Research and Training 19.300)

The program is designed to sustain and strengthen American expertise on the Commonwealth of Independent States, Georgia, the Baltic countries, and countries of Eastern Europe by supporting graduate training; advanced research; public dissemination of research data, methods, and findings; contact and collaboration among government and private specialists; and first hand experience of the (former) Soviet Union and Eastern European countries by American specialists, including on site conduct of advanced training and research. Graduate students interested in conducting research on the Commonwealth of Independent States, Georgia, the Baltic countries, and the countries of Eastern Europe can receive fellowships which can support a student while conducting research or training.

Funds are given to nonprofit organizations and institutions of higher learning who act as intermediaries for the federal funds by conducting their own competitions to make the awards. Grants in the past include grants for onsite independent short term research; individual exchange fellowships for American graduate students to pursue research in the region; and advanced in-country language training fellowships in Russian, Ukrainian, Hungarian, Polish, and more. Students must apply to those institutions that received the money. For a listing of institutions that received money contact the office listed below. Money available: $5,000,000. Contact Eurasian and East European Research and Training Program, INR/RES, U.S. Department of State, 2201 C St., NW, Room 2251, Washington, DC 20520; 202-736-4572; {www.state.gov/}.

Money For Criminal Justice Majors

(Criminal Justice Research and Development - Grant Research Fellowships 16.562)

The program objective is to improve the quality and quantity of knowledge about crime and the criminal justice system. Additionally, the program seeks to increase the number of persons who are qualified to teach in collegiate criminal justice programs, to conduct research related to criminal justice issues, and to perform more effectively within the criminal justice system. Students can receive a fellowship for a year, plus, two to three months to visit the National Institute of Justice to work with staff as an intern.

This competitive program provides fellowship stipends, major project costs and certain university fees, round trip travel expenses to the Institute, and housing costs. Detailed information can be received by requesting the NIJ Research Plan from the National Criminal Justice Reference Service, Box 6000, Rockville, MD 20850; 800-851-3420. Money available: $120,000. Maximum grant per student $15,000. Contact National Institute of Justice, 633 Indiana Ave., SW, Washington, DC 20531; 202-307-2942; {www.ncjrs.org}.

$3,000 A Year To Be A Merchant Marine

(State Marine Schools 20.806)

The program objective is to train merchant marine officers in State Marine Schools. You can receive $3,000 per year to train to be a merchant marine officer at a designated State Marine School. In exchange for this incentive payment program, you must commit yourself to a minimum of five years duty to the Maritime Administration, which can be satisfied by: serving as a merchant marine officer aboard vessels; as an employee in a U.S. maritime related industry, profession or marine science; or as a commissioned officer on active duty in an armed force of the U.S. or in the National Oceanic and Atmospheric Administration.

You must also remain in a reserve unit of an armed force for a minimum of eight years.

Students need to apply to one of the State Marine Schools. Money available: $7,457,000. Contact Office of Maritime Labor and Training, Maritime Administration, U.S. Department of Transportation, 400 7th St., SW, Washington, DC 20590; 202-366-5755; {www.marad.dot.gov}.

All Expenses Plus $558 A Month To Be A Merchant Marine

(U.S. Merchant Marine Academy – Kings Point 20.807)

This program trains merchant marine officers while they attend the Merchant Marine Academy in Kings Point, NY. Students receive training, subsistence, books, quarters, uniforms, medical care, and program travel without cost. In addition, the student will receive a monthly wage from their steamship company employer. Money available: $47,822,000. An allowance is prescribed for all personnel for uniforms and textbooks. During the sea year a midshipman will earn $600 per month from the steamship employer.

Contact Office of Maritime Labor and Training, Maritime Administration, U.S. Department of Transportation, 400 Seventh St., SW, Washington, DC 20590; 202-366-5755; {www.marad.dot.gov}.

Money For Social, Behavioral, And Economic Sciences Students

(Social, Behavioral, and Economic Sciences 47.075)

The program objective is to promote the progress of the social, behavioral, and economic science; to facilitate cooperative research activities with foreign scientists, engineers, and institutions and to support understanding of the resources invested in science and engineering in the U.S. Funds are provided for U.S. scientists and engineers to carry out studies abroad, to conduct research, to engage in joint research projects with foreign counterpart organizations, and to support international scientific workshops in the U.S. and abroad.

Money can be used for paying associated costs necessary to conduct research or studies for doctorate students; and more. Students must contact the office listed below for application information. Money available: $168,790,000. Contact Assistant Director, Social, Behavioral, and Economic Research, National Science Foundation, 4201 Wilson Blvd., Suite 935Arlington, VA 22230; 703-292-8710; {www.nsf.gov}.

Money For Disabled Veterans To Go To College

(Vocational Rehabilitation For Disabled Veterans 64.116)

The program objective is to provide all services and assistance necessary to enable service-disabled veterans and service persons hospitalized pending discharge to achieve maximum independence in daily living and, to the maximum extent possible, to become employable and to obtain and maintain suitable employment. The fund provides for the entire cost of tuition, books, fees, supplies, and other services to help the veteran live with a reduced dependency on others while staying in their homes and communities. The veteran also receives a monthly allowance, a work-study allowance, and more. Enrollment can be in a trade, business, or technical schools, colleges, apprenticeship programs, cooperative farming, special rehabilitation facilities, or at home when necessary.

Students must obtain an application from any Veterans Affairs office or regional office. Money available: Direct payments: $436,638,000; Loan advances: $2,726,000.

Monthly full time allowances per student range from $448 for a single veteran to $655 for a veteran with two dependents, plus $47.76 for each dependent in excess of two. Contact Veterans Benefits Administration, Department of Veterans Affairs, Washington, DC 20420; 202-273-7419, 800-827-1000; {www.va.gov}.

Money For Spouses And Children Of Deceased Or Disabled Veterans To Go To School

(Survivors and Dependents Educational Assistance 64.117)

The program provides partial support to those seeking to advance their education who are qualifying spouses, surviving spouses, or children of deceased or disabled veterans who, as a result of their military service, have a permanent and total (100 percent) service connected disability, or a service personnel who have been listed for a total of more than 90 days as currently Missing in Action, or as Prisoners of War. Spouse, surviving spouse, or child of a deceased or disabled veteran can receive monthly payments to be used for tuition, books, subsistence, for courses, training, or college. Financial assistance is $485 per month, and there is tutorial assistance, vocational counseling and testing, and a work-study allowance. Benefits may be awarded for pursuit of associate, bachelor, or graduate degrees at colleges and universities, as well as study at business, technical, or vocational schools.

Information on the program and application forms are available from your local or regional Veterans Affairs office. Money available: $179,043,000. Contact Department of Veterans Affairs, Central Office, Washington, DC 20420; 202-273-7132, 800-827-1000; {www.va.gov}.

Money For Retired Veterans To Go To School
(All-Volunteer Force Educational Assistance 64.124)

This program helps servicemen readjust to civilian life after their separation from military service, assists in the recruitment and retention of highly qualified personnel in the active and reserve components in the Armed Forces, and extends the benefits of a higher education to those who may not otherwise be able to afford it. Honorably discharged veterans can take advantage of the Montgomery GI Bill Active Duty benefits, which provides funds to pursue professional or vocational education, and even covers correspondence courses.

Veterans can receive a monthly stipend while attending school, with the amount varying depending upon date of entry into the service and length of service. Additional information and application materials are available through any regional Veterans Affairs office. Money available: $1,376,127,000. A maximum allowance of $28,800 as basic assistance is available per student, as well as a work-study allowance, and up to $1,200 in tutorial assistance. Contact Department of Veterans Affairs, Central Office, Washington, DC 20420; 202-273-7132, 800-827-1000; {www.gibill.va.gov}.

Money For Vietnam Veterans To Go To School
(Post-Vietnam Era Veterans' Educational Assistance 64.120)

Post-Vietnam veterans who entered the Armed Services between 1977 and 1985 may be eligible for funds to obtain a college degree or vocational training. Through this program, the government matches $2 for every $1 the serviceman contributes. Some contribution to the fund must have been made prior to April 1, 1987. Contact your local or regional Veterans Affairs office for additional information or application materials. Money available: $15,151,000.

Up to a maximum of $8,100 of basic benefits is available per student, as well as a work-study allowance of minimum wage and tutorial assistance up to a maximum of $1,200. Contact Department of Veterans Affairs, Central Office, Washington, DC 20420; 202-273-7132, 800-827-1000; {www.va.gov}.

Volunteer And Earn Money To Pay For School
(AmeriCorps 94.006)

AmeriCorps is an initiative designed to achieve direct results in addressing the nation's critical education, human, public safety, and environmental needs at the community level. The program provides meaningful opportunities for people to serve their country in organized efforts, fostering citizen responsibility, building their community, and providing education opportunities for those who make a serious commitment to service.

Stipends can be used to support the person while they volunteer. Health care and childcare benefits may also be provided. Participants will also receive an education award, which may be used to pay for higher education or for vocational training, and may also be used to repay any existing student loans. Contact the Corporation for National Service to locate programs in your area or to apply for programs at the national level. Money available: $233,395,000.

Contact Corporation for National and Community Service, 1201 New York Ave., NW, Washington, DC 20525 202-606-5000, ext. 474; {www.americorps.org}.

Fellowships for Creative Writers and Translators
(Promotion of the Arts-Grants to Organizations and Individuals 45.024)

The National Endowment for the Arts provides grants to support Literature Fellowships, Fellowships for Creative Writers, Fellowships awarded to writers of poetry, fiction, and creative nonfiction to allow them to devote time to writing, research, travel, and to advance their writing careers. Money available: $32,242,000. Fellowships are usually $20,000. For more information, contact National Endowment for the Arts, 1100 Pennsylvania Ave., NW, Washington, DC 20506; 202-682-5400; {www.arts.gov}.

Scholarships for Minorities
(Higher Education Multicultural Scholars Program 10.220)

This program is designed to increase the ethnic and cultural diversity of the food and agricultural scientific and professional work force, and to advance the educational achievement of minority Americans. Money is given to colleges and universities that have a demonstrable capacity to attract, educate, and graduate minority students for careers as agriscience and agribusiness professionals. Funds can be used to support full-time undergraduate students pursuing a baccalaureate degree in an area of food and agricultural sciences. Money available: $958,080.

Contact National Programs Leader, Education Programs, CSREES, U.S. Department of Agriculture, Stop 2251, 1400 Independence Ave., SW, Washington, DC 20250; 202-720-1973; {www.reeusda.gov}.

Money To Study The Drug Abuse Field

(Drug Abuse National Research Service Awards for Research Training 93.278)

Individual grants are made to fellows seeking predoctoral or postdoctoral support for full time research training in the drug abuse field. It can be used to cover tuition fees, and more. Postdoctoral researchers are obligated to pay back their first year of support through a period of research and/or teaching activities. Predoctoral stipends are $18,156 and postdoctoral awards range from $26,256 to $48,852. Money available: $17,988,000.

Contact National Institute on Drug Abuse, National Institutes of Health, U.S. Department of Health and Human Services, Neurosciences Building, 6001 Executive Blvd., Bethesda, MD 20892; 301-443-6710; {www.nih.gov}.

State College Money

After checking out what money programs are available from the federal government, your next task is to find out what's available at the state level. There are close to 400 programs worth almost $3 billion dollars in financial aid available thru all 50 states. Just because you or your parents don't have the money to pay for college, that doesn't mean your dream of a college degree will never happen. Even if you do have the money, financial assistance from one of these programs could make things a little easier for all concerned.

Did you know that there are state money programs which:

- Pay for a singing degree?
- Give you money to study wildlife?
- Give you $2000 to go to vocational school?
- Pay for your nursing, teaching or law degree?
- Give you $7,000 to study marine sciences?

The advantages of many of these programs are that most people don't even know they exist, so your competition will be less. Each state has different requirements for their various programs, so you may need to do some checking on what specific programs might fit your needs. Some programs are exclusive to residents of a particular state, whereas others have no limitation on what school the student chooses to attend. In some cases, for teachers or health professionals a service requirement may exist which says that the student will practice in a particular state after graduation for a certain period of time.

What follows is a concise and comprehensive state-by-state listing of available programs. It will allow you to shop around for the best program to suit your individual needs. By remaining flexible and adjusting your educational goals to fit the program that most appeals to you, chances are you might find yourself pursuing the college education that you always thought was beyond your reach. Using this information might be an important first step in building a successful future for yourself.

STATE AID

Alabama

Alabama Commission on Higher Education
100 North Union Street
P.O. Box 30200
Montgomery, AL 36130-2000
334-242-1998
Fax: 334-242-0265
www.ache.state.al.us

General requirements: Resident of Alabama and attending an in-state school.

Programs Available:

Grants To Students Who Can't Afford Tuition (Alabama Student Assistance Program)
Grants To Students Attending Private Colleges (Alabama Student Grant Program)
Join The National Guard And Get $1,000 A Year For College (Alabama National Guard Assistance Program)
Grants and Loans To Nursing Students (Alabama Nursing Scholarships)
Tuition, Fees, And Books To Spouses and Children Of Veterans (Alabama GI Dependents Educational Benefit Program)
Grants To Children and Grandchildren of Veterans (American Legion Scholarship and American Legion Auxiliary Scholarship Programs)
Free Tuition If You're Over 60 (Senior Adult Scholarships)
Money For Jocks Going To Junior College (Junior and Community College Athletic Scholarships)
Money For Dancers, Singers, and Actors Attending Junior College (Junior and Community College Performing Arts Scholarships)
Grants To Children Of The Blind (Alabama Scholarships for Dependents of Blind Parents)
Grants For Dependents Of Fire Fighters And Police Officers Killed In The Line Of Duty (Police Officers and Fire Fighters Survivor's Educational Assistance Program)
Loans That Guarantee The Price Of Your Future Tuition (Prepaid College Tuition Program)
School Technology Scholarship Program for Alabama Teachers (Two Year College Academic Scholarship Program)
Scholarships and Loans to Become a Math or Science Teacher (Mathematics and Science Scholarship Program for Alabama Teachers)

Other Alabama Assistance Awards:

University Station
1600 Eighth Ave., S.
Birmingham, AL 35294

Alabama Board of Dental Scholarship
Alabama Board of Medical Scholarship
Alabama Board of Optometric Scholarship
Alabama State Chiropractic Association

Alaska

Alaska Commission on Postsecondary Education
3030 Vintage Blvd.
Juneau, AK 99801
907-465-2962
TTY: 907-465-3143
Fax: 907-465-5316
www.state.ak.us/acpe

General requirements: Alaska resident and attending an in-state or out-of-state school.

Programs Available:

Free Money To Go To School If You Work In Law Enforcement (Michael Murphy Memorial Scholarship Loan)
Money For 8 Years Of College If You Study Food Or Wildlife (A.W. "Winn" Brindle Memorial Scholarship Loan)
$7,500 A Year and Travel Money If You Study To Be A Teacher In A Small Town (Teacher Scholarship Loan Program)
$7000 A Year To Go To College in Alaska (Gear Up Alaska Scholarship Program)

Arizona

Arizona Commission for Postsecondary Education
2020 North Central, Suite 550
Phoenix, AZ 85004
602-258-2345
Fax: 602-258-2483
www.acpe.asu.edu

General requirements: Arizona administers a "decentralized" form of student aid in higher education. Monies are allocated based on a formula to postsecondary schools, and each college or university sets their own individual funding limits. Students should contact the Financial Aid office at the college they plan to attend for applicable scholarship, grant, and loan information. State residency is required for the programs listed.

Programs Available:

$2,500 Grants For Students Having Trouble Paying Tuition (LEAP)
Money And Help To Educate Students With Physical and Mental Disabilities (Vocational Rehabilitation Assistance)
Reduced Tuition To Take Courses Not Offered In Arizona (Student Exchange Program)
$3,000 For Community College Graduates To Go To Private College

Arkansas

Arkansas Department of Higher Education
114 East Capitol
Little Rock, AR 72201
501-371-2000
Fax: 501-371-2003
www.arkansashighered.com

General requirements: Applicants must be current residents of Arkansas.

Programs Available:

$600 Per Year On First-Come, First-Served Basis (Student Assistance Grants)
$4,000 For High School Graduates With At Least 3.5 Averages (Governor's Scholars)
$2,500 For High School Graduates With At Least 2.5 Averages (Arkansas Academic Challenge Scholarship)
Free Money For School If You Become a Math, Science, or Special Education Teacher, or a Guidance Counselor (Emergency Secondary Education Loan)

Free Tuition, Room, Board, and Fees To Dependents and Spouses of MIA's and POW's (MIA/KIA Dependent's Scholarship)
Grants To Dependents Of Law Enforcement Officers Killed Or Totally Disabled In The Line Of Duty (Law Enforcement Officer's Dependents Scholarship)
$1,000 To Top Ten GED Scorers (Second Effort Scholarship)
Money To Go Out Of State To Study Chiropractic Medicine, Dentistry, Optometry, Osteopathic Medicine, Podiatric Medicine, Or Become A Vet (Arkansas Health Education Grant Program)
$5,000 For Minorities To Get Teaching Certificate (Minority Teachers Scholarship)
Money To Teachers To Take Classes (Teacher and Administrator Program)
$7,500 For Minorities To Study Math, Sciences, Or Foreign Languages (Minority Masters Fellows Program)

California

California Postsecondary Education Commission
1303 J Street, Suite 500
Sacramento, CA 95814
916-445-7933
888-224-7268
Fax: 916-526-8802
www.csac.ca.gov

General requirements: Applicants must be residents of California.

Programs Available:
Grants For Tuition, Living Expenses, Vocational Training and Teachers (Cal Grants A, B, C and T)
Help To Work Your Way Through College (State Work-Study Program)
$11,000 To Become A Teacher (Assumption Program of Loans for Education (APLE))
Grants To Graduate Students Who Want To Become College Teachers (Graduate APLE)
Grants To Dependents Of Fire Fighters, Police Officers, and Correctional Officials Killed Or Totally Disabled In The Line Of Duty (Law Enforcement Personnel Dependents Scholarship)
$9,700 Grant To Get Teaching Certificate (Cal Grant T)
$4,000 To Study Child Development (Child Development Grant Program)
$1,500 Each Year For Bright Students (Robert C. Byrd Honors Scholarship Program)

Colorado

Colorado Commission on Higher Education
1380 Lawrence Street, Suite 1200
Denver, CO 80204
303-866-2723
www.state.co.us/cche_dir/hecche.html

General requirements: Applicants must be residents of Colorado.

Programs Available:
Grants To Students From Families Who Don't Normally Go To College (Colorado Diversity Grants)
Grants To Students Who Are Having Trouble Paying For Tuition (CLEAP)
More Grants To Students Who Are Having Trouble Paying For Tuition (Colorado Student Grants (CSG))

Money For Students Going To College Part Time (Colorado Part time Grants)
State Jobs For Students Having Trouble Paying Tuition (Colorado Work-Study)
Money For Smart Students Going To College In Colorado (Undergraduate Merit Awards)
Money For Graduates Who Have Trouble Paying Tuition (Colorado Graduate Grants)
Money For Smart Graduate Students (Colorado Graduate Fellowships)
Grants To Dependents Of POW/MIA's or Fire Fighters, Police Officers, and Correctional Officials Killed Or Totally Disabled In The Line Of Duty (Law Enforcement/POW-MIA Dependents Tuition Assistance)
Money To Be A Nurse And Practice In Colorado (Colorado Nursing Scholarship)
100% Tuition For National Guard Members (Colorado National Guard Tuition Assistance Program)
Money for First-Time College Freshman with Financial Need (Governor's Opportunity Scholarship Program)

Connecticut

Department of Higher Education
61 Woodland St.
Hartford, CT 06105-2326
860-947-1800
www.ctdhe.org

General requirements: Applicants must be Connecticut residents for in-state and out-of-state schools programs.

Programs Available:

$2,000 A Year If You Are In Top 20% Of Your High School Class (Capitol Scholarship)
$8,950 A Year To Attend A Private College (Connecticut Independent College Student Grant)
Money For Students Who Need Help Paying Tuition At A Public University (Connecticut Aid for Public College Students)
Money To Dependents Of Deceased, Disabled, Or MIA Veterans (Aid to Dependents of Deceased, Disabled, or MIA Veterans)
Free Tuition To Veterans (Tuition Waiver for Veterans)
$1,500 Each Year For Bright Students (Robert C. Byrd Honors Scholarship Program)
$10,000 For Minorities To Become Teachers (CT Minority Teacher Incentive Program)
$5,000 A Year to Become a Special Education Teacher (Special Education Teacher Incentive Grant Program)

Delaware

Commission on Higher Education
Carvel State Office Building, Fifth Floor
820 N. French St.
302-577-3240
Wilmington, DE 19801
Fax: 302-577-6765

General requirements: Applicants must be Delaware residents for in-state or out-of-state colleges.

Programs Available:

Money To Be A Teacher In Delaware (Christa McAuliffe Teacher Scholarship Loan)
$1,250 A Year For Undergraduate Students (Diamond State Scholarship)
Full Tuition, Room and Board To Smart High School Seniors (B. Bradford Barnes Scholarship)
Money To Be A Registered Or Practical Nurse And Practice In A State-Owned Hospital (Delaware Nursing Incentive Program)

$2,220 each Year To Attend College For Financially Needy (Scholarship Incentive Program-ScIP)
100% Tuition For Dependents Of Deceased Veterans (Education Benefits for Children of Deceased Veterans and Others)
$1,500 Each Year To Attend College Part-Time (Governor's Workforce Development Grant)
100% Tuition For Bright Students To Study Humanities Or Social Sciences (Charles L. Hebner Memorial Scholarship)
100% Tuition To Study at Delaware State University (Herman M. Holloway, Sr. Memorial Scholarship)
$1,500 Each Year For Bright Students (Robert C. Byrd Honors Scholarship Program)
$500 To Write An Essay (Legislative Essay Scholarship)
Loan (With Loan Forgiveness Provisions) To Study Optometry (Optometry Scholarship Program)
Loan (With Loan Forgiveness Provisions) To Become Librarian And Archivist (Librarian and Archivist Incentive Program)
Loan (With Loan Forgiveness Provisions) To Become Speech/Language Pathologist (Speech/Language Pathologist Incentive Program)
Support For Medical Students To Study At Jefferson Medical College Or Pennsylvania College of Osteopathic Medicine (Delaware Institute for Medical Education and Research and Delaware State Loan Repayment Program For Physicians and Dentists)
Lower Tuition To Become Vet At University of Georgia (University of Georgia College of Veterinary Medicine)

District of Columbia

Office of Postsecondary Education
2100 Martin Luther King, Jr., Ave., SE, Suite 401
Washington, DC 20020
202-685-2400
www.dhs.dc.gov/info/postsecondary.sht m

General requirements: Applicants must be District of Columbia residents for in-state or out-of-state school programs.

Programs Available:

Money For College Anywhere (D.C. State Student Incentive Program)
D.C. State Student Incentive Program, $700 per student for the academic year. Applications available: March 1.

Florida

Florida Department of Education
Bureau of Student Financial Assistance
1940 N. Monroe St., Suite 70
Tallahassee, FL 32303-4759
850-488-3612
888-827-2004
Fax: 850-488-3612

General requirements: Applicants must be Florida residents for in-state or out-of-state school programs.

Programs Available:

Money For Students Who Have Trouble Paying Their Tuition (Florida Student Assistance Grants (FSAG))
Work Your Way Through College With A Job At A Local Elementary School

(Instructional Aide Scholarship Program)
Jobs For Full Or Part-Time Students Who Need Help Paying Tuition (Florida Work Experience Program (FWEP))
Money For Smart High School Graduates Who Want To Be Teachers In Florida ("Chappie" James Most Promising Teacher Scholarship Loan Program)
Money For College Students Who Want To Be Teachers (Critical Teacher Shortage Scholarship Loan Program)
$3,000 A Year To Smart High School Graduates (Mary McLeod Bethune Scholarship Challenge Grant Fund)
Grants For American Indians To Go To College (Seminole and Miccosukee Indian Scholarship Program)
Money For Dependents Of Deceased or Disabled Veterans And POW/MIA's (Scholarships for Children of Deceased or Disabled Veterans)
$2,000 For Hispanic Americans Who Want To Go To College (Jose Marti Scholarship Challenge Grant Fund)
Money For Teachers To Take Part-Time Graduate Courses (Critical Teacher Shortage Tuition Reimbursement Program)
Free College Money If You Teach In Florida Public Schools (Critical Teacher Shortage Student Loan Forgiveness Program)
Money For Teachers To Get Retrained (Exceptional Student Education Training Grant for Out-of-Field Teachers)
Loan Forgiveness Program For Occupational or Physical Therapist (Critical Occupational Therapist or Physical Therapist Shortage Student Loan Forgiveness Program)
Ethics In Business Scholarship
Scholarships For Bright Students (Florida Bright Futures Scholarship Program)
$1,500 Each Year For Bright Students (Robert C. Byrd Honors Scholarship Program)
Grants To Minorities To Go To College Or Vo-Tech Schools (Rosewood Family Scholarship)
Grants To Attend Private College (William L. Boyd, IV Florida Resident Access Grant)

Georgia

Student Finance Commission
2082 E. Exchange Place, Suite 200
Tucker, GA 30084
770-724-9000
770-724-9225
www.gsfc.org

General requirements: Georgia provides no state grants but does offer the merit-based Valedictorian Governors Scholarship Program. This program identifies and recognizes high school seniors who have achieved excellence in school and community life. Requirements include: a minimum score of 1300 on the SAT test; a score of 31 on the ACT; or a ranking in the upper 10% of his or her graduating class. As a recipient of the award, the student may receive a Governor's Scholarship if he or she continues their postsecondary education in an approved public or private college or the University of Georgia, and meets other program requirements. The scholarship is used to defray the cost of tuition for a maximum of four years eligibility. The maximum amount awarded is $1,575.

Programs Available:
Scholarship To Go To College (HOPE-Helping Outstanding Pupils Educationally)
Grants To Attend College Out Of State, But Near The Border (Georgia Tuition Equalization Grant)
Scholarship To Study Engineering (Scholarship For Engineering Education)
$1,500 Each Year For Bright Students (Robert C. Byrd Honors Scholarship Program)

Grants To Attend College For Dependents of Deceased Law Enforcement Officers, Firefighters, or Prison Guards (Law Enforcement Personnel Dependents Grant/Public Safety Memorial Grant)
Grants For Low Income Students To Attend College (Leveraging Educational Assistance Program)
100% Tuition To Attend North Georgia College and State University And Participate In Reserve Officers Training Corps (ROTC Grant) Or Georgia's Army National Guard (Military Scholarship)
100% Tuition To Attend Georgia Military College (Georgia Military College State Service Scholarship)
Scholarship To Become A Teacher (Charles McDaniel Teacher Scholarship)
Loan To Become Osteopathic Doctor (Osteopathic Medical Loan)

Hawaii

Hawaii State Postsecondary Education Commission
Bachman Hall, Room 209
University of Hawaii
2444 Dole Street
Honolulu, HI 96822
808-956-8207
Fax: 808-956-5156
www.hern.hawaii.edu/hern

General requirements: Applicants must be Hawaii residents. Money available: $780,000.

Programs Available:

Free Tuition (Hawaii Student Incentive Grants (HSIG))
Free Tuition And Travel To High School Graduates With 3.5 Grade Point Averages (Regents Scholarship for Academic Excellence)
Free Tuition And Travel To High School Graduates With 3.7 Grade Point Averages (Presidential Achievement Scholarship)
Money For Students Planning To Study Pacific/Asian Studies (Pacific Asian Scholarships)
Robert C. Byrd Honor Scholarship
$2,000 To Major In Art, Geophysics, Music, Oceanography, or Medical Records (Community Scholarship Program)

Idaho

Office of the State Board of Education
650 W. State St.
P.O. Box 83720
Boise, ID 83720-0037
208-334-2270
Fax: 208-334-2632
www.sde.state.id.us/osbe/board.htm

General requirements: Applicants must be Idaho residents.

Programs Available:

$3,000 For Student Activists (Idaho Governor's Challenge Scholarship)
Disadvantaged High School Students Can Get $2,500 To Go To College (Idaho Minority and "At-Risk" Student Scholarship)
Free Money For Students Studying To Be Teachers Or Nurses (Education Incentive Loan Forgiveness)
$250 Per Semester To Attend College (Idaho Promise Category B Scholarship)
$5,00 For Financially Needy To Attend College (Leveraging Educational Assistance State Partnership Program-LEAP)
Subsidy To Study Medicine, Dentistry, Or Veterinary Medicine In Other States
$3,000 For Bright Students To Attend College (Idaho Promise Category A Scholarship)
Attend College In Washington Or Utah At In-State Rates (Idaho-Washington Reciprocity Program/ Utah-Idaho Scholarship)
$1,500 Each Year For Bright Students (Robert C. Byrd Honors Scholarship Program)

$2,000 To Attend College For Emmett High School Graduates (Tschudy Family Scholarship)
Attend College In Western United States At Reduced Rates (Western Interstate Commission For Higher Education)
Work Study Program For financially Needy (Atwell J. Parry Work Study Program)

Illinois

Illinois Student Assistance Commission
1755 Lake Cook Drive
Deerfield, IL 60015-5209
847-948-8500
800-899-ISAC
www.isca-online.org

General requirements: Applicants must be Illinois residents.

Programs Available:

Grants Up To $4,968 No Matter What Your Grades Are (Monetary Award Program)
$1,000 For Students In The Top 5% Of Their Class (Illinois Merit Recognition Scholarship Program)
Join The National Guard For Free Tuition For Graduate Or Undergraduate Studies (National Guard/Naval Militia Grant Program)
Veterans Living In Illinois Can Get Free Tuition and Fees (Illinois Veteran Grant Program)
Grants To Dependents Of Fire Fighters Or Police Officers Killed In The Line Of Duty (Police Officer/Fire Officer Dependent's Grant Program)
Grants To Dependents Of Correctional Officers Killed Or Disabled In The Line Of Duty (Correctional Officer's Survivor's Grant Program)
$2,500 To Study IT Industry (Arthur F. Quern Information Technology (Quern IT) Grant)
Enroll or be enrolled, at least half time in an eligible program of undergraduate information technology

$500 To Attend College (Illinois Incentive for Access (IIA) Program (Need-Based))
$5,000 For Minorities to Become Teachers (Minority Teachers of Illinois (MTI) Scholarship Program)
$5,000 For Bright Students To Become Teachers (DeBolt Teacher Shortage Scholarship Program)
$1,500 Each Year For Bright Students (Robert C. Byrd Honors Scholarship Program)
100% Tuition To Become Special Ed Teacher (Illinois Special Education Teacher Tuition Waiver Program)

Indiana

State Student Assistance Commission of Indiana
150 W. Market St., Suite 500
Indianapolis, IN 46204
317-232-2350
888-528-4719
Fax: 317-232-3260
www.ai.org/ssaci

General requirements: Applicants must be Indiana residents.

Programs Available:

Indiana College Students Who Have Trouble Paying Tuition (Indiana Higher Education Grant)
$500 For Bright Students To Attend College (Hoosier Scholar Award)

100% Tuition For Financially Needy To Attend State College (Twenty-first Century Scholars Program)
Scholarship To Become A Nurse (Nursing Scholarship Fund Program)
Scholarship For Minorities To Become Teachers or Anyone To Become Special Ed Teacher (Minority Teacher/Special Education Scholarship)
$1,500 Each Year For Bright Students (Robert C. Byrd Honors Scholarship Program)
Get A Summer Job (Summer State Work Study Program)
Grant To Go To College For National Guard Members (Indiana National Guard Supplemental Grant)
Grants To Go To School Part-Time (SSACI's Higher Education Award and Freedom of Choice Grant)

Iowa

Iowa College Student Aid Commission
200 Tenth, 4th Floor
Des Moines, IA 50309-3609
515-242-3344
800-383-4222
Fax: 515-242-3388
www.state.ia.us/collegeaid

General requirements: Applicants must be Iowa residents.

Programs Available:
Up to $1,000 for Outstanding Seniors Who Participate in Iowa State Fair Activities (Governor Terry E. Branstad Iowa State Fair Scholarship)
Money For High School Graduates In The Top 15% Of Their Class (State of Iowa Scholarship Program)
Grants To Pay For Tuition At Private Colleges (Iowa Tuition Grants)
$650 To Take A Vocational Education Course (Iowa Vocational-Technical Tuition Grants)
Grants To Students Who Need Money For Education (Iowa Grants)

Kansas

Kansas Board of Regents
700 SW Harrison, Suite 1410
Topeka, KS 66603-3760
785-296-3421
Fax: 785-296-0983
www.kansasregents.org

General requirements: Applicants must be Kansas residents.

Programs Available:
$1,850 A Year For Minority Students (Kansas Ethnic Minority Scholarship)
$500 To Take A Vocational Training Course (Vocational Education Scholarship)
$5,000 A Year If You Study To Be A Teacher In Kansas (Kansas Teacher Service Scholarship)
$3,500 A Year To Be A Nurse (Kansas Nursing Scholarship)
$1,000 To High School Graduates Who Have Trouble Paying Tuition (Kansas State Scholarship)
$3,000 For Financially Needy To Go To College (Kansas Comprehensive Grants)
$15,000 To Study Osteopathy (Kansas Osteopathy Medical Service Scholarship)
Subsidy For Optometry Students Who Open Practices in Kansas (Kansas Optometry Service Scholarship)
Subsidy For Dental Students Who Open Practices in Kansas (Kansas Dentistry Assistance)
$2,456 To Study Abroad (James B. Pearson Fellowship)
Grants To Scholars For Graduate Study (Kansas Distinguished Scholarship Program)
Subsidy For Students To Study Out Of State (Midwest Student Exchange Program)

Kentucky

Kentucky Higher Education Assistance Authority
1050 U.S. 127 South
Frankfort, KY 40601
502-696-7200
800-928-8926
TTY: 800-855-2880
Fax: 502-696-7345
www.kheaa.com

General requirements: Applicants must attend an eligible Kentucky college; be enrolled in an undergraduate degree program; be state residents; establish financial need; and meet program requirements. Funds are limited, so students who file by April 1 have the best chance of receiving awards. Money available: Approximately $20,100,000.

Programs Available:

Grants To Financially Needy Full-Time and Part-Time Students (College Access Program Grants (CAP))
Up To $1,800 To Needy Students Attending Private Colleges (Kentucky Tuition Grants (KTG))
Scholarships For Good Students (Kentucky Educational Excellence Scholarship)
Scholarship To Become A Teacher (KHEAA Teacher Scholarship Program)
Scholarship To Study Child Development (Early Childhood Development Scholarship)

Scholarship To Study Osteopathic Medicine (Osteopathic Medicine Scholarship)
Jobs For Those In College (KHEAA Work-Study Program)

Louisiana

Office of Student Financial Assistance
P.O. Box 91202
Baton Rouge, LA 70821-9202
225-922-1023
800-259-5626, ext. 1012
Fax: 225-922-0790
www.osfa.state.la.us

General requirements: Applicants must be Louisiana residents.

Programs Available:

Maximum $7,000 Grant To Study Forestry Or Marine Sciences (Louisiana Rockefeller State Wildlife Scholarship)
Scholarships For Financially needy To Go To College (Leveraging Educational Assistance Partnership-LEAP)
$1,500 Each Year For Bright Students (Robert C. Byrd Honors Scholarship Program)

Maine

Maine Education Assistance Division
Finance Authority of Maine (FAME)
5 Community Drive
Augusta, ME 04332-0949
800-228-3734 (In Maine)
207-623-3263
207-626-2717
Fax: 207-632-0095
www.famemaine.com

General requirements: Applicants must be Maine residents.

Programs Available:

Free Tuition To Dependents Of Law Enforcement Officers And Fire Fighters Killed In The Line Of Duty (Tuition Waiver Program for Children of Fire

Fighters and Law Enforcement Officers Killed in the Line of Duty)

Robert C. Byrd Honor Scholarship

Up to $1,250 For Needy To Attend College (Maine State Grant Program)

$12,000 Forgivable Loan Program To Those Who Agree Teach (Educators For Maine Program)

Tuition Waiver For Foster Children (Foster Children Under The Custody of the Department of Human Services)

Tuition Waiver For Spouses And Children Of Deceased EMTs (Children and Spouses of Emergency Medical Services Personnel Killed in the Line of Duty)

Scholarships For Needy Who Attend University of Maine (The University of Maine System Scholarship)

$1,000 For Architectural or Engineering Students (Advancement of Construction Technology Scholarship)

Maryland

Maryland Higher Education Commission
State Scholarship Administration
The Jeffrey Building
16 Francis Street, Suite 209
Annapolis, MD 21401-1781
410-260-4500
800-974-0203
TTY: 800-735-2258
Fax: 410-974-5994
www.mhec.state.md.us

General requirements: Applicants must be Maryland residents, unless specified for in-state or out-of-state schools.

Programs Available:

$2,000 To Full- Or Part-Time Students (Senatorial Scholarship Program)

$200 To Full-Time Or Part-Time Students (House of Delegate Award)

$300 To Take A Vocational Education Course (Tolbert Grant)

$3,000 A Year For Smart Students (Distinguished Scholar Program)

$4,500 To Get A Degree In Nursing (Maryland State Nursing Scholarship)

$3,000 A Year To Become A Teacher In Maryland (Teacher Education Distinguished Scholar Program)

Grants To Dependents Of POW's, Fire Fighters, Police Officers, and Safety Personnel Killed Or Disabled In The Line Of Duty (Edward Conroy Grant)

Grants To Study Physical Therapy (Physical and Occupational Therapists and Assistants Scholarships)

$7,500 A Year To Study Family Practice Medicine (Family Practice Medical Scholarship)

Grants To Study Law, Dentistry, Medicine, Nursing Or Pharmacy (Professional Scholarship)

Tuition, Fees, Room and Board To Become A Teacher (Sharon Christa McAuliffe Critical Shortage Teacher Scholarship)

$2,000 To Study Child Care, Full or Part Time (Child Care Provider Scholarship)

Free Tuition To Fire Fighters and Rescue Squad Members Who Want To Study Full Or Part Time (Reimbursement of Fire Fighters and Rescue Squad Members)

Student Loans If You Work For A Non-Profit (Loan Assistance Repayment Program (LARP))

$3,000 For Science and Technology Majors (Science and Technology Scholarship)

Up to $9,200 Per Year To Students in Extreme Financial Need (Guaranteed Access Grant)
Up to $2,700 Per Year For Students From Low or Moderate Income Families (Educational Assistance Grant)
Up to $1,000 for Part-Time Students (Part-Time Grant Program

Massachusetts

Board of Higher Education
One Ashburton Place, Room 1401
Boston, MA 02108-1696
617-994-6950

General requirements: Applicants must be Massachusetts residents.

Programs Available:
Money To Attend Private Colleges In Massachusetts (Gilbert Matching Scholarship)
Free Tuition At State Schools (Tuition Waiver Program)
No Interest Loan Program, $10,000,000.
Tuition Wavers For Smart Students (Paul Tsongas Scholarship)
$5,212 For Smart Teachers (Tomorrow's Teachers Scholarship Program)
$12,000 For Computer, Math and Science Majors (Commonwealth Futures Grant Program)
$2,900 Per Year For Needy To Attend College (MASSGrant Program)
Money To Help Pay For Fees (Massachusetts Cash Grant Program)
Money To Go To School Part-Time (Massachusetts Part-Time Grant Program)
Tuition For Spouse or Child Of Person Killed Or Missing In Line Of Public Service (Massachusetts Public Service Grant Program)
Up To $2,00 For Needy Students Who Do Well In College (Performance Bonus Grant Program)
Free College Courses For Teachers (Career Advancement Program Tuition Waiver)

Tuition Waivers For Veterans, Seniors, Disabled, Military And Native Americans (Categorical Tuition Waivers)
Tuition Waivers To Teachers Who Mentor (Collaborative Teachers Tuition Waiver)
Tuition Waiver For Foster Care Children (Department of Social Services Tuition Waiver For Foster Care Children)
Tuition Waiver For Adopted Children (DSS Adopted Children Tuition Waiver)
Tuition Waiver For Graduate Students (Graduate Tuition Waivers)
Tuition Waiver For High Technology Majors (High Technology Scholar/Intern Tuition Waiver Program)
Tuition Waiver For Teacher Shortage (Incentive Program For Aspiring Teachers)
1/3 Tuition Waiver For Community College Students Who Attend Four-Year University (Joint Admissions Tuition Advantage Program Waiver)
Tuition Waiver For Smart Students (Stanley Z. Koplik Certificate of Mastery Tuition Waiver)
Tuition Waiver For Students To Attend Other Colleges (University of Massachusetts Exchange Program Tuition Waiver)
Tuition Waiver For Work/Learning Experiences (Washington Center Program Tuition Waiver)

Michigan

Michigan Department of Treasury
Bureau of Student Financial Assistance
Office of Information and Resources
P.O. Box 30466

Lansing, MI 48909-7966
517-373-3394
Fax: 517-335-5984
www.MI-StudentAid.org

General requirements: Applicants must be Michigan residents.

Programs Available:

Money For Smart Kids Who Have Trouble Paying Tuition (Michigan Competitive Scholarships)
Money For Students Attending Private Colleges (Michigan Tuition Grants)
Robert C. Byrd Honor Scholarship
Scholarships For Community College Students (Postsecondary Access Student Scholarship Program)

Minnesota

Minnesota Higher Education Services Office
1450 Energy Park Drive, Suite 350
St. Paul, MN 55108-5227
651-642-0533
800-433-3243
Fax: 651-642-0675
www.mheso.state.mn.us

General requirements: Applicants must be residents of Minnesota, unless otherwise specified.

Programs Available:

Money To Pay Half Your College Expenses (State Grant Program)
Money For Part-Time Students (State Part-Time Grant Program)
Money For Child Care While You Go To School Or Work Part Time (Non-AFDC Child Care Grant Program)
$1,000 For High School Students To Take Summer Courses At A College (Summer Scholarships for Academic Enrichment)
Grants To Dependents Of Safety Officers Killed In The Line Of Duty (Safety Officers' Survivor Program)
$1,500 Each Year For Bright Students (Robert C. Byrd Honors Scholarship Program)
$1,850 Per Year For Native Americans To Attend College (Minnesota Indian Scholarship Program)
100% Tuition For Smart Students (MN Academic Excellence Scholarship)
Scholarships For Farm Families
$500 For Student Service Scholars (MN Service Scholarship Matching Grant)

Mississippi

Mississippi Institution of Higher Education
5825 Ridgewood Rd.
Jackson, MS 39211-6453
601-432-6997
www.ihl.state.ms.us/index.asp

General requirements: Applicants must be Mississippi residents. Money available: $2,600,000.

Programs Available:

Money To Pursue Degrees In Another State That Are Not Offered In Mississippi (Academic Common Market Program)
Grants To Full-Time Students Who Have Trouble Paying Tuition (State Student Incentive Grant Program)
Graduate Students Can Make $1,000 A Month As Student Interns (Mississippi Public Management Graduate Internship Program)
Money To Dental Students (State Dental Education Loan/Scholarship Program)

Money To Full-Time Students Who Want To Become Teachers (William Winter Teacher Scholar Loan Program)
$10,000 A Year To African-American Ph.D. Students (African-American Doctoral Teacher Loan/ Scholarship Program)
Money To Study Optometry Or Osteopathic Medicine (Southern Regional Educational Board (SREB) Loan/ Scholarship Program)
Tuition, Room and Board and Fees To Dependents Of Police Officers and Fire Fighters Who Died Or Became Disabled In The Line Of Duty (Law Enforcement Officers and Firemen Scholarship Program)
Tuition, Room and Board and Fees To Dependents Of POW/MIA's (Southeast Asia POW/MIA Scholarship Program)
Money To Professional Students Who Have To Go Out Of State To Get Their Degrees (Graduate and Professional Degree Loan/Scholarship Program)
Money To Professional Students Who Study In Mississippi (State Medical Education Loan/ Scholarship Program)
Money For Registered Nurses Who Want To Go Back And Get A Bachelor's Degree In Nursing (Career Ladder Nursing Loan/Scholarship Program)
Up To $5,000 Per Year For Nursing Students (Nursing Education Loan/ Scholarship Program)
$4,000 For Nursing Students (Special Nursing Education Loan/Scholarship for Study in Baccalaureate Nursing Education Program)
Money For Studying Psychology, Speech Pathology, Occupational Therapy, and Physical Therapy (Health Care Professions Loan Scholarship Program)
Money For Medical Students (Special Medical Education Loan/Scholarship Program)
Mississippi Resident Tuition Grant Program
Mississippi Eminent Scholar Program
Mississippi Nursing Teacher (Stipend) Program
$6,000 A Year to Study Veterinary Medicine at MSUC of Veterinary Medicine (Veterinary Medicine Minority Loan Scholarship)

Nursing Education Loans/Scholarship Program:
$1,500 A Year For RN's Going To School To Get A BSN Degree Who Will Be A Nurse In Mississippi (RN To BSN Program)
Up To $4,000 For Nursing Students To Get A BSN Degree (BSN Program)
$3,000 Per Year To Study Full-Time For A MSN Degree (MSN Program)
$5,000 Per Year For To Get A DSN Degree And Work In Mississippi For One Year (DSN Program)

Missouri

Missouri Coordinating Board of Higher Education
P.O. Box 1438
3515 Amazonas Drive
Jefferson City, MO 65109
573-751-2361
Fax: 573-751-6635
www.cbhe.mo.us

General requirements: Applicants must be Missouri residents.

Programs Available:
$2,000 A Year To Students With ACT Scores In The Top 3% (Missouri Higher Education Academic Scholarship Program, "Bright Flight")

Tuition For Dependents Of Public Safety Officers Or Department Of Highway Officers Who Were Killed In The Line Of Duty (Public Service Officer or Employee's Child Survivor Grant Program)
$10,000 For Biomedical or Information Technology Majors (The Advantage Missouri Program)
$1,500 For Financially Needy To Attend College (Charles Gallagher Student Financial Assistance Program)
Scholarships For Working Students (Marguerite Ross Barnett memorial Scholarship)
Tuition Adjustment For Students Who Attend School Out-Of-State (Midwest Student Exchange Program)
Tuition For Financially Needy (Missouri College Guarantee Program)
Tuition Waiver For Spouses Or Children Of Deceased Vietnam Veterans (Vietnam Veterans Survivor Grant Program)

Montana

Montana University System
Board of Regents of Higher Education
2500 Broadway St.
P.O. Box 203101
Helena, MT 59620-3101
406-444-6570
800-537-7508
www.montana.edu/wwwbor

General requirements: Applicants must be Montana residents.

Programs Available:

Free Tuition For Senior Citizens, Veterans, War Orphans, Etc. (Fee Waivers)
Scholarships For National Merit Semi-Finalists (National Merit Semi-Finalist Scholarship)
First Year of College Free To Smart High School Students (High School Honor Scholarship)
Scholarship For Community College Graduates To Attend Four Year College (Community College Honor Scholarship)
Scholarships For Disadvantaged Students (GEAR UP Scholarship)
$600 For Needy Students (Montana Higher Education Grant)
Money To Working Students (MTAP Baker Grant)

Nebraska

Nebraska Coordinating Commission For Postsecondary Education
P.O. Box 95005
Lincoln, NE 68509-5005
402-471-2847
Fax: 402-471-2886
www.ccpe.state.ne.us/PublicDoc/CCPE/Default.asp

General requirements: Nebraska administers a "decentralized" form of student aid in higher education. Monies are allocated based on a formula to postsecondary schools. A limited number of state programs are administered directly through postsecondary schools. Students should contact the Financial Aid Office at the college they plan to attend for scholarship, grant, and loan information. State residency is required.

Programs Available

$2,000 for Women Pursuing a Degree in English (Norma Ross Walter Scholarship)
$1,000 For an Amateur Radio Operator to Get a BA in Electronics or Communications (Paul and Helen L Grauer Scholarship)

Nevada

Nevada Department of Education
Student Incentive Grant Program
700 E. 5th Street
Carson City, NV 98701-5096
775-687-9200
Fax: 775-687-91

www.nde.state.nv.us
General requirements: Nevada has no state scholarships. The Nevada Student Incentive Grant Program is the only source of state grants. It administers renewable, need-based awards of up to $2,500 per year. Students should contact the Financial Aid Office at the college they plan to attend for further information. State residency is required.

Programs Available:
Robert C. Byrd Honor Scholarship

New Hampshire

New Hampshire Postsecondary Education Commission
2 Industrial Park Drive
Concord, NH 03301
603-271-2555
Fax: 603-271-2696
www.state.nh.us/postsecondary
General requirements: Applicants must be New Hampshire residents, for programs involving colleges in and out of state.

Programs Available
Grants To Attend Colleges In The New England States (New Hampshire Incentive Program)
Money For Dependents Of Veterans Who Died In Service (Scholarships for Orphans of Veterans)

Robert C. Byrd Honor Scholarship
Scholarship For Students In Career Shortage Areas (NH Career Incentive Program)
Scholarships For Medical Students At Dartmouth (Dartmouth Medical Education Program)
Scholarships For Nursing Students (Nursing Leveraged Scholarship Loan Program)
Scholarship For Vet Students (Veterinary Education Program)
Money for Sophomores, Juniors and Seniors Based on Merit and Need (Governor's Success Program)

New Jersey

New Jersey Higher Education Student Assistance Authority
P.O. Box 540
Trenton, NJ 08625-0540
609-588-3226
800-792-8670
TTY: 609-588-2526
Fax: 609-588-3316
www.hesaa.org
General requirements: Applicants must be New Jersey residents.

Programs Available:
$4,580 A Year In Grants To Full-Time Students (Tuition Aid Grants)
Grants To Students With High SAT Scores (Edward J. Bloustein Distinguished Scholar Program)
Grants To Smart High School Juniors (Garden State Scholars Program)
$1,000 For Smart City Kids (Urban Scholars Program)
$7,500 For High Achieving Students (OSRP)
Scholarships For Spouses and Dependents Of Deceased Law, Fire, or Emergency Personnel (Survivor Tuition Benefits)
Money for Exceptional Civic Minded Leaders (Miss New Jersey Educational Scholarship Program)

New Mexico

New Mexico Commission On Higher Education
1068 Cerrillos Road
Santa Fe, NM 87501
505-827-7383
800-279-9777
TTY: 800-659-8331
Fax: 505-827-7392
www.nmche.org

General requirements: Applicants must be New Mexico residents, unless otherwise stated.

Programs Available:

Free Tuition To Students With "Good Moral Character" (Three Percent Scholarship Program)

Tuition, Books, and Fees For High School Students In Top 5% Of Class (New Mexico Scholars Program)

Part-Time Jobs To Undergraduate and Graduate Students (New Mexico Work-Study Program)

Money For Osteopathic Students Willing To Practice In New Mexico (Osteopathic Medical Student Loan Program)

Grants To Half-Time and Full-Time Students In Financial Need (New Mexico Student Incentive Grant)

Tuition, Books, And Fees To Vietnam Vets (Vietnam Veterans' Scholarship Program)

$12,000 For Nursing Students Willing To Practice In New Mexico (New Mexico Nursing Student Loan for Service Program)

$7,500 Per Year For Women And Minorities To Go To Graduate School (Graduate Scholarship Program)

Money For Students Attending Private Colleges (Student Choice)

Money For Medical Students Willing To Practice In New Mexico (New Mexico Physician and Physician Assistant Student Loan for Service Program)

$25,000 For Women And Minority Ph.D. Students (Minority Doctoral Assistance Loan for Service Program)

Money For Student Athletes (Athletic Scholarships)

Money For Child Care (Child Care Grants)

Scholarships For Children of Deceased Military and State Police (Children of Deceased Military and State Police Personnel Scholarship)

Go To School In New Mexico (Competitive Scholarship For Out Of State Students)

Scholarships For Minority Students (Gates Millennium Scholars)

$2,500 For Financially Needy (Legislative Endowment Scholarships)

100% Tuition Scholarships (Lottery Success Scholarships)

Reduced Tuition For Senior Citizens (Senior Citizens' Reduced Tuition Act)

Loans For Allied Health Students (Allied Health Student Loan-For-Service)

Loan Repayment Program For Health Professionals (Health Professional Loan Repayment Program)

Loans for Minority or Disabled Teaching Majors (Southeastern New Mexico Teachers' Loan-For-Service)

New York

New York Higher Education Services Corporation
Grants and Scholarship Information
99 Washington Ave.
Albany, NY 12255
518-473-7087

TDD: 800-445-5234
Fax: 518-473-3749
www.hesc.com

General requirements: Applicants must be residents of New York. Amounts awarded are determined by the type of school you are planning to attend, your financial status (net taxable income), year in which the award is received, and amount of tuition.

Programs Available:

Grants For Full-Time Students (Tuition Assistance Program (TAP))
Grants For Part-Time Students (Aid for Part-Time Study (APTS))
Money For Accounting, Veterinary, and Students Pursuing 19 Other Professional Careers (New York Regents Professional Opportunity Scholarships)
Money for Students Studying Medicine Or Dentistry (New York Regents Health Care Opportunity Scholarships)
Money for Students Studying To Be Dental Hygienists, Midwives, Therapists, And Speech-Language Pathologists (New York State Health Service Corps Scholarships)
Money for Native Americans To Attend College (State Aid to Native Americans)
Grants To Dependents Of Deceased Or Disabled Veterans (Regents Award for Children of Deceased or Disabled Veterans)
Tuition And Fees For Dependents Of Deceased Police Officers and Fire Fighters (Memorial Scholarships for Children of Deceased Police Officers and Fire Fighters)
$1,000 Per Semester For Vietnam Veterans (Vietnam Veterans and Persian Gulf Veterans Tuition Awards)
Robert C. Byrd Honor Scholarship
$4,000 to Attend a New York State Accredited College, University or Trade School (New York State Lottery Leaders of Tomorrow Scholarship)
$1,500 For Smart High School Students (Scholarships For Academic Excellence)

North Carolina

North Carolina State Education Assistance Authority
P.O. Box 14103
Research Triangle Park, NC 27709
919-549-8614
800-700-1775 (NC residents only)
Fax: 919-549-8481
www.ncseaa.edu

General requirements: Applicants must be residents of North Carolina.

Programs Available:

Grants For Full-Time And Part-Time Students (Appropriated Grants)
$5,000 A Year For Preschool, Elementary, Or Secondary Level Teachers (Paul Douglas Teacher Scholarship Program (PDTS))
$3,000 For Smart High School Students Active In Public Service (Incentive Scholarship Program)
Grants For Minorities Studying Part Time Or Full Time (Minority Presence Grant Program)
Grants For Minorities Studying Law, Veterinary Medicine, Or Working On A Ph.D. (Minority Presence Grant Program: Doctoral/Law/Veterinary Medicine Program)
Grants For Students Going Part Time To Junior Colleges (North Carolina Community College Scholarship Program)
$1,500 To Full-Time Undergraduate Students (North Carolina Student Incentive Grant)
Grants Given By State Legislators To Students Who Don't Even Need The Money (North Carolina Legislative Tuition Grant Program, Private College).
$8,500 A Year For Undergraduate Or Graduate Students In Health, Science, Or

Mathematics (North Carolina Student Loan Program for Health, Science, and Mathematics)
$6,500 A Year To Students Who Want To Be Teachers (North Carolina Teaching Fellows Scholarship Program)
Grants To Dependents Of Deceased Or Disabled Veterans Or POW/MIA's (North Carolina Veterans Scholarship)
Grants To Full-Time Or Part-Time Native American Students (American Indian Student Legislative Grant Program)
Money For Students In 2-Year Or 4-Year Nursing Programs (Nurse Education Scholarship Loan Program)
$6,000 A Year For Nursing Students Willing To Practice In North Carolina (Nursing Scholars Program)
$5,000 Plus Tuition And Fees For Dental Students (Board of Governors Dental Scholarship)
$5,000 Plus Tuition And Fees For Medical Students (Board of Governors Medical Scholarship Program)
Free Loans For Studying Psychology, Counseling, Or Speech (Prospective Teacher Scholarship Loans)
Grants To Part-Time Or Full-Time Students Attending Private Colleges (State Contractual Scholarship Program, Private Colleges)
Tuition, Fees, And Day Care For the Physically Or Mentally Disabled (Vocational Rehabilitation Program)

Tuition, Fees, Books and Supplies, and Reader Services to Full-Time Visually Impaired Students With Financial Need (Rehabilitation Assistance for the Blind and Visually Impaired)
$3,500 A Year For Teacher Assistants To Attend Community College (Teacher Assistant Scholarship Loan Two-Year Program)

North Dakota

University Systems
10th Floor, State Capitol
600 E. Boulevard Ave., Dept. 215
Bismarck, ND 58505-0230
701-328-2960
Fax: 701-328-2961
www.ndus.edu

General requirements: Applicants must be residents of North Dakota.

Programs Available:
$600 To Students Attending Any College (North Dakota State Student Incentive Grant Program)
100% Tuition Awarded To Top High School Students (North Dakota Scholars Program)
$2,000 For Students With 1/4 Indian Blood (North Dakota Indian Scholarship)
$2,000 For Teacher Training (Teacher Retraining Scholarship Program)
Loan Forgiveness For Teachers (Teacher Shortage Loan Forgiveness Program)
Tuition Waivers for Senior Citizens, Peace Officers and Fire Fighters (Tuition Waivers)

Ohio

Ohio Board of Regents
State Grants and Scholarship Department
P.O. Box 182452
Columbus, OH 43218-2451
888-833-1133
614-466-7420

Fax: 614-752-5903
www.regents.state.oh.us/sgs
General requirements: Applicants must be residents of Ohio.

Programs Available:
Grants For Middle Income Families To Pay Tuition (Ohio Instructional Grants)
Grants To Pay Tuition At Private Colleges (Ohio Student Choice Grant Program)
Grants To Dependents Of Deceased Or Disabled Veterans And POW/MIAs (Ohio War Orphans Scholarship Program)
$2,205 A Year To Smart High School Students Who Attend Ohio Colleges (Ohio Academic Scholarship Program)
$3,500 A Year For Graduate Students (Regents Graduate/Professional Fellowship Program)
Free Tuition To Dependents Of Fire Fighters And Police Officers Killed In The Line Of Duty (Ohio Safety Officers College Memorial Fund)
$3,000 Loan With Loan Forgiveness For Work For Nurses (Nurse Education Assistance Loan Program)
$1,500 For Smart Students (Robert C. Byrd Honors Scholarship Program)
$144 For Career School (Student Workforce Development Grant Program)
$500 to Pass the Ohio Proficiency Tests and Attend College in Ohio (Ohio 12th Grade Proficiency Tests Scholarship Program)

Oklahoma

Oklahoma State Regents for Higher Education
655 Research Parkway, Suite 200
Oklahoma City, OK 73104
405-225-9100
Fax: 405-225-9230
www.okhighered.org
General requirements: Applicants must be Oklahoma residents.

Programs Available:
Chiropractic Education Assistance Scholarship
Money For Students Having Trouble Paying Tuition (Oklahoma Tuition Aid Grant Program)
Grants To Top 15% High School Students Who Want To Be Teachers (Future Teachers Scholarship Program)
Robert C. Byrd Honor Scholarship
Scholarships For Smart Students (Academic Scholars Program)
$3,000 For National Merit Students (Regional University Baccalaureate Scholarship)
$500 For Public Works Students (American Public Works Association Scholarship)
$1,000 For Public Service Students (George and Donna Nigh Public Service Scholarship)
$5,500 For Dependent Children Of Oklahoma City Bombing Victims (Heartland Scholarship Fund)
Tuition Waiver For Foster Children (Independent Living Act)
Free Tuition for Members of the National Guard (National Guard Tuition Waiver)
$2,300 For AmeriCorps (Smart Start For Brain Gain)

Oregon

Oregon Student Assistance Commission
1500 Valley River Dr., Suite 100
Eugene, OR 97401
503-687-7400
Fax: 541-687-7419
www.osac.state.or.us
General requirements: Applicants must be residents of Oregon.

Programs Available:
Grants To College Students In Financial Need (Oregon Opportunity Grants)
State Scholarships For High School Seniors, Graduate, and Undergraduate Students

Student Loans Forgiven If You Become a Nurse In a Needed Area of Oregon (Nursing Services Program)

Pennsylvania

Pennsylvania Higher Education Assistance Agency
1200 N. 7th Street
Harrisburg, PA 17105
717-720-2800
www.pheaa.org

General requirements: Applicants must be Pennsylvania residents for in-state schools, unless otherwise specified.

Programs Available:

Up to $3,300 For Financially Needy Students (Pennsylvania State Grants)
$3,300 for Veterans Who Want To Go To School (Financial Aid For Veterans)
$3,792 For National Guard Members (Educational Assistance Program for the Pennsylvania National Guard)
Tuition Waivers for Dependents of Deceased Police, Firefighters, Rescue Workers, and Others (Postsecondary Educational Gratuity Program)
$3,000 A Year To Study Science and Technology (New Economy Technology Scholarship Program)
State Work Study Program
Loan Forgiveness For Nursing, Early Childhood and Agriculture Education Students (Loan Forgiveness Programs)

Rhode Island

Rhode Island Higher Education Assistance Authority
560 Jefferson Boulevard
Warwick, RI 02886
401-736-1100
TDD: 401-734-9481
Fax: 401-732-3541
www.riheaa.org

General requirements: Applicants must be residents of Rhode Island.

Programs Available:

Up to $750 For Part-Time And Full-Time Students (Rhode Island State Grant Program)

South Carolina

South Carolina Commission on Higher Education
1333 Main Street, Suite 200
Columbia, SC 29201
803-737-2260
Fax: 803-737-2297
www.sctuitiongrants.com

General requirements: Applicants must be residents of South Carolina.

Programs Available:

$3,500 For Students In Financial Need (South Carolina Tuition Grants)
$15,000 For Graduate Students (South Carolina Graduate Incentive Scholarship Program)
$1,000 For Minority Students (South Carolina "Other Race" Grant Program)
$6,700 For High School Seniors With High Test Scores (Palmetto Fellows Scholarship)
$10,000 A Year For Medical And Dental Students (South Carolina Medical and Dental Scholarship Fund)
Free Tuition For Students Over 60 Years Old (Tuition Waiver for Senior Citizens)
Free Tuition For Dependents Of Disabled Or

Deceased Veterans (Free Tuition for Children of Deceased or Disabled South Carolina Veterans)
Free Tuition For Dependents Of Deceased Or Disabled Fire Fighters, Law Officers, and Members Of The Civil Air Patrol (Free Tuition for Children of Deceased or Disabled South Carolina Fire Fighters, Law Officers, and Members of Civil Air Patrol or Organized Rescue Squad)
Robert C. Byrd Honor Scholarship
$5,000 For Smart Students (Legislative Incentive For Future Excellence (LIFE))

South Dakota

South Dakota Department of Education and Cultural Affairs
Office of the Secretary
700 Governor's Drive
Pierre, SD 57051
605-773-6139
www.ris.sdbor.edu

General requirements: Applicants must be residents of South Dakota.

Programs Available:
$600 Per Year For Students In Financial Need (South Dakota State Student Incentive Grant Program)
$300 For Students Attending Private Colleges (South Dakota Tuition Equalization Grant Program)
Robert C. Byrd Honor Scholarship

Tennessee

Tennessee Student Assistance Corporation
404 James Robertson Parkway
Suite 1900, Parkway Towers
Nashville, TN 37243-0820
615-741-3650
Fax: 615-741-6230
www.state.tn.us/tsac

General requirements: Applicants must be residents of Tennessee.

Programs Available:
$1,482 For Financially Needy Students (Tennessee Student Assistance Award)
$5,000 A Year For Minorities In The Top 25% Of Class To Become Teachers (Minority Teaching Fellows Program)
Robert C. Byrd Honor Scholarship Program
$6,000 For Smart Students (Ned McWherter Scholars Program)
$1,000 For Teachers (Christa McAuliffe Scholarship Program)
Scholarships For Dependents of Deceased Law, Emergency, Fire and Other Personnel (Dependent Children Scholarship Program)
Scholarships For Teachers (Tennessee Teaching Scholars Program)

Texas

Texas Higher Education Coordinating Board
Box 12788, Capitol Station
Austin, TX 78711-2788
512-427-6127
Fax: 512-427-6127

General requirements: Applicants must be residents of Texas, unless otherwise specified.

Programs Available:
Money To Attend Public Colleges In Texas (Texas Public Education Grant)
Money To Attend Private Colleges In Texas (Tuition Equalization Grant)

$1,250 For Half Time Or Full Time Students (LEAP-Leveraging Educational Assistance Partnership Program)
Grants To Financially Needy Students (Texas Tuition Assistance Grant)
Money To Study To Be A Nurse (Professional Nursing Scholarships)
Tuition And Fees For Blind Or Deaf Students
Money For Dependents Of Disabled Or Deceased Firemen, Peace Officers, Custodial Employees of the Department Of Corrections, Or Game Wardens
Money For Dependents Of POW/MIAs (Children of Prisoners of War or Persons Missing in Action)
Tuition And Fees For Fire Fighters To Take Science Courses (Fire Fighters Enrolled in Fire Science Courses)
Free Tuition And Fees For Veterans (Veterans and Dependents (The Hazelwood Act))
Money For The Smartest High School Students (Valedictorian Exemption)
Money For Foreign Students From Central America (Students from Other Nations of the American Hemisphere (Good Neighbor Scholarship))
Up To $1,500 For Undergraduates (Texas Educational Opportunity Grant)
Robert C. Byrd Honors Scholarship Program
Scholarships for Students Enrolled In Two Colleges (Concurrent Enrollment Waiver)
$1,000 Scholarships For Early High School Graduates (Early High School Graduation Scholarship)
$500 For Educational Aide (Educational Aide Exemption)
Tuition Waiver For High School Students Who Take College Classes (Exemption for Dual-Enrolled Students)
Tuition Waiver For Texas National Guard Members (Texas National Guard Tuition Assistance Program)
Tuition For Children of Deceased Military or National Guard Members (Orphans of Texas Members of the U.S. Armed Forces or National Guard)
Reduced Tuition For Those Who Take More Credit Hours (Reduction in Tuition Charges for Students Taking 15 or More Semester Credit Hours Per Term)
Reduced Tuition for Senior Citizens (Senior Citizen, 55 or Older Tuition Reduction Program)
Tuition Waiver For Foster Care Kids
Tuition Waiver For Children Whose Parents Receive TANF (Temporary Assistance To Needy Families Exemption Program)
$3,000 for Accounting Students (Fifth Year Accounting Student Scholarship)
Scholarship For Needy Students (License Plate Insignia Scholarship)
Scholarships for Rural EMS Training (Rural Emergency Medical Services Scholarship Incentive Program)
$15,000 Stipend For Physicians Willing To Work In Under-served Areas (Texas Health Service Corps Program)
Grants To Needy Community College Students (Toward Excellence, Access & Success Grant II Program)
Scholarships For Smart Students (Toward Excellence, Access, & Success Grant Program)
Grants For Associate's Degree (Toward Excellence, Access, & Success Grant Program)
Scholarships For Vocational Nurses (Vocational Nursing Scholarships)

Utah

Utah System of Higher Education
355 West North Temple
3 Triad, Suite 550
Salt Lake City, UT 84180-1205
801-321-7101
Fax: 801-321-7199
www.utahsbr.edu/welcome.html

General requirements: Utah administers funding to state residents. The state uses a decentralized system. Students should contact the Financial Aid Office at the college they plan to attend.

Programs Available:

Grants For Students In Financial Need (State Student Incentive Grant Program)

75% Tuition Scholarships For Those That Complete Associate Degree While In High School (New Century Scholarship Program)

$2,500 For Needy Students (Leveraging Educational Assistance Partnership (LEAP)

Scholarships For College (Utah Centennial Opportunity Program for Education Grant)

Loan and Loan Forgiveness Program For Students Who Want To Be Teachers (Terrel H. Bell Teaching Incentive Program)

Vermont

Vermont Student Assistance Corporation
P.O. Box 2000
Champlain Mill
Winooski, VT 05404
800-642-3177
802-655-9602
TDD: 802-665-4050
Fax: 802-654-3765
www.vsac.org

General requirements: Applicants must be Vermont residents, unless otherwise stated.

Programs Available:

Grants For Students In Financial Need (Vermont Incentive Grants)

Grants For Part Time Students (Vermont Part Time Student Grants)

$650 Per Course If You're NOT Working Toward A Degree (Vermont Non-Degree Student Grant Program)

Extra Loans For College Students (Vermont EXTRA Loans (Supplemental))

Virginia

Virginia State Council of Higher Education
Office of Financial Aid
James Monroe Building
101 North 14th St., 9th Floor
Richmond, VA 23219
804-225-2628
Fax: 804-225-2638
www.schev.edu

General requirements: Applicants must be Virginia residents.

Programs Available:

$5,000 For Students In Financial Need (Virginia College Assistance Program (CSAP))

Grants For Students Even Though They Don't NEED The Money (Virginia Tuition Assistance Grant Program (TAGP))

Free Tuition For White Students To Attend Black Colleges (Virginia Transfer Grant Program (VTGP))

Grants To Black Undergraduate Students (Last Dollar Program)

Nursing Students Receive $100 A Month For Every Month They Agree To Work In Virginia (Nursing Scholarship Program)

Money For Medical Students Who Agree To Work In Virginia (Medical Scholarship Program)

$5,000 To Dental Students Who Agree To Work In Small Virginia Towns (Rural Dental Scholarships)

$3,720 A Year For Teaching Students For Every Year They Agree To Work In Virginia (Virginia Teaching Scholarship)

Free Tuition, Fees, And Room and Board For State Cadets (State Cadetships)

Free Tuition For Dependents Of Deceased Or Disabled Veterans (Virginia War Orphan Education Act)

Free Tuition And Fees For Students Who Want To Study Soil Science (Soil Scientist Program)
Free Tuition For Students Over 60 (Senior Citizens Tuition Waiver)
Loans To Middle Class Families Having Trouble Paying For Tuition (EDVANTAGE)
Robert C. Byrd Honors Scholarship Program
Scholarships For Financially Needy Students (Virginia Guaranteed Assistance Program)
Scholarships For Good Students (Virginia Graduate and Undergraduate Assistance Program)

Washington

Higher Education Coordinating Board
917 Lakeridge Way
P.O. Box 43430
Olympia, WA 98504
360-753-7800
Fax: 360-753-7808
www.hecb.wa.gov

General requirements: Applicants must be Washington residents for in-state or out-of-state programs, when specified.

Programs Available:

College Students Who Have Trouble Paying Tuition (Washington State Need Grant Program)
Part Time Employment To Students Who Need Money (Washington State Work-Study Program)
Money to High School Students In The Top 1% (Washington Scholars Program)
Money To Study Optometry In Other States (Western Interstate Commission for Higher Education (WICHE) Professional Exchange Program)
Money To Get A Master's Or Ph.D. In Out-Of-State Schools (Western Interstate Commission for Higher Education (WICHE) Regional Graduate Program)
Robert C. Byrd Honors Scholarship Program

$2,500 For Financially Needy Students (Educational Opportunity Grant)
Scholarships and Loan Repayment for Health Professionals (Health Professional Loan Repayment and Scholarship Program)
Grants For Vocational Education (Washington Award for Vocational Excellence- WAVE)
$1,000 For Native Americans (American Indian Endowed Scholarship)
Up to $1,000 for Students in the Top 15% of Their Class (Washington Promise Scholarship)

West Virginia

West Virginia Higher Education Policy Commission
1018 Kanawha Blvd. East, Suite 700
Charleston, WV 25301-2827
304-558-2101
Fax: 304-558-2101
www.hepc.wvnet.edu

General requirements: Applicants must be residents of West Virginia. Money available: $10,995,000.

Programs Available:

Money For Financially Needy Students (West Virginia Higher Education Grant)
Money To Study Teaching At The Graduate Or Undergraduate Level (Underwood-Smith Teacher Scholarship Program)

Money For Medical Students (Central Office of the State College and University Systems Medical Student Loan Program)
Robert C. Byrd Honors Scholarship Program
Scholarships For Good Students (PROMISE-Providing Real Opportunities for Maximizing In-State Student Excellence)
$3,000 For Science and Technology Majors (West Virginia Engineering, Science and Technology Scholarship Program)
Scholarships For Part-Time Students ((Higher Education Adult Part-Time Student (HEAPS) Grant Program))

Wisconsin

State of Wisconsin Higher Educational Aids Board
P.O. Box 7885
Madison, WI 53707-7885
608-267-2206
Fax: 608-267-2808
www.heab.state.wi.us

General requirements: Applicants must be residents of Wisconsin.

Programs Available:

Grants To College Or Vocational Students (Wisconsin Higher Education Grant)
Grants To Students Attending Private Colleges In Wisconsin (Wisconsin Tuition Grant)
Grants For Deaf And Blind Students (Visual and Hearing Impaired Program)
Grants To Blacks, Hispanics, Native Americans, And Former Citizens Of Laos, Vietnam, and Cambodia (Minority Retention Grant)
Grants To Non-Traditional Students (Talent Incentive Program)
$2,200 A Year To Students With At Least 25% Native American Blood (Indian Student Assistance Grant)
Grants To Smart High School Students (Academic Excellence Scholarships)
$1,000 A Year For Every Year You Work As A Nurse In Wisconsin (Nursing Student Stipend Loans)
Cheap Tuition For Attending Minnesota Universities (Minnesota-Wisconsin Reciprocity Program)
Loan and Loan Forgiveness For Minority Teachers (Minority Teacher Loan Program)
$10,000 For Those Who Teach Visually Impaired (Teacher of the Visually Impaired Loan)
Go To Dental School At Marquette (Contract for Dental Education)
$10,000 for Med School (Medical College of Wisconsin Capitation Program)
Loan and Loan Forgiveness Program For Teachers (Teacher Education Loan)

Wyoming

Wyoming Department of Higher Education
Hathaway Building, 2nd Floor
Cheyenne, WY 82002-0050
307-777-6268
www.k12.wy.us/higher_ed.html

General requirements: Applicants must be residents of Wyoming.

Programs Available:

Grants and Loans To Education Majors (Scholarship/Loan Fund for Superior Students in Education)
Grants To Students With 25% Native American Blood (Bureau of Indian Affairs Scholarship and Loan)
Robert C. Byrd Honors Scholarship Program
$500 For First Generation American To Go To College (Douvas Memorial Scholarship)
$600 For Student Leaders (Student Leader Scholarship)
Scholarship For Shoshone Members (Shoshone Tribal Scholarship)
Scholarship for Arapaho Members (Northern Arapaho Tribal Scholarship)
Scholarship For Community College (County Commissioners' Scholarship)

Free Money for College

Scholarships abound if you know where to look. Some samplings include:

- $2,500 for Young Composers
- Scholarships for Mature Women
- $4,000 for Gardening Students
- $1,500 for Women over Age 35
- $5,000 for Broadcasters
- $1,500 for Veterinarian Students
- $2,500 for Architecture Majors
- $5,000 for Pharmacy Students
- $10,000 for Legally Blind Students
- $5,000 for Journalists
- $4,000 for Physical Therapists

Where do you find these kinds of scholarships? Everywhere! Some great starting places include:

General Financial Aid Information Websites

FinAid
http://www.finaid.org

The Financial Aid Resource Network
http://www.theoldschool.org

Employers

If you have a job, ask your own human resources department if they offer scholarships or tuition reimbursement programs. If you are still in high school, have your parents ask their employers.

Professional or Social Organizations

Of what professional or social organizations are you or your parents members? 4H, JayCees, Lions Club? Association for Internet Addiction? If you or your parents are a member of an organization, ask them and see if they offer any kind of scholarships. If you are NOT a member of any organizations, the next thing to check with is organizations that represent what you are planning on studying. Many such organizations offer scholarships to students who are studying what they support, even if you are not a member. For example, the American Medical Record Association offers several scholarships for those planning on making a career in medical record administration, but there is no requirement that you be a member. Many organizations that do permit non-members to apply for scholarships, however, do expect you to join the organization after receiving the scholarship.

Labor Unions

Are you or your parents a member of a union? All the major labor unions offer scholarships for members and their dependent children (AFL-CIO, Teamsters, etc.)

Church

Check with your church. Your local parish may or may not have any scholarships for their members, but the diocese or headquarters may have some available. And if you have been very active in your local church, they may be able to help you in other ways.

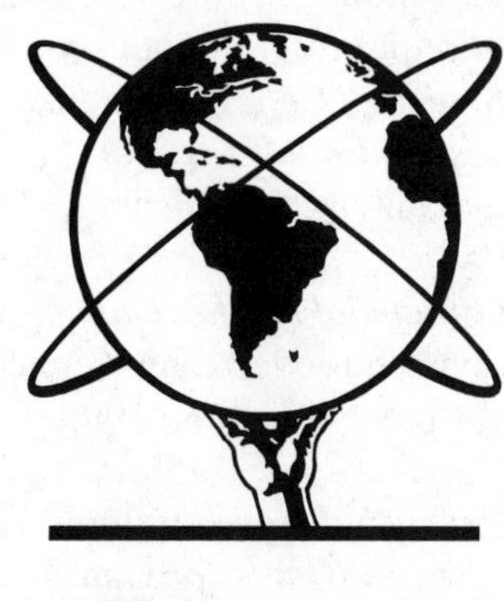

High School
If you are still in high school, it is very important that you speak with your guidance counselor or administration office and ask about scholarships that are available to students at your school.

College
If you are already attending college, or are planning on attending, the financial aid office at your college can be an excellent resource for scholarships and financial aid. You will also find applications for most of the state and federal level aid programs available at your financial aid office.

And if that weren't enough, scholarship books abound. We did a quick recent review of some of the more interesting options and found the following list. Most of these should be available in your local library, as well as at the bookstore.

- *The Black Student's Guide to Scholarships: 700+ Private Money Sources for Black and Minority Students* (5th Ed) by Barry Beckham, Madison Books, 1999.
- *The College Board Scholarship Handbook 2002* by College Board, College Entrance Examination Board, 2001.
- *Chronicle Financial Aid Guide 2002-2003: Scholarships and Loans for High School Students, College Students, Graduates, and Adult Learners*, Chronicle Guidance Publishing, 2002.
- *College Financial Aid for Dummies* by Herm Davis and Joyce Lain Kennedy, Hungry Minds Publishing, 1999.
- *The Complete Scholarship Book: The Biggest, Easiest Guide for Getting the Most Money for College by Fastweb.com*, Sourcebook Trade, 2000.
- *Directory of Financial Aid for Women, 2001-2003* by Gail Ann Schlachter, Reference Service Press, 2001.
- *Discounts and Deals at the Nation's 360 Best Colleges: The Parents Soup Financial Aid and College Guide* by Bruce G. Hammond, Golden Books Publishing Co., 1999
- *Get Free Cash for College* by Kelly Y. Tanabe and Gen S. Tanabe, Supercollege Publishing, 2001.
- *How to Go to College Almost for Free* by Benjamin R. Kaplan, HarperCollins, 2001.
- *The Minority and Women's Complete Scholarship Book* by Student Services L.L.C., Sourcebooks Trade, 1998.
- *Peterson's Basic Guidance Set 2003: 4 Year Colleges/Scholarships, Grants & Prizes* Petersons Guides, 2002.
- *Scholarships 2003 (Scholarships (Kaplan))* by Gail Schlachter, R. David Weber and Douglas Bucher, Kaplan, 2002.

- *The Scholarship Book 2002* by Daniel Cassidy, Prentice Hall Press, 2001.

- *The Scholarship Book 2003: The Complete Guide to Private-Sector Scholarships, Fellowships, Grants and Loans for the Undergraduate* by National Scholarship Research Service, Prentice Hall, 2002.

- *Winning Scholarships for College: An Insider's Guide* by Marianne Ragins, Owl Books, 1999.

- *The 2000 Hispanic Scholarship Directory* by Edward James Olmos, Nadres Tobar and Brenda Deal, WPR Publishing, 2000.

Free Money for Federal Employees and Their Families To Go To College

Over $2.75 million in college scholarships is awarded exclusively to federal and postal employees and their family members. The Federal Employee Education Assistance Program (FEEA) scholarship applications are available from January through March each year. You can get an application online at their web site. Applications are due back at FEEA headquarters by the end of March each year (see application for current deadline). Awards are announced in August in time for the fall school term and are paid in two installments — half in August/September and the balance in December/January. Awards generally range from $300 to $1,500.

Eligible applicants include current civilian federal and postal employees with at least three years of federal service and their dependent family members (children and spouses). Employee applicants may be part-time students; dependents must be full-time. All applicants must be enrolled or plan to enroll in an accredited post secondary school in a course of study that will lead to a two-year, four-year or graduate degree. All applicants must have at least a 3.0 grade point average on a 4.0 scale.

Applications are merit based. Criteria include the academic record of the applicant, a recommendation (character reference), extracurricular and community service activities, and an essay. The essay topic changes each year and is printed on the application. Applicants may be high school seniors or may already be in college or graduate school. FEEA scholarship awards are for one year. Although they are not renewable, recipients may reenter the competition each year. Applicants not selected for awards may also reapply. For more information send a self-addressed, stamped #10 business envelope to: FEEA Scholarships, Suite 200, 8441 W Bowles Ave, Littleton, CO 80123-9501; 303-933-7580; {http://www.feea.org/scholarships.shtml}.

Save Your Money

Don't spend money on something you can do yourself! Many scholarship search services will charge you $300 and guarantee you that they will find you a certain of scholarships for which you MAY qualify. You can do that yourself and save the $300 for your college textbooks. Search for scholarships on the web using any of these search engines for FREE!

Free Scholarship Information Service
{www.freschinfo.com}

The Scholarship Page
{www.scholarship-page.com}

FastAid
{www.fastaid.com}

Embark
{www.embark.com}

Go College
{www.gocollege.com}

FastWEB
{www.fastweb.com}

ASIS Arkansas Scholarship Information Service
{http://scholarships-ar-us.org}

College Planning Web Site
{http://collegeplan.org}

College Net
{www.collegenet.com}

OSAD Scholarship Search
(online study abroad directory)
{www.umabroad.umn.edu}

Arkansas Student Loan Authority
{www.asla.state.ar.us}

Free Money For Elementary and High School

Private Voucher Clearinghouse

CEO (Children's Educational Opportunity Foundation) serves as a national clearinghouse for privately funded voucher programs that provide everything from support services to new programs on videotapes for K-12 grades. These private tuition grants and tax funded options give families the power to choose the K-12 school that will best accomplish their needs.

The website has a map of the U.S. Just click on the area of the program that is located near or in your hometown. For example, click on Phoenix, AZ and the next screen will pop up indicating who is the contact person for AZ, the total amount invested in the voucher program, as well as other information. The website also gives you a history about school choice legislation, school choice research, and some testimonies on how you can make a difference in the program.

Contact: CEO America, P.O. Box 330, Bentonville, AR 72712; 501-273-6957; Fax: 501-273-9362; {www.ceoamerica.org}.

$1,700 Washington Scholarship Fund, Inc.

The Washington School Fund provides financial assistance for children to attend either private or parochial schools in the Washington, D.C. area for grades K through 8th. The maximum amount received per child is $1,700, and families of 4 with incomes up to $35,802 are eligible to apply.

Contact: Washington Scholarship Fund, Inc., 1133 15th Street, NW, Suite 580, Washington, DC 20005; 202-293-5560; Fax: 202-293-7893; {www.wsf-dc.org}.

$1,400 For Elementary Students In New York City

The School Choice Scholarships Foundation provides funds to cover the annual tuition costs up to $1,400 maximum per child and it is guaranteed for at least three years.

Scholarships are only for elementary school children who are currently enrolled in a New York City's public schools, and meet the income levels requirements. Students are selected by a lottery drawing with priority given to children who attend the lowest performing schools.

Contact: School Choice Scholarships Foundation, Inc., 730 Fifth Avenue, 9th Floor, New York, NY 10019; 212-338-8711; Fax: 212-307-3230; {www.nygroup.com}; Email: {scsf@nygroup.com}.

Dentist Offers Scholarships for Elementary School Children

For several years Dr. Albert Landucci has sponsored awards and scholarships to the less fortunate. Scholarships are based on academic excellence, community service, volunteering, science and mathematics excellence and dental assisting.

Scholarships are offered in the San Mateo Elementary School District at:

Abbott
Audubon
Bayside
Baywood
Beresford
Borel
Bowditch
Brewer Island
Central Elementary
Cipriani
Fiesta Gardens International
Foster City
Fox
George Hall
Highlands
Horrall
Immaculate Heart of MaryCounty College of San Mateo
Laurel
Laurel's Highly Gifted Program
Meadow Heights
Nesbit
North Shoreview
Notre Dame
Park
Parkside
Ralston
St. Gregory
St. Matthew
St. Timothy
Sandpiper
Sunnybrae
Turnball Learning Academy
All the high schools in San Mateo

For more information about the awards, scholarships and to see if your school is in the district, visit Dr. Landucci's website. Contact: Albert O. J. Landucci, D.D.S, 2720 Edison Street, San Mateo, CA 94403-2495; 650-574-4444; 650-574-4441 (voice mail); {www.drlanducci.com}; Email: (e@DrLanducci.com}.

Free Private Schools For Kids of Color

A Better Chance's mission is work with minority students from the 6th grade through college to open opportunity doors that otherwise would not be open without a helping hand. There are several programs that include helping students receive financial aid for attending private local

schools, boarding schools, or summer programs to help prepare for college.

Contact: A Better Chance, 88 Black Falcon Avenue, Suite 250, Boston, MA 02210-2414; 800-562-7865; 617-421-0950; Fax: 617-421-0965; {www.abetterchance.org}.

Tuition Assistance for Black Students

The Black Student Fund has provided financial assistance and support services to African American students and their families in the Washington, DC area for over 34 years. All financial assistance is based on a sliding scale. During the last several years, their scope has broadened to provide services to families in the greater Washington, DC area and the nation.

Contact them at Black Student Fund, 3636 16th Street, NW, 4th Floor, Washington, DC 20010; 202-387-1414; {www.blackstudentfund.org}; Email: {mail@blackstudentfund.org}.

Money For Future Writers

For those future award-winning writers, Amelia Magazine awards $200 for a high school student's first publication. First publications can be a previously unpublished poem, a nonfiction essay or a short story. Deadline for the contest is May 15.

Write or call for further information. Amelia Student Award, Amelia Magazine, 329 East Street, Bakersfield, CA 93304; 805-323-4064.

Education Loans Up To $20,000 For Grades K Thru 12

As with college loans, there are many financial institutions that provide loans for families to send their children to private or parochial schools at the elementary and secondary school levels. Listed below are some of the organizations that are providing these types of loans. Be sure to be aware that you can always contact your state banking commissioner by calling your state capitol operator listed in the Appendix.

1) ***Key Education Resources***
   745 Atlantic Ave., Suite 300
   Boston, MA 02111
   800-225-6783 (toll free)
   617-348-0010
   Fax: 617-348-0020
   {www.petersons.com/graduate/keylink.html}

2) ***USA Group Tuition Payment Plan***
   P.O. Box 7039
   Indianapolis, IN 46207-7039
   800-824-7044
   Fax: 317-951-5889
   {www.usagroup.com}

3) ***The Education Resources Institute (TERI)***
   800-255-TERI
   {www.teri.org}

4) ***First Marblehead Corporation***
   30 Little Harbor
   Marblehead, MA 01945
   781-639-2000

Fax: 781-639-4583
{http://gateloan.com}

5) ***FACTS SCHOLAR Loan Program***
P.O. Box 67037
100 N. 56th Street, Suite 306
Lincoln, NE 68504
800-624-7092
402-466-1063
Fax: 402-466-1136
{www.factsmgt.com}

$2,000 For Children In Arizona

Arizona children in K-12, with incomes up to $29,693 (for family of 4) can receive up to $2,000 per child per school year with a minimum three-year commitment to qualified children.

Contact: Arizona Scholarship Fund, P.O. Box 2576, Mesa, AZ 85214; 602-497-4564; Fax: 602-832-8853; Email: {ChamBria@ Azscholarships.org}; or Arizona Scholarship Fund, P.O. Box 31354, Tucson, AZ 85751-1354; 502-886-7248; Email: {ChamBria@Azscholarships.org}; {www. azscholarships.org}.

$10,000 for a 7th Grade Essay

The 53-year-old contest is open to parochial, private and home schooled 7th and 8th graders. Students should submit a 300-400 word, typed essay based on a patriotic theme established by VFW.

Contact your school counselor or principal to apply, or contact the VFW listed and they will tell you where your local chapter is located. First place national winners receive a $10,000 savings bond, 2nd place winners receive a $6,000 savings bond and 3rd place winners receive $5,000 savings bond.

Contact: VFW Voice of Democracy Essay Contest, Veterans of Foreign Wars of the United States, VFW Building, 406 West 34th Street, Kansas City, MO 64111; 816-756-3390; Fax: 816-968-1149; {www.vfw.org}; Email: {info@vfw.org}.

Money For Young Writers

Contestants receive a cash award for writing a short story that promotes brotherhood and is 4,000 words maximum. The money can be used for anything. For more information, contact Aim Magazine Short Story Contest, 7308 S Eberhart, Chicago, IL 60619.

$3,000 for Artists

Any high school students that need help with furthering their education can enter the VFW Ladies Auxiliary National Patriotic Creative Art Competition. Students should submit their entry through the VFW Ladies Auxiliary Local Chapter first.

Finalists from the local chapters are selected for the grand prize competition. First place grand prize winners receive $3,000, and an all expense paid trip to the VFW Ladies

Auxiliary Conference for Community Service in Washington, DC. Second place winners receive $2,000, 3rd place winners receive $1,500, 4th place winners receive $1,000 and 5th place winners receive $500.

Contact: VFW Ladies Auxiliary National Patriotic Creative Art Competition, Ladies Auxiliary to the VFW National Headquarters, 406 West 34th Street, Kansas City, MO 64111; 816-561-8655; Fax: 816-931-4753; {www.ladiesauxvfw.com}.

$1,500 For Young Science Types

Each year General Learning Communication with Dupont sponsors a science essay contest for children in grades 7-12. First place winners of each division receive $1,500, and an expense paid trip to Space Center Houston with their parents. This trip includes airfare, hotel and an allowance. Second place winners receive a $750 prize, 3rd place winners a $500 prize and honorable mentions receive $50. The deadline for the contest is January 29. Write or visit the website to obtain the entry application and mail first class in a 9x12 envelope.

Contact: Dupont Science Challenge, Science Essay Awards Program, c/o General Learning Communications, 900 Skokie Blvd, Suite 200, Northbrook, IL 60062; 847-205-3000; Fax: 847-564-8197; {www.glcomm.com/dupont}.

40,000 Scholarships For Kids From K to 8th Grade

That's how many scholarships were given out in 1999 by the Children's Scholarship Fund, but at press time it was not clear when the scholarships will be available again. The scholarships averaged $1,100 for children from K through 8th grade to attend private schools. There were income requirements, but the income level can go up to $44,415 for a family of 4. The awards are based on a lottery process.

To keep in touch to see when this program will be available again, contact Children's Scholarship Fund, 7 West 57th St. 3rd Floor, New York, N Y 10019; 212-751-8555; {www.scholarshipfund.org}.

Students in Grades 6-12 Can Win $20,000

Each year the **NSTA (National Science Teachers Association)** sponsors a scholarship competition for students in grades 6-12, who compete either individually or in pairs. The first place winner in the grades 6-9 receive a $20,000 savings bond, two 2nd place winners receive one $10,000 savings bonds each, and each 3rd place winner (5) receives one $3,000 savings bonds. The same awards disbursement will be done for grades 10-12. Deadline for the competition is in January.

Six teachers from the 1st and 2nd place winners will receive a $2000 gift certificate towards computer equipment. Ten teachers from the third place winners will receive a $200 certificate for NSTA publications. Contact: Duracell/NSTA Scholarship Competition, 1840 Wilson Blvd., Arlington, VA 22201; 888-255-4242 (toll free); {www.nsta.org}.

$1,000 For Writing About Technology

Students in K-12 from the U.S. and Canada can use their imagination and creative writing and illustrating skills to compose a ten page or less essay to indicate what technology would be like 20 years from now. There are four categories for students to participate: grades K-3, grades 4-6, grades 7-9 and grades 10-12. Final first place winners receive a $10,000 savings bond, second place winners receive a $5,000 savings bond, and teachers receive Toshiba prizes.

Contact: Toshiba/NSTA Explora Vision Awards Program, 1840 Wilson Boulevard, Arlington, VA 22201; 800-397-5679 (toll free); 703-243-7100; Email: {exploravision@nsta.org}.

$150 For Young Artists

American Automobile Association (AAA) awards prizes up to $150 for children in K to 12th grade and $5,000 for college students in their ***School Traffic Safety Program***. In the K-12 division, children submit posters. In the senior high division, students can submit essays, brochures, and even creative videos.

Contact your local AAA office and ask for the School Traffic Safety Division. You may also contact AAA School Traffic Safety Poster Program, Poster Program Manager, American Automobile Association (AAA), 1260 Fair Lakes Circle, Fairfax, VA 22033; 407-444-7916; Fax: 407-444-7956.

$10,000 For Young Inventors

Craftsman sponsors a program where students either invent or modify a tool independently. Two winners from grades 3-5 and 6-8 will receive a $10,000 savings bond. Ten finalists, five from each grade will receive a $5,000 savings bond. The teachers of these winners and their schools will receive prizes from Sears. Every contestant will receive a gift and certificate of appreciation.

Contact: Craftsman/NSTA Young Inventors Awards Program, National Science Teachers Association, 1840 Wilson Boulevard, Arlington, VA 22201; 888-494-4994 (toll free); Email: {younginventors@nsta.org}.

$1,000 a Year for 3 Years In Kentucky

School Choice Scholarships Inc. (SCSI) in Jefferson County, Kentucky awards its kids with 100 new partial-scholarships per year in addition to the 325 scholarships awarded just last year! If your Jefferson County child is in K-6 and your family meets the Federal School Lunch regulations, you can be awarded 50%-60% of all tuition (up to $1000) for THREE YEARS! SCSI is willing to make a three-year commitment to making sure your child can enjoy the freedom of school choice! Contact: SCSI, P.O. Box 221546, Louisville, KY 40252-1546; 502-254-7274.

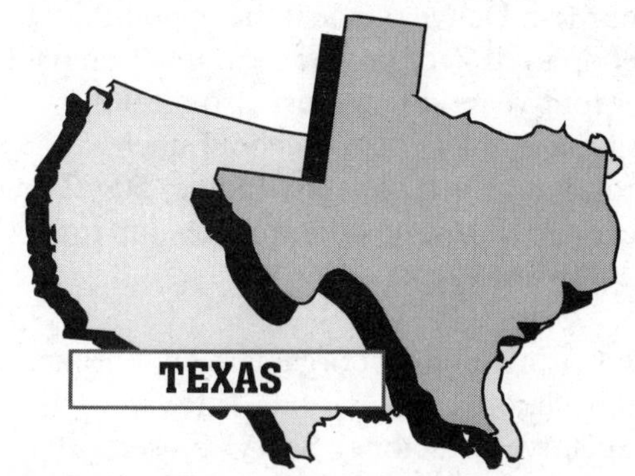

$1,450 For Families In Texas

The Childrens Educational Opportunity Foundation is a private scholarship program that will pay one-half of a child's tuition at any private school or out-of-district public school in Harris County (up to $1450). If your Harris County, TX family meets the Federal School Lunch Program requirements, your child enrolled in 1st to 8th grade may apply. This year, the Foundation hopes to award 550 students with the ability to practice school choice!

Contact: The Childrens Educational Opportunity Foundation, 952 Echo Lane, Suite 350, Houston, TX 77024; 713-722-8555; Fax: 713- 722-7442; {www.hern.org/ceo/index.html}.

$1,200 in Arizona

Arizona School Choice Trust (coupled with the Childrens Scholarship Fund) will grant 25%-75% towards your child's choice of educational institution (up to $1200). If you live in Maricopa County, meet the Federal School Lunch Program guidelines, and your child is in a grade from K-8, you are eligible to apply!

The Arizona School Choice Trust has awarded more than 500 four-year awards and through tax-deductible donations adds more students to the program each year. To ensure your child's success in the program, ASCT requires that while enrolled, your student must maintain a 90% attendance rate. Contact: Arizona School Choice Trust, Inc., 3737 E. Broadway Rd., Phoenix, AZ 85040-2966; 602-454-1360; Fax: 602-454-1362; {www.asct.org}.

$1,250 For 4 Years In Connecticut

CEO Connecticut offers your K-5 child, living in either Hartford or Bridgeport, CT, the extra help needed to attend any chosen private school in the area. Just meet the Federal School Lunch Program guidelines, apply, and you could be awarded up to half the tuition for four years (up to $1250). Just last year, CEO Connecticut awarded 200 four-year scholarships in Hartford and another 106 in Bridgeport! Plus, they're happy to help families stay together by making use of a sibling policy! Contact: CEO Connecticut, P.O. Box 6364, Bridgeport, CT 06606; 203-334-3003; Fax: 203-334-7358.

Up to $1,800 in Michigan

The Educational Choice Project assist K-8 students eligible for the Federal School Lunch Program by offering to pay half of the tuition needed to attend the child's school of choice (up to $1800). Last year alone, 149 students from Calhun County gladly accepted this generous opportunity! Contact: The Educational Choice Project, 34 W. Jackson, One River Walk Center, Battle Creek, MI 49017-3505; 616-962-2181; Fax: 616-962-2182.

Over $5 Million More For Texas Children

The Today Foundation of Dallas, Texas joins with the Childrens Education Fund and the Childrens Scholarship Fund (CSF) to be able to grant Dallas students in grades K-8 with help to attend their schools of choice. Just recently, the CSF agreed to donate 5 million dollars (over four years) to help these students (who must also be eligible for the Federal School Lunch Program).

Already, the Today Foundation has been able to award 500 students with half of their school choice tuition and due to this amazing gift from the CSF, many more students will be given a very special opportunity. For more information, contact Childrens Education Fund, P.O. Box 225748, Dallas, TX 75222-5748; 972-298-1811; Fax: 972-296-6369; Email: {today@todayfoundation.org}; {www.TodayFoundation.org}.

$2,000 For Elementary Students In Colorado

Educational Options for Children offers your K-6 Denver student the opportunity to get up to 65% of private school tuition paid for four years! (You must also meet the criteria of the Federal School Lunch Program.) Every 2 years, another 50-60 four year partial-tuition opportunities (up to $2000) are available!

EOC is a non-profit organization. For more information, contact Linda Tafoya, Executive Director or Sheryl Glaser, Program Administrator at c/o Adolph Coors Foundation, 3773 Cherry Creek North Dr., Denver, CO 80209; 303-380-6481; Fax: 303-477-9986.

Free Classes For Kids With A.D.D.

The nonprofit organization, *Children and Adults with Attention Deficit Disorder (CHADD),* identifies a number of federal laws that require the government to provide children with this disorder special educational services. It is only recently that these children became eligible for such services, so many eligible children may not be receiving what they deserve.

To learn more about these free educational services, or to find out more and how to treat a child with ADD, or what's good and bad about available treatments, contact: CHADD, 8181 Professional Place, Suite 201, Landover, MD 20785; 800-233-4050; Fax: 301-306-7090; {www.chadd.org}.

Save 50% On Elementary School Tuition

Gateway Educational Trust offers to pay half of your child's tuition (up to $1000) for up to three years to elementary school children. Your child must be entering K-4, live or attend school in St. Louis, and meet the regulations of the Federal Reduced Price Lunch Program. That's it! Simple!

If you'd like an application mailed to you, call 314-771-1998 and leave your name and address. For more information, you may contact Irene Allen, the Executive Director at Gateway Educational Trust, 7716 Forsyth Blvd., St. Louis, MO 63105-1810; 314-721-1375; Fax: 314-721-1857; Email: {ager2@aol.com}.

$$$ Pay Your Job Training Bills

Welfare-To-Work

If you are on welfare and are having trouble getting and keeping a job that will lead to self-sufficiency, the Welfare-to-Work program might just be the answer to help you get a great job. The Welfare-to-Work program provides grants to local agencies so they can provide for the needs of the local community.

You may be able to receive up to six months of pre-employment vocational training and other employment programs to help you get a job. After you have the job, there are post-employment services such as mentoring, English as a second language and job retention support available. Job retention and support services include such services as: transportation assistance, substance abuse treatment, childcare assistance, and emergency or short term housing assistance.

Contact your State Department of Labor listed in the appendix for information in your community. There is also a Welfare-to-Work service locator on the web at {http://wtw.doleta.gov/techassist/liaisonwtw.asp}. Contact National Office: U.S. Department of Labor, Frances Perkins Building, 200 Constitution Avenue, NW, Washington, DC 20210; 202-693-3900; {http://wtw.doleta.gov/}.

Supplement Your Retirement

If you are 55 years old or over, have a low-income and having trouble finding a job, the Senior Community Service Employment Program (SCSEP) may be able to help. The federal government provides job and educational training by placing seniors into community and government agency jobs for up to 20 hours a week. The job assignments may include positions at the library, schools, recreation facilities, maintenance and any other services essential for the community. These opportunities may then lead to non-subsidized jobs and higher pay.

To learn more about the opportunities in your area check the web site at {http://wdsc.doleta.gov/seniors/html_docs/grants.cfm}. You may also contact National Office: Division of Older Worker Programs, U.S. Department of Labor, Employment and Training Administration, 200 Constitution Ave. NW, Room N-4641, Washington, D.C. 20210; 202-693-3842; {http://wdsc.doleta.gov/seniors/}.

Learn New Technical Skills

The business world is in constant need of skilled technical workers, however, foreign workers under the H-1B visa program are filling many of those jobs in the U.S. today.

Because of this, the government has set aside millions of grant dollars for companies to train American workers for these technical jobs in hopes to lessen their dependency on skilled foreign workers. Businesses compete for grants to provide technical skills training for workers who have lost their jobs, or who want to upgrade their skills or change occupations.

Contact the US Labor Department for additional information at U.S. Department of Labor, Frances Perkins Building, 200 Constitution Avenue, NW, Washington, DC 20210; 202-693-3900; {http://www.doleta.gov/h-1b/}.

Become a Journeyman

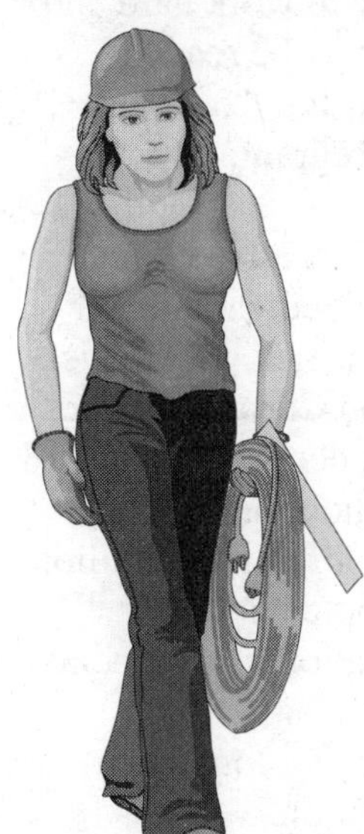

Getting a good job does not always mean that you have to go to college or a trade school. There are thousands of apprenticeship programs all over the country and in U.S. territories that will provide free on-the-job training, and best of all you earn while you learn.

Apprenticeship training is a system that can train you to be a highly skilled worker to meet the demands of employers competing in a global economy. Generally, apprentices need to be at least 18 years old and the programs can range in time commitment from 1-6 years depending on the chosen field. Program sponsors will pay most of the your training costs while at the same time paying you wages that increase as your skill level increases. For the apprentice, this can translate into an educational benefit worth $40,000 to $150,000.

Apprenticeships are for everyone; you can be rich, middle class, poor, man or women you just have to be willing to in the time and effort to become an expert at your new career. Programs may be sponsored by employers, a union or even the military and include construction, service, information technology, manufacturing, health care and public utilities apprenticeships.

For local offices and information, look in the blue pages of your phone book for the Bureau of Apprenticeship or the State Apprenticeship Council located in your state, or contact an employer or union engaged in the trade you want to enter.

To learn who to call in your area, contact National Office: Bureau of Apprenticeship and Training, Frances Perkins Building, 200 Constitution Avenue, NW, Room N4671; Washington, DC 20210; 202-693-2796; 202-693-3812; Fax: 202-693-2808; {http://www.doleta.gov/jobseekers/apprent.asp}; {http://bat.doleta.gov}.

Free Training and Money if You're Laid Off

If you have been laid off because of a plant closing or downsizing, apply for money and re-training from the government under the Economic Dislocation and Worker Adjustment Assistance Act (EDWAA). This money is not just for big business layoffs but includes long-term unemployed workers with limited job opportunities in their fields including farmers, ranchers and other self-employed persons who become unemployed due to general economic conditions. Under certain circumstances, states may even authorize service for displaced homemakers.

The Economic Dislocation and Worker Adjustment Assistance Act is administered by each state, and because of that, the program differs from state to state. The Governor of each state designates a Dislocated Worker Unit (DWU) that operates and administers the program at the local level to best service their states needs.

The programs may include retraining services: retraining classes, on-the-job training, occupational skills, literacy classes and even English as a second language. Readjustment services include outreach, testing and counseling, job search services, including child care and transportation allowances and relocation assistance. Dislocated workers in training who have exhausted all of their unemployment insurance may receive needs-related payments while they finish their training.

For additional information, contact your state Department of Labor or the Dislocated Workers Unit by using the blue pages of your local phone book. To learn more about services in your area contact National Office: Office of Worker Retraining and Adjustments Programs, U.S. Department of Labor, Room N-5426, 200 Constitution Avenue, NW; Washington, DC 20210; 202-693-3580; toll-free 877-US-2JOBS; {http://www.doleta.gov/programs/factsht/edwaa.asp}.

Job Corps

Just because you are a high school drop-out, have a low-income, need additional basic education, are homeless, a runaway or in foster care doesn't mean that you have to settle for a low paying job for the rest of your life. If you are ready to work hard and show commitment, you may be ready to participate successfully in Job Corps and gain the benefits of the program.

Job Corps is the nation's largest and most comprehensive residential, education and job training program for at-risk youth, ages 16 through 24. Today, Job Corps continues to serve nearly 70,000 students a year at 118 Job Corps centers throughout the country. Job Corps has provided more than 2 million disadvantaged young people with the integrated academic, vocational, and social skills training they need to gain independence and get quality, long-term jobs or further their education.

Job Corps has many career choices including agriculture, construction, food service, business management, health care, engineering, transportation and many more. The culinary arts students not only learn to sauté and broil, they also get to enter exciting Culinary Expos to show off their talents in the food industry.

To apply contact a Job Corps counselor at (800) 733-JOBS or apply on line at the web site listed below, or contact U.S. Department of Labor, 200 Constitution Ave., NW, Washington, DC 20210; 202-693-3900; 800-733-JOBS; {http://jobcorps.doleta.gov/}.

Free Help If You Lose Your Job Because of Increased Imports

As the business world becomes more and more competitive, many US businesses are moving their companies to other parts of the globe. U.S. workers may lose their jobs when this happens. The government however, is willing to help! The President signed into law the Trade Adjustment Assistance Reform Act of 2002 (TAA Reform Act) on August 6, 2002, which provides you with assistance if you lose your job because of increased imports. The Trade Adjustment Assistance Reform Act has consolidated the North America Free Trade Agreement (NAFTA) into the TAA Reform Act.

Any worker, no matter what their prior income level, can apply for assistance. The Trade Adjustment Assistance Reform Act of 2002 can help you learn marketable skills to move you on to new and better job opportunities. Workers may be eligible for up to 130 weeks of on-the-job and classroom training; you can receive 78 weeks of income benefits after your unemployment expires; you can receive $1,250 for job search and relocation

expenses; health care benefits may also be available. This program is also available to farmers who have been hurt by imports!

For more information contact U.S. Department of Labor, Employment and Training Administration, Division of Trade Adjustment Assistance, 200 Constitution Avenue, NW, Room C-5311, Washington, DC 20210; 202-693-3560; {www.doleta.gov}; {http://wdsc.doleta.gov/trade_act/petitions.asp}.

One-Stop Can Do It All

Are you looking for help in a career change or job skills training? If so, the government may have the help you need. The Workforce Investment Act (WIA), which replaces the Job Training Partnership Act (JTPA), provides a comprehensive workforce system to help Americans find the tools they need to manage their careers and to help U.S. companies find skilled workers.

You can find access to job search assistance, career guidance, salary data, training and education resources at your local One-Stop Service Center. The Workforce Investment Act (WIA) is now one of the main government program offering retraining funds to assist job seekers.

Contact your state One-Stop Career Center located in the appendix, check the web site to find the closest office, or contact National Office: Office of Career Transition Assistance, U.S. Department of Labor, 200 Constitution Avenue, NW, Room S-4231, Washington, DC 20210; 202-693-3900; {http://www.doleta.gov/usworkforce/onestop/}; {http://workforcesecurity.doleta.gov/}.

Free Job Training

Actually many state Departments of Labor offer a variety of job training programs to help employers train new hires or upgrade the skills of their current workers. Although these programs need to be initiated by the employer with the Labor Department, you can take the initiative and see what they have to offer. Then show your boss how eager you are to learn new skills, at no cost to them!

- California will reimburse you $20 per hour per student for training for mid-level Information Technology positions, as part of the TechForce program of the Employment Development Department.
- Ohio Training Tax Credit Program provides tax credits of up to $100,000 per year to help offset costs of training current workers.
- Pennsylvania offers Customized Job Training grants for specialized job training for existing or new employees; Guaranteed Free Training Program up to $700 per employee; and Critical Job Training Grants for high demand jobs or jobs with a shortage of skilled workers.
- Rhode Island has a Job Creation Grant Fund to offer customized training and a Competitiveness Improvement Program that provides grants up to $25,000 to upgrade and retrain existing employees.
- Arkansas' Business and Industry Training program will provide financial assistance to companies to recruit new workers, will provide customized training before employment, and will pay for more training once you hire the employee. They also offer the Existing Workforce Training Program which will pay for upgrading the skills of your current employees.

Contact your state Department of Labor listed in the Appendix to see what job training programs or tax credits they may offer to help you get the training or the employees you need.

The Little Extras

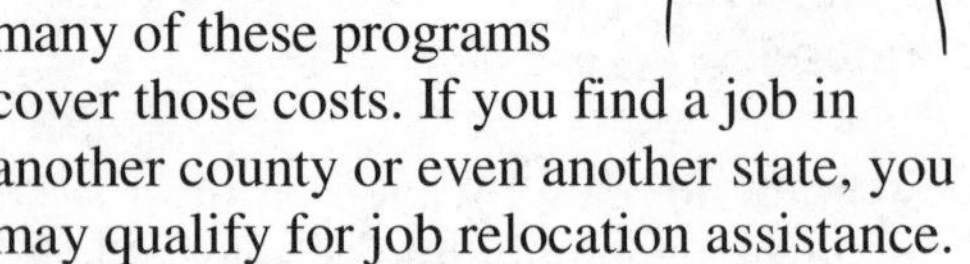

We talk about a great many different types of job training programs, but it is worth repeating about certain extras that many of these programs offer. If you have children and are in need of child care in order to seek employment, many of these programs cover those costs. If you find a job in another county or even another state, you may qualify for job relocation assistance.

Do you need help getting to the job training site? There may be funds to pay for transportation costs, as well as other supplies need to complete the training program. If you need something special, just ask your job counselor. You may be surprised!

Food Stamps-Not Just For Groceries Anymore!

The Food Stamp Program can do more than just help pay for your monthly food expenses; it can also help you train for a new job. On May 13, 2002, President Bush signed into law, a law that reauthorizes the Food Stamp Employment and Training Program (FSET) until 2007.

The U.S. Department of Agriculture requires each state to operate an employment and training program for Food Stamp recipients. The goal of the Food Stamp Employment and Training Program is to help recipients prepare for and become employed. Services may include an individual assessment of work-related strengths and barriers and an Employment Plan designed to help participants obtain or upgrade the skills necessary to gain employment.

Job training may also include General Equivalency Diploma (GED), English as a Second Language (ESL), high school diploma or short-term vocational training. FSET services are administered by each state, usually through service providers such as WorkForce Centers, community action agencies and county employment and training providers.

To apply for benefits or obtain information, contact your local Food Stamp program. Check your local phone book in the government pages under "Food Stamps". Contact National Headquarters, USDA Food and Nutrition Service, Food Stamp Program, 3101 Park Center Drive, Alexandria, VA 22302; 703-305-2026; {www.fns.usda.gov/fsp}.

On the Road to Independence

All kinds of free help is out there for teenagers in foster care, and young adults who have been raised in foster homes. Signed into law in 1999, the John H Chafee Foster Care Independence Program (CFCIP) offers assistance to current and former foster care youths achieve self-sufficiency.

Activities and programs include, but are not limited to help with education, employment, financial management, housing, emotional support and assured connections to caring adults for older youth in foster care as well as youth 18-21 who have aged out of the foster care system. This legislation helps ensure that young people involved in the foster care system get the tools they need to make the most of their lives.

Contact your state division of Child and Family Services for information on the Chafee Foster Care Independence Program. Contact Division of Child Welfare, Administration for Children and Families, 370 L'Enfant Promenade SW, Washington, DC 20447; 202-205-8575; {http://www.acf.hhs.gov/programs/cb/programs/indep_living.htm}.

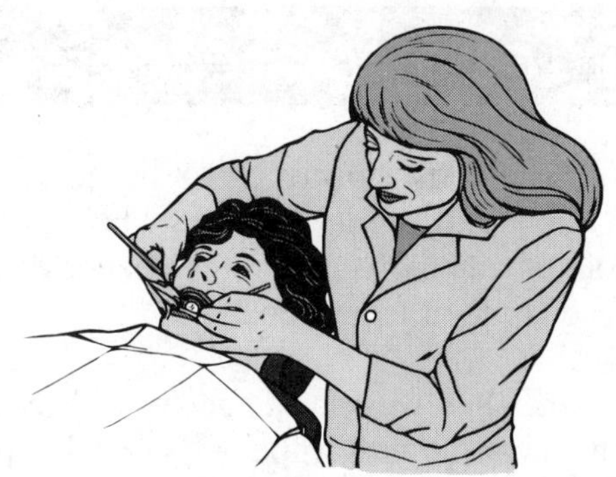

Cream of the Crop Programs for Seasonal Farmworkers

Migrant workers and seasonal laborers are some of the hardest working people in America. Yet when the crops are all picked or the economy sags, they are some of the first to be out of a job. Fortunately, the government has a special job-training program to help — The National Farmworker Jobs Program (NFJP).

The National Farmworker Jobs Program provides assistance, which includes, free skills assessment, basic education, job-training and short-term direct assistance. To obtain additional information and to see if you qualify, contact your local One-Stop Centers (the state One-Stops are listed in the Appendix). Contact Alicia Fernandez-Mott, Chief, Division of Seasonal Farmworker Programs, Employment and Training Administration, Room N-4641, 200 Constitution Avenue, NW, Washington, DC 20210; 202-693-3729; {http://wdsc.doleta.gov/msfw/}.

Tools for Teens

Bottom line: most construction jobs pay well. Many of the today's youths who dropout of school, would prefer a hands-on approach to their education.

Young men and women can get experience in construction trades while helping to build and restore affordable housing for low and moderate-income persons through the Youthbuild Program. Youthbuild provides grants to assist high-risk, very low-income youth between the ages of 16-24 to learn housing construction skills and to complete their high school education at the same time. Youthbuild teaches participants how to tear down or rehabilitate old houses and how to build new houses from the ground up.

Youthbuild programs offer educational and job training services, leadership training, counseling, living allowances, placement services and even driver's education courses. To obtain additional information, contact the HUD office or check their web site for a program in your area.

Contact U.S. Department of Housing and Urban Development, Office of Community Planning and Development, Jackie Mitchell, 451 7th Street, SW, Washington, DC 20410; 202-708-2290; {www.hud.gov/progdesc/youthb.cfm}; {www.youthbuildusa.org/}.

One-Stop Career Shopping

Are you tired of your old job? Do you need help training for a new career? Are you ready for a new exciting job? Well, the Department of Labor Employment and Training Administration's Career One-Stop may just be your ticket.

Career One Stop is a national online career development resource, which provides internet-based access for Americans, needing job search assistance, career guidance, salary data and training and education resources. You can find jobs from entry level to technical to professional to

CEO. In addition to the online program, there are also Comprehensive One-Stop Career Centers located throughout the country.

Each community has tailored their system to meet the needs of the citizens in their area. The centers may offer computers, career counseling, workshops and many other services. The number of centers is growing everyday.

To locate the Career One-Stop Program go to their web site. For additional information and to locate your closest Career One-Stop Center, go to the service locator web site or refer to the appendix of this book for a listing.

Contact U.S. Department of Labor, Frances Perkins Building, 200 Constitution Avenue, NW, Washington, DC 20210; 877-US-2JOBS; 877-889-5627 TTY; {http://www.doleta.gov/usworkforce/onestop/}; Career One-Stop: {http://www.careeronestop.org/}; Career One-Stop Center Locator: {http://www.servicelocator.org/nearest_onestop.asp}.

Earn Money While You Learn

Do you want to start your own business? You can take free business training classes while you collect unemployment benefits. If approved for this training, you may also be eligible for addition money for transportation and child care costs.

This program is offered through the Workforce Investment Act (formerly known as the Job Training Partnership Act- JTPA). The goal of this program is to help unemployed people stay gainfully employed, even if it in their own businesses. Local offices are located across the country to help you learn how to properly launch your new business.

The toll free number 877-US-2JOBS can help you locate your nearest job training or one-stop career center. You may also contact your local Workforce Investment Act office, or contact Office of Employment and Training Programs, U.S. Department of Labor, 200 Constitution Ave., NW, Room N4469, Washington, DC 20210; 202-693-3031; 877-US-2JOBS; {www.doleta.gov/usworkforce}.

Employment Help for Native Americans

If your ancestors were the some of the first people in our country, the Indian and Native American Program may be able to help you with valuable job skills. The Workforce Investment Act (WIA) provides help to Indians, Alaska Natives, and Native Hawaiians who are economically disadvantaged, unemployed, and underemployed.

Grants are distributed to organizations at a local level to provide the best quality of service to its customers. The goal of the program is to expand the occupational, academic, and literacy skills of Indians and Native Americans while enhancing their job prospects. The Workforce Investment Act also authorizes funds to provide employment and training programs for Indian youth on reservations.

Contact your local reservation, tribal government or One-Stop Career Center found in the appendix for additional information. You may also contact National Office: U.S. Department of Labor, Frances Perkins Building, 200 Constitution Avenue, NW, Washington, DC 20210; 202-693-3900; {http://wdsc.doleta.gov/dinap/}.

Training After the Harvest for Seasonal Farmworkers

We all depend on the fresh fruits and vegetables in our grocery stores and we thank seasonal farmworkers for picking them. The work however does not provide steady income throughout the year for the workers and their families and many migrant and seasonal workers become unemployed.

The National Farmworker Jobs Program (NFJP) assists migrant and other seasonally employed farmworkers and their families, achieve economic self-sufficiency through job training and other related services that address their employment related needs. Services available include skills assessment, basic education, job search, on-the-job training and other related assistance. The Migrant and Seasonal Farmworkers program also has a program to help farmworker youth ages 14 through 21.

Contact your local One-Stop Career Center listed in the appendix for additional information. Contact National Office: Alicia Fernandez-Mott, Chief, Division of Seasonal Farmworker Programs, Employment and Training Administration, Room N-4641, 200 Constitution Avenue, NW, Washington, DC 20210; 202-693-3729; {http://wdsc.doleta.gov/msfw/}.

Troubled Teen Training Right in Your Town

Troubled teens may need some guidance and support to get them through to adulthood. The Workforce Investment Act (WIA) provides funds to states and local communities to provide their 14-21 year olds with many opportunities. The program targets youth who are low income, basic skills deficient, drop outs, homeless, a parent or offender that requires additional help in completing their educational program or hold employment.

Local Workforce Investment Boards provide eligible youth the following services:

tutoring, study skill training, dropout prevention, summer employment opportunities and occupational skill training. The Department of Labor, in conjunction with the Department of Justice, also administers the Going Home: Serious and Violent Offender Reentry Initiative help violent offenders re-enter their communities through job placement and security.

To find the program closest to you contact your local One-Stop Career Center listed in the appendix. Contact National Office: U.S. Department of Labor, Frances Perkins Building, 200 Constitution Avenue, NW, Washington, DC 20210; 202-693-3900; {http://www.doleta.gov/youth_services/Programs_Services.asp}.

One Church, Ten Families

You may not think of churches and job skills in the same thought, but churches are a great place to connect with youth in need of help in finding and keeping employment.

The One Church Ten Families Faith-based Initiative (OCTF) project was developed to provide funds directly to the churches. Grants of $30,000 were awarded to each of the five pilot sites. One of the goals of the program is to provide youth participants career exploration opportunities, job preparation instruction and work experiences such as paid and non-paid internships, job-shadowing opportunities, job training, and volunteer experiences to facilitate long-term employment.

Contact National Office: DeEtta Roberson-Carter, Administrator, U.S. Department of Labor, Frances Perkins Building, 200 Constitution Avenue, NW, Washington, DC 20210; 202-693-3900; {http://www.doleta.gov/youth_services/octf.asp}.

One Church Ten Families Faith-based Initiative Sites:

New Canaan International
Pastor Owen Cardwell, Program Director
1708 Bryon Street
Richmond, VA; 23222
804-329-1680
Fax: 804-219-5059
mailto:octfncic@aol.com

Shiloh Baptist Church
Rev. Jacqueline Thompson, Program Director
Family Life Center Foundation
1510 Ninth Street, NW
Washington, DC 20001
202-232-4288 #23
Fax: 202-232-0782
Jackiethompson@shilohbaptist.org

New Psalmist Baptist Church
Cedric Easter, Program Director
Sankofa Community Corporation
4501 ½ Old Frederick Road
Baltimore, MD 21229
410-644-7080
Fax: 410-644-7081
Eastercc@comcast.net

Sumpter Community Church of God
Cynthia Mullen, Program Director
The Hope Program
16650 Sumpter Road
Belleville, MI 48111
734-697-7705
Fax: 734-697-7618
CynthiaJ2002@aol.com

Wheeler Avenue Baptist Church
Catherine Longino, Program Director

Central City Comprehensive Community Center
3826 Wheeler Avenue
Houston, TX. 77004
713-748-5240 #166
Fax: 713-748-2830
ICV@wheelerbc.org

Grant Money for Youths

Opportunities for youths living in high-poverty communities may be limited simply because of where they live, however the federal government provides millions of dollars every year to the Youth Opportunity Grant (YOG) Program.

The Workforce Investment Act authorized the Youth Opportunity Grant program to increase the high school graduation rate, college enrollment rate, and employment rate of youth living in high-poverty communities. The program targets any youth, 14-21, regardless of income, who lives in federally designated zones, enterprise communities, and other high-poverty areas. The Grants are funded annually so you need to check their web site for the most up to date information.

Contact National Office: U.S. Department of Labor, Frances Perkins Building, 200 Constitution Avenue, NW, Washington, DC 20210; 202-693-3900; {http://www.doleta.gov/youth_services/yog.asp}.

One Strike You're Not Out

Everyone makes mistakes, especially when we are young. That's why the Young Offender Initiative: Demonstration Grant Project was formed. The Department of Labor has funded projects to get youth at-risk of criminal involvement, youth offenders, and gang members between 14 and 24 into long-term employment at wage levels that prevent future dependency and break the cycle of crime and juvenile delinquency. The overall goal is to increase coordination between the One Stop Career System and other local agencies serving youth.

To obtain additional information contact your local One-Stop Career Center listed in the appendix. Contact National Office:, U.S. Department of Labor, Frances Perkins Building, 200 Constitution Avenue, NW, Washington, DC 20210; 202-693-3900; 202-693-2879; {http://www.doleta.gov/youth_services/youth_offender.asp}.

Loads of Youth Opportunities!!

Young people need guidance and direction to become successful in today's global world. The Department of Labor's Youth Opportunity appropriation includes millions for a Rewarding Youth Achievement (RYA) initiative to provide our youth with a variety of possibilities to explore career opportunities.

RYA provides positive incentives to youth by offering summer jobs, career assessment and counseling, mentoring, summer math and science classes, tutoring and college bound experiences to high school students who meet academic achievement and attendance standards. The goal of RYA is to increase high school graduation and college enrollment rates for the youth who participate. Participants include high school and middle school students, 14-21, who attend schools that serve the Youth Opportunity area.

For additional information contact your local One-Stop Career Center listed in the appendix or check their web site for specific grant locations. Contact National Office: U.S. Department of Labor, Frances Perkins Building, 200 Constitution Avenue, NW, Washington, DC 20210; 202-693-3900; {www.doleta.gov/youth_services/ryag.asp}.

Job Assistance Close to Home

Help finding a new job may be as close as your own back yard, or at least in your own town. Each state offers programs to get people the training and job counseling they need to earn a steady paycheck. Utilize your state's programs and soon you'll be laughing all the way to the bank!

Below is a state-by-state listing of State Employment Agencies for you to contact to find out about specific programs in your state. your state may offer free job training, tuition waivers, job listings, resume writing assistance, and maybe even child care during your job search. Don't forget to check the website for a wealth of information.

State Employment Agencies

Alabama
Department of Industrial Relations
State Employment Service
649 Monroe Street
Montgomery, AL 3613
334-242-8004
Monegomery local office: 334-286-3700
www.dir.state.al.us/es

Alaska
Employment Security Division
Alaska Department of Labor and Workforce Development
P.O. Box 25509
Juneau, AK 99802-5509
Juneau local office: 907-465-2711
www.labor.state.ak.us/esd/home.htm

Arizona
Department of Economic Security
DES Public Information Office
1789 W. Jefferson, 2nd Floor
Phoenix, AZ 85007
602-542-4791
www.de.state.az.us/links/esa/index.html

Arkansas
Arkansas Employment Security Department
#1 Pershing Circle
North Little Rock, AR 72114
501-682-2121
www.state.ar.us/esd/index.html

California
Employment Development Department
800 Capitol Mall, Room 5000
Sacramento, CA 95814
Mailing Address:
P.O. Box 826880
Sacramento, CA 94280-0001
916-653-0707
www.edd.ca.gov

Colorado
Colorado Department of Labor and Employment
Division of Employment and Training
1515 Arapahoe
Tower 2, Suite 400
Denver, CO 80202
303-318-8800
www.coworkforce.com

Connecticut
Connecticut Department of Labor

200 Folly Brook Boulevard
Wethersfield, CT 06109
860-263-6000
www.ctdol.state.ct.us

Delaware
Department of Labor
Employment and Training Division
P.O. Box 9499
Newark, DE 19714-9499
302-761-8129
www.delaware.gov/agencies/DeptLabor/Employment_Services

District of Columbia
Dept. of Employer Services
609 H. Street, NE
Washington, DC 20002
202-727-7000
http://does.ci.washington.dc.us/main.shtm

Florida
Department of Labor and Employment Security
3023 Capital Circle, SE
Suite 303, Hartman Bldg.
Tallahassee, FL 32399-2152
850-922-7021
www2.myflorida.com/les

Georgia
Employment Services Division
Department of Labor
148 Andrew Young International
Atlanta, GA 30303
404-656-6380
www.dol.state.ga.us

Hawaii
Hawaii State Employment Service
830 Punchbowl St., #112
Honolulu, HI 96813
808-586-8700
www.dlir.state.hi.us

Idaho
Access Idaho
999 Main St, W
Boise, ID 83702
208-332-3570
Boise local office: 208-334-6211
www.labor.state.id.us

Illinois
Department of Employment Security
401 South State Street
Chicago, IL 60605
312-793-5700
www.ides.state.il.us

Indiana
Department of Workforce Development
10 North Senate
Indianapolis, IN 46204
1-888-WorkOne
317-232-7670
Local Indianapolis office: 317-684-2400
www.state.in.us/dwd

Iowa
Job Service Program Bureau
Dept. of Employment Services
1000 East Grand Avenue
Des Moines, IA 50319
515-281-5387
800-JOB-IOWA
Des Moines local office: 512-281-9619
www.state.ia.us/government/des/index

Kansas
Division of Employment and Training
Dept. of Human Resources
401 Topeka Ave.
Topeka, KS 66603
785-296-7874
www.kansasjobs.org

Kentucky
Department for Employment Services
275 East Main Street, 2nd Floor
Frankfort, KY 40621
502-564-5331
Frankfort local office: 502-564-7046
www.desky.org

Louisiana
Office of Employment Security
Louisiana Department of Labor
P.O. Box 94094
Baton Rouge, LA 70804-9094
225-342-3111
www.ldol.state.la.us

Maine
Department of Labor
Bureau of Employment Services
20 Union Street
P.O. Box 259
Augusta, ME 04332-0259
202-287-3516
Augusta local office: 207-624-5120
www.state.me.us/labor

Maryland
Job Service
Department of Employment and Economic Development
1100 N. Eutaw St., Room 208
Baltimore, MD 21201
410-767-2000
www.dllr.state.md.us

Massachusetts
Division of Employment and Training
19 Staniford Street
Boston, MA 02114
617-626-5400
Boston local office: 617-626-6000
www.detma.org

Michigan
Michigan Department of Career Development
201 N. Washington Square
Victor Office Center, 7th Floor
Lansing, MI 48913
517-241-0592
866-MY GOALS
www.michigan.gov/mdcd

Minnesota
Minnesota Department of Economic Security
390 Roberts Street, 5th Floor
St. Paul, MN 55101
651-297-2177
888-GET-JOBS
St. Paul local office: 651-642-0363
www.mnwfc.org

Mississippi
Mississippi Employment Security Commission
1520 West Capitol St.
P.O. Box 1699

Jackson, MD 39203
601-354-8711
www.mesc.state.ms.us

Missouri
Employment Service
Division of Employment Security (DOLIR)
PO Box 59
Jefferson City, MO 65104
Gracia Yancey Backer, Director
573-751-8086
www.dolir.state.mo.us/es

Montana
Job Service/Employment and Training Division
P.O. Box 1728
Helena, MT 59624
406-444-2840
http://dli.state.mt.us

Nebraska
Job Training Program
Department of labor
P.O. Box 94600
Lincoln, NE 68509
402-471-2600
www.dol.state.ne.us

Nevada
Nevada Department of Employment, Training and Rehabilitation
Employment Security Division
500 East Third Street
Carson City, NV 89713
775-684-3849
http://detr.state.nv.us

New Hampshire
Employment Service Bureau
Department of Employment Security
32 South Main Street
Concord, NH 03301
603-224-3311
www.nhes.state.nh.us

New Jersey
Employment Services
New Jersey Department of Labor
P.O. Box 055
Trenton, NJ 08625
609-292-5005
www.state.nj.us/labor/index.html

New Mexico
New Mexico Dept. of Labor
401 Broadway NE
Albuquerque, NM 87102
505-841-8409
www.dol.state.nm.us

New York
New York State Dept. of Labor
State Office Building Campus
Room 500
Albany, NY 12240
518-457-9000
www.labor.state.ny.us

North Carolina
Employment Security Commission
700 Wade Ave.
P.O. Box 25903
Raleigh, NC 27611
919-733-4329
www.ncesc.com

North Dakota
Employment and Training Division
Job Service
PO Box 5507
Bismarck, ND 58506
701-328-2868
www.state.nd.us/jsnd

Ohio
Ohio Department of Job and Family Services
145 South Front St., 6th Floor
Columbus, OH 43215
614-752-3091
www.state.oh.us/odjfs

Oklahoma
Oklahoma Employment Service
Employment Security Commission
Will Rogers Memorial Office Bldg.
P.O. Box 52003
Oklahoma City, OK 73152
405-557-0200
www.oesc.state.ok.us

Oregon
Oregon Employment Department
875 Union St., NE
Salem, OR 97311
503 947-1387
www.emp.state.or.us

Pennsylvania
Pennsylvania Department of Labor and Industry
Seventh and Forster Sts., Room 1700
Harrisburg, PA 17120
717-787-5279
www.dli.state.pa.us

Rhode Island
Department of Labor and Training
101 Friendship St.
Providence, RI 02903
401-222-3682
www.det.state.ri.us

South Carolina
S.C. Employment Security Commission
P.O. Box 995
Columbia, SC 29202
803-737-9935
www.sces.org

South Dakota
South Dakota Department of Labor
700 Governors Drive
Pierre, SD 57501
605-773-3101
TTY: 605-773-3101
www.state.sd.us/dol/dol.asp

Tennessee
Department of Labor and Workforce
710 James Robertson Parkway
Andrew Jackson Tower, 4th Flr
Nashville, Tennessee 37243
615-253-1324
800-255-5872
www.state.tn.us/labor-wfd/esdiv.html

Texas
Texas Employment Commission
101 E. 15th Street
Austin, TX 78778
512-463-2236
www.twc.state.tx.us

Utah
Utah Department of Workforce Services
P.O. Box 45249
Salt Lake City, UT, 84115-0249
801-526-WORK
http://jobs.utah.gov

Vermont
Employment Service Administration
Deptartment of Employment and Training
P.O. Box 488
5 Green Mountain Drive
Montpelier, VT 05601
802-828-4000
www.det.state.vt.us

Virginia
Virginia Employment Commission
703 East Main Street
Richmond, VA 23219
804-786-1485
www.vec.state.va.us/index.cfm

Washington
Washington Employment Security Department
TRB2 Unit
PO Box 9046
Olympia, WA 98507-9046
360-438-4611
www.wa.gov/esd/

West Virginia
West Virginia Bureau of Employment Programs
112 California Ave.
Charleston, WV 25305-0112
304-558-2630
www.state.wv.us/bep

Wisconsin
Department of DILHR
Job Service, 2nd Floor
201 East Washington Ave., (GEF-1)
Madison, WI 53702
Mailing Address:
P.O. Box 7946
Madison, WI 53707-7946
608-266-3131
www.dwd.state.wi.us

Wyoming
Wyoming Department of Employment
122 West 25th Street
Cheyenne, WY 82002
307-777-7672
http://wydoe.state.wy.us

$$$ Pay With Lost Money & Gov't Bargains

Make $2,000 in 45 minutes. That's what the author, Mary Ann Martello, did when she searched state databases looking for old forgotten utility deposits and bank accounts set up by grandparents. Every state has an office that collects money in that state that has been abandoned, forgotten, or left unclaimed, including:

- Savings and checking accounts
- Uncashed payroll or cashiers checks
- Money orders and travelers checks
- Certificates of deposit
- Customer deposits or overpayment
- Paid up life insurance policies
- Health and accident insurance payments
- Uncashed death benefit checks
- Gift certificates and Christmas club accounts
- Stock and dividends
- Utility deposits
- Oil and gas royalty payments

The money could be a savings account that grandma set up for you when you were born. Or it could be a Christmas fund Great Aunt Rose contributed to before she passed away. Your father may have even had a safe deposit box he never told you existed.

According to reports, state agencies across the U.S. may be holding over $8 billion dollars in abandoned money. Although the rules vary from state to state, generally after two or more years without activity on an account (no deposits or withdrawals), the bank will try to contact you. If their efforts fail, the property is considered abandoned and transferred to the state of your last known address.

To locate funds, contact the unclaimed property office in the state (usually part of the state treasurer's department) where you or your benefactors have lived or conducted business. Most state agencies have websites, and many have searchable databases.

You can contact the National Association of Unclaimed Property Administrators, P.O. Box 7156, Bismarck, ND 58507; {www.unclaimed.org}. Not only does the website give you a listing of state offices, it also links you to those that have existing websites. A listing of state Unclaimed Property Offices is also listed in the Appendix.

$500 for Real Estate

Failed commercial banks often own businesses, land, or real estate that they must sell. Although a booklet of all available properties is not available, the Federal Deposit Insurance Corporation (FDIC) makes an effort to keep their website up-to-date showing available properties under the button, "**Asset Info**".

You can search the site for a specific location, business, price parameter, and more. A contact number is available for each listing. Look under ***Special Sales, FDIC Bargain Properties***, for the deals that go as low as $500. Property sales are handled through each regional FDIC office.

For more information on asset sales, contact Federal Deposit Insurance Corporation, 550 17th St., NW, Washington, DC 20429; 800-934-FDIC; {www.fdic.gov}.

Toys, Books, Videos, CDs, TVs, VCRs, etc. at 70% Off

Did you ever wonder what happens to undeliverable mail? The U.S. Postal Service auctions it to willing buyers. Everything from the Christmas sweater you never received from grandma to the latest infomercial diet craze that never found its rightful dieter. Some people attend these auctions and collect bundles of items that they then resell for a profit at flea markets, garage sales, or retail stores.

Contact the Mail Recovery Centers listed below to learn more about the auctions in your area. You can be put on a mailing list to receive advance notice about the auctions. These auctions are held every six to eight weeks, with lots of similar goods being offered together. Although what is available varies from auction to auction, you will generally find anything that can be mailed — from CDs to televisions and books to jewelry and clothes. Call ahead to find out about payment procedures. Some require cash only, while others allow checks for those pre-approved.

Central Region

U.S. Postal Service Mail Recovery Center, 443 E. Fillmore Ave., St. Paul, MN 55017-9617; 612-293-3083. Includes Minnesota, Michigan, Wisconsin, North Dakota, South Dakota, Nebraska, Iowa, Illinois, Northern New Jersey, New Hampshire, Maine, Vermont, Rhode Island, Massachusetts, Kansas, Missouri, Connecticut, and New York.

Western Region

U.S. Postal Service Mail Recovery Center, 390 Main St., 4th Floor, San Francisco, CA 94105; 415-543-1826. Includes Alaska, Oregon, Idaho, California, Washington, Nevada, Utah, Arizona, New Mexico, part of Texas, Hawaii, Wyoming, Colorado, Montana, Guam, and Samoa.

Southern Region

U.S. Postal Service Mail Recovery Center, 730 Great Southwest Parkway, Atlanta, GA 30336; 404-344-1625; Includes Georgia, Florida, Louisiana, Tennessee, Arkansas, Mississippi, Oklahoma, part of Texas, Alabama, Mississippi, Virgin Islands, Puerto Rico, Pennsylvania, Southern New Jersey,

Maryland, Delaware, Ohio, Kentucky, Indiana, Virginia, West Virginia, North Carolina, and South Carolina.

Seized Property DO AGAIN

The U.S. Customs and Treasury Department confiscate seized property and then sell it at regularly scheduled auctions, held approximately every nine weeks, at sales centers across the United States. Examples of property offered for sale include cars, boats, airplanes, real estate, commercial real estate opportunities, carpets, electronics, industrial goods, jewelry, and wearing apparel.

Contact EG&G, 3702 Pender Dr., Suite 400, Fairfax, VA 22030; 703-273-7373; {www.treas.gov/auctions/customs}.

Big Discounts on Boats, Limos, and Airplanes

The U.S. Marshals Service offers property for sale to the public that has been forfeited under laws enforced by the U.S. Department of Justice, the Drug Enforcement Administration, Federal Bureau of Investigation, and the Immigration and Naturalization Service. More than 6,000 items of forfeited real and personal property are sold annually with gross sales of $195 million.

The property offered for sale consists of residential and commercial real estate, business establishments, and a wide range of personal property such as motor vehicles, boats, aircraft, jewelry, art, antiques, collectibles, and livestock. The U.S. Marshals Service does not maintain a list of forfeited property for sale, nor a mailing list to notify prospective buyers of upcoming sales. The sales are handled through contract service providers.

The U.S. Marshals Service website provides information on the company/agency names, locations, and telephone numbers. This listing is also available by fax at 202-307-9777. For those without a fax or computer, the listing is available for 50 cents from the Consumer Information Center. To learn how to order a copy, call the Federal Information Center at 800-688-9889. For more information on the sales, contact U.S. Marshals Service, Seized Assets Division, U.S. Department of Justice, 600 Army-Navy Dr., Arlington, VA 22202; 202-307-9237; {www.usdoj.gov/marshals/}.

The IRS Has "GOOD NEWS" For 100,000 Taxpayers

Seems impossible, doesn't it? Close to 100,000 taxpayers are due a refund, yet their checks have been returned to the tune of over $62.6 million. The average check is $627.

What do you do if you think you or someone you love is missing a check? Contact the IRS toll-free hotline at 800-829-1040 and talk to a customer service representative. They can plug your name in the computer and see if your name pops up on their screen.

98% Discount on Gov't Surplus

If the U.S. Department of Defense buys a computer for $2,000, they sell it at auction for an average price of approximately $40 through the Defense Reutilization and Marketing Service (DRMS).

DRMS is responsible for the disposal of excess and surplus military personal property. Personal property is anything other than land, buildings, and real estate. It includes items such as tools, office furniture, camping equipment, appliances, furniture, computers, electronics, and much more.

DRMS offers four types of sales. Businesses can buy property in large quantities through the DRMS National Sales Office in Battle Creek, Michigan. Property is sold by auction, sealed bid sales, and in special circumstances, negotiated sales. These sales include such items as aircraft parts, ships, hazardous property, electronics, scrap bearing and hardware, and other property having wide commercial application.

Regional Sales offer deals for smaller businesses by selling smaller quantities of property through auction or sealed bids. This property includes vehicles and vehicular parts, furniture, appliances, material handling equipment, tools, and other property of interest.DRMS also maintains DRMS Retail Sales Outlet Stores, where property is offered at a fixed price. You can also purchase items via the World Wide Web. Sales schedules, catalogs, and bid submissions information can be found on the website.

For more information on any of these items, contact the Defense Reutilization Marketing Service (DRMS), Federal Center, 74 N. Washington, Battle Creek, MI 49107; 800-GOVT-BUY; 888-352-9333; {www.drms.com}.

Unclaimed Retirement Checks

Did you work some place twenty years ago that is no longer in business? What about an old pension fund that was in financial trouble? Don't give up. The Pension Benefit Guaranty Corporation (PBGC) monitors and sometimes takes over private sector-defined benefit plans. These are traditional pensions that promise a specified monthly benefit at retirement.

The PBGC operates a Pension Search Directory to find people who are owed pensions from the plans PBGC now controls. You can search by name, company worked for, or by state where the company is/was headquartered. In the last eighteen months, the directory found 1,400 people owed more that $4 million with the average benefit being $4,100. There is still $13 million just waiting to be claimed. For more

information, contact Pension Benefit Guaranty Corporation, Pension Search Program, 1200 K St., NW, Washington, DC 20005; 800-326-LOST; {www.pbgc.gov}.

165 Unclaimed Social Security Checks

Social Security checks go out to 92% of those over the age of 65, so once in awhile a check may go astray. If you think you are missing some checks, or if you find un-negotiated checks, contact your local Social Security Administration office. They can reissue the checks to the person or to the estate.

Social Security assures me that this occurs rarely, as they send out 612 million payments with only 165,000 checks that were not endorsed. Contact Social Security Hotline at 800-772-1213.

The same deal holds true with the Veterans Affairs Administration. If you feel you are missing checks or find checks that have not been endorsed, contact your local Veterans Affairs office so that checks can be reissued to you or to the estate of a loved one. Contact Veterans Affairs at 800-827-1000.

Pick Up Your Money in a Cheap Jeep

Well, not the actual mail, but you could be seen touring your town in a postal jeep. The U.S. Post Office sells used postal vehicles, including jeeps, sedans, trucks, buses, tractor-trailers, and more. These vehicles are sold through the more than 200 vehicle maintenance facilities throughout the country. Contact your local post office to find out which vehicle maintenance facility serves your area. Vehicles are put up for sale, and occasionally, several facilities will get together and hold an auction. For more information, contact Vehicle Maintenance Facility, U.S. Postal Service, 475 L'Enfant Plaza, SW, Washington, DC 20260.

Missing HUD Money is Waiting for You

If you ever purchased a home using a HUD/FHA insured mortgage, you may be eligible for a refund on part of your insurance premium or a share of the earnings. There are certain requirements you have to have met.

To be eligible for a premium refund, you must have purchased your home after September 1, 1983, have paid an up front mortgage insurance premium at closing, and have not defaulted on your mortgage. To be eligible for an earnings dividend, you must have purchased your home before September 1, 1983 and made mortgage payments for more than 7 years.
Many people known as "Tracers" are locating this money for people and charging a finder's fee. HUD does state that people

can do this for free, but many people are unaware that they are due a refund! You can search by a person's name or case number on the website.

For more information, contact U.S. Department of Housing and Urban Development, P.O. Box 23699, Washington, DC 20026; 800-697-6967; {www.hud.gov/refunds/index.cfm}.

$$$ Pay Your Bills If You Have A Disability

On separate occasions, two people recently came up to me and said how they received government money to pay their bills because they had a disability:

Case #1: Received $15,000 to pay college bills.
Disability: At 41 years she was suffering from low self esteem because she did not finish college.

Case #2: Received $7,000 to pay for the last 6 months of rent.
Disability: Developed a strange reaction to a prescription drug.

Over 43 million Americans have disabilities of one kind or another. Many of them dream of supporting themselves with good paying jobs but can't make this dream come true because of their disabilities or because their lack of job skills stand in the way of leading independent lives. It's the kind of discouragement felt by many, regardless of their age, ambition, or economic status.

The Federal Government has stepped in and funded programs across the country to help the disabled and handicapped reach their goals by providing them with all kinds of services to get them on their way. The help available ranges from free information services, self help groups (for specific disabilities and disabilities in general), free legal aid, and independent living programs, to free money for education, job training, living expenses, transportation, equipment, and mobility aids. You can even get money to have your home retrofitted to make it more accessible to you, given your specific handicap. And if you're denied any of these

programs or services, there are several free sources of legal help that can get you what you're legally entitled to.

Typical of the free services available in your state:

- medical examinations and treatment
- vocational evaluation, training, and placement
- disability counseling
- assistive devices
- transportation
- occupational equipment
- rehabilitation engineering
- postemployment services
- independent living training
- student services
- financial assistance
- supported employment
- deaf services

Your state Vocational Rehabilitation office will evaluate your skills, needs, and goals, and work with you to keep you a productive member of society. As their client, they will assist you in getting the equipment you need to do your job, and sometimes even help you with transportation to work. College is also an option. We know of a massage therapist who developed carpal tunnel syndrome and got a four year college degree paid for so she cold be trained for a new profession.

Terri Handshoe was the youngest member of her family, and was the only one who was deaf. In 1977, she dropped out of high school with no plans for the future. Sitting at home soon grew old, so she decided to work on getting her GED. She studied and passes, and a friend suggested that she contact the vocational rehabilitation office to see about furthering her education or vocational training. After working with her counselor, Terri attended a local college for a quarter. Her counselor was able to persuade Terri to transfer to Gallaudet University in Washington, DC, the world renowned school for students who are deaf. During school, vocational rehabilitation provided a much needed interpreter and books. "It was great! I had to study hard, but I didn't have to worry about those things," said Terri, referring to the assistance that she was provided that made getting her education so much easier. Terri went on to complete a graduate degree and is now a program coordinator for the deaf.

Sandy Smith lost her sight in high school because of an operation to treat a brain tumor. She worked with vocational rehabilitation upon her return to school. She liked office work and was very motivated to find a job that would put her new skills to good use. Sandy was hired as a switchboard operator for a major hotel. Because she couldn't see the blinking lights on the multi-line telephone keypad, Sandy couldn't determine which line was ringing. Vocational rehabilitation was able to custom design a plastic overlay which allows pins to pop out wherever a line is ringing. The device cost $3,000 which vocational rehabilitation paid for. They were also able to supply Sandy with a computer so she could put through calls on her own. Sandy is very satisfied with her job, and says, "If you don't try, you'll never know if you could do it."

The three best places where you should begin your search for information about services and money programs for the disabled and handicapped are:

- The Social Security Administration
- your State Office of Vocational Rehabilitation
- Client Assistance Programs

In this section, you'll find descriptions and listings of contacts for these three programs, along with several additional best places for self help and aid for handicapped or disabled individuals.

People Who Will Help You Find The Money

Clearinghouse on Disability Information
Office of Special Education and Rehabilitation Services
U.S. Department of Education
Room 3132 Switzer Building
Washington, DC 20202-2524
202-205-8241
www.ed.gov/offices/OSERS
The clearinghouse responds to inquiries,

provides referrals, and gives out information about services for individuals with disabilities at the national, state, and local levels. Free publications include:

- *Pocket Guide to Federal Help for Individuals with Disabilities*
- Brochure: *America needs us all, people with disabilities learning and earning.*
- *Clearinghouse on Disability Information* fact sheet

Higher Education and Adult Training for People With Handicaps
George Washington University HEATH Resource Center
2121 K Street, NW, Suite 220
Washington, DC 20037
202-973-0904
800-544-3284
www.health-resource-center.org/
The Higher Education and Adult Training for People with Handicaps (HEATH) Resource Center is a clearinghouse and information exchange center for resources on postsecondary education programs and the disabled. Topics include educational support services, policies, procedures, adaptations, and opportunities on American campuses, vocational-technical schools, adult education programs, independent living centers, and other training organizations after high school. Another clearinghouse, National Information Center for Children and Youth with Disabilities, handles the concerns of younger disabled persons through secondary school.

ERIC Clearinghouse on Disabilities and Gifted Education
The Council for Exceptional Children
1110 N. Glebe Rd., Suite 300
Arlington, VA 22201-5704
888-CDC-SPED
703-620-3660
TTY: 703-264-9446
www.cec.sped.org/
Topics cover all aspects of the education and development of children with disabilities, those who are gifted or both; including identification, assessment, intervention, and enrichment information.

National Association of Rehabilitation Agencies
National Association of Rehabilitation Agencies
11250 Roger Baron Dr., Suite 8
703-437-4377
Reston, VA 20190-5202
Fax: 703-435-4390
www.naranet.org/
A private membership organization of rehabilitation agencies and professionals. Refer inquiries to members.

National Clearinghouse for Professions in Special Education
National Clearinghouse for Professions in Special Education
1110 N. Glebe Rd., Suite 300
Arlington, VA 22201-5704
800-641-7824
TYY: 866-915-5000 (toll free)
Fax: 703-264-1637
www.special-ed-careers.org
The Clearinghouse provides information to those interested in pursuing the field of special education. They provide resources to people in high school and college including financial aid resources, job information, recruitment and retention, projection statistics, and more.

National Clearinghouse of Rehabilitation Training Materials
Oklahoma State University
5202 N. Richmond Hill Dr.
Stillwater, OK 74078-4080
800-223-5219
405-624-7650
www.nchrtm.okstate.edu

The Clearinghouse will supply rehabilitation training materials in print or on video.

National Information Center for Children and Youth with Disabilities

National Information Center for Children and Youth with Disabilities
P.O. Box 1492
Washington, DC 20013-1492
800-695-0285
202-884-8200 (Voice/TDD)
www.nichcy.org/
The Clearinghouse is an information and referral center that provides information on disabilities and disability related issues, as well as referrals to a wide network of specialists from agencies and organizations across the nation. They focus on children and youth ages birth to 22.

National Rehabilitation Association

633 South Washington St.
Alexandria, VA 22314
703-836-0850
703-836-0849 (TDD)
www.nationalrehab.org
A private membership organization of professionals, vendors and suppliers of rehabilitation services, consumers and family members, students and professors. Refer inquiries to members.

ABLEDATA

ABLEDATA
8630 Fenton St., Suite 930
Silver Spring, MD 20910
800-227-0216
TTY: 301-608-8912
www.abledata.com
National database containing information on assistive technology and rehabilitation equipment for persons with disabilities. Contains more than 25,000 products from over 2,700 manufacturers and distributors. Publications include the *Assistive Technology Directory*; *ABLEDATA thesaurus*; *ADA Source book*; Fact sheets and computer guides.

National Rehabilitation Information Center

National Rehabilitation Information Center
4200 Forbes Blvd., Suite 202
Lanham, MD 20706
301-459-5900
800-34-NARIC
800-346-2742 (V/TDD)
www.naric.com
Databases containing information on disability and rehabilitation research are available: REHABDATA; KnowledgeBase; *The NIDRR Directory; Guide to Periodicals.* For computer access: 301-589-3563.

Rehabilitation Information Hotline

National Rehabilitation Information Center (NARIC)
4200 Forbes Blvd., Suite 202
Lanham MD 20706
800-346-2742
301-459-5900
TTY: 301-495-5626
Fax: 301-562-2401
www.naric.com
The National Rehabilitation Information Center, a library and information center on disability and rehabilitation, collects and disseminates the results of federally funded research projects. NARIC also maintains a vertical file of pamphlets and fact sheets published by other organizations. NARIC

has documents on all aspects of disability and rehabilitation including, physical disabilities, mental retardation, psychiatric disabilities, independent living, employment, law and public policy and assistive technology.

Their user services include the ABLEDATA database which describes thousands of assistive devices from eating utensils to wheelchairs. A printed listing of fewer than 50 products is $5; NARIC charges $10 for 51 to 100 products, and $5 for each additional hundred products. ABLEDATA also provides an information specialist to answer simple information requests and provide referrals immediately at no cost. 800-227-0216.

Free Money for the Disabled Who Have Worked in the Past

Social Security Administration
6401 Security Blvd.
Baltimore, MD 21235-0001
800-772-1213
TTY: 800-325-0778
www.ssa.gov

If you're disabled and expect to be so for at least one year, and have worked long enough and recently enough under Social Security, you may be eligible for Social Security Disability Insurance Benefits (DIB). If you are found entitled to DIB, you will receive a monthly check in an amount based on your prior earnings.

If you start back to work after receiving DIB, you have nine months (not necessarily consecutive) to earn as much as you can without affecting your benefits. (The nine months of work must fall within a five-year period before your trial work period can end.) After your trial work period ends, your work is evaluated to see if it is "substantial." This means that your earnings are more than $700. For 36 months after a successful trial work period, if you are still disabled, you will be eligible to receive a monthly benefit without a new application for any month your earnings drop below $700 for people with disabilities, or $1,110 a month for the blind.

If you are still disabled, your Medicare coverage can continue for 39 months beyond the trial work period. If your Medicare coverage stops because of your work, you may purchase it for a monthly premium. For more information on "quarters of coverage" and the trial work period, contact the Social Security administration at the above listed number.

Impairment Related Work Expenses: Certain expenses for items you need for work due to your disability, can be deducted when calculating your earnings, which affects your disability insurance benefits. The amount of money you spends on such items is not counted as part of your income when determining your substantial work earnings.

Free and Low Cost Medical Insurance For the Disabled Who Have Worked In the Past

Medicare Hotline
Health Care Finance Administration
7500 Security Blvd.
Baltimore, MD 21244-1850
800-633-4227
TTY: 800-820-1220
410-786-3000
http://cms.hhs.gov

If you qualify for the Disability Insurance Benefits (DIB) described above, and have been receiving these payments for at least two years, you will also qualify to receive Medicare Part A for free which provides insurance coverage for hospitalization.

You can also receive Medicare Part B for a monthly premium of $45. This provides insurance coverage for your doctor visits and testing services. This is the same Medicare coverage those over 65 receive. Remember, there are deductibles and limits of coverage. For instance, doctor visits are covered after you meet the $100 deductible for the year, after which Medicare will pay 80% of the approved rate, and you are responsible for the other 20%.

To apply for this medical insurance or to receive the *Medicare Handbook* which provides detailed information on coverage, contact the hotline listed above.

Cash For Dependents Of the Disabled
Social Security Administration Hotline
800-772-1213
If you are eligible for Disability Insurance Benefits (DIB) described above, your dependents (wife, husband, children, or and in some cases, grandchildren) may also be eligible for payments on your record. To find out if your dependent is eligible, contact the hotline listed above.

Money For The Disabled Who Have Not Worked In The Past
Social Security Administration
6401 Security Blvd.
Baltimore, MD 21235-0001
800-772-1213
TTY: 800-325-0778
www.ssa.gov
If you are disabled but do not have enough work under Social Security for Disability Insurance Benefits (DIB), you may still be eligible to receive Supplemental Security Income (SSI) benefits if your income and resources are low enough. To see if you are eligible for SSI, contact the number listed above.

What To Do When Benefits Are Denied
If you are denied any of the above mentioned Social Security cash benefits — which often happens regardless of the disability or its severity — you can get free legal help to appeal the Social Security Administration's decision on your application. Contact your state or local Department of Welfare and request the name and address of the nearest Legal Services Corporation (LSC) program, and also contact your nearest State Client Assistance Program (CAP) office. Both programs offer low income individuals free legal help and representation in appealing application decisions.

The CAP program will either provide you with free legal help and representation for your appeal or they will help you find such aid. Unlike legal help offered under the Legal Services Corporation, CAP services are not determined by your income. On the chance that neither of these agencies are able to help you, contact the Disability Rights Education and Defense Fund (DREDF) at {www.dredf.org} or 510-644-2555.

Free Information for Employers Who Hire the Handicapped
Job Accommodation Network (JAN)
West VA University
P.O. Box 6080
Morgantown, WV 26506-6080
800-526-7234 (V/TTY)
800-526-2262 (Canada)
Fax: 304-293-5407
Email: jan@jan.icdi.wvu.edu

http://janweb.icdi.wvu.edu
The Job Accommodation Network (JAN) brings together free information about practical ways employers can make accommodations for employees and job applicants with disabilities. The Network offers comprehensive information on methods and available equipment that have proven effective for a wide range of accommodations, including names, addresses, and phone numbers of appropriate resources. They also provide information regarding the Americans with Disabilities Act (800-232-9675).

Free Money for Education and Job Training

If your disability stops you from being able to keep a full time job or from being able to competitively look for a job, your state's Office of Vocational Rehabilitation (OVR) can help. OVR can give you up to $6,000 each year for job training or education. You can use this grant money, which you do not have to repay, to cover any expenses related to your training or education, including tuition and fees, travel expenses, books, supplies, equipment (computers, motorized wheelchairs, etc.), food allowances, tutoring fees, photocopies, and so on.

For more information, contact your state's Office of Vocational Rehabilitation listed at the end of this section.

Help For the Handicapped to Find or Create a Job

Your state Office of Vocational Rehabilitation (OVR) also acts as an employment agency for the disabled and can contact employers for you who have looked favorably on hiring the disabled in the past. OVR will act as a liaison between you and a prospective employer and help them create a job for you by providing needed disability-related job equipment, provide needed transportation or other mobility equipment, or by providing any other help you might need to be able to work at a job for which you're qualified. For example, OVR has provided books in Braille and Braille-to-speech conversion equipment, and computer-robotics equipment that have allowed disabled individuals to work at a variety of jobs.

For more information, contact your state's Office of Vocational Rehabilitation listed at the end of this section.

Help For the Handicapped Already On the Job

If you are working and become disabled or handicapped, your state Office of Vocational Rehabilitation (OVR) can provide you with the equipment, transportation, education, training and other help you might need to keep your job. For example, many times an unexpected disability can put someone in a wheelchair. OVR may be able to provide you with a motorized wheelchair so you can continue in your current job.

Contact your state Office of Vocational Rehabilitation listed at the end of this section for more information.

Technical Assistance Project

Rehabilitation Engineering and Assertive Technology
Society of North America (RESNA)

1700 North Moore Street, #1540
Arlington, VA 22209
703-524-6686
TTY: 703-524-6639
Fax: 703-524-6630
www.resna.org
This project, funded by the U.S. Department of Education, has established an office in each state that provides information about how the latest technology can improve the lives of disabled persons. They also have an equipment loan program, which allows people to borrow new technology devices before purchasing them. They provide information on sources of funding for equipment and special loans.

For more information contact your state office listed at the end of this section.

Medical Help For the Disabled/Handicapped

Your state Office of Vocational Rehabilitation can pay for (or help you pay for) any medical testing or treatment that is expected to help you, as a handicapped or disabled individual, have a more healthy, prosperous and independent life. Contact your state Office of Vocational Rehabilitation listed at the end of this section for more information.

What To Do When OVR Benefits Are Denied

The first place to start when your state Office of Vocational Rehabilitation denies you handicap or disability benefits is your nearest state Client Assistance Program (CAP) office. CAP is a free information, referral, and legal service that helps disabled or handicapped individuals appeal a denial by OVR (or another agency). For a variety of reasons, it is not uncommon for a disabled individual to be turned down for services by OVR even when he/she is in fact eligible to receive them. It is often helpful to get a photocopy of section 103 of Chapter 34 of the *Code of Federal Regulations of the U.S. Department of Education* from your local or county library. These are the federal guidelines that each state OVR must follow when determining eligibility. This part of the code is only a few pages in length and can help you explain to the Client Assistance Program officer why you believe you are eligible even though you've been denied. CAP can take your appeal process from the first stages all the way to the U.S. Supreme Court if necessary — and it won't cost you a penny.

It is also sometimes helpful to contact the state Office of Vocational Rehabilitation (OVR) itself and make the executive director aware of your circumstances. When it appears that progress via CAP is stalled or has been dragging on for months, it can also be very helpful to contact the regional commissioner of the Rehabilitation Services Administration (RSA), a branch of the Office of Special Education Programs of the U.S. Department of Education. RSA is responsible for overseeing and funding the state OVR agencies and is generally receptive to a short explanatory phone call and letter from those who believe they can clearly show that they have been wrongly denied OVR services. If they think you've got a case, they'll contact the OVR in question and make sure that they review your application more favorably.

To get in touch with a Rehabilitation Services Administration official, contact the U.S. Department of Education, Office of Special Education and Rehabilitative Services, RSA, Washington, DC 20202: 202-205-5465, and ask for the address and phone number of the regional commissioner for the ED-OSERS-RSA office serving your area, or check the website {www.ed.gov/offices/OSERS}.

Three Important Tips When Appealing an OVR Denial Of Services

1. If your state Office of Vocational Rehabilitation (OVR) denies you services based on other similar cases in which they have denied other prospective clients, it is important and effective to argue that such reasons for denial are not allowable under federal regulations. The 34 Code of Federal Regulations Chapter III section 361.31(b)(1) states clearly that the barriers faced by a disabled individual are unique to each individual and to each individual set of circumstances.

2. If you have previously been accepted by your state Office of Vocational Rehabilitation (OVR) as a client and you have gained employment but your disability has not improved and you lose employment due to no fault of your own, then OVR can again provide you with their services to help you regain employment. For more specifics, consult again the 34 Code of Federal Regulations, Chapter III and check under the *Post-Employment Services* sections and *Supported Employment* sections.

3. If you're currently receiving Social Security Disability (SSD), make sure that your state Office of Vocational Rehabilitation (OVR) and Client Assistance Program (CAP) are aware of this fact. Because of the more restrictive SSD definition of what it means to be disabled (compared to OVR), being on SSD almost always automatically qualifies an SSD recipient for OVR services. It is very difficult for OVR to argue otherwise.

Free Legal Help and Information Services For the Handicapped

If you think you've been wrongly denied benefits or discriminated against because of a disability or handicap, the Client Assistance Program (CAP) will help you fight for your rights when you're denied various types of disability benefits from any disability program. They will help you directly and/or put you in contact with the agencies that can help you. Your state CAP office is listed at the end of this section.

More Free Legal Help for the Disabled

A national nonprofit law and policy center, the Disability Rights Education and Defense Fund (DREDF) can provide you with direct legal representation and act as co-counsel in cases of disability based discrimination. They also seek to educate legislators and policy makers on issues affecting the rights of people with disabilities.

Contact: Disability Rights Education and Defense Fund (DREDF), 2212 Sixth St., Berkeley, CA 94710; 510-644-2555 (Voice/TDD); {www.dredf.org}.

Help to Start a Business

SBA Answer Desk
6302 Fairview Rd., Suite 300
Charlotte, NC 28210
800-8-ASK-SBA
TTY: 703-344-6640
Email: answerdesk@sba.gov
www.sba.gov

If you dream of owning your own business, but need a little help, call the Small Business Administration (SBA). The SBA can help you think through your business plan, and give you some direction to help your business grow. They even have a Handicapped Assistance Loan program that provides low interest loans and loan guarantees to handicapped individuals or nonprofit organizations operating in the interest of disabled individuals.

To learn more about the qualifications and eligibility requirements for the loans, as well as other services available from the SBA, contact the Small Business Administration Answer Desk at 800-8-ASK-SBA or email {answerdesk@sba.gov}.

Plan for Achieving Self- Support (PASS)

Many people with disabilities want to work, and you're probably one of them. But maybe you need to go back to school before you can get a job. Or, maybe you'd like to start your own business, but you don't have the money. Whatever your work goal may be, a PASS can help you reach it. A PASS lets you set aside money and/or other things you own to help you reach your goal. For example, you could set aside money to start a business or to go to school or to get training for a job.

Your goal must be a job that will produce sufficient earnings to reduce your dependency on Supplemental Security Income (SSI) payments. A PASS is meant to help you acquire those items, services or skills you need so that you can compete with able-bodied persons for an entry level job in a professional, business or trade environment. If you have graduated from college or a trade/technical school, we usually consider you capable of obtaining such a position without the assistance of a PASS. You can contact your local Social Security office to find out whether a PASS is appropriate for you.

How Will A Plan Affect My SSI Benefit?

Under regular SSI rules, your SSI benefit is reduced by the other income you have. But the income you set aside for a PASS doesn't reduce your SSI benefit. This means you can get a higher SSI benefit when you have a PASS. But you can't get more than the maximum SSI benefit for the state where you live.

Money you save or things you own, such as property or equipment, that you set aside for a PASS won't count against the resource limit of $2,000 (or $3,000 for a couple). Under regular SSI rules, you wouldn't be eligible for SSI if your resources are above $2,000. But with a plan, you may set aside some resources so you would be eligible.

Who Can Have A PASS?

You can, if:

- you want to work;
- you get SSI (or can qualify for SSI) because of blindness or a disability; or
- you have or expect to receive income (other than SSI) and/or resources to set aside toward a work goal.

What Kinds Of Expenses Can A Plan Help Pay For?

A plan may be used to pay for a variety of expenses that are necessary to help you reach your work goal.

For example, your plan may help you save for:

- supplies to start a business;
- tuition, fees, books and supplies that are needed for school or training;
- employment services, such as payments for a job coach;
- attendant care or child care expenses;

- equipment and tools to do the job;
- transportation to and from work; or
- uniforms, special clothing and safety equipment.

These are only examples. Not all of these will apply to every plan. You might have other expenses depending on your goal.

How Will A Plan Affect Other Benefits I Get?

You should check with the agency that is responsible for those benefits to find out if the plan (and the extra SSI) might affect those benefits.

In many cases, income and resources set aside under a plan will not be counted for food stamps and housing assistance provided through the U.S. Department of Housing and Urban Development. But, it's important that you contact the particular agency to find out how your benefits will be affected.
For more information, ask Social Security for the booklet, *Working While Disabled—How We Can Help* (Publication No. 05-10095); {www.ssa.gov}.

5 States Give Money For Disability Insurance

California Disability Insurance
California Disability Insurance
Employment Development Department
800 Capitol Mall, MIC 83
Sacramento, CA 95814
800-480-3287
800-563-2441 TTY
http://www.edd.ca.gov/diind.htm
California State Disability Insurance (SDI) is a partial wage-replacement insurance plan

for California workers. The SDI program is State-mandated, and funded through employee payroll deductions. SDI provides affordable, short-term benefits to eligible workers who suffer a loss of wages when they are unable to work due to a NON WORK-RELATED illness or injury, or a medically disabling condition from pregnancy or childbirth. The majority of California employees, approximately 12 million workers, are covered by the SDI program. Disability is defined as any mental or physical illness or injury which prevents you from performing your regular or customary work. This includes elective surgery; illness or injury resulting from pregnancy, childbirth, or related conditions; or inability to work due to a written order of quarantine from a state or local health officer.

Hawaii Temporary Disability Insurance
State of Hawaii Department of Labor and Industrial Relations
Disability Compensation Division
Temporary Disability Insurance
P.O. Box 3769
Honolulu, HI 96812-3769
808-586-9188
808-586-9219
http://dlir.state.hi.us/
http://dlir.state.hi.us/dc_1.pdf
The state of Hawaii Temporary Disability Insurance (TDI) provides wage replacement benefits for non-work related illness or injury. Workers must have been in covered employment with any Hawaii employer for at least 14 weeks with 20 or more hours

each week and earned at least $400 during a 52 week period. You may obtain a claim from your employer.

New Jersey Temporary Disability Benefits
New Jersey Department of Labor
Division of Temporary Disability Insurance
P.O. Box 387
Trenton, NJ 08625-0387
609-292-7060
http://www.state.nj.us/labor/tdi/dtdi/dtdi.htm
Under the New Jersey Temporary Disability Benefits Law, cash benefits are payable when you cannot work because of sickness or injury NOT caused by your job. Workers who become disabled within 14 days of their last day of work in covered New Jersey employment may be covered for disability insurance under the State Plan. Contact the Division of Temporary Disability Insurance for more information.

New York State Insurance Fund
New York State Insurance Fund
Office of Temporary and Disability Assistance
225 Oak Street
Buffalo, NY 14203
800-866-NYSIFDB
http://www.nysif.com/disability/aboutdisabilitybenefitsPol.asp
The New York State Insurance Fund (NYSIF) is a non-profit agency of the State of New York consisting of The Disability Benefits Fund, established in 1949, which insures against disabling off-the-job sickness or injury sustained by employees. Employers with one or more employees are subject to the provisions of the New York State Disability Benefits Law. The law provides for the payment of cash benefits to employees who become disabled because of injuries or sicknesses which have no connection to their employment, and for disabilities arising from pregnancies. workers' compensation cases, the cost of medical treatment is borne by the insurance carrier.

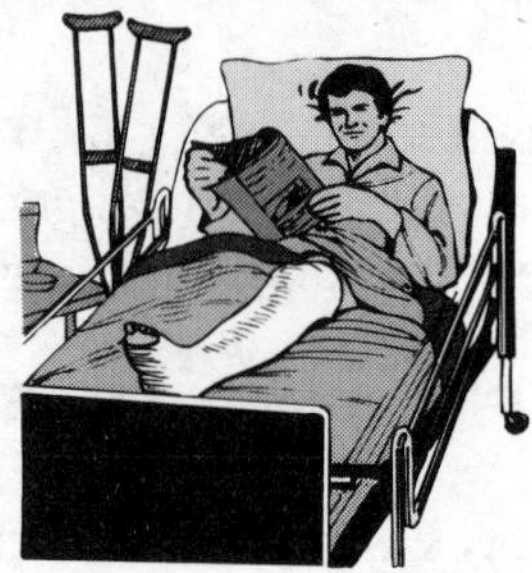

Rhode Island Disability Insurance
Rhode Island Department of Labor and Training
Temporary Disability Insurance
P.O. Box 20070
Cranston, RI 02920
401-462-8420
401-462-8466 FAX
http://www.dlt.state.ri.us/webdev/tdi/tdihome.htm
If you become ill or injured in Rhode Island and a doctor's examination shows that you cannot work for at least 7 consecutive days, you should apply for TDI benefits as soon as possible. To file for Temporary Disability Insurance (TDI), simply complete a TDI application form and mail it to Rhode Island Department of Labor and Training. Be sure to print or write carefully and answer all the questions completely and accurately. You can get an application form at any office of the Rhode Island Department of Labor and Training. You can also call (401) 462-8420 to have an application sent directly to you. Or, if you prefer, you can download an application at {http://www.dlt.state.ri.us/webdev/tdi/tdiapps.htm}. To be eligible for TDI, you must meet certain medical and earnings requirements. If you suffer a non-work related disability, apply for benefits. The office will determine if you qualify based on all facts relating to your claim and notify you as quickly as possible.

State Vocational Rehabilitation Offices

Alabama

Steven Shivers, Commissioner, Alabama Department of Rehabilitation Services, 2129 East South Boulevard, P.O. Box 11586, Montgomery, AL 36111-0586; 334-281-8780, 800-441-7607, TDD: 334-613-2249, Fax: 334-281-1973; {www.rehab.state.al.us}. Assistance offered:
- medical examinations and treatment
- psychological evaluation
- vocational evaluation, training and placement
- disability counseling
- assistive devices
- transportation
- occupational equipment
- rehabilitation engineering
- postemployment services
- independent living training
- student services
- Hemophilia Program
- OASIS Project (Older Alabamians System of Information and Services)
- in home care
- financial assistance
- Business Enterprise Program (BEP)
- supported employment
- deaf services

Alaska

Duane French, Director, Division of Vocational Rehabilitation, 801 West 10th St., Suite A, Juneau, AK 99801-1894; 907-465-2814, Email: {stevie.raleigh@educ.state.ak.us}, {www.labor.state.ak.us/dvr/home.html}. Assistance offered:
- medical and psychiatric examinations
- vocational evaluation, training, and placement
- medical treatment
- adaptive equipment
- transportation
- postemployment counseling

American Samoa

Peter P. Galea'i, Director, Division of Vocational Rehabilitation, Dept. Of Human Resources, American Samoa Government, Pago Pago, AS 96799, 011684-633-2336, {www.ipacific.com/samoa/samoa.html}

Arizona

Fred “Skip” Bingham, Administrator, Arizona Rehabilitation Services Administration, 1789 West Jefferson 2, NW, Phoenix, AZ 85007; 602-542-3651, 800-563-1221, TDD: 602-542-6049, Fax: 602-542-3778, Email: {mepps@mail.de.state.az.us}, {www.de.state.az.us/rsa}. Assistance offered:
- vocational evaluation, training, and evaluation
- independent living counseling
- Business Enterprise Program (BEP)
- deaf and Blind services
- communication devices
- adaptive equipment

Arkansas

John Wyvill, Director, Division of Vocational Rehabilitation, 1616 Brookwood Drive, Little Rock, AR 72203;, 501-296-1661, 800-285-7192, TDD: 501-296-1669, Fax: 501-296-1655, Email: {jcwyvill@ars.state.ar.us}, {www.arsinfo.org}. Assistance offered:
- individual and family counseling
- adaptive equipment
- in home care services
- vocational evaluation, training, and placement
- rehabilitation facilities

James C. Hudson, Director, Division of Services for the Blind, Dept. of Human Services, 522 Main Street, Little Rock, AR 72203; 501-682-0198, 800-960-9270, TTY: 501-682-0093, Fax: 501-682-0366; {www.state.ar.us/dhs/dsb/index.html}. Assistance offered:
- vocational training and placement
- medical diagnosis and treatment
- counseling on independent living
- personal adjustment counseling for family and children
- Vending Facility Program
- library materials
- radio reading service
- information referrals

California

Catherine Campisi, Director, Department of Rehabilitation, P.O. Box 944222, Sacramento,

CA 95815; 916-263-8981, TTY: 916-263-7477, {www.rehab.ca.gov/}. Assistance offered:
- medical and vocational evaluation
- medical treatment
- job training and placement
- transportation
- occupational licenses and equipment
- family services
- reader and interpreter services
- communication devices
- rehabilitation engineering
- adaptive equipment
- supported employment
- small business incentives
- postemployment services

Colorado

Diana Huerta, Director, Division of Vocational Rehabilitation, Dept. Of Social Services, 2211 West Evans, Bldg. B, Denver, Co 80223; 720-884-1234 (V/TDD), Fax: 720-884-1213, Email: {debbiepowell@state.co.us}, {www.cdhs.state.co.us/ods/dvr}. Assistance offered:
- vocational evaluation, training, and placement
- employer services
- rehabilitation engineering
- personal adjustment counseling
- Client Assistance Program (CAP)

Connecticut

Bureau of Rehabilitation Services, Department of Social Services, 25 Sigourney St., Hartford, CT 06106-5033, 800-842-4848, TDD: 860-424-4839, Fax: 860-424-4850, Email: {john.halliday@po.state.ct.us}, {www.dss.state.ct.us/svcs/rehab.htm}. Assistance offered:
- vocational counseling, training, and placement
- physical therapy
- adaptive technology
- psychotherapy
- academic training
- occupational tools and licenses
- architectural modifications to home and workplace
- rehabilitation employment
- supported employment
- transportation

Donna Balaski, Director, Board of Education and Services for the Blind, Vocational Rehabilitation Division, 184 Windsor Avenue, Windsor, CT 06095; 800-842-4510 (in CT), 860-602-4000, TTY: 860-602-4002, Fax: 860-602-4020, Email: {besb@po.state.ct.us}, {www.besb.state.ct.us}. Assistance offered:
- Radio Information Service
- individual and family counseling
- mobility instruction
- vocational training and placement
- industries opportunities
- financial counseling
- legal benefits
- recreation
- follow up services
- low vision exams and treatment
- home management training
- communication devices
- information and referral

Delaware

Andrea Guest, Director, Division of Vocational Rehabilitation, P.O. Box 9969, 4425 N. Market Street, Wilmington, DE 19809-0969; 302-761-8275, TDD: 302-761-8336, Fax: 302-761-6611, Email: {director@dvr.state.de.us}, {www.delawareworks.com/divisions/dvr/welcome.htm}. Assistance offered:
- vocational training and placement
- independent living counseling
- adaptive equipment
- family counseling
- home management training
- transportation
- financial assistance
- physical therapy
- occupational tools and licenses

Harry B. Hill, Director, Division for the Visually Impaired, Biggs Building, Health & Social Services Campus, 1901 N. Dupont Highway, New Castle, DE 19720; 302-255-9800, Fax: 302-255-4441, {www.state.de.us/dhss/dvi/dvihome.htm}. Assistance offered:
- low vision services
- counseling
- education
- mobility instruction
- job training and placement

- deaf/blind services
- independent living training
- personal adjustment counseling
- optical aids
- preventive examinations
- information and referral
- communication devices

District of Columbia
D.C. Rehabilitation Services Administration, Dept. of Human Services, 801 East Building, 2700 Martin Luther King Ave., SE, Washington, DC 20032; 202-279-6002, 202-729-6014, {http://dhs.dc.gov}. Assistance offered:
- vocational evaluation, training, and placement
- adaptive equipment
- personal adjustment counseling
- physical therapy
- transportation
- postemployment services
- occupational tools and licenses
- small business assistance

Florida
Tamira Bibb Allen, Director, Division of Vocational Rehabilitation, Dept. Of Labor and Employment, Security, Building A, 2002 Old St. Augustine Road, Tallahassee, FL 32399-0696; 904-488-6210, Information & Referral line: 800-451-4327, {www.rehabworks.org/}. Assistance offered:
- vocational and medical evaluation
- financial assistance
- job training and placement
- work adjustment training
- in home care
- postemployment counseling
- supported employment
- determination of benefit eligibility

Craig Kiser, Director, Division of Blind Services, Department of Education, 2551 Executive Center Circle, Tallahassee, FL 32399; 800-342-1330, 800-342-1828 (in FL), 850-488-1330, Fax: 850-487-1804, {www.state.fl.us/dbs/}. Assistance offered:
- medical, psychological, and vocational evaluation
- counseling
- medical services
- mobility instruction
- job training and placement
- rehabilitation facilities
- communication skills and equipment
- family and children services
- in home instruction
- Bureau of Business Enterprises
- library services

Georgia
Peggy Rosser, Director, Division of Rehabilitation Services, Georgia Department of Human Resources, 2 Peachtree Street, NW, 35th Floor, Atlanta, GA 30303-3142; 404-657-3000, Fax: 404-657-3086, Email: {Gradye@gomail.doas.state.ga.us}, {www.vorehabga.org/}. Assistance offered:
- vocational rehabilitation programs for competitive employment and sheltered employment
- independent living counseling
- evaluate clients to determine eligibility for health care and disability benefits
- refer clients to appropriate nearby facilities for rehabilitation services

Guam
Nobert Ungacto, Director, Dept. Of Vocational Rehabilitation, Government of Guam, 122 Harmon Plaza, Room B201, Harmon Industrial Park, Guam 96911; 011-671-646-9468, {www.gov.gu/}.

Hawaii
Neil Shim, Administrator, Division of Vocational Rehabilitation & Services for the Blind, Dept. Of Human Services, Bishop Trust Bldg., 1000 Bishop St., Room 615, Honolulu, HI 96813; 808-586-5366, Fax: 808-586-5377, {www.state.hk.us/dhs/}. Assistance offered:
- optical aids
- personal adjustment counseling
- independent living training
- communication devices
- low vision services
- preventive eye care
- vocational evaluation, training and placement
- job site modification

Idaho

Barry J. Thompson, Administrator, Division of Vocational Rehabilitation, P.O. Box 83720, 650 West State Street, Room 150, Boise, ID 83720-0096; 208-334-3390, TDD: 208-327-7040, Fax: 208-334-5305, Email: {pyoung@idvr.state.id.us}, {www2.state.id.us/idvr/idvrhome.htm}. Assistance offered:

- vocational evaluation, training, and placement
- medical treatment
- assistive devices
- occupational tools and licenses
- Business and Industry Program
- specialized rehabilitation
- personal adjustment counseling
- independent living training
- kidney program
- transportation
- recreation programs
- attendant care
- communication aids
- family services
- information and referral
- housing
- health maintenance

Michael Graham, Director, Idaho Commission for the Blind, Division of Vocational Rehabilitation, P.O. Box 83720, 341 West Washington, Boise, ID 83720, 208-334-3220, 800-542-8688 (in ID), Fax: 208-334-2963, Email: {mstarkov@icbvi.state.id.us}, {www.icbvi.state.id.us}. Assistance offered:

- Business Enterprise Program
- radio reading and taping
- independent living counseling
- information and referral
- job training and placement
- financial assistance
- orientation and adjustment center
- adaptive equipment
- prevention programs
- academic training
- home instruction

Illinois

Robert E. Davis, State Director, Illinois Office Rehabilitation Services, 100 South Grand Ave., E, 3rd Floor, Springfield, IL 62762, 217-785-0234, Fax: 217-558-4270, Email: {ors@dhs.state.il.us}, {www.state.il.us/agency/dhs}. Assistance offered:

- job training and placement
- educational assistance
- transportation
- independent living training
- in home care
- Illinois Children's School and Rehabilitation Center
- supported employment
- information and referral
- interpreter services
- personal adjustment counseling
- vending Facility Program
- Disability Determination Services

Indiana

Rita Martin, Deputy Director, Department of Human Services, Vocational Rehabilitation Services, Room W453, 402 West Washington St., P.O. Box 7083, Indianapolis, IN 46207-7083; 800-848-7763 (IN only), 317-232-1319, TDD: 317-232-1427, {www.state.in.us/fssa/servicedisable/vr/index.html}. Assistance offered:

- vocational evaluation, training and placement
- assistive devices
- rehabilitation engineering
- physical therapy
- information referral
- financial assistance
- transportation
- communication devices
- personal adjustment counseling
- independent living training

Linda Quarles, Deputy Director, Division of the Blind and Visually Impaired, Room W453, 402 W. Washington St., P.O. Box 7083, Indianapolis, IN 46207-7083; {www.ai.org/fssa/HTML/PROGRAMS/2bBVIS.html}.

Iowa

R. Creig Slayton, Director, Department for the Blind, 524 4th Street, Des Moines, IA 50309-2364; 515-281-1333, 800-362-2587 (IA only), TTY: 515-281-1355, {www.blind.state.ia.us}. Assistance offered:

- library services

- vocational evaluation, training and placement
- orientation and adjustment center
- independent living counseling
- Business Enterprises Program (BEP)
- adaptive equipment
- occupational tools
- registry of the blind
- information and referral
- communication training and equipment

Iowa Division of Vocational Rehabilitation Services, 510 East 12th Street, Des Moines, IA 50319, 515-281-4211 (V/TTY), 800-532-1486 (V/TTY); Email: {webmaster@dvrs.state.ia.us}, {www.dvrs.state.ia.us}.

Kansas

Vocational Rehabilitation, Department of Social and Rehabilitation Services, 915 Harrison Street, 6th Floor, Docking State Office Building, Topeka, Kansas 66612; 785-296-3959, Fax: 785-296-2173, {www.srskansas.org}.

Kentucky

Mr. Sam Serraglio, Commissioner, Kentucky Department of Vocational Rehabilitation, 209 St. Clair St., Frankfort, KY 40601; 800-372-7172 (KY), 502-564-4440, Fax: 502-564-6742, http://kydvr.state.ky.us. Assistance offered:

- Assessment for determining eligibility and vocational rehabilitation needs
- Counseling and guidance
- Information and referral to other agencies
- Physical and mental restoration services
- Vocational and other training services
- Supported employment
- Transportation and other services necessary to participate fully in your rehabilitation program
- Personal assistance services
- Interpreter and note taking services
- Telecommunications, sensory, and other technological aids and devices
- Rehabilitation technology
- Job Placement and Job Retention Services
- Employment follow-up and postemployment services

Department for the Blind, P.O. Box 757, 209 St. Clair Street, Frankfort, KY 40602; 502-564-4754, 800-321-6668, TDD: 502-564-2929, Fax: 502-564-2951, {www.kyblind.state.ky.us}. Assistance offered:

- diagnosis and evaluation
- counseling
- medical treatment
- vocational training and placement
- room and board
- transportation
- reader services
- orientation and mobility training
- optical aids
- communication technology
- occupational licenses, tools and equipment
- postemployment services
- Business Enterprises Program (BEP)
- Industries for the Blind

Louisiana

Mary Nelson, Director, Rehabilitation Services, Department of Social Services, 8225 Florida Blvd., Baton Rouge, LA 70806; 504-925-4131, 800-737-2958, Fax: 504-925-4481, {www.dss.state.la.us/offlrs/html/vocational_rehabilitation.html}. Assistance offered:

- vocational evaluation, training and placement
- assistive devices
- personal adjustment counseling
- independent living training
- in home care services
- deaf and blind services
- communication training
- transportation
- financial assistance
- occupational licenses and tools

Maine

Maine Bureau of Rehabilitation Services, 150 State House Station, Augusta, ME 04333, 207-624-5950, 800-698-4440, TTY: 888-755-0023, 207-624-5980, {www.state.me.us/rehab}.

Maryland

Division of Vocational Rehabilitation, State Department of Education, 2301 Argonne Drive, Baltimore, MD 21218-1696; 410/554-9385, 888-554-0334, TTY: 410/554-9411, Fax: 410-554-9412, Email: {dors@msde.state.lib.md.us}, {www.dors.state.md.us/voc_rehab.html}. Assistance offered:

- physical therapy
- vocational evaluation, training, and rehabilitation
- personal adjustment counseling
- transportation
- financial assistance
- occupational licenses and equipment
- assistive devices
- psychological evaluations
- independent living training

Massachusetts

Rehabilitation Commission, Fort Point Place, 27-43 Wormwood Street, Boston, MA 02210-1616; 800-245-6543, 617-204-3600, Fax: 617-727-1354, {www.state.ma.us/mrc}. Assistance offered:
- head injury program
- home based employment
- adaptive housing
- injured workers program
- supported employment
- deaf services
- bilingual specialty services
- independent living center
- transportation
- home care assistance program
- personal care assistance
- disability determination
- library services
- job training and placement
- job site modification
- information and referral

Commission for the Blind, 88 Kingston St., Boston, MA 02111-2227; 617-727-5550, 800-392-6450 (in MA), TDD: 617-727-9063, {www.state.ma.us/mcb}. Assistance offered:
- talking book and radio reading services
- administer Medicaid
- low vision and hearing aids
- information referral
- individual and family counseling
- homemaker services
- mobility instruction
- home management training
- protective services, including arranging guardianship
- interpreter services
- elder blind services
- recreation, housing assistance, and advocacy
- services for multi-handicapped individuals
- vocational training and placement
- Ferguson Industries program

Michigan

Patrick Cannon, Director, Commission for the Blind, 201 N. Washington Square, P.O. Box 30652, Lansing, MI 48909; 517-373-0262, TDD: 517-373-4025, Fax: 517-355-5140, {www.mfia.state.mi.us/mcb/home.asp}. Assistance offered:
- vocational evaluation
- financial aid
- academic instruction
- postemployment services
- medical treatment
- transportation
- reader services
- occupational licenses and equipment
- interpreter services
- daily living costs assistance
- disability determination

Michigan Rehabilitation Services, Michigan Department of Career Development, P.O. Box 30010, Lansing, MI 48909, 517-241-0377, 800-605-6722, Fax: 513-373-0565, {www.michigan.gov/mdcd}.

Minnesota

Paul Bridges, Ed.D., Department of Economic Security, Rehabilitation Services Branch, 390 North Robert Street, St. Paul, MN 55101; 651-296-9981, 800-328-9095, TTY: 651-296-3900, {www.mmwfc.org/rehab/vr/ main_vr.htm}. Assistance offered:
- vocational evaluation, training, and placement
- personal adjustment counseling
- independent living training
- assistive devices
- transportation
- information referral
- postemployment services
- physical therapy

Richard C. Davis, Minnesota Department of Economic Security, State Services for the Blind, 2200 University Ave. W. #240, St. Paul, MN 55114-1840; 651-642-0500, TTY: 651-642-0506, 800-652-9000, Email:

{Richard.Davis@state.mn.us}, {www.mnworkforcecenter.org/ssb}. Assistance offered:
- personal adjustment counseling
- training in independent living
- job training, placement and retention
- assistive technologies
- rehabilitation engineering
- low vision services
- blind vendor program
- child development
- parent support
- communication equipment and aids, including transcription to tape or braille

Mississippi
Mississippi Department of Rehabilitation Services, 1281 Highway 51 North, Madison, MS 39110, P.O. Box 1698, Jackson, MS 39215, 601-853-5100, 800-443-1000, {www.mdrs.state.ms.us}.

Missouri
Ronald Vessell, Director, Missouri Division of Vocational Rehabilitation, 3024 Dupont Circle, Jefferson City, MO 65109; 573-751-3251, 573-751-0881, TTY: 877-222-8963, {www.vr.dese.state.mo.us/vr/co/VRWebsite.nsf}. Assistance offered:
- medical examinations
- vocational evaluation, training, and placement
- health care
- assistive devices
- living expenses and transportation assistance
- occupational tools and licenses
- counseling in independent living
- Personal Care Assistance Program

Missouri Rehabilitation Services for the Blind, P.O. Box 88, Jefferson City, MO 65103-0088; 573-751-4249, 800-592-6004, Fax: 573-751-4984, Email: {mgiboney@mail.state.mo.us}, {www.dss.state.mo.us/dfs/rehab/vr.Htm}. Assistance offered:
- diagnosis and evaluation
- physical restoration
- instruction in daily living
- vocational training, including college
- job placement
- adaptive technology
- rehabilitation facilities
- Business Enterprise Program (BEP)
- counseling for children, adults, and families
- vision screening
- resource referrals

Montana
Joe Matthews, Administrator, Dept. Of Social and Rehabilitation Services, Rehabilitation/ Visual Services, 111 North Sanders, Helena, MT 59620; P.O. Box 4210, Helena, MT 59604-4210; 406-444-2590, TDD: 406-444-2590, Fax: 406-444-3632, {www.dphhs.state.mt.us/dsd/ index.htm}. Assistance offered:
- vocational evaluation, training and placement
- work adjustment training
- supported and sheltered employment
- counseling and training in independent living
- resource referrals
- adaptive equipment
- housing assistance
- Native American Vocational Rehabilitation Projects
- low vision treatment
- financial assistance

Nebraska
Director, Frank C. Lloyd, Vocational Rehabilitation Services, 301 Centennial Mall South, P.O. Box 94987, Lincoln, NE 68509; 402-471-3644, 800-742-7594, Fax: 402-471-0788, {www.vocrehab.state.ne.us}. Assistance offered:
- vocational evaluation, training, and placement
- transportation
- medical treatment
- personal adjustment counseling
- financial assistance
- postemployment services

Cheryl Puff, Director, Services for Visually Impaired, Dept. Of Public Institutions, 4600 Valley Road, Suite 420, Lincoln, NE 68510-4844; 402-471-3593, {www.ncbvi.state.ne.us/dbproject.htm}. Assistance offered:
- training for independent living
- educational assistance
- vocational evaluation, training and placement

- occupational equipment
- small business enterprises program
- medical services
- advocacy services
- individual and family counseling
- consultation services for employers
- computer training
- peer support groups

Nevada

Maynard Yasmer, Administrator, Department of Employment, Training and Rehabilitation, Rehabilitation Division, Bureau of Vocational Rehabilitation, 505 E. King St., #501, Carson City, NV 89701-3704; 775-684-4070, Fax: 775-684-4186, {www.state.nv.us/rehab/reh_vorh.htm}. Assistance offered:
- adaptive equipment
- physical and occupational therapy
- vocational training and placement
- occupational tools and licenses
- communication services and technology
- education for employers
- transportation
- counseling in independent living
- rehabilitation engineering
- resource referrals

New Hampshire

Paul K. Leather, Director, Division of Vocational Rehabilitation, 78 Regional Drive, Concord, NH 03301-9686; 603-271-3471, 800-299-1647, Email: {cfairneny@ed.state.nh.us}, {www.ed.state.nh.us/vrcopynew/index.htm}, Assistance offered:
- vocational evaluation, training, and placement
- independent living counseling
- physical and mental restoration
- assistive devices
- supported employment
- financial assistance
- postemployment services
- information and referral

New Jersey

Thomas G. Jennings, Director, 135 East State Street, P.O. Box 398, Trenton, NJ 08625-0398; 609-292-5987, TTY: 609-292-2919, Fax: 609-292-8347, Email: {dvradmin@dol.state.nj.us}, {www.state.nj.us/labor/dvrs/dvroff.htm}. Assistance offered:
- medical and psychological evaluation
- vocational counseling, training, and placement
- adaptive equipment
- financial assistance with equipment and transportation

Jamie Casabianca-Hilton, Director, Commission for the Blind and Visually Impaired, Dept. of Human Services, 153 Halsey Street, 6th Floor, P.O. Box 47017, Newark, NJ 07102; 973-648-2324, Email: {ddaniels@dhs.state.nj.us}, {www.state.nj.us/humanservices/cbvi/index.html }. Assistance offered:
- childcare
- individual and family counseling
- tutoring
- vocational evaluation, training, and placement
- high school and college counseling
- business enterprise programs
- instruction in independent living, including housing assistance
- eye health screenings and education
- community benefits for the disabled

New Mexico

Terry Brigance, Director, Division of Vocational Rehabilitation, 435 St. Michael's Drive, Building D, Santa Fe, NM 87505; 505-954-8500, 800-224-7005, Fax: 505-954-8562, Email: {SKelley@state.nm.us}, {http://public.dvrgetsjobs.com}. Assistance offered:
- vocational evaluation, training, and placement
- academic training
- work adjustment training
- adaptive equipment
- job site modification
- counseling
- postemployment services
- physical and psychological examination
- independent living counseling
- medical services
- occupational supplies
- meal allowance and transportation
- job coach assistance
- supported employment

- job seeking skills training
- postemployment counseling

New York
John A. Johnson, Commissioner, Dept. Of Social Services, Commission for the Blind and Visually Handicapped, 40 North Pearl Street, Albany, NY 11243--0001; 518-473-1675, TDD: 518-473-1698, Fax: 518-473-9255, Email: {CBVH@dfa.state.ny.us}, {www.ocfs.state.ny.us/main/cbvh}. Assistance offered:

- children services
- independent living training
- communications training and equipment
- mobility instruction
- vocational evaluation, training, and placement
- low vision aids
- medical exams
- counseling
- vending facility program
- academic instruction
- information and referral

North Carolina
George McCoy, Director, Division of Vocational Rehabilitation Services, 2801 Mail Service Center, Raleigh, NC 27699; 919-855-3500, Fax: 919-733-7968, {http://dvr.dhhs.state.nc.us}. Assistance offered:

- vocational evaluation, training, and placement
- assistive devices
- personal adjustment counseling
- independent living training
- financial assistance
- transportation

John DeLuca, Director, Division of Services for the Blind, 309 Ashe Ave., Raleigh, NC 27606; 919-733-9822, Fax: 919-733-9769, Email: {johndeluca@ ncmail.net}, {www.dhhs.state.nc/dsb}. Assistance offered:

- vision screening
- eye health education
- low vision services
- job evaluation, training, and placement
- small business assistance
- individual and family adjustment counseling
- housing and home improvement services
- home management training
- consultation and training for preschool visually impaired children and their families
- communication resources
- financial assistance

North Dakota
Gene Hysjulien, Director, N.D. Disability Services Division, Vocational Rehabilitation, 600 South 2nd Street, Suite 1B, Bismarck, ND 58504; 701-328-8950, 800-755-2745, TDD: 701-328-8968, Fax: 701-328-8969, Email: {dhsds@state.nd.us}, {http://notes.state.nd.us/dhs/dhsweb.nsf}. Assistance offered:

- diagnosis and evaluation
- vocational training and placement, including resume writing and interviewing workshops
- physical and mental retardation
- trade school/college training
- transportation
- rehabilitation engineering services
- postemployment services
- adaptive equipment

Ohio
John M. Connelly, Administrator, Ohio Rehabilitation Services Commission, 400 E. Campus View Blvd., Columbus, OH 43235-4604; 800-282-4536 (OH only), 614-438-1200, Fax: 614-438-1257, {www.state.oh.us/rsc/}. Assistance offered:

- determination of benefit eligibility
- vocational evaluation, training, and placement
- rehabilitation engineering
- medical and psychological evaluation
- personal care assistance
- independent living counseling
- community centers for the deaf
- peer counseling
- supported employment
- business enterprise programs
- head injury program
- communication technology and resources

Oklahoma
Linda Parker, Director, Dept. of Rehabilitation Services, 3535 NW 58th St., Suite 500, Oklahoma City, OK 73112-4815; 405-951-3400, 800-845-8476, Fax: 405-951-3529, Email:

{drspiowm@onenet.net}, {www.okrehab.org}. Assistance offered:
- medical examinations and treatment
- assistive devices
- job training and placement
- interpreter services
- maintenance and transportation
- occupational licenses and equipment
- initial inventory for small businesses
- rehabilitation engineering
- library services
- communication equipment
- independent living training
- supported employment
- work-study program
- school for the deaf
- school for the blind

Oregon

Gary K. Weeks, Director, Vocational Rehabilitation Division, Administration Office, 500 Summer Street NE, Salem, OR 97310-1012; 503-945-5880, TTY: 503-945-5894, Fax: 503-945-8991, Email: {dhr.info@state.or.us}, {http://vrdnet.hr.state.or.us/}. Assistance offered:
- vocational evaluation, training (including on-the-job), and placement
- education
- books, supplies, or tools
- transportation
- medical treatment
- adaptive equipment
- postemployment services
- independent living counseling
- Disability Determination Services (DDS)

Charles Young, Administrator, Commission for the Blind, 535 SE 12th Avenue, Portland, OR 97214; 503-731-3221, 888-202-5463, Email: {ocbmail@state.or.us}, {www.cfb.state.or.us}. Assistance offered:
- mobility instruction
- alternative communication skills and technology
- counseling on independent living
- optical and environmental aids
- individual, group, and family counseling
- employment counseling, training, and placement

Pennsylvania

Susan L. Aldrete, Executive Director, Office of Vocational Rehabilitation, Labor & Industry Building, 1521 N. 6th St., Harrisburg, PA 17102; 717-787-5244, 800-442-6351, TTY: 800-233-3008, Email: {ovr@dli.state.pa.us}, {www.dli.state.pa.us/ovr/index.htm}. Assistance offered:
- medical, psychological, and audiological exams
- vocational evaluation, training, and placement
- academic instruction
- counseling
- adaptive equipment
- occupational and physical therapy
- independent living training
- transportation
- occupational licenses and tools
- home and auto modifications
- attendant care
- communication devices

Rose Putric, Acting Director, Bureau of Blindness & Visual Services, Dept. of Public Welfare, 1521 N. 6th St., Harrisburg, PA 17102; 717-787-6176, {www.dli.state.pa.us/ovr/index.htm}. Assistance offered:
- optical aids
- low vision services
- communication devices and training
- transportation
- personal adjustment counseling
- vocational evaluation, training and placement

Rhode Island

Raymond A. Carroll, Administrator, Office of Vocational Rehabilitation Services, Department of Human Services, 40 Fountain St., Providence, RI 02908; 800-752-8088, ext. 2300, 401-421-7005, TDD: 401-421-7016, Fax: 401-421-9259, Email: {rcarroll@ors.state.ri.us}, {www.ors.state.ri.us/}. Assistance offered:
- optical aids
- low vision services
- transportation
- personal adjustment counseling
- communication training
- vocational and medical evaluation

- job training and placement
- information referral

South Carolina
South Carolina Vocational Rehabilitation Department, 1410 Boston Ave., P.O. Box 15, West Columbia, SC 29171-0015, 803-896-6503, TDD: 803-896-6635, Fax: 803-896-6529, Email: {scvrd@rehabnet.work.org}, {www.scvrd.net}.

South Dakota
Grady Kickul, Director, Division of Rehabilitation Services, East Highway 34, Hillsview Plaza, c/o 500 East Capitol Avenue, Pierre, SD 57501; 605-773-3195, Fax: 605-773-5483, Email: {infors@dhs.state.sd.us}, {www.state.sd.us/dhs/drs/}. Assistance offered:
- vocational and medical diagnosis
- family and individual personal adjustment counseling
- physical restoration through treatment and/or hospitalization
- orthotic and prosthetic devices
- job training and placement
- occupational licenses, tools, and equipment
- postemployment services
- transportation and financial assistance

Gaye Mattke, Director, Division of Service to the Blind and Visually Impaired, Hillsview Plaza, E. Hwy 34, c/o 500 East Capitol, Pierre, SD 57501-5070; 605-773-4644, Fax: 605-773-5483, Email: {infosbvi@dhs.state.sd.us}, {www.state.sd.us/dhs/sbvi}. Assistance offered:
- orientation and mobility counseling
- home management training and equipment
- communication skills training
- specialized library and radio reading services
- optical aids
- training for health care professionals and employers

Tennessee
Tennessee Division of Rehabilitation Services, 400 Deadrick St., Nashville, TN 78248, 615-313-4700, TTY: 800-270-1349, Fax: 615-741-4165, {www.state.tn.us/humanserv/DRS.html}.

Texas
Vernon M. Arrell, Commissioner, Texas Rehabilitation Commission, 4900 North Lamar Blvd, Austin, TX 78751; 800-628-5115, 512-424-4410, TDD: 512-424-4417, {www.rehab.state.tx.us/}. Assistance offered:
- vocational evaluation, training, and placement
- personal adjustment counseling
- independent living training
- physical therapy
- information referral

Terry Murphy, Executive Director, Texas Commission for the Blind, 4800 North Lamar, Austin, TX 78756-3175; 512-459-2500, Voice/TDD: 800-252-5204, Fax: 512-459-2685, {www.tcb.state.tx.us/}. Assistance offered:
- orientation and mobility instruction
- home management training
- communication skills and equipment
- occupational therapy
- low vision services
- college prep
- therapeutic recreation
- independent living counseling
- medical/health management
- optical aids
- vocational evaluation, training, and placement
- Business Enterprises Program (BEP)
- bilingual services

Utah
Blaine Petersen, Executive Director, Vocational Rehabilitation Services, 250 East 500 South, Salt Lake City, UT 84111; 801-538-7530, Fax: 801-538-7522, {www.usor.state.ut.us/}. Assistance offered:
- vocational evaluation, training, and placement
- personal adjustment counseling
- medical treatment
- psychotherapy
- physical and occupational therapy
- assistive devices
- academic instruction
- transportation
- occupational tools and licenses
- interpreter services
- postemployment services
- information and referral

Vermont

Diane P. Dalmasse, Director, Division of Vocational Rehabilitation, 103 South Main Street, Waterbury, VT 05671-2303; 802-241-2186, {www.dad.state.vt.us/dvr}. Assistance offered:

- vocational evaluation and placement
- transportation
- interpreter services
- adaptive equipment
- books, supplies, and tools
- financial support
- occupational and personal adjustment services
- upported employment

Division for the Blind and Visually Impaired, 103 S. Main St., Waterbury, VT 05671-2304; 802-241-2210, Fax: 802-241-3359, Email: {fred@dad.state.vt.us}, {www.dad.state.vt.us/dbvi}. Assistance offered:

- physical restoration
- adaptive aids
- vocational aassessment and training
- optical aids
- education
- personal adjustment through counseling
- job placement
- researching available financial benefits

Virgin Islands

Caterine Mall, Administrator, Division of Disabilities & Rehabilitation Services, Dept. Of Human Services, 1303 Hospital Road, St. Thomas, VI 00802; 340-774-0930, Email: {humanservices@usvi.org}, {www.usvi.org/humanservices}.

Virginia

Joseph Ashley, Director, Virginia Department of Rehabilitation Services, 8004 Franklin Farms Drive, P.O. Box K-300, Richmond, VA 23288; 800-552-5019, 804-662-7000, TTY: 800-464-9950, Fax: 804-662-9533, Email: {DRS@drs.state.va.us}, {www.vadrs.org/}. Assistance offered:

- physical, psychological, and vocational evaluation
- counseling
- restoration services
- job training and placement
- transportation
- interpreter services
- telecommunication aids
- occupational licenses and equipment
- supported employment
- postemployment services
- Long-Term Mentally Ill Program
- school-to-work transition programs
- personal assistance
- assistive devices
- independent living services
- Transitional Living Center

W. Roy Grizzard, Jr., Commissioner, Dept. For the Visually Handicapped, Commonwealth of Virginia, 397 Azalea Avenue, Richmond, VA 23227; 804-371-3140, 800-622-2155, {www.vdbvi.org}. Assistance offered:

- deaf-blind services
- independent living counseling
- information and referral
- low vision examinations and training
- determine eligibility for financial assistance
- youth programs
- instructional material center
- transportation
- medical, psychological, and vocational evaluation
- job training and placement
- medical treatment
- library services
- rehabilitation center
- small business assistance

Washington

Jeanne Munro, Director, Division of Vocational Rehabilitation, Dept. Of Social & Health Services, P.O. Box 45340, Olympia WA 98504; 612 Woodland Sq. Loop SE, Lacey, WA 98503-1044;, 800-637-5627, 360-438-8000, Fax: 360-438-8007, {www1.dshs.wa.gov/dvr}. Assistance offered:

- school-to-work transition program
- on-the-job training
- job placement
- supported employment
- independent living counseling
- attendant care
- assistive technology
- family counseling
- transportation

- medical treatment
- occupational supplies
- postemployment services

Bill Palmer, Acting Director, Dept. Of Services for the Blind, 402 Legion Way, SE, Suite 100, P.O. Box 40933, Olympia, WA 98504-0933; 360-586-1224, 800-552-7103, TDD: 360-586-6437, Fax: 360-586-7627, {www.wa.gov/dsb/}. Assistance offered:

- vocational evaluation, training and placement
- Business Enterprise Program (BEP)
- training center for independent living
- coordination of community and educational resources for adults and children
- in home training for the elderly
- recreation program

West Virginia

Janice Holland, Director, West Virginia Department of Education and the Arts, Division of Rehabilitation Services, State Capitol, P. O. Box 50890, Charleston, WV 25305-0890; 800-642-8207, 304-766-4600, Fax: 304-766-4690, Email: {penneyh@mail.drs.state.wv.us}, {www.wvdrs.org}. Assistance offered:

- vocational evaluation, training, and placement
- personal adjustment counseling
- communication devices
- physical, occupational, speech, and hearing therapy
- rehabilitation hospital
- low vision services
- medical treatment
- remedial education
- driver education
- counseling
- information and referral
- crisis intervention
- student financial aid

Wisconsin

Tom Dixon, Administrator, Division of Vocational Rehabilitation, 2917 International Lane, Suite 300, P.O. Box 7852, Madison, WI 53707-7852; 800-442-3477, 608-243-5600, TTY: 608-243-5601, Fax: 608-243-5680 or 608-243-5681, {www.dwd.state.wi.us/dvr}. Assistance offered:

- medical, psychological and vocational evaluation
- counseling
- job placement
- job training
- transportation
- job seeking skills
- job site modification
- technological aids and devices
- small business opportunities
- home based business development and marketing assistance
- occupational licenses and equipment
- independent living services
- training and education in approved schools
- cost of living benefits

Wyoming

Gary W. Child, Administrator, Division of Vocational Rehabilitation, Department of Employment, 1100 Herschler Building, Cheyenne, WY 82002; 307-777-7389, {http://wydoe.state.wy.us/doe.asp?10+5}. Assistance offered:

- evaluation of rehabilitation potential
- individual and family personal adjustment counseling
- information referrals
- physical and mental restoration
- job training and placement
- financial assistance
- communication aids and training
- transportation
- occupational licenses, tools, and equipment
- Business Enterprise Program (BEP)
- attendant services
- postemployment services

State Client Assistance Program (CAP)

The first place to start when your state Office of Vocational Rehabilitation denies your handicap or disability benefits is your nearest state Client Assistance Program (CAP) office. CAP is a free information, referral, and legal service that helps disabled or handicapped individuals appeal a denial by OVR (or other agency). CAP can take your appeal process from the first stages all the way to the U.S. Supreme Court if necessary — and it won't cost you a penny.

A CAP Specialist can help in many ways by:

- Providing assistance and advocacy services to help you resolve any problems you may have in applying for or receiving rehabilitation services;
- Explaining your rights and your responsibilities throughout the rehabilitation process;
- Helping you to communicate your concerns to DORS staff;
- Giving you accurate information on rehabilitation programs and services;
- Explaining DORS policies and procedures to you;
- Helping you when a service has been denied or when you are not satisfied with a service provided;
- Providing legal services when necessary to represent you in a formal hearing; and
- Providing information about your employment rights under the Americans With Disabilities Act.

State Client Assistance Program Offices

Alabama
Jerry Norsworthy, Director
Client Assistance Program
2125 East South Boulevard
Montgomery, AL 361116-2454
334-281-2276
In-State Toll Free: 800-228-3231
Email: sacap@hotmail.com
www.clik.to/SACAP

Alaska
Pam Stratton, Director
Client Assistance Program
2900 Boniface Parkway, #100
Anchorage, AK 99504-3195
907-333-2211
Fax: 907-333-1186
Email: akcap@alaska.com
http://home.gci.net/~alaskacap/

American Samoa
Hellene F. Stanley, Director
Client Assistance Program
P. O. Box 3937
Pago Pago, American Samoa
96799
011-684-633-2441
Fax: 011-684-633-7286
Email: opad@samoatelco.com

Arizona
Arizona Center for Disability Law
100 N. Stone Ave., Suite 305
Tucson, AZ 85701
520-327-9547 (V/TTY)
800-922-1447 (V/TTY)
Fax: 520-884-0992
Emaiol: center@acdl.com
www.acdl.com

Arkansas
Eddie Miller, Director
Client Assistance Program
Disability Rights Center, Inc.
Evergreen Place, Suite 201
1100 North University
Little Rock, AR 72207
501-296-1775
800-482-1174
Fax: 501-296-1779
Email:
panda@advocacyservices.org
www.advocacyservices.org

California
Sheila Conlen-Mentkowski, Director
Client Assistance Program
2000 Evergreen Street, 2nd Floor
Sacramento, CA 95815
916-263-8981
TTY: 916-263-7477
800-952-5544
Fax: 916-263-7464
Email:
smentkow@rehab.cahwnet.gov
www.rehab.cahwnet.gov

Colorado
Jeff Peterson, Director
Client Assistance Program
The Legal Center
455 Sherman Street, Suite 130
Denver, CO 80203
303-722-0300
800-288-1376

Fax: 303-722-0720
Email:
tlcmail@thelegalcenter.org
www.thelegalcenter.org

Connecticut
Susan Werboff, Director
Client Assistance Program
Office of P&A for Persons with Disabilities
60B Weston Street
Hartford, CT 06120-1551
860-297-4300
860-566-2102 (TDD)
800-842-7303 (statewide)
Fax: 860-566-8714
Email: hn2571@handsnet.org
www.state.ct.us/opapd

Delaware
Theresa Gallagher, Director
Client Assistance Program
United Cerebral Palsy, Inc.
254 East Camden-Wyoming Avenue
Camden, DE 19934
302-698-9336
800-640-9336
Fax: 302-698-9338
Email: capucp@magpage.com

District of Columbia
Joseph Cooney, Director
Client Assistance Program
University Legal Services
300 I Street, NE, Suite 202
Washington, DC 20002
202-547-0198
Fax: 202-547-2083
Email: jcooney@uls-dc.com

Florida
Ann Robinson, CAP Program
Advocacy Center for Persons with Disabilities
2671 Executive Ctr, Circle West
Webster Building, Suite 100
Tallahassee, FL 32301-5092
Phone: 850-488-9071
800-342-0823
800-346-4127 (TDD)
Fax: 850-488-8640
www.advocacycenter.org

Georgia
Charles Martin, Director
Client Assistance Program
123 N. McDonough
Decartur, GA 30030
404-373-2040
800-822-9727
Fax: 404-373-4110
Email: GaCAPDirector@
theOmbudsman.com
www.theOmbudsman.com/CAP/

Guam
Fidela Limtiacho
President of the Board
Client Assistance Program
Parent Agencies Network
P.O. Box 23474
GMF, Guam 96921
671-649-1948
Fax: 671-472-2568

Hawaii
Executive Director
Client Assistance Program
Protection & Advocacy Agency
900 Fort St. Mall, Suite 1040
Honolulu, HI 96814
808-949-2922
800-882-1057
Fax: 808-949-2928
Email: pahi@pixi.com
www.pixi.com/~pahi

Idaho
Shawn DeLoyola, Director
Client Assistance Program
Co-Ad, Inc.
4477 Emerald, Suite B-100
Boise, ID 83706
208-336-5353
800-632-5125
Fax: 208-336-5396
Email: coadinc@mcleodusa.net
http://users.moscow.com/co-ad

Illinois
Cynthia Grothaus, Director
Client Assistance Program
100 N. First Street, 1st Floor
Springfield, IL 62702
217-782-5374
800-641-3929
Fax: 217-524-1790
www.state.il.us/agency/dhs/capnp.html

Indiana
Amy Ames
Client Assistance Program
Indiana Protection and Advocacy Services
4701 N. Keystone Ave.
Suite 222
Indianapolis, IN 46204
317-722-5555
800-622-4845
Fax: 317-722-5564
Email:
tgallagher@ipas.state.in.us
www.in.gov/ipas/programs/cap.html

Iowa
Harlietta Helland, Director
Client Assistance Program
Division on Persons with Disabilities
Lucas State Office Building
Des Moines, IA 50319
515-281-3957
800-652-4298
Fax: 515-242-6119
Email:
dhr.disabilities@dhr.state.ia.us
www.state.ia.us/government/dhr/pd/pdfs/DisabilityRightsGuide.pdf

Kansas
Mary Reyer, Director
Client Assistance Program
3640 SW Topeka Blvd.
Suite 150
Topeka, KS 66611
785-266-8193
800-432-2326
Fax: 785-266-8574
Email: mreyer5175@aol.com
www.srskansas.org/CAP

Kentucky
Gerry Gordon-Brown, Consumer Advocate
Client Assistance Program
209 St. Clair, 5th Floor
Frankfort, KY 40601
502-564-8035; 800-633-6283
Fax: 502-564-2951
Email:
dianehigh@uky.campus.mci.net
http://kydvr.state.ky.us/index.htm

Louisiana
Susan Howard, CAP Director
Client Assistance Program
Advocacy Center for the Elderly and Disabled

225 Baronne, Suite 2112
New Orleans, LA 70112-1724
Phone: 504-522-2337
800-960-7705
Fax: 504-522-5507
Email: simplo@advocacyLA.org
www.advocacyla.org

Maine
Steve Beam, Director
Client Assistance Program
CARES, Inc.
4-C Winter Street
August, ME 04330
Phone: 207-622-7055
800-773-7055
Fax: 207-621-1869
Email: capsite@aol.com
www.caresinc.org

Maryland
Peggy Dew, Director
Client Assistance Program
Maryland Rehabilitation Center
Division of Rehabilitation Services
2301 Argonne Drive
Baltimore, MD 21208
410-554-9361
800-638-6243
Fax: 410-554-9362
Email: cap@dors.state.md.us
www.dors.state.md.us/services/client_assist.htm

Massachusetts
Barbara Lybarger
Client Assistance Program
Massachusetts Office on Disability
One Ashburton Place
Room 1305
Boston, MA 02108
617-727-7440
800-322-2020
Fax: 617-727-0965
Email:
blybarger@modi.state.ma.us
www.state.ma.us/mod/MSCAPBRO.html

Michigan
Amy Maes, Director
Client Assistance Program
Michigan P&A Service
106 West Allegan, Suite 300
Lansing, MI 48933
517-487-1755
CAP only: 800-292-5896
Fax: 517-487-0827
Email: ebauer@mpas.org
www.mpas.org

Minnesota
Pamela Hoopes, Director
Client Assistance Program
Minnesota Disability Law Center
430 First Avenue North
Suite 300
Minneapolis, MN 55401-1780
612-332-1441
800-292-4150
Fax: 612-334-5755
Email hn0518@handsnet.org
www.mnlegalservices.org/mdlc

Mississippi
Presley Posey, Director
Client Assistance Program
Easter Seal Society
3226 N. State Street
Jackson, MS 39216
601-982-7051
Fax: 601-981-1951
Email: pposey8803@aol.com
www.members.od.com/msess1/cap.htm

Missouri
Cecilia Callahan, Director of Advocacy
Client Assistance Project
Missouri P&A Services
925 S. Country Club Dr.
Unit B-1
Jefferson City, MO 65109
573-893-3333
800-392-8667
Fax: 573-893-4231
Email: mopasjc@socket.net
http://members.socket.net/~mopasjc/MOP&A.htm

Montana
Lynn Wislow, Director
Client Assistance Project
Montana Advocacy Program
316 N. Park, Room 211
P.O. Box 1680
Helena, MT 59624
406-449-2344
800-245-4743
800-245-4743
Fax: 406-444-0261
Email: advocate@mt.net
www.mtadv.org

Nebraska
Victoria L. Rasmussen, Director
Client Assistance Program
Division of Rehabilitation Services
Nebraska Dept. of Education
301 Centennial Mall South
Lincoln, NE 68509
402-471-3656
800-742-7594
Fax: 402-471-0117
Email:
Vicki_r@nde4.nde.state.ne.us
www.cap.state.ne.us/

Nevada
William E. Bauer, Director
Client Assistance Program
505 East King St.
Carson City, NV 89701-3705
775-688-1440
800-633-9879
Fax: 775-688-1627
Email: detrcap@nvdetr.org
www.detr.state.nv.us/rehab/reh_cap.htm

New Hampshire
Michael D. Jenkins
Executive Director
Client Assistance Program
Governor's Commission on Disability
57 Regional Drive
Concord, NH 03301-9686
603-271-4175
800-852-3405
Fax: 603-271-2837
Email: bhagy@gov.state.nh.us
www.state.nh.us/disability/caphomepage.html

New Jersey
Ellen Lence, Director
Client Assistance Program
New Jersey P&A, Inc.
210 S. Broad Street, 3rd Floor
Trenton, NJ 08608
609-292-9742
800-922-7233
Fax: 609-777-0187
Email: advoca@njpanda.org
www.njpanda.org

New Mexico
Barna Dean, CAP Coordinator
Protection & Advocacy, Inc
1720 Louisiana Blvd., NE
Suite 204
Albuquerque, NM 87106
505-256-3100
800-432-4682
Fax: 505-256-3184
Email: nmpanda@nmprotection-advocacy.com
www.nmprotection-advocacy.com

New York
Gary O'Brien, Director
Client Assistance Program
NY Commission on Quality of Care for the Mentally Disabled
401 State Street
Schenectody, NY 12305-2397
518-381-7098
800-624-4143 (TDD)
Fax: 518-381-7095
www.cqc.state.ny.us
michealp@cqc.state.ny.us

North Carolina
Kathy Brack, Director
Client Assistance Program
North Carolina Division of Vocational Rehabilitation Services
2801 Mail Service Center
Raleigh, NC 27699-2801
919-855-3600
800-215-7227
Fax: 919-715-2456
Email: kbrack@dhr.state.nc.us
http://dvr.dhhs.state.nc.us/DVR/CAP/ caphome.htm

North Dakota
Teresa Larsen, Director
Client Assistance Program
600 South 2nd Street, Suite 1B
Bismarck, ND 58504-5729
701-328-8964
800-207-6122
Fax: 701-328-8969
Email: panda@state.nd.us
www.ndpanda.org

N. Marianas Islands
Client Assistance Program
Northern Marianas Protection and Advocacy System, Inc.
P.O. Box 3529 C.K.
Saipan, MP 96950
011-670-235-7274/3
Fax: 011-670-235-7275
Email:
lbarcinasp&a@saipan.com
www.saipan.com/gov/branches/ovr/ service.htm

Ohio
Caroline Knight, Director
Client Assistance Program
Ohio Legal Rights Service
8 East Long Street, 5th Floor
Columbus, OH 43215
614-466-7264
800-282-9181
Fax: 614-644-1888
Email:
cknight@mail.olrs.ohio.gov
www.state.oh.us/olrs/

Oklahoma
Helen Kutz, Director
Client Assistance Program
Oklahoma Office of Handicapped Concerns
2712 Villa Prom
Oklahoma City, OK 73107
405-521-3756
800-522-8224
Fax: 405-943-7550
Email: cap@ohc.state.ok.us
www.state.ok.us/~ohc/cap.htm

Oregon
Barbara Fields, Director
Client Assistance Program
Oregon Advocacy Center
620 W. Fifth Ave., 5th Floor
Portland, OR 97204-1428
503-243-2081
TTY: 503-323-9161
800-452-1694
TTY: 800-556-5351
Email:
welcome@oradvocacy.org
www.oradvocacy.org

Pennsylvania
Stephen Pennington
Executive Director
Client Assistance Program
Center for Disability Law & Policy
1617 J.F.K. Blvd.
Suite 800
Philadelphia, PA 19103
215-557-7112
888-745-2357
Fax: 215-557-7602
Email: capcdkt@trfn.clpgh.org
www.equalemployment.org/cap.html

Puerto Rico
Enrique Rodriguez Otero, Director
Client Assistance Program
Office of the Governor
Ombudsman for the Disabled
P. O. Box 41309
San Juan, PR 00902-4234
787-725-2333
TTY: 787-725-4014
800-981-4125
Fax: 787-721-2455
Email:
erodriguez@oppi.gobierno.pr
www.oppi.prstar.net

Republic of Palau
Client Assistance Program
Bureau of Public Health
Ministry of Health
P.O. Box 6027
Koror, Republic of Palau 96940
011-680-488-2813
Fax: 011-680-488-1211
Email phpa@palaunet.com

Rhode Island
Raymond Bandusky, Director
Client Assistance Program
Rhode Island Disability Law Center Inc.
151 Broadway
Providence, RI 02903
401-831-3150
401-831-5335 (TDD)
800-733-5332
Fax: 401-274-5568
Email: hn7384@handsnet.org
http://ridlc.org/RIDLC/ridlc.html

South Carolina
Larry Barker, Director
Client Assistance Program
Office of the Governor
Division of Ombudsman and Citizen Services
1205 Pendleton St.
Columbia, SC 29205
803-734-0285

800-868-0040
TDD: 803-734-1147
Fax: 803-734-0546
Email:
mbutler@govoepp.state.sc.us
www.govoepp.state.sc.us/cap

South Dakota
Nancy Schade, Director
Client Assistance Program
South Dakota Advocacy
Services
221 South Central Avenue
Pierre, SD 57501
605-224-8294
800-658-4782
Fax: 605-224-5125
Email:sdas@sdadvocacy.com
www.sdadvocacy.com

Tennessee
Dann Suggs, Director
Client Assistance Program
Tennessee P&A, Inc.
P. O. Box 121257
Nashville, TN 37212
615-298-1080
TTY: 615-298-2471
800-342-1660
Fax: 615-298-2046
Email: shirleys@tpainc.org
www.state.tn.us/yumanserv/
VRServices.html#cap

Texas
Judy Sokolow, Coordinator
Client Assistance Program
Advocacy, Inc.
7800 Shoal Creek Blvd.
Suite 171-E
Austin, TX 78757
512-454-4816
800-252-9108
Fax: 512-323-0902
Email: hn2414@handsnet.org
www.advocacyinc.org

Utah
Nancy Friel, Director
Client Assistance Program
Disability Law Center
455 East 400 South
Suite 410
Salt Lake City, UT 84111
801-363-1347
800-662-9080
Fax: 801-363-1437
Email:
info@disabilitylawcenter.org
www.disabilitylawcenter.org

Vermont
Laura Phillips, Director
Client Assistance Program
57 North Main St., Suite 2
Rutland, VT 05401
802-775-0021
800-769-7459
Email: nbrieden@vtlegalaid.org
www.dad.state.vt.us/DVR/cap.ht
m

Virginia
Mary Hart, Manager
Client Assistance Program
Dept. for Rights of Virginians
with Disabilities
Ninth Street Office Bldg.
202 North 9th Street, 9th floor
Richmond, VA 23219
804-225-2042
800-552-3962
Fax: 804-225-3221
Email: fergusst@drvd.state.va.us
www.cns.state.va.us/drvd

Virgin Islands
Amelia Headley LeMont
Client Assistance Program
Virgin Islands Advocacy
Agency
63 Estate Cane Carlton
Frederiksted
St. Croix, USVI 00840
340-772-1200
340-776-4303
340-772-4641 (TDD)
Fax: 340-772-0609
Email: info@viadvocacy.org
www.viadvocacy.org

Washington
Jerry Johnsen, Director
Client Assistance Program
2531 Ranier Ave. South
Seattle, WA 98144
Phone: 206-721-5999
800-544-2121
Fax: 206-721-4537
Email: capseattle@att.net
www.wata.org/resource/legal/
agencies/cap.htm

West Virginia
Susan Edwards, Director
Client Assistance Program
West Virginia Advocates, Inc.
Litton Bldg, 4th Floor
1207 Quarrier Street
Charleston, WV 25301
304-346-0847
800-950-5250
Fax: 304-346-0867
Email:
wvadvocates@newwave.net
www.newwave.net/~wvadvocate
s

Wisconsin
Linda Vegoe
Department of Health and
Family Services
Client Assistance Program
2811 Agriculture Dr.
P.O. Box 8911
Madison, WI 53708-8911
608-224-5070
800-362-1290
Fax: 608-224-5069
Email:
linda.vegoe@datcp.state.wi.us
www.dwd.state.wi.us/dvr/cap.ht
m

Wyoming
Jeanne Thobro, Director
Client Assistance Program
Wyoming P&A System
320 West 25th St., 2nd Floor
Cheyenne, WY 82001
307-632-3496
800-821-3091 (Voice/TDD)
800-624-7648
Fax: 307-638-0815
Email: wypanda@vcn.com
http://wypanda.com

Additional Contacts For Resources

Alabama
Alabama Statewide Technology Access and Response Project (STAR) System For Alabamians with Disabilities
2125 East South Boulevard
P.O. Box 20752
Montgomery, AL 36120-0752
Project Director: Dr. Tom Gannaway
334-613-3480
800-STAR656 (In-State)
TDD: 334-613-2519
FAX: 334-613-3485
Email: jbanks@rehab.state.al.us
www.rehab.state.al.us/star

Alaska
Assistive Technologies of Alaska
2217 E. Tudor Rd., Suite 1
Anchorage, AK 99507
Director: Kathy Pivratsky
907-562-7372
TTD: 907-563-8284
Fax: 907-562-0545
Email: Kprivratsky@sesa.org
www.sesa.org/sesa/agency/at/at.html

American Samoa
American Samoa Assistive Technology Service Project (ASATS)
Division of Vocational Rehabilitation
Department of Human Resources
Pago Pago, American Samoa 96799
Project Director: Edmund Pereira
684-699-1529
TDD: 684-233-7874
Fax: 684-699-1376
Email: edperei@yahoo.com

Arizona
Arizona Technology Access Program (AZTAP)
Institute for Human Development
Northern Arizona University
4105 B, 20th St., Suite 260
Phoenix, AZ 85016
Jill Oberstein
602-728-9534
800-477-9921
TTY: 602-728-9536
Fax: 602-728-9353
www.nau.edu/ihd/aztap

Arkansas
Arkansas Increasing Capabilities Access Network (ICAN)
Arkansas Department of Workforce Education
Arkansas Rehabilitation Services
2201 Brookwood Drive
Suite 117
Little Rock, AR 72202
Project Director: Barbara Gullett
501-666-8868 (V/TDD)
800-828-2799 (V/TDD, In-State)
Fax: 501-666-5319
Email: sogaskin@ars.state.ar.us
www.arkansas-ican.org

California
California Assistive Technology System
California Department of Rehabilitation
2000 Evergreen
Sacramento, CA 95815
Mailing Address:
P.O. Box 944222
Sacramento, CA 94244-2220
Project Director: William Campagna
916-263-8687
TTY: 916-263-8685
Fax: 916-263-8683
Email: wcampagn@dor.ca.gov
www.atnet.org/cats.html

Colorado
Colorado Assistive Technology Partners
University of Colorado Health Sciences Center
Colorado University Affiliated Program
1245 E. Colfax Ave.
Denver, CO 80218
Project Director: Cathy Bodine
303-315-1280
TDD: 303-837-8964
Fax: 303-837-1208
Email:
cathy.bodine@UCHSC.edu
Homepage:
www.UCHSC.edu/atp

Connecticut
Connecticut Assistive Technology Project
Department of Social Services, BRS
25 Sigourney St., 11th Floor
Hartford, CT 06106
Project Director: John M. Ficarro
860-424-4881
800-537-2549 (In-State)
TDD: 860-424-4839
Fax: 860-424-4850
Email: jficarro@aol.com
www.techactproject.com

Delaware
Delaware Assistive Technology Initiative (DATI)
Center for Applied Science & Engineering
University of Delaware/duPont Hospital for Children
1600 Rockland Road, Room 117E
P.O. Box 269
Wilmington, DE 19899-0269
Director: Beth A. Mineo Mollica, Ph.D.
302-651-6790
800-870 DATI (3284) (In-State)
TDD: 302-651-6794
Fax: 302-651-6793
Email: dati@asel.udel.edu
www.asel.udel.edu/dati

District of Columbia
University Legal Services AT Program for the District of Columbia
Information Specialist: Gil Shamir
Program Manager: Alicia C. Johns
300 I Street, NE, Suite 200
Washington, DC 20002
202-547-0198
TDD: 202-547-2657

Fax: 202-547-2662
Email: atpdc@uls-dc.com
www.atpdc.org

Florida
Florida Alliance for Assistive Service and Technology
1020 E. Lafayette St., Suite 110
Tallahassee, FL 32301-4546
Project Director: Terry Ward
850-487-3278 (V/TDD)
Fax/TDD: 850-487-2805
Email: faast@faast.org
Homepage: www.faast.org

Georgia
Georgia Tools for Life
Division of Rehabilitation Services
1700 Century Circle B-4
Atlanta, GA 30345
Project Director: Joy Kniskern
404-657-3084
800-479-8665 (In-State)
TDD: 404-657-3085
Fax: 404-657-3086
Email: 102476.1737@compuserve.com
www.gatfl.org

Guam
Guam System for Assistive Technology (GSAT)
University Affiliated Program-Developmental Disabilities
303 University Drive
University of Guam
UOG Station
Mangilao, Guam 96923
Principal Investigator: Heidi E. Farra-San Nicolas, Ph.D.
Project Director: Ben Servino
671-735-2490-3
TDD: 671-734-8378
Fax: 671-734-5709
Email: gsat@ite.net

Hawaii
Hawaii Assistive Technology Training and Services (HATTS)
414 Kuwili Street, Suite 104
Honolulu, HI 96817
Information and Resource: Judith Clark
808-532-7114
Project Director: Barbara Fischlowitz-Leong, M.Ed.
808-532-7110 (V/TDD)
800-645-3007 (V/TDD, In-State)
Fax: 808-532-7120
Email: atrc@atrc.org
www.atrc.org

Idaho
Idaho Assistive Technology Project
129 W. Third Street
Moscow, ID 83844-4401
Information and Referral: Susan House
208-885-3771
Project Director: Ron Seiler
208-885-3559 (V/TDD)
Fax: 208-885-3628
Email: rseile861@uidaho.edu
www.et.uidaho.edu/idatech

Illinois
Illinois Assistive Technology Project (1989)
1 W. Old State Capitol Plaza
Suite 100
Springfield, IL 62701
Project Director: Wilhelmina Gunther
217-522-7985
TDD: 217-522-9966
Fax: 217-522-8067
Email: iatp@ilteh.org
www.iltech.org

Indiana
Indiana ATTAIN (Accessing Technology Through Awareness in Indiana) Project
2346 Lynhurst Dr.
Airport Office Center, Suite 507
Indianapolis, IN 46241
Project Manager: Cris Fulford
317-486-8808
800-528-8246 (In-State)
TDD: 800-486-8809 (National)
Fax: 317-486-8809
Email: attain@attaininc.org
www.attaininc.org

Iowa
Iowa Program for Assistive Technology
Iowa University Affiliated Program
Center for Disabilities
100 Hawkins Drive, Room 5295
Iowa City, IA 52242-1011
Information and Referral: Ann Dudler
319-356-0550
Directors: Jane Gay, 319-356-4463
800-331-3027 (V/TDD; National)
Fax: 319-356-8284
Email: infotech@uiowa.edu
www.uiowa.edu/infotech/

Kansas
Assistive Technology for Kansans Project
2601 Gabriel
P.O. Box 738
Parsons, KS 67357
Project Director: Charles R. Spellman
316-421-6550, ext. 1890
Email: chuck@ku.edu
Co-Director: Sara Sack
Project Coordinator: Sheila Simmons
316-421-8367
800-KAN DO IT
Fax/TDD: 316-421-0954
Email: ssack@ku.edu
www.atkilsi.ukans.edu

Kentucky
Kentucky Assistive Technology Services Network
Charles McDowell Rehabilitation Center
8412 Westport Road
Louisville, KY 40242
Information and Referral: Jim Syme
Project Director: J. Chase Forrester
502-327-0022
800-327-5287 (V/TDD, In-State)
Fax: 502-327-9974
TDD: 502-327-9855
Email: katsnet@iglou.com
www.katsnet.org

Louisiana
Louisiana Assistive Technology Access Network
P.O. Box 14115
Baton Rouge, LA 70898-4115
Executive Director: Julie Nesbit
225-925-9500 (V/TDD)
800-270-6185 (V/TDD)

Fax: 225-925-9560
Email: latanstate@aol.com
www.latan.org

Maine
Maine Consumer Information and Technology Training Exchange (MAINE CITE)
Maine CITE Coordinating Center
UMS Network for Education and Tech. Services
46 University Drive
Augusta, ME 04330
Project Director: Kathy Powers
207-621-3195
TDD: 207-621-3482
Fax: 207-621-3193
Email: iweb@doe.k12.me.us
www.mecite.org

Maryland
Maryland Technology Assistance Program
Governor's Office for Individuals with Disabilities
2301 Argonne Dr., Room T-17
Baltimore, MD 21218
Information Specialist :Patrick McCurdy
Project Director: Paul Rasinski
410-554-9230 (V/TDD)
Fax: 410-554-9237
Email: rasinski@mdtap.org

Massachusetts
Massachusetts Assistive Technology Partnership
MATP Center
Children's Hospital
1295 Boylston Street, Suite 310
Boston, MA 02115
Information and Referral: Patricia Hill
Project Director: Marylyn Howe
617-355-7167 (TDD)
800-848-8867 (V/TDD, In-State)
617-355-7820
TDD: 617-355-7301
Fax: 617-355-6345
Email: mhowe@matp.org
www.matp.org

Michigan
Michigan Tech 2000
Michigan Assistive Technology Project
740 W. Lake Lansing, Rd.
Suite 400
East Lansing, MI 48823
Project Director: Katherine Wyeth
Project Manager: Roanne Chaney
517-333-2477 (V/TDD)
800-760-4600 (In-State)
Fax: 517-333-2677
Email: kdwyeth@match.org
Homepage: www.match.org

Minnesota
Minnesota STAR Program
300 Centennial Building
658 Cedar Street
St. Paul, MN 55155
Acting Executive Director: Rona Linforth
800-657-3862 (In-State)
TDD: 800-657-3895 (In-State)
651-296-2771
TDD: 651-296-9478
Fax: 651-282-6671
Email:
star.program@state.mn.us
www.admin.state.mn.us/assistive technology

Mississippi
Mississippi Project START
P.O. Box 1698
Jackson, MS 39215-1000
Information and Referral: Albert Newsome
601-987-4872
Project Director: Stephen Power
601-987-4872
800-852-8328 (V/TDD; In-State)
Fax: 601-364-2349
Email:
contactus@msprojectstart.org
www.msprojectstart.org

Missouri
Missouri Assistive Technology Project
4731 South Cochise, Suite 114
Independence, MO 64055-6975
Project Director: Diane Golden, Ph.D.
800-647-8557 (In-State)
816-373-5193
TDD: 816-373-9315
Fax: 816-373-9314
Email: matpmo@swbell.net
Homepage:
www.dolir.state.mo.us/matp/

Montana
MONTECH
Rural Institute on Disabilities
The University of Montana
634 Eddy Avenue
Missoula, MT 59812
Project Director: Gail McGregor
406-243-5676
TDD: 800-732-0323 (National)
Fax: 406-243-4730
Email:
montech@selway.umt.edu
Homepage:
www.ruralinstitute.umt.edu

Nebraska
Nebraska Assistive Technology Partnership
5143 South 48th Street, Suite C
Lincoln, NE 68516-2204
Information and Referral: Kathryn Kruse
Project Director: Mark Schultz;
402-471-0735 (V/TDD)
402-471-0734 (V/TDD)
888-806-6287 (In-State)
Fax: 402-471-6052
Email: atp@atp.state.ne.us
www.nde.state.ne.us/ATP/

Nevada
Nevada Assistive Technology Collaborative
Rehabilitation Division
Community Based Services
711 South Stewart Street
Carson City, NV 89710
Project Administrator: Donny Loux
775-687-4452
TDD: 775-687-3388
Fax: 775-687-3292
Email:
pgowins@govmail.state.nv.us
http://detr.state.nv.us/rehab/reh_pgbs.htm

New Hampshire
New Hampshire Technology Partnership Project
Institute on Disability/UAP
#14 Ten Ferry Street
The Concord Center
Concord, NH 03301

Project Director: Jan Nisbet,
603-862-4320
Co-Project Director: Therese Willkomm
603-528-3060
800-427-3338 (V/TDD; In-State)
603-224-0630 (V/TDD)
Fax: 603-226-0389
Email: twillkomm@nhaat.mv.com
Homepage: http://iod.unh.edu

New Jersey
New Jersey Technology Assistive Resource Program (TARP)
New Jersey Protection and Advocacy, Inc.
210 South Broad St., 3rd Floor
Trenton, NJ 08608
Project Director: Ellen Lence
609-777-0945
Program Manager: Tim Montagano
609-292-7498
Lav42prg@concentric.net
800-342-5832 (In-State)
TDD: 609-633-7106
Fax: 609-777-0187
Email: rringh@njpanda.org
Homepage: www.njpanda.org

New Mexico
New Mexico Technology Assistance Program
435 St. Michael's Drive
Building D
Santa Fe, NM 87505
Information and Referral: Carol Cadena
Project Director: Alan Klaus
800-866-2253
Phone/TDD: 505-954-8539
Fax: 505-954-8562
Email: aklaus@state.mn.us
Homepage: www.nmtap.com

New York
New York State Traid Project
Office of Advocate for Persons with Disabilities
One Empire State Plaza
Suite 1001
Albany, NY 12223-1150
Project Director: Lisa Rosano-Kaczkowski;
518-474-2825
800-522-4369 (V/TDD; In-State)
TDD: 518-473-4231
Fax: 518-473-6005
Email: triad@emi.com
www.advoc4disabled.state.ny.us/TRIAD_Project/technolog.htm

North Carolina
North Carolina Assistive Technology Project
Department of Health and Human Services
Division of Vocational Rehabilitation Services
1110 Navaho Drive, Suite 101
Raleigh, NC 27609-7322
Project Director: Ricki Hiatt
919-850-2787 (V/TDD)
Fax: 919-850-2792
Email: ncatp@mindspring.com
www.ncatp.org

North Dakota
North Dakota Interagency Program for Assistive Technology (IPAT)
P.O. Box 743
Cavalier, ND 58220
Director: Judie Lee
701-265-4807 (V/TDD)
Fax: 701-265-3150
Email: jlee@polarcomm.com
Homepage: www.ndipat.org

N. Marianas Islands
Commonwealth of the Northern Mariana Islands Assistive Technology Project
Governor's Developmental Disabilities Council
Systems of Technology-Related Assistance for Individuals with Disabilities
P.O. Box 2565 CK
Saipan, MP 96950
Project Director: Celia Lamkin, MD
670-664-7000(V/TDD)
Fax: 670-664-7030
Email: clamkin@cnmiddcouncil.org
www.cnmiddcouncil.org/atstarid/atflash.htm

Ohio
Ohio TRAIN
J.L. Canera Center
2050 Kenny Rd., 9th Floor
Columbus, OH 43212
Executive Director: Douglas Huntt
614-292-2426 (V/TDD)
800-784-3425 (V/TDD, In-State)
TDD: 614-292-3162
Fax: 614-292-5866
Email: huntt.1@osc.edu
www.atohio.org

Oklahoma
Oklahoma Able Tech
Oklahoma State University
Wellness Center
1514 W. Hall of Fame Road
Stillwater, OK 74078-2026
Project Manager: Linda Jaco; (405) 744-9864
405-744-9748
800-257-1705 (V/TDD)
Fax: 405-744-2487
Email: okway.okstate.edu
www.okabletech.okstate.edu

Oregon
Oregon Technology Access for Life Needs Project (TALN)
c/o Access Technologies Inc.
3070 Lancaster Drive NE
Salem, OR 97305-1396
Project Director: Byron McNaught
800-677-7512 (In-State)
503-361-1201 (V/TDD)
Fax: 503-370-4530
Email: ati@orednet.org
www.taln.org

Pennsylvania
Pennsylvania's Initiative on Assistive Technology
Institute on Disabilities/UAP
Ritter Annex 423
Philadelphia, PA 19122-6090
Project Director: Amy Goldman
800-204-PIAT (7428)
TDD: 800-750-PIAT (TT)
Fax: 215-204-9371
Email: piat@astro.temple.edu
www.temple.edu/inst_disabilities/piat

Puerto Rico
Puerto Rico Assistive Technology Project
University of Puerto Rico

Medical Sciences Campus
College of Related Health Professions
Office of Project Investigation and
Development
Box 365067
San Juan, PR 00936-5067
Project Director: Maria I. Miranda, B.A.
800-496-6035 (National)
800-981-6033 (In PR)
787-758-2525 x4413
TDD/Fax: 787-754-8034
Email: pratp@coqui.net

Rhode Island
Rhode Island Assistive Technology Access Partnership
Office of Rehabilitation Services
40 Fountain Street
Providence, RI 02903
Project Director: Regina Connor
401-421-7005 x390
800-752-8088 x2608 (In-State)
TDD: 401-421-7016
Fax: 401-421-9259
Email: reginac@ors.state.ri.us
Homepage: www.atap.state.ri.us

South Carolina
South Carolina Assistive Technology Program
USC School of Medicine
Center for Developmental Disabilities
Columbia, SC 29208
Project Director: Evelyn Evans;
803-935-5263
803-935-5263 (V/TDD)
Fax: 803-935-5342
Email: jjendron@usit.net
www.sc.edu/scatp

South Dakota
South Dakota Assistive Technology Project
(DAKOTALINK)
1925 Plaza Blvd.
Pierre, SD 57501
Project Director: Dave Vogel
605-394-1876
800-645-0673 (V/TDD, In-State)
Fax: 605-224-8320
Email: atinfo@tie.net
www.datalink.tie.net

Tennessee
Tennessee Technology Access Project (TTAP)
Citizens Plaza Bldg.
400 Deadrick St.
Nashville, TN 37248
Project Director: Jacque Cundall
615-532-3122
800-732-5059
Fax: 615-532-4685
Email: ttap@mail.state.tn.us
www.state.tn.us/humanserv/ttap_index.htm

Texas
Texas Assistive Technology Partnership
University of Texas at Austin
4030 West Braker Lane
Building 1, Suite 180
Mail Code L4000
Austin, TX 78759
800-828-7839
Project Director: Susanne Elrod
512-232-0740
TDD: 512-232-0762
Fax: 512-232-0761
Email: techaccess@teachnet.edb.utexas.edu
http://techaccess.edb.utexas.edu

Virgin Islands
U.S. Virgin Island Technology-Related Assistance for Individuals with Disabilities
(TRAID)
University of the Virgin Islands/UAP
#2 John Brewers Bay
St. Thomas, VI 00801-0990
Executive Director: Dr. Yegin Habtes
809-693-1323
Fax: 809-693-1325
Email: yhabtey@ uvi.edu
Homepage: www.uvi.edu

Utah
Utah Assistive Technology Program
Center for Persons with Disabilities
6588 Old Main Hill
Logan, UT 84322-6588
Project Director: Martin Blari;
435-797-1982
Project Coordinator: Martin Blair,
435-797-3886
435-797-1981 (V/TDD)
Fax: 435-797-2355
Email: marv@cpd2.usu.edu
www.uatpat.org

Vermont
Vermont Assistive Technology Project
103 South Main Street
Weeks Building, First Floor
Waterbury, VT 05671-2305
Project Director: Julie Tucker
802-241-2620 (V/TDD)
800-750-6355
Fax: 802-241-2174
Email: jtucker@dad.state.vt.us
www.dad.state.vt.us/atp

Virginia
Virginia Assistive Technology System
8004 Franklin Farms Drive
Richmond, VA 23288-0300
Information and Referral: 800-435-8490
Project Director: Kenneth Knorr
804-552-5019
804-662-9990 (V/TDD)
Fax: 804-662-9478
Email: knorrkh@drs.state.va.us
www.vats.org

Washington
Washington Assistive Technology Alliance
DSHS/DVR
AT Resource Center
Univ. of Washington
Box 357920
Seattle, WA 98195-7920
Project Director: Debbie Cook
800-841-8345
206-685-4181
TDD: 206-616-1396
Fax: 206-543-4779
Email: uwctds@washington.edu
http://wata.org

West Virginia
West Virginia Assistive Technology System
University Affiliated Center for Developmental Disabilities
Airport Research and Office Park

955 Hartman Run Road
Morgantown, WV 26505
Project Manager: Jack Stewart
304-293-4692 (V/TDD)
800-841-8436 (In-State)
Fax: 304-293-7294
Email: jstewart@wvu.edu
www.ced.wvu.edu/wvats

Wisconsin
WISTECH
Wisconsin Assistive Technology Program
Office for Persons with Physical Disabilities
P.O. Box 7851
1 W. Wilson St., Room 450
Madison, WI 53707-7851
Project Director: Holly Laux O'Higgins
608-266-0421
TTY: 608-267-9880
Fax: 608-267-3203
Email: lauxhm@dhfs.state.wi.us
www.wistech.state.wi.us

Wyoming
Wyoming's New Options in Technology (WYNOT)
University of Wyoming
1465 North 4th Street, Suite 111
Laramie, WY 82072
Project Director: Kathleen Laurin
800-861-4312 (V/TTY)
307-766-2084 (V/TDD)
Fax: 307-721-2084
Email: wynot.uw@uwyo.edu
http://wind.uwyo.edu/wynot

State Disability Offices

Alabama
Governor's Committee on Employment of People with Disabilities
Department of Rehabilitation Service
P.O. Box 11586
2129 East South Boulevard
Montgomery, AL 36111-0586
Voice/TTY: 334-281-8780
800-441-7607
Fax: 334-288-1104
Email:
webinfo@rehab.state.al.us
www.rehab.state.al.us

Alaska
The Governor's Committee on Employment and Rehabilitation of People with Disabilities
801 W. 10th Street, Suite 200
Juneau, AK 99801
Voice/TTY: 907-465-2814
Fax: 907-465-2856
Email:
anne_knight@labor.state.ak.us
www.labor.state.ak.us/govscomm

Arizona
Governor's Committee on Employment of People with Disabilities
1012 E. Willetta, SRI-1Bb
Phoenix, AZ 85006
602-239-4762
Fax: 602-239-5256

Arkansas
Governor's Commission on People with Disabilities
1616 Brookwood Drive
Little Rock, AR 72203
501-296-1626
TTY: 501-296-1623
Fax: 501-296-1675
Email:
bmvuletich@ars.state.ar.us
www.arsinfo.org

California
The California Governor's Committee for Employment of Disabled Persons
P.O. Box 826880, MIC 41
Sacramento, CA 94280-0001
800 Capitol Mall
Room 5078, MIC 41
Sacramento, CA 95814
916-654-8055
800-695-0350
TTY: 916-654-9820
Fax: 916-654-9821
www.disabilityemployment.org

Colorado
Colorado Governor's Advisory Council for People with Disabilities
c/o Aging and Adult Services
P.O. Box 172
Denver, CO 80201-0172
303-485-5956
888-887-9135 (In CO)
Fax: 303-620-4191
http://pw1.netcom.com/~cliffmau/ability.html

Connecticut
Governor's Committee on Employment of People with Disabilities
Labor Department Building
200 Folly Brook Boulevard
Wethersfield, CT 06109
860-263-6000
TTY: 860-566-1345
Fax: 860-566-1629
www.ctdol.state.ct.us/ctbln/gov/bln.html

Delaware
Governor's Committee on Employment of People with Disabilities
DVR, P.O. Box 9969
Wilmington, DE 19809-0969
Street Address:
4425 North Market Street
Wilmington, DE 19802
302-761-8275
Fax: 302-761-6611
www.delawareworks.com/divisions/dvr/director.htm

District of Columbia
Mayor's Committee on Persons with Disabilities
810 First Street, NE, Room 1007
Washington, D.C. 20002
202-442-8464
Fax: 202-442-8742
http://does.ci.washington.dc.us/news/2000/10_23_00.shtm

Florida
The Governor's Alliance & The Able Trust

106 East College Ave., Suite 820
Tallahassee, FL 32301
850-224-4493
888-838-ABLE (in FL)
Fax: 850-224-4496
Email: info@abletrust.org
www.abletrust.org

Georgia
Georgia Committee on Employment of Persons with Disabilities
Division of Rehabilitation Services
2 Peachtree Street, NW
Suite 3-210
Atlanta, GA 30303-3142
404-657-2126
888-ASK-GCDD (in GA)
Fax: 404-657-2132
Email:
eejacobson@dhr.state.ga.us
www.gcdd.org

Guam
Governor's Commission on Persons with Disabilities
1313 Central Avenue
Tiyan, Guam 96913
671-475-4646
Fax: 671-477-2892

Hawaii
Disability Communication Access Board
919 Ala Moana Blvd.
Suite 101
Honolulu, HI 96814
Voice/TTY: 808-586-8121
Fax: 808-586-8129
www.state.hi.us/health/dcab

Idaho
Governor's Committee on Employment of People with Disabilities
Department of Employment
317 Main Street
Boise, ID 83735
208-334-6264
TTY: 208-334-6424
Fax: 208-334-6300

Illinois
James R. Thompson Center
Department of Rehabilitative Services
100 West Randolph St.
Suite 8-100
Chicago, IL 60601
312-814-4036
TTY: 312-814-5000 (TTY)
Fax: 312-814-5949
www.state.il.us/agency/dhs/rsnp.html

Indiana
Governor's Commission on Planning for People with Disabilities
150 West Market Street, #628
Indianapolis, IN 46204
317-232-7770
Fax: 317-233-3712
Email: gpcpd@gpcpd.org
www.state.in.us\gpcpd

Iowa
Iowa Commission of Persons with Disabilities
Lucas State Office Building
321 East 12th Street
Des Moines, IA 50319
515-242-6334
888-219-0471
Fax: 515-242-6119
Email:
dhr.disabilities@dhr.state.ia.us
www.state.ia.us/government/dhr/pd/

Kansas
Kansas Commission on Disability Concerns
1430 SW Topeka Blvd.
Topeka, KS 66612-1877
800-295-5232
785-296-1722
TTY: 877-340-5874 (toll-free)
TTY: 785-296-5044
Fax: 785-296-0466
Email: mkgabeha@hr.state.ks.us
www2.hr.state.ks.us/dc/index.html

Kentucky
Kentucky Committee on Employment of People with Disabilities
CHR Bldg., Second - West
275 E. Main Street
Frankfort, KY 40621
Voice/TTY: 502-564-5331
Fax: 502-564-7799

Louisiana
Governor's Office of Disability Affairs
Office of the Governor
P.O. Box 94004
Baton Rouge, LA 70806-9004
225-219-7550
877-668-2722 (toll free)
Fax: 225-219-7551
Email: brackin@idsmail.com
www.gov.state.la.us/disabilityaffairs

Maine
Maine Subcommittee on Disabilities
Maine Jobs Council
443 Congress St.
Portland, ME 04101
207-879-1140
Fax: 207-879-1146
www.state.me.us/labor/mjc

Maryland
Governor's Committee on Employment of People with Disabilities
1 Market Center, Box 10
300 West Lexington Street
Baltimore, MD 21201
800-637-4113
Voice/TTY: 410-333-2263
Fax: 410-333-6674
www.mdtap.org/oid.html

Massachusetts
Governor's Commission on Employment of People with Disabilities
Department of Employment and Training Policy Office
19 Stanford Street, 4th Floor
Boston, MA 02114
617-626-5400
Fax: 617-570-8581
www.detma.org

Michigan
Michigan Commission on Disability Concerns
P.O. Box 30659
Lansing, MI 48909
Street Address:
320 No. Washington Square
Suite 250
Lansing, MI 48933
Voice/TTY: 517-334-8000

Fax: 517-334-6637
www.mfia.state.mi.us/mcdc.htm

Minnesota
Minnesota State Council on Disability
121 E. 7th Place, Suite 107
St. Paul, MN 55101
651-296-6785
800-945-8913
Fax: 651-296-5935
Email: council.disability@state.mn.us
www.disability.state.mn.us

Mississippi
Mississippi Dept. of Rehabilitation Services
P.O. Box 1698
Jackson, MS 39215-1698
Street Address:
1281 Highway 51, North
Madison, MS 39110
601-853-5100
800-443-1000 (In MS)
Fax: 601-853-5325
www.mdrs.state.ms.us.

Missouri
Missouri Governor's Council on Disability
P.O. Box 1668
3315 West Truman Boulevard
Jefferson City, MO 65102
800-877-8249
Voice/TTY: 573-751-2600
Fax: 573-526-4109
Email: gcd@dolir.state.mo.us
www.dolir.state.mo.us/gcd

Montana
Governor's Advisory Council on Disability
State Personnel Division
Dept. of Administration
P.O. Box 200127
Helena, MT 59620-0127
Street Address:
125 Roberts Street
Helena, MT 59620
406-444-3794
800-243-4091 (Montana State Relay)
Fax: 406-444-0544
www.dphhs.state.mt.us/dsd/govt_programs/vrp/vrs/admin_info/GovCouncil

Nebraska
Governor's Committee on Employment of People with Disabilities
Nebraska Job Service
Department of Labor
550 South 16th Street
Box 94600
Lincoln, NE 68509
402-471-2600
Fax: 402-471-9687
Email: lmi_ne@dol.state.ne.us
www.dol.state.ne.us/nwd

Nevada
Governor's Committee on Employment of People with Disabilities
4600 Kietzke Lane
Suite A125
Reno, NV 89502
Voice/TTY: 775-688-1111
Fax: 775-688-1113
www.epd.state.nv.us

New Hampshire
Governor's Commission on Disability
57 Regional Drive
Concord, NH 03301-8518
800-852-3405
Voice/TTY: 603-271-2773
Fax: 603-271-2837
www.state.nh.us/disability

New Jersey
New Jersey Division of Vocational Rehabilitation Services
135 East State St.
P.O. Box 398
Trenton, NJ 08625
609-292-5987
TTY: 609-292-2912
Fax: 609-292-8347
Email: dvradmin@dol.state.nj.us
www.state.nj.us/labor/dvrs/dvr.html

New Mexico
Governor's Committee on Concerns of the Handicapped
Lamy Building, Room 117
491 Old Santa Fe Trail
Santa Fe, NM 87501
505-827-6465
TTY: 505-827-6329
Fax: 505-827-6328
www.state.nm.us/gcch/gcch.htm

New York
New York State Office of Advocate for Persons with Disabilities
One Empire State Plaza
Suite 1001
Albany, NY 12223-1150
518-473-4129
800-522-4369 (In NY)
TTY: 518-473-4231
Fax: 518-473-6005
www.advoc4disabled.state.ny.us

North Carolina
Governor's Advocacy Council for Persons with Disabilities
1314 Mail Service Center
Raleigh, NC 27699-1314
919-733-9250
877-235-4210 (in NC)
TTY: 888-268-5535
919-733-9173
www.doa.state.nc.us/doa/gacpd/gacpd.htm

North Dakota
Governor's Committee on Employment of People with Disabilities
600 South 2nd Street
Bismarck, ND 58504
701-328-8952
Fax: 701-328-8969
http://lnotes.state.nd.us/dhs/dhsweb.nsf

Ohio
Ohio Governor's Council on People with Disabilities
400 East Campus View Boulevard
Columbus, OH 43235-4604
614-438-1393
800-282-4536, ext. 1391 (Statewide)
Fax: 614-438-1274
www.state.oh.us/gcpd

Oklahoma
Governor's Committee on Employment of the Handicapped
Office of Handicapped Concerns
Shepherd Mall
2712 Villa Prom

Oklahoma City, OK 73107-2423
405-521-3756
800-522-8224
TDD: 405-522-6706
Fax: 405-943-7550
www.state.ok.us/~ohc

Oregon
Oregon Disabilities Commission
1257 Ferry Street SE
Salem, OR 97310
800-358-3117 (in OR)
Voice/TTY: 503-378-3142
Fax: 503-378-3599
www.odc.state.or.us

Pennsylvania
Governor's Committee on Employment of People with Disabilities
Office of Vocational Rehabilitation
1521 N. 6th St.
Harrisburg, PA 17102
717-787-5232
Fax: 717-783-5221

Puerto Rico
Governor's Committee on Employment of Persons with Disabilities
Office of the Ombudsman for Persons w/ Disabilities
P.O. Box 4234
San Juan, PR 00902-4234
Street Address:
670 Ponce De Leon Avenue
Miramar, San Juan 00902
787-725-2333, ext. 2021
TTY: 787-725-4014
Fax: 787-721-2455

Rhode Island
Governor's Commission on the Handicapped
Building 51, 3rd Floor
41 Cherry Dale Court
Cranston, RI 02920
401-462-0100
TTY: 401-462-0101
Fax: 401-462-0106
Email:
disabilities@gcd.state.ri.us
www.gcd.state.ri.us

South Carolina
Governor's Committee on Employment of the Handicapped
Vocational Rehabilitation Department
1410 Boston Avenue
P.O. Box 15
West Columbia, SC 29171-0015
803-896-6580
Fax: 803-896-6510
www.scvrd.net

South Dakota
Governor's Advisory Committee on Employment of People with Disabilities
Department of Human Services
221 South Central, Suite 34 A
Pierre, SD 57501
605-945-2207
Fax: 605-945-2422
www.state.sd.us/dhs/drs

Tennessee
Tennessee Committee for Employment of People with Disabilities
Division of Rehabilitation Services
Citizens Plaza Bldg., Room 1100
400 Deaderick Street
Nashville, TN 37248
615-313-4891
TTY: 615-313-5695
Fax: 615-741-6508
www.state.tn.us

Texas
Governor's Committee on People with Disabilities
P.O. Box 12428
Austin, TX 78711
Street Address:
1100 San Jacinto, Room 300
Austin, TX 78701
512-463-5739
TTY: 512-463-5746
Fax: 512-463-5745
www.governor.state.tx.us/disabilities/

Utah
Utah Governor's Committee on Employment of People with Disabilities
c/o BOOST
1595 West 500 South
Salt Lake City, UT 84104
801-887-9529
800-473-7530
Fax: 801-278-9844
www.usor.state.ut.us

Vermont
Governor's Committee on Employment of People with Disabilities
c/o Vermont D.D. Council
103 South Main Street
Waterbury, VT 05671-0206
Voice/TTY: 802-241-2612
Fax: 802-244-5075
www.hireus.org

Virginia
The Virginia Board for People with Disabilities
202 North 9th Street, 9th Floor
Richmond VA 23219
Voice/TTY: 804-786-0016
Voice/TTY: 800-846-4464 (In VA)
Fax: 804-786-1118
www.vaboard.org

Virgin Islands
Governor's Committee on Employment of the Handicapped
Administrator Disabilities & Rehabilitation Services
Department of Human Services
Barbel Plaza South
St. Thomas, VI 00802
340-774-0930, ext. 157
Fax: 340-774-3466

Washington
Governor's Committee on Disability Issues and Employment
State of Washington
Employment Security Dept.
P.O. Box 9046
Olympia, WA 98507-9046
Street Address:
605 Woodland Square Loop SE, 3rd Floor
Lacey, WA 98503
360-438-3168
TTY: 360-438-3167
Fax: 360-438-3208
Email: algoodwin@esd.wa.gov

West Virginia
Division of Rehabilitation Services
State Capitol Building

P.O. Box 50890
Charleston, WV 25305
304-766-4601
TTY: 304-766-4965
Fax: 304-766-4905
www.wvdrs.org

Wisconsin
Governor's Committee for
People with Disabilities
P.O. Box 7850
Madison, WI 53707-7850
Street Address:
1 West Wilson #558
Madison, WI 53707-7850
Voice/TTY: 608-266-5451
Fax: 608-264-9832
www.dhfs.state.wi.us/disabilities
/physical/facts.htm

Wyoming
Governor's Committee on
Employment of People with
Disabilities
1st Floor - East Wing
Herschler Building, Room 1126
Cheyenne, WY 82002
Voice/TTY: 307-777-7389
Fax: 307-777-5939
http://wydoe.state.wylus/doe.asp
?1D=119

Free Pet Care At Veterinary Teaching Hospitals

The International Association of Assistance Dog Partners (IAADP), a cross-disability advocacy organization, provides information on veterinary teaching hospitals and what they offer disabled clients with assistance dogs. After surveying 26 hospitals, the IAADP found nineteen hospitals which have adopted official policies to reduce the cost of health care for assistance dogs. Here are the listings:

- Auburn University waives fees for examinations, diagnosis surgery and hospitalization of assistance dogs.
- Cornell University offers up to a 20% discount for services.
- Iowa State University offers 50% reduced fee structure for assistance dogs.
- Louisiana State University offers a 40% reduction on all services, except pharmacy and central surgery supplies which are billed at cost plus 25%.
- Michigan State University offers 25% fee reduction across the board for all services, if the disabled client indicates financial need.
- Mississippi State University provides a 50% reduction in fees for all working dogs, including assistance dogs.
- Ohio State University has an unofficial policy of providing a 20% reduction for all assistance dogs.
- Oklahoma State University charges 10% above the actual cost of the service for assistance dogs.
- Purdue University offers a 50% reduction on all services for assistance dogs and a 23% reduction on pharmaceuticals.
- Tufts University does not charge for professional services,, visits or consultations. They offer a 20% discount on all other services.
- Tuskegee University provides whatever level of reduction that is needed to medically treat the assistance dog.
- University of Illinois offers a 50% discount for all services and 20% discount for laboratory work on an assistance dog.

- University of Minnesota has a 20% reduction of the professional examination fee.
- University of Missouri gives a 25% discount on all charges for assistance dogs.
- University of Pennsylvania does not charge for clinic examinations. There is a 25% reduction of all services for assistance dogs, including pharmaceuticals.
- Virginia Tech and University of Maryland does not charge for initial visit and consultation.
- Washington State University has a 20% discount on fees generated for goods and service related to the care of service dogs seen or admitted to the facility. This applies only if the bill is paid in full at the time of service.
- Animal Medical Center, New York is a teaching facility and not a teaching vet school hospital. They do not charge for guide dogs and there is a fee reduction on a case by case basis for hearing and service dogs.
- Nebraska Veterinary Medical Association will provide a $100 voucher for preventative vet care such as vaccines and heartworm for all assistance dog partners in the state.
- National Pet Care Centers offer a 20% discount on total billing for assistance dog partners. More than 70 veterinary hospitals are members of this group.

Other veterinary teaching hospitals provide funds for indigent clients or offer help on a case by case basis. For more information on what these hospitals offer, contact the International Association of Assistance Dog Partners (IAADP), 38691 Filly Drive, Sterling Heights, MI 48310; 586-826-3938; {www.iaadp.org}; Email: {info@iaadp.org}.

More Health Care Assistance For Disabled Clients With Assistance Dogs

Bayer, Fort Dodge Animal Health, Friskies, and Nutramax Laboratories, in cooperation with the International Association of Assistance Dog Partners (IAADP), provides grants to subsidize the veterinary care of assistance dogs. Grants are available for disabled clients unable to pay for expensive procedures required to treat and keep their dogs in full working condition.

Membership in IAADP (which is approximately $15/year) is required to apply for the subsidized vet care. Members also qualify for the following: a free AVID microchip and registration in PETtrac; free enrollment in the AKC Companion Recovery program; an Emergency Recovery Kit; free Advantage flea product ($50 value); plus various publications, brochures and newsletters. Veterinarians who are working with an IAADP member in need of subsidized pet care should call the Bayer Animal Hospital at 800-422-9874.

For more information on what these hospitals offer, contact the International

Association of Assistance Dog Partners (IAADP), 38691 Filly Drive, Sterling Heights, MI 48310; 586-826-3938; {www.iaadp.org}; Email: {info@iaadp.org}.

Assistance Dogs and Training Provided Free of Charge to the Blind (Valued at $5,700)

Pilot Dogs, Inc.
Pilot Dogs, Inc. is an organization providing guide dogs to the blind. The organization not only provides their trained dogs free of charge, they also provide four weeks of training so that the new owner is equipped to fully utilize and care for his or her new dog. The dog, the transportation to and from the Pilot Dog training school, the room and board during the four weeks of training and all necessary equipment are provided free of charge. Pilot Dogs pays for the $5,700 service. For more information, write to Pilot Dogs, Inc., 625 West Town St., Columbus, OH 43215; 614-221-6367; Fax: 614-221-1577; {www.pilotdogs.org/indes.shatml}.

The Guide Dog Foundation for the Blind
The Guide Dog Foundation for the Blind, Inc. offers free guide dogs to legally blind individuals of high school age or older. Individuals who qualify for the program travel to New York for 25 days of training with their new guide dogs. The training and transportation to and from the school are also provided free of charge. The free travel applies to applicants residing in the U.S., as well as those from Canada and Mexico. For an information packet and application, contact the Guide Dog Foundation For The Blind, 371 East Jericho Turnpike, Smithtown, NY 11787; 800-548-4337; 631-265-2121; fax: 631-361-5192; {www.guidedog.org}.

Southeastern Guide Dogs
Any legally blind person, 16 or older may apply for a free guide dog from Southeastern Guide Dogs, Inc. Also included free of charge are the 26-day training course (with room and board) and the dog harness. Southeastern Guide Dogs makes a lifetime commitment to the dog and its new owner and provides follow-up visits each year or as often as necessary. There is an outreach program where those who qualify, can receive in-home training. The training with this program lasts 2 weeks. You must speak to an admissions representative to see if you qualify for the program based on your circumstances. If you live in the North or South Carolina areas, call the outreach center at 704-721-5000. For those in the Georgia area, call 770-459-2051, and all others should call the main office at 800-944-3647. For more information contact Southeastern Guide Dogs, Inc., 4210 77th St. East, Palmetto, FL 34221; 941-729-5665; 800-944-DOGS (3647); fax: 941-729-6646; {www.guidedogs.org}; Email: {msergeant@guidedogs.org}.

$15,000 Service Dogs Available Free Of Charge

Support Dogs, Inc. offers free service dogs to eligible individuals with disabilities. The standard skills of the service dogs include opening heavy doors, loading wheelchairs into vehicles, pulling wheelchairs up inclines and over long distances, retrieving dropped or distant objects, and other tasks of daily living. The service dogs fall into the following categories:

- Street Certified: Dogs qualified to accompany their owners in public.
- Certified Facility-Based (Companion/Therapy): Dogs that provide emotional support for residents/clients of a treatment center. These dogs may also perform some tasks.
- Home Certified: Dogs that provide emotional support to individuals in their home environment only. These dogs also perform some tasks, such as retrieving.
- Certified Home-Based Companion: Dogs that provide emotional support to individuals in home settings.
- Pediatric Companion: Dogs provide emotional support assistance to a child. They also give a limited amount of assistance.

Support Dogs has programs that cover three different assistance areas; Service, TOUCH (Therapy), and Pediatric.

- Service- A service dog is trained to help in completing tasks. These dogs are certified at three different levels.
- Para-the dogs have the strength and physical structure to pull a wheelchair up steep embankments.
- Quad-the dog has been trained to perform a variety of tasks.
- Companion- these dogs provide emotional support and a variety of tasks in a home setting. They do not brace or support their partner during transfer.
- TOUCH- The Therapy of Unique Canine Helpers (TOUCH) dogs are trained to work with patients in long-term health facilities, hospitals, rehabilitation centers, children's hospitals, geriatric facilities, and trauma hospitals.
- Pediatric Companion- A dog for this program is trained to be a companion for a special needs child. It will become an active participant in the child's development and education. The cost to raise and train the dogs is approximately $27,000.

For more information, contact Support Dogs, inc., 9510 Page Ave., St. Louis, MO 63132; 314-423-1988; {www.supportdogs.org}; Email: {info@supportdogs.org}.

Canine Companions

Canine Companions for Independence (CCI) is a nonprofit organization that provides trained service and hearing dogs and continued support to people with disabilities who want to increase their independence with the aid of a dog. People interested in receiving a dog must pay a $100 training fee, which covers everything the dog will take home.

For more information, contact CCI, National Headquarters, P.O. Box 446, Santa Rosa,

CA 95402; 800-572-2275; 707-577-1770; TDD: 707-577-1756; {www.caninecompanions.org}.

Aid For Adults and Children

Independence Dogs Inc. trains dogs to assist adults and children with mobility problems. Dogs are specially trained to assist persons who are quadriplegic or use walkers or wheelchairs. The organization requests a minimum donation of $200. It cost between $10,00 and $12,000 to fully train the dogs.

For more information contact Independence Dogs, Inc., 146 State Line Road, Chadda Ford, PA 19317; 610-358-2723; Fax: 610-358-5314; {www.independencedogs.org}; Email: {idi@independencedogs.org}.

Canine Working Companions

A regional group serving New York State is Canine Working Companions, a not-for-profit organization providing specially trained dogs to assist people with disabilities. They also work diligently to educate the public about the rights of the disabled with companion assistance animals. They are funded through donations and memberships.

The dogs are raised and trained by the organization. There is a $25 application fee and $175 fee upon acceptance into the program. They also encourage the clients to try to raise funds on their own, but that is not a requirement. They serve the state of

New York except for the city of New York and the Buffalo areas.

For more information contact Canine Working Companions, P.O. Box 2128, Syracuse, NY 13220-2128; 315-656-3301; {www.cwccanine.cc}.

Assistance Dogs for the Disabled

"PAWS with a Cause" is a national charitable and non-profit organization, which trains dogs to assist the disabled. Since 49 million Americans are disabled in some way — and only 3% of the disabled are blind — these animals are more than just "seeing eye dogs." They are trained to help individuals with cerebral palsy, muscular dystrophy, spinal cord injuries, epilepsy, hearing impairment, vision loss and a host of other disabilities.

A disabled person seeking an assistance dog sends an application to PAWS, which then assesses the needs of the applicant. Once an applicant is accepted into the program, PAWS begins the fund-raising process to secure the financial support needed for the training of the assistance dog. Recipients of assistance dogs are not charged a fee of any kind; they are only encouraged to take an active role in the fund-raising process (and PAWS provides the information needed for them to do so). Once the training is complete, full ownership of the assistance dog is transferred to the disabled recipient.

If you are not disabled but want to help this commendable cause, you can enroll in the Foster puppy Program to raise a puppy until it begins its assistance training. To find out more about the possibility of acquiring a specially trained dog, contact PAWS WITH A CAUSE, National Headquarters, 4646 South Division, Wayland, MI 49348; 800-253-PAWS; 616-877-7297; Fax: 616-877-0248; {www.pawswithacause.org}.

Trained Dogs - Valued at $12,000 - Given Free To Disabled Youth

Disabled children under the age of 18 can now discover why dogs are called "man's best friend." Tr"ained assistance dogs can aid seriously disabled chi"ldren- those with muscular dystrophy, cerebral palsy, spina bifida, as well as other disabilities- in opening and closing doors, pulling wheelchairs, pushing elevator buttons, alerting a parent at night, or going for help in an emergency.

Loving Paws Assistance Dogs is a non-profit organization, which trains and provides dogs to care for disabled children. Although the trained dogs are valued at $12,000 each, recipients are asked to pay only a small application fee and the dog is given free of charge.

To find out more information, contact Loving Paws Assistance Dogs, P.O. Box 12005, Santa Rosa, CA 95406; 707-586-0798; Fax: 707-586-0799; {www.lovingpaws.com}; Email: {info@lovingpaws.com}.

372 Sources To Pay Emergency Expenses

Not sure where to turn or what resources exist for you? Bravekids.org has put together a resource directory that lists over 372 sources for financial and other types of assistance for those with disabled children or adults or low-income families in need of help. It could be anything from paying your utility bill to respite care or medical expenses.

No need to feel like help does not exist. Check out {www.bravekids.org}.

Financial Benefits For Caregivers

The Alexandria Division of Social Services offers financial benefits for caregivers of children and adolescents with disabilities. Check your local, city, county or state for financial benefits for which you may qualify if you care for someone who is disabled.

$$$ PAY YOUR BILLS IF YOU ARE A VETERAN

Veterans have served our country bravely for years. There are 25 million veterans currently alive and of those nearly 75% of them served during a war or official period of hostility. About a quarter of the nation's population – approximately 70 million people – are eligible for Veteran Benefits and Services because they are veterans, family members or survivors of veterans. The Veterans' Affairs office goal is to provide patient care, veterans' benefits and customer satisfaction. They are committed to help veterans get the services they have earned and deserve. If you think you might be eligible for one or more of the Veterans' Benefits take the time to apply. It may just bring you free money and free services.

Veteran's Hotlines

The Department of Veterans Affairs has toll-free numbers for the convenience of veterans and their dependents. In addition, the *Federal Benefits for Veterans and Dependents* booklet and other VA information is available to the public.

Education Benefits	888-442-4551
VA Benefits	800-827-1000
Life Insurance	800-669-8477
Debt Management Center	800-827-0648
Telecommunications Device for the Deaf (TDD)	800-829-4833
CHAMPVA	800-733-8387
Headstones and Markers	800-697-6947
Persian Gulf Helpline	800-PGW-VETS
Health Benefits	877-222-8387
Mammography Helpline	888-492-7844

Free Money For College

If you need help with your VA education benefits, you can contact the Veteran's Administration at 1-800-827-1000.

- The Veterans Administration has established a website devoted to providing general and detailed information about education benefits. Check it out at {www.gibill.va.gov}.
- Call 1-888-GIBILL-1 (1-888-442 -4551) for information concerning the GI Bill.
- You can apply for benefits online at {http://vabenefits.vba.va.gov/vonapp/main.asp}

Toll-free telephone service is available in all 50 states, Puerto Rico, and the U.S. Virgin Islands. For forms and additional information contact your VA Regional Office or Vet Center listing on page 635.

Veterans Administration
810 Vermont Ave NW
Washington, DC 20420
888-442-4551
www.va.gov

Get A "Kicker"

There are many benefits for veterans to receive money for all types of education. The Montgomery GI-Active Duty-MGIB program provides veterans who entered service after June 30, 1985, up to 36 months of assistance for college, technical or vocational school, correspondence courses, apprenticeships or flight training school. Remedial, deficiency, tutoring and refresher courses may also be available. You may even be eligible for a "kicker", additional money that increases your basic MGIB monthly benefit.

For additional information, contact your regional office or vet center listed on page 635, call 1-800-827-1000, or check their web site at {www.gibill.va.gov}.

Free Money for Reserves' Education

Money for education may be available to you if you are a member of the Selected Reserve. The Selected Reserve includes the Army Reserve, Navy Reserve, Air Force Reserve, Marine Corps Reserve, Coast Guard Reserve, and the Army National Guard and the Air National Guard.

The Montgomery Bill-Selected Reserve (MGIB-SR) is an education assistance program for degree programs, correspondence courses, cooperative training, independent study programs, apprenticeships and vocational flight training programs. Eligibility for this program is determined by the Selected Reserve components. The Veteran's Administration makes the payments for this program and determines the level of benefit.

For additional information, contact your regional office or vet center listed on page 635, call 1-800-827-1000, or check their web site at {www.gibill.va.gov}.

Get $2 for every $1 You Spend on Education

The Veterans Educational Assistance Program (VEAP) is available to you if you first entered active duty between January 1, 1977 and June 30, 1985 and you elected to make contributions from your military pay to participate in this education benefit program. Under this program, the government contributes $2 for every $1 the participant contributes.

You may use these benefits for degree and certificate programs, flight training, apprenticeships and correspondence courses. Remedial, deficiency, and refresher courses may also be approved under certain circumstances. You have 10 years from release from active duty to use the VEAP benefits.

For additional information, contact your regional office or vet center listed on page 635, call 1-800-827-1000, or check their web site at {www.gibill.va.gov}.

Education Assistance for Spouses and Children

Survivors' and Dependents' Educational Assistance Program (DEA) provides education and training to eligible dependents of veterans who are permanently and totally disabled due to a service-related condition, or who died while on active duty or as a result of a service related condition.

The program offers up to 45 months of educational benefits. These benefits may be used for degree and certificate programs, apprenticeship, and on-the-job training. If you are a son or daughter and wish to receive benefits, you must be between the ages 18 and 26 in most cases. If you are a spouse, these benefits must be used within 10 years from the date of eligibility.

For additional information, contact your regional office or vet center listed on page 635, call 1-800-827-1000, or check their web site at {www.gibill.va.gov}.

Earn While You Learn

If you are a student receiving any Veterans' Administration educational benefits, you may be eligible to work for the VA to earn some cash. Students attending school at least three-quarter time in need of money can apply. The student may work for the Veterans' Administration by working at the schools veterans' office, the VA Regional Office, a VA Medical Facilities or other approved State employment office.

For additional information, contact your regional office or vet center listed on page 635, call 1-800-827-1000, or check their web site at {www.gibill.va.gov}.

Get a Tutor to Help You with Calculus (or any other difficult class)

Tutorial Assistance is available for any student going to school at least half time and receiving VA educational benefits. The student can receive assistance if there is a deficiency in a subject matter making tutoring necessary.

For additional information, contact your regional office call 1-800-827-1000, or vet center listed on page 635, or check their web site at {www.gibill.va.gov}.

$2,000 for Taking A Test

You can receive reimbursement of up to $2,000 for some licensing and certification tests. The tests must be approved for the G.I. Bill. The Veterans' Administration will only pay for the costs of the tests and not for other fees connected with obtaining a license or certification.

For additional information, contact your regional office or vet center listed on page 635, call 1-800-827-1000, or check their web site at {www.gibill.va.gov}.

Veterans' Vocational Rehabilitation and Employment Services

The Veterans' Administration's Vocational Rehabilitation and Employment (VR&E) is a national employment resource to provide information about employment and independent living to disabled veterans, vocational counseling to service-members and veterans recently discharged and vocational counseling or special rehabilitation services to dependents of veterans who meet certain requirements.

This program's primary function is to help veterans who have service-connected disabilities to become employed and to maintain suitable employment. Services that you may be eligible for through the VR&E program include:

- Vocational counseling and planning
- Assistance finding and keeping a job, including special employer incentives
- Training such as on-the-job training, non-paid work experiences
- Educational training such as 2- or 4-year degree programs
- Supportive rehabilitation services and additional counseling

Everything You Need to Find and Get a Job as a Veteran

The Veterans' Vocational Rehabilitation and Employment Program offers a variety of employment services as a means to obtain suitable employment for veterans.

- assistance in finding employment
- job seeking skills training,
- on-the-job training and apprenticeships
- job development,
- vocational training,
- 1-year certification programs,
- 2-year diploma programs,
- 2 and 4 year post secondary training programs.

For additional information, contact your regional office or vet center listed on page 635, call 1-800-827-1000, check their web site at {www.vba.va.gov/bln/vre/emp_resources.htm}. You can also apply online at {http://vabenefits.vba.va.gov/vonapp/main.asp}.

Get Free Individualized Help

The Independent Living Program (ILP) is designed to be tailored for each individual's needs. A veteran whose service-oriented disability makes employment impossible can receive help.

An Independent Living Program will be designed with input from the veteran, medical professionals, family members and other consultants to provide the assistance needed by the veteran. Subsistence allowances are paid each month of enrollment in the ILP. You can receive money for yourself and your dependents.

If you believe your service-connected disabilities and overall condition are so serious that employment goals are impossible, you may qualify for the Independent Living Program. For additional information, contact your regional office or vet center listed on page 635, call 1-800-827-1000, or check their web site at {www.vba.va.gov/bln/vre/ilp.htm}.

Choose a Career For Free

Vocational Rehabilitation and Employment Service provides vocational-educational counseling to veterans and certain dependents. Eligibility for this service is based on having eligibility for a VA Education program such as the Montgomery Bill, Veterans' Education Assistance Program or Dependents Education Assistance. Vocational Rehabilitation and Education can provide a wide range of vocational and educational counseling services to veterans and dependents.

These services are designed to help an individual choose a vocational direction and determine the course needed to achieve the chosen goal. Assistance may include interest and aptitude testing; occupational exploration; setting occupational goals; locating the right type of training program and exploring educational or training facilities which might be utilized to achieve an occupational goal. Counseling services are provided to eligible persons at no charge. To provide a full service, the counseling may take more than one session. Request VA Form 28-8832.

For additional information, contact your regional office or vet center listed on page 635, call 1-800-827-1000, or check their web site at {www.vba.va.gov/bln/vre/vec.htm}.

Free Help to Start A Your Own Business

The Center for Veterans Enterprise (CVE) is a centralized program to help veterans start-up and succeed in business. Their goal is to support economic empowerment for every veteran entrepreneur and to provide assistance for veterans and service-disabled veterans who are considering business ownership. They provide assistance in management, marketing, financing and even provide a mentoring program.

The Center for Veterans Enterprise works in conjunction with the Small Business Administration (SBA) to maximize the benefits for veterans. There are SBA Veterans Business Development Offices in each state. To declare your firm as a veteran owned business, a veteran or group of veterans must have 51% ownership and control of the business. A similar 51% rule is applied to businesses owned by service-disabled veterans.

Contact U.S. Department of Veterans Affairs, The Center for Veterans Enterprise (00VE), 810 Vermont Avenue, NW, Washington, D.C. 20420; 202-565-8336; 866-584-2344 Toll free; Fax: 202-565-4255; Email: {VACVE@mail.va.gov}; {www.vetbiz.gov}.

Dream It, Find It, Get It

If you are looking for a dream job, you may find it on Job Seekers. Veterans may search online through the database of over one million jobs, post their resume online or set-up an automated job search. Go to {http://dva.jobsearch.org/} to begin your search.

Get Paid to Train for a New Career

You may be able to receive living expenses or training allowances for vocational rehabilitation training programs if you are a veteran who is required to take additional education or training to become employable.

A subsistence allowance is paid each month during training and is based on the rate of attendance (full-time or part-time) , the number of dependents, and the type of training. A full-time veteran training at an Institute of Higher Learning can receive $655 a month for their family of two dependents.

For additional information, contact your regional office or vet center listed on page 635, call 1-800-827-1000, or check their web site at {www.vba.va.gov/bln/vre/InterSubsistence0202.htm}.

Free Job Outreach Programs

Disabled Veterans' Outreach Program (DVOP) is managed by the Department of Labor and specializes in the development of job and training opportunities for veterans, with special emphasis on veterans with service-related disabilities.

DVOP specialists provide direct services to veterans enabling them to be competitive in the labor market. They provide outreach and offer assistance to disabled and other veterans by promoting community and employer support for employment and training opportunities, including apprenticeship and on-the-job training. DVOP specialists are available to those veterans and their employers to help ensure that necessary follow up services are provided to promote job retention.

To contact a DVOP specialist, call or visit the nearest State Employment Service (sometimes known as Job Service) agency listed in the State Government section of your phone book. Contact Office of the Assistant Secretary for Veterans' Employment and Training, U.S. Department of Labor, 200 Constitution Avenue, NW, Room S-1316, Washington, D.C. 20210; 202-693-4700; Fax: 202-693-4754; {www.dol.gov/vets/programs/fact/Employment_Services_fs01.htm#LVEP}.

Free Job Finding Assistance

If you need help finding a job, Local Veterans' Employment Representatives (LVERs) are available at state job service offices throughout the country. The LVER contact employers to develop job openings for veterans, and monitor job listings from federal contractors to assure that eligible veterans get priority in job referrals.

They provide free job counseling, testing, training, referral, and placement services to veterans. LVER works with the Department of Veterans' Affairs to identify and aid veterans who need work-related prosthetic devices, sensory aids, or other special equipment to improve their employability. They also contact community leaders, employers, unions, and training programs and veterans' service organizations to be sure eligible veterans receive the services to which they are entitled.

For additional information call or visit the nearest State Employment Service (sometimes known as Job Service) agency listed in the State Government section of your phone book. Contact Office of the Assistant Secretary for Veterans' Employment and Training, U.S. Department of Labor, 200 Constitution Avenue, NW, Room S-1316, Washington, D.C. 20210; 202-693-4700; Fax: 202-693-4754; {www.dol.gov/vets/programs/fact/Employment_Services_fs01.htm#LVEP}.

Get Your Old Job Back After Military Time With A Raise

When you have finished serving your country, The Uniformed Services Employment and Reemployment Rights Act of 1994 (USERRA) may be a big help in getting your previous job back. The USERRA was signed into law on October 13, 1994.

USERRA clarifies and strengthens the Veterans' Reemployment Rights (VRR) Statue. USERRA is intended to minimize the disadvantages to an individual that occur when that person needs to be absent from his or her civilian employment to serve in this country's uniformed service which includes the Armed Forces, the Army National Guard and the Air National Guard.

USERRA makes major improvements in protecting service member rights and benefits by clarifying the law and improving enforcement mechanisms. It also provides employees with Department of Labor assistance in processing claims. Specifically, USERRA expands the cumulative length of time that an individual may be absent from work for uniformed services duty and retain reemployment rights.

USERRA potentially covers every individual in the country who serves in or has served in the uniformed services and applies to all employers in the public and private sectors, including Federal employers. The law seeks to ensure that those who serve their country can retain their civilian employment and benefit, and can seek employment free from discrimination because of their service. USERRA provides enhanced protection for disabled veterans, requiring employers to make reasonable efforts to accommodate the disability

USERRA is administered by the United States Department of Labor, through the Veterans' Employment and Training Service (VETS). VETS provides assistance to those persons experiencing service connected problems with their civilian employment and provides information about the Act to employers. VETS also assists veterans who have questions regarding Veterans' Preference. For more information, please visit the Veterans' Preference Advisor at {www.dol.gov/elaws/vetspref.htm}.

This USERRA Advisor has been designed to answer questions about the rights and responsibilities for both the employee and employer. For additional information, contact your regional office or vet center listed on page 635, call 1-800-827-1000, or check their web site at {www.dol.gov/elaws/vets/userra/userra.asp}

Unemployment Compensation When Leaving The Military

Ex-service members are eligible for a weekly income for a limited period of time to help meet basic needs while searching for employment. The amount and duration of payments are governed by state laws, which vary considerably. Be sure to bring a copy of military discharge form DD-214 when you are applying. Contact your nearest state employment office listed in the blue pages of your telephone book under State Government.

Free Workshop Before Heading Back to Civilian Life

The Transition Assistance Program (TAP) was established to meet the needs of separating service members during their period of transition into civilian life by offering job-search assistance and related services. The law creating TAP established a partnership between the Departments of Defense, Veterans Affairs, Transportation and the Departments of Labor's Veterans' Employment and Training Service (VETS), to give employment and training information to armed forces members within 180 days of separation or retirement.

TAP consists of comprehensive three-day workshops at selected military installations nationwide. Professionally-trained workshop facilitators provide information about job searches, career decision-making, current occupational and labor market conditions, and resume and cover letter preparation and interviewing techniques. Participants also are provided with an evaluation of their employability relative to the job market and receive information on the most current veterans' benefits.

Service members leaving the military with a service-connected disability are offered the Disabled Transition Assistance Program (DTAP). DTAP includes the normal three-day TAP workshop plus additional hours of individual instruction to help determine job readiness and address the special needs of disabled veterans.

For additional information about U.S. Department of Labor employment and training programs for veterans contact Office of the Assistant Secretary for Veterans' Employment and Training, U.S. Department of Labor, 200 Constitution Avenue, NW; Room S-1316, Washington, D.C. 20210; 202-693-4700; Fax: 202-693-4754; {www.dol.gov/vets/programs/fact/TAPFS_02.htm}.

Government Contractors That Have to Hire a Vet

When you are looking for a job, you should consider applying at companies that have contracts and subcontracts with the Federal government. Any contractor or subcontractor with a contract of $25,000 or more with the Federal Government must take affirmative action to hire and promote qualified targeted veterans which includes, special disabled veterans, veterans of the Vietnam-era, or recently separated veterans.

Contractors and subcontractors with openings for jobs, other than executive or top management positions, positions which are to be filled from within the contractor's organization, and positions lasting 3 days or less, must list them with the nearest State Job Service (also known as State Employment Service) office. Qualified targeted veterans receive priority for referral to Federal contractor job openings listed at those offices. Federal contractors are not required to hire those referred, but must have affirmative action plans.

Companies must file an annual VETS-100 report, which shows the number of targeted veterans in their work force by job category, hiring location, and number of new hires. Instructions, information and follow-up assistance is provided at VETS-100 Internet site at {http://vets100.cudenver.edu/} or employers may contact the VETS-100 Processing Center at 703-461-2460 or Email at {helpdesk@vets100.com}.

For copies of Affirmative Action Obligations of Contractors and Subcontractors for Disabled Veterans and Veterans of the Vietnam Era, Rules and Regulations, contact Office of Federal Contract Compliance Programs, Employment Standards Administration, 200 Constitution Ave., NW, U.S. Department of Labor, Washington, DC 20210.

e-VETS Resource Advisor to the Rescue

If you are a veteran in need of help preparing to enter the job market, e-VETS may be a just what you need. It includes information on a broad range of topics, such as job search tools and tips, employment openings, career assessment, education and training, and benefits and special services available to veterans.

E-VETS was developed by the US Department of Labor to help employees and employers understand their rights and responsibilities under numerous Federal employment laws. There are two sections on e-VETS Resource Advisor, General Services and Personal Profile. If you are a veteran, use both to achieve the best results.

Contact Veterans' Employment and Training, U.S. Department of Labor, 200 Constitution Avenue, NW, Room S-1316, Washington, D.C. 20210; 202-693-4700; Fax: 202-693-4754; {www.dol.gov/elaws/evets.htm}.

Receive a $10,000 Bonus

WOW, a $10,000 bonus to teach school. Troops to Teachers (TTT) was established in 1994 as a Department of Defense program. The National Defense Authorization Act for FY 2000 transferred the responsibility for program oversight and funding to the U.S. Department of Education but continued operation by the Department of Defense. TTT is managed by the Defense Activity for Non-Traditional Education Support (DANTES). The "No Child Left Behind Act of 2001" provides for the continuation of the Troops to Teachers program.

Troops to Teacher's primary objective is to help recruit quality teachers for schools that serve low-income families throughout America. TTT helps relieve teacher shortages, especially in math, science, special education and other high-needs subject areas, and assists military personnel in making successful transitions to second careers in teaching.

Financial assistance may be provided to eligible individuals as stipends up to $5K to help pay for teacher certification costs or as bonuses of $10K. Stipend and bonus recipients must agree to teach for three years in school locations that meet certain

Department of Education criteria. Contact DANTES Troops to Teachers, 6490 Saufley Field Road, Pensacola, FL 32509-5243; 850-452-1320; 800-231-6242; {www. voled.doded.mil/dantes/ttt/index.htm}.

An Umbrella of Protection

The nature of military service can often compromise the ability of service members to fulfill their financial obligations. Congress and the state legislatures have long recognized the need for "umbrella" protective legislation. The Soldiers' and Sailors' Relief Act (SSCRA) protects active duty, reservists and members of the National Guard while on active duty. However, some protections extend for a limited time beyond discharge. Additionally, some of the Act's protections extend to the members' dependents. Benefits include:

- Reduced interest rates on mortgage payments
- Reduced interest rates on credit cards
- Protection from eviction if your rent is $1,200 or less
- Delay of all civil court actions

Contact your local unit or installation legal assistance office or {http://usmilitary.about.com/cs/sscra/} for additional information.

Get a Job Without Any Competition

Get your foot in the door by applying for civil service appointments. The Veterans Readjustment Appointment (VRA) is a special authority by which agencies can employ eligible veterans without competition.

VRA appointees are initially hired for a 2-year period. Successful completion of the VRA leads to a permanent civil service appointment. You must have served on active duty for more than 180 days, except if you were released due to a service-connected disability.

For additional information, veterans should contact the personnel office at the Federal agency where they wish to work or contact the Office of Personnel Management at 202-606-1848 or online at {www.opm.gov/index.htm}.

VA Medical Care Promote, Preserve and Restore Your Health

In October 1996, Congress passed the Veterans' Health Care Eligibility Reform Act of 1996. This legislation paved the way for the creation of a Medical Benefits Package, a standard health care benefits plan available to all enrolled veterans. Only 15% of eligible veterans take advantage of this service and you must apply to receive benefits.

The Medical Benefits Package provides veterans' with hospital care and outpatient care that are needed to promote, preserve, and restore your health. Medical care is provided at a VA health facility. Veterans pay for medical benefits depending on their service-connected level in the military and an assigned Priority Group.

You can apply by completing Form 10-10EZ. The form may be obtained by visiting, calling or writing any VA health care facility or veterans' benefits office. You may also receive a form by calling (877) 222-VETS or accessing the form from the internet at {www.10-10EZ.med.va.gov}.

For more information contact Veterans' Health Administration, 810 Vermont Ave., NW, Washington, DC 20420; 202-273-5400; 877-222-3887; {www.va.gov/elig/}.

To Copay or not to Copay

There are three outpatient copayment levels. The first level is no copayment. These services are for publicly announced VA health initiatives (i.e.: health fairs) or an outpatient visit consisting solely of preventative screening and immunizations. These may include flu immunization, alcohol or tobacco screenings, breast and cervical cancer screenings and certain blood tests.

In the second level, the VHA provides primary care outpatient preventative care, which includes periodic exams, health education, maintenance of drug-use profiles, mental health and substance abuse prevention services. Depending on your Priority group, you may be required to pay a $15 copayment for primary care visits.

The third level is a $50 copay to see a specialist. Many veterans apply for a needs test, which allows them to receive many if not all medical benefits at no cost to them.

For additional information contact your local VA health care facility or contact the Veteran's Health Administration. Contact Veterans' Health Administration, 810 Vermont Ave., NW, Washington, DC 20420; 202-273-5400; 877-222-3887; {www.va.gov/elig/}.

Coverage While You're Lying in the Hospital

Basic care for inpatient services include: medical, surgical and mental health care, including care for substance abuse. If you are required to remain in the hospital, Congress determined the inpatient copayment should be the current inpatient Medicare deductible rate plus $10 for the first 90 days that you are confined to the hospital.

For additional information contact your local VA health care facility or contact the

Veteran's Health Administration. Contact Veterans' Health Administration, 810 Vermont Ave., NW, Washington, DC 20420; 202-273-5400; 877-222-3887; {www.va.gov/elig/}.

At Home or in a Nursing Home You're Covered

The Veterans' Administration provides coverage for home health care as well as respite, hospice and palliative care. Congress determined the copayment should be the current Medicare deductible rate plus $5.00 for each day.

For additional information contact your local VA health care facility or contact the Veteran's Health Administration. Contact Veterans' Health Administration, 810 Vermont Ave., NW, Washington, DC 20420; 202-273-5400; 877-222-3887; {www.va.gov/elig/}.

Prescriptions

Prescriptions are available at Veterans' Administration pharmacies. Congress has established the copayment cost to be $7 for a 30 day or less supply of medications provided on an outpatient basis for nonservice-connected condition. Medication copays apply to medications and over-the-counter medications (aspirin, cough syrup, vitamins etc) that are dispensed from a VA pharmacy.

For additional information contact your local VA health care facility or contact the Veteran's Health Administration. Contact Veterans' Health Administration, 810 Vermont Ave., NW, Washington, DC 20420; 202-273-5400; 877-222-3887; {www.va.gov/elig/}.

Help! It's an Emergency

Emergency care is available through VA medical facilities. If a Federal facility is not feasibly available at the time of the emergency and your emergency is a service-connected disability you may be eligible for reimbursement for treatment at another medical facility.

For additional information contact your local VA health care facility or contact the Veteran's Health Administration. Contact Veterans' Health Administration, 810 Vermont Ave., NW, Washington, DC 20420; 202-273-5400; 877-222-3887; {www.va.gov/elig/}.

Free Medical Care For Veterans

The Veterans Health Administration (VHA) provides a broad spectrum of medical, surgical, and rehabilitative care to Veterans under the Veterans' Health Care Eligibility Reform Act of 1996. This legislation paved the way for the creation of a Medical Benefits Package — a standard enhanced health benefits plan available to all enrolled veterans. Eligible veterans may obtain medical care at facilities throughout the country.

Listed are the Regional and VA Medical Centers. In addition to these facilities, many states also have Outpatient Clinics and Community Outpatient Clinics to serve veterans. Contact the closest VA Medical facility to find an outpatient office near your home or check their web site at {www.va.gov/sta/guide/home.asp}. Veterans Health Administration, 800 Vermont Ave., NW, Washington, DC 20420; 202-273-5400; Benefits: 877-222-VETS.

Alabama

Birmingham VA Medical Center
700 S. 19th Street
Birmingham, AL 35233
205-933-8101
Fax: 205-933-4484

Central Alabama Veterans
Health Care System
West Campus
215 Perry Hill Road
Montgomery, AL 36109-3798
334-272-4670
Fax: 334-260-4143

Tuscaloosa VA Medical Center
3701 Loop Road, East
Tuscaloosa, AL 35404
205-554-2000
Fax: 205-554-2034

Central Alabama Veterans
Health Care System
East Campus
2400 Hospital Road
Tuskegee, AL 36083-5001
334-727-0550
Fax: 334-724-2793

VA Gulf Coast Health Care
System
Mobile Outpatient Center
1504 Springhill Ave.
Mobile, AL 36604
251-219-3900

Alaska

VA Healthcare System and
Regional Office
2925 DeBarr Road
Anchorage, AK 99508-2989
907-257-4700
Fax: 907-257-6774

Fairbanks VA Medical Clinic
Bassett Army Community
Hospital, Building 4065,
Gaffney Road, Room 169/176
Fort Wainwright, AK 99703
Toll Free-(888-353-5242
907-353-6370
Fax: 907-353-6372

Arizona

VISN 18: VA Southewest Health
Care Network
6950 E. Williams Field Road
Mesa, AZ 85212-6033
602-222-2681
Fax: 602-222-2686
http://www.va.gov/visn18/

Northern Arizona VA Health
Care System
500 N. Hwy 89
Prescott, AZ 86313
928-445-4860
Fax: 928-768-6076

Southern Arizona VA Health
Care System
3601 South 6th Avenue
Tucson, AZ 85723
520-792-1450
http://www.va.gov/678savahcs/

Carl T. Hayden VA Medical
Center
650 E. Indian School Road
Phoenix, AZ 85012
602-277-5551
http://www.phoenix.med.va.gov/

Arkansas

Fayetteville VA Medical Center
1100 N. College Avenue
Fayetteville, AR 72703
479-443-4301

Central Arkansas Veterans
Healthcare System
John L. McClellan Memorial
Veterans Hospital
4300 West 7th Street
Little Rock, AR 72205-5484
501-257-1000

Eugene J. Towbin Healthcare
Center
2200 Fort Roots Drive
North Little Rock, AR 72114-
1706
501-257-1000

California

VISN 22: Desert Pacific
Healthcare Network
5901 E. 7th Street
Long Beach, CA 90822
562-826-5963
Fax: 562-826-5987
http://www.visn22.med.va.gov/

VISN 21: Sierra Pacific Network
201 Walnut Avenue
Mare Island, CA 94592
707-562-8350
Fax: 707-562-8369
http://www.visn21.med.va.gov/

VA Central California Health
Care System
2615 E. Clinton Avenue
Fresno, CA 93703
559-225-6100
Fax: 559-228-6903
700-466-5000

Livermore
4951 Arroyo Road
Livermore, CA 94550
925-477-2560

VA Loma Linda Healthcare
System
11201 Benton Street
Loma Linda, CA 92357
800-741-8387
Fax: 909-422-3106
FTS: (909-825-7084
FTS Fax: 909-422-3106
http://www.lom.med.va.gov/

VA Long Beach Healthcare
System

5901 E. 7th Street
Long Beach, CA 90822
562-826-8000
Fax: 562-826-5972
http://www.long-beach.med.va.gov/

VA Greater Los Angeles Healthcare System (GLA)
11301 Willshire Boulevard
Los Angeles, CA 90073
310-478-3711
Fax: 310-268-4848
http://www.gla.med.va.gov/

Martinez Center for Rehab and Extended Care
150 Muir Rd.
Martinez, CA 94553
925-370-4701

VA Northern California Health Care System
150 Muir Road
Martinez, CA 94553
925-372-2000
Fax: 925-372-2020

Sacramento VA Medical Center
10535 Hospital Way
Mather, CA 95655
916-366-5366
Fax: 916-366-5328

Menlo Park
795 Willow Road
Menlo Park, CA 94025
650-493-5000
http://www.palo-alto.med.va.gov/

VA Palo Alto Health Care System
3801 Miranda Avenue
Palo Alto, CA 94304-1290
650-493-5000
Fax: 650-852-3228
FTS: (700-463-5000
http://www.palo-alto.med.va.gov/

VA San Diego Health Care System
3350 La Jolla Village Drive
San Diego, CA 92161
858-552-8585
FTS: (700-897-3100
FTS Fax: 700-897-7509
http://www.san-diego.med.va.gov/start.htm

San Francisco VA Medical Ctr
4150 Clement Street
San Francisco, CA 94121-1598
415-221-4810
Fax: 415-750-2185

Colorado

VA Health Administration Ctr
300 S. Jackson St.
Denver, CO 80206
303-331 7500
Fax: 303-331 7800
http://www.va.gov/hac/

VISN 19: Rocky Mountain Network
4100 E. Mississippi Ave.
Suite 510
Glendale, CO 80246
303-756-9279
Fax: 303-756-9243

Southern Colorado Healthcare System
4112 Outlook Blvd.
Pueblo, CO 81008
719-553-1003
FTS: 1-888-544-6724
FTS Fax: 719-553-1102

Denver VA Medical Center
1055 Clermont Street
Denver, CO 80220
303-399-8020
Fax: 303-393-2861

Grand Junction VA Medical Center
2121 North Avenue
Grand Junction, CO 81501
970-242-0731
Fax: 970-244-1331

Connecticut

VA Connecticut Healthcare System
Newington Campus
555 Willard Avenue
Newington, CT 06111
860-666-6951
Fax: 860-667-6764
http://www.visn1.med.va.gov/vact/

VA Connecticut Healthcare System
West Haven Campus
950 Campbell Avenue
West Haven, CT 06516
203-932-5711
Fax: 203-937-3868
http://www.visn1.med.va.gov/vact/

Delaware

Wilmington VA Medical and Regional Office Center
1601 Kirkwood Highway
Wilmington, DE 19805
302-994-2511
Fax: 302-633-5516

District of Columbia

Washington D.C. VA Medical Center
50 Irving Street, NW
Washington, DC 20422
202-745-8000
Fax: 202-754-8530
http://www.washington.med.va.gov/

Florida

VISN 8: VA Sunshine Healthcare Network
VISN Office: P.O. Box 406
Bay Pines, FL 33744
727-319-1125
Fax: 727-319-1135

North Florida/South Georgia Veterans Health System
Gainesville Division
1601 S.W. Archer Road
Gainesville, FL 32608-1197
352-376-1611
Fax: 352-374-6113
http://www.va.gov/north-florida/

North Florida/South Georgia Veterans Health System
City Division
801 S. Marion Street
Lake City, FL 32025-5898
386-755-3016
Fax: 386-758-3209
http://www.va.gov/north-florida/

Miami VA Medical Center
1201 N.W. 16th Street
Miami, FL 33125

305-324-4455
Fax: 305-324-3232
http://www.va.gov/546miami/

Bay Pines VA Medical Center
10,000 Bay Pines Blvd
St. Petersburg, FL 33708
727-398-6661
Fax: 727-398-9442

Tampa (James A. Haley-VA Medical Center
13000 Bruce B. Downs Blvd.
Tampa, FL 33612
813-972-2000
Fax: 813-972-7673

West Palm Beach VA Medical Center
7305 N. Military Trail
West Palm Beach, FL 33410-6400
561-882-8262
Fax: 561-882-6707

Georgia

VISN 7: The Atlanta Network
3700 Crestwood Parkway, NW, Suite 500
Duluth, GA 30096-5585
678-924-5700
Fax: 678-924-5757

Augusta VA Medical Center
1 Freedom Way
Augusta, GA 30904-6285
706-733-0188
Fax: 706-823-3934

Atlanta VA Medical Center
1670 Clairmont Road
Decatur, GA 30033
404-321-6111
Fax: 404-728-7734

Carl Vinson VA Medical Center
1826 Veteran's Boulevard
Dublin, GA 31021
478-272-1210
Fax: 478-277-2717

Guam

Guam Outpatient Clinic
222 Chalan Santo Papast, Reflection Center, Ste. 102
Agana, GU 96910
705-475-7161

Hawaii

Spark M. Matsunaga VA Medical and Regional Office Center
459 Patterson Road
Honolulu, HI 96819-1522
808-433-1000
Fax: 808-433-0390
http://www.va.gov/hawaii/

Idaho

Boise VA Medical Center
500 West Fort Street
Boise, ID 83702
208-422-1000
Fax: 208-422-1326

Illinois

VISN 12: Great Lakes Health Care System
P.O. Box 5000, Building 18
Hines, IL 60141-5000
708-202-8400
Fax: 708-202-8424
http://www.vagreatlakes.org/

VA Chicago Health Care System-Lakeside Division
333 East Huron Street
Chicago, IL 60611
312-569-8387
Fax: 312-469-2248
http://www.vagreatlakes.org/

VA Chicago Health Care System-West Side Division
820 South Damen Avenue
Chicago, IL 60612
312-569-8387
http://www.vagreatlakes.org/

VA Illiana Health Care System
1900 East Main Street
Danville, IL 61832-5198
217-442-8000
Fax: 217-554-4552

Edward Hines Jr. VA Hospital
5th & Roosevelt Rd. P.O. Box 5000
Hines, IL 60141
708-202-8387
Fax: 708-202-2721
http://www.vagreatlakes.org/

Marion VA Medical Center
2401 West Main Street
Marion, IL 62959
618-997-5311

North Chicago VA Medical Ctr
3001 Green Bay Road
North Chicago, IL 60064
847-688-1900
Fax: 847-578-3806
http://www.n-chicago.med.va.gov/

Indiana

VA Northern Indiana Health Care System-Fort Wayne Campus
2121 Lake Ave.
Fort Wayne, IN 46805
260-426-5431
Fax: 260-460-1336

Richard L. Roudebush VA Medical Center
1481 W. Tenth Street
Indianapolis, IN 46202
317-554-0000
Fax: 317-554-0127

VA Northern Indiana Health Care System-Marion Campus
1700 East 38th Street
Marion, IN 46953-4589
765-674-3321
Fax: 765-677-3124

Iowa

Des Moines Division- VA Central Iowa Health Care System
3600 30th Street
Des Moines, IA 50310-5774
515-699-5999
Fax: 515-699-5862

Iowa City VA Medical Center
601 Highway 6 West
Iowa City, IA 52246-2208
319-338-0581
Fax: 319-339-7135
http://www.iowa-city.med.va.gov/

Knoxville Division-VA Central Iowa Health Care System
1515-W. Pleasant Street
Knoxville, IA 50138
641-842-3101
Fax: 641-828-5124

Kansas
VA Eastern Kansas Health Care System
Dwight D. Eisenhower VA Medical Center
4101 S. 4th Street
Leavenworth, KS 66048-5055
913-682-2000

VA Eastern Kansas Health Care System
Colmery-O'Neil VA Medical Center
2200 SW Gage Boulevard
Topeka, KS 66622
785-350-3111
Fax: 785-350-4336

Robert J. Dole Department of Veteran Affairs Medical and Regional Office Center
5500 E. Kellogg
Wichita, KS 67218
316-685-2221
Fax: 316-651-3666

Kentucky
Lexington VA Medical Center
1101 Veterans Drive
Lexington, KY 40502-2236
859-233-4511

Louisville VA Medical Center
800 Zorn Avenue
Louisville, KY 40206
502-895-3401

Louisiana
Alexandria VA Medical Center
P. O. Box 69004
Alexandria, LA 71360
318-473-0010
Fax: 318-483-5029
http://www.alexandria.med.va.gov/

New Orleans VA Medical Center
1601 Perdido Street
New Orleans, LA 70112-1262
504-568-0811
Fax: 504-589-5210

Overton Brooks VA Medical Center
510 E. Stoner Ave.
Shreveport, LA 71101-4295
318-221-8411
Fax: 318-424-6156

Maine
Togus VA Medical/Regional Office Center
1 VA Center
Augusta, ME 04330
207-623-8411
Fax: 207-623-5722
http://www.visn1.med.va.gov/togus/

Maryland
VISN 5: VA Capitol Health Care Network
849 International Dr., Suite 275
Linthicum, MD 21090
410-691-1131
Fax: 410-684-3189
http://www.va.gov/visn5/

Baltimore VA Rehabilitation and Extended Care Center (BRECC)
3900 Loch Raven Boulevard
Baltimore, MD 21218
410-605-7000
Fax: 410-605-7900

Baltimore VAMC-VA Maryland Health Care System
10 North Greene Street
Baltimore, MD 21201
410-605-7000
Fax: 410-605-7901
http://www.vamhcs.med.va.gov/

Fort Howard VAMC-VA Maryland Health Care System
9600 North Point Road
Fort Howard, MD 21052
410-477-1800
Fax: 410-477-7177
http://www.vamhcs.med.va.gov/

Perry Point VAMC-VA Maryland Health Care System
Perry Point, MD 21902
410-642-2411
Fax: 410-642-1161
http://www.vamhcs.med.va.gov/

Massachusetts
VISN 1: VA New England Healthcare System
200 Springs Road Building 61
Bedford, MA 01730
781-687-3400
Fax: 781-687-3470
http://www.visn1.med.va.gov/

Edith Nourse Rogers Memorial Veterans Hospital
200 Springs Rd.
Bedford, MA 01730
781-687-2000
Fax: 781-687-2101
http://www.visn1.med.va.gov/bedford/

VA Boston Healthcare System, Brockton Campus
940 Belmont Street
Brockton, MA 02301
508-583-4500
Fax: 700-885-1000
http://www.visn1.med.va.gov/boston/

VA Boston Healthcare System, Jamaica Plain Campus
150 South Huntington Avenue
Jamaica Plain, MA 02130
617-232-9500
Fax: 617-278-4549
http://www.visn1.med.va.gov/boston/

Northampton VA Medical Center
421 North Main Street
Leeds, MA 01053-9764
413-584-4040
Fax: 413-582-3121

VA Boston Healthcare System, West Roxbury Campus
1400 VFW Parkway
West Roxbury, MA 02132
617-323-7700
http://www.visn1.med.va.gov/boston/

Michigan
VISN 11: Veterans In Partnership
P.O. Box 134002
Ann Arbor, MI 48113-4002
734-930-5950
Fax: 734-930-5932

VA Ann Arbor Healthcare System
2215 Fuller Road

Ann Arbor, MI 48105
734-769-7100
Fax: 734-761-7870

Battle Creel VA Medical Center
5500 Armstrong Road
Battle Creek, MI 49015
616-966-5600
Fax: 616-966-5483

John D. Dingell VA Medical Center
4646 John R
Detroit, MI 48201
313-576-1000
Fax: 313-576-1025

Iron Mountain VA Medical Center
325 East H Street
Iron Mountain, MI 49801
906-774-3300
Fax: 906-779-3114
FTS: (700-769-3300
http://www.vagreatlakes.org/

Alesa E. Lutz VA Medical Center
1500 Weiss Street
Saginaw, MI 48602
989-497-2500
Fax: 989-791-2428

Minnesota

VISN 23: Lincoln and Minneapolis Offices
Minneapolis Office
5445 Minnehaha Ave S.
Second Floor
Minneapolis, MN 55417-2300
612-725-1968
FAX:(612)-727-5967
http://www.visn23.med.va.gov/

Minneapolis VA Medical Center
One Veterans Drive
Minneapolis, MN 55417
612-725-2000
Fax: 612-725-2049

St. Cloud VA Medical Center
4801 Veterans Drive
St. Cloud, MN 56303
320-252-1670
Fax: 320-255-6494

Mississippi

VISN 16: South Central VA Healthcare Network
1600 East Woodrow Wilson
3rd Floor, Suite A
Jackson, MS 39216
601-364-7900
Fax: 601-364-7996
FTS: (601-364-7900
http://www.visn16.med.va.gov/

VA Gulf Coast Veterans Health Care System
400 Veterans Avenue
Biloxi, MS 39531
228-523-5000
Fax: 228-523-5719

Jackson VA Medical Center
1500 E. Woodrow Wilson Drive
Jackson, MS 39216
601-362-4471
Fax: 601-364-1359

Missouri

VISN 15: VA Heartland Network
4801 Linwood Blvd.
Kansas City, MO 64128
816-922-2908
Fax: 816-922-3392

Harry S. Truman Memorial
800 Hospital Drive
Columbia, MO 65201-5297
573-814-6000
Fax: 573-814-6600

Kansas City VA Medical Center
4801 Linwood Boulevard
Kansas City, MO 64128
816-861-4700
Fax: 816-922-3303
FTS: (700-754-1700

John J. Pershing VA Medical Center
1500 N. Westwood Blvd.
Poplar Bluff, MO 63901
573-686-4151
Fax: 573-778-4559

St. Louis VA Medical Center
Jefferson Barracks Division #1
Jefferson Barracks Drive
St. Louis, MO 63125
314-652-4100
Fax: 314-894-6682
http://www.va.gov/stlouis/

Montana

VA Montana Health Care System
William Street off Highway 12 West
Fort Harrison, MT 59636
406-442-6410
Fax: 406-447-7965

Fort Harrison Medical and Regional Office
William Street off Highway
Fort Harrison, MT 59636
800-827-1000

Nebraska

VISN 23: Lincoln and Minneapolis Offices
Lincoln Office
Building 5
600 South 70th Street
Lincoln, NE 68510
402-484-3200
Fax: 402-484-3232
http://www.visn23.med.va.gov/

Grand Island Division VA Nebraska Western Iowa Health Care System
2201 No. Broadwell Avenue
Grand Island, NE 68803-2196
308-382-3660

Omaha Division-VA Nebraska Western Iowa Health Care
4101 Woolworth Avenue
Omaha, NE 68105
402-346-8800
Fax: 402-449-0684

Nevada

VA Southern Nevada Healthcare System (VASNHS)
1700 Vegas Drive
Las Vegas, NV 89106
702-636-3000
Fax: 702-636-4000

VA Sierra Nevada Health Care System
1000 Locust Street
Reno, NV 89502
775-786-7200
Fax: 775-328-1447

New Hampshire
Manchester VA Medical Center
718 Smyth Road
Manchester, NH 03104
603-624-4366
http://www.visn1.med.va.gov/manchester/

New Jersey
East Orange Campus of the VA New Jersey Health Care System
385 Tremont Avenue
East Orange, NJ 07018
973-676-1000
Fax: 973-676-4226
http://www.va.gov/visns/visn03/default.asp

VA Mobile Clinic
Serving NY and NJ Veterans
800-269-8749

Lyons Campus of the VA New Jersey Health Care System
151 Knollcroft Road
Lyons, NJ 0793
908-647-0180
Fax: 908-647-3452
http://www.va.gov/visns/visn03/default.asp

New Mexico
New Mexico VA Health Care System
1501 San Pedro Drive, SE
Albuquerque, NM 87108-5153
505-265-1711
Fax: 505-256-2855

New York
VISN 2: VA Healthcare Network Upstate New York
P.O. Box 8980
Albany, NY 12208-8980
518-626-7300
Fax: 518-626-7333
http://www.va.gov/visns/visn02/

VISN 3: VA NY/NJ Veterans Healthcare Network
Building 16, 130 W. Kingsbridge Road
Bronx, NY 10486
718-741-4110
Fax: 718-741-4141
http://www.va.gov/visns/visn03/default.asp

VA Mobile Clinic
Serving NY and NJ Veterans
800-269-8749

Albany VA Medical Center: Samuel S. Stratton
113 Holland Avenue
Albany, NY 12208
518-626-5000
Fax: 518-626-5500
http://www.va.gov/visns/visn02/

VA Western New York Healthcare System at Batavia
222 Richmond Avenue
Batavia, NY 14020
716-343-7500
Fax: 716-344-3305
http://www.va.gov/visns/visn02/

Bath VA Medical Center
76 Veterans Avenue
Bath, NY 14810
607-664-4000
Fax: 607-664-4511
http://www.va.gov/visns/visn02/

Bronx VA Medical Center
130 West Kingsbridge Road
Bronx, NY 10468
718-584-9000
Fax: 718-741-4260
http://www.va.gov/visns/visn03/default.asp

Brooklyn Campus of the VA NY Harbor Healthcare System
800 Poly Place
Brooklyn, NY 11209
718-836-6600
http://www.va.gov/visns/visn03/default.asp

VA Western New York Healthcare System at Buffalo
3495 Bailey Avenue
Buffalo, NY 14215
716-834-9200
Fax: 716-862-8759

Canandaigua VA Medical Center
400 Fort Hill Avenue
Canandaigua, NY 14424
585-394-2000
Fax: 585-393-8328
http://www.va.gov/visns/visn02/

Castle Point Campus of the VA Hudson Valley Healthcare System
Castle Point, NY 12511
845-831-2000
Fax: 845-838-5180
http://www.va.gov/visns/visn03/default.asp

Franklin Delano Roosevelt Campus of the VA Hudson Valley Healthcare System
622 Albany Post Rd., Route 9A,
P.O. Box 100
Montrose, NY 10548
914-737-4400 ext. 2400
Fax: 914-788-4244
http://www.va.gov/visns/visn03/default.asp

New York Campus of the NY Harbor Healthcare System
423 East 23rd Street
New York, NY 10010
212-686-7500
Fax: 212-951-3487
FTS: (700-662-7500
FTS Fax: 700-662-3487
http://www.va.gov/visns/visn03/default.asp

Northport VA Medical Center
79 Middleville Road
Northport, NY 11768
631-261-4400
Fax: 631-754-7933
http://www.va.gov/visns/visn03/default.asp

Syracuse VA Medical Center
800 Irving Avenue
Syracuse, NY 13210
315-476-7461
Fax: 315-477-4547
http://www.va.gov/visns/visn02/

North Carolina
VISN 6: The Mid-Atlantic Network
Dept. of Veterans Affairs
300 W. Morgan St., Suite 1402
Durham, NC 27701
919-956-5541
Fax: 919-956-5172

Asheville VA Medical Center
1100 Tunnel Road

Asheville, NC 28805
828-298-7911
Fax: 828-299-2502

Durham VA Medical Center
508 Fulton Street
Durham, NC 27705
919-286-0411
Fax: 919-286-6825

Fayetteville VA Medical Center
2300 Ramsey Street
Fayetteville, NC 28301
910-488-2120
Fax: 910-822-7927

Salisbury-W.G. (Bill-Hefner VA Medical Center
1601 Brenner Avenue
Salisbury, NC 28144
704-638-9000
Fax: 704-638-3395

North Dakota

Fargo VA Medical/Regional Office Center
2101 Elm Street
Fargo, ND 58102
701-232-3241
Fax: 701-239-3705

Ohio

VISN 10: VA Healthcare System of Ohio
11500 Northlake Drive, Suite 200
Cincinnati, OH 45249
513-247-4621
Fax: 513-247-4620

Chillicothe VA Medical Center
17273 State Route 104
Chillicothe, OH 45601
740-773-1141
Fax: 740-772-7023
http://www.bright.net/~vachilli/

Cincinnati VA Medical Center
3200 Vine Street
Cincinnati, OH 45220
513-861-3100
Fax: 513-475-6500
http://www.gcfeb.com/vaweb/

Louis Stokes VA Medical Center
10701 East Boulevard
Cleveland, OH 44106
216-791-3800
Fax: 216-421-3217
http://www.cleveland.med.va.gov/

Dayton VA Medical Center
4100 W. 3rd Street
Dayton, OH 45428
937-268-6511
Fax: 937-262-2179
http://www.dayton.med.va.gov/

Oklahoma

Muskogee VA Medical Center
1011 Honor Heights Drive
Muskogee, OK 74401
918-683-3261
Fax: 918-680-3648
FTS: (918-683-3261

Oklahoma City VA Medical Center
921 N.E. 13th Street
Oklahoma City, OK 73104
405-270-0501
Fax: 405-270-1560

Oregon

VISN 20: Northwest Network
P.O. Box 1035
Portland, OR 97207
360-690-1832
Fax: 360-737-1405
http://www.visn20.med.va.gov/

VA Roseburg Healthcare System
913 NW Garden Valley Blvd.
Roseburg, OR 97470-6513
541-440-1000
Fax: 541-440-1225

Portland VA Medical Center
3710 S. W. US Veterans Hospital Road
PO Box 1034
Portland, OR 97207
503-220-8262
Fax: 503-273-5319
http://www.portland.med.va.gov/

Pennsylvania

VISN 4: VA Stars and Stripes Healthcare Network
c/o VAMC, Delafield Road
Pittsburgh, PA 15240
412-784-3939
Fax: 412-784-3940
http://www.starsandstripes.med.va.gov/visn4/

James E. Van Zandt VA Medical Center-Altoona
2907 Pleasant Valley Boulevard
Altoona, PA 16602-4377
814-943-8164
Fax: 814-940-7898

Butler VA Medical Center
325 New Castle Road
Butler, PA 16001-2480
724-287-4781
Fax: 724-282-4408
http://www.va.gov/butlerva/

Coatesville VA Medical Center
1400 Black Horse Hill Road
Coatesville, PA 19320-2096
610-384-7711
Fax: Not Provided
http://www.coatesville.med.va.gov/

Erie VA Medical Center
135 East 38 Street
Erie, PA 16504
814-868-8661
Fax: 814-860-2135

Lebanon VA Medical Center
1700 South Lincoln Avenue
Lebanon, PA 17042
717-272-6621
Fax: 717-228-6045
http://www.starsandstripes.med.va.gov/visn4/

Philadelphia VA Medical Center
University and Woodland Avenues
Philadelphia, PA 19104
215-823-5800

VA Pittsburgh Healthcare System, Highland Drive Division
7180 Highland Drive
Pittsburgh, PA 15206
412-365-4900
http://www.va.gov/pittsburgh/

VA Pittsburgh Healthcare System, University Drive Division
University Drive

Pittsburgh, PA 15240
412-688-6000
Fax: 412-688-6121
http://www.va.gov/pittsburgh/

Wilkes-Barre VA Medical Center
1111 East End Blvd.
Wilkes-Barre, PA 18711
570-824-3521
Fax: 570-821-7278

Puerto Rico
San Juan VA Medical Center
10 Casia Street
San Juan, PR 00921-3201
787-641-7582
Fax: 787-641-4557

Rhode Island
Providence VA Medical Center
830 Chalkstone Avenue
Providence, RI 02908-4799
401-273-7100
Fax: 401-457-3370
http://www.visn1.med.va.gov/providence/

South Carolina
Ralph H. Johnson VA Medical Center
109 Bee Street
Charleston, SC 29401-5799
843-577-5011
Fax: 843-937-6100

Wm. Jennings Bryan Dorn VA Medical Center
6439 Garners Ferry Road
Columbia, SC 29209-1639
803-776-4000
Fax: 803-695-6739

South Dakota
The VA Black Hills Health Care System-Fort Meade Campus
113 Comanche Road
Fort Meade, SD 57741
605-347-2511
Fax: 605-347-7171

The VA Black Hills Health Care System-Hot Springs Campus
500 North 5th Street
Hot Springs, SD 57747
605-745-2000
Fax: 605-745-2091

Sioux Falls VA Medical/Regional Office Center
2501 W. 22nd Street
PO Box 5046
Sioux Falls, SD 57117-5046
605-336-3230
Fax: 605-333-6878

Tennessee
VISN 9: VA Mid South Healthcare Network
1310-24th Avenue South
Nashville, TN 37212-2637
615-340-2380
Fax: 615-340-2398 (fax)

Mountain Home VA Medical Center
Johnson City, TN 37684
423-926-1171

Memphis VA Medical Center
1030 Jefferson Avenue
Memphis, TN 38104
901-523-8990

Alvin C. York VA Medical Center
3400 Lebanon Road
Murfreesboro, TN 37129
615-893-1360
Fax: 615-898-4872

Nashville VA Medical Center
1310 24th Avenue, South
Nashville, TN 37212-2637
615-327-4751
Fax: 615-321-6350

Texas
VISN 17: VA Heart of Texas Health Care Network
1901 N. Highway 360, Suite 350
Grand Prairie, TX 75050
817-649-2991
Fax: 817-633-2272

Amarillo VA Health Care System
6010 Amarillo Boulevard, West
Amarillo, TX 79106
806-355-9703
Fax: 806-354-7869

Big Texas VA Health Care System
300 Veterans Blvd.
Big Spring, TX 79720
915-263-7361
Fax: 915-264-4834

El Paso VA Health Care System
5001 North Piedras Street
El Paso, TX 79930-4211
915-564-6100
Fax: 915-564-7920

Central Texas VA Health Care System
1901 Veterans Memorial Drive
Temple, TX 76504
254-778-4811
Fax: 254-771-4588

VA North Texas Health Care System: Sam Rayburn Memorial Veterans Center
1201 E. 9th Street
Bonham, TX 75418
903-583-2111
Fax: 903-583-6688

VA North Texas Health Care System: Dallas VA Medical Center
4500 South Lancaster Road
Dallas, TX 75216
214-742-8387
Fax: 214-857-1171

Houston VA Medical Center
2002 Holcombe Blvd.
Houston, TX 77030-4298
713-791-1414
Fax: 713-794-7218
http://www.houston.med.va.gov/

Kerrville VA Medical Center
3600 Memorial Blvd
Kerrville, TX 78028
830-896-2020

South Texas Veterans Health Care System
7400 Merton Minter Blvd.
San Antonio, TX 78229
210-617-5300
http://www.vasthcs.med.va.gov/

Central Texas Veterans Health Care System
1901 Veterans Memorial Drive
Temple, TX 76504

254-778-4811
Fax: 254-771-4588
http://www.central-texas.med.va.gov/main/

Utah
VA Salt Lake City Health Care System
500 Foothill Drive
Salt Lake City, UT 84148
801-582-1565
Fax: 801-584-1289

Vermont
White River Junction VA Medical and Regional Center
215 North Main Street
White River Junction, VT 05009
802-295-9363
Fax: 802-296-6354

Virgin Islands
St. Croix CBOC
Box 12, RR-02
The Village Mall #113
Kings Hill, VI 00850-4701
340-778-5553
Fax: 340-778-5554

Virginia
Hampton VA Medical Center
100 Emancipation Drive
Hampton, VA 23667
757-722-9961
Fax: 757-723-6620

Hunter Holmes McGuire VA Medical Center
1201 Broad Rock Boulevard
Richmond, VA 23249
804-675-5000
Fax: 804-675-5585

Salem VA Medical Center
1970 Roanoke Boulevard
Salem, VA 24153
540-982-2463
Fax: 540-983-1096

Washington
VA Puget Sound Health Care System
1660 S. Columbian Way
Seattle, WA 98108
800-329-8387
http://www.puget-sound.med.va.gov/

Spokane VA Medical Center
4815 N. Assembly Street
Spokane, WA 99205-6197
509-434-7000
Fax: 509-434-7119

Jonathon M. Wainwright VA Memorial Center
77 Wainwright Drive
Walla Walla, WA 99362
509-525-5200
Fax: 509-527-3452

West Virginia
Beckley VA Medical Center
200 Veterans Avenue
Beckley, WV 25801
304-255-2121
Fax: 304-255-2431

Louis A Johnson VA Medical Center
One Medical Center Drive
Clarksburg, WV 26301
304-623-3461
Fax: 304-626-7026

Huntington VA Medical Center
1540-Spring Valley Drive
Huntington, WV 25704
304-429-6741
Fax: 304-429-6713

Martinsburg VA Medical Center
Route 9/Charles Town Road
Martinsburg, WV 25401
304-263-0811
Fax: 304-262-7433

Wisconsin
William S. Middleton Memorial Veterans Hospital
2500 Overlook Terrace
Madison, WI 53705
608-256-1901
Fax: 608-280-7095

Clement J. Zablocki Veterans Affairs Medical Center
5000 West National Avenue
Milwaukee, WI 53295-1000
414-384-2000
Fax: 414-382-5319
http://www.va.gov/milwaukee/

Tomah VA Medical Center
500 E. Veterans Street
Tomah, WI 54660
608-372-3971
http://www.vagreatlakes.org/

Wyoming
Cheyenne VA Medical Center/Regional Office Center
2360 E. Pershing Blvd.
Cheyenne, WY 82001
307-778-7550
Fax: 307-778-7336

Sheridan VA Medical Center
1898 Fort Road
Sheridan, WY 82801
307-672-3473
Fax: 307-672-1900

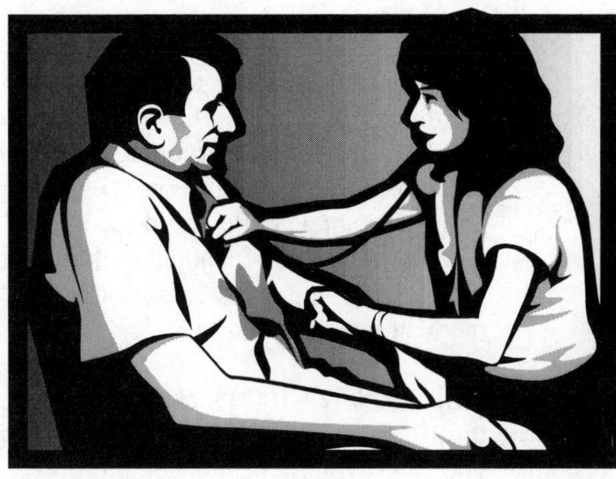

Compensation and Pension Services

The Compensation and Pension Service administers a variety of benefits and services for veterans, their dependents and survivors, including, but not limited to: service-connected compensation, DIC, non-service connected pension, burial and accrued benefits, guardianship and public contact services. You may also apply online at {http://vabenefits.vba.va.gov/vonapp/main.asp}.

Contact Veterans Benefits Administration, 810 Vermont Ave. NW, Washington, DC 20420; 800-827-1000; {www.vba.va.gov/bln/21/index.htm}.

$935 Month for Surviving Spouses

Dependency and Indemnity Compensation (DIC) is a monthly check paid to eligible survivors of certain deceased veterans. To get DIC, you must be an eligible survivor of a veteran who died because of a service-related illness or injury. If the veteran's death was not service-related, you may still be eligible if certain conditions apply.

There are many other benefits for surviving spouses which include Death Pension, Survivors' Educational Assistance, Home Loan Guaranty, Medical Benefits and Burial Benefits. Call 1-800-827-1000 for additional information or check the web site at {www.vba.va.gov/bln/dependents/Spouse.htm}.

Veterans' Benefits for Dependent Parents

Parents of disabled or deceased veterans may be eligible for certain benefits. Parents who are dependents of a veteran may be eligible for Dependency and Indemnity Compensation (DIC). Servicemember Group Life Insurance (SGLI) and financial counseling may also be obtained. In the event of the death of a veteran, parents may be eligible for Burial Benefits and a Burial Flag.

Call 1-800-827-1000 for additional information or check the web site at {www.vba.va.gov/bln/dependents/parent.htm}.

Benefits for Dependent Children

If you are a surviving unmarried child with no eligible parent and a counted yearly income limit is less than $1630 you may be eligible for Death Pension Benefits. The VA pays the difference between the countable income and the yearly limit.

Dependency and Indemnity Compensation (DIC) is also available to dependent children. DIC is a monthly check paid to eligible survivors of certain deceased veterans. If the surviving spouse is not entitled, a single child could receive up to $397 per month. Dependent children may also be eligible for education assistance and medical benefits.

Call 1-800-827-1000 for additional information or check the web site at {www.vba.va.gov/bln/dependents/child.htm}.

Burial and Memorial Benefits

On December 27, 2001, the Veterans Education and Benefit Expansion Act of 2001 became law which includes a provision that allows the Department of Veterans Affairs to furnish an appropriate headstone or marker for the graves of eligible veterans buried in private cemeteries regardless of whether the grave is already marked with a non-government marker. The death must have occurred on or after December 27, 2001.

Contact 1-800-827-1000 for additional information or check the web site at {www.cem.va.gov/hmlaw.htm}.

"A Sacred Trust"

The video "A Sacred Trust: The Story of the National Cemetery Administration" provides an overview of the National Cemetery Administration and the many services it provides to our Nation's veterans.

Through a dramatic presentation of one family's experience, this program depicts the entire burial process, covering such topics as eligibility requirements, military funeral honors, headstones and markers, and the Presidential Memorial Certificate that is given to the next of kin.

You can view this video on your computer at {www.cem.va.gov/sacred.htm} or call 1-800-827-1000 for information.

Get Free Burial Benefits

Many Burial Benefits are available for veterans from the National Cemetery Administration. Veterans are eligible for a gravesite in any of the 120 national cemeteries with space available, opening and closing of the grave, perpetual care, a government headstone or marker, a grave liner for casketed remains, a U.S. burial flag. And a Presidential Memorial Certificate at no cost to the family.

Minorities in the Military

The Center for Minority Veterans ensures the Department of Veterans' Affairs addresses the unique circumstances and special needs of minority veterans without regard to racial, ethnic, religious or gender distinctions. The Center promotes the use of existing programs, services and benefits by minority veterans, assesses the needs of minority veterans and proposes new programs to meet the specific needs of minority veterans.

Contact Department of Veteran Affairs, Center for Minority Veterans, 810 Vermont Ave., NW, Washington, DC 20420; 800-827-1000; {www.va.gov/minority_new/main/index.asp}.

Women Veterans

Women Veterans' should be aware of The Center for Women Veterans because it helps to insure that women veterans receive benefits and services on par with male veterans, encounter no discrimination in their attempt to access these services, and are treated with respect and dignity by VA service providers. They also act as the primary advisor to the Secretary for Veteran Affairs on all matters related to programs, issues, and initiatives for and affecting women.

Contact The Center For Women Veterans, 810 Vermont Ave. NW, Washington, DC 20420; 202-273-6193; Fax: 202-273-7092; {www.va.gov/womenvet/}.

Homeless Vets

One-third of the adult homeless male population and nearly one-quarter (23%) of all homeless adults have served their country in the armed services. While there is no true measure of the number of homeless veterans, it has been estimated that more than 250,000 veterans may be homeless on any given night and that twice as many veterans experience homelessness over the course of a year.

VA is the only federal agency that provides substantial hands-on assistance directly to homeless persons, specifically homeless veterans. The VA's Health Care for Homeless Veterans Program (HCHV) operates 135 sites, where extensive outreach, physical and psychiatric health exams, treatment, referrals, and ongoing case management are provided to homeless veterans with mental health problems, including substance abuse.

The VA's Domiciliary Care for Homeless Veterans (DCHV) Program provides medical care and rehabilitation in a residential setting on VA medical center grounds to eligible ambulatory veterans disabled by medical or psychiatric disorders, injury or age and who do not need hospitalization or nursing home care. Veterans Benefits Assistance is provided at Regional Offices by designated staff who serve as coordinators and points of contact for homeless veterans.

The Homeless Eligibility Clarification Act enables eligible veterans without fixed addresses to receive VA benefit checks at the VA regional office.

There are many other homeless programs that provide many valuable benefits for veterans. For additional information contact; VA's Homeless Veterans Program Office; 810 Vermont Ave. NW; Washington, DC 20420; 202-273-5764; Email: {homelessvets@mail.va.gov}; {www.va.gov/homeless/index.cfm}.

Home Loan Guaranty Service

More than 29 million veterans and service personnel are eligible for VA financing. Even though many veterans have already used their loan benefits, it may be possible for them to buy homes again with VA financing using remaining or restored loan entitlement.

The more you know about the home loan program, the more you will realize how little "red tape" there really is in getting a VA loan. These loans are often made without any downpayment at all, and frequently offer lower interest rates than ordinarily available with other kinds of loans.

Aside from the veteran's certificate of eligibility and the VA-assigned appraisal, the application process is not much different than any other type of mortgage loan. And if the lender is approved for automatic processing, as more and more lenders are now, a buyer's loan can be processed and closed by the lender without waiting for VA's approval of the credit application.

Before arranging for a mortgage to finance a home purchase, veterans should consider some of the advantages of VA home loans.

- No downpayment is required in most cases.
- Loan maximum may be up to 100 percent of the VA of the VA-established reasonable value of the property. Generally not to exceed $250,000.
- No monthly mortgage insurance premium.
- Limitations on buyer's closing costs.
- An appraisal which informs the buyer of the property value.
- Thirty year loans with a choice of repayment plans.
- For most loans for new houses, construction is inspected at appropriate stages to ensure compliance with the approved plans, and a 1-year warranty is required from the builder.
- An assumable mortgage.
- Right to prepay loan without penalty.
- VA performs personal loan servicing and offers financial counseling to help veterans avoid losing their homes during temporary financial difficulties.

If you live in one of the following states: Alaska, Arizona, Arkansas, California, Colorado, Hawaii, Idaho, Illinois, Iowa, Kansas, Louisiana, Minnesota, Missouri, Montana, Nebraska, Nevada, New Mexico, North Dakota, Oklahoma, Oregon, South Dakota, Texas, Utah, Washington, Wisconsin or Wyoming, please send your request for determination of Eligibility VA Form 26-1880, along with proof of military service) to:

Los Angeles Eligibility Center
P.O. Box 240097
Los Angeles, CA 90024
Toll free number: 1-888-487-1970
Email: {vavbalan/lgyeli@vba.va.gov}
LA Website:
{www.vahomes.org/la/home.htm}. To obtain VA Form 26-1880 online {http://www.vba.va.gov/pubs/forms1.htm}.

If you live in one of the following states: Alabama, Connecticut, District of Columbia, Delaware, Florida, Georgia, Indiana, Kentucky, Maine, Maryland, Massachusetts, Michigan, Mississippi, New Hampshire, New Jersey, New York, North Carolina, Ohio, Pennsylvania, Puerto Rico, Rhode Island, South Carolina, Tennessee, Vermont, Virginia or West Virginia, please send your request for determination of Eligibility VA Form 26-1880, along with proof of military service) to:

Winston-Salem Eligibility Center
VA Loan Eligibility Center

PO Box 20729
Winston-Salem, NC 27120
To obtain VA Form 26-1880 online
{http://www.vba.va.gov/pubs/forms1.htm}

For overnight delivery:
VA Loan Eligibility Center
251 N. Main St.
Winston-Salem, NC 27155
Toll free number: 1-888-244-6711
Email: NCELIGIB@vba.va.gov
Note: If you are located outside the U.S., you may use either Eligibility Center.

Veterans' Employment and Training Service and Regional Administrators

The Veterans' Employment and Training Service has 10 regional offices, as well as, at least one service office in each state. The regional offices are administered by Regional Administration (RAVET) and the state offices are administered by a Director for Veterans' Employment and Training. These offices can give you information about veterans employment and training programs and reemployment rights for veterans reservists and members of the National Guard.

Veterans Employment and Training Services Offices

Veterans' Employment and Training Service National Office
U.S. Department of Labor
200 Constitution Avenue, NW, Room S-1316
Washington, DC 20210
Assistant Secretary, Frederico Juarbe Jr.
Deputy Assistant Secretary, Charles S. Ciccolella
202-693-4754
202-693-4700
www.dol.gov/vets/

Region I
(Connecticut, Maine, Massachusetts, New Hampshire, Rhode Island, Vermont)
Regional Administrator, David Houle
Email: houle-david@dol.gov
Veterans' Employment and Training Service
U.S. Department of Labor
J.F. Kennedy Federal Building, Room E-315
Government Center
Boston, MA 02203
617-565-2080
Fax: 617-565-2082

Region II
(New Jersey, New York, Puerto Rico, Virgin Islands)
Regional Administrator, Vacant
Veterans' Program Specialist, Tim Hays
Email: Hays-Timothy@dol.gov
Veterans' Employment and Training Service
U.S. Department of Labor
201 Varick Street, Room 766
New York, NY 10014
212-337-2211
Fax: 212-337-2634

Region III
(Delaware, District of Columbia, Maryland, Pennsylvania, Virginia, West Virginia)
Regional Administrator, Joseph W. Hortiz. Jr.
Email: Hortiz-Joseph@dol.gov
Veterans' Employment and Training Service
U.S. Department of Labor
The Curtis Center
VETS/770 West
170 S. Independence Mall

Philadelphia, PA 19106-3310
215-861-5390
Fax: 215-861-5389

Region IV
(Alabama, Florida, Georgia, Kentucky, Mississippi, North Carolina, South Carolina, Tennessee)
Regional Administrator, William J. Bolls, Jr.
Email: bolls-william@dol.gov
Veterans' Employment and Training Service
U.S. Department of Labor
Sam Nunn Atlanta Federal Center
61 Forsyth Street, SW, Room 6-T85
Atlanta, GA 30303
404-562-2305
Fax: 404-562-2313

Region V
(Illinois, Indiana, Michigan, Minnesota, Ohio, Wisconsin)
Regional Administrator, Ronald G. Bachman
Email: bachman-ronald@dol.gov
Veterans' Employment and Training Service
U.S. Department of Labor
230 South Dearborn, Room 1064
Chicago, IL 60604
312-353-4942
312-353-0970 (ans. machine)
Fax: 312-886-1184

Region VI
(Arkansas, Louisiana, New Mexico, Oklahoma, Texas)
Regional Administrator, Lester L. Williams, Jr.
Email: williams-lester@dol.gov
Veterans' Employment and Training Service
U.S. Department of Labor
525 Griffin Street, Room 858
Dallas, TX 75202
214-767-4987
Fax: 214-767-2734

Region VII
(Iowa, Kansas, Missouri, Nebraska)
Regional Administrator, Lester L. Williams, Jr.
Email: williams-lester@dol.gov
Veterans' Employment and Training Service
U.S. Department of Labor
City Center Square Building
1100 Main Street, Suite 850
Kansas City, MO 64105-2112
Mailing Address:
P.O. Box 1087
Jefferson City, MO 65102-1087
816-426-7151
Fax: 816-426-7259

Region VIII
(Colorado, Montana, North Dakota, South Dakota, Utah, Wyoming)
Regional Administrator, Ronald G. Bachman
Email: bachman-ronald@dol.gov
Veterans' Employment and Training Service
U.S. Department of Labor
P.O. Box 4730
420 South Roosevelt Street
Aberdeen, SD 57402-4730
303-844-1175
303-844-1176/78
605-626-2325
Fax: 605-626-2322

Region IX
(Arizona, California, Hawaii, Nevada)
Regional Administrator, Vacant
Management Services Assistant, Nelia Bedia Nacor
Email: Nacor-Canosa-Nelia@dol.gov
Veterans' Employment and Training Service
U.S. Department of Labor
71 Stevenson Street, Suite 705
San Francisco, CA 94105
415-975-4701
415-975-4700 (ans. machine)
Fax: 415-975-4704

Region X
(Alaska, Idaho, Oregon, Washington)
Regional Administrator, Vacant
Veterans' Program Specialist, Karen Marin
Email: Marin-Karen@dol.gov
Veterans' Employment and Training Service
U.S. Department of Labor
1111 Third Avenue, Suite 800
Seattle, WA 98101-3212
206-553-4831
Fax: 206-553-6853

Veterans' Employment And Reemployment Rights Assistance And Information

Alabama
Director, Thomas M. Karrh
Email: Karrh-Thomas@dol.gov
Veterans' Employment and Training Service
U.S. Department of Labor
649 Monroe Street, Room 2218
Montgomery, AL 36131-6300
334-223-7677, 242-8115
Fax: 334-242-8927

Alaska
Director, Dan Travis
Email: Travis-Dan@dol.gov
Veterans' Employment and Training Service

U.S. Department of Labor
P.O. Box 25509
1111 West 8th Street
Juneau, AK 99802-5509
907-465-2723
Fax: 907-465-5528

Arizona
Director, Michael Espinosa
Email: Espinosa-Michael@dol.gov
Veterans' Employment and Training Service
U.S. Department of Labor
P.O. Box 6123-SC760E
1400 West Washington
Phoenix, AZ 85005
602-379-4961
Fax: 602-542-4103

Arkansas
Director, Billy R. Threlkeld
Email: Threlkeld-Billy@dol.gov
Veterans' Employment and Training Service
U.S. Department of Labor
Employment Security Building #2
State Capitol Mall, Room G-12
Little Rock, AR 72201
Mailing address:
P.O. Box 128
Little Rock, AR 72203
501-324-5502
501-682-3786
Fax: 501-682-3752

California
Director, Rosendo A. "Alex" Cuevas
Email: Cuevas-Rosendo@dol.gov
Veterans' Employment and Training Service
U.S. Department of Labor
800 Capitol Mall, Room W1142
P.O. Box 826880
Sacramento, CA 94280-0001
916-654-8178
Fax: 916-654-9469

Assistant Director, Steven L. Bragman
Email: Bragman-Steven@dol.gov
Veterans' Employment and Training Service
U.S. Department of Labor
2550 Mariposa Mall, Room 1080
Fresno, CA 93721-2296
559-445-5193
Fax: 559 445-5023

Assistant Director, Christopher D. Still
Email: still-christopher@dol.gov
Veterans' Employment and Training Service
U.S. Department of Labor
363 Civic Drive
Pleasant Hills, CA 94523-1987
925-602-1541
Fax: 925-602-5023

Assistant Director, Kevin D. Nagel
Email: Nagel-Kevin@dol.gov
EDD, Redlands Field Office
814 W. Colton Avenue
Redlands, CA 92374-2930
909-335-6763
Fax: 909-335-8303

Assistant Director, Linda Jacobe
Email: Jacobe-Linda@dol.gov
Veterans' Employment and Training Service
U.S. Department of Labor
320 Campus Lane
Suisun, CA 94583
707-863-3583
Fax: 707-864-3216

Assistant Director, Carolyn C. McMillan
Email: McMillan-Carolyn@dol.gov
Veterans' Employment and Training Service
U.S. Department of Labor
1501 East Arrow Highway
Pomona, CA 91767-2198
909-392-2675
Fax:-909 593-8913

Assistant Director, Michael S. Beadle
Email: Beadle-Michael@dol.gov
Veterans' Employment and Training Service
U.S. Department of Labor
932 Broadway
Santa Monica, CA 90401-2383
310-576-6444
Fax: 310-395-4819

Assistant Director, Nancy Ise
Email: Ise-Nancy@dol.gov
Veterans' Employment and Training Service
U.S. Department of Labor
2450 E. Lincoln Avenue
Anaheim, CA 92806-4175
714 687-4845
Fax: 714-518-2391

Assistant Director, Edward J. Scheer
Email: scheer-edward@dol.gov
Veterans' Employment and Training Service
U.S. Department of Labor
8977 Activity Road
San Diego, CA 92126-4427
619-689-6008
Fax: 619-689-6012

Colorado
Director, Mark A. McGinty
Email: McGinty-Mark@dol.gov
Veterans' Employment and Training Service
U.S. Department of Labor
1515-Arapahoe St. Tower #2, Suite 400
P.O. Box 46550
Denver, CO 80202
303-844-2151, 844-2152
Fax: 303-620-4257

Assistant Director, Donald Rincon
Email: Rincon-Donald@dol.gov
Veterans' Employment and Training Service
U.S. Department of Labor
2555 Airport Road
CO Springs, CO 80910-3176
719-475-3750
Fax: 719-636-1682

Connecticut
Director, William Mason, Jr.
Email: Mason-William@dol.gov
Veterans' Employment and Training Service
U.S. Department of Labor
Connecticut Department of Labor Building
200 Folly Brook Boulevard
Wethersfield, CT 06109
860-263-6490
Fax: 860-263-6498

Delaware
Director, David White
Email: white-david@dol.gov
U.S. Department of Labor
Veterans' Employment and Training Service
4425 North Market Street, Room 420
Wilmington, DE 19809-0828
302-761-8138/9
Fax: 302-761-6621 (temp)

District of Columbia
Director, Stanley K. Williams
Email: Williams-Stanley@dol.gov
Veterans' Employment and Training Service
U.S. Department of Labor
1500 Franklin Street, NE
Washington, D.C. 20018
202-576-3082
Fax: 202-576-3113

Florida
Director, Derek W. Taylor
Email: taylor-derek@dol.gov
Mailing address:
Veterans' Employment and Training Service
U.S. Department of Labor
P.O. Box 1527
Tallahassee, FL 32301- 5008
Located at:
Marathon Building, Suite 205
2574 Seagate Drive
Tallahassee, FL 32399-0676
850-942-8800
850-877-4164
850-488-2967
Fax: 904-922-2690

Assistant Director, Richard Bate
Email: bate-richard@dol.gov
Mailing address:
Veterans' Employment and Training Service
U.S. Department of Labor
P.O. Box 17747
Jacksonville, FL 32245-7747
Located at:
215 Market Street, Suite 300
Jacksonville, FL 32202-2851
904-359-6080 Ext. 2191 - 3191
Fax: 904-359-6151

Assistant Director, Oscar G. Fuentes
Email: fuentes-oscar@dol.gov
Veterans' Employment and Training Service
U.S. Department of Labor
Ft. Lauderdale Jobs & Benefits Office
P.O. Box 5124
Ft. Lauderdale, Fl, 32814-9084
Located at:
2660 West Oakland Parks Boulevard
Ft. Lauderdale, FL 33311-1347
954-677-5400
Fax: 954-457-2889

Assistant Director, Ronnie L. Carter
Email: carter-ronnie@dol.gov
Veterans' Employment and Training Service
U.S. Department of Labor
P.O. Box 149084
Orlando, FL 32814-9084
Located at:
1001 Executive Center Drive, Suite
Orlando, FL 32803
954-677-5818
Fax: 954-677-5820 (call ahead)

Assistant Director, Craig K. Spry
Email: spry-craig@dol.gov
Veterans' Employment and Training Service
U.S. Department of Labor
P.O. Box 12528
St. Petersburg, FL 33733-2528
Located at:
3160 - 5th Avenue North, Suite 200

Plaza 300 North Building
St. Petersburg, FL 33713
727-893-2415
Fax: 727-893-2378

Georgia
Director, Ed Gresham
Email: gresham-ed@dol.gov
Veterans' Employment and Training Service
U.S. Department of Labor
Georgia State Employment Service
Sussex Place, Suite 504
148 International Boulevard, N.E.
Atlanta, GA 30303-1751
404-656-3127, -3138
404-331-3893
Fax: 404-657-7403

Hawaii
Director, Gilbert "Gil" N. Hough
Email: hough-gilbert@dol.gov
Veterans' Employment and Training Service
U.S. Department of Labor
P.O. Box 3680
Honolulu, HI 96811
Located at:
830 Punchbowl Street, Rm. 315
Honolulu, HI 96813
808-522-8216 (ans. service)
Fax: 808-586-9258

Idaho
Director, Vacant
Assistant Director, Pamela "Pam" Langley
Email: Lengley-Pamela@dol.gov
Veterans' Employment and Training Service
U.S. Department of Labor
P.O. Box 2697
Boise, ID 83701
Located at:
317 Main Street, Room 303
Boise, ID 83735
208-334-6163
Fax: 208-334-6389, 334-6430

Illinois
Director, Samuel Parks
Email: Parks-Samuel@dol.gov
Veterans' Employment and Training Service
U.S. Department of Labor
401 South State Street, Room 744-North
Chicago, IL 60605
312-793-3433
Fax: 312-793-4795

Assistant Director, David Lyles
Email: lyles-davidl@dol.gov
Veterans' Employment and Training Service
U.S. Department of Labor
555 S. Pasfield
Springfield, IL 62704
217-524-7769
Fax: 217-785-9715

Assistant Director, James R. Harris
Email: harris-james@dol.gov
Veterans' Employment and Training Service
U.S. Department of Labor
800 Lancer Lane - suite E-107
Grayslake, IL 60030
847-523-7400
Fax: 847-543-7465

Assistant Director, James R. Harris
Email: harris-james@dol.gov
Veterans' Employment and Training Service
U.S. Department of Labor
221 N. Genesee Street
Waukegan, IL 60085
847-543-7400 Ext. 273
Fax: 847-543-7465

Indiana
Bruce Redman, Director
Director, David "Bruce" Redman
Email: redman-david@dol.gov
Veterans' Employment and Training Service
U.S. Department of Labor
10 North Senate Ave., Room SE 103
Indianapolis, IN 46204
317-232-6804
317-232-6805
Fax: 317-232-4262

Iowa
Director, Anthony J. Smithhart
Email: Smithhart-Anthony@dol.gov
Veterans' Employment and Training Service
U.S. Department of Labor
150 Des Moines Street
Des Moines, IA 50309-5563
515-281-9061
Fax: 515-281-9063

Kansas
Director, Gayle A. Gibson
Email: Gibson-Gayle@dol.gov
Veterans' Employment and Training Service
U.S. Department of Labor
401 Topeka Boulevard
Topeka, KS 66603-3182
785-296-5032
Fax: 785-296-0264

Kentucky
Director, Charles R. "Rick" Netherton
Email: Netherton-Charles@dol.gov
Veterans' Employment and Training Service
U.S. Department of Labor
Department for Employment Services
275 East Main Street
2nd Floor West - 2WD
Frankfort, KY 40621-2339
502-564-7062
Fax: 502-564-1476

Veterans' Program Specialist, Robert Kuenzli
Email: Kuenzli-Robert@dol.gov
Veterans' Employment and Training Service
U.S. Department of Labor
320 Garrard Street
Covington, KY 41011
859-292-6666 Ext. 253
Fax: 859-292-6708

Louisiana
Director, Lester L. Parmenter
Email: Parmenter-Lester@dol.gov
Veterans' Employment and Training Service
U.S. Department of Labor
Louisiana Department of Labor
Administration Building, Room 184
1001 North 23rd Street
Baton Rouge, Louisiana 70802
Mailing address:
P.O. Box 94094, Room 184
Baton Rouge, LA 70804-9094
225-389-0339
225-389-0440
Fax: 225-342-3152

Maine
Director, Jon Guay
Email: Guay-Jon@dol.gov
Veterans' Employment and Training Service
U.S. Department of Labor
P.O. Box 3106
Lewiston, ME 04243
Located at:
5 Mollison Way
Lewiston, ME 04240
207-753-9090
Fax: 207-783-5304

Maryland
Director, Gary D. Lobdell
Email: Lobdell-Gary@dol.gov
U.S. Department of Labor
Veterans' Employment and Training Service
1100 North Eutaw Street, Room 210
Baltimore, MD 21201
410-767-2110, -2111
Fax: 410-333-5136

Assistant Director, Larry Mettert
Email: mettert-larry@dol.gov
U.S. Department of Labor
Veterans' Employment and Training Service
201 Baptist Street
Salisbury, MD 21801
410-334-6897

Assistant Director, James Theriault
Email: theriault-james@dol.gov
U.S. Department of Labor
Veterans' Employment and Training Service
P.O. Box 1317
Wheaton, MD 20915
301-929-4379
Fax: 301-929-4383

Massachusetts
Director, Paul Desmond
Email: desmond-paul@dol.gov
Veterans' Employment and Training Service
U.S. Department of Labor
C.F. Hurley Building, 5th Floor
19 Staniford Street
Boston, MA 02114
617-626-6699
Fax: 617-727-2330

Assistant Director, Reginald E. Dupuis
Email: Dupuis-Reginald@dol.gov
Veterans' Employment and Training Service
U.S. Department of Labor
Division of Employment Security
72 School Street
Taunton, MA 02780
508-977-1414
Fax: 617-727-2112

Michigan
Director, Kim Fulton
Email: Fulton-Kim@dol.gov
Veterans' Employment and Training Service
U.S. Department of Labor
Candillac Place
3032 West Grand Boulevard, Suite 48202
Detroit, MI 48202
313-456-3180
Fax: 313-456-3181

Assistant Director, Edgar J. Hekman
Email: hekman-edgar@dol.gov
Veterans' Employment and Training Service
U.S. Department of Labor
Employment Security Commission

3391 Plainfield, N.E.
Grand Rapids, MI 49505
616-361-3254

Minnesota
Director, Michael Graham
Email: graham-michael@dol.gov
Veterans' Employment and Training Service
U.S. Department of Labor
390 Robert Street North, 1st Floor
St. Paul, MN 55101-1812
651-296-3665
Fax: 651-282-2711

Assistant Director, Vacant
Veterans' Employment and Training Service
U.S. Department of Labor
c/o Job Service
320 West 2nd Street, Rm. 205
Duluth, MN 55802
218-723-4766

Mississippi
Director, Angelo Terrell
Email: Terrell-Angelo@dol.gov
Veterans' Employment and Training Service
U.S. Department of Labor
P.O. Box 1699
1520 West Capitol Street
Jackson, MS 39215-1699
601-965-4204, 961-7588
Fax: 601-961-7717

Missouri
Director, Mick Jones
Email: Jones-Mickey@dol.gov
Veterans' Employment and Training Service
U.S. Department of Labor
421 East Dunklin Street
Jefferson City, MO 65104-3138
Mailing address:
P.O. Box 1087
Jefferson City, MO 65102-1087059
573-751-3921
Fax: 573-751-6710

Montana
Director, H. Polly LaTray-Halmes
Email: Latray-Halmes-Hazel@dol.gov
Veterans' Employment and Training Service
U.S. Department of Labor
1215 8th Avenue
Helena, MT 59601
406-449-5431, 442-2541
Fax: 406-444-3365

Nebraska
Director, Richard "Rick" Nelson
Email: Nelson-Richard@dol.gov
Veterans' Employment and Training Service
U.S. Department of Labor
550 South 16th Street
Lincoln, NE 68508
Mailing address:
P.O. Box 94600
Lincoln, NE 68509-4600
402-471-9833
Fax: 402-471-2092

Nevada
Director, Darrol Brown
Email: brown-darrol@dol.gov
Veterans' Employment and Training Service
U.S. Department of Labor
1923 North Carson Street, Room 205
Carson City, NV 89702
702-687-4632
Fax: 702-687-3976

New Hampshire
Director, John Gagne
Email: gagne-john@dol.gov
Veterans' Employment and Training Service
U.S. Department of Labor
143 North Main Street, Room 208
Concord, NH 03301
603-225-1424
Fax: 603-225-1545

New Jersey
Director, Alan E. Grohs
Email: grohs-alan@dol.gov
U.S. Department of Labor
Veterans' Employment and Training Service
Labor Building, 11th Floor
P.O. Box 058
Trenton, NJ 08625
609-292-2930
609-989-2305 and 989-2396
Fax: 609-292-9070

Assistant Director, James J. Curcio
Email: curcio-james@dol.gov
U.S. Department of Labor
Veterans' Employment and Training Service
2600 Mt. Ephraim Avenue
Camden, NJ 08104
856-614-3163
Fax: 856-614-3156

New Mexico
Director, Sharon I Mitchell
Email: Mitchell-Sharon@dol.gov

Veterans' Employment and Training Service
U.S. Department of Labor
501 Mountainroad N.E.
Albuquerque, NM 87102
Mailing address:
P.O. Box 25085
Albuquerque, NM 87125-5085
505-346-7502
Fax: 505-346-7503

New York
Director, James H. Hartman
Email: Hartman-James@dol.gov
U.S. Department of Labor
Veterans' Employment and Training Service
Harriman State Campus Bldg. 12, Room 518
Albany, NY 12240-0099
518-457-7465, 435-0831
Fax: 518-435-0833

Veterans' Program Specialist, Frank Carey
Email: Carey-Frank@dol.gov
Veterans' Employment and Training Service
U.S. Department of Labor
Leo O'Brien Federal Bldg., Room 819
Albany, NY 12207
518-431-4276
Fax: 518-431-4283
Aux Office: 518-270-5872

Assistant Director, Alice F. Jones
J Email: ones-Alice@dol.gov
212-352-6183 (M-Tu-W-F)
212-227-5213 (Thursday only)
Assistant Director, Daniel A. Friedman
Friedman-Daniel@dol.gov
212-352-6184 (M-F)
Fax: 212-352-6185
212-227-5213 (M-F only)
Veterans' Employment and Training Service
U.S. Department of Labor
345 Hudson Street, Rm. 8209
P.O. Box 668, Mail Stop 8C
New York, NY 10014-0668

Assistant Director, Vacant
U.S. Department of Labor
Veterans' Employment and Training Service
State Office Building, Room 702
207 Genesee Street
Utica, NY 13501
315-793-2323
Fax: 315-793-2303

Assistant Director, James C. Donahue
Email: donahue-james@dol.gov
U.S. Department of Labor
Veterans' Employment and Training Service
290 Main Street, Room 231
Buffalo, NY 14202-4076
716-851-2748
Fax: 716-851-2792

Assistant Director, Frank J. Policastri
Email: Policastri-Frank@dol.gov
U.S. Department of Labor
Veterans' Employment and Training Service
450 South Salina St., 2nd Floor, Rm. 200
Syracuse, NY 13202-2402
315-479-3381
Fax: 315-479-3421

North Carolina
Director, Steven W. Guess
Email: Guess-Steven@dol.gov
Veterans' Employment and Training Service
U.S. Department of Labor
P.O. Box 27625
Raleigh, NC 27611-7625
Located at:
700 Wade Avenue, Building M
Raleigh, NC 27605 – 1154
919-856-4792
919-733 -7402
Fax: 919-733-1508

Assistant Director, Thomas E. West
Email: west-tom@dol.gov
Veterans' Employment and Training Service
U.S. Department of Labor
c/o North Carolina Employment
Security Commission
3301 Hwy US 70, S.E.
Newton, NC 28658
828-466-5535
Fax: 828-466-5545

North Dakota
Director, Gerald (Jerry) H. Meske
Email: Gerald-Meske@dol.gov
Veterans' Employment and Training Service
U.S. Department of Labor
P.O. Box 1632
1000 E. Divide Avenue
Bismarck, ND 58502-1632
701-250-4337
701-328-2865
Fax: 701-328-2890

Ohio
Director, Carl Price
Email: Price-Carl@dol.gov
Veterans' Employment and Training Service
U.S. Department of Labor

P.O. Box 1618
Columbus, OH 43216
Located at:
145 South Front Street, Room 523
Columbus, OH 43215
614-466-2768/2769
Fax: 614-752-5007

Assistant Director, Kevin Patterson
Email: patterson-kevin@dol.gov
Veterans' Employment and Training Service
U.S. Department of Labor
684 N. Park Avenue
P.O. Box 1188
Warren, Ohio 44482-1188
330-399-8114
Fax: 330-399-1957

Assistant Director, William Forester
Email: forester-william@dol.gov
Veterans' Employment and Training Service
U.S. Department of Labor
1841 Prospect Ave.
Cleveland, OH 44115
216-787-5164
Fax: 216-787-5213

Assistant Director, John E. Moon
Email: moon-john@dol.gov
Veterans' Employment and Training Service
U.S. Department of Labor
1935 East Second Street, Suite B
Defiance, OH 43512-2503
419-782-6050 (Temporary Tele. No.)
Fax: 419-782-4755

Oklahoma
Director, Darrell H. Hill
Email: Hill-Darrell@dol.gov
Veterans' Employment and Training Service
U.S. Department of Labor
2401 North Lincoln Blvd., Rm. 304-2
Oklahoma City, OK 73105
Mailing address:
P. O. Box 52003
Oklahoma City, OK 73152-2003
405-231-5088, 557-7189
Fax: 405-557-7123

Oregon
Director, Ron Cannon
Email: Cannon-Ron@dol.gov
Veterans' Employment and Training Service
U.S. Department of Labor
Employment Division Building, Rm. 108
875 Union Street, N.E.
Salem, OR 97311-0100
503-947-1490
Fax: 503-947-1492

Assistant Director, Tonja Pardo
Email: pardo-tonja@dol.gov
Veterans' Employment and Training Service
U.S. Department of Labor
1433 Southwest 6th Avenue
Portland, OR 97201
503-731-3478
Fax: 503-229-5829

Pennsylvania
Director, Larry Babitts
Email: babitts-lawrence@dol.gov
U.S. Department of Labor
Veterans' Employment and Training Service
Labor and Industry Bldg., Room 1108
Seventh and Forster Streets
Harrisburg, PA 17121
717-787-5834, 5835
Fax: 717-783-2631

Assistant Director, Dennis M. Ero
Email: Ero-Dennis@dol.gov
Capitol Region Career Link
2971 North 7th Street (Suite A)
Harrisburg, PA 17101
717-783-3272 x129

Director, Darrell R. Fritzinger
Email: fritzinger-darrell@dol.gov
U.S. Department of Labor
Veterans' Employment and Training Service
10th Floor 640 Hamilton Street
Allentown, PA 18103
610-821-6571

Veterans' Program Specialist, Denise M. Adair
Email: adair-denise@dol.gov
U.S. Department of Labor
Veterans' Employment and Training Service
State Office Building
300 Liberty Avenue, Room 1307
Pittsburgh, PA 15222
412-565-2469
Fax: 412-565-2518

Assistant Director, Wayne E. Faith
Email: faith-wayne@dol.gov
U.S. Department of Labor
Veterans' Employment and Training Service
Job Service Office
135 Franklin Avenue
Scranton, PA 18503
717-963-4735

Assistant Director, Richard P. Schaffer
Email: schaffer-richard@dol.gov
Veterans' Employment and Training Service
U.S. Department of Labor
71 South Union Avenue
Lansdowne, PA 19050
610-284-7588

Puerto Rico
Director, Angel Mojica
Email: Mojica-Angel@dol.gov
U.S. Department of Labor
Veterans' Employment and Training Service
Puerto Rico Department of Labor and Human Resources
#198 Calle Guayama
Hato Rey, PR 00917
787-754-5391, 751-0731,
766-6425
Fax: 787-754-2983

Rhode Island
Director, John F. Dunn
Email: Dunn-John@dol.gov
Veterans' Employment and Training Service
U.S. Department of Labor
Oliver Stedman Government Center
4808-Tower Hill Road
Wakefield, RI 02879
401-528-5134
Fax: 401-528-5106

South Carolina
Director, William C. Plowden, Jr.
Email: plowden-william@dol.gov
Veterans' Employment and Training Service
U.S. Department of Labor
P.O. Box 1755
Columbia, SC 29202-1755
Located at:
Lem Harper Building
631 Hampton Street, Suite 141
Columbia, SC 29201
803-765-5195, 253-7649
Fax: 803-253-4153

South Dakota
Director, Earl R. Schultz
Email: Schultz-Earl@dol.gov
Veterans' Employment and Training Service
U.S. Department of Labor
P.O. Box 4730
420 South Roosevelt Street
Aberdeen, SD 57402-4730
605-626-2325
Fax: 605-626-2322

Tennessee
Director, Richard E. Ritchie
Email: Ritchie-Richard@dol.gov
Veterans' Employment and Training Service
U.S. Department of Labor
P.O. Box 280656
Nashville, TN 37228-0656
615-736-7680, 741-2135
Fax: 615-741-4241
615-736-5037

Clarksville Montgomery County Career Center
350 Pageant Lane, Suite 406
Clarksville, TN 37040
931-572-1688
Fax: 931-648-5564

Assistant Director, Jim George Pearson
Email: Pearson-Jim@dol.gov
Veterans' Employment and Training Service
U.S. Department of Labor
1309 Poplar Avenue
Memphis, TN 38104-2006
901-543-7853
Fax: 901-543-7882

Texas
Director, John D. McKinny
Email: McKinny-John@dol.gov
Veterans' Employment and Training Service
U.S. Department of Labor
TwC Building, Room 516-T
1117 Trinity Street
Austin, TX 78701
Mailing address:
P.O. Box 1468
Austin, TX 78767
512-463-2207
512-463-2815
512-463-2814
Fax: 512-475-2999

Assistant Director, Ronny J. Hays
Email: hays-ronny@dol.gov
Veterans' Employment and Training Service
U.S. Department of Labor
1602 16th Street
Lubbock, Texas 79401
Mailing address:
P.O. Box 2858
Lubbock, TX 79408-2858
806-763-6416
Fax: 806-747-8629

Assistant Director, Randy W. Walker
Email: walker-randolph@dol.gov
Veterans' Employment and Training Service

U.S. Department of Labor
8323 Culebra Road Suite #103
San Antonio, TX 78251
210-684-1051 Ext 241
Fax: 210-684-1822

Assistant Director, Alberto Navarro
Email: mailto:walker-randolph@dol.gov
Veterans' Employment and Training Service
U.S. Department of Labor
5425 Polk Street, G-20
Houston, TX 77023
713-767-2022
Fax: 713-767-2489

Assistant Director, Albert L. Arredondo
Email: arredondo-albert@dol.gov
Veterans' Employment and Training Service
U.S. Department of Labor
412 South High Street
Longview, TX 75606
Mailing address:
P.O. Box 2152
Longview, TX 75606-2152
903-758-1783 Ext. 211
Fax: 903-757-7835

Assistant Director, Vacant
Veterans' Employment and Training Service
U.S. Department of Labor
3649 Leopard Street, Suite 600
Corpus Christi, TX 78408
512-882-3994
Fax: 512-882-1621

Assistant Director, Robert A. Marterella
Email: marterella-robert@dol.gov
Veterans' Employment and Training Service
U.S. Department of Labor
301 W. 13th Street, Room 407
Ft. Worth, TX 76102-4699
Mailing address:
P.O. Box 591
FT. Worth, TX 76101-0591
817-335-5111 Ext. 404
Fax: 817-336-8723

Assistant Director, (vacant)
Veterans' Employment and Training Service
U.S. Department of Labor
8300 Gateway East, Suite 400
El Paso, TX 79915
Mailing address:
Texas Workforce Commission
P.O. Box 26960
El Paso, TX 79926-6950
915-594-8211
Fax: 915-594-3529

Utah

Director, Howard "Dale" Brockbank
Email: Brockbank-Howard@dol.gov
Veterans' Employment and Training Service
U.S. Department of Labor
140 East 300 South, Suite 209
Salt Lake City, UT 84111-2333
801-524-5703
Fax: 801-524-3099

Vermont

Director, Richard Gray
Email: gray-richard@dol.gov
Veterans' Employment and Training Service
U.S. Department of Labor
P.O. Box 603
Montpelier, VT 05601
Located at:
Post Office Building
87 State Street, Room 303
Montpelier, VT 05602
802-828-4441
Fax: 802-828-4445

Virginia

Director, Roberto L. Pineda
Email: Pineda-Roberto@dol.gov
U.S. Department of Labor
Veterans' Employment and Training Service
703-East Main Street, Room 118
Richmond, VA 23219
804-786-7270, 7269, 6599
Fax: 804-786-4548

Assistant Director, Heather Higgins
Email: Higgins-heather@dol.gov
U.S. Department of Labor
Veterans' Employment and Training Service
13370 Minnieville Road
Woodbridge, VA 22192
703-897-0433
Fax: 703-897-0440

Assistant Director, Michael T. Skidmore
Email: SkidmoreMichael@dol.gov
U.S. Department of Labor
Veterans' Employment and Training Service
Virginia Employment Commission
P.O. Box 40008
Roanoke, VA 24022
Located at:
5060 Valleyview Boulevard, NW
Roanoke, VA 24012

540-561-7494
Fax: 540-561-7510

Virgin Islands
Director, Angel Mojica
Email: Mojica-Angel@dol.gov
U.S. Department of Labor
Veterans' Employment and Training Service
Puerto Rico Department of Labor and Human Resources
#198 Calle Guayama
Hato Rey, PR 00917
787-754-5391, 751-0731,
766-6425
Fax: 787-754-2983

Washington
Director, Thomas "Tom" Pearson
Email: Pearson-Thomas@dol.gov
Veterans' Employment and Training Service
U.S. Department of Labor
P.O. Box 165
Olympia, WA 98507-0165
360-438-4600
Fax: 360-438-3160

West Virginia
Director, Charles W. Stores, Jr.
Email: Stores-Charles@dol.gov
U.S. Department of Labor
Veterans' Employment and Training Service
Capitol Complex, Room 204
112 CA Avenue
Charleston, WV 25305-0112
304-558-4001
Fax: 304-344-4591

Wisconsin
Director, James Gutowski
Email: Gutowski-James@dol.gov
Veterans' Employment and Training Service
U.S. Department of Labor
P.O. Box 8310
Madison, WI 53708-8310
Located at:
Jeff Building, Room G-201A
201 East Washington Ave.
Madison, WI 53703
608-266-3110
Fax: 608-261-6710

Wyoming
Director, David McNulty
Email: McNulty-David@dol.gov
Veterans' Employment and Training Service
U.S. Department of Labor
P.O. Box 2760
100 West Midwest Avenue
Casper, WY 82602-2760
307-261-5454,
235-3281, 3282
Fax: 307-473-2642

U.S. Department of Veterans Affairs Regional Offices and Vet Centers

Department of Veterans Affairs Headquarters
810 Vermont Ave, NW
Washington, D.C. 20420
800-827-1000
www.va.gov

Alabama
Regional Office:
Montgomery Regional Office
345 Perry Hill Rd.
Montgomery, AL 36109
800-827-1000

Vet Centers:
Birmingham Vet Center
1500 5th Avenue South
Birmingham, AL 35205
205-731-0550
Fax: 205-731-0654

Mobile Vet Center
Festival Center
3725 Airport Blvd.
Suite 143
Mobile, AL 36608
205-304-0108

Alaska
Regional Office:
Anchorage Regional Office
2925 DeBarr Road
Anchorage, AK 99508-2989
800-827-1000

Vet Centers:
Anchorage Vet Center
4201 Tutor Center Dr.
Suite 115
Anchorage, AK 99508
907-563-6966
Fax: 907-561-7183

Fairbanks Vet Center
540-4th Avenue, Suite 100
Fairbanks, AK 99701
907-456-4238
Fax: 907-456-0475

Kenai Vet Center
4335 K- Beach Rd.
Building F, Suite 4
Diamond Center
Soldotna, AK 99611
907-260-7640

Wasila Vet Center
851 E. Westpoint Ave., Suite 111
Wasila, AK 99654
907-376-4318
907-373-1883

Arizona

Regional Office:
Phoenix Regional Office
3225 N. Central Ave.
Phoenix, AZ 85012
800-827-1000

Vet Centers:
Phoenix Vet Center
77 E Weldon
Phoenix, AZ 85012
602-640-2981
Fax: 602-640-2967

Prescott Vet Center
161 S Granite Street, Suite B
Prescott, AZ 86303
520-778-3469
Fax: 520-776-6042

Tucson Vet Center
3055 North 1st Avenue
Tucson, AZ 85719
520-882-0333

Arkansas

Regional Office:
North Little Rock Regional Center
Building 65, Fort Roots
P.O. Box 1280
Little Rock, AR 72115
800-827-1000

Vet Centers:
North Little Rock Vet Center
201 W Broadway, Suite A
Little Rock, AR 72114
501-324-6395

California

Regional Offices:
Los Angeles Regional Office
Federal Office
11000 Wilshire Boulevard
Los Angeles, CA 90024
800-827-1000

Oakland Regional Office
1301 Clay Street, Room 1300 North
Oakland, CA 94612
800-827-1000

San Diego Regional Office
8810 Rio San Diego Drive
San Diego, CA 92108
800-827-1000

Vet Centers:
Anaheim Vet Center
859 S. Harbor Blvd.
Anaheim, CA 92805
714-776-0161

Chico Vet Center
25 Main Street
Chico, CA 95926
916-899-8549

Commerce Vet Center
VA East L.A. Clinic
5400 E. Olympic Blvd., #140
Commerce, CA 90022
213-728-9966

Concord Vet Center
1899 Clayton Rd., Suite 140
Concord, CA 94520
925-680-4526

Culver City Vet Center
5730 Uplander Way, Suite 100
Culver City, CA 90230
310-641-0326

Eureka Vet Center
2839 G. Street, Suite A
Eureka, CA 95501
707-444-8271

Fresno Vet Center
3636 N 1st Street, Suite 112
Fresno, CA 93726
559-437-5660

Los Angeles Vet Center
S. Central LA
251 W. 85th Place
Los Angeles, CA 90003

Oakland Vet Center
1504 Franklin St, Suite 200
Oakland, CA 94612
510-763-3904

Peninsula Vet Center
2946 Broadway St
Redwood City, CA 94062
650-299-0672

Riverside Vet Center
4954-Arlington Ave., Suite A
Riverside, CA 94928
Rohnert Park, CA 92571
909-276-6342

Rohnert Park Vet Center
6225 State Farm Drive
Suite 101
Rohnert Park, CA 94928
707-586-3295

Sacramento Vet Center
111 Howe Ave., Suite 390
Sacramento, CA 95825
916-566-7430

San Diego Vet Center
2900 6th Ave.
San Diego, CA 92103
858-294-2040

San Francisco Vet Center
505 Polk Street
San Francisco, CA 94102
415-441-5051

Santa Cruz Vet Center
1350 41st Avenue, Suite 102
Capitola, CA 95010
831-464-4575

Colorado

Regional Offices:
Denver Regional Office
155 Van Gordon St.
Lakewood, CO 80228
800-827-1000

Western Mountain Regional Office
789 Sherman Street
Suite 570
Denver, CO 80203
303-393-2897
Fax: 303-860-7614

Vet Centers:
Boulder Vet Center
2336 Canyon Blvd.
Suite 103
Boulder, CO 80302
303-440-7306

Colorado Springs Vet Center
416 E. Colorado Avenue
Colorado Springs, CO 80903
719-471-9992

Denver Vet Center
7465 E First Avenue, Suite B
Denver, CO 80230
303-326-0645

Fort Collins Vet Center
1100 Poudre River Dr
Fort Collins, CO 80524
970-221-5176

Pueblo Vet Center
909 N. Elizabeth St.
Pueblo, CO 81003
719-543-8343

Connecticut
Regional Office:
Hartford Regional Office
450 Main Street
Hartford, CT 06103
800-827-1000

Vet Centers:
Hartford Vet Center
30 Jordan Lane
Wethersfield, CT 06109
860-240-3542

New Haven Vet Center
141 Captain Thomas Blvd.
New Haven, CT 06516
203-932-9899

Norwich Vet Center
100 Main Street
Norwich, CT 06360
203-887-1755

Delaware
Regional office:
Wilmington Regional Office
1601 Kirkwood Highway
Wilmington, DE 19805
800-827-1000

Vet Centers:
Wilmington Vet Center
VAMROC Bldg. 2
1601 Kirkwood Highway
Wilmington, DE 19805
302-994-1660

District of Columbia
Regional Office:
Washington DC Regional Office
1120 Vermont Avenue, NW
Washington, DC 20421
800-827-1000

Vet Center:
Washington DC Vet Center
911 Second Street, NE
Washington, DC 20003
202-543-8821
Fax: 202-745-8648

Florida
Regional Office:
St. Petersburg Regional Office
9500 Bay Pines Blvd.
Bay Pines, FL 33708
800-827-1000

Vet Centers:
Ft. Lauderdale Vet Center
713 NE 3rd Ave
Ft. Lauderdale, FL 33304
954-356-7926

Jacksonville Vet Center
1833 Boulevard St.
Jacksonville, FL 32206
904-232-3621

Miami Vet Center
2700 SW 3rd Ave., Suite 1A
Miami, FL 33129
305-859-8387

Orlando Vet Center
5001 Orange Ave., Suite A
Orlando, FL 32809
407-857-2800

Palm Beach Vet Center
2311 10th Ave., North #13
Lake Worth, FL 33461
561-585-0441

Pensacola Vet Center
4501 Twin Oaks Dr., Suite 104
Pensacola, FL 32506
805-456-5886
Fax: 850-456-9403

Sarasota Vet Center
4801 Swift Rd
Sarasota, FL 34231
941-927-8285

Georgia
Regional Office:
Atlanta Regional Office
1700 Clairmont Rd.
Decatur, GA 30033
800-827-1000

Vet Centers:
Atlanta Vet Center
77 Peachtree Pl., NW
Atlanta, GA 30309
404-347-7264

Savannah Vet Center
8110 White Bluff Road
Savannah, GA 31406
912-652-4097

Guam
Vet Center:
Guam Vet Center
222 Chalan Santo Papast
Reflection Center, Suite 102
Agana, GU 96910
705-475-7161

Hawaii
Regional Office:
Hawaii Regional Center
459 Patterson Rd., E-Wing
Honolulu, HI 96819
800-827-1000

Vet Centers:
Hilo Vet Center
120 Keawe St., Suite 201
Hilo, HI 96720
808-969-3833

Honolulu Vet Center
1680 Kapiolani Blvd.
Suite F
Honolulu, HI 96814
808-566-1764

Kallua-Kona Vet Center
Pottery Terrace
Fern Bldg.
75-5995 Kuakini Hwy., #415

Kallua-Kona, HI 96740
808-329-0574

Kauai Vet Center
3367 Kuhio Hwy., Suite 101
Lihue, HI 96766
808-246-1163

Maui Vet Center
35 Lunaliho St., Suite 101
Wailuku, HI 96793
808-242-8557

Idaho

Regional Office:
Boise Regional Center
805 W. Franklin St.
Boise, ID 83702
800-827-1000

Vet Centers:
Boise Vet Center
5440 Franklin Rd.
Suite 100
Boise, ID 83705
208-342-3612

Pocatello Vet Center
1800 Garrett Way
Pocatello, ID 83201
208-232-0316

Illinois

Regional Office:
Chicago Regional Office
536 S. Clark St
Chicago, IL 60605
800-827-1000

Vet Centers:
Chicago Vet Center
1514 E. 63rd Street
Chicago, IL 60637
312-684-5500

Chicago Heights Vet Center
1600 Halsted Street
Chicago Heights, IL 60411
708-754-0340

Evanston Vet Center
565 Howard Street
Evanston, IL 60202
847-332-1019

Oak Park Vet Center
155 S. Oak Park Avenue
Oak Park, IL 60302
708-383-3325

Peoria Vet Center
3310 N. Prospect Street
Peoria, IL 61603
309-671-7300

Springfield Vet Center
624 S. 4th Street
Springfield, IL 62701
217-492-4955

East St. Louis Vet Center
1269 N. 89th Street, Suite 1
St. Louis, IL 62203
618-397-6602

Indiana

Regional Office:
Indianapolis Regional Office
575 N. Pennsylvania St.
Indianapolis, IN 46204
800-827-1000
317-226-7860

Vet Centers:
Fort Wayne Vet Center
528 West Berry St.
Fort Wayne, IN 46802
219-460-1465

Indianapolis Vet Center
3833 Meridian
Indianapolis, IN 46408
317-927-6440

Merillville Vet Center
6505 Broadway
Merillville, IN 46410
219-736-5633
Fax: 219-736-5936

Iowa

Regional Office:
Des Moines Regional Office
210 Walnut Street
Des Moines, IA 50309
800-827-1000
Cedar Rapids 319-378-0016
Des Moines 515-284-4929
Sioux City 712-255-3808

Kansas

Regional Office:
Wichita Regional Office
5500 E. Kellogg
Wichita, KS 67211
800-827-1000

Vet Center:
Wichita Vet Center
413 S. Pattie
Wichita, KS 67211
800-478-3381
316-265-3260

Kentucky

Regional Office:
Louisville Regional Office
545 S 3rd St.
Louisville, KY 40202
800-827-1000

Vet Centers:
Lexington Vet Center
301 East Vine St.
Suite C
Lexington, KY 40503
606-253-0717

Louisville Vet Center
1347 South 3rd St.
Louisville, KY 40208
502-634-1916

Louisiana

Regional Office:
New Orleans Regional Office
701 Loyola Regional Office
New Orleans, LA 70113
800-827-1000

Vet Centers:
New Orleans Vet Center
1529 N. Claiborne Avenue
New Orleans, LA 70116
504-943-8386

Shreveport Vet Center
2800 Youree Drive
LA Suite 1-105
Shreveport, LA 71104
318-861-1776

Maine

Medical and Regional Office:
Togus VA Medical/Regional
Office Center
Togus, ME 04330
207-623-8411
Bangor: 207-947-3391
Caribou: 207-496-3900
Lewiston: 207-783-0068

Portland: 207-780-3584
Sanford: 207-490-1513

Maryland
Regional Office:
Baltimore Regional Office
31 Hopkins Plaza Federal Building
Baltimore, MD 21201
800-827-1000

Vet Centers:
Baltimore Vet Center
6666 Security Blvd., Suite 2
Baltimore, MD 21207
410-277-3604

Cambridge Vet Center
5510 West Shore Drive
Cambridge, MD 21613
410-228-6305 ext 4123
Fax: 410-901-4011

Elkton Vet Center
103 Chesapeake Blvd., Suite A
Elkton, MD 21921
410-392-4485

Silver Spring Vet Center
1015 Spring Street, Suite 101
Silver Spring, MD 20910
301-589-1073

Massachusetts
Regional Office:
Boston VA Regional Office
JFK Federal Building,
Government Center
Boston, MA 02114
800-827-1000

Vet Centers:
Boston Vet Center
665 Beacon Street, Suite 100
Boston, MA 02215
617-424-0655

Brockton Vet Center
1041-L Pearl Street
Brockton, MA 02401
508-580-2730

Lowell Vet Center
Community Care Center
81 Bridge Street
Lowell, MA 01103
508-737-5167

Worchester Vet Center
1985 Lincoln Street
Worchester, MA 01605
508-856-7046

Michigan
Regional Office:
Detroit Regional Office
Patrick V. McNamara Federal Bldg.
477 Michigan Ave.
Detroit, MI 48226
800-827-1000

Vet Centers:
Dearborn Vet Center
2881 Monroe St.
Dearborn, MI 48124
313-277-1428
Fax: 313-277-5471

Detroit Vet Center
4161 Cass Ave.
Detroit, MI 48201
313-831-6509

Grand Rapids Vet Center
1940 Eastern Ave., SE
Grand Rapids, MI 49507
616-243-0385

Minnesota
Regional Office:
St. Paul Regional Office
1 Federal Drive, Fort Snelling
St. Paul, MN 55111
800-827-1000
Fax: 612-970-5415

Vet Centers:
Duluth Vet Center
405 East Superior St.
Duluth, MN 55802
218-722-8654

St. Paul Vet Center
2480 University Ave.
St. Paul, MN 5514
612-644-4022

Mississippi
Regional Office:
Jackson Regional Office
1600 E. Woodrow Wilson Ave.
Jackson, MS 39216
800-827-1000
601-364-7000

Vet Centers:
Biloxi Vet Center
313 Abbey Ct.
Biloxi, MS 39531
228-388-9938

Jackson Vet Center
4436 N. State St., Suite A3
Jackson, MS 39206
601-965-5727

Missouri
Regional Office:
St. Louis Regional Office
Federal Building
400 South 18th Street
St. Louis, MO 63103
800-827-1000

Vet Centers:
Kansas City Vet Center
3931 Main Street
Kansas, MO 64111
816-753-1866

St. Louis Vet Center
2345 Pine Street
St. Louis, MO 63103
314-231-1260
Fax: 314-289-6539

Montana
Regional Office:
Fort Harrison Medical and Regional Office
William Street off Highway
Fort Harrison, MT 59636
800-827-1000

Vet Centers:
Billings Vet Center
1234 Ave C
Billings, MT 59102
406-657-6071

Missoula Vet Center
500 N. Higgins Avenue
Missoula, MT 59802
406-721-4918

Nebraska
Regional Office:
Lincoln Vet Center
5631 South 48th Street
Lincoln, NE 68516
800-827-1000

Vet Centers:
Lincoln Vet Center
920 L. Street
Lincoln, NE 685008
402-476-9736

Omaha Vet Center
2428 Cuming St.
Omaha, NE 68131-1600
402-346-6735

Nevada
Regional Office:
Reno Regional Office
1201 Terminal Way
Reno, NV 89520
800-827-1000

Vet Centers:
Las Vegas Vet Center
704 S 6th Street
Las Vegas, NV 89101
702-388-6368
702-388-6369

Reno Vet Center
1155 W 4th Street, Suite 101
Reno, NV 89503
702-323-1294

New Hampshire
Regional Office:
Manchester Regional Office
Norris Cotton Federal Building
275 Chestnut ST.
Manchester, NH 03101
800-827-1000

Vet Center:
Manchester Vet Center
103 Liberty St.
Manchester, NH 03104
603-668-7060

New Jersey
Regional Office:
Newark Regional Office
20 Washington Place
Newark, NJ 07102
800-827-1000

Vet Centers:
Jersey City Vet Center
115 Christopher Columbus Dr., Room 200
Jersey, NJ 07302
201-645-2038

Newark Vet Center
157 Washington St.
Newark, NJ 07102
201-645-5954
Fax: 201-645-5932

Trenton Vet Center
171 Jersey St., Bldg 36A
Trenton, NJ 08611
609-989-2260

Ventnor Vet Center
6601 Ventnor Ave., Suite 401
Ventnor, NJ 08406
609-927-8387

New Mexico
Regional Office:
Albuquerque Regional Office
Danis Chavez Federal Building
500 Gold Avenue, SW
Albuquerque, NM 87102
800-827-1000

Vet Centers:
Albuquerque Vet Center
1600 Mountain Road NW
Albuquerque, NM 87104
505-766-6562

Farmington Vet Center
4251 E. Main, Suite B
Farmington, NM 87402
505-327-9684

Santa Fe Vet Center
2209 Brothers Rd.
Suite 110
Santa Fe, NM 87505
505-988-6562
Fax: 505-988-6564

New York
Regional Office:
Buffalo Regional Office
Federal Regional
111 W Huron St.
Buffalo, NY 14202
800-827-1000
Serves Counties not served by the New York, NY Regional Office.

New York Regional Office
245 W Houston St.
New York, NY 10014
800-827-1000
Serves the counties of Albany, Bronx, Clinton, Columbia, Delaware, Dutchess, Essex, Franklin, Fulton, Greene, Hamilton, Kings, Montgomery, Nassau, New York, Orange, Otsego Putnam, Queens, Rensselaer, Richmond, Rockland, Saratoga, Schenectady, Schoharie, Suffolk, Sullivan, Ulster, Warren, Washington, and Westchester.

Vet Centers:
Albany Vet Center
875 Central Ave.
Albany, NY 12206
518-438-2505

Babylon Vet Center
116 West Main Street
Babylon, NY 11702
516-661-3930

Bronx Vet Center
226 East Fordham Road
Bronx, NY 10468
718-367-3500

Brooklyn Vet Center
25 Chapel St.
Suite 604
Brooklyn, NY 11201
718-330-2825

Buffalo Vet Center
564 Franklin St.
Buffalo, NY 14202
716-882-0505

Manhattan Vet Center
201 Varick St., Room 707
New York, NY 10014
212-620-3306

Rochester Vet Center
134 South Fitzhugh St.
Rochester, NY 14614
716-263-5710

Staten Island Vet Center
150 Richmond Terrace
Staten Island, NY 10301
718-816-4499

Syracuse Vet Center
716 East Washington St.

Syracuse, NY 13203
315-478-7127

White Plains Vet Center
300 Hamilton Avenue
White Plains, NY 10601
914-682-6250

Queens Vet Center
75-108 91st Avenue
Woodhaven, NY 11421
718-296-2871

North Carolina
Regional Office:
Winston-Salem Regional Office
Federal Building, 251 N. Main St.
Winston-Salem, NC 27155
800-827-1000

Vet Centers:
Charlotte Vet Center
223 S. Brevard St., Suite 103
Charlotte, NC 28202
704-333-6107

Fayetteville Vet Center
4140 Ramsey Street
Suite 110
Fayetteville, NC 28311
910-488-6252

Greensboro Vet Center
2009 Elm-Eugene St.
Greensboro, NC 27406
910-333-5366

Greenville Vet Center
150 Arlington Blvd., Suite B
Greenville, NC 27858
919-355-7920

North Dakota
Medical and Regional Office:
Fargo VA Medical/Regional Office Center
2101 Elm Street
Fargo, ND 58102
800-827-1000

Vet Centers:
Bismarck Vet Center
1684 Capitol Way
Bismarck, ND 58501
701-224-9751

Fargo Vet Center
3310 Fiechtner Dr.
Suite 100
Fargo, ND 58103
701-237-0942

Minot Vet Center
3041 3rd Street, NW
Minot, ND 58703
701-852-0177

Ohio
Regional Office:
Cleveland Regional Office
A.J. Celebrezze Federal Building
1240 East 9th Street
Cleveland, OH 44199
800-827-1000

Vet Centers:
Cincinnati Vet Center #204
801 B. West 8th Street
Suite 126
Cincinnati, OH 45203
513-763-3500
Fax: 513-763-3505

Cleveland Vet Center
11511 Lorain Ave.
Cleveland, OH 44111
440-845-5023

Cleveland Heights Vet Center
2134 Lee Road
Cleveland Heights, OH 44118
216-932-8476

Columbus Vet Center #221
30 Spruce Street
Columbus, OH 43215
614-257-5550
Fax: 614-257-5551

Dayton Vet Center #225
111 W 1st Street
Dayton, OH 45402
937-461-9150
Fax 937-461-9371

Oklahoma
Regional Office:
Muskogee Regional Office
125 South Main Street
Muskogee, OK 74401
800-827-1000
Oklahoma City: 405-270-5184
Tulsa: 918-748-5105

Oregon
Regional Office:
Portland Regional Office
1220 SW 3rd Avenue
Portland, OR 97204
800-827-1000

Vet Centers:
Eugene Vet Center
1225 Pearl St., Suite 200
Eugene, OR 97401
541-465-6656

Grants Pass Vet Center
211 SE 10th Street
Grants Pass, OR 97526
541-479-6912

Portland Vet Center
8383 N.E. Sandy Blvd.
Suite 110
Portland, OR 97220
503-273-5370

Salem Vet Center
617 Chemeketa St. NE
Salem, OR 97301
503-362-9911

Pennsylvania
Regional Offices:
Philadelphia Regional Office and Insurance Center
5000 Wissahickon Avenue
Philadelphia, PA 19101
800-827-1000

Pittsburgh Regional Office
1000 Liberty Avenue
Pittsburgh, PA 15222
800-827-1000

Vet Centers:
Erie Vet Center
1000 State Street
Suite 1-2
Erie, PA 16501
814-453-7955

Harrisburg Vet Center
1500 North Second St.
Harrisburg, PA 17102
717-782-3954

McKeesport Vet Center
2001 Lincoln Way
Oak Park Mall (White Oak)

McKeesport, PA 15132
412-678-7704

Philadelphia Vet Center
801 Arch Street
Philadelphia, PA 19107
215-627-0238

Philadelphia Vet Center
101 E Olney Ave.
Box C-7
Philadelphia, PA 19120
215-924-4670

Pittsburgh Vet Center
954-Penn Ave.
Pittsburgh, PA 15222
412-765-1193

Scranton Vet Center
959 Wyoming Ave.
Scranton, PA 18509
570-344-2676

Philippines
Regional Office:
Manila Regional Office
1131 Roxas Blvd.
Pasay City, PI 96440
800-827-1000

Puerto Rico
Regional Office:
San Juan Regional Office
150 Carlos Chardon Avenue
Hato Ray, PR 00918
800-827-1000

Vet Centers:
Arecibo Vet Center
52 Gonzalo Marin St.
Arecibo, PR 00616
809-879-4510
809-879-4581

Ponce Vet Center
35 Mayor Street
Ponce, PR 00731
809-841-3260

San Juan/Rio Piedros Vet Center
Condomino Medical Center
Plaza
Suite LCBA, LC9, La Riviera
San Juan, PR 000921
787-783-8794

Rhode Island
Regional Office:
Providence Regional Office
380 Westminster Mall
Providence, RI 02903
800-827-1000

Vet Centers:
Cranston Vet Center
789 Park Avenue
Cranston, RI 09210
401-528-5271

Providence Vet Center
909 N. Main St.
Providence, RI 02904
401-528-5271

South Carolina
Regional Office:
Columbia Regional Office
1801 Assembly Street
Columbia, SC 29201
800-827-1000

Vet Centers:
Columbia Vet Center
1513 Pickens St.
Columbia, SC 29201
803-765-9944

Greenville Vet Center
14 Lavinia St.
Greenville, SC 29601
864-271-2711

North Charleston Vet Center
5603 A Rivers Ave.
North Charleston, SC 29418
803-747-8387

South Dakota
Regional Office:
Sioux Falls Regional Office
P.O. Box 5046
2501 W 22nd Street
Sioux Falls, SD 57117
800-827-1000

Vet Centers:
Rapid City Vet Center
621 Sixth St., Suite 101
Rapid City, SD 55701
605-348-0077

Sioux Falls Vet Center
601 South Cliffs Ave., Suite C
Sioux Falls, SD 57104
605-332-0856

Tennessee
Regional Office:
Nashville Regional Office
110 9th Avenue South
Nashville, TN 37203
800-827-1000

Vet Centers:
Chattanooga Vet Center
425 Cumberland St., Suite 140
Chattanooga, TN 37404
423-855-6570

Johnson City Vet Center
1615 A Market St.
Johnson City, TN 37604
615-928-8387

Knoxville Vet Center
2817 E. Magnolia Ave.
Knoxville, TN 37914
423-545-4680

Memphis Vet Center
1835 Union, Suite 100
Memphis, TN 38104
901-722-2510

Texas
Regional Offices:
Houston Regional Office
6900 Almeda Road
Houston, TX 77030
800-827-1000

Waco Regional Office
1 Veterans Plaza
701 Clay Ave.
Waco, TX 76799
800-827-1000

Vet Centers:
Amarillo Vet Center
3414 E. Olsen Blvd., Suite E
Amarillo, TX 79109
806-354-9779

Austin Vet Center
1110 W. William Canon Dr.
Austin, TX 78723
512-416-1314

Corpus Christi Vet Center
3166 Reid Dr., Suite 1

Corpus Christi, TX 78404
512-854-9961

Dallas Vet Center
5232 Forest Lane, Suite 111
Dallas, TX 75244
214-361-5896

El Paso Vet Center
Sky Park II
6500 Boeing, Suite L-112
El Paso, TX 79925
915-722-0013

Fort Worth Vet Center
1305 W. Magnolia, Suite B
Fort Worth, TX 76104
817-921-9095

Houston Vet Center
503 Westheimer
Houston, TX 77006
713-523-0884

Houston Vet Center
701 N. Post Oak Road
Houston, TX 77024
713-682-2288

Laredo Vet Center
6020 McPherson Road
Laredo, TX 78041
956-723-4680

Lubbock Vet Center
3208-34th St.
Lubbock, TX 79410
806-792-99782

McAllen Vet Center
1317-E. Hackberry Street
McAllen, TX 78501
956-631-2147

Midland Vet Center
3404-W. Illinois, Suite 1
Midland, TX 79703
915-697-8222

San Antonio Vet Center
231 W. Cypress Street
San Antonio, TX 78212
210-472-4025

Utah
Regional Office:
Salt Lake City Regional Office
125 South State Street
Salt Lake City, UT 84147
800-827-1000

Vet Centers:
Provo Vet Center
750 North 200 West, Suite 105
Provo, UT 84601
801-377-1117

Salt Lake City Vet Center
1354 East 3300 South
Salt Lake City, UT 84106
801-584-1294

Vermont
Regional Office:
White River Regional Office
N. Hartland Road
White River Junction, VT 05009
800-827-1000

Vet Centers:
South Burlington Vet Center
359 Dorset St.
Burlington, VT 05403
802-862-1806

Whit River Junction Vet Center
2 Holiday Drive
Gilman Office Building #2
White River Junction, VT 05001
802-295-2908

Virginia
Regional Office:
Roanoke Regional Office
210 Franklin Rd. SW
Roanoke, VA 24011
800-827-1000

Vet Centers:
Alexandria Vet Center
8796 D Sacramento Dr.
Alexandria, VA 22309
703-360-8633

Norfolk Vet Center
2200 Colonial Ave.
Suite 3
Norfolk, VA 23517
804-623-7584

Richmond Vet Center
3022 West Clay St.
Richmond, VA 23517
804-353-8958

Roanoke Vet Center
320 Mountain Ave. SW
Roanoke, VA 24016
703-342-9726

Virgin Islands
Vet Centers:
St. Croix Vet Center
Box 12, R.R. 02
Village Mall, #113
St. Croix, VI 00850
809-778-5553

St. Thomas Vet Center
Buccaneer Mall
St. Thomas, VI 00801
809-774-6674

Washington
Regional Office:
Seattle Regional Office
Federal Building
915 2nd Avenue
Seattle, WA 98174
800-827-1000

Vet Centers:
Bellingham Vet Center
3800 Byron, Suite 124
Bellingham, WA 98226
360-733-9226
Fax: 360-733-9117

Seattle Vet Center
2030 9th Avenue, Suite 210
Seattle, WA 98121
206-553-2706

Spokane Vet Center
100 N. Mullian Rd., Suite 102
Spokane, WA 99206
509-444-VETS

Tacoma Vet Center
4916 Center St., Suite E
Tacoma, WA 98409
253-565-7038

West Virginia
Regional Office:
Huntington Regional Office
640 Fourth Ave.
Huntington, WV 25701
800-827-1000

Vet Centers:
Beckley Vet Center

101 Ellison Ave.
Beckley, WV 25801
304-252-8220

Charleston Vet Center
512 Washington St. West
Charleston, WV 25302
304-343-3825

Huntington Vet Center
1005 6th Avenue
Huntington, WV 25701
304-523-8387

Martinsburg Vet Center
900 Winchester Ave.
Martinsburg, WV 25401
304-263-6776

Morgantown Vet Center
1083 Greenbag Rd.
Morgantown, WV 26508
304-291-4303

Mt. Gay Vet Center
Mt Gay, WV 25637
304-752-4453

Princeton Vet Center
905 Mercer St.
Princeton, WV 24740
304-232-0587

Wisconsin

Regional Office:
Milwaukee Regional Office
5000 West National Avenue
Milwaukee, WI 53295
800-827-1000

Vet Centers:
Madison Vet Center
147 S. Butler Street
Madison, WI 53703
608-264-5342

Milwaukee Vet Center
3400 Wisconsin
Milwaukee, WI 53208
414-344-5504

Wyoming

Medical and Regional Office:
Cheyenne VA Medical/Regional Office Center
2360 E. Pershing Blvd.
Cheyenne, WY 82001
800-827-1000

Vet Centers:
Casper Vet Center
111 S. Jefferson
Casper, WY 82601
307-261-5355

Cheyenne Vet Center
2424 Pioneer Ave.
Suite 103
Cheyenne, WY 82001
307-778-7370

APPENDIX

Don't know who to call or where to turn for assistance? Never fear; the Appendix is here! This is a state-by-state listing of starting places for any problem, concern, or issue you may have. We have included address, phone number and website wherever possible. Each listing should be able to either answer your question or direct you to an office near you. Happy hunting!

The ***Federal Information Center*** can connect you with the appropriate federal government agency that handles your topic of interest.

The ***State Information Operator*** can connect you to the correct state government office that can answer your question.

State Departments on Aging focus on issues and concerns of the senior population. If you are looking for nutrition, transportation, housing, financial assistance, nursing home resources, or anything else having to do with seniors, then contact this office. They will direct you to local services and resources, as well as tell you about programs offered by the state.

Attorney General's Offices have Consumer Protection Offices where you can call to complain or seek assistance for a problem dealing with a business in the state. Many of these offices have special automobile hotlines that handle car complaints.

Banking Commissioners are in charge of state banks. If you feel a state bank has not treated you fairly or you would like to do research on a bank before you hand over your life savings, then call the Banking Commissioner.

Child Care and Development Block Grant Agencies give money to states to help families meet their child care needs. Each state sets up their eligibility requirements and programs offered. To find out what your state provides in the way of child care assistance contact this office.

Child Support Enforcement Agencies are the people to contact if your ex has not been paying all of the child support payment. These offices can help track down your ex and get what you are owed — even across state lines.

The ***Cooperative Extension Service*** has offices located in almost every county across the U.S. and has a wealth of information regarding finances, child care, home economics, gardening, and more. Many operate special horticulture hotlines where you can find information concerning your garden, plants, and grass. They offer free or cheap courses and publications in cooking, sewing, financial planning and more.

Corporation Division Offices are the people that incorporate businesses in their state. If you are starting a business, you need to talk to this office. If you have a concern about a corporation in your state, they can provide you with information about the corporation's status. You can also find out who owes money to whom through the Uniform Commercial Code.

Day Care Licensing Agencies license daycare facilities in the state. Each state has their own rules the agencies must follow. Contact this agency to learn if a child care setting has had any violations or problems, and to inquire about the rules and regulations they must follow.

Economic Development Offices are a good place to start to learn about business assistance and financing programs offered through the state. Many have one-stop business assistance centers that will answer your licensing questions as well.

State Departments of Education are responsible for the elementary and secondary schools in the state. They can provide you with the amount spent per child, student-teacher ratio, test scores, experiences, and more concerning the different school districts.

The ***Departments of Higher Education*** are responsible for colleges and universities in the state and can tell you about accreditation concerns. This office usually has information regarding state scholarship and loan programs.

The ***Health Departments*** are in charge of various health programs offered by the state. They can direct you to local community services, and can answer questions regarding health statistics and other health information. If you cannot afford health insurance, this office can direct you to resources your state may have to provide coverage.

State Housing Offices have a variety of programs to help with the construction and purchase of homes. Contact this office to learn more, and to be referred to county and city offices that may have additional programs. If you are having a problem with your housing needs, call this office for assistance. This office can also refer you to rental assistance programs.

Insurance Commissioners enforce the laws and regulations for all kinds of insurance, and they also handle complaints from consumers. If you have a complaint about your insurance company's policies, and the company won't help you, contact the Insurance Commission in the state. This office can also let you know what insurance companies can do business in the state, and most have informative booklets to help you learn how to choose the best insurance coverage for you.

Labor Departments are in charge of the state's work force. They offer special job training programs to help people get the training they need and offer incentives to companies often in the form of training subsidies. Call this department if you are looking for a job to see what kinds of assistance programs your state offers.

Licensing Offices can provide you with information concerning various licensed professionals, and can direct you to the appropriate office for those professions covered by other agencies or boards. If you are having trouble with your beautician, contractor, veterinarian, or other professional, call this office.

One Stop Career Centers are located throughout the U.S. and offer career services to those looking for a job. Services vary from site to site, but most include help with resume writing, job skills training, job hunting assistance, and more.

Security Regulators license and regulate stock brokers and investment advisers in their state, as well as the securities these people offer and sell. This office can provide information on these various professionals, such as their current standing and will accept complaints, although they will usually only investigate to make sure no laws were broken. These offices usually have information for investors for assistance in making sound investment decisions.

Small Business Development Centers are located in over 700 cities across the U.S. and offer free or very low cost consulting services on most aspects of business ownership, including how to write a business plan, sell your idea, get government contracts, and more.

Social Services Offices are the ones in charge of child care programs, welfare, Medicaid, and other programs designed to help individuals and families get back on their feet. If you are struggling to make ends meet, contact this office to be directed to resources and services in your area.

Temporary Assistance to Needy Families (TANF) is the new office that replaced Aid to Families With Dependent Children (AFDC). This program helps people who need funds to pay for basic necessities as they enter job training programs, finish their education, or care for small children. Welfare-To-Work is often part of this program.

Transportation Departments are in charge of highways, road construction, and can direct you to those in charge of transportation systems and programs throughout their state. Many of these departments offer funds to local organizations to help fill some transportation needs in the community.

Unclaimed Property Offices hold money and other valuables that go unclaimed in the state. Unclaimed funds include savings and checking accounts, certificates of deposit, health insurance payments, stock and dividends, and more. If you think you or someone in your family may have missing funds, contact this office and they can do a search for you.

Unemployment Insurance Offices are the ones that distribute unemployment checks. Contact this office if you are eligible for the checks, want to appeal a denial, or need an extension of your benefits.

Utility Commissioners are in charge of the utility companies in the state. Many companies offer discounts and other special services to seniors or those in need. Contact your local utility company or this office to learn what is available.

In almost every state, there are ***Women's Commissions*** and similar groups that provide direction or assistance to women. Missions and programs vary, but these groups all share the goal of working toward eliminating the inequities that affect women at home and in the workplace. Some commissions are simply advocacy groups, bringing attention to issues that affect women and working to bring about legislative changes that would improve situations that women face. Others provide information and referrals to help women get ahead and some even provide direct services to help women get the training, education, and financial help they need to succeed.

ALABAMA

Federal Information Center
1-800-FED-INFO
www.firstgov.gov
www.pueblo.gsa.gov/call/

State Information Office
334-242-8000
www.state.al.us

Department on Aging
Department of Senior Services
770 Washington Ave., Suite 470
Montgomery, AL 36130
334-242-5743
877-425-2243
www.adss.state.al.us

Attorney General's Office
Office of the Attorney General
Alabama State House
11 South Union Street, 3rd Floor
Montgomery, AL 36130
334-242-7300
800-392-5658
www.ago.state.al.us

Banking Commissioner
State Banking Department
Center for Commerce
401 Adams Ave.
Montgomery, AL 36130
334-242-3452
www.bank.state.al.us

Child Care and Development Block Grant Lead Agency
Department of Human Resources
Family Services Division
50 Ripley St.
Montgomery, AL 36130
334-242-9500
www.dhr.state.al.us/fsd

Child Support Enforcement Agency
Department of Human Resources
Child Support Enforcement Division
P.O. Box 30400
Montgomery, AL 36130
334-242-9300
800-284-4347 (in AL and GA)
Fax: 334-242-0606
www.dhr.state.al.us/csed

Cooperative Extension Offices
Dr. W. Gaines Smith, Interim Director
Alabama Cooperative Extension Service
122 Duncan Hall
Auburn University
Auburn, AL 36849-5612
334-844-5690
www.aces.edu

Chinelle Henderson, Administrator
Alabama A&M University
Cooperative Extension Service
P.O. Box 222
Normal, AL 35762
205-851-5710
http://saes.aamu.edu/

Dr. Moore, Director
Cooperative Extension Program
U.S. Department of Agriculture
Tuskegee University
207 N. Main St., Suite 400
Tuskegee, AL 36083-1731
334-727-8808
www.tusk.edu/academics/cooperative_ext//

Corporation Division Office
Corporations Division
Secretary of State
11 S. Union St., Suite 207
Montgomery, AL 36103
334-242-5324
www.sos.state.al.us/business/corporations.cfm

Day Care Licensing Agency
Alabama Department of Human Resources
Office of Child Care
50 Ripley St.
Montgomery, AL 36130
334-242-9500
www.dhr.state.al.us/fsd/child_care.asp

Economic Development Office
Alabama Development Office
401 Adams Avenue, Suite 670
Montgomery, AL 36130-4106
800-248-0033
334-242-0400
Fax: 334-242-0415
www.ado.state.al.us

Alabama Department of Revenue
50 N. Ripley
Montgomery, AL 36132-7123
334-242-1170
www.ador.state.al.us/

Department of Education
Alabama Department of Education
50 N. Ripley
P.O. Box 302101
Montgomery, AL 36104
334-242-9700
www.alsde.edu/

Department of Higher Education
Alabama Commission on Higher Education
100 N. Union St.
P.O. Box 30200
Montgomery, AL 36130-2000
334-242-1998
Fax: 334-242-0268
www.ache.state.al.us

Health Department
Alabama Dept. of Public Health
RSA Tower
201 Monroe Street
Montgomery, AL 36104
MAILING ADDRESS:
RSA Tower
P.O. Box 303017
Montgomery, AL 36130-3017
334-206-5300
www.adph.org
Email:
webmaster@alapubhealth.org

Housing Office
Alabama Housing Finance Authority
P.O. Box 230909
Montgomery, AL 36123-0909
334-244-9200
800-325-AHFA
www.ahfa.com

Insurance Commissioner
Insurance Commissioner

201 Monroe St., Suite 1700
Montgomery, AL 36104
334-269-3550
800-243-5463
www.aldoi.org

Labor Department
Alabama Department of Economic Security
100 N. Union St.
P.O. Box 6123
Montgomery, AL 36130-3500
334-242-3460
www.alalabor.state.al.us

Licensing Office
Alabama Career Information Network System (ACINS)
401 Adams Ave.
P.O. Box 5690
Montgomery, AL 36103
334-242-5591
www.adeca.state.al.us/soicc/soicc/WEBSTAR3.0/SOICC/default.html

One-Stop Career Center
Department of Industrial Relations
649 Monroe Street
Montgomery, AL 36131
334-242-8990
Fax: 334-242-8843
www.dir.state.al.us
Email: webmaster@dir.state.al.us

Security Regulators
Alabama Securities Commission
770 Washington Ave., Suite 570
Montgomery, AL 36130-4700
334-242-2984
800-222-1253
www.nasdr.com/3450/3450_alabama.htm

Small Business Development Center
Alabama Small Business Development Consortium
University of Alabama at Birmingham
2800 Milan Ct.
Birmingham, AL 35211
205-943-6750
Email: sandefur@uab.edu
www.asbdc.org

Social Services Offices
Alabama Department of Human Resources
Office of Governmental Affairs and Public Information
Gordon Pearson Building
Suite 2104
50 N. Ripley St.
Montgomery, AL 36130
334-242-1850
www.dhr.state.al.us

Temporary Assistance to Needy Families (TANF)
Temporary Aid to Needy Families
Joel Sander
Alabama Department of Human Resources
Family Assistance Division
Gordon Pearson Bldg.
50 Ripley St.
Montgomery, AL 36130
334-242-1773
www.dhr.state.al.us/fad

Transportation Department
Alabama Department of Transportation
1409 Coliseum Blvd.
P.O. Box 303050
Montgomery, AL 36130-3050
334-242-6358
www.dot.state.al.us

William Luckerson
Alabama Department of Transportation
1409 Coliseum Blvd.
Montgomery, AL 36130-3050
334-242-6083
www.dot.state.al.us

Unclaimed Property Office
Unclaimed Property Division
RSA Union Bldg., Room 636
Montgomery, AL 31630
334-242-9614
888-844-8400
www.treasury.state.al.us/

Unemployment Insurance Office
Unemployment Compensation Division
Alabama Department of Industrial Relations
649 Monroe St., Room 3430H
Montgomery, AL 36131-0378
334-242-7953
www.dir.state.al.us/uc.htm
Weekly benefit range: $45-190
Duration of benefits: 15-26 weeks

Utility Commission (Energy Division)
Public Service Commission
P.O. Box 991
RSAUnion
100 N. Union St.
Montgomery, AL 36101-0991
334-242-5868
800-392-8050 (AL only)
www.psc.state.al.us

Women's Commission
Alabama Women's Commission
P.O. Box 10582
Birmingham, AL 35202
205-934-5286
Yvonne Agee, Chair
Email: yagee@FMS.uab.edu

Your Senator
United States Senate
Washington, DC 20510
202-224-3121
www.senate.gov

Your Representative
United States House of Representatives
Washington, DC 20515
202-224-3121
www.house.gov

ALASKA

Federal Information Center
1-800-FED-INFO
www.firstgov.gov
www.pueblo.gsa.gov/call/

State Information Office
907-465-2111
www.state.ak.us

Department on Aging
Alabama Commission on Aging
Division of Senior Services
Commission on Aging
P.O. Box 110209
Juneau, AK 99811-0209
907-465-3250
www.alaskaaging.org

Attorney General's Office
Office of the Attorney General
1031 West 4th Avenue, Suite 200
Juneau, AK 99501
P.O. Box 110300
Juneau, AK 99811-0300
907-465-3500
www.law.state.ak.us
Email: Attorney_General@law.
state.ak.us

Banking Commissioner
Division of Banking, Securities and
Corporations
P.O. Box 110807
Juneau, AK 99811-0807
907-465-2521
www.dced.state.ak.us/bsc/
contact.htm

Child Care and Development Block Grant Lead Agency
Alaska Department of Health and
Social Services
Division of Public Assistance
350 Main St., #311
Juneau, AK 99801
907-465-3329
Fax: 907-465-5254
www.hss.state.ak.us

Child Support Enforcement Agency
Barbar Miklos
Child Support Enforcement Division
550 West 7th Ave., Suite 310
Anchorage, AK 99501-6699
907-269-6900
800-478-3300
Fax: 907-269-6650
www.csed.state.ak.us/

Cooperative Extension Office
Hollis D. Hall, Director
Alaska Cooperative Extension
University of Alaska Fairbanks
P.O. Box 756180
Fairbanks, AK 99775-6180
907-474-7246
www.uaf.edu/coop-ext/

Corporation Division Office
State of Alaska
Division of Banking, Securities and
Corporation
Corporation Section
P.O. Box 110808
Juneau, AK 99811-0808
907-465-2530
www.dced.state.ak.us/bsc/
corps.htm

Day Care Licensing Agency
Department of Health and Social
Services
Office of Day Care Licensing
P.O. Box 110630
Juneau, AK 99811-0630
907-465-3170
www.hss.state.ak.us

Economic Development Office
Alaska Department of Commerce,
Community and Business
Development, and Economic
Development
P.O. Box 110800
Juneau, AL 98111
907-465-2017
800-478-LOAN
Fax: 907-465-3767
www.dced.state.ak.us/cbd/

Department of Education
Alaska Department of Education
Public Information
801 W. 10th St., Suite 200
Juneau, AK 99801-1894
907-465-2800
www.eed.state.ak.us

Department of Higher Education
Alaska Commission on
Postsecondary Education
3030 Vintage Boulevard
Juneau, AK 99801-7100
800-441-2962
907-465-2962
Fax: 407-465-5316
www.state.ak.us/acpe/home.html

Health Department
Alaska Department of Health &
Social Services
350 Main Street, Room 503
Juneau, AK 99801
MAILING ADDRESS:
P.O. Box 110610
Juneau, AK 99811-0610
907-465-3090
Fax: 907-586-1877
www.hss.state.ak.us/dph

Housing Office
Alaska Housing Finance Corporation
P.O. Box 101020
4300 Boniface Parkway
Anchorage, AK 99510-1020
907-330-8447
www.ahfc.state.ak.us

Insurance Commissioner
Director of Insurance
P.O. Box 110805
Juneau, AK 99811-0805
907-465-2515
Fax: 907-465-3422
www.dced.state.ak.us/insurance

Labor Department
Alaska Department of Labor
P.O. Box 21149
Juneau, AK 99802-1149
907-456-4855
www.labor.state.ak.us/

Licensing Office
Division of Occupational Licensing

Department of Commerce and
Economic Development
State of Alaska
P.O. Box 110806
Juneau, AK 99811-0806
907-465-2534
www.dced.state.ak.us/

One-Stop Career Center
Alaska Job Center Network
Department of Labor
P.O. Box 21149
Juneau, AK 99802-1149
907-456-4855
www.jobs.state.ak.us

Security Regulators
Division of Banking, Securities and Corporations
P.O. Box 110807
Juneau, AK 99801
907-465-2521
www.dced.state.ak.us/

Small Business Development Center
Alaska Small Business Development Center
University of Alaska Anchorage
510 L Street, Suite 310
Anchorage, AK 99501-3550
907-271-4022
Fax: 907-271-4545
www.sba.gov/ak/

Social Services Offices
Alaska Department of Health and Social Services
3601 "C" Street, Suite 578
P.O. Box 240249
Anchorage, AK 99524-0249
907-269-8950
Fax: 907-562-1619
www.hss.state.ak.us

Temporary Assistance to Needy Families (TANF)
Temporary Aid to Needy Families
Jim Nordlund
Alaska Department of Health and Social Services
P.O. Box 110640
Juneau, AK 99811-0640
907-465-3347
www.hss.state.ak.us/dpa

Transportation Department
Bruce Wells
Alaska Department of Transportation and Public Facilities
3132 Channel Dr., Room 200
Juneau, AK 99801
907-465-3900
www.dot.state.ak.us

Tom Brigham
Alaska Department of Transportation and Public Facilities
3132 Channel Dr., Room 200
Juneau, AK 99801
907-465-3900
www.dot.state.ak.us

Unclaimed Property Office
Department of Revenue
Unclaimed Property Unit
P.O. Box 110405
Juneau, AK 99811-0405
907-465-3726
www.revenue.state.ak.us

Unemployment Insurance Office
Unemployment Insurance Program Manager
Employment Security Division
P.O. Box 25510
Juneau, AK 99802-5510
907-465-5552
888-252-2557
www.labor.state.ak.us
Weekly benefit range: $44-248
Duration of benefits: 16-26 weeks

Utility Commission
Regulatory Commission of Alaska
701 West 8th Ave., Suite 300
Anchorage, AK 99501
907-276-6222
www.state.ak.us/apuc/

Women's Commission
Safe City
Anchorage Women's Commission
Dept. of Health and Human Services
P.O. Box 196650
Anchorage, AK 99519-6650
907-343-6589
Fax: 907-343-6730
www.muni.org

Your Senator
United States Senate
Washington, DC 20510
202-224-3121
www.senate.gov

Your Representative
United States House of Representatives
Washington, DC 20515
202-224-3121
www.house.gov

ARIZONA

Federal Information Center
1-800-FED-INFO
www.firstgov.gov
www.pueblo.gsa.gov/call/

State Information Office
602-542-4900
www.state.az.us

Department on Aging
Aging and Adult Administration
Arizona Dept. of Economic Security
1789 W. Jefferson
Phoenix, AZ 85007
602-542-4446
Fax: 602-542-6474
www.de.state.az.us

Attorney General's Office
Office of the Attorney General
Department of Law
1275 West Washington Street
Phoenix, AZ 85007
602-542-5025
800-352-8431
www.ag.state.az.us
Email: ag.inquiries@ag. state.az.us

Banking Commissioner
Superintendent of Banks
2910 N. 44th St., Suite 310
Phoenix, AZ 85018
602-255-4421
800-544-0708 (toll free in AZ)
www.azbanking.com

Child Care and Development Block Grant Lead Agency
Department of Economic Security
Child Care Administrator
3150 E. Union Hills
Phoenix, AZ 85020
602-569-4719
Fax: 602-542-4197
www.de.state.az.us/

Child Support Enforcement Agency
Nancy Mendoza
Division of Child Support Enforcement
Department of Economic Security
P.O. Box 40458
Site Code 021A
Phoenix, AZ 85067
602-252-4045
800-882-4151
www.de.state.az.us/

Cooperative Extension Office
Jim Christenson, Director
Cooperative Extension Office
University of Arizona, Forbes 301
Tucson, AZ 85721
520-621-7205
http://ag.arizona.edu/extension

Corporation Division Office
Arizona Corporation Commission
Secretary of State
1300 W. Washington
Phoenix, AZ 85007
602-542-3026
www.cc.state.az.us/corp/ index.htm

Day Care Licensing Agency
State Department of Health Services
Office of Child Care Licensure
1647 E. Morten Ave., Suite 230
Phoenix, AZ 85020
602-674-4340
www.hs.state.az.us/als/ childcare/ index.htm

Economic Development Office
Department of Commerce
3800 N. Central, Suite 1500
Phoenix, AZ 85012
602-280-1300
800-542-5684
Fax: 620-280-1339
www.commerce.state.az.us/

Department of Education
Arizona Department of Education
Research and Policy Division
1535 W. Jefferson
Phoenix, AZ 85007
602-542-5151
www.ade.state.az.us/

Department of Higher Education
Arizona Commission for Postsecondary Education
2020 North Central, Suite 550
Phoenix, AZ 85004-4503
602-258-2435
Fax: 602-258-2483
www.acpe.asu.edu

Health Department
Arizona Department of Health Services
Office of Women's and Children's Health
411 North 24th Street
Phoenix, AZ 85008
602-220-6550
Fax: 602-220-6551
TDD: 602-256-7577
www.hs.state.az.us/cfhs/owch/ index.html

Housing Office
Arizona Dept. of Commerce
Office of Housing Development
3800 N. Central, Suite 1500
Phoenix, AZ 85012
602-280-1300
www.state.az.us/ commerce

Insurance Commissioner
Director of Insurance
2910 N. 44th St., Suite 210
Phoenix, AZ 85018
602-912-8444
800-325-2548
www.state.az.us/id/

Labor Department
Arizona Department of Economic Security
1789 West Jefferson, 1 NE
Phoenix, AZ 85007
602-542-3871
www.de.state.az.us

Licensing Office
Registrar of Contractors
800 W. Washington St., 6th Floor
Phoenix, AZ 85007
602-542-1525
www.rc.state.az.us

One-Stop Career Center
One Stop Career Center

Arizona Department of Economic Security
P.O. Box 6123
Site Code 901A
Phoenix, AZ 85005
602-542-1250
www.de.state.az.us/oscc/ index.html
Email: onestop@de.state.az.us

Security Regulators
Arizona Corporation Commission
1300 W. Washington St.. 3rd Floor
Phoenix, AZ 85007
602-542-4242
www.ccsd.cc.state.az.us

Small Business Development Center
Arizona Small Business Development Center Network
Maricopa County Community Colleges
Small Business Development Center
2411 West 14th Street
Tempe, AZ 85281
480-731-8720
Fax: 480-230-7989
Email: york@maricopa.edu
www.dist.maricopa.edu/sbdc

Social Services Offices
Arizona Department of Economic Security
P.O. Box 6123
Site Code 0862
Phoenix, AZ 85005
602-542-4296
www.de.state.az.us

Temporary Assistance to Needy Families (TANF)
Temporary Aid to Needy Families
Social Services Block Grant
Arizona Department of Economic Security
1717 West Jefferson St.
Box 6123
Phoenix, AZ 85005
602-542-3678
www.de.state.az.us

Transportation Department
Katie Dusenberry
Arizona Department of Transportation
206 South 17th Ave.
Suite 340-B
Phoenix, AZ 85007
520-747-1400
www.dot.state.az.us

Ingo Radicke
Arizona Department of Transportation
206 South 17th Ave.
Suite 340-B
Phoenix, AZ 85007
540-425-6280
www.dot.state.az.us

Unclaimed Property Office
Department of Revenue
Unclaimed Property Unit
1600 West Monroe
Phoenix, AZ 85007
602-364-0380
877-492-9957
www.revenue.state.az.us/unclm/unclprop.htm

Unemployment Insurance Office
ESA Administrator
P.O. Box 29225
Phoenix, AZ 85038
602-364-2722
www.de.state.az.us/links/esa/index.html
Weekly benefit range: $40-205
Duration of benefits: 12-26 weeks

Utility Commission
Corporation Commission
1200 W. Washington St.
Phoenix, AZ 85007-2996
602-542-4251
800-222-7000 (AZ only)
www.cc.state.az.us/utility/ index.htm

Women's Commission
Phoenix Women's Commission
Equal Opportunity Department
251 West Washington, 7th Floor
Phoenix, AZ 85003-6211
602-261-8242
Fax: 602-256-3389
www.ci.phoenix.az.us/PHXWOMEN/index.html

Tucson Women's Commission
240 North Court Ave.
Tucson, AZ 85701
520-624-8318
Fax: 520-624-5599
Email: tctwc@starnet.com
Neema Caughran, Exec. Director
Louisa Hernandez, Chair

Your Senator
United States Senate
Washington, DC 20510
202-224-3121
www.senate.gov

Your Representative
United States House of Representatives
Washington, DC 20515
202-224-3121
www.house.gov

ARKANSAS

Federal Information Center
1-800-FED-INFO
www.firstgov.gov
www.pueblo.gsa.gov/call/

State Information Office
501-682-3000
www.state.ar.us

Department on Aging
Division of Aging and Adult Services
Box 1437, Slot S-530
Little Rock, AR 72203
501-682-2441
Fax: 501-682-8155
www.state.ar.us/dhs/aging/index.html

Attorney General's Office
Office of the Attorney General
323 Center Street, Suite 200
Little Rock, AR 72201
501-682-2007
800-482-8982
www.ag.state.ar.us
Email: oag@ag.state.ar.us

Banking Commissioner
Bank Commissioner
400 Hardin Rd., Suite 100
Little Rock, AR 72201
501-324-9019
www.state.ar.us/bank/

Child Care and Development Block Grant Lead Agency
Arkansas Department of Human Services
Division of Child Care and Early Childhood Education
P.O. Box 1437, Slot S-140
Little Rock, AR 72203
501-682-4891
Fax: 501-682-4897/2317
www.state.ar.us/childcare

Child Support Enforcement Agency
Dan McDonald
Office of Child Support Enforcement
Division of Revenue
400 E. Capitol
P.O. Box 8133
Little Rock, AR 72203
501-682-6169
800-264-2445 (in AR)
Fax: 501-682-6002
www.state.ar.us/dfa/childsupport/index.html

Cooperative Extension Offices
David Foster, Director
Cooperative Extension Service
P.O. Box 391
Little Rock, AR 72203
501-671-2000
www.uaex.edu

Corporation Division Office
Secretary of State
Corporations Division
Aegon Bldg., Suite 310
501 Woodlane
Little Rock, AR 72201
501-682-3409
888-233-0325
www.sosweb.state.ar.us

Day Care Licensing Agency
State Department of Human Services
Child Care Licensing Unit
P.O. Box 1437
Slot 720
Little Rock, AR 72203-1437
501-682-8590
www.state.ar.us/childcare

Economic Development Office
Arkansas Economic Development Commission
1 State Capitol Mall
Little Rock, AR 72201
501-682-1121
Fax: 501-682-7394
www.aedc.state.ar.us

Department of Education
Arkansas Department of Education
Office of Accountability
4 State Capitol Mall, 204-B
Little Rock, AR 72201
501-682-4475
http://arkedu.state.ar.us

Department of Higher Education
Arkansas Department of Higher Education
114 East Capitol
Little Rock, AR 72201
501-371-2000
Fax: 501-371-2001
www.arkansashighered.com

Health Department
Arkansas Department of Health
4815 West Markham
Little Rock, AR 72201
501-661-2000
800-482-5400
www.healthyarkansas.com/
Email: wbankson@ mail.doh.state.ar.us

Housing Office
Arkansas Development Finance Authority
P.O. Box 8023
100 Main St., Suite 200
Little Rock, AR 77201
501-682-5900
www.accessarkansas.org/adfa

Insurance Commissioner
Insurance Commissioner
Arkansas Insurance Department
1200 W. 3rd St.
Little Rock, AR 72201
501-371-2640
800-852-5494
www.state.ar.us/insurance/

Labor Department
Arkansas Department Of Labor
10421 West Markham
Little Rock, AR 72205
501-682-4500
Fax: 501-682-4535
www.ark.org/labor

Licensing Office
Boards and Commissions
Governor's Office
State Capitol Building
Little Rock, AR 72201
501-682-3570
www.state.ar.us/governor

One-Stop Career Center
Arkansas Career Development Network
Arkansas Employment Security Department
#1 Pershing Circle
Little Rock, AR 72114
501-682-2121
Fax: 501-682-2273
www.state.ar.us/esd/

Security Regulators
Arkansas Securities Department
Heritage West Building
201 East Markham, Suite 300
Little Rock, AR 72201
501-324-9260
www.accessarkansas.org/arsec

Small Business Development Center
Arkansas Small Business Development Center
University of Arkansas at Little Rock
Little Rock Technology Center Building
100 South Main, Suite 401
Little Rock, AR 72201
501-324-9043
Fax: 501-324-9049
Email: jmnye@ualr.edu
www.asbac.ualr.edu

Social Services Offices
Arkansas Department of Human Services
Donaghey Plaza West
Slot 5201
P.O. Box 1437
Little Rock, AR 72203-1437
501-682-8650
www.state.ar.us/dhs/

Temporary Assistance to Needy Families (TANF)
Temporary Aid to Needy Families
Arkansas Department of Human Services
TEA Support Center
101 East Capitol
P.O. Box 1437, Slot 1230
Little Rock, AR 72203-1437
501-682-8299
www.state.ar.us/dhs/tea/

Transportation Department
James Gilbert
Arkansas State Highway and Transportation Department
P.O. Box 2261
Little Rock, AR 72203
501-569-2000
Fax: 501-569-2400
www.ahtd.state.ar.us

Unclaimed Property Office
Auditor of State
Unclaimed Property Division
1400 West 3rd, Suite 100
Little Rock, AR 72201
501-682-6000
800-252-4648
www.accessarkansas.org/auditor

Unemployment Insurance Office
Unemployment Insurance Director
Arkansas Employment Security Department
P.O. Box 2981
Little Rock, AR 72203
501-682-3200
www.accessarkansas.org/esd
Weekly benefit range: $47-264
Duration of benefits: 9-26 weeks

Utility Commission
Public Service Commission
1000 Center St.
P.O. Box 400
Little Rock, AR 72203-0400
501-682-2051
800-482-1164 (AR only)
www.accessarkansas.org/psc

Women's Commission
Closed 96-99

Your Senator
United States Senate
Washington, DC 20510
202-224-3121
www.senate.gov

Your Representative
United States House of Representatives
Washington, DC 20515
202-224-3121
www.house.gov

CALIFORNIA

Federal Information Center
1-800-FED-INFO
www.firstgov.gov
www.pueblo.gsa.gov/call/

State Information Office
916-322-9900
www.state.ca.us

Department on Aging
California Department of Aging
1600 K St.
Sacramento, CA 95814
916-322-3887
Fax: 916-324-4989
www.aging.state.ca.us/

Attorney General's Office
Office of the Attorney General
P.O. Box 944255
Sacramento, CA 94244-2550
916-322-3360
800-952-5225
http://caag.state.ca.us

Banking Commissioner
Department of Financial Institutions
111 Pine St., Suite 1100
San Francisco, CA 94111-5613
415-263-8500
800-622-0620 (toll free in CA)
www.dfi.ca.gov

Child Care and Development Block Grant Lead Agency
Child Development Division
California Dept. of Education
560 J Street, Room 220
Sacramento, CA 95814-4785
916-322-6233
Fax: 916-323-6853
www.cde.ca.gov/cyfsbranch/child_development/

Child Support Enforcement Agency
Leslie Frye
California Department of Child Support Services
P.O. Box 419064
Rancho Cordova, CA 95741-9064
916-464-5050
866-249-0773 (in CA)
www.childsup.cahwnet.gov

Cooperative Extension Office
Kenneth Farrell, Vice President
University of California
Division of Agriculture and Natural Resources
300 Lakeside Drive, 6th Floor
Oakland, CA 94612-3560
510-987-0060
www.ucanr.org
(programs are at county level)

Corporation Division Office
Corporations Unit
Secretary of State
1500 11th St.
Sacramento, CA 95814
916-657-5448
www.ss.ca.gov/business/business.htm

Day Care Licensing Agency
Department of Social Services
Community Care Licensing Division
744 P St., Mail Station 19-50
Sacramento, CA 95814
916-657-3667
www.dss.cahwnet.gov/ default.htm

Economic Development Office
California Trade and Commerce Agency
1102 Q Street, Suite 6000
Sacramento, CA 95814
916-324-3788
http://commerce.ca.gov

Department of Education
California Department of Education
721 Capitol Mall
P.O. Box 944272
Sacramento, CA 95814
916-657-2676
www.cde.ca.gov/

Department of Higher Education
California Student Aid Commission
P.O. Box 419026
Rancho Cordova, CA 95741-9026
916-526-7590
Fax: 916-526-8002
www.csac.ca.gov

Health Department
California Department of Health Services
Office of Women's Health
714 P Street, Room 792
Sacramento, CA 95814
906-653-3330
Fax: 916-653-3535
www.dhs.ca.gov/director/ouh/index

Housing Offices
California Housing Finance Agency
1121 L St., 7th Floor
Sacramento, CA 95814
916-322-3991
www.chfa.ca.gov

California Department of Housing and Community Development
P.O. Box 952054
Sacramento, CA 94252-2054
916-445-4782
http://housing.hcd.ca.gov

Insurance Commissioner
Commissioner of Insurance
300 S. Spring St., 13th Floor
Los Angeles, CA 90013
916-492-3500 (Sacramento)
213-897-8921
800-927-HELP (complaints)
www.insurance.ca.gov/

Labor Department
California Employment Development Department
800 Capital Mall
Sacramento, CA 95814
800-758-0398
www.edd.cahwnet.gov/

Licensing Office
State of California
Department of Consumer Affairs
400 R St.
Sacramento, CA 95814

916-445-1254
800-952-5210
www.dca.ca.gov

One-Stop Career Center
One-Stop Office
800 Capitol Mall, MIC 83
Sacramento, CA 95814
800-758-0398
Fax: 916-654-9863
www.sjtcc.cahwnet.gov/SJTCCWEB/ONE-STOP/
Email: onestop@edd.ca.gov

Security Regulators
Department of Corporations
1515 K Street, Suite 200
Sacramento, CA 95814-4052
916-445-7205
www.corp.ca.gov

Small Business Development Center
California Small Business Development Center
California Trade and Commerce Agency
801 K Street, Suite 1700
Sacramento, CA 95814
916-324-5068
800-303-6600
Fax: 916-322-5084
www.sbdc.net

Social Services Offices
California Department of Social Services
Office of Community Relations
744 P Street
M.S. 17-02
Sacramento, CA 95814
916-657-3667
www.dss.cahwnet.gov

Temporary Assistance to Needy Families (TANF)
Temporary Aid to Needy Families
Eloise Anderson
California Department of Social Services
744 P Street
Mail Station 17-11
Sacramento, CA 95814
916-657-3661
www.dss.cahwnet.gov/cdssweb

Transportation Department
Jeff Morales
California Department of Transportation - CALTRANS
P.O. Box 942873
Sacramento, CA 94273-0001
916-654-5266
www.dot.ca.gov

Tory Harris
California Department of Transportation - CALTRANS
P.O. Box 942873
Sacramento, CA 94273-0001
916-654-5266
www.dot.ca.gov

Unclaimed Property Office
Division of Collections
Bureau of Unclaimed Property
P.O. Box 942850
Sacramento, CA 94250
916-445-2636
800-992-4647
www.sco.ca.gov

Unemployment Insurance Office
Unemployment Insurance
Employment Development Department
800 Capitol Mall, MIC 83
Sacramento, CA 95814
800-758-0398
www.edd.ca.gov/uifc.htm
Weekly benefit range: $40-230
Duration of benefits: 12-26 weeks

Utility Commission
Public Utilities Commission
505 Van Ness Ave.
San Francisco, CA 94102
415-703-2782
www.cpuc.ca.gov

Women's Commission
California Commission on the Status of Women
1303 J St., Suite 400
Sacramento, CA 95814-2900
916-445-3173
Fax: 916-322-9466
Email: csw@sna.com
www.statusofwomen.ca.gov
Elmy Bermejo, Chair

Your Senator
United States Senate
Washington, DC 20510
202-224-3121
www.senate.gov

Your Representative
United States House of Representatives
Washington, DC 20515
202-224-3121
www.house.gov

COLORADO

Federal Information Center
1-800-FED-INFO
www.firstgov.gov
www.pueblo.gsa.gov/call/

State Information Office
303-866-5000
www.state.co.us

Department on Aging
Office of Adult and Veterans Services
Social Services Department
1575 Sherman St., Room 816
Denver, CO 80203
303-866-2557
Fax: 303-866-4214
www.cdhs.state.co.us/

Attorney General's Office
Office of the Attorney General
Department of Law
1525 Sherman Street, 7th Floor
Denver, CO 80203
303-866-4500
Fax: 303-866-5691
www.ago.state.co.us

Banking Commissioner
State Bank Commissioner
Division of Banking
Denver Post Bldg.
1560 Broadway, Suite 1175
Denver, CO 80202
303-894-7575
Fax: 303-894-7570
www.dora.state.co.us/banking

Child Care and Development Block Grant Lead Agency
Office of Child Care Services
Colorado Dept. of Human Services
1575 Sherman St.
Denver, CO 80203-1714
303-866-5958
Fax: 303-866-4453
www.cdhs.state.co.us/childcare/home.html

Child Support Enforcement Agency
Pauline Burton
Division of Child Support Enforcement
Department of Human Services
1575 Sherman St., Second Floor
Denver, CO 80203
303-866-5992
303-866-2214
www.childsupport.state.co.us/

Cooperative Extension Office
Milan Rewets, Director
Colorado State University Cooperative Extension
1 Administration Building
Fort Collins, CO 80523
970-491-6281
www.ext.colostate.edu

Corporation Division Office
Corporate Division
Secretary of State
1560 Broadway, Suite 200
Denver, CO 80202
303-894-2200
www.sos.state.co.us/

Day Care Licensing Agency
State Department of Human Services
Office of Social Services
Child Care Licensing
1575 Sherman St.
Denver, CO 80203-1714
303-866-5958
www.cdhs.state.co.us/childcare/licensing.htm

Economic Development Office
Office of Economic Development and International Trade
1625 Broadway, Suite 1710
Denver, CO 80202
303-892-3840
Fax: 303-892-3848
TDD: 800-659-2656
www.state.co.us/gov_dir/oed.html

Department of Education
Colorado Department of Education
Planning and Evaluation Unit
201 E. Colfax
Denver, CO 80203-1799
303-866-6600
www.cde.state.co.us/

Department of Higher Education
Colorado Commission on Higher Education
1380 Lawrence St., Suite 1200
Denver, CO 80204
303-866-2723
www.state.co.us/cche_dir/hecche.html

Health Department
Colorado Department of Public Health & Environment
4300 Cherry Creek Drive South
Denver, CO 80246-1530
303-692-2035
www.cdphe.state.co.us/

Housing Office
Colorado Housing and Finance Authority
1981 Blake St.
Denver, CO 80202-1272
303-297-2432
www.colohfa.org

Insurance Commissioner
Commissioner of Insurance
1560 Broadway, Suite 850
Denver, CO 80202
303-894-7499
800-930-3745
Fax: 303-894-7455
www.dora.state.co.us/insurance/index.htm

Labor Department
Colorado Department of Labor and Employment
1515 Arapahoe
Tower 2, Suite 400
Denver, CO 80202
303-318-8000
www.cdle.state.co.us

Licensing Office
Department of Regulatory Agencies
State Services Building

1560 Broadway, Suite 1550
Denver, CO 80202
303-894-7855
Fax: 303-894-7885
www.dora.state.co.us

One-Stop Career Center
Job Service Centers
Colorado Department of Labor and Employment
Office of Employment and Training
1515 Arapahoe Street
Tower 2, Suite 400
Denver, CO 80202-2117
303-318-8000
Fax: 303-620-4257
http://navigator.cdle.state.co.us

Security Regulators
Division of Securities
1580 Lincoln St.
Suite 420
Denver, CO 80203
303-894-2320
www.dora.state.co.us/Securities/index.htm

Small Business Development Center
Colorado Small Business Development Center
Office of Business Development
1625 Broadway, Suite 1710
Denver, CO 80202
303-892-3864
800-333-7798
Fax: 303-892-3848
www.state.co.us/oed/sbdc

Social Services Offices
Colorado Department of Human Services
1575 Sherman Street
Denver, CO 80203-1714
303-866-5700
Fax: 303-866-4740
www.cdhs.state.co.us

Temporary Assistance to Needy Families (TANF)
Temporary Aid to Needy Families
Sue Tuffin
Colorado Department of Human Services
1575 Sherman St., Third Floor
Denver, CO 80203
303-866-5981
www.cdhs.state.co.us/oss/Self_Sufficiency.html

Transportation Department
Pat Loose
Colorado Department of Transportation
4201 East Arkansas Ave.
Room 212
Denver, CO 80222
303-757-9769
www.dot.state.co.us

Unclaimed Property Office
Unclaimed Property Division
The Great Colorado Payback
1120 Lincoln St., Suite 1004
Denver, CO 80203
303-894-2448
800-825-2111
www.treasurer.state.co.us/payback/index.htm

Unemployment Insurance Office
Office of Unemployment Insurance
1515 Arapahoe St.
Tower 2, Suite 400
Denver, CO 80202
303-318-8000
http://unempben.cdle. state.co.us
Weekly benefit range: $25 -272
Duration of benefits: 13-26 weeks

Utility Commission
Public Utilities Commission
1580 Logan St.
Logan Tower, Office Level 2
Denver, CO 80203
303-894-2000
800-888-0170 (CO only)
Fax: 303-894-2065
www.dora.state.co.us/PUC/index.htm

Women's Commission
Denver Women's Commission
303 West Colfax, Suite 1600
Denver, CO 80204
720-913-8450
Fax: 303-640-4627
www.denvergov.org/
Chaer Robert, Director

Fort Collins City Commission on the Status of Women
c/o Human Resources
City of Ft. Collins
P.O. Box 580
Fort Collins, CO 80522
970-221-6871
970-224-6050
www.ci.fort-collins.co.us
Laurie Fonken-Joseph, Chair

Your Senator
United States Senate
Washington, DC 20510
202-224-3121
www.senate.gov

Your Representative
United States House of Representatives
Washington, DC 20515
202-224-3121
www.house.gov

CONNECTICUT

Federal Information Center
1-800-FED-INFO
www.firstgov.gov
www.pueblo.gsa.gov/call/

State Information Office
860-240-0222
www.state.ct.us

Department on Aging
Elderly Services
Department of Social Services
25 Sigourney St.
Hartford, CT 06106-5033
860-424-5277
800-994-9422
www.ctelderlyservices.state.ct.us

Attorney General's Office
Office of the Attorney General
55 Elm Street
P.O. Box 120
Hartford, CT 06141-0120
860-808-5318
Fax: 860-808-5387
www.cslib.org/attygenl
Email: attorney.general@
po.state.ct.us

Banking Commissioner
Banking Commissioner
260 Constitution Plaza
Hartford, CT 06103-1800
860-240-8100
800-831-7225 (toll free in CT)
www.state.ct.us/ dob/

Child Care and Development Block Grant Lead Agency
Office of Child Care
Connecticut Dept. of Social Services
25 Sigourney St., 10th Floor
Hartford, CT 06106-5033
860-424-5598
Fax: 860-951-2996
www.dss.state.ct.us/ccare/
ccare.htm

Child Support Enforcement Agency
Diane Fray
Bureau of Child Support
Enforcement
Department of Social Services
25 Sigourney St.
Hartford, CT 06106
860-424-5251
860-951-2996
800-228-5437
www.dss.state.ct.us/csrc/csrc.htm

Cooperative Extension Office
Associate Director
Cooperative Extension System
University of Connecticut
1376 Storrs Road
Storrs, CT 06269-4036
860-486-6271
www.canr.uconn.edu/ces/ index.html

Corporation Division Office
Office of Secretary of State
Commercial Recording Division
30 Trinity St.
Hartford, CT 06106
860-509-6001
www.sots.state.ct.us

Day Care Licensing Agency
State of Connecticut Department of
Public Health
Child Day Care Licensing
410 Capital Ave.
MS #12DAC
P.O. Box 340308
Hartford, CT 06134-3038
860-509-8045
www.dph.state.ct.us

Economic Development Office
Economic Resource Center
Department of Economic and
Community Development
805 Brooks St., Bldg. 4
Rocky Hill, CT 06067-3405
860-571-7136
800-392-2122
Fax: 860-571-7150
www.cerc.com

Department of Education
Connecticut Department of Education
Public Information Office
165 Capitol Ave.
Hartford, CT 06145
860-713-6548
www.state.ct.us/sde/

Department of Higher Education
Department of Higher Education
61 Woodland Street
Hartford, CT 06105-2326
860-947-1800
Fax: 860-947-1310
www.ctdhe.org

Health Department
Connecticut Dept. of Public Health
410 Capitol Avenue
P.O. Box 340308
Hartford, CT 06134-0308
860-509-8000
TDD: 860-509-7191
www.state.ct.us/dph/

Housing Office
Connecticut Housing Finance
Authority
999 West St.
Rocky Hill, CT 06067-4005
860-721-9501
www.chfa.org

Insurance Commissioner
Insurance Commissioner
P.O. Box 816
Hartford, CT 06142-0816
860-297-3800
800-203-3447
Fax: 860-560-7410
www.state.ct.us/cid/

Labor Department
Connecticut Department of Labor
200 Folly Brook Blvd.
Wethersfield, CT 06109-1114
860-263-6000
www.ctdol.state.ct.us

Licensing Office
Occupational Licensing Division
Department of Consumer Protection
165 Capitol Ave.
Hartford, CT 06106
860-713-6000
Fax: 860-713-7239
www.dcp.state.ct.us/licensing

One-Stop Career Center
Connecticut Works
Connecticut Department of Labor
200 Folly Brook Boulevard
Wethersfield, CT 06109
860-263-6000
www.ctdol.state.ct.us/ctworks/
ctworks.htm
Email: dol.help@po.state.ct.us

Security Regulators
Department of Banking
260 Constitution Plaza
Hartford, CT 06013-1800
860-240-8230
800-831-7225
www.state.ct.us/dob

Small Business Development Center
Connecticut Small Business
Development Center
University of Connecticut
School of Business Administrtion
2100 Hillside Rd., Unit 1094
Storrs, CT 06269-1094
860-486-4135
Fax: 860-486-1576
Email: CSBDinformation@
sba.uconn.edu
www.sbdc.uconn.edu

Social Services Offices
Connecticut Department of Social
Services
25 Siqourney Street
Hartford, CT 06106
860-424-5010
www.dss.state.ct.us

Temporary Assistance to Needy Families (TANF)
Temporary Aid To Needy Families
Patricia Wilson-Cooker
Connecticut Department of Social
Services
25 Sigourney St.
Hartford, CT 06106
860-424-5008
800-842-1508
www.dss.state.ct.us/svcs/tanf.htm

Transportation Department
Lynn DiNallo
Connecticut Department of
Transportation
P.O. Box 317546
2800 Berlin Turnpike
Newington, CT 06131-7546
806-594-2000
www.state.ct.us/dot

Unclaimed Property Office
Unclaimed Property Unit
Office of State Treasurer
55 Elm ST.
Hartford, CT 06106
860-702-3050
www.state.ct.us/ott

Unemployment Insurance Office
State Labor Department
200 Folley Brook Blvd.
Wethersfield, CT 06109
860-263-6785
www.ctdol.state.ct.us/
Weekly benefit range: $15-362
Duration of benefits: 26 weeks

Utility Commission
Department of Public Utility Control
10 Franklin Square
New Britain, CT 06051
860-827-1553
888-922-3782
Fax: 860-827-2613
800-382-4586 (CT only)
www.state.ct.us/dpuc/

Women's Commission
Connecticut Permanent Commission
of the Status of Women
18-20 Trinity St.
Hartford, CT 06106
860-240-8300
Fax: 860-240-8314
Email: pcsw@po.state.ct.us
www.cga.state.ct.us/pcsw/
Leslie Brett, Ph.D, Exec. Director
Barbara DeBaptiste, Chair

Your Senator
United States Senate
Washington, DC 20510
202-224-3121
www.senate.gov

Your Representative
United States House of
Representatives
Washington, DC 20515
202-224-3121
www.house.gov

DELAWARE

Federal Information Center
1-800-FED-INFO
www.firstgov.gov
www.pueblo.gsa.gov/call/

State Information Office
302-739-4000
www.state.de.us

Department on Aging
Aging Division
Health and Social Services Department
1901 N. Dupont Hwy.
New Castle, DE 19720
302-577-4791
www.dsaapd.com

Attorney General's Office
Office of the Attorney General
Carvel State Office Building
820 North French Street
Wilmington, DE 19801
302-577-8400
800-220-5424
www.state.de.us/attgen/index.htm
Email:
Attorney.General@state.DE.US

Banking Commissioner
State Bank Commissioner
555 E. Lockerman St., Suite 210
Dover, DE 19901
302-739-4235
302-739-4235 (complaints only)
Fax: 302-739-2356
www.state.de.us/ bank/

Child Care and Development Block Grant Lead Agency
Social Services Administrator
Delaware Department of Health and Social Services
1901 N. DuPont Highway
Lewis Building
New Castle, DE 19720
302-577-4400
Fax: 302-577-4405
www.state.de.us/dhss/irm/ dhss.htm

Child Support Enforcement Agency
Charles E. Hayward
Division of Child Support Enforcement
Department of Health and Social Services
1901 N. DuPont Highway
Biggs Building
New Castle, DE 19720
302-577-4863
Fax: 302-577-4873
www.state.de.us/dhss/dcse/index.html

Cooperative Extension Office
Dr. Starlene Taylor
Assistant Administrator
Delaware State College
Cooperative Extension Service
1200 N. DuPont Highway
Dover, DE 19901
302-739-5157
http://ag.udel.edu/extension/index.html#

Corporation Division Office
Delaware Department of State
Division of Corporations
Secretary of State
P.O. Box 898
Dover, DE 19903
302-739-3073
www.state.de.us/corp/ index.htm

Day Care Licensing Agency
Department of Health and Social Services
Office of Child Care Licensing
DSCYF, 1825 Falkland Rd.
Wilmington, DE 19805
302-892-5800
www.state.de.us/dhss

Economic Development Office
Delaware Economic Development Office
John D. Wilk
99 Kings Highway
P.O. Box 1401
Dover, DE 19901
302-739-4271
Fax: 302-739-2028
www.state.de.us/dedo/ index.htm

Department of Education
Delaware Department of Education
401 Federal St.
P.O. Box 1402
Dover, DE 19903-1402
302-739-4601
Fax: 302-739-4654
www.doe.state.de.us/

Department of Higher Education
Delaware Higher Education Commission
820 North French Street
Carvel State Office Building
Wilmington, DE 19801
800-292-7935
302-577-3240
Fax: 302-577-6765
www.doe.state.de.us/high-ed

Health Department
Delaware Division of Public Health
P.O. Box 637
Federal & Water Streets
Dover, DE 19903
302-739-4701
Fax: 302-739-6659
www.state.de.us/dhss/dph/index.htm

Housing Office
Delaware State Housing Authority
Division of Housing and Community Development
18 the Green
Dover, DE 19901
302-739-4263
www2.state.de.us/dsah/

Insurance Commissioner
Insurance Commissioner
841 Silver Lake Blvd.
Rodney Bldg.
Dover, DE 19904
302-739-4251
800-282-8611
Fax: 302-739-6278
www.state.de.us/inscom/index.html

Labor Department
Delaware Department of Labor
4425 North Market Street

Wilmington, DE 19802
302-761-8085
www.delawareworks.com/
DeptLabor

Licensing Office
Division of Professional Regulation
861 Silver Lake Blvd.
Cannon Building
Suite 203
Dover, DE 19904
302-739-4522

One-Stop Career Center
Delaware Career Network
Department of Labor, Employment and Training
4425 North Market Street
Wilmington, DE 19809-0828
302-761-8102
Fax: 302-761-6617
www.vcnet.net
Email: rclarkin@state.de.us

Security Regulators
Delaware Division of Securities
Carvel State Office Building
820 North French St., 5th Floor
Wilmington, DE 19801
302-577-8424
www.state.de.us/securities

Small Business Development Center
Delaware Small Business Development Center
University of Delaware
1318 N. Market St.
Wilmington, DE 19801
302-571-1555
Fax: 302-571-5222
Email:
wilmington@delawareesbdc.org
www.delawaresbdc.org

Social Services Offices
Delaware Department of Health and Social Services
Health and Social Service Campus
1901 North DuPont Highway
Main Building
New Castle, DE 19720
302-577-4500
www.state.de.us/dhss/

Temporary Assistance to Needy Families (TANF)
Temporary Aid to Needy Families
Nina Licht
Delaware Social Services
Lewis Building
1901 North Dupont Highway
New Castle, DE 19720
302-577-4500
www.state.de.us/dhss

Transportation Department
Alton Hillis
Delaware Administration for Specialized Transit Corp.
400 S. Madison
Wilmington, DE 19801
302-739-3278, ext. 3124
www.state.de.us/deldot/

Delaware Department of Transportation
800 S. Bay Rd.
P.O. Box 778
Dover, DE 19903
800-652-5600
302-760-2080
www.state.de.us/deldot/

Unclaimed Property Office
Delaware State Escheater
P.O. Box 8931
Wilmington, DE 19899
302-577-8667
www.state.de.us/revenue/escheat/escheat.htm

Unemployment Insurance Office
Division of Unemployment Insurance
4425 N. Market Street
Wilmington, DE 19802
302-761-8446
www.delawareworks.com/divisions/unemployment/ welcome.htm
Weekly benefit range: $20-300
Duration of benefits: 24-26 weeks

Utility Commission
Public Service Commission
861 Silver Lake Blvd.
Suite 100, Cannon Bldg.
Dover, DE 19904
302-739-4247
800-282-8574 (DE only)
www.state.de.us/delpsc/index.html

Women's Commission
Delaware Commission for Women
4425 N. Market St.
Wilmington, DE 19802
302-761-8005
Fax: 302-761-6652
Email: cgomez@state.de.us
Romona S. Fullman, Esq., Director

Your Senator
United States Senate
Washington, DC 20510
202-224-3121
www.senate.gov

Your Representative
United States House of Representatives
Washington, DC 20515
202-224-3121
www.house.gov

DISTRICT OF COLUMBIA

Federal Information Center
1-800-FED-INFO
www.firstgov.gov
www.pueblo.gsa.gov/call/

District of Columbia Information Office
202-727-6161
www.dc.gov/

Department on Aging
Aging Office
441 4th St., NW, Suite 900S
Washington, DC 20001
202-724-5626
Fax: 202-724-4979
www.dcoa.dc.gov

Attorney General's Office
Office of the Corporation Counsel
441 4th Street, NW, Suite 1060N
Washington, DC 20001
202-727-3400
http://occ.dc.gov/main.shtm

Banking Commissioner
Superintendent of Banking and Financial Institutions
1400 L Street, NW
Suite 400
Washington, DC 20005
202-727-1563
Fax: 202-727-1290
www.obfi.dc.gov

Child Care and Development Block Grant Lead Agency
Office of Early Childhood Development
Department of Human Services
801 E Building
2700 Martin Luther King Ave., SE
Washington, DC 20032
202-279-6002
Fax: 202-279-6014
www.dhs.dc.gov

Child Support Enforcement Agency
Bureau of Paternity and Child Support Enforcement
John A. Wilson Building
1350 Pennsylvania Ave., NW
Suites 407 & 409
Washington, DC 20004
202-727-3400
Fax: 202-347-8922
www.occ.dc.gov

Cooperative Extension Office
Reginald Taylor, Acting Director
Cooperative Extension Service
University of the District of Columbia
4340 Connecticut Ave., NW
Washington, DC 20008
202-274-7100
www.udc.edu/coes/index.html

Corporation Division Office
Corporations Division
Consumer and Regulatory Affairs
941 N. Capitol St., NE
Washington, DC 20002
202-442-4400
Fax: 202-442-9445
www.dcra.dc.gov

Day Care Licensing Agency
Department of Social Services
Consumer and Regulatory Affairs
941 N. Capitol St., NE
Washington, DC 20002
202-442-4400
www.dcra.dc.gov

Economic Development Office
Office of Economic Development
1350 Pennsylvania Ave., NW
Suite 317
Washington, DC 20004
202-727-6365
www.dcbiz.dc.gov

Department of Education
Public Schools
825 North Capitol Street, NE
Washington, DC 20002-4232
202-442-4289
www.K12.dc.us

Department of Higher Education
Office of Postsecondary Education
John A. Wilson Building
1350 Pennsyhlvania Ave., NW
Washington, DC 20004
202-727-1000
www.dhs.dc.gov

Health Department
District of Columbia Department of Health
825 N. Capitol St., NE
Washington, DC 20002
202-442-5999
Fax: 202-442-4788
www.dchealth.dc.gov/index.asp

Housing Offices
DC Housing Finance Agency
815 Florida Ave., NW
Washington, DC 20001
202-777-1600
Fax: 202-986-6705
www.dchfa.org

District of Columbia Department of Housing and Community Development
801 N. Capitol St., NE
Suite 8000
Washington, DC 20002
202-442-7200
http://dhcd.dc.gov

Insurance Commissioner
Commissioner of Insurance
801 First St., NE, Suite 701
Washington, DC 20001
202-727-8000
www.disr.dc.gov

Labor Department
Department of Employment Services
600 H Street, NE
Washington, DC 20002
202-724-7000
www.does.dc.gov

Licensing Office
Department of Consumer and Regulatory Affairs
941 N. Capitol St., NE
Washington, DC 20002
202-442-4400
Fax: 202-442-9445
www.dcra.dc.gov

One-Stop Career Center
DOES One-Stop Career Center
Department of Employment Services
609 H Street, NE
Washington, DC 20002
202-724-7000
www.does.dc.gov

Security Regulators
Securities Bureau of the District of Columbia
810 First Street, NE, Suite 701
Washington, DC 20002
202-727-8000
www.disr.dc.gov

Small Business Development Center
Small Business Development Center
1110 Vermont Ave., NW, 9th Floor
Washington, DC 20005
202-606-4000
www.sba.gov/dc

Social Services Offices
Department of Human Services
Martin Luther King Ave., SE
Building 801E
Washington, DC 20032
202-279-6002
Fax: 202-279-6014
www.dhs.dc.gov

Temporary Assistance to Needy Families (TANF)
Welfare Reform
Patricia Handy
Washington DC Department of Human Services
801 East Building
2700 M.L. King Ave., SE
Washington, DC 20032
202-279-6002
www.dhs.dc.gov

Transportation Department
Radamese Cabrera
Washington DC Department of Public Works
2000 14th St., 6th Floor
Washington, DC 20009
202-673-6813
Fax: 202-671-0642
www.ddot.dc.gov

Unclaimed Property Office
Office of Chief Financial officer
Unclaimed Property Unit
1350 Pennsylvania Ave., NW
Room 209
Washington, DC 20004
202-727-2476
www.cfo.dc.gov

Unemployment Insurance Office
Office of Unemployment Compensation
Department of Employment Services
609 H. Street, NE
Washington, DC 20002
202-724-7000
Fax: 202-724-5683
www.does.dc.gov
Weekly benefit range: $50-359
Duration of benefits: 20-26 weeks

Utility Commission
Public Service Commission
1333 H St., NW
Suite 200 West Tower
Washington, DC 20005
202-626-5110
www.dcpsc.org

Women's Commission
Women's Bureau
U.S. Department of Labor
200 Constitution Ave., NW
Washington, DC 20210
866-4-USA-DOL
202-693-6710
Fax: 202-219-5529
www.dol.gov/dol.wb
Shinae Chun, Director
Lillian M. Long, Chair

Your Senator
United States Senate
Washington, DC 20510
202-224-3121
www.senate.gov

Your Representative
United States House of Representatives
Washington, DC 20515
202-224-3121
www.house.gov

FLORIDA

Federal Information Center
1-800-FED-INFO
www.firstgov.gov
www.pueblo.gsa.gov/call/

State Information Office
850-488-1234
www.state.fl.us

Department on Aging
Department of Elder Affairs
4040 Esplanade Way, Suite 315
Tallahassee, FL 32399-7000
850-414-2000
Elder Helpline:
800-96-ELDER (in FL)
www.state.fl.us/doea/

Attorney General's Office
Office of the Attorney General
The Capitol
Tallahassee, FL 32399-1050
850-487-1963
800-HELPFLA(435-7352)
Fax: 850-487-2564
http://legal.firn.edu

Banking Commissioner
State Comptroller
Division of Banking and Finance
101 E. Gaines St.
Tallahassee, FL 32399-0350
850-410-9286
800-848-3792 (toll free in FL)
www.dbf.state.fl.us

Child Care and Development Block Grant Lead Agency
Chief, Child Care Services
Florida Department of Children and Families
1317 Winewood Blvd.
Building 1, Room 202
Tallahassee, FL 32399-0700
850-487-1111
Fax: 850-488-9584
www.state.fl.us/cf_web/

Child Support Enforcement Agency
Patricia Piller
Child Support Enforcement Program
Department of Revenue
P.O. Box 8030
Tallahassee, FL 32314
800-622-5437
Fax: 850-488-4401
http://sun6.dms.state.fl.us/dor/childsupport/

Cooperative Extension Offices
Christine Taylor-Stephens, Dean
Florida Cooperative Extension Service
P.O. Box 110210
University of Florida
Gainesville, FL 32611-0210
352-392-1761
www.ifas.ufl.edu/www/extension/ces.htm

Lawrence Carter, Director
Cooperative Extension Service
215 Perry Paige Building
Florida A&M University
Tallahassee, FL 32307
850-599-3546
www.famu.edu

Corporation Division Office
Division of Corporations
Secretary of State
409 Gaines St.
Tallahassee, FL 32399
850-488-9000
www.dos.state.fl.us/doc/ index.html

Day Care Licensing Agency
Florida Department of Children and Families
Family Safety and Preservation/Child Care
1317 Winewood Blvd.
Building 8, Room 213
Tallahassee, FL 32399-0700
850-488-8762
www.state.fl.us/cf_web/

Economic Development Office
Florida Economic Development Council
P.O. Box 3186
Tallahassee, FL 32315
850-201-FEDC
Fax: 850-201-3330
www.fedc.net

Enterprise Florida
390 N. Orange Ave.
Suite 1300
Orlando, FL 32801
407-316-4600
Fax 407-316-4599
www.floridabusiness.com

Department of Education
Florida Department of Education
Education Information and Accountability Services
325 W. Gaines St., Room 852
Tallahassee, FL 32399-0400
850-487-2280
www.firn.edu/doe/index.html

Department of Higher Education
Florida Office of Student Financial Assistance
1940 N. Monroe St., Suite 70
Tallahassee, FL 32303-4759
850-410-5321
Fax: 850-488-3612
www.firn.edu/doe/bin00065/home0065.htm

Health Department
Florida Department of Health
4052 Bald Cypress Way
Tallahassee, FL 32399-1701
850-245-4443
www.doh.state.fl.us
Email: dhs@doh.state.fl.us
Email: health@doh.state.fl.us

Housing Office
Florida Housing Finance Agency
227 N. Bronough St.
Suite 5000
Tallahassee, FL 32301-1329
850-488-4197
www.floridahousing.org

Insurance Commissioner
Insurance Commissioner
200 E. Gaines St.
Tallahassee, FL 32399-0300
850-413-3100
800-342-2762
www.doi.state.fl.us/

Labor Department
Florida Department of Labor and Employment Security
2012 Capital Circle SE, Suite 306
Tallahassee, FL 32399-2156
866-487-9243
www2.myflorida.com/les

Licensing Office
Florida Department of Business and Professional Regulation
1940 N. Monroe St.
Tallahassee, FL 32399
850-487-1395
www.state.fl.us/dbpr

One-Stop Career Center
Workforce Florida
Department of Labor and Employment Security
Division of Jobs and Benefits
3800 Inverrary Blvd., Suite 400
Lauderhill, FL 33319
954-535-2345
http://workforce.floridajobs.org

Security Regulators
Division of Securities
101 East Gaines St.
Tallahassee, FL 32399
850-410-9805
800-848-3792
www.dbf.state.fl.us/index.html

Small Business Development Center
Florida Small Business Development Center
University of West Florida
19 West Garden Street, Suite 302
Pensacola, FL 32501
850-595-6060
800-644-SBDC
Fax: 850-595-6070
Email: fsbdc@uwf.edu
www.sbdc.uwf.edu

Social Services Offices
Florida Department of Children and Families
1317 Winewood Boulevard
Building 1, Room 206
Tallahassee, FL 32399-0770
904-488-4855
www.state.fl.us/cf_web/

Temporary Assistance to Needy Families (TANF)
Temporary Aid to Needy Families
Christy Moore
Florida Department of Children and Families
1317 Winewood Blvd.
Tallahassee, FL 32399-0770
907-488-4855
www.state.fl.us/cf_web

Transportation Department
Catherine Kelly
Department of Transportation
605 Suwannee St.
Mail Stop 26
Tallahassee, FL 32399
850-414-4100
www.dot.state.fl.us

Unclaimed Property Office
Department of Banking and Finance
Abandoned Property Division
101 East Gaines St.
Tallahassee, FL 32399-0350
850-488-7777
http://up.dbf.state.fl.us/

Unemployment Insurance Office
Division of Unemployment Compensation
201 Caldwell Building
Tallahassee, FL 32399
904-921-3889
www2.myflorida.com/awi/unemployment
Weekly benefit range: $10-250
Duration of benefits: 10-26 weeks

Utility Commission
Public Service Commission
2540 Shumard-Oak Blvd.
Tallahassee, FL 32399-0850
850-413-6100
800-342-3552 (FL only)
www.psc.state.fl.us

Women's Commission
Florida Commission on the Status of Women
Office of the Attorney General
The Capitol
Tallahassee, FL 32399-1050
850-414-3300
Fax: 850-921-4131
Email: Michele-Manning@oag.state.fl.us
http://legal.firn.edu/units/fcsw
Kate Gooderham, Chair
Susan Gilbert, Vice Chair

Your Senator
United States Senate
Washington, DC 20510
202-224-3121
www.senate.gov

Your Representative
United States House of Representatives
Washington, DC 20515
202-224-3121
www.house.gov

GEORGIA

Federal Information Center
1-800-FED-INFO
www.firstgov.gov
www.pueblo.gsa.gov/call/

State Information Office
404-656-2000
www.state.ga.us

Department on Aging
Division of Aging Services
Georgia Department of Human Resources
2 Peachtree St., NW, Suite 9-385
Atlanta, GA 30303-3142
404-657-5258
Fax: 404-657-5285
www2.state.ga.us/departments/dhr/aging.html

Attorney General's Office
Office of the Attorney General
40 Capitol Square, SW
Atlanta, GA 30334
404-656-3300
http://ganet.org/ago

Banking Commissioner
Commissioner of Banking and Finance
2990 Brandywine Rd., Suite 200
Atlanta, GA 30341-5565
707-986-1633
www.ganet.org/dbf/dbf.html

Child Care and Development Block Grant Lead Agency
Family Support Unit
Division of Family and Children Services
Georgia Department of Human Resources
Two Peachtree St., NW
Suite 19-490
Atlanta, GA 30303-3142
404-657-7600
Fax: 404-657-3489
www2.state.ga.us/Departments/DHR

Child Support Enforcement Agency
Robert Riddle
Child Support Enforcement
Department of Human Resources
2 Peachtree St.
Atlanta, GA 30303
404-657-3851
800-227-7993 (in GA)
Fax: 404-657-3326
www.cse.dhr.state.ga.us

Cooperative Extension Offices
Bob Isaac, Interim Director
Cooperative Extension Service
University of Georgia
1111 Conner Hall
Athens, GA 30602
706-542-3824
www.ces.uga.edu

Dr. Fred Harrison, Jr., Director
Cooperative Extension Service
P.O. Box 4061
Fort Valley State College
Fort Valley, GA 31030
4785-6269
www.aginfo.fvsu.edu/ces/overview.htm

Corporation Division Office
Corporations Division
Secretary of State
315 West Tower
#2 M.L. King Dr.
Atlanta, GA 30334-1530
404-656-2817
Fax: 404-657-2248
www.sos.state.ga.us/corporations/

Day Care Licensing Agency
Department of Human Resources
Child Care Licensing Unit
2 Peachtree St., NW, 32nd Floor
Atlanta, GA 30303-3142
404-657-5562
www2.state.ga.us/Departments/DHR

Economic Development Office
Office of Economic Development
60 Executive Park South, NE
Suite 250
Atlanta, GA 30329-2231
404-679-4940
Fax: 800-736-1155
www.dca.state.ga.us

Department of Education
Georgia Department of Education
205 Jesse Hill Jr. Dr.
Twin Towers East, Suite 1654
Atlanta, GA 30334
404-656-2800
800-311-3627 (in GA)
www.doe.k12.ga.us/

Department of Higher Education
Student Finance Commission
2082 East Exchange Place
Tucker, GA 30084
800-776-6878
770-724-9000
Fax: 770-724-9089
www.gsfc.org

Health Department
Georgia Division of Public Health
Two Peachtree Street, NW
Atlanta, GA 30303-3186
404-657-2700
www.ph.dhr.state.ga.us/
Email: gdphinfo@ dhr.state.ga.us

Housing Office
Georgia Residential Finance Authority
60 Executive Park South, Suite 250
Atlanta, GA 30329
404-679-4940
www.dca.state.ga.us

Insurance Commissioner
Insurance Commissioner
West Tower, Suite 704
2 Martin Luther King, Jr. Dr.
Atlanta, GA 30334
404-656-2070
800-656-2298
www.gainsurance.org

Labor Department
Georgia Department of Labor
148 International Boulevard
Atlanta, GA 30303-1751
404-656-6380
www.dol.state.ga.us

Licensing Office
Examining Board Division
Secretary of State
237 Coliseum Dr.
Macon, GA 31217
478-207-1300
www.sos.state.ga.us/plb

One-Stop Career Center
Department of Labor
Employment Services
148 International Boulevard, NE
Atlanta, GA 30303-1751
404-656-6380
Fax: 404-657-8285
www.state.ga.us/index/gaemp. html

Security Regulators
Securities and Business Regulation Division
802 West Tower
Suite 802
2 Martin Luther King Jr. Dr., SE
Atlanta, GA 30334
404-656-3920
Fax: 404-657-8410
www.sos.state.ga.us/Securities/default.htm

Small Business Development Center
Georgia Small Business Development Center
University of Georgia
Chicopee Complex
1180 East Broad Street
Athens, GA 30602-5412
706-542-6762
Fax: 706-542-6776
Email:SBDCDIR@ sbdc.uga.edu
www.sbdc.uga.edu

Social Services Offices
Georgia Department of Human Resources
2 Peachtree St., NW
Atlanta, GA 30303
404-656-4937
www.state.ga.us/Departments/ DHR

Temporary Assistance to Needy Families (TANF)
Temporary Aid to Needy Families
Tommy Olmstead
Georgia Department of Human Resources
2 Peachtree St., NW
Suite 16-200
Atlanta, GA 30303
404-656-5680
www2.state.ga.us/departments/dhr/tanf.html

Transportation Department
Tom Coleman
Georgia Dept. of Transportation
276 Memorial Dr., SW
Atlanta, GA 30303
404-656-5206
www.dot.state.ga.us

Unclaimed Property Office
Department of Revenue
Property Tax Division
Unclaimed Property
4245 International Parkway
Hapeville, GA 30354-3903
404-968-0490
www2.state.ga.us/departments/dor/ptd/ucp/index.html

Unemployment Insurance Office
Assistance Commissioner
Unemployment Insurance
Georgia Department of Labor
148 International Blvd.,NE
Suite 718
Atlanta, GA 30303
404-656-3050
www.dol.state.ga.us/ui/
Weekly benefit range: $39-274
Duration of benefits: 8-26 weeks

Utility Commission
Public Service Commission
244 Washington Street, SW
Atlanta, GA 30334
404-656-4501
800-282-5813 (GA only)
www.psc.state.ga.us

Women's Commission
GA State Commission of Women
148 International Blvd., NE
Atlanta, GA 30303
404-657-9260
Fax: 404-657-2963
Email: gawomen@mindspring.com
www.mindspring.com/~gawomen
Nellie Duke, Chair
Juliana McConnell, Vice Chair

Your Senator
United States Senate
Washington, DC 20510
202-224-3121
www.senate.gov

Your Representative
United States House of Representatives
Washington, DC 20515
202-224-3121
www.house.gov

HAWAII

Federal Information Center
1-800-FED-INFO
www.firstgov.gov
www.pueblo.gsa.gov/call/

State Information Office
808-548-6222
www.state.hi.us

Department on Aging
Aging Office
205 S. Hotel St., Suite 109
Honolulu, HI 96813-2831
808-586-0100
www2.state.hi.us/eoa

Attorney General's Office
Dept. of the Attorney General
425 Queen Street
Honolulu, HI 96813
808-586-1500
Fax: 808-586-1239
www.state.hi.us/ag

Banking Commissioner
Commissioner of Financial Institutions
P.O. Box 2054
1010 Richards St., Room 602A
Honolulu, HI 96805
808-586-2820
www.state.hi.us/dcca/dfi

Child Care and Development Block Grant Lead Agency
Hawaii Department of Human Services
Benefits, Employment and Support Services Division
Child Care Program Office
1390 Miller St., Room 209
Honolulu, HI 96813
808-586-4890
Fax: 808-586-5180
www.state.hi.us/dhs

Child Support Enforcement Agency
Mike Meaney
Child Support Enforcement Agency
Department of Attorney General
601 Kamokila Blvd., Suite 251
Kapolei, HI 96707
808-692-8265
Fax: 808-587-3716
www.state.hi.us/csea/csea.htm

Cooperative Extension Office
Dr. Po'Yung Lai, Assistant Director
Cooperative Extension Service
3050 Maile Way
Honolulu, HI 96822
808-956-8397
www.hawaii.edu

Corporation Division Office
Business Registration Division
Department of Commerce and Consumer Affairs
1010 Richards St.
P.O. Box 40
Honolulu, HI 96813
808-586-2850
www.state.hi.us/dcca

Day Care Licensing Agency
Department of Human Services
Employment/Child Care Program Office
1390 Miller St., Room 209
Honolulu, HI 96813
808-586-4890
www.hawaii.gov/dhs

Economic Development Office
Department of Business and Economic Development and Tourism
P.O. Box 2359
Honolulu, HI 96804
No. 1 Capitol District Bldg.
250 S. Hotel Street
Honolulu, HI 96813
808-586-2423
Fax: 808-587-2790
www.hawaii.gov/dbedt/

Department of Education
Hawaii Department of Education
Information Branch
P.O. Box 2360
Honolulu, HI 96804
808-586-2320
Fax: 808-586-3234
www.doe.k12.hi.us

Department of Higher Education
Hawaii State Postsecondary Education Commission
2444 Dole Street, Room 209
Honolulu, HI 96882-2302
808-956-8213
www.hern.hawaii.edu/hern

Health Department
Hawaii Department of Health
1250 Punchbowl Street
Honolulu, HI 96813
808-586-4400
Fax: 808-586-4444
www.state.hi.us/health/
Email: pijohnst@ health.state.hi.us

Housing Office
Housing and Community Development
1002 N. School St.
P.O. Box 17907
Honolulu, HI 96817
808-587-0641
www.hcdch.state.hi.us

Insurance Commissioner
Insurance Commissioner
Department of Commerce and Consumer Affairs
250 S. King Street, 5th Floor
Honolulu, HI 96813
808-586-2790
www.state.hi.us/dcca/ins

Labor Department
Hawaii Department of Labor and Industrial Relations
830 Punchbowl Street
Honolulu, HI 96813
808-586-8865
http://dlir.state.hi.us/

Licensing Office
Office of the Director
Department of Commerce and Consumer Affairs
P.O. Box 3469
Honolulu, HI 96801
808-586-3000
www.hawaii.gov/dcca/

One-Stop Career Center
Workforce Development
Department of Labor
Workforce Development Division
830 Punchbowl Street, #112
Honolulu, HI 96813
808-586-8700
Fax: 808-586-8724
http://dlir.state.hi.us/

Security Regulators
Hawaii Corporate & Securities Commission
P.O. Box 40
Honolulu, HI 96810
808-586-2744
www.state.hi.us/dcca/breg-seu/compliance.html

Small Business Development Center
Hawaii Small Business Development Center Network
University of Hawaii at Hilo
200 West Kawili Street
Hilo, HI 96720-4091
808-974-7515
Fax: 808-974-7683
Email: darrylm@interpac.net
www.hawaii-sbdc.org

Social Services Offices
Hawaii Department of Human Services
P.O. Box 339
Honolulu, HW 96809
808-586-5701
www.state.hi.us/dhs

Temporary Assistance to Needy Families (TANF)
Temporary Aid to Needy Families
Kathleen Stanley
Hawaii Department of Human Services
P.O. Box 339
Honolulu, HI 96809
808-586-4999
www.state.hi.us/dhs/

Transportation Department
Brian Minaai
Hawaii Department of Transportation
Aliiaimoku Bldg.
869 Punchbowl St.
Honolulu, HI 96813
808-587-2150
www.hawaii.gov/dot/

Unclaimed Property Office
Unclaimed Property Section
P.O. Box 150
Honolulu, HI 96810
808-586-1589
www.state.hi.us/budget/uncprop/uncprop.htm

Unemployment Insurance Office
Administrator
Unemployment Insurance Division
Department of Labor and Industrial Relations
830 Punchbowl Street, Room 325
Honolulu, HI 96813
808-586-9069
http://dlir.state.hi.us
Weekly benefit range: $5-395
Duration of benefits: 26 weeks

Utility Commission
Public Utilities Commission
P.O. Box 150
Honolulu, HI 96810
808-586-2020
www.state.hi.us/budget/puc/puc.htm

Women's Commission
Hawaii State Commission on the Status of Women
235 S. Beretaniast, Suite 401
Honolulu, HI 96813
808-586-5757
Fax: 808-586-5756
Email: hscsw@pixi.com
www.state.hi.us/hscsw
Alicynttikida Tasaka, Executive Director

Your Senator
United States Senate
Washington, DC 20510
202-224-3121
www.senate.gov

Your Representative
United States House of Representatives
Washington, DC 20515
202-224-3121
www.house.gov

IDAHO

Federal Information Center
1-800-FED-INFO
www.firstgov.gov
www.pueblo.gsa.gov/call/

State Information Office
208-334-2411
www.state.id.us

Department on Aging
Aging Office
P.O. Box 83720
Boise, ID 83720-0007
208-334-3833
www.idahoaging.com/abouticoa/ind
ex.htm

Attorney General's Office
Office of the Attorney General
Statehouse
700 West Jefferson Street
P.O. Box 83720
Boise, ID 83720-0100
208-334-2400
800-432-3545
Fax: 208-334-2530
www2.state.id.us/ag/

Banking Commissioner
Department of Finance
P.O. Box 83720
700 W. State St.
Boise, ID 83720-0031
208-332-8000
www2.state.id.us/ finance/dof.htm

Child Care and Development Block Grant Lead Agency
Department of Health and Welfare
Policy
P.O. Box 83720
Boise, ID 83720-0036
208-334-5500
Fax: 208-334-6558
www2.state.id.us/dhw/index.htm

Child Support Enforcement Agency
Jo An Silva
Bureau of Child Support Services
Department of Health and Welfare
P.O. Box 83720
Boise, ID 83720
208-324-8144
800-356-9868
Fax: 208-334-0666

Cooperative Extension Office
Dr. LeRoy D. Luft, Director
Cooperative Extension System
College of Agriculture
University of Idaho
Moscow, ID 83844-2338
208-885-6639
www.uidaho.edu/ag/extension/

Corporation Division Office
Corporate Division
Secretary of State
Room 203, Statehouse
Boise, ID 83720
208-334-2300
www.idsos.state.id.us/

Day Care Licensing Agency
Department of Health and Welfare
Bureau of Family and Children's
Services
450 W. State St., 10th Floor
Boise, ID 83720-0036
208-334-5500
www2.state.id.us/dhw/index.htm

Economic Development Office
Idaho Department of Commerce
700 West State Street
P.O. Box 83720
Boise, ID 83720-0093
208-334-2470
Fax: 208-334-2631
www.idoc.state.id.us/

Department of Education
Idaho Department of Education
P.O. Box 83720
Boise, ID 83720-0027
208-332-6800
www.sde.state.id.us/dept/

Department of Higher Education
Office of the State Board of
Education
P.O. Box 83720
Boise, ID 83720-0037
208-334-2270
www.sde.state.id.us/osbe/
board.htm

Health Department
Idaho Department of Health &
Welfare
450 W. State St., 10th Floor
P.O. Box 83720
Boise, ID 83720-0036
208-334-5500
Fax: 208-334-6558
TDD: 208-334-4921
www2.state.id.us/dhw/index.htm

Housing Office
Idaho Housing Agency
565 W. Myrtle
P.O. Box 7899
Boise, ID 83707-1899
208-331-4887
www.ihfa.org

Insurance Commissioner
Director of Insurance
P.O. Box 83720
Boise, ID 83720-0043
208-334-4250
www.doi.state.id.us/

Labor Department
Idaho Department of Labor
317 Main Street
Boise, ID 83735-0001
208-332-3570
www.labor.state.id.us

Licensing Office
State of Idaho
Department of Self-Governing
Agencies
Bureau of Occupational Licenses
Owyhee Plaza
1109 Main, #220
Boise, ID 83720
208-334-3233
www2.state.id.us/ibol

One-Stop Career Center
Idaho Works
Idaho Department of Labor
317 Main Street

Boise, ID 83735-0600
208-334-6303
Fax: 208-332-7417
www.idahoworks.state.id.us

Security Regulators
Idaho Securities Bureau
P.O. Box 83720
Boise, ID 83720
208-332-8004
www.finance.state.id.us/home.asp

Small Business Development Center
Idaho Small Business Development Center
Boise State University
College of Business
1910 University Drive
Boise, ID 83725-1655
208-426-1640
800-225-3815
Fax: 208-385-3877
Email: jhogge@bsu.idbsu.edu
www.idahosbdc.org

Social Services Offices
Idaho Department of Health and Welfare
450 West State Street
Boise, ID 83720-0036
208-334-5500
www2.state.id.us/dhw/index.htm

Temporary Assistance to Needy Families (TANF)
Temporary Aid to Needy Families
Social Services Block Grant
Linda Caballero
Idaho Department of Health and Welfare
P.O. Box 83720
Boise, ID 83720
208-334-5500
www2.state.id.us/dhw/index.htm

Transportation Department
Dwight Bower
Idaho Department of Transportation
P.O. Box 7129
Boise, ID 83707
208-334-8848
www2.state.id.us/itd/index.htm

Linda Collins
Idaho Department of Transportation
P.O. Box 7129
Boise, ID 83707
208-334-8808
www2.state.id.us/itd/index.htm

Unclaimed Property Office
Unclaimed Property Division
P.O. Box 36
Boise, ID 83722
208-334-7500
www2.state.id.us/tax/unclaimed_idaho.htm

Unemployment Insurance Office
Administrator
Unemployment Insurance Division
Department of Employment
317 Main St.
Boise, ID 83735
208-334-3570
www.labor.state.id.us
Weekly benefit range: $44-248
Duration of benefits: 10-26 weeks

Utility Commission
Public Utilities Commission
P.O. Box 83720
Boise, ID 83720-0074
208-334-0300
www.puc.state.id.us

Women's Commission
Idaho Commission on the Women's Program
P.O. Box 8915
Moscow, ID 83843
208-885-3758
Fax: 208-885-3759
Email: ehurlbudt@women.state.id.us
www.state.id.us/women
Linda Hurlbudt, Director
Cindy Agidius, Chair

Your Senator
United States Senate
Washington, DC 20510
202-224-3121
www.senate.gov

Your Representative
United States House of Representatives
Washington, DC 20515
202-224-3121
www.house.gov

ILLINOIS

Federal Information Center
1-800-FED-INFO
www.firstgov.gov
www.pueblo.gsa.gov/call/

State Information Office
217-782-2000
www.state.il.us

Department on Aging
Aging Department
421 E. Capitol Ave. #100
Springfield, IL 62701-1789
217-785-3356
www.state.il.us/aging/

Attorney General's Office
Office of the Attorney General
100 West Randolph Street
Chicago, IL 60601
312-814-3000
TTY: 312-814-3374
www.ag.state.il.us

Banking Commissioner
Commissioner of Banks and Trust Companies
500 E. Monroe St.
Springfield, IL 62701
217-782-3000
www.obre.state.il.us/

Child Care and Development Block Grant Lead Agency
Office of Child Care and Family Services
Illinois Dept. of Human Services
300 Iles Park Place
Suite 270
Springfield, IL 62762
217-785-2559
Fax: 217-524-6030
www.state.il.us/agency/dhs/

Child Support Enforcement Agency
Jackie Garner
Child Support Enforcement Division
Illinois Department of Public Aid
509 South 6th St., 6th Floor
Springfield, IL 62701
217-524-4602
800-447-4278
Fax: 217-524-4608
www.state.il.us/ dpa/

Cooperative Extension Office
Dennis Campion, Director
University of Illinois
Cooperative Extension Service
214 Mumford Hall
1301 W. Gregory Drive
Urbana, IL 61801
217-333-5900
www.extension.uiuc.edu/welcome.html

Corporation Division Office
Department of Business Services
Centennial Building, Room 328
Springfield, IL 62756
217-782-6961
www.sos.state.il.us/

Day Care Licensing Agency
Department of Children and Family Services
406 E. Monroe St.
Springfield, IL 62701-1498
217-785-2509
www.state.il.us/dcfs/index.shtml

Economic Development Office
Department of Commerce and Community Affairs
620 E. Adams
Springfield, IL, 62701
100 West Randolph St.
Suite 3-400
Chicago, IL 60601
217-782-7500
Fax: 217-524-3701
www.commerce.state.il.us

Department of Education
Illinois State Board of Education
100 N. First St.
Springfield, IL 62777-0001
217-782-4321
www.isbe.state.il.us/

Department of Higher Education
Illinois Student Assistance Commission
1755 Lake Cook Drive
Deerfield, IL 60015-5209
847-948-8550 ext.3503
Fax: 847-831-8549
www.isac-online.org

Health Department
Illinois Department of Public Health
535 West Jefferson Street
Springfield, IL 62761
217-782-4977
Fax: 217-782-3987
TTY: 800-547-0466
www.idph.state.il.us

Housing Office
Illinois Housing Development Authority
401 N. Michigan Ave., Suite 900
Chicago, IL 60611
312-836-5362
800-942-8439
www.ihda.org

Insurance Commissioner
Director of Insurance
320 W. Washington St., 4th Floor
Springfield, IL 62767-0001
217-782-4515
800-548-9034
www.state.il.us/ins/

Labor Department
Illinois Department of Labor
State of Illinois Building
160 North LaSalle, SuiteC-1300
Chicago, IL 60601
312-793-2800
www.state.il.us/agency/idol

Licensing Office
State of Illinois
Department of Professional Regulations
320 W. Washington, Third Floor
Springfield, IL 62786
217-785-0800
www.dpr.state.il.us/

One-Stop Career Center
Illinois Employment and Training Center (IETC) Network

Dept. of Employment Security
Employment Services
400 West Monroe Street
Springfield, IL 62704
217-785-5069
www.ides.state.il.us/program/employer.htm

Security Regulators
Illinois Securities Department
Lincoln Tower, Suite 200
520 South Second St.
Springfield, IL 62701
217-782-2256
800-628-7937
www.sos.state.il.us/

Small Business Development Center
Illinois Small Business Development Center
Department of Commerce & Community Affairs
620 East Adams Street, 3rd Floor
Springfield, IL 62701
217-782-7500
Fax: 217-785-1627
www.commerce.state.il.us/

Social Services Offices
Illinois Department of Human Services
Office of Communications
401 South Clinton, 7th Floor
Chicago, IL 60607
312-793-2343
www.state.il.us/agency/dhs

Temporary Assistance to Needy Families (TANF)
Temporary Aid to Needy Families
Amina Everett
Illinois Department of Human Services
Harris Bldg.
100 South Grand Ave.
Springfield, IL 62762
217-782-1210
www.state.il.us/agency/dhs/tanfnp.html

Transportation Department
Kirk Brown
Illinois Department of Transportation
2300 S. Dirksen Pkwy.
Springfield, IL 62764
217-782-5597
www.dot.state.il.us

Joseph Banks
Illinois Department of Transportation
2300 S. Dirksen Pkwy.
Springfield, IL 62764
217-793-2242
www.dot.state.il.us

Unclaimed Property Office
Unclaimed Property Division
Office of State Treasurer
P.O. Box 19495
Springfield, IL 62794
217-785-6992
www.cashdash.net

Unemployment Insurance Office
Unemployment Insurance Manager
Illinois Department of Employment Security
401 S. State St., Room 622
Chicago, IL 60615
312-793-1900
www.ides.state.il.us
Weekly benefit range: $51-269
Duration of benefits: 26 weeks

Utility Commission
Commerce Commission
527 E. Capitol Ave.
P.O. Box 19280
Springfield, IL 62794-9280
217-782-7295
www.icc.state.il.us

Women's Commission
Governor's Commission on the Status of Women
100 W. Randolph, Suite 16-100
Chicago, IL 60601
312-814-5743
Fax: 312-814-3823
Ellen Solomon, Executive Director

Your Senator
United States Senate
Washington, DC 20510
202-224-3121
www.senate.gov

Your Representative
United States House of Representatives
Washington, DC 20515
202-224-3121
www.house.gov

INDIANA

Federal Information Center
1-800-FED-INFO
www.firstgov.gov
www.pueblo.gsa.gov/call/

State Information Office
317-232-1000
www.state.in.us

Department on Aging
Aging and Rehabilitative Services Division
Family and Social Services Administration
402 W. Washington St.
Room W454
Indianapolis, IN 46207
317-232-7020

Attorney General's Office
Office of the Attorney General
Indiana Government Center South
5th Floor
402 West Washington Street
Indianapolis, IN 46204
317-232-6201
800-382-5516
www.in.gov/attorneygeneral

Banking Commissioner
Department of Financial Institutions
402 W. Washington, Suite W066
Indianapolis, IN 46204
317-232-3955
800-382-4880 (toll free in IN)
www.dfi.state.in.us/

Child Care and Development Block Grant Lead Agency
Indiana Family and Social Services Administration
Division of Family and Children
402 W. Washington St.
Room W386
P.O. Box 7083
Indianapolis, IN 46204-7083
317-233-1148
Fax: 317-232-4436
www.ai.org/fssa/index.html

Child Support Enforcement Agency
Joe Mamlin
Child Support Bureau
402 W. Washington St.
Room W360
Indianapolis, IN 46204
317-232-4885
Fax: 317-233-4925
www.ai.org/fssa/

Cooperative Extension Office
Dr. Wadsworth, Director
1140 AGAD
CES Administration
Purdue University
West Lafayette, IN 47907-1140
317-494-8489
888-398-4636
www.ces.purdue.edu

Corporation Division Office
Office of Corporation
Secretary of State
Room E018
302 West Washington St.
Indianapolis, IN 46204
317-232-6576
www.state.in.us/sos/

Day Care Licensing Agency
Indiana Family and Social Services Administration
Division of Family and Children
Child Care Licensing Unit
402 W. Washington St., Room 386
Indianapolis, IN 46204
317-232-4468 for centers
317-232-4521 for family care
www.ai.org/fssa/index.html

Economic Development Office
Indiana Department of Commerce
One North Capitol, Suite 700
Indianapolis, IN 46204
317-232-8800
800-463-8081
Fax: 317-232-4146
www.state.in.us/doc/index.html

Department of Education
Indiana Department of Education
Education Information Systems
Room 229, State House
Indianapolis, IN 46204-2798
317-232-0808
www.doe.state.in.us/

Department of Higher Education
State Student Assistance Commission of Indiana
150 West Market Street, Suite 500
Indianapolis, IN 46204-2811
317-232-2350
Fax: 317-232-3260
www.in.gov/ssaci

Health Department
Indiana State Department of Health
2 North Meridian Street
Indianapolis, IN 46204
317-233-1325
www.state.in.us/isdh
Email: OPA@isdh.state.in.us

Housing Office
Indiana Housing Finance Authority
115 W. Washington
South Tower, Suite 1350
Indianapolis, IN 46204-3413
317-232-7777
www.state.in.us/ihfa

Insurance Commissioner
Commissioner of Insurance
311 W. Washington St., Suite 300
Indianapolis, IN 46204-2787
317-232-2385
800-622-4461
www.in.gov/idoi/

Labor Department
Indiana Department of Labor
Indiana Government Center-South
402 W. Washington St.
Room W 195
Indianapolis, IN 46204
317-232-2655
www.in.gov/labor

Licensing Office
Indiana Professional Licensing Agency
Indiana Government Center S.
302 W. Washington St.
Room E-034
Indianapolis, IN 46204

317-232-2980
www.in.gov/pla

One-Stop Career Center
Workforce Development
Indiana Department of Workforce Development
Indiana Government Center
10 North Senate Avenue
Indianapolis, IN 46204
317-232-4259
Fax: 317-233-4793
www.dwd.state.in.us
Email: workone@dwd-is.state.in.us

Security Regulators
Securities Division
302 W. Washington St.
Room E-111
Indianapolis, IN 46204
317-232-6681
www.state.in.us/sos

Small Business Development Center
Small Business Development Center
One North Capitol, Suite 900
Indianapolis, IN 46204
317-234-2082
Email: sbdc@isbdcorp.org
www.isbdcorp.org/

Social Services Offices
Indiana Family and Social Services Administration
402 West Washington Street
P.O. Box 7083
Indianapolis, IN 46204
317-233-4454
www.state.in.us/fssa/index.html

Temporary Assistance to Needy Families (TANF)
Temporary Aid to Needy Families
James Hmurovich
Indiana Division of Family and Children
402 West Washington St., Room W392
Indianapolis, IN 46204
317-232-4705
www.state.in.us/fssa/families

Transportation Department
Brian Jones
Indiana Department of Transportation
100 N. Senate Ave.
Room IGCN755
Indianapolis, IN 46204
317-232-5533
www.in.gov/dot/

Rebecca Rowley
Indiana Institute for Urban Transportation
825 East 8th St.
Bloomington, IN 47408
812-855-8143
www.indiana.edu/~iutrans/iut.html

Unclaimed Property Office
Attorney General's office
Unclaimed Property Division
402 West Washington St.
Suite C-531
Indianapolis, IN 46204
317-232-6348
800-447-5598
www.state.in.us/attorneygeneral/ucp/index.htm

Unemployment Insurance Office
Dept. of Workforce Development
Indiana Government Center South
10 N. Senate Ave., Room 302
Indianapolis, IN 46204
317-233-5724
Weekly benefit range: $87-217
Duration of benefits: 8-26 weeks

Utility Commission
Utility Regulatory Commission
302 W. Washington St., Suite E306
Indianapolis, IN 46204
317-232-2700
www.in.gov/iurc/

Women's Commission
Indiana State Commission for Women
100 N. Senate Ave., Room SE205
Indianapolis, IN 46204
317-232-6720
Fax: 317-232-6580
Email: icw@state.in.us
www.state.in.us/icw

Your Senator
United States Senate
Washington, DC 20510
202-224-3121
www.senate.gov

Your Representative
United States House of Representatives
Washington, DC 20515
202-224-3121
www.house.gov

IOWA

Federal Information Center
1-800-FED-INFO
www.firstgov.gov
www.pueblo.gsa.gov/call/

State Information Office
515-281-5011
www.state.ia.us

Department on Aging
Elder Affairs Department
Clemens Building
200 W. 10th St., Third Floor
Des Moines, IA 50309
515-242-3333
www.state.ia.us/elderaffairs/

Attorney General's Office
Office of the Attorney General
1305 East Walnut Street
Des Moines, IA 50319
515-281-5164
515-281-5926 (consumer advocate)
Fax: 515-281-4209
www.state.ia.us/government/ag/
index.html
Email: webteam@ag.state.ia.us

Banking Commissioner
Superintendent of Banking
200 E. Grand, Suite 300
Des Moines, IA 50309
515-281-4014
www.idob.state.ia.us/

Child Care and Development Block Grant Lead Agency
Federal Day Care Program Manager
Iowa Dept. of Human Services
Hoover State Office Bldg., 5th Flr.
Des Moines, IA 50319-0114
515-281-6212
Fax: 515-281-4597
www.dhs.state.ia.us/

Child Support Enforcement Agency
Jim Hennessey
Bureau of Collections
Department of Human Services
Hoover Building- 5th Floor
Des Moines, IA 50319
515-242-5530
515-281-8854
800-374-KIDS (in IA)
www.dhs.state.ia.us/boc/boc.asp

Cooperative Extension Office
Dr. Nolan R. Hartwig
Interim Director
Cooperative Extension Service
315 Beardshear Hall
Iowa State University
Ames, IA 50011
515-294-9434
www.extension.iastate.edu

Corporation Division Office
Corporate Division
Secretary of State
Lucas Building
321 E. 12th St.
Des Moines, IA 50319
515-281-5204
www.sos.state.ia.us

Day Care Licensing Agency
Department of Human Services
Child Care Licensing Department
Hoover State Office Bldg., 5th Floor
Des Moines, IA 50319
515-281-4357
www.dhs.state.ia.us/

Economic Development Office
Department of Economic Development
200 East Grand Ave.
Des Moines, IA 50309-1827
515-242-4700
Fax: 515-242-4809
TTY: 800-735-2942
www.state.ia.us/ided

Department of Education
Iowa Department of Education
Grimes State Office Bldg.
Des Moines, IA 50319-0146
515-281-5294
www.state.ia.us/educate/

Department of Higher Education
Iowa College Student Aid Commission
200 Tenth Street, 4th Floor
Des Moines, IA 50309-2036
515-281-3501
www.state.ia.us/collegeaid

Health Department
Iowa Department of Public Health
Lucas Building
321 East 12th Street
DesMoines, IA 50319
517-281-5787
www.idph.state.ia.us

Housing Office
Iowa Finance Authority
100 E. Grand Ave.
Suite 250
Des Moines, IA 50309
515-242-4990
www.ifahome.com

Insurance Commissioner
Insurance Commissioner
330 E. Maple St.
Des Moines, IA 50319
515-281-5705
877-955-1212
www.iid.state.ia.us/

Labor Department
Iowa Workforce Development
1000 East Grand Avenue
DesMoines, IA 50319-0209
515-281-5387
www.iowaworkforce.org

Licensing Office
Bureau of Professional Licensing
Iowa Department of Health
Lucas State Office Building
1918 SE Hulsizer
Ankeny, IA 50021
515-281-3183
www.state.ia.us/government/
com/prof/pdl1.htm

One-Stop Career Center
Workforce Development
Department of Workforce Development
1000 East Grand Avenue
Des Moines, IA 50319-0209

515-281-5387
800-JOB-IOWA
www.iowaworkforce.org

Security Regulators
Securities Division
340 East Maple St.
Des Moines, IA 50319
515-281-4441
www.iid.state.ia.us/

Small Business Development Center
Iowa Small Business Development Center
Iowa State University
College of Business Administration
2501 N. Loop Drive
Building 1, Suite 615
Ames, IA 50010-8283
515-296-7828
800-373-7232
Fax: 515-292-0020
Email: rmanning@iastate.edu
www.iabusnet.org/sbdc/index.html

Social Services Offices
Iowa Dept. of Human Services
Hoover Street Office Building
5th Floor NW
1305 East Walnut
DesMoine, IA 50319
515-281-4847
www.dhs.state.ia.us

Temporary Assistance to Needy Families (TANF)
Temporary Aid to Needy Families
Chuck Palmer
Iowa Department of Human Services
Hoover State Office Building E
13th and Walnut
Des Moines, IA 50319
515-281-5452
www.dhs.state.ia.us/

Transportation Department
Mark Wandro
Iowa Dept. of Transportation
800 Lincoln Way
Ames, IA 50010
515-239-1111
www.dot.state.ia.us/

Unclaimed Property Office
Treasurer
Unclaimed Property Division
State Capitol Bldg.
Des Moines, IA 50319
515-281-5368

Unemployment Insurance Office
Bureau Chief of Job Insurance
Dept. of Employment Services
1000 E. Grand Ave.
Des Moines, IA 50319
515-281-5387
www.state.ia.us/iwd/ui/index.html
Weekly benefit range: $33-274
Duration of benefits: 11-26 weeks

Utility Commission
Iowa Utilities Board
350 Maple St.
Des Moines, IA 50319
515-281-5979
www.state.ia.us/government/com/util/util.htm

Women's Commission
Iowa Commission on the Status of Women
Lucas State Office Building
Des Moines, IA 50319
515-281-4461
Fax: 515-242-6119
Email: icsw@compuserve.com
www.state.ia.us/dhr/sw
Charlotte Nelson, Exec. Director
Kathryn Burt, Chair

Your Senator
United States Senate
Washington, DC 20510
202-224-3121
www.senate.gov

Your Representative
United States House of Representatives
Washington, DC 20515
202-224-3121
www.house.gov

KANSAS

Federal Information Center
1-800-FED-INFO
www.firstgov.gov
www.pueblo.gsa.gov/call/

State Information Office
913-296-0111
www.accesskansas.org

Department on Aging
Kansas Department on Aging
New England Building
503 S. Kansas Ave.
Topeka, KS 66603-3404
800-432-3535
785-296-4986
Fax: 785-296-0256
www.agingkansas.org/kdoa

Attorney General's Office
Office of the Attorney General
120 SW 10th Avenue, 2nd Floor
Topeka, KS 66612-1597
785-296-2215
800-432-2310
Fax: 785-296-6296
www.ink.org/public/ksag
Email: General@ksag.org

Banking Commissioner
State Bank Commissioner
700 Jackson St., Suite 300
Topeka, KS 66603-3714
785-296-2266
Fax: 785-296-0168
www.osbckansas.org

Child Care and Development Block Grant Lead Agency
Coordinator of Child Care Services
Kansas Department of Social and
Rehabilitation Services
915 SW Harrison, Room 681W
Topeka, KS 66612
785-368-6354
Fax: 785-296-0146
www.srskansas.org

Child Support Enforcement Agency
John Badger
Child Support Enforcement Program
Department of Social and
Rehabilitation Services
P.O. Box 497
Topeka, KS 66601
785-296-3237
800-432-0152
Fax: 785-296-5206
www.srskansas.org/
srslegalservice.html

Cooperative Extension Office
Mark Johnson, Interim Director
Cooperative Extension Service
Kansas State University
123 Umberger Hall
Manhattan, KS 66506
913-532-5820
www.oznet.ksu.edu

Corporation Division Office
Corporate Division
Secretary of State
Capitol Building, Second Floor
Topeka, KS 66612
785-296-7456
www.kssos.org

Day Care Licensing Agency
Kansas Department of Health and
Environment
Child Care Licensing and
Registration
1000 SW Jackson, Suite 200
Topeka, KS 66612-1274
785-296-1270
Fax: 785-296-0803
www.kdhe.state.ks.us/kidsnet

Business Development Division
Department of Commerce and
Housing
1000 SW Jackson St., Suite 100
Topeka, KS 66612-1357
785-296-5298
Fax 785-296-3490
TTY 785-296-3487
http://kdoch.state.ks.us

Department of Education
Kansas State Department of
Education
120 SE 10th Ave.
Topeka, KS 66612-1182
785-296-3201
Fax: 785-296-7933
www.ksbe.state.ks.us/

Department of Higher Education
Kansas Board of Regents
1000 SW Jackson St., Suite 520
Topeka, KS 66612-1368
785-296-3421
Fax: 785-296-0983
www.kansasregents.org

Health Department
Kansas Division of Health &
Environment
1000 SW Jackson St.
Suite 300
Topeka, KS 66612-1365
785-296-1343
Fax: 785-296-1560
www.kdhe.state.ks.us

Housing Development Division
Kansas Department of Commerce
and Housing
1000 SW Jackson St., Suite 100
Topeka, KS 66612-1354
785-296-5865
Fax: 785-296-8985
http://kdoch.state.ks.us

Insurance Commissioner
Commissioner of Insurance
420 SW 9th St.
Topeka, KS 66612-1678
785-296-3071
800-432-2484
www.ksinsurance.org

Labor Department
Kansas Department of Human
Resources
401 SW Topeka Boulevard
Topeka, KS 66603-3182
785-296-5000
Fax: 785-296-5286
www.hr.state.ks.us

Licensing Office
Governor's Office
State Capitol, 2nd Floor

Topeka, KS 66612
785-296-3232

One-Stop Career Center
Kansas Job Service Career Centers
Department of Human Resources
Division of Employment and Training
401 SW Topeka Boulevard
Topeka, KS 66603-3182
785-296-5000
http://entkdhr.state.ks.us

Security Regulators
Kansas Securities Commission
618 S. Kansas Ave., 2nd Floor
Topeka, KS 66603
785-296-3307
800-232-9580
Fax: 785-296-6872
www.ink.org/public/ksecom

Small Business Development Center
Fort Hays State University
Kansas Small Business Development Center
214 SW 6th Street, Suite 301
Topeka, KS 66603-3179
785-296-6514
Fax: 785-291-3261
Email: ksbdc.boqorman@fhsu.edu
www.fhsu.edu/ksbdc

Social Services Offices
Kansas Department of Social and Rehabilitation Services
915 Harrison Street, SW
Docking State Office Building
Topeka, KS 66612
785-296-3959
Fax: 785-296-2173
www.srskansas.org

Temporary Assistance to Needy Families (TANF)
Temporary Aid to Needy Families
Rochelle Chronister
Kansas Department of Social and Rehabilitation Services
Docking State Office Bldg.
915 Harrison St.
Topeka, KS 66612
785-296-3271
www.srskansas.org

Transportation Department
James Van Sickel
Kansas Department of Transportation
915 Harrison, Room 754
Docking State Office Bldg.
Topeka, KS 66612-1568
785-296-3585
www.ink.org/public/kdot

Unclaimed Property Office
Unclaimed Property Division
900 Jackson, Suite 201
Topeka, KS 66612-1235
785-296-4165
800-432-0386
www.treasurer.state.ks.us

Unemployment Insurance Office
Director
Division of Employment Security
Department of Human Resources
401 Topeka Ave.
Topeka, KS 66603
785-296-5025
www.hr.state.ks.us/ui/html/ enui.htm
Weekly benefit range: $65-260
Duration of benefits: 10-26 weeks

Utility Commission
Kansas Corporation Commission
1500 SW Arrowhead Rd.
Topeka, KS 66604-2425
785-271-3100
800-662-0027 (KS only)
Fax: 785-271-3354
www.kcc.state.ks.us

Women's Commission
Wichita Commission on the Status of Women
Human Services Dept., 2nd Floor
455 North Main St.
Wichita, KS 67202
316-268-4691
Fax: 316-268-4219
Susan K. Leiker, Contact Person

Your Senator
United States Senate
Washington, DC 20510
202-224-3121
www.senate.gov

Your Representative
United States House of Representatives
Washington, DC 20515
202-224-3121
www.house.gov

KENTUCKY

Federal Information Center
1-800-FED-INFO
www.firstgov.gov
www.pueblo.gsa.gov/call/

State Information Office
502-564-3130
www.kydirect.net

Department on Aging
Aging Services Division
Cabinet for Families and Children
275 E. Main St., 5th Floor
Frankfort, KY 40621
502-564-6930
Fax: 502-564-4595
http://chs.state.ky.us/aging

Attorney General's Office
Office of the Attorney General
700 Capital Center Dr., Suite 118
Frankfort, KY 40601-3499
502-696-5300
502-696-5389 (consumer protection)
www.law.state.ky.us
Email: attorney.general@law.state.ky.us

Banking Commissioner
Commissioner
Department of Financial Institutions
1025 Capital Center Dr., Suite 200
Frankfort, KY 40601
502-573-3390
800-223-2579
Fax: 502-573-8787
www.dfi.state.ky.us/

Child Care and Development Block Grant Lead Agency
Department for Social Services
Cabinet for Families and Children
275 E. Main St., 6W
Frankfort, KY 40621
502-564-0850
Fax: 502-564-2467
http://cfc.state.ky.us

Child Support Enforcement Agency
Steven Veno
Division of Child Support Enforcement
Cabinet for Families and Children
275 East Main St., 6th Floor East
Frankfort, KY 40621
502-564-2285, ext.4403
800-248-1163
http://cfc.state.ky.us

Cooperative Extension Offices
Dr. Absher, Director
Cooperative Extension Service
310 W.P. Garrigus Building
University of Kentucky
Lexington, KY 40546
606-257-1846
www.ca.uky.edu

Dr. Harold Benson, Director
Kentucky State University
Cooperative Extension Program
Frankfort, KY 40601
502-227-5905
www.kysu.edu/landgrant/CEP/cep.htm

Corporation Division Office
Corporate Division
Secretary of State
Capitol Building, Room 154
700 Capitol Ave.
Frankfort, KY 40601
502-564-2848
Fax: 502-564-4075
www.sos.state.ky.us/

Day Care Licensing Agency
Cabinet for Health Services
Office of Inspector General
Division of Licensed Child Care
275 E. Main St., 5E-A
Frankfort, KY 40621
502-564-2800
Fax: 502-564-6546
http://chs.state.ky.us/oig/childcare

Economic Development Office
Kentucky Cabinet for Economic Development
2300 Capital Plaza Tower
500 Mero Street
Frankfort, KY 40601
502-564-7670
www.edc.state.ky.us/

Department of Education
Kentucky Department of Education
Education Technology Assistance Center
15 Fountain Place
Frankfort, KY 40601
502-564-2020
www.kde.state.ky.us/

Department of Higher Education
Kentucky Higher Education Assistance Authority
1050 U.S. 127 South, Suite 102
Frankfort, KY 40601-4323
800-928-8926, ext. 3963
502-564-7990
www.kheaa.com

Health Department
Kentucky Cabinet for Health Services
275 East Main Street
Frankfort, KY 40621
502-564-3970
Fax: 502-564-2556
http://chs.state.ky.us

Housing Office
Kentucky Housing Corporation
1231 Louisville Rd.
Frankfort, KY 40601-6191
502-564-7630
800-633-8896
www.kyhousing.org

Insurance Commissioner
Insurance Commissioner
215 W. Main St.
P.O. Box 517
Frankfort, KY 40602
502-564-3630
800-595-6053
www.doi.state.ky.us/

Labor Department
Kentucky Cabinet for Workforce Development
500 Mero Street
Frankfort, KY 40601
502-564-6606
Fax: 502-564-7967
www.kycwd.org

Licensing Office
Division of Occupations and Professions
P.O. Box 1360
Frankfort, KY 40602
502-564-3296
Fax: 502-696-1922
www.state.ky.us/agencies/finance/occupations

One-Stop Career Center
One-Stop Career Centers System
Department for Employment Services
275 East Main Street, 2 West
Frankfort, KY 40601
502-564-5331
Fax: 502-564-7452
www.kycwd.org

Security Regulators
Kentucky Department of Financial Institutions
1025 Capital Center Dr., Suite 200
Frankfort, KY 40601
502-573-3390
800-223-2579
Fax: 502-573-8787
www.dfi.state.ky.us

Small Business Development Center
Kentucky Small Business Development Center
University of Kentucky
Center for Entrepreneurship
225 College of Business and Economics
Lexington, KY 40056-0034
859-257-7668
www.ksbdc.org

Social Services Offices
Kentucky Cabinet for Families and Children
275 East Main Street
Frankfort, KY 40621
502-564-7130
Fax: 502-564-3866
http://cfc.state.ky.us/

Temporary Assistance to Needy Families (TANF)
Temporary Aid to Needy Families
Dietra Paris
Dept. of Community Based Services
275 East Main St., Third Floor, West
Frankfort, KY 40621
502-564-3703
Fax: 502-564-6907
http://cfc.state.ky.us

Transportation Department
James Codell
Kentucky Transportation Cabinet
501 High Street
Frankfort, KY 40622
502-564-4890
Fax: 502-564-4809
www.kytc.state.ky.us

Unclaimed Property Office
Unclaimed Property Branch
Kentucky State Treasury Department
Suite 183, Capitol Annex
Frankfort, KY 40601
502-564-4722
800-465-4722
www.kytreasury.com

Unemployment Insurance Office
Director, Division for Unemployment Insurance
Dept. of Employment Services
275 E. Main St., 2nd Floor
Frankfort, KY 40621
502-564-2900
www.des.state.ky.us/agencies/wforce/des/ui/ui.htm
Weekly benefit range: $32-180
Duration of benefits: 15-26 weeks

Utility Commission
Public Service Commission
211 Sower Boulevard
P.O. Box 615
Frankfort, KY 40602-0615
502-564-3940
800-772-4636
Fax: 502-564-3460
www.psc.state.ky.us/

Women's Commission
Kentucky Commission on Women
312 West Main Street
Frankfort, KY 40601
502-564-6643
Fax: 502-564-2315
Email: kcw@mail.state.ky.us
http://women.state.ky.us
Betsy Nowland-Curry, Executive Director

Your Senator
United States Senate
Washington, DC 20510
202-224-3121
www.senate.gov

Your Representative
United States House of Representatives
Washington, DC 20515
202-224-3121
www.house.gov

Louisiana

Federal Information Center
1-800-FED-INFO
www.firstgov.gov
www.pueblo.gsa.gov/call/

State Information Office
504-342-6600
www.state.la.us

Department on Aging
Elderly Affairs
412 N. 4th St.
Baton Rouge, LA 70802
225-342-7100
Fax: 225-342-7133
www.gov.state.la.us/depts/elderly.htm

Attorney General's Office
Office of the Attorney General
One American Place
301 Main Street, 12th Floor
P.O. Box 94095
Baton Rouge, LA 70804-9095
225-342-7900
800-351-4889 (consumer hotline)
Fax: 225-342-9637
www.ag.state.la.us

Banking Commissioner
Commissioner of Financial Institutions
8660 United Plaza Blvd., 2nd Floor
P.O. Box 94095
Baton Rouge, LA 70804-9095
504-925-4660
Fax: 225-925-4548
www.ofi.state.la.us

Child Care and Development Block Grant Lead Agency
Child Care Assistance Program
Louisiana Dept. of Social Services
Office of Family Support
P.O. Box 94065
Baton Rouge, LA 70804
225-342-3947
Fax: 225-342-4252
www.dss.state.la.us

Child Support Enforcement Agency
Lisa Woodruff-White
Support Enforcement Services
Office of Family Support
P.O. Box 94065
Baton Rouge, LA 70804-9065
225-342-4780
800-256-4650
Fax: 225-342-7397

Cooperative Extension Offices
Dr. Jack Bagent, Director
Cooperative Extension Service
Louisiana State University
P.O. Box 25100
Baton Rouge, LA 70894-5100
225-388-4141
www.agctr.lsu.edu/nav/extension.extension.asp

Dr. Leadrey Williams, Administrator
Cooperative Extension Program
Southern University and A&M College
P.O. Box 10010
Baton Rouge, LA 70813
225-771-2242
www.subr.edu

Corporation Division Office
Commercial Division
Secretary of State
3851 Essen Lane
Baton Rouge, LA 70809
225-925-4704
www.sec.state.la.us/

Day Care Licensing Agency
Department of Social Services
Child Care Licensing Division
P.O. Box 3078
Baton Rouge, LA 70821
225-922-0015
Fax: 225-922-0014
www.dss.state.la.us/

Economic Development Office
Department of Economic Development
P.O. Box 94185
Baton Rouge, LA 70804-9185
225-342-3000
www.lded.state.la.us

Department of Education
Louisiana Department of Education
P.O. Box 94064
Baton Rouge, LA 70804-9064
225-342-4667
877-453-2721
Fax: 225-342-0193
www.doe.state.la.us/

Department of Higher Education
Office of Student Financial Assistance
P.O. Box 91202
Baton Rouge, LA 70821-9202
225-922-1011
Fax: 225-922-0790
www.osfa.state.la.us

Health Department
Louisiana Department of Health and Hospitals
1201 Capitol Access Road
P.O. Box 629
Baton Rouge, LA 70821-0629
225-342-9500
Fax: 225-342-5568
www.dhh.state.la.us
Email: Webmaster@dhhmail.dhh.state.la.us

Housing Office
Louisiana Housing Finance Agency
200 Lafayette St., Suite 300
Baton Rouge, LA 70801
225-342-1320
Fax: 225-342-1310
www.lhfa.state.la.us

Insurance Commissioner
Commissioner of Insurance
P.O. Box 94214
Baton Rouge, LA 70804-9214
225-342-5900
800-259-5300
www.ldi.state.la.us/

Labor Department
Louisiana Department of Labor
1001 North 23rd
P.O. Box 94094
Baton Rouge, LA 70804-9094
225-342-3202
www.ldol.state.la.us

Licensing Office
First Stop Shop
Secretary of State
P.O. Box 94125
Baton Rouge, LA 70804-9125
225-922-2675
800-259-0001
www.sec.state.la.us

One-Stop Career Center
Louisiana Works
Louisiana Occupational Information System (L.O.I.S.)
P.O. Box 94094
Baton Rouge, LA 70804-9094
225-342-3141
888-302-7662
www.ldol.state.la.us

Security Regulators
Louisiana Commission of Securities
3445 N. Causeway, Suite 509
Metairie, LA 70002
504-846-6970
www.ofi.state.la.us

Small Business Development Center
Louisiana Small Business Development Center
University of Louisiana at Monroe
Administration, Room 2-57
Monroe, LA 71209-6435
318-342-5506
Fax: 318-342-5510
Email: brwilkerson@ulm.edu
http://lsbdc.net1.nlu.edu

Social Services Offices
Louisiana Department of Human Services
P.O. Box 3776
Baton Rouge, LA 70821
225-342-0286
www.dss.state.la.us

Temporary Assistance to Needy Families (TANF)
Temporary Aid to Needy Families
Louisiana Dept. of Social Services
P.O. Box 3776
Baton Rouge, LA 70821
225-342-0286
www.dss.state.la.us/offofs/html/tanf_state_plan.html

Transportation Department
Carol Cranshaw, Public Transportation Administrator
Louisiana Department of Transportation and Development
P.O. Box 94245
Baton Rouge, LA 70804
225-379-1436
www.dotd.state.la.us

Unclaimed Property Office
Louisiana Department of Treasury
Unclaimed Property Section
P.O. Box 91010
Baton Rouge, LA 70821
225-219-9400
888-925-4127 (in state)
www.treasury.state.la.us

Unemployment Insurance Office
Director, Unemployment Insurance
Louisiana Department of Labor
P.O. Box 94094
Baton Rouge, LA 70804-9094
225-342-3013
Fax: 225-342-5208
www.ldol.state.la.us/laworksweb/uibenefits.asp
Weekly benefit range: $10-258
Duration of benefits: 26 weeks

Utility Commission
Public Service Commission
One American Place
Suite 1630
P.O. Box 91154
Baton Rouge, LA 70821-9154
225-342-4404
800-228-9368 (LA only)
Fax: 225-342-2831
www.lpsc.org

Women's Commission
Governor's Office of Women's Services
1885 Woodale Blvd., 9th Floor
Baton Rouge, LA 70806
504-922-0960
Fax: 504-922-0959
Email: owsbradm@cmq.com
www.ows.state.la.us/

Your Senator
United States Senate
Washington, DC 20510
202-224-3121
www.senate.gov

Your Representative
United States House of Representatives
Washington, DC 20515
202-224-3121
www.house.gov

MAINE

Federal Information Center
1-800-FED-INFO
www.firstgov.gov
www.pueblo.gsa.gov/call/

State Information Office
207-582-9500
www.state.me.us

Department on Aging
Elder and Adult Services
Human Services Department
11 State House Station
35 Anthony Ave.
Augusta, ME 04333-0011
207-624-5335
800-262-2232
www.state.me.us/dhs/beas/

Attorney General's Office
Office of the Attorney General
6 State House Station
Augusta, ME 04333
207-626-8800
TTY: 207-626-8865
www.state.me.us/ag/homepage. htm

Banking Commissioner
Bureau of Financial Institutions
#36 State House Station
Augusta, ME 04333-0036
207-624-8570
Fax: 207-624-8590
www.state.me.us/
pfr/bkg/bkghome2.htm

Child Care and Development Block Grant Lead Agency
Office of Child Care and Head Start
Maine Dept. of Human Services
221 State St.
Augusta, ME 04333-0011
207-287-5060
Fax: 207-287-5031
www.state.me.us/dhs/

Child Support Enforcement Agency
Stephen Hussey
Division of Support Enforcement
and Recovery
Bureau of Income Maintenance
Department of Human Services
State House Station 11
Whitten Rd.
Augusta, ME 04333
207-287-3110
800-371-3101 (in ME)
Fax: 207-287-2334
www.state.me.us/dhs/bfi/dser

Cooperative Extension Office
Vaughn Holyoke, Director
Cooperative Extension Service
University of Maine
5741 Libby Hall, Room 102
Orono, ME 04469-5741
207-581-3188
www.umext.maine.edu

Corporation Division Office
Information and Report Section
Bureau of Corporations
Secretary of State
State House Station 101
Augusta, ME 04333-0101
207-624-7736
Fax: 207-287-5428
www.state.me.us/sos/

Day Care Licensing Agency
Bureau of Child and Family Services
221 State St., Station 11
Augusta, ME 04333
207-287-5060
Fax: 207-287-5031
TTY: 207-287-5048
www.state.me.us/dhs/ welcome.htm

Economic Development Office
Office of Business Development
Department of Economic and
Community Development
59 State House Station
Augusta, ME 04333
207-624-9804
Fax: 207-287-5701
www.econdevmaine.com

Department of Education
Maine Department of Education
Educational Bldg.
Station No. 23
Augusta, ME 04333
207-624-6620
Fax: 207-624-6601
www.state.me.us/education/
homepage.htm

Department of Higher Education
Finance Authority of Maine (FAME)
Maine Education Assistance
Division
5 Community Drive
P.O. Box 949
Augusta, ME 04332-0949
207-623-3263
800-228-3734
TDD: 207-626-2717
Fax: 207-623-0095
www.famemaine.com

Health Department
Maine Dept. of Human Services
221 State Street
Augusta, ME 04333
207-287-8016
www.state.me.us/dhs/ welcome.htm

Housing Office
Maine State Housing Authority
353 Water St.
Augusta, ME 04330-4633
207-626-4600
800-452-4668
Fax: 207-626-4678
TTY: 800-452-4603
www.mainehousing. org

Insurance Commissioner
Superintendent of Insurance
34 State House Station
Augusta, ME 04333-0034
207-624-8475
800-300-5000 (in state)
Fax: 207-624-8599
www.state.me.us/pfr/ins/
inshome2.htm

Labor Department
Maine Department of Labor
Bureau of Employment Services
54 State House Station
Augusta, ME 04333-0054
207-287-3516
Fax: 207-287-8394
www.state.me.us/labor/

Licensing Office
Department of Professional and Financial Regulation
State House Station 35
August, ME 04333
207-624-8500
Fax: 207-624-8690
TTY: 207-624-8563
www.state.me.us/pfr/ pfrhome.htm

One-Stop Career Center
Maine Career Centers
Department of Labor
Bureau of Employment Services
54 State House Station
Augusta, ME 04333-0054
888-457-8883
TTY: 800-794-1110
www.mainecareercenter.com

Security Regulators
Maine Securities Division
121 State House Station
Augusta, ME 04333
207-624-8551
Fax: 207-624-8590
www.state.me.us/pfr/sec/sec_index.htm

Small Business Development Center
Small Business Development Center
University of Southern Maine
15 Surrenden Street
Portland, ME 04103
MAILING ADDRESS:
96 Falmouth Street
P.O. Box 3000
Portland, ME 04104-9300
207-780-4420
Fax: 207-780-4810
TTY: 207-780-4420
Email: msbdc@usm.maine.edu
www.mainesbdc.org

Social Services Offices
Maine Dept. of Human Services
221 State Street
Augusta, ME 04333
207-287-2546
www.state.me.us/dhs/

Temporary Assistance to Needy Families (TANF)
Temporary Aid to Needy Families
Kevin Concannon
Maine Dept. of Human Services
Bureau of Family Independence
11 Statehouse Station
Augusta, ME 04333
207-287-2736
Fax: 207-287-3005
TTY: 207-287-4479
www.state.me.us/dhs/

Transportation Department
Kim King
Office of Passenger Transportation
16 Statehouse Station
Augusta, ME 043333
207-287-2551
www.state.me.us/mdot/homepage.htm

Ronald Roy
Office of Passenger Transportation
16 Statehouse Station
Augusta, NE 04333
207-287-3318
www.state.me.us/mdot/homepage.htm

Unclaimed Property Office
Treasury Department
Abandoned Property Division
39 State House Station
Augusta, ME 043333
207-624-7470
888-283-2808 (in state)
www.state.me.us/treasurer/property.htm

Unemployment Insurance Office
Director, Unemployment Compensation Division
Maine Department of Labor
P.O. Box 309
Augusta, ME 04332
207-287-2316
www.state.me.us/labor/uibennys/index.html
Weekly benefit range: $47-272
Duration of benefits: 21-26 weeks

Utility Commission
Public Utilities Commission
18 State House Station
Augusta, ME 04333-0018
207-287-3831
800-452-4699 (ME only)
Fax: 207-287-1039
TTY: 800-437-1220
www.state.me.us/mpuc

Women's Commission
Maryland Commission for Women
45 Calvert Street
Annapolis, MD 21401
410-260-6047
Fax: 410-974-2307
TTY: 800-925-4434
Email: mcw@dhr.state.md.us
www.dhr.state.md.us/mcw

Your Senator
United States Senate
Washington, DC 20510
202-224-3121
www.senate.gov

Your Representative
United States House of Representatives
Washington, DC 20515
202-224-3121
www.house.gov

MARYLAND

Federal Information Center
1-800-FED-INFO
www.firstgov.gov
www.pueblo.gsa.gov/call/

State Information Office
800-449-4347
www.state.md.us

Department on Aging
Aging Office
301 W. Preston St., Suite 1004
Baltimore, MD 21201-2374
410-767-1100
800-AGE-DIAL
Fax: 410-333-7943
TTY: 410-767-1083
www.mdoa.state.md.us

Attorney General's Office
Office of the Attorney General
200 St. Paul Place
Baltimore, MD 21202
410-576-6300
888-743-0023
TDD: 410-576-6372
www.oag.state.md.us
Email: consumer@oag. state.md.us

Banking Commissioner
Commissioner of Financial Regulation
500 North Calvert St., Room 402
Baltimore, MD 21202-2272
410-230-6100
Email: finreg@dllr.state.md.us

Child Care and Development Block Grant Lead Agency
Child Care Administration
Maryland Department of Human Resources
311 W. Saratoga St., 1st Floor
Baltimore, MD 21201
410-767-7128
Fax: 410-333-8699
www.dhr.state.md.us/dhr

Child Support Enforcement Agency
Clifford Layman
Child Support Enforcement Administration
311 West Saratoga St.
Baltimore, MD 21201
410-767-7043
800-332-6347 (in MD)
Fax: 410-333-0774
TTY: 800-925-4434
www.dhr.state.md.us/csea/index.ht
m

Cooperative Extension Offices
Dr. Thomas Fretz
Regional Directors Office
Cooperative Extension Service
Room 1202, Simons Hall
University of Maryland
College Park, MD 20742
301-405-2907
www.agnr.umd.edu/MCE/index.cfm

Dr. Henry Brookes, Administrator
Cooperative Extension Service
UMES
Princess Anne, MD 21853
410-651-6206
http://umesde.umes.edu/ 1890-mce/

Corporation Division Office
Corporate Charter Division
Dept. of Assessments and Taxation
301 W. Preston St.
Baltimore, MD 21201
410-767-1184
Fax: 410-333-5873
www.dat.state.md.us/

Day Care Licensing Agency
Department of Human Resources
Child Care Administration
Licensing Division
311 W. Saratoga St.
Baltimore, MD 21201
410-767-7128
www.dhr.state.md.us/

Economic Development Office
Department of Business and Economic Development
217 East Redwood St.
Baltimore, MD 21202
800-541-8549
Fax: 410-333-8628
TDD/TTY: 410-333-6926
www.dbed.state.md.us/

Department of Education
Maryland Department of Education
Office of Planning
Results and Information Management
200 W. Baltimore St.
Baltimore, MD 21201
410-767-0073
888-246-0016
www.msde.state.md.us/

Department of Higher Education
Maryland Higher Education Commission
State Scholarship Administration
The Jeffery Building
16 Francis Street, Suite 209
Annapolis, MD 21401-1781
410-260-4565
800-974-1024
Fax: 410-974-5994
TTY: 800-735-2258
www.mhec.state.md.us

Health Department
Maryland Department of Health & Mental Hygiene
State Office Building Complex
201 West Preston Street
Baltimore, MD 21201-2399
410-767-6860
877-463-3464 (in state)
TDD: 800-735-2258
www.dhmh.state.md.us/index.html

Housing Office
Department of Housing and Community Development
100 Community Place
Crownsville, MD 21032-2023
410-514-7000
800-756-0229 (in state)
www.dhcd.state.md.us

Insurance Commissioner
Insurance Commissioner
525 St. Paul Place
Baltimore, MD 21202
410-468-2000
800-492-6116

Fax: 410-468-2020
TTY: 800-735-2258
www.mdinsurance.state.md.us

Labor Department
Maryland Department of Labor, Licensing and Regulation
1100 North Eutaw Street
Baltimore, MD 21201-000
410-767-2357
www.dllr.state.md.us

Licensing Office
Division of Occupational and Professional Licensing
Department of Labor, Licensing and Regulation
500 N. Calvert St., 3rd Floor
Baltimore, MD 21202
410-230-6100
www.dllr.state.md.us/license/occprof/index.html

One-Stop Career Center
CareerNet
Department of Labor, Licensing and Regulation
Employment Services
500 North Calvert Street
Baltimore, MD 21202-2272
410-767-2800
TTY: 410-767-2986
www.careernet.state.md.us/
Email: pflowers@careernet.state.md.us

Security Regulators
Maryland Division of Securities
200 St. Paul Place, 20th Floor
Baltimore, MD 21202
410-576-6360
www.oag.state.md.us/Securities

Small Business Development Center
Maryland Small Business Development Center
7100 Baltimore Avenue, Suite 401
College Park, MD 20740
877-787-7232
www.bsos.umd.edu/sbdc

Social Services Offices
Maryland Department of Human Resources
Saratoga State Center
311 West Saratoga Street
Baltimore, MD 21201-1000
410-767-7758
800-332-6347
TTY: 800-925-4434
www.dhr.state.md.us/

Temporary Assistance to Needy Families (TANF)
Temporary Aid to Needy Families
Maryland Department of Human Resources
311 W. Saratoga St., Room 1045
Baltimore, MD 21201
410-767-7338
www.dhr.state.md.us/fia/p_assist.htm

Transportation Department
Maryland Mass Transit Administration
6 St. Paul St.
Baltimore, MD 21201
410-767-3765
www.mtamaryland.com

Unclaimed Property Office
Unclaimed Property Section
301 West Preston St.
Baltimore, MD 21201
410-767-1700
800-782-7383
http://in1.comp.state.md.us/unclaim/default.asp

Unemployment Insurance Office
Executive Director
Office of Unemployment Insurance
Department of Labor, Licensing, and Regulation
1100 N. Eutaw St., Room 501
Baltimore, MD 21201
410-767-2444
Fax: 410-333-7099
www.dllr.state.md.us/employment/unemployment.html
Weekly benefit range: $25-250
Duration of benefits: 26 weeks

Utility Commission
Public Service Commission
6 St. Paul St., 16th Floor
Baltimore, MD 21202
410-767-8000
800-492-0474 (MD only)
www.psc.state.md. us/psc/

Women's Commission
Maryland Commission for Women
45 Calvert Street
Baltimore, MD 21401
410-260-6047
877-868-2196
Fax: 410-974-2307
TTY: 800-925-4434
Email: mcw@dhr.state.md.us
www.dhr.state.md.us/mcw/index.htm
Carol A. Silberg, PhD, Exec. Director
Kathleen E. Schafer, Chair

Your Senator
United States Senate
Washington, DC 20510
202-224-3121
www.senate.gov

Your Representative
United States House of Representatives
Washington, DC 20515
202-224-3121
www.house.gov

MASSACHUSETTS

Federal Information Center
1-800-FED-INFO
www.firstgov.gov
www.pueblo.gsa.gov/call/

State Information Office
617-722-2000
www.state.ma.us

Department on Aging
Elder Affairs Department
1 Ashburton Place
5th Floor, Room 506
Boston, MA 02108
617-727-7750
800-882-2003
TTY: 800-872-0166
www.state.ma.us/elder

Attorney General's Office
Office of the Attorney General
One Ashburton Place
Boston, MA 02108-1698
617-727-2200
617-727-8400 (consumer hotline)
www.ago.state.ma.us

Banking Commissioner
Commissioner of Banks
One South Station
Boston, MA 02110
617-956-1500
800-495-2265 (in state)
Fax: 617-956-1599
TDD: 617-956-1577
www.state.ma.us/ dob/

Child Care and Development Block Grant Lead Agency
Office of Child Care Services
One Ashburton Place, Room 1105
Boston, MA 02108
617-626-2000
Fax: 617-626-2028
www.qualitychildcare.org

Child Support Enforcement Agency
Jerry Fay
Child Support Enforcement Division
Department of Revenue
51 Sleeper Street
Boston, MA 02205
617-577-7200
617-621-4991
800-332-2733
TDD: 800-255-5587
www.cse.state.ma.us/

Cooperative Extension Office
Dr. John Gerber, Associate Director
212C Stockbridge Hall
University of Massachusetts
Amherst, MA 01003
413-545-4800
www.umass.edu/umext/

Corporation Division Office
Corporate Division
Secretary of State
1 Ashburton Place, 17th Floor
Boston, MA 02108
617-727-9640
Fax: 617-742-4525
www.state.ma.us/sec/cor/coridx.htm

Day Care Licensing Agency
Department of Health
Office of Child Care Services
Day Care Licensing Division
1 Ashburton Place, Room 1105
Boston, MA 02108
617-626-2000
Fax: 617-626-2028
www.qualitychildcare.org

Economic Development Office
Massachusetts Office of Business Development
10 Park Plaza, 3rd Floor
Boston, MA 02116
617-973-8600
800-5-CAPITAL
Fax: 617-727-8797
www.state.ma.us/mobd

Department of Education
Massachusetts Department of Education
Information and Outreach
350 Main St.
Malden, MA 02148-0523
781-388-3000
www.doe.mass.edu

Department of Higher Education
Board of Higher Education
Office of Student Financial Assistance
454 Broadway, Suite 200
Revere, MA 02151
617-727-9420
Fax: 617-727-0667
www.osfa.mass.edu

Health Department
Massachusetts Department of Public Health
250 Washington Street
Boston, MA 02108-4619
617-624-6000
Fax: 617-624-5206
www.state.ma.us/dph/ dphhome.htm

Housing Offices
Massachusetts Housing Finance Agency
1 Beacon St.
Boston, MA 02108
617-854-1000
Fax: 617-854-1029
TDD: 617-854-1025
www.mhfa.com/

Massachusetts Department of Housing and Community Development
One Congress Street, 10th Floor
Boston, MA 02114
617-727-7765
Fax: 617-727-5060

Insurance Commissioner
Division of Insurance
One South Station, 5th Floor
Boston, MA 02210-2208
617-521-7794
Consumer Hotline: 617-521-7777
Fax: 617-521-7772
www.state.ma.us/doi

Labor Department
Massachusetts Division of Employment and Training
19 Staniford Street
Boston, MA 02114
617-626-5400

Fax: 617-570-8581
www.detma.org

Licensing Office
Division of Professional Licensure
239 Causeway St.
Boston, MA 02114
617-727-3074
Fax: 617-727-2197
TTY: 617-727-2099
www.state.ma.us/reg

One-Stop Career Center
Massachusetts One-Stop Career Center Network
Division of Employment and Training
19 Staniford Street
Boston, MA 02114
617-626-5400
Fax: 617-570-8581
www.detma.org/jobseeker/centers/careercenters.htm

Security Regulators
Massachusetts Securities Division
One Ashburton Place, 17th Floor
Boston, MA 02108
617-727-3548
800-269-5428 (in state)
Fax: 617-248-0177
www.state.ma.us/sec/sct/ sctidx.htm

Small Business Development Center
Massachusetts Small Business Development Center
University of Massachusetts Amherst
205 Isenberg School of Management
1221 President's Drive
Amherst, MA 01003-9310
413-545-6301
Fax: 413-545-1273
http://msbdc.som.umass.edu

Social Services Offices
Massachusetts Health and Human Services
1 Ashburton Place, Room 1109
Boston, MA 02108-1818
617-727-7600
Fax: 617-727-5134
www.masscares.org

Temporary Assistance to Needy Families (TANF)
Temporary Aid to Needy Families
Claire McIntire
Massachusetts Department of Transitional Assistance
600 Washington St.
Boston, MA 02111
617-348-8500
www.state.ma.us/dta

Transportation Department
Kevin J. Sullivan
Massachusetts Executive Office of Transportation and Construction
10 Park Plaza
Boston, MA 02116
617-973-7000
Fax: 617-523-6454
www.eotc.org

Unclaimed Property Office
Abandoned Property Division
1 Ashburton Place, 12th Floor
Boston, MA 02108
617-367-0400
800-647-2300
Fax: 617-227-1622
www.state.ma.us/treasury

Unemployment Insurance Office
Unemployment Insurance Director
Department of Employment and Training
19 Staniford St., 2nd Floor
Boston, MA 02114
617-626-5400
Fax: 617-870-8591
www.detma.org/claimant/
Weekly benefit range: $14-402
Duration of benefits: 10-30 weeks

Utility Commission
Department of Telecommunications and Energy
One South Station
Boston, MA 02110
617-305-3500
www.magnet.state.ma.us/dpu

Women's Commission
Massachusetts Governor's Advisory Committee on Women's Issues
Statehouse Governor's Office
Room 111
Boston, MA 02133
617-727-3600
Fax: 617-727-9725
Joanne Thompson, Chair
www.state.ma.us/womenissues

Your Senator
United States Senate
Washington, DC 20510
202-224-3121
www.senate.gov

Your Representative
United States House of Representatives
Washington, DC 20515
202-224-3121
www.house.gov

MICHIGAN

Federal Information Center
1-800-FED-INFO
www.firstgov.gov
www.pueblo.gsa.gov/call/

State Information Office
517-373-1837
www.state.mi.us

Department on Aging
Michigan Office of Services to the Aging
P.O. Box 30676
Lansing, MI 48909-8176
517-373-8230
www.miseniors.net

Attorney General's Office
Office of the Attorney General
G. Mennen Williams Bldg., 7th Fl.
525 West Ottawa Street
P.O. Box 30212
Lansing, MI 48909
517-373-1110
517-373-1140 (consumer protection)
Fax: 517-373-3042
www.ag.state.mi.us
Email: miag@michigan.gov

Banking Commissioner
Commissioner of Financial Institutions Bureau
P.O. Box 30220
Lansing, MI 48909-7720
517-373-0220
877-999-6442
Fax: 517-335-4978
www.cis.state.mi.us/ofis

Child Care and Development Block Grant Lead Agency
Office of Children's Services
Michigan Department of Social Services
235 S. Grand Ave., Suite 1302
P.O. Box 30037
Lansing, MI 48909-7537
517-373-0356
Fax: 517-241-7843

Child Support Enforcement Agency
Wallace Dutkowski
Office of Child Support
Department of Social Services
P.O. Box 30478
235 S. Grand Ave.
Suite 1215
Lansing, MI 48909-7978
517-373-7570
Fax: 517-373-4980

Cooperative Extension Office
Arlen Leholm, Director
Michigan State University Extension
Room 108, Agriculture Hall
Michigan State University
East Lansing, MI 48824
517-355-2308
www.msue.msu.edu/home

Corporation Division Office
Corporation Division
Corporation and Securities Bureau
Michigan Department of Commerce
P.O. Box 30054
6546 Mercantile
Lansing, MI 48909
517-241-6470
www.cis.state.mi.us/corp

Day Care Licensing Agency
Division of Child Day Care Licensing
CIS-BRS
7109 W. Saginaw, 2nd Floor
P.O. Box 30650
Lansing, MI 48917-8150
517-373-8300
Fax: 517-335-6121
www.cis.state.mi.us/brs/cdc/home.htm

Economic Development Corporation
Michigan Jobs Commission
300 North Washington Square
Lansing MI 48913
517-373-9808
http://medc.michigan.org

Department of Education
Michigan Department of Education
Information Center Data Services
P.O. Box 30008
Lansing, MI 48909
517-373-3324
www.mde.state.mi.us/

Department of Higher Education
Michigan Department of Treasury
Higher Education Assistance Authority
P.O. Box 30468
Lansing, MI 48909-7962
888-447-2687
517-373-3394
www.michigan.gov/mistudentaid

Health Department
Michigan Department of Community Health
Lewis Cass Building, Sixth Floor
320 South Walnut Street
Lansing, MI 48913
517-373-3500
www.michigan.gov/mdch
Email: arias@michigan.gov

Housing Office
Michigan State Housing Development Authority
735 E. Michigan Ave.
P.O. Box 30044
Lansing, MI 48912
517-373-8370
Fax: 517-335-4797
TTY: 800-382-4568
www.mshda.org

Insurance Commissioner
Office of Financial and insurance Services
P.O. Box 30220
Lansing, MI 48909-7720
517-373-0220
877-999-6442
Fax: 517-335-4978
www.cis.state.mi.us/ofis

Labor Department
Michigan Jobs Commission
201 North Washington Square
Victor Office Center, 4th Floor
Lansing, MI 48913
800-946-6829
http://jobs.michigan.org

Licensing Office
Michigan Department of Consumer and Industry Services
P.O. Box 30018
Lansing, MI 48909
517-241-9223
Fax: 517-241-9280
www.cis.state.mi.us

One-Stop Career Center
Michigan Works!
Michigan Jobs Commission
201 North Washington Square
Victor Office Center, 7th Floor
Lansing, MI 48913
800-285-WORKS
866-MY-GOALS
Email: Customer-Assistance@state.mi.us
www.michiganworks.org

Security Regulators
Michigan Corporation & Securities Bureau
P.O. Box 30220
Lansing, MI 48909-7220
517-373-0220
877-999-6442
Fax: 517-335-4978
www.cis.state.mi.us/ofis

Small Business Development Center
Michigan Small Business Development Center
Grand Valley State University
510 W. Fulton St.
Grand Rapids, MI 49504
616-336-7480
Fax: 616-336-7485
Email: sbdcq@gvsu.edu
www.mi-sbdc.org

Social Services Offices
Michigan Family Independence Agency
235 South Grand Avenue
Lansing, MI 48933
517-373-7394
General Info: 517-373-2035
www.mfia.state.mi.us

Temporary Assistance to Needy Families (TANF)
Temporary Aid to Needy Families
Douglas Howard, Director
Michigan Family Independence Agency
P.O. Box 30037
Lansing, MI 48909
517-373-2000
General Info: 517-373-2035
Fax: 517-335-6101
www.mfia.state.mi.us/ 1997fact.htm

Transportation Department
Gus Lluberes
Michigan Department of Transportation
425 West Ottawa St.
P.O. Box 30050
Lansing, MI 48909
517-373-8820
General Info: 517-373-2090
www.mdot.state.mi.us/

Al Johnson
Michigan DOT, UPTRAN
P.O. Box 30050
Lansing, MI 48909
517-335-2549
www.mdot.state.mi.us/ uptran/

Unclaimed Property Office
Department of Treasury
Abandoned & Unclaimed Property Division
Lansing, MI 48922
517-335-4327
Fax: 517-335-4400
www.treas.state.mi.us/

Unemployment Insurance Office
Unemployment Agency
Consumer and Industry Services
Cadillac Place
3024 W. Grand Blvd.
Detroit, MI 48202
313-456-2400
800-638-3995
Fax: 313-456-2424
www.cis.state.mi.us/ua/homepage.htm
Weekly benefit range: $42-300
Duration of benefits: 15-26 weeks

Utility Commission
Public Service Commission
6545 Mercantile Way, Suite 7
P.O. Box 30221
Lansing, MI 48909
517-241-6180
800-292-9555 (MI only)
Fax: 517-241-6181
http://cis.state.mi.us/mpsc/

Women's Commission
Michigan Women's Commission
124 W. Allegan Street
Lansing, MI 48933
517-373-2884
Fax: 517-355-1649
Email: mwci1@michigan.gov
www.michigan.gov/mdcr
Anne Norlander, Chair

Your Senator
United States Senate
Washington, DC 20510
202-224-3121
www.senate.gov

Your Representative
United States House of Representatives
Washington, DC 20515
202-224-3121
www.house.gov

MINNESOTA

Federal Information Center
1-800-FED-INFO
www.firstgov.gov
www.pueblo.gsa.gov/call/

State Information Office
612-296-6013
www.state.mn.us

Department on Aging
Minnesota Board on Aging
Department of Human Services
444 LaFayette Rd. North
St. Paul, MN 55155-3843
651-296-2770
800-882-6262
www.mnaging.org

Attorney General's Office
Office of the Attorney General
1400 NCL Tower
445 Minnesota Street
St. Paul, MN 55101
651-296-3353
800-657-3787
www.ag.state.mn.us
Email: attorney.general@
state.mn.us

Banking Commissioner
Department of Commerce
Division of Financial Examinations
85 7th Place East, Suite 500
St. Paul, MN 55101-2198
651-296-2135
www.commerce.state.mn.us/

Child Care and Development Block Grant Lead Agency
Child Care Program Administrator
Minnesota Department of Children,
Families and Learning
1500 Highway 36 West
Roseville, MN 55113
651-582-8390
http://children.state.mn.us

Child Support Enforcement Agency
Laura Kadwell
Child Support Enforcement Division
Department of Human Services
444 Lafayette Rd., 4th Floor
St. Paul, MN 55155
651-296-2542
www.dhs.state.mn.us/ecs/
program/csed.htm

Cooperative Extension Office
Catherine Fennelly, Director
Minnesota Extension Service
University of Minnesota
240 Coffey Hall
1420 Eckles Avenue
St. Paul, MN 55108
612-624-1222
www.extension.umn.edu

Corporation Division Office
Business Services Division
Secretary of State
180 State Office Building
St. Paul, MN 55155
651-296-2803
877-551-6SOS (6767)
www.sos.state.mn.us/business/
index.html

Day Care Licensing Agency
Department of Human Services
Licensing Division
444 Lafayette Rd. North
St. Paul, MN 55155-3842
651-296-3971
www.dhs.state.mn.us/Licensing/
ChildCareCenters.htm

Economic Development Office
Department of Trade and Economic
Development
500 Metro Square Bldg.
121 7th Place East
St. Paul, MN 55101-2146
651-297-1291
800-657-3858
www.dted.state.mn.us

Department of Education
Minnesota Department of Children,
Families & Learning
1500 Highway 36 West
Roseville, MN 55113
651-582-8200
http://children.state.mn.us/

Department of Higher Education
Minnesota Higher Education
Programs
1450 Energy Park Dr.
Suite 350
St. Paul, MN 55108-5227
651-642-0567
www.mheso.state.mn.us

Health Department
Minnesota Department of Health
717 Delaware Street Southeast
P.O. Box 64975
Minneapolis, MN 55440-9441
651-215-5800
www.health.state.mn.us

Housing Office
Minnesota Housing Finance Agency
400 Sibley St.
Suite 300
St. Paul, MN 55101-1998
651-296-7608
800-657-3769
www.mhfa.state.mn.us

Insurance Commissioner
Commissioner of Commerce
85 7th Place East
Suite 500
St. Paul, MN 55101-2362
651-297-7161
800-657-3602
800-657-3978 (license status)
www.commerce.state.mn.us/pages/
InsuranceMain.htm

Labor Department
Minnesota Economic Security
390 North Robert Street
St.Paul, MN 55101
651-296-3644
800-GET-JOBS
www.mnwfc.org

Licensing Office
Office of Consumer Services
Office of Attorney General
1400 NCL Tower
445 Minnesota St.
St. Paul, MN 55101
651-296-3353

800-657-3787
www.ag.state.mn.us

One-Stop Career Center
Minn WorkForce Center
Department of Economic Security
390 North Robert Street
St. Paul, MN 55101
888-GET-JOBS
www.mnwfc.org

Security Regulators
Department of Commerce
85 7th Place East, Suite 500
St. Paul, MN 55101
651-296-4973
www.commerce.state.mn.us/
pages/SecuritiesMain.htm

Small Business Development Center
Minnesota Small Business
Development Center
Minnesota Department of Trade and
Economic Development
500 Metro Square Bldg.
121 7th Place East
St. Paul, MN 55101-2146
651-297-5773
Fax: 651-296-1290
Email: mary.kruger@state.mn.us
www.dted.state.mn.us

Social Services Offices
Minnesota Department of Human
Services
444 Lafayette Road North
St.Paul, MN 555155
651-297-3933
www.dhs.state.mn.us

Temporary Assistance to Needy Families (TANF)
Temporary Aid to Needy Families
David Doth
Minnesota Department of Human
Services
444 Lafayette Rd. North
St. Paul, MN 55155
651-296-4776
www.dhs.state.mn.us/
ecs/Welfare/default.htm

Transportation Department
Elwyn Tinkenberg
Minnesota Department of
Transportation
Transportation Bldg.
395 John Ireland Blvd.
St. Paul, MN 55155
800-657-3774
651-296-3000
www.dot.state.mn.us

Unclaimed Property Office
Minnesota Commerce Department
Unclaimed Property Division
85 7th Place East, Suite 600
St. Paul, MN 55101-3165
651-296-2568
800-925-5668
www.commerce.state.mn.us/
pages/UnclaimedMain.htm

Unemployment Insurance Office
Director Jack Weidenbach
Minnesota Department of Economic
Security
Workforce Wage Assistance Branch
390 N. Robert St.
St. Paul, MN 55101
651-296-3611
888-438-5627 (888-GET-JOBS)
www.mnwfc.org/ui/index.htm
Weekly benefit range: $38-452
Duration of benefits: up to 26 weeks

Utility Commission
Public Utilities Commission
121 7th Place East, Suite 350
St. Paul, MN 55101-2147
612-296-0406
800-657-3782 (MN only)
www.puc.state.mn.us

Women's Commission
Minnesota Commission on the
Economic Status of Women
85 State Office Building
St. Paul, MN 55155
651-296-8590
800-657-3949
Email: lcesw@commissions.
leg.state.mn.us
www.commissions.leg.state.
mn.us/lcesw
Diane Cushman, Director
Cheryl Hoium, Asst. Director

Your Senator
United States Senate
Washington, DC 20510
202-224-3121
www.senate.gov

Your Representative
United States House of
Representatives
Washington, DC 20515
202-224-3121
www.house.gov

MISSISSIPPI

Federal Information Center
1-800-FED-INFO
www.firstgov.gov
www.pueblo.gsa.gov/call/

State Information Office
601-359-1000
www.state.ms.us

Department on Aging
Aging and Adult Services Division
Human Services Department
750 North State Street
Jackson, MS 39202
601-359-4929
800-948-3090
Email: icraig@mdhs.state.ms.us
www.mdhs.state.ms.us/aas.html

Attorney General's Office
Office of the Attorney General
P.O. Box 220
Jackson, MS 39205
601-359-3680
800-281-4418
www.ago.state.ms.us
Email: msag05@ago.state.ms.us

Banking Commissioner
Commissioner of Banking and
Consumer Finance
501 N. West St.
901 Woolfolk Bldg., Suite A
P.O. Box 23729
Jackson, MS 39225-3729
601-359-1031
800-844-2499
www.dbcf.state.ms.us/

Child Care and Development Block Grant Lead Agency
Office for Children and Youth
Mississippi Dept. of Human Services
750 N. State St.
Jackson, MS 39202
601-359-4544
800-877-7882 (in state)
Fax: 601-359-4422
www.mdhs.state.ms.us/ocy.html

Child Support Enforcement Agency
Alsee McDaniel
Division of Child Support
Enforcement
Department of Human Services
750 N. State St.
Jackson, MS 39205
601-359-4861
800-948-4010 (in MS)
www.mdhs.state.ms.us/cse.html

Cooperative Extension Offices
Ronald A. Brown, Director
Cooperative Extension Service
Mississippi State University
P.O. Box 9601
Mississippi State, MS 39762
601-325-3034
http://msucares.com

LeRoy Davis, Dean
Cooperative Extension Service
1000 ASU Dr., #479
Lorman, MS 39096
601-877-6128
www.alcorn.edu/academic/
academ/ags.htm

Corporation Division Office
Office of Corporations
Secretary of State
202 N. Congress St.
Suite 601
P.O. Box 136
Jackson, MS 39205
800-256-3493
601-359-1633
www.sos.state.ms.us/busserv/
corp/corporations.html

Day Care Licensing Agency
Mississippi State Dept. of Health
Child Care Facilities Licensure
Branch
570 E. Woodrow Wilson Dr.
Jackson, MS 39216
601-576-7400
800-227-7308
www.mdhs.state.ms.us/

Economic Development Office
Mississippi Development Authority
P.O. Box 849
Jackson, MS 39205-0849
601-359-3155
Fax: 601-359-2832
www.decd.state.ms.us

Department of Education
Mississippi Dept. of Education
Central High School
359 N. West St.
P.O. Box 771
Jackson, MS 39205-0771
601-359-3513
www.mde.k12.ms.us

Department of Higher Education
Mississippi Institution of Higher
Learning
3825 Ridgewood Road
Jackson, MS 39211-6453
601-432-6430
www.ihl.state.ms.us

Health Department
Mississippi State Dept of Health
570 E. Woodrow Wilson Dr.
P.O. Box 1700
Jackson, MS 39215-1700
601-576-7400
www.msdh.state.ms.us/
Email: info@msdh.state.ms.us

Housing Office
Mississippi Home Corporation
P.O. Box 23369
Jackson, MS 39225-3369
601-718-INFO
601-718-4642
Email: emailus@mshc.com
www.mshomecorp. com

Insurance Commissioner
Commissioner of Insurance
1001 Woolfolk State Office Bldg.
501 N. West St.
P.O. Box 79
Jackson, MS 39205
601-359-3569
800-562-2957
www.doi.state.ms.us

Labor Department
Mississippi Employment Security
Commission

1520 W. Capitol St.
MESC P.O. Box 1699
Jackson, MS 31295-1699
601-354-8711
www.mesc.state.ms.us

Licensing Office
Secretary of State
P.O. Box 136
Jackson, MS 39205
601-359-3123
www.sos.state.ms.us

One-Stop Career Center
Employment Security Commission
1520 W. Capitol St.
P.O. Box 1699
Jackson, MS 39215
601-354-8711
www.mesc.state.ms.us

Security Regulators
Securities Division
202 N. Congress St., Suite 601
P.O. Box 136
Jackson, MS 39205
601-359-1633
800-804-6364
www.sos.state.ms.us/busserv/securities/securities.html

Small Business Development Center
Mississippi Small Business Development Center
University of Mississippi
B19 Jeanette Philips Dr.
P.O. Box 1848
University, MS 38677-1848
662-915-5001
800-725-7232 (in state)
Fax: 662-915-5650
Email: msbdc@olemiss.edu
www.olemiss.edu/depts/mssbdc

Social Services Offices
Mississippi Department of Human Services
750 North State Street
Jackson, MS 39202
601-359-4500
800-345-6347 (in state)
www.mdhs.state.ms.us

Temporary Assistance to Needy Families (TANF)
Temporary Aid To Needy Families
Division of Economic Assistance
Department of Human Services
750 State St.
Jackson, MS 39202
601-359-4800
800-948-4060
Email: leden@mdhs.state.ms.us
www.mdhs.state.ms.us/ea_tanf.html

Transportation Department
Dick Hall
Mississippi Department of Transportation
401 N. West St.
P.O. Box 1850
Jackson, MS 39215-1850
601-359-7001
Email: paffairs@mdot.state.ms.us
www.mdot.state.ms.us

Unclaimed Property Office
Unclaimed Property Division
P.O. Box 138
Jackson, MS 39205-0138
601-359-3600
www.treasury.state.ms.us/

Unemployment Insurance Office
Director, Unemployment Insurance Division
Employment Security Commission
1520 W. Capitol St.
P.O. Box 1699
Jackson, MS 39215
601-961-7755
www.mesc.state.ms.us
Weekly benefit range: $30-200
Duration of benefits: 13-26 weeks

Utility Commission
Public Service Commission and Public Utilities Staff
501 N. West Street
201-A Woolfolk State Office Bldg.
Jackson, MS 39201
601-961-5400
www.psc.state.ms.us/mpsc/psc-home.htm

Women's Commission
Inactive

Your Senator
United States Senate
Washington, DC 20510
202-224-3121
www.senate.gov

Your Representative
United States House of Representatives
Washington, DC 20515
202-224-3121
www.house.gov

MISSOURI

Federal Information Center
1-800-FED-INFO
www.firstgov.gov
www.pueblo.gsa.gov/call/

State Information Office
573-751-2000
www.state.mo.us

Department on Aging
Aging Division
615 Howerton Ct.
P.O. Box 1337
Jefferson City, MO 65102
573-751-3082
800-235-5503 (aging information referral)
www.dss.state.mo.us/da/ index.htm

Attorney General's Office
Office of the Attorney General
Supreme Court Bldg.
207 West High Street
P.O. Box 899
Jefferson City, MO 65102
573-751-3321
800-392-8222 (consumer protection hotline)
Fax: 573-751-0774
Email: attgenmail@moago.org
www.ago.state.mo.us

Banking Commissioner
Commissioner of Finance
Harry S. Truman Office Bldg., Room 630
P.O. Box 716
Jefferson City, MO 65102
573-751-3242
800-722-3321
Email: finance@mail.state.mo.us
www.ecodev.state.mo.us/finance/finhome.htm

Child Care and Development Block Grant Lead Agency
Division of Family Services
Missouri Department of Social Services
P.O. Box 88
Jefferson City, MO 65103
573-751-3221
800-735-2466
Email: askdss@mail.state.mo.us
www.dss.state.mo.us/dfs/ index.htm

Child Support Enforcement Agency
Teresa Kaiser
Division of Child Support Enforcement
Department of Social Services
3418 Knipp Dr., Suite F
P.O. Box 2320
Jefferson City, MO 65102
573-751-4301
800-859-7999
Fax: 573-751-8450
Email: askcse@mail.state.mo.us
www.dss.state.mo.us/cse/ index.htm

Cooperative Extension Offices
Ronald J. Turner, Interim Director
Cooperative Extension Service
University of Missouri
309 University Hall
Columbia, MO 65211
573-882-7754
http://extension.missouri.edu

Dyremple Marsh, Director
Cooperative Extension Service
Lincoln University, 110A Allen Hall
P.O. Box 29
Jefferson City, MO 65102-0029
573-681-5550
www.lincolnu.edu

Corporation Division Office
Business Services Department
Corporate Division
Secretary of State
James C. Kirkpatrick State Information Center
P.O. Box 778
Jefferson City, MO 65102
573-751-4153
www.sos.state.mo.us/business/corporations

Day Care Licensing Agency
State Department of Health and Senior Services
Bureau of Child Care, Safey and Licensure
P.O. Box 570
Jefferson City, MO 65102
573-751-2450
www.dhss.state.mo.us

Economic Development Office
Department of Economic Development
301 W. High St., Room 680
P.O. Box 1157
Jefferson City, MO 65102
573-751-4962
Email: ecodev@mail.state.mo.us
www.ecodev.state.mo.us

Department of Education
Missouri Department of Elementary and Secondary Education
P.O. Box 480
Jefferson City, MO 65102-0480
573-751-4212
Email:
pubinfo@mail.dese.state.mo.us
http://services.dese.state.mo.us/

Department of Higher Education
Missouri Department of Higher Education
P.O. Box 1438
3515 Amazonas Drive
Jefferson City, MO 65109-5717
573-751-2361
800-473-6757
Fax: 573-751-6635
www.cbhe.state.mo.us

Health Department
Missouri Department of Health
920 Wildwood
P.O. Box 570
Jefferson, MO 65102-0570
573-751-6400
Fax: 573-751-6041
www.dhss.state.mo.us

Housing Office
Missouri Housing Development Commission
3435 Broadway
Kansas City, MO 64111-2415
816-759-6600

Email: info@mhdc.com
www.mhdc.com

Insurance Commissioner
Director of Insurance
301 W. High St.
P.O. Box 690
Jefferson City, MO 65102-0690
573-751-4126
800-726-7390 (consumer hotline)
www.insurance.state.mo.us/

Labor Department
Missouri Department of Labor and Industrial Relations
3315 West Truman Boulevard, Room 213
P.O. Box 504
Jefferson, MO 65102
573-751-4091
www.dolir.state.mo.us

Licensing Office
Division of Professional Registration
Department of Economic Development
3605 Missouri Blvd.
Jefferson City, MO 65102
573-751-0293
Email: profreg@mail.state.mo.us
www.ecodev.state.mo.us/pr

One-Stop Career Center
Missouri Works
Division of Workforce Development
421 E. Dunklin St.
P.O. Box 1087
Jefferson City, MO 65102-1087
573-751-3999
Fax: 573-751-4088
www.works.state.mo.us

Security Regulators
Securities Division
Missouri State Information Center
600 W. Main
P.O. Box 1276
Jefferson City, MO 65101
573-751-4136
800-721-7996 (investor hotline)
www.sos.state.mo.us/securities

Small Business Development Center
Missouri Small Business Development Center
University of Missouri-System
1205 University Avenue
Suite 300
Columbia, MO 65211
573-882-0344
Fax: 573-884-4297
Email: websbdc@ext.missouri.edu
www.mo-sbdc.org/index.shtml

Social Services Offices
Missouri Department of Social Services
221 West High Street
P.O. Box 1527
Jefferson City, MO 65102-1527
573-751-4815
800-735-2466
Email: askdss@mail.state.mo.us
www.dss.state.mo.us

Temporary Assistance to Needy Families (TANF)
Temporary Assistance
Missouri Department of Social Services
Division of Family Services
P.O. Box 88
Jefferson City, MO 65103
573-751-3221
800-735-2466
www.dss.state.mo.us/dfs/tempa.htm

Transportation Department
Don Hall
Missouri Department of Transportation
105 W. Capitol Ave.
P.O. Box 270
Jefferson City, MO 65102
573-751-2551
888-ASK-MODOT
Email: comments@mail.modot.state.mo.us
www.modot.state.mo.us

Henry Hungerbeder
Missouri Department of Transportation
105 W. Capitol Ave.
P.O. Box 270
Jefferson City, MO 65102
573-751-7480
888-ASK-MODOT
www.modot.state.mo.us

Unclaimed Property Office
Unclaimed Property Division
P.O. Box 1004
Jefferson City, MO 65102
573-751-0840
Email: ucp@mail.sto.state.mo.us
www.sto.state.mo.us/ucp/ucp.htm

Unemployment Insurance Office
Director
Unemployment Insurance
Division of Employment Security
421 E. Dunklin St.
P.O Box 59
Jefferson City, MO 65102-0059
573-751-3670
www.dolir.state.mo.us/es/
Weekly benefit range: $40-250
Duration of benefits: up to 26 weeks

Utility Commission
Public Service Commission
Governor Office Bldg.
200 Madison St.
P.O. Box 360
Jefferson City, MO 65102
573-751-3234
800-392-4211 (MO only)
Email: pscinfo@mail.state.mo.us
www.psc.state.mo.us

Women's Commission
Missouri Women's Council
Division of Workforce Development
421 E. Dunklin St.
P.O. Box 1684
Jefferson City, MO 65102
573-751-0810
877-426-9284 (in state)
Fax: 573-751-8835
Email: wcouncil@mail.state.mo.us
www.womenscouncil.org
Katherine Emke, Chair

Your Senator
United States Senate
Washington, DC 20510
202-224-3121
www.senate.gov

Your Representative
United States House of Representatives
Washington, DC 20515
202-224-3121
www.house.gov

MONTANA

Federal Information Center
1-800-FED-INFO
www.firstgov.gov
www.pueblo.gsa.gov/call/

State Information Office
406-444-2511
www.discoveringmontana.com

Department on Aging
Senior and Long Term Care Division
Department of Public Health and Human Services
111 North Sanders, Room 210
Helena, MT 59604
406-444-4077
800-332-2272 (aging hotline)
www.dphhs.state.mt.us/sltc/index.ht m

Attorney General's Office
Office of the Attorney General
P.O. Box 201401
Helena, MT 59620-1401
406-444-2026
Fax: 406-444-3549
www.doj.state.mt.us/ago/ index.htm

Banking Commissioner
Commissioner of Banking and Financial Institutions
846 Front St.
Helena, MT 59601
MAILING ADDRESS:
P.O. Box 200546
Helena, MT 59620-0546
406-444-2091
Fax: 406-444-4186
www.discoveringmontana.com/doa/banking

Child Care and Development Block Grant Lead Agency
Human and Community Services Division
Montana Dept. of Public Health and Human Services
1400 Broadway
Helena, MT 59620
MAILING ADDRESS:
P.O. Box 202952
Helena, MT 59620-2952
406-444-5901
Fax: 406-444-2547
Email: hhudson@state.mt.us
www.dphhs.state.mt.us

Child Support Enforcement Agency
Mary Ann Wellbank
Child Support Enforcement Division
Department of Social and Rehabilitation Services
3075 N. Montana Ave.
Helena, MT 59601
MAILING ADDRESS:
P.O. Box 202943
Helena, MT 59620-2943
406-444-9855
800-346-5437 (in MT)
Fax: 406-444-1370
www.dphhs.state.mt.us

Cooperative Extension Office
Vice Provost for Outreach and Director of Extension
212 Montana Hall
Montana State University
Bozeman, MT 59717
406-994-4371
http://extn.msu.montana.edu

Corporation Division Office
Business Bureau
Secretary of State
Room 260, Capitol
P.O. Box 202801
Helena, MT 59620-2801
406-444-3665
Email: sos@state.mt.us
http://sos.state.mt.us/css/BSB/BSB.asp

Day Care Licensing Agency
Department of Health and Human Services
Quality Assurance Division
Licensure Bureau
1400 Broadway
P.O. Box 202951
Helena, MT 59620-2951
406-444-2037
Email: mdalton@state.mt.us
www.dphhs.state.mt.us

Economic Development Office
Department of Commerce
Economic Development Division
1429 Ninth Ave.
PO Box 200505
Helena, MT 59620-0505
406-444-3814
Fax: 406-444-1872
http://commerce.state.mt.us/EconDev/index.html

Department of Education
Montana Office of Public Instruction
P.O. Box 202501
Helena, MT 59620-2501
406-444-3095
888-231-9393
www.opi.state.mt.us

Department of Higher Education
Office of the Commissioner of Higher Education
2500 Broadway St.
P.O. Box 203101
Helena, MT 59620-3101
406-444-6570
Fax: 404-444-1469
www.montana.edu/wwwoche

Health Department
Montana Department of Public Health & Human Services
111 North Sanders
Helena, MT 59620
MAILING ADDRESS:
P.O. Box 4210
Helena, MT 59604-4210
406-444-5622
Fax: 406-444-1970
www.dphhs.state.mt.us
Email: kpekoc@state.mt.us

Housing Office
Department of Commerce
Housing Division
836 Front St.
Helena, MT 59601
MAILING ADDRESS:
P.O. Box 200528
Helena, MT 59620-0528
406-444-3040
Fax: 406-444-4688

http://commerce.state.mt.us/Housing/hous_home.html

Insurance Commissioner
Commissioner of Insurance and Securities
State Auditor's Office
840 Helena Ave.
Helena, MT 59601
MAILING ADDRESS:
P.O. Box 4009
Helena, MT 59604-4009
406-444-2040
800-332-6148
www.discoveringmontana.com/sao/default.htm

Labor Department
Montana Department of Labor and Industry
P.O. Box 1728
Helena, MT 59624
406-444-9091
Email: dwest@state.mt.us
http://dli.state.mt.us/

Licensing Office
Business Standards Division
Licensing, Business Regulation
Department of Commerce
301 S. Park, 4th Floor
Helena, MT 59602
406-841-2300
www.discoveringmontana.com/dli/bsd/license/bus_index.htm

One-Stop Career Center
Job Service Workforce Centers
Department of Labor and Industry
Workforce Services Division
1327 Lockey
Walt Sullivan Bldg.
P.O. Box 1728
Helena, MT 59624
406-444-2645
http://jsd.dli.state.mt.us

Security Regulators
Montana State Auditor's Office
Securities Department
840 Helena Ave.
Helena, MT 59601
406-444-2040
800-332-6148
www.discoveringmontana.com/sao/securities/secintro.htm

Small Business Development Center
Montana Small Business Development Center
Montana Dept. of Commerce
1424 Ninth Avenue
Helena, MT 59601
MAILING ADDRESS:
P.O. Box 200501
Helena, MT 59620
406-444-4780
Fax: 406-444-1872
http://commerce.state.mt.us/BRD/BRD_SBDC.html

Social Services Offices
Montana Department of Public Health and Human Services
111 North Sanders
Helena, MT 59620
MAILING ADDRESS:
P.O. Box 4210
Helena, MT 59604
406-444-5622
Fax: 406-444-1970
www.dphhs.state.mt.us
Email: dphhstech@state.mt.us

Temporary Assistance to Needy Families (TANF)
Temporary Aid to Needy Families
Montana Department of Public Health and Human Services
1400 Broadway
P.O. Box 202952
Helena, MT 59620
406-444-5901
Fax: 406-444-2547
www.dphhs.state.mt.us

Transportation Department
Janis Winston
Montana Dept. of Transportation
2701 Prospect Ave.
P.O. Box 201001
Helena, MT 59620-1001
406-444-6200
www.mdt.state.mt.us

Unclaimed Property Office
Unclaimed Property
Department of Revenue
P.O. Box 5805
Helena, MT 59604-5805
406-444-6900
Fax: 406-444-0629
www.state.mt.us/revenue/css/2forindividuals/08unclaimedproperty.asp

Unemployment Insurance Office
Administrator
Unemployment Insurance Division
P.O. Box 1728
Helena, MT 59624
406-444-2749
http://uid.dli.state.mt.us
Weekly benefit range: $68-286
Duration of benefits: 8-26 weeks

Utility Commission
Public Service Commission
1701 Prospect Ave.
P.O. Box 202601
Helena, MT 59620-2601
406-444-6199
www.psc.state.mt.us

Women's Commission
Interdepartmental Coordinating Committee for Women (ICCW)
P.O. Box 1728
Helena, MT 59624
406-444-4521
Email: jabranscum@state.mt.us
www.mdt.state.mt.us/iccw
Jean Branscum, Chair
Diane West, Vice Chair

Your Senator
United States Senate
Washington, DC 20510
202-224-3121
www.senate.gov

Your Representative
United States House of Representatives
Washington, DC 20515
202-224-3121
www.house.gov

NEBRASKA

Federal Information Center
1-800-FED-INFO
www.firstgov.gov
www.pueblo.gsa.gov/call/

State Information Office
402-471-2311
www.state.ne.us

Department on Aging
Aging and Disability Services
P.O. Box 95044
Lincoln, NE 68509-5044
402-471-2307
800-942-7830
www.hhs.state.ne.
us/ags/agsindex.htm
Email: mark.Intermill@hhss.
state.ne.us

Attorney General's Office
Office of the Attorney General
State Capitol, Room 2115
Lincoln, NE 68509-8920
402-471-2682
800-727-6432 (consumer protection)
Fax: 402-471-3297
www.ago.state.ne.us

Banking Commissioner
Director of Banking and Finance
P.O. Box 95006
1200 N. Street
The Atrium, Suite 311
Lincoln, NE 68509-5006
402-471-2171
www.ndbf.org

Child Care and Development Block Grant Lead Agency
Child Care and Development Fund
Nebraska Department of Health and
Human Services
P.O. Box 95044
Lincoln, NE 68509-5044
402-471-9676
Fax: 402-471-7763
www.hhs.state.ne.us/
chs/chc/chcindex.htm

Child Support Enforcement Agency
Child Support Enforcement Office
Department of Health and Human
Services
P.O. Box 94728
Lincoln, NE 68509-4728
402-441-8715
877-631-9973
www.hhs.state.ne.us/cse/cseindex.h
tm

Cooperative Extension Office
Randall Cantrell, Director
University of Nebraska
S.E. Research and Extension Center
Room 211, Mussehl Hall
East Campus
Lincoln, NE 68583-0714
402-472-2966
http://extension.unl.edu/

Corporation Division Office
Corporations Division
Secretary of State
State Capitol
Room 1305
Lincoln, NE 68509-4608
402-471-4079
Fax: 402-471-3666
www.nol.org/home/SOS/htm/
services.htm
Email: corpol@nol.org

Day Care Licensing Agency
Nebraska Health and Human
Services System
Department of Services
P.O. Box 95044
Lincoln, NE 68509-5044
402-471-9278
800-600-1289
Fax: 402-471-7763
www.hhs.state.ne.us/
crl/childcare.htm

Economic Development Office
Department of Economic
Development
P.O. Box 94666
301 Centennial Mall South
Lincoln, NE 68509-4666
402-471-3111
800-426-6505 (in NE)
Fax: 402-471-3778
TDD: 800-833-7352
www.neded.org

Department of Education
Nebraska Department of Education
301 Centennial Mall South
Lincoln, NE 68509
402-471-2295
www.nde.state.ne.us/

Department of Higher Education
Nebraska Coordinating Commission
for Postsecondary Education
P.O. Box 95005
Lincoln, NE 68509-5005
402-471-2847
Fax: 402-471-2886
www.ccpe.state.ne.us/
PublicDoc/CCPE/Default.asp

Health Department
Nebraska Health & Human Services
System
Department of Services
P.O. Box 95044
Lincoln, NE 68509-5044
402-471-2306
www.hhs.state.ne.us/index.htm
Email: hhsinfo@ www.hhs.
state.ne.us

Housing Office
Nebraska Investment Finance
Authority
200 Commerce Court
1230 O St.
Lincoln, NE 68508-1402
402-434-3900
800-204-NIFA (6432)
www.nifa.org

Insurance Commissioner
Director of Insurance
941 O St., Suite 400
Lincoln, NE 68508-3639
402-471-2201
TDD: 800-833-7352
www.nol.org/home/ndoi/

Labor Department
Nebraska Workforce Development
550 South 16th Street

P.O. Box 94600
Lincoln, NE 68509-4600
402-471-9000
Fax: 402-471-2318
TDD: 402-471-9924
www.dol.state.ne.us

Licensing Office
Regulation and Licensure
Credentialing Division
Nebraska Department of Health and Human Services
301 Centennial Mall South
Third Floor
Lincoln, NE 68509-9486
402-471-2115
Fax: 402-471-3577
www.hhs.state.ne.us/crl/crlindex.htm
Email: marie.mcclatchey@hhss.state.ne.us

One-Stop Career Center
Nebraska Office of Workforce Services
Department of Labor
550 South 16th Street
Lincoln, NE 68509
402-471-1939
Fax: 402-471-3050
www.dol.state.ne.us

Security Regulators
Nebraska Securities Bureau
Department of Banking & Finance
1200 "N" Street
The Atrium, Suite 311
P.O. Box 95006
Lincoln, NE 68509-5006
402-471-3445
www.ndbf.org/sec.htm

Small Business Development Center
Nebraska Business Development Center
College of Business Administration
Roskens Hall, Room 415
University of Nebraska at Omaha
Omaha, NE 68182-0248
402-554-2521
Email:
robert_bernier@unomaha.edu
http://nbdc.unomaha.edu

Social Services Offices
Nebraska Health and Human Services System
Department of Services
P.O. Box 95044
Lincoln, NE 68509-5044
402-471-9106
Email:
hhsinfo@www.hhs.state.ne.us
www.hhs.state.ne.us

Temporary Assistance to Needy Families (TANF)
Temporary Aid to Needy Families
Dan Cillessen
Nebraska Department of Health and Human Services
P.O. Box 95044
Lincoln, NE 68509-5044
402-471-9270
www.hhs.state.ne.us/ fia/adc.htm

Transportation Department
Jerry Wray
Nebraska Department of Roads
1500 Highway 2
Lincoln, NE 68502
MAILING ADDRESS:
P.O. Box 94759
Lincoln, NE 68509
402-471-4567
www.dor.state.ne.us

Unclaimed Property Office
Unclaimed Property Division
P.O. Box 94788
Lincoln, NE 68509
402-471-2455
www.nebraska.treasurer.org

Unemployment Insurance Office
Unemployment Insurance Director
Nebraska Department of Labor
P.O. Box 94600
550 S. 16th St.
Lincoln, NE 68509
402-471-9979
800-725-9918 (to file a claim)
www.dol.state.ne.us/
Weekly benefit range: $36-262
Duration of benefits: 20-26 weeks

Utility Commission
Public Service Commission
300 The Atrium
1200 N St.
Lincoln, NE 68508
MAILING ADDRESS:
P.O. Box 94927
Lincoln, NE 68509-4927
402-471-3101
800-526-0017
www.nol.org/home/NPSC

Women's Commission
Nebraska Commission on the Status of Women
301 Centennial Mall South
Box 94985
Lincoln, NE 65809
402-471-2039
Fax: 402-471-5655
Email: ncswmail@mail. state.ne.us
www.women.state.ne.us
Carlene Bourn, Executive Director

Your Senator
United States Senate
Washington, DC 20510
202-224-3121
www.senate.gov

Your Representative
United States House of Representatives
Washington, DC 20515
202-224-3121
www.house.gov

NEVADA

Federal Information Center
1-800-FED-INFO
www.firstgov.gov
www.pueblo.gsa.gov/call/

State Information Office
702-687-5000
www.state.nv.us

Department on Aging
Aging Services Division
Human Resources Dept.
3416 Goni Rd., Bldg. D 132
Carson City, NC 89706
775-687-4210
http://aging.state.nv.us

Attorney General's Office
Office of the Attorney General
100 North Carson Street
Carson City, NV 89701-4717
775-684-1100
Fax: 775-684-1108
http://ag.state.nv.us
Email: aginfo@ag.state.nv.us

Banking Commissioner
Commissioner of Financial Institutions
406 E. Second St., Suite 3
Carson City, NV 89701-4758
775-684-1830
Fax: 775-684-1845
Email: fid@govmail.state.nv.us
http://fid.state.nv.us

Child Care and Development Block Grant Lead Agency
CCDBG Coordinator
Nevada Department of Human Resources
Welfare Division
1470 E. College Pkwy.
Carson City, NV 89710
775-684-0500
http://welfare.state.nv.us

Child Support Enforcement Agency
Nancy Kathryn Ford
Child Support Enforcement Program
Nevada State Welfare Division
1470 E. College Pkwy.
Carson City, NV 89706-7924
775-687-0704
800-922-0900, ext. 0704 (in NV)
http://welfare.state.nv.us/child.htm

Cooperative Extension Office
Janet Usinger, Director
Nevada Cooperative Extension
2345 Redrock
Las Vegas, NV 89102
702-251-7531
www.unce.unr.edu

Corporation Division Office
Corporations Division
Secretary of State
555 E. Washington Blvd.
Suite 2900
Las Vegas, NV 89101
702-486-2880
http://sos.state.nv.us

Day Care Licensing Agency
Division of Child and Family Services
Bureau of Services for Child Care
711 E. 5th Street
Carson City, NV 89701
775-684-4400
Fax: 775-684-4464
http://dcfs.state.nv.us/page23.html

Economic Development Office
State of Nevada Commission on Economic Development
108 E. Proctor St.
Carson City, NV 89701
775-687-4325
800-336-1600
Fax: 775-687-4450
www.expand2nevada.com/index2.html

555 E. Washington Avenue
Suite 5400
Las Vegas, NV 89101
702-486-2700
Fax: 702-486-2701

Department of Education
Nevada Department of Education
700 E. Fifth St.
Carson City, NV 89701-5096
775-687-9200
Fax: 775-687-9101
www.nde.state.nv.us

Department of Higher Education
University and Community College System of Nevada
System Administration North
2601 Enterprise Rd.
Reno, NV 89512
775-784-4905
Fax: 775-784-1127
www.nevada.edu

University and Community College System of Nevada
System Administration South
5550 West Flamingo Rd.
Suite C-1
Las Vegas, NV 89103
702-889-8426
Fax: 702-889-8492
www.nevada.edu

Health Department
Nevada State Health Division
505 East King Street, Room 201
Carson City, NV 89710-4797
775-684-4200
http://health2k.state.nv.us

Housing Offices
Department of Business & Industry
Housing Division
1802 N. Carson St., Suite 154
Carson City, NV 89701
775-687-4258
800-227-4960
Fax: 775-687-4040
Email: nhd@govmail.state.nv.us
http://nvhousing.state.nv.us

Nevada Rural Housing Authority
2100 California St.
Carson City, NV 89701
702-887-1795

Insurance Commissioner
Commissioner of Insurance
788 Fairview Dr., Suite 300
Carson City, NV 89701-5491

775-687-4270
800-992-0900
Fax: 775-687-3937
http://doi.state.nv.us

Labor Department
Nevada Department of Employment, Training and Rehabilitation
500 East Third Street
Carson City, NV 89713
702-687-4550
Email: detradmn@nvdetr.org
www.detr.state.nv.us

Licensing Office
Consumer Affairs Division
Department of Business and Industry
1850 E. Sahara Ave., Suite 101
Las Vegas, NV 89104
702-486-7355
800-326-5202
Fax: 702-486-7371
www.fyiconsumer.org

One-Stop Career Center
Nevada Department of Employment, Training and Rehabilitation
Job Connect
500 East Third Street
Carson City, NV 89713-0021
702-687-4550
www.nevadajobconnect.com
Email: detradmn@nvdetr.org

Security Regulators
Securities Division
Secretary of State
555 E. Washington St., Suite 5200
Las Vegas, NV 89101
702-486-2440
Fax: 702-486-2452
Email: nvsec@govmail.state.nv.us
http://sos.state.nv.us/securities/index.htm

Small Business Development Center
Nevada Small Business Development Center
University of Nevada, Reno
College of Business Administration
Business Building, Room 411
Reno, NV 89557-0100
775-784-1717
Fax: 775-784-4337
Email: nsbdc@unr.nevada.edu
www.nsbdc.org

Social Services Offices
Nevada Department of Human Resources
505 East King Street, Room 600
Carson City, NV 89701-3708
775-684-4000
www.hr.state.nv.us

Temporary Assistance to Needy Families (TANF)
Temporary Aid to Needy Families
Welfare Division
1470 E. College Pkwy.
Carson City, NV 89701
775-684-0500
welfare.state.nv.us/elig_pay/tanf_home.htm

Transportation Department
Tom Stephens, P.E.
Nevada Department of Transportation
1263 South Stewart St.
Carson City, NV 89712
775-888-7000
Fax: 775-888-7115
www.nevadadot.com
Email: info@dot.state.nv.us

Unclaimed Property Office
Unclaimed Property Division
2501 East Sahara Ave.
Suite 304
Las Vegas, NV 89104
702-486-4140
800-521-0019
Fax: 702-486-4177
www.unclaimed.state.nv.us
Email:
unclaimed@nevadatreasurer.com

Unemployment Insurance Office
Unemployment Insurance
Employment Security Department
500 E. Third St.
Carson City, NV 89713
775-687-4550
www.detr.state.nv.us/uiben/uiben_uiben.htm
Email: detrui@nvdetr.org
Weekly benefit range: $16-301
Duration of benefits: up to 26 weeks
Automated telephone system for unemployment
Northern Nevada: 775-684-0350
Southern Nevada: 702-486-0350
Rural Nevada: 888-890-8211

Utility Commission
Public Service Commission
1150 E. William St.
Carson City, NV 89701
771-687-6001
800-992-0900
Fax: 775-687-6110
www.puc.state.nv.us

Women's Commission
Nevada Women's Fund
770 Smithridge Dr.
Suite 300
Reno, NV 89502
775-786-2335
Fax: 775-786-8152
www.nwfonline.org
Email:
info@nevadawomensfund.org

Your Senator
United States Senate
Washington, DC 20510
202-224-3121
www.senate.gov

Your Representative
United States House of Representatives
Washington, DC 20515
202-224-3121
www.house.gov

NEW HAMPSHIRE

Federal Information Center
1-800-FED-INFO
www.firstgov.gov
www.pueblo.gsa.gov/call/

State Information Office
603-271-1110
www.state.nh.us

Department on Aging
Elderly and Adult Services Division
129 Pleasant St.
Concord, NH 03301-3843
603-271-4384
800-351-1888
www.dhhs.state.nh.us/
index.nsf?open

Attorney General's Office
Office of the Attorney General
33 Capitol Street
Concord, NH 03301
603-271-3658
TDD: 800-735-2964
Fax: 603-271-2110
http://webster.state.nh.us/nhdoj

Banking Commissioner
Bank Commissioner
64B Old Suncook Rd.
Concord, NH 03301
603-271-3561
Fax: 603-271-1090
webster.state.nh.us/banking

Child Care and Development Block Grant Lead Agency
Child Development Bureau
Division for Children, Youth and Families
New Hampshire Department of Health and Human Services
129 Pleasant St., Brown Bldg.
Concord, NH 03301
603-271-7983
800-852-3345
Fax: 603-271-4729
www.dhhs.state.nh.us

Child Support Enforcement Agency
Division of Child Support Services
Dept. of Health and Human Services
129 Pleasant St.
Concord, NH 03301-3857
603-271-4427
800-852-3345, ext 4427 (in NH)
Fax: 603-271-4787
www.dhhs.state.nh.us/

Cooperative Extension Office
Peter J. Horne, Dean and Director
UNH Cooperative Extension
59 College Road, Taylor Hall
Durham, NH 03824
603-862-1520
http://ceinfo.unh.edu/

Corporation Division Office
Corporate Division
Secretary of State
25 Capitol Street
State House, Room 204
Concord, NH 03301
603-271-3244
www.state.nh.us/sos/corporate/index.htm

Day Care Licensing Agency
State Department of Health and Human Service
Program Support
Office, Child Care Licensing Unit
129 Pleasant St.
Health and Human Services Building
Concord, NH 03301-3857
603-271-4625
www.dhhs.state.nh.us/

Economic Development Office
State of New Hampshire
Department of Resources and Economic Development
172 Pembroke Road
Concord, NH 03302-1856
603-271-2341
Fax: 603-271-6784
www.nheconomy.com
Email: info@nheconomy.com

Department of Education
New Hampshire Dept. of Education
101 Pleasant St.
Concord, NH 03301-3860
603-271-3494
Fax: 603-271-1953
www.ed.state.nh.us

Department of Higher Education
New Hampshire Postsecondary Education Commission
2 Industrial Park Drive
Concord, NH 03301-8512
603-271-2555
TDD: 800-735-2964
Fax: 603-271-2696
webster.state.nh.us/ postsecondary

Health Department
New Hampshire Department of Health & Human Services
Office of Community and Public Health
129 Pleasant St.
Concord, NH 03301-6527
603-271-4501
Fax: 603-271-4827
www.healthynh2010.org
Email: healthynh2010@dhhs.state.nh.us

Housing Office
Housing Finance Authority
32 Constitution Dr.
Bedford, NH
MAILING ADDRESS:
P.O. Box 5087
Manchester, NH 03108
603-472-8623
800-640-7239
TDD: 603-472-2089
www.nhhfa.org

Insurance Commissioner
Insurance Commissioner
56 Old Suncook Rd.
Concord, NH 03301-5151
603-271-2261
800-852-3416
webster.state.nh.us/insurance/

Labor Department
New Hampshire Department of Labor
95 Pleasant Street

Concord, NH 03301
603-271-3176
www.labor.state.nh.us

Licensing Office
New Hampshire Joint Board of Licensure and Certification
57 Regional Dr.
Concord, NH 03301
603-271-2219
Fax: 603-271-6990
Email: llavertu@nhsa.state.nh.us
www.state.nh.us/jtboard/ home.htm

One-Stop Career Center
New Hampshire Works
Dept. of Employment Security
32 South Main Street
Concord, NH 03301
603-224-3311
800-852-3400
www.nhworks.state.nh.us
Email: webmaster@nhes.state.nh.us

Security Regulators
Bureau of Securities Regulation
State House, Room 204
Concord, NH 03301-4989
603-271-1463
Fax: 603-271-7933
http://webster.state.nh.us/sos/securities

Small Business Development Center
New Hampshire Small Business Development Center
University of New Hampshire
The Whittemore School of Business
108 McConnell Hall
Durham, NH 03824-3593
603-862-2200
Fax: 603-862-4876
Email: mec@christa.unh.edu
http://.nhsbdc.org

Social Services Offices
New Hampshire Department of Health and Human Services
129 Pleasant St.
Concord, NH 03301
603-271-4688
800-852-3345, ext. 4688 (in NH)
www.dhhs.state.nh.us/

Temporary Assistance to Needy Families (TANF)
Temporary Aid to Needy Families
Division of Family Services
New Hampshire Department of Health and Human Services
129 Pleasant St.
Concord, NH 03301-6506
603-271-4580
800-852-3345, ext. 4580 (in NH)
www.dhhs.state.nh.us/familyservices/famservc.nsf/vmain?openview

Transportation Department
New Hampshire Department of Transportation
John O. Morton Bldg.
1 Hazen Dr.
P.O. Box 483
Concord, NH 03302-0483
603-271-3434
Fax: 603-271-3914
webster.state.nh.us/dot

Unclaimed Property Office
Abandoned Property Division
Treasury Department
25 Capitol St., Room 205
Concord, NH 03301
603-271-2619
800-791-0920
Email: aptreasury@treasury.state.nh.us
www.state.nh.us/treasury/appage.html

Unemployment Insurance Office
Unemployment Compensation Bureau
Dept. of Employment Security
32 South Main St.
Concord, NH 03301
603-228-4031
www.nhworks.state.nh.us
Weekly benefit range: $32-331
Duration of benefits: 26 weeks

Utility Commission
Public Utilities Commission
8 Old Suncook Rd.
Concord, NH 03301
603-271-2431
800-852-3793 (NH only)
Fax: 603-271-3878
TDD: 800-735-2964
Email: puc@puc.state.nh.us
www.puc.state.nh.us/

Women's Commission
New Hampshire Commission on the Status of Women
State House Annex, Room 334
Concord, NH 03301-6312
603-271-2660
Fax: 603-271-4032
Email: cmswweb@admin.state.nh.us
www.state.nh.us/csw
Theresa deLangis, Exec. Director
Molly Kelly, Chair

Your Senator
United States Senate
Washington, DC 20510
202-224-3121
www.senate.gov

Your Representative
United States House of Representatives
Washington, DC 20515
202-224-3121
www.house.gov

New Jersey

Federal Information Center
1-800-FED-INFO
www.firstgov.gov
www.pueblo.gsa.gov/call/

State Information Office
609-292-2121
www.state.nj.us

Department on Aging
Division of Senior Affairs
Dept. of Health and Senior Services
P.O. Box 807
Trenton, NJ 08625-0807
609-558-3141
800-792-8820 (hotline)
www.state.nj.us/health/senior/sraffair.htm

Attorney General's Office
Office of the Attorney General
Hughes Justice Complex
25 Market Street
P.O. Box 080
Trenton, NH 08625-0080
609-292-4925
Fax: 609-292-3508
Email: lpaciti@smtp.lps.state.nj.us
www.state.nj.us/lps

Banking Commissioner
Commissioner of Banking and Insurance
20 W. State St.
P.O. Box 040
Trenton, NJ 08625
609-292-5360
www.state.nj.us/dobi/index.html

Child Care and Development Block Grant Lead Agency
Division of Family Development
New Jersey Department of Human Services
Quakerbridge Plaza, Bldg. 6
P.O. Box 716
Trenton, NJ 08625-0716
609-588-2400
www.state.nj.us/humanservices/

Child Support Enforcement Agency
Child Support
Division of Family Development
Department of Human Services
Quakerbridge Plaza
Building 6
P.O. Box 716
Trenton, NJ 08625-0716
609-588-2400
877-NJKIDS1
www.njchildsupport.org

Cooperative Extension Office
Zane Helsel, Director
Rutgers Cooperative Extension
P.O. Box 231
New Brunswick, NJ 08903
732-932-9306
www.rce.rutgers.edu

Corporation Division Office
Commercial Recording Division
Secretary of State
225 W. State St.
P.O. Box 308
West Trenton, NJ 08625
609-292-9292
www.state.nj.us/treasury/revenue/dcr/dcrpg1.html

Day Care Licensing Agency
Division of Youth and Family Services
Bureau of Licensing
P.O. Box 717
Trenton, NJ 08625-0717
609-292-1018
800-331-3937
www.state.nj.us/humanservices/dyfs/licensing.html

Economic Development Office
New Jersey Economic Development Authority
P.O. Box 990
Trenton, NJ 08625-0990
609-292-1800
www.njeda.com
Email: njeda@njeda.com

Department of Education
New Jersey Department of Education
Office of Public Information
100 River View Executive Dr.
CN 500
Trenton, NJ 08625
609-292-4041
Fax: 609-984-6756
www.state.nj.us/education/

Department of Higher Education
New Jersey Commission of Higher Education
20 West State St.
P.O. Box 542
Trenton, NJ 08625-0542
609-292-4310
Fax: 609-292-7225
www.state.nj.us/highereducation
Email: nj_che@che.state.nj.us

Health Department
New Jersey Department of Health & Senior Services
P.O. Box 360
John Fitch Plaza
Trenton, NJ 08625-0360
609-292-7837
Fax: 609-292-0053
www.state.nj.us/health/

Housing Office
New Jersey Housing and Mortgage Finance Agency
637 S. Clinton Ave.
P.O. Box 18550
Trenton, NJ 08650-2085
609-278-7400
800-NJ-HOUSE
www.state.nj.us/dca/hmfa/ index.html

Insurance Commissioner
Commissioner
Department of Banking and Insurance
20 W. State St.
P.O. Box 325
Trenton, NJ 08625-0325
609-292-5360
www.state.nj.us/dobi

Labor Department
New Jersey Department of Labor
John Fitch Plaza
P.O. Box 110
Trenton, NJ 08625
609-292-2323

Email: cmycoff@dol.state.nj.us
www.state.nj.us/labor

Licensing Office
Division of Consumer Affairs
124 Halsey St.
Newark, NJ 07102
973-504-6200
800-242-5846 (complaints)
Fax: 973-648-3538
www.state.nj.us/lps/ca/ nonmed.htm
Email: askconsumeraffairs@
smtp.lps.state.nj.us

One-Stop Career Center
Workforce New Jersey
Division of Employment and
Training
P.O. Box 940
Trenton, NJ 08625
609-292-1906
www.wnjpin.state.nj.us

Security Regulators
Bureau of Securities
P.O. Box 47029
153 Halsey St.
Newark, NJ 07101
973-504-3600
www.state.nj.us/lps/ca/bos.htm

Small Business Development Center
New Jersey Small Business
Development Center
Rutgers Graduate School of
Management
49 Bleeker Street
Newark, NJ 07102-1993
973-353-1927
800-432-1565
Email:
sbdcinfo@yourbizpartner.com
www.nj.com/njsbdc_new/
index.ssf?main.html

Social Services Offices
New Jersey Department of Human
Services
P.O. Box 700
Trenton, NJ 08625-0700
609-292-3717
www.state.nj.us/humanservices/

Temporary Assistance to Needy Families (TANF)
Temporary Aid to Needy Families
New Jersey Department of Human
Services
Quakerbridge Plaza, Bldg. 6
P.O. Box 716
Trenton, NJ 08625-0716
609-588-2400
www.state.nj.us/humanservices/
DFD/wfnjws.html

Transportation Department
Jeffrey Warsh
New Jersey Transit Corporation
1 Penn Plaza East
Newark, NJ 07105
973-491-9400
800-772-3606 (in NJ)
www.njtransit.com

Unclaimed Property Office
Department of the Treasury
Unclaimed Property Section
CN 214
Trenton, NJ 08646
609-984-8234
Email: taxation@tax.state.nj.us
www.state.nj.us/treasury/
taxation/unclaimsrch.htm

Unemployment Insurance Office
Director, Division of Unemployment
Insurance
New Jersey Department of Labor
John Fitch Plaza
P.O. Box 955
Trenton, NJ 08625-0955
609-292-2460
www.state.nj.us/labor/uiex/
main2.html
Weekly benefit range: $60-475
Duration of benefits: up to 26 weeks

Utility Commission
Board of Public Utilities
Two Gateway Center
Newark, NJ 07102
973-648-2026
800-624-0241 (NJ only)
www.state.nj.us/bpu

Women's Commission
New Jersey Department of
Community Affairs
Division of Women
101 South Broad St.
P.O. Box 801
Trenton, NJ 08625-0801
609-292-8840
Fax: 609-633-6821
www.state.nj.us/dca/dow
Linda B. Bowker

Your Senator
United States Senate
Washington, DC 20510
202-224-3121
www.senate.gov

Your Representative
United States House of
Representatives
Washington, DC 20515
202-224-3121
www.house.gov

New Mexico

Federal Information Center
1-800-FED-INFO
www.firstgov.gov
www.pueblo.gsa.gov/call/

State Information Office
505-827-4011
www.state.nm.us

Department on Aging
State Agency on Aging
228 E. Palace Ave.
Santa Fe, NM 87501
505-827-7640
800-432-2080 (in NM)
www.nmaging.state.nm.us
Email: nmaoa@state.nm.us

Attorney General's Office
Office of the Attorney General
407 Galisteo Street
Bataan Memorial Bldg.
Room 260
Santa FE, NM 87501
P.O. Drawer 1508
Santa Fe, NM 87504-1508
505-827-6000
800-678-1508 (in NM)
Fax: 505-827-5826
www.ago.state.nm.us

Banking Commissioner
Financial Institutions Division
Regulation and Licensing Department
725 St. Michael's Dr.
Santa Fe, NM 87501
505-827-7100
Fax: 505-827-7107
www.rld.state.nm.us/fid/index.htm

Child Care and Development Block Grant Lead Agency
Bureau Chief
Child Care Services Bureau
Department of Children, Youth and Families
P.O. Drawer 5160
PERA Bldg., Room 111
Santa Fe, NM 87502-5160
505-827-9932
Fax: 505-827-7361

Child Support Enforcement Agency
J. Barry Bitzer
Child Support Division
Department of Human Services
P.O. Box 25110
2009 S. Pacheco
Pollen Plaza
Santa Fe, NM 87504
505-476-7040
800-288-7207 (in NM)
800-585-7631 (in NM)
www.state.nm.us/hsd/csed.html

Cooperative Extension Office
Dr. Jerry Schickenanz
New Mexico State University
Box 3AE
Las Cruces, NM 88003
505-646-3016
http://cahe.nmsu.edu/ces/

Corporation Division Office
New Mexico Public Regulation Commission
Corporations Bureau
1120 Paseo De Peralta
P.O. Drawer 1269
Santa Fe, NM 87504
505-827-4508
800-947-4722
www.nmprc.state.nm.us/corporation.htm

Day Care Licensing Agency
Children, Youth and Families Department
Prevention and Intervention Division
Child Care Licensing Bureau
P.O. Drawer 5160
Santa Fe, NM 87502-5160
505-827-3839
800-832-1321
www.state.nm.us/cyfd/index.htm

Economic Development Office
Economic Development Department
Joseph M. Montoya Bldg.
1100 S. St. Francis Drive
Santa Fe, NM 87503
505-827-0300
800-374-3061
Fax: 505-827-0407
www.edd.state.nm.us

Department of Education
New Mexico Department of Education
Education Bldg.
Public Outreach Office
300 Don Gaspar Ave.
Santa Fe, NM 87501-2786
505-827-6045
Email: webmaster@sde.state. nm.us
http://sde.state.nm.us/

Department of Higher Education
New Mexico Commission On Higher Education
1068 Cerrillos Road
Santa Fe, NM 87501
505-827-7383
Fax: 505-827-7392
www.nmche.org

Health Department
New Mexico Department of Health
1190 St. Francis Drive
P.O. Box 26110
Sante Fe, NM 87502-6110
505-827-2613
Fax: 505-827-2530
www.health.state.nm.us

Housing Offices
Mortgage Finance Authority
344 4th Street, SW
Albuquerque, NM 87102
505-843-6880
800-444-6880
www.nmmfa.org

Insurance Commissioner
Superintendent of Insurance
P.O. Drawer 1269
Santa Fe, NM 87504-1269
505-827-4601
800-947-4722 (in NM)
www.nmprc.state.nm.us/inshm.htm

Labor Department
New Mexico Department of Labor
401 Broadway NE
Albuquerque, NM 87102
505-841-8409
www.dol.state.nm.us

Licensing Office
Regulation and Licensing Department
725 St. Michael's Drive
Santa Fe, NM 87505
505-827-7000
Email: RDL@state.nm.us
www.rld.state.nm.us

One-Stop Career Center
New Mexico Works
Department of Labor
401 Broadway, NE
Albuquerque, NM 87102
505-841-8513
www.dol.state.nm.us/nmworks/front.asp
Email: clissance@state.nm.us

Security Regulators
New Mexico Securities Division
Regulation and Licensing Department
725 St. Michael's Drive
P.O. Box 25101
Santa Fe, NM 87505
505-827-7140
800-704-5533 (in NM)
www.rld.state.nm.us/sec

Small Business Development Center
New Mexico Small Business Development Center
Santa Fe Community College
6401 Richards Avenue
Santa Fe, NM 87508
505-428-1362
800-281-7232
Fax: 505-428-1469
Email: info@nmsbdc.org
www.nmsbdc.org

Social Services Offices
New Mexico Human Services Dept.
P.O. Box 2348
Santa Fe, NM 87504
505-827-7750
800-432-6217
TDD: 800-609-4TDD
Email: marty.eckert@state.nm.us
www.state.nm.us/hsd/home.htm

Temporary Assistance to Needy Families (TANF)
Temporary Aid to Needy Families
Tom Clayton
New Mexico Department of Human Services
P.O. Box 2348
Santa Fe, NM 87504
505-827-7250
888-473-3676
Email: marty.eckert@state.nm.us
www.state.nm.us/hsd/isd.html

Transportation Department
Peter Rahn
New Mexico Highway and Transportation Department
P.O. Box 1149
1120 Cerrillos Rd.
Santa Fe, NM 87504-1149
505-827-5100
www.nmshtd.state.nm.us

Unclaimed Property Office
Dept. of Revenue & Taxation
Special Tax Programs and Services
P.O. Box 25123
Santa Fe, NM 87504-5123
505-827-0769
www.state.nm.us/tax/

Unemployment Insurance Office
Chief, Unemployment Insurance Bureau
New Mexico Department of Labor
401 Broadway Blvd., NE
P.O. Box 1928
Albuquerque, NM 87103
505-841-8431
www.dol.state.nm.us/dol_UIclaims.html
Weekly benefit range: $42-212
Duration of benefits: 19-26 weeks

Utility Commission
Public Utility Commission
224 E. Palace Ave.
Santa Fe, NM 87501-2013
505-827-6940
800-663-9782
www.nmprc.state.nm.us/utility.htm

Women's Commission
New Mexico Commission on the Status of Women
4001 Indian School Rd., NE
Suite 300
Albuquerque, NM 87110
505-841-8920
800-432-9168
Fax: 505-841-8926
Email: womenscommission@state.nm.us
Darlene Smart-Herrera, Chair
www.state.nm.us/womenscommission

Your Senator
United States Senate
Washington, DC 20510
202-224-3121
www.senate.gov

Your Representative
United States House of Representatives
Washington, DC 20515
202-224-3121
www.house.gov

NEW YORK

Federal Information Center
1-800-FED-INFO
www.firstgov.gov
www.pueblo.gsa.gov/call/

State Information Office
518-474-2121
www.state.ny.us

Department on Aging
Office for the Aging
2 Empire State Plaza
Albany, NY 12223-1251
518-474-5731
800-342-9871 (NY only)
Email: nysofa@ofa.state.ny.us
http://aging.state.ny.us/nysofa/

Attorney General's Office
Office of the Attorney General
The Capitol
Albany, NY 12224-0341
518-474-7330
800-771-7755
www.oag.state.ny.us

Banking Commissioner
Superintendent of Banks
New York State Banking Department
Two Rector St.
New York, NY 10006-1894
212-618-6553
800-522-3330 (consumer)
800-832-1838 (small business)
www.banking.state. ny.us/

Child Care and Development Block Grant Lead Agency
Office of Children and Family Services
Child Day Care Services
52 Washington St.
Rensselaer, NY 12144-2735
518-474-9324
www.ocfs.state.ny.us/main/becs/default.htm

Child Support Enforcement Agency
Robert Doar
Office of Child Support Enforcement
Office of Temporary and Disability Services
40 N. Pearl St.
Albany, NY 12243
518-474-9081
518-486-3127
800-342-3009
800-343-8859 (in NY)
www.otda.state.ny.us/csms/default.htm

Cooperative Extension Office
William Lacy, Director
Cornell Cooperative Extension
276 Roberts Hall
Ithaca, NY 14853
607-255-2237
www.cce.cornell.edu/

Corporation Division Office
New York State
Department of State
Division of Corporations, State Records, and UCC
41 State St.
Albany, NY 12231-0001
518-473-2492
Fax: 518-474-1418
Email: corporations@dos.state.ny.us
www.dos.state.ny.us/corp/corpwww.html

Day Care Licensing Agency
State Department of Family Assistance
Bureau of Early Childhood Services
Office of Children and Family Services
Child Day Care Services
52 Washington St.
Rensselaer, NY 12144-2735
518-474-9454
www.ocfs.state.ny.us/main/becs/default.htm

Economic Development Office
Empire State Development
30 S. Pearl St.
Albany, NY 12245
and
633 Third Ave.
New York, NY 10017-6706
518-474-7756
800-STATE-NY (782-8369)
Email: esd@empire.state.ny.us
www.empire.state.ny.us

Department of Education
New York Department of Education
Education Building
89 Washington Ave.
Albany, NY 12234
518-474-3852
www.nysed.gov/

Department of Higher Education
New York Higher Education Services Corporation
Grants and Scholarship Information
99 Washington Avenue
Albany, NY 12255
518-473-1574
888-NYSHESC
Email: webmail@hesc.com
www.hesc.com

Health Department
New York Department of Health
Corning Tower Building
Empire State Plaza
Albany, NY 12237
518-474-2011
www.health.state.ny.us
Email: nyhealth@health.state. ny.us

Housing Offices
State of New York
Division of Housing and Community Renewal
Hampton Plaza
38-40 State St.
Albany, NY 12207
518-473-2517

State of New York
Division of Housing and Community Renewal
25 Beaver St.
New York, NY 10004
212-480-6700
866-ASK-DHCR (3427)
Email: DHCRInfo@dhcr.state.ny.us
www.dhcr.state.ny.us

Insurance Commissioner
Superintendent of Insurance
25 Beaver St.
New York, NY 10004
212-480-6400
800-342-3736 (in NY)
www.ins.state.ny.us

Labor Department
New York Department of Labor
State Office Bldg. Campus
Room 500
Albany, NY 12240-0003
518-457-9000
www.labor.state.ny.us

Licensing Office
New York State Education Dept.
Office of the Professions
State Education Building, 2nd Floor
89 Washington Ave.
Albany, NY 12234
518-474-3817
800-442-8106
Email: op4info@mail.nysed.gov
www.op.nysed.gov

One-Stop Career Center
Workforce Development and Training
Department of Labor
Workforce Development
Building 12, State Campus
Albany, NY 12240
518-457-0380
Email: onestop@labor.state.ny.us
www.wdsny.org

Security Regulators
New York Bureau of Investor Protection and Securities
120 Broadway, 23rd Floor
New York, NY 10271
212-416-8222
Fax: 212-416-8816
www.oag.state.ny.us

Small Business Development Center
New York Small Business Development Centers
State University of New York (SUNY)
41 State St.
Albany, NY 12246
518-443-5398
800-732-SBDC (in NY)
Fax: 518-465-4992
Email: kingjl@nysbdc.org
www.smallbiz.suny.edu/

Social Services Offices
New York State Department of Family Assistance
52 Washington St.
Rensselaer, NY 12144-2735
518-473-8437
www.dfa.state.ny.us

Temporary Assistance to Needy Families (TANF)
Temporary Aid to Needy Families
John Johnson
Office of Temporary and Disability Assistance
40 North Pearl St.
Albany, NY 12243
518-474-9222
800-342-3009
www.otda.state.ny.us

Transportation Department
Joseph H. Boardman
New York Department of Transportation
5-504 Harriman State Office Campus
1220 Washington Ave., Room 115
Albany, NY 12232
518-457-4422
www.dot.state.ny.us

Unclaimed Property Office
Office of Unclaimed Funds
Office of State Comptroller
110 State St.
Albany, NY 12236
518-474-4038
800-221-9311 (in NY)
Email: nysouf@osc.state.ny.us
www.osc.state.ny.us

Unemployment Insurance Office
Director
Unemployment Insurance Division
New York State Dept. of Labor
State Office Building Campus, Room 500
Albany, NY 12240-0003
518-457-9000
888-209-8124 (to file a claim)
www.labor.state.ny.us/working_ny/unemployment_insurance/unemployment_insurance.html
Weekly benefit range: $40-405
Duration of benefits: 26 weeks

Utility Commission
Public Service Commission
Empire State Plaza
Agency Bldg. 3
Albany, NY 12223-1350
518-474-3280
800-342-3377 (NY only)
Email: csd@dps.state.ny.us
www.dps.state.ny.us

Women's Commission
New York State Division for Women
633 Third Ave., 38th Floor
New York, NY 10017
212-681-4547
Fax: 212-681-7626
Email: women@www.women.state.ny.us
www.women.state.ny.us
Elaine Wingate Conway, Director

Your Senator
United States Senate
Washington, DC 20510
202-224-3121
www.senate.gov

Your Representative
United States House of Representatives
Washington, DC 20515
202-224-3121
www.house.gov

North Carolina

Federal Information Center
1-800-FED-INFO
www.firstgov.gov
www.pueblo.gsa.gov/call/

State Information Office
919-733-1110
www.ncgov.com

Department on Aging
Aging Division
Human Resources Dept.
693 Palmer Dr.
MAILING ADDRESS:
2101 Mail Service Center
Raleigh, NC 27699-2101
Raleigh, NC 27603
919-733-3983
Fax: 919-733-0443
www.dhhs.state.nc.us/aging

Attorney General's Office
Office of the Attorney General
Department of Justice
P.O. Box 629
Raleigh, NC 27602-0629
919-716-6400
919-716-6000 (consumer protection)
Fax: 919-716-6050
www.jus.state.nc.us
Email: agjus@mail.jus.state.nc.us

Banking Commissioner
Commissioner of Banks
316 Edenton St.
Raleigh, NC 27603
MAILING ADDRESS:
4309 Mail Service Center
Raleigh, NC 27699-4309
919-733-3016
Fax: 919-733-6918
www.banking.state. nc.us/

Child Care and Development Block Grant Lead Agency
Department of Health and Human Services
Division of Child Development
2201 Mail Service Center
Raleigh, NC 27699-2201
919-662-4499
800-859-0829 (in NC)
Fax: 919-662-4568
Email: webmasterdcd@ncmail.net
www.dhhs.state.nc.us/dcd/

Child Support Enforcement Agency
Michael Adams
Child Support Enforcement Section
Division of Social Services
Albemarle Bldg.
325 N. Salisbury St.
Raleigh, NC 27603
MAILING ADDRESS:
2401 Mail Service Center
Raleigh, NC 27699-2401
919-571-4114
919-571-4126
800-992-9457 (in NC)
www.dhhs.state.nc.us/dss/cse/cse_hm.htm

Cooperative Extension Offices
Dr. Jon F. Ort, Director
Cooperative Extension Service
North Carolina State University
Box 7602
Raleigh, NC 27695-7602
919-515-2811
www.ces.ncsu.edu/

Dr. Dalton McAfee, Director
Cooperative Extension Program
North Carolina A&T State University
P.O. Box 21928
Greensboro, NC 27420-1928
336-334-7956
www.ag.ncat.edu/extension/index.htm

Corporation Division Office
Division of Corporation
Secretary of State
P.O. Box 29622
Raleigh, NC 27626-0622
919-807-2225
Fax: 919-807-2039
www.secretary.state.nc.us/corporations

Day Care Licensing Agency
Department of Family Assistance
Division of Child Development
Child Care Licensing
319 Chapanoke Rd., Suite 120
Raleigh, NC 27603
MAILING ADDRESS:
2201 Mail Service Center
Raleigh, NC 27699-2201
919-662-4499
800-859-0829
www.dhhs.state.nc.us/dcd

Economic Development Office
Department of Commerce
Commerce Finance Center
301 N. Wilmington St.
Raleigh, NC 27601
MAILING ADDRESS:
4301 Mail Service Center
Raleigh, NC 27699-4301
919-733-4151
Fax: 919-715-9265
www.commerce.state.nc.us/

Department of Education
North Carolina Department of Public Instruction
301 N. Wilmington St.
Raleigh, NC 27601-2825
919-807-3300
www.dpi.state.nc.us/

Department of Higher Education
North Carolina State Education Assistance Authority
P.O. Box 14103
Research Triangle Park, NC 27709
919-549-8614
Fax: 919-549-8481
Email: information@ncseaa.edu
www.ncseaa.edu

Health Department
North Carolina State Center for Health Statistics
Cotton Classing Building
222 North Dawson Street
Raleigh, NC 27603-1392
MAILING ADDRESS:
1908 Mail Service Center
Raleigh, NC 27699-1908
919-733-4728
Fax: 919-733-8485
www.schs.state.nc.us/SCHS

Housing Office
North Carolina Housing Finance Agency
3508 Bush St.
Raleigh, NC 27609-7509
919-877-5700
Email: webmaster@nchfa.com
www.nchfa.state.nc.us

Insurance Commissioner
Commissioner of Insurance
Dobbs Bldg.
P.O. Box 26387
Raleigh, NC 27611
919-733-2032
800-JIM-LONG
Email: consumer@ncdoi.net
www.ncdoi.com/

Labor Department
North Carolina Dept. of Labor
4 West Edenton Street
Raleigh, NC 27601
919-733-7166
800-LABOR-NC
www.dol.state.nc.us/

Licensing Office
Department of the Secretary of State
111 Hillsborough St.
Raleigh, NC 27603
919-807-2166
800-228-8443 (in NC)
www.secretary.state.nc.us/blio/default.asp

One-Stop Career Center
Joblink Career Centers
Commission on Workforce Development
NC Department of Commerce
301 N. Wilmington St.
4327 Mail Service Center
Raleigh, NC 27699-4327
919-715-3300
Fax: 919-715-3974
Email: hlaffler@nccommerce.com
www.joblink.state.nc.us

Security Regulators
North Carolina Securities Division
300 N. Salisbury St., Room 302
Raleigh, NC 27603
MAILING ADDRESS:
P.O. Box 29622
Raleigh, NC 27626-0622
919-733-3924
800-688-4507 (complaints)
www.secretary.state.nc.us/sec

Small Business Development Center
North Carolina Small Business and Technology Development Center
University of North Carolina
5 West Hargett St.
Suite 600
Raleigh, NC 27601-0862
919-715-7272
800-2580-UNC
Fax: 919-715-7777
Email: info@sbtdc.org
www.sbtdc.org

Social Services Offices
North Carolina Department of Health and Human Services
Albemarle Bldg.
325 N. Salisbury St.
Raleigh, NC 27603
MAILING ADDRESS:
2401 Mail Service Center
Raleigh, NC 27699-2401
919-733-3055
www.dhhs.state.nc.us/dss

Temporary Assistance to Needy Families (TANF)
Temporary Aid to Needy Families
Pheon Beal
Division of Social Services
325 North Salisbury St.
Raleigh, NC 27603
MAILING ADDRESS:
2401 Mail Service Center
Raleigh, NC 27699-2401
919-733-3055
www.dhhs.state.nc.us/dss/ tanf.htm

Transportation Department
Lynda Tippett
North Carolina Department of Transportation
1500 Mail Service Center
Raleigh, NC 27699-1500
919-733-2520
www.ncdot.org

Gene Conti
North Carolina Department of Transportation
1500 Mail Service Center
Raleigh, NC 27699-1500
919-733-2520
www.ncdot.org

Unclaimed Property Office
Escheat & Unclaimed Property
325 North Salisbury St.
Raleigh, NC 27603
919-508-5979
http://ncdst-webt.treasurer.state.nc.us/asd/frescheat.htm

Unemployment Insurance Office
Unemployment Insurance Division
Employment Security Commission of North Carolina
700 Wade Ave.
Raleigh, NC 27605
919-733-3121
www.esc.state.nc.us/
Email: esc.ui.customerservice@ncmail.net
Weekly benefit range: $15-396
Duration of benefits: 13-26 weeks

Utility Commission
Utilities Commission
430 N. Salisbury St.
Dobbs Bldg.
4325 Mail Service Center
Raleigh, NC 27699-4325
919-733-7328
www.ncuc.commerce.state.nc.us

Women's Commission
North Carolina Council for Women
1320 Mail Service Center
Raleigh, NC 27699-1320
919-733-2455
Fax: 919-733-2464
www.doa.state.nc.us/doa/cfw/cfw.htm
Leslie Starsoneck, Exec. Director
Jane Carver, Chair

Your Senator
United States Senate
Washington, DC 20510
202-224-3121
www.senate.gov

Your Representative
United States House of Representatives
Washington, DC 20515
202-224-3121
www.house.gov

NORTH DAKOTA

Federal Information Center
1-800-FED-INFO
www.firstgov.gov
www.pueblo.gsa.gov/call/

State Information Office
701-224-2000
http://discovernd.com

Department on Aging
Aging Services Division
Human Services Dept.
600 South 2nd St., Suite 1-C
Bismarck, ND 58504-5729
701-328-8910
800-451-8693 (senior info)
Email: dhsaging@state.nd.us
http://lnotes.state.nd.us/dhs/dhsweb.nsf/ServicePages/AgingServices

Attorney General's Office
Office of the Attorney General
State Capitol Building
600 East Boulevard Ave.
Department 125
Bismarck, ND 58505-0040
701-328-2210
800-472-2600
TDD: 701-328-3409
www.ag.state.nd.us

Banking Commissioner
Commissioner of Banking and Financial Institutions
2000 Schafer St., Suite G
Bismarck, ND 58501-1204
701-328-9933
TDD: 800-366-6888
www.state.nd.us/bank/
Email: dfi@state.nd.us

Child Care and Development Block Grant Lead Agency
Early Childhood Services
Children and Family Services
North Dakota Department of Human Services
600 E. Boulevard Ave.
Bismarck, ND 58505-0250
701-328-2316
800-245-3736
Fax: 701-328-2359
http://lnotes.state.nd.us/dhs/dhsweb.nsf/ServicePages/ChildrenandFamilyServices
Email: sobenc@state.nd.us

Child Support Enforcement Agency
Child Support Enforcement Division
Department of Human Services
1929 N. Washington St.
P.O. Box 7190
Bismarck, ND 58507-7190
701-328-3582
Fax: 701-328-6575
TDD: 800-366-6888
http://lnotes.state.nd.us/dhs/dhsweb.nsf/ServicePages/ChildSupportEnforcement

Cooperative Extension Office
Dr. Sharon Anderson, Director
Cooperative Extension Service
North Dakota State University
Morrill Hall, Room 311, Box 5437
Fargo, ND 58105
701-231-8944
www.ext.nodak.edu/

Corporation Division Office
Business Info/Registration Division
Secretary of State
Capitol Building
600 E. Boulevard Ave.
Bismarck, ND 58505
701-328-4284
800-352-0867, ext. 4284
Email: sosbir@state.nd.us
www.state.nd.us/sec/Business/businessinforegmnu.htm

Day Care Licensing Agency
Department of Human Services
Children and Family Services
Early Childhood Services
600 E. Boulevard
Bismarck, ND 58505-0250
701-328-2316
800-245-3736
Email: sobenc@state.nd.us
http://lnotes.state.nd.us/dhs/dhsweb.nsf/ServicePages/ChildrenandFamilyServices

Economic Development Office
Department of Economic Development and Finance
400 E. Broadway, Suite 50
Bismarck, ND 58502-2057
701-328-5300
Fax: 701-328-5320
TTY: 800-366-6888
www.growingnd.com

Department of Education
Department of Public Instruction
600 E. Boulevard Ave.
Department 201
Floors 9, 10, and 11
Bismarck, ND 58505-0440
701-328-2260
Fax: 701-328-2461
www.dpi.state.nd.us/

Department of Higher Education
University Systems
10th Floor, State Capitol
600 East Boulevard Ave.
Department 215
Bismarck, ND 58505-0230
701-328-2960
Fax: 701-328-2961
Email: ndus.office@ndus.nodak.edu
www.ndus.nodak.edu

Health Department
North Dakota Department of Health
600 East Boulevard Avenue
Bismarck, ND 58505-0200
701-328-2372
Fax: 701-328-4727
www.health.state.nd.us
Email: tdwelle@state.nd.us

Housing Office
Housing Finance Agency
P.O. Box 1535
Bismarck, ND 58502-1535
701-328-8080
800-292-8621
Fax: 701-328-8090
TTY: 800-366-6888
www.ndhfa.state.nd.us

Insurance Commissioner
Commissioner of Insurance

Capitol Bldg., 5th Floor
600 E. Boulevard Ave.
Department 401
Bismarck, ND 58505-0320
701-328-2440
800-247-0560 (in ND)
Email: insuranc@state.nd.us
www.state.nd.us/ndins

Labor Department
600 E. Boulevard Ave.
Department 406
Bismarck, ND 58505-0340
701-328-2660
800-582-8032 (in ND)
Email: labor@state.nd.us
www.state.nd.us/labor

Licensing Office
Licensing Section
Office of the Attorney General
600 East Boulevard
Department 125
Bismarck, ND 58505-0040
701-328-2329
www.ag.state.nd.us/

One-Stop Career Center
Job Service North Dakota
P.O. Box 5507
Bismarck, ND 58506-5507
800-732-9787
701-328-2868
TTY; 800-366-6888
Fax: 701-328-4193
www.state.nd.us/jsnd/
Email: jsndweb@state.nd.us

Security Regulators
North Dakota Securities
Commissioner's Office
State Capitol Building, 5th Floor
600 East Boulevard Ave.
Bismarck, ND 58505-0510
701-328-2910
800-297-5124 (in ND)
Email: seccom@state.nd.us
www.state.nd.us/securities

Small Business Development Center
North Dakota Small Business
Development Center
University of North Dakota
118 Gamble Hall, Box 7308
Grand Forks, ND 58202-7308
701-777-3700
800-445-7232 (SBDC)
Fax: 701-777-3225
Email: ndsbdc@sage.und.
nodak.edu
http://bpa.und.nodak.edu/sbdc

Social Services Offices
Department of Human Services
State Capitol, Judicial Wing
600 E. Boulevard Ave.
Department 325
Bismarck, ND 58505-0250
701-328-2310
800-472-2622
Fax: 701-328-2359
TTY: 800-366-6888
Email: sosteh@state.nd.us
http://lnotes.state.nd.us/dhs/
dhsweb.nsf

Temporary Assistance to Needy Families (TANF)
Temporary Aid to Needy Families
Public Assistance Division
Department of Human Services
600 East Boulevard Ave.
Department 325
Bismarck, ND 58505-0269
701-328-3513
800-755-2716
Email: sooppj@state.nd.ud
http://lnotes.state.nd.us/dhs/
dhsweb.nsf/ServicePages/
PublicAssistance

Transportation Department
David A. Sprynczynatyk
North Dakota Department of
Transportation
608 East Boulevard Ave.
Bismarck, ND 58505
701-328-2500
Email: dot@state.nd.us
www.state.nd.us/dot

Unclaimed Property Office
Unclaimed Property Division
State Land Department
P.O. Box 5523
Bismarck, ND 58506
701-328-2800
Email: lfisher@state.nd.us
www.land.state.nd.us

Unemployment Insurance Office
Director, Job Insurance Division
Job Service North Dakota
P.O. Box 5507
Bismarck, ND 58506
701-328-2868
800-732-9787
Email: jsapps@state.nd.us
www.state.nd.us/jsnd/
Weekly benefit range: $43-290
Duration of benefits: 12-26 weeks

Utility Commission
Public Service Commission
600 E. Boulevard, Dept. 408
Bismarck, ND 58505-0480
701-328-2400
Fax: 701-328-2410
TTY: 800-366-6888
www.psc.state.nd.us/

Women's Commission
North Dakota Governor's
Commission on the Status of
Women
P.O. Box 1913
Bismarck, ND 58502
701-328-3159
Fax: 701-328-1255
Carol Reed, Chairman
www.governor.state.nd.us/boards
Email: BoardMember@
statusofwomen.com

Your Senator
United States Senate
Washington, DC 20510
202-224-3121
www.senate.gov

Your Representative
United States House of
Representatives
Washington, DC 20515
202-224-3121
www.house.gov

Ohio

Federal Information Center
1-800-FED-INFO
www.firstgov.gov
www.pueblo.gsa.gov/call/

State Information Office
614-466-2000
www.state.oh.us

Department on Aging
Department of Aging
50 W. Broad St., 9th Floor
Columbus, OH 43215-3363
614-466-5500
Fax: 614-466-5741
Email: ODAMAIL@age.state. oh.us
www.state.oh.us/age/index.htm

Attorney General's Office
Office of the Attorney General
Montgomery State Office Tower
30 East Broad Street, 17th Floor
Columbus, OH 43215-3428
614-466-4320
800-282-0515 (OH)
(consumer protection)
www.ag.state.oh.us

Banking Commissioner
Superintendent of Financial
Institutions
77 S. High St., 21st Floor
Columbus, OH 43266-0121
614-728-8400
Email: webdfi@dfi.com.state.oh.us
www.com.state.oh.us/ODOC/dfi

Child Care and Development Block Grant Lead Agency
Department of Job and Family
Services
Office for Children and Families
30 E. Broad St., 32nd Floor
Columbus, OH 43266-0423
614-466-6282
Fax: 614-466-2815
www.state.oh.us/odjfs/
ocf/fund_plan2002.stm

Child Support Enforcement Agency
Joseph Pilat
Office of Child Support
Department of Jobs and Family
Services
30 East Broad St., 31st Floor
Columbus, OH 43215-3414
614-752-6561
800-686-1556 (in OH)
Fax: 614-752-9760
www.state.oh.us/odhs/ocs/index.htm

Cooperative Extension Office
Keith Smith, Director
OSU Extension
2120 Fiffe Road
Agriculture Administration Building
Columbus, OH 43210
614-292-6181
www.ag.ohio-state.edu/

Corporation Division Office
Corporation Division
Secretary of State
30 East Broad St., 14th Floor
Columbus, OH 43266
MAILING ADDRESS:
P.O. Box 1390
Columbus, OH 43216
614-466-3910
877-SOS-FILE
www.state.oh.us/sos/business_servi
ces_information.htm
Email: busserv@sos.state.oh.us

Day Care Licensing Agency
Department of Jobs and Family
Services
Child Care Licensing Section
255 E. Main St., 3rd Floor
Columbus, OH 43215
614-466-3822
Fax: 614-728-6803
Email: childcare@odjfs.state.oh.us
www.state.oh.us/odhs/cdc/

Economic Development Office
Ohio Department of Development
77 S. High St.
P.O. Box 1001
Columbus, OH 43216-1001
614-466-2317
800-848-1300
Fax: 614-463-1789
www.odod.state.oh.us

Department of Education
Ohio Department of Education
25 S. Front St.
Columbus, OH 43215-4183
614-995-1545
877-644-6338
Email:
contact.center@ods.state.oh.us
www.ode.state.oh.us

Department of Higher Education
Ohio Board of Regents
State Grants and Scholarship
Department
30 East Broad St., 36th Floor
Columbus, OH 43215-3414
MAILING ADDRESS:
P.O. Box 182452
Columbus, OH 43218-2452
888-833-1133
614-466-7420
Fax: 614-752-5903
Email: regents@regents.state.oh.us
www.regents.state.oh.us

Health Department
Ohio Department of Health
246 North High Street
P.O. Box 118
Columbus, OH 43216-0118
614-466-2253
www.odh.state.oh.us
Email:
webmaster@gw.odh.state.oh.us

Housing Office
Ohio Housing Finance Agency
57 E. Main St.
Columbus, OH 43215-5135
614-466-7970
TDD: 614-466-1940
www.odod.state.oh.us/ohfa/default.ht
m

Insurance Commissioner
Director of Insurance
2100 Stella Court
Columbus, OH 43215-1067
614-644-2658
800-686-1526 (consumer)
800-686-1527 (fraud)

800-686-1578 (senior health)
www.ohioinsurance.gov

Labor Department
Workforce Development
Department of Jobs and Family Services
145 South Front Street
Columbus, OH 43215
614-752-3091
www.state.oh.us/odjfs/0001OurServices.stm

Licensing Office
State of Ohio
Dept. of Administrative Services
State Information Office
30 East Broad St., 40th Floor
Columbus, OH 43215
614-466-2000

One-Stop Career Center
One-Stop Systems
One-Stop Employment and Training System
Bureau of Employment Services
145 Front Street, 6th Floor
Columbus, OH 43215
614-466-3817
Fax: 614-728-5938
www.state.oh.us/odjfs/onestop/

Security Regulators
Department of Commerce
Ohio Division of Securities
77 South High St., 22nd Floor
Columbus, OH 43215
614-644-7381
800-788-1194
(Investor Protection Hotline)
www.securities.state.oh.us

Small Business Development Center
Ohio Small Business Development Center
Department of Development
77 South High Street, 28th Floor
Columbus, OH 43216-1001
614-466-2711
800-848-1300
Fax: 614-466-0829
Email: dshupe@odod.state.oh.us
www.ohiosbdc.org

Social Services Offices
Ohio Department of Jobs and Family Services
30 East Broad Street, 32nd Floor
Columbus, OH 43266-0423
614-466-6650
www.state.oh.us/odjfs/index.stm

Temporary Assistance to Needy Families (TANF)
Ohio Works First
Office of Workforce Development
145 S. Front St., 6th Floor
Columbus, OH 43266
614-752-3091
www.state.oh.us/odhs/owf/Tanf/index.htm

Transportation Department
Gordon Proctor
Ohio Department of Transportation
1980 W. Broad St.
Columbus, OH 43223
614-466-7170
www.dot.state.oh.us

Lynn Rathke
Ohio Department of Transportation
1980 W. Broad St.
Columbus, OH 43215
614-644-7362
www.dot.state.oh.us

Unclaimed Property Office
Division of Unclaimed Funds
77 South High St., 20th Floor
Columbus, OH 43215-6108
614-466-4433
Email: unfd.claims@com.state.oh.us
www.com.state.oh.us/ODOC/unfd/default.htm

Unemployment Insurance Office
Director
Unemployment Insurance
Ohio Bureau of Employment Services
Office of Unemployment Compensation
145 S. Front St., 5th Floor
Columbus, OH 43215
614-995-7066
www.state.oh.us/odjfs/ouc
Weekly benefit range: $66-414
Duration of benefits: 20-26 weeks

Utility Commission
Public Utilities Commission
180 E. Broad St.
Columbus, OH 43215-3793
614-466-3016
800-686-7826 (OH only)
TTD/TTY: 800-686-1570
www.puc.state.oh.us/

Women's Commission
Closed June 15, 2001

Your Senator
United States Senate
Washington, DC 20510
202-224-3121
www.senate.gov

Your Representative
United States House of Representatives
Washington, DC 20515
202-224-3121
www.house.gov

OKLAHOMA

Federal Information Center
1-800-FED-INFO
www.firstgov.gov
www.pueblo.gsa.gov/call/

State Information Office
405-521-2011
www.state.ok.us

Department on Aging
Aging Services Division
Human Services Dept.
P.O. Box 25352
Oklahoma City, OK 73125
405-521-2327
800-211-2116 (senior info)
www.okdhs.org/aging

Attorney General's Office
Office of the Attorney General
112 State Capitol Building
Oklahoma City, OK 73105
405-521-3921
405-521-2029 (consumer protection)
www.oag.state.ok.us/

Banking Commissioner
Bank Commissioner
4545 N. Lincoln Blvd.
Suite 164
Oklahoma City, OK 73105-3427
405-521-2782
Fax: 405-522-2993
www.state.ok.us/ ~osbd/

Child Care and Development Block Grant Lead Agency
Administrator of CCDF
Office of Child Care
Oklahoma Department of Human Services
Sequoyah Memorial Office Bldg.
2400 N. Lincoln Blvd.
P.O. Box 25325
Oklahoma City, OK 73125
405-521-3561
800-347-2276
Fax: 405-521-0391
www.okdhs.org/childcare

Child Support Enforcement Agency
Herbert Jones
Child Support Enforcement Division
Department of Human Services
P.O. Box 53552
Oklahoma City, OK 73152
405-522-5871
800-522-2922 (in OK) (kids line)
Fax: 405-522-2753
www.okdhs.org/childsupport

Cooperative Extension Offices
Dr. C.B. Browning, Director
Oklahoma Cooperative Extension Service
Oklahoma State University
139 Agriculture Hall
Stillwater, OK 74078
405-744-5398
www.dasnr.okstate.edu/oces

Corporation Division Office
Secretary of State
Business Filing Department
101 State Capitol Building
2300 N. Lincoln Blvd.
Room 101
Oklahoma City, OK 73105-4897
405-522-4560
Fax: 405-521-3771
www.sos.state.ok.us/

Day Care Licensing Agency
Department of Human Services
Division of Child Care
Sequoyah Memorial Office Bldg.
2400 N. Lincoln Blvd.
P.O. Box 25352
Oklahoma City, OK 73125
405-521-3561
800-347-2276
www.okdhs.org/childcare

Economic Development Office
Department of Commerce
900 North Stiles
P.O. Box 26980
Oklahoma City, OK 73126-0980
405-815-6552
800-879-6552.
Fax: 405-815-5199
www.locateok.com
www.odoc.state.ok.us/index.html

Department of Education
Oklahoma State Department of Education
2500 N. Lincoln Blvd.
Oklahoma City, OK 73105-4599
405-521-3301
www.sde.state.ok.us/

Department of Higher Education
Oklahoma State Regents for Higher Education
655 Research Pkwy., Suite 200
Oklahoma City, OK 73104
405-225-9100
Fax: 405-225-9230
Email: tsimonton@osrhe.edu
www.okhighered.org

Health Department
Oklahoma State Department of Health
1000 NE 10th Street
Oklahoma City, OK 73117
405-271-5600
800-522-0203
www.health.state.ok.us
Email:
webmaster@health.state.ok.us

Housing Office
Oklahoma Housing Finance Agency
100 NW 63rd Street
Suite 200
P.O. Box 26720
Oklahoma City, OK 73116
405-848-1144
800-256-1489
TDD: 405-848-7471
Email: webteam@ohfa.org
www.ohfa.org

Insurance Commissioner
Insurance Commissioner
2401 NW 23rd, Suite 28
P.O. Box 53408
Oklahoma City, OK 73152-3408
405-521-2828
800-522-0071
www.oid.state.ok.us

Labor Department
Oklahoma Department of Labor

4001 North Lincoln Boulevard
Oklahoma City, OK 73105-5212
405-528-1500
888-269-5353
Fax: 405-528-5751
www.oklaosf.state.ok.us/~okdol

Licensing Office
Governor's Office
State Capitol
Oklahoma City, OK 73105
405-521-2342

One-Stop Career Center
Oklahoma Workforce Centers
Employment Security Commission
218 Will Rogers Building
P.O. Box 52003
Oklahoma City, OK 73152
405-557-7201
www.oesc.state.ok.us

Security Regulators
Oklahoma Dept. of Securities
First National Center
120 North Robinson, Suite 860
Oklahoma City, OK 73102
405-280-7700
Fax: 405-280-7742
www.securities.state.ok.us

Small Business Development Center
Oklahoma Small Business Development Center
Southeastern Oklahoma State University
517 University
Station A, Box 2584
Durant, OK 74701
580-924-0277
800-522-6154
Fax: 580-920-7471
www.osbdc.org

Social Services Offices
Oklahoma Department of Human Services
2400 North Lincoln Boulevard
P.O. Box 25352
Oklahoma City, OK 73125
405-521-3646
www.okdhs.org

Temporary Assistance to Needy Families (TANF)
Temporary Aid to Needy Families
Peggy Butcher
Oklahoma Department of Human Service
Family Support Services Division
P.O. Box 25352
Oklahoma City, OK 73125
405-521-3076
Fax: 405-521-4158
www.okdhs.org/fssd/ProgramInformation.htm#Temporary
Email: Peggy.Butcher@okdhs.org

Transportation Department
Gary Ridley
Oklahoma Dept. of Transportation
Transportation Bldg.
200 NE 21st St.
Oklahoma City, OK 73015-3204
405-521-2631
Email: webinfo@odot.org
www.okladot.state.ok.us

Unclaimed Property Office
Oklahoma Tax Commission
Unclaimed Property Section
2501 Lincoln Blvd.
Oklahoma City, OK 73194
405-521-4273
www.oktax.state.ok.us

Unemployment Insurance Office
Unemployment Insurance Director
Employment Security Commission
P.O. Box 52003
218 Will Rogers Building
Oklahoma City, OK 73152
405-557-0200
www.oesc.state.ok.us/ui/ default.htm
Weekly benefit range: $16-293
Duration of benefits: 20-26 weeks

Utility Commission
Corporation Commission
201 N. Lincoln Blvd.
P.O. Box 52000
Oklahoma City, OK 73152-2000
405-521-2211
www.occ.state.ok.us

Women's Commission
Oklahoma Governor's Commission on the Status of Women
101 State Capitol Bldg.
2300 North Lincoln Blvd.
Oklahoma City, OK 73105-4897
918-492-4492
Fax: 918-492-4472
Sydney Hill, Chair
Cathrine Haynes, Senior Vice Chair

Lawton Mayor's Commission on the Status of Women
102 SW 5th St.
Lawton, OK 73501
405-581-3260
Janet Childress, Chair
Emma Crowder, Vice Chair

Tulsa Mayor's Commission on the Status of Women
c/o Department of Human Rights
200 Civic Center
Tulsa, OK 74103
918-582-0558
918-592-7818

Your Senator
United States Senate
Washington, DC 20510
202-224-3121
www.senate.gov

Your Representative
United States House of Representatives
Washington, DC 20515
202-224-3121
www.house.gov

OREGON

Federal Information Center
1-800-FED-INFO
www.firstgov.gov
www.pueblo.gsa.gov/call/

State Information Office
503-378-3111
http://oregon.gov

Department on Aging
Seniors and People with Disabilities
500 Summer St., NE, E02
Salem, OR 97301-1073
503-945-5811
800-282-8096
Email: sdsd.info@state.or.us
www.sdsd.hr.state.or.us/

Attorney General's Office
Office of the Attorney General
Department of Justice
1162 Court Street, NE
Salem, OR 97310
503-378-4400
877-877-9392 (OR consumer hotline)
www.doj.state.or.us
Email: doj.info@state.or.us

Banking Commissioner
Administrator
Division of Finance and Corporate Securities
350 Winter St., NE, Room 410
Salem, OR 97301-3881
503-378-4140
Fax: 503-947-7862
Email: dcbs.dfcsmail@state.or.us
www.cbs.state.or.us/dfcs/

Child Care and Development Block Grant Lead Agency
Child Care Division
Department of Employment
875 Union St., NE
Salem, OR 97311
503-947-1400
800-556-6616
Fax: 503-947-1428
Email: child_care@emp.state. or.us
http://findit.emp.state.or.us/childcare/ccdf.cfm

Child Support Enforcement Agency
Phil Yarnell
Oregon Child Support Program
Children, Adult and Family Services Division
Department of Human Resources
500 Summer St., E46
Salem, OR 97301-1066
503-945-5600
TTY: 503-945-5896
www.afs.hr.state.or.us/childsupp.html

Cooperative Extension Office
Dr. Lyla Houghlum, Director
Oregon State Extension
Service Administration
Oregon State University
Ballard Extension Hall #101
Corvallis, OR 97331-3606
541-737-2711
www.osu.orst.edu/extension/

Corporation Division Office
Corporation Division
Secretary of State
Public Service Bldg.
255 Capitol St., NE, Suite 151
Salem, OR 97310
503-986-2200
www.sos.state.or.us/corporation

Day Care Licensing Agency
Employment Department
Child Care Division
875 Union Street, NE
Salem, OR 97311
503-947-1400
800-556-6616
Email: child_care@emp.state. or.us
www.emp.state.or.us

Economic Development Office
Economic and Community Development Department
775 Summer St., Suite 200
Salem, OR 97301-1280
503-986-0123
800-233-3306 (in OR)
www.econ.state.or.us/

Department of Education
Oregon Department of Education
255 Capitol St., NE
Salem, OR 97310-0203
503-378-3569
TDD: 503-378-2892
Fax: 503-378-5156
www.ode.state.or.us/

Department of Higher Education
Oregon Student Assistance Commission
1500 Valley River Drive, Suite 100
Eugene, OR 97401
800-452-8807
503-687-7400
www.osac.state.or.us

Health Department
Oregon Health Division
800 NE Oregon Street
Portland, OR 97232
503-731-4000
www.ohd.hr.state.or.us
Email: ohd.info@state.or.us

Housing Office
Oregon Housing and Community Services Department
1600 State St.
Salem, OR 97301-4246
503-986-2000
TTY: 503-986-2100
Email: info@hcs.state.or.us
www.hcs.state.or.us

Insurance Commissioner
Department of Consumer and Business
Insurance Commissioner
350 Winter St., NE, Room 440
Salem, OR 97301-3883
503-947-7980
800-722-4134
Fax: 503-378-4351
Email: dcbs.insmail@state.or.us
www.cbs.state.or.us/external/ins/index.html

Labor Department
Oregon Employment Department
875 Union Street NE

Salem, OR 97311
503-947-1470
800-327-3710
TTY: 503-947-1391
Email: info@emp.state.or.us
www.emp.state.or.us/

Licensing Office
Business Information Center
Corporations Division
Public Service Bldg.
255 Capitol St., NW, Suite 151
Salem, OR 97310
503-986-2200
www.sos.state.or.us/corporation/bic/bicintro.htm

One-Stop Career Center
Oregon Career Network
Oregon Employment Department
875 Union Street, NE
Salem, OR 97311
503-947-1470
800-237-3710
www.emp.state.or.us
Email: info@emp.state.or.us

Security Regulators
Division of Finance and Corporate Securities
Department of Consumer & Business Services
350 Winter St., NE, Room 410
Salem, OR 97301-3881
503-378-4140
Fax: 503-947-7862
Email: dcbs.dfcsmail@state.or.us
www.cbs.state.or.us/external/ dfcs/

Small Business Development Center
Oregon Business Development Center
Lane Community College
1445 Willamette St., Suite 1
Eugene, OR 97401-4087
541-687-0611
Fax: 541-686-0096
Email: contact@lanebdc.com
www.lanebdc.com

Social Services Offices
Oregon Department of Human Services
500 Summer Street, NE, E25
Salem, OR 97301-1098
503-945-5944
TTY: 503-945-5928
Fax: 503-378-2897
Email: dhr.info@state.or.us
www.hr.state.or.us/

Temporary Assistance to Needy Families (TANF)
Temporary Aid to Needy Families
Sandie Hoback
Oregon Department of Human Resources
500 Summer St., NE
Salem, OR 97310-1013
503-945-5601
800-359-9517
www.afs.hr.state.or.us/

Transportation Department
Karen Elliott
Oregon Department of Transportation
355 Capitol St., NE
Salem, OR 97301-3871
503-986-3450
888-ASK-DOT
www.odot.state.or.us/

Unclaimed Property Office
Unclaimed Property Unit
775 Summer St., NE
Salem, OR 97301
503-378-3805, ext. 450
Email: claims@dsl.state.or.us
http://statelands.dsl.state.or.us/upintro.htm

Unemployment Insurance Office
Programs and Methods
Employment Department
875 Union St., NE
Salem, OR 97311
503-947-1470
Email: ui_info@emp.state.or.us
http://findit.emp.state.or.us/uiinfo.cfm
Weekly benefit range: $93-400
Duration of benefits: 4-26 weeks

Utility Commission
Public Utility Commission
550 Capital St., NE, Suite 215
Salem, OR 97301-2551
503-378-6611
800-522-2404 (OR only)
www.puc.state.or.us

Women's Commission
Oregon Commission for Women
P.O. Box 751-CW
Portland, OR 97207
503-725-5889
Fax: 503-725-5889
Email: ocfw@pdx.edu
Roslyn Farrington, Executive Director

Your Senator
United States Senate
Washington, DC 20510
202-224-3121
www.senate.gov

Your Representative
United States House of Representatives
Washington, DC 20515
202-224-3121
www.house.gov

PENNSYLVANIA

Federal Information Center
1-800-FED-INFO
www.firstgov.gov
www.pueblo.gsa.gov/call/

State Information Office
717-787-2121
www.state.pa.us

Department on Aging
Department of Aging
555 Walnut St., 5th Floor
Harrisburg, PA 17101-1919
717-783-1550
Fax: 717-783-6842
Email: aging@state.pa.us
www.aging.state.pa.us/aging/site/default.asp

Attorney General's Office
Office of the Attorney General
16th Floor, Strawberry Square
Harrisburg, PA 17120
717-787-3391
800-441-2555
www.attorneygeneral.gov
Email: info@attorneygeneral.gov

Banking Commissioner
Secretary of Banking
333 Market St., 16th Floor
Harrisburg, PA 17101-2290
717-787-2665
800-PA-BANKS (toll free in PA)
www.banking.state.pa.us/

Child Care and Development Block Grant Lead Agency
CCDBG Administrator
Office of Children, Youth and Families
Pennsylvania Department of Public Welfare
Health and Welfare Bldg.
Room 131
P.O. Box 2675
Harrisburg, PA 17105-2675
717-783-3856
877-4-PA-KIDS
www.dpw.state.pa.us/ocyf/dpwocyf.asp

Child Support Enforcement Agency
Daniel Richard
Office of Income Maintenance
Department of Public Welfare
Health and Welfare Bldg, Room 432
P.O. Box 2675
Harrisburg, PA 17105-2675
717-787-1894
800-932-0211
www.dpw.state.pa.us/oim/dpwoim.asp

Cooperative Extension Office
Dr. Ted Alter, Director
Pennsylvania State University
Room 201, A.G. Administration
University Park, PA 16802
814-863-3438
www.extension.psu.edu

Corporation Division Office
Corporation Bureau
Department of State
206 N. Office Building
Harrisburg, PA 17120
MAILING ADDRESS:
P.O. Box 8722
Harrisburg, PA 17105-8721
717-787-1057
www.dos.state.pa.us/corps/

Day Care Licensing Agency
Child Care Works
Office of Children, Youth and Families
Health and Welfare Bldg, Room 131
P.O. Box 2675
Harrisburg, PA 17105-2675
717-783-3856
877-4-PA-KIDS
www.dpw.state.pa.us/ocyf/dpwocyf.asp

Economic Development Office
Department of Community and Economic Development
4th Floor, Commonwealth Keystone Bldg.
Harrisburg, PA 17120-0225
800-379-7448
Email: fa-DCEDCS@state.pa.us
www.inventpa.com

Governor's Action Team
100 Pine Street, Suite 100
Harrisburg, PA 17101
717-787-8199
888-4TEAMPA
Fax: 717-772-5419
www.teampa.com

Department of Education
Pennsylvania Dept. of Education
333 Market St.
Harrisburg, PA 17126-0333
717-783-6788
www.pde.psu.edu

Department of Higher Education
Office of Postsecondary and Higher Education
333 Market St.
Harrisburg, PA 17126-0333
717-787-5041
www.pdehighered.state.pa.us/higher/site/default.asp?g=O

Pennsylvania Higher Education Assistance Agency
1200 North 7th Street
Harrisburg, PA 17102
717-720-2850
800-692-7392
TTY: 800-654-5988
Fax: 717-720-3907
www.pheaa.org

Health Department
Pennsylvania Dept. of Health
P.O. Box 90
Health & Welfare Building
Harrisburg, PA 17108
877-PA-HEALTH
webserver.health.state.pa.us/health/site
Email:
webmaster@heath.state.pa.us

Housing Office
Pennsylvania Housing Finance Agency
2101 North Front St.
P.O. Box 8029
Harrisburg, PA 17105-8029
717-780-3800

TDD: 717-780-1869
www.phfa.org

Insurance Commissioner
Insurance Commissioner
1326 Strawberry Square
Harrisburg, PA 17120
717-787-6174
877-881-6388 (hotline)
TTY/TDD: 717-783-3898
www.insurance.state.pa.us

Labor Department
Pennsylvania Department of Labor and Industry
Room 1700, 7th and Forster Sts.
Harrisburg, PA 17120
717-787-5279
www.dli.state.pa.us/

Licensing Office
Bureau of Professional and Occupational Affairs
618 Transportation and Safety Building
Harrisburg, PA 17120
MAILING ADDRESS:
P.O. Box 2649
Harrisburg, PA 17105-2649
717-787-8503
800-822-2113 (PA only) (complaints)
www.dos.state.pa.us/

One-Stop Career Center
Team Pennsylvania CareerLink
Department of Labor and Industry
Room 1720, Seventh & Foster St.
Harrisburg, PA 17120
717-787-5279
Email: careerlink@dli.state.pa.us
www.pacareerlink.state.pa.us

Security Regulators
Pennsylvania Securities Commission
Eastgate Office Building, 2nd Floor
1010 N. 7th St.
Harrisburg, PA 17102-1410
717-787-8061
800-600-0007 (in PA)
Email: pscwebmaster@ state.pa.us
www.psc.state.pa.us

Small Business Development Center
Pennsylvania Small Business Development Center
Vance Hall, 4th Floor
3733 Spruce Street
Philadelphia, PA 19104-6374
215-898-1219
Fax: 215-573-2135
Email: pasbdc@ wharton.upenn.edu
www.pasbdc.org

Social Services Offices
Pennsylvania Department of Public Welfare
333 Health and Welfare Building
Harrisburg, PA 17105
717-787-4592
www.dpw.state.pa.us/general/program.asp

Temporary Assistance to Needy Families (TANF)
Temporary Aid to Needy Families
Feather Houston
Pennsylvania Department of Public Welfare
Health and Welfare Bldg, Room 432
P.O. Box 2675
Harrisburg, PA 17105
717-787-1894
800-692-7462
TDD: 800-451-5886
www.dpw.state.pa.us/oim/oimcash.asp

Transportation Department
Pennsylvania Department of Transportation
Keystone Bldg., 400 North St.
Harrisburg, PA 17120
717-787-2838
Fax: 717-787-1738
www.dot.state.pa.us

Brad Mallory
Pennsylvania Department of Transportation
Keystone Bldg., 400 North St.
Harrisburg, PA 17120
717-787-5574
www.dot.state.pa.us

Unclaimed Property Office
Pennsylvania State Treasury
Office of Unclaimed Property
P.O. Box 1837
Harrisburg, PA 17105
800-222-2046
Email: tupmail@tre.state.pa.us
www.treasury.state.pa.us/unclaimed.html

Unemployment Insurance Office
Bureau of U.C. Benefits and Allowances
Department of Labor and Industry
Labor and Industry Bldg., 6th Floor
Seventh and Forster Sts.
Harrisburg, PA 17121
717-783-3140
Email: 4C-news@dli.state.pa.us
www.dli.state.pa.us
Weekly benefit range: $33-442
Duration of benefits: 16-26 weeks

Utility Commission
Public Utility Commission
Commonwealth Keystone Bldg.
400 North St.
Harrisburg, PA 17120
MAILING ADDRESS:
P.O. Box 3265
Harrisburg, PA 17105
717-783-1740
800-782-1110 (complaints-PA only)
http://puc.paonline.com/

Women's Commission
Pennsylvania Commission for Women
Finance Building, Room 205
Harrisburg, PA 17120
888-615-7477
717-787-8128
Fax: 717-772-0653
Email: lesbn@oa.state.pa.us
Email: ra_pcwwebe-mail@state.pa.us
www.pcw.state.pa.us
Loida Esbri, Executive Director

Your Senator
United States Senate
Washington, DC 20510
202-224-3121
www.senate.gov

Your Representative
United States House of Representatives
Washington, DC 20515
202-224-3121
www.house.gov

Rhode Island

Federal Information Center
1-800-FED-INFO
www.firstgov.gov
www.pueblo.gsa.gov/call/

State Information Office
401-222-2000
www.state.ri.us

Department on Aging
Department of Elderly Affairs
160 Pine St.
Providence, RI 02903
401-222-2858
www.dea.state.ri.us

Attorney General's Office
Office of the Attorney General
150 South Main Street
Providence, RI 02903
401-274-4400
800-852-7776
TDD: 401-222-2354
www.riag.state.ri.us
Email: contactus@riag.state.ri.us

Banking Commissioner
Director and Superintendent of Banking
Department of Business Regulation
233 Richmond St., Suite 231
Providence, RI 02903-4231
401-222-2405
Fax: 401-222-5628
TDD: 401-222-2223
www.dbr.state.ri.us

Child Care and Development Block Grant Lead Agency
Rhode Island Department of Human Services
Individual and Family Support Services
Louis Pasteur Bldg.
600 New London Ave.
Cranston, RI 02920
401-462-2423
www.dhs.state.ri.us/dhs/dserfch.htm

Child Support Enforcement Agency
John Murphy
Department of Administration
Child Support Enforcement
77 Dorrance St.
Providence, RI 02903
401-222-2847
800-638-5434

Cooperative Extension Office
Marsha Morreira, Director
Cooperative Extension Education Center
University of Rhode Island
East Alumni Avenue
Kingston, RI 02881-0804
401-874-2900
www.uri.edu/ce/index1.html

Corporation Division Office
Corporations Division
Secretary of State
100 North Main St., 1st Floor
Providence, RI 02903-1335
401-222-3040
Fax: 401-222-1309
Email: corporations@sec.state. ri.us
http://155.212.254.78/corporations.htm

Day Care Licensing Agency
Department of Children, Youth and Families
Louis Pasteur Bldg.
600 New London Ave.
Cranston, RI 02902
401-272-7510
800-244-8700

Economic Development Office
Economic Development Corporation
One West Exchange St.
Providence, RI 02903
401-222-2601
Fax: 401-222-2102
Email: riedc@riedc.com
www.riedc.com

Department of Education
Rhode Island Department of Education
255 Westminster St.
Providence, RI 02903-3400
401-222-4600
www.ridoe.net

Department of Higher Education
Rhode Island Office of Higher Education
301 Promenade St.
Providence, RI 02909-5748
401-222-2088
Fax: 401-222-2545
Email: ribghe.etal.uri.edu
www.ribghe.org/riohe.htm

Health Department
Rhode Island Department of Health
3 Capitol Hill
Providence, RI 02908
401-222-2231
Fax: 401-222-6548
TTY: 711
www.health.state.ri.us/
Email: library@doh.state.ri.us

Housing Office
Rhode Island Housing and Mortgage Finance Corporation
44 Washington St.
Providence, RI 02903-1721
401-751-5566
TDD: 401-427-9799
www.rihousing.com

Insurance Commissioner
Insurance Commissioner
Department of Business Regulation
233 Richmond St., Suite 233
Providence, RI 02903
401-222-2223
Fax: 401-222-5475
TDD: 401-222-2999
www.dbr.state.ri.us

Labor Department
Rhode Island Department of Labor and Training
Pastore Government Center
1511 Pontiac Ave.
Cranston, RI 02920-4407
401-462-8000
www.dlt.state.ri.us

Licensing Office
Department of Labor and Training
Professional Regulation Division
Howard Center

1511 Pontiac Ave.
Cranston, RI 02920
401-462-8526
www.dlt.state.ri.us/

One-Stop Career Center
NetWorkri
Department of Labor and Training
1511 Pontiac Ave.
Cranston, RI 02920-4407
401-462-8000
Email: brutherford@networkri.org
www.networkri.org

Security Regulators
Department of Business Regulation
Division of Securities Regulation
233 Richmond St., Suite 232
Providence, RI 02903
401-222-3048
www.dbr.state.ri.us

Small Business Development Center
Bryant College
Small Business Development Center
1150 Douglas Pike
Smithfield, RI 02197-1284
401-232-6111
Fax: 401-232-6933
www.RISBDC.org

Social Services Offices
Rhode Island Department of Human Services
600 New London Avenue
Cranston, RI 02920
401-462-5300
www.dhs.state.ri.us

Temporary Assistance to Needy Families (TANF)
Family Independence Program
Louis Pasture Bldg.
600 New London Ave.
Cranston, RI 02920
401-464-2423
800-DHS-3322
www.dhs.state.ri.us/dhs/famchild/dfipgm.htm

Transportation Department
Robert Letourneau
Rhode Island Department of Transportation
Two Capitol Hill
Providence, RI 02903
401-222-1362
www.dot.state.ri.us

Unclaimed Property Office
Unclaimed Property Division
P.O. Box 1435
Providence, RI 02901
401-222-6505
TDD: 401-222-3399
Email: ups@treasury.state.ri.us
www.state.ri.us/treas/ moneylst.htm

Unemployment Insurance Office
Assistant Director
Unemployment Insurance
Department of Employment and Training
1511 Pontiac Ave.
Cranston, RI 02920-4407
401-243-9100
www.dlt.state.ri.us/webdev/ui/default.htm
Weekly benefit range: $56-415
Duration of benefits: 15-26 weeks

Utility Commission
Public Utilities Commission
89 Jefferson Blvd.
Warwick, RI 02888
Providence, RI 02903
401-941-4500
www.ripuc.org

Women's Commission
Rhode Island Advisory Commission on Women
260 W. Exchange St., Suite 4
Providence, RI 02093
401-222-6105
Fax: 401-222-5638
Email: ricw@doa.state.ri.us
www.ricw.state.ri.us
Toby Ayers, Ph.D., Director

Your Senator
United States Senate
Washington, DC 20510
202-224-3121
www.senate.gov

Your Representative
United States House of Representatives
Washington, DC 20515
202-224-3121
www.house.gov

SOUTH CAROLINA

Federal Information Center
1-800-FED-INFO
www.firstgov.gov
www.pueblo.gsa.gov/call/

State Information Office
803-734-1000
www.myscgov.com

Department on Aging
Office of Senior and Long Term Care Services
South Carolina Department of Health and Human Services
P.O. Box 8206
Columbia, SC 29202-8206
803-898-2850
www.dhhs.state.sc.us/offices/long_term_care/ltcindex.htm

Attorney General's Office
Office of the Attorney General
Rembert Dennis Building
1000 Assembly Street
Room 501
P.O. Box 11549
Columbia, SC 29211
803-734-3970
www.scattorneygeneral.org
Email: info@scattorneygeneral.org

Banking Commissioner
Commissioner of Banking
309 Calhoun St.
Columbia, SC 29201
803-734-2001

Child Care and Development Block Grant Lead Agency
Advocates for Better Care
South Carolina Health and Human Services
Bureau of Community Services
P.O. Box 8206
Columbia, SC 29202-8206
803-253-6154
800-476-0199
800-763-ABCD
Fax: 803-253-6152
www.dhhs.state.sc.us/FAQ/child_care.htm

Child Support Enforcement Agency
Larry McKeown
Child Support Enforcement Division
Department of Social Services
P.O. Box 1469
Columbia, SC 29202-1469
803-898-9210
800-768-5858 (in SC)
www.state.sc.us/dss/csed/index.html

Cooperative Extension Offices
Carroll Culvertson, Director
Clemson University
Cooperative Extension Service
P.O. Box 995
Pickens, SC 29671
864-656-3382
http://virtual.clemson.edu/groups/extension/

Director
Cooperative Extension Office
P.O. Box 8103
South Carolina State University
Orangeburg, SC 29117-8103
803-536-8928
www.1890.scsu.edu/

Corporation Division Office
Division of Corporations
Secretary of State
P.O. Box 11350
Columbia, SC 29211
803-734-2158
www.scsos.com/

Day Care Licensing Agency
Department of Social Services
Division of Child Day Care Licensing and Regulation
P.O. Box 1520, Room 520
Columbia, SC 29202-1520
803-898-7345
877-886-2384
Fax: 803-898-7179
Email: daycare@dss.state.sc.us
www.state.sc.us/dss/cdclrs/index.html

Economic Development Office
Department of Commerce
P.O. Box 927
Columbia, SC 29202
803-737-0400
800-868-7232
Fax: 803-737-0418
www.callsouthcarolina.com

Department of Education
South Carolina Dept. of Education
1429 Senate St.
Columbia, SC 29201
803-734-8500
www.sde.state.sc.us/

Department of Higher Education
South Carolina Commission on Higher Education
Tuition Grants Commission
101 Business Park Blvd.
Suite 2100
Columbia, SC 29203-9498
803-896-1120
Fax: 803-896-1126
Email: info@sctuitiongrants.org
www.sctuitiongrants.com

Commission on Higher Education
1333 Main St., Suite 200
Columbia, SC 29201
803-737-2660
Fax: 803-737-2297
www.che400.state.sc.us

Health Department
South Carolina Department of Health & Environmental Control
2600 Bull Street
Columbia, SC 29201
803-898-3432
www.scdhec.net
Email: houghmh@columb20.dhec.state.sc.us

Housing Office
South Carolina State Housing Financing and Development Authority
919 Bluff Rd.
Columbia, SC 29201
803-734-2000
www.sha.state.sc.us

Insurance Commissioner
Chief Insurance Commissioner
300 Arbor Lark Dr., Suite 1200
Columbia, SC 29223
MAILING ADDRESS:
P.O. Box 100105
Columbia, SC 29202-3105
803-737-6212
800-768-3467
Email: cnsmmail@doi.state.sc.us
www.state.sc.us/doi/

Labor Department
South Carolina Department of Labor, Licensing and Regulation
Public Information Office
110 Centerview Drive
P.O. Box 11329
Columbia, SC 29211-1329
803-896-4300
Email: contactllr@mail.llr.state.sc.us
www.llr.state.sc.us

Licensing Office
South Carolina Department of Labor, Licensing, and Regulation
110 Centerview Dr.
P.O. Box 11329
Columbia, SC 29211
803-896-4363
www.llr.state.sc.us/

One-Stop Career Center
1 Stop Partnership
Employment Security Commission
P.O. Box 995
1550 Gadsden Street
Columbia, SC 29202
803-737-9935
Fax: 803-737-0202
www.sces.org/1stop/ 1stopmain.htm
Email: jobs@sces.org

Security Regulators
Office of the SC Attorney General
Securities Division
P.O. Box 11549
Columbia, SC 29211
803-734-9916
www.scsecurities.org/index.html

Small Business Development Center
South Carolina Small Business Development Center
University of South Carolina
College of Business Administration
Columbia, SC 29208
803-777-4907
Fax: 803-777-4403
Email: sbdc@darla.badm.sc.edu
http://sbdcweb.badm.sc.edu

Social Services Offices
South Carolina Department of Social Services
1535 Confederate Ave.
P.O. Box 1520
Columbia, SC 29202-1520
803-898-7601
800-311-7220
TTY: 800-311-7219
www.state.sc.us/dss

Temporary Assistance to Needy Families (TANF)
Temporary Aid to Needy Families
South Carolina Department of Social Services
P.O. Box 1520, Room 605
Columbia, SC 29202
803-898-7825
Email: lmason@dss.state.sc.us
www.state.sc.us/dss/

Transportation Department
Elizabeth S. Marby
South Carolina Department of Transportation
P.O. Box 191
955 Park St.
Columbia, SC 29202-0191
803-737-2314
www.dot.state.sc.us

Unclaimed Property Office
State Treasurer's Office
Unclaimed Property Division
P.O. Box 11778
Columbia, SC 29211
803-734-4771
Email: payback@sto.state.sc.us
www.state.sc.us/treas/

Unemployment Insurance Office
Deputy Executive Director
Unemployment Compensation
Employment Security Commission
P.O. Box 995
Columbia, SC 29202
803-737-2474
Email: claimantinfo@sces.org
www.sces.org/ui/index.htm
Weekly benefit range: $20-268
Duration of benefits: 15-26 weeks

Utility Commission
Public Service Commission
101 Executive Center Dr.
Columbia, SC 29210
803-896-5100
800-922-1531 (SC only)
www.psc.state.sc.us

Women's Commission
Governor's Office Commission on Women
1205 Pendleton St., Room 366
Columbia, SC 29201
803-734-1609
Fax: 803-734-0241
www.govoepp.state.sc.us/cow.htm
Rebecca Collier, Executive Director

Your Senator
United States Senate
Washington, DC 20510
202-224-3121
www.senate.gov

Your Representative
United States House of Representatives
Washington, DC 20515
202-224-3121
www.house.gov

SOUTH DAKOTA

Federal Information Center
1-800-FED-INFO
www.firstgov.gov
www.pueblo.gsa.gov/call/

State Information Office
605-773-3011
www.state.sd.us

Department on Aging
Adult Services on Aging Office.
Social Services Department
700 Governors Dr.
Pierre, SD 57501
605-773-3656
www.state.sd.us/social/ASA/index.ht
m

Attorney General's Office
Office of the Attorney General
500 East Capitol Avenue
Pierre, SD 57501-5070
605-773-3215
800-300-1986 (SD consumer hotline)
Fax: 605-773-4106
www.state.sd.us/attorney/index.html
Email: consumerhelp@state.sd.us

Banking Commissioner
Director of Banking and Finance
State Capitol Bldg.
217 1/2 West Missouri
Pierre, SD 57501-4590
605-773-3421
Fax: 605-773-5367
Email: tammi.watkins@state.sd.us
www.state.sd.us/dcr/bank/BANK-HOM.htm

Child Care and Development Block Grant Lead Agency
Child Care Services
South Dakota Department of Social Services
700 Governors Dr.
Pierre, SD 57501-2291
605-773-4766
800-227-3020
Fax: 605-773-6834
Email: csc@dss.state.sd.us
www.state.sd.us/social/ccs/ccshome
.htm

Child Support Enforcement Agency
Terry Walter
Office of Child Support Enforcement
Department of Social Services
700 Governors Dr.
Pierre, SD 57501
605-773-3641
Fax: 605-773-6834
www.state.sd.us/social/CSE/index.ht
m

Cooperative Extension Office
Mylo Hellickson, Director
SDSU
Box 2207D
AG Hall 154
Brookings, SD 57007
605-688-4792
http://sdces.sdstate.edu

Corporation Division Office
Corporate Division
Secretary of State
Capitol Bldg.
500 East Capitol Ave., Suite 204
Pierre, SD 57501-5070
605-773-4845
www.state.sd.us/sos/corporations/co
rpcover.htm

Day Care Licensing Agency
Department of Social Services
Child Care Services
Child Care Licensing Division
700 Governors Dr.
Pierre, SD 57501-2291
605-773-3383
800-227-3020
Email: ccs@dss.state.sd.us
www.state.sd.us/state/social/

Economic Development Office
Governor's Office of Economic Development
711 East Wells Ave.
Pierre, SD 57501-3369
605-773-5032
800-872-6190
Fax: 605-773-3256
Email: goedinfo@state.sd.us
www.sdgreatprofits.com

Department of Education
South Dakota Department of Education and Cultural Affairs
Office of Finance Management
Kneip Bldg.
700 Governors Dr.
Pierre, SD 57501-2291
605-773-3248
605-773-6139
www.state.sd.us/deca/

Department of Higher Education
South Dakota Board of Regents
306 E. Capitol Ave., Suite 200
Pierre, SD 57051-2545
605-773-3455
Email: info@ris.sdbor.edu
www.ris.sdbor.edu

Health Department
South Dakota Department of Health
Health Building
600 East Capitol
Pierre, SD 57501-2563
605-773-3361
800-738-2301 (in SD)
Fax: 605-773-5683
www.state.sd.us/doh
Email: doh.info@state.sd.us

Housing Office
South Dakota Housing Development Authority
221 S. Central Ave.
P.O. Box 1237
Pierre, SD 57501-1237
605-773-3181
www.sdhda.org

Insurance Commissioner
Director of Insurance
Insurance Bldg.
118 W. Capitol St.
Pierre, SD 57501
605-773-3563
www.state.sd.us/insurance/

Labor Department
South Dakota Dept. of Labor
700 Governors Drive
Pierre, SD 57501-2291
605-773-3101

Fax: 605-773-4211
www.state.sd.us/dol/dol.htm

Licensing Office
Department of Commerce and Regulation
Professional and Occupational Licensing
118 E. Capitol Ave.
Pierre, SD 57501-2000
605-773-3178
Fax: 605-773-3018
www.state.sd.us/dcr/boards/boardhom.htm

One-Stop Career Center
Job Service of South Dakota
SD Department of Labor
Kneip Building
700 Governors Drive
Pierre, SD 57501-2291
605-773-3101
Fax: 605-773-4211
www.state.sd.us/dol/sdjob/js-home.htm
Email: infor@dol-pr.state.sd.us

Security Regulators
Department of Commerce and Regulation
Division of Securities
118 W. Capitol Ave.
Pierre, SD 57501
605-773-4823
Fax: 605-773-5953
Email: secur@crpr1.state.sd.us
www.state.sd.us/dcr/securities/

Small Business Development Center
South Dakota Small Development Center
University of South Dakota
School of Business
414 East Clark Street/
Vermillion, SD 57069-2390
605-677-5287
Fax: 605-677-5427
Email: stracy@charlie.usd.edu
Email: wdruin@usd.edu
www.usd.edu/brbinfo/sbdc

Social Services Offices
South Dakota Department of Social Services
700 Governors Drive
Pierre, SD 57501-2291
605-773-3165
www.state.sd.us/social

Temporary Assistance to Needy Families (TANF)
TANF Work Program
Judy Thompson
South Dakota Department of Social Services
700 Governors Dr.
Pierre, SD 57501
605-773-4678
Email: tanf@dss.state.sd.us
www.state.sd.us/social/tanf/index.htm

Transportation Department
Ronald W. Wheeler
South Dakota Department of Transportation
Becker-Hansen Bldg.
700 E. Broadway Ave.
Pierre, SD 57501
605-773-3265
www.sddot.com

Dennis Landguth
South Dakota Department of Transportation
Becker-Hansen Bldg.
700 E. Broadway Ave.
Pierre, SD 57501
605-773-3265
www.sddot.com

Unclaimed Property Office
Unclaimed Property Division
State Capitol Bldg., Suite 212
500 East Capitol Ave.
Pierre, SD 57501
605-773-3379
Email: unclaimed.property@state.sd.us
www.state.sd.us/treasurer/ prop.htm

Unemployment Insurance Office
Director, Unemployment Insurance Division
Department of Labor
P.O. Box 4730
420 S. Roosevelt St.
Aberdeen, SD 57402-4730
605-626-2452
Fax: 605-626-2322
www.state.sd.us/dol/dol.asp
Weekly benefit range: $28-234
Duration of benefits: 15-26 weeks

Utility Commission
Public Utilities Commission
Capitol Bldg., 1st Floor
500 E. Capitol Ave.
Pierre, SD 57501
605-773-3201
800-332-1782
www.state.sd.us/puc

Women's Commission
Abolished

Your Senator
United States Senate
Washington, DC 20510
202-224-3121
www.senate.gov

Your Representative
United States House of Representatives
Washington, DC 20515
202-224-3121
www.house.gov

TENNESSEE

Federal Information Center
1-800-FED-INFO
www.firstgov.gov
www.pueblo.gsa.gov/call/

State Information Office
615-741-3011
www.state.tn.us

Department on Aging
Aging Commission
500 Deaderick St., 9th Floor
Nashville, TN 37243-0860
615-741-2056
www.state.tn.us/comaging

Attorney General's Office
Office of the Attorney General & Recorder
425 5th Avenue
Nashville, TN 37243
P.O. Box 20207
Nashville, TN 37202-0207
615-741-3491
www.attorneygeneral.state.tn.us

Banking Commissioner
Commissioner of Financial Institutions
500 Charlotte Ave.
John Sevier Bldg., 4th Floor
Nashville, TN 37243-0705
615-741-2236
www.state.tn.us/financialinst/

Child Care and Development Block Grant Lead Agency
Child Care Services
Tennessee Department of Human Services
Citizens Plaza - 14th Floor
400 Deaderick St.
Nashville, TN 37248
615-313-4778
Fax: 615-532-9956
www.state.tn.us/humanserv/

Child Support Enforcement Agency
Joyce McClaran
Child Support Services
Department of Human Services
Citizens Plaza Bldg., 12th Floor
400 Deaderick St.
Nashville, TN 37248
615-313-4880
800-838-6911
www.state.tn.us/humanserv/child_support.htm

Cooperative Extension Offices
Dr. Billy G. Hicks, Dean
Agricultural Extension Service
University of Tennessee
P.O. Box 1071
Knoxville, TN 37901-1071
423-974-7114
www.utextension.utk.edu

Cherry Lane Zon Schmittou, Extension Leader
Davidson County Agricultural Service
Tennessee State University
3500 John A. Merritt Blvd.
Nashville, TN 37209
615-963-5491
www.tnstate.edu/cep/

Corporation Division Office
Office of Secretary of State
Business Services Division
Suite 1800, James K. Polk Bldg.
Nashville, TN 37243
615-741-2286
www.state.tn.us/sos/soshmpg.htm

Day Care Licensing Agency
Department of Human Services
Day Care Licensing Division
400 Deaderick St.
Nashville, TN 37248-9800
615-313-4778
www.state.tn.us/humanserv/

Economic Development Office
Department of Economic and Community Development
Rachel Jackson Bldg., 8th Floor
320 Sixth Avenue North
Nashville, TN 37243-0405
615-741-3282
800-342-8470 (in TN)
800-251-8594
Fax: 615-741-7306
www.state.tn.us/ecd

Department of Education
Tennessee Dept. of Education
Office of Accountability
Gateway Plaza
710 James Robertson Parkway
Nashville, TN 37243-0381
615-741-2731
www.state.tn.us/education

Department of Higher Education
Tennessee Student Assistance Corporation
404 James Robertson Pkwy.
Suite 1950
Nashville, TN 37243-0820
615-741-3605
Fax: 615-741-6230
www.state.tn.us/thec/

Health Department
Tennessee Department of Health
425 5th Avenue North
Nashville, TN 37247
615-741-3111
www.state.tn.us/health
Email: DDenton@mail.state.tn.us

Housing Office
Tennessee Housing Development Agency
404 James Robertson Pkwy.
Suite 1114
Nashville, TN 37243-0900
615-741-2400
www.state.tn.us/thda

Insurance Commissioner
Commissioner of Insurance
500 James Robertson Parkway
Nashville, TN 37243-0565
615-741-2218
800-342-4029
www.state.tn.us/commerce

Labor Department
Tennessee Department of Labor
2nd Floor Andrew Johnson Tower
710 James Robertson Parkway
Nashville, TN 37213-0658
615-741-2582
www.state.tn.us/labor-wfd/

Licensing Office
Division of Regulatory Boards
Department of Commerce and Insurance
500 James Robertson Parkway
Nashville, TN 37243
615-741-3449
www.state.tn.us/commerce

One-Stop Career Center
Tennessee Career Center
Office of Workforce Development
Andrew Johnson Bldg., 8th Floor
710 James Robertson Parkway
Nashville, TN 37243
615-741-7973
800-576-3467
Fax: 615-741-1500
www.state.tn.us/labor-wfd/
Email: jfite@mail.state.tn.us

Security Regulators
Tennessee Securities Division
Volunteer Plaza, Suite 680
500 James Robertson Pkwy.
Nashville, TN 37243
615-741-2947
800-863-9117
www.state.tn.us/commerce/securdiv.html

Small Business Development Center
Tennessee Small Business Development Center
University of Memphis
South Campus (Getwell Road)
Building #1
Memphis, TN 38152-0001
901-678-2500
Fax: 901-678-4072
Email:gmickle@cc.memphis.edu
www.tsbdc.org

Social Services Offices
Tennessee Department of Human Services
Citizens Plaza Building
400 Deaderick Street
Nashville, TN 37248-0001
615-313-4707
www.state.tn.us/humanserv

Temporary Assistance to Needy Families (TANF)
Temporary Aid to Needy Families
Wanda Moore
Tennessee Department of Human Services
400 Deaderick St., 12th Floor
Nashville, TN 37248
615-313-4867
888-863-6178
www.state.tn.us/humanserv/famfir.htm

Transportation Department
Tennessee Department of Transportation
505 Deaderick
JK Polk Bldg., Suite 400
Nashville, TN 37243
615-741-2848
www.tdot.state.tn.us

Unclaimed Property Office
Unclaimed Property Division
Andrew Jackson Bldg., 9th Floor
Nashville, TN 37243
615-741-6499
www.treasury.state.tn.us

Unemployment Insurance Office
Deputy Commissioner
Tennessee Department of Employment Security
500 James Robertson Parkway
12th Floor
Nashville, TN 37245
615-741-2131
www.state.tn.us/labor_wfd/esdiv.html
Weekly benefit range: $30-200
Duration of benefits: 12-26 weeks

Utility Commission
Tennessee Regulatory Authority
460 James Robertson Parkway
Nashville, TN 37243
615-741-2904
800-342-8359 (TN only)
www.state.tn. us/tra/

Women's Commission
Abolished

Your Senator
United States Senate
Washington, DC 20510
202-224-3121
www.senate.gov

Your Representative
United States House of Representatives
Washington, DC 20515
202-224-3121
www.house.gov

TEXAS

Federal Information Center
1-800-FED-INFO
www.firstgov.gov
www.pueblo.gsa.gov/call/

State Information Office
512-463-4630
www.state.tx.us

Department on Aging
Aging Department
Box 12786
Austin, TX 78711
512-424-6840
www.tdoa.state.tx.us

Attorney General's Office
Office of the Attorney General
P.O. Box 12548
Austin, TX 78711-2548
512-463-2100
800-621-0508 (consumer protection)
www.oag.state.tx.us
Email: cac@oag.state.tx.us

Banking Commissioner
Banking Commissioner
2601 N. Lamar Blvd.
Austin, TX 78705
512-475-1300
877-276-5554
www.banking.state. tx.us

Child Care and Development Block Grant Lead Agency
Texas Workforce Commission
Child Care Services
Work and Family Clearinghouse
101 E. 15th St., Suite 416T
Austin, TX 78778-0001
512-463-3659
Fax: 512-936-3255
www.twc.state.tx.us/

Child Support Enforcement Agency
David Vela
Child Support Division
Office of the Attorney General
P.O. Box 12017
Austin, TX 78711
512-460-6000
512-479-6478
800-252-8014
www.oag.state.tx. us/child/
mainchil.htm

Cooperative Extension Offices
Dr. Zerle Carpenter, Director
Texas Agricultural Extension Service
Texas A&M University
Administration Building, Room 106-A
College Station, TX 77843
979-845-7967
http://agextension.tamu.edu

Dr. Linda Willis, Director
Cooperative Extension Program
P.O. Box 3059
Prairie View, TX 77446-3059
936-857-2023
http://pvcep.pvamu.edu

Corporation Division Office
Corporation Section
Statue Filing Division
Secretary of State
P.O. Box 13697
Austin, TX 78711
512-463-9856
www.sos.state.tx.us/

Day Care Licensing Agency
Department of Protective and Regulatory Services
Child Care Licensing
P.O. Box 149030
M.C.E-550
Austin, TX 78714-9030
512-438-4800
800-862-5252
www.tdprs.state.tx.us/child_care

Economic Development Office
Department of Economic Development
P.O. Box 12728
Austin, TX 78711
512-936-0260
800-888-0511
www.tded.state.tx.us

Department of Education
Texas Education Agency
Division of Public Information
1701 N. Congress
Austin, TX 78701-1494
MAILING ADDRESS:
P.O. Box 13817
Austin, TX 78711-3817
512-463-9734
www.tea.state.tx.us/

Department of Higher Education
Texas Higher Education Coordinating Board
Box 12788, Capitol Station
Austin, TX 78711-2788
512-427-6101
www.thecb.state.tx.us/

Health Department
Texas Department of Health
1100 West 49th Street
Austin, TX 78756-3199
512-458-7111
888-963-7111
www.tdh.texas.gov/

Housing Office
Texas Housing Agency
507 Saveine St.
Austin, TX 78701
512-475-3800
www.tdhca.state. tx.us

Insurance Commissioner
Director
Claims and Compliance Division
State Board of Insurance
P.O. Box 149104
Austin, TX 78714-9104
512-463-6464
800-252-3439
www.tdi.state.tx.us

Labor Department
Texas Workforce Commission
101 East 15th Street
Austin, TX 78778
512-463-2222
800-832-2829
www.twc.state.tx.us

Licensing Office
Department of Licensing and Regulation

P.O. Box 12157
Austin, TX 78711
512-463-6599
800-803-9202
www.license.state.tx.us

One-Stop Career Center
Texas Workforce Information System (TWIST)
Texas Workforce Commission
101 East 15th Street
Austin, TX 78778
512-463-6438
800-832-2829
www.twc.state.tx.us
Email: ombudsman@twc. state.tx.us

Security Regulators
State Securities Board
P.O. Box 13167
Austin, TX 78711
512-305-8300
www.ssb.state.tx.us

Small Business Development Center
North Texas Small Business Development Center
Dallas County Community College
1402 Corinth Street
Dallas, TX 75215
214-860-5831
Fax: 214-860-5813
Email: daw1404@dcccd.edu
www.bizcoach.org

Social Services Offices
Texas Department of Human Services
701 West 51st Street
Austin, TX 78751
512-438-3045
888-834-7406
www.dhs.state.tx.us

Temporary Assistance to Needy Families (TANF)
Temporary Aid to Needy Families
Eric Bost
Texas Department of Human Services
P.O. Box 149030
Austin, TX 78714
512-438-3280
888-834-7406
www.dhs.state.tx.us/programs/TexasWorks/TANF-FAQ.html

Transportation Department
Bobby Killebrew
Texas Department of Transportation
125 East 11th St.
Austin, TX 78701
512-416-2816
www.dot.state.tx.us

Unclaimed Property Office
Comptroller of Public Accounts
Unclaimed Property Section
P.O. Box 12019
Austin, TX 78711
512-463-3120
800-321-2274
www.window.state.tx.us/up

Unemployment Insurance Office
Director
Unemployment Insurance
Texas Workforce Commission
15th and Congress, Room 668
Austin, TX 78778
512-463-0735
www.twc.state.tx.us/ui/bnfts/claimantinfo.html
Weekly benefit range: $47-287
Duration of benefits: 9-26 weeks

Utility Commission
Public Utility Commission
1701 N. Congress Ave.
Austin, TX 78701
512-936-7000
888-782-8477
www.puc.state.tx.us

Women's Commission
Texas Governor's Commission for Women
P.O. Box 12428
Austin, TX 78711
512-475-2615
800-834-5323
Fax: 512-463-1832
www.governor.state.tx.us/women/
Ashley Horton, Executive Director

Your Senator
United States Senate
Washington, DC 20510
202-224-3121
www.senate.gov

Your Representative
United States House of Representatives
Washington, DC 20515
202-224-3121
www.house.gov

Utah

Federal Information Center
1-800-FED-INFO
www.firstgov.gov
www.pueblo.gsa.gov/call/

State Information Office
801-538-3000
www.state.ut.us

Department on Aging
Aging and Adult Services Division
Human Services Dept.
120 North, 200 West
Salt Lake City, UT 84107
801-538-3910
www.hsdaas.state.ut.us

Attorney General's Office
Office of the Attorney General
Room 236 State Capitol
160 East 300 South, 6th Floor
Salt Lake City, UT 84114
801-538-9600
800-244-4636
Fax: 801-538-1121
www.attygen.state.ut.us
Email: uag@state.ut.us

Banking Commissioner
Commissioner of Financial Institutions
P.O. Box 89
Salt Lake City, UT 84110-0089
801-538-8830
www.dfi.state.ut.us

Child Care and Development Block Grant Lead Agency
Utah Dept. of Workforce Services
Policy and Program Unit
140 East 3rd South
Salt Lake City, UT 84111
801-526-4341
800-622-7390
Fax: 801-526-4349
http://occ.dws.state.ut.us

Child Support Enforcement Agency
James Kidder
Bureau of Child Support Services
Department of Human Services
P.O. Box 45011
Salt Lake City, UT 84145
801-536-8500/8509
800-662-8525
www.ors.state.ut.us/

Cooperative Extension Office
Dr. Robert Gilliland
Vice President for Extension and Continuing Education
U.M.S. 4900
Utah State University
Logan, UT 84322-4900
435-797-2200
http://extension.usu.edu/coop/index.htm

Corporation Division Office
Corporations and UCC
Division of Business Regulations
P.O. Box 45801
160 East 300 South St., 2nd Floor
Salt Lake City, UT 84145
801-530-4849
www.commerce.utah.gov

Day Care Licensing Agency
Bureau of Licensing
Child Care Unit
288 N. 1460 West
P.O. Box 142003
Salt Lake City, UT 84114-2003
801-538-9299
www.dhs.state.ut.us/

Economic Development Office
Business and Economic Development Division
324 South State St., Suite 500
Salt Lake City, UT 84111
801-538-8800
Fax: 801-538-8889
www.utah.org/dbed/welcome.htm

Department of Education
Utah Board of Education
Department of Finance
250 E. 500 S.
Salt Lake City, UT 84111
801-538-7500
www.usoe.k12.ut.us/

Department of Higher Education
Utah System of Higher Education
3 Triad Center, Suite 550
Salt Lake City, UT 84180-1205
801-321-7101
www.utahsbr.edu

Health Department
Utah Department of Health
P.O. Box 1010
Salt Lake City, UT 84114-1010
801-538-5101
www.health.state.ut.us
Email: pwightma@doh.state.ut.us

Housing Office
Utah Housing Corporation
554 South, 300 East
Salt Lake City, UT 84111
801-521-6950
800-284-6950 (in UT)
www.utahhousing.corp

Insurance Commissioner
Commissioner of Insurance
3110 State Office Bldg.
Salt Lake City, UT 84114
801-538-3800
800-439-3805
www.insurance.state.ut.us

Labor Department
Utah Department of Workforce Services
P.O. Box 45249
Salt Lake City, UT 84145-0249
801-526-9675
http://jobs.utah.gov

Licensing Office
Division of Occupational and Professional Licensing
Department of Commerce
160 East 300 South
P.O. Box 45802
Salt Lake City, UT 84145
801-530-6628
866-275-3675
www.commerce.state.ut.us

One-Stop Career Center
Career Centers
Department of Workforce Services
140 East 300 South
Salt Lake City, UT 84111

801-531-3780
Fax: 801-531-3785
http://jobs.utah.gov

Security Regulators
Securities Division
P.O. Box 146760
Salt Lake City, UT 84114
801-530-6600
www.commerce.state.ut.us/

Small Business Development Center
Small Business Development Ctr.
Salt Lake Community College
1623 South State Street
Salt Lake City, UT 84115
801-957-3480
Fax: 801-957-3489
Email: FinnerMi@slcc.edu
www.slcc.edu/sbdc

Social Services Offices
Utah Dept. of Human Services
P.O. Box 45500
120 North 200 West
Salt Lake City, UT 84145-0500
801-538-3991
www.dhs.state.ut.us

Temporary Assistance to Needy Families (TANF)
Temporary Aid to Needy Families
Robin Arnold Williams
Utah Dept. of Human Services
120 North 200 West, Suite 319
Salt Lake City, UT 84103
801-538-3998
www.dhs.state.ut.us

Transportation Department
Glenda Seelos
Utah Department of Transportation
P.O. Box 143600
4501 South 2700 West
Salt Lake City, UT 84119
801-965-4141
www.dot.state.ut.us

Unclaimed Property Office
State Treasurer's Office
Unclaimed Property Division
341 South Main St., 5th Floor
Salt Lake City, UT 84111
801-320-5360
888-217-1203
www.treasurer.state.ut.us

Unemployment Insurance Office
Director Unemployment Insurance
Workforce Services
140 East 300 South
P.O. Box 11249
Salt Lake City, UT 84147
801-536-7423
http://ui.dws.state.ut.us
Weekly benefit range: $20-284
Duration of benefits: 10-26 weeks

Utility Commission
Public Service Commission
160 East, 300 South
P.O. Box 45585
Salt Lake City, UT 84145
801-530-6716
www.psc.state.ut.us

Women's Commission
Utah Governor's Commission for Women and Families
1160 State Office Bldg.
Salt Lake City, UT 84114
801-538-1736
Fax: 801-538-3027
www.governor.state.ut.us/women/
Email:
women&families@gov.state.ut.us
Michael Neider, Chair

Your Senator
United States Senate
Washington, DC 20510
202-224-3121
www.senate.gov

Your Representative
United States House of Representatives
Washington, DC 20515
202-224-3121
www.house.gov

VERMONT

Federal Information Center
1-800-FED-INFO
www.firstgov.gov
www.pueblo.gsa.gov/call/

State Information Office
802-828-1110
www.state.vt.us

Department on Aging
Vermont Department of Aging and Disabilities
103 S. Main St.
Waterbury, VT 05676
802-241-2400
www.dad.state.vt.us/

Attorney General's Office
Office of the Attorney General
109 State Street
Montpelier, VT 05609-1001
802-828-3171
TTY: 802-828-3171
Fax: 802-828-2154
www.state.vt.us/atg
Email: consumer@uvm.edu

Banking Commissioner
Commissioner of Banking and Insurance Securities
89 Main St., Drawer 20
Montpelier, VT 05620-3101
802-828-3301
www.bishca.state.vt.us

Child Care and Development Block Grant Lead Agency
Child Care Services Division
Vermont Department of Social and Rehabilitation Services
103 S. Main St., 2nd Floor
Waterbury, VT 05671-2401
802-241-3110
Fax: 802-241-1220
www.state.vt.us/srs/childcare

Child Support Enforcement Agency
Jeffery Cohen
Office of Child Support
103 South Main St.
Waterbury, VT 05671
802-241-2319
800-786-3214
Fax: 802-244-1483
www.ocs.state.vt.us

Cooperative Extension Office
Dr. Larry Forchier, Dean
Division of Agriculture, Natural Resources, and Extension
University of Vermont
601 Main
Burlington, VT 05401-3439
802-656-2990
http://ctr.uvm.edu/ext/

Corporation Division Office
Corporate Division
Secretary of State
109 State St.
Montpelier, VT 05602
802-828-2386
www.sec.state.vt.us

Day Care Licensing Agency
Department of Social and Rehabilitation Services
Child Care Licensing Unit
103 S. Main St.
Montpelier, VT 05761-2901
802-241-2131
www.state.vt.us/srs/

Economic Development Office
Dept. of Economic Development
National Life Building, Drawer 20
Montpelier, VT 05620-0501
802-828-3221
800-341-2211
Fax: 802-828-3258
www.thinkvermont.com

Department of Education
Vermont Department of Education
School Finance Department
State Office Bldg.
120 State St.
Montpelier, VT 05620-2501
802-828-3135
www.state.vt.us/educ/

Department of Higher Education
Vermont Student Assistance Corporation
P.O. Box 2000
Champlain Mill, 4th Floor
Winooski, VT 05404
800-798-8722
802-655-4050
www.vsac.org

Health Department
Vermont Department of Health
108 Cherry Street
Burlington, VT 05402-0070
802-863-7200
800-464-4343
Fax: 802-863-7475
www.state.vt.us/health

Housing Offices
Vermont Housing Finance Agency
One Burlington Sq.
164 St. Paul St.
Burlington, VT 05402-0408
802-864-5743
800-287-8432
www.vhfa.org

Vermont State Housing Authority
1 Prospect St.
Montpelier, VT 05602-3556
802-828-3295
800-820-5119
www.vsha.org

Insurance Commissioner
Commissioner of Banking and Insurance
89 Main St., Drawer 20
Montpelier, VT 05620-3101
802-828-3301
800-642-5119
www.bishca.state.vt.us/

Labor Department
Vermont Department of Employment and Training
5 Green Mountain Drive
P.O. Box 488
Montpelier, VT 05601-0488
802-828-4000
www.det.state.vt.us

Licensing Office
Office of Professional Regulation

Secretary of State
Pavilion Office Building
Montpelier, VT 05609
802-828-2363
http://vtprofessionals.org

One-Stop Career Center
One-Stop Career Resource
Department of Employment and Training
Division of Jobs and Training
5 Green Mountain Drive
P.O. Box 488
Montpelier, VT 05602
802-828-4000
TDD: 802-828-4203
Fax: 802-828-4022
www.det.state.vt.us

Security Regulators
Department of Banking, Insurance, Securities & Health Care Administration
Securities Division
89 Main St., Drawer 20
Montpelier, VT 05620
802-828-3420
www.bishca.state.vt.us

Small Business Development Center
Vermont Small Business Devlopment Center
Vermont Technical College
Randolph Center, VT 05060
MAILING ADDRESS:
P.O. Box 422
Randolph, VT 05060-0422
802-728-9101
800-464-SBDC
Fax: 802-728-3026
www.vtsbdc.org
Email: dkelpins@vtc.vsc.edu

Social Services Offices
Vermont Agency of Human Services
103 South Main Street
Waterbury, VT 05671-2401
802-241-2220
www.ahs.state.vt.us

Temporary Assistance to Needy Families (TANF)
Temporary Aid to Needy Families
Jane Kitchel
Vermont Department of Social Welfare
103 South Main St.
Waterbury, VT 05671
802-241-2853
www.dsw.state.vt.us/wrp/tanf_stp.htm

Transportation Department
William Peabody
Vermont Agency of Transportation
133 State St.
Montpelier, VT 05633
802-828-2828
www.aot.state.vt.us

Unclaimed Property Office
Abandoned Property Division
State Treasurer's Office
133 State St.
Montpelier, VT 05633
802-828-2301
800-642-3191
www.tre.state.vt.us

Unemployment Insurance Office
Unemployment Insurance
Dept. of Employment and Training
5 Green Mountain Dr.
P.O. Box 488
Montpelier, VT 05602
802-828-4100
www.det.state.vt.us/
Weekly benefit range: $25-275
Duration of benefits: 26 weeks

Utility Commission
Public Service Board
112 State St.
Chittenden Bank Bldg.
4th Floor, Drawer 20
Montpelier, VT 05620-2701
802-828-2358
www.state.vt.us/psb

Women's Commission
Vermont Governor's Commission on the Status of Women
126 State St., Drawer 33
Montpelier, VT 05602
802-828-2851
800-881-1561
Fax: 802-828-2930
www.state.vt.us/wom
Email: info@women.state.vt.us
Judith Sutphen, Executive Director

Your Senator
United States Senate
Washington, DC 20510
202-224-3121
www.senate.gov

Your Representative
United States House of Representatives
Washington, DC 20515
202-224-3121
www.house.gov

VIRGINIA

Federal Information Center
1-800-FED-INFO
www.firstgov.gov
www.pueblo.gsa.gov/call/

State Information Office
804-786-0000
www.state.va.us

Department on Aging
Aging Department
1600 Forest Ave., Suite 102
Richmond, VA 23229
804-662-9333
800-552-3402
www.aging.state.va.us/

Attorney General's Office
Office of the Attorney General
900 East Main Street
Richmond, VA 23219
804-786-2071
800-552-9963
TDD: 804-371-8946
www.oag.state.va.us
Email: mail@oag.state.va.us

Banking Commissioner
Bureau of Financial Institutions
1300 E. Main St., Suite 800
P.O. Box 640
Richmond, VA 23218-0640
804-371-9657
800-552-7945 (toll free in VA)
www.state.va.us/scc/division/
banking/index.htm

Child Care and Development Block Grant Lead Agency
Virginia Department of Social
Services
Child Day Care
730 E. Broad St.
Richmond, VA 23219-1849
804-692-1210
Fax: 804-692-2209
www.dss.state.va.us/

Child Support Enforcement Agency
Nathaniel Young
Asst. Commissioner for Child
Support Enforcement
Department of Social Services
730 East Broad St.
Richmond, VA 23219
804-692-1428
800-468-8894 (in VA)
Fax: 804-692-1438
www.dss.state.va.us/family/dcse.ht
ml

Cooperative Extension Offices
Dr. Clark Jones, Interim Director
Virginia Cooperative Extension
Virginia Tech
Blacksburg, VA 24061-0402
540-231-5299
www.ext.vt.edu/

Lorenza Lyons, Administrator
Cooperative Extension
Virginia State University
Petersburg, VA 23806-9081
804-524-5961
www.vsu.edu/ext/

Corporation Division Office
Clerk of Commission
State Corporation Commission
Secretary of State
P.O. Box 1197
Richmond, VA 23209
804-371-9967
800-552-7945
www.state.va.us/scc/index.html

Day Care Licensing Agency
Department of Social Services
Child Care Licensing Division
730 Broad St., 7th Floor
Richmond, VA 23219-1849
804-692-1787
www.dss.state.va.us/

Economic Development Office
Economic Development Partnership
P.O. Box 798
Richmond, VA 23206
804-371-8100
Fax: 804-371-8112
www.yesvirginia.org/

Department of Education
Virginia Department of Education
Management Information Office
101 N. 14th St., 22nd Floor
Richmond, VA 23219
804-225-2540
800-292-3820
www.pen.k12.va.us/

Department of Higher Education
Virginia State Council of Higher
Education
Office of Financial Aid
James Monroe Building
101 North 14th Street, 9th Floor
Richmond, VA 23219
804-225-2628
TDD: 804-371-8017
Fax: 804-225-2638
www.schev.edu/schevhome.html

Health Department
Virginia Department of Health
Main Street Station
Richmond, VA 23219
804-786-5916
Fax: 804-371-4110
www.vdh.state.va.us/
Email: rnash@vdh.state.va.us

Housing Office
Virginia Housing Development
Authority
601 S. Belvedere St.
Richmond, VA 23220-6504
804-782-1986
800-968-7837
www.vhda.com

Insurance Commissioner
Commissioner of Insurance
1300 E. Main St.
P.O. Box 1157
Richmond, VA 23218
804-371-9741
800-552-7945
www.state.va.us/scc/division/
boi/index.htm

Labor Department
Virginia Department of Labor and
Industry
Powers - Taylor Building
13 South Thirteenth Street

Richmond, VA 23219
804-371-2327
www.dli.state.va.us

Licensing Office
Virginia Dept. of Professional and Occupational Regulation
3600 W. Broad St.
Richmond, VA 23230
804-367-8500
www.state.va.us/dpor/ indexne.html

One-Stop Career Center
Workforce Development System
Employment Commission
P.O. Box 1358
Richmond, VA 23218-1358
804-786-4832
Fax: 804-786-6091
www.vec.state.va.us/
Email: vaemployment@aol.com

Security Regulators
Virginia Division of Securities
P.O. Box 1197
Richmond, VA 23218
804-371-9051
800-552-7945
www.state.va.us/scc/division/srf/index.htm

Small Business Development Center
Virginia Small Business Development Center
Dept. of Economic Development
901 East Byrd Street, Suite 1400
Richmond, VA 23219
804-371-8253
Fax: 804-225-3384
www.dba.state.va.us/
Email: rwilburn@dba.state.va.us

Social Services Offices
Virginia Dept. of Social Services
730 East Broad Street
Richmond, VA 23219
804-692-1906
www.dss.state.va.us

Temporary Assistance to Needy Families (TANF)
Temporary Aid to Needy Families
Marsha Sharpe
Department of Social Services
730 East Broad St., 7th Floor
Richmond, VA 23229
804-692-1730
www.dss.state.va.us/benefit/tanf.html

Transportation Department
Neil Sherman
Virginia Department of Rail and Public Transportation
1401 East Broad St., Room 1401
Richmond, VA 23219
804-786-1154
http://virginiadot.org

Metropolitan Planning Organization
Darrel Feasel
Virginia Department of Rail and Public Transportation
1401 East Broad St., Room 1401
Richmond, VA 23219
804-786-4440
www.drpt.state.va.us

Unclaimed Property Office
Division of Unclaimed Property
Department of Treasury
P.O. Box 2478
Richmond, VA 23218
804-225-2142
www.trs.state.va.us/

Unemployment Insurance Office
Field Operations
Virginia Employment Commission
703 E. Main St.
Richmond, VA 23219
804-786-3004
www.vec.state.va.us
Weekly benefit range: $55-228
Duration of benefits: 12-26 weeks

Utility Commission
State Corporation Commission
P.O. Box 1197
Richmond, VA 23218-1197
804-371-9967
800-552-7945 (VA only)
www.state.va.us/scc/division/puc/index.htm

Women's Commission
Alexandria Council on the Status of Women
110 North Royal St., Suite 201
Alexandria, VA 22314
703-838-5030
Fax: 703-838-4976
http://ci.alexandria.va.us/alexandria.html
Norma Gattsek, Exec. Director
Tara Hardiman, Chair

Arlington Commission on the Status of Women
2100 Clarendon Blvd., Suite 310
Arlington, VA 22201
703-228-3257
Fax: 703-228-3295
www.co.arlington.va.us/cmo
Email: publicaffairs@co.arlington.va.us
Katherine Hoffman

Fairfax City Commission for Women
10455 Armstrong St.
Fairfax, VA 22030
703-385-7894
Fax: 703-385-7811
www.ci.fairfax.va.us/host/women/cfw.html
Louise Armitage, Director

Fairfax County Commission for Women
12000 Government Center Pkwy.
Suite 318
Fairfax, VA 22035
703-324-5720
Fax: 703-324-3959
TTY: 703-222-3504
Leia Francisco, Executive Director

Richmond Mayor's Committee on the Concerns of Women
City Hall, 900 East Marshall St.
Room 302
Richmond, VA 23219
804-646-5987
Nancy Ownes, Admin. Assistant
Caroline Adams, Chair

Your Senator
United States Senate
Washington, DC 20510
202-224-3121
www.senate.gov

Your Representative
United States House of Representatives
Washington, DC 20515
202-224-3121
www.house.gov

WASHINGTON

Federal Information Center
1-800-FED-INFO
www.firstgov.gov
www.pueblo.gsa.gov/call/

State Information Office
360-753-5000
www.state.wa.us

Department on Aging
Aging and Adult Services
P.O. Box 45050
Olympia, WA 98504-5600
360-586-8753
800-422-3263
www.aasa.dshs.wa.gov

Attorney General's Office
Office of the Attorney General
P.O. Box 40100
1125 Washington Street, SE
Olympia, WA 98504-0100
360-753-6200
800-551-4636
TDD: 800-276-9883
www.wa.gov/ago
Email: protect@atg.wa.gov

Banking Commissioner
Department of Financial Institutions
Division of Banking
210 11th Ave., SW
Third Floor, Room 300
P.O. Box 41200
Olympia, WA 98504-1200
360-902-8700
800-372-8303
www.wa.gov/dfi/banks

Child Care and Development Block Grant Lead Agency
Office of Child Care Policy
Washington Department of Social and Health Services
P.O. Box 5700
Olympia, WA 98504-5700
360-902-8038
800-446-1114
Fax: 360-902-7903
www.wa.gov/dshs/

Child Support Enforcement Agency
Meg Sollenberger
Division of Child Support, DSHS
P.O. Box 9162
Olympia, WA 98507
360-586-3162
360-586-3274
800-457-6202
www.wa.gov/dshs/

Cooperative Extension Office
Dr. Harry Burcalow, Director
Cooperative Extension
411 Hulbert
Washington State University
Pullman, WA 99164-6230
509-335-2811
http://ext.wsu.edu

Corporation Division Office
Corporate Division
Secretary of State
Republic Bldg.
520 Union Ave., 2nd Floor
Mail Stop PM-21
Olympia, WA 98504
360-902-4151
www.secstate.wa.gov

Day Care Licensing Agency
Office of Child Care Policy
Child Care Licensing Division
P.O. Box 45700
Olympia, WA 98504-5710
360-902-8038
www.wa.gov/dshs

Economic Development Office
Office of Trade and Economic Development
128 10th Ave., SW
P.O. Box 42525
Olympia, WA 98504
360-725-4000
800-237-1233
www.oted.wa.gov

Department of Education
Washington State Board of Education
600 S. Washington St.
Olympia, WA 98504
360-725-6025
www.sbe.wa.gov

Department of Higher Education
Higher Education Coordinating Board
917 Lakeridge Way
P.O. Box 43430
Olympia, WA 98504-3430
360-753-7800
TTY: 360-753-7809
Fax: 360-753-7808
www.hecb.wa.gov

Health Department
Washington State Department of Health
1112 SE Quince Street
P.O. Box 47890
Olympia, WA 98504-7890
360-236-4010
www.doh.wa.gov/
Email: gkm0303@doh.wa.gov

Housing Office
Washington State Housing Finance Commission
1000 Second Ave., Suite 2700
Seattle, WA 98104-1046
206-464-7139
800-767-4663
www.wshfc.org

Insurance Commissioner
Insurance Commissioner
Insurance Bldg. AQ21
P.O. Box 40255
Olympia, WA 98504-0255
360-753-7300
800-562-6900
www.insurance.wa.gov

Labor Department
Washington Workforce Training and Education Coordinating Board
Building 17 Airdustrial Park
Olympia, WA 98504-3105
360-753-5662
www.wtb.wa.gov

Licensing Office
Department of Licensing
P.O. Box 9020
Olympia, WA 98507
360-902-3600
www.wa.gov/dol/

One-Stop Career Center
Washington One-Stop Career Center System
Employment Security Department
212 Maple Park
P.O. Box 9046
Olympia, WA 98507-9046
360-438-4611
360-438-3224
www.wa.gov/esd/1stop
Email: btarrow@esd.wa.gov

Security Regulators
Department of Financial Institutions
Securities Division
P.O. Box 9033
Olympia, WA 98507
360-902-8760
800-372-8303
www.wa.gov/dfi

Small Business Development Center
Washington State Small Business Development Center
Washington State University
College of Business and Economics
501 Johnson Tower
MAILING ADDRESS:
P.O. Box 644851
Pullman, WA 99164-4851
509-335-1576
Fax: 509-335-0949
Email: riesenbe@wsu.edu
www.sbdc.wsu.edu/wsbdc.htm

Social Services Offices
Washington Department of Social and Health Services
DSHS Constituent Services
P.O. Box 45130
Olympia, WA 98504-5130
360-902-7892
www.wa.gov/dshs

Temporary Assistance to Needy Families (TANF)
Temporary Aid to Needy Families
Roxane Lowe
Department of Social and Health Services
1009 College St., SE
P.O. Box 45400
Olympia, WA 98504
360-413-3010
www.wa.gov/dshs/

Transportation Department
Barbara Savary
Washington State Department of Transportation
P.O. Box 47387
Olympia, WA 98504
306-705-7919
www.wsdot.wa.gov/

Unclaimed Property Office
Unclaimed Property Section
Department of Revenue
P.O. Box 448
Olympia, WA 98507
360-586-2736
http://dor.wa.gov/

Unemployment Insurance Office
Assistant Commissioner
Employment Security Department
P.O. Box 9046
Olympia, WA 98507
360-902-9303
www.wa.gov/esd/ui.htm
Weekly benefit range: $82-384
Duration of benefits: 10-30 weeks

Utility Commission
Utilities and Transportation Commission
1300 S. Evergreen Park Dr. SW
Olympia, WA 98504
360-753-6423
800-562-6150 (WA only)
www.wutc.wa.gov/

Women's Commission
Seattle Women's Commission
c/o Seattle Office for Civil Rights
700 Third Ave, Suite 250
Seattle WA 98104
206-684-4500
Fax: 206-684-0332
Email: diane.pina@ci.seattle. wa.us
www.ci.seattle.wa.us/civilrights/swc/swc.htm

Your Senator
United States Senate
Washington, DC 20510
202-224-3121
www.senate.gov

Your Representative
United States House of Representatives
Washington, DC 20515
202-224-3121
www.house.gov

West Virginia

Federal Information Center
1-800-FED-INFO
www.firstgov.gov
www.pueblo.gsa.gov/call/

State Information Office
304-558-3456
www.state.wv.us

Department on Aging
Aging Commission
1900 Kanawha Blvd.
State Capitol
Holly Grove
Charleston, WV 25305
304-558-3317
www.wvdhhr.org/

Attorney General's Office
Office of the Attorney General
1900 Kanawha Blvd., Room 26E
Charleston, WV 25305
304-558-2021
800-368-8808
www.state.wv.us/wvag

Banking Commissioner
Commissioner of Banking
State Capitol Complex
1900 Kanawha Blvd. East
Bldg. 3, Room 311
Charleston, WV 25305-0240
304-558-2294
800-642-9056
www.wvdob.org

Child Care and Development Block Grant Lead Agency
Day Care and Licensing
DHHR, Bureau of Social Services
Building 6, Room B-850
State Capitol Complex
Charleston, WV 25305
304-558-0938
Fax: 304-558-8800
www.wvdhhr.org/

Child Support Enforcement Agency
Jeff Matherly
Child Support Enforcement Division
Department of Health and Human Resources
Building 6, Room 817
State Capitol Complex
1900 Kanawa Blvd., East
Charleston, WV 25305
304-558-3780
800-249-3778
Fax: 304-558-2059
www.wrdhhr.org/bcse

Cooperative Extension Office
Robert Maxwell, Interim Director
Cooperative Extension
8th Floor, Knapt Hall
P.O. Box 6031
West Virginia University
Morgantown, WV 26506-6031
304-293-3408
www.wvu.edu/~exten

Corporation Division Office
Corporate Division
Secretary of State
Room 139 West, State Capitol
Charleston, WV 25305
304-558-8000
866-SOS-VOTE
www.wvsos.com

Day Care Licensing Agency
Department of Health and Human Resources
Day Care Licensing
P.O. Box 2590
Fairmont, WV 26555
304-363-3261
www.wvdhhr.org/oss/

Economic Development Office
West Virginia Development Office
1900 Kanawha Blvd., East
Charleston, WV 25305-0311
304-558-2234
800-982-3386
Fax: 304-558-0449
www.wvdo.org

Department of Education
West Virginia Dept. of Education
Dept. of Statistical Information
Bldg. 6, Room B-346
1900 Kanawha Blvd. E.
Charleston, WV 25305-0330
304-558-8869
http://wvde.state.wv.us/

Department of Higher Education
State College and University Systems Central Office
1018 Kanawha Boulevard East, Suite 700
Charleston, WV 25301
304-558-2101
www.hepc.wvnet.edu

Health Department
West Virginia Bureau for Public Health
Building 3, Room 518
State Capitol Complex
Charelston, WV 25305
304-558-2971
Fax: 304-558-1035
www.wvdhhr.org/bph/index.htm

Housing Office
West Virginia Housing Development Fund
814 Virginia St., East
Charleston, WV 25301
304-345-6475
800-933-9843
www.wvhdf.com/

Insurance Commissioner
Insurance Commissioner
2019 Washington St., E.
P.O. Box 50540
Charleston, WV 25305-0540
304-558-3394
800-642-9004
www.state.wv.us/insurance/

Labor Department
West Virginia Bureau of Employment Programs
112 California Avenue
Charleston, WV 25305-0112
304-558-2630
www.state.wv.us/bep

Licensing Office
Secretary of State
State Capitol
Charleston, WV 25305

304-558-6000
www.wvsos.com

One-Stop Career Center
Job Service
Bureau of Employment Programs
Jobs/Job Training
112 California Avenue
Charleston, WV 25305-0112
304-558-1138
Fax: 304-558-1136
www.state.wv.us/bep/jobs/
Email: haydep@wvnvm. wvnet.edu

Security Regulators
West Virginia Securities Division
State Capitol
Kanawha Blvd., East
Room 118 West
Charleston, WV 25305
304-558-2257
www.wvauditor.com

Small Business Development Center
West Virginia Small Business Development Center
West Virginia Development Office
950 Kanawha Boulevard
Charleston, WV 25301
304-558-2960
Fax: 304-558-0127
Email: palmeh@mail.wvnet.edu
www.wvsbdc.org

Social Services Offices
West Virginia Department of Health and Human Resources
State Capital Complex
Building 3, Room 218
Charleston, WV 25305
304-558-8886
www.wvdhhr.org

Temporary Assistance to Needy Families (TANF)
Temporary Aid to Needy Families
Sharon Paterno
West Virginia Department of Health and Human Resources
Building 6, Room 650
State Capitol Complex
Charleston, WV 25305
304-558-4069
www.wvdhhr.org/ofs/

Transportation Department
Toni Boyd
West Virginia Department of Transportation
1900 Kanawha Boulevard
East Building 5, Room 803
Charleston, WV 25305
304-558-0428
www.wvdot.com

Unclaimed Property Office
West Virginia State Treasurer
1900 Kanawha Blvd., East
State Capitol Bldg. 1, Room E-145
Charleston, WV 25305
304-558-5000
www.wvtreasury.com

Unemployment Insurance Office
Director, Unemployment Compensation Division
Bureau of Employment Programs
112 California Ave.
Charleston, WV 25305
304-558-2624
www.state.wv.us/bep/uc/ default.htm
Weekly benefit range: $24-290
Duration of benefits: 26 weeks

Utility Commission
Public Service Commission
201 Brooks St.
P.O. Box 812
Charleston, WV 25323-0812
304-340-0300
800-344-5113 (WV only)
www.psc.state.wv.us

Women's Commission
West Virginia Women's Commission
Building 6, Room 637
Capitol Complex
Charleston, WV 25305
304-558-0070
Fax: 304-558-5767
Email: vrobinson@wvdhhr.org
www.wvdhhr.org/women/index.asp
Joyce M. Stover, Acting Executive Director
Sally Riley, Chair

Your Senator
United States Senate
Washington, DC 20510
202-224-3121
www.senate.gov

Your Representative
United States House of Representatives
Washington, DC 20515
202-224-3121
www.house.gov

Wisconsin

Federal Information Center
1-800-FED-INFO
www.firstgov.gov
www.pueblo.gsa.gov/call/

State Information Office
608-266-2211
www.wisconsin.gov

Department on Aging
Aging and Long Term Care Board
217 S. Hamilton St., Suite 300
Madison, WI 53703
608-266-2536
www.dhfs.state.wi.us

Attorney General's Office
Office of the Attorney General
Department of Justice
State Capitol, Suite 114 East
P.O. Box 7857
Madison, WI 53707-7857
608-266-1221
800-422-7128
www.doj.state.wi.us

Banking Commissioner
Commissioner of Banking
345 W. Washington Ave., 4th Floor
Madison, WI 53703
608-266-1621
800-452-3328
www.wdfi.org/

Child Care and Development Block Grant Lead Agency
Wisconsin Department of Workforce Development
Office of Child Care
1 West Wilson St.
P.O. Box 7935
Madison, WI 53707-7935
608-267-3708
Fax: 608-261-6968
www.dwd.state.wi.us/des/childcare/default.htm

Child Support Enforcement Agency
Mary Southwick
Bureau of Child Support
Division of Economic Support
P.O. Box 7935
Madison, WI 53707
608-266-9909
Fax: 608-627-2824
www.dwd.state.wi.us/bcs/

Cooperative Extension Office
Dr. Aeyse Somersan, Director
432 North Lake Street, Room 601
Madison, WI 53706
608-262-7966
www1.uwex.edu/ces/

Corporation Division Office
Corporate Division
Secretary of State
P.O. Box 7846
Madison, WI 53707
608-266-3590
www.state.wi.us/agencies/sos/

Day Care Licensing Agency
Department of Health and Social Services
Child Care Licensing Division
P.O. Box 8916
Madison, WI 53708-8916
608-266-9314
www.dhfs.state.wi.us

Economic Development Office
Department of Commerce
201 W. Washington Avenue
Madison, WI 53707
Business Helpline:
1-800-HELP-BUSiness
Fax Request Hotline:
608-264-6154
Export Helpline:
1-800-XPORT-WIsconsin
www.commerce.state.wi.us

Department of Education
Wisconsin Department of Public Instruction
Center for Education Statistics
125 S. Webster
P.O. Box 7841
Madison, WI 53707-7841
608-266-3390
800-441-4563
www.dpi.state.wi.us/

Department of Higher Education
State of Wisconsin Higher Educational Aids Board
P.O. Box 7885
Madison, WI 53707-7885
608-267-2206
Fax: 608-267-2808
http://heab.state.wi.us

Health Department
Wisconsin Department of Health & Family Services
1 West Wilson Street
Madison, WI 53702-0007
608-266-1865
TTY: 608-267-7371
www.dhfs.state.wi.us

Housing Office
Wisconsin Housing and Economic Development Authority
P.O. Box 1728
Madison, WI 53701-1728
608-266-7884
800-334-6873
www.wheda.com

Insurance Commissioner
Commissioner of Insurance
P.O. Box 7873
Madison, WI 53707-7873
608-266-3585
800-236-8517
http://oci.wi.gov/oci_home.htm

Labor Department
Wisconsin Department of Workforce Development
201 East Washington Avenue
P.O. Box 7946
Madison, WI 53707-7946
608-267-4400
www.dwd.state.wi.us

Licensing Office
Department of Regulation and Licensing
P.O. Box 8935
Madison, WI 53708
608-266-7482
http://badger.state.wi.us/agencies/drl

One-Stop Career Center
Partnership for Full Employment (PFE)
Department of Workforce Development
201 East Washington Avenue
P.O. Box 7946
Madison, WI 53707-7946
608-266-3131
888-258-9966
Fax: 608-261-7979
www.dwd.state.wi.us/dwe/Directory.htm
Email: DWDINFO@dwd.state.wi.us

Security Regulators
Division of Securities
P.O. Box 1768
Madison, WI 53701
608-266-1064
www.wdfi.org

Small Business Development Center
Wisconsin Small Business Development Center
University of Wisconsin
432 North Lake St., Room 423
Madison, WI 53706
608-263-7794
Fax: 608-262-3878
http://cf.uwex.edu/sbdc/
Email: Kauten@admin.uwex.edu

Social Services Offices
Wisconsin Department of Health and Family Services
1 West Wilson Street
Madison, WI 53702
608-266-1683
www.dhfs.state.wi.us

Temporary Assistance to Needy Families (TANF)
Temporary Aid to Needy Families
Linda Stewart
Work Force Development
P.O. Box 7946
Madison, WI 53707
608-266-7553
www.dwd.state.wi.us/desw2/

Transportation Department
Elizabeth Trautsch
Wisconsin Bureau of Transit and Local Roads
P.O. Box 7913
Madison, WI 53606
608-266-0560
www.dot.state.wi.us

Unclaimed Property Office
Unclaimed Property Division
State Treasurer's Office
P.O. Box 2114
Madison, WI 53701
608-267-7977
www.ost.state.wi.us/static/html/unclaim.html

Unemployment Insurance Office
Administrator
Division of Unemployment Insurance
201 E. Washington Ave.
Room 371
P.O. Box 7905
Madison, WI 53707
608-266-7074
www.dwd.state.wi.us/ui/
Weekly benefit range: $52-274
Duration of benefits: 12-26 weeks

Utility Commission
Public Service Commission
610 North Whitney Way
Madison, WI 53707
608-266-2001
800-225-7729
www.psc.state.wi.us

Women's Commission
Wisconsin Women's Council
16 North Carroll St., Suite 720
Madison, WI 53703
608-266-2219
Fax: 608-261-2432
Email: Katie.Mnuk@wwc.state.wi.us
http://wwc.state.wi.us
Katie Mnuk, Executive Director

Your Senator
United States Senate
Washington, DC 20510
202-224-3121
www.senate.gov

Your Representative
United States House of Representatives
Washington, DC 20515
202-224-3121
www.house.gov

Wyoming

Federal Information Center
1-800-FED-INFO
www.firstgov.gov
www.pueblo.gsa.gov/call/

State Information Office
307-777-7011
www.state.wy.us

Department on Aging
Division on Aging
Department of Health
117 Hathaway Bldg.
Room 139
Cheyenne, WY 82002
307-777-7986
800-442-2766
http://wdhfs.state.wy.us/aging

Attorney General's Office
Office of the Attorney General
123 Capitol Building
200 West 24th Street
Cheyenne, WY 82002
307-777-7841
800-438-5799 (consumer complaints)
TDD: 307-777-5351
http://attorneygeneral.state.wy.us

Banking Commissioner
Banking Commissioner
Division of Banking
Department of Audit
Herschler Bldg., 3rd Floor E.
Cheyenne, WY 82002
307-777-7797
http://audit.state.wy.us/banking/banking.htm

Child Care and Development Block Grant Lead Agency
CCDBG Administrator
Wyoming Department of Family Services
Hathaway Building
2300 Capitol Ave.
Cheyenne, WY 82002-0490
307-777-6848
Fax: 307-777-3693
http://dfsweb.state.wy.us/

Child Support Enforcement Agency
James Mohler
Child Support Enforcement Program
Department of Family Services
Hathaway Building
2300 Capital Ave.
Cheyenne, WY 82002
307-777-6948
Fax: 307-777-3693
http://dfsweb.state.wy.us/csehome/cs.htm

Cooperative Extension Office
Darryl Kautzman, Director
CES
University of Wyoming
Box 3354
Laramie, WY 82071-3354
307-766-5124
www.uwyo.edu/ces/ceshome.htm

Corporation Division Office
Corporate Division
Secretary of State
State of Wyoming
Capitol Building
Cheyenne, WY 82002
307-777-5334
http://soswy.state.wy.us

Day Care Licensing Agency
Department of Family Services
Office of Child Care Licensing
Hathaway Building, Room 323
2300 Capitol Ave.
Cheyenne, WY 82002-0490
307-777-6285
http://dfsweb.state.wy.us/

Economic Development Office
Wyoming Business Council
214 W. 15th St.
Cheyenne, WY 82002
307-777-2800
800-262-3425
Fax: 307-777-2838
www.wyomingbusiness.org

Department of Education
Wyoming Department of Education
Statistical Department
Hathaway Bldg., 2nd Floor
2300 Capitol Ave.
Cheyenne, WY 82002-0050
307-777-7673
www.k12.wy.us/ wdehome.html

Department of Higher Education
Wyoming Department of Higher Education
Hathaway Building
2300 Capitol Avenue
Cheyenne, WY 82002
307-777-6213

Health Department
Wyoming Department of Health
2300 Capitol Avenue
MAILING ADDRESS:
117 Hathaway Building
Cheyenne, WY 82002
307-777-7657
Fax: 307-777-7439
TTY: 307-777-5648
http://wdhfs.state.wy.us/wdh/
Email: wdh@missc.state.wy.us

Housing Office
Wyoming Community Development Authority
155 North Beach
Casper, WY 82602
307-265-0603
www.wyomingcda.com

Insurance Commissioner
Commissioner of Insurance
Herschler Bldg. 3 East
122 W. 25th St.
Cheyenne, WY 82002
307-777-7401
800-438-5768
http://insurance.state.wy.us

Labor Department
Wyoming Dept. of Employment
122 West 25th Street
Cheyenne, WY 82002
307-777-7672
http://wydoe.state.wy.us/

Licensing Office
Governor's Office

State Capitol
Cheyenne, WY 82002
307-777-7434
www.state.wy.us/governor/governor_home.html

One-Stop Career Center
Employment Resource Centers
Department of Employment
Employment Resource Division
100 West Midwest
Casper, WY 82602
307-235-3254
http://wydoe.state.wy.us/erd

Security Regulators
Securities Division
Secretary of State
24th Street & State Capitol Ave.
Cheyenne, WY 82002
307-777-7370
http://soswy.state.wy.us

Small Business Development Center
Wyoming Small Business Development Center
University of Wyoming
P.O. Box 3922
Laramie, WY 82071-3922
307-766-3505
800-348-5194
Fax: 307-766-3406
Email: DDW@uwyo.edu
www.uwyo.edu/sbdc

Social Services Offices
Wyoming Department of Family Services
Hathaway Building
Cheyenne, WY 82002-0490
307-777-3679
dfsweb.state.wy.us

Temporary Assistance to Needy Families (TANF)
Temporary Aid to Needy Families
Marianne Lee
Department of Family Services
2300 Capitol Ave.
Hathaway Building, 3rd Floor
Cheyenne, WY 82002
307-777-7531
http://dfsweb.state.wy.us/

Transportation Department
John Black
State Highway Department
P.O. Box 1708
Cheyenne, WY 82003
307-777-4375
http://wydotweb.state.wy.us

Unclaimed Property Office
Unclaimed Property Division
State Treasurer's Office
1st Floor West, Herschler Bldg.
122 West 25th St.
Cheyenne, WY 82008
307-777-5590
http://treasurer.state.wy.us

Unemployment Insurance Office
Administrator, Division of Unemployment Insurance
Department of Employment
P.O. Box 2760
Casper, WY 82602
307-235-3254
http://wydoe.state.wy.us/
Weekly benefit range: $18-250
Duration of benefits: 12-26 weeks

Utility Commission
Public Service Commission
2515 Warren Ave.
Hansen Bldg., Suite 300
Cheyenne, WY 82002
307-777-7427
http://psc.state.wy.us

Women's Commission
Wyoming State Government
Commission for Women
c/o Department of Employment
Herschler Building
122 West 25th St.
Cheyenne, WY 82002
307-777-7671
http://wydoe.state.wy.us
Amy McClure, Chair

Your Senator
United States Senate
Washington, DC 20510
202-224-3121
www.senate.gov

Your Representative
United States House of Representatives
Washington, DC 20515
202-224-3121
www.house.gov

INDEX

A

B

C

G

I

L

M

N

O

P

T

U

V

W

Y